UNITED STATES ARMY IN THE KOREAN WAR

SOUTH TO THE NAKTONG, NORTH TO THE YALU

(June–November 1950)

by

Roy E. Appleman

CENTER OF MILITARY HISTORY

UNITED STATES ARMY

WASHINGTON, D.C., 1992

Published by Books Express Publishing
Copyright © Books Express, 2012
ISBN 978-1-78266-080-4

Books Express publications are available from all good retail and online booksellers. For publishing proposals and direct ordering please contact us at: info@books-express.com

UNITED STATES ARMY IN THE KOREAN WAR

Stetson Conn, General Editor

Advisory Committee
(As of 15 March 1960)

Fred Harvey Harrington University of Wisconsin	Maj. Gen. Ben Harrell U.S. Continental Army Command
Oron J. Hale University of Virginia	Maj. Gen. Evan M. Houseman Industrial College of the Armed Forces
W. Stull Holt University of Washington	Brig. Gen. Bruce Palmer, Jr. U.S. Army War College
Bell I. Wiley Emory University	Brig. Gen. William A. Cunningham III U.S. Army Command and General Staff College
T. Harry Williams Louisiana State University	Col. Vincent J. Esposito United States Military Academy

C. Vann Woodward
Johns Hopkins University

Office of the Chief of Military History
Brig. Gen. James A. Norell, Chief of Military History

Chief Historian	Stetson Conn
Chief, Histories Division	Lt. Col. James C. Griffin
Chief, Publication Division	Lt. Col. James R. Hillard
Editor in Chief	Joseph R. Friedman

. . . to Those Who Served

Foreword

At the outbreak of the Korean War in June 1950, the U.S. Army combat units nearest the scene were the four infantry divisions performing occupation duties in Japan. When the Army of the Republic of Korea, supported only by U.S. air and naval forces, was unable to halt the North Korean aggressors, these divisions, seriously understrength and only partially trained and equipped for fighting, provided the troops that were committed initially to action in response to the call of the United Nations Security Council.

Colonel Appleman's narrative portrays vividly the grimness of "limited war" against a fanatical enemy, and the tragic consequences of unpreparedness. His writing recaptures the dismay that most Americans experienced in the realization that a small, little-known country could achieve military success against a coalition that included this, the world's most powerful nation.

Here is the story of how U.S. Army combat units, thrown piecemeal into the battle to slow Communist advances, fought a desperate and heroic delaying action, buying time until the United Nations forces could attain the military strength necessary to take the offensive. When that offensive was launched, it quickly crushed the North Korean forces, only to be met with the massive intervention of a more formidable adversary, Communist China.

This volume covers U.S. Army action in Korea from the outbreak of war to the full-scale intervention of the Chinese Communists. It is the first of five volumes now planned for inclusion in UNITED STATES ARMY IN THE KOREAN WAR, a series patterned on the much more voluminous UNITED STATES ARMY IN WORLD WAR II. Subsequent volumes will complete the Korean combat narrative as well as deal with related problems of command, strategy, logistics, handling of prisoners of war, and the armistice negotiations.

Washington, D. C.
15 March 1960

JAMES A. NORELL
Brigadier General, U.S.A.
Chief of Military History

The Author

Roy E. Appleman, a graduate of Ohio State University, *magna cum laude*, continued his education at Yale Law School and Columbia University, receiving from the latter the M.A. degree in History and completing all requirements for the Ph.D. degree except the publication of a dissertation.

He entered the United States Army as a private in the infantry in 1942 during World War II and after completing Officer Candidate School the following year was commissioned a 2d lieutenant. After a number of assignments, he was sent overseas to the Pacific theater in 1944, assigned as a combat historian with the United States Tenth Army and subsequently attached to the XXIV Corps. Coauthor of *Okinawa: The Last Battle*, first combat volume to be published in the series UNITED STATES ARMY IN WORLD WAR II, he received the Army Commendation Ribbon in 1945 for performance of duties as combat historian in the Okinawa campaign and his subsequent contribution to the Okinawa volume.

Early in 1951 Colonel Appleman (then a major) was ordered from reserve status to active duty with the Army and sent to Korea as a combat historian for the purpose of studying the action there and preparing the Army's history of the Korean War. A lieutenant colonel, he returned to civilian life in the autumn of 1954. Upon completion of the manuscript for the present work, he received the Secretary of the Army's Certificate of Appreciation for Patriotic Civilian Service.

Author of *Abraham Lincoln: From His Own Words and Contemporary Accounts*, published by the Government Printing Office; coauthor of *Great Western Indian Fights*, being published by Doubleday & Company, Inc.; and coauthor of *History of the United States Flag and Symbols of Sovereignty*, being published by Harper & Brothers, Mr. Appleman is presently Staff Historian in the National Park Service, U.S. Department of the Interior, and holds a commission as lieutenant colonel in the U. S. Army Reserve.

Preface

William Napier, upon finishing after seventeen years of painful toil the six volumes of his *Peninsular War,* wrote in a parody of Chaucer:
*"Easy ys myne boke to rede and telleth of moche fyte,
But then your easy rede is damned hard to wryte. . . ."*

True it is that a historian's first business is grinding toil and drudgery. All of this it has been to the writer of this book. Nevertheless it was a labor willingly undertaken, but accompanied throughout by the apprehension that he might fail in doing justice to the story of his countrymen who fought in Korea.

First and always, within the limits of his knowledge and ability, the author has neglected no effort nor passed over any evidence that seemed likely to further his purpose of writing a true history of the Korean War. He accepted Parkman's dictum that faithfulness to the truth of history involves far more than research, that one who is to write it "must study events in their bearings near and remote; in the character, habits, and manners of those who took part in them . . . and must himself be, as it were, a sharer or a spectator of the action he describes."

During the first four of the nine years he devoted to writing this book, from 1951 to 1954, the writer was on active duty in the United States Army and completed a first draft of the manuscript. In the following five years, as a civilian in Army reserve status, he devoted the time he could salvage from earning a living to several revisions and final completion of the work.

The writer was not entirely a stranger to Korea when he arrived there early in July 1951. Six years earlier, as a staff officer, he had accompanied Lt. Gen. John R. Hodge's U. S. XXIV Army Corps from Okinawa to Korea in early September 1945. This was at the beginning of United States commitment in Korea, when General Hodge accepted the surrender of the Japanese there at the end of World War II and began the occupation of that country below the 38th Parallel. But it was in 1951 that the writer saw Korea's hills at close quarter and felt his knees tremble and buckle as he climbed the steeply pitched ridges.

Korea was at the same time both beautiful and sordid. The green hills and patchwork-patterned rice paddies have an enchanting beauty when seen from a distance or the relative comfort of a vehicle on the roads. Slogging over this same ground carrying a load of weapons and pack in scorching heat or pelting rain, or in the numbing cold of a Siberian-type winter, with the enemy waiting around the next bend or over the next rise of ground, is another matter. Then the landscape loses its charm and becomes harsh and deadly to the spirit and exhausting to mind and body.

From Pusan in the south to the United Nations line north of the 38th Parallel, from the Imjin River in the west to the Iron Triangle, to the mountain line above the Hwach'on Reservoir, to Heartbreak Ridge and the Punchbowl, and on to the high Taebaek Mountains near the east coast in the ROK sector, the writer traveled from command post to command post and often up to battalions and rifle companies on the line. His companion during these travels in Korea was Capt. (now Major) Russell A. Gugeler, an experienced soldier who subsequently wrote *Combat Actions in Korea*. Whenever possible the earlier, 1950 battlefields were visited. Where lack of time or other circumstances did not permit this, critical terrain was studied from liaison planes that could dip low and circle at leisure around points of interest.

The writer came to know the stifling dust, the heat, the soaking rains, the aching legs, the exhausted body that was the common experience of the men who fought in Korea, although he seldom had to run any risk of known personal danger as did they, and he could always look forward to food at night and a safe place to sleep at some command post, which most of them could not. It is easy for him now to close his eyes and see the rushing torrents in the mountain gorges and everywhere the hills, scantily covered, if at all, in the south, and green with pine in the higher mountains of the north. In the lower ground were the rice paddies, small vegetable patches, the mud-walled and thatched-roof huts. How could one forget this Asiatic land where so many of his countrymen died or were maimed, where they enacted their roles of bravery and fortitude. In a sense, the Korean War experience became a part of him.

Official records are indispensable for fixing dates and time of major events and troop movements. But anyone familiar with the way the records of combat units during battle are made up will know that they seldom tell the essential facts of what happened, and how, and why. They are often the products of indifferent clerks transcribing, at places remote from the scene of action, a minimum of messages for something—anything—that will satisfy the official requirement for a report. Those who know the most about an action or an event seldom take the time to tell, or write, about it. They are too tired, or too nearly dead, or they are dead.

In the early months of the Korean War there was little time for the military organizations committed there to keep adequate records of what they did, even had there been the desire to do so. Always they were stopping only briefly, fighting hazardous rear-guard actions, and then on the run again. No one had time to write down what had happened and why, even if he knew. And no one in the various headquarters had the time or the energy or the will to search out those who survived each action and from them learn firsthand of the event. Everyone was too much concerned with survival or of getting a moment of respite from exhaustion. A record for posterity, for history, weighed the least of many things on their minds. Even when reports of military organizations are models of official records, the author agrees wholly with Marshal Erich von Manstein, who believes that a historian of military matters and campaigns "cannot get the truth from files and documents alone . . . the answer . . . will seldom be found—certainly not in a complete form—in files or war diaries."

How easy it would have been to write a story of the war based on the records alone, never stopping to get beneath that gloss! Such a book might have read smoothly and had a tone of plausibility to all except those whose personal knowledge would have branded it as inadequate at best and as almost wholly false at worst. Rather than produce such a book, the author chose the nine years of work that resulted in this one.

Since it was only from survivors of the early battles in Korea that one could hope to reconstruct the narrative of the first months of the conflict, the writer undertook to get their story. When he arrived in Korea in early July 1951, on active duty with the Army, he had orders from Maj. Gen. Orlando Ward, then Chief of Military History, to study the terrain of the action and to interview as many participants, of all ranks, as he could find. He began then a process continued almost to the hour that this manuscript went to press. He talked with hundreds of soldiers, from privates to three- and four-star generals, about particular actions and decisions affecting the action of which each had personal knowledge in some degree. One interview would result in leads to others. Thus the snowball grew. Many officers and soldiers who had information were now in distant lands on reassignment, or otherwise out of reach for personal discussion. To them went letters. Over the years, information came back from many corners of the globe. The response was remarkable. The author had only to ask and he received. The men were eager to tell their story—from the private in the ranks to General of the Army Douglas MacArthur. Without this willing help of those who toiled, suffered, bled, and lost their comrades the story of the Korean War in 1950 could never have been told satisfactorily. If this narrative carries the mark of truth, it is to these men largely that it is due. My debt to them is great.

Some major events almost defied comprehension. Such was the battle of Taejon. The author spent seven years in attempting to solve that puzzling and bizarre action. The first draft of the Taejon chapter, based on the official records, was nothing. Knowing this, the author sought out survivors and throughout the years searched for, and gradually accumulated, more information. Missing pieces of the puzzle came to light that made it possible to fit others into place. The author rewrote this chapter eight times. Finally he obtained from Maj. Gen. William F. Dean his comments on the manuscript and a statement of his contemporary thoughts and actions bearing on the events described. Some of them were not calculated to raise him to the level of an all-seeing military commander, but they marked Dean as a man of truth and honor. Then, with General Dean's contributions, the author felt at last that he had salvaged about all that ever would be learned concerning Taejon from American sources. Many other chapters reached their final form in much the same manner as this one.

The scope and scale of treatment change as the narrative proceeds. At first only two reinforced rifle companies were committed to battle, then a battalion, then a regiment, then a division, finally the Eighth Army and the reconstituted ROK Army. Against them was the might of the initially victorious North Korean Army, and later the light infantry masses of the Chinese Communist Forces. Gradually, United Nations troops from many parts of the world entered the lists, usually in small numbers to be sure, but in the case of Great Britain the force rose from two battalions to a Commonwealth division. As the larger forces came into action against each other the focus of action necessarily broadened and detail diminished. Task Force Smith, for example, in the first week of July 1950, received a detail of treatment that could not possibly be continued for all of the Eighth Army late in the year, nor even in August and September at the Naktong Perimeter. The use of detail necessarily had to be more selective. The ROK Army is treated in less detail than the American organizations, but enough is told to relate its part in the over-all operations. Reliable information on ROK action was nearly always very difficult to obtain, and sometimes impossible.

Throughout, the writer's sympathies have been with the troops who fought the battles at close range—the men who handled the rifles, who threw the grenades, who caught the enemy's bullets, who fought their own fears in the face of the unknown, who tried to do their duty as United States soldiers even though they were fighting for a cause they did not understand, and in a country to whose culture and interests they were strangers. He tried to be there with them.

The writer is indebted to many officers who, while serving in the Office of the Chief of Military History, Department of the Army, have read the manuscript in its various stages and offered comments and criticisms. They include Maj. Gen. Richard W. Stephens, a leading participant in the action; Col. George G. O'Connor; Col. S. W. Foote; Col. Carl D. McFerren; Col. Joseph Rockis; Col. Warren H. Hoover; and Lt. Col. Eugene J. White.

The sympathetic and generous viewpoint of Dr. Kent Roberts Greenfield, who gave valuable help in directing the critical panel review of the manuscript and evaluating needed final revisions, is gratefully acknowledged. Dr. Louis Morton gave detailed and critical review to the manuscript. Dr. Stetson Conn, who succeeded Dr. Greenfield as Chief Historian, and his Deputy, Dr. John Miller, jr., have been most helpful in reviewing the final draft of the manuscript.

To Miss Ruth Stout, the editor, and Mr. Thomas J. Seess, the copy editor, the writer especially wants to express his appreciation for their friendly, necessary, and painstaking editing of the manuscript and guiding it through the printer. Mr. Joseph R. Friedman, as Editor in Chief, has contributed from his wide editorial experience and wisdom. Mrs. Norma

Heacock Sherris assisted in finding suitable illustrations for the volume.

Mr. Billy Mossman, assisted by Mr. Elliot Dunay and the draftsmen who worked under his supervision, produced the maps in this volume. The author turned over to Mr. Mossman a large number of sketch maps and overlays which he had prepared while writing the text. Mr. Mossman, a former infantry officer with World War II experience in the Pacific Theater, and later on active duty in Korea during the Korean War, has a wide knowledge of military matters and of Korea itself. This background combined with his training in military cartography made him an ideal choice for the layout and supervision of the map work on this volume.

Mr. Israel Wice and his staff in the General Reference Section, Office of the Chief of Military History, cheerfully and efficiently gave their services in obtaining official records and other materials requested by the writer for his use. Mr. Stanley Falk prepared a useful digest of the Far East Command Daily Intelligence Summary, July through November 1950, relative to the Korean War. In an early stage of the work, Mrs. Gwendolyn Taylor as typist and general assistant gave valuable help.

The writer is much indebted to Mrs. Joy B. Kaiser. Many a complicated troop movement she has reconstructed on an overlay from coordinate readings given in S–3 and G–3 journals and periodic reports. The author never tried to write up the story of an action until after it had been plotted on a terrain map. Thus, Mrs. Kaiser in a two-year period saved him much labor, doubling as typist for an early draft of the manuscript, preparing overlays from journal co-ordinates, and otherwise contributing to the work.

Another whose dedication benefited the writer is Mrs. Edna W. Salsbury. She assumed the task of typing what turned out to be the last two revisions of the manuscript, and she performed that task ably. Throughout the tedious work of typing a heavily footnoted manuscript she made many suggestions that resulted in improving readability and her careful attention to detail contributed much in maintaining accuracy.

Notwithstanding the considerable assistance given the author by so many individuals and organizations, he alone is responsible for interpretations made and conclusions drawn in this volume as well as for any errors of omission or commission.

The person to whom the author owes most is Maj. Gen. Orlando Ward. As Chief of Military History, Department of the Army, in 1951, he ordered him to Korea to start this work. He opened the door for him to all commanders in Korea and the Far East Command. His experience as Secretary of the General Staff from 1938 to 1941, and subsequently as commander of the 1st Armored Division in North Africa, had given him broad knowledge of military matters and firsthand experience of battle and how it affects men.

General Ward's constant injunction to the author was to seek the truth of the Korean War and to tell it, no matter whom it might touch unfavorably. He wanted the facts made known, because only from them, he thought, could the United States build a better army for its defense. How well the writer remembers his statement one day in casual conversation, "Truth is the first casualty in battle." He has tried not to have it the first casualty in this account of the Korean War.

Washington, D.C.
15 March 1960

ROY E. APPLEMAN
Lieutenant Colonel, USAR

Contents

Chapter	Page
I. KOREA AND THE BACKGROUND OF CONFLICT	1
II. ARMED FORCES OF NORTH AND SOUTH KOREA	7
The North Korea People's Army	8
The Republic of Korea Armed Forces	12
III. 'INVASION ACROSS THE PARALLEL	19
Invasion	21
The ROK Counterattack at Uijongbu	28
The Fall of Seoul	30
IV. THE UNITED STATES AND THE UNITED NATIONS REACT	36
U.S. and U.N. Action	37
Evacuation of U.S. Nationals From Korea	38
KMAG Starts To Leave Korea	40
ADCOM in Korea	42
MacArthur Flies to Korea	44
The President Authorizes Use of U.S. Ground Troops in Korea	46
V. THE NORTH KOREANS CROSS THE HAN RIVER	49
Deployment of U.S. Forces in the Far East, June 1950	49
The River Crossing	52
ADCOM Abandons Suwon	55
VI. AMERICAN GROUND FORCES ENTER THE BATTLE	59
Task Force Smith Goes to Korea	60
Task Force Smith at Osan	65
VII. DELAYING ACTION: P'YONGT'AEK TO CHOCH'IWON	77
The Retreat From P'yongt'aek	79
Night Battle at Ch'onan	82
The 21st Infantry Moves Up	88
The Fight at Chonui	90
Choch'iwon	96
VIII. IN THE CENTRAL MOUNTAINS AND ON THE EAST COAST	101

Chapter	Page
IX. EIGHTH ARMY IN COMMAND	109
General Walker Assumes Command in Korea	110
Troop Training and Logistics	113
The Port of Pusan and Its Communications	116
American Command Estimate	117
X. DISASTER AT THE KUM RIVER LINE	121
The N.K. 4th Division Crosses the Kum Below Kongju	123
The 63d Field Artillery Battalion Overrun	126
The N.K. 3d Division Crosses the Kum Against the 19th Infantry	130
Roadblock Behind the 19th Infantry	137
XI. TAEJON	146
Dean's Plan at Taejon	147
Taejon—The First Day	151
Taejon—The Second Day	155
Withdrawal From Taejon—Roadblock	164
The 24th Division After Taejon	179
XII. THE FRONT LINE MOVES SOUTH	182
Yongdok and the East Coastal Corridor	182
Reorganization of the ROK Army	188
The U.S. 25th Division at Sangju	190
The 1st Cavalry Division Sails for Korea	195
The 1st Cavalry Division Loses Yongdong	197
The 27th Infantry's Baptism of Fire	199
Retreat	203
"Stand or Die"	205
XIII. THE ENEMY FLANKS EIGHTH ARMY IN THE WEST	210
Walker Acts	211
The Trap at Hadong	215
The N.K. 4th Division Joins the Enveloping Move	222
The N.K. 4th Division Seizes the Koch'ang Approach to the Naktong	225
Chinju Falls to the Enemy—31 July	227
Three Pershing Tanks at Chinju	231
Colonel Wilson Escapes With the 1st Battalion, 29th Infantry	233
XIV. BLOCKING THE ROAD TO MASAN	235
The Two Roads to Masan	235
The Battle at the Notch	239
Colonel Check's Reconnaissance in Force Toward Chinju	242
The Affair at Chindong-ni	244

Chapter	Page
XV. ESTABLISHING THE PUSAN PERIMETER	248
The 25th Division Moves South	248
United Nations Forces Withdraw Behind the Naktong	249
The Pusan Perimeter	252
U.S. Air Action and Build-up in the First Month	255
Strength of the Opposing Forces at the Pusan Perimeter	262
XVI. THE FIRST AMERICAN COUNTERATTACK—TASK FORCE KEAN	266
Who Attacks Whom?	270
The 5th Marines on the Coastal Road	274
Bloody Gulch—Artillery Graveyard	276
Task Force Kean Ended	286
XVII. THE FIRST BATTLE OF THE NAKTONG BULGE	289
The Naktong Bulge	290
The N.K. 4th Division Attacks Into the Naktong Bulge	291
The Enemy Gains Cloverleaf—Obong-ni	298
Yongsan Under Attack	302
Battle at Cloverleaf—Obong-ni	304
Marines Attack Obong-ni	310
24th Division Attack Gains Cloverleaf	313
Obong-ni Falls	315
The Enemy Bridgehead Destroyed	316
XVIII. BATTLE FOR THE EASTERN CORRIDOR TO PUSAN	319
The Kyongju Corridor to Pusan	319
The North Koreans Reach P'ohang-dong	320
The Air Force Abandons Yonil Airfield	329
The ROK 3d Division Evacuated by Sea	330
The North Koreans Turned Back From the Kyongju Corridor	331
XIX. THE TAEGU FRONT	334
The North Koreans Cross the Naktong for the Attack on Taegu	335
Triangulation Hill	340
The Enemy 10th Division's Crossing at Yongp'o	342
Hill 303 at Waegwan	345
Tragedy on Hill 303	347
Carpet Bombing Opposite Waegwan	350
Bowling Alley—the Sangju-Taegu Corridor	353

Chapter	Page
XX. STALEMATE WEST OF MASAN	364
The Southern Anchor of the Army Line	364
The N.K. 6th Division Regroups West of Masan	365
Enemy Attacks at Komam-ni (Saga)	366
Battle Mountain	368
XXI. AUGUST BUILD-UP AND SEPTEMBER PORTENTS	376
The Far East Air Forces in August	376
Ground Build-up	379
Korean Augmentation to the United States Army	385
Eighth Army Realignment and Extension Eastward	389
The North Korean Plan	392
XXII. PERIMETER BATTLE	397
Action in the East—Task Force Jackson	397
Enemy Breakthrough at Yongch'on	408
Back on Taegu	411
Crisis in Eighth Army Command	415
The 7th Cavalry's Withdrawal Battle	417
Troopers in the Mountains—Walled Ka-san	421
Hill 314	432
XXIII. NORTH KOREAN BREAKTHROUGH IN THE SOUTH	437
Midnight Near Masan	438
Agok	443
Task Force Manchu Misfires	446
The North Koreans Split the U.S. 2d Division	448
General Walker's Decisions on 1 September	451
XXIV. THE NORTH KOREAN GREAT NAKTONG OFFENSIVE	454
The End of Task Force Manchu	456
The Battle of Yongsan	459
The 23d Infantry in Front of Changnyong	466
A North Korean Puzzle	469
The 35th Infantry—The Rock of the Nam	470
Counterattack at Haman	479
Battle Mountain and Sobuk-san	483
XXV. THE LANDING AT INCH'ON	488
MacArthur's Early Plans	488
X Corps Troops Assembled	489
The Landing Controversy	492
Naval Plans	497
Intelligence Estimate	500
The Ships Load Out	501
Preliminary Bombardment	502
Securing the Inch'on Beachhead	503
Capture of Kimpo Airfield and Advance to the Han River	509

Chapter	Page
XXVI. THE CAPTURE OF SEOUL	515
The Capture of Yongdungp'o	516
Securing the Southern Flank	520
Seoul's Western Rampart	523
The 32d Infantry Enters Seoul	527
Battle of the Barricades	531
MacArthur Re-establishes Syngman Rhee in Seoul	536
The Blocking Force South of Seoul	538
The X Corps Situation	540
XXVII. BREAKING THE CORDON	542
The Eighth Army Plan	542
The Enemy Strength	545
United Nations' Perimeter Strength	547
The 38th Infantry Crosses the Naktong	548
The 5th Regimental Combat Team Captures Waegwan	552
The 24th Division Deploys West of the Naktong	554
The Indianhead Division Attacks West	558
Encirclement Above Taegu	560
The Right Flank	567
The Left Flank—The Enemy Withdraws From Sobuk-san	568
XXVIII. PURSUIT AND EXPLOITATION	573
The 25th Division Crosses Southwest Korea	574
The 2d Division Pushes West	579
Taejon Regained	582
From Tabu-dong to Osan—Eighth Army Link-up With X Corps	588
The ROK Army Arrives at the 38th Parallel	598
The Invaders Expelled From South Korea	600
XXIX. THE PLAN FOR COMPLETE VICTORY	607
MacArthur's Plan of Operations in North Korea	609
Eighth Army Deploys for the Attack	612
The ROK I Corps Captures Wonsan and Hungnam	614
The X Corps Prepares To Move Amphibiously to Northeast Korea	618
XXX. EIGHTH ARMY AND X CORPS ENTER NORTH KOREA	622
Eighth Army Crosses the Parallel—The Kumch'on Pocket	622
The X Corps Moves to Northeast Korea	631
Mines at Wonsan Harbor	633
The X Corps Ashore	635
XXXI. THE CAPTURE OF P'YONGYANG	638
The Logistical Situation	638
Sariwon Scramble	640
Into P'yongyang	646

Chapter	Page
XXXII. UP TO THE CH'ONGCH'ON	654
Airborne Attack: Sukch'on and Sunch'on	654
The Enemy Blocking Force Destroyed	658
Death in the Evening	661
The Advance Continues	663
XXXIII. THE CHINESE INTERVENE	667
American Optimism at End of October	669
Continuation of the Pursuit	671
ROK Troops Reach the Yalu	672
Chinese Strike the ROK II Corps	673
Unsan—Prelude	675
On the West Coastal Road	681
The X Corps' Changing Mission	684
The CCF Block Way to Changjin Reservoir	686
XXXIV. UNSAN	689
North of the Town	691
Roadblock South of Town	696
Ordeal Near Camel's Head Bend	700
XXXV. EIGHTH ARMY HOLDS THE CH'ONGCH'ON BRIDGEHEAD	709
Action North of the River	709
MIG's and Jets Over the Yalu	715
XXXVI. THE CHINESE APPRAISE THEIR FIRST PHASE KOREAN ACTION	717
XXXVII. GUERRILLA WARFARE BEHIND THE FRONT	721
XXXVIII. THE X CORPS ADVANCES TO THE YALU	729
ROK I Corps Attacks up the Coastal Road	729
U.S. 7th Infantry Division Reaches Manchurian Border	732
3d Infantry Division Joins X Corps	738
7th Marines Clear Road to Reservoir	741
The Gap Between Eighth Army and X Corps	745
XXXIX. THE BIG QUESTION	749
The Chinese Communist Forces	749
Eighth Army Estimate of CCF Intervention	751
The X Corps Estimate	755
The Far East Command's and MacArthur's Estimates	757
Actuality	765
Conclusion	769
The Pregnant Military Situation	770

	Page
SOURCES	777
GLOSSARY	779
BASIC MILITARY MAP SYMBOLS	783
INDEX	785

Tables

No.		
1.	ROK Combat Divisions, 1 June 1950	15
2.	ROK Army, 26 July 1950	191
3.	Estimated U.N. Strength as of 30 September 1950	605
4.	Postwar Tabulation of U.N. Strength in Korea as of 30 September 1950	606
5.	Organization of the XIII Army Group	768

Maps

No.		
1.	The North Koreans Cross the Han, 28 June–4 July 1950	54
2.	Task Force Smith at Osan, 5 July 1950	67
3.	Delaying Action, 34th Infantry, 5–8 July 1950	78
4.	Delaying Action, 21st Infantry, 8–12 July 1950	91
5.	The U.S.-ROK Front, 13 July 1950	103
6.	Defense of the Kum River Line, 34th Infantry, 14 July 1950	124
7.	Defense of the Kum River Line, 19th Infantry, 13–16 July 1950	131
8.	Task Force Kean, 7–12 August 1950	268
9.	North Korean Forces Enter the Naktong Bulge, 5–6 August 1950	292
10.	Destroying the Enemy Bridgehead, 17–19 August 1950	311
11.	The Threat to the Eastern Corridor, 10 August 1950	322
12.	Eliminating the Threat, 11–20 August 1950	328
13.	The N.K. Attacks on Taegu, 4–24 August 1950	336
14.	The N.K. Attacks in the East, 27 August–15 September 1950	399
15.	The N.K. Attacks on Taegu, 2–15 September 1950	412
16.	The Inch'on Landing, 15–16 September 1950	504
17.	Breaking the Cordon, 16–22 September 1950	549
18.	The Kumch'on Pocket, 9–14 October 1950	624
19.	The Capture of P'yongyang, 15–19 October 1950	641
20.	Airborne Attack on Sukch'on and Sunch'on, 187th Airborne RCT, 20 October 1950	655

No.		Page
21.	Advance of United Nations Command Forces, 20–24 October 1950	665
22.	The Chinese Intervene in the West, 25 October–1 November 1950	673
23.	The Unsan Engagement, 8th Cavalry Regiment, Night, 1–2 November 1950	692
24.	The Ch'ongch'on Bridgehead, 3–6 November 1950	710
25.	X Corps Advances to the Yalu River, 25 October–26 November 1950	730

Color Maps

No.		
I.	The North Korean Invasion, 25–28 June 1950	21
II.	The Fall of Taejon, 20 July 1950	150
III.	The Front Moves South, 14 July–1 August 1950	182
IV.	The Pusan Perimeter, 4 August 1950	236
V.	The North Korean Naktong Offensive, U.S. 25th Division Sector, 31 August–1 September 1950	438
VI.	The North Korean Naktong Offensive, U.S. 2d Division Sector, 31 August–1 September 1950	443
VII.	The Capture of Seoul, 19–28 September 1950	511
VIII.	The Pursuit, 23–30 September 1950	574

Illustrations

South Korean Troops	14
Uijongbu Corridor	25
Brig. Gen. John H. Church	42
General of the Army Douglas MacArthur	45
Maj. Gen. William F. Dean	60
American Combat Troops Arriving at Taejon	63
Road Leading to Suwon	64
Task Force Smith Position	66
Traffic Jam	85
South of Ch'onan	87
Lt. Gen. Walton H. Walker	89
Defense of Choch'iwon	97
General Walker and Col. Alfred G. Katzin	111
Main Rail Line out of Taejon	117
Moving Across the Kum River Bridge	125
Kum River Bridge Explosion	127
Dike Position near Taep'yong-ni	132

	Page
Aerial View of Taejon Airfield	148
Machine Gun Emplacement	149
Aerial View of Taejon City	151
The A-Frame	183
Strafing Attack	188
Naktong River at Andong	189
Cavalrymen Preparing for Action	198
Hadong	218
Hadong Pass	219
Moving Up From Chinju	237
Pier 2 at Pusan	260
60-Ton Crane at Pusan	261
Fox Hill Position	273
Point of a Combat Column	305
Marines on Hill 311	317
Aerial View of P'ohang-dong	326
Triangulation Hill	341
Waegwan Bridge	346
Maj. Gen. Paik Sun Yup	350
The Bowling Alley	356
Tank Action in the Bowling Alley	358
Enemy Side of the Rocky Crags	372
Rocket and Napalm Attack	378
Exploding Phosphorus Bombs	379
South Korean Recruit	387
Assault Troops of Company K	403
1st Cavalry Observation Post	413
General Walker Crossing the Naktong	418
Ruins of Ancient Fortress on Ka-san	422
D Company, 8th Engineer Combat Battalion	423
Mountain Mass West of Haman	439
Defensive Position in Front of Changnyong	451
U.N. Troops Cross Rice Paddies	463
Battle Trophy	471
2d Battalion, 27th Infantry	474
27th Infantry Command Post	481
Veteran of the 5th Regimental Combat Team	486
Wolmi-do	505
Landing Craft and Bulldozers	507
Marines on Wolmi-do	508
Destroyed Enemy Tanks	510
Kimpo Runway	513
Top-Level Briefing	514
Marines on Hill 125	517
American Troops Move on Seoul	526

	Page
Seoul as Seen From the Air	529
Tanks Entering Seoul	533
The Battle for Hill 201	552
Crossing the Kumho River	557
Ponton Treadway Bridge	558
Advancing to the Crest of Hill 201	560
View From the Crest of Hill 201	561
40-mm. Antiaircraft Battery	564
Enemy-Held Area	569
Kumch'on From the Air	584
On the Outskirts of Kumch'on	585
Col. Lee Hak Ku	589
Captured Enemy Equipment	601
Tank Troops of 1st Cavalry Division	613
3d ROK Division Officers and KMAG Advisers	617
ROK Troops	618
Kumch'on, North Korea	631
Landing Craft Approaching Beach	636
Tank-Supported Convoy	648
Burning Enemy Tank	649
5th Cavalry Troops	650
Capitol Building in P'yongyang	651
Kim Il Sung's Desk	653
Mass Airdrop Near Sunch'on	656
Artillery Airdrop Near Sukch'on	657
North Korean Atrocity Site	662
The Middlesex 1st Battalion	664
Supply by Air in Unsan Area	678
The 1st Battalion, 17th Infantry	734
Looking Across the Yalu	735
On the Banks of the Yalu	738
Ox-Drawn Sleds	739
Chinese Communist POW's	743
Chinese Communist Flag	751
Chu Teh	752
Lin Piao	753
Chou En-lai	758
Kim Il Sung	767
Peng Teh-huai	769
General MacArthur	771
Insignia of Major U.S. Ground Force Units	775

Illustrations are from Department of Defense files.

SOUTH TO THE NAKTONG,
NORTH TO THE YALU

CHAPTER I

Korea and the Background of Conflict

> One should not forget . . . that the earth is round and that "every road leads to Rome."
> WALDEMAR ERFURTH, *Surprise*

Every now and then in the history of mankind, events of surpassing importance take place in little-known areas of the earth. And men and women in countries distant from those events whose lives turn into unexpected and unwanted channels because of them can but wonder how it all happened to come about. So it was with Korea in 1950. In this ancient land of high mountains and sparkling streams the United Nations fought its first war.

For decades it has been axiomatic in Far Eastern politics that Russia, China, and Japan could not be indifferent to what happened in Korea, and, to the extent that they were able, each consistently has tried to shape the destinies of that peninsula. For Korea lies at the point where the Russian, Chinese, and Japanese spheres meet—the apex of the three great power triangles in Asia. Korea, the ancient invasion route of Japan into the Asian continent, in turn has always been the dagger thrust at Japan from Asia.

Korea is a mountainous peninsula of the Asiatic land mass and has natural water boundaries for almost the entire distance on all sides. The Yalu and Tumen Rivers are on the north, the Sea of Japan on the east, the Korea Strait on the south, and the Yellow Sea on the west. The only countries of the Asiatic mainland having boundaries with Korea are China across the Yalu and Tumen Rivers for 500 miles and the Union of Soviet Socialist Republics (USSR) for a distance of approximately eleven miles along the lower reaches of the Tumen River.

Korea embraces a little more than 85,000 square miles, is about the size of Utah, and in shape resembles Florida. It has more than 5,400 miles of coast line. High mountains come down abruptly to deep water on the east where there are few harbors, but on the south and west a heavily indented shoreline provides many. There is almost no tide on the east coast. On the west coast at Inch'on the tidal reach of thirty-two feet is the second highest in the world.

Korea varies between 90 and 200 miles in width and 525 to 600 miles in length. The mountains are highest in the north, some reaching 8,500 feet.

The high Taebaek Range extends down the east coast like a great spine, gradually falling off in elevation to the south. Practically all of Korea south of the narrow waist from P'yongyang to Wonsan slopes westward from the high Taebaek Range. This determines the drainage basins and direction of flow of all sizable rivers within Korea—generally to the southwest.

Only about 20 percent of Korea is arable land, most of it in the south and west. But every little mountain valley throughout Korea is terraced, irrigated, and cultivated. The principal food crops are rice, barley, and soybeans, in that order. Most of the rice is raised in the south where the warm and long growing season permits two crops a year. In 1950 the country's population of about 30,000,000 was divided between 21,000,000 south and 9,000,000 north of the 38th Parallel, with 70 percent engaged in agriculture.[1] The population density of South Korea, 586 per square mile, was one of the highest in the world for an agricultural people. Although having less than one third of the population, North Korea in 1950 comprised more than half (58 percent) the country.

Despite the fact that Korea has the sea on three sides, in climate it is continental rather than oceanic. Summers are hot and humid with a monsoon season generally lasting from June to September. In winter, cold winds come from the interior of Asia.

The Hermit Kingdom or Chosen, the "Land of the Morning Calm," has an ancient history. Its recorded history begins shortly before the time of Christ. An invasion from China, about one hundred years after the beginning of the Christian era, established a Chinese influence that has persisted to the present time. Many of China's cultural and technical advances, however, were borrowed from early Korea.

In a short war of a few months' duration in 1894–1895, known as the Sino-Japanese War, Japan ended Chinese political influence in Korea. Thereafter, Russian ambitions in Manchuria clashed with Japanese ambitions in Korea. This rivalry led to the Russo-Japanese War of 1904–1905, which ended with Japan dominant in Korea. Despite the bitter opposition of the Korean people, Japan proceeded step by step to absorb Korea within her empire and in 1910 annexed it as a colony. During World War II, in 1942, Korea became an integral part of Japan and came under the control of the Home Ministry.

All the critical events which occurred in Korea after 1945 grew out of the joint occupation of the country at the end of World War II by the United States and the USSR. The boundary between the two occupation forces was the 38th Parallel.

While all the influences operating on the decision to divide Korea for purposes of accepting the surrender of the Japanese forces there at the end of World War II cannot here be explored, it appears that American military consideration of an army boundary line in Korea began at the Potsdam Conference in July 1945. One day during the conference, General of the Army George C. Marshall called in Lt. Gen. John E. Hull, then Chief of the Operations Divi-

---

[1] Central Intelligence Agency, National Intelligence Survey (NIS), Korea, 1949, ch. 4, pp. 41–42, and ch. 6, pp. 61–66. Figures are from 1949 census.

KOREA AND THE BACKGROUND OF CONFLICT

sion, U.S. Army, and a member of the U.S. military delegation, and told him to be prepared to move troops into Korea. General Hull and some of his planning staff studied a map of Korea trying to decide where to draw a line for an army boundary between U.S. and Soviet forces. They decided that at least two major ports should be included in the U.S. zone. This led to the decision to draw a line north of Seoul which would include the port of Inch'on. Pusan, the chief port of Korea, was at the southeastern tip of the country. This line north of Seoul, drawn at Potsdam by the military planners, was not on the 38th Parallel but was near it and, generally, along it. The American and Russian delegates, however, did not discuss a proposed boundary in the military meetings of the Potsdam Conference.[2]

The matter lay dormant, apparently, in the immense rush of events following hard on the heels of the Potsdam Conference, which terminated 26 July—the dropping of atomic bombs on Hiroshima and Nagasaki in the first part of August, the Russian declaration of war against Japan on 8 August, and the Japanese offer of surrender on 10 August. The latter event brought the question of a demarcation line in Korea to the fore. It was settled in General Order 1, approved by President Harry S. Truman on 15 August 1945 and subsequently cleared with the British and Soviet Governments. It provided that U.S. forces would receive the surrender of Japanese forces in Korea south of the 38th Parallel; Soviet forces would receive the surrender of Japanese forces north of the Parallel. General of the Army Douglas MacArthur issued General Order 1 on 2 September as the directive under which Japanese forces throughout the Far East would surrender after the Japanese signed the Instrument of Surrender that day at Tokyo Bay in obedience to the Imperial Rescript by Emperor Hirohito.

It seems that the Soviet Army reached the 38th Parallel in Korea on 26 August. On 3 September, just as XXIV Corps was loading at Okinawa 600 miles away for its movement to Korea, Lt. Gen. John R. Hodge, commander of XXIV Corps and designated U.S. Commander in Korea, received a radio message from Lt. Gen. Yoshio Kozuki, commander of the Japanese *17th Area Army in Korea*, reporting that Soviet forces had advanced south of the 38th Parallel only in the Kaesong area. They evacuated the town on 8 September, evidently in anticipation of an early American entry.[3]

Two weeks after he had accepted the surrender of the Japanese south of the 38th Parallel in Seoul on 9 September 1945, General Hodge reported to General MacArthur in Tokyo, "Dissatisfaction with the division of the country grows." The 38th Parallel had nothing to commend it as a military or political

---

[2] Interv, author with Gen John E. Hull, Vice CofS, USA, 1 Aug 52. Dept of State Pub 4266, *The Conflict in Korea*, gives the diplomatic and legal background of U.S. commitments on Korea. A detailed discussion of the division of Korea at the 38th Parallel will be found in Lt. Col. James F. Schnabel, Theater Command: June 1950–July 1951, a forthcoming volume in the series UNITED STATES ARMY IN THE KOREAN WAR. TERMINAL Conference: Papers and Minutes of Meetings (July, 1945), U.S. Secy CCS, 1945, pp. 320–21 (hereafter cited, TERMINAL Conf: Papers and Min).

[3] GHQ FEC, History of U.S. Army Occupation in Korea, ch. IV, MS in OCMH Files.

boundary. It crossed Korea at the country's widest part without respect to terrain features; it came close to several important towns; and it cut off the Ongjin Peninsula in the west from the rest of Korea south of the Parallel.

For a few days at least after the American landing at Inch'on on 8 September 1945 the Koreans lived in a dream world. They thought this was the end of fifty years of bondage and the beginning of an era of peace, plenty, and freedom from interference by foreign peoples in their lives.

And for the Americans, too, who experienced those memorable September days in Korea there was little at the moment to suggest the disillusionment that onrushing events of the next few years would bring. A composite company, made up of elements of each rifle company of the 7th Infantry Division, paraded proudly and happily out of the courtyard at the Government House in Seoul at the conclusion of the ceremonies attending the Japanese surrender. The wide thoroughfare outside was so densely packed with the throng there was scarcely room for it to pass. These men had fought across the Pacific from Attu to Okinawa.[4] They thought that war was behind them for the rest of their lives. Five years later this same division was to assault this same capital city of Seoul where many of its men were to fall in the streets.

In an effort to reunite the country and to end the ever-mounting hostilities between the two parts of divided Korea, the General Assembly of the United Nations in November 1947 voted to establish a nine-nation United Nations Temporary Commission on Korea (UNCOK) to be present in Korea and to supervise elections of representatives to a National Assembly which would establish a national government. But the Soviet Union denied the U.N. Commission permission to enter North Korea, thus preventing that part of the country from participation in the free election.

South Korea held an election on 10 May 1948 under the auspices of the United Nations, sending 200 representatives to the National Assembly. The National Assembly held its first meeting on 31 May, and elected Syngman Rhee Chairman. On 12 July the Assembly adopted the Constitution of the Republic of Korea and formally proclaimed it the next day. Three days later the Assembly elected Syngman Rhee President. On 15 August 1948 the government of the Republic of Korea was formally inaugurated and the U.S. Army Military Government in Korea terminated. President Rhee and General Hodge on 24 August signed an interim military agreement to be in effect until such time as the United States withdrew its troops. The withdrawal of these troops began about three weeks later on 15 September. The United States recognized the new Republic of Korea on New Year's Day, 1949. Mr. John J. Muccio, special representative of the United States to the new government of South Korea since 12 August 1948, became the first U.S. Ambassador to the Republic of Korea on 21 March 1949.[5]

---

[4] The author witnessed this scene.

[5] Text of agreement in Dept of State Pub 3305, *Korea: 1945–1948*, Annex 26, pp. 103–04; *Ibid.*, Annex 23, pp. 100–101; George M. McCune, *Korea Today* (Cambridge: Harvard University Press, 1950), p. 231, n. 25.

Meanwhile, events in North Korea took a course which seems to have been guided by a deliberately planned political purpose. On 10 July 1948 the North Korean People's Council adopted a draft resolution and set 25 August as the date for an election of members of the Supreme People's Assembly of Korea. This assembly on 8 September adopted a constitution of the Democratic People's Republic of Korea and, the next day, claimed for this government jurisdiction over all Korea.[6] Kim Il Sung took office 10 September as Premier of the Democratic People's Republic of Korea.

Thus, three years after U.S. military authorities accepted the surrender of the Japanese south of the 38th Parallel there were two Korean governments in the land, each hostile to the other and each claiming jurisdiction over the whole country. Behind North Korea stood the Soviet Union; behind South Korea stood the United States and the U.N. Temporary Commission on Korea.

The General Assembly of the United Nations on 12 December 1948 recognized the lawful nature of the government of the Republic of Korea and recommended that the occupying powers withdraw their forces from Korea "as early as practicable." Russia announced on 25 December that all her occupation forces had left the country. But North Korea never allowed the U.N. Commission to enter North Korea to verify this claim. On 23 March 1949 President Truman approved the withdrawal of the remaining U.S. troops from Korea, a regiment of the 7th Infantry Division. Ambassador Muccio notified the U.N. Commission on 8 July 1949 that the United States had completed withdrawal of its forces on 29 June and that the U.S. Army Forces in Korea (USAFIK) had been deactivated as of midnight 30 June.[7]

While these events were taking place, internal troubles increased in South Korea. After the establishment of the Syngman Rhee government in the summer of 1948, civil disorder spread below the 38th Parallel. There began a campaign of internal disorders directed from North Korea designed to overthrow the Rhee government and replace it by a Communist one. Armed incidents along the 38th Parallel, in which both sides were the aggressors and crossed the boundary, became frequent.[8]

North Korea did not stop at inciting revolt within South Korea and taking military action against the border, it made threats as well against the United Nations. On 14 October 1949 the Foreign Minister of North Korea sent a letter to the Secretary General of the United Nations denying the legality of U.N. activity in Korea and declaring that the U.N. Commission in Korea would be driven out of the country. Eight days later the General Assembly of the United Nations decided to continue the Commission and charged it with investigat-

---

[6] *Korea: 1945-1948*, p. 21; McCune, *Korea Today*, p. 220.

[7] Lt Col Joseph Rockis, Notes on United States Occupation Force in Korea, OCMH Files; *The Conflict in Korea*, pp. 7, 20; McCune, *Korea Today*, pp. 267-68; Interv, author with Maj Gen Orlando Ward (CG US 6th Inf Div in Korea 1948), 31 Jan 52.

[8] See Capt Robert K. Sawyer, The U.S. Military Advisory Group to the Republic of Korea, pt. II, a monograph in the files of OCMH, for an extended treatment of this subject. (Hereafter cited as Sawyer, KMAG MS.) This MS is in three parts: I: 1 Sep 45-30 Jun 49; II: 1 Jul 49-24 Jun 50; III: 25 Jun-30 Jul 51.

ing matters that might lead to military action in Korea.[9] The United Nations supplemented this action on 4 March 1950 by the Secretary General's announcement that eight military observers would be assigned to observe incidents along the 38th Parallel.

During the month there were rumors of an impending invasion of South Korea and, in one week alone, 3–10 March, there occurred twenty-nine guerrilla attacks in South Korea and eighteen incidents along the Parallel.[10] Beginning in May 1950, incidents along the Parallel, and guerrilla activity in the interior, dropped off sharply. It was the lull preceding the storm.

---

[9] *The Conflict in Korea*, p. 21.

[10] DA Wkly Intel Rpts, 17 Mar 50, Nr 56, p. 14; U.S. Military Advisory Group, Semi-Annual Report to the Republic of Korea, 1 January–15 June 1950 (hereafter cited as Rpt, USMAG to ROK, 1 Jan–15 Jun 50), sec. IV, pp. 14–15.

CHAPTER II

Armed Forces of North and South Korea

> It was not Lacedaemon alone that gave birth to warriors, . . . they were produced in all countries where men were found capable of instructing others in the art of war.
>
> NICCOLO MACHIAVELLI, *The Discourses*

The North Korea People's Army had been from the beginning under the supervision of the Soviets. At first the Peace Preservation Corps had undertaken the organization and training of a military force. Then, when the Soviets began to withdraw their occupation forces in February 1948, the North Korean Government established a Ministry of Defense and activated the North Korea People's Army. Soviet instruction and supervision of the Army continued, however, after the withdrawal of Soviet forces from North Korea. One prisoner stated that every training film he ever saw or used had been made in the USSR. About three thousand Russians were active in the Army program before June 1950. In some instances as many as fifteen Soviet officers served as advisers on an N.K. infantry division staff. The adviser to a division commander reportedly was a Soviet colonel.[1]

The Soviet diplomatic mission to North Korea, apparently organized in January 1949, became the postoccupation body for Soviet control of the country. By June 1950 every member of the Soviet diplomatic staff in North Korea was either an army or an air force officer. Col. Gen. Terenty F. Shtykov, commander of the Soviet occupation forces in North Korea and, after their withdrawal, the Soviet Ambassador there, apparently functioned as the senior Soviet officer in the country. Intelligence reports indicate that Premier Kim Il Sung received weekly instructions from the USSR through Ambassador Shtykov.[2]

In June 1950 Kim Il Sung was Commander in Chief of the North Korean armed forces. His deputy was Marshal Choe Yong Gun. Both had left Korea in their youth, resided in China for long periods of time, and, ultimately, gone to Moscow for training. Kim Il Sung returned to Korea on 25 September 1945 under Soviet sponsorship, landing at Wonsan on that date with a group of Soviet-trained guerrillas.

---

[1] DA Intel Rev, Mar 51, Nr 178, p. 32; *Ibid.*, Aug 50, Nr 171, pp. 16–17; *Ibid.*, Mar 51, Nr 178, p. 36; 24th Div G–2 PW Interrog File, 6–22 Jul 50; GHQ FEC MIS GS, History of the North Korean Army, 31 July 1952 (hereafter cited as GHQ FEC, History of the N.K. Army), pp. 8–24.

[2] DA Intel Rev, Apr 51, Nr 179, p. 32; GHQ FEC, History of the N.K. Army.

For all practical purposes the North Korean ground forces in June 1950 comprised two types of units: (1) the Border Constabulary (BC or *Bo An Dae*) and (2) the North Korea People's Army (NKPA or *In Min Gun*). The Border Constabulary, an internal security force, was organized, trained, and supervised by Soviet officials. It was uncommonly strong in political indoctrination and supported and promoted the Communist party line throughout North Korea. All officer training for the Border Constabulary was under the direct supervision of Soviet advisers on the school staffs.[3]

The Border Constabulary had its beginnings as early as September 1945, when anti-Japanese and Communist Koreans, guerrillas who had fled from Korea and Manchuria to Soviet territory, came back to Korea and formed the nucleus of what was called the Peace Preservation Corps. It numbered about 18,000 men and drew its personnel mostly from Communist youth groups. Its officers were usually active Communists. In May 1950 the effective strength of the North Korean internal security forces was approximately 50,000, divided among the Border Constabulary, the regular police, and the "thought" police.[4]

The Border Constabulary in June 1950 consisted of five brigades of uneven size and armament—the *1st*, *2d*, *3d*, *5th*, and *7th*. The *1st Brigade* numbered 5,000 men; the *3d* and *7th* each had a strength of 4,000. These three brigades were stationed just north of the 38th Parallel. The *7th* was in the west, deployed from Haeju to the coast, just above the Ongjin Peninsula; the *3d* was east of the *7th*, in the center from Haeju to the vicinity of Chorwon; and the *1st* was at Kansong on the east coast. These three brigades, totaling 13,000 men, were armed and equipped to combat-infantry standards. The brigades each had six or seven battalions composed of three rifle companies each, together with machine gun and mortar companies, an antitank platoon, and the usual headquarters and service units.

The BC *2d Brigade*, with a total strength of only 2,600, was divided into seven battalions. It held positions along the Yalu and Tumen River boundaries separating North Korea from Manchuria and the USSR. This brigade had little heavy equipment and few mortars, machine guns, or antitank guns. The BC *5th Brigade*, with a strength of about 3,000 men, had headquarters at Pyongyang, the North Korean capital. It was responsible for railroad security.[5]

The North Korea People's Army

The North Korea People's Army in June 1950 constituted a ground force of eight infantry divisions at full strength, two more infantry divisions activated at an estimated half strength, a separate infantry regiment, a motorcycle reconnaissance regiment, and an armored brigade. Five of the infantry divisions and the armored brigade had well-trained combat personnel. Many of these soldiers were hardened veterans who had fought with the Chinese Com-

---
[3] DA Intel Rev, Jun 50, Nr 169, pp. 20–23.
[4] *Ibid.*

[5] Future reference to the two opposed Korean forces generally will be North Korean or N.K. and South Korean or ROK. The abbreviation N.K. will precede a numbered NKPA unit; ROK will precede a numbered South Korean unit.

munist and Soviet Armies in World War II.

The North Korea People's Army was officially activated on 8 February 1948. Its first full infantry divisions, the *3d* and *4th*, were established between 1947 and 1949; and its first armored unit, the *105th Armored Battalion*, was established in October 1948. The latter increased to regimental strength in May 1949. Conscription for replacements and build-up of the North Korea People's Army apparently began about July 1948. After a meeting of USSR and Communist China officials, reportedly held in Peiping early in 1950 to explore the advisability of using the North Korea People's Army for an invasion of South Korea, there was a rapid build-up of that Army. It increased its training program, transferred ordnance depots from urban to isolated rural sites, and readied hidden dump areas to receive supplies, weapons, and munitions of war from the USSR. At the beginning of this build-up there were in Korea about 16,000 repatriated North Koreans from the Chinese Communist Forces (CCF). In April 1950 Communist China returned 12,000 more veterans of the CCF to Korea where they formed the N.K. *7th Division* (redesignated the *12th* about 2 July 1950).[6]

The Korean veterans of the Chinese Communist Forces made up about one third of the North Korea People's Army in June 1950 and gave it a combat-hardened quality and efficiency that it would not otherwise have had. Five of the eight divisions in the North Korea People's Army—the *1st, 4th, 5th, 6th,* and *7th (12th) Divisions*—had in their ranks substantial numbers of CCF soldiers of Korean extraction. The *5th, 6th,* and *7th (12th) Divisions* had the largest number of them. Also, many of the NKPA units that did not have rank and file soldiers from the CCF did have officers and noncommissioned officers from it.[7]

Special mention needs to be made of the N.K. *5th, 6th,* and *7th Divisions*. In July 1949 the Chinese Communist Forces transferred all non-Koreans in the CCF *164th Division*, then stationed in Manchuria, to other Chinese divisions and filled the *164th* with Korean replacements. Near the end of the month the division, about 7,500 strong, moved by rail to Korea where it reorganized into the *10th, 11th,* and *12th Rifle Regiments* of the N.K. *5th Division.*[8]

At the same time, in July 1949, the CCF *166th Division* moved to Korea and reorganized into the *13th, 14th,* and *15th Regiments* of the N.K. *6th Division*. The story of the Koreans in this division goes back to 1942 when the Chinese Communists formed a Korean Volunteer Army largely with deserters from the Japanese *Kwantung Army.* This division had a strength of about 10,000 men when it entered Korea; there 800 replacements brought it to full strength.[9]

---

[6] GHQ FEC, History of the N.K. Army, pp. 3, 8–24; DA Intel Rev, Sep 51, Nr 184, p. 18; *Ibid.,* Mar 51, Nr 178, p. 36; ATIS Res Supp Interrog Rpts, Issue 99 (N.K. *12th Div*), p. 41. PW Interrog estimates of number of CCF veterans in the N.K. *1st, 4th, 5th,* and *6th Divisions*. See ATIS Res Supp Interrog Rpts, Issues 94, 95, 100.

[7] ATIS Res Supp Interrog Rpts, Issue 100 (N.K. *6th Div*), p. 29; Issue 94 (N.K. *4th Div*), p. 41; GHQ FEC, History of the N.K. Army, pp. 23–24.

[8] ATIS Res Supp Interrog Rpts, Issue 96 (N.K. *5th Div*), p. 37; GHQ FEC, History of the N.K. Army, p. 23.

[9] ATIS Res Supp Interrog Rpts, Issue 100 (N.K. *6th Div*), pp. 27–29; GHQ FEC, History of the N.K. Army, p. 23.

In February 1950 all Korean units in the Chinese Manchurian Army assembled in Honan Province. They numbered about 12,000 men drawn from the CCF *139th*, *140th*, *141st*, and *156th Divisions*. Some of them had participated in the Chinese Communist advance from Manchuria to Peiping, and all were veteran troops. In the first part of April these troops moved by rail to Korea. In the Wonsan area these CCF veterans reorganized into the *1st*, *2d*, and *3d Regiments* of the N.K. *7th Division*.[10]

In addition to these three divisions, the N.K. *1st* and *4th Divisions* each had one regiment of CCF veterans. All the units from the CCF Army upon arrival in North Korea received Soviet-type arms and North Korean uniforms and were retrained in North Korean tactical doctrine, which closely followed the Russian.

In March 1950 North Korea activated two new divisions: the *10th*, around Manchurian-trained units, and the *15th*, with men from three youth-training schools and veteran Communist officers and noncommissioned officers. Although activated in March, the *15th Division* received most of its troops near the end of June—after the invasion had started. In early June the *13th Division* was activated; the last one to be activated before the invasion of South Korea.[11]

By June 1950, the *105th Armored Regiment* had become the *105th Armored Brigade* with a strength of 6,000 men and 120 T34 tanks. Its equipment —tanks, weapons, and vehicles—was Russian-made. The brigade had three tank regiments—the *107th*, *109th*, and *203d*—each with 40 tanks, and a mechanized infantry regiment, the *206th*, with a strength of about 2,500 men. A tank regiment had three medium tank battalions, each having 13 tanks. The battalions each had three tank companies with 4 tanks to a company. Tank crews consisted of five men. Battalion, regimental, and division tank commanders each had a personal tank. The *105th Armored Brigade* was raised to division status in Seoul at the end of June 1950 before it crossed the Han River to continue the attack southward.[12]

In addition to the 120 tanks of the *105th Armored Brigade*, the better part of another tank regiment appears to have been available to North Korea in late June. Thirty tanks reportedly joined the N.K. *7th (12th) Division* at Inje in east central Korea just before it crossed the Parallel.[13] This gave North Korea a total of 150 Russian-built T34 tanks in June 1950.

In the six months before the invasion, a defensive-type army of 4 divisions and an armored regiment had doubled in strength to form 7 combat-ready divisions and an armored brigade. And there were in addition 3 other newly activated and trained divisions, and 2 independent regiments.[14]

The North Korean ground forces—the NKPA and the Border Constabulary—in June 1950 numbered about 135,000 men. This estimated total included 77,838 men in seven assault infantry divi-

---

[10] ATIS Res Supp Interrog Rpts, Issue 99 (N.K. *12th Div*), pp. 41–44; GHQ FEC, History of the N.K. Army, p. 23.

[11] GHQ FEC, History of the N.K. Army, p. 24; ATIS Res Supp Interrog Rpts, Issue 104 (N.K. *10th* and *13th Divs*), pp. 43, 57.

[12] ATIS Res Supp Interrog Rpts, Issue 4 (N.K. *105th Armd Div*), pp. 27–37.

[13] *Ibid.*, Issue 99 (N.K. *12th Div*), p. 42.

[14] DA Intel Rev, Mar 51, Nr 178, p. 38.

sions, 6,000 in the tank brigade, 3,000 in an independent infantry regiment, 2,000 in a motorcycle regiment, 23,000 in three reserve divisions, 18,600 in the Border Constabulary, and 5,000 in Army and I and II Corps Headquarters.[15]

The North Korean infantry division at full strength numbered 11,000 men. It was a triangular division composed of three rifle regiments, each regiment having three battalions.[16] The division had as integral parts an artillery regiment and a self-propelled gun battalion.

---

[15] The estimate of 135,000 is based on the following tabulation, drawn principally from N.K. PW interrogation reports:

Total	135,438
1st Div	11,000
2d Div	10,838
3d Div	11,000
4th Div	11,000
5th Div	11,000
6th Div	11,000
7th (12th) Div	12,000
10th Div	6,000
13th Div	6,000
15th Div	11,000
766th Ind Inf Unit	3,000
12th MTsP (Motorcycle Regt)	*2,000
105th Armored Brig	6,000
B.C. 1st Brig	5,000
B.C. 2d Brig	*2,600
B.C. 3d Brig	*4,000
B.C. 5th Brig	*3,000
B.C. 7th Brig	*4,000
Army, I and II Corps Hq	*5,000

* Indicates the figure is based on U.S. military intelligence or strong inferential data but not on extensive PW reports or order of battle documents. No figure for the strength of II Corps, organized about 12 June 1950, has been found. The strength for Army, I, and II Corps Headquarters possibly should be increased to 6,000–7,000. N.K. I Corps was activated about 10 June 1950. See GHQ FEC, History of the N.K. Army, pp. 41–43. According to some PW reports, there was a 17th Motorcycle Regiment in the enemy's order of battle at the beginning of the invasion.

The KMAG report for the semiannual period ending 15 June 1950 gives a total North Korean ground force estimate of 117,357 men, including 64,372 for the North Korea People's Army and 27,600 for the Border Constabulary. The ROK Army G-2 estimate of North Korean strength, according to Capt. Frederick C. Schwarze (Asst G-2 adviser to ROK Army in Seoul when the invasion occurred) was 175,000. Schwarze, Notes for author.

[16] The 12th Division had a strength of 12,000.

There were also medical, signal, antitank, engineer, and training battalions, and reconnaissance and transport companies.

The artillery support of the North Korean division in 1950 closely resembled that of the older type of Soviet division in World War II. A division had 12 122-mm. howitzers, 24 76-mm. guns, 12 SU-76 self-propelled guns, 12 45-mm. antitank guns, and 36 14.5-mm. antitank rifles. In addition, the regiments and battalions had their own supporting weapons. Each regiment, for instance, had 6 120-mm. mortars, 4 76-mm. howitzers, and 6 45-mm. antitank guns. Each battalion had 9 82-mm. mortars, 2 45-mm. antitank guns, and 9 14.5-mm. antitank rifles. The companies had their own 61-mm. mortars. A North Korean rifle regiment at full strength numbered 2,794 men—204 officers, 711 noncommissioned officers, and 1,879 privates.[17]

From the beginning the Soviet Union had been the sponsor for the NKPA and had provided it with the sinews of war. Most important at first were the Russian-built T34 tanks of the *105th Armored Brigade*. The T34 was a standard medium tank in the Soviet Army at the end of World War II. The Russians first used this tank against the Germans in July 1941. Guderian gives it the credit for stopping his drive on Tula and Moscow.[18] The T34 weighed 32 tons, was of low silhouette, had a

---

[17] ATIS Res Supp Interrog Rpts, Issue 106 (N.K. Arty), Chart, p. 32; Issue 100 (N.K. 9th Div), p. 49; GHQ FEC, History of the N.K. Army, Charts 3b–8.

[18] General Heinz Guderian, *Panzer Leader* (New York: E. P. Dutton & Co., Inc., 1952), pp. 162, 233–38.

broad tread, and was protected by heavy armor plate. It mounted an 85-mm. gun and carried two 7.62-mm. machine guns, one mounted on the bow and the other coaxially with the gun.[19]

Other ordnance items supplied to the NKPA by the Soviets included 76-mm. and 122-mm. howitzers; 122-mm. guns; 76-mm. self-propelled guns; 45-mm. antitank guns; 61-mm., 82-mm., and 120-mm. mortars; small arms; ammunition for these weapons; and grenades. From the Soviet Union North Korea also received trucks, jeeps, radios, and fire control, signal, and medical equipment.[20]

In the spring of 1950 the Soviet Union made particularly large shipments of arms and military supplies to North Korea. One captured North Korean supply officer stated that in May 1950, when he went to Ch'ongjin to get supplies for the N.K. *5th Division*, Soviet merchant ships were unloading weapons and ammunition, and that trucks crowded the harbor waterfront area. Korean-speaking crew members told him the ships had come from Vladivostok. Markings on some of the North Korean equipment captured in the first few months of the Korean War show that it was manufactured in the Soviet Union in 1949–50 and, accordingly, could not have been matériel left behind in 1948 when the occupation forces withdrew from North Korea, as the Soviets have claimed.[21]

North Korea began the war with about 180 aircraft, all supplied by Russia. Of these about 60 were YAK trainers; 40, YAK fighters; 70, attack bombers; and 10, reconnaissance planes. The North Korean Navy had approximately 16 patrol craft of various types and a few coastwise steamers reportedly equipped with light deck guns.[22]

The Republic of Korea Armed Forces

In June 1950 President Syngman Rhee was Commander in Chief of the South Korean Army. Under him was Sihn Sung Mo, the Minister of National Defense. The Deputy Commander in Chief actually in command of the Army was Maj. Gen. Chae Byong Duk.

The origins and development of an

---

[19] Not until the end of the third week of the war did American intelligence settle on the identification of the T34 tank.

Characteristics of the Russian-built T34 medium tank used by the North Koreans:

```
Weight (combat-loaded)_____35 short tons
Length (not including gun)_____19.7 feet
Width (over-all)_____9.8 feet
Width (between track centers)_____8.0 feet
Height (to top of turret)_____7.9 feet
Ground clearance_____1.3 feet
Turret traverse_____360° hand and electric
Rate of fire (85-mm. gun)_____7–8 rounds per minute
Ammunition carried_____85-mm. 55 rounds
                                      7.62-mm., 2,745 rounds
Engine
    Type_____12 cylinder, Diesel
    Horsepower_____493
Fuel
    Type_____Diesel
    Capacity (main tanks)_____143 gallons
Performance
    Maximum speed_____30–34 miles per hour
Source: EUSAK WD, 8 Sep 50, an. 1, to G–2 PIR 58.
```

[20] ATIS Res Supp Interrog Rpts, Issue 106 (N.K. Arty), pp. 1–40; DA Intel Rev, Mar 51, Nr 178, pp. 54, 56; *Ibid.*, Jun 51, Nr 181, pp. 26–27; Rpt, USMAG to ROK, 1 Jan–15 Jun 50, sec. III, p. 6.

[21] ATIS Res Supp Interrog Rpts, Issue 96 (N.K. *5th Div*), p. 38; GHQ FEC, History of the N.K. Army, p. 24; DA Intel Rev, Mar 51, Nr 178, pp. 54–56.

[22] Rpt, USMAG to ROK, 1 Jan–15 Jun 50, sec. III, p. 6; Capt Walter Karig, Comdr Malcolm W. Cagle, and Lt. Comdr Frank A. Manson, "Battle Report Series," vol. VI, *Battle Report, The War in Korea* (New York and Toronto: Farrar and Rinehart, 1952), p. 67.

armed force in South Korea had their roots, as in North Korea, in the occupation period after World War II. At first the principal objects of the U.S. occupation were to secure the surrender of the Japanese troops south of the 38th Parallel, return them to Japan, and preserve law and order until such time as the Koreans could do this for themselves.

In January 1946 a Korean constabulary was authorized and established. This organization took form so slowly that a year later it numbered only 5,000 men. By April 1947, however, it had doubled in strength and by July of that year it had reached 15,000. The constabulary became the Republic of Korea (ROK) Army in August 1948 and grew so rapidly in the next few months that by January 1949 it numbered more than 60,000 men.[23] In March 1949 the Republic of Korea had an Army of 65,000, a Coast Guard of 4,000, and a police force of 45,000—a total security force of about 114,000 men. The United States had equipped about 50,000 men in the Army with standard infantry-type weapons and matériel, including the M1 rifle and 60-mm. and 81-mm. mortars.[24]

Upon withdrawal of the last of the U.S. occupation force at the end of June 1949 a group of 482 United States military advisers began working with the South Korean Army. This small group of U.S. Army officers and enlisted men, established on 1 July 1949 with an authorized strength of 500 men, was called the United States Korean Military Advisory Group to the Republic of Korea (KMAG). Its mission was "to advise the government of the Republic of Korea in the continued development of the Security Forces of that government."[25] KMAG was an integral part of the American Mission in Korea (AMIK) and, as such, came under the control of Ambassador Muccio. In matters purely military, however, it was authorized to report directly to the Department of the Army and, after co-ordinating with Ambassador Muccio, to inform General MacArthur, the Commander in Chief, Far East (CINCFE), of military matters.

In April 1950 the South Korean Government began the formation of combat police battalions to relieve the Army of internal security missions, but of twenty-one battalions planned only one, that activated at Yongwol on 10 April 1950 to provide protection for the power plant, coal mines, and other vital resources in that vicinity, was in existence when the war started.

By June 1950 the Republic of Korea armed forces consisted of the following: Army, 94,808; Coast Guard, 6,145; Air

---

[23] Sawyer, KMAG MS, pts. I and II. This is the best available study on KMAG policies and operations in Korea.

[24] *The Conflict in Korea*, p. 9.

[25] Rpt, USMAG to ROK, 1 Jan–15 Jun 50, Annex I. The Department of the Army in a message to General MacArthur dated 10 June 1949 established KMAG. It became operational in Korea on 1 July 1949. Msg, G-3 Plans and Opns to CINCFE WARX90049, 10 Jun 49. The KMAG personnel present for duty 1 July 1949 numbered 482: 165 officers, 4 warrant officers, and 313 enlisted men. Sawyer, KMAG MS; Msg, WX90992, DA to CG USAFIK, 2 Jul 49, cited in General Headquarters Support and Participation, 25 June 1950–30 April 1951, by Maj. James F. Schnabel (hereafter cited as Schnabel, FEC, GHQ Support and Participation in Korean War), ch. I, pp. 4–5. This is Volume I of Far East Command, United Nations Command, History of the Korean War, in OCMH.

SOUTH KOREAN TROOPS *stand for inspection by the Korean Minister of Defense and members of KMAG at Ch'unch'on in July 1949.*

Force, 1,865; National Police, 48,273. When the war began nearly a month later the Army had a strength of about 98,000, composed of approximately 65,000 combat troops and 33,000 headquarters and service troops.[26]

In June 1950 the combat troops of the ROK Army were organized into eight divisions: the 1st, 2d, 3d, 5th, 6th, 7th, 8th, and Capital Divisions. Five of them, the 1st, 2d, 6th, 7th, and Capital, had 3 regiments; two divisions, the 3d and 8th, had 2 regiments; and one division, the 5th, had 2 regiments and 1 battalion. Only four divisions, the 1st, 6th, 7th, and Capital, were near full strength of 10,000 men.

The organization of the combat divisions and their present-for-duty strength are shown in Table 1. For some unknown reason the ROK Army headquarters report, on which Table 1 is based, does not include the 17th Regiment. It numbered about 2,500 men and was

---

[26] Schnabel, FEC, GHQ Support and Participation in Korean War, sec. V, p. 16; Interv, author with Maj James W. Hausman, 12 Jan 52. Major Hausman was KMAG adviser to the ROK Army Chief of Staff in June 1950. KMAG figures for 1 June give a total of about 67,000 in the eight infantry divisions.

ARMED FORCES OF NORTH AND SOUTH KOREA

TABLE 1—ROK COMBAT DIVISIONS, 1 JUNE 1950

Unit	Present	Division Total
Total	-----	64,697
1st Infantry Division	1,882	9,715
Col. Paik Sun Yup, CO		
11th Regiment	2,527	
12th Regiment	2,728	
13th Regiment	2,578	
2d Infantry Division	1,397	7,910
Brig. Gen. Lee Hyung Koon, CO		
5th Regiment	1,895	
16th Regiment	2,408	
25th Regiment	2,210	
3d Infantry Division	1,826	7,059
Col. Yu Sung Yul, CO (Brig. Gen. Lee Joon Shik took command of 3d Div on 10 Jul 50).		
22d Regiment	2,646	
23d Regiment	2,587	
5th Infantry Division	2,274	7,276
Maj. Gen. Lee Ung Joon, CO		
15th Regiment	2,119	
20th Regiment	2,185	
1st Separate Battalion	698	
6th Infantry Division	2,245	9,112
Col. Kim Chong O, CO		
7th Regiment	2,411	
8th Regiment	2,288	
19th Regiment	2,168	
7th Infantry Division	2,278	9,698
Brig. Gen. Yu Jae Hung, CO		
1st Regiment	2,514	
3d Regiment	2,487	
9th Regiment	2,419	
8th Infantry Division	1,923	6,866
Col. Lee Jung Il, CO		
10th Regiment	2,476	
21st Regiment	2,467	
Capital Infantry Division	1,668	7,061
Col. Lee Chong Chan, CO		
2d Regiment	2,615	
18th Regiment	2,778	
17th Regiment	(2,500)	
Col. Paik In Yup, CO		

Source: ROK Army Hq, Consolidated Morning Rpt, 1 Jun 50.

part of the Capital Division in the paper organization of the Army.[27]

In the early summer of 1950 the 1st, 7th, 6th, and 8th Divisions, considered the best in the ROK Army, held positions along the Parallel in the order named, from west to east. Beyond the 1st Division at the extreme western end of the line was the 17th Regiment of the Capital Division on the Ongjin Peninsula. The other four divisions were scattered about the interior and southern parts of the country, three of them engaged in antiguerrilla activity and training in small unit tactics. The Capital Division's headquarters was at Seoul, the 2d's at Ch'ongju near Taejon, the 3d's at Taegu, and the 5th's at Kwangju in southwest Korea.[28]

The South Korean divisions along the Parallel were equipped mostly with the United States M1 rifle, .30-caliber carbine, 60-mm. and 81-mm. mortars, 2.36-in. rocket launchers, 37-mm. antitank guns, and 105-mm. howitzers M3. The howitzers had been used in the U.S. infantry cannon companies in World War II. They had a shorter barrel than the regular 105-mm. howitzer M2, possessed no armor shield, and had an effective range of only 7,250 yards (8,200 yards maximum range) as compared to 12,500 yards for the 105-mm. howitzer M2. There were five battalions of these howitzers organized into the usual headquarters and service companies and three firing batteries of five howitzers each. The 1st, 2d, 6th, 7th, and 8th Divisions each had a battalion of the howitzers. A sixth battalion was being formed when the war started.[29] Of 91 howitzers on hand 15 June 1950, 89 were serviceable. The South Korean armed forces had no tanks, no medium artillery, no 4.2-in. mortars, no recoilless rifles, and no fighter aircraft or bombers. The divisions engaged in fighting guerrillas in the eastern and southern mountains had a miscellany of small arms, including many Japanese Model 99 World War II rifles.

In October of 1949 the ROK Minister of Defense had requested 189 M26 tanks but the acting chief of KMAG told him the KMAG staff held the view that the Korean terrain and the condition of roads and bridges would not lend themselves to efficient tank operations. About the same time a KMAG officer pointed out to Ambassador Muccio that the equipment provided the

---

[27] Interv, author with Maj Gen Chang Chang Kuk (Military Attaché, Korean Embassy, Washington), 14 Oct 53. General Chang was G-3 of the ROK Army in June 1950. Rpt, USMAG to ROK, 1 Jan-15 Jun 50, Annex IX.

Major Hausman says he always considered 10,000 as the table of organization strength of a South Korean division. Some references give the figure as 9,500. General Chang said the ROK Army considered 9,000-9,500 as T/O strength of a division in June 1950. Spelling of names and rank as of June 1950 checked and corrected by General Chang and by General Paik Sun Yup, ROK Chief of Staff, in MS review comments, 11 July 1958. In accordance with Korean usage, the surnames come first, the name Syngman Rhee is one of the rare exceptions to this rule. Korean personal names ordinarily consist of three monosyllables.

[28] Rpt, USMAG to ROK, 1 Jan-15 Jun 50; EUSAK WD, Prologue, 25 Jun-12 Jul 50; Interv, author with Col Rollins S. Emmerich, 5 Dec 51 (Emmerich was KMAG senior adviser to the ROK 3d Division in 1950).

[29] Rpt, USMAG to ROK, 1 Jan-30 Jun 50, Annex X; Interv, author with Maj Hausman; Col William H. S. Wright, Notes for author, 1952 (Wright was CofS and Acting CO of KMAG at the time of the invasion).

ARMED FORCES OF NORTH AND SOUTH KOREA

ROK's was not adequate to maintain the border, and he cited the fact that North Korean artillery outranged by several thousand yards the ROK 105-mm. howitzer M3 and shelled ROK positions at will while being out of range of retaliatory fire.

The ROK Army in June 1950 had among its heavier weapons 27 armored cars; something more than 700 artillery pieces and mortars, including 105-mm. howitzers and 81-mm. and 60-mm. mortars; about 140 antitank guns; and approximately 1,900 2.36-in. bazookas. In June 1950 it had about 2,100 serviceable U.S. Army motor vehicles for transportation, divided between about 830 2½-ton trucks and 1,300 ¼-ton trucks (jeeps). Motor maintenance was of a low order.[30]

The South Korean Air Force in June 1950 consisted of a single flight group of 12 liaison-type aircraft and 10 advance trainers (AT6). Maj. Dean E. Hess, KMAG adviser to the South Korean Air Force, had a few (approximately 10) old F-51 (Mustang) planes under his control but no South Korean pilots had yet qualified to fly combat missions. These planes were given to the ROK Air Force on 26 June 1950.

On 25 June the South Korean Navy consisted of a patrol craft (PC701) recently purchased in the United States from surplus vessels, 3 other similar patrol craft at Hawaii en route to Korea, 1 LST, 15 former U.S. mine sweepers, 10 former Japanese mine layers, and various other small craft.[31]

In June 1950 the ROK Army supply of artillery and mortar ammunition on hand was small and would be exhausted by a few days of combat. An estimated 15 percent of the weapons and 35 percent of the vehicles in the ROK Army were unserviceable. The six months' supply of spare parts originally provided by the United States was exhausted.[32]

The state of training of the ROK Army is reflected in the Chief of KMAG's report that a majority of the units of the South Korean Army had completed small unit training at company level and were engaged in battalion training.

In summary, the North Korean Army in June 1950 was clearly superior to the South Korean in several respects: the North Koreans had 150 excellent medium tanks mounting 85-mm. guns, the South Koreans had no tanks; the North Koreans had three types of artillery—the 122-mm. howitzer, the 76-mm. self-propelled gun, and the 76-mm. divisional gun with a maximum range of more than 14,000 yards which greatly outranged the 105-mm. howitzer M3 of the ROK Army with its maximum range of about 8,200 yards. In number of divisional artillery pieces, the North Koreans exceeded the South Korean on an

---

[30] The original U.S. commitment in July 1949 was to supply the Korean Army with an issue of equipment and a six months' supply of spare parts for a force of 50,000. See Memo, Gen Roberts to All Advisers, KMAG, 5 May 50, sub: Korean Army Logistical Situation. The Department of State gives $57,000,000 as the value of military equipment given to South Korea before its invasion by North Korea, with a replacement cost at time of delivery to South Korea of $110,000,000. See *The Conflict in Korea*, p. 10.

[31] Karig, et al., *Battle Report, The War in Korea*, p. 68.

[32] Rpt, USMAG to ROK, 1 Jan–15 Jun 50, sec. VI, pp. 18–22.

average of three to one.³³ The North Koreans had a small tactical air force, the South Koreans had none. In the North Korean assault formations there were 89,000 combat troops as against approximately 65,000 in the South Korean divisions. Also, North Korea had an additional 18,600 trained troops in its Border Constabulary and 23,000 partially trained troops in three reserve divisions. In comparison, South Korea had about 45,000 national police, but they were not trained or armed for tactical use. The small coast guard or navy of each side just about canceled each other and were relatively unimportant.

The superiority of the North Korean Army over the South Korean in these several respects was not generally recognized, however, by United States military authorities before the invasion. In fact, there was the general feeling, apparently shared by Brig. Gen. William L. Roberts, Chief of KMAG, on the eve of invasion that if attacked from North Korea the ROK Army would have no trouble in repelling the invaders.

---

³³ The maximum range of the Soviet artillery used by the N.K. Army in June 1950 was as follows: 122-mm. howitzer, 12,904 yards; 76-mm. SP gun, 12,400 yards; 76-mm. divisional gun, 14,545 yards. The average North Korean division had 48 122-mm. howitzers, 76-mm. SP and non-SP guns; the ROK division had 15 105-mm. howitzers M3.

CHAPTER III

Invasion Across the Parallel

> He, therefore, who desires peace, should prepare for war. He who aspires to victory, should spare no pains to train his soldiers. And he who hopes for success, should fight on principle, not chance. No one dares to offend or insult a power of known superiority in action.
>
> VEGETIUS, *Military Institutions of the Romans*

On 8 June 1950 the P'yongyang newspapers published a manifesto which the Central Committee of the United Democratic Patriotic Front had adopted the day before proclaiming as an objective a parliament to be elected in early August from North and South Korea and to meet in Seoul on 15 August, the fifth anniversary of the liberation of Korea from Japanese rule.[1] It would appear from this manifesto that Premier Kim Il Sung and his Soviet advisers expected that all of Korea would be overrun, occupied, and "elections" held in time to establish a new government of a "united" Korea in Seoul by mid-August.

During the period 15–24 June the North Korean Command moved all Regular Army divisions to the close vicinity of the 38th Parallel, and deployed them along their respective planned lines of departure for the attack on South Korea. Some of these units came from the distant north. Altogether, approximately 80,000 men with their equipment joined those already along the Parallel. They succeeded in taking their positions for the assault without being detected. The attack units included 7 infantry divisions, 1 armored brigade, 1 separate infantry regiment, 1 motorcycle regiment, and 1 Border Constabulary brigade. This force numbered approximately 90,000 men supported by 150 T34 tanks. General Chai Ung Jun commanded it. All the thrusts were to follow major roads. In an arc of forty miles stretching from Kaesong on the west to Ch'orwon on the east the North Koreans concentrated more than half their infantry and artillery and most of their tanks for a converging attack on Seoul. The main attack was to follow the Uijongbu Corridor, an ancient invasion route leading straight south to Seoul.[2]

In preparation for the attack the chief

---

[1] New York *Times*, June 27, 1950. An enterprising *Times* employee found this manifesto and accompanying *Tass* article in *Izvestia*, June 10, 1950, datelined Pyong [P'yongyang], in the Library of Congress and had it translated from the Russian.

[2] GHQ FEC, History of the N.K. Army; ATIS Res Supp Interrog Rpts for the various North Korean divisions.

of the NKPA Intelligence Section on 18 June issued Reconnaissance Order 1, in the Russian language, to the chief of staff of the N.K. *4th Division,* requiring that information of enemy defensive positions guarding the approach to the Uijongbu Corridor be obtained and substantiated before the attack began.[3] Similar orders bearing the same date, modified only to relate to the situation on their immediate front, were sent by the same officer to the *1st, 2d, 3d, 6th,* and *7th Divisions,* the *12th Motorcycle Regiment,* and the BC *3d Brigade.* No doubt such orders also went to the *5th Division* and possibly other units.[4]

On 22 June Maj. Gen. Lee Kwon Mu, commanding the N.K. *4th Division,* issued his operation order in the Korean language for the attack down the Uijongbu Corridor. He stated that the *1st Division* on his right and the *3d Division* on his left would join in the attack leading to Seoul. Tanks and self-propelled artillery with engineer support were to lead it. Preparations were to be completed by midnight 23 June. After penetrating the South Korean defensive positions, the division was to advance to the Uijongbu–Seoul area.[5] Other assault units apparently received their attack orders about the same time.

The North Korean attack units had arrived at their concentration points generally on 23 June and, by 24 June, were poised at their lines of departure for attack. Officers told their men that they were on maneuvers but most of the latter realized by 23–24 June that it was war.[6]

Destined to bear the brunt of this impending attack were elements of four ROK divisions and a regiment stationed along the south side of the Parallel in their accustomed defensive border positions. They had no knowledge of the impending attack although they had made many predictions in the past that there would be one. As recently as 12 June the U.N. Commission in Korea had questioned officers of General Roberts' KMAG staff concerning warnings the ROK Army had given of an imminent attack. A United States intelligence agency on 19 June had information pointing to North Korean preparation for an offensive, but it was not used for an estimate of the situation. The American officers did not think an attack was imminent. If one did come, they expected the South Koreans to repel it.[7] The South Koreans themselves did not share this optimism, pointing to the fighter planes, tanks, and superior artillery possessed by the North Koreans, and their numerically superior Army. In June 1950, before and immediately after the North Korean attack, several published articles based on interviews with KMAG officers reflect the opinion held apparently by General Roberts and most of his KMAG advisers that the ROK Army would be able to meet any test the

---

[3] ATIS Res Supp Interrog Rpts, Issue 2 (Documentary Evidence of N.K. Aggression), pt. 2; *The Conflict in Korea,* pp. 26–28, 32–36.

[4] ATIS Res Supp Interrog Rpts, Issue 2, pt. 2, pp. 12–23.

[5] *Ibid.,* Opn Orders *4th Inf Div,* 22 Jun 50, Transl 200045. This document includes an annex giving a breakdown of regimental attack plans. *The Conflict in Korea,* pages 28–32, gives part of the document.

[6] *The Conflict in Korea,* pp. 12–69; ATIS Enemy Documents, Korean Opns, Issue 1, item 3, p. 37; *Ibid.,* item 6, p. 43.

[7] Schnabel, Theater Command, ch. IV, p. 5; *New York Times,* Sept. 15, 1950.

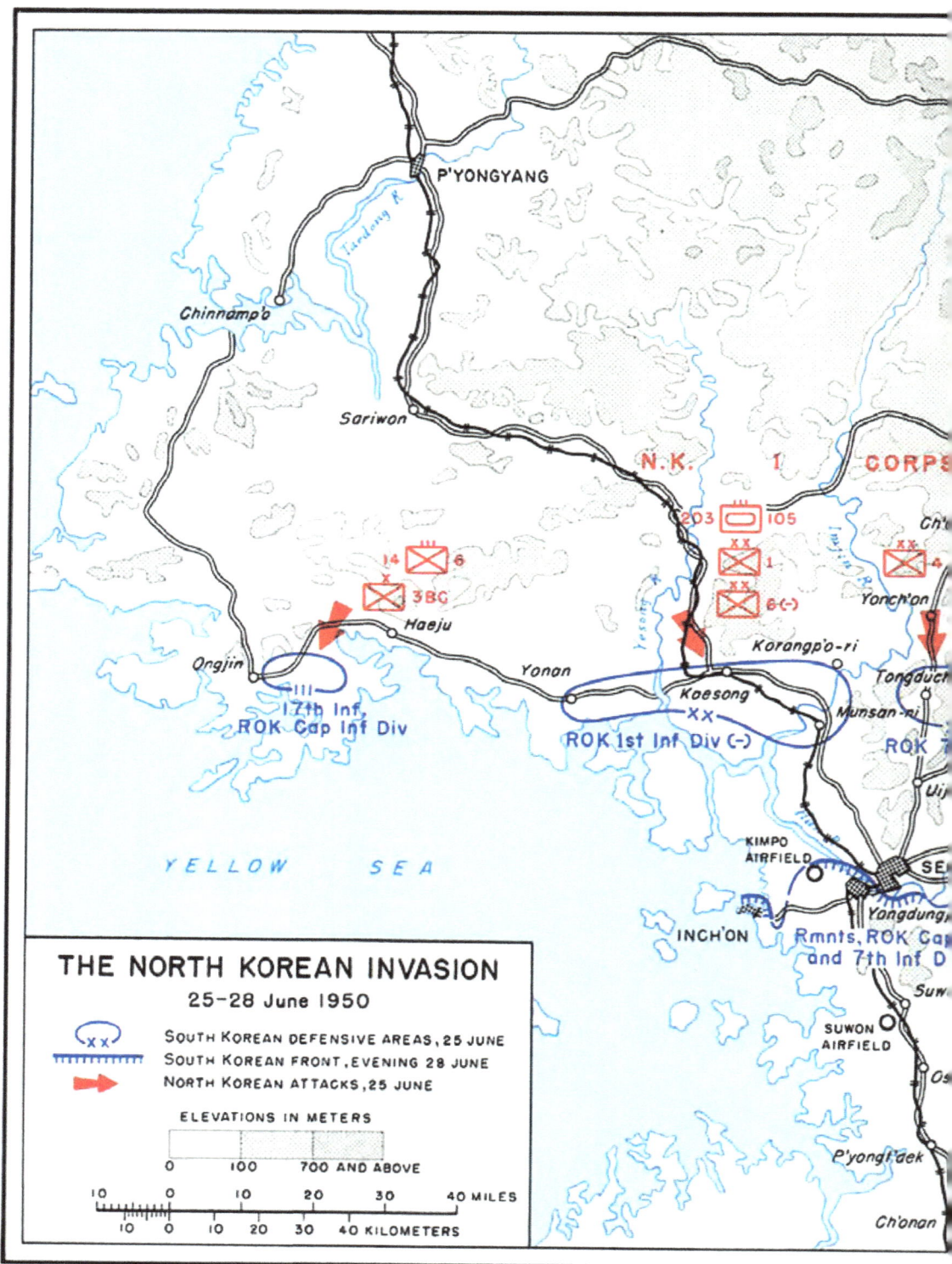

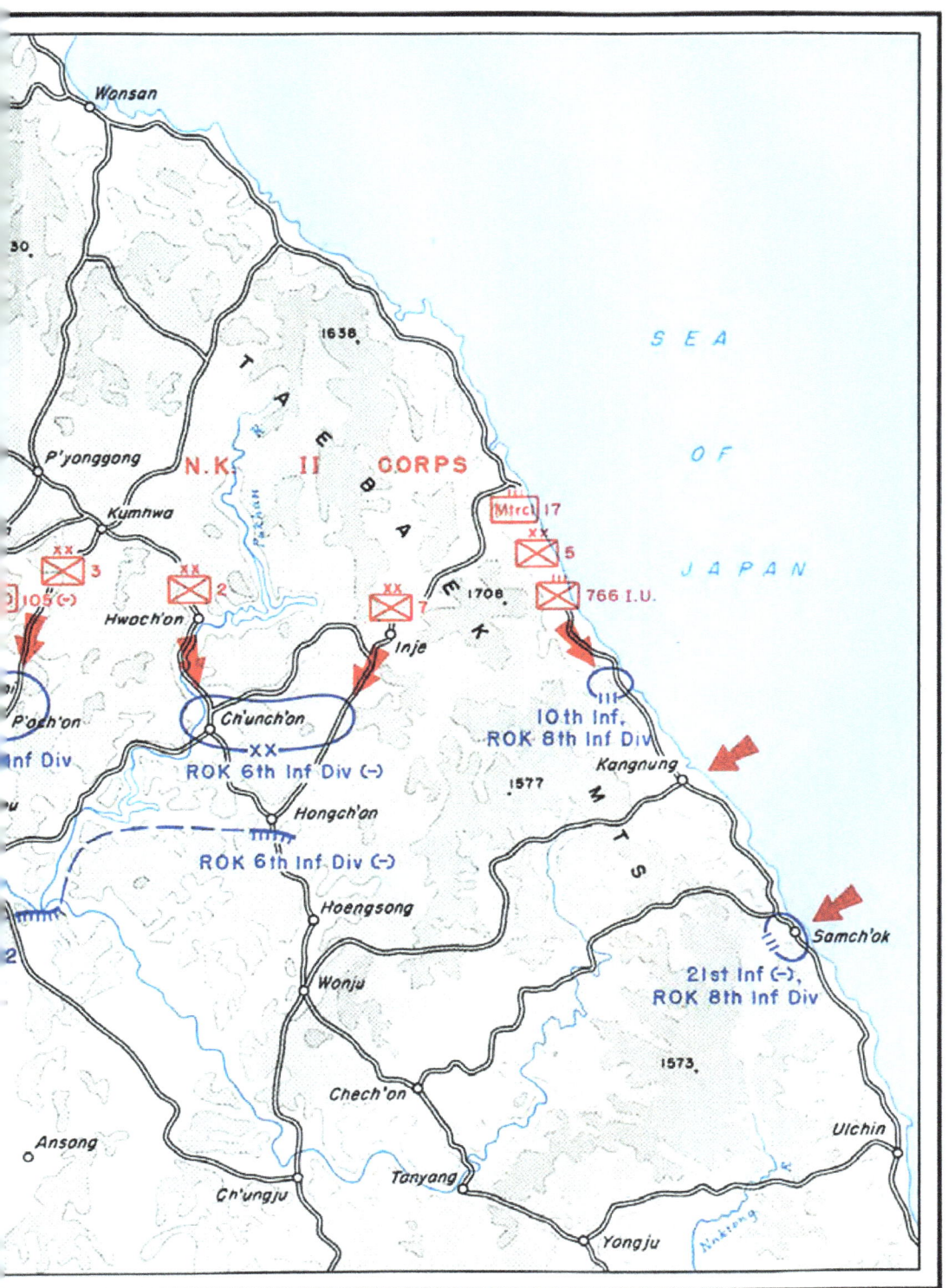

MAP I

North Korean Army might impose on it.[8]

Invasion

Scattered but heavy rains fell along the 38th Parallel in the predawn darkness of Sunday, 25 June 1950. Farther south, at Seoul, the day dawned overcast but with only light occasional showers. The summer monsoon season had just begun. Rain—heavy rain—might be expected to sweep over the variously tinted green of the rice paddies and the barren gray-brown mountain slopes of South Korea during the coming weeks.

Along the dark, rain-soaked Parallel, North Korean artillery and mortars broke the early morning stillness. It was about 0400. The precise moment of opening enemy fire varied perhaps as much as an hour at different points across the width of the peninsula, but everywhere it signaled a co-ordinated attack from coast to coast. The sequence of attack seemed to progress from west to east, with the earliest attack striking the Ongjin Peninsula at approximately 0400.[9] (*Map I*)

The blow fell unexpectedly on the South Koreans. Many of the officers and some men, as well as many of the KMAG advisers, were in Seoul and other towns on weekend passes.[10] And even though four divisions and one regiment were stationed near the border, only one regiment of each division and one battalion of the separate regiment were actually in the defensive positions at the Parallel. The remainder of these organizations were in reserve positions ten to thirty miles below the Parallel. Accordingly, the onslaught of the North Korea People's Army struck a surprised garrison in thinly held defensive positions.

After the North Korean attack was well under way, the P'yongyang radio broadcast at 1100 an announcement that the North Korean Government had declared war against South Korea as a result of an invasion by South Korean puppet forces ordered by "the bandit traitor Syngman Rhee."[11] The broadcast said the North Korea People's Army had struck back in self-defense and had begun a "righteous invasion." Syngman Rhee, it stated, would be arrested and executed.[12] Shortly after noon, at 1335, Premier Kim Il Sung, of North Korea, claimed in a radio broadcast that South Korea had rejected every North Korean proposal for peaceful unification, had attacked North Korea that morning in the area of Haeju above the Ongjin Peninsula, and would have to take the conse-

---

[8] Norman Bartlett, *With the Australians in Korea* (Canberra: Australian War Memorial, 1954), p. 166; *Time* Magazine, June 5, 1950, pp. 26–27. The New York *Times*, June 26, 1950, gives General Roberts' views as reported by Lindsay Parrott in Tokyo.

[9] The time used is for the place where the event occurred unless otherwise noted. Korean time is fourteen hours later than New York and Washington EST and thirteen hours later than EDT. For example, 0400 25 June in Korea would be 1400 24 June in New York and Washington EST.

[10] Col Walter Greenwood, Jr., Statement of Events 0430, 25 June–1200, 28 June 1950, for Capt Robert K. Sawyer, with Ltr to Sawyer, 22 Feb 54. Colonel Greenwood was Deputy Chief of Staff, KMAG, June 1950.

[11] GHQ FEC, Annual Narrative Historical Report, 1 Jan–31 Oct 50, p. 8; New York *Times*, June 25, 1950. That the North Korean Government actually made a declaration of war has never been verified.

[12] Transcript of the radio broadcast in 24th Div G–2 Jnl, 25 Jun.

quences of the North Korean counterattacks.[13]

The North Korean attack against the Ongjin Peninsula on the west coast, northwest of Seoul, began about 0400 with a heavy artillery and mortar barrage and small arms fire delivered by the *14th Regiment* of the N.K. *6th Division* and the BC *3d Brigade*. The ground attack came half an hour later across the Parallel without armored support. It struck the positions held by a battalion of the ROK 17th Regiment commanded by Col. Paik In Yup.[14]

The first message from the vicinity of the Parallel received by the American Advisory Group in Seoul came by radio about 0600 from five advisers with the ROK 17th Regiment on the Ongjin Peninsula. They reported the regiment was under heavy attack and about to be overrun.[15] Before 0900 another message came from them requesting air evacuation. Two KMAG aviators, Maj. Lloyd Swink and Lt. Frank Brown, volunteered to fly their L-5 planes from Seoul. They succeeded in bringing the five Americans out in a single trip.[16]

The Ongjin Peninsula, cut off by water from the rest of South Korea, never had been considered defensible in case of a North Korean attack. Before the day ended, plans previously made were executed to evacuate the ROK 17th Regiment. Two LST's from Inch'on joined one already offshore, and on Monday, 26 June, they evacuated Col. Paik In Yup and most of two battalions—in all about 1,750 men. The other battalion was completely lost in the early fighting.[17]

The *14th Regiment, 6th Division*, turned over the Ongjin Peninsula area to security forces of the BC *3d Brigade* on the second day and immediately departed by way of Haeju and Kaesong to rejoin its division.[18]

East of the Ongjin Peninsula, Kaesong, the ancient capital of Korea, lay two miles south of the Parallel on the main Seoul-P'yongyang highway and railroad. Two battalions of the 12th Regiment, ROK 1st Division, held positions just north of the town. The other battalion of the regiment was at Yonan, the center of a rich rice-growing area some twenty miles westward. The 13th Regiment held Korangp'o-ri, fifteen air miles east of Kaesong above the Imjin River, and the river crossing below the city. The 11th Regiment, in reserve, and division headquarters were at Suisak, a small village and cantonment area a few miles north of Seoul. Lt. Col. Lloyd H. Rockwell, senior adviser to the ROK 1st Division, and its youthful commander, Col. Paik Sun Yup, had decided some time earlier that the only defense line the division could hold in case of attack was south of the Imjin River.[19]

Songak-san (Hill 475), a mountain shaped like a capital T with its stem running east-west, dominated Kaesong

---

[13] Dept of State Pub 3922, *United States Policy in the Korean Crisis*, Document 10 (U.N. Commission on Korea, Report to the Secretary-General), pp. 18–20.

[14] ATIS Res Supp Interrog Rpts, Issue 100 (N.K. *6th Div*), p. 32; Interv, author with Hausman, 12 Jan 52; KMAG G-2 Unit Hist, 25 Jun 50.

[15] Sawyer, KMAG MS, pt. III.

[16] *Ibid.*; Statement, Greenwood for Sawyer.

[17] Interv, Schnabel with Schwarze; DA Wkly Intel Rpt, 30 Jun 50, Nr 71, p. 10.

[18] ATIS Res Supp Interrog Rpts, Issue 100 (N.K. *6th Div*), p. 33.

[19] Ltr, Col Rockwell to author, 21 May 54; Gen Paik Sun Yup, MS review comments, 11 Jul 58.

which lay two miles to the south of it. The 38th Parallel ran almost exactly along the crest of Songak-san, which the North Koreans had long since seized and fortified. In Kaesong the northbound main rail line linking Seoul-P'yongyang-Manchuria turned west for six miles and then, short of the Yesong River, bent north again across the Parallel.

Capt. Joseph R. Darrigo, assistant adviser to the ROK 12th Regiment, 1st Division, was the only American officer on the 38th Parallel the morning of 25 June. He occupied quarters in a house at the northeast edge of Kaesong, just below Songak-san. At daybreak, approximately 0500, Captain Darrigo awoke to the sound of artillery fire. Soon shell fragments and small arms fire were hitting his house. He jumped from bed, pulled on a pair of trousers, and, with shoes and shirt in hand, ran to the stairs where he was met by his Korean houseboy running up to awaken him. The two ran out of the house, jumped into Darrigo's jeep, and drove south into Kaesong. They encountered no troops, but the volume of fire indicated an enemy attack. Darrigo decided to continue south on the Munsan-ni Road to the Imjin River.

At the circle in the center of Kaesong small arms fire fell near Darrigo's jeep. Looking off to the west, Darrigo saw a startling sight—half a mile away, at the railroad station which was in plain view, North Korean soldiers were unloading from a train of perhaps fifteen cars. Some of these soldiers were already advancing toward the center of town. Darrigo estimated there were from two to three battalions, perhaps a regiment, of enemy troops on the train. The North Koreans obviously had relaid during the night previously pulled up track on their side of the Parallel and had now brought this force in behind the ROK's north of Kaesong while their artillery barrage and other infantry attacked frontally from Songak-san. The *13th* and *15th Regiments* of the N.K. *6th Division* delivered the attack on Kaesong.

Most of the ROK 12th Regiment troops at Kaesong and Yonan were killed or captured. Only two companies of the regiment escaped and reported to the division headquarters the next day. Kaesong was entirely in enemy hands by 0930. Darrigo, meanwhile, sped south out of Kaesong, reached the Imjin River safely, and crossed over to Munsan-ni.[20]

Back in Seoul, Colonel Rockwell awakened shortly after daylight that Sunday morning to the sound of pounding on the door of his home in the American compound where he was spending the weekend. Colonel Paik and a few of his staff officers were outside. They told Rockwell of the attack at the Parallel. Paik phoned his headquarters and ordered the 11th Regiment and other units to move immediately to Munsan-ni–Korangp'o-ri and occupy prearranged defensive positions. Colonel Rockwell and Colonel Paik then drove directly to Munsan-ni. The 11th Regiment moved rapidly and in good order from Suisak and took position on the left of the 13th

---

[20] Interv, author with Capt Joseph R. Darrigo, 5 Aug 53; Ltr, Maj William E. Hamilton to author, 29 Jul 53. Major Hamilton on 25 June 1950 was adviser to the ROK 12th Regiment. He said several ROK officers of the 12th Regiment who had escaped from Kaesong, including the regimental commander with whom he had talked, confirmed Darrigo's story of the North Korean entrance into Kaesong by train. See also, Ltr, Rockwell to author, 21 May 54; ATIS Res Supp Interrog Rpts, Issue 100 (N.K. *6th Div*), p. 32; 24th Div G-3 Jnl, 25 Jun 50.

Regiment, both thereby protecting the approaches to the Imjin bridge. There they engaged in bitter fighting, the 13th Regiment particularly distinguishing itself.[21]

Upon making a reconnaissance of the situation at Munsan-ni, Colonel Rockwell and Colonel Paik agreed they should blow the bridge over the Imjin River according to prearranged plans and Paik gave the order to destroy it after the 12th Regiment had withdrawn across it. A large body of the enemy so closely followed the regiment in its withdrawal, however, that this order was not executed and the bridge fell intact to the enemy.[22]

The *N.K. 1st Division* and supporting tanks of the *105th Armored Brigade* made the attack in the Munsan-ni–Korangp'o-ri area. At first some ROK soldiers of the 13th Regiment engaged in suicide tactics, hurling themselves and the high explosives they carried under the tanks. Others approached the tanks with satchel or pole charges. Still others mounted tanks and tried desperately to open the hatches with hooks to drop grenades inside. These men volunteered for this duty. They destroyed a few tanks but most of them were killed, and volunteers for this duty soon became scarce.[23]

The ROK 1st Division held its positions at Korangp'o-ri for nearly three days and then, outflanked and threatened with being cut off by the enemy divisions in the Uijongbu Corridor, it withdrew toward the Han River.

On 28 June, American fighter planes, under orders to attack any organized body of troops north of the Han River, mistakenly strafed and rocketed the ROK 1st Division, killing and wounding many soldiers. After the planes left, Colonel Paik got some of his officers and men together and told them, "You did not think the Americans would help us. Now you know better." [24]

The main North Korean attack, meanwhile, had come down the Uijongbu Corridor timed to coincide with the general attacks elsewhere. It got under way about 0530 on 25 June and was delivered by the *N.K. 4th* and *3d Infantry Divisions* and tanks of the *105th Armored Brigade*.[25] This attack developed along two roads which converged at Uijongbu and from there led into Seoul. The *N.K. 4th Division* drove straight south toward Tongduch'on-ni from the 38th Parallel near Yonch'on. The *N.K. 3d Division* came down the Kumhwa-Uijongbu-Seoul road, often called the P'och'on Road, which angled into Uijongbu from the northeast. The *107th Tank Regiment* of the *105th Armored Brigade* with about forty T34 tanks supported the *4th Division;* the *109th Tank*

---

[21] Ltr, Rockwell to author, 21 May 54; Interv, author with Darrigo, 5 Aug 53; Ltr, Hamilton to author, 21 Aug 53; Gen Paik, MS review comments, 11 Jul 58.

[22] Ltr, Rockwell to author, 21 May 54; Ltr, Hamilton to author, 21 Aug 53; Gen Paik, MS review comments, 11 Jul 58.

[23] Ltr, Rockwell to author, 21 May 54; Interv, author with Hausman, 12 Jan 52. Colonel Paik some days after the action gave Hausman an account of the Imjin River battle. Paik estimated that about ninety ROK soldiers gave their lives in attacks on enemy tanks.

[24] Interv, author with Hausman, 12 Jan 52 (related by Paik to Hausman).

[25] DA Intel Rev, Mar 51, Nr 178, p. 34; ATIS Res Supp Interrog Rpts, Issue 2 (Documentary Evidence of N.K. Aggression), pt. II, Opn Ord Nr 1, 4th Inf Div, 22 Jun 50; *Ibid.*, Issue 3 (Enemy Documents), p. 65; G–2 Periodic Rpt, 30 Jun 50, Reserve CP (N.K.); *The Conflict in Korea*, p. 28.

ENEMY APPROACH ROUTES *through Uijongbu Corridor.*

Regiment with another forty tanks supported the *3d Division* on the P'och'on Road.[26]

The 1st Regiment of the ROK 7th Division, disposed along the Parallel, received the initial blows of the N.K. *3d* and *4th Divisions*. In the early fighting it lost very heavily to enemy tanks and self-propelled guns. Behind it at P'och'on on the eastern road was the 9th Regiment; behind it at Tongduch'on-ni on the western road was the 3d Regiment. At 0830 a ROK officer at the front sent a radio message to the Minister of Defense in Seoul saying that the North Koreans in the vicinity of the Parallel were delivering a heavy artillery fire and a general attack, that they already had seized the contested points, and that he must have immediate reinforcements—that all ROK units were engaged.[27] The strong armored columns made steady gains on both roads, and people in Uijongbu, twenty miles north of Seoul, could hear the artillery fire of the two converging columns before the day ended.

At midmorning reports came in to

---

[26] ATIS Res Supp Interrog Rpts, Issue 4 (Enemy Forces), p. 37; *Ibid.*, Issue 2 (Documentary Evidence of N.K. Aggression), p. 45; Opn Plan, N.K. *4th Inf Div*, Opn Ord Nr 1, 221400 Jun 50; *Ibid.*, Issue 94 (N.K. *4th Div*); *Ibid.*, Issue 96 (N.K. *3d Div*).

[27] Interv, author with Gen Chang, 14 Oct 53; ATIS Res Supp Interrog Rpts, Issue 3 (Enemy Documents), p. 5, file 25 Jun–9 Jul 50.

Seoul that Kimpo Airfield was under air attack. A short time later, two enemy Russian-built YAK fighter planes appeared over the city and strafed its main street. In the afternoon, enemy planes again appeared over Kimpo and Seoul.[28]

Eastward across the peninsula, Ch'unch'on, like Kaesong, lay almost on the Parallel. Ch'unch'on was an important road center on the Pukhan River and the gateway to the best communication and transport net leading south through the mountains in the central part of Korea. The attacks thus far described had been carried out by elements of the N.K. *I Corps*. From Ch'unch'on eastward the N.K. *II Corps*, with headquarters at H'wachon north of Ch'unch'on, controlled the attack formations. The N.K. *2d Division* at H'wach'on moved down to the border, replacing a Border Constabulary unit, and the N.K. *7th Division* did likewise some miles farther eastward at Inje. The plan of attack was for the *2d Division* to capture Ch'unch'on by the afternoon of the first day; the *7th Division* was to drive directly for Hongch'on, some miles below the Parallel.[29]

The 7th Regiment of the ROK 6th Division guarded Ch'unch'on, a beautiful town spread out below Peacock Mountain atop which stood a well-known shrine with red lacquered pillars. Another regiment was disposed eastward guarding the approaches to Hoengsong. The third regiment, in reserve, was with division headquarters at Wonju, forty-five miles south of the Parallel.

The two assault regiments of the N.K. *2d Division* attacked Ch'unch'on early Sunday morning; the *6th Regiment* advanced along the river road, while the *4th Regiment* climbed over the mountains north of the city. From the outset, the ROK artillery was very effective and the enemy *6th Regiment* met fierce resistance. Before the day ended, the *2d Division's* reserve regiment, the *17th*, joined in the attack.[30] Lt. Col. Thomas D. McPhail, adviser to the ROK 6th Division, proceeded to Ch'unch'on from Wonju in the morning after he received word that the North Koreans had crossed the Parallel. Late in the day the ROK reserve regiment arrived from Wonju. A factor of importance in Ch'unch'on's defense was that no passes had been issued to ROK personnel and the positions there were fully manned when the attack came.

The battle for Ch'unch'on was going against the North Koreans. From dug-in concrete pillboxes on the high ridge just north of the town the ROK 6th Division continued to repel the enemy attack. The failure of the N.K. *2d Division* to capture Ch'unch'on the first day, as ordered, caused the N.K. *II Corps* to change the attack plans of the N.K. *7th Division*. This division had started from the Inje area, 30 miles farther east, for Hongch'on, an important town southeast of Ch'unch'on. The *II Corps* now diverted it to Ch'unch'on, which it reached on the evening of 26 June. There

---

[28] Statement, Greenwood for Sawyer; Schwarze, Notes for author, 13 Oct 53; 24th Div G-2 Jnl, 25 Jun 50; New York *Times*, June 26, 1950.
[29] ATIS Res Supp Interrog Rpts, Issue 9 (N.K. Forces), pp. 158–74, Interrog Nr 1468 (Sr Col Lee Hak Ku, N.K. *II Corps* Opns Off at time of invasion).

[30] *Ibid.*, Issue 94 (N.K. *2d Div*), p. 33; 24th Div G-2 Jnl, 25 Jun 50; Ltr, Lt Col Thomas D. McPhail to author, 28 Jun 54; New York *Times*, June 25, 1950.

the *7th Division* immediately joined its forces with the *2d Division* in the battle for the city.[31]

Apparently there were no enemy tanks in the Ch'unch'on battle until the *7th Division* arrived. The battle continued through the third day, 27 June. The defending ROK 6th Division finally withdrew southward on the 28th on orders after the front had collapsed on both sides of it. The North Koreans then entered Ch'unch'on. Nine T34 tanks apparently led the main body into the town on the morning of 28 June.[32]

The enemy *2d Division* suffered heavily in the battle for Ch'unch'on; its casualty rate reportedly was more than 40 percent, the *6th Regiment* alone having incurred more than 50 percent casualties. According to prisoners, ROK artillery fire caused most of the losses. ROK counterbattery fire also inflicted heavy losses on enemy artillery and supporting weapons, including destruction of 7 of the division's 16 self-propelled SU–76-mm. guns, 2 45-mm. antitank guns, and several mortars of all types.[33] The N.K. *7th Division* likewise suffered considerable, but not heavy, casualties in the Ch'unch'on battle.[34]

Immediately after the capture of Ch'unch'on the *7th Division* pressed on south toward Hongch'on, while the N.K. *2d Division* turned west toward Seoul.

On the east coast across the high Taebaek Range from Inje, the last major concentration of North Korean troops awaited the attack hour. There the N.K. *5th Division*, the *766th Independent Unit*, and some guerrilla units were poised to cross the Parallel. On the south side of the border the 10th Regiment of the ROK 8th Division held defensive positions. The ROK division headquarters was at Kangnung, some fifteen miles down the coast; the division's second regiment, the 21st, was stationed at Samch'ok, about twenty-five miles farther south. Only a small part of the 21st Regiment actually was at Samch'ok on 25 June, however, as two of its battalions were engaged in antiguerrilla action southward in the Taebaek Mountains.[35]

About 0500 Sunday morning, 25 June, Koreans awakened Maj. George D. Kessler, KMAG adviser to the 10th Regiment, at Samch'ok and told him a heavy North Korean attack was in progress at the 38th Parallel. Within a few minutes word came that enemy troops were landing at two points along the coast nearby, above and below Samch'ok. The commander of the 10th Regiment and Major Kessler got into a jeep and drove up the coast. From a hilltop they saw junks and sampans lying offshore and what looked like a battalion of troops milling about on the coastal road. They drove back south, and below Samch'ok they saw much the same scene. By the time the two officers returned to Samch'ok

---

[31] ATIS Res Supp Interrog Rpts, Issue 99 (N.K. *12th Div*), p. 43; *Ibid.*, Issue 2 (Documentary Evidence of N.K. Aggression), p. 22; KMAG G–2 Unit Hist, 25 Jun 50; DA Intel Rev, Mar 51, p. 34; Rpt, USMAG to ROK, 1 Jan–15 Jun 50, Annex IV, 15 Jun 50.

[32] Ltr, McPhail to author, 28 Jun 54; KMAG G–2 Unit Hist, 28 Jun 50; 24th Div G–3 Jnl, 30 Jun 50.

[33] ATIS Res Supp Interrog Rpts, Issue 94 (N.K. *2d Div*), pp. 33–34; *Ibid.*, Issue 106 (N.K. Arty), p. 51.

[34] *Ibid.*, Issue 99 (N.K. *12th Div*), p. 43.

[35] Interv, Sawyer with Col George D. Kessler, 24 Feb 54; ATIS Res Supp Interrog Rpts, Issue 96 (N.K. *5th Div*), p. 39; KMAG G–2 Unit Hist, 25 Jun 50.

enemy craft were circling offshore there. ROK soldiers brought up their antitank guns and opened fire on the craft. Kessler saw two boats sink. A landing at Samch'ok itself did not take place. These landings in the Samch'ok area were by guerrillas in the approximate strength of 400 above and 600 below the town. Their mission was to spread inland into the mountainous eastern part of Korea.[36]

Meanwhile, two battalions of the *766th Independent Unit* had landed near Kangnung. Correlating their action with this landing, the N.K. *5th Division* and remaining elements of the *766th Independent Unit* crossed the Parallel with the *766th Independent Unit* leading the attack southward down the coastal road.[37]

The American advisers to the ROK 8th Division assembled at Kangnung on 26 June and helped the division commander prepare withdrawal plans. The 10th Regiment was still delaying the enemy advance near the border. The plan agreed upon called for the 8th Division to withdraw inland across the Taebaek Range and establish contact with the ROK 6th Division, if possible, in the central mountain corridor, and then to move south toward Pusan by way of Tanyang Pass. The American advisers left Kangnung that night and drove southwest to Wonju where they found the command post of the ROK 6th Division.[38]

On 28 June the commander of the 8th Division sent a radio message to the ROK Army Chief of Staff saying that it was impossible to defend Kangnung and giving the positions of the 10th and 21st Regiments. The ROK 8th Division successfully executed its withdrawal, begun on 27-28 June, bringing along its weapons and equipment.[39]

The ROK Counterattack at Uijongbu

By 0930 Sunday morning, 25 June, the ROK Army high command at Seoul had decided the North Koreans were engaged in a general offensive and not a repetition of many earlier "rice raids."[40]

Acting in accordance with plans previously prepared, it began moving reserves to the north of Seoul for a counterattack in the vital Uijongbu Corridor. The 2d Division at Taejon was the first of the divisions distant from the Parallel to move toward the battle front. The first train with division headquarters and elements of the 5th Regiment left Taejon for Seoul at 1430, 25 June, accompanied by their American advisers. By dark, parts of the 5th Division were on their way north from Kwangju in southwest Korea. The 22d Regiment, the 3d Engineer Battalion, and the 57-mm. antitank company of the ROK 3d Division

---

[36] Interv, Sawyer with Kessler 24 Feb 54; 24th Div G-3 Jnl, 25 Jun 50; DA Wkly Intel Rpt, Nr 72, 7 Jul 50, p. 18.

[37] ATIS Res Supp Interrog Rpts, Issue 2 (Documentary Evidence of N.K. Aggression), pp. 46-50; *Ibid.*, Issue 96 (N.K. *5th Div*), p. 39; 24th Div G-3 Jnl, 25 Jun 50; DA Wkly Intel Rpt, Nr 72, 7 Jul 50, p. 18; KMAG G-2 Unit Hist, 25 Jun 50. According to North Korean Col. Lee Hak Ku, the *17th Motorcycle Regiment* also moved to Kangnung but the terrain prevented its employment in the attack. See ATIS Res Supp Interrog Rpts, Issue 9 (N.K. Forces), pp. 158-74, Nr 1468.

[38] Interv, Sawyer with Kessler, 24 Feb 54.

[39] *Ibid.*; ATIS Res Supp Interrog Rpts, Issue 3 (Enemy Documents), pp. 28, 45, file 25 Jun-9 Jul 50. On the 29th the 8th Division reported its strength as 6,135.

[40] Interv, author with Gen Chang, 14 Oct 53.

also started north from Taegu that night.

During the 25th, Capt. James W. Hausman, KMAG adviser with General Chae, ROK Army Chief of Staff, had accompanied the latter on two trips from Seoul to the Uijongbu area. General Chae, popularly known as the "fat boy," weighed 245 pounds, and was about 5 feet 6 inches tall. General Chae's plan, it developed, was to launch a counterattack in the Uijongbu Corridor the next morning with the 7th Division attacking on the left along the Tongduch'on-ni road out of Uijongbu, and with the 2d Division on the right on the P'och'on road. In preparing for this, General Chae arranged to move the elements of the 7th Division defending the P'och'on road west to the Tongduch'on-ni road, concentrating that division there, and turn over to the 2d Division the P'och'on road sector. But the 2d Division would only begin to arrive in the Uijongbu area during the night. It would be impossible to assemble and transport the main body of the division from Taejon, ninety miles below Seoul, to the front above Uijongbu and deploy it there by the next morning.

Brig. Gen. Lee Hyung Koon, commander of the 2d Division, objected to Chae's plan. It meant that he would have to attack piecemeal with small elements of his division. He wanted to defer the counterattack until he could get all, or the major part, of his division forward. Captain Hausman agreed with his view. But General Chae overruled these objections and ordered the attack for the morning of 26 June. The Capital Division at Seoul was not included in the counterattack plan because it was not considered tactical and had no artillery. It had served chiefly as a "spit and polish" organization, with its cavalry regiment acting as a "palace guard."

Elements of the 7th Division which had stopped the N.K. *3d Division* at P'och'on withdrew from there about midnight of 25 June. The next morning only the 2d Division headquarters and the 1st and 2d Battalions of the 5th Regiment had arrived at Uijongbu.[41]

During the first day, elements of the 7th Division near Tongduch'on-ni on the left-hand road had fought well, considering the enemy superiority in men, armor, and artillery, and had inflicted rather heavy casualties on the *16th Regiment* of the N.K. *4th Division*. But despite losses the enemy pressed forward and had captured and passed through Tongduch'on-ni by evening.[42] On the morning of 26 June, therefore, the N.K. *4th Division* with two regiments abreast and the N.K. *3d Division* also with two regiments abreast were above Uijongbu with strong armor elements, poised for the converging attack on it and the corridor to Seoul.

On the morning of 26 June Brig. Gen. Yu Jai Hyung, commanding the ROK 7th Division, launched his part of the counterattack against the N.K. *4th Division* north of Uijongbu. At first the counterattack made progress. This early success apparently led the Seoul broadcast in the afternoon to state that the 7th Division had counterattacked, killed

---

[41] Interv, author with Hausman, 12 Jan 52; ATIS Res Supp Interrog Rpts, Issue 96 (N.K. *3d Div*), p. 29; EUSAK WD, G-2 Sec, 20 Jul 50, ATIS Interrog Nr 89 (2d Lt Pak Mal Bang, escapee from North Korea, a member of the ROK 5th Regt at Uijongbu on 26 Jun).

[42] ATIS Res Supp Interrog Rpts, Issue 94 (N.K. *4th Div*), p. 44; Ibid., Issue 2 (Documentary Evidence of N.K. Aggression), Recon Ord Nr 1 to *4th Div*.

1,580 enemy soldiers, destroyed 58 tanks, and destroyed or captured a miscellany of other weapons.[43]

Not only did this report grossly exaggerate the success of the 7th Division, but it ignored the grave turn of events that already had taken place in front of the 2d Division. The N.K. *3d Division* had withdrawn from the edge of P'och'on during the night, but on the morning of the 26th resumed its advance and re-entered P'och'on unopposed. Its tank-led column continued southwest toward Uijongbu. General Lee of the ROK 2d Division apparently believed a counterattack by his two battalions would be futile for he never launched his part of the scheduled counterattack. Visitors during the morning found him in his command post, doing nothing, surrounded by staff officers.[44] His two battalions occupied defensive positions about two miles northeast of Uijongbu covering the P'och'on road. There, these elements of the ROK 2d Division at 0800 opened fire with artillery and small arms on approaching North Koreans. A long column of tanks led the enemy attack. ROK artillery fired on the tanks, scoring some direct hits, but they were unharmed and, after halting momentarily, rumbled forward. This tank column passed through the ROK infantry positions and entered Uijongbu. Following behind the tanks, the enemy *7th Regiment* engaged the ROK infantry. Threatened with encirclement, survivors of the ROK 2d Division's two battalions withdrew into the hills.[45]

This failure of the 2d Division on the eastern, righthand, road into Uijongbu caused the 7th Division to abandon its own attack on the western road and to fall back below the town. By evening both the N.K. *3d* and *4th Divisions* and their supporting tanks of the *105th Armored Brigade* had entered Uijongbu. The failure of the 2d Division above Uijongbu portended the gravest consequences. The ROK Army had at hand no other organized force that could materially affect the battle above Seoul.[46]

General Lee explained later to Col. William H. S. Wright that he did not attack on the morning of the 26th because his division had not yet closed and he was waiting for it to arrive. His orders had been to attack with the troops he had available. Quite obviously this attack could not have succeeded. The really fatal error had been General Chae's plan of operation giving the 2d Division responsibility for the P'och'on road sector when it was quite apparent that it could not arrive in strength to meet that responsibility by the morning of 26 June.

The Fall of Seoul

The tactical situation for the ROK Army above Seoul was poor as evening

---

[43] 24th Div G-2 Jnl, 26 Jun 50. The New York Times, June 26, 1950, carries an optimistic statement by the South Korean cabinet.

[44] Interv, Dr. Gordon W. Prange and Schnabel with Lt Col Nicholas J. Abbott, 6 Mar 51; EUSAK WD G-2 Sec, 20 Jul 50, ATIS Interrog Nr 89 (Lt Pak Mal Bang).

[45] EUSAK WD, G-2 Sec, 20 Jul 50, ATIS Interrog 89 (Lt Pak Mal Bang); ATIS Res Supp Interrog Rpts, Issue 96 (N.K. *3d Div*), p. 29.

[46] Interv, author with Col Wright, 3 Jan 52; Interv, Prange and Schnabel with Abbott, 6 Mar 51; Statement, Greenwood for Sawyer, 22 Feb 54; ATIS Res Supp Interrog Rpts, Issue 1 (Enemy Documents), item 6, p. 43; 24th Div G-2 Jnl, 26 Jun 50.

fell on the second day, 26 June. Its 1st Division at Korangp'o-ri was flanked by the enemy *1st Division* immediately to the east and the *4th* and *3d Divisions* at Uijongbu. Its 7th Division and elements of the 2d, 5th, and Capital Divisions were fighting un-co-ordinated delaying actions in the vicinity of Uijongbu.

During the evening the Korean Government decided to move from Seoul to Taejon. Members of the South Korean National Assembly, however, after debate decided to remain in Seoul. That night the ROK Army headquarters apparently decided to leave Seoul. On the morning of the 27th the ROK Army headquarters left Seoul, going to Sihung-ni, about five miles south of Yongdungp'o, without notifying Colonel Wright and the KMAG headquarters.[47]

Ambassador Muccio and his staff left Seoul for Suwon just after 0900 on the 27th. Colonel Wright and KMAG then followed the ROK Army headquarters to Sihung-ni. There Colonel Wright persuaded General Chae to return to Seoul. Both the ROK Army headquarters and the KMAG headquarters were back in Seoul by 1800 27 June.[48]

The generally calm atmosphere that had pervaded the Seoul area during the first two days of the invasion disappeared on the third. The failure of the much discussed counterattack of the ROK 7th and 2d Divisions and the continued advance of the North Korean columns upon Seoul became known to the populace of the city during 27 June, and refugees began crowding the roads. During this and the preceding day North Korean planes dropped leaflets on the city calling for surrender. Also, Marshal Choe Yong Gun, field commander of the North Korean invaders, broadcast by radio an appeal for surrender.[49] The populace generally expected the city to fall during the night. By evening confusion took hold in Seoul.

A roadblock and demolition plan designed to slow an enemy advance had been prepared and rehearsed several times, but so great was the terror spread by the T34 tanks that "prepared demolitions were not blown, roadblocks were erected but not manned, and obstacles were not covered by fire." But in one instance, Lt. Col. Oum Hong Sup, Commandant of the ROK Engineer School, led a hastily improvised group that destroyed with demolitions and pole charges four North Korean tanks at a mined bridge on the Uijongbu-Seoul road.[50] A serious handicap in trying to stop the enemy tanks was the lack of antitank mines in South Korea at the time of the invasion—only antipersonnel mines were available.[51]

Before midnight, 27 June, the defenses

---

[47] Interv, author with Col Robert T. Hazlett, 14 Jun 54 (Hazlett was adviser to the ROK Infantry School, June 1950); Statement, Greenwood for Sawyer, 22 Feb 54; Sawyer, KMAG MS, pt. III; Col Wright, Notes for author, 1952; Soon-Chun Pak, "What Happened to a Congress Woman," in John W. Riley, Jr., and Wilbur Schram, *The Reds Take a City* (New Brunswick, N.J.: Rutgers University Press, 1951), p. 193. Sihung-ni had been a cantonment area of the ROK Infantry School before the invasion.

[48] Sawyer, KMAG MS; Wright, Notes for author, 1952.

[49] The New York *Times*, June 27, 1950; DA Intel Rev, Aug 50, Nr 171, p. 18.

[50] Wright, Notes for author, 1952.

[51] Maj. Richard I. Crawford, Notes on Korea, 25 June–5 December 1950, typescript of talk given by Crawford at Ft. Belvoir, Va., 17 Feb 51. (Crawford was senior engineer adviser to the ROK Army in June 1950.)

of Seoul had all but fallen. The *9th Regiment, N.K. 3d Division*, was the first enemy unit to reach the city. Its leading troops arrived in the suburbs about 1930 but heavy fire forced them into temporary withdrawal.[52] About 2300 one lone enemy tank and a platoon of infantry entered the Secret Gardens at Chang-Duk Palace in the northeast section of the city. Korean police managed to destroy the tank and kill or disperse the accompanying soldiers.[53]

Lt. Col. Peter W. Scott at midnight had taken over temporarily the G-3 adviser desk at the ROK Army headquarters. When reports came in of breaks in the line at the edge of Seoul he saw members of the ROK Army G-3 Section begin to fold their maps. Colonel Scott asked General Chae if he had ordered the headquarters to leave; the latter replied that he had not.[54]

About midnight Colonel Wright ordered some of the KMAG officers to go to their quarters and get a little rest. One of these was Lt. Col. Walter Greenwood, Jr., Deputy Chief of Staff, KMAG. Soon after he had gone to bed, according to Colonel Greenwood, Maj. George R. Sedberry, Jr., the G-3 adviser to the ROK Army, telephoned him that the South Koreans intended to blow the Han River bridges. Sedberry said that he was trying to persuade General Kim Paik Il, ROK Deputy Chief of Staff, to prevent the blowing of the bridges until troops, supplies, and equipment clogging the streets of Seoul could be removed to the south side of the river. There had been an earlier agreement between KMAG and General Chae that the bridges would not be blown until enemy tanks reached the street on which the ROK Army headquarters was located. Greenwood hurried to the ROK Army headquarters. There General Kim told him that the Vice Minister of Defense had ordered the blowing of the bridges at 0130 and they must be blown at once.[55]

Maj. Gen. Chang Chang Kuk, ROK Army G-3 at the time, states that General Lee, commander of the 2d Division, appeared at the ROK Army headquarters after midnight and, upon learning that the bridges were to be blown, pleaded with General Kim to delay it at least until his troops and their equipment, then in the city, could cross to the south side of the Han. It appears that earlier, General Chae, the Chief of Staff, over his protests had been placed in a jeep and sent south across the river. According to General Chang, General Chae wanted to stay in Seoul. But with Chae gone, General Kim was at this climactic moment the highest ranking officer at the ROK Army headquarters. After General Lee's pleas, General Kim turned to General Chang and told him to drive to the river and stop the blowing of the bridge.

---

[52] Diary found on dead North Korean, entry 27 Jun 50, in 25th Div G-2 PW Interrog File, 2-22 Jul 50; ATIS Res Supp Interrog Rpts, Issue 96 (N.K. *3d Div*), p. 30.

[53] Intervs, author with Gen Chang, 14 Oct 53, Schwarze, 3 Feb 54, and Hausman, 12 Jan 54. Statement, Greenwood for Sawyer, 22 Feb 54. The rusting hulk of this tank was still in the palace grounds when American troops recaptured the city in September.

[54] Copy of Ltr, Col Scott to unnamed friend, n.d. (ca. 6-7 Jul 50). Colonel Scott was the G-1 adviser to ROK Army.

[55] Statement, Greenwood for Sawyer, 22 Feb 54; Ltr, Greenwood to author, 1 Jul 54; Interv, author with Col Lewis D. Vieman (KMAG G-4 adviser), 15 Jun 54. Sedberry said he did not remember this conversation relating to blowing the Han River bridge. Ltr, Sedberry to author, 10 Jun 54.

General Chang went outside, got into a jeep, and drove off toward the highway bridge, but he found the streets so congested with traffic, both wheeled and pedestrian, that he could make only slow progress. The nearest point from which he might expect to communicate with the demolition party on the south side of the river was a police box near the north end of the bridge. He says he had reached a point about 150 yards from the bridge when a great orange-colored light illumined the night sky. The accompanying deafening roar announced the blowing of the highway and three railroad bridges.[56]

The gigantic explosions, which dropped two spans of the Han highway bridge into the water on the south side, were set off about 0215 with no warning to the military personnel and the civilian population crowding the bridges.

Two KMAG officers, Col. Robert T. Hazlett and Captain Hausman, on their way to Suwon to establish communication with Tokyo, had just crossed the bridge when it blew up—Hausman said seven minutes after they crossed. Hazlett said five minutes. Hausman places the time of the explosion at 0215. Several other sources fix it approximately at the same time. Pedestrian and solid vehicular traffic, bumper to bumper, crowded all three lanes of the highway bridge. In Seoul the broad avenue leading up to the bridge was packed in all eight lanes with vehicles of all kinds, including army trucks and artillery pieces, as well as with marching soldiers and civilian pedestrians. The best informed American officers in Seoul at the time estimate that between 500 and 800 people were killed or drowned in the blowing of this bridge. Double this number probably were on that part of the bridge over water but which did not fall, and possibly as many as 4,000 people altogether were on the bridge if one includes the long causeway on the Seoul side of the river. Three American war correspondents—Burton Crane, Frank Gibney, and Keyes Beech—were just short of the blown section of the bridge when it went skyward. The blast shattered their jeep's windshield. Crane and Gibney in the front seat received face and head cuts from the flying glass. Just ahead of them a truckload of ROK soldiers were all killed.[57]

There was a great South Korean uproar later over the premature destruction of the Han River bridges, and a court of inquiry sat to fix the blame for the tragic event. A Korean army court martial fixed the responsibility and blame on the ROK Army Chief Engineer for the "manner" in which he had prepared the bridges for demolition, and he was summarily executed. Some American advisers in Korea at the time believed that General Chae ordered the bridges blown and that the Chief Engineer merely carried out his orders. General Chae denied that he had given the order. Others in a good position to ascertain all the facts available in the prevailing confusion believed that the Vice Minister of

---

[56] Interv, author with Gen Chang, 14 Oct 53.

[57] Wright, Notes for author, 1952; Statement, Greenwood for Sawyer, 22 Feb 54; Lt Col Lewis D. Vieman, Notes on Korea, typescript, 15 Feb 51; Interv, author with Hausman, 12 Jan 52; Interv, author with Keyes Beech, 1 Oct 51; Interv, author with Hazlett, 11 Jun 54. The New York Times, June 29, 1950, carries Burton Crane's personal account of the Han bridge destruction.

Defense ordered the blowing of the bridges. The statements attributed to General Kim support this view.

The utter disregard for the tactical situation, with the ROK Army still holding the enemy at the outskirts of the city, and the certain loss of thousands of soldiers and practically all the transport and heavy weapons if the bridges were destroyed, lends strong support to the view that the order was given by a ROK civilian official and not by a ROK Army officer.

Had the Han River bridges not been blown until the enemy actually approached them there would have been from at least six to eight hours longer in which to evacuate the bulk of the troops of three ROK divisions and at least a part of their transport, equipment, and heavy weapons to the south side of the Han. It is known that when the KMAG party crossed the Han River at 0600 on 28 June the fighting was still some distance from the river, and according to North Korean sources enemy troops did not occupy the center of the city until about noon. Their arrival at the river line necessarily must have been later.

The premature blowing of the bridges was a military catastrophe for the ROK Army. The main part of the army, still north of the river, lost nearly all its transport, most of its supplies, and many of its heavy weapons. Most of the troops that arrived south of the Han waded the river or crossed in small boats and rafts in disorganized groups. The disintegration of the ROK Army now set in with alarming speed.

ROK troops held the North Koreans at the edge of Seoul throughout the night of 27-28 June, and the North Koreans have given them credit for putting up a stubborn resistance. During the morning of the 28th, the North Korean attack forced the disorganized ROK defenders to withdraw, whereupon street fighting started in the city. Only small ROK units were still there. These delayed the entry of the N.K. *3d Division* into the center of Seoul until early afternoon.[58] The *16th Regiment* of the N.K. *4th Division* entered the city about midafternoon.[59] One group of ROK soldiers in company strength dug in on South Mountain within the city and held out all day, but finally they reportedly were killed to the last man.[60] At least a few North Korean tanks were destroyed or disabled in street fighting in Seoul. One captured North Korean tanker later told of seeing two knocked-out tanks in Seoul when he entered.[61] The two North Korean divisions completed the occupation of Seoul during the afternoon. Within the city an active fifth column met the North Korean troops and helped them round up remaining ROK troops, police, and South Korean government officials who had not escaped.

In the first four days of the invasion, during the drive on Seoul, the N.K. *3d* and *4th Divisions* incurred about 1,500 casualties.[62] Hardest hit was the *4th Di-*

---

[58] ATIS Res Supp Interrog Rpts, Issue 96 (N.K. *3d Div*), p. 30. The time given for the entry into Seoul is 1300.

[59] *Ibid.*, Issue 94 (N.K. *4th Div*), p. 44. GHQ FEC, History of the N.K. Army, p. 44, claims that the *18th Regiment*, N.K. *4th Division*, entered Seoul at 1130, 28 June. The P'yongyang radio broadcast that the North Korea People's Army occupied Seoul at 0300, 28 June. See 24th Div G-2 Msg File, 28 Jun 50.

[60] Interv, author with Schwarze, 3 Feb 54; KMAG G-2 Unit Hist, 28 Jun 50.

[61] ORO-R-1 (FEC), 8 Apr 51, The Employment of Armor in Korea, vol. I, p. 156.

[62] ATIS Res Supp Interrog Rpts, Issue 94 (N.K. *4th Div*), p. 44; *Ibid.*, Issue 96 (N.K. *3d Div*), p. 30; *Ibid.*, Issue 1 (Enemy Documents), p. 37.

vision, which had fought the ROK 7th Division down to Uijongbu. It lost 219 killed, 761 wounded, and 132 missing in action for a total of 1,112 casualties.[63]

In an order issued on 10 July, Kim Il Sung honored the N.K. *3d* and *4th Divisions* for their capture of Seoul by conferring on them the honorary title, "*Seoul Division.*" The *105th Armored Brigade* was raised by the same order to division status and received the same honorary title.[64]

Of the various factors contributing to the quick defeat of the ROK Army, perhaps the most decisive was the shock of fighting tanks for the first time. The North Koreans had never used tanks in any of the numerous border incidents, although they had possessed them since late 1949. It was on 25 June, therefore, that the ROK soldier had his first experience with tanks. The ROK soldier not only lacked experience with tanks, he also lacked weapons that were effective against the T34 except his own handmade demolition charge used in close attack.[65]

Seoul fell on the fourth day of the invasion. At the end of June, after six days, everything north of the Han River had been lost. On the morning of 29 June, General Yu Jai Hyung with about 1,200 men of the ROK 7th Division and four machine guns, all that was left of his division, defended the bridge sites from the south bank of the river. In the next day or two remnants of four South Korean divisions assembled on the south bank or were still infiltrating across the river.[66] Colonel Paik brought the ROK 1st Division, now down to about 5,000 men, across the Han on 29 June in the vicinity of Kimpo Airfield, twelve air miles northwest of Seoul. He had to leave his artillery behind but his men brought out their small arms and most of their crew-served weapons.[67]

Of 98,000 men in the ROK Army on 25 June the Army headquarters could account for only 22,000 south of the Han at the end of the month.[68] When information came in a few days later about the 6th and 8th Divisions and more stragglers assembled south of the river, this figure increased to 54,000. But even this left 44,000 completely gone in the first week of war—killed, captured, or missing. Of all the divisions engaged in the initial fighting, only the 6th and 8th escaped with their organization, weapons, equipment, and transport relatively intact. Except for them, the ROK Army came out of the initial disaster with little more than about 30 percent of its individual weapons.[69]

---

[63] GHQ FEC, History of the N.K. Army (*4th Div*), p. 58. These figures are based on a captured enemy casualty report.

[64] GHQ FEC, History of the N.K. Army, p. 56.

[65] On Friday, 30 June, the sixth day of the invasion, the first antitank mines arrived in Korea. Eight hundred of them were flown in from Japan. Crawford, Notes on Korea.

[66] Ltr, Greenwood to author, 1 Jul 54.

[67] Interv, author with Hazlett, 11 Jun 54. Hazlett was at Sihung-ni, reconnoitering a crossing, when Colonel Paik arrived there the evening of 28 June, and talked with him later about the division's crossing.

[68] Interv, author with Hausman, 12 Jan 54.

[69] *Ibid.*; Vieman, Notes on Korea, 15 Feb 51; Interv, author with Gen Chang, 14 Oct 53. General Chang estimated there were 40,000 soldiers under organized ROK Army command 1 July. General MacArthur on 29 June placed the number of ROK Army effectives at 25,000.

CHAPTER IV

The United States and the United Nations React

> Thus we see that war is not only a political act, but a true instrument of politics, a continuation of politics by other means.
> CARL VON CLAUSEWITZ, *On War*

The first official word of the North Korean attack across the border into South Korea reached Tokyo in an information copy of an emergency telegram dispatched from Seoul at 0925, 25 June, by the military attaché at the American Embassy there to the Assistant Chief of Staff, G–2, Department of the Army, in Washington.[1] About the same time the Far East Air Forces in Tokyo began receiving radio messages from Kimpo Airfield near Seoul stating that fighting was taking place along the 38th Parallel on a scale that seemed to indicate more than the usual border incidents. Northwest Airlines, with Air Force support, operated Kimpo Airfield at this time. Brig. Gen. Jared V. Crabb, Deputy Chief of Staff for Far East Air Forces, telephoned Brig. Gen. Edwin K. Wright, Assistant Chief of Staff, G–3, Far East Command, about 1030 and the two compared information. Thereafter throughout the day the two men were in constant communication with each other on the direct line they maintained between their offices. Most of the messages to Tokyo during 25 June came to the U.S. Air Force from Kimpo Airfield, and there was a constant stream of them. By 1500 in the afternoon both Crabb and Wright were convinced that the North Koreans were engaged in a full-scale invasion of South Korea.[2]

About the time the military attaché in Seoul sent the first message to the Department of the Army, representatives of press associations in Korea began sending news bulletins to their offices in the United States. It was about eight o'clock Saturday night, 24 June, Washington time, when the first reports reached that city of the North Korean attacks that had begun five hours earlier. Soon afterward, Ambassador Muccio sent his first radio message from Seoul to the Department of State, which received it at 9:26 p.m., 24 June. This would correspond to 10:26

---

[1] Schnabel, FEC, GHQ Support and Participation in Korean War, ch. II, p. 24.

[2] Ltr, Gen Wright to author, 12 Feb 54.

a.m., 25 June, in Korea. Ambassador Muccio said in part, "It would appear from the nature of the attack and the manner in which it was launched that it constitutes an all-out offensive against the Republic of Korea." [3]

The North Korean attack surprised official Washington. Maj. Gen. L. L. Lemnitzer in a memorandum to the Secretary of Defense on 29 June gave what is undoubtedly an accurate statement of the climate of opinion prevailing in Washington in informed circles at the time of the attack. He said it had been known for many months that the North Korean forces possessed the capability of attacking South Korea; that similar capabilities existed in practically every other country bordering the USSR; but that he knew of no intelligence agency that had centered attention on Korea as a point of imminent attack.[4] The surprise in Washington on Sunday, 25 June 1950, according to some observers, resembled that of another, earlier Sunday–Pearl Harbor, 7 December 1941.

U.S. and U.N. Action

When Trygve Lie, Secretary-General of the United Nations, at his Long Island home that night received the news of the North Korean attack he reportedly burst out over the telephone, "This is war against the United Nations." [5] He called a meeting of the Security Council for the next day. When the Council met at 2 p.m., 25 June (New York time), it debated, amended, and revised a resolution with respect to Korea and then adopted it by a vote of nine to zero, with one abstention and one absence. Voting for the resolution were China, Cuba, Ecuador, Egypt, France, India, Norway, the United Kingdom, and the United States. Yugoslavia abstained from voting; the Soviet Union was not represented. The Soviet delegate had boycotted the meetings of the Security Council since January 10, 1950, over the issue of seating Red China's representative in the United Nations as the official Chinese representative.[6]

The Security Council resolution stated that the armed attack upon the Republic of Korea by forces from North Korea "constitutes a breach of the peace." It called for (1) immediate cessation of hostilities; (2) authorities of North Korea to withdraw forthwith their armed forces to the 38th Parallel; and, finally, "all Members to render every assistance to the United Nations in the execution of this resolution and to refrain from giving assistance to the North Korean authorities." [7]

President Truman had received the news at his home in Independence, Mo. He started back to Washington by plane in the early afternoon of 25 June. At a meeting in Blair House that night, with

---

[3] This radio message is reproduced in full in Dept of State Pub 3922, *United States Policy in the Korean Crisis*, Doc. 1, p. 11.

[4] Memo, Maj Gen L. L. Lemnitzer, Director, Off of Mil Assistance, for Secy Defense, 29 Jun 50; S. Comm. on Armed Services and S. Comm. on Foreign Relations, 82d Cong., 1st Sess., 1951, Joint Hearings, *Military Situation in the Far East* (MacArthur Hearings), pt. III, pp. 1990–92, Testimony of Secretary of State Acheson.

[5] Albert L. Warner, "How the Korea Decision was Made," *Harper's Magazine*, June 26, 1950, pp. 99–106; Beverly Smith, "Why We Went to War in Korea," *Saturday Evening Post*, November 10, 1951.

[6] *United Staes Policy in the Korean Crisis*, p. 1, n. 5, and Docs. 3, 4, and 5, pp. 12–16.

[7] *Ibid.*, Doc. 5, p. 16.

officials of the State and Defense Departments present, President Truman made a number of decisions. The Joint Chiefs of Staff established a teletype conference with General MacArthur in Tokyo at once and relayed to him President Truman's decisions. They authorized General MacArthur to do the following: (1) send ammunition and equipment to Korea to prevent loss of the Seoul-Kimpo area with appropriate air and naval cover to assure their safe arrival; (2) provide ships and planes to evacuate American dependents from Korea and to protect the evacuation; and (3) dispatch a survey party to Korea to study the situation and determine how best to assist the Republic of Korea. President Truman also ordered the Seventh Fleet to start from the Philippines and Okinawa for Sasebo, Japan, and report to the Commander, U.S. Naval Forces, Far East (NAVFE), for operational control.[8]

In the evening of 26 June President Truman received General MacArthur's report that ROK forces could not hold Seoul, that the ROK forces were in danger of collapse, that evacuation of American nationals was under way, and that the first North Korean plane had been shot down. After a short meeting with leading advisers the President approved a number of measures.

Further instructions went to MacArthur in another teletype conference that night. They authorized him to use the Far East naval and air forces in support of the Republic of Korea against all targets south of the 38th Parallel. These instructions stated that the purpose of this action was to clear South Korea of North Korean military forces. On 27 June, Far Eastern time, therefore, General MacArthur had authorization to intervene in Korea with air and naval forces.[9]

During the night of 27 June the United Nations Security Council passed a second momentous resolution calling upon member nations to give military aid to South Korea in repelling the North Korean attack. After a statement on the act of aggression and the fruitless efforts of the United Nations to halt it, the Security Council resolution ended with these fateful words: "*Recommends* that the Members of the United Nations furnish such assistance to the Republic of Korea as may be necessary to repel the armed attack and to restore international peace and security in the area." [10]

Thus, events on the international stage by the third day of the invasion had progressed swiftly to the point where the United States had authorized its commander in the Far East to use air and naval forces below the 38th Parallel to help repel the aggression and the United Nations had called upon its member nations to help repel the attack. The North Koreans were now in Seoul.

Evacuation of U.S. Nationals From Korea

From the moment United States KMAG officers in Korea and responsible

---

[8] Telecon TT3418, 25 Jun 50. For a detailed discussion of the Department of the Army and Far East Command interchange of views and instructions concerning the Korean crisis and later conduct of the war following intervention see Maj James F. Schnabel, Theater Command.

[9] Telecon TT3426, 27 Jun 50.
[10] *United States Policy in the Korean Crisis*, p. 4, and Doc. 16, p. 24; The vote was seven in favor, one opposed, two abstentions, and one absence; the Soviet Union was absent. Two days later India accepted the resolution. See Doc. 52, pp. 42-43.

officers in General MacArthur's Far East Command headquarters accepted the North Korean attack across the Parallel as an act of full-scale war, it became imperative for them to evacuate American women and children and other nonmilitary persons from Korea.

Almost a year earlier, on 21 July 1949, an operational plan had been distributed by the Far East Command to accomplish such an evacuation by sea and by air. NAVFE was to provide the ships and naval escort protection for the water lift; the Far East Air Forces was to provide the planes for the airlift and give fighter cover to both the water and air evacuation upon orders from the Commander in Chief, Far East.[11] By midnight, 25 June, General Wright in Tokyo had alerted every agency concerned to be ready to put the evacuation plan into effect upon the request of Ambassador Muccio.[12] About 2200, 25 June, Ambassador Muccio authorized the evacuation of the women and children by any means without delay, and an hour later he ordered all American women and children and others who wished to leave to assemble at Camp Sobinggo, the American housing compound in Seoul, for transportation to Inch'on.[13]

The movement of the American dependents from Seoul to Inch'on began at 0100, 26 June, and continued during the night. The last families cleared the Han River bridge about 0900 and by 1800 682 women and children were aboard the Norwegian fertilizer ship, the *Reinholt,* which had hurriedly unloaded its cargo during the day, and was under way in Inch'on Harbor to put to sea. At the southern tip of the peninsula, at Pusan, the ship *Pioneer Dale* took on American dependents from Taejon, Taegu, and Pusan.[14] American fighter planes from Japan flew twenty-seven escort and surveillance sorties during the day covering the evacuation.

On 27 June the evacuation of American and other foreign nationals continued from Kimpo and Suwon Airfields at an increased pace. During the morning 3 North Korean planes fired on four American fighters covering the air evacuation and, in the ensuing engagement, the U.S. fighters shot down all 3 enemy planes near Inch'on. Later in the day, American fighter planes shot down 4 more North Korean YAK-3 planes in the Inch'on-Seoul area. During 27 June F-80 and F-82 planes of the 68th and 339th All-Weather Fighter Squadrons and the 35th Fighter-Bomber Squadron of the Fifth Air Force flew 163 sorties over Korea.[15]

During the period 26-29 June sea and air carriers evacuated a total of 2,001 persons from Korea to Japan. Of this number, 1,527 were U.S. nationals—718 of them traveled by air, 809 by water.

---

[11] Schnabel, FEC, GHQ Support and Participation in the Korean War, ch. II, pp. 11-12.

[12] Ltr, Gen Wright to author, 12 Feb 54.

[13] Sawyer, KMAG MS; John C. Caldwell, *The Korea Story* (Chicago: H. Regnery Co., 1952), p. 170.

[14] Sawyer, KMAG MS; Statement, Greenwood for Sawyer, 22 Feb 54.

[15] GHQ FEC, Ann Narr Hist Rpt, 1 Jan-31 Oct 50, pp. 8-9; Capt Robert L. Gray, Jr., "Air Operations Over Korea," *Army Information Digest*, January 1952, p. 17; USAF Opns in the Korean Conflict, 25 Jun-1 Nov 50, USAF Hist Study 71, pp. 5-6; 24th Div G-3 and G-2 Jnl Msg files, 27 Jun 50; New York *Herald-Tribune*, June 27, 1950.

The largest single group of evacuees was aboard the *Reinholt*.

KMAG Starts To Leave Korea

On Sunday, 25 June, while Colonel Wright, KMAG Chief of Staff, was in church in Tokyo (he had gone to Japan to see his wife, the night before, board a ship bound for the United States, and expected to follow her in a few days), a messenger found him and whispered in his ear, "You had better get back to Korea." Colonel Wright left church at once and telephoned Colonel Greenwood in Seoul. Colonel Wright arrived at Seoul at 0400, Monday, after flying to Kimpo Airfield from Japan.[16]

Colonel Wright reached the decision, with Ambassador Muccio's approval, to evacuate all KMAG personnel from Korea except thirty-three that Colonel Wright selected to remain with the ROK Army headquarters. Most of the KMAG group departed Suwon by air on the 27th. Strangely enough, the last evacuation plane arriving at Kimpo that evening from Japan brought four correspondents from Tokyo: Keyes Beech of the Chicago *Daily News*, Burton Crane of the New York *Times*, Frank Gibney of *Time* Magazine, and Marguerite Higgins of the New York *Herald-Tribune*. They joined a KMAG group that returned to Seoul. In the east and south of Korea, meanwhile, some fifty-six KMAG advisers by 29 June had made their way to Pusan where they put themselves under the command of Lt. Col. Rollins S. Emmerich, KMAG adviser to the ROK 3d Division.[17]

Shortly after midnight of 26 June the State Department ordered Ambassador Muccio to leave Seoul and, accordingly, he went south to Suwon the morning of the 27th.[18] Colonel Wright with his selected group of advisers followed the ROK Army headquarters to Sihung on the south side of the river. Colonel Wright had with him the KMAG command radio, an SCR–399 mounted on a 2½-ton truck. Soon after crossing the Han River en route to Sihung Colonel Wright received a radio message from General MacArthur in Tokyo stating that the Joint Chiefs of Staff had directed him to take command of all U.S. military personnel in Korea, including KMAG, and that he was sending an advance command and liaison group from his headquarters to Korea.[19] After he arrived at Sihung, Colonel Wright received another radio message from General MacArthur, intercepted by the radio station at Suwon Airfield. It said in effect, "Personal MacArthur to Wright: Repair to your former locations. Momentous decisions are in the offing. Be of good cheer."[20] Aided by the import of these messages, Colonel Wright persuaded General Chae to return the ROK Army headquarters to Seoul that evening.

---

[16] Sawyer, KMAG MS; Col Wright, Notes for author, 1952; Ltr, Gen Wright to author, 12 Feb 54; Statement, Greenwood for Sawyer.

[17] Wright, Notes for author; Statement, Greenwood for Sawyer; Sawyer, KMAG MS; Ltr, Rockwell to author, 21 May 54; Ltr, Scott to friend, ca. 6–7 Jul 50; Col Emmerich, MS review comments, 26 Nov 57.

[18] Msg 270136Z, State Dept to Supreme Commander, Allied Powers (U.S. Political Adviser), cited in Schnabel, FEC, GHQ Support and Participation in the Korean War, ch. 2, p. 17.

[19] Col Wright, Notes for author; Sawyer, KMAG MS.

[20] Col Wright, Notes for author; Gen MacArthur, MS review comments, 15 Nov 57.

UNITED STATES AND UNITED NATIONS REACT

That night the blowing of the 'Han River bridges cut off the KMAG group in Seoul. Colonel Wright had had practically no rest since Sunday and, accompanied by Lt. Col. William J. Mahoney, he had retired to his quarters before midnight to get some sleep. Beginning about 0100, 28 June, KMAG officers at ROK Army headquarters tried repeatedly to telephone him the information that the ROK Army headquarters was leaving Seoul. This would necessitate a decision by Colonel Wright as to whether KMAG should also leave. But the telephone message never got to Colonel Wright because Colonel Mahoney who took the calls refused to disturb him. Finally, after the ROK Army headquarters staff had departed, Lt. Col. Lewis D. Vieman went to Colonel Wright's quarters for the second time, found the houseboy, and had him awaken Colonel Wright. Colonel Vieman then informed Colonel Wright of the situation.[21]

The latter was just leaving his quarters when the Han River bridges blew up. Colonel Wright assembled all the Americans in a convoy and started for a bridge east of the city.[22] En route they learned from Korean soldiers that this bridge too had been blown. The convoy turned around and returned to the KMAG housing area at Camp Sobinggo. About daylight a small reconnaissance party reported that ferries were in operation along the Han River east of the highway bridge. At this juncture Lt. Col. Lee Chi Yep, a member of the ROK Army staff, long friendly with the Americans and in turn highly regarded by the KMAG advisers, walked up to them. He volunteered to help in securing ferry transportation across the river.

Upon arriving at the river bank, Colonel Wright's party found a chaotic melee. ROK soldiers and unit leaders fired at the boatmen and, using threats, tried to commandeer transportation from among the ferries and various kinds of craft engaged in transporting soldiers and refugees across the river. Colonel Lee adopted this method, persuading a boatman to bring his craft alongside by putting a bullet through the man's shirt. It took about two hours for the party to make the crossing. Colonel Wright, two other officers, and two or three enlisted men stayed behind and finally succeeded in getting the command radio vehicle across the river. It provided the only communication the KMAG group had with Japan, and Colonel Wright would not leave it behind. Enemy artillery fire was falling some distance upstream and tank fire had drawn perceptibly closer when the last boatload started across the river.[23]

After reaching the south bank, about 0800, the KMAG party struck out and walked the 15-mile cross-country trail to Anyang-ni, arriving there at 1500, 28 June. Waiting vehicles, obtained by an advance party that had gone ahead in a jeep, picked up the tired men and carried them to Suwon. Upon arriving at Suwon they found Colonel Wright and

---

[21] Vieman, Notes on Korea, 15 Feb 51; Interv, author with Vieman, 15 Jun 54; Interv, author with Hausman, 12 Jan 52; Interv, author with Col Wright, 3 Jan 52; Ltr, Col George R. Sedberry, Jr., to Capt Sawyer, 22 Dec 53.

[22] Greenwood estimates there were 130-odd men in the convoy, other estimates are as low as sixty.

[23] Vieman, Notes on Korea, 15 Feb 51; Statement, Greenwood for Sawyer; Ltr, Maj Ray B. May to Capt Sawyer, 23 Apr 54; Ltr, Scott to friend; Marguerite Higgins, *War in Korea* (Garden City, N.Y.: Doubleday and Company, Inc., 1951), pp. 27–30.

GENERAL CHURCH *(left)* being met at Suwon Airfield by *(left to right)* Mr. E. F. Drumwright, Counselor of U.S. Embassy at Seoul, President Rhee, and Ambassador Muccio.

his command radio already there. After getting across the river Wright had turned through Yongdungp'o, which, contrary to rumors, proved to be free of enemy and had then traveled the main road.[24]

---

[24] Vieman, Notes on Korea, 15 Feb 51; Higgins, *War in Korea*; Statement, Greenwood for Sawyer; Ltr, May to Sawyer, 23 Apr 54.

The British Minister to South Korea, Capt. Vyvyan Holt, members of his staff, and a few other British subjects remained in Seoul and claimed diplomatic immunity. Instead of getting it they spent almost three years in a North Korean prison camp. The North Koreans finally released Captain Holt and six other British subjects to the Soviets in April 1953 for return to Britain during the prisoner exchange negotiations. Two, Father Charles Hunt and Sister Mary Claire, died during the internment. See the New York *Times*, April 21 and 22, 1953; the Washington *Post*, April 10, 1953.

Although in the first few days some members of the KMAG group reportedly were cut off and missing, all reached safety by the end of the month, and up to 5 July only three had been slightly wounded.[25]

ADCOM in Korea

General MacArthur as Commander in Chief, Far East, had no responsibility in Korea on 25 June 1950 except to support KMAG and the American Embassy logistically to the Korean water line. This situation changed when President Truman authorized him on 26 June, Far

---

[25] Crawford, Notes on Korea.

Eastern Time, to send a survey party to Korea.

General MacArthur formed at once a survey party of thirteen GHQ General and Special Staff officers and two enlisted men, headed by Brig. Gen. John H. Church. Its mission upon arrival in Korea was to help Ambassador Muccio and KMAG to determine logistical requirements for assisting the ROK Army. The party left Haneda Airfield at 0400, 27 June, and arrived at Itazuke Air Base in southern Japan two hours later. While there awaiting further orders before proceeding to Seoul, General Church received telephone instructions from Tokyo about 1425 changing his destination from Seoul to Suwon because it was feared the former might be in enemy hands by the time he got there. MacArthur had by this time received the Joint Chiefs of Staff directive which instructed him to assume operational control of all U.S. military activities in Korea. Accordingly, he redesignated the survey group as GHQ Advance Command and Liaison Group in Korea (ADCOM), and gave it an expanded mission of assuming control of KMAG and of lending all possible assistance to the ROK Army in striving to check the Red drive southward.[26]

The ADCOM group arrived at Suwon Airfield at 1900, 27 June, where Ambassador Muccio met it. General Church telephoned Colonel Wright in Seoul, who advised him not to come into the city that night. The ADCOM group thereupon set up temporary headquarters in the Experimental Agriculture Building in Suwon.[27]

The next day about 0400 Colonel Hazlett and Captain Hausman, KMAG advisers, arrived at Suwon from Seoul. They told General Church that the Han River bridges were down, that some North Korean tanks were in Seoul, that the South Korean forces defending Seoul were crumbling and fleeing toward Suwon, and that they feared the majority of KMAG was still in Seoul and trapped there.[28] Such was the dark picture presented to General Church before dawn of his first full day in Korea, 28 June.

General Church asked Hazlett and Hausman to find General Chae, ROK Chief of Staff. Several hours later General Chae arrived at ADCOM headquarters. Church told him that MacArthur was in operational control of the American air and naval support of the ROK forces, and that the group at Suwon was his, MacArthur's, advance headquarters in Korea. At Church's suggestion Chae moved the ROK Army headquarters into the same building with Church's ADCOM headquarters.

General Church advised General Chae to order ROK forces in the vicinity of Seoul to continue street fighting in the city; to establish straggler points be-

---

[26] Gen Church, Memo for Record, ADCOM Activities in Korea, 27 Jun–15 July 1950, GHQ FEC G–3, Ann Narr Hist Rpt, 1 Jan–31 Oct 51, Incl 11, pt. III. The Church ADCOM document grew out of stenographic notes of an interview by Major Schnabel with General Church, 17 July 1950. General Church was not satisfied with the notes thus produced and rewrote the draft himself a few days later. This source will hereafter be cited as Church MS. Lt Col Olinto M. Barsanti (G–1 ADCOM Rep), contemporary handwritten notes on ADCOM activities; Interv, author with Col Martin L. Green, ADCOM G–3, 14 Jul 51; Schnabel, FEC, GHQ Support and Participation in the Korean War, ch. 2, pp. 18–19.

[27] Church MS; Barsanti Notes; Statement, Greenwood for Sawyer.

[28] Church MS; Interv, author with Col Robert T. Hazlett, 11 Jun 54; Interv, author with Hausman, 12 Jan 52.

tween Seoul and Suwon and to collect all ROK troops south of the Han River and reorganize them into units, and to defend the Han River line at all cost.[29] During the day, KMAG and ROK officers collected about 1,000 ROK officers and 8,000 men and organized them into provisional units in the vicinity of Suwon. General Chae sent them back to the Han River.

General Church sent a radio message to General MacArthur on the 28th, describing the situation and stating that the United States would have to commit ground troops to restore the original boundary line.[30] That evening he received a radio message from Tokyo stating that a high-ranking officer would arrive the next morning and asking if the Suwon Airfield was operational. General Church replied that it was.

MacArthur Flies to Korea

The "high-ranking officer" mentioned in the radio message of the 28th was General of the Army Douglas MacArthur. Shortly before noon on 28 June, General MacArthur called Lt. Col. Anthony F. Story, his personal pilot, to his office in the Dai Ichi Building in Tokyo and said he wanted to go to Suwon the next day to make a personal inspection. Colonel Story checked the weather reports and found them negative—storms, rains, low ceiling, and heavy winds predicted for the morrow.[31]

At 0400, 29 June, MacArthur was up and preparing for the flight to Suwon. At 0600 he arrived at Haneda and, with the assembled group, climbed aboard the *Bataan*, his personal C-54 plane. A total of fifteen individuals made the trip, including seven high-ranking officers of General MacArthur's staff. Rain was falling when the *Bataan* took off from Haneda at 0610. About 0800 General MacArthur dictated a radiogram to Maj. Gen. Earl E. Partridge, commanding FEAF in Lt. Gen. George E. Stratemeyer's absence. General Stratemeyer wrote it out and handed it to Story to send. It said, "Stratemeyer to Partridge: Take out North Korean Airfield immediately. No publicity. MacArthur approves." [32]

The weather had now improved sufficiently to permit fighter planes to take off, and at 1000 four of them intercepted and escorted the *Bataan* to Suwon. That morning North Korean fighter planes had strafed the Suwon Airfield and set on fire a C-54 at the end of the runway. This wrecked plane constituted a 20-foot obstacle on an already short runway, but Colonel Story succeeded in setting the *Bataan* down without mishap. Waiting at the airfield were President Rhee, Ambassador Muccio, and General Church. The party got into an old black sedan and drove to General Church's headquarters. In the conversation there Church told MacArthur that that morning not more than 8,000 ROK's could be accounted for; that at that moment, noon, they had 8,000 more; and that by night he expected to have an additional

---

[29] Church MS; Barsanti Notes.
[30] Church MS. Church gives the date as 27 June, but this is a mistake.
[31] Interv, Dr. Gordon W. Prange with Col Story, 19 Feb 51, Tokyo. Colonel Story referred to his logbook of the flight for the details related in this interview.

[32] *Ibid.*

GENERAL MACARTHUR, *accompanied by Maj. Gen. Edward M. Almond, discusses the military situation with Ambassador Muccio at ROK Army Headquarters.*

8,000; therefore at day's end they could count on about 25,000.[33]

Colonel Story, in the meantime, took off from the Suwon Airfield at 1130 and flew to Fukuoka, Japan where he refueled and made ready to return to Suwon. During the afternoon North Korean planes bombed the Suwon Airfield and a YAK fighter destroyed a recently arrived C-47 plane.[34]

General MacArthur insisted on going up to the Han River, opposite Seoul, to form his own impression of the situation. On the trip to and from the Han, MacArthur saw thousands of refugees and disorganized ROK soldiers moving away from the battle area. He told General Church that in his opinion the situation required the immediate commitment of American ground forces. He said he would request authority from Washington that night for such action.[35]

Colonel Story brought the *Bataan* back to Suwon at 1715. Within an hour General MacArthur was on his way back to Japan.

---

[33] Interv, Prange with Story; Church MS; Ltr, Lt Gen Edward M. Almond to author, 18 Dec 53. (Almond was a member of the party.)
[34] Interv, Prange with Story.

[35] Church MS; Ltr, Gen Wright to author, 8 Feb 54. (Wright was a member of the party.)

Other than KMAG and ADCOM personnel, the first American troops to go to Korea arrived at Suwon Airfield on 29 June, the day of MacArthur's visit. The unit, known as Detachment X, consisted of thirty-three officers and men and four M55 machine guns of the 507th Antiaircraft Artillery (Automatic Weapons) Battalion. At 1615 they engaged 4 enemy planes that attacked the airfield, shooting down 1 and probably destroying another, and again at 2005 that evening they engaged 3 planes.[36]

The President Authorizes Use of U.S. Ground Troops in Korea

Reports coming into the Pentagon from the Far East during the morning of 29 June described the situation in Korea as so bad that Secretary of Defense Louis A. Johnson telephoned President Truman before noon. In a meeting late that afternoon the President approved a new directive greatly broadening the authority of the Far East commander in meeting the Korean crisis.

This directive, received by the Far East commander on 30 June, Tokyo time, authorized him to (1) employ U.S. Army service forces in South Korea to maintain communications and other essential services; (2) employ Army combat and service troops to ensure the retention of a port and air base in the general area of Pusan-Chinhae; (3) employ naval and air forces against military targets in North Korea but to stay well clear of the frontiers of Manchuria and the Soviet Union; (4) by naval and air action defend Formosa against invasion by the Chinese Communists and, conversely, prevent Chinese Nationalists from using Formosa as a base of operations against the Chinese mainland; (5) send to Korea any supplies and munitions at his disposal and submit estimates for amounts and types of aid required outside his control. It also assigned the Seventh Fleet to MacArthur's operational control, and indicated that naval commanders in the Pacific would support and reinforce him as necessary and practicable. The directive ended with a statement that the instructions did not constitute a decision to engage in war with the Soviet Union if Soviet forces intervened in Korea, but that there was full realization of the risks involved in the decisions with respect to Korea.[37] It is to be noted that this directive of 29 June did not authorize General MacArthur to use U.S. ground combat troops in the Han River area—only at the southern tip of the peninsula to assure the retention of a port.

Several hours after this portentous directive had gone to the Far East Command, the Pentagon received at approximately 0300, 30 June, General MacArthur's report on his trip to Korea the previous day. This report described the great loss of personnel and equipment in the ROK forces, estimated their effective military strength at not more than 25,000 men, stated that everything possible was being done in Japan to establish and maintain a flow of supplies to the ROK Army through the Port of Pusan and Suwon Airfield, and that every effort was being made to establish

---

[36] Det X, 507th AAA AW Bn Act Rpt, 1 Jul 50.

[37] JCS 84681 DA (JCS) to CINCFE, 29 Jun 50; Schnabel, FEC, GHQ Support and Participation in the Korean War, ch. 2, p. 26; MacArthur Hearings, pt. I, pp. 535-36, Secy of Defense George C. Marshall's testimony; New York *Times*, May 12, 1951.

a Han River line but the result was problematical. MacArthur concluded:

> The only assurance for the holding of the present line, and the ability to regain later the lost ground, is through the introduction of U.S. ground combat forces into the Korean battle area. To continue to utilize the forces of our Air and Navy without an effective ground element cannot be decisive.
>
> If authorized, it is my intention to immediately move a U.S. regimental combat team to the reinforcement of the vital area discussed and to provide for a possible build-up to a two division strength from the troops in Japan for an early counteroffensive.[38]

General J. Lawton Collins, Army Chief of Staff, notified Secretary of the Army Frank Pace, Jr., of MacArthur's report and then established a teletype connection with MacArthur in Tokyo. In a teletype conversation MacArthur told Collins that the authority already given to use a regimental combat team at Pusan did not provide sufficient latitude for efficient operations in the prevailing situation and did not satisfy the basic requirements described in his report. MacArthur said, "Time is of the essence and a clear-cut decision without delay is essential." Collins replied that he would proceed through the Secretary of the Army to request Presidential approval to send a regimental combat team into the forward combat area, and that he would advise him further, possibly within half an hour.[39]

Collins immediately telephoned Secretary Pace and gave him a summary of the conversation. Secretary Pace in turn telephoned the President at Blair House. President Truman, already up, took the call at 0457, 30 June. Pace informed the President of MacArthur's report and the teletype conversations just concluded. President Truman approved without hesitation sending one regiment to the combat zone and said he would give his decision within a few hours on sending two divisions. In less than half an hour after the conclusion of the MacArthur-Collins teletype conversations the President's decision to send one regiment to the combat zone was on its way to MacArthur.[40]

At midmorning President Truman held a meeting with State and Defense Department officials and approved two orders: (1) to send two divisions to Korea from Japan; and (2) to establish a naval blockade of North Korea. He then called a meeting of the Vice President, the Cabinet, and Congressional and military leaders at the White House at 1100 and informed them of the action he had taken.

That afternoon Delegate Warren Austin addressed the Security Council of the United Nations telling them of the action taken by the United States in conformity with their resolutions of 25 and 27 June. On the afternoon of 30 June, also, the President announced his momentous decision to the world in a terse and formal press release.[41]

The die was cast. The United States was in the Korean War.

Meanwhile, the Secretary-General of the United Nations on 29 June had sent

---

[38] Msg, CINCFE to JCS, 30 Jun 50.
[39] Schnabel, FEC, GHQ Support and Participation in the Korean War, ch. 2, pp. 27–28, citing and quoting telecons.
[40] Ibid., ch. 2, p. 28.
[41] United States Policy in the Korean Crisis, Doc. 17, pp. 24–25, and Doc. 18, pp. 25–26; Smith, "Why We Went to War in Korea," op. cit.

a communication to all member nations asking what type of assistance they would give South Korea in response to the Security Council resolution of 27 June. Three members—the Soviet Union, Poland, and Czechoslovakia—declared the resolution illegal. Most of the others promised moral or material support. Material support took the form chiefly of supplies, foodstuffs, or services that were most readily available to the particular countries.

The United Kingdom Defense Committee on 28 June placed British naval forces in Japanese waters (1 light fleet carrier, 2 cruisers, and 5 destroyers and frigates) under the control of the U.S. naval commander. This naval force came under General MacArthur's control the next day. On 29 June, the Australian Ambassador called on Secretary of State Dean Acheson and said that his country would make available for use in Korea a destroyer and a frigate based in Japan, and that a squadron of short-range Mustang fighter planes (77th Squadron Royal Australian Air Force) also based in Japan would be available.[42] Canada, New Zealand, and the Netherlands said they were dispatching naval units.

Only Nationalist China offered ground troops—three divisions totaling 33,000 men, together with twenty transport planes and some naval escort. General MacArthur eventually turned down this offer on 1 August because the Nationalist Chinese troops were considered to be untrained and had no artillery or motor transport.

---

[42] *United States Policy in the Korean Crisis*, Docs. 20–90, pp. 28–60.

CHAPTER V

The North Koreans Cross the Han River

> The nature of armies is determined by the nature of the civilization in which they exist.
> BASIL HENRY LIDDELL HART, *The Ghost of Napoleon*

Deployment of U.S. Forces in the Far East, June 1950

At the beginning of the Korean War, United States Army ground combat units comprised 10 divisions, the European Constabulary (equivalent to 1 division), and 9 separate regimental combat teams.[1] The Army's authorized strength was 630,000; its actual strength was 592,000. Of the combat units, four divisions—the 7th, 24th, and 25th Infantry Divisions and the 1st Cavalry Division (infantry)—were in Japan on occupation duty. Also in the Pacific were the 5th Regimental Combat Team in the Hawaiian Islands and the 29th Regiment on Okinawa. The divisions, with the exception of the one in Europe, were understrength, having only two instead of the normal three battalions in an infantry regiment, and they had corresponding shortages in the other combat arms. The artillery battalions, for instance, were reduced in personnel and weapons, and had only two of the normal three firing batteries. There was one exception in the organizations in Japan. The 24th Regiment, 25th Division, had a normal complement of three battalions, and the 159th Field Artillery Battalion, its support artillery, had its normal complement of three firing batteries.

The four divisions, widely scattered throughout the islands of Japan, were under the direct control of Eighth Army, commanded by Lt. Gen. Walton H. Walker. The 7th Division, with headquarters near Sendai on Honshu, occupied the northernmost island at Hokkaido and the northern third of Honshu. The 1st Cavalry Division held the populous central area of the Kanto Plain in Honshu, with headquarters at Camp Drake near Tokyo. The 25th Division was in the southern third of Honshu with headquarters at Osaka. The 24th Division occupied Kyushu, the southernmost island of Japan, with headquarters at Kokura, across the Tsushima (Korea) Strait from Korea. These divisions averaged about 70 percent of full war strength, three of them numbering between 12,000 and 13,000 men and one

---

[1] Memo from Troop Control Br, DA, May 51, OCMH files.

slightly more than 15,000.[2] They did not have their full wartime allowances of 57-mm. and 75-mm. recoilless rifles and 4.2-inch mortars. The divisional tank units then currently organized had the M24 light tank. Nearly all American military equipment and transport in the Far East had seen World War II use and was worn.

In June 1950, slightly more than one-third of the United States naval operating forces were in the Pacific under the command of Admiral Arthur W. Radford. Only about one-fifth of this was in Far Eastern waters. Vice Adm. Charles Turner Joy commanded U.S. Naval Forces, Far East. The naval strength of the Far East Command when the Korean War started comprised 1 cruiser, the *Juneau;* 4 destroyers, the *Mansfield, Dehaven, Collett,* and *Lyman K. Swenson;* and a number of amphibious and cargo-type vessels. Not under MacArthur's command, but also in the Far East at this time, was the Seventh Fleet commanded by Vice Adm. Arthur D. Struble. It comprised 1 aircraft carrier, the *Valley Forge;* 1 heavy cruiser, the *Rochester;* 8 destroyers, a naval oiler, and 3 submarines. Part of the Seventh Fleet was at Okinawa; the remainder was in the Philippines.[3]

The Fleet Marine Force was mostly in the United States. The 1st Marine Division was at Camp Pendleton, Calif.; the 2d Marine Division at Camp Lejeune, N.C. One battalion of the 2d Marine Division was in the Mediterranean with fleet units.

At the beginning of hostilities in Korea, the U.S. Air Force consisted of forty-eight groups. The largest aggregation of USAF strength outside continental United States was the Far East Air Forces (FEAF), commanded by General Stratemeyer. On 25 June, there were 9 groups with about 350 combat-ready planes in FEAF. Of the 18 fighter squadrons, only 4, those based on Kyushu in southern Japan, were within effective range of the combat zone in Korea.[4] There were a light bomb wing and a troop carrier wing in Japan. The only medium bomb wing (B-29's) in the Far East was on Guam.

At the end of May 1950, FEAF controlled a total of 1,172 aircraft, including those in storage and being salvaged, of the following types: 73 B-26's; 27 B-29's; 47 F-51's; 504 F-80's; 42 F-82's; 179 transports of all types; 48 reconnaissance planes; and 252 miscellaneous aircraft. The Far East Air Forces, with an authorized personnel strength of 39,975 officers and men, had 33,625 assigned to it.[5]

Commanding the United States armed forces in the Far East on 25 June 1950 was General MacArthur. He held three command assignments: (1) as Supreme Commander for the Allied Powers (SCAP) he acted as agent for the thirteen nations of the Far Eastern Commis-

---

[2] EUSAK WD, Prologue, 25 Jun-12 Jul 50, pp. ii, vi. The aggregate strength of the four divisions in Japan as of 30 June 1950 was as follows: 24th Infantry Division, 12,197; 25th Infantry Division, 15,018; 1st Cavalry Division, 12,340; 7th Infantry Division, 12,907. Other troops in Japan included 5,290 of the 40th Antiaircraft Artillery, and 25,119 others, for a total of 82,871.

[3] Memo, Navy Dept for OCMH, Jun 51.

[4] Memo, Off Secy Air Force for OCMH, Jun 50. Other fighter squadrons were located as follows: 7 in the industrial area of central and northern Honshu, 4 on Okinawa, and 3 in the Philippines.

[5] U.S. Air Force Operations in the Korean Conflict 25 Jun-1 Nov 50, USAF Hist Study 71, 1 Jul 52, pp. 2-4.

sion sitting in Washington directing the occupation of Japan; (2) as Commander in Chief, Far East (CINCFE), he commanded all U.S. military forces—Army, Air, and Navy—in the western Pacific of the Far East Command; and (3) as Commanding General, U.S. Army Forces, Far East, he commanded the U.S. Army in the Far East. On 10 July, General MacArthur received his fourth command assignment—Commander in Chief, United Nations Command. The General Headquarters, Far East Command (GHQ FEC), then became the principal part of General Headquarters, United Nations Command (GHQ UNC).

Nearly a year before, General MacArthur had established on 20 August 1949 the Joint Strategic Plans and Operations Group (JSPOG), composed of Army, Navy, and Air Force representatives. This top planning group, under the general control of General Wright, G-3, Far East Command, served as the principal planning agency for the U.N. Command in the Korean War.

In the two or three days following the North Korean crossing of the Parallel, air units moved hurriedly from bases in Japan distant from Korea to those nearest the peninsula. Most of the fighter and fighter-bomber squadrons moved to Itazuke and Ashiya Air Bases, which had the most favorable positions with respect to the Korean battle area. Bombers also moved closer to the combat zone; twenty B-29's of the 19th Bombardment Group, Twentieth Air Force, had moved from Guam to Kadena Airfield on Okinawa by 29 June.[6]

The air action which began on 26 June continued during the following days. One flight of U.S. planes bombed targets in Seoul on the 28th. Enemy planes destroyed two more American planes at Suwon Airfield during the day.[7]

Land-based planes of the Far East Air Forces began to strike hard at the North Koreans by the end of June. On the 29th, the Fifth Air Force flew 172 combat sorties in support of the ROK Army and comparable support continued in ensuing days. General Stratemeyer acted quickly to augment the number of his combat planes by taking approximately 50 F-51's out of storage. On 30 June he informed Washington that he needed 164 F-80C's, 21 F-82's, 23 B-29's, 21 C-54's, and 64 F-51's. The Air Force informed him that it could not send the F-80's, but would substitute 150 F-51's in excellent condition. The F-51 had a greater range than the F-80, used less fuel, and could operate more easily from the rough Korean airfields.[8]

Of immediate benefit to close ground support were the two tactical air control parties from the Fifth Air Force that arrived at Taejon on 3 July. These two TACP were being formed in Japan for an amphibious maneuver when the war started. They went into action on 5 July and thereafter there was great improvement in the effectiveness of U.N. air support and fewer mistaken strikes by friendly planes on ROK forces which, unfortunately, had characterized the air effort in the last days of June and the first days of July.

---

[6] *Ibid.*, p. 14.

[7] 24th Div WD, G-2 Jnl Msg File, 28 Jun 50.
[8] USAF Hist Study 71, p. 16; Hq X Corps, Staff Study, Development of Tactical Air Support in Korea, 25 Dec 50, p. 7.

Concurrently with the initiation of air action, the naval forces in the Far East began to assume their part in the conflict. On 28 June the American cruiser *Juneau* arrived off the east coast of Korea, and the next day shelled the Kangnung-Samch'ok area where North Korean amphibious landings had occurred.[9] American naval forces from this date forward took an active part in supporting American and ROK forces in coastal areas and in carrying out interdiction and bombardment missions in enemy rear areas. Naval firepower was particularly effective along the east coastal corridor.

Acting on instructions he had received from Washington on 1 July to institute a naval blockade of the Korean coast, General MacArthur took steps to implement the order. Just after midnight, 3 July, he dispatched a message to Washington stating that an effective blockade required patrolling the ports of Najin, Ch'ongjin, and Wonsan on the east coast, Inch'on, Chinnamp'o, Anju, and Sonch'on on the west coast, and any South Korean ports that might fall to the North Koreans. In order to keep well clear of the coastal waters of Manchuria and the USSR, General MacArthur said, however, that he would not blockade the ports of Najin, Ch'ongjin, and Sonch'on. On the east coast he planned naval patrols to latitude 41° north and on the west coast to latitude 38° 30′ north. General MacArthur said his naval forces would be deployed on 4 July to institute the blockade within the limits of his existing naval forces.[10]

Admiral Joy received from General MacArthur instructions with respect to the blockade and instituted it on 4 July.[11]

Three blockade groups initially executed the blockade plan: (1) an east coast group under American command, (2) a west coast group under British command, and (3) a south coast group under ROK Navy command.

Before the organization of these blockade groups, the cruiser U.S.S. *Juneau* and 2 British ships at daylight on 2 July sighted 4 North Korean torpedo boats escorting 10 converted trawlers close inshore making for Chumunjin-up on the east coast of Korea. The *Juneau* and the two British ships turned to engage the North Korean vessels, and the torpedo boats at the same time headed for them.

The first salvo of the naval guns sank 2 of the torpedo boats, and the other 2 raced away. Naval gunfire then sank 7 of the 10 ships in the convoy; 3 escaped behind a breakwater.[12]

The first U.N. carrier-based air strike of the war came on 3 July by planes from the U.S.S. *Valley Forge* and the British *Triumph,* of Vice Admiral Struble's Seventh Fleet, against the airfields of the P'yongyang-Chinnamp'o west coast area.[13]

The River Crossing

While United States air and naval forces were delivering their first blows

---

[9] Memo, Navy Dept for OCMH, Jun 51.
[10] Msg, CINCFE to DA, dispatched Tokyo 030043, received Washington 021043 EDT.
[11] Schnabel, FEC, GHQ Support and Participation in Korean War, ch. III, p. 11.
[12] Karig, et al., *Battle Report: The War In Korea,* pp. 58–59.
[13] USAF Hist Study 71, pp. 9–13; Hq X Corps, Staff Study, Development of Tactical Air Support in Korea, 25 Dec 50, pp. 7–8; Memo, Navy Dept for OCMH, Jun 51; Karig, et al., op. cit., pp. 75, 83.

of the war, the South Koreans were trying to reassemble their scattered forces and reorganize them along the south bank of the Han River. (*See Map I*). On the 29th, when General MacArthur and his party visited the Han River, it seemed to them that elements of only the ROK 1st and 7th Divisions there might be effective within the limits of the equipment they had salvaged. Parts of the 5th Division were in the Yongdungp'o area opposite Seoul, and, farther west, elements of the Capital Division still held Inch'on. Remnants of the 2d Division were eastward in the vicinity of the confluence of the Han and Pukhan Rivers; the 6th Division was retreating south of Ch'unch'on in the center of the peninsula toward Wonju; and, on the east coast, the 8th Division had started to withdraw inland and south. The 23d Regiment of the ROK 3d Division had moved from Pusan through Taegu to Ulchin on the east coast, sixty-five miles above Pohang-dong, to block an anticipated enemy approach down the coastal road.[14]

On the last day of the month, American planes dropped pamphlets over South Korea bearing the stamp of the United Nations urging the ROK soldiers, "Fight with all your might," and promising, "We shall support your people as much as we can and clear the aggressor from your country."

Meanwhile, the victorious North Koreans did not stand idle. The same day that Seoul fell, 28 June, elements of the enemy's *6th Division* started crossing the Han River west of the city in the vicinity of Kimpo Airfield and occupied the airfield on the 29th.[15] (*Map 1*) After capturing Seoul the North Korean *3d* and *4th Divisions* spent a day or two searching the city for South Korean soldiers, police, and "national traitors," most of whom they shot at once. The North Koreans at once organized "People's Committees" from South Korean Communists to assume control of the local population. They also took steps to evacuate a large part of the population. Within a week after occupying Seoul, the victors began to mobilize the city's young men for service in the North Korean Army.[16]

The N.K. *3d Division*, the first into Seoul, was also the first to carry the attack to the south side of the Han River opposite the city. It spent only one day in preparation. North Korean artillery fire which had fallen on the south side of the Han sporadically on 28 and 29 June developed in intensity the night of the 29th. The next morning, 30 June, under cover of artillery and tank fire the *8th Regiment* crossed from Seoul to the south side of the Han in the vicinity of the Sobinggo ferry. Some of the men crossed in wooden boats capable of carrying a 2½-ton truck or twenty to thirty men. Others crossed the river by wading and swimming.[17] These troops drove the South Koreans from the south bank in

---

[14] Telecon 3441, FEC, Item 27, 1 Jul 50, Lt Gen M. B. Ridgway and Maj Gen C. A. Willoughby; Ltr, Lt Col Peter W. Scott to friend, ca. 6–7 Jul 50; Interv, author with Col Emmerich, 5 Dec 51; 24th Div WD, G–2 Jnl, 1 Jul 50.

[15] ATIS, Enemy Docs, Issue 4, Diary of N.K. soldier (unidentified), 16 Jun–31 Aug 50, entrys for 28–29 Jun, p. 10; ATIS Res Supp Interrog Rpts, Issue 100 (N.K. 6th Div), p. 33; Gen Paik Sun Yup, MS review comments, 11 Jul 58.

[16] There are extensive discussions of this subject in many prisoner interrogations in the ATIS documents.

[17] Church MS; ATIS Res Supp Interrog Rpts, Issue 96 (N.K. *3d Div*), p. 30.

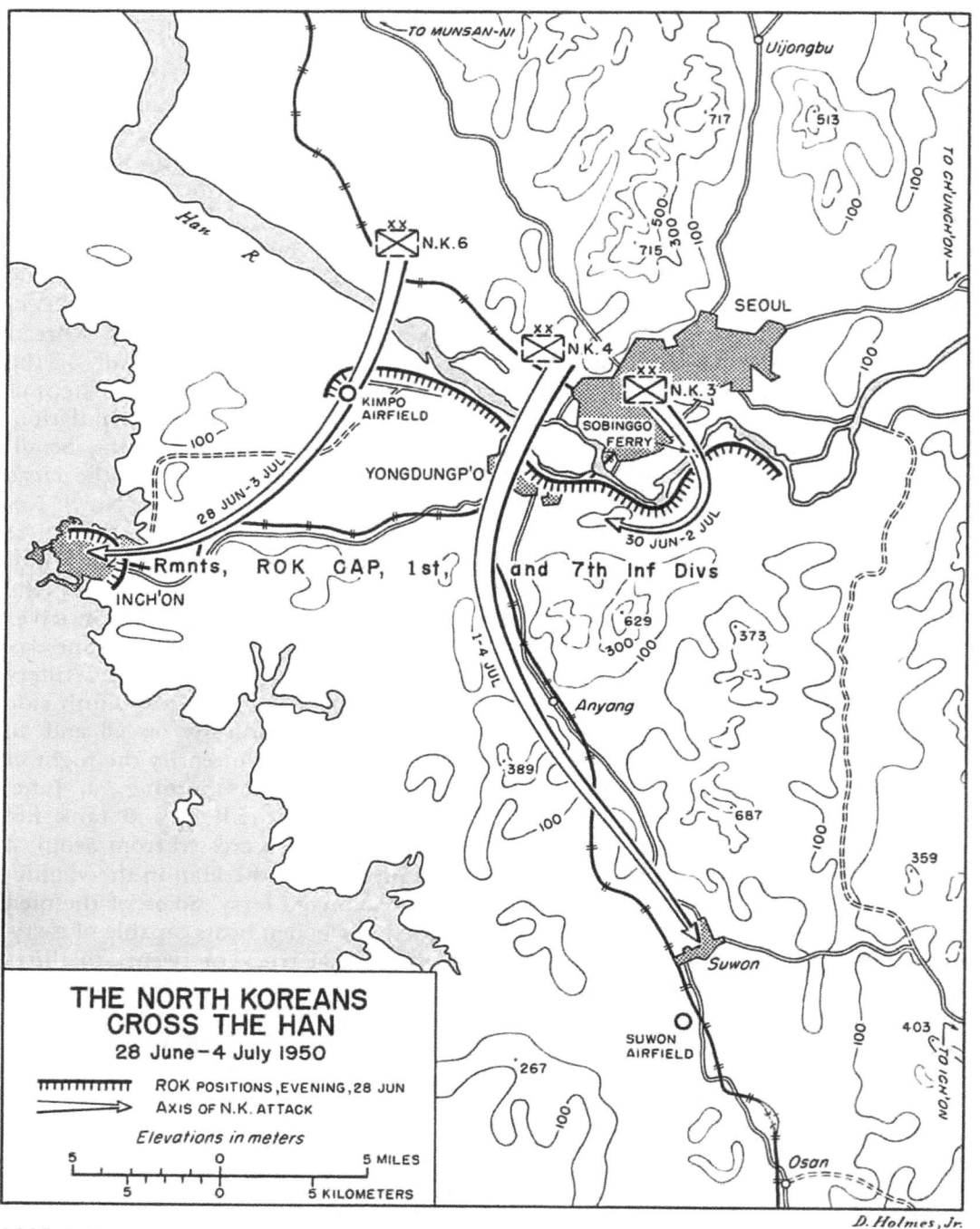

MAP 1

some places and began to consolidate positions there. But they did not penetrate far that first day nor did they occupy Yongdungp'o, the big industrial suburb of Seoul south of the river and the key to the road and rail net leading south. General Church directed General Chae to counterattack the North Koreans at the water's edge, but enemy artillery prevented the ROK troops from carrying out this order.

The enemy's main crossing effort, aimed at Yongdungp'o, came the next morning. The *4th Division* prepared to make the attack. For the assault crossing, it committed its *5th Regiment* which had been in reserve all the way from the 38th Parallel to Seoul. The *3d Battalion* of the regiment started crossing the river southwest of Seoul at 0400 1 July, and upon reaching the south side it immediately began a two-day battle for Yongdungp'o. The remainder of the *4th Division* followed the lead battalion across the river and joined in the battle. Yongdungp'o fell to the division about 0800 3 July. ROK troops waged a bitter battle and North Korean casualties were heavy. The enemy *4th Division* lost 227 killed, 1,822 wounded, and 107 missing in action at Yongdungp'o.[18]

The North Koreans fought the battle for Yongdungp'o without tank support and this may account in large part for the ROK troops' stubborn defense and excellent showing there. The first North Korean tanks crossed the Han River on 3 July after one of the railroad bridges had been repaired and decked for tank traffic. Four enemy tanks were on the south side by midmorning.[19] While the battle for Yongdungp'o was in progress, the remainder of the N.K. *3d Division* crossed the Han on 3 July. As the battle for Yongdungp'o neared its end, part of the N.K. *6th Division* reached the edge of Inch'on. That night an enemy battalion and six tanks entered the port city.

By the morning of 4 July two of the best divisions of the North Korean People's Army stood poised at Yongdungp'o. With tank support at hand they were ready to resume the drive south along the main rail-highway axis below the Han River.

ADCOM Abandons Suwon

On the first day of the invasion, President Syngman Rhee, Ambassador Muccio, and KMAG notified United States authorities of the need for an immediate flow of military supplies into Korea for the ROK Army.[20] General MacArthur with Washington's approval, ordered Eighth Army to ship to Pusan at once 105,000 rounds of 105-mm. howitzer, 265,000 rounds of 81-mm. mortar, 89,000 rounds of 60-mm. mortar, and 2,480,000 rounds of .30-caliber ball ammunition. The *Sergeant Keathley*, a Military Sea Transportation Service (MSTS) ship, left North Pier, Yokohama, at midnight 27 June bound for

---

[18] ATIS Res Supp Interrog Rpts, Issue 94 (N.K. *4th Div*), pp. 44–45; GHQ FEC, History of the N.K. Army, p. 58. The N.K. *6th Division* claims to have entered Yongdungp'o 1 July, but this could have been only an approach to the city's edge. *Ibid.*, Issue 100 (N.K. *6th Div*), p. 33.

[19] *Ibid.*, Issue 4 (Enemy Forces), p. 37; ADCOM G–3 Log, 3 Jul 50. Colonel Green, the ADCOM G–3 from GHQ, made this handwritten log available to the author in Tokyo in 1951. KMAG G–2 Unit History, 4 Jul 50.

[20] Schnabel, FEC, GHQ Support and Participation in Korean War, ch. IV, p. 5.

Pusan, Korea, with 1,636 long tons of ammunition and twelve 105-mm. howitzers on board. Early the next day, 28 June, a second ship, the MSTS *Cardinal O'Connell,* feverishly loaded a cargo from the Ikego Ammunition Depot. Airlift of ammunition began also on the 28th from Tachikawa Air Base near Tokyo. The first C-54 loaded with 105-mm. howitzer shells took off at 0600 28 June for Suwon, Korea.[21] By 1517 in the afternoon, transport planes had departed Japan with a total of 119 tons of ammunition.

In ground action the situation deteriorated. At noon, 30 June, American observers at the Han River sent word to General Church that the ROK river line was distintegrating. About this time, Lt. Gen. Chung Il Kwon of the South Korean Army arrived from Tokyo to replace General Chae as ROK Army Chief of Staff.

At 1600 General Church sent a radio message to Tokyo describing the worsening situation. Three hours later he decided to go to Osan (Osan-ni), twelve miles south of Suwon, where there was a commercial telephone relay station, and from there call Tokyo. He reached Maj. Gen. Edward M. Almond, MacArthur's Chief of Staff, who told him that the Far East Command had received authority to use American ground troops, and that if the Suwon airstrip could be held the next day two battalions would be flown in to help the South Koreans. General Church agreed to try to hold the airstrip until noon the next day, 1 July.[22]

Back at Suwon, during General Church's absence, affairs at the ADCOM headquarters took a bad turn. A series of events were contributory. An American plane radioed a message, entirely erroneous, that a column of enemy was approaching Suwon from the east. Generals Chae and Chung returned from the Han River line with gloomy news. About dusk ADCOM and KMAG officers at the Suwon command post saw a red flare go up on the railroad about 500 yards away. To one observer it looked like an ordinary railroad warning flare. However, some ADCOM officers queried excitedly, "What's that? What's that?" Another replied that the enemy were surrounding the town and said, "We had better get out of here." There was some discussion as to who should give the order. Colonel Wright and General Church were both absent from the command post. In a very short time people were running in and out of the building shouting and loading equipment. This commotion confused the Korean officers at the headquarters who did not understand what was happening. One of the ADCOM officers shouted that the group should assemble at Suwon Airfield and form a perimeter. Thereupon all the Americans drove pell-mell down the road toward the airfield, about three miles away.[23]

When this panic seized the ADCOM group, communications personnel began destroying their equipment with thermite grenades. In the resultant fire the schoolhouse command post burnt to the ground. At the airfield, the group started

---

[21] EUSAK WD, 25 Jun–12 Jul 50, G–4 Unit Hist, 25–30 Jun 50, pp. 4–5.
[22] Church MS.

[23] Statement, Greenwood for Sawyer, 22 Feb 54; Ltr, Scott to friend, ca. 6–7 Jul 50; Church MS.

to establish a small defensive perimeter but before long they decided instead to go on south to Taejon. ADCOM officers ordered the antiaircraft detachment at the airfield to disable their equipment and join them. About 2200, the column of ADCOM, KMAG, AAA, and Embassy vehicles assembled and was ready to start for Taejon.[24]

At this point, General Church returned from Osan and met the assembled convoy. He was furious when he learned what had happened, and ordered the entire group back to Suwon. Arriving at his former headquarters building General Church found it and much of the signal equipment there had been destroyed by fire. His first impulse was to hold Suwon Airfield but, on reflection, he doubted his ability to keep the field free of enemy fire to permit the landing of troops. So, finally, in a downpour of rain the little cavalcade drove south to Osan.[25]

General Church again telephoned General Almond in Tokyo to acquaint him with the events of the past few hours, and recommended that ADCOM and other American personnel withdraw to Taejon. Almond concurred. In this conversation Almond and Church agreed, now that Suwon Airfield had been abandoned, that the American troops to be airlifted to Korea during 1 July should come to Pusan instead.[26] In the monsoon downpour General Church and the American group then continued on to Taejon where ADCOM established its new command post the morning of 1 July.

At Suwon everything remained quiet after the ADCOM party departed. Colonels Wright and Hazlett of the KMAG staff returned to the town near midnight and, upon learning of ADCOM's departure, drove on south to Choch'iwon where they stayed until morning, and then continued on to Taejon. The ROK Army headquarters remained in Suwon. After reaching Taejon on 1 July, Colonel Wright sent five KMAG officers back to ROK Army headquarters. This headquarters remained in Suwon until 4 July.[27]

After securing Yongdungp'o on 3 July, the N.K. *4th Division* prepared to continue the attack south. The next morning, at 0600, it departed on the Suwon road with the *5th Regiment* in the lead. Just before noon on 4 July, eleven enemy tanks with accompanying infantry were in Anyang-ni, halfway between Yongdungp'o and Suwon. The road from Suwon through Osan toward P'yongt'aek was almost solid with ROK Army vehicles and men moving south the afternoon and evening of 4 July. The 5th Regiment of the ROK 2d Division attempted to delay the enemy column between Anyang-ni and Suwon, but fourteen T34 tanks penetrated its positions, completely disorganized the

---

[24] Statement, Greenwood for Sawyer; Ltr, Scott to friend, ca. 6–7 Jul 50; Det X, 507th AAA AW Bn, Action Rpt, 30 Jun–3 Jul 50; 24th Div WD, G–2 Jnl, 25 Jun–3 July 50, verbal rpt by Lt Bailey of verbal orders he received to destroy AAA weapons and equipment at Suwon Airfield.

[25] Church MS; Interv, Capt Robert K. Sawyer with Lt Col Winfred A. Ross, 17 Dec 53. Ross was GHQ Signal member of ADCOM and was with General Church on the trip to Osan and during the night of 30 June.

[26] Church MS.

[27] Sawyer, KMAG MS; KMAG G–2 Jnl, 4 Jul 50; ATIS Res Supp Interrog Rpt, Issue 94 (N.K. *4th Div*), p. 45; Ltr, Scott to friend. Colonel Scott was one of the five officers who returned to Suwon on 1 July.

regiment, and inflicted on it heavy casualties. The Australian and U.S. Air Forces, striving to slow the North Korean advance, did not always hit enemy targets. On that day, 4 July, friendly planes strafed ROK troops several times in the vicinity of Osan. The ROK Army headquarters left Suwon during the day. At midnight the N.K. *4th Division* occupied the town.[28]

---

[28] ATIS Res Supp Interrog Rpts, Issue 94 (N.K. *4th Div*), pp. 44-45; GHQ FEC, History of N.K. Army, p. 58; EUSAK WD, 20 Jul 50, G-2 Sec, ATIS Interrog Nr 89, 2d Lt Pak Mal Bang; ADCOM G-3 Log, 4 Jul 50.

CHAPTER VI

American Ground Forces Enter the Battle

> If you know the enemy and know yourself, you need not fear the result of a hundred battles. If you know yourself, but not the enemy, for every victory gained you will also suffer a defeat. If you know neither the enemy nor yourself, you will succumb in every battle.
>
> SUN TZU, *The Art of War*

Across the Korea Strait events of importance were taking place in Japan that would soon have an impact on the Korean scene. In Tokyo, General MacArthur on 30 June instructed General Walker, commander of Eighth Army, to order the 24th Infantry Division to Korea at once. Its proximity to Korea was the principal reason General MacArthur selected it for immediate commitment.[1] General Walker gave Maj. Gen. William F. Dean, Commanding General, 24th Division, preliminary verbal instructions concerning the division. These instructions were formalized in an Eighth Army Operation Order at 0315 1 July which provided that (1) a delaying force of two rifle companies, under a battalion commander, reinforced by two platoons of 4.2-inch mortars and one platoon of 75-mm. recoilless rifles was to go by air to Pusan and report to General Church for orders; (2) the division headquarters and one battalion of infantry were to go to Pusan by air at once; (3) the remainder of the division would follow by water; and (4) a base was to be established for early offensive operations. The mission of the advance elements was phrased as follows: "Advance at once upon landing with delaying force, in accordance with the situation, to the north by all possible means, contact enemy now advancing south from Seoul towards Suwon and delay his advance."[2] The order also stated that General Dean would assume command of all U.S. Army Forces in Korea (USAFIK) upon his arrival there.

In the next few days Eighth Army transferred a total of 2,108 men to the 24th Division from other units to bring it up to full authorized strength, most of them from the other three infantry divisions. The division, thus readied for the movement to Korea, numbered 15,965 men and had 4,773 vehicles.[3]

---

[1] Schnabel, FEC, GHQ Support and Participation in Korean War, ch. III, p. 1, citing Msg CX 56978, CINCFE to CG 8th Army, 30 Jun 50.

[2] EUSAK WD, Opns Ord 2, 010315K Jul 50.

[3] *Ibid.*, troop list accompanying Opns Ord 2; *Ibid.*, Prologue, 25 Jun–13 Jul 50, Incl 1, Rpt of G–1 Activities, 1–12 Jul 50, pp. 1–2.

GENERAL DEAN *studies the map of Korea.*

Task Force Smith Goes to Korea

On the evening of 30 June, Lt. Col. Charles B. Smith, Commanding Officer, 1st Battalion, 21st Infantry Regiment, 24th Infantry Division, went to bed at 9 o'clock in his quarters at Camp Wood near Kumamoto, Kyushu, tired and sleepy after having been up all the previous night because of an alert. An hour and a half later his wife awakened him, saying, "Colonel Stephens is on the phone and wants you." At the telephone Smith heard Col. Richard W. Stephens, Commanding Officer, 21st Infantry, say to him, "The lid has blown off—get on your clothes and report to the CP." Thus began Task Force Smith as seen by its leader.[4] Colonel Smith had been at Schofield Barracks, Oahu, on 7 December 1941 when the Japanese hit Pearl Harbor, causing him hurriedly to take D Company, 35th Infantry, to form a defense position on Barbers Point. Now, this call in the night vividly reminded him of that earlier event.

At the regimental command post, Colonel Stephens told Smith to take his battalion, less A and D Companies, to Itazuke Air Base; it was to fly to Korea at once. General Dean would meet him at the airfield with further instructions.

Colonel Stephens quickly arranged to lend Smith officers from the 3d Battalion to fill gaps in the rifle platoons of B and C Companies. By 0300 1 July Colonel Smith and his men were on trucks and started on the seventy-five mile drive from Camp Wood to Itazuke. They rode in a downpour of rain, the same monsoon deluge that descended on General Church and his ADCOM party that night on the road from Suwon to Taejon. Smith's motor convoy reached Itazuke at 0805.

General Dean was waiting for Smith at the airfield. "When you get to Pusan," he said to him, "head for Taejon. We want to stop the North Koreans as far from Pusan as we can. Block the main road as far north as possible. Contact General Church. If you can't locate him, go to Taejon and beyond if you can. Sorry I can't give you more information. That's all I've got. Good luck to you, and God bless you and your men."[5]

Thus, the fortunes of war decreed that Colonel Smith, a young infantry officer of the West Point Class of 1939 who had served with the 25th Division in the Pacific in World War II, would command the first American ground troops

---

[4] Interv, author with Smith, 7 Oct 51.

[5] *Ibid.*

to meet the enemy in the Korean War. Smith was about thirty-four years of age, of medium stature, and possessed a strong, compact body. His face was friendly and open.

Assembled at Itazuke, Colonel Smith's force consisted of the following units and weapons of the 1st Battalion, 21st Infantry Regiment: 2 understrength rifle companies, B and C; one-half of Headquarters Company; one-half of a communications platoon; a composite 75-mm. recoilless rifle platoon of 4 guns, only 2 of which were airlifted; and 4 4.2-inch mortars, only 2 airlifted. The organization of B and C Companies included 6 2.36-inch bazooka teams and 4 60-mm. mortars. Each man had 120 rounds of .30-caliber rifle ammunition and 2 days of C rations. In all, there were about 440 men, of whom only 406 were destined to be in the group airlanded in Korea that day.[6]

Smith's force had a liberal sprinkling of combat veterans from World War II. About one-third of the officers had had combat experience either in Europe or in the Pacific. About one-half of the noncommissioned officers were World War II veterans, but not all had been in combat. Throughout the force, perhaps one man in six had had combat experience. Most of the men were young, twenty years old or less.

Only six C-54 planes were available for the transport job. The first plane was airborne at 0845. The first and second planes upon arrival over the small runway near Pusan found it closed in with fog and, unable to land, they returned to Japan. Colonel Smith was on the second plane but he could not land in Korea until the tenth flight—between 1400 and 1500. Colonel Emmerich, who the previous afternoon had received instructions to have the airstrip ready, a few other KMAG officers, and a great number of South Korean civilians met the first elements when they landed about 1100.[7]

A miscellaneous assortment of about a hundred Korean trucks and vehicles assembled by Colonel Emmerich transported the men of Task Force Smith the seventeen miles from the airstrip to the railroad station in Pusan. Cheering crowds lined the streets and waved happily to the American soldiers as they passed. The city was in gay spirits—flags, banners, streamers, and posters were everywhere. Korean bands at the railroad station gave a noisy send-off as the loaded train pulled out at 2000.

The train with Task Force Smith aboard arrived at Taejon the next morning, 0800 2 July. There Lt. Col. LeRoy Lutes, a member of ADCOM, met Colonel Smith and took him to General Church's headquarters where the general was in conference with several American and ROK officers. Church greeted Smith and, pointing to a place on the map, explained, "We have a little action up here. All we need is some men up there who won't run when they see tanks. We're going to move you up to support the ROKs and give them moral support." [8]

Colonel Smith then suggested that he would like to go forward and look over

---

[6] Ltr, Smith to author, 4 May 52.

[7] Intervs, author with Smith, 7 Oct 51, and Emmerich, 5 Dec 51. The 24th Division War Diary, 1 July 1950, erroneously states that 24 C-54 planes were available for the airlift. Smith denies this.

[8] Interv, author with Smith, 7 Oct 51.

the ground. While his men went to their bivouac area, Smith and his principal officers got into jeeps and set out over the eighty miles of bad, bumpy roads to Osan. All along the way they saw thousands of ROK soldiers and refugees cluttering the roads and moving south.

Three miles north of Osan, at a point where the road runs through a low saddle, drops down, and bends slightly northwest toward Suwon, Smith found an excellent infantry position which commanded both the highway and the railroad. An irregular ridge of hills crossed the road at right angles, the highest point rising about 300 feet above the low ground which stretched northward toward Suwon. From this high point both the highway and railroad were in view almost the entire distance to Suwon, eight miles to the north.

After looking over the ground, Smith issued verbal orders for organizing a position there. A flight of enemy fighters, red stars plainly visible on their wings, passed overhead, but their pilots apparently did not see the few men below. Its purpose accomplished, the group returned to the Taejon airstrip well after dark.

That night, 2 July, Smith received an order to take his men north by train to P'yongt'aek and Ansong. The former is 15 miles south, and the latter 20 miles southeast, of Osan. Smith loaded his men into trains and they rolled north into the night. One company dug in at P'yongt'aek; the other at Ansong 12 miles away. Smith established his command post with the group at P'yongt'aek on the main highway.

The next day at P'yongt'aek Colonel Smith and his men witnessed a demonstration of aerial destructiveness. A northbound ammunition train of nine boxcars on its way to ROK units pulled into P'yongt'aek. While the train waited for further instructions, four Mustangs flown by Royal Australian Air Force pilots made six strafing runs over it firing rockets and machine guns. The train was blown up, the station demolished, and parts of the town shot up. All night ammunition kept exploding. Many residents of P'yongt'aek died or were injured in this mistaken air strike.[9]

That same afternoon friendly air also attacked Suwon and strafed a South Korean truck column near the town. ROK rifle fire damaged one plane and forced the pilot to land at Suwon Airfield. There, KMAG and ROK officers "captured" a highly embarrassed American pilot. One KMAG officer with the ROK Army headquarters at Suwon said he was under attack by friendly planes five different times on 3 July. This same officer in a letter to a friend a few days later wrote of these misplaced air attacks, "The fly boys really had a field day! They hit friendly ammo dumps, gas dumps, the Suwon air strip, trains, motor columns, and KA [Korean Army] Hq." In the afternoon, four friendly jet planes made strikes on Suwon and along the Suwon-Osan highway setting fire to gasoline at the railroad station in Suwon and destroying buildings and injuring civilians. On the road they strafed and burned thirty South Korean trucks and killed 200 ROK soldiers. Because of these incidents throughout the day, General Church sent a strong protest to

---

[9] *Ibid.;* 24th Div WD, G–2 Jnl, 25 Jun–3 Jul 50, Msg 239, msg from Gen Church to FEAF, 3 Jul 50; N. Bartlett, ed., *With the Australians in Korea* (Canberra: Australian War Memorial, 1954), p. 174.

AMERICAN COMBAT TROOPS *arriving at Taejon, 2 July. These were 21st Infantry men of Task Force Smith.*

FEAF asking that air action be held to Han River bridges or northward.[10]

The next day, 4 July, Smith's divided command reunited at P'yongt'aek, and was joined there by a part of the 52d Field Artillery Battalion. This artillery contingent comprised one-half each of Headquarters and Service Batteries and all of A Battery with 6 105-mm. howitzers, 73 vehicles, and 108 men under the command of Lt. Col. Miller O. Perry. It had crossed from Japan on an LST 2 July, disembarking at Pusan late that night. Two trains the next day carried the unit to Taejon. There General Church ordered Perry to join Smith at P'yongt'aek, and about 2100 that night Perry's artillery group entrained and departed northward. Because of the destroyed railroad station at P'yongt'aek, the train stopped at Songhwan-ni, where the artillerymen unloaded and drove on the six miles to P'yongt'aek before daylight.[11]

Meanwhile, the 34th Infantry Regiment loaded at Sasebo during the night of 1 July, and arrived at Pusan the next night. After Task Force Smith had left Japan the rest of the 21st Infantry Regiment, except A and D Companies which sailed from Moji, loaded at Sasebo 3

---

[10] Ltr, Scott to friend, ca. 6–7 Jul 50; Interv, author with Hazlett, 11 Jun 54 (Colonel Hazlett was in the Suwon area on 3 July); Msg 239, 24th Div G–2 Jnl, 25 Jun–3 Jul 50.

[11] Ltr, Col Perry to author, 25 May 52; Intervs, author with 1st Lt Edwin A. Eversole, 52d FA Bn, 1 Aug 51, and Perry, 13 Dec 51.

ROAD LEADING TO SUWON *is visible for eight miles from the Task Force Smith position near Osan.*

July and departed for Pusan, arriving there early the next morning.[12]

General Dean also was on his way to Korea. Failing on 2 July to land at Taejon because his pilot could not find the airstrip in the dark, General Dean the next morning at Ashiya Air Base joined Capt. Ben L. Tufts on his way to Korea by General Almond's order to act as liaison between Army and the press. Tufts' pilot knew the Taejon airstrip and landed his plane there about 1030, 3 July. General Dean and Captain Tufts went directly to the two-story yellow brick building serving as General Church's ADCOM Headquarters.[13]

That afternoon a message from General MacArthur notified General Dean that United States Army Forces in Korea was activated under his command as of 0001 4 July. General Dean assumed command of USAFIK during the day and appointed General Church as Deputy Commander. Twenty-two other officers were named General and Special Staff officers of USAFIK.[14] ADCOM pro-

---

[12] Schnabel, FEC, GHQ Support and Participation in Korean War, ch. III, pp. 4-5; Maj Gen Richard W. Stephens, MS review comments, Dec 57.

[12] Interv, author with Capt Tufts, 6 Aug 51; Capt Tufts, notes for author, 8 Aug 51 (8 typescript pages); W. F. Dean and W. L. Worden, *General Dean's Story* (New York: Viking Press, 1954), pp. 18-19.

[14] 24th Div WD, G-3 Jnl, Msg 242, 3 Jul 50; USAFIK GO 1, 4 Jul 50, and SO 1, 4 Jul 50.

AMERICAN GROUND FORCES ENTER THE BATTLE

vided most of the officers for the USAFIK staff, but some KMAG officers also served on it. Most of the KMAG officers who had left Korea by air on 27 June returned aboard the ammunition ship *Sergeant Keathley* on 2 July.[15] By this time the ROK Army had assembled and partly reorganized about 68,000 men.

Task Force Smith at Osan

Colonels Smith and Perry, and some others, went forward in the late afternoon of 4 July to make a final reconnaissance of the Osan position. At this time Perry selected the positions for his artillery. On the road ROK engineer groups were preparing demolitions on all bridges.

Back at Taejon General Dean, a big six-footer with a bristling crew cut cropping his sand-colored hair, and beanpole General Church, slightly stooped, always calm seemingly to the point of indifference, discussed the probability of imminent American combat with the enemy. The third general officer to come to the forward area in Korea, Brig. Gen. George B. Barth, acting commanding general of the 24th Division artillery, now arrived in Taejon in the early afternoon. General Dean decided to send Barth forward to represent him, and with instructions for Task Force Smith. So, at 1500 4 July, General Barth started north by jeep for P'yongt'aek.[16] When he found Smith, General Barth relayed his orders to "take up those good positions near Osan you told General Church about." [17]

A little after midnight the infantry and artillery of Task Force Smith moved out of P'yongt'aek. Colonel Smith had to commandeer Korean trucks and miscellaneous vehicles to mount his men. The native Korean drivers deserted when they found that the vehicles were going north. American soldiers took over in the drivers' seats. General Barth and Colonel Smith followed the task force northward. On the way, General Barth tried to halt the ROK demolition preparations by telling the engineer groups that he planned to use the bridges. At one bridge, after talk failed to influence the ROK engineers, Barth threw the boxes of dynamite into the river. It was only twelve miles to Osan, but it took two and a half hours to get there because ROK soldiers and civilians fleeing south filled the road and driving was under blackout conditions.[18]

About 0300 on 5 July, the delaying force reached the position which Smith had previously selected. The infantry units started setting up weapons and digging in at the predesignated places. Colonel Perry moved his guns into the positions behind the infantry that he had selected the previous afternoon. All units were in place, but not completely dug in, before daylight.[19] (*Map 2*)

---

[15] Church MS; Sawyer, KMAG MS; Schnabel FEC, GHQ Support and Participation in Korean War, ch. IV, pp. 8–9.
[16] Brig Gen G. B. Barth, 25th Div Unit Hist, Tropic Lightning and Taro Leaf in Korea (prepared in 1951), MS in OCMH (hereafter cited as Barth MS); Gen Barth, MS review comments, 24 Feb 58.
[17] Interv, author with Smith, 7 Oct 51; Dean and Worden, *General Dean's Story*, p. 20. Barth says Smith had already started his men forward when he arrived at P'yongt'aek. MS review comments, 24 Feb 58.
[18] Interv, author with Smith, 7 Oct 51; Barth MS, p. 1; Barth, MS review comments, 24 Feb 58.
[19] Intervs, author with Smith, 7 Oct 51, Perry, 13 Dec 51, and Eversole, 1 Aug 51.

TASK FORCE SMITH POSITION *straddling the Osan-Suwon road.*

In seeking the most favorable place to pass through the ridge, the railroad bent eastward away from the highway until it was almost a mile distant. There the railroad split into two single-track lines and passed over low ground between hills of the ridge line. On his left flank Colonel Smith placed one platoon of B Company on the high knob immediately west of the highway; east of the road were B Company's other two rifle platoons. Beyond them eastward to the railroad tracks were two platoons of C Company. This company's third platoon occupied a finger ridge running south, forming a refused right flank along the west side of the railroad track. Just east of the highway B Company emplaced one 75-mm. recoilless rifle; C Company emplaced the other 75-mm. recoilless rifle just west of the railroad. Colonel Smith placed the 4.2-inch mortars on the reverse, or south, slope of the ridge about 400 yards behind the center of B Company's position. The infantry line formed a 1-mile front, not counting the refused right flank along the railroad track.[20] The highway, likely to be the critical axis of enemy advance, passed through the shallow saddle at the infantry position and then zigzagged gently downgrade northward around several knoblike spurs to low ground a little more than a mile away. There it crossed to the east side of the railroad track and continued on over semilevel ground to Suwon.

Two thousand yards behind the infantry, Colonel Perry pulled four 105-mm. howitzers 150 yards to the left (west) off the highway over a small trail that only jeeps could travel. Two jeeps in tandem pulled the guns into place. Near a cluster of houses with rice

---

[20] Interv, author with Smith, 7 Oct 51.

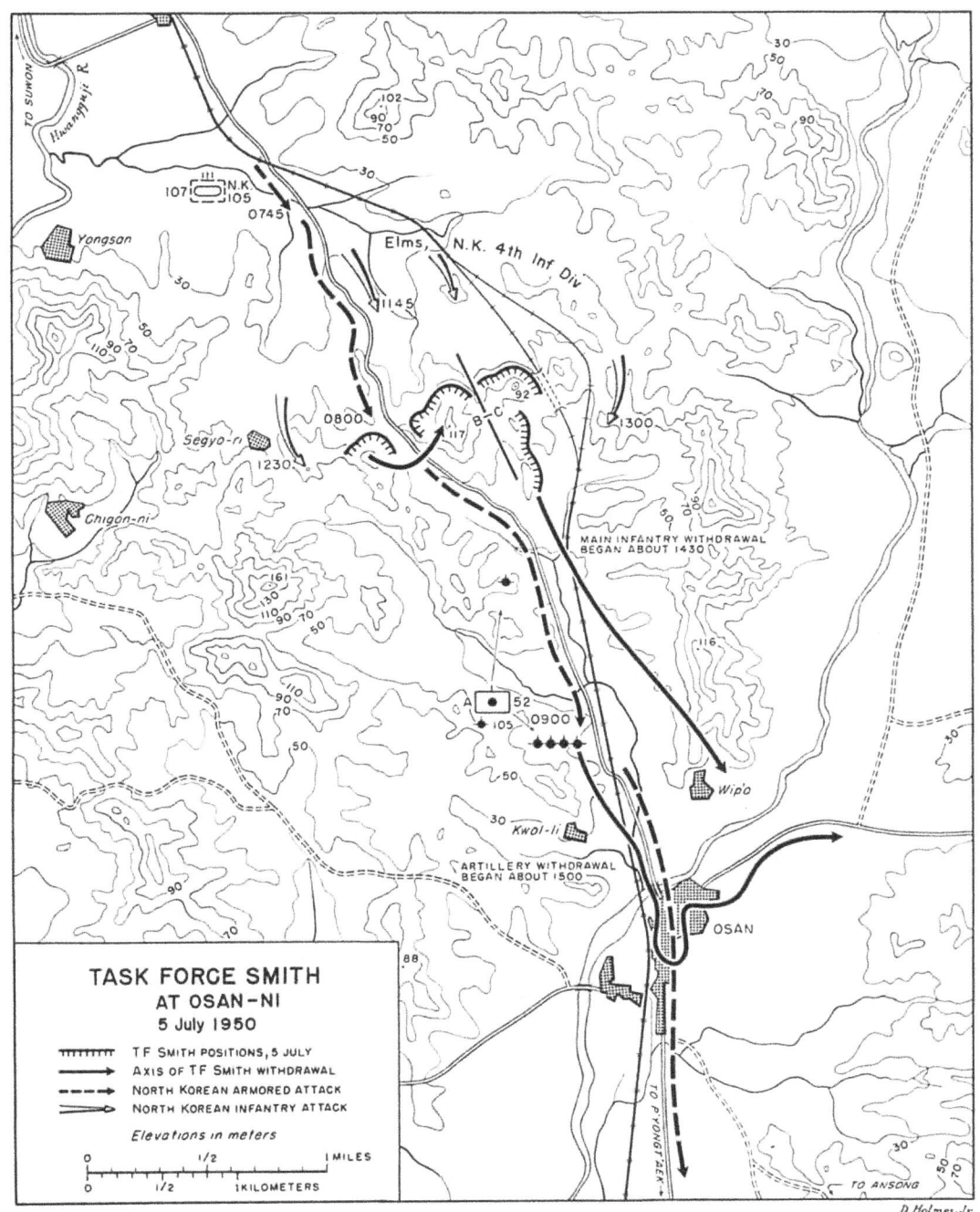

MAP 2

paddies in front and low hills back of them, the men arranged the guns in battery position. Perry emplaced the fifth howitzer as an antitank gun on the west side of the road about halfway between the main battery position and the infantry. From there it could place direct fire on the highway where it passed through the saddle and the infantry positions.[21]

Volunteers from the artillery Headquarters and Service Batteries made up four .50-caliber machine gun and four 2.36-inch bazooka teams and joined the infantry in their position.

The infantry parked most of their miscellaneous trucks and jeeps along the road just south of the saddle. The artillerymen left their trucks concealed in yards and sheds and behind Korean houses along the road just north of Osan. There were about 1,200 rounds of artillery ammunition at the battery position and in two trucks parked inside a walled enclosure nearby. One or two truckloads more were in the vehicles parked among the houses just north of Osan. Nearly all this ammunition was high explosive (HE); only 6 rounds were high explosive antitank (HEAT), and all of it was taken to the forward gun.[22] When the 52d Field Artillery was loading out at Sasebo, Japan, the battalion ammunition officer drew all the HEAT ammunition available there—only 18 rounds.[23] He issued 6 rounds to A Battery, now on the point of engaging in the first battle between American artillery and the Russian-built T34 tanks.

At the Osan position as rainy 5 July dawned were 540 Americans: 389 enlisted men and 17 officers among the infantry and 125 enlisted men and 9 officers among the artillerymen.[24] When first light came, the infantry test-fired their weapons and the artillerymen registered their guns. Then they ate their C ration breakfasts.

In spite of the rain Smith could see almost to Suwon. He first saw movement on the road in the distance near Suwon a little after 0700. In about half an hour a tank column, now easily discernible, approached the waiting Americans. In this first group there were eight tanks. About 0800 the men back in the artillery position received a call from the forward observer with the infantry for a fire mission.[25]

---

[21] Intervs, author with Perry, 13 Dec 51, and Eversole, 1 Aug 51; Ltr, Perry to author, 5 Dec 51. The sixth howitzer had been left at P'yongt'aek because of trouble with the prime mover.
[22] Ltr, Perry to author, 5 Dec 51; Intervs, author with Perry, 13 Dec 51, and Eversole, 1 Aug 51.
[23] Interv, author with 1st Lt Percy R. Hare, 5 Aug 51. (Hare was Ammunition and Trains Officer, 52d Field Artillery Battalion, when the battalion left for Korea.)
[24] Interv, author with Smith, 7 Oct 51; Ltr, Perry to author, 5 Dec. 51. The official army records contain many inaccuracies with respect to Task Force Smith. To note only a few: one FEC G-2 report gives the date of the Osan action as 6 July, the 24th Division War Diary gives it as 4 July. Both are wrong. Several sources state that enemy tank fire destroyed all the American 105-mm. howitzers at Osan; only one was destroyed.
[25] Ltr, Smith to author, 4 May 52; Intervs, author with Smith, 7 Oct 51, and Eversole, 1 Aug 51. Eversole says he looked at his watch when the request for a fire mission came in from the forward observer and noted the time as 0745. Barth thinks the time was closer to 0800. Smith told the author he first saw the enemy column about 0700 and that it was about half an hour in moving up in front of his position. In an interview with the 24th Division G-2 on 7 July 1950, two days after the action, Colonel Smith gave the time as 0745 when the tank column approached his position. See 24th Div G-3 Jnl, 6-10 Jul 50, entry 64, 071720. A telephone call from USAFIK headquarters in Taejon to GHQ in Tokyo at 1105, 5 July, gave the time of initial contact as 0818. Memo, Gen Wright, FEC G-3, for CofS ROK, 051130 Jul 50.

AMERICAN GROUND FORCES ENTER THE BATTLE

At 0816 the first American artillery fire of the Korean War hurtled through the air toward the North Korean tanks. The number two howitzer fired the first two rounds, and the other pieces then joined in the firing. The artillery took the tanks under fire at a range of approximately 4,000 yards, about 2,000 yards in front of the American infantry.[26] The forward observer quickly adjusted the fire and shells began landing among the tanks. But the watching infantrymen saw the tanks keep on coming, undeterred by the exploding artillery shells.

To conserve ammunition Colonel Smith issued orders that the 75-mm. recoilless rifle covering the highway should withhold fire until the tanks closed to 700 yards. The tanks stayed in column, displayed little caution, and did not leave the road. The commander of the enemy tank column may have thought he had encountered only another minor ROK delaying position.

General Barth had gone back to the artillery just before the enemy came into view and did not know when he arrived there that an enemy force was approaching. After receiving reports from the forward observer that the artillery fire was ineffective against the tanks, he started back to alert the 1st Battalion of the 34th Infantry, whose arrival he expected at P'yongt'aek during the night, against a probable breakthrough of the enemy tanks.[27]

When the enemy tank column approached within 700 yards of the infantry position, the two recoilless rifles took it under fire. They scored direct hits, but apparently did not damage the tanks which, firing their 85-mm. cannon and 7.62-mm. machine guns, rumbled on up the incline toward the saddle. When they were almost abreast of the infantry position, the lead tanks came under 2.36-inch rocket launcher fire. Operating a bazooka from the ditch along the east side of the road, 2d Lt. Ollie D. Connor, fired twenty-two rockets at approximately fifteen yards' range against the rear of the tanks where their armor was weakest. Whether they were effective is doubtful. The two lead tanks, however, were stopped just through the pass when they came under direct fire of the single 105-mm. howitzer using HEAT ammunition. Very likely these artillery shells stopped the two tanks, although the barrage of close-range bazooka rockets may have damaged their tracks.[28]

The two damaged tanks pulled off to the side of the road, clearing the way for those following. One of the two caught fire and burned. Two men emerged from its turret with their hands up. A third jumped out with a burp gun in his hands and fired directly into a machine gun position, killing the assistant gunner. This unidentified machine gunner probably was the first American ground soldier killed in action in Korea.[29] American fire killed the

---

[26] Intervs, author with Perry, 13 Dec 51, and Eversole, 1 Aug 51; Barth, MS review comments, 28 Feb 58. Knowing the action was of historic importance, Barth looked at his watch when the artillery opened fire. He says it was 0816.

[27] Barth MS; Interv, author with Capt Ben M. Huckabay, 2 Aug 51. (Huckabay was a corporal at Osan with the 52d Field Artillery.)

[28] Intervs, author with Smith, 7 Oct 51, and Perry, 13 Dec 51. Smith told the author that the bazooka ammunition had deteriorated because of age.

[29] Interv, author with 1st Lt Lawrence C. Powers, 2 Aug 51. Powers was Headquarters Company Communications Officer, 1st Battalion, 21st Infantry, at Osan, 5 July. He said he saw this action.

three North Koreans. The six rounds of HEAT ammunition at the forward gun were soon expended, leaving only the HE shells which richocheted off the tanks. The third tank through the pass knocked out the forward gun and wounded one of its crew members.

The tanks did not stop to engage the infantry; they merely fired on them as they came through. Following the first group of 8 tanks came others at short intervals, usually in groups of 4. These, too, went unhesitatingly through the infantry position and on down the road toward the artillery position. In all, there were 33 tanks in the column. The last passed through the infantry position by 0900, about an hour after the lead tanks had reached the saddle. In this hour, tank fire had killed or wounded approximately twenty men in Smith's position.[30]

Earlier in the morning it was supposed to have been no more than an academic question as to what would happen if tanks came through the infantry to the artillery position. Someone in the artillery had raised this point to be answered by the infantry, "Don't worry, they will never get back to you." One of the artillerymen later expressed the prevailing opinion by saying, "Everyone thought the enemy would turn around and go back when they found out who was fighting."[31] Word now came to the artillerymen from the forward observer that tanks were through the infantry and to be ready for them.

The first tanks cut up the telephone wire strung along the road from the artillery to the infantry and destroyed this communication. The radios were wet and functioning badly; now only the jeep radio worked. Communication with the infantry after 0900 was spotty at best, and, about 1100, it ceased altogether.

The tanks came on toward the artillery pieces, which kept them under fire but could not stop them. About 500 yards from the battery, the tanks stopped behind a little hill seeking protection from direct fire. Then, one at a time, they came down the road with a rush, hatches closed, making a run to get past the battery position. Some fired their 85-mm. cannon, others only their machine guns. Their aim was haphazard in most cases for the enemy tankers had not located the gun positions. Some of the tank guns even pointed toward the opposite side of the road. Only one tank stopped momentarily at the little trail where the howitzers had pulled off the main road as though it meant to try to overrun the battery which its crew evidently had located. Fortunately, however, it did not leave the road but instead, after a moment, continued on toward Osan. The 105-mm. howitzers fired at ranges of 150–300 yards as the tanks went by, but the shells only jarred the tanks and bounced off. Altogether, the tanks did not average more than one round each in return fire.[32]

Three bazooka teams from the artillery had posted themselves near the road before the tanks appeared. When word came that the tanks were through the infantry, two more bazooka teams, one led by Colonel Perry and the other by

---

[30] Intervs, author with Smith, 7 Oct 51, Perry, 13 Dec 51, and Huckabay, 2 Aug 51, and Sgt Jack L. Ruffner, 2 Aug 51.

[31] Interv, author with Eversole, 1 Aug 51.

[32] Intervs, author with Perry, 13 Dec 51, and Huckabay, 2 Aug 51; Ltr, Perry to author, 5 Dec 51.

AMERICAN GROUND FORCES ENTER THE BATTLE

Sgt. Edwin A. Eversole, started to move into position. The first tank caught both Perry and Eversole in the rice paddy between the howitzers and the highway. When Eversole's first bazooka round bounced off the turret of the tank, he said that tank suddenly looked to him "as big as a battleship." This tank fired its 85-mm. cannon, cutting down a telephone pole which fell harmlessly over Eversole who had flung himself down into a paddy drainage ditch. A 105-mm. shell hit the tracks of the third tank and stopped it. The other tanks in this group went on through. The four American howitzers remained undamaged.[33]

After these tanks had passed out of sight, Colonel Perry took an interpreter and worked his way up close to the immobilized enemy tank. Through the interpreter, he called on the crew to come out and surrender. There was no response. Perry then ordered the howitzers to destroy the tank. After three rounds had hit the tank, two men jumped out of it and took cover in a culvert. Perry sent a squad forward and it killed the two North Koreans.[34]

During this little action, small arms fire hit Colonel Perry in the right leg. Refusing to be evacuated, he hobbled around or sat against the base of a tree giving orders and instructions in preparation for the appearance of more tanks.[35]

In about ten minutes the second wave of tanks followed the last of the first group. This time there were more—"a string of them," as one man expressed it. They came in ones, twos, and threes, close together with no apparent interval or organization.

When the second wave of tanks came into view, some of the howitzer crew members started to "take off." As one present said, the men were "shy about helping." [36] The officers had to drag the ammunition up and load the pieces themselves. The senior noncommissioned officers fired the pieces. The momentary panic soon passed and, with the good example and strong leadership of Colonel Perry and 1st Lt. Dwain L. Scott before them, the men returned to their positions. Many of the second group of tanks did not fire on the artillery at all. Again, the 105-mm. howitzers could not stop the oncoming tanks. They did, however hit another in its tracks, disabling it in front of the artillery position.[37] Some of the tanks had one or two infantrymen on their decks. Artillery fire blew off or killed most of them; some lay limply dead as the tanks went by; others slowly jolted off onto the road.[38] Enemy tank fire caused a building to burn near the battery position and a nearby dump of about 300 rounds of artillery shells began to explode. The last of the tanks passed the artillery position by 1015.[39] These tanks were from

---

[33] Intervs, author with Perry, 13 Dec 51, Eversole, 1 Aug 51, and Huckabay, 2 Aug 51.
[34] Intervs, author with Perry, 13 Dec 51, and Eversole, 1 Aug 51.
[35] Intervs, author with Eversole, 1 Aug 51, and Huckabay, 2 Aug 51. Special Order 76, 20 September 1950, awarded Colonel Perry the Distinguished Service Cross.

[36] Interv, author with Eversole, 1 Aug 51.
[37] Intervs, author with Eversole, 1 Aug 51, and Perry, 13 Dec 51. The 24th Division General Order 111, 30 August 1950, awarded Lieutenant Scott the Silver Star for action at Osan, 5 July 1950.
[38] Intervs, author with Eversole, 1 Aug 51, and Perry, 13 Dec 51.
[39] Ibid.

the *107th Tank Regiment* of the *105th Armored Division*, in support of the N.K. *4th Division*.[40]

Colonel Perry estimates that his four howitzers fired an average of 4 to 6 rounds at each of the tanks, and that they averaged perhaps 1 round each in return. After the last tank was out of sight, rumbling on toward Osan, the score stood as follows: the forward 105-mm. howitzer, and 2.36-inch bazookas fired from the infantry position, had knocked out and left burning 1 tank and damaged another so that it could not move; the artillery had stopped 2 more in front of the battery position, while 3 others though damaged had managed to limp out of range toward Osan. This made 4 tanks destroyed or immobilized and 3 others slightly damaged but serviceable out of a total of 33.

For their part, the tanks had destroyed the forward 105-mm. howitzer and wounded one of its crew members, had killed or wounded an estimated twenty infantrymen, and had destroyed all the parked vehicles behind the infantry position. At the main battery position the tanks had slightly damaged one of the four guns by a near miss.[41] Only Colonel Perry and another man were wounded at the battery position.

Task Force Smith was not able to use any antitank mines—one of the most effective methods of defense against tanks —as there were none in Korea at the time. Colonel Perry was of the opinion that a few well-placed antitank mines would have stopped the entire armored column in the road.[42]

After the last of the tank column had passed through the infantry position and the artillery and tank fire back toward Osan had subsided, the American positions became quiet again. There was no movement of any kind discernible on the road ahead toward Suwon. But Smith knew that he must expect enemy infantry soon. In the steady rain that continued throughout the morning, the men deepened their foxholes and otherwise improved their positions.

Perhaps an hour after the enemy tank column had moved through, Colonel Smith, from his observation post, saw movement on the road far away, near Suwon. This slowly became discernible as a long column of trucks and foot soldiers. Smith estimated the column to be about six miles long.[43] It took an hour for the head of the column to reach a point 1,000 yards in front of the American infantry. There were three tanks in front, followed by a long line of trucks, and, behind these, several miles of marching infantry. There could be no doubt about it, this was a major force of the North Korean Army pushing south—the *16th* and *18th Regiments* of the N.K. *4th Division*, as learned later.[44]

Whether the enemy column knew that American ground troops had arrived in Korea and were present in the battle area is unknown. Later, Sr. Col. Lee Hak Ku, in early July operations officer of the N.K. *II Corps*, said he had no idea

---

[40] ATIS Res Supp Interrog Rpts, Issue 4 (Enemy Forces), p. 37.

[41] Ltr, Perry to author, 5 Dec 51; Interv, author with Perry, 13 Dec 51.

[42] Intervs, author with Perry, 13 Dec 51, and Powers, 2 Aug 51; Ltr, Smith to author, 4 May 52.

[43] Interv, author with Smith, 7 Oct 51.

[44] ATIS Res Supp Interrog Rpts, Issue 94 (N.K. *4th Div*), p. 45. The division's third regiment, the *5th*, remained behind in Suwon.

AMERICAN GROUND FORCES ENTER THE BATTLE

that the United States would intervene in the war, that nothing had been said about possible U.S. intervention, and that he believed it came as a surprise to North Korean authorities.[45]

With battle against a greatly superior number of enemy troops only a matter of minutes away, the apprehensions of the American infantry watching the approaching procession can well be imagined. General MacArthur later referred to his commitment of a handful of American ground troops as "that arrogant display of strength" which he hoped would fool the enemy into thinking that a much larger force was at hand.[46]

When the convoy of enemy trucks was about 1,000 yards away, Colonel Smith, to use his own words, "threw the book at them." Mortar shells landed among the trucks and .50-caliber machine gun bullets swept the column. Trucks burst into flames. Men were blown into the air; others sprang from their vehicles and jumped into ditches alongside the road. The three tanks moved to within 200–300 yards of the American positions and began raking the ridge line with cannon and machine gun fire. Behind the burning vehicles an estimated 1,000 enemy infantry detrucked and started to deploy. Behind them other truckloads of infantry stopped and waited. It was now about 1145.[47]

The enemy infantry began moving up the finger ridge along the east side of the road. There, some of them set up a base of fire while others fanned out to either side in a double enveloping movement. The American fire broke up all efforts of the enemy infantry to advance frontally. Strange though it was, the North Koreans made no strong effort to attack the flanks; they seemed bent on getting around rather than closing on them. Within an hour, about 1230, the enemy appeared in force on the high hill to the west of the highway overlooking and dominating the knob on that side held by a platoon of B Company. Smith, observing this, withdrew the platoon to the east side of the road. Maj. Floyd Martin, executive officer of the 1st Battalion, meanwhile supervised the carrying of available ammunition stocks to a central and protected area back of the battalion command post. The 4.2-inch mortars were moved up closer, and otherwise the men achieved a tighter defense perimeter on the highest ground east of the road.[48] In the exchange of fire that went on an increasing amount of enemy mortar and artillery fire fell on the American position. Enemy machine guns on hills overlooking the right flank now also began firing on Smith's men.

Earlier, Colonel Perry had twice sent wire parties to repair the communications wire between the artillery and the infantry, but both had returned saying they had been fired upon. At 1300 Perry sent a third group led by his Assistant S–3. This time he ordered the men to put in a new line across the paddies east of the road and to avoid the area where

---

[45] ATIS Interrog Rpts, Issue 9 (N.K. Forces), pp. 158–74, Interrog of Sr Col Lee Hak Ku.

[46] Senate MacArthur Hearings, pt. I, p. 231.

[47] ATIS Res Supp Interrog Rpts, Issue 94 (N.K. 4th Div), p. 45; 24th Div G–3 Jnl, Rpt of Interrog of Col Smith, 071720, entry 64; Interv, author with Smith, 7 Oct 51.

[48] 21st Inf Regt WD, 5 Jul 50; Intervs, author with Smith, 7 Oct 51, and Powers, 2 Aug 51.

the earlier parties said they had received fire.⁴⁹

About 1430, Colonel Smith decided that if any of his command was to get out, the time to move was at hand. Large numbers of the enemy were now on both flanks and moving toward his rear; a huge enemy reserve waited in front of him along the road stretching back toward Suwon; and his small arms ammunition was nearly gone. A large enemy tank force was already in his rear. He had no communications, not even with Colonel Perry's artillery a mile behind him, and he could hope for no reinforcements. Perry's artillery had fired on the enemy infantry as long as the fire direction communication functioned properly, but this too had failed soon after the infantry fight began. The weather prevented friendly air from arriving at the scene. Had it been present it could have worked havoc with the enemy-clogged road.⁵⁰

Smith planned to withdraw his men by leapfrogging units off the ridge, each jump of the withdrawal covered by protecting fire of the next unit ahead. The selected route of withdrawal was toward Osan down the finger ridge on the right flank, just west of the railroad track. First off the hill was C Company, followed by the medics, then battalion headquarters, and, finally, B Company, except its 2d Platoon which never received the withdrawal order. A platoon messenger returned from the company command post and reported to 2d Lt. Carl F. Bernard that there was no one at the command post and that the platoon was the only group left in position. After confirming this report Bernard tried to withdraw his men. At the time of the withdrawal the men carried only small arms and each averaged two or three clips of ammunition. They abandoned all crew-served weapons—recoilless rifles, mortars, and machine guns. They had no alternative but to leave behind all the dead and about twenty-five to thirty wounded litter cases. A medical sergeant, whose name unfortunately has not been determined, voluntarily remained with the latter. The slightly wounded moved out with the main units, but when enemy fire dispersed some of the groups many of the wounded dropped behind and were seen no more.⁵¹

Task Force Smith suffered its heaviest casualties in the withdrawal. Some of the enemy machine gun fire was at close quarters. The captain and pitcher of the regimental baseball team, 1st Lt. Raymond "Bodie" Adams, used his pitching arm to win the greatest victory of his career when he threw a grenade forty yards into an enemy machine gun position, destroying the gun and killing the crew. This particular gun had caused heavy casualties.

About the time B Company, the initial covering unit, was ready to withdraw, Colonel Smith left the hill, slanted off to the railroad track and followed it south to a point opposite the artillery position. From there he struck off west through the rice paddies to find Colonel Perry and tell him the infantry was leaving. While crossing the rice paddies Smith met Perry's wire party and to-

---

⁴⁹ Ltr, Perry to author, 25 May 52.

⁵⁰ Intervs, author with Perry, 13 Dec 51, and Smith, 7 Oct 51.

⁵¹ Intervs, author with Smith, 7 Oct 51, Eversole, 1 Aug 51, and Powers, 2 Aug 51; Capt Carl Bernard, MS review comments, 24 Feb 58.

gether they hurried to Perry's artillery battery. Smith had assumed that the enemy tanks had destroyed all the artillery pieces and had made casualties of most of the men. His surprise was complete when he found that all the guns at this battery position were operable and that only Colonel Perry and another man were wounded. Enemy infantry had not yet appeared at the artillery position.[52]

Upon receiving Smith's order to withdraw, the artillerymen immediately made ready to go. They removed the sights and breech locks from the guns and carried them and the aiming circles to their vehicles.[53] Smith, Perry, and the artillerymen walked back to the outskirts of Osan where they found the artillery trucks as they had left them, only a few being slightly damaged by tank and machine gun fire.

Perry and Smith planned to take a road at the south edge of Osan to Ansong, assuming that the enemy tanks had gone down the main road toward P'yongt'aek. Rounding a bend in the road near the southern edge of the town, but short of the Ansong road, Smith and Perry in the lead vehicle came suddenly upon three enemy tanks halted just ahead of them. Some or all of the tank crew members were standing about smoking cigarettes. The little column of vehicles turned around quickly, and, without a shot being fired, drove back to the north edge of Osan. There they turned into a small dirt road that led eastward, hoping that it would get them to Ansong.

The column soon came upon groups of infantry from Smith's battalion struggling over the hills and through the rice paddies. Some of the men had taken off their shoes in the rice paddies, others were without head covering of any kind, while some had their shirts off. The trucks stopped and waited while several of these groups came up and climbed on them. About 100 infantrymen joined the artillery group in this way. Then the vehicles continued on unmolested, arriving at Ansong after dark.[54]

There was no pursuit. The North Korean infantry occupied the vacated positions, and busied themselves in gathering trophies, apparently content to have driven off the enemy force.

The next morning, 6 July, Colonel Smith and his party went on to Ch'onan. Upon arrival there a count revealed that he had 185 men. Subsequently, Capt. Richard Dashmer, C Company commander, came in with 65 men, increasing the total to 250. There were about 150 men killed, wounded, or missing from Colonel Smith's infantry force when he took a second count later in the day. The greatest loss was in B Company.[55] Survivors straggled in to American lines at P'yongt'aek, Ch'onan, Taejon, and other points in southern Korea during the next several days. Lieutenant Bernard and twelve men of the reserve

---

[52] Intervs, author with Smith, 7 Oct 51, and Huckabay, 2 Aug 51.

[53] Ltr, Perry to author, 25 May 52; Intervs, author with Perry, 13 Dec 51, and Eversole, 1 Aug 51.

[54] Intervs, author with Smith, 7 Oct 51, and Huckabay, 2 Aug 51.

[55] Interv, author with Smith, 7 Oct 51. Smith estimated his losses at 155 men. A verbal report by the 24th Division G-1, recorded in a penciled journal entry in the division G-3 Journal, entry 71, 071500, gave the total missing from the 1st Battalion, 21st Infantry, as 148 enlisted men and 5 officers. This total included 63 enlisted men and 2 officers from B Company, and 32 enlisted men and 2 officers from C Company.

platoon of B Company reached Ch'onan two days after the Osan fight. Five times he and his men had encountered North Korean roadblocks. They arrived at Ch'onan only half an hour ahead of the enemy. A few men walked all the way from Osan to the Yellow Sea and the Sea of Japan. One man eventually arrived at Pusan on a Korean sampan from the west coast.[56]

None of the 5 officers and 10 enlisted men of the artillery forward observer, liaison, machine gun, and bazooka group with the infantry ever came back. On 7 July 5 officers and 26 enlisted men from the artillery were still missing.[57]

The N.K. *4th Division* and attached units apparently lost approximately 42 killed and 85 wounded at Osan on 5 July.[58] A diary taken from a dead North Korean soldier some days later carried this entry about Osan: "5 Jul 50 . . . we met vehicles and American PWs. We also saw some American dead. We found 4 of our destroyed tanks. Near Osan there was a great battle." [59]

---

[56] Bernard, MS review comments, 24 Feb 58; Lt. Bernard as told to Sgt. Al Mullikin, "The First Brutal Weeks in Korea," the Washington *Post*, June 24, 1951; Interv, author with Smith, 7 Oct 51.

[57] Ltr, Perry to author, 25 May 52; Interv, author with Huckabay, 2 Aug 51; 24th Div G-3 Jnl, Msg 67, 071935; 24th Div G-2 PW Interrog file, 6-22 Jul 50 (Paik In Soo); New York *Times*, July 6, 1950. One group of 36 Americans led by 2d Lt. Jansen C. Cox was captured on 6 July southeast of Osan.

---

[58] ATIS Interrog Rpts, Issue 4 (Enemy Docs), p. 3, Casualty Rpt for *16th, 17th, 18th Regts*, Arty Regt and attached units, 25 Jun-10 Jul 50. A few of the enemy casualties given for Osan may have occurred at P'yongt'aek the next day, but their losses at the latter place could not have been numerous.

[59] 24th Div G-2 PW Interrog File, 6-22 Jul 50. On 11 July an enemy radio broadcast from Seoul first used PW's for propaganda purposes. Capt. Ambrose H. Nugent, of the 52d Field Artillery Battalion, read a statement of about a thousand words in English. The Seoul radio said Nugent was one of seventy-two Americans captured at Osan from the 21st Infantry and the 52d Field Artillery Battalion. See New York *Times*, July 6, 1950, and the New York *Herald-Tribune*, July 12, 1950.

CHAPTER VII

Delaying Action: P'yongt'aek to Choch'iwon

> No speech of admonition can be so fine that it will at once make those who hear it good men if they are not good already; it would surely not make archers good if they had not had previous practice in shooting; neither could it make lancers good, nor horsemen; it cannot even make men able to endure bodily labour, unless they have been trained to it before.
>
> Attributed to Cyrus the Great, in XENOPHON, *Cyropaedia*

Elements of the 34th Infantry began arriving at Pusan by ship late in the afternoon of 2 July. The next afternoon two LST's arrived with equipment. All that night loading went on at the railroad station. Just after daylight of 4 July the 1st Battalion started north by rail; by evening the last of the regiment was following. Col. Jay B. Lovless commanded the regiment, which had a strength of 1,981 men.[1]

When Colonel Lovless saw General Dean at Taejon early on 5 July the General told him that Lt. Col. Harold B. Ayres (an experienced battalion combat officer of the Italian campaign in World War II), whom Lovless had never seen and who had just flown to Korea from Japan, had been placed in command of his 1st Battalion at P'yongt'aek. Colonel Ayres had arrived at P'yongt'aek that morning about 0500 with the 1st Battalion. Dean told Lovless that he would like the 3d Battalion to go to Ansong, if possible, and that the 34th Regimental command post should be at Songhwan-ni. As requested by General Dean, the 3d Battalion, commanded by Lt. Col. David H. Smith, went to Ansong, twelve miles east of P'yongt'aek to cover the highway there. Colonel Lovless set up his regimental headquarters that day, 5 July, at Songhwan-ni, six miles south of P'yongt'aek, on the main highway and rail line. (*Map 3*)

General Dean placed great importance on holding the P'yongt'aek-Ansong line. On the west, an estuary of the Yellow Sea came up almost to P'yongt'aek and offered the best barrier south of Seoul to an enemy that might try to pass around the west (or left) flank of a force defending the main highway and rail line.

---

[1] 24th Div WD, G-3 Jnl, Msg 10, 030930 Jul 50; 34th Inf WD, Summ, 28 Jun–22 Jul 50; Col Jay B. Lovless, MS review comments, 7 Aug 58.

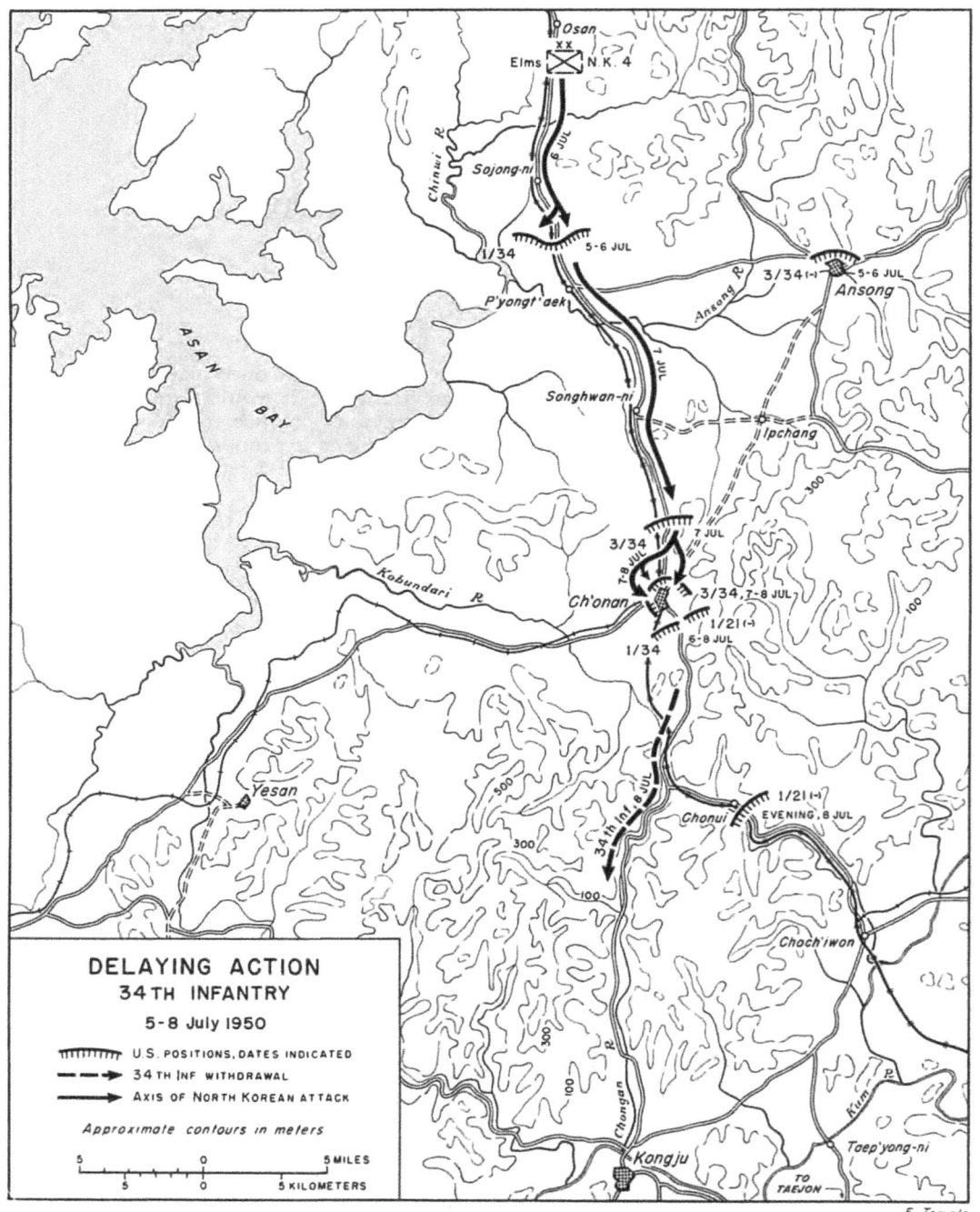

MAP 3

Once south of P'yongt'aek, the Korean peninsula broadens out westward forty-five miles and a road net spreads south and west there permitting the outflanking of the Seoul-Taegu highway positions. East of Ansong, mountains come down close to that town, affording some protection there to a right (east) flank anchored on it. P'yongt'aek and Ansong were key points on the two principal highways running south between the Yellow Sea and the west central mountains. If enemy troops succeeded in penetrating south of P'yongt'aek, delaying and blocking action against them would become infinitely more difficult in the western part of Korea.[2] General Dean was expecting too much, however, to anticipate that one battalion in the poor state of training that characterized the 1st Battalion, 34th Infantry, and without artillery, tank, or antitank weapon support, could hold the P'yongt'aek position more than momentarily against the vastly superior enemy force that was known to be advancing on it.

The Retreat From P'yongt'aek

When General Barth reached P'yongt'aek from the Osan position the morning of 5 July he found there, as he had expected, Colonel Ayres and the 1st Battalion, 34th Infantry. He told Ayres of the situation at Osan and said that probably enemy tanks would break through there and come on down the road. He asked Ayres to send some bazooka teams on ahead to intercept the expected tanks.

Lt. Charles E. Payne with some infantrymen started north. Approaching the village of Sojong they discovered tank tracks in the muddy road where an enemy tank had turned around. Payne stopped the trucks and dismounted his men. A South Korean soldier on horseback, wearing foliage camouflage on his helmet, rode up to them and yelled, "Tanks, tanks, go back!" Payne eventually located the enemy tank on the railroad track about a mile ahead at the edge of Sojong-ni, five miles south of Osan. In an exchange of fire about 1600 between his bazooka teams and the tank at long range, enemy machine gun fire killed Pvt. Kenneth Shadrick. The bazooka teams withdrew, bringing Shadrick's body with them. The group returned to P'yongt'aek and reported the futile effort to Barth and Ayres.[3]

That evening after dark General Dean and his aide, 1st Lt. Arthur M. Clarke, drove to P'yongt'aek. There was still no word from Smith and his men, but the presence of enemy tanks south of Osan raised all sorts of conjectures in Dean's mind. After midnight, he started back to Taejon full of forebodings about Task Force Smith.[4]

Four survivors of the Osan fight arrived at Ayres' command post at P'yongt'aek shortly after General Dean had left it and told an exaggerated story of the destruction of Task Force Smith. A few minutes later, Colonel Perry arrived from Ansong and made his report of

---

[2] 24th Div WD, 5 Jul 50; 34th Inf WD, Summ, 28 Jun–22 Jul 50; Dean and Worden, *General Dean's Story*, pp. 19–21.

[3] 34th Inf WD, 5 Jul 50; Barth MS, pp. 2–3; Higgins, *War in Korea*, pp. 58–65; New York *Times*, July 6, 1950, p. 3; *Time* Magazine, July 17, 1950, p. 12. Miss Higgins erroneously publicized Shadrick as being the first American infantryman killed in the Korean War.

[4] Dean and Worden, *General Dean's Story*, pp. 21–23; Barth MS, p. 3.

what had happened to Task Force Smith. Barth and Ayres then decided to keep the 1st Battalion in its blocking position but to destroy the highway bridge just north of the town now that enemy tanks must be expected momentarily. Members of the 1st Battalion blew the bridge at 0300, 6 July. General Barth instructed Colonel Ayres to hold as long as he could but to withdraw if his battalion was in danger of being outflanked and cut off. He was "not to end up like Brad Smith."

General Barth left the 1st Battalion command post at P'yongt'aek about 0130, 6 July, and started south. He arrived at Colonel Lovless' regimental command post at Songhwan-ni about an hour later. Already Colonel Smith with the remnant (about eighty-six men) of his task force had passed through there from Ansong on the way to Ch'onan, leaving four badly wounded men with Lovless. Colonel Lovless had not received any instructions from General Dean about General Barth, yet now he learned from the latter that he was giving orders to the regiment, and also independently to its battalions. General Barth told Lovless about the position of his 1st Battalion at P'yongt'aek. According to Colonel Lovless, Barth then told him to consolidate the regiment in the vicinity of Ch'onan. Barth directed that the 3d Battalion, less L Company (the regimental reserve) which was near P'yongt'aek, should move from Ansong to Ch'onan. Colonel Lovless thereupon directed L Company to act as a rear guard and delay on successive positions when the 1st Battalion should withdraw from P'yongt'aek. As events later proved, the company did not carry out that order but closed directly on Ch'onan when the withdrawal began. Barth left the 34th Infantry command post for Ch'onan before daylight.[5]

The men of the 1st Battalion, 34th Infantry, in their positions at the river line two miles north of P'yongt'aek had an uncomfortable time of it as dawn broke on 6 July in fog and rain. With water in their foxholes, the men huddled in small groups beside them as they broke open C ration cans for an early breakfast. Colonel Ayres came down the road and stopped where a group of them manned a roadblock, and then he climbed the hill west of the highway to the A Company command post.

On the hill, Platoon Sgt. Roy F. Collins was eating his C ration breakfast when the sound of running motors caused him suddenly to look up. He saw in the fog the outline of tanks on the far side of the blown bridge. From the company command post, Colonel Ayres and Capt. Leroy Osburn, A Company commander, saw the tanks about the same time. Beyond the first tanks, a faint outline of soldiers marching in a column of twos on the left side of the road and a line of more tanks and trucks on the right side, came into view. Some of those watching speculated that it might be part of the 21st Infantry Task Force Smith coming back from Osan. But others immediately said that Task Force Smith had no tanks. It required only a minute or two for everyone to realize that the force moving up to the blown bridge was

---

[5] Interv, author with Col Harold B. Ayres, 13 Jul 54; Barth, MS review comments, 24 Feb 57; Barth MS, pp. 2–3 (a part of this MS was published in *Combat Forces Journal*, March, 1952, as "The First Days in Korea"); Lovless, MS review comments, 7 Aug 58.

North Korean. It was, in fact, elements of the North Korean *4th Division*.[6]

The lead tank stopped at the edge of the blown bridge and its crew members got out to examine the damage. Other tanks pulled up behind it, bumper to bumper, until Sergeant Collins counted thirteen of their blurred shapes. The North Korean infantry came up and, without halting, moved around the tanks to the stream, passing the blown bridge on both sides. Colonel Ayres by this time had ordered the 4.2-inch mortars to fire on the bridge area. Their shells destroyed at least one enemy truck. The enemy tanks opened fire with their tank guns on A Company's position. American return fire was scattered and ineffective.

After watching the first few minutes of action and seeing the enemy infantry begin fanning out on either flank, Colonel Ayres told Captain Osburn to withdraw A Company, leaving one platoon behind briefly as a screening force. Ayres then started back to his command post, and upon reaching it telephoned withdrawal orders to B Company on the other (east) side of the highway.

The 4.2-inch mortar fire which had started off well soon lapsed when an early round of enemy tank fire stunned the mortar observer and no one else took over direction of fire. Within half an hour after the enemy column had loomed up out of the fog and rain at the blown bridge, North Korean infantrymen had crossed the stream and worked sufficiently close to the American positions for the men in A Company to see them load their rifles.

When he returned to his command post, Colonel Ayres talked with Maj. John J. Dunn, S-3 of the 34th Infantry, who had arrived there during his absence. About 0300 that morning, Dunn had awakened at the regimental command post to find everyone in a state of great excitement. News had just arrived that the enemy had overrun Task Force Smith. The regiment had no communication with its 1st Battalion at P'yongt'aek. The distances between Ansong, P'yongt'aek, and Songhwan-ni were so great the command radios could not net. Land lines were laid from Songhwan-ni to P'yongt'aek but it was impossible to keep them intact. Retreating South Korean soldiers and civilian refugees repeatedly cut out sections of the telephone wire to improvise harness to carry packs and possessions. The only communication was liaison officers or messengers. Accordingly, orders and reports often were late and outdated by events when received. Dunn asked Colonel Lovless for, and got, permission to go forward and determine the situation. Before he started, Dunn asked for any instructions to be delivered to Colonel Ayres. Lovless spread a map on a table and repeated General Barth's instructions to hold as long as possible without endangering the battalion and then to withdraw to a position near Ch'onan, which he pointed out on the map. Dunn set out in a jeep, traveling northward through the dark night along a road jammed with retreating ROK soldiers and refugees. In his conversation with

---

[6] Interv, author with Ayres, 13 Jul 54; Capt Russell A. Gugeler, *Combat Actions in Korea: Infantry, Artillery, Armor* (Washington: Combat Forces Press, 1954), "Withdrawal Action," pp. 5-8. Gugeler's book, notable for its detail of incident and action, is based largely on interviews with soldiers engaged in the actions described. ATIS Res Supp Interrog Rpts, Issue 94 (N.K. *4th Div*), p. 45.

Ayres at the 1st Battalion command post, Major Dunn delivered the instructions passed on to him. The decision as to when to withdraw the 1st Battalion was Ayres'; the decision as to where it would go to take up its next defensive position apparently was General Barth's as relayed by Lovless.[7]

Colonel Ayres started withdrawing his battalion soon after his conversation with Major Dunn. By midmorning it was on the road back to Ch'onan. That afternoon it began arriving there. Last to arrive in the early evening was A Company. Most of the units were disorganized. Discarded equipment and clothing littered the P'yongt'aek-Ch'onan road.

Night Battle at Ch'onan

When General Barth arrived at Ch'onan that morning he found there two troop trains carrying A and D Companies and a part of Headquarters Company, 1st Battalion, 21st Infantry. They were the parts of the battalion not airlifted to Korea on 1 July with Task Force Smith. Barth put them in a defensive position two miles south of Ch'onan.

When General Barth returned to Ch'onan in the early afternoon the advance elements of the 1st Battalion, 34th Infantry, were already there. He ordered the 1st Battalion to join elements of the 21st Infantry in the defensive position he had just established two miles south of the town. Lovless had already telephoned from Ch'onan to Dean at Taejon giving him the P'yongt'aek news.[8] Familiar aspects of war were present all day in Ch'onan. Trains going south through the town were loaded with ROK soldiers or civilians. Everyone was trying to escape southward.

Dean that evening started for Ch'onan. There he presided over an uncomfortable meeting in Colonel Lovless' command post Dean was angry. He asked who had authorized the withdrawal from P'yongt'aek. Colonel Ayres finally broke the silence, saying he would accept the responsibility. Dean considered ordering the regiment back north at once, but the danger of a night ambuscade caused him to decide against it. Instead, he ordered a company to go north the next morning after daylight. General Barth remained at Ch'onan overnight and then started for Taejon. He remained in command of the 24th Division artillery until 14 July when he assumed command of his regular unit, the 25th Division artillery.[9]

As ordered, the 3d Battalion, 34th Infantry, had arrived at Ch'onan from Ansong the afternoon of 6 July and during that night. Colonel Lovless gave its L Company the mission of advancing north of Ch'onan to meet the North Koreans the morning of the 7th. With the regimental Intelligence and Reconnaissance Platoon in the lead, the little force started out at 0810. Only some South Korean police were in the silent town. The civilian population had fled. At

---

[7] Ltr, Dunn to author, 17 Jun 54; Intervs, author with Ayres, 13 Jul 54 and 16 Sep 55; Lovless, MS review comments, 7 Aug 58; Gugeler, *Combat Actions in Korea*, pp. 10–12; New York *Herald Tribune*, July 12, 1950; ATIS Res Supp Interrog Rpts, Issue 94 (N.K. *4th Div*), p. 45.

[8] Barth MS, pp. 3–4; Lovless, MS review comments, 7 Aug 58.

[9] Barth MS, p. 4; Interv, author with Ayres, 13 Jul 54; Ltr, Dunn to author, 17 Jun 54; Dean and Worden, *General Dean's Story*, p. 23.

this point Lovless received a message from General Dean. It read, "Time filed 1025, date 7 July 50. To CO 34th Inf. Move one Bn fwd with minimum transportation. Gain contact and be prepared to fight delaying action back to recent position. PD air reports no enemy armor south of river. CG 24 D." [10] Pursuant to these instructions, the 3d Battalion moved up behind L Company.

Col. Robert R. Martin had now arrived at Ch'onan from Taejon. He was wearing low-cut shoes, overseas cap, and had neither helmet, weapons, nor equipment. General Dean and Colonel Martin had been good friends since they served together in the 44th Division in Europe in World War II. Dean had the highest opinion of Martin as a regimental commander and knew him to be a determined, brave soldier. As soon as he was ordered to Korea, General Dean requested the Far East Command to assign Martin to him. Arriving by air from Japan, Colonel Martin had been at Taejon approximately one day when on the morning of 7 July Dean sent him northward to the combat area.

As the 3d Battalion moved north out of Ch'onan it passed multitudes of South Koreans going south on foot and on horseback. Lovless and others could see numerous armed troops moving south on the hills to the west. Lovless asked the interpreter to determine if they were North or South Koreans. The latter said they were South Koreans. Some distance beyond the town, men in the point saw enemy soldiers on high ground where the road dipped out of sight. The time was approximately 1300. These enemy troops withdrew several times as the point advanced cautiously. Finally, about four or five miles north of Ch'onan enemy small arms fire and some mortar shells came in on the I & R Platoon. The advance halted. It was past midafternoon. An artillery officer reported to Lovless and Martin (the latter accompanied Lovless during the day) that he had one gun. Lovless had him emplace it in a gap in the hills about three miles north of Ch'onan; from there he could place direct fire in front of L Company.

A liaison plane now came over and dropped a message for Lovless which read, "To CO 34th Infantry, 1600 7 July. Proceed with greatest caution. Large number of troops on your east and west flanks. Near Ansong lots of tanks (40–50) and trucks. Myang-Myon large concentration of troops. Songhwan-ni large concentration of troops trying to flank your unit. [Sgd] Dean." [11]

Lovless and Martin now drove to the command post of the 1st Battalion, 34th Infantry, to acquaint Colonel Ayres with this intelligence and the situation north of Ch'onan. When they arrived there they found Brig. Gen. Pearson Menoher, Assistant Division Commander, 24th Division, and General Church. General Menoher gave Colonel Lovless an order signed by General Dean relieving him of command of the 34th Infantry and directing that he turn over command to Colonel Martin. Martin

---

[10] Lovless, MS review comments, 7 Aug 58, quoting order, original in his possession.

[11] Lovless, MS review comments, 7 Aug 58. This order is in Lovless' possession. It and the message dated at 1025 were the only two orders Lovless received from Dean during the action at Ch'onan before his relief. 24th Div WD, G-2 Jnl, entry 55, 071045 Jul 50; Ibid., WD, 7 Jul 50; New York Times, July 7, 1950.

likewise received an order to assume command. The change of command took place at 1800. Lovless had been in command of the regiment only a month or two before the Korean War started. He had replaced an officer who had failed to bring the regiment to a desired state of training. It appears that Lovless inherited a chaotic situation in the regiment; the state of training was unsatisfactory and some of the officers wholly unfitted for troop command. Before the regiment's initial commitment in Korea, Lovless had not had time to change its condition appreciably.

While the change of command scene was taking place at the 1st Battalion command post, Major Dunn had gone forward from the regimental command post to find the 3d Battalion moving into a good defensive position north of Ch'onan with excellent fields of fire. While he talked with Colonel Smith, the battalion commander, the I&R Platoon leader drove up in a jeep. There were bullet holes in his canteen and clothing. He reported that an estimated forty enemy soldiers had ambused his platoon in a small village a mile ahead. The platoon had withdrawn, he said, but three of his men were still in the village.

Dunn started forward with the leading rifle company, intending to attack into the village to rescue the men. As he was making preparations for this action, Maj. Boone Seegars, the battalion S–3, came from the direction of the village with several soldiers and reported that he had found the missing men. Dunn then canceled the planned attack and directed the company to take up a blocking position. As the company started back to do this a small group of North Koreans fired on it from the west. The company returned the fire at long range. Dunn kept the company moving and got it into the position he had selected, but he had trouble preventing it from engaging in wild and indiscriminate firing. Friendly mortar fire from the rear soon fell near his position and Dunn went back to find Colonel Smith and stop it. Upon arriving at the 3d Battalion defensive position he found the battalion evacuating it and falling back south along the road. He could find neither the battalion commander nor the executive officer.[12]

Dunn went to the command post and explained to the group that the 3d Battalion was abandoning its position. One of the colonels (apparently Colonel Martin) asked Dunn if the regiment would take orders from him. Dunn replied, "Yes." The colonel then ordered, "Put them back in that position."

Dunn headed the retreating 3d Battalion back north. Then with Major Seegars, two company commanders, and a few men in a second jeep, Dunn went on ahead. Half a mile short of the position that Dunn wanted the battalion to reoccupy, the two jeeps were fired on from close range. Majors Dunn and Seegars were badly wounded; others were also hit. Dunn crawled to some roadside bushes where he worked to stop blood flowing from an artery in a head wound. An enlisted man pulled Seegars to the roadside. Dunn estimates there were about thirty or forty enemy advance scouts in the group that ambushed his party. An unharmed officer ran to the rear, saying he was going for help.

---

[12] Ltr, Dunn to author, 17 Jun 54; Interv, 1st Lt Fred Mitchell with SFC Charles W. Menninger, 31 Jul 50 (Menninger was Opns Sgt, 3d Bn, 34th Inf), copy in OCMH.

TRAFFIC JAM *occurs when the 34th Infantry, moving up, crosses the path of ROK troops and civilians retreating from Ch'onan.*

From his position on a little knoll, Dunn could see the leading rifle company behind him deploy when the firing began, drop to the ground, and return the enemy fire. The men were close enough that he could recognize them as they moved into line. But they did not advance, and their officers apparently made no attempt to have them rescue the wounded men. After a few minutes, Dunn heard an officer shout, "Fall back! Fall back!" and he saw the men leave the skirmish line and move to the rear. This exhibition of a superior force abandoning wounded men without making an effort to rescue them was, to Dunn, "nauseating." Dunn, who was captured and held thirty-eight months a prisoner in North Korea, said the main enemy body did not arrive for two hours. Major Seegars apparently died that night.[13]

The battalion, in withdrawing to Ch'onan, abandoned some of its mortars. By the time the battalion reached the town its units were mixed up and in considerable disorder. South of the town, Colonel Smith received an order to return to Ch'onan and defend it. Colonel Martin led a Headquarters Company patrol north of Ch'onan and recovered jeeps and other abandoned 3d Battalion equipment.

By 1700, 7 July, the 3d Battalion was in a defensive position along the railroad tracks west of Ch'onan and along the

---

[13] Ltr, Dunn to author, 17 Jun 54.

northern edge of the town. Some of the troops organized the concrete platform of the railroad station as a strongpoint. Others mined a secondary road running from the northwest into the town to prevent a surprise tank attack from that direction.

In the early part of the evening some enemy pressure developed from the west. At 2000 a battery of the 63d Field Artillery Battalion, newly arrived in Korea, emplaced south of Ch'onan to support the 34th Infantry. Soon thereafter it fired its first fire mission, employing high explosive and white phosphorus shells, against a column of tanks and infantry approaching the town from the east, and reportedly destroyed two tanks. This enemy force appears to have made the first infiltration into Ch'onan shortly before midnight.[14]

After midnight, reports to the regimental command post stated that approximately eighty men and Colonel Martin, who had gone into the town, were cut off by enemy soldiers. Lt. Col. Robert L. Wadlington, the regimental executive officer, reported this to General Dean at Taejon, and, at the same time, said the regimental ammunition supply was low and asked for instructions. Dean instructed Wadlington to fight a delaying action and to get word to Martin in Ch'onan to bring his force out under cover of darkness. Dean learned with great relief from a message sent him at 0220 8 July that Colonel Martin had returned from the town and that the supply road into Ch'onan was open.[15]

Sometime before daylight Colonel Martin went back into Ch'onan. About daylight a 2½-ton truck came from the town to get ammunition. Returning, the driver saw an enemy tank approaching on the dirt road running into Ch'onan from the northwest. Others were following it. They came right through the mine field laid the day before. Enemy soldiers either had removed the mines under cover of darkness or the mines had been improperly armed; none exploded. The driver of the truck turned the vehicle around short of the road intersection and escaped.[16]

This group of five or six tanks entered Ch'onan and opened fire on the railroad station, the church, several buildings suspected of harboring American soldiers, and all vehicles in sight. In the street fighting that followed, members of the 3d Battalion reportedly destroyed two tanks with bazookas and grenades. Pvt. Leotis E. Heater threw five grenades onto one tank and set it burning. Enemy infantry penetrated into the city about 0600 and cut off two rifle companies.

In this street fighting, Colonel Martin met his death about 0800. Martin had obtained a 2.36-inch rocket launcher when the tanks entered Ch'onan and

---

[14] Interv, Mitchell with Menninger, 31 Jul 50; 34th Inf WD, 7 Jul 50; Interv, Mitchell with SFC Leonard J. Smith (Ch Comp, Fire Direction Center, Hq Btry, 63d FA Bn), 29 Jul 50; 24th Div WD, G-3 Jnl, entry 175, 091125 Jul 50; New York *Herald Tribune*, July 9, 1950, Bigart dispatch from Ch'onan.

[15] 24th Div WD, G-3 Jnl, entries 93, 080220, and 97, 080200 Jul 50.

[16] Interv, author with Col Stephens, 8 Oct 51; Interv, Mitchell with Smith, 29 Jul 50; Interv, Mitchell with Lt Col Robert H. Dawson (CO 63d FA Bn), 27 Jul 50; Interv, Mitchell with Menninger, 31 Jul 50.

SOUTH OF CH'ONAN, *a battery of 155's fires on the enemy-held town, 10 July.*

posted himself in a hut on the east side of the main street. He acted as gunner and Sgt. Jerry C. Christenson of the regimental S-3 Section served as his loader. Sergeant Christenson told Major Dunn a month later when both were prisoners at the North Korean prison camp at P'yongyang that an enemy tank came up and pointed its gun at their building. Colonel Martin aimed the rocket launcher but the tank fired its cannon first, or at the same time that Martin fired the rocket launcher. Its 85-mm. shell cut Martin in two. Concussion from the explosion caused one of Christenson's eyes to pop from its socket but he succeeded in getting it back in place. On 11 July, the Far East Command awarded Martin posthumously the first Distinguished Service Cross of the Korean War.[17]

After Martin's death, the enemy tanks and increasing numbers of infiltrating enemy soldiers quickly caused confusion in the thinning ranks of the 3d Battalion. It soon became a question whether any appreciable number of the men would escape from the town. Artillery laid down a continuous white phosphorus screen and under its cloak some of the 3d Battalion escaped from Ch'onan

---

[17] Ltr, Dunn to author, 17 Jun 54; Ltr and Comments, Col Wadlington to author, 1 Apr 53; Interv, author with Col Green (G-3 of ADCOM staff in Korea and temporarily on Dean's staff), 28 Sep 51; 34th Inf WD, 8 Jul 50; 24th Div WD, 8 Jul 50; FEC GO 12, 11 Jul 50. According to Dunn, Sergeant Christenson died in a North Korean prison camp in December 1950.

between 0800 and 1000. The battalion commander, Colonel Smith, was completely exhausted physically and was evacuated a day or two later. Colonel Wadlington placed Maj. Newton W. Lantron, the senior officer left in the battalion, in charge of the men at the collecting point. At 1000 the artillery began to displace southward. The 1st Battalion still held its blocking position south of the town.

Back at Taejon, Dean had spent a sleepless night as the messages came in from the 34th Regiment. In the morning, General Walker flew in from Japan and told Dean that the 24th Division would soon have help—that the Eighth Army was coming to Korea. Walker and Dean drove north to the last hill south of Ch'onan. They arrived in time to watch the remnants of the 3d Battalion escape from the town. There they learned the news of Martin's death.

Dean ordered Wadlington to assume command of the regiment and to withdraw it toward the Kum River. Just south of Ch'onan the highway splits: the main road follows the rail line southeast to Choch'iwon; the other fork runs almost due south to the Kum River at Kongju. Dean ordered the 21st Infantry to fight a delaying action down the Choch'iwon road; the 34th Infantry was to follow the Kongju road. The two roads converged on Taejon. Both had to be defended.[18]

In the afternoon, a count at the collecting point showed that 175 men had escaped from Ch'onan—all that were left of the 3d Battalion. The 34th Regimental Headquarters also had lost many officers trapped in the town. Survivors were in very poor condition physically and mentally. The North Korean radio at P'yongyang claimed sixty prisoners at Ch'onan. The 3d Battalion lost nearly all its mortars and machine guns and many individual weapons. When the 34th Infantry began its retreat south toward the Kum in the late afternoon, enemy troops also moving south were visible on the ridge lines paralleling its course.[19]

The enemy units that fought the battle of Ch'onan were the *16th* and *18th Regiments* of the N.K. *4th Division*, supported by tank elements of the *105th Armored Division*. The third regiment, called up from Suwon, did not arrive until after the town had fallen. Elements of the *3d Division* arrived at Ch'onan near the end of the battle and deployed east of the town.[20]

The 21st Infantry Moves Up

The 21st Infantry Regiment of the 24th Division had now crossed from Japan to Korea. Colonel Stephens, commanding officer of the regiment, arrived at Taejon with a trainload of his troops before noon on 7 July. Stephens, a bluff, rugged soldier, reported to General Dean for instructions. Within the hour Dean sent him northward to take up a delaying position at Choch'iwon, support the

---
[18] Dean and Worden, *General Dean's Story*, pp. 25-26; Comments, Wadlington to author, 1 Apr 53.

[19] Comments, Wadlington to author, 1 Apr 53; Ltr, Wadlington to author, 25 Jun 53; 34th Inf WD, 8 Jul 50; Interv, author with Ayres, 5 Apr 55; *New York Herald Tribune*, July 9, 1950, Bigart dispatch; *New York Times*, July 9, 1950.

[20] ATIS Res Supp Interrog Rpts, Issue 94 (N.K. *4th Div*), p. 45; Ibid., Issue 96 (N.K. *3d Div*), p. 31.

GENERAL WALKER *(left)* is greeted on arrival at Taejon by General Dean.

34th Infantry, and keep open the main supply road to that regiment.[21]

At Choch'iwon all was confusion. There were no train schedules or train manifests. Supplies for the 24th Division and for the ROK I Corps troops eastward at Ch'ongju arrived all mixed together. The South Korean locomotive engineers were hard to manage. At the least alarm they were apt to bolt south with trains still unloaded, carrying away the supplies and ammunition they had just brought up to the front. American officers had to place guards aboard each locomotive.[22]

Colonel Stephens placed his 3d Battalion, commanded by Lt. Col. Carl C. Jensen, in position along the highway six miles north of Choch'iwon. A little more than a mile farther north, after they withdrew from their Ch'onan positions, he placed A and D Companies of the 1st Battalion in an advanced blocking position on a ridge just east of the town of Chonui. Chonui is approximately twelve miles south of Ch'onan and three miles below the point where the Kongju road forks off from the main highway.[23] *(Map 4)*

---

[21] 21st Inf WD, 6–7 Jul 50; *Ibid.*, Summ, 29 Jun–22 Jul 50; 24th Div WD, G–3 Jnl, msgs 73, 74, 86, 7 Jul 50.
[22] 24th Div WD, 7 Jul 50.

[23] 21st Inf WD, 7–8 Jul 50; Ltr, with sketch map showing positions of A and D Companies at Chonui, Brig Gen Richard W. Stephens to author, 24 Mar 52.

Late in the day on 8 July, General Dean issued an operational order confirming and supplementing previous verbal and radio instructions. It indicated that the 24th Division would withdraw to a main battle position along the south bank of the Kum River, ten miles south of Choch'iwon, fighting delaying actions at successive defensive positions along the way. The order stated, "Hold Kum River line at all costs. Maximum repeat maximum delay will be effected." The 34th Infantry was to delay the enemy along the Kongju road to the river; the 21st Infantry was to block in front of Choch'iwon. Dean ordered one battery of 155-mm. howitzers of the 11th Field Artillery Battalion to Choch'iwon for direct support of the 21st Infantry. Also in support of the regiment were A Company, 78th Heavy Tank Battalion (M24 light tanks), less one platoon of four tanks, replacing the 24th Reconnaissance Company tanks, and B Company of the 3d Engineer Combat Battalion. The 3d itself was to prepare roadblocks north of Kongju along the withdrawal route of the 34th Infantry and to prepare all bridges over the Kum River for demolition.[24]

Messages from General Dean to Colonel Stephens emphasized that the 21st Infantry must hold at Choch'iwon, that the regiment must cover the left flank of the ROK forces eastward in the vicinity of Ch'ongju until the latter could fall back, and that he could expect no help for four days. General Dean's intent was clear. The 34th and 21st Infantry Regiments were to delay the enemy's approach to the Kum River as much as possible, and then from positions on the south side of the river make a final stand. The fate of Taejon would be decided at the Kum River line.

The Fight at Chonui

On the morning of 9 July, the 3d Battalion, 21st Infantry, completed moving into the positions north of Choch'iwon, and Colonel Jensen began registering his 81-mm. and 4.2-inch mortars. Engineers blew bridges in front of Chonui.[25] By noon the 21st Regimental Headquarters received a report that enemy tanks were moving south from Ch'onan.

In midafternoon, Capt. Charles R. Alkire, in command at the forward blocking position at Chonui, saw eleven tanks and an estimated 200–300 enemy infantry move into view to his front. He called for an air strike which came in a few minutes later. Artillery also took the tanks under observed fire. Five of the eleven tanks reportedly were burning at 1650. Enemy infantry in Chonui came under 4.2-inch mortar and artillery fire. Observers could see them running from house to house. The men on the low ridge east of Chonui saw columns of black smoke rise beyond the hills to the northwest and assumed that the planes and artillery fire had hit targets there. Aerial observers later reported that twelve vehicles, including tanks, were burning just north of Chonui. At dusk another air report stated that of about 200 vehicles on the road from P'yongt'aek to Chonui approximately 100 were destroyed or burning. The third and fourth tactical air control parties to operate in

---

[24] 24th Div Opn Order 3, 082145 Jul 50; 78th Tk Bn WD, 8 Jul 50; 24th Div WD, 8 Jul 50.

[25] 24th Div WD, G-3 Jnl, entry 169, 090935 Jul 50.

DELAYING ACTION: P'YONGT'AEK TO CHOCH'IWON

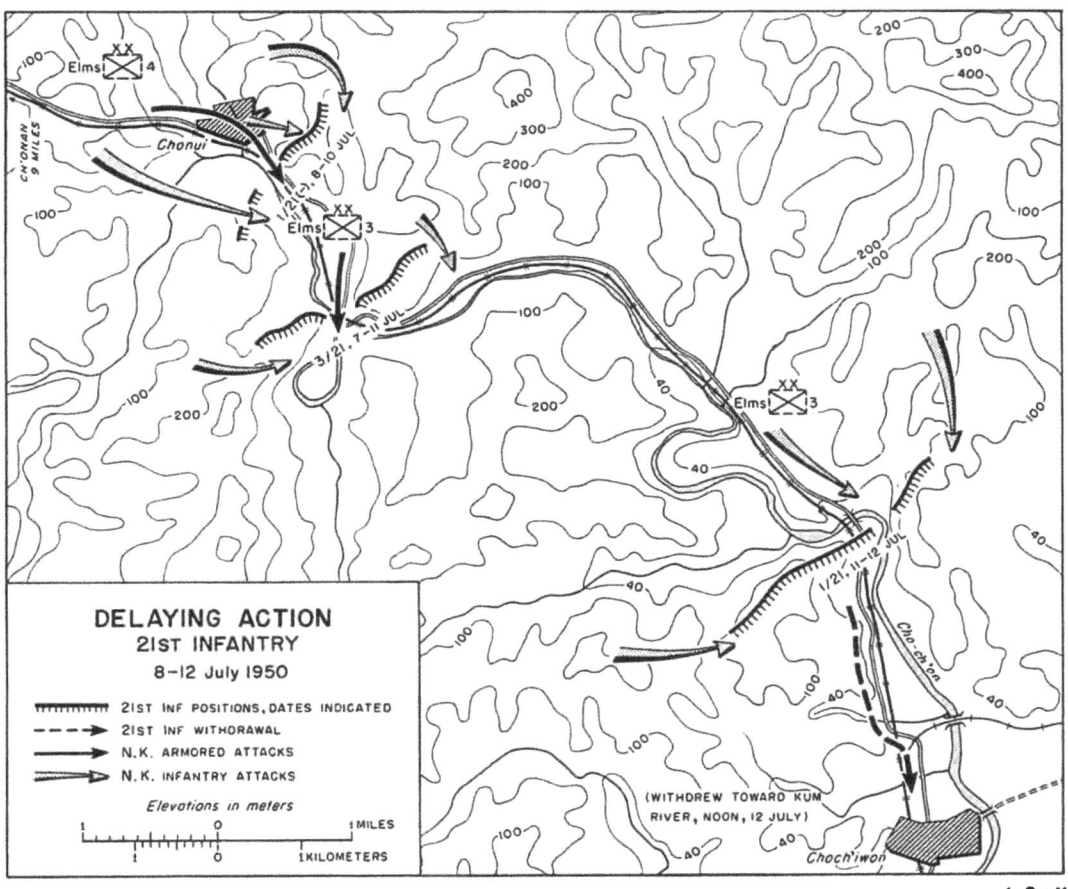

MAP 4

the Korean War (Air Force personnel) directed the strikes at Chonui.[26]

While this heavy bombardment of the enemy column was still in progress, Colonel Stephens arrived at the forward position about dusk and announced he was going to stay overnight.[27] In their front,

---

[26] 21st Inf WD, 9 Jul 50; 24th Div WD, G-2 Jnl, entries 315, 091900 and 317, 091950 Jul 50; *Ibid.*, G-3 Jnl, entries 211, 091820, and 217, 091945 Jul 50; Ltr, Stephens to author, 17 Apr 52; ATIS Res Supp Interrog Rpts, Issue 4 (Enemy Forces), p. 39. Captured North Koreans said later this aerial and artillery action destroyed twenty of their tanks north of Chonui. New York *Herald Tribune*, July 12, 1950, Bigart dispatch; USAF Hist Study 71, p. 25.

[27] New York *Herald Tribune*, July 12, 1950, article by H. Bigart, "From a Foxhole in Korea." This account is a delayed dispatch written by Bigart on 10 July. He occupied a foxhole with Stephens, Alkire, and 1st Lt. Earl Babb, commanding officer of A Company, on the ridge east of Chonui. Bigart kept a log of events as they occurred, describing what he saw and heard from his foxhole and consulting his watch for each recording.

burning Chonui relieved the blackness of the night. Enemy patrols probed their position. Unless all signs failed there would be action on the morrow.

About 500 men of A and D Companies and fillers for B and C Companies who had arrived at Pusan too late to join Task Force Smith for the Osan action comprised the composite battalion of the 21st Infantry at the Chonui position. They occupied a three-quarter mile front on a low ridge 500 yards east of Chonui and on a higher hill 800 yards south of the town. Rice paddy land lay between this high ground and Chonui. The railroad and highway passed between the ridge and the hill. Still another hill westward dominated the left flank but there were too few troops to occupy it.[28]

From the low ridge east of Chonui one normally could see the road for a mile beyond the town, but not on the morning of 10 July. The day dawned with a ground fog billowing up from the rice paddies. With it came the North Koreans. At 0555 the American soldiers could hear enemy voices on their left. Fifteen minutes later those on the ridge at the center of the position heard an enemy whistle at the left; then firing began in that direction. Soon, some of the men near Colonel Stephens began shooting blindly into the fog. He promptly stopped them. At 0700, enemy mortar fire began falling on the ridge.

Lt. Ray Bixler with a platoon of A Company held the hill on the left. The rate of small arms fire increased and those in the center could hear shouting from Bixler's platoon. It was apparent that the main enemy attack centered there, coming from the higher hill beyond it. A concentration of friendly registered mortar fire covered the little valley between the two hills and in the early part of the morning prevented the enemy from closing effectively with Bixler's platoon. But an enemy force passed to the rear around the right flank of the battalion and now attacked the heavy mortar positions. At the same time, enemy tanks came through Chonui on the highway and passed through the infantry position. The men on the ridge could hear the tanks but could not see them because of fog.[29]

At 0800 the fog lifted. Chonui was still burning. Four tanks came into view from the north and entered the village. Stephens radioed for an air strike. Then the men heard tank fire to their rear. The enemy tanks that had passed through the lines earlier were joining their flanking infantry force in an attack on the American heavy mortar position. Stephens had already lost wire communication with the mortarmen; now he lost radio communication with them. The mortars fell silent, and it seemed certain that the enemy had overrun and destroyed them. Although artillery still gave support, loss of the valuable close-in support of the 4.2-inch mortars proved costly.[30]

North Korean infantry came from Chonui at 0900 and began climbing the ridge in a frontal attack against the cen-

---

[28] Ltr, Stephens to author, 24 Mar 52.

[29] Ltrs, Stephens to author, 24 Mar, 17 Apr 52.
[30] Bigart, "From a Foxhole in Korea," op. cit.; 24th Div WD, G-3 Jnl, entry 239, 101000 Jul 50.

ter of the position. The artillery forward observers adjusted artillery fire on them and turned them back. Men watching anxiously on the ridge saw many enemy fall to the ground as they ran. The T34's in Chonui now moved out of the town and began spraying the American-held ridge with machine gun fire.

Shortly after 1100, intense small arms fire erupted again at Lieutenant Bixler's position on the left. The absence of the former heavy mortar fire protecting screen enabled the enemy to close with him. The fog had lifted and men in the center could see these enemy soldiers on the left. Bixler radioed to Stephens at 1125 that he needed more men, that he had many casualties, and asked permission to withdraw. Stephens replied that he was to stay—"Relief is on the way." Five minutes later it came in the form of an air strike. Two American jet planes streaked in, rocketed the tanks without any visible hits, and then strafed the enemy infantry on the left. The strafing helped Bixler; as long as the planes were present the enemy kept under cover. Soon, their ammunition expended, the planes departed. Then the enemy infantry resumed the attack.

While the air strike was in progress, survivors from the overrun recoilless rifle and mortar positions in the rear climbed the ridge and joined the infantry in the center of the position. At 1132, according to Bigart's watch, friendly artillery fire began falling on the ridge. Apparently the artillerymen thought that enemy troops had overrun the forward infantry position and they were firing on them. Enemy fire and tanks had destroyed wire communication from the battle position to the rear, and the artillery forward observer's radio had ceased working. There was no communication. Stephens ran to his radio jeep, 100 yards to the rear of the foxholes, and from there was able to send a message to the regiment to stop the artillery fire; but it kept falling nevertheless.[31]

As the men on the ridge crouched in their foxholes under the shower of dirt and rocks thrown into the air by the exploding artillery shells, Stephens at 1135 received another report from Bixler that enemy soldiers surrounded him and that most of his men were casualties. That was his last report. The enemy overran Bixler's position and most of the men there died in their foxholes.

Even before the friendly artillery fire began falling, some of the men on the north (right) end of the ridge had run off. About the time of Bixler's last radio message, someone yelled, "Everybody on the right flank is taking off!" Stephens, looking in that direction, saw groups running to the rear. He yelled out, "Get those high priced soldiers back into position! That's what they are paid for." A young Nisei from Hawaii, Cpl. Richard Okada, tried to halt the panic on the right but was able to get only a few men together. With them he formed a small perimeter.

At 1205 Colonel Stephens decided that those still on the ridge would have to fall back if they were to escape with their lives. On a signal from him, the small group leaped from their foxholes and ran across open ground to an orchard and rice paddies beyond. There they learned, as thousands of other American

---

[31] Bigart, "From a Foxhole in Korea," op. cit.; 24th Div WD, G-3 Jnl, entry 255, 101530 Jul 50; Ltr, Stephens to author, 17 Apr 52.

soldiers were to learn, that crossing flooded rice paddies in a hurry on the narrow, slippery dikes was like walking a tightrope. While they were crossing the paddies, two American jet planes strafed them, thinking them enemy soldiers. There were no casualties from the strafing but some of the men slipped knee-deep into mud and acquired a "lifelong aversion to rice." Stephens and his small group escaped to American lines.[32]

In this action at Chonui, A Company had 27 wounded and 30 missing for a total of 57 casualties out of 181 men; D Company's loss was much less, 3 killed and 8 wounded. The Heavy Mortar Company suffered 14 casualties. Of the total troops engaged the loss was about 20 percent.[33]

Upon reaching friendly positions, Stephens ordered Colonel Jensen to counterattack with the 3d Battalion and regain the Chonui positions. Jensen pressed the counterattack and regained the ridge in front of the town, but was unable to retake Bixler's hill south of the railroad. His men rescued about ten men of A and D Companies who had not tried to withdraw under the shell fire.

Jensen's counterattack in the afternoon uncovered the first known North Korean mass atrocity perpetrated on captured American soldiers. The bodies of six Americans, jeep drivers and mortarmen of the Heavy Mortar Company, were found with hands tied in back and shot through the back of the head. Infiltrating enemy soldiers had captured them in the morning when they were on their way to the mortar position with a resupply of ammunition. An American officer farther back witnessed the capture. One of the jeep drivers managed to escape when the others surrendered.[34]

American tanks on the morning of 10 July near Chonui engaged in their first fight of the Korean War. They performed poorly. In the afternoon, tanks participated in the 3d Battalion counterattack and did better. One of them got in a first shot on an enemy tank and disabled it. Two American light tanks were lost during the day.[35]

Elements of the N.K. *4th Division* had pressed on south after the capture of Ch'onan and they had fought the battle of Chonui. Leading elements of the N.K. *3d Division*, following the *4th* by one day, apparently came up to Chonui late on the 10th. They found the town such a mass of rubble that the reserve regiment bypassed it.[36]

On the afternoon of 10 July American

---

[32] Bigart, "From a Foxhole in Korea," *op. cit.*; 24th Div WD, G-3 Jnl, entry 255 gives Stephens' message to Dean immediately after his return to American lines.

[33] Dr. J. O'Sullivan, the Rand Corp., Casualties of United States Eighth Army in Korea, Battle of Chochiwon, 10–11 July 1950.

[34] 24th Div WD, G-2 Jnl, entry 420, 101445 and entry 424, 101505 Jul 50; Ltr, Stephens to author, 17 Apr 52; Bernard, MS review comments, 24 Feb 57; New York *Herald Tribune*, July 11, 12, 1950, Bigart dispatches.

[35] 21st Inf WD, 10 Jul 50; Interv, author with Stephens, 8 Oct 51; Ltr, Stephens to author, 17 Apr 52; TAS, Employment of Armor in Korea—the First Year (Ft. Knox, 1952), p. 49. Signal Corps Photo 50-3965, taken 10 July 1950, shows a tank named "Rebels Roost," captioned as the first American tank to see action in Korea.

[36] ATIS Res Supp Interrog Rpts, Issue 94 (N.K. *4th Div*), p. 46; *Ibid.*, Issue 96 (N.K. *3d Div*), p. 31; ORO-R-1 (FEC), The Employment of Armor in Korea, vol. I, p. 138.

air power had one of its great moments in the Korean War. Late in the afternoon, a flight of jet F-80 planes dropped down through the overcast at P'yongt'aek, twenty-five air miles north of Chonui, and found a large convoy of tanks and vehicles stopped bumper to bumper on the north side of a destroyed bridge. Upon receiving a report of this discovery, the Fifth Air Force rushed every available plane to the scene—B-26's, F-80's, and F-82's—in a massive air strike. Observers of the strike reported that it destroyed 38 tanks, 7 half-track vehicles, 117 trucks, and a large number of enemy soldiers. This report undoubtedly exaggerated unintentionally the amount of enemy equipment actually destroyed. But this strike, and that of the previous afternoon near Chonui, probably resulted in the greatest destruction of enemy armor of any single action in the war.[37]

Perhaps a word should be said about the close air support that aided the ground troops in their hard-pressed first weeks in Korea. This support was carried out by United States Air Force, Navy, Marine, and Australian fighter planes and some U.S. fighter-bombers. Beginning early in the war, it built up as quickly as resources would permit. On 3 July the Far East Air Forces established a Joint Operations Center at Itazuke Air Base, on Kyushu in Japan, for control of the fighter planes operating over the Korean battlefield. This center moved to Taejon in Korea on 5 July, and on 14 July to Taegu, where it

established itself near Eighth Army headquarters. By 19 July, heavy communications equipment arrived and a complete tactical air control center was established in Korea, except for radar and direction-finding facilities. Advance Headquarters, Fifth Air Force, opened at Taegu on 20 July.

The forward element in the control system of the close air support was the tactical air control party, consisting of a forward air controller (usually an officer and an experienced pilot), a radio operator, and a radio repair man who also served as jeep driver. Six of these parties operated with the 24th Division in Korea in the early days of the war. As soon as others could be formed, one joined each ROK corps and division, and an Air Liaison Officer joined each ROK corps to act as adviser on air capabilities for close support.

The Fifth Air Force began using T-6 trainer aircraft to locate targets on and behind enemy lines. The controllers in these planes, using the call sign "Mosquito," remained over enemy positions and directed fighter planes to the targets. Because of the call sign the T-6's soon became known in Army and Air Force parlance as Mosquitoes. The Mosquito normally carried an Air Force pilot and a ground force observer. The plane was equipped with a Very High Frequency radio for contact with tactical air control parties and fighter aircraft in the air. It also had an SCR-300 radio for contact with front-line ground troops. The ground force observer and the pilot in the Mosquito, the control party, and the forward infantry elements co-ordinated their information to bring fighter aircraft to targets where they delivered their

---

[37] USAF Hist Study 71, p. 40.

strikes, and also to direct ground fire on enemy targets in front of the infantry.[38]

In the early part of the war the F-51 (Mustang), a propeller-driven fighter, predominated in the Air Force's close support effort. This plane had shown to good advantage in World War II in low-level close support missions. It had greater range than the jet F-80 and could use the rough, short fields in Korea. Most important of all, it was available. For close support of Marine troops when they were committed later, a tried and tested plane, the Marine F4U Corsair, was used. The F-51 was capable of carrying 6 5-inch rockets and 2 110-gallon napalm tanks, and it mounted 6 .50-caliber machine guns. The F-80 could carry 2 110-gallon napalm tanks, and mounted 6 .50-caliber machine guns with about the same ammunition load as the F-51. It could also carry 2 5-inch rockets if the target distance was short. Both the F-51 and the F-80 could carry 2,000 pounds of bombs if the mission required it. The F4U could carry 8 5-inch rockets, 2 110-gallon napalm tanks, and it mounted 4 20-mm. cannon with 800 rounds of ammunition. If desired it could carry a 5,200-pound bomb load. The F-51 had a 400-mile operating radius, which could be increased to 760 miles by using external gas tanks. The F-80's normal radius was 125 miles, but it could be increased to 550 miles with external tanks. The F4U had a shorter operating range. With external tanks it reached about 335 miles.[39]

Choch'iwon

Just before midnight of 10 July Colonel Jensen began to withdraw the 3d Battalion from the recaptured ridge east of Chonui, bringing along most of the equipment lost earlier in the day. When the battalion arrived at its former position it received a surprise: enemy soldiers occupied some of its foxholes. Only after an hour's battle did K Company clear the North Koreans from its old position.[40]

In a message to Colonel Stephens at 2045 General Dean suggested withdrawing the 3d Battalion from this position. But he left the decision to Stephens, saying, "If you consider it necessary, withdraw to your next delaying position prior to dawn. I am reminding you of the importance of the town of Choch'iwon. If it is lost, it means that the SKA [South Korean Army] will have lost its MSR [Main Supply Route]." An hour later, in talking to a regimental staff officer, Dean authorized falling back four miles to the next delaying position two miles north of Choch'iwon, but ordered, "Hold in your new position and fight like hell. I expect you to hold it all day tomorrow."[41]

Meanwhile, Task Force Smith, re-

---

[38] "Air War in Korea," *Air University Quarterly Review*, IV, No. 3 (Spring, 1951), 56; Hq X Corps, Analysis of the Air-Ground Operations System, 28 Jun-8 Sep 50, Staff Study, 25 Dec 50; Maj Louis H. Aten, Debriefing Rpt 75, Arty School, Ft. Sill, Okla, 5 Mar 52.

[39] X Corps Study, p. 14; Operations Research Office, Close Air Support Operations in Korea, ORO-R-3 (FEC), pp. 13-14.
[40] 21st Inf WD, 11 Jul 50.
[41] 24th Div WD, G-3 Jnl, entries 275 at 102045, 277 at 102040, and 278 at 102130 Jul 50.

DEFENSE OF CHOCH'IWON. *Engineer troops prepare to mine a bridge.*

equipping at Taejon, had received 205 replacements and on 10 July it received orders to rejoin the 21st Regiment at Choch'iwon. Smith arrived there with B and C Companies before dawn of 11 July. A and D Companies had re-equipped at Choch'iwon and they joined with B and C Companies to reunite the 1st Battalion. Colonel Smith now had his battalion together in Korea for the first time. At 0730, 11 July, the 1st Battalion was in position along the highway two miles north of Choch'iwon.[42] Four miles north of it Colonel Jensen's 3d Battalion was already engaged with the North Koreans in the next battle.

At 0630 that morning, men in the 3d Battalion position heard tanks to their front on the other side of a mine field, but could not see them because of fog. Within a few minutes four enemy tanks crossed the mine field and loomed up in the battalion area. Simultaneously, enemy mortar fire fell on the battalion command post, blowing up the communications center, the ammunition supply point, and causing heavy casualties among headquarters troops. Approximately 1,000 enemy infantry enveloped both flanks of the position. Some for-

---

[42] 21st Inf WD, 9 and 11 Jul 50.

ward observers had fine targets but their radios did not function. In certain platoons there apparently was no wire communication. Consequently these forward observers were unable to call in and direct mortar and artillery fire on the North Koreans.

This attack on the 3d Battalion, 21st Infantry, was one of the most perfectly co-ordinated assaults ever launched by North Koreans against American troops. The North Koreans who had been driven from the 3d Battalion's position shortly after midnight, together no doubt with other infiltrators, apparently had provided detailed and accurate information of the 3d Battalion's defenses and the location of its command post. The attack disorganized the battalion and destroyed its communications before it had a chance to fight back. Enemy roadblocks behind the battalion prevented evacuation of the wounded or resupplying the battalion with ammunition. For several hours units of the battalion fought as best they could. Many desperate encounters took place. In one of these, when an enemy machine gun placed a band of fire on K Company's command post, Pvt. Paul R. Spear, armed with only a pistol, charged the machine gun emplacement alone, entered it with his pistol empty and, using it as a club, routed the enemy gunners. Enemy fire seriously wounded him.[43]

The North Koreans overran the 3d Battalion. Before noon, survivors in small groups made their way back toward Choch'iwon. Enemy fire killed Colonel Jensen, the battalion commander, and Lt. Leon J. Jacques, Jr., his S-2, when they tried to cross a stream in the rear of their observation post. The battalion S-1 and S-3, Lieutenants Cashe and Lester, and Capt. O'Dean T. Cox, commanding officer of L Company, were reported missing in action. The 3d Battalion, 21st Infantry, lost altogether nearly 60 percent of its strength in this action. Of those who escaped, 90 percent had neither weapons, ammunition, nor canteens, and, in many instances, the men had neither helmets nor shoes. One officer of L Company who came out with some men said that after he and others had removed an enemy machine gun blocking their escape route many uninjured men by the side of the road simply refused to try to go on. One noncom said, "Lieutenant, you will have to go on. I'm too beat up. They'll just have to take me." A remnant of 8 officers and 142 men able for duty was organized into a provisional company of three rifle platoons and a heavy weapons company. But by 15 July a total of 322 out of 667 men had returned to the battalion. Four tanks of A Company, 78th Heavy Tank Battalion, were lost to enemy action north of Choch'iwon on 10 and 11 July.[44] The 21st Infantry on 10 and 11 July north of Choch'iwon lost maté-

---

[43] 21st Inf WD, 11 Jul 50; 24th Div WD, G-3 Jnl, entry 292, 110650 Jul 50; Bernard (1st Plat Ldr L Co at time), MS review comments, 24 Feb 57. General Order 55, awarded the Distinguished Service Cross to Private Spear. EUSAK WD, 7 Sep 50.

[44] Ltr, Stephens to author, 24 Mar 52; Bernard, MS review comments, 24 Feb 57; 21st Inf WD, 11 Jul 50; Ibid., 12 Jul 50, Incl III, Activities Rpt, 3d Bn; 24th Div WD, 11 Jul 50. When it regained this ground on 29 September 1950, the 5th Cavalry Regiment, 1st Cavalry Division, found many American dead. See Hist, 5th Cav Regt, 1st Cav Div, Msg 49; 291825 Sep 50.

riel and weapons sufficient to equip two rifle battalions and individual and organic clothing for 975 men.

At Chonui the *3d Division* had passed the *4th* on the main highway. It struck the blow against the 3d Battalion, 21st Infantry. The *4th Division* turned back from Chonui and took the right fork toward Kongju, following the retreating 34th Infantry.[45]

Toward evening of the 11th, after he had full information of the fate of the 3d Battalion, 21st Infantry, General Dean ordered A Company, 3d Engineer Combat Battalion, to prepare every possible obstacle for the defense of the Choch'iwon area and to cover, if necessary, the withdrawal of the regiment. Dean also started the 19th Infantry Regiment and the 13th Field Artillery Battalion from Taegu and P'ohang-dong for Taejon during the day.[46]

That night the 1st Battalion, 21st Infantry, rested uneasily in its positions two miles north of Choch'iwon. It had to expect that the North Koreans would strike within hours. At dawn an enemy patrol approached C Company's position, and members of the battalion saw hostile movement on both flanks. At 0930 an estimated enemy battalion, supported by artillery fire, attacked Smith's left flank. Very quickly a general attack developed by an estimated 2,000 enemy soldiers. Colonel Stephens decided that the understrength 1st Battalion, with its large percentage of replacement and untried troops, would have to withdraw. At noon, 12 July, he sent the following message to General Dean: "Am surrounded. 1st Bn left giving way. Situation bad on right. Having nothing left to establish intermediate delaying position am forced to withdraw to river line. I have issued instructions to withdraw." [47]

Colonel Smith disengaged the 1st Battalion by moving one company at a time Regimental trucks loaded the troops near Choch'iwon. While the infantry were displacing southward, enemy artillery began shelling the regimental command post in Choch'iwon. The retreat was orderly and there was no close pursuit. By 1530 the 1st Battalion occupied new defensive positions on the south bank of the Kum River where the highway crossed it at Taep'yong-ni. The 21st Infantry Regiment completed its withdrawal across the Kum at 1600, but straglers were still crossing the river five hours later. A thin line of approximately 325 men held the new blocking position at the river—64 men from the 3d Battalion, the rest from the 1st Battalion.[48]

In the series of battles between Chonui and Choch'iwon the understrength two-battalion 21st Infantry Regiment had delayed two of the best North Korean divisions for three days. It was the most impressive performance yet of American troops in Korea, but the regiment paid heavily for it in loss of personnel and equipment.

---

[45] ATIS Res Supp Interrog Rpts, Issue 94 (N.K. *4th Div*), p. 46; *Ibid.*, Issue 96 (N.K. *3d Div*), p. 31.
[46] 24th Div WD, 11 Jul 50.

[47] 21st Inf WD, 12 Jul 50; 24th Div WD, G-3 Jnl, entry 353, 121200 Jul 50; Interv, author with Col Charles B. Smith, 7 Oct 51; Interv, author with Stephens, 8 Oct 51.
[48] 21st Inf WD, 12 Jul 50; 24th Div WD, G-2 Jnl, entry 703, 11-13 Jul 50; *Ibid.*, G-3 Jnl, entries 361, 121545, and 372, 122120 Jul 50.

The 1st Battalion, 34th Infantry, meanwhile, had covered the retreat on the Kongju road and fought a series of minor delaying actions against the leading elements of the N.K. *4th Division* which had taken up the pursuit there. Four light M24 tanks of the 78th Tank Battalion joined the battalion, and D Company of the 3d Engineer Combat Battalion prepared demolitions along the road. In the afternoon of 11 July, enemy action destroyed three of the four tanks, two of them by artillery fire and the third by infantry close attack when the tank tried to rescue personnel from a litter jeep ambushed by enemy infiltrators. Remnants of the 3d Battalion had led the retreat. Reorganized as a composite company and re-equipped at Taejon, it returned to Kongju on the 11th. The next day the 63d Field Artillery Battalion and the 34th Infantry crossed the Kum. The last of the infantry and Colonel Ayres, the 1st Battalion commander, crossed at dusk. General Dean's instructions were to "leave a small outpost across the river. Blow the main bridge only when enemy starts to cross." To implement this order Colonel Wadlington had L Company hold the bridge and outpost the north bank for 600 yards.[49]

---

[49] Comments, Wadlington to author, 1 Apr 53; 24th Div WD, 9-12 Jul 50, and G-3 Jnl, entries 158, 032300, 292, 110650, and 356, 121818 Jul 50; G-2 Jnl, entries 555, 111520, and 572, 111630 Jul 50; 34th Inf WD, 12 Jul 50, and Summ, 28 Jun-22 Jul 50; Interv, Mitchell with Sgt Justin B. Fleming, I Co, 34th Inf, 1 Aug 50; Interv, Mitchell with 2d Lt James B. Bryant, B Co, 34th Inf, 30 Jul 50; ATIS Res Supp Interrog Rpts, Issue 9 (N.K. *4th Div*), p. 46. The 34th Infantry War Diary for this period, made up at a later date, is poor and unreliable. It rarely agrees with the 24th Division War Diary on the time for the same event.

CHAPTER VIII

In the Central Mountains and on the East Coast

> He supposes all men to be brave at all times and does not realize that the courage of the troops must be reborn daily, that nothing is so variable, and that the true skill of a general consists in knowing how to guarantee it by his dispositions, his positions, and those traits of genius that characterize great captains.
>
> MAURICE DE SAXE, *Reveries on the Art of War*

Eastward, in the central mountains of Korea, aerial observation on 8 July, the day Ch'onan fell, showed that enemy armor, truck, and infantry columns were moving south and were already below Wonju. This led to speculation at the Far East Command that the North Koreans were engaged in a wide envelopment designed to cut the main north-south line of communications in the Taejon area.[1] South of the Han River only one enemy division, the *6th*, initially was west of the Seoul-Pusan highway.

The area defended by the ROK Army after American troops of the U.S. 24th Division entered action on 5 July was everything east of the main Seoul-Taegu railroad and highway. In the mountainous central part of Korea there are two main north-south axes of travel and communication. The first, from the west, is the Wonju - Ch'ungju - Mun'gyong- Kumch'on corridor running almost due south from Wonju. The second, farther east, is the Wonju-Chech'on-Tanyang-Yongju-Andong-Uisong-Yongch'on corridor slanting southeast from Wonju.

The critical military terrain of both corridors is the high watershed of a spur range which runs southwest from the east coastal range and separates the upper Han River on the north from the upper Naktong on the south. Both rivers have their sources in the western slope of the Taebaek Range, about twenty miles from the Sea of Japan. The Han River flows south for forty miles, then turns generally northwest to empty into the Yellow Sea; the Naktong flows first south, then west, then again south to empty into the Korea Strait. Mun'gyong is at the pass on the first corridor over the high plateau of this dividing watershed. Tanyang is on the south side of the upper Han and at the head of the

---

[1] Telecon TT3486, FEC with Washington, 8 Jul 50.

long, narrow pass through the watershed on the second corridor.

On the south side of this watershed, and situated generally at its base, from southwest to northeast are the towns of Sangju, Hamch'ang, Yech'on, and Yongju in the valley of the Naktong. Once these points were reached, enemy units could turn down that valley for a converging attack on Taegu. Or, the more eastern units could cross the relatively wide valley of the Naktong to enter another east-west spur range of the southern Taebaeks at a number of points —the most important being Andong—and cut across to the east-west corridor between Taegu and P'ohang-dong and the Kyongju corridor leading south to Pusan.

After the initial success of the North Korean Army in driving ROK forces from their 38th Parallel positions, the South Koreans east of the U.S. 24th Division were badly disorganized and fighting separate regimental and division actions. In the first part of July the ROK Army was generally disposed from west to east as follows: 17th Regiment, 2d, Capital, 6th, and 8th Divisions, and the 23d Regiment of the 3d Division.

The North Korean Army advanced southward on a wide front. (*Map 5*) The N.K. *1st Division* followed the *4th* and the *3d* south out of Seoul, but then turned off on the next major road east of the Seoul-Pusan highway. This led through Ich'on and Umsong. Ahead of it was the N.K. *2d Division* which had moved westward to this road after the fall of Ch'unch'on. At Ich'on, ROK forces cut off an enemy regiment and destroyed or captured many mortars and several pieces of artillery. Farther west on the Yongin road another enemy regiment suffered heavy casualties at the same time, on or about 5 July, the day of Task Force Smith's fight at Osan. After these actions, the N.K. *1st Division* left the path of the *2d* and slanted southeast toward Ch'ungju. This left the *2d* the first division east of U.S. 24th Division troops on the Seoul-Taejon highway and in a position to join with the N.K. *4th* and *3d Divisions* in a converging attack on Taejon.

Despite losses and low morale among its troops, officers drove the *2d Division* southward toward Chinch'on, twenty miles east of Ch'onan. There on 9 July, one day after Ch'onan had fallen, the ROK Capital Division and South Korean police ambushed one of its battalions, capturing four pieces of artillery and twenty-seven vehicles. This began a three-day battle between the enemy division and the ROK Capital Division. The ROK's withdrew on 11 July after other enemy divisions had outflanked them on the west by the capture of Ch'onan and Chonui. The N.K. *2d Division,* exhausted and depleted by heavy casualties, then entered Chinch'on. Despite its condition, its commander allowed it no rest and drove it on toward Ch'ongju, headquarters of the ROK I Corps. At the edge of the town, ROK artillery took it under fire and inflicted another estimated 800 casualties. Only when the ROK troops at Ch'ongju were forced to fall back after the U.S. 24th Division, on 12 July, lost Choch'iwon, twelve miles westward, did the enemy division enter the town.[2]

[2] ATIS Res Supp Interrog Rpts, Issue 106 (N.K. Arty), p. 60; *Ibid.*, Issue 94 (N.K. *2d Div*), pp. 34-36; 24th Div WD, G-2 Jnl, entry 281, 091230 Jul 50; *Ibid.*, G-3 Jnl, entry 153, 081605 Jul 50; 24th Div Opns Rpt 4, 9 Jul 50; FEC Telecons TT3487, 9 Jul, and TT3489, 10 Jul 50.

IN THE CENTRAL MOUNTAINS AND ON THE EAST COAST

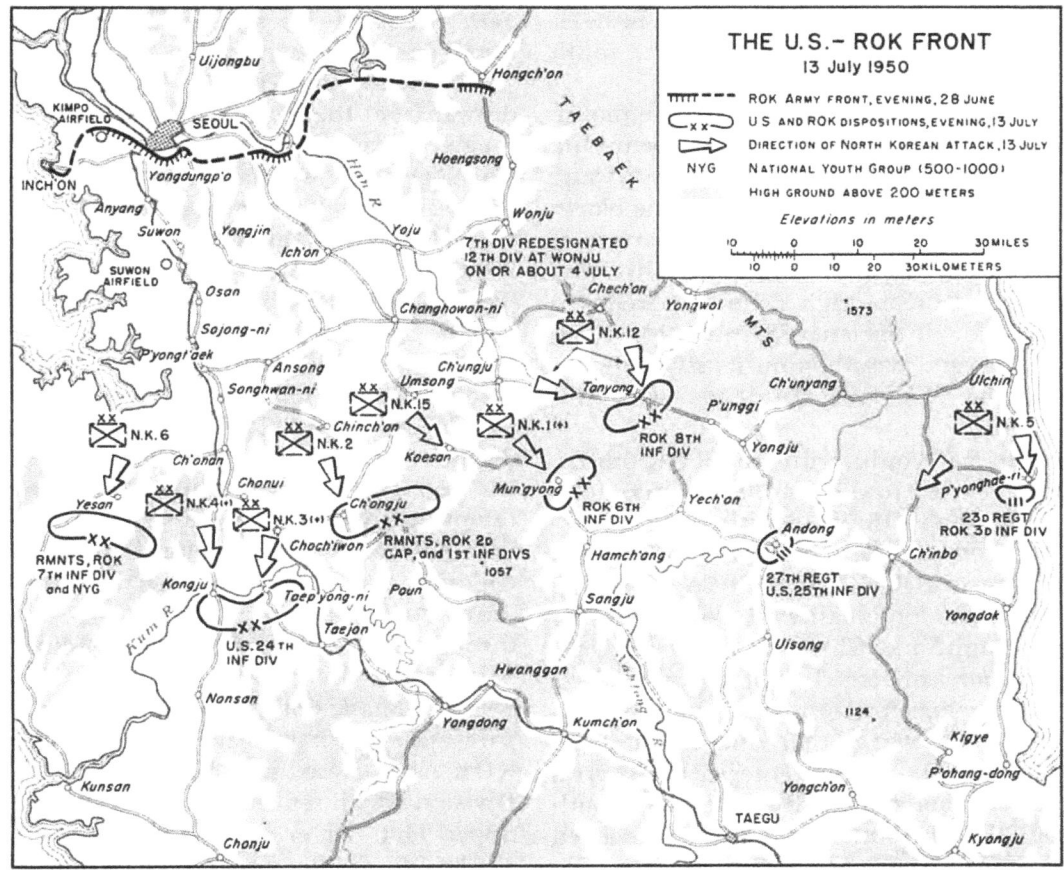

MAP 5

Eastward, the N.K. *7th Division* advanced down the mountainous central corridor of Korea after it had helped the *2d Division* capture Ch'unch'on in the opening days of the invasion. Retiring slowly in front of it and fighting effectively was the ROK 6th Division. Between Ch'unch'on and Hongch'on, the 6th Division inflicted approximately 400 casualties on the enemy division and knocked out a number of its T34 tanks. From Hongch'on the battle continued on down the road toward Wonju, the action reaching the edge of that rail and road center on or about 2 July. There, the North Korean High Command relieved Maj. Gen. Chon U, commander of the *7th Division*, because his division was behind schedule in its advance. At the same time, the North Korean high command redesignated the *7th Division* the *12th*, and activated a new *7th Division*. After the fall of Wonju on or about 5 July, the newly designated *12th Divi-*

sion split its forces—part going southeast toward Chech'on, the remainder south toward Ch'ungju.[3]

These enemy operations in the mountainous central part of the peninsula were conducted by Lt. Gen. Kim Kwang Hyop, commanding general of the North Korean *II Corps,* with headquarters at Hwach'on. On or about 10 July, the North Korean high command relieved him for inefficiency because his corps was several days behind its schedule, replacing him with Lt. Gen. Kim Mu Chong.[4]

Below Wonju, while the ROK 6th Division tried to defend the Ch'ungju corridor, the ROK 8th Division upon arriving from the east coast tried to establish a line to defend the Tanyang corridor, the next one eastward. After seizing Ch'ungju and Chech'on, the N.K. *12th Division* converged on Tanyang and on 12 July encountered the ROK 8th Division just north of that village. The N.K. *1st Division,* having entered the central sector from the northwest, turned south at Ch'ungju and on the 12th approached positions of the ROK 6th Division just above Mun'gyong. The N.K. *15th Division,* meantime, joined the attack after following the *7th Division* from Ch'unch'on to Wonju. At Wonju, the *15th* veered westward, passed through Yoju, then turned south, clearing the town of Changhowon-ni after a stiff battle with ROK forces. By 12 July, the *15th* occupied Koesan, eighteen miles northwest of Mun'gyong.

The ROK 8th Division in its withdrawal from the east coast was supposed to concentrate in the vicinity of Wonju-Chech'on. For several days the ROK Army headquarters had only vague and fragmentary information concerning its location. Eventually, in moving from Tanyang toward Ch'ungju on Army order the division found the enemy blocking its way. Instead of trying to fight through to Ch'ungju or to make a detour, the ROK 8th Division commander decided, in view of the exhaustion of his troops and the time involved in attempting a detour over mountain trails, that he would transfer the division to Ch'ungju by rail on a long haul southward to Yongch'on, thence to and through Taegu. A KMAG adviser found part of the division at Yongch'on, between P'ohang-dong and Taegu; other parts appear to have reached Taegu. The ROK Army issued new orders to the 8th Division which sent it back by rail to the upper Han River area. There on the south side of the upper Han River in the Tanyang area the 8th Division had concentrated by 10 July to defend the Yongju-Andong corridor.[5]

American and ROK strategy and tactics in this part of Korea now centered on holding the Mun'gyong and Tanyang passes of the Han-Naktong watershed. Both offered excellent defensive terrain.

---

[3] ATIS Res Supp Interrog Rpts, Issue 99 (N.K. *12th Div*), p. 43; 24th Div WD, G-2 Jnl, entry 112, 080912 Jul 50; FEC Telecon TT3486, 8 Jul 50; ATIS Supp, Enemy Documents, Issue 3, p. 62; KMAG G-2 Unit Hist, p. 3, copy in OCMH; New York *Times*, July 9, 1950.

[4] GHQ FEC, History of the North Korean Army, p. 43.

[5] FEC Telecons TT3489, 10 Jul, TT3499, 11 Jul, TT3510, 12 Jul, and TT3515, 13 Jul 50; 24th Div WD, G-2 Jnl, entry 340, 092400 and G-3 Jnl, entry 133, 081615 Jul 50; Interv, Sawyer with Col Kessler (KMAG adviser with ROK 8th Div May-Dec 50), 24 Feb 54, copy in OCMH; Gen Paik Sun Yup, MS review comments, 8 Jul 58.

IN THE CENTRAL MOUNTAINS AND ON THE EAST COAST

The major part of the North Korean Army was striking in a great attack on a wide front against the southern tip of the peninsula. Five divisions moved south over the two mountain corridors, while a sixth followed a western branch of the first corridor, the road from Ch'ongju through Poun to Hwanggan where it entered the Seoul-Taegu highway.

Over the first mountain corridor and across the Mun'gyong plateau came three North Korean divisions, the *1st, 13th,* and *15th,* supported by the *109th Tank Regiment* of the *105th Armored Division.*[6] Over the second, or eastern, corridor came two North Korean divisions, the *12th* and *8th.* In the eastern mountains there were also 2,000-3,000 partisan guerrillas who had landed in the Ulchin area at the beginning of the war with the mission of operating as an advance element to prepare for the easy conquest of that part of South Korea. This group functioned poorly and was a big disappointment to the North Korean Army.

The battles in the mountains between the North and South Koreans in July were often bitter and bloody with losses high on both sides. One of the most critical and protracted of these began about the middle of the month near Mun'gyong between the N.K. *1st Division* and the ROK 6th Division for control of the Mun'gyong pass and plateau.

On the next corridor eastward, the N.K. *12th Division* carried the main burden of the attack all the way south from the Parallel to the upper Han River. Some of its advanced troops crossed the river on 12 July and the division captured the river crossing at Tanyang on the 14th. The *12th* then fought the ROK 8th Division for control of the Tanyang Pass near the village of P'unggi, northwest of Yongju. It outflanked the ROK positions astride the road at Tanyang Pass and forced the 8th Division to withdraw southward. By the middle of July the North Koreans were forcing the Taebaek Mountain passes leading into the valley of the upper Naktong River [7]

On the east coast along the Sea of Japan the N.K. *5th Division* and the *766th Independent Infantry Unit* after crossing the 38th Parallel moved south with virtually no opposition. The high and all but trackless Taebaek Range, with almost no lateral routes of communication through it, effectively cut off the east coast of Korea below the 38th Parallel from the rest of the country westward. Geography thus made it an isolated field of operations.

At Kangnung, on the coastal road, twenty miles below the Parallel, the *11th Regiment* of the *5th Division* swung inland on an 8-day 175-mile march through some of the wildest and roughest country in Korea. It passed through P'yongch'ang, Yongwol, and Ch'unyang. At the last place the regiment met and fought a hard battle with elements of the ROK

---

[6] ATIS Res Supp Interrog Rpts, Issue 104 (N.K. *13th Div*), pp. 60-61; *Ibid.,* Issue 3 (N.K. *1st* and *15th Divs*), pp. 32-33, 42; *Ibid.,* Issue 4 (*105th Armored Div*), p. 38; *Ibid.,* Issue 99 (N.K. *12th Div*), pp. 44-45; ATIS Supp, Enemy Documents, Issue 38, pp. 31-33, notebook of Maj Kim Hak Son, *12th Div.*

[7] FEC Telecons TT3489, 10 Jul, TT3499, 11 Jul, TT3510, 13 Jul, TT3514, 13 Jul, TT3518, 14 Jul, and TT3526, 15 Jul 50; ATIS Supp, Enemy Documents, Issue 3, p. 72; ATIS Res Supp Interrog Rpts, Issue 3 (N.K. *1st Div*), pp. 32-33.

8th Division which were withdrawing inland to the Tanyang area.[8] The regiment then turned east and joined the rest of the division at Ulchin on the coast on or about 10 July. In this arduous march through and along the mountains bordering the east coast, the N.K. *5th Division* lost from all causes about 1,800 men.

Meanwhile, the North Koreans succeeded in landing amphibiously a large party of civilians at Ulchin. They had been specially trained at P'yongyang to take charge of the civil government in this eastern province. When it reached Ulchin, the *766th Independent Infantry Unit* separated from the *5th Division* and started westward into the mountains with the mission, as reported by prisoners, of infiltrating southward in small units and cutting communications between Pusan and Taegu.

One of the enemy's major tactical mistakes of the Korean War was failure to press rapidly south on the east coastal road after crossing the Parallel. By sending strong reconnaissance parties out into the wild and rugged mountains inland from the coast to make sure its rear would not be threatened, the N.K. *5th Division* dissipated some of its strength and lost valuable time. There seems little doubt that had it pressed south with all possible speed and effort the division could have been in P'ohang-dong within two weeks after the war began and thus have turned, on this flank, the entire ROK and American line across the peninsula. Once in P'ohang-dong it would have been in a position to advance directly on Pusan.

After the ROK 8th Division withdrew inland the only troops on the east coast to oppose the enemy were the ROK 23d Regiment of the 3d Division. Col. Kim Chong Won, better known as "Tiger Kim," an unusually big and strong man for a Korean, commanded this regiment. The regiment went into action against Communist guerrillas in the vicinity of Ulchin and P'yonghae-ri in early July. Beginning on 10 July it engaged the N.K. *5th Division* in battle on the coastal road in the vicinity of P'yonghae-ri. From this time on through July there was hard fighting on the coastal road for control of Yongdok and the northern approaches to P'ohang-dong.[9]

General MacArthur was aware of the enemy division advancing down the coastal road, and he knew that unless halted it would constitute a grave menace. On 7 July, he ordered General Dean to halt hostile troops moving south along the east coast near Yongdok, and instructed him to provide security for Col. Robert Witty and his 35th Fighter Group at the air base being established at Yonil, five miles south of P'ohang-dong. Pursuant to these instructions, General Dean ordered the 3d Battalion, 19th Infantry Regiment, then assembling at Taegu, to proceed to P'ohang-dong, where it arrived on 8 July. By 9 July an antiaircraft company also was at P'ohang-dong and heavy engineering equipment was en route by LST to im-

---

[8] ATIS Res Supp Interrog Rpts, Issue 96 (N.K. *5th Div*), pp. 39–41; 24th Div WD, G–2 Jnl, entry 125, 081025 Jul 50; DA Wkly Intel Rpt 72, 7 Jul 50, p. 19; ADCOM G–3 Log, 4 Jul 50; Interv, author with Emmerich, 5 Dec 51.

[9] ATIS Res Supp Interrog Rpts, Issue 96 (N.K. *5th Div*), p. 41.

prove and extend the Yonil air strip by 3,000 feet.[10]

Reports of strong unidentified enemy or guerrilla forces moving south along the Taebaek Range now reached the ROK Army and 24th Division headquarters. They assumed that these forces intended to attack P'ohang-dong in conjunction with the main enemy force moving down the coastal road.

Colonel "Tiger Kim," feeling the force of the N.K. *5th Division* for the first time, requested that he be sent reinforcements. Colonel Emmerich, senior KMAG adviser with the ROK 3d Division, in turn requested that the ROK Army release immediately the ROK 1st Separate Battalion and the Yongdungp'o Separate Battalion from their antiguerrilla operations in the Chiri Mountains of southwest Korea. This was granted and the two battalions, numbering about 1,500 men armed with Japanese rifles and carbines, moved by rail and motor transport to the east coast.[11]

Meanwhile, Capt. Harold Slater, KMAG adviser with the ROK 23d Regiment, sent to Colonel Emmerich at Taegu a radio message that the ROK situation near P'yonghae-ri had grown critical. Emmerich started for that place accompanied by the G-3 of the ROK 3d Division. Some fifty miles below the front, at P'ohang-dong, they found retreating ROK soldiers. They also found there the regimental executive officer in the act of setting up a rear command post. Emmerich, through the ROK G-3, ordered them all back north to Yongdok and followed them himself.

Already U.S. naval and air forces had joined in the fight along the coastal road. Ships came close in-shore on the enemy flank to bombard with naval gunfire the North Korean troop concentrations and supply points on the coastal corridor. The newly arrived 35th Fighter Group at Yonil Airfield joined in the fight. Weather permitting, aircraft bombed and strafed the N.K. *5th Division* daily. Capt. Gerald D. Putnam, a KMAG adviser with the ROK 23d Regiment, served as an observer with the fighter group in identifying targets and in adjusting naval gunfire. Heavy monsoon rains created landslides on the mountain-flanked coastal road and helped to slow the North Korean advance.[12]

Late in the afternoon of 11 July the command post of the ROK 23d Regiment withdrew south into Yongdok. When the 3d Division commander arrived at P'ohang-dong, pursuant to Colonel Emmerich's request that he take personal command of his troops, he ordered the military police to shoot any ROK troops found in the town. That proved effective for the moment. The next day, young Brig. Gen. Lee Chu Sik arrived on the east coast to assume command of the division.

On or about 13 July, the N.K. *5th Division* entered P'yonghae-ri, twenty-two miles above Yongdok and fifty miles from P'ohang-dong. There the *10th Regiment* turned westward into the mountains and headed for Chinbo, back of

---

[10] Interv, author with Emmerich, 5 Dec 51; Interv, author with Maj Gen Chang Chang Kuk, 14 Oct 53; ATIS Supp, Enemy Documents, Issue 3, pp. 57–58; 24th Div WD, G-3 Jnl, entries 182, 071714; 124, 072051; 151, 081245; 153, 081605; 336, 092335; 355, 092125; and entry at 102055 Jul 50.

[11] Col Emmerich, MS review comments, 30 Nov 57.

[12] GHQ FEC, History of the North Korean Army, p. 60; ATIS Res Supp Interrog Rpts, Issue 96 (N.K. *5th Div*), p. 41; 24th Div WD, G-3 Jnl entry 336, 092335 Jul 50; New York *Times*, July 29, 1950.

Yongdok. The enemy advances down the mountain backbone of central Korea and on the east coast had assumed alarming proportions. The attack on Yongdok, the first critical and major action on the east coast, was at hand.

General Dean tried to give this front additional strength by assembling there the advanced units of the 25th Infantry Division, commanded by Maj. Gen. William B. Kean. It was the second United States division to be committed in the war and arrived in Korea between 10 and 15 July. On the 8th, General Kean and an advance party flew from Osaka, Japan, to Taejon for a conference with General Dean. Two days later the 27th Infantry Regiment (Wolfhound) landed at Pusan. There the regiment learned that its new commander was Lt. Col. John H. "Mike" Michaelis. On the 12th, a second regiment, the 24th Infantry, an all-Negro regiment and the only regiment in the Eighth Army having three battalions, arrived in Korea. Col. Horton V. White commanded it. Lastly, the 35th Infantry Regiment, commanded by Col. Henry G. Fisher, arrived at Pusan between 13 and 15 July.[13]

The 27th Infantry at first went to the Uisong area, thirty-five miles north of Taegu. General Kean opened his first 25th Division command post in Korea at Yongch'on, midway between Taegu and P'ohang-dong. On 12 July General Dean ordered him to dispose the 25th Division, less one battalion which was to secure Yonil Airfield, so as to block enemy movement south from Ch'ungju. One regiment was to be in reserve at Kumch'on ready to move either to the Taejon or the Ch'ongju area.[14] The next day, 13 July, the 27th Infantry moved from Uisong to Andong on Eighth Army orders to take up blocking positions north of the town behind ROK troops.

On 13 July, with the U.S. 24th Division in defensive positions along the south bank of the Kum River, the front extended along that river to a point above Taejon, eighty miles south of Seoul, where it bent slightly north of east to pass through Ch'ongju and across the high Taebaek passes south of Ch'ungju and Tanyang, and then curved slightly south to the east coast at P'yonghae-ri, 110 air miles north of Pusan at the southern tip of the peninsula. On all the principal corridors leading south from this line heavy battles were immediately in prospect.

---

[13] 25th Div WD, Summ, Jul 50; 27th Inf WD, 6-31 Jul 50; 35th Inf WD, 6-31 Jul 50.

[14] USAFIK Ltr of Instr 4, 120900 Jul 50.

CHAPTER IX

Eighth Army in Command

> The conduct of war resembles the workings of an intricate machine with tremendous friction, so that combinations which are easily planned on paper can be executed only with great effort.
>
> CARL VON CLAUSEWITZ, *Principles of War*

By 6 July it was known that General MacArthur planned to have Eighth Army, with General Walker in command, assume operational control of the campaign in Korea. General Walker, a native of Belton, Texas, already had achieved a distinguished record in the United States Army. In World War I he had commanded a machine gun company and won a battlefield promotion. Subsequently, in the early 1930's he commanded a battalion of the 15th Infantry Regiment in China. Before Korea he was best known, perhaps, for his command of the XX Corps of General Patton's Third Army in World War II. General Walker assumed command of Eighth Army in Japan in 1948. Under General MacArthur he commanded United Nations ground forces in Korea until his death in December 1950.

During the evening of 6 July General Walker telephoned Col. William A. Collier at Kobe and asked him to report to him the next morning at Yokohama. When Collier arrived at Eighth Army headquarters the next morning General Walker told him that Eighth Army was taking over command of the military operations in Korea, and that he, Walker, was flying to Korea that afternoon but was returning the following day. Walker told Collier he wanted him to go to Korea as soon as possible and set up an Eighth Army headquarters, that for the present Col. Eugene M. Landrum, his Chief of Staff, would remain in Japan, and that he, Collier, would be the Eighth Army combat Chief of Staff in Korea until Landrum could come over later.

General Walker and Colonel Collier had long been friends and associated in various commands going back to early days together at the Infantry School at Fort Benning. They had seen service together in China in the 15th Infantry and in World War II when Collier was a member of Walker's IV Armored Corps and XX Corps staffs. After that Collier had served Walker as Chief of Staff in command assignments in the United States. Colonel Collier had served in Korea in 1948 and 1949 as Deputy Chief of Staff and then as Chief of Staff of United States Army forces there. During that time he had come to know the country well.

On the morning of 8 July Colonel Collier flew from Ashiya Air Base to Pusan and then by light plane to Taejon. After some difficulty he found General Dean with General Church between Taejon and the front. The day before, General Walker had told Dean that Collier would be arriving in a day or two to set up the army headquarters. General Dean urged Collier not to establish the headquarters in Taejon, adding, "You can see for yourself the condition." Collier agreed with Dean. He knew Taejon was already crowded and that communication facilities there would be taxed. He also realized that the tactical situation denied the use of it for an army headquarters. Yet Colonel Collier knew that Walker wanted the headquarters as close to the front as possible. But if it could not be at Taejon, then there was a problem. Collier was acquainted with all the places south of Taejon and he knew that short of Taegu they were too small and had inadequate communications, both radio and road, to other parts of South Korea, to serve as a headquarters. He also remembered that at Taegu there was a cable relay station of the old Tokyo-Mukden cable in operation. So Collier drove to Taegu and checked the cable station. Across the street from it was a large compound with school buildings. He decided to establish the Eighth Army headquarters there. Within two hours arrangements had been made with the Provincial Governor and the school buildings were being evacuated. Collier telephoned Colonel Landrum in Yokohama to start the Eighth Army staff to Korea. The next day, 9 July at 1300, General Walker's advance party opened its command post at Taegu.[1]

General Walker Assumes Command in Korea

As it chanced, the retreat of the U.S. 24th Infantry Division across the Kum River on 12 July coincided with the assumption by Eighth United States Army in Korea (EUSAK) of command of ground operations. General Walker upon verbal instructions from General MacArthur assumed command of all United States Army forces in Korea effective 0001 13 July.[2] That evening, General Church and his small ADCOM staff received orders to return to Tokyo, except for communications and intelligence personnel who were to remain temporarily with EUSAK. A total American and ROK military force of approximately 75,000 men, divided between 18,000 Americans and 58,000 ROK's, was then in Korea.[3]

General Walker arrived in Korea on the afternoon of 13 July to assume personal control of Eighth Army operations. That same day the ROK Army headquarters moved from Taejon to Taegu to be near Eighth Army headquarters. General Walker at once established tactical objectives and unit responsibility.[4] Eighth Army was to delay the enemy advance, secure the current defensive line,

[1] Brig Gen William A. Collier, MS review comments, 10 Mar 58; EUSAK WD, 25 Jun–12 Jul 50, Prologue, p. xiv.
[2] EUSAK GO 1, 13 Jul 50; EUSAK WD, G–3 Sec, 13 Jul 50; Church MS.
[3] ADCOM reached Tokyo the afternoon of 15 July. See EUSAK WD, 13 Jul 50, for American organizations' strength ashore. ROK strength is approximate.
[4] EUSAK WD, G–3 Sec, 13 Jul 50, Opn Ord 100.

GENERAL WALKER *talks with Colonel Katzin, who has just presented him with the United Nations flag.*

stabilize the military situation, and build up for future offensive operations. The 24th Division, deployed along the south bank of the Kum River in the Kongju-Taejon area on the army's left (west) was to "prevent enemy advance south of that line." To the east, in the mountainous central corridor, elements of the 25th Division were to take up blocking positions astride the main routes south and help the ROK troops stop the North Koreans in that sector. Elements of the 25th Division not to exceed one reinforced infantry battalion were to secure the port of P'ohang-dong and Yonil Airfield on the east coast.

On 17 July, four days after he assumed command of Korean operations, General Walker received word from General MacArthur that he was to assume command of all Republic of Korea ground forces, pursuant to President Syngman Rhee's expressed desire. During the day, as a symbol of United Nations command, General Walker accepted from Col. Alfred G. Katzin, representing the United Nations, the United Nations flag and hung it in his Eighth Army headquarters in Taegu.[5]

A word should be said about General MacArthur's and General Walker's com-

---

[5] EUSAK GO 3, 17 Jul 50; EUSAK WD and G-3 Sec, 17 Jul 50.

mand relationship over ROK forces. President Syngman Rhee's approval of ROK forces coming under United Nations command was never formalized in a document and was at times tenuous. This situation grew out of the relationship of the United Nations to the war in Korea.

On 7 July the Security Council of the United Nations took the third of its important actions with respect to the invasion of South Korea. By a vote of seven to zero, with three abstentions and one absence, it passed a resolution recommending a unified command in Korea and asked the United States to name the commander. The resolution also requested the United States to provide the Security Council with "appropriate" reports on the action taken under a unified command and authorized the use of the United Nations flag.[6]

The next day, 8 July, President Truman issued a statement saying he had designated General Douglas MacArthur as the "Commanding General of the Military Forces," under the unified command. He said he also had directed General MacArthur "to use the United Nations flag in the course of operations against the North Korean forces concurrently with the flags of the various nations participating.[7]

The last important act in establishing unified command in Korea took place on 14 July when President Syngman Rhee of the Republic of Korea placed the security forces of the Republic under General MacArthur, the United Nations commander.[8]

Although there appears to be no written authority from President Rhee on the subject, he verbally directed General Chung Il Kwon, the ROK Army Chief of Staff, to place himself under the U.N. Command. Under his authority stemming from General MacArthur, the U.N. commander, General Walker directed the ROK Army through its own Chief of Staff. The usual procedure was for General Walker or his Chief of Staff to request the ROK Army Chief of Staff to take certain actions regarding ROK forces. That officer or his authorized deputies then issued the necessary orders to the ROK units. This arrangement was changed only when a ROK unit was attached to a United States organization. The first such major action took place in September 1950 when the ROK 1st Division was attached to the U.S. I Corps. About the same time the ROK 17th Regiment was attached to the U.S. X Corps for the Inch'on landing. Over such attached units the ROK Army Chief of Staff made no attempt to exercise control. Actually the ROK Army authorities were anxious to do with the units remaining nominally under their control whatever the commanding general of Eighth Army wanted. From a military point of view there was no conflict on this score.[9]

---

[6] Dept of State Pub 4263, *United States Policy in the Korean Conflict, July 1950–February 1951*, p. 8. Abstentions in the vote: Egypt, India, Yugoslavia. Absent: Soviet Union. For text of the Security Council resolution of 7 July see Document 99, pages 66–67.

[7] *Ibid.*, Doc. 100, p. 67, gives text of the President's statement. The JCS sent a message to General MacArthur on 10 July informing him of his new United Nations command.

[8] *Ibid.*, p. 47.

[9] Ltr, Lt Gen Francis W. Farrell to author, 11 Jun 58. General Farrell was Chief of KMAG and served as ranking liaison man for Generals Walker, Ridgway, and Van Fleet with the ROK Army for most of the first year of the war. He confirms the author's understanding of this matter.

When political issues were at stake during certain critical phases of the war it may be questioned whether this command relationship would have continued had certain actions been taken by the U.N. command which President Syngman Rhee considered inimical to the political future of his country. One such instance occurred in early October when U.N. forces approached the 38th Parallel and it was uncertain whether they would continue military action into North Korea. There is good reason to believe that Syngman Rhee gave secret orders that the ROK Army would continue northward even if ordered to halt by the U.N. command, or that he was prepared to do so if it became necessary. The issue was not brought to a test in this instance as the U.N. command did carry the operations into North Korea.

Troop Training and Logistics

General Walker had instituted a training program beginning in the summer of 1949 which continued on through the spring of 1950 to the beginning of the Korean War. It was designed to give Eighth Army troops some degree of combat readiness after their long period of occupation duties in Japan. When the Korean War started most units had progressed through battalion training, although some battalions had failed their tests.[10] Regimental, division, and army levels of training and maneuvers had not been carried out. The lack of suitable training areas in crowded Japan constituted one of the difficulties.

If the state of training and combat readiness of the Eighth Army units left much to be desired on 25 June 1950, so also did the condition of their equipment. Old and worn would describe the condition of the equipment of the occupation divisions in Japan. All of it dated from World War II. Some vehicles would not start and had to be towed on to LST's when units loaded out for Korea. Radiators were clogged, and overheating of motors was frequent. The poor condition of Korean roads soon destroyed already well-worn tires and tubes.[11]

The condition of weapons was equally bad. A few examples will reflect the general condition. The 3d Battalion of the 35th Infantry Regiment reported that only the SCR–300 radio in the battalion command net was operable when the battalion was committed in Korea. The 24th Regiment at the same time reported that it had only 60 percent of its Table of Equipment allowance of radios and that four-fifths of them were inoperable. The 1st Battalion of the 35th Infantry had only one recoilless rifle; none of its companies had spare barrels for machine guns, and most of the M1 rifles and M2 carbines were reported as not combat serviceable. Many of its 60-mm. mortars were unserviceable because the bipods and the tubes were worn out. Cleaning rods and cleaning and preserving supplies often were not available to the first troops in Korea. And there were shortages in certain types of ammunition that became critical in July. Trip flares, 60-mm. mortar illuminating shells, and grenades were very scarce. Even the 60-mm. illuminating shells that were

---

[10] Schnabel, Theater Command, treats this subject in some detail.

[11] 24th Div WD, G–4 Daily Summ, 7–8 Jul 50.

available were old and on use proved to be 50 to 60 percent duds.[12]

General Walker was too good a soldier not to know the deficiencies of his troops and their equipment. He went to Korea well aware of the limitations of his troops in training, equipment, and in numerical strength. He did not complain about the handicaps under which he labored. He tried to carry out his orders. He expected others to do the same.

On 1 July the Far East Command directed Eighth Army to assume responsibility for all logistical support of the United States and Allied forces in Korea.[13] This included the ROK Army. When Eighth Army became operational in Korea, this logistical function was assumed by Eighth Army Rear which remained behind in Yokohama. This dual function of Eighth Army—that of combat in Korea and of logistical support for all troops fighting in Korea—led to the designation of that part of the army in Korea as Eighth United States Army in Korea. This situation existed until 25 August. On that date the Far East Command activated the Japan Logistical Command with Maj. Gen. Walter L. Weible in command. It assumed the logistical duties previously held by Eighth Army Rear.

The support of American troops in Korea, and indeed of the ROK Army as well, would have to come from the United States or Japan. Whatever could be obtained from stocks in Japan or procured from Japanese manufacturers was so obtained. Japanese manufacturers in July began making antitank mines and on 18 July a shipment of 3,000 of them arrived by boat at Pusan.

That equipment and ordnance supplies were available to the United States forces in Korea in the first months of the war was largely due to the "roll-up" plan of the Far East Command. It called for the reclamation of ordnance items from World War II in the Pacific island outposts and their repair or reconstruction in Japan. This plan had been conceived and started in 1948 by Brig. Gen. Urban Niblo, Ordnance Officer of the Far East Command.[14] During July and August 1950 an average of 4,000 automotive vehicles a month cleared through the ordnance repair shops; in the year after the outbreak of the Korean War more than 46,000 automotive vehicles were repaired or rebuilt in Japan.

The Tokyo Ordnance Depot, in addition to repairing and renovating World War II equipment for use in Korea, instituted a program of modifying certain weapons and vehicles to make them more effective in combat. For instance, M4A3 tanks were modified for the replacement of the 75-mm. gun with the high velocity 76-mm. gun, and the motor carriage of the 105-mm. gun was modified so that it could reach a maximum elevation of 67 degrees to permit high-angle fire over the steep Korean mountains. Another change was in the half-track M15A1, which was converted to a T19 mounting a 40-mm. gun instead of the old model 37-mm. weapon.[15]

---

[12] 24th Inf WD, 6-31 Jul 50; 1st Bn, 35th Inf (25th Div) Unit Rpt, 12-31 Jul, and 1-6 Aug 50; 24th Div WD, G-4 Sec, Daily Summ, 3-4 Aug 50, p. 113, and Hist Rpt, 23 Jul-25 Aug 50.

[13] GHQ FEC, Ann Narr Hist Rpt, 1 Jan-31 Oct 50, p. 43.

[14] GHQ FEC, Ann Narr Hist Rpt, 1 Jan-31 Oct 50, p. 50; Brig. Gen. Gerson K. Heiss, "Operation Roll-up," *Ordnance* (September–October, 1951), 242-45.

[15] Heiss, "Operation Roll-up," *op. cit.*, pp. 242-45.

EIGHTH ARMY IN COMMAND

Of necessity, an airlift of critically needed items began almost at once from the United States to the Far East. The Military Air Transport Service (MATS), Pacific Division, expanded immediately upon the outbreak of the war. The Pacific airlift was further expanded by charter of civil airlines planes. The Canadian Government lent the United Nations a Royal Canadian Air Force squadron of 6 transports, while the Belgian Government added several DC-4's.[16] Altogether, the fleet of about 60 four-engine transport planes operating across the Pacific before 25 June 1950 was quickly expanded to approximately 250. In addition to these, there were MATS C-74 and C-97 planes operating between the United States and Hawaii.

The Pacific airlift to Korea operated from the United States over three routes. These were the Great Circle, with flight from McChord Air Force Base, Tacoma, Washington, via Anchorage, Alaska and Shemya in the Aleutians to Tokyo, distance 5,688 miles and flying time 30 to 33 hours; a second route was the Mid-Pacific from Travis (Fairfield-Suisun) Air Force Base near San Francisco, Calif., via Honolulu and Wake Island to Tokyo, distance 6,718 miles and flying time 34 hours; a third route was the Southern, from California via Honolulu, and Johnston, Kwajalein, and Guam Islands to Tokyo, distance about 8,000 miles and flying time 40 hours. The airlift moved about 106 tons a day in July 1950.[17]

From Japan most of the air shipments to Korea were staged at Ashiya or at the nearby secondary airfields of Itazuke and Brady.

Subsistence for the troops in Korea was not the least of the problems to be solved in the early days of the war. There were no C rations in Korea and only a small reserve in Japan. The Quartermaster General of the United States Army began the movement at once from the United States to the Far East of all C and 5-in-1 B rations. Field rations at first were largely World War II K rations.

Subsistence of the ROK troops was an equally important and vexing problem. The regular issue ration to ROK troops was rice or barley and fish. It consisted of about twenty-nine ounces of rice or barley, one half pound of biscuit, and one half pound of canned fish with certain spices. Often the cooked rice, made into balls and wrapped in cabbage leaves, was sour when it reached the combat troops on the line, and frequently it did not arrive at all. Occasionally, local purchase of foods on a basis of 200 won a day per man supplemented the issue ration (200 won ROK money equaled 5 cents U.S. in value).[18]

An improved ROK ration consisting of three menus, one for each daily meal, was ready in September 1950. It provided 3,210 calories, weighed 2.3 pounds, and consisted of rice starch, biscuits, rice cake, peas, kelp, fish, chewing gum, and condiments, and was packed in a waterproofed bag. With slight changes, this ration was found acceptable to the ROK troops and quickly put into production. It became

---

[16] Maj. Gen. Lawrence S. Kuter, "The Pacific Airlift," *Aviation Age*, XV, No. 3 (March, 1951), 16–17.

[17] Maj. James A. Huston, Time and Space, pt. VI, pp. 93–94, MS in OCMH.

[18] Interv, author with Capt Darrigo, 5 Aug 53. (Darrigo lived with ROK troops for several months in 1950.)

the standard ration for them during the first year of the war.[19]

On 30 June, Lt. Col. Lewis A. Hunt led the vanguard of American officers arriving in Korea to organize the logistical effort there in support of United States troops. Less than a week later, on 4 July, Brig. Gen. Crump Garvin and members of his staff arrived at Pusan to organize the Pusan Base Command, activated that day by orders of the Far East Command. This command was reorganized on 13 July by Eighth Army as the Pusan Logistical Command, and further reorganized a week later. The Pusan Logistical Command served as the principal logistical support organization in Korea until 19 September 1950 when it was redesignated the 2d Logistical Command.[20]

The Port of Pusan and Its Communications

It was a matter of the greatest good fortune to the U.N. cause that the best port in Korea, Pusan, lay at the southeastern tip of the peninsula. Pusan alone of all ports in South Korea had dock facilities sufficiently ample to handle a sizable amount of cargo. Its four piers and intervening quays could berth twenty-four or more deepwater ships, and its beaches provided space for the unloading of fourteen LST's, giving the port a potential capacity of 45,000 measurement tons daily. Seldom, however, did the daily discharge of cargo exceed 14,000 tons because of limitations such as the unavailability of skilled labor, large cranes, rail cars, and trucks.[21]

The distance in nautical miles to the all-important port of Pusan from the principal Japanese ports varied greatly. From Fukuoka it was 110 miles; from Moji, 123; from Sasebo, 130; from Kobe, 361; and from Yokohama (via the Bungo-Suido strait, 665 miles), 900 miles. The sea trip from the west coast of the United States to Pusan for personnel movement required about 16 days; that for heavy equipment and supplies on slower shipping schedules took longer.

From Pusan a good railroad system built by the Japanese and well ballasted with crushed rock and river gravel extended northward. Subordinate rail lines ran westward along the south coast through Masan and Chinju and northeast near the east coast to P'ohang-dong. There the eastern line turned inland through the east-central mountain area. The railroads were the backbone of the U.N. transportation system in Korea.

The approximately 20,000 miles of Korean vehicular roads were all of a secondary nature as measured by American or European standards. Even the best of them were narrow, poorly drained, and surfaced only with gravel or rocks broken laboriously by hand, and worked into the dirt roadbed by the traffic passing over it. The highest classification placed on any appreciable length of road in Korea by Eighth Army engineers was for a gravel or crushed rock road with gentle grades and curves and one and a

---

[19] Capt. Billy C. Mossman and 1st Lt. Harry J. Middleton, Logistical Problems and Their Solutions, pp. 50–51, MS in OCMH.

[20] Pusan Logistical Command Monthly Activities Rpt, Jul 50, Introd and p. 1; Schnabel, FEC, GHQ Support and Participation in Korean War, ch. III, pp. 3, 6, and ch. 4, pp. 8–9.

[21] Pusan Log Comd Rpt, Jul 50.

MAIN RAIL LINE, *Pusan to Seoul, and highway north out of Taejon.*

half to two lanes wide. According to engineer specifications there were no two-lane roads, 22 feet wide, in Korea. The average width of the best roads was 18 feet with numerous bottlenecks at narrow bridges and bypasses where the width narrowed to 11-13 feet. Often on these best roads there were short stretches having sharp curves and grades up to 15 percent. The Korean road traffic was predominately by oxcart. The road net, like the rail net, was principally north-south, with a few lateral east-west connecting roads.[22]

---

[22] EUSAK WD, 10 Sep 50, Annex to G-3 Hist Rpt.

American Command Estimate

Almost from the outset of American intervention, General MacArthur had formulated in his mind the strategical principles on which he would seek victory. Once he had stopped the North Koreans, MacArthur proposed to use naval and air superiority to support an amphibious operation in their rear. By the end of the first week of July he realized that the North Korean Army was a formidable force. His first task was to estimate with reasonable accuracy the forces he would need to place in Korea to stop the enemy and fix it in place, and then the strength of the force he would need in reserve to land behind the enemy's line. That the answer to these problems was not easy and clearly discernible at first will become evident when one sees how the unfolding tactical situation in the first two months of the war compelled repeated changes in these estimates.

By the time American ground troops first engaged North Koreans in combat north of Osan, General MacArthur had sent to the Joint Chiefs of Staff in Washington by a liaison officer his requests for heavy reinforcements, most of them already covered by radio messages and teletype conferences. His requests included the 2d Infantry Division, a regimental combat team from the 82d Airborne Division, a regimental combat team and headquarters from the Fleet Marine Force, the 2d Engineer Special Brigade, a Marine beach group, a Marine antiaircraft battalion, 700 aircraft, 2 air squadrons of the Fleet Marine Force, a Marine air group echelon, 18 tanks and crew personnel, trained personnel to operate LST's, LSM's, and LCVP's, and 3 medium tank battalions, plus authorization to expand existing heavy tank units in the Far East Command to battalion strength.[23]

On 6 July, the Joint Chiefs of Staff requested General MacArthur to furnish them his estimate of the total requirements he would need to clear South Korea of North Korean troops. He replied on 7 July that to halt and hurl back the North Koreans would require, in his opinion, from four to four and a half full-strength infantry divisions, an airborne regimental combat team complete with lift, and an armored group of three medium tank battalions, together with reinforcing artillery and service elements. He said 30,000 reinforcements would enable him to put such a force in Korea without jeopardizing the safety of Japan. The first and overriding essential, he said, was to halt the enemy advance. He evaluated the North Korean effort as follows: "He is utilizing all major avenues of approach and has shown himself both skillful and resourceful in forcing or enveloping such road blocks as he has encountered. Once he is fixed, it will be my purpose fully to exploit our air and sea control, and, by amphibious maneuver, strike him behind his mass of ground force."[24]

By this time General MacArthur had received word from Washington that bomber planes, including two groups of B-29's and twenty-two B-26's, were expected to be ready to fly to the Far East before the middle of the month. The carrier *Boxer* would load to capacity with F-51 planes and sail under forced draft for the Far East. But on 7 July Far East hopes for a speedy build-up of fighter plane strength to tactical support of the ground combat were dampened by a message from Maj. Gen. Frank F. Everest, U.S. Air Force Director of Operations. He informed General Stratemeyer that forty-four of the 164 F-80's requested were on their way, but that the

---

[23] FEC, G-3 Opns, Memo for Record, 5 Jul 50, sub: CINCFE Immediate Requirements, cited in Schnabel, FEC, GHQ Support and Participation in the Korean War, ch. III, p. 17.

[24] Schnabel, FEC, GHQ Support and Participation in the Korean War, ch. III, p. 16, citing Msg JCS 85058 to CINCFE, 6 Jul and Msg C 57379, CINCFE to DA, 7 Jul 50.

rest could not be sent because the Air Force did not have them.²⁵

To accomplish part of the build-up he needed to carry out his plan of campaign in Korea, MacArthur on 8 July requested of the Department of the Army authority to expand the infantry divisions then in the Far East Command to full war strength in personnel and equipment. He received this authority on 19 July.²⁶

Meanwhile, from Korea General Dean on 8 July had sent to General MacArthur an urgent request for speedy delivery of 105-mm. howitzer high-explosive antitank shells for direct fire against tanks. Dean said that those of his troops who had used the 2.36-inch rocket launcher against enemy tanks had lost confidence in the weapon, and urged immediate air shipment from the United States of the 3.5-inch rocket launcher. He gave his opinion of the enemy in these words, "I am convinced that the North Korean Army, the North Korean soldier, and his status of training and quality of equipment have been under-estimated." ²⁷

The next day, 9 July, General MacArthur considered the situation sufficiently critical in Korea to justify using part of his B-29 medium bomber force on battle area targets. He also sent another message to the Joint Chiefs of Staff, saying in part:

The situation in Korea is critical . . . His [N.K.] armored equip[ment] is of the best and the service thereof, as reported by qualified veteran observers, as good as any seen at any time in the last war. They further state that the enemy's inf[antry] is of thoroughly first class quality.

This force more and more assumes the aspect of a combination of Soviet leadership and technical guidance with Chinese Communist ground elements. While it serves under the flag of North Korea, it can no longer be considered as an indigenous N.K. mil[itary] effort.

I strongly urge that in add[ition] to those forces already requisitioned, an army of at least four divisions, with all its component services, be dispatched to this area without delay and by every means of transportation available.

The situation has developed into a major operation.²⁸

Upon receiving word the next day that the 2d Infantry Division and certain armor and antiaircraft artillery units were under orders to proceed to the Far East, General MacArthur replied that same day, 10 July, requesting that the 2d Division be brought to full war strength, if possible, without delaying its departure. He also reiterated his need of the units required to bring the 4 infantry divisions already in the Far East to full war strength. He detailed these as 4 heavy tank battalions, 12 heavy tank companies, 11 infantry battalions, 11 field artillery battalions (105-mm. howitzers), and 4 antiaircraft automatic weapons battalions (AAA AW), less four batteries.²⁹

After the defeat of the 24th Division on 11 and 12 July north of Choch'iwon,

---

²⁵ Schnabel, FEC, GHQ Support and Participation in Korean War, ch. V, pp. 18–19, citing Msg JCS 84876, JCS to CINCFE, 3 Jul 50; USAF Hist Study 71, p. 16.

²⁶ GHQ FEC, Ann Narr Hist Rpt, 1 Jan–31 Oct 50, p. 11.

²⁷ Schnabel, FEC, GHQ Support and Participation in the Korean War, ch. III, p. 8, citing Ltr, Dean to CINCFE, 080800 Jul 50, sub: Recommendations Relative to the Employment of U.S. Army Troops in Korea.

²⁸ Msg, CINCFE to JCS, 9 Jul 50; Hq X Corps, Staff Study, Development of Tactical Air Support in Korea, 25 Dec 50, p. 8.

²⁹ Schnabel, FEC, GHQ Support and Participation in Korean War, ch. III, pp. 19–20, citing Msg CX57573, CINCFE to DA, 10 Jul 50.

General Walker decided to request immediate shipment to Korea of the ground troops nearest Korea other than those in Japan. These were the two battalions on Okinawa. Walker's chief of staff, Colonel Landrum, called General Almond in Tokyo on 12 July and relayed the request. The next day, General MacArthur ordered the Commanding General, Ryukyus Command, to prepare the two battalions for water shipment to Japan.[30]

The worsening tactical situation in Korea caused General MacArthur on 13 July to order General Stratemeyer to direct the Far East Air Forces to employ maximum B-26 and B-29 bomber effort against the enemy divisions driving down the center of the Korean peninsula. Two days later he advised General Walker that he would direct emergency use of the medium bombers against battle-front targets whenever Eighth Army requested it.[31]

It is clear that by the time the 24th Division retreated across the Kum River and prepared to make a stand in front of Taejon there was no complacency over the military situation in Korea in either Eighth Army or the Far East Command. Both were thoroughly alarmed.

---

[30] Schnabel, FEC, GHQ Support and Participation in the Korean War, ch. III, p. 21; Digest of fonecon, Landrum and Almond, FEC G-3, 12 Jul 50.

[31] USAF Hist Study 71, pp. 22-23.

CHAPTER X

Disaster at the Kum River Line

> Continual exercise makes good soldiers because it qualifies them for military duties; by being habituated to pain, they insensibly learn to despise danger. The transition from fatigue to rest enervates them. They compare one state with another, and idleness, that predominate passion of mankind, gains ascendancy over them. They then murmur at every trifling inconvenience, and their souls soften in their emasculated bodies.
>
> MAURICE DE SAXE, *Reveries on the Art of War*

The Kum River is the first large stream south of the Han flowing generally north from its source in the mountains of southwestern Korea. Ten miles east of Taejon, the river in a series of tight loops slants northwest, then bends like an inverted letter U, and 12 miles northwest of the city starts its final southwesterly course to the sea. For 25 miles upstream from its mouth, the Kum River is a broad estuary of the Yellow Sea, from 1 to 2 miles wide. In its semicircle around Taejon, the river constitutes in effect a great moat, much in the same manner as the Naktong River protects Taegu and Pusan farther south and the Chickahominy River guarded Richmond, Virginia, during the American Civil War.

Protected by this water barrier, generally 10 to 15 miles distant, Taejon lies at the western base of the Sobaek Mountains. To the west, the coastal plain stretches northward to Seoul and southwestward to the tip of Korea. But south and southeastward all the way to the Naktong and on to Pusan lie the broken hills and ridges of the Sobaek Mountains. Through these mountains in a southeasterly course from Taejon passes the main Seoul-Pusan railroad and highway. Secondary roads angle off from Taejon into all of southern Korea. Geographical and communication factors gave Taejon unusual military importance.

The Seoul-Pusan railroad crossed the Kum River 8 air miles due north of Taejon. Nine air miles westward and downstream from the railroad, the main highway crossed the river. The little village of Taep'yong-ni stood there on the southern bank of the Kum 15 air miles northwest of Taejon. At Kongju, 8 air miles farther westward downstream from Taep'yong-ni and 20 air miles northwest of Taejon, another highway crossed the Kum.

Engineers blew the highway bridges across the Kum at Kongju and Taep'yong-ni and the railroad bridge at Sinch'on the night and morning of 12-13

July. On the approaches to Taejon, engineer units placed demolitions on all bridges of small streams tributary to the Kum.[1]

Downstream from Kongju the 24th Reconnaissance Company checked all ferries and destroyed all native flat-bottomed boats it found in a 16-mile stretch below the town. Checking below this point for another twenty miles it came to the south side of the river. In the arc of the river from Kongju eastward to the railroad crossing, General Menoher, the assistant division commander of the 24th Division, then ordered all similar boats seized and burned.[2]

General Dean and his 24th Division staff had a fairly clear idea of the situation facing them. On 13 July, the division intelligence officer estimated that two enemy divisions at 60 to 80 percent strength with approximately fifty tanks were closing on the 24th Division. Enemy prisoners identified them as the *4th Division* following the 34th Infantry and the *3d Division* following the 21st Infantry. This indicated a two-pronged attack against Taejon, and perhaps a three-pronged attack if the *2d Division* moving south next in line to the east could drive ROK forces out of its way in time to join in the effort.[3]

Behind the moat of the Kum River, General Dean placed his 24th Division troops in a horseshoe-shaped arc in front of Taejon. The 34th Infantry was on the left, the 19th Infantry on the right, and the 21st Infantry in a reserve defensive blocking position southeast of Taejon. On the extreme left, the 24th Reconnaissance Company in platoon-sized groups watched the principal river crossing sites below Kongju. Thus, the division formed a two-regiment front, each regiment having one battalion on the line and the other in reserve.[4]

The 24th Division was in poor condition for what was certain to be its hardest test yet. In the first week, 1,500 men were missing in action, 1,433 of them from the 21st Regiment. That regiment on 13 July had a strength of about 1,100 men; the 34th Infantry had 2,020 men; and the 19th Infantry, 2,276 men. There were 2,007 men in the division artillery. The consolidated division strength on 14 July was 11,440 men.[5]

Action against the Kum River Line began first on the left (west), in the sector of the 34th Infantry.

From Seoul south the N.K. *4th Division* had borne the brunt of the fighting against the 24th Division and was now down to 5,000–6,000 men, little more than half strength. Approximately 20 T34 tanks led the division column, which included 40 to 50 pieces of artillery. Just before midnight of 11 July the *16th Regiment* sent out scouts to make a reconnaissance of the Kum, learn the depth and width of the river, and report back before 1000 the next morning. An outpost of the 34th Infantry I&R Platoon

---

[1] 24th Div WD, G–2 Jnl, entry 406, 101115 Jul 50; 3d Engr (C) Bn WD, 14 Jul 50.

[2] 24th Recon Co WD, 12 Jul 50; ADCOM G–3 Log, 202513 Jul 50; 24th Div G–2 Jnl, entry 778, 131330 Jul 50.

[3] 24th Div WD, Narr Summ, 13 Jul 50; *Ibid.,* G–2 Jnl, entries 681 and 790, 122200 and 131445 Jul 50; EUSAK WD, G–2 Sec, 13 Jul 50.

[4] Ltr and Comments, Wadlington to author, 1 Apr 53 (Wadlington commanded the 34th Infantry at the time); 24th Div WD, Narr Summ, 13 Jul 50.

[5] 24th Div WD, G–3 Jnl, entry 413, 131535 Jul 50; *Ibid.,* G–1 Stf Hist Rpt, 14 Jul 50.

during the night captured one of the scouts, an officer, 600 yards north of the river opposite Kongju. The regiment's mission was the capture of Kongju.[6]

U.N. air attacks on North Korean armor, transport, and foot columns had become by now sufficiently effective so that the enemy no longer placed his tanks, trucks, and long columns of marching men on the main roads in broad daylight. The heavy losses of armor and equipment to air attack in the vicinity of P'yongt'aek, Chonui, and Ch'onan in the period of 7 to 10 July had wrought the change. Now, in approaching the Kum, the enemy generally remained quiet and camouflaged in orchards and buildings during the daytime and moved at night. The North Koreans also used back roads and trails more than in the first two weeks of the invasion, and already by day were storing equipment and supplies in railroad tunnels.[7]

The N.K. 4th Division Crosses the Kum Below Kongju

On the high ground around Kongju, astride the Kongju-Nonsan road, the 3d Battalion, 34th Infantry, was in its defensive positions. On line from left to right were L, I, and K Companies, with the mortars of M Company behind them. The 63d Field Artillery Battalion was about two and a half miles south of the Kum in their support. Three miles farther south, the 1st Battalion, 34th Infantry, was in an assembly area astride the road.[8] *(Map 6)*

Communication between the 3d Battalion units was practically nonexistent. For instance, L Company could communicate with only one of its squads, and it served as a lookout and was equipped with a sound power telephone. The L Company commander, 1st Lt. Archie L. Stith, tried but failed at the 3d Battalion headquarters to obtain a radio that would work. He had communication with the battalion only by messenger. Procurement of live batteries for Signal Corps radios SCR-300's and 536's was almost impossible, communication wire could not be obtained, and that already laid could not be reclaimed.[9]

At 0400 hours 13 July, D Company of the 3d Engineer Combat Battalion blew the steel truss bridge in front of Kongju. A few hours after daybreak an enemy squad walked to the water's edge, 700 yards from a 34th Infantry position across the river, and set up a machine gun. On high ground north of this enemy machine gun squad, a North Korean tank came into view.[10] The men of the 3d Battalion, 34th Infantry, now had only the water barrier of the Kum between them and the enemy. That after-

---

[6] ATIS Res Supp, Issue 2 (Documentary Evidence of N.K. Aggression), Interrog 118; ATIS Res Supp Interrog Rpts, Issue 94 (N.K. *4th Div*), p. 46; 24th Div WD, G-2 Sec, PW Interrog file, interrog of 2d Lt Bai Jun Pal, 12 and 13 Jul 50.

[7] EUSAK WD, G-2 Stf Rpt, 13 and 22 Jul 50; 24th Div WD, G-2 PW Interrog File, interrog of Lee Ki Sup, 20 Jul 50.

[8] Interv, Mitchell with MSgt Milo W. Garman (Plat Sgt, 2d Plat, K Co, 34th Inf), 1 Aug 50; Interv, Mitchell with 2d Lt James B. Bryant (Plat Ldr, B Co, 34th Inf), 30 Jul 50; Wadlington Comments; Ltr, Lt Col Harold B. Ayres to author, 3 Oct 52.

[9] Interv, 1st Lt Billy C. Mossman with Stith, 31 Jul 50; Wadlington Comments.

[10] 24th Div WD, 13 Jul 50; 3d Engr (C) Bn Unit WD, 13 Jul 50; Interv, Mitchell with MSgt Wallace A. Wagnebreth (Plat Ldr, L Co, 34th Inf), 31 Jul 50, copy in OCMH.

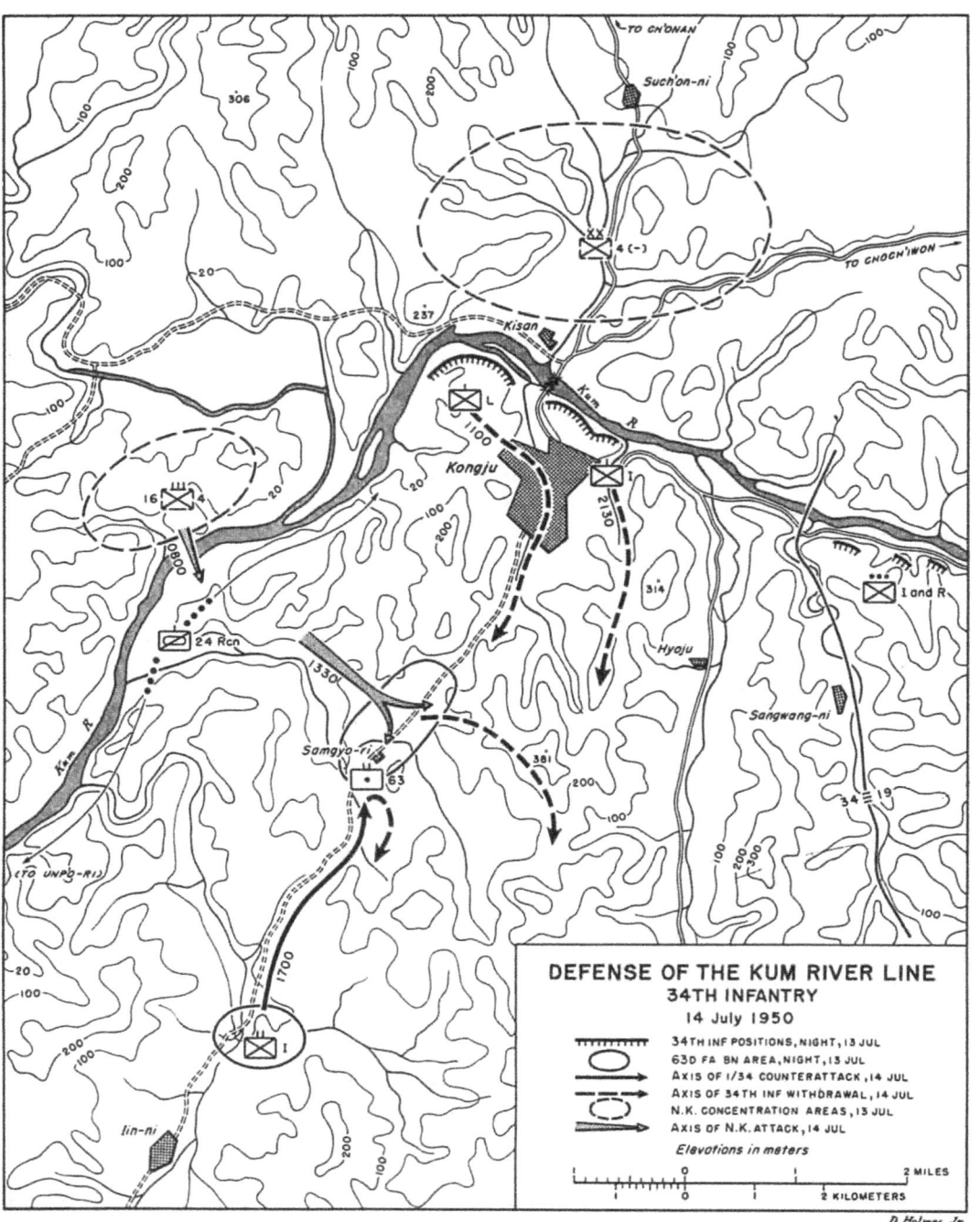

MAP 6

Moving South *across the Kum River bridge on 14 July.*

noon, the North Koreans began shelling Kongju from across the river.

The command situation for Colonel Wadlington continued to worsen as both the regimental S-2 and S-3 were evacuated because of combat fatigue. Then, that night, K Company, a composite group of about forty men of the 3d Battalion in such mental and physical condition as to render them liabilities in combat, was withdrawn from the Kum River Line with division approval and taken to Taejon for medical disposition.[11]

There were now only two understrength rifle companies of the 34th Infantry in front of Kongju—L Company on the left and I Company on the right of the road on the river hills, with some mortars of the Heavy Weapons Company behind. These troops knew of no friendly units on their left (west). From the 19th Infantry on their right, Capt. Melicio Montesclaros had visited the I Company position and told the men there was a 2-mile gap between that flank and his outpost position eastward on the regimental boundary.

Shortly after daybreak of the 14th, American troops on the south side of the Kum at Kongju heard enemy tanks in the village across the river. By 0600, enemy flat trajectory weapons, possibly tank guns, were firing into I Company's area. Their target apparently was the mortars back of the rifle company. Simultaneously, enemy shells exploded in air bursts over L Company's position but were too high to do any damage. Soon thereafter, L Company lookouts sent word that enemy soldiers were crossing

---

[11] Interv, Mitchell with Garman, 1 Aug 50; Wadlington Comments.

the river in two barges, each carrying approximately thirty men, about two miles below them. They estimated that about 500 North Koreans crossed between 0800 and 0930.

The weather was clear after a night of rain. The 63d Field Artillery Battalion sent aloft a liaison plane for aerial observation. This aerial observer reported by radio during the morning that two small boats carrying men were crossing the Kum to the south side and gave the map co-ordinates of the crossing site. Apparently this was part of the same enemy crossing seen by L Company men. The battalion S-3, Maj. Charles T. Barter, decided not to fire on the boats but to wait for larger targets. One platoon of the 155-mm. howitzers of A Battery, 11th Field Artillery Battalion, in position east of Kongju fired briefly on the enemy troops. But Yak fighter planes soon drove away the liaison observation planes, and artillery fire ceased.[12]

Soon after the enemy crossed the river below L Company, Lieutenant Stith, the company commander, unable to find the machine gun and mortar sections supporting the company and with his company coming under increasingly accurate enemy mortar and artillery fire, decided that his position was untenable. He ordered L Company to withdraw. The men left their positions overloking the Kum shortly before 1100. When Sgt. Wallace A. Wagnebreth, a platoon leader of L Company, reached the positions of the 63d Field Artillery Battalion, he told an unidentified artillery officer of the enemy crossing, but, according to him, the officer paid little attention. Lieutenant Stith, after ordering the withdrawal, went in search of the 3d Battalion headquarters. He finally found it near Nonsan. Learning what had happened, the battalion commander relieved Stith of his command and threatened him with court martial.[13]

The 63d Field Artillery Battalion Overrun

Three miles south of the river, the 63d Field Artillery Battalion had emplaced its 105-mm. howitzers along a secondary road near the village of Samyo. The road at this point was bordered on either side by scrub-pine-covered hills. From north to south the battery positions were A, Headquarters, B, and Service. The artillery battalion had communication on the morning of the 14th with the 34th Regimental headquarters near Nonsan but none with the infantry units or the artillery forward observers with them on the Kum River Line. The day before, the commanding officer of the 63d Field Artillery Battalion, Lt. Col. Robert H. Dawson, had been evacuated to Taejon because of illness, and Maj. William E. Dressler assumed command of the battalion.

About 1330 an outpost of the artillery battalion reported enemy troops coming up the hill toward them. It received instructions not to fire unless fired upon as the men might be friendly forces. As

---

[12] Interv, Mossman with Stith, 31 Jul 50; Interv, Mitchell with Wagnebreth, 31 Jul 50; Interv, Mossman with Pfc Doyle L. Wilson, L Co, 34th Inf, 2 Aug 50; Interv, author with Maj Clarence H. Ellis, Jr. (S-3 Sec, 11th FA Bn, Jul 50), 22 Jul 54; Interv, Mossman with SFC Clayton F. Gores (Intel Sgt, Hq Btry, 63d FA Bn), 31 Jul 50.

[13] Intervs, Mossman with Stith, 31 Jul 50, and Wilson, 2 Aug 50; Interv, Mitchell with Wagnebreth, 31 Jul 50.

KUM RIVER BRIDGE EXPLOSION

a result, this group of enemy soldiers overran the machine gun outpost and turned the captured gun on Headquarters Battery.[14] Thus began the attack of the North Korean *16th Regiment* on the 63d Field Artillery Battalion. Enemy reconnaissance obviously had located the support artillery and had bypassed the river line rifle companies to strike at it and the line of communications running to the rear.

Now came enemy mortar fire. The first shell hit Headquarters Battery switchboard and destroyed telephone communication to the other batteries. In rapid succession mortar shells hit among personnel of the medical section, on the command post, and then on the radio truck. With the loss of the radio truck all means of electrical communication vanished. An ammunition truck was also hit, and exploding shells in it caused further confusion in Headquarters Battery.[15]

Almost simultaneously with the attack on Headquarters Battery came another directed against A Battery, about 250 yards northward. This second force of about a hundred enemy soldiers started running down a hill from the west toward an A Battery outpost "squealing like a bunch of Indians," according to one observer. Some of the artillerymen opened up on them with small arms fire and they retreated back up the hill. Soon, however, this same group of soldiers came down another slope to the road and brought A Battery under fire

---

[14] Interv, Mitchell with Cpl Lawrence A. Ray (A Btry, 63d FA Bn), 29 Jul 50.

[15] Interv, Mitchell with SFC Leonard J. Smith (Chief Computer, FDC, Hq Btry, 63d FA Bn), 29 Jul 50; 24th Div WD, G-2 Jnl, entry 1056, statement of Lee Kyn Soon.

at 150 yards' range. Mortar fire began to fall on A Battery's position. This fire caused most of the artillerymen to leave their gun positions. Some of them, however, fought courageously; Cpl. Lawrence A. Ray was one of these. Although wounded twice, he continued to operate a BAR and, with a few others, succeeded in holding back enemy soldiers while most of the men in the battery sought to escape. Soon a mortar burst wounded Ray and momentarily knocked him unconscious. Regaining consciousness, he crawled into a ditch where he found fifteen other artillerymen—not one of them carrying a weapon. All of this group escaped south. On the way out they found the body of their battery commander, Capt. Lundel M. Southerland.[16]

Back at Headquarters Battery, enemy machine guns put bands of fire across both the front and the back doors of the building which held the Fire Direction Center. The men caught inside escaped to a dugout, crawled up a ravine, and made their way south toward Service Battery. In the excitement of the moment, apparently no one saw Major Dressler. More than two and a half years later his remains and those of Cpl. Edward L. McCall were found together in a common foxhole at the site.[17]

After overrunning A and Headquarters Batteries, the North Koreans turned on B Battery. An enemy force estimated at 400 men had it under attack by 1415. They worked to the rear of the battery, set up machine guns, and fired into it. The battery commander, Capt. Anthony F. Stahelski, ordered his two machine guns on the enemy side of his defense perimeter to return the fire. Then enemy mortar shells started falling and hit two 105-mm. howitzers, a radio jeep, and a 2½-ton prime mover. A group of South Korean cavalry rode past the battery and attacked west toward the enemy, but the confusion was so great that no one in the artillery position seemed to know what happened as a result of this intervention. The North Koreans kept B Battery under fire. At 1500 Captain Stahelski gave the battery march order but the men could not get the artillery pieces onto the road which was under fire. The men escaped as best they could.[18]

An hour and a half after the first enemy appeared at the artillery position the entire 63d Field Artillery Battalion, with the exception of Service Battery, had been overrun, losing 10 105-mm. howitzers with their ammunition and from 60 to 80 vehicles. The 5 guns of A Battery fell to the enemy intact. In B Battery, enemy mortar fire destroyed 2 howitzers; artillerymen removed the sights and firing locks from the other 3 before abandoning them.

Meanwhile, Service Battery had received word of the enemy attack and prepared to withdraw at once. A few men from the overrun batteries got back to it and rode its trucks fifteen miles south to Nonsan. Stragglers from the overrun artillery battalion came in to

---

[16] Intervs, Mossman with Pvt Fred M. Odle (A Btry, 63d FA Bn), 28 Jul 50, and Sgt Leon L. Tucker (Hq Btry, 63d FA Bn), 31 Jul 50; interv, Mitchell with Ray, 29 Jul 50. General Order 55, 7 September 1950, awarded the Distinguished Service Cross to Corporal Ray. EUSAK WD.

[17] Interv, Mitchell with Smith, 29 Jul 50; Washington *Post*, April 9, 1953.

[18] Interv, Mitchell with Pvt William R. Evans, 29 Jul 50; 24th Div WD, G-2 Jnl, entry 1056, 15-19 Jul 50, statement of Capt Stahelski.

the Nonsan area during the night and next morning. Eleven officers and 125 enlisted men of the battalion were missing in action.[19]

It is clear from an order he issued that morning that General Dean did not expect to hold Kongju indefinitely, but he did hope for a series of delaying actions that would prevent the North Koreans from accomplishing an early crossing of the Kum River at Kongju, a quick exploitation of a bridgehead, and an immediate drive on Taejon.[20]

Pursuant to General Dean's orders, Colonel Wadlington, the acting regimental commander, left his headquarters at Ponggong-ni on the main road running south out of Kongju the morning of the 14th to reconnoiter the Nonsan area in anticipation of a possible withdrawal. He was absent from his headquarters until midafternoon.[21] Shortly after his return to the command post, between 1500 and 1600, he learned from an escaped enlisted man who had reached his headquarters that an enemy force had attacked and destroyed the 63d Field Artillery Battalion. Wadlington at once ordered Lt. Col. Harold B. Ayres to launch an attack with the 1st Battalion, 34th Infantry, to rescue the men and equipment in the artillery area and drive the North Koreans westward. According to Ayres, Wadlington's order brought him his first word of the enemy attack.[22]

The 1st Battalion a little after 1700 moved out northward in a column of companies in attack formation. The three-mile movement northward was without incident until C Company approached within a hundred yards of the overrun artillery position. Then, a few short bursts of enemy machine gun and some carbine fire halted the company. Dusk was at hand. Since his orders were to withdraw if he had not accomplished his mission by dark, Colonel Ayres ordered his battalion to turn back. At its former position, the 1st Battalion loaded into trucks and drove south toward Nonsan.[23]

As soon as the 24th Division received confirmation of the bad news about the 63d Field Artillery Battalion it ordered an air strike for the next morning, 15 July, on the lost equipment—a practice that became standard procedure for destroying heavy American equipment lost or abandoned to enemy in enemy-held territory.[24]

During the day I Company, 34th In-

---

[19] Interv, Mossman with Tucker, 31 Jul 50; 24th Div WD, 14 July 50. Enemy sources indicate the N.K. *4th Division* occupied Kongju by 2200, 14 July, and claim that the *16th Regiment* in overrunning the 63d Field Artillery Battalion captured 86 prisoners, 10 105-mm. howitzers, 17 other weapons, 86 vehicles, and a large amount of ammunition. See ATIS Res Supp Interrog Rpts, Issue 94 (N.K. *4th Div*), p. 46.

[20] 24th Div WD, G-3 Jnl, entry 457, 141025 Jul 50; Wadlington Comments; Ltr, Maj David A. Bissett, Jr. (Sr Aide to Gen Dean, Jul 50), 14 Jul 52.

[21] Wadlington Comments; Ltr, Wadlington to author, 2 Jun 55.

[22] Wadlington Comments and Ltr to author, 1 Apr 53; Ltr, Ayres to author, 3 Oct 52; Interv, Mossman with Gores, 31 Jul 50; 24th Div WD, G-2 Jnl, entry 1056, 15-19 Jul 50. The communications officer of the 63d Field Artillery Battalion, 1st Lt. Herman W. Starling, however, has stated that about 1400 he went to the 1st Battalion command post and reported that the artillery was under attack and asked for help. Ayres says he has no knowledge of this but that it might have occurred in his absence since he was away from his post command most of the day. He says no one on his staff reported such an incident to him.

[23] Ltr, Ayres to author, 3 Oct 52; Interv, Mitchell with Bryant, 30 Jul 50; Wadlington Comments; 24th Div WD, G-2 Jnl, entry 1056, 15-19 Jul 50.

[24] 24th Div Arty WD, 15 Jul 50; Barth MS, p. 5.

fantry, had stayed in its position on the river line. Enemy mortar fire had fallen in its vicinity until noon. In the early afternoon, artillery from across the river continued the shelling. The acting commander, Lt. Joseph E. Hicks, tried but failed to locate L Company and the 3d Battalion Headquarters. A few men from the Heavy Weapons Company told him that enemy roadblocks were in his rear and that he was cut off. Except for the enemy shelling, all was quiet in I Company during the day. That night at 2130, pursuant to orders he received, Hicks led I Company over the mountains east and southeast of Kongju and rejoined the regiment. The 34th Infantry occupied new positions just east of Nonsan early in the morning of 15 July.[25]

In their first day of attack against it, the North Koreans had widely breached the Kum River Line. Not only was the line breached, but the 19th Infantry's left flank was now completely exposed. The events of 14 July must have made it clear to General Dean that he could not long hold Taejon.

Nevertheless, Dean tried to bolster the morale of the defeated units. After he had received reports of the disaster, he sent a message at 1640 in the afternoon saying, "Hold everything we have until we find where we stand—might not be too bad—may be able to hold—make reconnaissance—may be able to knock those people out and reconsolidate. Am on my way out there now."[26] Informing Colonel Stephens that the 34th Infantry was in trouble, he ordered him to put the 21st Infantry Regiment in position on selected ground east of Taejon. Something of Dean's future intentions on operations at Taejon was reflected in his comment, "We must coordinate so that the 19th and 34th come out together." General Dean closed his message by asking Stephens to come to his command post that night for a discussion of plans.[27]

Although an aerial observer saw two tanks on the south side of the Kum River southwest of Kongju early in the morning of the 15th, enemy armor did not cross in force that day. Other parts of the *4th Division* continued to cross, however, in the Kongju area. Air strikes destroyed some of their boats and strafed their soldiers. By nightfall of 15 July some small groups of North Korean soldiers had pressed south from the river and were in Nonsan.[28]

The N.K. 3d Division Crosses the Kum Against the 19th Infantry

The third and last regiment of the 24th Division, the 19th Infantry, commanded by Col. Guy S. Meloy, Jr., began to arrive in Korea on 4 July. Nearly ninety years earlier the 19th Infantry Regiment had won the sobriquet, "The Rock of Chickamauga," in a memorable stand in one of the bloodiest of Civil War battles. Now, on 11 and 12 July General Dean moved the 1950 version of the regiment to Taejon as he concentrated the 24th Division there for the defense of the city. Before dark of the

---

[25] Wadlington Comments; Interv, Mitchell with Sgt Justin B. Fleming (2d Plat, I Co, 34th Inf), 1 Aug 50.
[26] 24th Div WD, G-3 Jnl, entry 495, 141830 Jul 50.
[27] *Ibid.*, entry 487, 141640 Jul 50; Ltr, Stephens to author, 17 Apr 52.
[28] 24th Div WD, G-2 Jnl, entry 936, 150830 Jul 50; *Ibid.*, G-3 Jnl, entry 562, 151945 Jul 50; *Ibid.*, Narr Summ, 25 Jun-22 Jul 50.

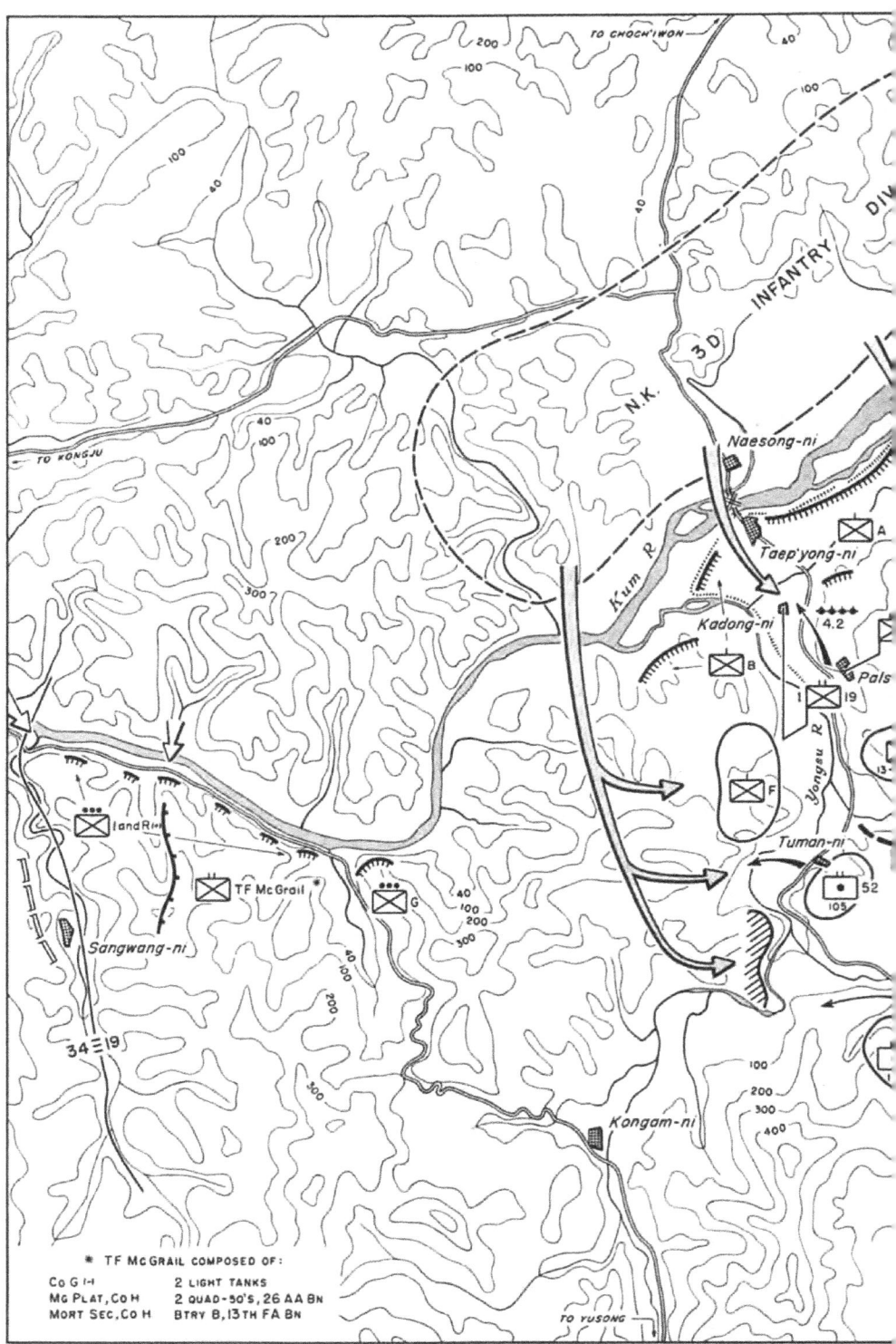

MAP 7

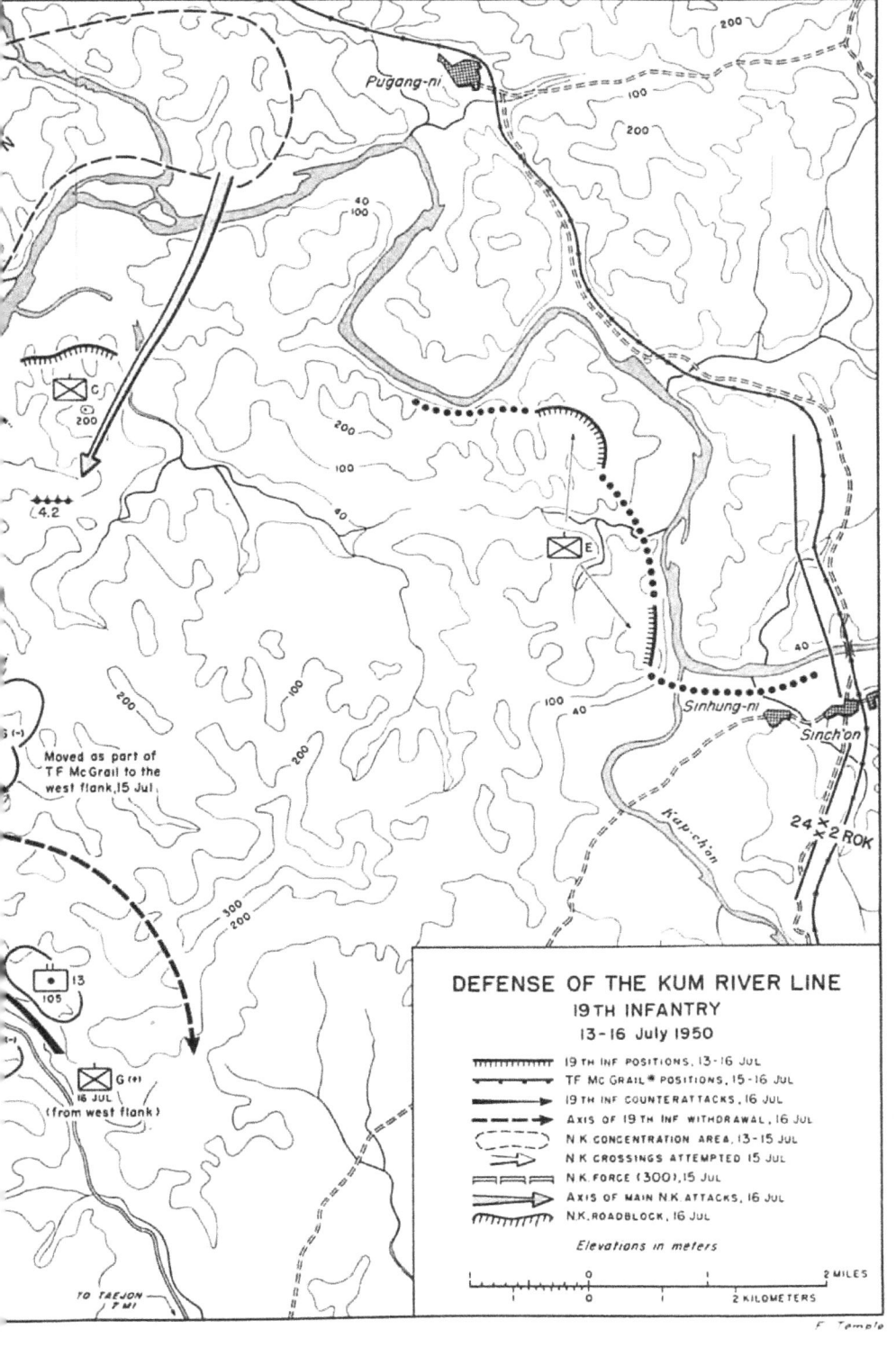

DISASTER AT THE KUM RIVER LINE

12th, the 19th Infantry was in position to relieve the 21st Infantry Regiment on the south bank of the Kum, but the formal relief and transfer of responsibility for the regimental sector did not take place until 0930 the next day. Fourteen years earlier General Dean had served as captain in the regiment in Hawaii.[29]

The 19th Infantry's zone of responsibility was a wide one, extending from high ground just east of the railroad bridge, 8 miles due north of Taejon, westward along the river to within 3 miles of Kongju. This was an airline distance of 15 miles or a river distance of almost 30 miles because of the stream's numerous deep folds. Necessarily, there were wide gaps between some of the units in disposing a regiment—a 2-battalion regiment at that—over this distance. The main regimental position was astride the Seoul-Pusan highway where it crossed the Kum River at Taep'yong-ni, about midway of the regimental sector. (*Map 7*)

Engineer demolition troops had blown, but only partially destroyed, the highway bridge over the Kum at 2100, 12 July. The next morning they dynamited it again, and this time two spans dropped into the water. On the 15th, engineers destroyed the railroad bridge upstream at Sinch'on.[30]

At Taep'yong-ni the Kum River in mid-July 1950 was 200 to 300 yards wide, its banks 4 to 8 feet high, water 6 to 15 feet deep, and current 3 to 6 miles an hour. Sandbars ran out into the streambed at almost every bend and the channel shifted back and forth from the center to the sides. The river, now swollen by rains, could be waded at many points when its waters fell.

On the regimental right, the railroad bridge lay just within the ROK Army zone of responsibility. A mile and a half west of the railroad bridge a large tributary, the Kap-ch'on, empties into the Kum. On high ground west of the railroad and the mouth of the Kap-ch'on, E Company in platoon-sized units held defensive positions commanding the Kum River railroad crossing site. West of E Company there was an entirely undefended 2-mile gap. Beyond this gap C Company occupied three northern fingers of strategically located Hill 200 three miles east of Taep'yong-ni.[31] Downstream from C Company there was a 1,000-yard gap to where A Company's position began behind a big dike along the bank of the Kum. The A Company sector extended westward beyond the Seoul-Pusan highway at Taep'yong-ni. One platoon of A Company was on 500-foot high hills a mile south of the Taep'yong-ni dike and paddy ground.

West of the highway, the 1st Platoon of B Company joined A Company behind the dike, while the rest of the company was on high ground which came down close to the river. West of B Company for a distance of five air miles to the regimental boundary there was little protection. One platoon of G Company manned an outpost two miles away. The I&R Platoon of about seventy men, together with a platoon of engineers and a battery of artillery, all under the com-

---

[29] 21st Inf WD, 13 Jul 50; 19th Inf WD, 13 Jul 50.
[30] Interv, Mitchell with Col Meloy, 30 Jul 50. Standard practice was to blow the spans adjacent to the friendly side of a stream.

[31] There were two 600-foot high hills (Hills 200) in the 1st Battalion, 19th Infantry, zone. The second is close to the highway and just east of the village of Palsan.

DIKE POSITION *in Taep'yong-ni area. The BAR man is from the 19th Regiment.*

mand of Capt. Melicio Montesclaros, covered the last three miles of the regimental sector in the direction of Kongju.

The command post of Lt. Col. Otho T. Winstead, commander of the 1st Battalion, was at the village of Kadong, about a mile south of the Kum on the main highway. Colonel Meloy's regimental command post was at the village of Palsan, about a mile farther to the rear on the highway.[32]

The 2d Battalion with two of its rifle companies was in reserve back of the 1st Battalion. Behind A Company, east of the highway, were two platoons of G Company; behind B Company, west of the highway, was F Company. The 4.2-inch mortars of the Heavy Mortar Company were east of the highway.

Artillery supporting the 19th Infantry consisted of A and B Batteries, 52d Field Artillery Battalion; A and B Batteries of the 11th Field Artillery Battalion (155-mm. howitzers); and two batteries of the 13th Field Artillery Battalion. Lt. Col. Charles W. Stratton, commanding officer of the 13th Field Artillery Battalion, coordinated their firing. The 52d Field Artillery Battalion, in position along the main highway at the village of Tumanni, about three miles south of the Kum, was farthest forward. Behind it two

[32] The positions given for the 19th Infantry at the Kum River are based on 19th Inf WD, 13 Jul 50; Ltr, Brig Gen Guy S. Meloy, Jr., to author, 6 Jul 52; Notes and overlays of 19th Inf position 14–16 Jul 50 prepared by Lt Col Edward O. Logan (S–3, 19th Inf, at Kum River) for author, Jun 52; Interv, author with Maj Melicio Montesclaros, 20 Aug 52; Intervs, Capt Martin Blumenson with 2d Lt Charles C. Early (Plat Ldr, 3d Plat, B Co, 19th Inf), 26 Aug 51, with 2d Lt Augustus B. Orr (Plat Ldr, C Co, 19th Inf), 26 Aug 51, and with Capt Elliot C. Cutler, Jr. (CO Hv Mort Co, 19th Inf at Kum River), 27 Aug. 51.

miles farther south were the 11th and the 13th Field Artillery Battalions.[33]

The larger parts of the 26th Antiaircraft Artillery (Automatic Weapons) Battalion and of A Company, 78th Heavy Tank Battalion (light M24 tanks), were at Taejon.

Aerial strikes on the 14th failed to prevent the build-up of enemy armor on the north side of the Kum opposite Taep'yong-ni. Tanks moved up and dug in on the north bank for direct fire support of a crossing effort. Their fire started falling on the south bank of the Kum in the 19th Infantry's zone at 1300, 14 July. Late in the day an aerial observer reported seeing eleven enemy tanks dug in, camouflaged, and firing as artillery. There were some minor attempted enemy crossings during the day but no major effort. None succeeded.[34]

The afternoon brought the bad news concerning the left flank—the collapse of the 34th Infantry at Kongju.

The next morning, at 0700, Colonel Meloy received word from his extreme left flank that North Koreans were starting to cross there. An aerial strike and the I&R Platoon's machine gun fire repelled this crossing attempt. But soon thereafter enemy troops that had crossed lower down in the 34th Infantry sector briefly engaged the Reconnaissance Platoon when it tried to establish contact with the 34th Infantry.[35]

These events on his exposed left flank caused Colonel Meloy to reinforce the small force there with the remainder of G Company, 1 machine gun platoon and a section of 81-mm. mortars from H Company, 2 light tanks, and 2 quad-50's of the 26th Antiaircraft Artillery Battalion—in all, two thirds of his reserve. Lt. Col. Thomas M. McGrail, commanding officer of the 2d Battalion, accompanied these troops to the left flank. Meloy now had only F Company in reserve behind the 1st Battalion in the main battle position.[36]

The morning of 15 July, Colonel Stephens at 0600 started his 21st Infantry Regiment from the Taejon airstrip for Okch'on, ten miles east of the city on the main Seoul-Pusan highway. This organization was now only a shadow of a regiment. Its 1st Battalion had a strength of 517 men. The 132 men of the 3d Battalion were organized into K and M Companies and attached to the 1st Battalion. A separate provisional group numbered 466 men. As already noted, the regiment so organized numbered little more than 1,100 men of all ranks.[37]

General Dean had ordered the move to the Okch'on position. He feared there might be a North Korean penetration through ROK Army forces east of Taejon, and he wanted the 21st Infantry deployed on the high hills astride the

---

[33] Overlay, Logan for author, Jun 52; Ltr and sketch map, Col Perry (CO 52d FA Bn at Kum River) for author, 8 Jun 52.
[34] 24th Div WD, G-2 Jnl, entry 911, 142105 Jul 50; 19th Inf WD, 14 Jul 50.
[35] Ltr, Meloy to author, 4 Dec 52; Overlay, Logan for author, Jun 52.

[36] Ltr, Meloy to author, 29 May 52; Ltr, Capt Michael Barszcz (CO G Co, 19th Inf) to author, 3 Jul 52; Notes and overlay, Logan for author, Jun 52; 19th Inf WD, 14–15 Jul 50; 24th Div WD, 15 Jul 50; EUSAK WD, G-3 Sec, Msg at 151700 Jul 50.
[37] 21st Inf WD, 29 Jun–22 Jul 50 and Incl II, Activities Rpt 1st Bn; 24th Div WD, G-3 Jnl, entry 408, 131440 Jul 50; Ltr, Gen Stephens to author, 17 Apr 52.

highway in that vicinity to protect the rear of the 24th Division. The regiment went into position five miles east of Taejon, beyond the railroad and highway tunnels, with the command post in Okch'on. From its new position the 21st Infantry also controlled a road running south from a Kum River ferry site to the highway. One battery of the 11th Field Artillery Battalion accompanied the 21st Infantry. A company of attached engineer troops prepared the tunnels and bridges east of Taejon for demolition.[38]

As evening of 15 July approached, Colonel Meloy alerted all units in battle positions for an enemy night crossing. Supporting mortars and artillery fired on the enemy-held villages across the river. This and air strikes during the evening set the flimsy Korean wood-adobe-straw huts on fire and illuminated the river front with a reddish glow.

Enemy sources indicate that all day the N.K. *3d Division* had made preparations for an attack on the river line, and that repeated air attacks seriously hampered the movement of its heavy equipment and instilled fear in the minds of its soldiers. Political officers tried to raise the lowering morale of the troops by promising them a long rest after the capture of Taejon and by saying that when the city fell the Americans would surrender.[39]

Just before dusk, 2d Lt. Charles C. Early, platoon leader of the 3d Platoon, B Company, from his position above the Kum, saw an enemy T34 tank come around a bend in the highway across the river. While he telephoned this information to his company commander, he counted eight more tanks making the turn in the road. He could see them distinctly with the naked eye at a distance of about two miles. Three of the tanks pulled off the road, swung their turrets, and fired on Early's position. Most of their rounds passed overhead. Enemy artillery began firing at the same time. The 1st Battalion had called for an air strike when the enemy tanks opened fire, and now two planes appeared. When the planes arrived over the river all the tanks except one took cover in a wooded area. The strike left the exposed tank burning on the road. The two planes stayed over the area until dark. Upon their departure, enemy infantry in trucks moved to the river's edge.[40]

Small groups of enemy soldiers tested the American river defenses by wading into the river; others rushed out to the end of the blown bridge, jumped into the water, and began swimming across. Recoilless rifle and machine gun fire of the Heavy Weapons Company inflicted heavy casualties on this crossing attempt at and near the bridge, but some of the North Koreans got across under cover of tank fire.

Upstream in front of Hill 200 another enemy crossing attempt was under way in front of C Company. The combined fire from all company weapons supported by that from part of the Heavy Weapons Company repelled this attack and two more that followed after short intervals.

---

[38] Ltr, Stephens to author, 17 Apr 52; Ltr, Perry to author, 8 Jun 52; 21st Inf WD, 15–16 Jul 50.
[39] ATIS Res Supp Interrog Rpts, Issue 96 (N.K. *3d Div*), p. 32.

[40] Ltr, Meloy to author, 30 Dec 52; Intervs, Blumenson with Early, 26 Aug 51, and Orr, 26 Aug 51; 19th Inf WD, 15 Jul 50.

Some rounds falling short from friendly 81-mm. mortars knocked out two of the company's 60-mm. mortars and broke the base plate of the remaining one. Corporal Tabor improvised a base plate and, holding the tube in his hand, fired an estimated 300 rounds.

With his first river crossing attacks repulsed, the enemy made ready his major effort. At 0300 Sunday, 16 July, an enemy plane flew over the Kum and dropped a flare. It was the signal for a co-ordinated attack. The intensity of the fire that now came from enemy guns on the north bank of the river was as great, General Meloy has said, as anything he experienced in Europe in World War II. Under cover of this intense fire the North Koreans used boats and rafts, or waded and swam, and in every possible way tried to cross the river. American artillery, mortar, and supporting weapons fire met this attack.[41]

Representative of the accidents that weigh heavily in the outcome of most battles was one that now occurred. One of the 155-mm. howitzers of the 11th Field Artillery Battalion had been assigned to fire flares over the river position on call. At the most critical time of the enemy crossing, the 1st Battalion through the regiment requested a slight shift of the flare area. Normally this would have taken only a few minutes to execute. But the artillery personnel misunderstood the request and laid the howitzer on an azimuth that required moving the trails of the piece. As a result of this mishap there were no flares for a considerable period of time. Colonel Winstead, the 1st Battalion commander, said that mishap and the resulting lack of flares hurt his men more than anything else in their losing the south bank of the river.[42]

Enemy troops succeeded in crossing the river at 0400 in front of the gap between C and E Companies on the regimental right and struck the 1st Platoon of C Company for the fourth time that night. In the midst of this attack, Lt. Henry T. McGill called Lt. Thomas A. Maher, the 1st Platoon leader, to learn how things were going. Maher answered, "We're doing fine." Thirty seconds later he was dead with a burp gun bullet in his head. North Koreans in this fourth assault succeeded in overrunning the platoon position. The platoon sergeant brought out only about a dozen men. C Company consolidated its remaining strength on the middle finger of Hill 200 and held fast. But the North Koreans now had a covered route around the east end of the 1st Battalion position. They exploited it in the next few hours by extensive infiltration to the rear and in attacks on the heavy mortar position and various observation and command posts.[43]

Simultaneously with this crossing at the right of the main regimental position, another was taking place below and on the left flank of the main battle position. This one lasted longer and apparently was the largest of all. At daybreak,

---

[41] Ltr, Meloy to author, 29 May 52; 19th Inf WD, 16 Jul 50; 13th FA Bn WD, 16 Jul 50. The journal of the 19th Infantry was lost in action on the 16th. The summary of events in the regimental war diary for 16 July was compiled later from memory by the regimental staff.

[42] Notes, Logan for author, Jun 52, quoting his conversation with Winstead on 16 Jul 50.

[43] Interv, Blumenson with Orr, 26 Aug 51.

men in B Company saw an estimated 300 to 400 North Korean soldiers on high ground southwest of them—already safely across the river. And they saw that crossings were still in progress downstream at a ferry site. Enemy soldiers, 25 to 30 at a time, were wading into the river holding their weapons and supplies on their heads, and plunging into neck-deep water.[44]

From his observation post, Colonel Meloy could see the crossing area to the left but few details of the enemy movement. Already B Company had called in artillery fire on the enemy crossing force and Colonel Meloy did likewise through his artillery liaison officer. Capt. Monroe Anderson of B Company noticed that while some of the enemy moved on south after crossing the river, most of them remained in the hills camouflaged as shrubs and small trees. Lieutenant Early, fearing an attack on his rear by this crossing force, left his 3d Platoon and moved back to a better observation point. There for an hour he watched enemy soldiers bypass B Company, moving south.[45]

By this time it seemed that the North Koreans were crossing everywhere in front of the regiment. As early as 0630 Colonel Winstead had reported to the regiment that his command post and the Heavy Mortar Company were under attack and that the center of his battalion was falling back. The enemy troops making this attack had crossed the river by the partly destroyed bridge and by swimming and wading. They made deep penetrations and about 0800 overran part of the positions of A Company and the right hand platoon of B Company behind the dike. They then continued on south across the flat paddies and seized the high ground at Kadong-ni. Lt. John A. English, Weapons Platoon leader with B Company, seeing what had happened to the one platoon of B Company along the dike, ran down from his hill position, flipped off his helmet, swam the small stream that empties into the Kum at this point, and led out fourteen survivors.[46]

This enemy penetration through the center of the regimental position to the 1st Battalion command post had to be thrown back if the 19th Infantry was to hold its position. Colonel Meloy and Colonel Winstead immediately set about organizing a counterattack force from the 1st Battalion Headquarters and the Regimental Headquarters Companies, consisting of all officers present, cooks, drivers, mechanics, clerks, and the security platoon. Colonel Meloy brought up a tank and a quad-50 antiaircraft artillery half-track to help in the counterattack. This counterattack force engaged the North Koreans and drove them from the high ground at Kadong-ni by 0900. Some of the enemy ran to the river and crossed back to the north side. In leading this attack, Maj. John M. Cook, the 1st Battalion Executive Officer, and Capt. Alan Hackett, the Battalion S-1, lost their lives.[47]

Colonel Meloy reported to General Dean that he had thrown back the North

---

[44] Interv, Blumenson with Early, 26 Aug 51.
[45] Ibid.; Ltrs, Meloy to author, 4, 30 Dec 52.

[46] Ltrs, Meloy to author, 4, 30 Dec 52; Notes, Logan for author, Jun 52; Ltr, Meloy to author, 29 May 52.
[47] Notes, Logan for author, Jun 52; Ltr, Meloy to author, 29 May 52; Interv, Mitchell with Meloy, 30 Jul 50; Intervs, Blumenson with Early, 26 Aug 51, and Cutler, 27 Aug 51; 24th Div WD, G-3 Jnl, entry 583, 160730, Jul 50.

Koreans, that he thought the situation was under control, and that he could hold on until dark as he, General Dean, had requested. It was understood that after dark the 19th Infantry would fall back from the river to a delaying position closer to Taejon.[48]

Roadblock Behind the 19th Infantry

But events were not in reality as favorable as they had appeared to Colonel Meloy when he made his report to General Dean. Colonel Winstead, the 1st Battalion commander, soon reported to Colonel Meloy that while he thought he could hold the river line to his front he had no forces to deal with the enemy in his rear. Fire from infiltrated enemy troops behind the main line was falling on many points of the battalion position and on the main supply road. Then came word that an enemy force had established a roadblock three miles to the rear on the main highway. Stopped by enemy fire while on his way forward with a resupply of ammunition for the 1st Battalion, 2d Lt. Robert E. Nash telephoned the news to Colonel Meloy who ordered him to go back, find Colonel McGrail, 2d Battalion commander, and instruct him to bring up G and H Companies to break the roadblock. Almost simultaneously with this news Colonel Meloy received word from Colonel Stratton that he was engaged with the enemy at the artillery positions.[49]

All morning the hard-pressed men of the 19th Infantry had wondered what had happened to their air support. When the last two planes left the Kum River at dark the night before they had promised that air support would be on hand the next morning at first light. Thus far only six planes, hours after daylight, had made their appearance over the front. Now the regiment sent back an urgent call for an air strike on the enemy roadblock force.

Scattered, spasmodic firing was still going on in the center when Colonel Meloy and his S–3, Maj. Edward O. Logan, left the regimental command post about an hour before noon to check the situation at the roadblock and to select a delaying position farther back. Before leaving the Kum River, Meloy gave instructions to Colonel Winstead concerning withdrawal of the troops after dark.[50]

The enemy soldiers who established the roadblock behind the regiment had crossed the Kum below B Company west of the highway. They bypassed B and F Companies, the latter the regiment's reserve force. Only enough enemy soldiers to pin it down turned off and engaged F Company. During the morning many reports had come into the regimental command post from F Company that enemy troops were moving south past its position. Once past F Company, the enemy flanking force turned east toward the highway.[51]

About 1000, Colonel Perry, commanding officer of the 52d Field Artillery Battalion, from his command post near Tuman-ni three miles south of the Kum River, saw a long string of enemy soldiers in white clothing pass over a moun-

---

[48] Ltrs, Meloy to author, 29 May, 20 Aug, and 30 Dec 52.

[49] 19th Inf WD, Summ, 16 Jul 50; 52d FA Bn WD, 16 Jul 50; 24th Div WD, G–3 Jnl, entry 160910 Jul 50; Ltr, Meloy to author, 30 Dec 52.

[50] Ltrs, Meloy to author, 29 May, 20 Aug, and 30 Dec 52.

[51] Notes and overlay, Logan for author, Jun 52.

tain ridge two miles westward and disappear southward over another ridge. He ordered A Battery to place fire on this column, and informed the 13th Field Artillery Battalion below him that an enemy force was approaching it. A part of this enemy force, wearing regulation North Korean uniforms, turned off toward the 52d Field Artillery Battalion and headed for B Battery.

Men in B Battery hastily turned two or three of their howitzers around and delivered direct fire at the North Koreans. The North Koreans set up mortars and fired into B Battery position. One of their first rounds killed the battery commander and his first sergeant. Other rounds wounded five of the six chiefs of sections. The battery executive, 1st Lt. William H. Steele, immediately assumed command and organized a determined defense of the position. Meanwhile, Colonel Perry at his command post just south of B Battery assembled a small attack force of wire, medical, and fire direction personnel not on duty, and some 19th Infantry soldiers who were in his vicinity. He led this group out against the flank of the North Koreans, directing artillery fire by radio as he closed with them. The combined fire from B Battery, Colonel Perry's group, and the directed artillery fire repelled this enemy attack. The North Koreans turned and went southward into the hills.[52]

Before noon the enemy force again turned east to the highway about 800 yards south of the 52d Field Artillery position. There it opened fire on and halted some jeeps with trailers going south for ammunition resupply. Other vehicles piled up behind the jeeps. This was the beginning of the roadblock, and this was when Colonel Meloy received the telephone message about it. South of the roadblock the 11th and 13th Field Artillery Battalions came under long-range, ineffective small arms fire. The artillery continued firing on the Kum River crossing areas, even though the 13th Field Artillery Battalion Fire Direction Center, co-ordinating the firing, had lost all communication about 1100 with its forward observers and liaison officers at the infantry positions.[53]

The North Korean roadblock, a short distance below the village of Tuman where the highway made a sharp bend going south, closed the only exit from the main battle position of the 19th Infantry. At this point a narrow pass was formed by a steep 40-foot embankment which dropped off on the west side of the road to a small stream, the Yongsu River, and a steep hillside that came down to the road on the other side. There was no space for a vehicular by-pass on either side of the road. South of this point for approximately four miles high hills approached and flanked the highway on the west. As the day wore on, the enemy built up his roadblock force and extended it southward into these hills.

When Colonel Meloy and Major Logan arrived at the roadblock they found conditions unsatisfactory. Small groups

---

[52] Ltr, Col Perry to author, 8 Jun 52; Notes, Logan for author, Jun 52; Ltr, Meloy to author, 30 Dec 52; 52d FA Bn WD, 16 Jul 50; 13th FA Bn WD, 16 Jul 50. General Order 120, 5 September 1950, 24th Division, awarded the Silver Star to Lieutenant Steele for action on 16 July.

[53] Ltr, Perry to author, 8 Jun 52; Notes, Logan for author, Jun 52, quoting Maj Leon B. Cheek, S-3, 13th FA Bn; Interv, Blumenson with Lt Nash (S-4, 2d Bn, 19th Inf), 1 Aug 51.

of soldiers, entirely disorganized and apathetic, were returning some fire in the general direction of the unseen enemy. While trying to organize a group to attack the enemy on the high ground overlooking the road Colonel Meloy was wounded. He now gave to Colonel Winstead command of all troops along the Kum River.

Major Logan established communication with General Dean about 1300. He told him that Meloy had been wounded, that Winstead was in command, and that the regimental situation was bad. Dean replied that he was assembling a force to try to break the roadblock but that probably it would be about 1530 before it could arrive at the scene. He ordered the regiment to withdraw at once, getting its personnel and equipment out to the greatest possible extent. Soon after this conversation, enemy fire struck and destroyed the regimental radio truck, and there was no further communication with the division. Colonel Winstead ordered Major Logan to try to reduce the roadblock and get someone through to establish contact with the relief force expected from the south. Winstead then started back to his 1st Battalion along the river. Shortly after 1330 he ordered it to withdraw. In returning to the Kum, Winstead went to his death.[54]

During the previous night the weather had cleared from overcast to bright starlight, and now, as the sun climbed past its zenith, the temperature reached 100 degrees. Only foot soldiers who have labored up the steep Korean slopes in midsummer can know how quickly exhaustion overcomes the body unless it is inured to such conditions by training and experience. As this was the initial experience of the 19th Infantry in Korean combat the men lacked the physical stamina demanded by the harsh terrain and the humid, furnacelike weather. And for three days and nights past they had had little rest. This torrid midsummer Korean day, growing light at 0500 and staying light until 2100, seemed to these weary men an unending day of battle.

When the 1st Battalion began to withdraw, some of the units were still in their original positions, while others were in secondary positions to which enemy action had driven them. In the withdrawal from Hill 200 on the battalion right, officers of C Company had trouble in getting the men to leave their foxholes. Incoming mortar fire pinned them down. Cpl. Jack Arawaka, a machine gunner, at this time had his gun blow up in his face. Deafened, nearly blind, and otherwise wounded from the explosion, he picked up a BAR and continued fighting. Arawaka did not follow the company off the hill.

As 2d Lt. Augustus B. Orr led a part of the company along the base of the hill toward the highway he came upon a number of North Korean soldiers lying in rice paddy ditches and partly covered with water. They appeared to be dead. Suddenly, Orr saw one of them who was clutching a grenade send air bubbles into the water and open his eyes. Orr shot

---

[54] Ltrs, Meloy to author, 29 May, 7 Jul, 4 Dec, and 30 Dec 52; Notes, Logan for author, Jun 52; 24th Div WD, G-2 Jnl, entry 1031, 161300 Jul 50. The message in the G-2 Journal reporting Logan's conversation with General Dean reads, "Colonel Meloy hit in calf of leg. Winstead in command. Vehicles badly jammed. Baker Battery is no more [apparently referring to B Battery, 52d Field Artillery Battalion, but in error]. Will fight them and occupy position in rear. Both sides of road. Vehicles jammed. Taking a pounding in front. Air Force does not seem able to find or silence tanks."

him at once. He and his men now discovered that the other North Koreans were only feigning death and they killed them on the spot.[55]

When C Company reached the highway they saw the last of A and B Companies disappearing south along it. Enemy troops were starting forward from the vicinity of the bridge. But when they saw C Company approaching from their flank, they ran back. Upon reaching the highway, C Company turned south on it but soon came under enemy fire from the hill east of Palsan-ni. An estimated six enemy machine guns fired on the company and scattered it. Individuals and small groups from the company made their way south as best they could. Some of those who escaped saw wounded men lying in the roadside ditches with medical aid men heroically staying behind administering to their needs. On the west side of the highway, F Company was still in position covering the withdrawal of B Company. At the time of the withdrawal of the 1st Battalion, F Company was under fire from its left front, left flank, and the left rear.[56]

As elements of the withdrawing 1st Battalion came up to the roadblock, officers attempted to organize attacks against the enemy automatic weapons firing from the high ground a few hundred yards to the west. One such force had started climbing toward the enemy positions when a flight of four friendly F-51's came in and attacked the hill. This disrupted their efforts completely and caused the men to drop back off the slope in a disorganized condition. Other attempts were made to organize parties from drivers, mechanics, artillerymen, and miscellaneous personnel to go up the hill—all to no avail. Two light tanks at the roadblock fired in the general direction of the enemy. But since the North Koreans used smokeless powder ammunition, the tankers could not locate the enemy guns and their fire was ineffective. Lt. Lloyd D. Smith, platoon leader of the 81-mm. mortar platoon, D Company, was one of the officers Major Logan ordered to attack and destroy the enemy machine guns. He and another platoon leader, with about fifty men, started climbing toward the high ground. After going several hundred feet, Smith found that only one man was still with him. They both returned to the highway. Men crowded the roadside ditches seeking protection from the enemy fire directed at the vehicles.[57]

Several times men pushed vehicles blocking the road out of the way, but each time traffic started to move enemy machine guns opened up causing more driver casualties and creating the vehicle block all over again. Strafing by fighter planes seemed unable to reduce this enemy automatic fire of three or four machine guns. Ordered to attack south against the enemy roadblock force, F Company, still in its original reserve position, was unable to do so, being virtually surrounded and under heavy attack.

About 1430, Major Logan placed Capt. Edgar R. Fenstermacher, Assistant S–3, in command at the roadblock, and taking twenty men he circled eastward and then southward trying to determine

---

[55] Interv, Blumenson with Orr, 26 Aug 51.

[56] *Ibid.;* Ltr, Meloy to author, 4 Dec 52, citing comments provided him by Capt Anderson, CO, B Co.

[57] Notes, Logan for author, Jun 52; Interv, Blumenson with Lt Smith (D Co, 19th Inf), 25 Aug 51.

the extent of the roadblock and to find a bypass. Approximately two hours later, he and his group walked into the positions of the 13th Field Artillery Battalion which had started to displace southward. A few minutes later Logan met General Dean. With the general were two light tanks and four antiaircraft artillery vehicles, two of them mounting quad .50-caliber machine guns and the other two mounting dual 40-mm. guns.[58]

In carrying out Meloy's instructions and going back down the road to find Colonel McGrail and bring G and H Companies to break the roadblock, Nash ran a gantlet of enemy fire. His jeep was wrecked by enemy fire, but he escaped on foot to the 13th Field Artillery Battalion position. There he borrowed a jeep and drove to McGrail's command post at Sangwang-ni on the regimental extreme left flank near Kongju. After delivering Meloy's orders, Nash drove back to Taejon airstrip to find trucks to transport the troops. It took personal intercession and an order from the assistant division commander, General Menoher, before the trucks went to pick up G Company. Meanwhile, two tanks and the antiaircraft vehicles started for the roadblock position. Colonel McGrail went on ahead and waited at the 13th Field Artillery Battalion headquarters for the armored vehicles to arrive. They had just arrived when Logan met General Dean.[59]

Logan told General Dean of the situation at the roadblock and offered to lead the armored vehicles to break the block. Dean said that Colonel McGrail would lead the force and that he, Logan, should continue on south and form a new position just west of Taejon airfield. While Logan stood at the roadside talking with General Dean, a small group of five jeeps came racing toward them. Lt. Col. Homer B. Chandler, the 19th Infantry Executive Officer, rode in the lead jeep. He had led four jeeps loaded with wounded through the roadblock. Every one of the wounded had been hit again one or more times by enemy fire during their wild ride.[60]

McGrail now started up the road with the relief force. One light tank led, followed by the four antiaircraft vehicles loaded with soldiers; the second light tank brought up the rear. About one mile north of the former position of the 13th Field Artillery Battalion, enemy heavy machine gun and light antitank fire ripped into the column just after it rounded a bend and came onto a straight stretch of the road. Two vehicles stopped and returned the enemy fire. Most of the infantry in the antiaircraft vehicles jumped out and scrambled for the roadside ditches. As McGrail went into a ditch he noticed Colonel Meloy's and Major Logan's wrecked jeeps nearby. Enemy fire destroyed the four antiaircraft vehicles. After expending their ammunition, the tanks about 1600 turned around and headed back down the road. McGrail crawled back along the roadside ditch and eventually got out of enemy fire. The personnel in the four antiaircraft vehicles suffered an estimated 90 percent casualties. The location of the wrecked

---

[58] Notes, Logan for author, Jun 52; Interv, author with Col Thomas M. McGrail, 24 Oct 52.

[59] Interv, Blumenson with Nash, 1 Aug 51; Interv, author with McGrail, 24 Oct 52.

[60] Notes, Logan for author, Jun 52; Interv, author with McGrail, 24 Oct 52.

Meloy and Logan jeeps would indicate that McGrail's relief force came within 300 to 400 yards of the regimental column piled up behind the roadblock around the next turn of the road.[61]

Back near Kongju on the regimental west flank, G Company came off its hill positions and waited for trucks to transport it to the roadblock area. Elements of H Company went on ahead in their own transportation. Captain Montesclaros stayed with the I&R Platoon, and it and the engineers blew craters in the road. They were the last to leave. At Yusong General Menoher met Capt. Michael Barszcz, commanding officer of G Company, when the company arrived there from the west flank. Fearing that enemy tanks were approaching, Menoher ordered him to deploy his men along the river bank in the town.

Later Barszcz received orders to lead his company forward to attack the enemy-held roadblock. On the way, Barszcz met a small convoy of vehicles led by a 2½-ton truck. A Military Police officer riding the front fender of the truck yelled, "Tanks, Tanks!" as it hurtled past. Barszcz ordered his driver to turn the jeep across the road to block it and the G Company men scrambled off their vehicles into the ditches. But there were no enemy tanks, and, after a few minutes, Barszcz had G Company on the road again, this time on foot. Some distance ahead, he met General Dean who ordered him to make contact with the enemy and try to break the roadblock.[62]

About six miles north of Yusong and two miles south of Tuman-ni, G Company came under long-range enemy fire. Barszcz received orders to advance along high ground on the left of the road. He was told that enemy troops were on the hill half a mile ahead and to the left. While climbing the hill the company suffered several casualties from enemy fire. They dug in on top at dusk. A short time later a runner brought word for them to come down to the road and withdraw. That ended the effort of the 19th Infantry and the 24th Division to break the roadblock behind the regiment.[63]

Efforts to break the enemy roadblock at both its northern and southern extremities disclosed that it covered about a mile and a half of road. The enemy soldiers imposing it were on a Y-shaped hill mass whose two prongs dropped steeply to the Yongsu River at their eastern bases and overlooked the Seoul-Pusan highway.

Behind the roadblock, the trapped men had waited during the afternoon. They could not see either of the two attempts to reach them from the south because of a finger ridge cutting off their view. Not all the troops along the river line, however, came to the roadblock; many groups scattered into the hills and moved off singly or in small units south and east toward Taejon.

About 1800, several staff officers decided that they would place Colonel Meloy in the last tank and run it through the roadblock. The tank made four efforts before it succeeded in pushing aside the pile of smoldering 2½-ton trucks

---

[61] *Ibid.*; 19th Inf WD, 16 Jul 50; 78th Hv Tk Bn, A Co, WD, 16 Jul 50.

[62] Ltr, Barszcz to author, 3 Jul 52; Interv, author with Montesclaros, 20 Aug 52. Interv, Blumenson with 2d Lt Robert L. Herbert (Plat Ldr, 2d Plat, G Co, 19th Inf), 20 Aug 51.

[63] Ltr, Barszcz to author, 3 Jul 52; Interv, Blumenson with Herbert, 20 Aug 51.

DISASTER AT THE KUM RIVER LINE

and other equipment blocking the road. Then it rumbled southward. About twenty vehicles followed the tank through the roadblock, including a truck towing a 105-mm. howitzer of the 52d Field Artillery Battalion, before enemy fire closed the road again and for the last time. A few miles south of the roadblock the tank stopped because of mechanical failure. There Captain Barszcz and G Company, withdrawing toward Yusong, came upon it and Colonel Meloy. No one had been able to stop any of the vehicles for help that had followed the tank through the roadblock. Instead, they sped past the disabled tank. The tank commander, Lt. J. N. Roush, upon Colonel Meloy's orders, dropped a thermite grenade into the tank and destroyed it. Eventually, an officer returned with a commandeered truck and took Colonel Meloy and other wounded men to Yusong.[64]

About an hour after the tank carrying Colonel Meloy had broken through the roadblock, Captain Fenstermacher, acting under his authority from Major Logan, ordered all personnel to prepare for cross-country movement. The critically wounded and those unable to walk were placed on litters. There were an estimated 500 men and approximately 100 vehicles at the roadblock at this time. Captain Fenstermacher and others poured gasoline on the vehicles and then set them afire. While so engaged, Captain Fenstermacher was shot through the neck. About 2100 the last of the men at the roadblock moved eastward into the hills.[65]

One group of infantrymen, artillerymen, engineers, and medical and headquarters troops, numbering approximately 100 men, climbed the mountain east of the road. They took with them about 30 wounded, including several litter cases. About 40 men of this group were detailed to serve as litter bearers but many of them disappeared while making the ascent. On top of the mountain the men still with the seriously wounded decided they could take them no farther. Chaplain Herman G. Felhoelter remained behind with the wounded. When a party of North Koreans could be heard approaching, at the Chaplain's urging, Capt. Linton J. Buttrey, the medical officer, escaped, though seriously wounded in doing so. From a distance, 1st Sgt James W. R. Haskins of Headquarters Company saw through his binoculars a group of what appeared to be young North Korean soldiers murder the wounded men and the valiant chaplain as the latter prayed over them.[66]

All night long and into the next day, 17 July, stragglers and those who had escaped through the hills filtered into Yusong and Taejon. Only two rifle companies of the 19th Infantry were relatively intact—G and E Companies. On the eastern flank near the railroad bridge, E Company was not engaged

---

[64] Ltrs, Meloy to author, 20 Aug and 30 Dec 52; Notes, Logan for author, Jun 52; Intervs, Blumenson with Early, 26 Aug 51 and Herbert, 20 Aug 51; 52d FA Bn WD, 16 Jul 50; 13th FA Bn WD, 16 Jul 50; Intervs, author with Huckabay and Eversole, 52d FA Bn, 4 Aug 51.

[65] Notes, Logan for author, Jun 52; Ltr, Meloy to author, 4 Dec 52 (both Meloy and Logan quote information from Fenstermacher on the departure from the roadblock); Interv, Blumenson with Early, 26 Aug 51; 19th Inf WD, 16 Jul 50.

[66] Interv, Blumenson with Early, 26 Aug 51; Ltr, Meloy to author, quoting Fenstermacher, 4 Dec 52; Notes, Logan to author, Jun 52; New York *Herald Tribune*, July 19, 1950.

during the Kum River battle and that night received orders to withdraw.

When Captain Barszcz encountered Colonel Meloy at the stalled tank the latter had ordered him to dig in across the road at the first good defensive terrain he could find. Barszcz selected positions at Yusong. There G Company dug in and occupied the most advanced organized defense position of the U.S. 24th Division beyond Taejon on the morning of 17 July.[67]

The North Korean *3d Division* fought the battle of the Kum River on 16 July without tanks south of the river. Most of the American light tanks in the action gave a mixed performance. At the roadblock on one occasion, when Major Logan ordered two tanks to go around a bend in the road and fire on the enemy machine gun positions in an attempt to silence them while the regimental column ran through the block, the tankers refused to do so unless accompanied by infantry. Later these tanks escaped through the roadblock without orders. An artillery officer meeting General Dean at the south end of the roadblock asked him if there was anything he could do. Dean replied, "No, thank you," and then with a wry smile the general added, "unless you can help me give these tankers a little courage."[68]

The 19th Infantry regimental headquarters and the 1st Battalion lost nearly all their vehicles and heavy equipment north of the roadblock. The 52d Field Artillery Battalion lost 8 105-mm. howitzers and most of its equipment; it brought out only 1 howitzer and 3 vehicles. The 13th and 11th Field Artillery Battalions, two miles south of the 52d, withdrew in the late afternoon to the Taejon airstrip without loss of either weapons or vehicles.[69]

The battle of the Kum on 16 July was a black day for the 19th Infantry Regiment. Of the approximately 900 men in position along the river only 434 reported for duty in the Taejon area the next day. A count disclosed that of the 34 officers in the regimental Headquarters, Service, Medical, and Heavy Mortar Companies, and the 1st Battalion, 17 were killed or missing in action. Of these, 13 later were confirmed as killed in action. All the rifle companies of the 1st Battalion suffered heavy casualties, but the greatest was in C Company, which had total casualties of 122 men out of 171. The regimental headquarters lost 57 of 191 men. The 1st Battalion lost 338 out of 785 men, or 43 percent, the 2d Battalion, 86 out of 777 men; the 52d Field Artillery Battalion had 55 casualties out of 393 men, or 14 percent. The total loss of the regiment and all attached and artillery units engaged in the action was 650 out of 3,401, or 19 percent.[70]

---

[67] Ltr, Barszcz to author, 3 Jul 52.

[68] Ltr, Meloy to author, 29 May 52; Notes, Logan for author, Jun 52; Interv, author with Maj Leon B. Cheek, 5 Aug 51.

[69] Ltr, Col Perry to author, 6 Nov 52; 52d FA Bn WD, 16 Jul 50; 13th FA Bn WD, 16 Jul 50; Interv, author with Maj Jack J. Kron (Ex Off, 13th FA Bn), 4 Aug 51. The 11th Field Artillery Battalion on 14 July received a third firing battery, thus becoming the first U.S. artillery battalion in action in the Korean War to have the full complement of three firing batteries. Interv, author with Cheek, 5 Aug 51; 19th Inf WD, 16 Jul 50.

[70] Table, Confirmed KIA as of August 1, 1951, 19th Infantry, for 16 Jul 50, copy supplied author by Gen Meloy; Intervs, Blumenson with Early and Orr, 26 Aug 51; The Rand Corporation, Dr. J. O'Sullivan, Statistical Study of Casualties 19th Infantry at Battle of Taep'yong-ni, 16 July 1950.

During 17 July, B Company of the 34th Infantry relieved G Company, 19th Infantry, in the latter's position at Yusong, five miles northwest of Taejon. The 19th Infantry that afternoon moved to Yongdong, twenty-five air miles southeast of Taejon, to re-equip.[71]

In the battle of the Kum River on 16 July one sees the result of a defending force lacking an adequate reserve to deal with enemy penetrations and flank movement. Colonel Meloy never faltered in his belief that if he had not had to send two-thirds of his reserve to the left flank after the collapse of the 34th Infantry at Kongju, he could have prevented the North Koreans from establishing their roadblock or could have reduced it by attack from high ground. The regiment did repel, or by counterattack drive out, all frontal attacks and major penetrations of its river positions except that through C Company on Hill 200. But it showed no ability to organize counterattacks with available forces once the roadblock had been established. By noon, demoralization had set in among the troops, many of whom were near exhaustion from the blazing sun and the long hours of tension and combat. They simply refused to climb the hills to attack the enemy's automatic weapons positions.

The N.K. *3d Division,* for its part, pressed home an attack which aimed to pin down the 19th Infantry by frontal attack while it carried out a double envelopment of the flanks. The envelopment of the American left flank resulted in the fatal roadblock three miles below the Kum on the main supply road. This North Korean method of attack had characterized most other earlier actions and it seldom varied in later ones.

---

[71] 19th Inf WD, 17 Jul 50; 24th Div WD, G–4 Summ, 17–18 Jul 50.

CHAPTER XI

Taejon

> For it is by being often carried to the well that the pitcher is finally broken.
> GUSTAVUS ADOLPHUS

Both North Korean divisions were now across the Kum River, both were ready to advance to the attack of Taejon itself. The *3d Division* was closer to the city and approaching it from the northwest. The *4th Division*, in the Kongju-Nonsan area, was northwest and west of the city and in a position to join with the *3d Division* in a frontal attack or to move south and then east in a flanking movement that would bring it to the rear of Taejon. The road net from Kongju and Nonsan permitted both these possibilities, or a combination of them. After its successful crossing of the Kum on the 14th, the *4th Division* apparently had been gathering its forces and waiting on the *3d* to complete its crossing effort so that the two could then join in a co-ordinated attack.

In the North Korean plan, a third division, the *2d*, was supposed to join the *4th* and the *3d* in the attack on Taejon. This division was advancing on the east of the other two and had been heavily engaged for some days with ROK troops in the Chinch'on-Ch'ongju area, where it suffered crippling casualties. As events turned out, this division did not arrive in time to join in the attack, nor did the other two need it. Had it come up as planned it would have appeared on the east and southeast of Taejon, a thing that General Dean very much feared and which he had to take into account in his dispositions for the defense of the city.

If past practice signified anything for the future, the North Koreans would advance against Taejon frontally with a force strong enough to pin down the defenders and attack first with tanks in an effort to demoralize the defenders. Thus far, their tanks had led every advance and nothing had been able to stop them. While this frontal action developed, strong flanking forces would be moving to the rear to cut off the main escape routes. This North Korean maneuver had been standard in every major action. The N.K. *4th Division* was in a favored position to execute just such a flanking maneuver against Taejon from the west and southwest. Had the *2d Division* arrived on the scene as planned it would have been in a position to do the same thing from the east and southeast. The *3d Division* was in position between these two divisions and undoubtedly was expected to exert the main frontal pressure in the forthcoming attack.

TAEJON

In any deployment of his forces against the North Koreans in front of Taejon, General Dean faced the fact that he had only remnants of three defeated regiments. Each of them could muster little more than a battalion of troops. Osan, Chonui, and Choch'iwon had reduced the 21st Infantry to that state; P'yongt'aek, Ch'onan, and the Kum River had left only a decimated 34th Infantry; and 16 July at the Kum River had sadly crippled the 19th Infantry. In addition to numerical weakness, all the troops were tired and their morale was not the best. General Dean braced himself for the job ahead. He himself was as worn as his troops; for the past two weeks he had faced daily crises and had pushed himself to the limit.

Dean's Plan at Taejon

After dark on 16 July, the 34th Infantry on orders from General Dean fell back approximately twenty miles from the vicinity of Nonsan to new defensive positions three miles west of Taejon. Col. Charles E. Beauchamp, who had flown to Korea from Japan to take command of the regiment, established his command post at the Taejon airstrip just to the northwest of the city. General Dean consolidated all remaining elements of the divisional artillery, except the 155-mm. howitzers of the 11th Field Artillery Battalion, into one composite battalion and emplaced it at the airstrip for the defense of the city. The airstrip itself closed to ordinary traffic. Early in the afternoon of the 17th the 34th Infantry took over the entire defensive line north and west of Taejon. Except for General Dean and three or four other officers, the 24th Division headquarters left for Yongdong, 28 miles southeast on the main highway and rail line. Remaining with Dean at Taejon were Lieutenant Clarke, an aide; Capt. Richard A. Rowlands, Assistant G-3; Capt. Raymond D. Hatfield, Transportation Officer and Assistant G-4; and two drivers. Dean instructed Maj. David A. Bissett to establish an office for him at the 21st Infantry command post at Okch'on so that he could from there more easily keep informed of affairs east of Taejon. Dean said that he would spend nights at Okch'on. "But," commented Bissett, "he never did, and indeed none of us there expected him to." [1]

Before the battle of the Kum, Dean had selected two regimental positions three miles west of Taejon for the close-in defense of the city. These positions were on a 500-foot high, 3-mile long ridge behind (east of) the Kap-ch'on River. Each extremity covered a bridge and a road immediately to its front. The position was a strong one and well suited to a two-regimental front. It was known as the Yusong position. A village of that name lay across the Kap-ch'on River about a mile from the northern end of the ridge. Dean's plan had been to place the 19th Infantry on the northern part of the line covering the main Seoul-Pusan highway where it curved around the northern end of the ridge and to place the 34th Infantry on the southern part to cover the Nonsan-Taejon road where it passed along a narrow strip of low ground at the southern end of the

---

[1] Ltr, Bissett to author, 14 May 52; Ltr, Capt Arthur M. Clarke to author, 30 Jun 52; Interv, author with Col Beauchamp, 1 Aug 52; 24th Div WD, 16–17 Jul 50, and G–3 Jnl, entry 599, 1615o Jul 50; EUSAK WD, G-3 Sec, Msg at 2245, 16 Jul 50.

AERIAL VIEW OF TAEJON AIRFIELD, *looking south.*

ridge. But with the 19th Infantry combat-ineffective after the ordeal of the 16th and at Yongdong for re-equipping, the defense of the entire line fell upon the 34th Infantry.[2]

General Dean had no intention of fighting a last-ditch battle for Taejon. He looked upon it as another in the series of delaying actions to which the 24th Division had been committed by General MacArthur to slow the North Korean advance, pending the arrival of sufficient reinforcements to halt and then turn back the enemy. Expecting that the North Koreans would arrive before the city just as soon as they could get their tanks across the Kum River and carry out an envelopment with ground forces, General Dean on 18 July made plans to evacuate Taejon the next day. Anticipating an early withdrawal, engineer demolition teams with Colonel Stephens' 21st Infantry at the Okch'on position prepared the tunnels east of Taejon for destruction.

But Dean's plan was changed by the arrival of General Walker at the Taejon airstrip before noon of the 18th. After the North Korean crossing of the Kum River, General Walker had asked his Chief of Staff, Colonel Landrum, to as-

---

[2] Interv, author with Beauchamp, 1 Aug 52; Ltr, Stephens to author, 24 Mar 52.

semble troop and logistical data bearing on Eighth Army's capability in the face of the growing crisis in Korea. At his office in Yokohama, Colonel Landrum and his staff spent a hectic day on the telephone gathering the information Walker wanted. Then Landrum called Walker at Taegu and relayed to him the status of all troops in Korea or en route there; an estimate of United States military build-up in Korea during the next ten days, with particular emphasis on the 1st Cavalry Division; the status of supplies and especially of ammunition; and a report on General Garvin's progress in organizing the supply base at Pusan.

During the conversation Walker had at hand a set of terrain maps and terrain estimates of the roads, railroads, and corridors running from north to south and from south to north and their relationship to enemy operations and Eighth Army's build-up in Korea. He repeatedly interjected the question, "When and where can I stop the enemy and attack him?" General Walker's final decision in this conference was that the 24th Division and the ROK Army should execute maximum delay on the North Koreans in order to assure stopping them west and north of the general line Naktong River to Yongdok on the east coast. He hoped to get the 1st Cavalry Division deployed in the Okch'on area and south of Taejon along the Kumsan road, thinking this might provide the opportunity to stop the enemy between Taejon and Taegu. Walker felt that if he was forced to fall back behind the Naktong River he could stand there until Eighth Army's troop and equipment build-up would permit him to take the offensive. Upon concluding this conference with Lan-

MACHINE GUN EMPLACEMENT *in the Yusong position overlooking the Kap-ch'on River and the main highway. View is southwest over the bridge.*

drum, General Walker particularly instructed him to keep this estimate to himself, although authorizing him to consider it in reviewing staff plans.[3]

General Walker had this concept of future operations in Korea in his mind when he talked with General Dean at the 34th Infantry command post. He spoke of the 1st Cavalry Division landing which had started that morning at P'ohang-dong on the southeast coast. Walker said he would like to hold Taejon until the 1st Cavalry Division could move up to help in its defense or get into battle position alongside the 24th Division in the mountain passes southeast of Taejon. He said he needed two

---

[3] Ltr and Comments, Maj Gen Eugene M. Landrum to author, n.d., but received 23 Nov 53; Collier, MS review comments, 10 Mar 58.

days' time to accomplish this. After his conference with Dean, Walker flew back to Taegu. He informed Colonel Landrum that he had told General Dean he needed two days' delay at Taejon to get the 1st Cavalry Division up and into position. Landrum asked Walker how much latitude he had given Dean. Walker replied, in substance, "Dean is a fighter; he won't give an inch if he can help it. I told him that I had every confidence in his judgment, and that if it became necessary for him to abandon Taejon earlier, to make his own decision and that I would sustain him."[4]

This conference changed Dean's plan to withdraw from Taejon the next day, 19 July. Shortly after noon Dean informed the headquarters of the 21st Infantry that the withdrawal from Taejon planned for the 19th would be delayed 24 hours. The regiment passed this information on to the engineer demolition teams standing by at the tunnels.

At this point it is desirable to take a closer look at the geography and communications which necessarily would affect military operations at Taejon.

In 1950 Taejon, with a population of about 130,000 was in size the sixth city of South Korea, a rapidly growing inland commercial center, 100 miles south of Seoul and 130 miles northwest of Pusan.[5] A long and narrow city, Taejon lay in the north-south valley of the Taejon River at the western base of the middle Sobaek range of mountains. Extensive rice paddy ground adjoined the city on the north and west. The railroad ran along its eastern side with the station and extensive yards in the city's northeast quarter. Two arms of the Taejon River, the main one flowing northwest through the center of the city and the other curving around its eastern side, joined at its northern edge. Two miles farther north the Yudung River emptied into it and the Taejon then flowed into the Kap-ch'on, a large tributary of the Kum. (*Map II*)

The highway net can be visualized readily if one imagines Taejon as being the center of a clock dial. Five main routes of approach came into the city. The main rail line and a secondary road ran almost due south from the Kum River to it. On this approach, 3 miles north of the city, a platoon of I Company, 34th Infantry, established a road and rail block. From the east at 4 o'clock the main Pusan highway entered the city, and astride it some 6 miles eastward the 21st Infantry held a defensive blocking position in front of Okch'on with the regimental command post in that town. There were two railroad and two highway tunnels between Taejon and Okch'on. One of each of them was between Taejon and the 21st Infantry position. From the south, the Kumsan road entered Taejon at 5 o'clock. General Dean had the Reconnaissance Company at Kumsan to protect and warn the division of any enemy movement from that direction in its rear. At 8 o'clock the Nonsan road from the southwest slanted into the Seoul-Pusan highway a mile west of the city. Astride this road 3

---

[4] Ltr and Comments, Landrum to author, received 23 Nov 53; Comments, Landrum to author, received 4 Jan 54; Interv, author with Beauchamp, 1 Aug 52 (Beauchamp overheard part of the conversation on the 18th between Walker and Dean); Ltr, Clarke to author, 30 Jun 52; Ltr, Lt Col Layton C. Tyner (aide to Gen Walker) to author, 22 Aug 52; Interv, author with Lt Col Paul F. Smith (Comb Opn G–3, EUSAK, Jul 50), 1 Oct 52.

[5] National Intelligence Survey (NIS), Korea, 41, (1950) p. 4; JANIS 75 (1945) ch. VIII, pp. 23–24.

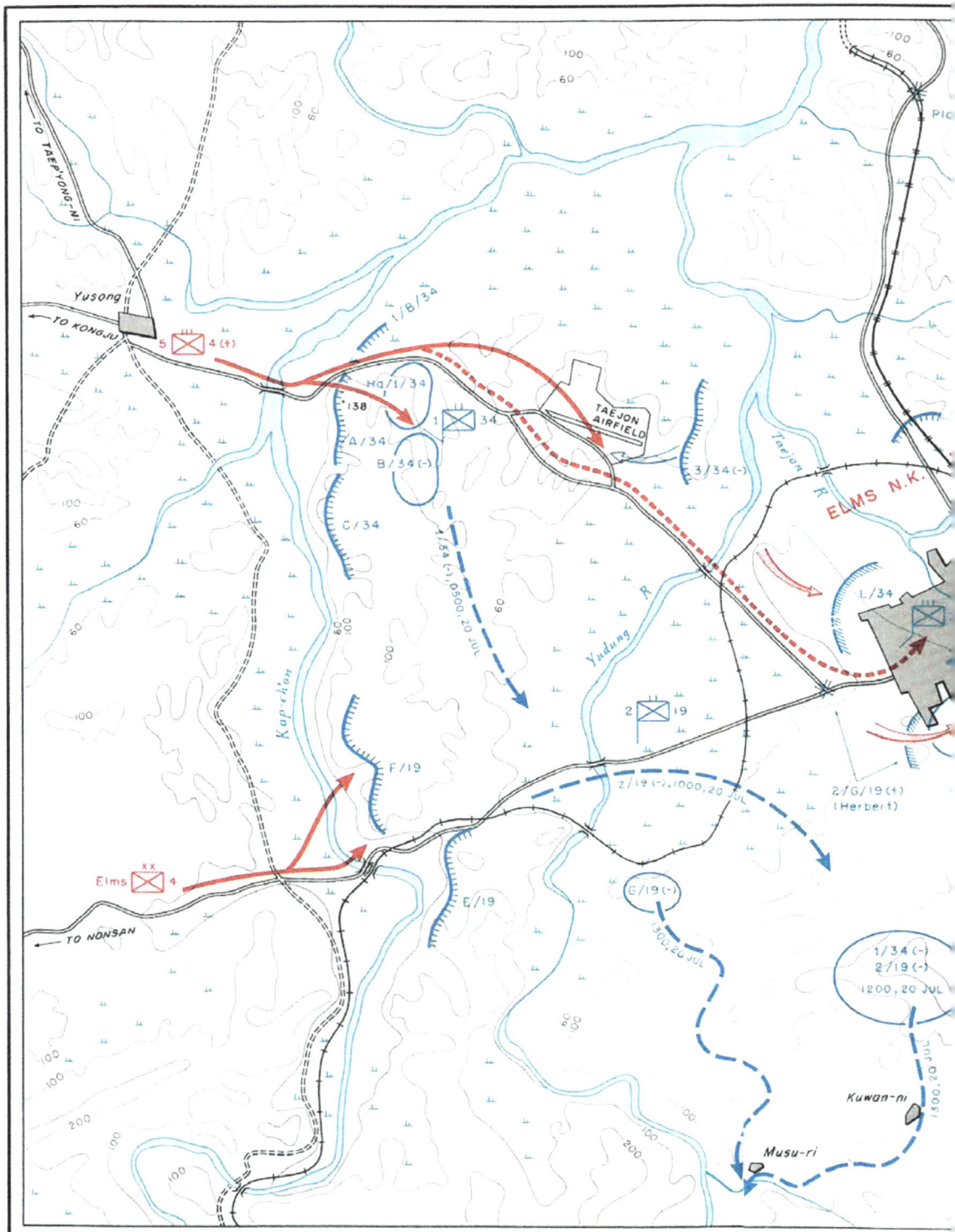

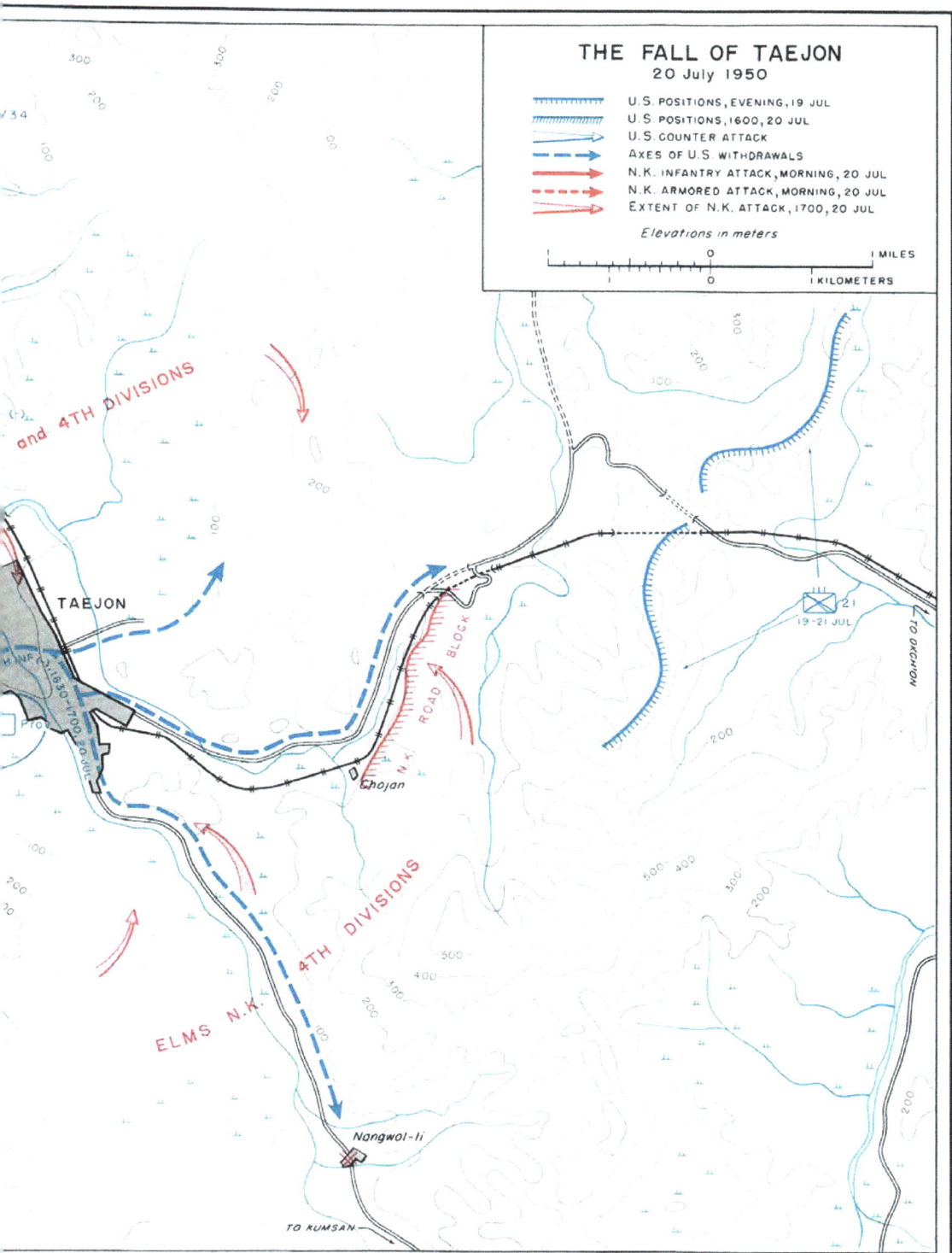

AERIAL VIEW OF TAEJON CITY

miles southwest of Taejon a platoon of L Company, 34th Infantry, held a roadblock at the bridge over the Kap-ch'on River at the southern end of the 34th Infantry defense position. The Seoul highway slanted toward the city from the northwest at 10 o'clock, and of all approaches it had to be considered the most important. At the western edge of Taejon (700 yards from the densely built-up section) where the Nonsan road joined it, the highway turned east to enter the city. The Taejon airstrip lay on a little plateau north of the road two miles from the city. A mile in front of the airstrip the 1st Battalion, 34th Infantry, was in battle position astride the highway at Hill 138 just east of the Kap-ch'on River. A mile farther west B Company occupied an advanced position.

Behind the 1st Battalion, a mile and a half away, the 3d Battalion, 34th Infantry, held a ridge east of the airfield and between it and the city. The composite battalion of artillery supporting the infantry was emplaced at the airfield where it could fire on the expected avenues of enemy approach.[6]

Taejon—The First Day

In the afternoon of 18 July General Dean went to the 24th Division com-

---

[6] Interv, author with Beauchamp, 1 Aug 52; Overlay of 34th Inf positions 18 Jul 50, prepared by Beauchamp for author, Aug 52; Ltr, Ayres to author, 3 Oct 52; Ltr, Maj Jack E. Smith (Actg CO 3d Bn, 34th Inf, 20 Jul 50) to author, 21 Jul 55.

mand post at Yongdong and there in the evening he took steps to bolster the defense of Taejon for an extra day, as desired by General Walker. He ordered the 2d Battalion, 19th Infantry, to move back to Taejon from Yongdong and B Battery of the 13th Field Artillery Battalion to return to the Taejon airstrip from the vicinity of Okch'on. At the same time he ordered the Reconnaissance Company to be released from division control and attached to the 34th Infantry Regiment. Up to this time the Reconnaissance Company had been based at Kumsan. The division order to the Reconnaissance Company releasing it to regimental control moved it to Taejon the next day. As a result, the division became blind to what the enemy was doing on its southern flank. General Dean subsequently considered his releasing the Reconnaissance Company to the regiment as one of his most serious errors at Taejon. His purpose in releasing it to Colonel Beauchamp's command was to ensure the 34th Infantry getting direct and immediate information as to conditions on its southern flank; he had not anticipated that the division order would send it to Taejon.[7]

General Dean also discussed again with Colonel Stephens the role of the 21st Infantry in the next few days. It was to keep open the withdrawal road out of Taejon. Stephens pointed out that his troops were astride that road and on the hills between Taejon and Okch'on and asked if he should change their disposition. General Dean answered no, that he did not want that done, as he also feared an enemy penetration behind his Taejon position from the east through the ROK Army area there and he had to guard against it. Dean decided that the 21st Infantry should stay where it was but patrol the terrain north of the Taejon-Okch'on road and send patrols periodically up the road into Taejon.[8]

The North Korean attack against Taejon got under way the morning of 19 July. The first blow was an air strike against communication lines in the rear of the city. At 0720, six YAK's flew over the lines of the 21st Infantry and dropped four bombs on the railroad bridge two miles northwest of Okch'on. One bomb damaged the bridge, but by noon B Company of the 3d Engineer Combat Battalion had repaired it and restored rail traffic in both directions. The YAK's strafed near the regimental command post and dropped propaganda leaflets signed by three American officers and three noncommissioned officers captured at Osan two weeks earlier. Four planes then strafed the Taejon airstrip. Later in the day, the crews of A Battery, 26th Antiaircraft Battalion, supporting the 1st Battalion, 34th Infantry, shot down two YAK's near Yusong, just west of Taejon.[9]

The U.S. Air Force also went into

---

[7] Dean, MS review comments, 20 Jan 58; 21st Inf WD, 18 Jul 50; 19th Inf WD, 18 Jul 50; Interv, author with Maj Leon B Cheek (Ex Off, 13th FA Bn, Jul 50), 7 Aug 51; 24th Recon Co WD, 18–20 Jul 50.

[8] Ltr, Stephens to author, 24 Mar 52; Gen Dean, MS review comments, 20 Jan 58.

[9] 24th Div WD, 19 Jul 50, Narr Summ of Enemy Info; 21st Inf WD, 19 Jul 50, includes copies of this enemy leaflet; Btry A, 26th AAA (AW) Bn WD, 19 Jul 50; *Antiaircraft Journal* (January–February, 1951), article by Cpl John S. Aaron on 24th Div AAA claims three YAK's shot down; 3d Engr (C) Bn WD, 19 Jul 50, Narr Summ, Opn Highlights.

TAEJON

action early on the 19th. It bombed and burned known and suspected points of enemy concentration west and southwest of Taejon. Aerial observers at noon reported that the enemy had partially repaired the bridge across the Kum River at Taep'yong-ni, ten miles north of Taejon, and that tanks and artillery were moving south of the river. The Air Force operated at considerable disadvantage at this time, however, for there were only two strips in Korea suitable for use by F–51 and C–47 types of aircraft—the K–2 dirt strip at Taegu and the similar K–3 strip at Yonil near P'ohang-dong. South of Chinju, the K–4 strip at Sach'on was available as an emergency field. Most of the tactical planes flew from Japan.[10]

After completing its crossing at Kongju, the N.K. *4th Division* split its forces for a two-pronged attack on Taejon. The bulk of the division, comprising the *16th* and *18th Infantry Regiments*, the *Artillery Regiment*, and most of the tanks, went south to Nonsan and there turned east toward Taejon. Some of the infantry of these regiments may have moved south out of Nonsan in a wheeling movement through Kumsan to the rear of Taejon. Others apparently moved across back country trails to strike the Kumsan road south of and below Taejon. The *5th Infantry Regiment*, supported by one tank company, left Kongju on the secondary road running southeast through a mountainous area to Yusong, and apparently was the first enemy unit to arrive at the outskirts of Taejon.[11]

At 1000, after the 24th Reconnaissance Company had arrived at Taejon, Colonel Beauchamp sent its 2d Platoon, consisting of thirty-nine men, southwest along the Nonsan road. Half an hour later, three miles west of the Kap-ch'on River, enemy fire struck the patrol from both sides of the road. It withdrew to the river and there joined the platoon of L Company on the east bank of the stream. The remainder of L Company arrived and deployed.[12]

General Dean had left Taejon that morning intending to go briefly to Yongdong. On the way he stopped at the 21st Infantry command post at Okch'on. There he said suddenly about 1000 that he was worried about the disposition of the 34th Infantry and was going back to Taejon.[13] When he arrived there, action already had started at the L Company roadblock on the Nonsan road. The battle of Taejon had begun. Dean stayed in Taejon.

The 2d Battalion, 19th Infantry, arrived at Taejon from Yongdong about this time, just after noon. By 1300, Colonel McGrail, the battalion commander, had the unit ready to move out at the railroad station. There he received an order saying the North Koreans were breaking through L Company's blocking position at the Kap-ch'on River and he was to attack there immediately and

---

[10] 24th Div WD, G–3 Jnl, entry 106, 190825 Jul 50; *Ibid.*, G–2 Jnl, entry 1222, 191315 Jul 50; Hq X Corps, Staff Study, Development of Tactical Air Support in Korea, 25 Dec 50, p. 8; EUSAK WD, G–2 Daily Stf Rpt, 19 Jul 50, p. 2; FEAF Opn Hist, I, 25 Jun–1 Nov 50, 58–59.

[11] ATIS Res Supp Interrog Rpts, Issue 94 (N.K. *4th Div*), pp. 46–47.

[12] 24th Recon Co WD, 19 Jul 50; 24th Div WD, 19 Jul 50; Interv, author with Beauchamp, 1 Aug 52; Situation Overlay 34th Inf, 19 Jul 50, prepared by Beauchamp for author, Aug 52.

[13] Interv, author with Col Ned D. Moore, 20 Aug 52. (Moore was with Dean.)

restore the position. When he arrived at the scene of fighting McGrail found General Dean there with two tanks, directing fire.[14]

McGrail's battalion attacked immediately with two companies abreast astride the Nonsan road, E on the left (south) and F on the right (north). On the right an enemy force was in the act of enveloping the north flank of L Company, 34th Infantry. F Company raced this enemy force for possession of critical high ground, taking and holding it in the ensuing fight. On the left, E Company moved up south of the road, and G Company occupied a hill position a mile behind it. Even with the newly arrived battalion now deployed covering the Nonsan road, there was still a mile-wide gap of high ground between it and the left of the 1st Battalion, 34th Infantry, to the north.[15]

Co-ordinated with the North Korean advance along the Nonsan road was an enemy approach on the main Seoul highway. There in the Yusong area, B Company of the 1st Battalion, 34th Infantry, came under heavy attack. Enemy flanking parties cut off two platoons half a mile north of Yusong. In the fighting there both platoon leaders were wounded and several men killed. Colonel Ayres from his observation post east of the Kap-ch'on River could see large groups of North Koreans assembling and artillery going into position in the little valley northwest of Yusong. He directed artillery fire and called in air strikes on these concentrations. In the afternoon he requested and received authority from Colonel Beauchamp to withdraw B Company from its exposed position at Yusong to the main battalion position back of the Kap-ch'on River. The company successfully withdrew in the evening.[16]

Meanwhile, just before noon, the North Koreans began shelling the Taejon airstrip with counterbattery fire. This fire, coming from the north and northwest, built up to great intensity during the afternoon. That evening, General Dean told Major Bissett that he had seen as much incoming artillery fire at the Taejon Airfield that day as he had ever seen in one day in Europe in World War II. Frequent artillery concentrations also pounded the main battle positions of the 34th Infantry.[17]

By early afternoon, Colonel Ayres was convinced that a major enemy attack was impending. At 1400 he recommended to Colonel Beauchamp that the regiment withdraw that night. Beauchamp rejected this, thinking they could hold the enemy out of Taejon another day, and he so told General Dean. After dark, however, Beauchamp moved his 34th Infantry command post from the airfield into Taejon. At the same time all the supporting artillery displaced from the

---

[14] 19th Inf WD, 19 Jul 50; Interv, author with McGrail, 20 Aug 52; Interv, author with Montesclaros (S-3 Sec, 2d Bn, 19th Inf, Jul 50), 20 Aug 52.

[15] Intervs, author with McGrail and Montesclaros, ~ Aug 52; Situation Overlay, 1st Bn, 34th Inf, 19 Jul 50, prepared by Col Ayres for author.

[16] Ltr, Ayres to author, 3 Oct 52; Interv, Mitchell with Bryant, 30 Jul 50.

[17] Interv, author with Beauchamp, 1 Aug 52; Ltr, Ayres to author, 3 Oct 52; Ltr, Bissett to author, 14 May 52. General Order 112, 30 August 1950, 24th Division, awarded the Bronze Star Medal to Cpl Robert D. Jones, Headquarters Battery, 63d Field Artillery Battalion.

airfield to positions on the south edge of the city.[18]

As darkness fell, Colonel Ayres ordered his motor officer to move the 1st Battalion vehicles into Taejon. He did not want to run the risk of losing them during a night attack. Only one jeep for each rifle company, two jeeps for the Heavy Weapons Company, the battalion command jeep, and the radio vehicle were left at the battle positions.

On the left of the defense position F Company of the 19th Infantry had been under attack all afternoon. After dark men there heard noises on their right flank, and it became apparent that enemy soldiers were moving into, and possibly through, the mile-wide gap between them and the 1st Battalion, 34th Infantry.[19]

Taejon was ominously quiet during the evening. Occasional showers from the edge of a typhoon that had narrowly missed the area settled the stifling dust raised by the vehicular traffic in the city. As the night wore on the quiet gave way to ominous noises. At his command post Colonel Ayres about 2200 heard the rumble of tanks on his right. He sent a patrol out to investigate. It never reported back. Ayres telephoned Beauchamp and told him he thought enemy troops were moving around the city and again recommended withdrawal.[20]

Before midnight a report came in to the 34th Infantry command post that an enemy unit was six miles south of Taejon on the Kumsan road. With nine members of the 24th Reconnaissance Company 1st Lt. George W. Kristanoff started down the road on a jeep patrol to investigate. Six miles below Taejon an enemy roadblock stopped them. Kristanoff reported the beginning of the action by radio. At 0300, 20 July, a platoon of the Reconnaissance Company drove cautiously out of Taejon down the same road to check on security. Enemy fire stopped the platoon at the same roadblock. There platoon members saw the bodies of several men of the earlier patrol and their four destroyed jeeps. A little earlier, at 0200, word had come in to Taejon that a jeep had been ambushed on the Okch'on road.[21]

It would seem clear from these incidents that enemy units were moving around to the rear of Taejon during the night—in just what strength might only be guessed. But for reasons that cannot now be determined these events were not so evaluated at the time of their occurrence. General Dean has stated that he did not know of the enemy roadblock on the Kumsan road—apparently it was not reported to him. He did learn of the jeep incident on the Okch'on road but dismissed it as the work of a few infiltrators and of no special importance because the road subsequently seemed to be clear.[22]

Taejon—The Second Day

Shortly after 0300, 20 July, the S-2 of the 1st Battalion, 34th Infantry, who

---

[18] Ltr, Ayres to author, 3 Oct 52; Interv, author with Beauchamp, 1 Aug 52; Comments, Beauchamp to author, 7 Jan 53.
[19] Intervs, author with McGrail and Montesclaros, 20 Aug 52.
[20] Ltrs, Ayres to author, 3 Oct 52 and 20 Feb 53; Interv, author with Ayres, 13 Jul 54.

[21] 24th Recon Co WD, 19-20 July 50; 24th Div WD, G-2 Jnl, entry 1313, 201040 Jul 50; General Order 111, 30 August 1950, 24th Division, awarded the Silver Star to Lieutenant Kristanoff.
[22] Dean, MS review comments, 20 Jan 58.

since dark had remained in the battalion forward observation post, ran into Colonel Ayres' command post and said that the North Koreans had overrun the observation post and penetrated the battalion main line of resistance. Ayres has said that this was his first knowledge of the enemy's general attack. He could now hear small arms fire to the front and right and see flares bursting at many points over the battalion position. There seemed to be no action on the battalion left in C Company's position.[23]

The enemy attack, infantry and armor, came down both sides of the highway and rolled up the battalion right flank. Other enemy infantry attacked from the north against this flank. The North Koreans penetrated to the 81-mm. and 4.2-inch mortar positions behind the rifle companies and then struck Headquarters Company. About 0400 small arms fire hit the Korean house in which the 1st Battalion command post was located and riflemen from the overrun front line began coming into the Headquarters Company area. Ayres tried, and failed, to communicate with his front line companies. He sent a message to the regimental headquarters that tanks had penetrated his position and were headed toward the city. There is some evidence that the infantry bazooka teams abandoned their positions along the road when the attack began. And rifle companies certainly did not fight long in place. In the growing confusion that spread rapidly, Ayres decided to evacuate the command post. Maj. Leland R. Dunham, the battalion executive officer, led about 200 men from the Heavy Mortar Company, the Heavy Weapons Company, and the 1st Battalion Headquarters southward from the Yudung valley away from the sound of enemy fire. Colonel Ayres and his S–3 followed behind the others. Day was dawning.[24]

In Taejon, Colonel Beauchamp received Ayres' report that enemy tanks were in the 1st Battalion position. Later, telephone communication to the 1st Battalion ended and Beauchamp sent linemen out to check the wires. They came back and said they could not get through —that enemy infantry were on the road near the airfield. The regimental S–3 did not believe this report. Beauchamp went to his jeep and started down the road toward the 1st Battalion command post to find out for himself just what the situation was. At the road junction half a mile west of Taejon, where the main Seoul highway comes in from the northwest to join the Nonsan road, an enemy tank suddenly loomed up out of the darkness. The tank fired its machine gun just as Beauchamp jumped from his jeep; one bullet grazed him, others set the vehicle afire. Beauchamp crawled back some hundreds of yards until he found a 3.5-inch bazooka team. He guided it back to the road junction. This bazooka team from C Company, 3d Engineer Combat Battalion, set the enemy tank on fire with rockets and captured the crew members. It then took a position to guard the road intersection. Later in the morning this rocket launcher team and one from the 24th Reconnaissance Company destroyed two more T34 tanks

---

[23] Ltrs, Ayres to author, 3 Oct 52 and 20 Feb 53; Interv, author with Ayres, 13 Jul 54.

[24] *Ibid.*; Interv, Blumenson with 2d Lt George H. Wilcox (Plat Ldr, D Co, 34th Inf), 25 Aug 51; Gugeler, *Combat Actions in Korea*, "Withdrawal Action," pp. 16–17, recording interview with MSgt Zack C. Williams of A Co, 34th Inf.

approaching from the direction of the airfield.²⁵

This action at the crossroads just west of Taejon in the predawn of 20 July is the first verifiable use of the 3.5-inch rocket launcher against the T34 tanks. This rocket launcher had been under development since the end of World War II, but none had been issued to troops because of the difficulty in perfecting its ammunition. The ammunition had been standardized and in production only fifteen days when the Korean War started. General MacArthur on 3 July requested that the new rocket launcher be airlifted to Korea. The first of the launchers, together with an instruction team, left Travis Air Force Base in California on 8 July and arrived at Taejon on the 10th. The first delivery of the new weapon arrived at Taejon on 12 July. That same day selected members of the 24th Infantry Division began to receive instructions in its use. The 3.5-inch rocket launcher was made of aluminum and weighed about fifteen pounds. It looked like a 5-foot length of stovepipe. It was electrically operated and fired a 23-inch-long, eight-and-a-half-pound rocket from its smooth bore, open tube. The rocket's most destructive feature was the shaped charge designed to burn through the armor of any tank then known.²⁶

When Beauchamp returned to his command post after his encounter with the enemy tanks he found that there was still no communication with the 1st Battalion. A little later, however, a regimental staff officer told him radio communication with the battalion had been re-established and that it reported its condition as good. It was learned afterward that the 1st Battalion had no communication with the regiment after Ayres reported the enemy penetration of his position. The only plausible explanation of this incident is that North Koreans used Colonel Ayres' captured radio jeep to send a false report to the regiment.

Disturbed by reports of enemy penetrations of the regimental defense position, Colonel Beauchamp after daylight ordered the 3d Battalion to attack into the gap between the 1st Battalion, 34th Infantry, and the 2d Battalion, 19th Infantry. K Company with part of M Company started to execute this order but it never reached the designated area. On the road leading to the airfield it had a sharp encounter with an enemy force. Six T34 tanks and an estimated battalion of enemy infantry scattered part of the troops. In this action, SFC Robert E. Dare of K Company courageously covered and directed the withdrawal of the advanced platoon at the cost of his own life. The entire force withdrew to its former 3d Battalion position.²⁷

In its defensive positions on the ridge

---

²⁵ Interv, author with Beauchamp, 1 Aug 52; 3d Engr (C) Bn WD, 20 Jul 50; 24th Recon Co WD, 20 Jul 50.

²⁶ EUSAK WD, Prologue, G-4 Sec, 25 Jun-Jul 50, and WD, G-4 Sec, 17 Jul 50; 24th Div WD, Div Ordnance Off Stf Hist Rpt, 15 Jun-22 Jul 50; 24th Div WD, G-4 Daily Summ, Jnl entries 13-16 Jul 50; Schnabel, FEC, GHQ Support and Participation in Korean War, ch. 4, p. 15.

²⁷ Ltr, Maj Jack E. Smith to author, 18 Jun 55; Comments, Wadlington for author, 1 Apr 53; Ltr, Wadlington to author, 23 Jun 53; Comments, Beauchamp for author, 3 Jan 53. Department of the Army General Order 16, 20 March 1951, awarded the Distinguished Service Cross posthumously to SFC Robert E. Dare, K Company, 34th Infantry, for heroism at Taejon, 20 July 1950.

east of the airfield, the 3d Battalion remained undisturbed by enemy action throughout the morning except for a small amount of mortar and artillery fire. A peculiar incident had occurred, however, which no one in the battalion could explain. The battalion commander, Major Lantron, disappeared. Lantron got into his jeep about 0930, drove off from his command post, and simply did not return. Colonel Wadlington learned of Lantron's disappearance about 1100 when he visited the 3d Battalion. In Lantron's absence, Wadlington ordered Capt. Jack E. Smith to assume command of the battalion. Some weeks later it was learned that Lantron was a prisoner in North Korea.[28]

The predawn attack against the 1st Battalion, 34th Infantry, the first tank approaches to the edge of Taejon, and the subsequent North Korean repulse of the K and M Companies' attack force near the airfield apparently were carried out by the *5th Regiment, N.K. 4th Division*, together with its attached armored support. This regiment claims to have captured the Taejon airfield by 0400, 20 July.[29] But after these spectacular successes which started the wholesale withdrawal of the 1st Battalion from its positions west of the city, the enemy force apparently halted and waited for certain developments elsewhere. This probably included completion of the enveloping maneuver to the rear of the city. Only tanks and small groups of infiltrators, most of the latter riding the tanks, entered Taejon during the morning. All these actions appeared to be related parts of the enemy plan.

Neither Colonel Beauchamp nor his executive officer at the time knew of the North Korean repulse of the K and M Company attack force that was supposed to close the gap between the 1st Battalion, 34th Infantry, and the 2d Battalion, 19th Infantry. About the time this event was taking place near the airfield, Colonel Beauchamp told General Dean of his early morning experience with tanks at the edge of the city, and Dean also was informed erroneously that the 1st Battalion was holding in its original battle positions. From the vantage point of Taejon everything seemed all right. At this time, however, General Dean instructed Beauchamp to plan a withdrawal after dark on the Okch'on road. Dean then telephoned this information to the 24th Division command post at Yongdong.[30]

In the 2d Battalion, 19th Infantry, positions covering the Nonsan road there had been alarms during the night, and some false reports had reached Taejon that the enemy had overrun the battalion position. Actually, E Company held its position near the bridge, but north of the road F Company under enemy pressure withdrew approximately 200 yards about daylight.[31]

When Major Dunham led the 1st Battalion and the 34th Infantry Headquarters group south, followed at a short

---

[28] ATIS Interrog Rpts, Issue 12, Rpt 1708, p. 26, 1st Lt Bill M. McCarver, and Rpt 1775, p. 214, 1st Lt Henry J. McNichols, Jr.
[29] ATIS Res Supp Interrog Rpts, Issue 94 (N.K. 4th Div), pp. 46-47.
[30] Interv, author with Beauchamp, 1 Aug 52; Dean, MS review comments, 20 Jan 58.
[31] Intervs, author with McGrail and Montesclaros, 20 Aug 52; Intervs, Blumenson with 2d Lt Joseph S. Szito (81-mm. Mortar Plat, H Co, 19th Inf), 25 Aug 51, and 2d Lt Robert L. Herbert (G Co, 19th Inf), 31 Jul 51.

TAEJON

interval by Colonel Ayres and his small party, it was just after daylight. These men passed along a protected route behind the high ground held by F Company, 19th Infantry. They had expected to reach the Nonsan road about three miles away and there turn east on it to enter Taejon. As Ayres neared the road he could see F Company on the hill mass to his right (west) engaged in what he termed a "heavy fire fight." As he watched he saw the company begin to leave the hill. He continued on and saw ahead of him the main body of his headquarters group climbing the mountain on the other side of the Nonsan road.

Major Dunham, on reaching the road with this group, met and talked briefly there with Colonel McGrail who told him he had had reports that enemy tanks had cut that road into Taejon. Upon hearing this, Dunham led his party across the road into the mountains. When Ayres reached the road enemy machine gun fire was raking it and the bridge over the Yudung. Ayres led his party under the bridge, waded the shallow stream, and followed the main group into the mountains southward. These two parties of the 1st Battalion, 34th Infantry, united on high ground south of Taejon about an hour before noon. Even earlier, the rifle companies of the battalion, for the most part, had scattered into these mountains.[32]

The rumor of enemy tanks on the Nonsan road that caused the 1st Battalion, 34th Infantry, group to go into the mountains instead of into Taejon had come to Colonel McGrail soon after daylight. A jeep raced up to his command post east of the Yudung bridge. The men in it said that three enemy tanks blocked the road junction just outside the city (they had seen the tanks from a distance, apparently, and had not known they had been knocked out) and that they had seen three more tanks approaching the junction from the airfield. Colonel McGrail could see smoke hanging over Taejon and hear explosions and gunfire. He turned to 2d Lt. Robert L. Herbert and ordered him to take his G Company's 2d Platoon and open the road into the city. On the way Herbert encountered a bazooka team which he persuaded to accompany him. He also passed a rifle company getting water in a streambed. This unit identified itself as Baker Company, 34th Infantry; it continued south toward the mountains. Upon arriving at the road junction, Herbert found two T34 tanks burning and a third one that had been destroyed earlier. Lieutenant Little and a reinforced squad armed with two bazookas held the road fork. The burning wreckage of the Heavy Mortar Company, 34th Infantry, littered the road back toward the airfield. A mile to the north three enemy tanks stood motionless. Some men of H Company, 19th Infantry, passed the road fork on their way into Taejon. Herbert's platoon joined Little's squad.[33]

After Herbert's platoon had departed on its mission, Colonel McGrail lost communication with Colonel Beauchamp's command post. He had now learned from Major Dunham that the enemy had overrun the 1st Battalion, 34th Infantry, on the Yusong road to the north of him. His own F Company had started to fall back. The general feeling

---

[32] Ltrs, Ayres to author, 3 Oct 52, and 20 Feb 53; Interv, author with Ayres, 13 Jul 54; Interv, author with McGrail, 20 Aug 52.

[33] Interv, Blumenson with Herbert, 25 Aug 51.

of McGrail's 2d Battalion staff was that enemy troops had cut the road between the battalion and Taejon and were probably in the city itself. About 1100 Captain Montesclaros of the S-3 Section volunteered to try to get into Taejon and reach the regimental headquarters for instruction. Colonel McGrail gave him his jeep and driver for the trip.[34]

Montesclaros reached the road junction without incident, saw the burning enemy tanks, met Lieutenant Herbert's platoon at the roadblock, and, much to his surprise, found the road into the city entirely open. At the edge of the city, Montesclaros encountered General Dean. Montesclaros reported to him, gave the position of the 2d Battalion, 19th Infantry, and asked for instructions. General Dean patted Montesclaros on the back and replied, "My boy, I am not running this show, Beauchamp is." Dean took Montesclaros to the 34th Infantry command post. Beauchamp was not present, but from a member of his staff Montesclaros obtained a written order. Before placing it in his shirt pocket, Montesclaros glanced at the order. It directed McGrail to bring his battalion back to the west edge of Taejon.[35]

Montesclaros drove back down the road to the 2d Battalion command post. He found it deserted. Not a living person was in sight; a dead Korean lay in the courtyard. Puzzled, Montesclaros turned back toward Taejon. After driving a short distance, he turned back to the command post to make sure no one was there; he found it the same as before. No one, neither friend nor foe, was in sight. A strange stillness hung over the spot. Again he turned back toward Taejon. He overtook E Company on the road and instructed it to go into position there. At the edge of Taejon, Montesclaros met 1st Lt. Tom Weigle, S-2 of the battalion, who told him that McGrail had established a new command post on a high hill south of the road, and pointed out the place. Montesclaros set out for it and after walking and climbing for forty-five minutes reached the place. Colonel McGrail and his command post were not there, but a few men were; they knew nothing of Colonel McGrail's location.

Montesclaros started down the mountain with the intention of returning to Taejon. On his way he met Lieutenant Lindsay and E Company climbing the slope. They said the enemy had overrun them on the road. Looking in that direction, Montesclaros saw an estimated battalion of North Korean soldiers marching toward the city in a column of platoons. A T34 tank was traveling west on the road out of Taejon. As it approached the enemy column, the soldiers scurried for the roadside and ducked under bushes, apparently uncertain whether it was one of their own. Montesclaros decided not to try to get into Taejon but to join E Company instead.

What had happened at the command post of the 2d Battalion, 19th Infantry? Simply this, believing that the enemy had cut him off from Taejon, Colonel McGrail decided to move his command post to high ground south of the Nonsan road. He instructed E Company to fall back, and then his radio failed. McGrail and his battalion staff thereupon abandoned the command post shortly before noon and climbed the mountain

---
[34] Intervs, author with McGrail and Montesclaros, 20 Aug 52.
[35] Interv, author with Montesclaros, 20 Aug 52.

south of Taejon.³⁶ Already F Company had given way and was withdrawing into the hills.

Soon not a single unit of the 2d Battalion, 19th Infantry, was in its battle position west of Taejon. Nearest to the city, G Company was the last to leave its place. From his hill position, Captain Barszcz, the company commander, had seen enemy tanks two and a half miles away enter Taejon just after daylight and had reported this by radio to Colonel McGrail's headquarters. Later in the morning he lost radio communication with McGrail. Shortly after noon, Capt. Kenneth Y. Woods, S-3, 2d Battalion, 19th Infantry, arrived at G Company's position and gave Captain Barszcz instructions to join the 1st Battalion, 34th Infantry, group that had passed him in the morning headed south, and to withdraw with it. The G Company 60-mm. mortars were firing at this time. About 1300 Barszcz issued his orders for the withdrawal. The 3d Platoon was to follow the Weapons Section and bring up the rear. In the withdrawal, however, unknown to Captain Barszcz, the Weapons Platoon leader asked the 3d Platoon leader to precede him, as he had some mortar ammunition he wanted to expend. The Weapons Section never got out—the entire section of one officer and eighteen enlisted men was lost to enemy action.³⁷

Except for the small group at the road junction half a mile west of the city, all the infantry and supporting weapons units of the two battalions in the battle positions west of Taejon had been driven from or had left those positions by 1300. All of them could have come into Taejon on the Nonsan road. Instead, nearly all of them crossed this road approximately two miles west of the city and went south into the mountains.

Back at Taejon, the first North Korean tanks had reached the edge of the city before dawn. They came from the northwest along the Yusong road and from the airfield. There is no evidence that the 3.5-inch bazooka teams of the 1st Battalion, 34th Infantry, posted along the Yusong road engaged these tanks.

Soon after daylight two enemy tanks entered the city from somewhere to the northwest. They were soon followed by a third. Enemy soldiers crowded their decks. These tanks drove to the center of Taejon and there unloaded soldiers who spread quickly into buildings and began the sniping that continued throughout the day. The two tanks then turned back past the large compound where the Service Company of the 34th Infantry had established the regimental kitchen and motor pool. The 2d Battalion, 19th Infantry, also had its kitchen trucks in this compound. Approximately 150 men were there when the two enemy tanks opened fire on it with their tank cannon. This fire killed several men, destroyed vehicles, and set an ammunition truck on fire. After shooting up the compound, the tanks rumbled away and fired at various targets of opportunity.³⁸

---

³⁶ Interv, author with McGrail, 20 Aug 52.
³⁷ Ltr, Capt. Michael Barszcz to author, 6 Sep 52.

³⁸ 3d Engr (C) Bn WD, 20 Jul 50; 24th Div WD, G-2 Jnl, entry 1367, 19-20 Jul 50 (I&R Plat Rpt with sketch map); Interv, author with Beauchamp, 1 Aug 52; Interv, Blumenson with 2d Lt Robert E. Nash (S-4, 2d Bn, 19th Inf, July 50), 22 Aug 51. Nash was in the compound at the time of the tank attack.

Not until after the tanks had left the compound area did any of the men there locate a 3.5-inch bazooka. Then, in trying to drive out snipers from nearby buildings, someone fired a 3.5-inch white phosphorus rocket into a building setting it afire. The fire spread rapidly to other wood and straw structures in the city until large parts of Taejon were burning, from this and other causes.

Bazooka teams from the 24th Reconnaissance Company set out after the two tanks. These tanks, meanwhile, encountered two jeeploads of men at the Medical Company headquarters, killed all but two, and wounded them. One tank ran over one of the wounded as he lay helpless in the road. A bazooka man finally got in a shot against one of these tanks, hitting it in the side and bouncing it off the ground, but the tank kept on going. At the railroad station, this tank fired into supplies and equipment, starting large fires. There, with a track off, it came to the end of its journeys. Rifle fire killed the tank commander. A rocket hit the second tank and knocked a piece of armor three feet square from its front plate. A third tank for a period survived a rocket that penetrated the top turret. Pfc. Jack E. Lowe and Cpl. Robert B. Watkins of the 24th Reconnaissance Company were the bazooka men who scored the destructive hits on these tanks.[39]

General Dean and his aide, Lieutenant Clarke, had awakened about 0530 to the sound of small arms fire. As Clarke made the bed rolls he remarked to General Dean, "I don't think we'll sleep here again tonight." The general agreed. Sometime later an enemy tank passed close to the 34th Infantry command post headed west out of the city. General Dean immediately started in pursuit of this tank accompanied by two 2.36-inch rocket launcher teams. The tank went through Lieutenant Herbert's roadblock without being fired on. It was mistaken for a friendly tank until too late for action. When General Dean's party arrived at the road fork, Herbert explained what had happened. Subsequently this tank re-entered the city and was destroyed, apparently by a 155-mm. howitzer, at the southwest edge of Taejon. During the morning, Dean and his party lost an opportunity against 2 other tanks on the airfield road when the bazooka man with them missed with his only rocket.[40] By 0900, 4 of the 5 tanks known to have entered Taejon had been destroyed.

At noon another tank entered Taejon. A 3.5-inch bazooka team from the 3d Engineer Combat Battalion hunted it down and destroyed it. Soon afterward still another penetrated into the city and rumbled past the regimental command post. General Dean led a group, joined later by a 3.5-inch bazooka team from the 3d Engineer Combat Battalion, in pursuit of this tank. After an hour or more of climbing over walls and fences

---

[39] 24th Recon Co WD, 20 Jul 50 and Summ, 25 Jun-22 Jul 50; 24th Div WD, G-2 Jnl, entry 1304, 200850.

[40] Ltr, Capt Arthur M. Clarke to author, 31 May 52 (consists mostly of a copy of notes Clarke made shortly after he returned to friendly lines, on 23 July, while events were fresh in his mind); Field Artillery School, Fort Sill, Debriefing Rpt 42, Dept of Training Pubs and Aids, 11 Dec 51 (contains some of Clarke's recollections of Taejon); Dean and Worden, *General Dean's Story*, pp. 30-33; Interv, Blumenson with Herbert, 25 Aug 51; 24th Recon WD, 20 Jul 50; 24th Div WD, G-2 Jnl, entry 1304, 200850 Jul 50.

and dodging through houses stalking it, with enemy snipers firing at them frequently, General Dean and his party brought this tank to bay. About 1400 a group including General Dean, a corporal carrying the bazooka, an ammunition bearer, and two or three riflemen entered a 2-story business building through a back courtyard and climbed to the second story. Looking out from the edge of a window, they saw the tank immediately below them. General Dean has since written that the muzzle of the tank gun was no more than a dozen feet away and he could have spat down its tube. Under General Dean's directions the bazooka team fired into the tank. Captain Clarke has described what followed: "I remained by the corner of the building in front of the tank to use my Molotov cocktail on it if it began to move. The first round [3.5-inch rocket] hit the tank, and the occupants began to scream and moan. The second round quieted most of the screaming and the third made it all quiet. We all then withdrew to a better observation post and observed the tank burning." [41] This was the incident that led to the much-quoted remark attributed to General Dean that day, "I got me a tank."

General Dean's personal pursuit of enemy tanks in Taejon was calculated to inspire his men to become tank killers. He was trying to sell to his shaky troops the idea that "an unescorted tank in a city defended by infantry with 3.5-inch bazookas should be a dead duck." [42]

The number of enemy tanks that entered Taejon during the day cannot be fixed accurately. Most of them apparently entered Taejon singly or in small groups. It appears that American troops had destroyed 8 enemy tanks in Taejon or its immediate vicinity by 1100, 6 of them by 3.5-inch rockets and 2 by artillery fire. Engineer bazooka teams destroyed 2 more T34 tanks in the afternoon. If this is a correct count, United States soldiers destroyed 10 enemy tanks in Taejon on 20 July, 8 of them by the new 3.5-inch rocket launcher, first used in combat that day. [43]

Not every round from a 3.5-inch bazooka stopped a T34 tank in the Taejon street fighting as has been so often stated. Three bazooka teams of the 24th Reconnaissance Company, for instance, made seven hits at close range (30 to 70 yards) on 3 tanks and stopped only 1 of them.

Fifth Air Force planes also destroyed an undetermined number of enemy tanks at Taejon. In the morning, soon after the initial penetration of approximately 15 tanks along the Yusong road, the Air Force knocked out 5 before they reached the city. An enemy tank crew member captured during the day re-

---

[41] 3d Engr (C) Bn WD, 20 Jul 50; Ltr, Clarke to author, 31 May 52; Dean and Worden, *General Dean's Story*, pp. 34-35; New York *Herald Tribune*, July 24, 1950, Bigart interview with Clarke. The author saw three T34 tanks still standing in Taejon in July 1951, each bearing a bold inscription painted in white on its sides reading, "Knocked out 20 Jul 50 under the supervision of Maj Gen W. F. Dean." One tank was in the center of Taejon at a street corner; this apparently was the one destroyed under General Dean's direction. The other two were at the Yusong and Nonsan roads' juncture west of the city.

[42] Dean, MS review comments, 20 Jan 58.

[43] 34th Inf WD, 20 Jul 50; 24th Div WD, G-2 Jnl, entries 1315, 201107, and 1367, 202225 Jul 50; 24th Div Ordnance Off Stf Hist Rpt, 20 Jul 50. A 24th Division report of 19 July erroneously states that by that date the 3.5-inch bazooka had destroyed several enemy tanks. 24th Div WD, G-4 Daily Summ, 181800-198000 Jul 50.

ported that planes destroyed others north of Taejon. It appears that the North Koreans lost at least 15 tanks at Taejon, and possibly more.[44]

The enemy tanks largely failed in their mission within Taejon itself. They did not cause panic in the city, nor did they cause any troops to leave it. They themselves lost heavily, mostly to the new 3.5-inch bazooka which they encountered for the first time. Taejon demonstrated that for the future there was at hand an infantry weapon that, if used expertly and courageously, could stop the dreaded T34.

Withdrawal From Taejon—Roadblock

The sequence of events and the time of their occurrence in Taejon on the afternoon of 20 July have been impossible to establish with certainty in all instances. Participants and survivors have different recollections of the same event and of the time it occurred. Some recall incidents that others do not remember at all. Battalion and regimental records were all lost during the day and night and, except for an occasional message entry in the 24th Division journals made at Yongdong many miles to the rear, there is no contemporary record extant to fix time. Yet despite these difficulties in reconstructing the story of that eerie and bizarre afternoon, it is believed the jigsaw puzzle has yielded to the long and laborious efforts to solve it.

When he returned to the 34th Infantry command post after stalking and destroying the tank in the center of Taejon, General Dean joined Colonel Beauchamp for a lunch of cooked C ration. They discussed the situation, which did not seem particularly alarming to them at the time. It would be difficult to find a parallel to the bizarre situation—the two commanders quietly eating their late lunch in the belief that their combat forces were still in battle position a mile or two west of the city, while actually the two battalions were scattered in the hills, completely ineffective for any defense of Taejon. Except for a few scattered enemy infiltrator-snipers in Taejon, the city was quiet. During the conversation, Dean told Beauchamp that instead of waiting for dark as they had planned earlier, he wanted him to initiate a daylight withdrawal because the chances would be better of getting the transportation out safely. The time of this instruction was about 1400.[45]

Colonel Beauchamp immediately set about implementing the order. He instructed Maj. William T. McDaniel, the regimental operations officer, to send messages by radio or telephone to all units to prepare to withdraw. He then wrote out on paper duplicate orders and sent them by runners to the three infantry battalions. There was then no telephone or radio communication with the 1st Battalion, 34th Infantry, or the 2d Battalion, 19th Infantry. The runners, of course, never reached these two battalions. But it appears that neither Dean nor Beauchamp received any report on this. The 3d Battalion, 34th Infantry, did receive the withdrawal order. It and the other miscellaneous

---

[44] 24th Div WD, 20 Jul 50; *Ibid.*, G-2 PW Interrog File, interrog of Kim Chong Sun, 202300 Jul 50.

[45] Dean, MS review comments, 20 Jan 58; Interv, author with Beauchamp, 1 Aug 52.

units in and about the city received the withdrawal instructions about 1500. The planned march order for the movement out of Taejon gave the 3d Battalion, 34th Infantry, the lead, followed by the artillery; the Medical Company; the 34th regimental command group; 2d Battalion, 19th Infantry; and last, the 1st Battalion, 34th Infantry.[46]

After watching Beauchamp get off the orders to his units to withdraw, General Dean stepped out of the command post. He could see and hear friendly fighter planes overhead. He walked down to the end of the schoolhouse command post building where Lieutenant Hillery had set up the tactical air control party's equipment. In conversation with Hillery, Dean found that the former was having difficulty in getting target assignments from the 34th Infantry even though the planes reported many below them. In the confusion of getting out the withdrawal orders and making ready for it themselves the command group apparently did not give much attention to the TACP reports. Then there was also a reluctance to give targets close to Taejon because of the many mistaken attacks in recent days and weeks on American and ROK troops. General Dean remained with the TACP for some time and called several strikes on North Korean artillery and tank concentrations reported by the planes.

About this time a young lieutenant of the 1st Cavalry Division Tank Company arrived in Taejon with a platoon of tanks. Dean expressed to him his surprise at seeing him there and asked what had brought him. He replied that he had come in response to a request received at Yongdong from the 34th Infantry for tank escort out of Taejon for administrative vehicles. The young officer in turn told what a start he had received on seeing the smoldering T34 tanks in the center of Taejon. Various units had begun to form in the streets around the command post for the withdrawal, and the tank officer started with the first of them for Yongdong. This was about 1530 or 1600.[47]

Several incidents took place shortly after noon that, properly interpreted, should have caused deep alarm in Taejon. There was the urgent telephone call from an artillery observer who insisted on talking to the senior commander present. Beauchamp took the call. The observer reported a large column of troops approaching Taejon from the east. He said he was positive they were enemy soldiers. The "road from the east" Beauchamp interpreted to be the Okch'on road. Beauchamp had misunderstood a conversation held with General Dean that morning to mean that Dean had ordered the 21st Infantry to leave its Okch'on position and come up to Taejon to cover the planned withdrawal. What Dean had meant was that he expected the 21st Infantry to cover the withdrawal from its Okch'on positions in such a way as to keep open the pass and the tunnels east of the city. (With respect to the pass and tunnels, Dean miscalculated.) Now, receiving the report of the artillery observer, Beauchamp, with the erroneous concept in mind, thought the column was the 21st

---

[46] Interv, author with Beauchamp, 1 Aug 52; Ltr, Smith to author, 18 Jun 55; 24th Div WD, 20 Jul 50; 34th Inf WD, 20 Jul 50.

[47] Dean, MS review comments, 20 Jan 58.

Infantry approaching Taejon to protect the exit from the city. He told the observer the troops were friendly and not to direct fire on them. Events proved that this column of troops almost certainly was not on the Okch'on road but on the Kumsan road southeast of Taejon and was an enemy force.[48]

Later in the afternoon, just after the 1st Cavalry Division platoon of tanks led the first vehicles out toward Yongdong, General Dean received an aerial report through the TACP of a truck column of about twenty vehicles moving north toward Taejon on the Kumsan road. Dean inquired of the 34th Infantry operations officer if they could be friendly and received the reply that they were the 24th Reconnaissance Company and not to direct an air strike on them. Dean later became convinced that these were North Koreans who had come up from the rear through Kumsan.[49] But this is not certain because a Reconnaissance Company group did drive in to Taejon from its patrol post about this time.

The movements of large bodies of men on the Kumsan road toward Taejon in the early afternoon of 20 July actually were seen at close hand by Colonel Ayres, the commanding officer of the 1st Battalion, 34th Infantry, but he could not get the information to the men in the city. Just before noon, on the mountain southwest of Taejon, he had turned over command of the approximately 150 men of the battalion with him to the executive officer, Major Dunham, with instructions to take them down to the Kumsan road three miles south of Taejon and there establish a blocking position to protect the rear of Taejon. Then he set off with a small party including Maj. Curtis Cooper, his S–3; Capt. Malcolm C. Spaulding of the Heavy Weapons Company; a runner; his radio operator; an interpreter; and Wilson Fielder, Jr., a *Time* Magazine correspondent. About 400 yards short of the Kumsan road Ayres' party encountered North Korean soldiers on the hillside. In the scramble that followed, four men escaped—Ayres, Cooper, Spaulding, and the interpreter; the others were either killed or captured. Fielder's body was found some months later. Ayres and those with him who escaped hid in some bushes and during the afternoon watched North Koreans set up machine guns near them. They also saw an estimated battalion of enemy troops march north toward Taejon along the Kumsan road below them. That night the group escaped.[50]

Nor was this the only encounter with North Koreans close to the Kumsan road that afternoon. Major Dunham led his men down toward the Kumsan road, as directed by Ayres. On the way they had a fire fight with what they took to be a band of guerrillas. They disengaged and moved into the draw at Kuwan-ni about three miles south of Taejon. Enemy troops there fired on Dunham's party from nearby finger ridges. This fire hit Dunham in the neck, mortally wounding him, and there were other casualties. All in this party who could do so now fled west to the Yudung valley at Masu-

---

[48] Interv, author with Beauchamp, 1 Aug 52; Interv, author with Ayres, 13 Jul 54; Ltr, Ayres to author, 3 Oct 52; Dean, MS review comments, 20 Jan 58. Ayres watched a large column march along the Kumsan road toward Taejon about this time.

[49] Dean, MS review comments, 20 Jan 58.

[50] Ltr, Ayres to author, 3 Oct 52; Interv, author with Ayres, 13 Jul 54.

ri. But none of these incidents were known to Dean, Beauchamp, and the men in Taejon.[51]

Although the purpose was not apparent to the men in Taejon, enemy troops to the west and northwest of the city shortly after noon began to close on the city and exert increased frontal pressure to coincide with the movement of the enemy forces that by now had had time to get to the rear of the city. In the early afternoon, Lieutenant Herbert's platoon sergeant called his attention to a large column of troops on high ground westward from their roadblock position just west of Taejon. Herbert watched them for a while and decided that they were enemy troops. He then moved his men to a knoll south of the road and into defensive positions already dug there. The enemy force, which Herbert estimated to be in battalion strength, stopped and in turn watched Herbert's force from a distance of about 600 yards.[52] This probably was the same column that Montesclaros had seen on the Nonsan road about noon.

Back of Herbert's knoll position at the southwestern edge of the city was a battery of 155-mm. howitzers. A runner from the battery arrived to ask Herbert about the situation, and Herbert went back with him to talk with the battery commander. At the artillery position he found howitzers pointing in three different directions but none toward the southwest, where the enemy force had just appeared. Herbert asked that the pieces be changed to fire on the enemy in front of him. The battery commander said he could not change the howitzers without authority from the battalion operations officer. Herbert talked to this officer on the field telephone but failed to secure his approval to change the howitzers.

By this time the North Koreans in front of Herbert's men had set up mortars and begun to shell his position and also the howitzers. This fire killed several artillerymen and caused casualties in the infantry group. Herbert sent a runner into Taejon to report and ask for instructions. At the 34th Infantry command post a group of fifty men was assembled from Headquarters Company and sent back under Lt. William Wygal, S-2 of the 2d Battalion, 19th Infantry, with instructions to Herbert to hold where he was until the artillery could be evacuated. So Herbert's augmented force exchanged fire with the North Koreans and held them to their ridge position.

General Dean observed this fire fight from the command post and thought it was going well for the American troops. He mistakenly thought, however, that it was McGrail's 2d Battalion troops that were engaged. About this time, Dean walked back from the TACP to the 34th Infantry command post and asked for Colonel Beauchamp. It was about 1700. To his surprise he was told that no one had seen Beauchamp since about 1500. Like Major Lantron in the morning, he had just disappeared. Dean remembered that he had expressed a great deal of concern to Beauchamp about the loss of communications with the 1st Battalion, 34th Infantry, and that he had directed someone to get through and find Ayres. When he learned that Beauchamp had

---

[51] Ltr, Barszcz to author, 6 Sep 52 (he met the group in the Yudung valley); Interv, Blumenson with 2d Lt George W. Wilcox, Plat Ldr, 75-mm. Rec Rifle, D Co, 34th Inf, 25 Aug 51 (Wilcox was a member of Dunham's group).

[52] Interv, Blumenson with Herbert, 25 Aug 51.

left the command post shortly after 1500 he concluded that Beauchamp had personally gone forward to contact Ayres. It was not until some three years later after he was repatriated from North Korea that General Dean discovered that this was not the fact.[53]

What had happened to Beauchamp? About the time the first of the vehicles started to form into convoy at the command post and the tanks from Yongdong led the first of them out of Taejon, Colonel Beauchamp got into his jeep and drove to the southeast edge of the city along the withdrawal route. There he came upon four light tanks of the 24th Reconnaissance Company and ordered the tankers to defend the southeast side of the city and the Okch'on road exit. Starting back into Taejon, Beauchamp discovered on glancing back that the tanks were leaving their positions. He turned around and caught up with them on the Okch'on road. But in running after the tanks he came under enemy small arms fire. After stopping the tanks, Beauchamp decided to climb a nearby knoll and reconnoiter the situation. From this eminence he saw numerous groups of enemy troops moving across country south of Taejon toward the Okch'on road. Because he had been under fire on the road he knew that some of them had already arrived there. Knowing that the convoys for the withdrawal were forming and that the first vehicles already had gone through, Beauchamp decided to go on with the two tanks he had with him to the pass four miles east of the city and to organize there a defensive force to hold that critical point on the withdrawal road. At the pass, Beauchamp put the tanks in position and stopped some antiaircraft half-track vehicles mounting quad .50-caliber machine guns as they arrived in the early phase of the withdrawal. Some artillery passed through, and then a company of infantry. Beauchamp tried to flag down the infantry commander's vehicle, intending to stop the company and keep it at the pass. But the officer misunderstood his intent, waved back, and kept on going.

Enemy sniper fire built up sporadically on the road below the pass. From his vantage point Beauchamp saw a locomotive pulling a few cars halted by enemy small arms fire at the tunnel. This locomotive had departed Iwon-ni at 1620, so the time of this incident must have been approximately 1630. Still expecting the 21st Infantry to cover the withdrawal route, Beauchamp decided that the best thing he could do would be to hurry up its arrival. He drove eastward to the command post of the 1st Battalion, 21st Infantry, and from there telephoned the 21st Infantry regimental command post in Okch'on. It chanced that General Menoher was there. He instructed Beauchamp to come on in to Okch'on and give a detailed report.[54] But again, none of these happenings were known in Taejon.

The locomotive had been sent to Taejon as the result of General Dean's telephone request to the 24th Division a little earlier. In midafternoon, Captain Hatfield tried to send a rolling sup-

---

[53] Dean, MS review comments, 20 Jan 58.

[54] Interv, author with Beauchamp, 1 Aug 52; Beauchamp, Comments for author, 7 Jan 53; 24th Div WD, G–4 Daily Summ, 20 Jul 50.

ply point of ten boxcars of ammunition out of the Taejon railroad yard to Yongdong. Returning to the rail yard at the northeast side of Taejon, Hatfield discovered that the Korean crew had uncoupled the locomotive from the supply train and fled south in it. It was then that Dean had telephoned the division to dispatch a locomotive immediately to Taejon to pull out this train. The nearest rail yard was at Iwon-ni, fifteen miles southeast of Taejon. Only armed guards had kept the Korean train crews there on the job. Enemy fire on the locomotive from Iwon-ni punctured the water tender.

Though under sniper fire at the railroad yards, Hatfield awaited the arrival of the locomotive. When it pulled into the yards more enemy fire hit it. The engineer said the locomotive was so damaged that it could not pull the train out. To Hatfield's dismay, the Korean engineer threw the locomotive in reverse and backed speedily southward out of the yard. At the tunnel southeast of Taejon enemy fire again swept over the locomotive and grenades struck it, killing the engineer. The fireman, although wounded, took the train on into Okch'on. Some American soldiers rode the train out of Taejon. According to 24th Division records, the time was 1645. Informed of this untoward incident, Dean again telephoned the division, and at 1700 he received a telephone call that it was sending another locomotive, this time under guard. Dean informed Hatfield of this and the latter waited at the rail yard. Hatfield was killed by enemy soldiers there while waiting for the locomotive that never arrived. The next morning at 0830 a U.S. Air Force strike destroyed the trainload of ammunition and supplies still standing in the Taejon rail yard.[55]

About 1700 in the afternoon when he discovered that Colonel Beauchamp was not at the command post and that no one there knew where he was, General Dean turned to Colonel Wadlington, the regimental executive officer, and told him to get the withdrawal under way in earnest.

Wadlington called in the 3d Platoon of the 24th Reconnaissance Company which had held a position a few miles down the Kumsan road on the north side of the enemy roadblock that had been discovered during the night. For their own reasons the enemy forces in that vicinity had seen fit not to attack this platoon and thereby alert the 34th Infantry to the enemy strength in its rear. In coming in to Taejon to join the withdrawal convoy, the platoon drew machine gun fire near the rail station. Pvt. James H. Nelson engaged this enemy weapon with a .50-caliber machine gun mounted on a 2½-ton truck and knocked it out.[56]

In response to the earlier withdrawal order, Capt. Jack Smith had brought the 3d Battalion, 34th Infantry, in trucks to the designated initial point at the street corner in front of the regimental command post. When he arrived there, Major McDaniel told him that General Dean wanted a perimeter defense established to protect the initial point and to support an attempt to recover a battery

---

[55] Dean, MS review comments, 20 Jan 58; 24th Div WD, G-4 Daily Summ, 20 Jul 50; *Ibid.*, G-2 Jnl, entry 1372, 202140 (interv with personnel on locomotive); entry 1350, 201907; and entry 1401, 210950 Jul 50; Dean and Worden, *General Dean's Story*, p. 37.

[56] 24th Recon Co WD, 20 Jul 50.

of 155-mm. howitzers. Smith unloaded L Company for the perimeter defense and sent the rest of the battalion on to join the convoy that was forming.

Instead of withdrawing their howitzers while Herbert's force held off the enemy force at the west edge of Taejon, the artillerymen had shown no desire to limber up the pieces under fire. When Herbert left his position to fall back to join the withdrawal he noticed the howitzers. The North Koreans quickly moved up and occupied Herbert's old position when he withdrew from it, and some advanced to the battery position. From these places they began firing into the city. Learning of the impending loss of the 155-mm. howitzers, General Dean ordered Colonel Wadlington to organize a counterattack force from personnel at the command post to rescue the pieces. Major McDaniel, the regimental S-3, volunteered to organize and lead the counterattack. He drove the enemy soldiers from the battery position and kept down hostile fire until he could bring up tractor prime movers, hitch them to the howitzers, and pull out the pieces. Lack of tractor drivers prevented taking them all out; those left were rendered inoperative.[57]

By this time word came back to the command post that enemy small arms fire had knocked out and set afire two or three trucks at the tail end of the first group of vehicles to leave the city, and that they blocked the street at the southeast edge of Taejon. Flames could be seen in that corner of the city, and the sound of small arms fire came from there. Dean then rewrote a radio message to be sent to the 24th Division. It said in effect, "Send armor. Enemy roadblock eastern edge City of Taejon. Signed Dean." Dean directed that the message be sent in the clear.

The general then went over to the Capitol Building with his interpreter to see if he could find a northward route out of the city that would pass over the tableland east of the railroad station and swing around to hit the Okch'on road some miles from the city. The Koreans in the building were panic-stricken and he could get no information from them. Dean hastened back to the command post and, being informed that Beauchamp had still not returned, he directed Colonel Wadlington to close station and move out.

Enemy fire into and within the city had increased considerably. One result was that an enemy mortar shell scored a direct hit on the collecting station of the 34th Infantry, wounding ten men. Captain Smith from his perimeter defense post reported that he could see North Koreans advancing from the airfield. Wadlington told him to hold them off until the convoy could escape. Wadlington showed General Dean his place in the convoy. He told Dean that he was going to lead the convoy with two jeeps, each carrying five men, and that Major McDaniel was going to be at the tail of the column. With L Company already engaging approaching North Koreans, Captain Smith asked Dean how long he was to hold the company in position as a covering force.

---

[57] Dean, MS review comments, 20 Jan 58; Comments, Wadlington to author, 1 Apr 53; Ltr and Comments, Wadlington to author, 1 Jun 53; Interv, Blumenson with Herbert, 25 Aug 51; 24th Div Arty WD, 20 Jul 50; 3d Engr (C) Bn WD, 20 Jul 50. General Order 121, 5 September 1950, 24th Division, awarded the Silver Star to McDaniel.

Dean told him to give them forty-five minutes and then to withdraw.[58]

Dean looked at his watch as he drove out the gate of the command post. It was 1755. Outside in the street he talked briefly with Wadlington and the senior officers riding the lead vehicles. He told them that very likely they would get sniper fire in the city, but that once outside he thought they would be all right. He instructed that if sniper fire was encountered and the column stopped for any reason, everyone was to dismount and clean out the snipers. It was a few minutes after 1800 when the large, main convoy started to move.[59]

With Wadlington at its head the convoy rolled down the street. Some parts of the city were now blazing furnaces, and in places swirling smoke clouds obscured the streets. Soon the convoy stopped while those in the lead removed a burning ammunition trailer and telephone poles from the way. Then it continued on and swung into a broad boulevard. There the convoy encountered heavy enemy fire, both machine gun and small arms, sweeping up and down the avenue. Colonel Wadlington and the men in the two lead jeeps dismounted and opened fire. In about five minutes enemy fire slackened. Wadlington ordered the men in the second jeep to lead out, saying he would join them as soon as he saw that the convoy was moving. After the head of the convoy passed him, Wadlington and his men got into their jeep and started forward to overtake the head of the column. Not able to pass the trucks, however, they swung off at a corner to go around a block. This route led them to a series of misadventures—they found themselves in dead-end streets, cut off by enemy fire, and eventually in a dead-end schoolyard on the east side of the city. There Wadlington and his companions destroyed their vehicle and started up the nearby mountain.

Meanwhile, the convoy hurried through the city, drawing enemy sniper fire all the way. One 2½-ton truck in the convoy smashed into a building at an intersection and almost blocked the street for the rest of the vehicles. Then the first part of the convoy took a wrong turn through an underpass of the railroad and wound up in the same dead-end schoolyard as had Colonel Wadlington. There were approximately fifty vehicles in this part of the convoy. These men abandoned their vehicles. Led by an artillery major and other officers the group of about 125 started into the hills, first going north away from the sound of firing and later turning south. During the night the group became separated into several parts. Some of the men reached friendly lines the next morning, others on 22 July; some just disappeared and were never heard of again.[60]

---

[58] Ltr, Smith to author, 18 Jun 55; Ltr, Wadlington to author, 1 Apr 53.

McDaniel was among those captured at Taejon. In prisoner of war camps McDaniel strove to protect the rights of American prisoners. According to accounts brought back by repatriated prisoners in 1953, the North Koreans, unable to break his will, finally took McDaniel away and he disappeared from view. Dean and Worden, *General Dean's Story*, pp. 36-37; 32d Inf WD (7th Div), 26 Sep 50. McDaniel's name was on a roster of prisoners' names captured at Seoul, 26 September 1950.

[59] Dean, MS review comments, 20 Jan 58.

[60] Ltrs, Wadlington to author, 1 Apr, 1 Jun 53. General Order 116, 3 September 1950, 24th Division, awarded the Silver Star to Wadlington for action on 20 July 1950. Interv, Blumenson with Herbert, 25 Aug 51. Herbert was in the part of the convoy that took the wrong turn into the schoolyard.

After the first part of the convoy took the wrong turn, the remainder kept on the street leading to the Okch'on road. A little farther on they drove through walls of fire as buildings burned fiercely on both sides. Just beyond this point, General Dean's vehicle and an escort jeep sped past an intersection. They were scarcely past it when Lieutenant Clarke said to Dean that they had missed the Okch'on turn. Enemy fire prevented them from stopping to turn around, so they kept on going south down the Kumsan road.[61]

Just outside the city on the Okch'on highway the convoy encountered enemy mortar fire. A shell hit the lead vehicle and it began to burn. A half-track pushed it out of the way. The convoy started again. Enemy fire now struck the half-track, killed the driver, and started the vehicle burning. Machine gun fire swept the road. Everyone left the vehicles and sought cover in the roadside ditches. Some in the convoy saw North Korean soldiers rise from rice paddies along the road and spray the column with burp gun fire.

When the enemy mortar fire stopped the column, SFC Joseph S. Szito of the Heavy Weapons Company, 2d Battalion, 19th Infantry, set up a 60-mm. mortar in the roadside ditch and fired at a group of North Koreans on a hill just south of the road. A little later he set up an 81-mm. mortar and fired about thirty rounds of smoke shells in an effort to cloak a proposed attempt to push the destroyed half-track off the road so the undamaged vehicles could proceed. But enough men would not go out into the stream of enemy fire to clear the road. Enemy mortars soon hit and destroyed three more vehicles. The men then poured gasoline on most of their still undamaged vehicles, set them afire, and started for high ground to the north.[62]

Enemy mortars searched up and down the highway, making a shambles of everything on it. The latter part of the convoy now came up to the stalled and burning vehicles. These men scrambled out of their vehicles, sought cover in the ditches, and prayed for darkness. One survivor of this group estimates that there must have been 250 men bunched together in an area fifty yards square.

When darkness came, 2d Lt. Ralph C. Boyd, commanding a truck platoon of the 24th Quartermaster Company, with the help of some others, located six vehicles that appeared to be undamaged and still able to run. They were a full-track artillery prime mover, two half-track vehicles, two 2½-ton trucks, and a jeep. Boyd had the driver of the prime mover push vehicles to the side of the road and clear a path while he and others loaded the seriously wounded onto the half-tracks.

When the prime mover had cleared a path, the other vehicles started forward with most of the men walking in the roadside ditches. Boyd told them to maintain silence and not to return any enemy fire. Boyd's group turned into a narrow dirt road running north from the main highway and traveled on it for some time without trouble. Then, sud-

---

[61] Ltr, Clarke to author, 11 Dec 52; Dean and Worden, *General Dean's Story*, p. 39.

[62] Interv, author with Maj Clarence H. Ellis, Jr. (S-3 Sec, 11th FA Bn Jul 50), 22 Jul 54; Interv, Blumenson with Szito, 31 Jul 51.

TAEJON

denly, enemy machine gun fire ripped into the little group. It knocked Boyd off the prime mover. In falling, he struck a rock and lost consciousness. When he regained it sometime later everything was quiet and the vehicles were gone. Upon discovering that a bullet had only creased his knee, he got to his feet and ran two and a half miles into the lines of the 21st Infantry.[63]

Engineer troops of C Company, 3d Engineer Combat Battalion performed well in the withdrawal from the city, but they suffered heavy losses. Two examples of their heroism should be mentioned. Enemy mortar fire destroyed Pvt. Charles T. Zimmerman's jeep and wounded Zimmerman. Enemy soldiers then directed small arms fire at his group. Although wounded by a mortar fragment and eleven bullets, Zimmerman killed five enemy soldiers and destroyed two machine guns.[64]

Another member of the engineers, Sgt. George D. Libby, was awarded the Medal of Honor posthumously for his heroic behavior that evening. Enemy fire at the roadblock area disabled the truck in which he was riding and killed or wounded everyone in it except him. Libby got into the roadside ditch and engaged the enemy. Twice he crossed the road to give medical aid to the wounded. He stopped an M-5 artillery tractor going through the roadblock, put the wounded on it, and then placed himself on the enemy side of the driver. He wished to protect the driver as he realized that no one else present could drive the tractor out. In this position Libby "rode shotgun" for the tractor and its load of wounded, returning enenemy fire. The tractor stopped several times so that he could help other wounded on to it. In passing through the main enemy roadblock, Libby received several wounds in the body and arms. Later, the tractor came to a second roadblock and there he received additional wounds in shielding the driver. Libby lost consciousness and subsequently died from loss of blood, but the tractor driver lived to take his load of wounded through to safety.[65]

Just after dark an effort was made to break the roadblock from the Okch'on side. When Colonel Beauchamp reached the 21st Infantry command post that afternoon he told General Menoher of the threatened roadblock. Menoher directed him to take the rifle company that had come through the pass and a platoon of light tanks at the 21st Infantry command post and go back and hold the pass open. Beauchamp took the five tanks and on the way picked up approximately sixty men of I Company, 34th Infantry. It was getting dark when the group passed through the lines of the 21st Infantry.

Short of the pass, one of the tanks hit an enemy mine. Then a hidden enemy soldier detonated electrically a string of mines. The riflemen moved cautiously forward. From a position near

---

[63] General Order 126, 12 September 1950, 24th Division, awarded the Silver Star to Lieutenant Boyd. Interv, Capt John G. Westover with 1st Lt Ralph C. Boyd, 13 Mar 52, copy in OCMH. This interview was published in *U.S. Army Combat Forces Journal* (September, 1952), pp. 26–27.

[64] 3d Engr (C) Bn WD, 20 Jul 50.

[65] Department of the Army General Order 62, 2 August 1951, awarded the Medal of Honor to Libby.

the pass they could see enemy mortars firing from both sides of the road, but mostly from the western side. Some of the riflemen worked their way as far forward as the highway tunnel, but they never got control of the pass or any part of the highway west of it. In about two hours the tankers and the men of I Company had expended their ammunition and withdrawn.[66]

While at the pass area, Beauchamp saw that most of the men in the engineer platoon he had left there in the afternoon had been killed defending the pass—their bodies lay strewn about on the ground. Among them was the lieutenant he had instructed only a few hours before not to blow the tunnel but to hold it open for the Taejon troops. The two tanks and the antiaircraft vehicles had driven to the rear.

Although there were enemy troops scattered all along the escape route out of Taejon, their principal roadblock began about two miles east of the city on the Okch'on road near the little village of Chojon. The roadblock extended a mile from there to the first railroad and highway tunnels east of Taejon. In this stretch, the Seoul-Pusan highway and the double-track Mukden-Pusan railroad parallel each other along a little stream with high ground closing in from both sides. Most of the enemy fire came from the west side of the defile, but in the later stages of the roadblock action there were also enemy mortars, automatic weapons, and riflemen firing from the east side.[67]

All night long the several hundred men caught in the roadblock walked south and east through the mountains. During the night the 1st Battalion, 21st Infantry, aid station near Okch'on exhausted its medical supplies in treating wounded men arriving from the Taejon area. Many finally reached safety at the 24th Division lines twenty miles farther east near Yongdong on 22 and 23 July. They came through singly and in small groups, but, in one or two instances, in groups of approximately a hundred men. Colonel Wadlington was among those who reached friendly lines on the morning of 22 July near Yongdong.[68]

While this disaster was taking place during the evening and night of 20 July just east of Taejon, the 21st Infantry Regiment held its defense positions undisturbed only three or four miles away. Only when Beauchamp telephoned the regimental command post at Okch'on and talked with General Menoher there, and later, in person, reported in detail, did Colonel Stephens and his staff know of the serious trouble developing in Taejon and on the escape road eastward.[69] It would have taken several

---

[66] Interv, author with Beauchamp, 1 Aug 52; Ltr, Stephens to author, 24 Mar 52; 24th Div WD, G-3 Jnl, entry 196, 201930 Jul 50; 21st Inf WD, 20 Jul 50; New York *Herald Tribune*, July 21 and 23, 1950.

[67] Various interviews with survivors from the roadblock and the records of the 21st Infantry and the 24th Division place the eastern limit of the enemy roadblock at the first railroad tunnel southeast of Taejon.

[68] 21st Inf WD, 20 Jul 50; 24th Div WD, 20 and 23 Jul 50; *Ibid.*, G-2 Jnl, entry 4, 230115 Jul 50; Ltr, Stephens to author, 24 Mar 52; Ltr, Lt Col Charles B. Smith to author, 6 Nov 51; 34th Inf WD, 25 Jul 50; Interv, Blumsenson with Szito, 31 Jul 51; Interv, author with Pfc Alvin Moore, 34th Inf, 23 Jul 51; Ltrs, Wadlington to author, 1 Apr and 1 Jun 53.

[69] Ltr, Stephens to author, 24 Mar 52; Ltr, Bissett to author, 14 May 52.

hours to get the 21st Infantry troops down from their hill positions for any effort to clear the Taejon exit road. And it was well after dark before it was known definitely at Okch'on that the enemy had in fact successfully established a roadblock and that the Taejon troops were being decimated. It was too late then for the 21st Infantry to act in relief of the situation. To have accomplished this the regiment would have needed an order during the morning to move up to the eastern exit of Taejon and secure it.

That night at the 21st Infantry command post in Okch'on, General Menoher and Colonel Stephens discussed the situation. Stephens said he thought the North Koreans would try to cut off his regiment the next day and that if the regiment was to survive he wanted authority to withdraw it in a delaying action rather than to "hold at all costs." Menoher agreed with Stephens and left it to his discretion when and how he would withdraw. General Menoher returned to Yongdong about midnight.[70]

At daybreak, 21 July, engineer troops set off demolition charges at the railroad and highway tunnels just north of Okch'on that only partially blocked them. When full light came, observers and patrols from the 21st Infantry reported enemy troops in estimated regimental strength moving south around their west flank at a distance of two miles. Before long, an automatic weapons and small arms fight was in progress on that flank.[71]

Colonel Stephens gave the order for the regiment to withdraw. The 21st Infantry and 52d Field Artillery Battalion began leaving their Okch'on positions shortly after 1100. Engineer troops destroyed the last bridge across the Kum River east of Okch'on to give some temporary security to ROK forces on the east side of the river. The regiment successfully withdrew twenty miles to prepared positions on the east side of the Kum River, about four miles northwest of Yongdong. There it also established a strong roadblock on the road running southwest from Yongdong to Kumsan.[72]

Not all the troops withdrawing from Taejon followed the main Okch'on highway, although they were supposed to. Many missed the tricky turn at the southeast edge of the city and found themselves on the Kumsan road. Once on this road and under fire they kept going. After holding off the enemy at the Taejon command post perimeter while the convoy got away, Captain Smith quickly loaded his L Company, 34th Infantry, into waiting trucks and started it on its way through the city. By this time enemy machine guns were firing across nearly every street intersection. Passing the Okch'on turn inadvertently, Smith kept on down the Kumsan road. Outside the city he found the road littered with trucks, jeeps, and various kinds of abandoned equipment. At an enemy roadblock he organized approximately 150 men, including about fifty wounded, and salvaged a prime mover, two 2½-ton trucks, and four

---

[70] Ltr, Bissett to author, 14 May 52.

[71] Ltr, Stephens to author, 24 Mar 52; Ltr, Lt Col Charles B. Smith to author, 10 May 52; 21st Inf WD, 21 Jul 50; 24th Div WD, 21 Jul 50.

[72] Ltr, Stephens to author, 24 Mar 52; Ltr, Smith to author, 10 May 52; 24th Div WD, 21 Jul 50.

jeeps. The group fought its way south through several miles of small roadblocks, clearing the last one just before dark. In this group Smith had men from practically every unit that had been in Taejon. Some of them had been with General Dean earlier in the evening.

Smith led his group south through Kumsan, Anui, and on to Chinju near the southern tip of Korea. From there he telephoned Pusan and a hospital train was dispatched to him at Chinju. Smith left the wounded in Pusan, but continued on with the others to Taegu, where they joined other elements of the 3d Battalion that had escaped. At Taegu on 23 July Colonel Wadlington had assembled approximately 300 men who had escaped through the hills from Taejon.[73]

Of all the incidents in the withdrawal, none was more dramatic or attended by such gripping subsequent drama as the adventures of General Dean. They began on the Kumsan road. When he missed the Okch'on turn, it was probable that General Dean would not get far. There had been enemy roadblocks on the Kumsan road since the night before. A mile from the city Dean stopped his jeep where a wrecked truck lay on its side in the ditch with several wounded soldiers in it. He loaded these into his two jeeps and waved them on. He and two or three other soldiers soon clambered on to an artillery half-track that came south on the road. Riding in one of the jeeps ahead, Lieutenant Clarke was hit in the shoulder by enemy fire a mile farther down the road. Another mile ahead his group came to a knocked out truck blocking the road. There an enemy force had established a roadblock with machine gun and rifle fire. Clarke and the other men tumbled from the jeeps into the righthand ditch. Dean and those on the half-track did the same when they arrived a few minutes later.

General Dean and the others crawled through bean patches and a garden to the bank of the Taejon River where they lay concealed until darkness came. It must have been at this time that Captain Smith and his L Company party fought their way through that roadblock. After dark Dean's party crossed to the west side of the river and started climbing a high mountain. This was just north of the little village of Nangwol. General Dean and others in the party took turns in helping a badly wounded man up the steep slope. Once, Clarke dissuaded Dean from going back down the mountain for water. A little after midnight, at a time when he was leading the group, Lieutenant Clarke suddenly discovered that no one was following him. He turned back and found several men asleep. He called for General Dean. Someone replied that General Dean had gone for water. Clarke estimated that an unencumbered man could go to the bottom and back up to where they were in an hour. He decided to wait two hours. Dean did not return. At 0315 Clarke awakened the sleeping men and the party climbed to the top of the mountain, arriving there just before dawn. There they waited all day, four or five miles south of Taejon, hoping to see General Dean. That night, Clarke

---

[73] Ltrs, Smith to author, 18 Jun and 21 Jul 55. General Order 123, 9 September 1950, 24th Division, awarded the first Oak Leaf Cluster to the Silver Star to Capt. Jack E. Smith for gallantry and leadership on 20 July 1950.

led his party back down the mountain, recrossed the Taejon River in a rainstorm near the village of Samhoe, climbed eastward into the mountains, and then turned south. He eventually led his party to safety through the lines of the 1st Cavalry Division at Yongdong on 23 July.[74]

It was some years before the mystery of what had happened to Dean that night after Taejon was finally cleared up. In going after water for the wounded men, General Dean fell down a steep slope and was knocked unconscious. When he regained consciousness he found he had a gashed head, a broken shoulder, and many bruises. For thirty-six days General Dean wandered in the mountains trying to reach safety, but this was the period when the North Koreans were advancing southward as rapidly as he was. On 25 August, two South Koreans who pretended to be guiding him toward safety led him into a prearranged ambush of North Korean soldiers, and they captured the emaciated, nearly starved, and injured general, who now weighed only 130 pounds instead of his normal 190. His capture took place near Chinan, thirty-five miles due south of Taejon and sixty-five air miles west of Taegu. Then began his more than three years of life as a prisoner of the North Koreans that finally ended on 4 September 1953 when he was repatriated to American officials at P'anmunjom.[75] General Dean's heroic and fascinating chronicle as told in his book, *General Dean's Story*, is one of the great documents to come out of the Korean War. That war was destined to add many illustrious names to the roll of honor in United States military annals. But posterity probably will accord to none as high a place as to General Dean in the example he set as a soldier and leader in great adversity and as an unbreakable American in Communist captivity.

A word needs to be said about the men of the 1st Battalion, 34th Infantry, and the 2d Battalion, 19th Infantry, who were driven from or left their positions west of Taejon during the morning of 20 July and climbed into the hills south of the Nonsan road. Most of them escaped. These men traveled all night. One large party of 1st Battalion, 34th

---

[74] Interv, author with Capt Ben Tufts, 2 Aug 51; Ltrs, Clarke to author, 11 and 22 Dec 52, together with sketch map of escape route he followed; New York *Herald Tribune*, July 24, 1950, dispatch by Homer Bigart.

[75] The Department of the Army awarded General Dean the Medal of Honor for his courage and exploits at Taejon on 20 July. DA GO No. 7, 16 Feb 51. The first information that Dean might be alive as a prisoner of war came from a North Korean soldier, Lee Kyu Hyun, who escaped to American lines (his claim) or was captured near P'yongyang in North Korea in late October 1950. He had been assigned to live with General Dean and to serve as interpreter. Col. William A. Collier of the Eighth Army Staff who had established the Advanced Headquarters in P'yongyang was the first American officer to interview Lee. He was convinced that Lee had lived with Dean and made a detailed report to Maj. Gen. Leven C. Allen, then Chief of Staff, Eighth Army. Capt. Ben Tufts also interviewed Lee extensively, first at P'yongyang and subsequently early in 1951 at Pusan. In the summer of 1951 Tufts furnished the author with a copy of his interview notes with Lee. Lee's story proved to be substantially in agreement with the account given later by Dean himself. But in 1951 the author could find scarcely anyone in Eighth Army or in the Far East Command who believed that General Dean might still be alive.

Infantry, troops, which included Captain Barszcz' G Company, 19th Infantry, was led by Captain Marks. It passed through Kumsan, where a few small parties turned east toward Yongdong. But the main party continued south, believing the enemy might have cut the road eastward. On the 23d this group encountered some ROK trucks and shuttled south in them until they broke down. The next day the entire party loaded into a boxcar train it met and rode the last 50 miles into the south coast port of Yosu, 110 air miles south of Taejon and 80 air miles west of Pusan. From Yosu they traveled by boat the next day, 25 July, to Pusan. From there they returned north to rejoin their parent organizations.[76]

Most of the 2d Battalion, 19th Infantry, reached Kumsan and there turned eastward to come through friendly lines at Yongdong. Included in these parties were Colonels McGrail and Ayres and Captains Montesclaros and Slack. They arrived at Yongdong on 21 and 22 July.

Taejon must be considered a major victory for the North Koreans, even though two divisions with T34 tanks were operating against only about 4,000 men of the U.S. 24th Division in and around the city. It appears that credit should go to the N.K. *4th Division* for carrying out the envelopment of Taejon from the west and south by strong elements of its *16th* and *18th Regiments* and imposing the disastrous roadblock on the Okch'on highway east of Taejon. These elements had no tanks or artillery with them; theirs was a light infantry maneuver and tactic. Whether they came around by road through Kumsan from Nonsan or marched across country over the mountains south and southwest of Taejon from the Nonsan-Taejon road is not definitely known. There is some evidence that at least part of the enveloping force came through Kumsan.

The N.K. *3d Division* joined the *5th Regiment* of the N.K. *4th Division* in maintaining frontal pressure against Taejon in the afternoon of the 20th and enveloped it on the north and northeast. The *3d* infiltrated the city heavily in the latter part of the afternoon. The enemy tanks that penetrated Taejon in the morning apparently belonged to the *107th Tank Regiment* of the *105th Armored Division*, attached to the N.K. *4th Division* ever since the crossing of the 38th Parallel. Some of the tanks that entered the city later in the day were probably from the *203d Tank Regiment* attached to the N.K. *3d Division*.[77]

The N.K. *2d Division*, which was supposed to have joined the *3d* and *4th* in the attack on Taejon, failed to come up in time. This all but exhausted division did not leave Ch'ongju until on or about the 18th. It then moved through Pugang-ni southwest toward Taejon, apparently intending to cross the Kum River in the vicinity of the railroad bridge. It had yet to cross the Kum when it received word on 21 July that Taejon had fallen. The *2d Division* thereupon altered its course and turned southeast through Poun, headed for Kumch'on.[78]

---

[76] Ltr, Barszcz to author, 6 Sep 52; Interv, Blumenson with Wilcox, 25 Aug 51.

[77] ATIS Res Supp Interrog Rpts, Issue 106 (N.K. Arty), p. 66; *Ibid.*, Issue 94 (N.K. *4th Div*), pp. 46–47; *Ibid.*, Issue 96 (N.K. *3d Div*), pp. 31–32; ORO-R-1, FEC, Employment of Armor in Korea (8 Apr 51), vol. 1, p. 127, citing Sr Capt Kwon Jae Yon, and pp. 112–13, citing 2d Lt Kim Ji Soon.

[78] ATIS Res Supp Interrog Rpts, Issue 94 (N.K. *2d Div*), p. 36.

It is difficult to estimate enemy losses at Taejon. The North Korean infantry losses apparently were light. Their losses in armor and artillery were considerable. The N. K. *4th Division,* according to prisoner reports later, lost 15 76-mm. guns and 6 122-mm. mortars, together with 200 artillerymen. The tank losses were relatively heavy; at least 15 of them were destroyed, and possibly the number may have been 20 or more.

Within five days the enemy, employing numerically superior forces, had executed two highly successful envelopments of American positions at the Kum River and at Taejon. In each case the North Koreans moved around the left flank to impose roadblocks covering the rear routes of escape. In each instance the result was catastrophic for the units cut off. These enemy operations must stand as excellent examples of this type of military tactic.

On the American side, the lack of information of the true state of affairs caused by the almost complete breakdown in all forms of comunication was the major factor leading to the disaster. In battle, communication is all important.

The 24th Division After Taejon

When all the men who escaped from Taejon had rejoined their units, a count showed 1,150 casualties out of 3,933 of the U.S. 24th Division forces engaged there on 19–20 July—nearly 30 percent. Of these casualties, 48 were known dead, 228 wounded, and 874 missing in action. Most of the last were presumed killed and this was borne out by subsequent information. Among the rifle companies, L Company, 34th Infantry, the rear guard unit, lost the most with 107 casualties out of 153 men (70 percent).[79]

The equipment loss also was very great. Virtually all the organic equipment of the troops in Taejon was lost there. Only B Battery, 13th Field Artillery Battalion, B Battery, 63d Field Artillery Battalion, and I Company, 34th Infantry, brought out their equipment substantially intact. They escaped just before the enemy enforced the roadblock which caught everything behind them. Approximately only 35 regimental vehicles escaped from Taejon. The 24th Quartermaster Company lost 30 of 34 trucks; A Battery, 11th Field Artillery Battalion, lost all 5 of its 155-mm. howitzers.

At noon on 22 July the 24th Infantry Division turned over the front-line positions at Yongdong to the 1st Cavalry Division. The division's consolidated strength on that day was 8,660 men. Seventeen days had elapsed since division troops had first met North Koreans in combat at Osan on 5 July. In that time,

---

[79] Casualties of some of the major units at Taejon were as follows:

Unit	Casualties	Percentage
Hq, 34th Inf	71 of 171	41.5
1st Bn, 34th Inf	203 of 712	28.5
3d Bn, 34th Inf	256 of 666	38.4
2d Bn, 19th Inf	211 of 713	29.5
C Co, 3d Engr (C) Bn	85 of 161	53.0
A Btry, 11th FA Bn	39 of 123	31.7

See 24th Div Arty WD, 20 Jul 50; 24th Div WD, 20 Jul 50 and G–3 Jnl, entry 198, 202000 Jul 50; A Btry, 26th AAA Bn WD, 21 Jul 50; 24th Div WD, G–1 Stf Hist Rpt, 22 Jul 50; 3d Engr (C) Bn WD, Narr Summ, Opnl Highlights, 20 Jul 50, and Unit Hist, 23 Jul–25 Aug 50; 34th Inf WD, 22 Jul–26 Aug, Logistical Rpt; The Rand Corp., Dr. J. O'Sullivan, 24th Division Casualties at Taejon.

two enemy divisions had driven it back 100 miles in a southeasterly direction. In these two and a half weeks, the division had suffered more than 30 percent casualties. More than 2,400 men were missing in action. It had lost enough matériel to equip a division. Losses in senior officers of field grade had been unusually severe. And then finally, at Taejon, the commanding general of the division was missing in action. Charged with carrying out a delaying action, the division had held the enemy on its front to an average gain of about six miles a day. On 22 July, with General Dean still missing in action, Eighth Army ordered Maj. Gen. John H. Church to assume command of the 24th Division.[80]

Soldiers of the 24th Division faced many handicaps in their early battles with the North Koreans. Often the unit commanders were new to the units and did not know their officers and men; there were few qualified officer replacements for those lost; communication was a most serious and continuing problem —there was a lack of telephone wire, and the batteries for radios were outdated and lasted only an hour or so in operation or they did not function at all; there was a shortage of ammunition, particularly for the 60-mm., 81-mm., and 4.2-inch mortars; dysentery at times affected a fourth of the men; and always there were the rumors, generally absurd and groundless, which kept the men agitated and uneasy. The maps, based on the Japanese survey of 1918–32, were often unreliable, resulting in inaccurate artillery fire unless directed and adjusted by an observer. Road and convoy discipline was poor. Driver maintenance was poor.

There were many heroic actions by American soldiers of the 24th Division in these first weeks in Korea. But there were also many uncomplimentary and unsoldierly ones. Leadership among the officers had to be exceptional to get the men to fight, and several gave their lives in this effort. Others failed to meet the standard expected of American officers. There is no reason to suppose that any of the other three occupation divisions in Japan would have done better in Korea than did the U.S. 24th Division in July 1950. When committed to action they showed the same weaknesses.

A basic fact is that the occupation divisions were not trained, equipped, or ready for battle. The great majority of the enlisted men were young and not really interested in being soldiers. The recruiting posters that had induced most of these men to enter the Army mentioned all conceivable advantages and promised many good things, but never suggested that the principal business of an army is to fight.

When the first American units climbed the hills in the Korean monsoon heat and humidity, either to fight or to escape encirclement by the enemy, they "dropped like flies," as more than one official report of the period states. Salt tablets became a supply item of highest priority and were even dropped to troops by plane.

One participant and competent observer of the war in those first days has expressed the conditions well. He said,

---

[80] 24th Div WD, Summ, 23 Jul–25 Aug 50; Ltr, Smith to author, 6 Nov 51; 21st Inf WD, 25 Jun–22 Jul 50, Incl III, Act Rpt, 3d Bn, 24 Jul 50; 34th Inf WD, 22 Jul–26 Aug 50, Logistical Rpt; EUSAK WD, 13–31 Jul 50, Summ, Sec II, 22 Jul 50. Church was promoted from brigadier general to major general on 18 July 1950.

TAEJON

"The men and officers had no interest in a fight which was not even dignified by being called a war. It was a bitter fight in which many lives were lost, and we could see no profit in it except our pride in our profession and our units as well as the comradeship which dictates that you do not let your fellow soldiers down." [81]

As part of the historical record, it may be worthwhile to record General Dean's own judgment after turning over in his mind for several years the events of Taejon, and after having read this chapter in manuscript. Many of the things related in this chapter he did not, of course, know at the time. Here are the words of this brave and honest soldier, written seven and a half years after the event.

Hostile and friendly dispositions, which are now quite clear, were much more obscure at the time. I stayed in Taejon for a number of reasons: (1) In an effort to stimulate the fighting spirit of the 34th Infantry and attached troops there in the city. The second reason was as an example to the ROK leaders and also to give confidence to the ROK forces. The third was to see at close hand just what kind of a fighter the North Korean was. It is now clear to me that I was too close to the trees to see the forest, and therefore was at the time blind to the envelopment that the North Koreans were engineering. Not until we turned off on the road to Kumsan and we ran into the North Korean detachment dug in at intervals along that highway did I realize what had happened. I was disturbed about the infiltrators into the City of Taejon itself, but I was not alarmed and I was sanguine of extricating the 34th Infantry until I had left the city on the Kumsan road and realized that there had been an envelopment of major proportions. But even then, I did not realize the extent of the envelopment and my earnest prayer at the time was that the majority of the 34th Infantry would not take the Kumsan road but would leave by way of the Okch'on road. Subsequent events have proved that it would have been better if we had all headed down the Kumsan road because I am certain we could have cleared that and gotten a greater number through. . . .

In retrospect, it would appear that the 21st Infantry Regiment should have been employed to secure the exit from Taejon. But I never issued such an order and my reason for not doing so was that I was convinced that the 21st Infantry Regiment should hold the commanding terrain just west of Okch'on to prevent an envelopment from the north, which would cut off both the 21st Infantry Regiment and the 34th Infantry Regiment and permit the enemy to drive through Yongdong and south through Yongdong to Kumch'on and hence south. My big two errors were: (1) Not withdrawing the 34th Infantry Regiment the night of the 19th of July, as originally planned; (2) releasing the 24th Reconnaissance Company to the 34th Infantry Regiment.[82]

After the fall of Taejon the war was to enter a new phase. Help in the form of the 1st Cavalry Division had arrived. No longer would the 24th Division and the ROK Army have to stand alone.

---

[81] Ltr, Stephens to author, 17 Sep 52. The author has heard essentially the same thing from many others who fought in Korea during the summer of 1950.

[82] Ltr and MS review comments, Dean to Maj Gen Richard W. Stephens, Chief of Military History, 20 Jan 58.

CHAPTER XII

The Front Line Moves South

There is no one but yourself to keep your back door open. You can live without food, but you cannot last long without ammunition.

Lt. Gen. Walton H. Walker to Maj. Gen.
Hobart R. Gay, Korea, July 1950

Yongdok and the East Coastal Corridor

While the battles of the Kum River and Taejon were being fought on the main axis south from Seoul, many miles eastward, the enemy *5th Division* pressed forward against Yongdok, a key point where a lateral road came in from the mountains to meet the coastal road. *(Map III)* The ROK 3d Division had orders to hold Yongdok. It was certain that heavy battles would be fought there.

On 13 July Colonel Emmerich and the KMAG detachment with the ROK 3d Division forwarded to Eighth Army a demolition plan for use on the coastal road and bridges. Maj. Clyde Britton, one of the KMAG officers, was to be responsible for giving authority to blow any of the bridges. The long bridge at Yongdok was recognized as the most important feature on the coastal road, and it was to be held intact unless enemy armor was actually crossing it.

At this time interrogation of an enemy prisoner disclosed that the North Koreans had a plan to blow a bridge near An'gang-ni, on the lateral corridor from Taegu to P'ohang-dong and to blow both ends of the Ch'ongdo railroad tunnel between Pusan and Taegu. Destruction of the tunnel would constitute a serious blow to the logistical support for the front-line troops. Two American officers with two platoons of ROK troops went to the tunnel to protect it.

On 14 July, Brig. Gen. Lee Chu Sik, Commanding General, ROK 3d Division, indicated that he wanted to move the division command post to P'ohang-dong and to withdraw his troops south of Yongdok. Colonel Emmerich told him this could not be done—that the east coast road had to be held at all costs. General Walker had given a great deal of attention to the east coast situation because he knew it was isolated from the rest of the ROK command and needed close watching, and Col. Allan D. MacLean of the Eighth Army G–3 staff was in constant communication with Colonel Emmerich.

Support of the ROK 3d Division had stabilized to the extent that large fishing vessels moved from Pusan up and down the coast, supplying the ROK's with ammunition and food, without

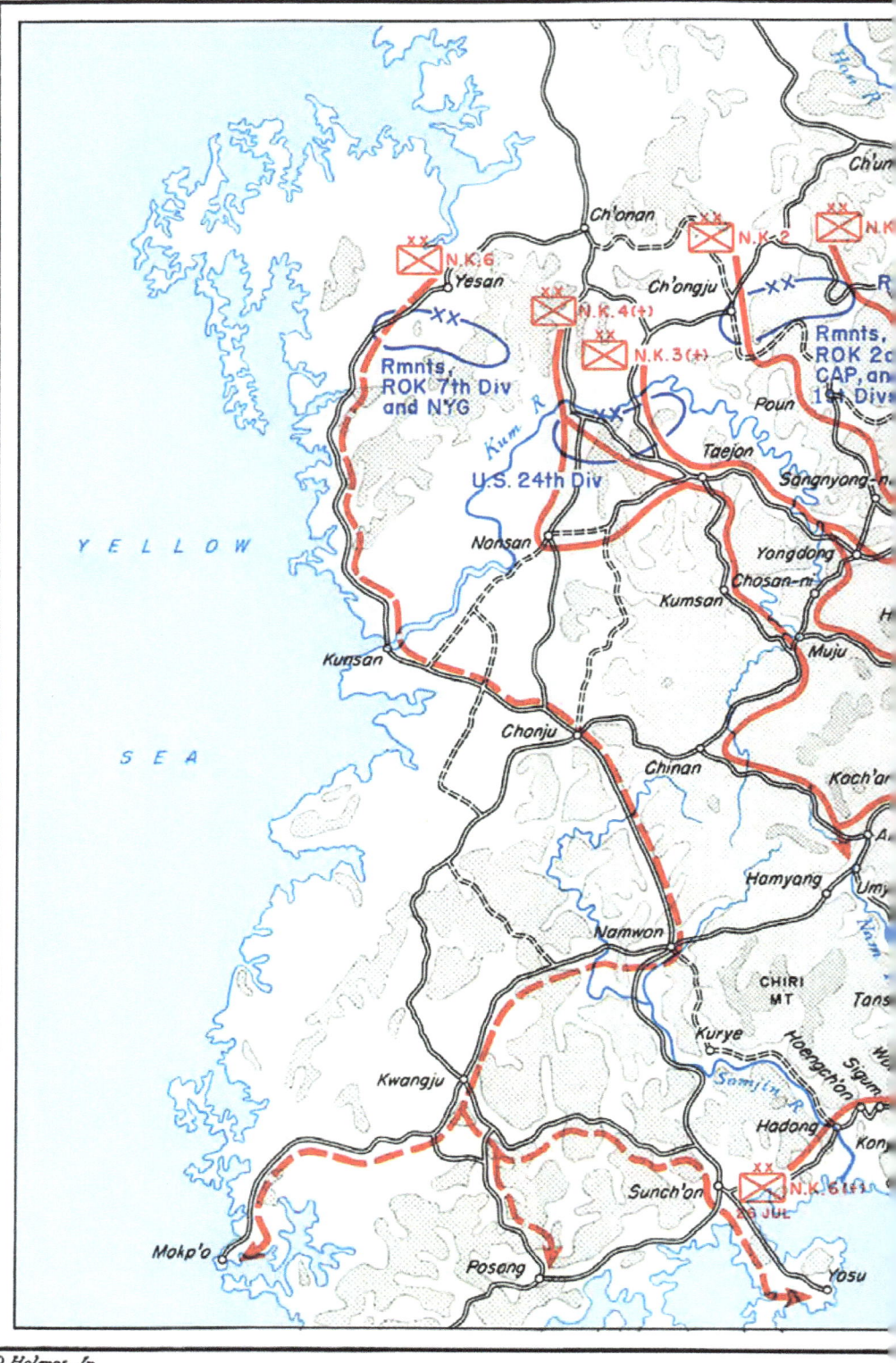

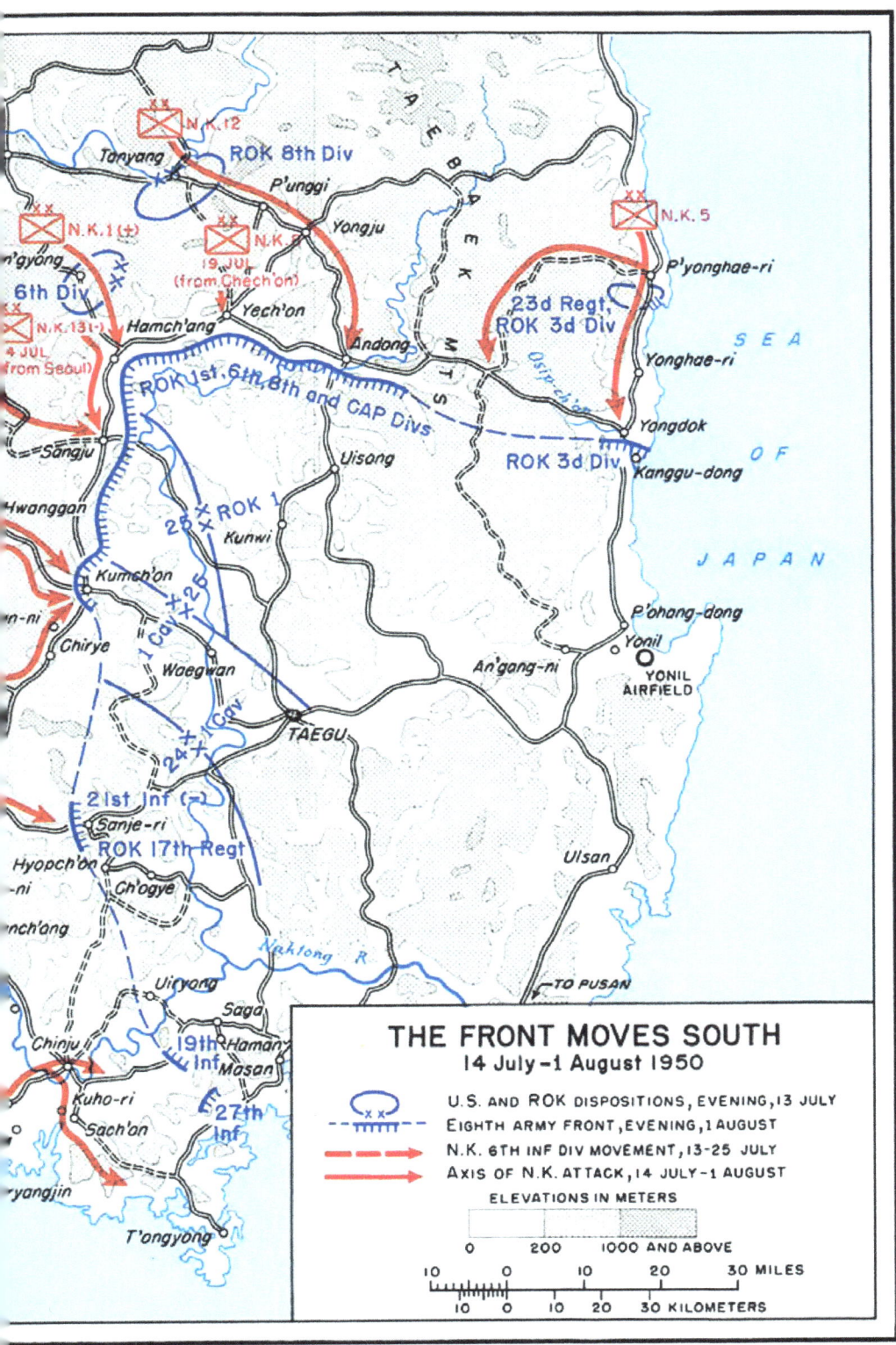

THE FRONT LINE MOVES SOUTH

THE A-FRAME, *a familiar sight in Korea and the most commonly used method of packing supplies.*

being targets of the United States Navy. News that a railhead would be established at P'ohang-dong and a daily supply train would arrive there from Pusan promised soon to relieve the situation still further. On land, each ROK commander had his own system of recruiting help and had large numbers of untrained combat troops and labor groups carrying supplies into the hills on A-frames. At this stage of the war, typical food of the ROK soldier was three rice balls a day —one for each meal—supplemented along the coast by fish. The rice was usually cooked behind the lines by Korean women, then scooped out with a large cup which served as a measuring device, pressed into a ball about the size of an American softball, and wrapped in a boiled cabbage leaf. Whether his rice was warm or cold or whether flies and other insects had been on it, seemed to have little effect on the ROK soldier. Apparently the Korean people had become immune to whatever disease germs, flies, and other insects carry.[1]

As the east coast battle shaped up, it became apparent that it would be of the utmost importance to have a fire direction center to co-ordinate the 81-

[1] Col Rollins S. Emmerich, MS review comments, 30 Nov 57; Interv, author with Darrigo (KMAG adviser to ROK 17th Regt, Jul–Aug 50), 5 Aug 53.

mm. mortars, the artillery, the fighter aircraft, and the naval gunfire. Such a center was set up in a schoolhouse south of Yongdok with Capt. Harold Slater, the KMAG G-3 adviser to the 3d Division, in charge of it and Capt. John Airsman as artillery adviser. The ROK 3d Division artillery at this time consisted of three batteries of four 75-mm. pack howitzers and one battery of 105-mm. howitzers.

On 14 July ROK troops withdrew in front of the advancing North Koreans and set off demolitions at two bridges, two tunnels, and two passes between Yonghae and Yongdok on the coastal road. United States naval vessels bombarded roadside cliffs next to the sea to produce landslides that would block the road and delay the North Koreans.

Two days later the ROK 23d Regiment gave way and streamed south. The KMAG advisers considered the situation grave. In response to an inquiry from Colonel Collier of Eighth Army, Colonel Emmerich sent the following message:

> Situation deplorable, things are popping, trying to get something established across the front, 75% of the 23d ROK Regiment is on the road moving south. Advisers threatening and shooting in the air trying to get them assembled, Commanding General forming a straggler line. If straggler line is successful we may be able to reorganize and re-establish the line. If this fails I am afraid that the whole thing will develop in complete disintegration. The Advisory Group needs food other than Korean or C rations and needs rest.[2]

On 17 July the North Koreans drove the disorganized regiment south of Yongdok. The loss of this town so quickly was a demoralizing blow, and Eighth Army became at once concerned about it. During the day the first United States artillery to support the ROK's on the east coast, C Battery of the 159th Field Artillery Battalion, entered the fight.[3]

The enemy entry into Yongdok began three weeks of fighting for this key coastal town, with first one side and then the other holding it. Two or three miles of ground immediately south of it became a barren, churned up, fought-over no man's land. The first ROK counterattack came immediately. On 18 July at 0545 an air strike came in on the enemy front lines. Heavy naval gunfire pounded the Yongdok area after the strike. At 0600 the United States light cruiser *Juneau* fired two star shells over the ROK line of departure. Newly arrived reinforcements took part in the attack as ROK troops advanced behind the screen of naval gunfire to close rifle range with the North Koreans. At the same time, other naval guns placed interdiction fire on the North Korean rear areas. These heavy support fires were largely responsible for a North Korean withdrawal to a point about three miles north of Yongdok for reorganization.[4]

But this success was short lived. Elements of the N.K. *5th Division* regained the town the next day, driving the ROK's back to their former positions south of it.

On 20 July Colonel Emmerich went to Yonil Airfield to discuss with Col. Robert Witty, commanding the 35th Fighter-Interceptor Group, the co-ordination of air strikes at Yongdok. These promised to become more numerous, because on that day the 40th

---

[2] Emmerich, MS review comments, 30 Nov 57.
[3] 159th FA Bn WD (25th Div), 17 Jul 50.
[4] Emmerich, MS review comments, 30 Nov 57.

Fighter-Interceptor Squadron became operational at Yonil. General Walker and General Partridge flew to Yonil Airfield from Taegu to join in the discussions, and General Kean of the 25th Division also joined the group there. Emmerich briefed the commanders thoroughly on the situation. General Walker ordered that the 3d ROK Division must retake Yongdok. When Colonel Emmerich relayed Walker's orders to General Lee of the ROK division the latter was upset, but he received instructions from higher ROK authority to obey the Eighth Army commander.[5]

The second battle for Yongdok began on the morning of 21 July. This was a savage and bloody fight at close quarters. Naval reinforcements had arrived off the coast during the night of 19 July, and Rear Adm. J. M. Higgins informed Emmerich that the destroyers *Higbee, Mansfield, DeHaven,* and *Swenson,* and the British cruiser *Belfast* would add their gunfire to the battle. This naval gunfire, U.S. artillery and mortar fire, and air strikes enabled the ROK's to retake the town, only to be driven out again by nightfall. In this action unusually accurate enemy mortar and artillery fire caused very heavy ROK casualties. The second battle of Yongdok left the area from Kanggu-dong to a point about two miles north of Yongdok a smoldering no man's land. The pounding of the artillery, naval gunfire, and air strikes had stripped the hills of all vegetation and reduced to rubble all small villages in the area.

In the attack on the 21st, observers estimated that naval gunfire from the *Juneau* alone killed 400 North Korean soldiers. Even though enemy troops again held Yongdok they were unable to exploit their success immediately because they were held under pulverizing artillery and mortar fire, naval gunfire, and almost continuous daylight air strikes. In their efforts to execute wide enveloping moves around the flank of the ROK troops over mountainous terrain, barren of trees and other cover, they came under decimating fire. On 24 July alone the North Koreans lost 800 casualties to this gunfire, according to prisoners. One enemy battalion was virtually destroyed when naval gunfire from the east and air strikes from the west pocketed it and held it under exploding shells, bombs, and strafing fires.[6]

The reconstituted ROK 22d Regiment arrived from Taegu, and about 500 men of the ROK naval combat team and its engineer battalion were sent to buttress the east coast force.[7] All the troops on the east coast were now reorganized into a new ROK 3d Division.

Beginning on 9 July a succession of American units had performed security missions at Yonil Airfield below P'ohang-dong; first the 3d battalion of the 19th Infantry, then the 2d Battalion of the 27th Infantry, next the 1st Battalion of the 35th Infantry, and that in turn gave way to the 1st Battalion of the 7th Cavalry Regiment. Thus, in the course

---

[5] *Ibid.*

[6] EUSAK WD, G-3 Sec, 20-24 Jul 50; EUSAK POR 26, 21 Jul 50; GHQ FEC Sitrep, 21 Jul 50; 35th Inf Regt WD, Unit Rpt, 1st Bn, 22 Jul 50; 159th FA Bn WD, 23-24 Jul 50; Emmerich, MS review comments, 30 Nov 57; Karig, *et al., Battle Report: The War in Korea,* p. 101.

[7] EUSAK WD, G-3 Jnl, 24 Jul 50; GHQ FEC G-3 Opn Rpt 30, 24 Jul 50 and 31, 25 Jul 50.

of two weeks, battalion-size units of all three United States divisions then in Korea had constituted a security force in the P'ohang-dong area behind the ROK 23d Regiment.

Lt. Col. Peter D. Clainos' 1st Battalion, 7th Cavalry, had orders to support the ROK troops with fire only. But on 23 July, North Koreans surrounded the 81-mm. mortar platoon of D Company, forcing it to fight at close range. That same day, C Company on Round Top (Hill 181), at the southern outskirts of Yongdok, watched in silence as North Korean and ROK troops fought a seesaw battle in its vicinity. That night North Koreans surrounded the hill and C Company troops spent a sleepless night. The next day when the ROK's regained temporary possession of Yongdok the 21st Infantry Regiment of the 24th Division replaced Colonel Clainos' battalion in the blocking mission behind the ROK's at Yongdok.[8]

Despite the savage pounding it received from naval, artillery, and mortar fire and aerial bombardments, the N.K. *5th Division* held on to the hills two miles south of Yongdok. The ROK's adopted a plan of making counter and probing attacks during the day and withdrawing to prepared positions in an all-around perimeter for the night. The saturation support fires delivered by the United States Navy, Air Force, and Army day and night outside this perimeter caused many enemy casualties. Certain key pieces of terrain, such as Hill 181, often changed hands several times in one day. Unfortunately, many civilians were killed in this area as they tried to move through the lines and were caught by the supporting fires. Just south of Hill 181 and its surrounding rough ground, a small river, the Osipch'on, descends the coastal range to the Sea of Japan. South of it, sheer mountain walls press the coastal road against the shoreline for ten miles in the direction of P'ohang-dong, twenty-five miles away. If the ROK's lost control of the Yongdok area, this bottleneck on the coastal road would be the scene of the next effort to stop the North Koreans.

At this time the KMAG advisers had serious trouble with "Tiger" Kim, the commander of the ROK 23d Regiment. He was extremely brutal in his disciplinary methods. In the presence of several advisers he had his personal bodyguard shoot a young 1st lieutenant of his regiment whose unit had been surrounded for several days. This incident took place on 26 July. The next day Kim used the butt of an M1 rifle on some of the enlisted men of this unit. The KMAG advisers remonstrated at this action, and in order to avoid possible personal trouble with Kim they asked for his removal. "Tiger" Kim was removed from command of the regiment and the commander of the 1st Separate Battalion, Colonel Kim, replaced him.[9]

ROK troops regrouped for another desperate counterattack, to be supported by all available U.N. sea, air, and ground weapons, in an effort to hurl the North Koreans back to the north of Yongdok. At this time General Walker required hourly reports sent to his headquarters

---

[8] EUSAK WD, G-3 Sec, 16-22 Jul 50; *Ibid.*, Summ, 13-31 Jul 50; Clainos, Notes for author, May 1954; 24th Div WD, G-2 Jnl, entry 1533, 230935 Jul 50.

[9] Emmerich, MS review comments, 30 Nov 57.

at Taegu. In action preliminary to the main attack, planned for the morning of 27 July, ROK troops during the night of the 26th captured seventeen machine guns, but took only eight prisoners. The preparatory barrages began at 0830. Then came the air strikes. The battle that then opened lasted until 2 August without letup. On that date at 1800 the ROK 3d Division recaptured Yongdok and pursued the enemy north of the town. North Korean prisoners said that U.S. naval, artillery, and mortar fire and the air strikes gave them no rest, day or night. They said that in the two weeks' battle for Yongdok the N.K. *5th Division* had lost about 40 percent of its strength in casualties.[10]

During the last half of July 1950, this holding battle on the east coast by the ROK 3d Division was the only one that succeeded in all Korea. It was made possible by American air, sea, and ground fire power and the physical features of the east coast, which hampered North Korean freedom of movement and aided effective employment of American fire power.

Of particular note among the battles during the last part of July in the central mountains was the duel between the N.K. *12th Division* and the ROK 8th Division for control of Andong and the upper Naktong River crossing there. This series of battles was closely related to the fighting on the east coast and the North Korean efforts to gain control of P'ohang-dong and the east coast corridor to Pusan.

After crossing the upper Han River at Tanyang, the N.K. *12th Division* advanced on the road through Yongju to Andong. The ROK 8th Division attacked the *12th* on 21 July between the two towns. From then on to the end of the month these two divisions on the road to Andong engaged in one of the bloodiest fights of the first month of the war.

Just when it was encountering this stubborn resistance from the ROK 8th Division, the *12th* received orders from the N.K. *II Corps* to capture P'ohang-dong by 26 July. This order doubtless was occasioned by the failure of the *5th Division* to advance as rapidly along the east coast as had been expected. Ever since the invasion began, the N.K. Army Command had criticized its *II Corps* for failure to meet its schedule of advance. The Army reportedly demoted the *II Corps* commander, Maj. Gen. Kim Kwang Hyop, to corps chief of staff, about 10 July, replacing him with Lt. Gen. Kim Mu Chong. The order given to the *12th Division* was almost impossible to carry out. The distance from Yongju to P'ohang-dong was about seventy-five air miles, and the greater part of the route, that beyond Andong, lay across high mountain ranges traversed only by foot and oxcart trails. Just to march across these mountains by 26 July would have been no mean feat.[11]

In an effort to meet the deadline given it for the capture of P'ohang-dong,

---

[10] EUSAK WD, G-3 Jnl, 27 Jul 50 and 3 Aug 50; 159th FA Bn (25th Div) WD, 27 Jul 50; GHQ UNC G-3 Opn Rpts 36 and 37, 30-31 Jul, and 40, 3 Aug 50; ATIS Res Supp Interrog Rpts, Issue 96 (N.K. *5th Div*), p. 42; Emmerich, MS review comments, 30 Nov 57.

[11] ATIS Res Supp Interrog Rpts, Issue 99 (N.K. *12th Div*), p. 45; G-2 PW Interrog file, interrog of Col Lee Hak Ku; FEC, telecon TT3559, 21 Jul 50.

Strafing Attack *by an F-80 fighter.*

the N.K. *12th Division* resumed daylight marches. U.N. aerial attacks struck it daily. The ROK 8th Division at the same time fought it almost to a halt. But, despite these difficulties the enemy division pressed slowly on toward Andong. At the end of the month it was engaged in a hard battle with the ROK 8th Division for the control of that key town and the upper Naktong River crossing site.

The battle for Andong lasted five days. The river town finally fell on 1 August. The N.K. Army communiqué for 3 August, broadcast by the P'yongyang radio and monitored in Tokyo, claimed the capture of Andong on 1 August with 1,500 enemy killed and 1,200 captured. It alleged that captured equipment included 6 105-mm. howitzers, 13 automatic guns, 900 rifles, and a large number of vehicles.[12]

The ROK 8th Division, and some elements of the Capital Division which had joined it, lost very heavily in these battles. Enemy losses also were heavy. Prisoners reported that air attacks had killed an estimated 600 North Korean soldiers; that the *31st Regiment* alone lost 600 men in the Andong battles; that the *2d Battalion* of the division artillery had expended all its ammunition and, rather than be burdened with useless weapons and run the risk of their capture or destruction, it had sent them back to Tanyang; that of the original 30 T34 tanks only 19 remained; and, also, that a shell fragment had killed their division commander. This enemy crack division, made up of veterans of the Chinese wars, was so exhausted by the Andong battle that it had no recourse but to rest where it was for several days in early August.[13]

Reorganization of the ROK Army

To a considerable extent the reorganization of the ROK Army influenced the disposition of ROK troops and the U.S. 25th Division along the front.

Throughout the first part of July there had been a continuing effort by American commanders to assemble the surviving men and units of the ROK Army that had escaped south of the Han River and to reorganize them for combat operations. Generals Church, Dean, and Walker each took an active interest in

---

[12] New York *Times*, August 4, 1950.
[13] ATIS Res Supp Interrog Rpts, Issue 99 (N.K. *12th Div*), pp. 45-46; GHQ UNC G-3 Opn Rpt 37, 31 Jul 50; FEC telecon to DA TT3597, 30 Jul 50; TT3600, 31 Jul 50; TT3605, 1 Aug 50.

NAKTONG RIVER AT ANDONG, *showing the Andong bridge.*

this necessary objective. As a part of this reorganization, the ROK Army activated its I Corps and with it directed ROK operations on the right flank of the U.S. 24th Division in the first part of July. The 1st, 2d, and Capital Divisions had carried the fight for the ROK I Corps in the central mountains east of the Seoul-Taejon highway. By the time Taejon fell, these ROK divisions were each reduced to a strength of between 3,000 and 3,500 men. The ROK I Corps at that time had only one 3-gun and two 4-gun batteries of artillery. The three divisions reportedly each had ten 81-mm. mortars without sights.[14]

On 14 July the ROK Army activated its II Corps with headquarters at Hamch'ang. It was composed of the 6th and 8th Divisions and the 23d Regiment. This corps controlled ROK operations in the eastern mountains and, to the extent that it could, it tried to control the 23d Regiment on the east coast.[15] But this latter effort never amounted to very much.

Finally, on 24 July, the ROK Army reorganized itself with two corps and five divisions. ROK I Corps controlled the 8th and Capital Divisions; ROK II Corps controlled the 1st and 6th Divisions. The 2d Division was inactivated

---

[14] 24th Div WD, G-3 Jnl, 16-20 Jul 50, entry 148, Rpt of Opns with I Corps, ROK Army.

[15] GHQ FEC G-3 Opn Rpt 22, 16 Jul 50.

and its surviving elements were integrated into the 1st Division. A reconstituted ROK 3d Division was placed under direct ROK Army control. The principal reason for doing this was the division's isolated position on the east coast, away from effective co-ordinated control by I Corps with the 8th and Capital Divisions westward across the main Taebaek Range.

The ROK divisions held the east central and eastern parts of the United Nations line. To the right (east) of the American troops was, first, the ROK II Corps headquarters at Hamch'ang, with the 1st and 6th Divisions on line in that order from west to east. Next, eastward, was I Corps headquarters at Sangju (briefly at Andong), with the 8th and Capital Divisions on line from west to east; and, lastly, the 3d Division was on the east coast under direct ROK Army control. This ROK Army organization and position on line remained relatively stable for the next two months.[16]

On 26 July, after large numbers of recruits and replacements had entered the ROK Army, it had an effective assigned strength of 85,871 men, with a total assigned strength of 94,570. The combat divisions at that time varied in strength from just under 6,000 to almost 9,000 men. Table 2 shows the organization and unit strengths of the ROK Army after the reorganization.

The U.S. 25th Division at Sangju

On the next major axis west of the Andong road, where at the end of the month the N.K. *12th Division* was recuperating from its heavy battles, lay the town of Sangju. It was a crossroads center for all the mountain roads in that part of Korea. Situated south of the Mun'gyong plateau and the dividing watershed between the Han and the Naktong Rivers, it had a commanding position in the valley of the Naktong, forty-five air miles northeast up that valley from Taegu. Sangju was a place of both confusion and activity during the third week of July. Refugees and stragglers poured south into and through the town. Many ROK units were retreating to Sangju and some had passed south through it. Fighting had already been joined between North Koreans and ROK forces for control of the Mun'gyong plateau when the U.S. 25th Division received orders from General Walker to concentrate there to bolster ROK defenses of the central mountain corridors.[17] General Walker looked to the 25th Division to help the ROK forces in central Korea prevent a movement of major enemy forces into the valley of the upper Naktong.

The first action between elements of the 25th Division and enemy forces appears to have occurred at Yech'on on 20 July. Company K, 24th Infantry, led by 1st Lt. Jasper R. Johnson, entered the town during the afternoon. When other units of the 3d Battalion failed to take a ridge overlooking the town on the left, he requested and received permission to withdraw from the town for the night.[18]

---

[16] GHQ UNC Sitrep, 27 Jul 50; EUSAK WD, G-3 Rpt., 4 Jul 50, and G-3 Jnl, 25 Jul 50. The reorganization was effective 241800 Jul 50.

[17] 24th Inf Regt WD, 17-20 Jul 50; 35th Inf Regt WD, Narr, 19-20 Jul 50.

[18] Interv, author with Capt Johnson, 11 Jul 52.

THE FRONT LINE MOVES SOUTH

TABLE 2—ROK ARMY, 26 JULY 1950

	Strength
Total assigned	94,570
Total effective assigned	85,871
Wounded and nonbattle casualties	8,699
I Corps Headquarters	3,014
Capital Division (1st, 17th, 18th Regiments)	6,644
8th Division (10th, 16th, 21st Regiments)	8,864
II Corps Headquarters	976
1st Division (11th, 12th, 15th Regiments)	7,601
6th Division (2d, 7th, 19th Regiments)	5,727
ROK Army Headquarters	3,020
3d Division (1st Cavalry, 22d, 23d Regiments)	8,829
ROK Troops	11,881
Replacement Training Command	9,016
Chonju Training Command	8,699
Kwangju Training Command	6,244
Pusan Training Command	5,356

Meeting at the battalion command post, the commanders of the various units planned a renewed assault for 0500 the next morning. Artillery and mortars zeroed in as scheduled, and soon the town was in flames. By this time, however, Yech'on may already have been abandoned by the enemy. At Hamch'ang, Col. Henry G. Fisher, commanding the 35th Infantry, received early that morning an erroneous message that the North Koreans had driven the 3d Battalion, 24th Infantry from Yech'on. He started for the place at once. He found the battalion commander about five miles west of the town, but was dissatisfied with the information that he received from him. Fisher and a small party then drove on into Yech'on, which was ablaze with fires started by American artillery shells. He encountered no enemy or civilians. The 3d Platoon, 77th Engineer Combat Company, attached to Company K, entered the town with the infantrymen and attempted to halt the spread of flames—unsuccessfully, because of high, shifting winds. By 1300 Yech'on was secured, and 3d Battalion turned over control to the ROK 18th Regiment of the Capital Division the task of holding the town. The Capital Division now concentrated there the bulk of its forces and opposed the N.K. *8th Division* in that vicinity the remainder of the month.[19]

General Kean and his 25th Division had to guard two main approaches to Sangju if he was to secure the town. First was the main road that crossed the Mun'gyong plateau and passed through Hamch'ang at the base of the plateau about fifteen miles due north of Sangju. Next, there was the secondary mountain road that crossed the plateau farther west and, once through the mountains, turned east toward Sangju.

On the first and main road, the 2d Battalion, 35th Infantry, held a block-

---
[19] Fisher, MS review comments, 27 Oct 57; 35th Inf WD and 24th Inf WD, 20–21 Jul 50.

ing position northwest of Hamch'ang, supported by a platoon of tanks from A Company, 79th Tank Battalion, and A Battery, 90th Field Artillery Battalion. Colonel Fisher was unable to concentrate his two-battalion regiment here for the defense of Sangju because the 1st Battalion had no sooner arrived on 25 July from P'ohang-dong than it was sent posthaste the next day to reinforce the 27th Infantry Regiment on the next north-south line of communications westward. Thus, in effect, one battalion of U.S. troops stood behind ROK units on the Hamch'ang approach. On the second road, that leading into Sangju from the west, the 24th Infantry Regiment assembled two, and later all three, of its battalions.

The 2d Battalion of the 35th Infantry took up a hill position northwest of Hamch'ang and south of Mun'gyong on the south side of a stream that flowed past Sangju to the Naktong. On the north side of the stream a ROK battalion held the front line. Brig. Gen. Vennard Wilson, Assistant Division Commander, insisted that F Company of the battalion should be inserted in the center of the ROK line north of the stream, and this was done over the strong protests of Colonel Fisher and the battalion commander, Lt. Col. John L. Wilkins. Wilson thought the American troops would strengthen the ROK defense; Fisher and Wilkins did not want the untried company to be dependent upon ROK stability in its first engagement. Behind the ROK and F Company positions the ground rose in another hill within small arms range. Heavy rains had swollen the stream behind the ROK's and F Company to a torrent that was rolling large boulders along its channel.

On 22 July the North Koreans attacked. The ROK's withdrew from their positions on either side of F Company without informing that company of their intentions. Soon enemy troops were firing into the back of F Company from the hill behind it. This precipitated an unorganized withdrawal. The swollen stream prevented F Company from crossing to the south side and the sanctuary of the 2d Battalion positions. Walking wounded crowded along the stream where an effort to get them across failed. Two officers and a noncommissioned officer tied a pair of twisted telephone wires about their bodies and tried to swim to the opposite bank and fasten a line, but each in turn was swept downstream where they floundered ashore a hundred yards away on the same bank from which they had started. Some men drowned in trying to cross the swollen river. The covering fire of a platoon of tanks on the south side held off the enemy and allowed most of the survivors eventually to escape. In this fiasco, F Company lost 6 men killed, 10 wounded, and 21 missing.[20]

The next morning five enemy tanks crossed the river and moved toward Hamch'ang. Artillery fire from a battery of the 90th Field Artillery Battalion knocked out four of the tanks. The fifth turned back across the river, and there an air strike later destroyed it.

The 2d Battalion, 35th Infantry, was still in its position when it received orders on 23 July to withdraw to a point 5 miles north of Sangju. On the 29th the battalion fell back 2 miles more, and the next day it moved to a position south of

---

[20] 35th Inf Regt WD, 22 Jul 50; Fisher, MS review comments, 27 Oct 57.

Sangju. On the last day of July the 35th Infantry was ordered to a blocking position on a line of hills 8 miles south of Sangju on the Kumch'on road. In eleven days it had fallen back about thirty miles on the Sangju front. In these movements it did little fighting, but executed a series of withdrawals on division orders as the front around it collapsed.[21]

The ROK 6th Division continued its hard-fought action on the road through the mountains from Mun'gyong, but gradually it fell back from in front of the N.K. *1st Division*. In the mountains above Hamch'ang the ROK 6th Division on 24 July destroyed 7 enemy T34 tanks. Three days later the ROK 1st Division, now relieved northwest of Sangju by the U.S. 24th Infantry and redeployed on the Hamch'ang front, reportedly destroyed 4 more tanks there with 2.36-inch bazookas and captured 1 tank intact. The decimated remnants of the ROK 2d Division, relieved by the 27th Infantry Regiment on the Hwanggan-Poun road, were incorporated into the ROK 1st Division. Thus, by 24 July the U.S. 25th Division had taken over from the ROK 1st and 2d Divisions the sector from Sangju westward to the Seoul-Taegu highway, and these ROK troops were moving into the line eastward and northward from Sangju on the Hamch'ang front.[22]

By 27 July all the Mun'gyong divide was in North Korean possession and enemy units were moving into the valley of the upper Naktong in the vicinity of Hamch'ang. Prisoners taken at the time and others captured later said that the N.K. *1st Division* lost 5,000 casualties in the struggle for control of the divide, including the division commander who was wounded and replaced. The *13th Division*, following the *1st*, suffered about 500 casualties below Mun'gyong, but otherwise it was not engaged during this period.[23]

Simultaneously with his appearance on the Hamch'ang road at the southern base of the Mun'gyong plateau north of Sangju, the enemy approached on the secondary mountain road to the west. On 22 July, the same day that F Company of the 35th Infantry came to grief north of Hamch'ang, elements of the 24th Infantry Regiment had a similar unhappy experience west of Sangju. On that day the 2d Battalion, 24th Infantry, and elements of the ROK 17th Regiment were advancing into the mountains twenty miles northwest of the town. With E Company leading, the battalion moved along the dirt road into a gorge with precipitous mountain walls. Suddenly, an enemy light mortar and one or two automatic weapons fired on E Company. It stopped and the men dispersed along the sides of the road. ROK officers advised that the men deploy in an enveloping movement to the right and to the left, but the company commander apparently did not understand. Soon enemy rifle fire came in on the dispersed

---

[21] 35th Inf Regt WD, 23-31 Jul 50; 25th Div POR 28, 23 Jul 50; 25th Div WD, Narr Rpt, 8-31 Jul 50; 35th Inf Opn Instr, 25 Jul 50; ATIS Res Supp Interrog Rpts, Issue 104 (N.K. *13th Div*), p. 60.

[22] FEC telecons with DA, TT3566, 23 Jul 50; TT3567, 24 Jul 50; TT3577, 25 Jul 50; TT3579, 26 Jul 50; ATIS Supp, Enemy Docs, Issue 1, pp. 42-48, Battle Rpts 23 Jun-3 Aug 50, by NA unit, Ok Chae Min and Kim Myung Kap; 34th Div WD, G-2 Sec, entry 1616, 271900 Jul 50.

[23] ATIS Res Supp Interrog Rpts, Issue 3 (N.K. *1st Div*), pp. 32-33; *Ibid.*, Issue 104 (N.K. *13th Div*), p. 60.

men and E and F Companies began withdrawing in a disorderly manner.

Col. Horton V. White, the regimental commander, heard of the difficulty and drove hurriedly to the scene. He found the battalion coming back down the road in disorder and most of the men in a state of panic. He finally got the men under control. The next day the ROK 17th Regiment enveloped the enemy position that had caused the trouble and captured two light machine guns, one mortar, and about thirty enemy who appeared to be guerrillas.[24] The ROK 17th Regiment fought in the hills for the next two days, making some limited gains, and then it moved back to Sangju in the ROK Army reorganization in progress. This left only the U.S. 24th Infantry Regiment guarding the west approach to Sangju from the Mun'gyong plateau.

The tendency to panic continued in nearly all the 24th Infantry operations west of Sangju. Men left their positions and straggled to the rear. They abandoned weapons on positions. On one occasion the 3d Battalion withdrew from a hill and left behind 12 .30-caliber and 3 .50-caliber machine guns, 8 60-mm. mortars, 3 81-mm. mortars, 4 3.5-inch rocket launchers, and 102 rifles. On another occasion, L Company took into position 4 officers and 105 enlisted men; a few days later, when the company was relieved in its position, there were only 17 men in the foxholes. The number of casualties and men evacuated for other reasons in the interval had been 1 officer and 17 enlisted men, leaving 3 officers and 88 enlisted men unaccounted for. As the relieved unit of 17 men moved down off the mountain it swelled in numbers to 1 officer and 35 enlisted men by the time it reached the bottom.[25]

By 26 July the 24th Infantry had all three of its battalions concentrated in battle positions astride the road ten miles west of Sangju. Elements of the N.K. *15th Division* advancing on this road had cleared the mountain passes and were closing with the regiment. From 26 July on to the end of the month the enemy had almost constant contact with the 24th Infantry, which was supported by the 159th and 64th Field Artillery Battalions and one battery of the 90th Field Artillery Battalion.[26]

The general pattern of 24th Infantry action during the last days of July was to try to hold positions during the day and then withdraw at night. On the evening of 29 July the 1st Battalion got out of hand. During the day the battalion had suffered about sixty casualties from enemy mortar fire. As the men were preparing their perimeter defense for the night, an inexplicable panic seized them and the battalion left its positions. Colonel White found himself, the 77th Combat Engineer Company, and a battery of the 159th Field Artillery Battalion all that was left in the front line. He had to reorganize the battalion himself. That night the supporting artillery fired 3,000 rounds, part of it direct fire, in holding back the North Koreans.

In these last days west of Sangju, Maj. John R. Woolridge, the regimental S–1, set up a check point half a mile west of

---

[24] 24th Inf Regt WD, 22 Jul 50; 25th Div WD, Incl 3, 22 Jul 50; EUSAK IG Rept on 24th Inf Regt, 1950, testimony of bn and regtl off, 2d Bn and 24th Inf Regt.

[25] EUSAK IG Rpt, 24th Inf Regt, 1950.

[26] 24th Inf Regt WD, 23–26 Jul 50; 159th FA Bn WD, Jul 50.

the town and stopped every vehicle coming from the west, taking off stragglers. He averaged about seventy-five stragglers a day and, on the last day, he collected 150.[27]

By 30 July, the 24th Infantry had withdrawn to the last defensible high ground west of Sangju, three miles from the town. The regiment had deteriorated so badly by this time that General Kean recalled the 1st Battalion, 35th Infantry, and placed it in blocking positions behind the 24th Infantry. The next day North Koreans again pressed against the regiment and forced in the outpost line of resistance. In this action, 1st Lt. Leon A. Gilbert, commanding A Company, quit the outpost line with about fifteen men. Colonel White and other ranking officers ordered Lieutenant Gilbert back into position, but he refused to go, saying that he was scared. The senior noncommissioned officer returned with the men to their positions.[28]

Finally, during the night of 31 July the 24th Infantry Regiment withdrew through Sangju. The 1st Battalion, 35th Infantry, covered the withdrawal. In eleven days of action in the Sangju area the regiment had suffered 323 battle casualties—27 killed, 293 wounded, 3 missing.[29]

In reaching the upper Naktong valley at the end of July, the enemy divisions engaged in this part of the North Korean drive southward had not gone unharmed. The N.K. *1st Division* in battling across the Mun'gyong plateau against the ROK 6th Division not only suffered great losses in the ground battle but also took serious losses from U.N. aerial attack. Prisoners reported that by the time it reached Hamch'ang at the end of July it was down to 3,000 men. The N.K. *15th Division,* according to prisoners, also lost heavily to artillery and mortar fire in its drive on Sangju against ROK troops and the U.S. 24th Infantry Regiment, and was down to about half strength, or approximately 5,000 men, at the end of July. In contrast, the N.K. *13th Division* had bypassed Hamch'ang on the west and, save for minor skirmishes with ROK troops and the 2d Battalion, 35th Infantry, it had not been engaged and consequently had suffered relatively few casualties.[30]

The 1st Cavalry Division Sails for Korea

At first General MacArthur and the staff of the Far East Command had expected that the 24th and 25th Divisions in support of the ROK Army would be able to check the North Korean advance. Based on this expectation, initial preliminary planning called for a third United States division, the 1st Cavalry, to land in the rear of the enemy forces and, together with a counterattack from in front by the combined American and ROK forces, to crush and destroy the North Korean Army.

In furtherance of this plan, the Far

---

[27] EUSAK IG Rpt, 24th Inf Regt, 1950; 24th Inf WD, 29 Jul 50; 159th FA Bn WD, 29-30 Jul 50.

[28] 24th Inf WD, 30-31 Jul 50; EUSAK WD, G-3 Jnl, Msg 301355 Jul 50; JAG CM-343472, U.S. *vs.* 1st Lt Leon A. Gilbert, O-1304518, (includes all legal action taken in the case up to commutation of sentence on 27 Nov 50); Washington *Post*, September 20, 1952.

[29] 24th Inf Regt WD, 31 Jul 50 and app. V.

[30] ATIS Res Supp Interrog Rpts, Issue 3 (N.K. *1st Div*), pp. 32-33; *Ibid.*, Isssue 104 (N.K. *13th Div*), p. 61; and p. 42 (N.K. *15th Div*); *Ibid.*, Issue 4 (*105th Armored Div*), p. 38; EUSAK WD, G-2 Sec, 2 Aug 50, ATIS Interrog Rpt 339.

East Command called Maj. Gen. Hobart R. Gay, Commanding General, 1st Cavalry Division, to General MacArthur's headquarters on 6 July and informed him of plans for the 1st Cavalry Division to make an amphibious landing at Inch'on. From this briefing General Gay went to the G-2, Far East Command office, where he was told, "You must expedite preparations to the utmost limit because if the landing is delayed all that the 1st Cavalry Division will hit when it lands will be the tail end of the 24th Division as it passes north through Seoul." [31]

The transfer to the 24th and 25th Infantry Divisions, in strengthening them for their combat missions in Korea, of approximately 750 noncommissioned officers from the 1st Cavalry Division had weakened the latter. It had been stripped of practically every first grader except the first sergeants of companies and batteries.

Between 12 and 14 July the division loaded on ships in the Yokohama area. But, by this time, the steady enemy successes south of the Han River had changed the objective from a landing in the enemy's rear at Inch'on to a landing on the east coast of Korea at P'ohang-dong, a fishing town sixty air miles northeast of Pusan. Its mission was to reinforce at once the faltering 24th Division. A landing at P'ohang-dong would not congest still further the Pusan port facilities, which were needed to land supplies for the troops already in action; also, from P'ohang-dong the division could move promptly to the Taejon area in support of the 24th Division. The date of the landing was set for 18 July.[32]

The command ship *Mt. McKinley* and final elements of the first lift sailed for Korea on 15 July in Task Force 90, commanded by Rear Adm. James H. Doyle. The landing at P'ohang-dong was unopposed. Lead elements of the 8th Cavalry Regiment were ashore by 0610 18 July, and the first troops of the 5th Cavalry Regiment came in twenty minutes later. Typhoon Helene swept over the Korean coast and prevented landing of the 7th Cavalry Regiment and the 82d Field Artillery Battalion until 22 July. For three days ships could not be unloaded at Pusan and Eighth Army rations dropped to one day's supply.[33]

Even though it had received 1,450 replacements before it left Japan, 100 of them from the Eighth Army stockade, the division was understrength when it landed in Korea and, like the preceding divisions, it had only 2 battalions in the regiments, 2 firing batteries in the artillery battalions, and 1 tank company (light M24 tanks).

On 19 July, the 5th Cavalry Regiment started toward Taejon. The next day the 8th Cavalry Regiment followed by rail and motor, and closed in an assembly area east of Yongdong that evening. Brig. Gen. Charles D. Palmer, division artillery commander, commanded these two forward regiments. On 22 July the 8th Cavalry Regiment relieved the 21st Infantry, 24th Division, in its positions at Yongdong and the 1st Cavalry Division thereby assumed responsibility for

---

[31] Ltr and Comments, Gen Gay to author, 24 Aug 53.

[32] Comdr, Amphibious Group One, Task Force 90, Attack Force Opn Order 10-50, 131200 Jul 50, Tokyo; Notes, Harris for author, 18 May 54.

[33] 1st Cav Div WD, 12-22 Jul 50, and Summ, 25 Jun-Jul 50.

blocking the enemy along the main Taejon-Taegu corridor.[34]

In a conference at Taegu General Walker gave General Gay brief instructions. In substance, Walker told Gay: "Protect Yongdong. Remember there are no friendly troops behind you. You must keep your own back door open. You can live without food but you cannot last long without ammunition, and unless the Yongdong-Taegu road is kept open you will soon be without ammunition." In the week that followed, these words of Walker's rang constantly in General Gay's ears.[35]

Leaving Taegu, General Gay joined his troops and General Palmer at Yongdong. Colonel MacLean, from the Eighth Army G-3 Section, was present and had given instructions that one battalion should be posted four miles northwest of Yongdong on the south side of the Kum River, and that another battalion should be placed two miles southwest of Yongdong. The first would cover the approach along the main Taejon-Taegu highway, the second the approach on the Chosan-ni–Muju–Kumsan road. General Palmer had protested this disposition of troops to Colonel MacLean on the ground that the enemy could encircle and cut off one battalion at a time and that neither battalion could support the other. Palmer wanted to place the 1st Cavalry Division on a line of hills just east of Yongdong and then have the 24th Division withdraw through it. General Gay agreed with General Palmer and stated that he could not comply with Colonel MacLean's instructions unless Eighth Army confirmed them over the telephone. The army headquarters did confirm the orders, and the two battalions of the 8th Cavalry Regiment went into the two blocking positions, the 1st Battalion on the Taejon road northwest of Yongdong and the 2d Battalion southwest of Yongdong. General Gay placed the 5th Cavalry Regiment on the high ground east of the town in a blocking position.[36]

The strength of the Eighth Army at this time, with the 1st Cavalry Division in the line, was about 39,000 men. Less than three weeks earlier, when there were no American troops in Korea, such a number would have seemed a large force indeed.[37]

The 1st Cavalry Division Loses Yongdong

The enemy paused but briefly after the capture of Taejon. After a day's rest in that town, which it had helped to capture, the N.K. *3d Division* departed the city on 22 July, advancing down the main highway toward Taegu. The next morning, 23 July, the 1st Battalion, 8th

---

[34] *Ibid.*, 21–22 Jul 50; *Ibid.*, G-3 Sec, 20 Jul 50; 24th Div WD, G-4 Daily Summ, 22 Jul 50; EUSAK WD, Summ, 13–31 Jul 50; 8th Cav Regt Opn Jnl, 21 Jul 50.

[35] Comments, Gen Gay to author, 24 Aug 53.

[36] *Ibid.*

[37] The strength of the major units in USAFIK is shown in the following:

Total	39,439
EUSAK	2,184
KMAG	473
1st Cav Div (Inf)	10,027
24th Inf Div	10,463
25th Inf Div	13,059
Pusan Base	2,979
ADCOM	163
Misc Personnel	91

Source: GHQ FEC G-3 Opn Rpt 34, 19 Jul 50; *Ibid.*, Sitrep, 19 Jul 50.

CAVALRYMEN PREPARING FOR ACTION *in the bitter fighting at Yongdong. Artillery bursts on enemy positions are visible in the background.*

Cavalry Regiment, in front of Yongdong, reported it had destroyed three enemy T34 tanks with 3.5-inch rocket launchers in its first use of that weapon.[38] The enemy division was closing with the 1st Cavalry Division for the battle for Yongdong.

During 23 July the *7th* and *9th Regiments* of the N.K. *3d Division* began their attack on the Yongdong positions. The enemy made his first penetration southwest of Yongdong, establishing a roadblock a mile and a half behind the 2d Battalion, 8th Cavalry, at the same time other units heavily engaged the 1st Battalion northwest of Yongdong in frontal attack.

The next day four different attempts by three American light tanks failed to dislodge the enemy behind the 2d Battalion, and Lt. Col. Eugene J. Field, the 2d Battalion commander, was wounded at the roadblock. General Palmer sent the 1st Battalion, 5th Cavalry Regiment, and the 16th Reconnaissance Company toward the cutoff battalion. By noon, enemy troops were attacking the 99th and 61st Field Artillery Battalions

---

[38] ATIS Res Supp Interrog Rpts, Issue 96 (N.K. *3d Div*), p. 32; EUSAK WD, 23 Jul 50; 8th Cav Regt Opn Jnl. The 1st Battalion, 8th Cavalry, had enemy contact at 222100.

which were supporting the 2d Battalion, 8th Cavalry Regiment, indicating that the infiltration had been extensive.[39]

On the other approach road, northwest of Yongdong, heavy automatic fire from quad-50's, 37-mm. fire from A Battery of the 92d Antiaircraft Artillery Battalion, and artillery fire from the 77th Field Artillery Battalion helped the 1st Battalion there to repel enemy attacks.

The large numbers of Korean refugees crowding the Yongdong area undoubtedly helped the enemy infiltrate the 1st Cavalry Division positions. On 24 July, for example, a man dressed in white carrying a heavy pack, and accompanied by a woman appearing to be pregnant, came under suspicion. The couple was searched and the woman's assumed pregnancy proved to be a small radio hidden under her clothes. She used this radio for reporting American positions. Eighth Army tried to control the refugee movement through the Korean police, permitting it only during daylight hours and along predetermined routes.[40]

By the morning of 25 July enemy forces had infiltrated the positions of the 1st Cavalry Division so thoroughly that they forced a withdrawal. Northwest of Yongdong, Lt. Col. Robert W. Kane's 1st Battalion executed an orderly and efficient withdrawal, covered by the fire of the Heavy Mortar Company and the two batteries of Lt. Col. William A. Harris' 77th Field Artillery Battalion. The mortar men finally lost their mortars and fought as infantry in the withdrawal.[41]

Meanwhile, the situation worsened on the road southwest of Yongdong. Concentrated artillery support—with the shells falling so close to the 2d Battalion positions that they wounded four men—together with an attack by the battalion, briefly opened the enemy roadblock at 0430, 25 July, and the bulk of the battalion escaped to Yongdong. But F Company, 8th Cavalry, the 16th Reconnaissance Company, and the 1st Platoon, A Company, 71st Tank Battalion, at the rear of the column were cut off. Only four of eleven light tanks broke through the enemy positions. Crews abandoned the other seven tanks and walked over the hills in a two days' journey as part of a group of 219 men, most of them from F Company. All equipment except individual arms was abandoned by this group. Others escaped in the same manner.[42]

On this same road, but closer to Yongdong, the 2d Battalion, 5th Cavalry, in trying to help the cutoff units of the 8th Cavalry, ran into trouble. Through some error, its F Company went to the wrong hill and walked into a concentration of enemy soldiers. Only twenty-six men returned. Altogether, the 5th

---

[39] 1st Cav Div WD, 23–24 Jul 50; 8th Cav Regt Opn Jnl, 24 Jul 50. Overlay 36 to 8th Cav Opn Jnl shows location of enemy roadblock.

[40] 8th Cav Regt Opn Jnl, 24 Jul 50; 1st Cav Div WD, G-3 Sec, serial 80, 26 Jul 50.

[41] 1st Cav Div WD, 25 Jul 50; Interv, author with Maj Rene J. Giuraud, 21 Apr 54 (Giuraud commanded the mortar company at Yongdong); Interv, author with Harris, 30 Apr 54; Notes, Harris for author, 18 May 54.

[42] 1st Cav Div WD, 25–27 Jul 50; Ltr, Gay to author, 24 Aug 53; 8th Cav Regt Opn Jnl, 25 Jul 50; Capt Charles A. Rogers, History of the 16th Reconnaissance Company in Korea, 18 July 1950–April 1951, typescript MS, May 51, copy in OCMH; New York Times, July 29, 1950, dispatch by William H. Lawrence from 1st Cavalry Division.

Cavalry Regiment had 275 casualties on 25 July.[43]

The N.K. *3d Division* used against the 1st Cavalry Division at Yongdong essentially the same tactics it had employed against the 24th Division at Taejon—a holding attack frontally, with the bulk of its force enveloping the American left flank and establishing strongly held roadblocks behind the front positions. The enemy division entered Yongdong the night of 25 July; at least one unit was in the town by 2000. The North Koreans expected a counterattack and immediately took up defensive positions at the eastern edge of the town. Prisoners reported later that the division suffered about 2,000 casualties, mostly from artillery fire, in the attack on Yongdong on 24-25 July.[44] This brought it down to about 5,000 men, approximately half-strength.

The 27th Infantry's Baptism of Fire

Closely related to the Yongdong action was the enemy advance southward on the next road eastward, the Poun-Hwanggan road. The N.K. *2d Division*, arriving too late on the east of Taejon to help in the attack on that city, turned toward Poun. Unless checked it would pass through that town and come out on the main Seoul-Pusan highway at Hwanggan, about ten miles east of Yongdong. This would place it in the rear of the 1st Cavalry Division on the latter's main supply road.

The task of defending this road fell to the 27th Infantry Regiment of the U.S. 25th Division. Upon first arriving in Korea that regiment went to the Uisong area, thirty-five air miles north of Taegu. On 13 July it moved from there to Andong to support ROK troops, but before it entered action in the heavy battles then taking place in that area it suddenly received orders to move to Sangju. En route to that place it received still other orders to change its destination to Hwanggan, and it closed there in an assembly area the night of 22-23 July. General Walker had begun the quick and improvised shifting of troops to meet emergencies that was to characterize his defense of the Pusan Perimeter. The 27th Infantry's mission at Hwanggan was to relieve the decimated ROK troops retreating down the Poun road.[45]

In carrying out Eighth Army's orders to block the Poun road, Colonel Michaelis assigned the 1st Battalion of the 27th Infantry the task of making contact with the enemy. On the morning of 23 July, Lt. Col. Gilbert J. Check moved the 1st Battalion northward toward Poun from the Hwanggan assembly area. He took up defensive positions in the evening near the village of Sangyong-ni, south of Poun. The battalion assumed responsibility for that sector at 1700 after ROK troops fell back through its position.[46] Colonel Check was unable to obtain from the retreating ROK troops any information on the size of the North Korean force following them or how close it was.

That night he sent 1st Lt. John A. Buckley of A Company with a 30-man

---

[43] 1st Cav Div WD, 25 Jul 50.

[44] ATIS Res Supp Interrog Rpts, Issue 96 (N.K. *3d Div*), pp. 32-33; *Ibid.*, Enemy Docs, Issue 2, pp. 66-67 (Choe Song Hwan diary, 21 Jul-10 Aug 50).

[45] 27th Inf WD, an. 2, 13 Jul, and Opn sec, 6-31 Jul 50; *Ibid.*, Summ of Activities, 2d Bn, Opn Rpt, 1st Bn, and an. 2, 21-22 Jul 50.

[46] EUSAK WD, G-3 Sec, 22 Jul 50; 27th Inf WD, Opn Rpt, 1st Bn, 23 Jul-3 Aug 50.

patrol northward to locate the enemy. Near Poun Buckley saw an enemy column approaching. He quickly disposed his patrol on hills bordering both sides of the road, and, when the column was nearly abreast, opened fire on it with all weapons. This fire apparently caused the enemy advanced unit to believe it had encountered a major position, for it held back until daylight. When the enemy turned back, Buckley and his patrol returned to the 1st Battalion lines, arriving there at 0400, 24 July. Six men were missing.[47]

Check's 1st Battalion prepared to receive an attack. It came at 0630, 24 July, shortly after daybreak in a heavy fog that enabled the North Koreans to approach very close to the battalion positions before they were observed. Two rifle companies, one on either side of the road on low ridges, held the forward positions. Enemy mortar and small arms fire fell on the men there, and then tanks appeared at the bend in the road and opened fire with cannon and machine guns as they approached. Enemy infantry followed the tanks. Although the two rifle companies stopped the North Korean infantry, the tanks penetrated their positions and fired into the battalion command post which was behind B Company. This tank fire destroyed several vehicles and killed the medical officer. Capt. Logan E. Weston, A Company commander, armed himself with a bazooka and knocked out one of the tanks within the position. In this close action, tank fire killed a man near Weston and the concussion of the shell explosion damaged Weston's ears so that he could not hear. Weston refused to leave the fight, and Colonel Check later had to order him to the rear for medical treatment.

On the right (north) of the road the enemy overran the battalion observation post and B Company's outpost line. This high ground changed hands three times during the day. While the infantry fight was in progress, and shortly after the first tank penetration, five more T34's came around the road bend toward the 1st Battalion. When the first tanks appeared Colonel Check had called for an air strike. Now, at this propitious moment, three F–80 jet planes arrived and immediately dived on the approaching second group of tanks, destroying 3 of them with 5-inch rockets. Altogether, bazooka, artillery, and air strikes knocked out 6 enemy tanks during the morning, either within or on the edge of the 1st Battalion position. In this, its first engagement with American troops, the N.K. *2d Division* lost all but 2 of the 8 tanks that had been attached to it a few days earlier at Chongju.[48]

Late in the evening after dark the 1st Battalion disengaged and withdrew through the 2d Battalion immediately behind it. Both Check and the regimental commander, Colonel Michaelis, expected the enemy to encircle the 1st Battalion position during the night if it stayed where it was.

The North Koreans apparently were unaware of the 1st Battalion withdrawal, for the next morning, 25 July, two en-

---

[47] 27th Inf WD, Opn Rpt, 1st Bn, 23 Jul–3 Aug 50; 25th Div WD, G–3 Sec, 24 Jul 50; ATIS Res Supp Interrog Rpts, Issue 94 (N.K. *2d Div*) p. 36.

[48] EUSAK WD, G–3 Jnl, 24 Jul 50; 27th Inf WD, Opn Rpt, 1st Bn 24 Jul 50; ATIS Res Supp Interrog Rpts, Issue 94 (N.K. *2d Div.*), p. 36; Col Gilbert J. Check, MS review comments, 25 Nov 57.

emy battalions in a double envelopment came in behind its positions of the evening before but in front of Maj. Gordon E. Murch's 2d Battalion. There they were surprised and caught in the open by the combined fire of American tanks, artillery, and mortar, and the 2d Battalion's automatic and small arms fire. The North Koreans suffered severely in this action. Surviving remnants of the two enemy batalions withdrew in confusion. The 2d Battalion took about thirty prisoners.[49]

Despite this costly setback, the enemy division pushed relentlessly forward, and that afternoon elements of it were flanking the regimental position. Colonel Michaelis issued an order about 2200 for another withdrawal to high ground near Hwanggan. The withdrawal started near midnight with heavy fighting still in progress on the right flank. Major Murch took control of all tanks and put them on line facing north. There the nine tanks of A Company, 79th Tank Battalion, fired into visible enemy troops approaching on the road. Enemy mortar fire, estimated to be eight or ten rounds a minute, fell along the battalion line and the road behind it. F Company and the nine tanks covered the 2d Battalion withdrawal.[50]

The next day, 26 July, the arrival of the 1st Battalion, 35th Infantry, on the 27th Infantry's right flank eased the precarious situation. But the following day the regimental left flank came under attack where a large gap existed between C Company, the lefthand (west) unit of the 27th Infantry, and the 7th Cavalry Regiment, the nearest unit of the 1st Cavalry Division. C Company lost and regained a peak three times during the day. More than 40 casualties reduced its strength to approximately 60 men. B Company also lost heavily in action, falling to a strength of about 85 men. By the morning of 28 July the enemy had penetrated the 1st Battalion's line, forcing C Company to withdraw.[51]

At this point Colonel Michaelis went to the 1st Cavalry Division command post in Hwanggan and asked General Gay for permission to withdraw his hard-pressed regiment through that division. General Gay telephoned Colonel Landrum, Eighth Army Chief of Staff, and described the situation. He asked if he should attack in an effort to relieve the enemy pressure on the 27th Infantry, or if that regiment should withdraw into the 1st Cavalry Division's area, move south to Kumch'on, and then turn toward Sangju to rejoin the 25th Division. Colonel Landrum called back later and said, "Let Mike withdraw through you." Colonel Collier drove from Taegu to Hwanggan to discuss the situation with General Gay who said, "We are in what they call a military mousetrap."[52]

Before dawn, 29 July, the 27th Infantry Regiment withdrew through the 1st Cavalry Division lines at Hwanggan to a position about a mile east of Kumch'on. That afternoon Colonel Michaelis received orders from Eighth Army to move to Waegwan on the Naktong River near Taegu, as army reserve, instead of

---

[49] 27th Inf WD, 25 Jul 50; Lt Col Gordon E. Murch, Notes for author, 7 Apr 54.
[50] Murch, Notes for author, 7 Apr 54; 27th Inf WD, Summ of Activities, 2d Bn, 25 Jul 50.
[51] EUSAK WD, G-3 Sec, 26 Jul 50; 27th Inf WD, Opn Rpt, 1st Bn, 27 Jul 50; 27th Inf WD, Hist Rpt, 27-28 Jul 50.
[52] Comments, Gay for author, 24 Aug 53; Collier, MS review comments, 10 Mar 58.

joining the 25th Division in the Sangju area.

In its five days of delaying action on the Poun-Hwanggan road, the 27th Infantry Regiment lost 53 men killed, 221 wounded, and 49 missing, a total of 323 battle casualties. The N.K. *2d Division* suffered heavily during this time, some estimates placing its loss above 3,000 men.[53]

Retreat

During the battle for Yongdong the 7th Cavalry Regiment headquarters and the 2d Battalion arrived from P'ohang-dong and took up a position west of Kumch'on. Reports reached them the night of 25–26 July of enemy gains in the 27th Infantry sector northward, which increased the uneasiness of the untested staff and troops. After midnight there came a report that the enemy had achieved a breakthrough. Somehow, the constant pressure under which the 27th Infantry fought its delaying action on the Poun road had become magnified and exaggerated. The 7th Cavalry Regiment headquarters immediately decided to arouse all personnel and withdraw. During the withdrawal the 2d Battalion, an untried unit, scattered in panic. That evening 119 of its men were still missing.[54]

In this frantic departure from its position on 26 July, the 2d Battalion left behind a switchboard, an emergency lighting unit, and weapons of all types. After daylight truck drivers and platoon sergeants returned to the scene and recovered 14 machine guns, 9 radios, 120 M1 rifles, 26 carbines, 7 BAR's, and 6 60-mm. mortars.[55]

While this untoward incident was taking place in their rear, other elements of the 1st Cavalry Division held their defensive positions east of Yongdong. The *7th Regiment* of the N.K. *3d Division,* meanwhile, started southwest from Yongdong on the Muju road in a sweeping flank movement through Chirye against Kumch'on, twenty air miles eastward. That night, elements of the enemy division in Yongdong attacked the 1st Cavalry troops east of the town. Four enemy tanks and an infantry force started this action by driving several hundred refugees ahead of them through American mine fields. Before daybreak the 1st Cavalry Division had repulsed the attack.[56]

Patrols reported to General Gay's headquarters that enemy troops were moving around the division's left flank in the direction of Chirye. On his right flank at the same time there was a question whether the 27th Infantry could hold. These developments caused General Gay to decide that although he was under no immediate enemy pressure he would have to withdraw or his division would be cut off from Taegu. Accordingly, he ordered a withdrawal to the vicinity of Kumch'on where he considered the terrain excellent for defense. This withdrawal began on 29 July after

---

[53] 27th Inf WD: Hist Rpt 28–29 Jul 50; Opn Rpt, 1st Bn, 27–29 Jul 50; an. 2, 29–31 Jul 50; Opn Sec, 6–31 Jul 50; S–1 Sec, Cumulative Casualties; S–2 Sec, Act Rpt, Jul 50; 1st Cav Div WD, 28–29 Jul 50; ATIS Res Supp Interrog Rpts, Issue 94, p. 36.
[54] 7th Cav Regt WD, 26 Jul 50; 1st Cav Div WD, 26 Jul 50; Ltr, Gay to author, 24 Aug 53.

[55] 7th Cav Regt WD, 26 Jul 50.
[56] ATIS Res Supp Interrog Rpts, Issue 96 (N.K. *3d Div*), p. 33; 1st Cav Div WD, 26–27 Jul 50; Ltr, Gay to author, 24 Aug 53; New York *Times,* July 27, 1950.

the 27th Infantry had passed east through the division's lines.[57]

The 1st Cavalry Division took up new defensive positions around Kumch'on, an important road center thirty air miles northwest of Taegu. The 8th Cavalry Regiment went into position astride the Sangju road north of the town; the 5th Cavalry blocked the Chirye road southwest of it; the 7th Cavalry Regiment remained in its Hwanggan position until the other units had withdrawn, and then it fell back to a position on the Yongdong road about six miles northwest of Kumch'on.

The enemy flanking movement under way to the southwest through the Chirye area threatened the division's rear and communications with Taegu. Eighth Army strengthened the 1st Cavalry Division against this threat by attaching to it the 3d Battalion, 21st Infantry. This battalion had the mission of establishing a roadblock ten miles southwest of Kumch'on near Hawan-ni on the Chirye road.[58] This proved to be a timely and wise move, for, on this very day, the enemy *7th Regiment* began arriving at Chirye, only a few miles farther down the road.

That morning, 29 July, a platoon-sized patrol of the 16th Reconnaissance Company under Lt. Lester Lauer drove southwest through Chirye. Later in the morning, Korean police informed Lauer that an enemy battalion was in Chirye. He radioed this information to the Reconnaissance Company and asked for instructions. The company commander, Capt. Charles V. H. Harvey, decided to take another platoon to the assistance of the one beyond Chirye. He set out immediately from Kumch'on with the platoon and fourteen South Korean police. At the outskirts of Chirye this force surprised and killed three enemy soldiers. Beyond Chirye the little column drew scattered rifle fire. The two platoons joined forces at noon and started back.

In the northern part of Chirye, which Harvey's column entered cautiously, the lead vehicles came upon a partially built roadblock from which an estimated enemy platoon opened fire on the column. Harvey ordered his little column to smash through the roadblock. The M39 vehicle pushed aside the wagon and truck that constituted the partially built block, but only one jeep was able to follow it through. Enemy machine gun fire disabled the next vehicle in line; thus the northern exit from Chirye was closed.[59] Several hundred enemy were now in view, moving to surround the patrol.

The patrol pulled back to the south edge of town, set up three 81-mm. mortars, and began firing on the enemy machine gun positions. Cpl. Harry D. Mitchell, although wounded four times and bleeding profusely, stayed with his mortar and fired it until his ammunition was expended. Captain Harvey early in the fight had received a bullet through one hand, and now machine gun fire struck him again, this time cutting his jugular vein. He did not respond to first aid treatment and died in a few

---

[57] ATIS Res Supp Interrog Rpts, Issue 96 (N.K. *3d Div*), p. 33; 1st Cav Div WD, 26–27 Jul 50; Ltr, Gay to author, 24 Aug 53.

[58] 1st Cav Div WD, 28–29 Jul 50; Ltr, Gay to author, 24 Aug 53.

[59] 1st Cav Div WD, 29 Jul 50; Rogers, History of the 16th Reconnaissance Company in Korea.

minutes. His last order was for the company to withdraw.

Three officers and forty-one enlisted men, abandoning their vehicles and heavier equipment, gained the nearest hill. They walked all night—an estimated thirty-five miles—and reached 1st Cavalry Division lines the next morning. The 16th Reconnaissance Company in this incident lost 2 killed, 3 wounded, and 11 missing.

The Chirye action made clear that a strong enemy force was approaching the rear of, or passing behind, the 1st Cavalry Division positions at Kumch'on. The next day, 30 July, General Gay ordered the 1st Battalion, 5th Cavalry; the 3d Battalion, 21st Infantry; and the 99th Field Artillery Battalion to Chirye. This strong force was able to enter the town, but the enemy held the hills around it. The next day North Koreans shelled Chirye, forcing the Americans to withdraw to a position northeast of the town.[60] The enemy *8th Regiment* together with its artillery now joined the other North Koreans already at Chirye. This meant that the bulk of the division was engaged in the enveloping move.

On 31 July the N.K. *3d Division* was closing on Kumch'on. About daylight a squad of North Koreans infiltrated into the command post of the 8th Engineer Combat Battalion, 1,000 yards from the 1st Cavalry Division command post, and killed four men and wounded six others. Among the latter was the battalion executive officer who died subsequently of his wounds. The 7th Cavalry also came under attack. But in pressing forward the North Koreans exposed their tanks. Air and ground fire power reportedly destroyed thirteen of them and set six more on fire.[61]

During its first ten days of action in Korea the 1st Cavalry Division had 916 battle casualties—78 killed, 419 wounded, and 419 missing.[62]

The N.K. *3d Division* in forcing the 1st Cavalry Division from Yongdong and back on Kumch'on apparently suffered nearly 2,000 casualties, which reduced it to a strength of about 5,000 men. Nevertheless, it had effectively and quickly driven the 1st Cavalry Division toward the Naktong. For its operations in the Yongdong-Kumch'on area the N.K. *3d Division* received the honorary title of Guards.[63]

"Stand or Die"

On Wednesday, 26 July, Eighth Army had issued an operational directive indicating that the army would move to prepared positions, stabilize the front line, and maintain a position from which it could initiate offensive action. The time of the movement was to be announced later. During the withdrawal, units were to maintain contact with the enemy.[64] Three days later, on 29 July, General Walker issued his much discussed "stand or die" order and seemingly ruled out

---

[60] 1st Cav Div WD, 30-31 Jul 50; ATIS Supp, Enemy Docs, Issue 4, p. 69 (Battle Rpt of Arty Opns, N.K. *8th Regt, 3d Div*, 3 Aug 50); *Ibid.*, Issue 2, pp. 66-67 (Choe Song Hwan diary, 21 Jul-10 Aug 50).

[61] 1st Cav Div WD, 31 Jul 50; *Ibid.*, G-2 Narr Rpt, 31 Jul 50.
[62] *Ibid.*, Summ, Jul 50.
[63] ATIS Res Supp Interrog Rpts, Issue 96 (N.K. *3d Div*), p. 33; GHQ FEC, History of the N.K. Army, p. 57.
[64] EUSAK WD, G-3 Stf Sec Rpt, 26 Jul 50.

the previously announced withdrawal. The actual withdrawal of Eighth Army behind the Naktong River in the first days of August further confused the issue.

What prompted General Walker to issue his 29 July "stand or die" order?

For several days both the 25th Infantry and the 1st Cavalry Divisions had been withdrawing steadily in the face of North Korean attacks, often in circumstances that seemed not to justify it, and with troops in panic and out of control. General Walker was disappointed and upset over the performance of the 25th Division in the Sangju area and he made this feeling known to General Kean, the division commander.[65]

General Walker was also disappointed over the inability of the 1st Cavalry Division to check the advance of the enemy on the Taejon-Taegu axis. This was apparent on the afternoon on 29 July when he visited the division command post in a little schoolhouse at Kumch'on. He questioned the withdrawals and ordered that there be no more. General Gay replied that he himself did not know whether the withdrawals had been sound, but that he had feared his communications to the rear would be cut. General Gay had served as Chief of Staff for General Patton's Third Army in Europe in World War II. This, his initial experience in Korea, was a defensive operation and, as he has since said, "he didn't know what to do about it." And always General Walker's earlier admonition to him in Taegu rang in his ears.[66]

General Walker himself was a most determined commander. His bulldog tenacity became a byword in Korea and it was one of the decisive factors in the summer battles of 1950. These characteristics caused him to smart all the more under the poor showing of many of the American units. He understood well the great problem of maintaining morale in his command at a time when Eighth Army was retreating rapidly toward its base of supply and, unless checked, would soon have its back to the sea.

On 26 July, the day Eighth Army issued its warning order for a planned withdrawal to a defensive position, General Walker telephoned General MacArthur's headquarters in Tokyo. General Almond, MacArthur's Chief of Staff, took the call. General Walker asked for authority to move Eighth Army headquarters from Taegu to Pusan immediately for security of the army communications equipment which was virtually irreplaceable if destroyed or lost. He said the enemy was approaching too close to Taegu for its safety there. There was no indication in this conversation that General Walker contemplated having the army's tactical units themselves fall back on Pusan. The withdrawals to a planned position Walker then had in mind would bring the enemy to the Naktong River. General Almond told Walker over the telephone that he would transmit the request to General MacArthur, but that he personally thought such a move at that time would have a very bad effect on Eighth Army units and

---

[65] Interv, author with Lt Col Paul F. Smith 1 Oct 52; Ltr, Landrum to author, recd 23 Nov 53; Colllier, MS review comments, Mar 58.

[66] Ltr, Gay to author, 24 Aug 53.

THE FRONT LINE MOVES SOUTH

also on the ROK troops. It might lead to the belief that Eighth Army could not stay in Korea and might be the forerunner of a general debacle.[67]

At the conclusion of the telephone conversation with Walker, General Almond related the substance of it to General MacArthur, strongly recommending that the latter fly to Korea at once —the next day—to talk with Walker. Almond said he felt the situation in Korea was critical and demanded the personal attention of the Far East commander. MacArthur said he would think about it. Half an hour later he directed Almond to arrange for the flight to Korea the next morning. Almond notified Walker that evening of the projected trip.

Thursday morning early, 27 July, the *Bataan* departed Haneda Airfield and landed at Taegu about 1000. A small group of officers, including General Almond, accompanied MacArthur. Met by Generals Walker and Partridge and Colonel Landrum, the party went directly to Eighth Army headquarters.

During a ninety-minute conference between General MacArthur and General Walker only one other person was present—General Almond. In this lengthy conversation General MacArthur never mentioned Walker's request of the day before, nor did he in any way criticize Walker. But he did emphasize the necessity of Eighth Army standing its ground. He said withdrawals must cease. Later, after lunch and in the presence of several members of the army staff, MacArthur said there would be no evacuation from Korea—that there would be no Korean Dunkerque. He praised the 24th Division and the ROK Capital Division.[68]

Two days later, on Saturday, 29 July, General Walker visited the 25th Division command post at Sangju. There he conferred with General Kean and afterward spoke to the division staff and issued his order to hold the line. The press widely reported this as a "stand or die" order to Eighth Army. A paraphrase of Walker's talk, recorded in notes taken at the time, gives a clear version of what he said:

General MacArthur was over here two days ago; he is thoroughly conversant with the situation. He knows where we are and what we have to fight with. He knows our needs and where the enemy is hitting the hardest. General MacArthur is doing everything possible to send reinforcements. A Marine unit and two regiments are expected in the next few days to reinforce us. Additional units are being sent over as quickly as possible. We are fighting a battle against time. There will be no more

---

[67] Interv, author with Almond, 13 Dec 51. Even the principal members of General Walker's Eighth Army staff knew nothing of this matter. General Landrum and Colonel Collier, on intimate personal terms with General Walker, indicate that there was no plan in the Eighth Army staff or in the Signal Section for such a move to Pusan at that time; that, in the long-range planning initiated some days later, the proposed site of a rear command post was Ulsan on the east coast and not Pusan; that General Walker would not discuss a removal of the command post from Taegu with his staff until late August, when considerable danger existed that the signal equipment might be destroyed; and that no responsible member of the Army staff had at that time proposed a move of the command post to Pusan. See Ltr, Landrum to author, rec'd 23 Nov 53; Colllier, MS review comments, Mar 58; Interv, author with Col Albert K. Stebbins (EUSAK G-4 at the time), 4 Dec 53.

[68] Interv, author with Almond, 13 Dec 51; Ltr, Landrum to author, rec'd 23 Nov 53; EUSAK WD, G-3 Stf Sec Rpt, 27 Jul 50; New York *Times*, July 27, 1950. General MacArthur read this passage in MS form and offered no comment on it.

retreating, withdrawal, or readjustment of the lines or any other term you choose. There is no line behind us to which we can retreat. Every unit must counterattack to keep the enemy in a state of confusion and off balance. There will be no Dunkirk, there will be no Bataan, a retreat to Pusan would be one of the greatest butcheries in history. We must fight until the end. Capture by these people is worse than death itself. We will fight as a team. If some of us must die, we will die fighting together. Any man who gives ground may be personally responsible for the death of thousands of his comrades.

I want you to put this out to all the men in the Division. I want everybody to understand that we are going to hold this line. We are going to win.[69]

General Walker said much the same thing to his other division commanders at this time, but he did not repeat it to the other division staffs.

General Walker's words reached down quickly to every soldier, with varying results. Many criticized the order because they thought it impossible to execute. One responsible officer with troops at the time seems to have expressed this viewpoint, saying that the troops interpreted it as meaning, "Stay and die where you are." They neither understood nor accepted this dictum in a battle situation where the enemy seldom directed his main effort at their front but moved around the flanks to the rear when, generally, there were no friendly units on their immediate flanks.[70]

A contrary viewpoint about the order was expressed by a regimental commander who said he and the men in his command had a great sense of relief when the order reached them. They felt the day of withdrawals was over, and "a greater amount of earth came out with each shovelful" when the troops dug in.[71]

Whatever the individual viewpoint about the order might have been, General Walker was faced with the fact that soon there would be no place to go in the next withdrawal except into the sea. And it must be said, too, that the troops very often were not fighting in position until they were threatened with encirclement—they left their positions long before that time had arrived. It was actually this condition to which General Walker had addressed his strong words. But they did not immediately change the course of events.

Two days after Walker had spoken at Sangju, the 25th Division ordered its troops to withdraw to positions three miles east of the town—another withdrawal. On the Kumch'on front an observer saw elements of the 1st Cavalry Division come off their positions—leaving behind heavy equipment—load into trucks, and once again move to the rear.[72]

A New York *Times* article on General Walker's talk to the 25th Division staff commented that it apparently ruled out the possibility of a strategic withdrawal to the Pusan Perimeter. William H. Lawrence of the New York *Times* asked General Walker if he thought the battle had reached a critical point. General Walker replied, "very certainly, very definitely." The next day the *Times* ran an edi-

---

[69] 25th Div WD, G-3 Jnl, 29 Jul 50, Div Historian's Notes; Barth MS, p. 9.

[70] Interv, author with Maj Leon B. Cheek, 7 Aug 51. The author has listened to many similar comments among officers and men of the Eighth Army with respect to this order.

[71] Fisher, MS review comments, 27 Oct 57.

[72] 25th Div WD, 31 Jul 50; Charles and Eugene Jones, *The Face of War* (New York: Prentice-Hall Inc., 1951), p. 22.

torial headed, "Crisis in Korea." It said the "critical point in the defense of Korea has already been reached or will shortly be upon us. For five weeks we have been trading space for time. The space is running out for us. The time is running out for our enemies." [73]

On 30 July General Walker softened somewhat the impact of his recent order and statements by expressing confidence that the United States would hold "until reinforcements arrive" and that "ultimate victory will be ours." But, he added, the simple truth was that the "war had reached its critical stage." [74]

A few days later, Hanson W. Baldwin, the military critic of the New York *Times*, referred to Walker's "stand or die" order as a "well merited rebuke to the Pentagon, which has too often disseminated a soothing syrup of cheer and sweetness and light since the fighting began." [75] It is clear that by the end of July the reading public in the United States should have realized that the country was in a real war, that the outcome was in doubt, and that many uncertainties lay ahead.

The optimistic forecasts of the first days of the war as to the American military strength needed to drive the invaders northward had now given way to more realistic planning. By 22 July, some Eighth Army staff officers had even suggested that it might be necessary to deploy ground troops in Korea until the spring of 1951, to accomplish the objectives stated in the U.N. Security Council resolutions.[76]

---

[73] New York *Times*, July 29, 30 (Lawrence dispatch), and 31, 1950.
[74] New York *Times*, July 31, 1950.

[75] New York *Times*, August 2, 1950.
[76] EUSAK WD, G-4 Sec, 22 Jul 50, Basis for Planning Supply Requisitions and Service Support for Military Operations in Korea to 1 July 1951.

CHAPTER XIII

The Enemy Flanks Eighth Army in the West

The smallest detail, taken from the actual incident in war, is more instructive for me, a soldier, than all the Thiers and Jominis in the world. They speak, no doubt, for the heads of states and armies but they never show me what I wish to know—a battalion, a company, a squad, in action.

ARDANT DU PICQ, *Battle Studies*

The N.K. *6th*, farthest to the west of the enemy divisions, had a special mission. After the fall of Seoul, it followed the N.K. *3d* and *4th* Divisions across the Han as far as Ch'onan. There the N.K. Army issued new orders to it, and pursuant to them on 11 July it turned west off the main highway toward the west coast. For the next two weeks the division passed from the view of Eighth Army intelligence. Various intelligence summaries carried it as location unknown, or placed it vaguely in the northwest above the Kum River.

Actually, the *6th Division* was moving rapidly south over the western coastal road net. Its shadow before long would turn into a pall of gloom and impending disaster over the entire U.N. plan to defend southern Korea. Its maneuver was one of the most successful of either Army in the Korean War. It compelled the redisposition of Eighth Army at the end of July and caused Tokyo and Washington to alter their plans for the conduct of the war.

Departing Yesan on 13 July, the N.K. *6th Division* started south in two columns and crossed the lower Kum River. (*See Map III.*) The larger force appeared before Kunsan about the time the *3d* and *4th Divisions* attacked Taejon. The port town fell to the enemy without resistance. The division's two columns united in front of Chonju, thirty miles to the southeast, and quickly reduced that town, which was defended by ROK police.[1]

The N.K. *6th Division* was now poised to make an end run through southwest Korea toward Pusan, around the left flank of Eighth Army. In all Korea southwest of the Taejon-Taegu-Pusan highway, at this time, there were only a few hundred survivors of the ROK 7th

---
[1] ATIS Res Supp Interrog Rpts, Issue 100 (N.K. 6th Div), pp. 33-35; GHQ FEC Sitrep, 20 Jul 50.

Division, some scattered ROK marines, and local police units.[2]

The *6th Division* departed Chonju on or about 20 July. At Kwangju on 23 July the three regiments of the division separated. The *13th* went southwest to Mokp'o on the coast, the *14th* south to Posong, and the *15th* southeast through Sunch'on to Yosu on the southern coast. The division encountered little resistance during this week of almost constant movement. About 25 July, it reassembled at Sunch'on, ninety air miles west of Pusan, and made ready for its critical drive eastward toward that port. Logistically, the division was poorly prepared for this operation. Its supply was poor and rations were cut in half and on some days there were none.[3]

Advancing next on Chinju, General Pang Ho San, commander of the N.K. *6th Division,* proclaimed to his troops on the eve of the advance, "Comrades, the enemy is demoralized. The task given us is the liberation of Masan and Chinju and the annihilation of the remnants of the enemy. . . . The liberation of Chinju and Masan means the final battle to cut off the windpipe of the enemy.[4]

Everywhere refugees fled the terror sweeping over southwest Korea with the advance of the North Korean Army and guerrilla units. An entry on 29 July in the diary of a guerrilla tellingly illustrates the reasons for panic: "Apprehended 12 men; National Assembly members, police sergeants and Myon leaders. Killed four of them at the scene, and the remaining eight were shot after investigation by the People's court."[5]

Walker Acts

During the battle for Taejon, U.N. aerial observers had reported enemy movements south of the Kum River near the west coast. U.N. intelligence mistakenly concluded that these troops were elements of the N.K. *4th Division*. A report from the Far East Command to Washington on 21 July noted this enemy movement and attributed it to that division. The next day a similar report from the Far East Command stated, "The 4th North Korean Division . . . has been picked up in assemblies in the vicinity of Nonsan." Enemy forces in battalion and regimental strength, the report said, were moving in a "southward trend, colliding with local police forces." General MacArthur's headquarters considered this "a very bold movement, evidently predicated on the conviction of the enemy high command that the Allied units are potentially bottled up in the mountainous areas northeast of the headwaters of the Kum River. . . . The potential of the advance of the enemy *4th Division* to the south is altogether uncomfortable, since at the moment, except for air strikes, there is no organized force capable of firm resistance, except local police units."[6]

---

[2] EUSAK WD, Briefing for CG and G-3 Sec, 20 Jul 50.
[3] ATIS Res Supp Interrog Rpts, Issue 100 (N.K. 6th Div), p. 36. The dates given in the enemy interrogations are often erroneous by one to several days, dependent as they are on human memory. They always have to be checked against U.S. records.
[4] ATIS Res Supp Interrog Rpts, Issue 100 (N.K. 6th Div), p. 37.

[5] ATIS Res Supp Interrog Rpts, Issue 2, pp. 86–89, Notebook, Itinerary of Guerrilla Band, 4 Jul–3 Aug 50.
[6] Telecons, Tokyo to Washington, TT 3559, 21 Jul 50, and TT 3563, 22 Jul 50.

General Walker knew enemy units were moving south of the Kum River into southwest Korea and maintained aerial observation of the roads there when flying weather conditions permitted. His intelligence section wanted distant armored reconnaissance of this region, but the armored vehicles and personnel to carry it out were not available. In addition to aerial reconnaissance, however, there were the many reports from local South Korean police units. These often were vague, conflicting, and, it was thought, exaggerated [7]

On 21-22 July, heavy overcast prevented aerial reconnaissance and permitted the enemy to put his columns on the road during daylight and to move rapidly without fear of aerial attack. Alarm at Eighth Army headquarters began to grow. The Fifth Air Force had moved its advance headquarters from Itazuke, Japan, to Taegu on 16 July. The most advanced air bases in Japan—Itazuke and Ashiya—were hardly close enough to the battle area of early and middle July to allow more than fifteen to twenty minutes of support by jet fighters. When weather was bad the F-80 jets could scarcely fly a mission at the front and get back to Itazuke. Effective 24 July, the advance group of the Air Force was designated as the Fifth Air Force in Korea. Fair weather returned on 23 July, and General Walker requested the Fifth Air Force to fly an armed reconnaissance of the Kwangju-Nonsan area.[8]

When General Walker asked for aerial reconnaissance of southwest Korea on 23 July, he had at hand a G-2 estimate of the enemy situation in the west below the Kum, just provided at his request. This estimate postulated that elements of one division were in the southwest. It estimated the rate of progress at two miles an hour and calculated that if the enemy turned east he could reach the Anui-Chinju line in the Chiri Mountains by 25 July.[9] This proved to be an accurate forecast.

The air reconnaissance carried out on 23 July was revealing. It showed that enemy forces had indeed begun a drive south from the estuary of the Kum River and were swinging east behind the left (west) flank of Eighth Army.[10]

On the basis of the time and space estimate given him on the 23d and the aerial reconnaissance of the same date, General Walker realized that a major crisis was developing in a section far behind the lines, and at a time when constant enemy attack was pushing his front back. On 24 July, Eighth Army made its first move to counter the threatened enemy envelopment in the southwest. General Walker decided to send the 24th Division posthaste southward to block the enemy enveloping move. He also directed his chief of staff, Colonel Landrum, personally to make sure that the Fifth Air Force made a major effort

---

[7] Telephone interv, author with Lt Col James C. Tarkenton, Jr. (Eighth Army G-2 in 1950), 3 Oct 52. Colonel Tarkenton said that at this time he used two L-4 planes to fly daily reconnaissance to the west coast below the Kum River. Information also came from aerial combat missions.

[8] EUSAK WD, G-3 Sec, 23 Jul 50; Landrum, Notes for author, n.d., but received 8 Mar 54; New York Times, July 23, 1950; USAF Hist Study 71, pp. 15-16, 20.

[9] EUSAK WD, G-2 Stf Rpt, 23 Jul 50; Interv, author with Tarkenton, 3 Oct 52.

[10] EUSAK WD, G-3 Sec, 24 Jul 50.

against the enemy forces in southwest Korea.[11]

At noon on the 24th, General Walker asked General Church, the new commander of the 24th Division, to come to Eighth Army headquarters in Taegu. There Walker informed him of the threat in the southwest and told him that he would have to move the 24th Division to the sector. "I am sorry to have to do this," he said, "but the whole left flank is open, and reports indicate the Koreans are moving in. I want you to cover the area from Chinju up to near Kumch'on."[12] The two places General Walker mentioned are sixty-five air miles apart and separated by the wild Chiri Mountains.

General Church had assumed command of the 24th Division just the day before, on 23 July, after General Dean had been three days missing in action. The division had been out of the line and in army reserve just one day. It had not had time to re-equip and receive replacements for losses. The division supply officer estimated that 60 to 70 percent of the division's equipment would have to be replaced. All three regiments were far understrength.[13]

General Church immediately ordered the 19th Infantry to move to Chinju, and it started from Kumch'on shortly before midnight, 24 July. The next day, 25 July, at 1700, Eighth Army formally ordered the division, less the 21st Regiment, to defend the Chinju area.[14]

Eighth Army now had reports of 10 enemy tanks and 500 infantry in Mok'po at the southwest tip of the peninsula; 26 trucks and 700 soldiers in Namwon; tanks, trucks, and 800 soldiers in Kurye; and 500 enemy troops engaging South Korean police in Hadong.[15] The Eighth Army G-2 estimated at this time that the N.K. *4th Division* was dispersed over 3,300 square miles of southwest Korea.

On the morning of 25 July, Col. Ned D. Moore arrived at Chinju about 0600, preceding his 19th Infantry Regiment headquarters and the 2d Battalion, which reached the town at 1500 in the afternoon. Lt. Col. Robert L. Rhea, following with the 1st Battalion, remained behind on the Kumch'on road north of Chinju. There, at Anui, where a road came in from the west, Colonel Rhea placed A Company in a defensive position. The remainder of the battalion continued south eight miles to a main road junction at Umyong-ni (Sanggam on some old maps and Hwasan-ni on others), just east of Hamyang.[16]

The next day, 26 July, Col. Charles E. Beauchamp's 34th Infantry Regiment, on orders from General Church, moved from the Kunwi-Uisong area north of Taegu to Koch'ang. At the same time the 24th Division headquarters and divisional troops moved to Hyopch'on, where General Church established his

---

[11] Interv, author with Lt Col Paul F. Smith, 1 Oct 52; Landrum, Notes for author, recd 8 Mar 54.
[12] Interv, author with Church, 25 Sep 52.
[13] EUSAK WD, Summ, 12-31 Jul 50; 24th Div GO 52, 23 Jul 50; 24th Div WD, G-4 Hist Rpt, 23 Jul-25 Aug 50, p. 16.
At one point in his career, General Church had commanded the 157th Regiment at Anzio in World War II.

[14] 24th Div WD, Jul 50, 25-26 Jul; *Ibid.*, G-2 Jnl, entries 53, 241440 Jul 50, and 104, 2517000 Jul 50; EUSAK WD POR 36, 24 Jul 50.
[15] EUSAK PIR 13, 25 Jul 50; *Ibid.*, G-3 Jnl, 25 Jul 50; 24th Div WD, G-2 Jnl, entry 81, 250215, entry 1513, 251700, and entry 1491, 250530 Jul 50; Telecon, Tokyo to Washington, TT 3567, 24 Jul 50.
[16] Ltr, Col Robert L. Rhea to author, 21 Sep 53; Moore, Notes for author, Jul 53; 24th Div WD, 25-26 Jul 50.

command post. Hyopch'on is 12 air miles west of the Naktong River, 25 miles north of Chinju, and 15 miles southeast of Koch'ang. It was reasonably well centered in the vast area the division had to defend.[17]

Of the eleven infantry battalions requested by General MacArthur in early July to make up shortages within the infantry divisions of the Far East Command, two battalions from the 29th Infantry Regiment on Okinawa were the first to arrive in Korea. The history of these units between the time they were alerted for probable combat use in Korea and their commitment in battle shows the increasing sense of urgency that gripped the Far East Command in July, and how promises and estimates made one day in good faith had to be discarded the next because of the growing crisis in Korea. And it also shows how troops not ready for combat nevertheless suddenly found themselves in it.

About the middle of July, Maj. Tony J. Raibl, Executive Officer, 3d Battalion, 29th Infantry, learned in Tokyo that the Far East Command expected that the regiment would have at least six weeks' training before being sent to Korea.[18]

Yet, immediately after making that estimate, the Far East Command issued orders to the regiment on 15 July to prepare for movement. All troops were placed in two battalions, the 1st and 3d. Lt. Col. Wesley C. Wilson commanded the 1st Battalion and Lt. Col. Harold W. Mott, the 3d Battalion. The regimental headquarters was to remain behind as a nucleus for a new regiment that would assume responsibility for the ground defense of Okinawa.

The USS *Walker* arrived at Okinawa on the 20th with about 400 recruits. They were hastily disembarked and allowed to take with them only their toilet articles, driven to the battalion areas, assigned to companies, issued arms and field equipment, and moved back to the Naha docks. On 21 July the two battalions, now at full strength, loaded on board the *Fentriss* and *Takasago Maru* during a heavy rain and sailed for Pusan.

On 20 July at Yokohama, Major Raibl learned that the two battalions would not come to Japan but would sail directly for Korea, where they would receive at least ten days of intensive field training in the vicinity of Pusan before they would be committed. When Major Raibl arrived at Taegu on 22 July, he found Col. Allan D. MacLean, Eighth Army Assistant G–3, in no mood to listen to or discuss the lack of combat readiness of the 29th Infantry. Raibl talked at length with General Walker, who was sympathetic but indicated that the situation was urgent. When he left Taegu, Raibl understood that the two battalions would have a minimum of three days at Pusan to draw equipment and zero-in and test fire their weapons.[19]

---

[17] Interv, author with Beauchamp, 24 Sep 52; 24th Div WD, 26 Jul 50.

[18] Interv, author with Raibl, 7 Oct 53; Raibl, 10-page typescript statement prepared for author, 19 Oct 53, on events leading up to and participation of 3d Bn, 29th Inf, in action at Hadong; Ltr, Capt James E. Townes (S–4, 3d Bn, 29th Inf, Jul 50) to author, 8 Oct 53.

[19] Raibl, Statement for author, 19 Oct 53 Interv, author with Lt Col Charles E. Arnold (Ex Off, 1st Bn, 29th Inf, Jul 50), 22 Jul 51; Capt Sam C. Holliday, Notes prepared for author, 31 Mar 53, on 1st Bn, 29th Inf, 21 Jul–4 Aug 50 (Holliday was S–2, 1st Bn, in Jul 50); Ltr, Gen Wright to author, 9 Mar 54; 3d Bn, 27th Inf, Hist Rpt, 24 Jul–31 Aug 50 (3d Bn, 29th Inf, in Jul 50).

Instead, when the two battalions disembarked at Pusan the morning of 24 July orders from Eighth Army awaited them to proceed to Chinju. There they would be attached to the 19th Infantry Regiment. The next afternoon the two battalions arrived at Chinju. Instead of the six weeks of training first agreed upon, they found themselves now in a forward position, rifles not zeroed, mortars not test-fired, and new .50-caliber machine guns with cosmoline rubbed off but not cleaned.[20]

That evening, 25 July, Colonel Mott received orders from Colonel Moore, commanding the 19th Infantry at Chinju, to seize Hadong, a road junction point thirty-five miles southwest of Chinju. Colonel Moore said that about 500 N.K. troops were moving on Hadong and comprised the nearest enemy organized resistance. Maj. Gen. Chae Byong Duk, formerly ROK Army Chief of Staff and now in Chinju, urged on Colonel Moore the importance of Hadong in controlling the western approach to Chinju and the desirability of holding it. He offered to accompany any force sent to Hadong. Colonel Moore gave Chae permission to accompany the troops; he had no command function—he was merely to serve as an interpreter, guide, and adviser to Colonel Mott.[21]

The Trap at Hadong

At dusk, 25 July, the 3d Battalion issued a warning order to its units to be prepared to move at 2230 that night, with the mission of seizing Hadong. Colonel Mott and Major Raibl based their plans on the assumption that the battalion would reach Hadong before daylight. They expected that some enemy troops would already be in the town.

Half an hour after midnight the motorized battalion started for Hadong. General Chae and some other ROK officers guided the column south out of Chinju through Konyang, where it turned north to strike the main Chinju-Hadong road at Wonjon. In taking this route they had detoured from the direct road because of an impassable ford. The column spent the entire night trying to negotiate the narrow road and pulling vehicles out of rice paddies.[22]

A little after daylight, the battalion encountered a truck traveling south containing 15 to 20 badly shot-up South Koreans. They claimed to be the only survivors of about 400 local militia at Hadong, which the North Koreans had attacked the night before. Pondering this grave information, Colonel Mott led the battalion on to Wonjon on the main road. There he halted the battalion for breakfast and set up security positions. Mott and Raibl decided that Colonel Moore should know about the happenings at Hadong and, since the battalion did not have radio communication with the 19th Infantry in Chinju, Raibl set out by jeep to tell him.

At Chinju, Raibl told Colonel Moore and Major Logan the story related by the wounded South Koreans. He requested authority for the 3d Battalion,

---

[20] EUSAK WD, POR 36, 24 Jul 50; *Ibid.*, G-4 Sec, 24 Jul 50.

[21] Raibl Statement, 19 Oct 53; Interv, author with Raibl, 7 Oct 53; Interv, author with Maj George F. Sharra (CO L Co, 29th Inf, Jul 50), 20 Oct 53; Interv, author with Col Moore, 20 Aug 52.

[22] Raibl Statement, 19 Oct 53; Intervs, author with Raibl, 7 Oct 53, and Sharra, 20 Oct 53.

29th Infantry, to dig in on a defensive position west of Chinju to cover the Hadong road. After considerable discussion, Colonel Moore told Raibl that the battalion should continue on and seize Hadong. Major Raibl accepted the order reluctantly since he thought the battalion could not accomplish this mission. Major Raibl returned to Wonjon shortly after noon and informed Colonel Mott of the instructions.

Colonel Mott stopped the battalion at dusk at the village of Hoengch'on, situated about three miles from Hadong on a bend of the tortuous mountain road.

An Air Force captain with a radio jeep and a tactical air control party arrived a little later. His mission was to direct air strikes the next day and provide communication for the battalion. But en route his radio had become defective and now he could not establish communication with Chinju.

The battalion moved out from Hoengch'on-ni at approximately 0845, 27 July. Capt. George F. Sharra and L Company, with a platoon of the Heavy Weapons Company, were in the lead, followed by the battalion command group and K, M, and I Companies, in that order. Sharra was an experienced rifle company commander, having seen action in Africa, Sicily, France, and Germany in World War II.

When he was about 1,000 yards from the top of the Hadong pass, Sharra saw a patrol of ten or twelve enemy soldiers come through the pass and start down toward him. The Heavy Weapons platoon fired their two 75-mm. recoilless rifles at the patrol but the rounds passed harmlessly overhead. The enemy patrol turned and ran back over the pass. Captain Sharra ordered L Company to dash to the top of the pass and secure it. His men reached the top and deployed on either side of the pass. It was now about 0930. Sharra received orders for L Company to dig in and wait for an air strike on Hadong scheduled for 0945.[23]

The road climbed to the top of the pass along the southern shoulder of a high mountain in a series of snakelike turns, and then started downward to Hadong a mile and a half westward. A high peak on the right (north) towered over the road at the pass; to the left the ground dropped away rapidly to flat paddy land along the Sumjin River.

The command group, including Colonel Mott, Captain Flynn, and most of the battalion staff, now hurried forward to the pass. General Chae and his party accompanied Colonel Mott. Captain Sharra pointed out to Colonel Mott unidentified people moving about on the higher ground some distance to the north. Mott looked and replied, "Yes, I have K Company moving up there." Raibl, at the rear of the column, received orders from Mott to join him at the pass, and he hurried forward.

As the battalion command group gathered in the pass, Captain Sharra, thinking that it made an unusually attractive target, walked over to the left and dropped to the ground beside the gunner of a light machine gun.

Raibl arrived at the pass. He saw that L Company was deployed with two platoons on the left of the pass and one platoon on the right, and that K Com-

---

[23] Raibl Statement, 19 Oct 53; Interv, author with Maj Robert M. Flynn, 5 Nov 53 (Flynn was S-3, 3d Bn, 29th Inf, in Jul 50); 25th Div WD, 3d Bn, 27th Inf, Hist Rpt, 24 Jul-31 Aug 50.

pany was climbing toward higher ground farther to the north.

Colonel Mott directed Raibl's attention down the road toward Hadong. Around a curve came a column of enemy soldiers marching on either side of the road. Sharra also saw it. He directed his machine gunner to withold fire until the column was closer and he gave the word. The enemy soldiers seemed unaware that American troops were occupying the pass.

Standing beside Raibl in the pass, General Chae watched the approaching soldiers, apparently trying to determine their identity. Some appeared to be wearing American green fatigue uniforms and others the mustard brown of the North Korean Army. When the approaching men were about 100 yards away, General Chae shouted to them in Korean, apparently asking their identity. At this, they scampered to the ditches without answering. The machine guns of L Company then opened fire. Sharra, who had the column in clear view, estimates it comprised a company.[24]

Almost simultaneously with the opening of American fire, enemy machine gun, mortar, and small arms fire swept over the pass from the high ground to the north. The first burst of enemy machine gun fire struck General Chae in the head and a great stream of blood spurted from the wound. He died instantly. Korean aides carried his body back to a vehicle. The same machine gun fire hit Major Raibl. He rolled down the incline to get out of the line of fire. Colonel Mott, the S–2, and the Assistant S–2 were also wounded by this initial enemy fire into the pass. Enemy mortars apparently had been registered on the pass, for their first rounds fell on the road and knocked out parked vehicles, including the TACP radio jeep. Captain Flynn, unhurt, dropped to the ground and rolled down from the pass. In the first minute of enemy fire the 3d Battalion staff was almost wiped out.

Just after the fight opened, Major Raibl saw two flights of two planes each fly back and forth over the area, apparently trying vainly to contact the TACP below. They finally flew off without making any strikes. Raibl was wounded again by mortar fragments and went down the hill seeking a medical aid man. Meanwhile, Colonel Mott, wounded only slightly by a bullet crease across the back, got out of the line of fire. He was just below the pass helping to unload ammunition when a box dropped, breaking his foot. A soldier dug him a foxhole. As the fighting developed, everyone in Mott's vicinity was either killed or wounded, or had withdrawn down the hill. Very soon, it appears, no one knew where Mott was.[25]

In the pass a hard fight flared between L Company and the North Koreans higher up the hill. On the righthand (north) side of the road, 2d Lt. J. Morrissey and his 1st Platoon bore the brunt of this fight. The enemy was just above them and the machine gun that had all but wiped out the battalion group in the road was only 200 yards from the pass. Enemy soldiers immediately came in be-

---

[24] Raibl statement, 19 Oct 53; Intervs, author with Raibl, 7 Oct 53, Sharra, 20 Oct 53, and Flynn, 5 Nov 53; Interv, author with Capt Kenneth W. Hughes (who commanded the advanced mortar platoon at Hadong), 21 Jul 51. All these men saw the incident described and agree on the essentials.

[25] Intervs, author with Raibl, 7 Oct 53, Flynn, 5 Nov 53, and Sharrra, 20 Oct 53.

HADONG

tween them and elements of K Company that were trying to climb the hill higher up. These North Koreans attacked Morrissey's men in their foxholes, bayoneting two of them. Morrissey proved a capable leader, however, and his men held their position despite numerous casualties.

Across the road on the south side of the pass, Captain Sharra and the 2d Platoon gave supporting fire to Morrissey's men. Sharra had only voice communication with his three platoons. It is a tribute to the officers, the noncommissioned officers, and the rank and file, half of them young recruits freshly arrived from the United States, that L Company held steadfast in its positions on both sides of the pass against enemy fire and attack from commanding terrain. The North Korean soldiers exposed themselves recklessly and many must have been killed or wounded.

Captain Flynn hastened down from the pass at the beginning of the fight to hurry up the supporting elements of the battalion. Down the road he found part of the Heavy Weapons Company and part of K Company. He ordered a platoon of K Company to attack up the hill, and talked by radio with the company commander, Capt. Joseph K. Donahue, who was killed later in the day. Flynn continued on down the road looking for I Company.

Coming to the battalion trains, Flynn had the wounded, including Major Raibl, loaded on the trucks and started them back to Chinju. Farther in the rear, Flynn found 1st Lt. Alexander G. Makarounis and I Company. He ordered Makarounis to move the company

HADONG PASS *where men of the 29th Regiment were ambushed.*

into the gap between L and K Companies. Flynn started one of its platoons under MSgt. James A. Applegate into the rice paddies on the left of the road, where he thought it could get cover from the dikes in crossing a large, horseshoe-shaped bowl in its advance toward the enemy-held hill mass.[26]

About noon, 2d Lt. Ernest Philips of L Company came to Captain Sharra in the pass and told him he had found Colonel Mott, wounded, a short distance away. Philips went back and carried Mott to Sharra's position. Mott told Sharra to take over command of the battalion and to get it out.

Sharra sent instructions to his three platoons to withdraw to the road at the foot of the pass. His runner to Lieutenant Morrissey and the 1st Platoon on the north side of the pass never reached them. As the L Company men arrived at the trucks they loaded on them, and at midafternoon started for Chinju.

On the way back to Chinju this group met B Battery, 13th Field Artillery Battalion, which had started for Hadong on Colonel Moore's orders at 0800 that morning. The artillery battery had moved slowly with many stops for reconnaissance. It now turned around and went back to Chinju, abandoning one 105-mm. howitzer and four 2½-ton trucks that became bogged down in rice paddies.[27]

Meanwhile, a radio message from Colo-

---

[26] Interv, author with Flynn, 5 Nov 53.

[27] 13th FA Bn WD, 27 Jul 50.

nel Mott reached Flynn near the top of the pass, ordering all elements still on the hill to withdraw. Flynn climbed to a point where he could call to Lieutenant Morrissey, still holding out on the right of the pass, and told him to withdraw.

Morrissey had twelve men left; he and one other were wounded. The unidentified Air Force captain with the TACP had fought all day as a rifleman with Morrissey's platoon and had distinguished himself by his bravery. Now he was either dead or missing. Captain Mitchell, the battalion S-2, likewise had fought all day as a rifleman but he lived to withdraw. Morrissey's riflemen fell back down the road to the waiting vehicles and wearily climbed in. When all were accounted for, Captain Flynn started them for Chinju. Then, getting into his own jeep, he found it would not run.

Flynn clambered down to the low ground south of the road. In the rice paddies he saw many men of I Company. Looking back at the pass he saw enemy troops coming down off the hill, perhaps a battalion or more of them. Mortar and machine gun fire now swept the paddy area. The men caught there had to cross a deep, 20-foot-wide stream to escape, and many drowned in the attempt. Most men rid themselves of helmet, shoes, nearly all clothing, and even their weapons in trying to cross this stream.

Flynn got across and, in a little valley about a mile and a half away, he found perhaps sixty to seventy other American soldiers. While they rested briefly, enemy fire suddenly came in on them from pursuers and they scattered like quail seeking cover. Flynn and three companions walked all night. The next afternoon his party, now numbering ten men, entered the lines of the 19th Infantry.

The largest single group of survivors escaped by going south to the seacoast, only a few miles distant. Sergeant Applegate of I Company led one group of ninety-seven men to the coast, where a Korean fishing vessel took them on board at Noryangjin, five miles south of Hadong. From there the vessel went west to a point near Yosu, where it transferred the men to a Korean naval patrol vessel which returned them to Pusan.[28]

The morning that Mott's battalion approached Hadong, 27 July, Captain Barszcz received orders to take his G Company, 19th Infantry, from Chinju on a motorized patrol along secondary roads northeast of Hadong. He mounted his seventy-eight men in vehicles and conducted the patrol about fourteen miles northeast of Hadong without encountering the enemy. In the afternoon Barszcz returned to the main Hadong-Chinju road near the village of Sigum, about twelve miles east of Hadong.

While he stopped there, an officer with about fifty men came down the road from the direction of Hadong. They told him they were all that were left of L Company. Most of the men were without clothing except for their shorts and boots. One M1 rifle, which apparently had not been fired, and a .45-caliber pistol were their only weapons. The L Company group explained their condition by saying they had to swim a river and wade through rice paddies. Barszcz relieved the group of the weapons, put the men on two trucks, and sent them down the road to Chinju.

---

[28] New York *Times*, July 29, 1950, R. J. H. Johnston dispatch.

THE ENEMY FLANKS EIGHTH ARMY IN THE WEST

Expecting more American stragglers from Hadong, Barszcz put G Company astride the road in a defensive position to cover their withdrawal. He had sent a message with the Chinju-bound trucks explaining what he had done and asked for further orders.[29] Barszcz held his roadblock east of Hadong until 0400 the morning of 28 July, when Captain Montesclaros from the staff of 2d Battalion, 19th Infantry, arrived with orders and trucks to take G Company back to a line of hills just west of the Nam River, about four miles from Chinju.[30]

At first, Colonel Moore had thought that the Hadong fight was going well. Major Raibl arrived at Chinju with the first wounded in the early afternoon of 27 July, and reported that the 3d Battalion was fighting well and that he thought it would win the battle. But, when other survivors came in later, the real outcome of the engagement became clear. News of the disaster at Hadong reached higher headquarters with unexpected and startling impact. A message from Major Logan, 19th Infantry, to General Church that night reporting on the condition of the 3d Battalion, 29th Infantry, said, "No estimate on total number of casualties. Over 100 WIA now in aid station" [31] A count the next day of the assembled 3d Battalion showed there were 354 officers and men, including some walking wounded, able for duty. When all the stragglers had come in, casualties were listed as 2 killed, 52 wounded, and 349 missing. An enemy soldier captured later said the North Koreans took approximately 100 American prisoners at Hadong. When American forces rewon the Hadong area in late September a search uncovered 313 American bodies, most of them along the river and in the rice paddies.[32]

The loss of key officers in the battalion was severe. It included the battalion executive officer, the S-1, the S-2, and the Assistant S-3. The company commanders of Headquarters, I, K, and M Companies were lost, Donahue of K and Capt. Hugh P. Milleson of M were killed, Makarounis of I was captured. (He escaped from the North Koreans in October near P'yongyang.) Approximately thirty vehicles and practically all the crew-served weapons, communication equipment, and even most of the individual weapons were lost.[33]

On 28 July, the day after Hadong, the 3d Battalion, 29th Infantry, was reorganized, all remaining personnel being grouped in K and L Companies. The next day, K Company was attached to the 2d Battalion, 19th Infantry, at Chinju, and L Company to the 1st Battalion, 19th Infantry, two miles to the south of Chinju.[34]

---

[29] Ltrs, Capt Michael Barszcz to author, 30 Jul and 21 Aug 52; Interv, Blumenson with Herbert (Plat Ldr, 1st Plat, G Co, 19th Inf, in Jul 50), 31 Jul 51, in OCMH files as Chinju Action.
[30] Ltrs, Barszcz to author, 30 Jul and 21 Aug 52; Intervs, author with McGrail and Montesclaros, 20 Aug 52.
[31] 24th Div WD, G-3 Jnl, entry 159, 27 Jul 50.

[32] 24th Div G-2 Jnl, entry, 1583, 272210 Jul 50; EUSAK WD, Br for CG, 27 Jul 50; 24th Div WD, G-3 Jnl, entry 206, 281245 Jul 50; 25th Div WD, 3d Bn, 27th Inf, Hist Rpt, 24 Jul-31 Aug 50; Ltr, Townes to author, 8 Oct 53; 25th Div WD, Aug 50, 35th Inf Interrog PW's (Ko Hei Yo). Major Sharra gave the author the figure of 313 American dead.
[33] 25th Div WD, 3d Bn, 27th Inf Hist Rpt, 24 Jul-31 Aug 50.
[34] 24th Div WD, 30 Jul 50.

The N.K. 4th Division Joins the Enveloping Move

After the fall of Taejon, the N.K. *4th Division* rested in the city for two days and took in 1,000 untrained replacements. On the morning of 23 July, it started south from Taejon on the Kumsan road. It was joining the *6th Division* in an envelopment of the United Nations' left flank. The *N.K. 6th Division* moved on an outer arc around the left of the U.N. position, the N.K. *4th Division* on an inner arc. The two divisions were engaging in a co-ordinated movement on a theater scale.[35] (*See Map III.*)

At Kumsan the *4th Division* received another 1,000 replacements that had trained only a few days. Departing Kumsan on or about 25 July, the division reportedly left behind the tank regiment that had accompanied it ever since they had crosssed the 38th Parallel together a month earlier. The tanks were to remain in Kumsan until the division had crossed the Naktong.[36]

On 28 July the first indication appeared in American intelligence estimates that elements of the N.K. *6th Division* might have moved south. The next day the Eighth Army intelligence section conjectured that the enemy had shifted troops southward. It stated that major parts of one enemy division probably were in the Chinju area and major elements of another in the Koch'ang area. While the estimate did not identify the enemy unit in the Koch'ang area, it erroneously repeated that "all elements of this division [the *4th*] are attacking eastward along the axis Chinju—Masan."[37] Even after the Hadong battle on the 27th, Eighth Army did not know that these troops were from the *6th Division*.

The 34th Infantry of the 24th Division, defending the Koch'ang approach to the Naktong, had a regimental strength at this time of about 1,150 men, with the 1st and 3d Battalions averaging approximately 350 men each. It was in position at Koch'ang on 27 July.

Koch'ang is about midway on the main road between Kumch'on and Chinju and is strategically located near the point where two lateral east-west roads, one from Namwon and Hamyang and the other from Chinan, cross the Kumch'on-Chinju road and continue eastward through Hyopch'on and Ch'ogye to the Naktong River. Chinju is thirty-five air miles south of Koch'ang.

On 27 July, Colonel Moore sent Colonel Wilson with the 1st Battalion, 29th Infantry, north from Chinju to relieve Colonel Rhea in the Anui area. Colonel Rhea was then to bring his battalion south to Chinju, where Colonel Moore planned to concentrate the 19th Infantry.

The relief took place at Umyong-ni in the early afternoon of 27 July. Wilson's battalion had no artillery, armor, or air support. A platoon of 4.2 mortars had only two rounds of white phosphorous shells for ammunition. Mounted messengers traveling over thirty-five miles of road were the only means of communication between Wilson and Colonel Moore's command post.[38]

In the early afternoon, Colonel Rhea

---

[35] ATIS Res Supp Interrog Rpts, Issue 100 (N.K. *6th Div*), pp. 35–37; *Ibid.*, Issue 94 (N.K. *4th Div*), pp. 46–47.
[36] *Ibid.*, Issue 94 (N.K. *4th Div*), p. 47.

[37] EUSAK WD, G–2 Stf Sec Rpt, 29 Jul 50.
[38] Holliday, Notes for author, 31 Mar 53.

guided 1st Lt. John C. Hughes with B Company, 29th Infantry, reinforced by approximately thirty-five men and their weapons from the Heavy Weapons Company, from Umyong-ni to relieve A Company, 19th Infantry, at Anui. A Company was engaged in a small arms fight and its relief could not be accomplished at once. Colonel Rhea returned to Umyong-ni, leaving instructions that the company should follow him as soon as possible, which he expected would be shortly. At Umyong-ni Rhea waited about five hours for A Company. Then, when reconnaissance toward Anui showed that an enemy force had cut the road, he started just before dusk with the rest of the battalion for Chinju as ordered.[39]

Meanwhile, Colonel Wilson had sent 2d Lt. Frank Iwanczyk, Assistant S-3, with two jeeps from Umyong-ni to make contact with the 34th Infantry at Koch'ang; 1st Lt. Sam C. Holliday, S-2, went to make contact with the ROK troops at Hamyang.

Iwanczyk set off northward. At the Anui crossroads he checked his map and then led off toward Koch'ang, waving the other jeep to follow. Because of the heavy dust the second jeep kept well behind the first.

A mile north of the crossroads, an enemy machine gun, hidden in a native hut on a turn of the road, suddenly poured devastating fire into the lead jeep. The bodies of all four men fell from the wrecked vehicle into a rice field. The second jeep stopped with a jerk and the men jumped into the ditch by the road. After three or four minutes of silence, seven or eight North Korean soldiers started down the road. They passed the first jeep and, when nearing the second, they shouted and started to run toward it. Pvt. Sidney D. Talley stood up and fired his M1 at the North Koreans. He killed two of them. His three companions now joined in firing. The surviving North Koreans turned and ran back.

One of the Americans scrambled up the bank, turned the jeep around, the others jumped in, and the driver raced back to the Anui crossroads. There, they excitedly told members of B Company about the roadblock. At the battalion command post they repeated their story.[40]

By this time, Lieutenant Holliday had returned from Hamyang. There he had found somewhat less than 600 men of the ROK 7th Division and 150 fresh South Korean marines from Mokp'o. Holliday with three men now set off for Anui. Two and a half miles short of the town, enemy fire from a roadblock destroyed their jeep and wounded one man in the chest. Holliday covered the withdrawal of his three men with BAR fire, and then followed them.

Relieved finally at Anui about 1600, A Company, 19th Infantry, loaded into trucks and started south to join Rhea's battalion. A mile below the town the company ran into a fire fight between North and South Korean troops and was stopped. After enemy fire wrecked six of its vehicles, the company destroyed the others, abandoned its heavy equipment, and started on foot through the hills toward the 34th Infantry positions at Koch'ang. The next morning 64 Ameri-

---

[39] Ltrs, Col Rhea to author, 9 Apr and 21 Sep 53.

[40] Holliday, Notes for author, 31 Mar 53.

can and 60 ROK soldiers came in to Colonel Beauchamp's positions there. Why this force did not return to Anui and join Lieutenant Hughes is not known.[41]

Meanwhile at Anui, Lieutenant Hughes' B Company, 29th Infantry, was under attack from superior numbers closing in from three sides, and by nightfall it had been forced back into the town. Hughes made plans to withdraw across the upper Nam River to a high hill east of the town. Two officers and sixteen men got across before enemy automatic fire cut off the rest. After vainly trying to help the rest of the company to break out eastward, the eighteen men went over the hills to the 34th Infantry position at Koch'ang. In Anui the cutoff troops engaged in street fighting until midnight. Those who escaped walked out through the hills during the next several days. Approximately half of the 215 men of B and D Companies, 29th Infantry, taking part in the Anui battle, were either killed or listed as missing in action.[42]

Colonel Wilson and the rest of the battalion at Umyong-ni meanwhile knew nothing of the fate of B Company at Anui except that enemy forces had engaged it, and that roadblocks were above and below it. Wilson made two unsuccessful attempts to send help to B Company.

The enemy troops that had closed on Anui were advanced units of the N.K. *4th Division*. They were well aware that a mixed force of American and South Korean troops was only a few miles below them. To deal with this force, elements of the division turned south from Anui early on 28 July.

In defensive positions about Umyong-ni and Hamyang, Colonel Wilson's men were on the east side of the Nam River. Col. Min Ki Sik's remnants of the ROK 7th Division and a small force of South Korean marines were on the west side. American mortar fire turned back the small enemy force that approached Umyong-ni. On the west side of the river near Hamyang a hard fight developed. There, the South Koreans seemed about to lose the battle until their reserve marines fought through to the enemy's flank. This caused the North Koreans to withdraw northward. From prisoners captured in this battle Wilson learned of the American defeat at Anui the day before.[43]

Learning that evening that the enemy was moving around his battalion on back trails in the direction of Chinju, Colonel Wilson began, after dark, the first of a series of withdrawals. On 30 July the battalion reached the vicinity of Sanch'ong, twenty miles north of Chinju, and went into defensive positions there on orders from Colonel Moore. Colonel Min's ROK troops also withdrew southward, passed through Wilson's positions, and continued on into Chinju.[44]

---

[41] Holliday, Notes for author, 31 Mar 53; 24th Div WD, G-3 Jnl, entry 159, 27 Jul, and entries 217 at 281120 and 219 at 281407 Jul 50; *Ibid.*, G-2 Jnl, entry 1570, 27 Jul, and entries 1614 and 1621, 28 Jul 50; 24th Div WD, 29 Jul 50.

[42] Holliday, Notes for author, 31 Mar 53. The account of B Company action at Anui is based largely on information supplied by Lieutenant Hughes in the Notes.

[43] Holliday, Notes for author, 31 Mar 53.

[44] *Ibid*. The author has been unable to find the 1st Battalion, 29th Infantry, records for July 1950.

The N.K. 4th Division Seizes the Koch'ang Approach to the Naktong

Having brushed aside the American and ROK force at Anui, in what it called a "small engagement," the N.K. *4th Division* turned northeast toward Koch'ang. A patrol from the 34th Infantry on 27 July had, from a distance, seen and heard the fighting in progress at Anui. Its report alerted Colonel Beauchamp to the possibility of an early attack.[45]

Colonel Beauchamp had disposed the 34th Infantry in a three-quarter circle around Koch'ang, which lay in the middle of a two-and-a-half-mile-wide oval-shaped basin in a north-south mountain valley. The 3d Battalion was on high ground astride the Anui road two miles west of the town, the 1st Battalion about the same distance east of it on the Hyopch'on road, a reinforced platoon of I Company at a roadblock across the Kumch'on road four miles north of the town, while the Heavy Mortar Company was at its northern edge. Artillery support consisted of A Battery, 13th Field Artillery Battalion, which had five 105-mm. howitzers in position two miles southeast of the town.[46]

The 34th Infantry, not having been able to re-equip since Taejon, did not have a regimental switchboard. There were only a few radios. The regiment was short of mortars, bazookas, and machine guns. Some of the men did not have complete uniforms, many had no helmets, most did not have entrenching tools. Every man, however, did have his individual weapon.

Before dusk of 28 July, forward observers could see a long line of enemy traffic piled up behind a roadblock that the 34th Infantry had constructed at a defile on the Anui road west of the town. They directed artillery fire on this column until darkness fell.[47] Colonel Beauchamp then brought his two infantry battalions closer to Koch'ang for a tighter defense.

About dark, Beauchamp received orders to report to the 24th Division command post at Hyopch'on. There he told General Church of an anticipated enemy attack and of his plan to withdraw the 3d Battalion to a previously selected position three miles southeast of Koch'ang. General Church did not agree and told Beauchamp to hold the town.[48] Beauchamp thereupon telephoned his executive officer and told him to stop the withdrawal of the 3d Battalion. When Beauchamp returned to Koch'ang at 0300 everything was quiet.

In darkness an hour later (about 0400 29 July), a North Korean attack came from two directions. One force, striking from the north, cut off I Company. Another moved around the town on the north and then struck southward across the road east of Koch'ang. The 1st Battalion repulsed this attack, but then, without orders, fell back toward the secondary position three miles east of Ko-

---

[45] ATIS Res Supp Interrog Rpts, Issue 94 (N.K. *4th Div*), p. 47; Interv, author with Beauchamp, 24 Sep 52.

[46] *Ibid.*; 24th Div WD, 28 Jul 50; *Ibid.*, G-3 Jnl, 23-29 Jul 50, entries 219, 281407, and 220, 281415; 34th Inf WD, 25 Jul 50; Interv, author with Beauchamp, 24 Sep 52; Interv, author with Cheek (Ex Off, 13th FA Bn, and with A Btry at Koch'ang in Jul 50), 7 Aug 51.

[47] Intervs, author with Beauchamp, 24 Sep 52, and Cheek, 7 Aug 51; 24th Div WD, 28 Jul 50; *Ibid.*, G-3 Jnl, 23-29 Jul 50, entry 220, 281415.

[48] Interv, author with Beauchamp, 24 Sep 52.

ch'ang. Colonel Beauchamp met the battalion on the road and stopped it.

Before daylight the 3d Battalion, also without orders, fell back through Koch'ang, leaving I Company isolated to the north. This battalion ran a gantlet of enemy automatic and small arms fire for a mile, but in the protecting darkness suffered few casualties. After daylight the 1st Battalion rescued all but one platoon of I Company. The men of this platoon were either killed or captured.[49]

During the predawn attack some small arms fire struck in the howitzer positions of A Battery, 13th Field Artillery Battalion, from a ridge 500 yards eastward. Maj. Leon B. Cheek, the battalion executive officer, awoke to the sound of the firing. Hurrying to the road he saw the battery commander, who said the enemy had overrun the artillery. The battery executive officer came up and told Cheek that everyone had "taken off," although he had ordered the men to their foxholes. When the firing began, he said, someone yelled, "Run for your life!" Two squads of infantry attached to the artillery to provide security had joined the stampede.[50]

Cheek stopped the wild shooting in his vicinity and started toward the howitzers. He ordered all prime movers driven back to the gun positions. Twelve men from the artillery and the drivers of the prime movers obeyed. From the infantry, a BAR man and three riflemen volunteered to go forward to cover the artillerymen while they pulled out the howitzers. Cheek placed these four men in firing positions and they soon almost silenced the enemy. A small enemy patrol of six or seven men apparently had caused the debacle. Cheek and the twelve artillerymen loaded the equipment and ammunition, hitched the prime movers to the guns, and, one by one, pulled the five howitzers to the road. They then withdrew eastward.

During 29 July the 34th Infantry Regiment withdrew eastward 15 miles to hill positions near Sanje-ri on the road to Hyopch'on. From a point 3 miles southeast of Koch'ang the road for the next 10 miles is virtually a defile. The withdrawing 34th Infantry and its engineer troops blew all the bridges and at many points set off demolition charges in the cliffs overhanging the road.

The *18th Regiment* of the enemy division pressed on after the retreating 34th Infantry. The N.K. *4th Division* left its artillery behind at Koch'ang because of the destroyed bridges ahead of it. In advancing to the Naktong River on the Hyopch'on road, it employed only small arms and mortar fire.[51]

It was anticipated that the enemy force which had captured Koch'ang would soon approach the Naktong River for a crossing below Taegu. This prospect created another difficulty for Eighth Army. To meet it, General Walker told General Church he would send to him the ROK 17th Regiment, one of the best South Korean units at that time. He also shifted the 1st Battalion, 21st Infantry Regiment, from the P'ohang-dong-

---

[49] 34th Inf WD, 29 Jul 50.
[50] Interv, author with Cheek, 7 Aug 51; Ltr, Ayres to author, 5 Jun 53 (Ayres commanded the 1st Bn, 34th Inf, at Koch'ang); 13th FA Bn WD, 29 Jul 50; Interv, author with Beauchamp, 24 Sep 52.

[51] Interv, author with Beauchamp, 24 Sep 52; 34th Inf WD, 29 Jul 50; 24th Div WD, 30 Jul 50; ATIS Res Supp Interrog Rpts, Issue 94 (N.K. *4th Div*), p. 48.

Yongdok area on the east coast to Hyopch'on, where it took up defensive positions back of the 34th Infantry west of the town. The ROK 17th Regiment, 2,000 strong, arrived at the 34th Infantry position in the dead of night at 0200 30 July. It went at once into positions on the high ground on either flank.[52]

Only after the Koch'ang action did Eighth Army finally, on 31 July, identify the enemy unit in this area as the *4th Division*. This led it to conclude in turn that the enemy force in the Chinju area was the *6th Division*. Eighth Army then decided that the enemy effort against the United Nations' left flank was in reality being carried out by two widely separated forces: the N.K. *4th Division* from the Anui-Koch'ang area, to envelop the main battle positions on Eighth Army's left flank, and the N.K. *6th Division* from the Chinju area, to cut lines of communication in the rear, drive through Masan, and capture the port of Pusan.[53]

Chinju Falls to the Enemy—31 July

On 28 July, Colonel Rhea arrived at Chinju from Anui with the 1st Battalion, 19th Infantry, less A Company. He passed through the town with orders to take up blocking positions ten miles south. Rhea proceeded to the vicinity of Kuho-ri, about two miles west of the Sach'on Airfield. There his battalion of only 200 riflemen went into position to block a secondary road approach to Chinju along the coast from Hadong.[54]

Colonel McGrail's 2d Battalion, 19th Infantry, that same morning occupied defensive positions on high ground astride the Chinju-Hadong road just west of the Nam River. Remnants of the 3d Battalion, 29th Infantry, that had escaped from the Hadong fight and numerous ROK troops were in and around Chinju.

Aerial reconnaissance during that day and the next showed heavy enemy traffic entering Hadong from all roads and noted movement northeast on the Chinju road. American intelligence estimated that two enemy regiments with tanks were in the Hadong area.[55]

Before noon, 29 July, an enemy column with three motorcycles in the lead approached the 2d Battalion's advanced blocking position about six miles southwest of Chinju. Although there was an automatic weapon available, it did not fire on the column. The few rounds of artillery that fell were inaccurate and ineffective. The advanced unit, F Company, then withdrew to join the main battalion position just west of the Nam River four miles from Chinju. An air strike on the enemy column reportedly inflicted considerable damage, halting it temporarily.[56]

Early the next morning an enemy unit moved around the right flank (north) of the 2d Battalion and cut the road running northwest out of Chinju to the 1st Battalion, 29th Infantry.

Captain Barszcz, from G Company's

---

[52] 24th Div WD, 30 Jul 50; Interv, author with Church, 25 Sep 52. The 34th Infantry War Diary for 29 July says that the ROK 17th Regiment was in position that day.

[53] EUSAK WD, PIR 19, 31 Jul 50.

[54] 24th Div WD, G-3 Jnl, entry 206, 281245 Jul 50; Ltrs, Rhea to author, 9 Apr and 21 Sep 53.

[55] 24th Div WD, G-2 Jnl, entries 1651, 290755, and 1753, 290818 Jul 50; *Ibid.*, G-3 Jnl, entries 247, 29100, and 260, 291145 Jul 50.

[56] Interv, author with Montesclaros, 20 Aug 52; 24th Div WD, 29 Jul 50; 19th Inf WD, 29 Jul 50.

position across the Nam River west of Chinju, saw and reported at least 800 enemy troops moving across his front. Small arms fire did not disperse them. He called for an aerial observer, but the observer overhead reported he saw no enemy. The reason was clear: the North Koreans were all wearing foliage camouflage and they squatted quietly on the ground while the plane was overhead. Captain Barszcz directed artillery fire on the column, but after about twenty rounds the artillery stopped firing because of ammunition shortage. Rain and low overcasts during the day hampered efforts of aerial reconnaissance to report on enemy movements.[57]

That afternoon, 30 July, E and F Companies of the 19th Infantry fell back across the Nam River to the hills two miles west of Chinju. Just before evening, G Company crossed the river from its isolated position. Once on the east side it took up a defensive position in the flat ground near the river bank, with the mission of preventing enemy infiltration into Chinju between the road and the river. The hill positions of the rest of the battalion were beyond the road to its right (north). There was no physical contact between G Company and these troops.[58]

The 19th Infantry faced the critical test of the defense of Chinju pitifully understrength. Its unit report for 30 July gives the regiment a strength of 1,895, with 300 men in the 1st Battalion and 290 men in the 2d Battalion. Colonel Moore, however, states that the strength of the 19th Infantry on 30 July, including the replacements that arrived that afternoon, was 1,544. The 3d Battalion, 29th Infantry, still disorganized as a result of the Hadong battle, had a reported strength that day of 396 men. On 30 July, all ROK forces in the Chinju area came under Colonel Moore's command, including the remnants of the 7th Division, now known as Task Force Min, which during the day arrived at Chinju from the Hamyang area with 1,249 men.[59]

Several hundred replacements arrived at Chinju for the 19th Infantry at this time—175 on 28 July and 600 on 30 July—but it is doubtful if they contributed much to the combat effectiveness of the regiment in the Chinju battle. Of the 600 that arrived on 30 July, 500 went to the 19th Infantry and most of the remainder to the 13th Field Artillery Battalion. About 1600 these replacements started forward from the regimental command post in Chinju for distribution by the battalions to the rifle companies that evening. Although the rifle companies were then engaged with the enemy, Colonel Moore decided that they needed replacements at the front to help in the fighting, and that it would be best to send them forward at once rather than to wait for an opportunity to integrate them into the units during a lull in the battle.[60]

---

[57] Ltr, Barszcz to author, 30 Jul 52; 24th Div WD, 30 Jul 50; 19th Inf WD, 30 Jul 50. Civilians in the Chinju area seemed openly hostile to American troops and friendly to the enemy. Refugees had to be watched closely. Interv, Blumenson with Herbert, 31 Jul 51.

[58] Ltr, Barszcz to author, 30 Jul 52; Notes, Montesclaros (Asst S–3, 2d Bn, 19th Inf) for author, n.d.; Interv, Blumenson with Herbert, 31 Jul 51.

[59] 19th Inf Unit Rpt 21, 30 Jul 50; 24th Div WD, G–3 Jnl, entry 386, 312325 Jul 50; EUSAK WD POR 53, 30 Jul 50; GHQ UNC G–3 Opn Rpt, 31 Jul 50.

[60] 19th Inf WD, Narr Summ, 22 Jul–25 Aug 50; Intervs, author with Moore, 20 Aug 52, and McGrail, 24 Oct 52.

The 1st Battalion received about 150 of the replacements just before dark and Colonel Rhea immediately assigned them to companies. Some died without ever appearing on the company rosters. The 2d Battalion received an approximately equal number of replacements, and they, too, reached the rifle companies about dusk. Of the sixty replacements assigned to G Company, four or five became casualties before they reached the company position. Captain Barszcz had pleaded in vain with the battalion executive against sending replacements to him in the midst of action. He believed that they not only would be a burden to him but that many of them would be casualties. In the battle that night both fears became reality.[61]

After dark the enemy moved in for close-quarter attack. Before midnight, G Company killed several North Korean soldiers inside its perimeter. Out of communication with battalion headquarters, and with friendly artillery fire falling near, Barszcz tried to join the other rifle companies on his right, but he found North Koreans on the road in strength and had to move around them. About midnight he crossed the road to the north side. There he and his men lay hidden in bushes for two or three hours. During this time several enemy tanks loaded with infantry passed along the road headed in the direction of Chinju.[62]

The North Koreans directed their main attack against E and F Companies in front of Chinju. This began about 0215, 31 July, with artillery barrages. Forty-five minutes later whistles signaled the infantry attack and enemy soldiers closed in, delivering small arms fire. The main effort was against F Company on the hill overlooking the river. There a crisis developed about 0500.[63]

Back of the F Company hill, members of the Heavy Weapons Company watched the battle as it developed in front of them. One of the youngsters in H Company said, "Here comes the cavalry just like in the movies," as a platoon of F Company came off the hill followed by North Koreans. Other members of F Company ran toward E Company's position. At least one platoon of the Heavy Weapons Company opened fire on the intermingled American and North Korean soldiers. Within a few minutes, however, this platoon withdrew toward Chinju. At the edge of the town, Colonel McGrail met H Company and put it in a defensive position around the battalion command post. The organized parts of E and F Companies also fell back on Chinju about daylight.[64]

While this battle was in progress, Captain Barszcz received radio orders to move to Chinju. He took his company north over high ground and then circled eastward. On the way he picked up stragglers and wounded men from E, F, and H Companies, 19th Infantry, and K Company, 29th Infantry. By daylight his group was two or three miles northeast of Chinju. Around noon, Barszcz joined Colonel Moore and elements of the 19th

---

[61] Ltr, Rhea to author, 9 Apr 53; Ltr, Barszcz to author, 21 Aug 52; Interv, Blumenson with 2d Lt Joseph Szito, 25 Aug 51, Action in Chinju, in OCMH. Szito, in July 1950, was in the Mortar Platoon, H Company, 19th Infantry.

[62] Ltr, Barszcz to author, 30 Jul 52; Interv, Blumenson with Herbert, 31 Jul 51.

[63] 19th Inf Unit Rpt 22, 31 Jul 50; Interv, author with McGrail, 24 Oct 52; Interv, Blumenson with Szito, 25 Aug 51.

[64] Interv, Blumenson with Szito, 25 Aug 51.

Infantry east of the town. During the night, G Company had suffered about 40 casualties, but of this number it brought approximately 20 wounded through the hills with it—10 were litter cases.[65]

The 1st Battalion, 19th Infantry, also had come under attack during the night. It held a strong defensive position below the Nam River on high ground four miles south of Chinju, overlooking the Sach'on-Chinju road near its juncture with the road east to Masan.

Colonel Rhea and his men at dusk on 30 July could clearly see North Koreans out in the open going into position, but they were forbidden to fire because a ROK Marine battalion attack was scheduled to sweep across in front of them. But the ROK's never entered the fight there, and the enemy used this three-to four-hour period unmolested for maneuvering against the 1st Battalion.[66]

That night, enemy mortars and self-propelled weapons supported efforts of the N.K. *15th Regiment* to infiltrate the 1st Battalion's position. But it was on terrain hard to attack, and the enemy effort failed. The North Koreans in front of the 1st Battalion withdrew before dawn, apparently veering off to the northwest.

After daylight, 31 July, Colonel Rhea, on orders from Colonel Moore, began moving his battalion ten miles eastward on the Masan road to occupy a defensive position at the Chinju pass. The 1st Battalion withdrew to this position without enemy contact and went into defensive perimeter there astride the road before nightfall.[67]

Within Chinju itself, Colonel Moore, shortly after daybreak, prepared to evacuate the town. By 0600 enemy small arms fire was striking in its western edge, and six North Korean armored vehicles, which Colonel Moore believed to be three tanks and three self-propelled guns, were in Chinju firing at American targets. At 0640 Moore ordered heavy equipment withdrawn from the town. Fifty minutes later the 13th Field Artillery Battalion (less A Battery) and B Battery, 11th Field Artillery Battalion, started to displace and move eastward. Enemy mortar, machine gun, and small arms fire fell in Chinju during the withdrawal. Enemy snipers were also inside the town.[68]

By 0745, 31 July, Maj. Jack R. Emery, regimental S-4, had dispatched eastward out of Chinju the last of five trains totaling twenty-five cars evacuating the 19th Infantry supplies. Colonel Moore and his command post stayed in Chinju until about 0800.

The withdrawal from Chinju was relatively orderly, although slow and laborious, with refugees, animal-drawn wagons, and American and ROK foot soldiers intermingled in the streets. There was some tendency to panic, however, and Colonel Moore himself had occasion

---

[65] Ltr, Barszcz to author, 30 Jul 52; Interv, Blumenson with Herbert, 31 Jul 51; Moore, Notes for author, Jul 53.

[66] Ltrs, Rhea to author, 9 Apr and 21 Sep 53, together with sketch map of 1st Bn positions, 28–31 Jul 50.

[67] *Ibid.*; Ltr, Maj Elliot C. Cutler, Jr., to author, 9 Mar 53. Cutler was Acting S-3, 19th Infantry, at the time.

[68] Intervs, author with Moore and Montesclaros, 20 Aug 52; 24th Div WD, 31 Jul 50; 25th Div WD, 3d Bn, 27th Inf, Hist Rpt, Aug 50; *New York Times*, August 1, 1950, W. H. Lawrence dispatch from southwestern front; 13th FA Bn WD, 31 Jul 50.

to stop some cars that started to "take off" east of Chinju.[69]

The main highway bridge over the Nam at the southern edge of Chinju was under enemy fire and considered unusable. In the withdrawal, therefore, the 2d Battalion followed the road north of the Nam to Uiryong, where it assembled on the evening of 31 July. The regimental command post moved eastward out of Chinju, crossed the Nam about 3 miles northeast of the town, and then went east on the Masan road to Chiryong-ni, a small village 12 air miles east of Chinju and 1 mile beyond the Much'on-ni–Masan road fork. The artillery, accompanied by the 3d Battalion, 29th Infantry, withdrew from Chinju north of the Nam River, crossing to the south side at Uiryong, and went into an assembly area at Komam-ni (Saga) shortly after noon. There it received an airdrop message from General Church ordering it to return to the vicinity of Chinju. During the afternoon the five 105-mm. howitzers of B Battery, 13th Field Artillery Battalion, and the eight 155-mm. howitzers of B Battery, 11th Field Artillery Battalion, rolled west and went into position at the Chinju pass in support of Colonel Rhea's 1st Battalion, 19th Infantry.[70]

The 19th Infantry estimated enemy strength in the Chinju area, when the city fell on the morning of 31 July, as 2,000 troops, with an unknown number of tanks and artillery pieces. American aerial strikes on Chinju during the day left it in flames. Late that night a Korean source sent a message that 4,000 enemy troops were in Chinju setting up communications and weapons.[71]

A ROK Army source reported that North Koreans had secured Chinju at 0900, 31 July. This may very well have been true for the main part of the town north of the Nam River, but it was not true for that part south of the Nam, where 1st Lt. Samuel R. Fowler and fourteen enlisted men still stayed by three M26 Pershing medium tanks.

Three Pershing Tanks at Chinju

One little drama was enacted in Chinju on 31 July after the 19th Infantry withdrew from the town that should be told. It is the story of the first three medium tanks in Korea and their brave commander. On 28 June, the fourth day of the war, Col. Olaf P. Winningstad, Eighth Army Ordnance chief, found three M26 Pershing medium tanks at the Tokyo Ordnance Depot in bad condition and needing extensive repairs, including rebuilt engines. The repair work began at once and was completed on 13 July. The three tanks were shipped to Pusan where they arrived on 16 July, the first American medium tanks in Korea. With them were Lieutenant Fowler and fourteen enlisted crew members. Trained to operate M24 light tanks, they were now expected to become familiar with the Pershing tank.

The tanks gave trouble because of improper fan belts that would stretch and permit the motors to overheat. Belts made in Japan were either too short or

---

[69] Interv, author with Moore, 20 Aug 52; Interv, Blumenson with Szito, 25 Aug 51.
[70] Intervs, author with Moore, 20 Aug 52, and McGrail, 24 Oct 52; Ltr, Cutler to author, 9 Mar 53; 13th FA Bn WD, 31 Jul 50.

[71] 19th Inf Unit Rpt 22, 31 Jul 50; 24th Div WD, G-2 Jnl, entry 10, 010255 Aug 50; *Ibid.*, G-3 Jnl, entry 421, 011800 Aug 50.

too long despite emergency orders for corrections in them.⁷²

Eighth Army hoped to use these tanks to help stop the North Korean drive in the southwest. It sent them by rail to Chinju where they arrived at 0300, 28 July. They were unloaded at the Rail Transportation Office on the south side of the Nam River where the rail line terminated. There they awaited new belts. When the N.K. *6th Division* entered Chinju on the morning of 31 July, these tanks took no part in the battle.

Flatcars from Pusan to evacuate the tanks passed through Masan the morning of 31 July but never got beyond Chungam-ni, about twenty-five miles short of Chinju. Snarled rail traffic caused by evacuation of the 19th Infantry supplies blocked the way.

At daybreak, Lieutenant Fowler went to Colonel Moore for instructions. Moore told him that if the enemy overran the 19th Infantry positions on the northwest side of Chinju and he could not evacuate the tanks under their own power, he was to destroy them and evacuate his tank crews by truck. Lieutenant Fowler telephoned Masan and apparently learned that the flatcars had departed there for Chinju to get the tanks. He decided to stay.⁷³

Gradually the firing in Chinju died down. A ROK soldier who passed the rail station about noon told Fowler that only a very few ROK soldiers were still in the town.

A little later, William R. Moore, an Associated Press correspondent, suddenly appeared and suggested to Fowler that he should check a body of men coming up the rail track. It was now perhaps an hour past noon. Fowler had an interpreter call to the approaching men. They were North Koreans. Fowler ordered his tank crews to open fire. In the fire fight that immediately flared between the tank .30- and .50-caliber machine guns and the enemy small arms fire, Fowler received a bullet in his left side. In this close-range fight the tank machine gun fire killed or wounded most of the enemy group, which was about platoon size. The tankers put Fowler into his tank and started the three tanks east on the road to Masan.

Two miles down the road the tanks came to a blown bridge. The men prepared to abandon the tanks and proceed on foot. They removed Fowler from his tank and made a litter for him. Fowler ordered the men to destroy the tanks by dropping grenades into them. Three men started for the tanks to do this. At this moment an enemy force lying in ambush opened fire. A number of men got under the bridge with Fowler. MSgt. Bryant E. W. Shrader was the only man on the tanks. He opened fire with the .30-caliber machine gun. A North Korean called out in English for the men to surrender.

Shrader left the machine gun, started the tank, and drove it close to one of the other tanks. He dropped the escape hatch and took in six men. He then drove back toward Chinju and stopped the tank a few feet short of the bridge over the Nam, undecided whether to cross to the other side. There the overheated engine stopped and would not start again. The seven men abandoned the tank and ran into the bamboo thickets fringing the

---

⁷² EUSAK Inspector General Rpt (Col William O. Perry), Three M26 Tanks at Chinju, 31 Jul 50, dated 10 Sep 50.
⁷³ *Ibid.*, testimonies of Col Moore, Maj Emery, Capt Applegate (RTO Off, Masan), Pvt Harold Delmar; Interv, author with Moore, 20 Aug 52.

river. After many close calls with enemy forces Shrader and his group finally reached safety and passed through the lines of the 25th Division west of Masan.[74]

The men back at the blown bridge had no chance. Some were killed or wounded at the first fire. Others were killed or wounded under the bridge. A few ran into nearby fields trying to escape but were killed or captured. One of those captured said later he saw several bodies floating in the stream and recognized two as Fowler and Moore.[75]

Colonel Wilson Escapes With the 1st Battalion, 29th Infantry

On the morning of 31 July, the 1st Battalion, 29th Infantry, was at Sanch'ong. It was unaware that Chinju, twenty air miles to the southeast, had fallen and that the 19th Infantry Regiment had withdrawn eastward.

The mess trucks that went to Chinju the day before from the battalion had not returned. During the morning local villagers suddenly disappeared, a sure sign that enemy forces were approaching. Colonel Wilson drove south to Tansong, ten air miles from Chinju, where he had a roadblock. While he talked with Lieutenant Griffin, who was in command of a platoon there, about 700 refugees streamed through the roadblock. All agreed that enemy troops were behind them.[76]

Colonel Wilson now decided to send the battalion's heavy vehicles out eastward before the roads were cut. His executive officer, Maj. Charles E. Arnold, brought the vehicular convoy to Tansong and there it turned east over a trail through the mountains in the direction of Uiryong. The trail was passable only to jeeps. But by the labors of his own men and all the Koreans he could assemble, Arnold improved it to the extent that all vehicles got through and reached Chungam-ni, except one that broke through an improvised bridge and was abandoned.

At 1700, Colonel Wilson and the battalion troops started withdrawing southward from Sanch'ong. They had marched about an hour when a liaison plane flew over the column and dropped a message. Opening it, Colonel Wilson was astonished to read, "Yesterday you were ordered to report to the concentration area of Haman. What are you doing here?" Haman was thirty-five miles away as the crow flies and much farther by the roads and mountain trails.

Wilson led his battalion on down to Tansong. There, a South Korean naval lieutenant detached himself from a group of refugees and came over to Wilson with a map. He said he had been at Chinju and that the American troops had left there, retreating eastward. He continued, "The Reds are just seven miles behind us and will get here tonight." Wilson talked to him at length and became convinced that his story was reliable. After consulting some of the battalion staff, Wilson decided to leave the Chinju road and head for Haman across the mountains.

The men discarded all personal effects. Three or four sick and injured

---

[74] EUSAK IG Rpt, testimony of Capt John W. Coyle, Jr. (CO 8066th Mech Rec Det), 2d Lt Vincent P. Geske, Sgt Francis A. Hober, and MSgt Bryant E. W. Shrader (C Co, 89th Tk Bn), Pfc Carl Anderson; ATIS Res Supp Interrog Rpts, Issue 1, Rpt 1, p. 119, Capt Pak Tong Huk.

[75] EUSAK IG Rpt, testimony of Pfc Anderson.

[76] Ltr, Col Wesley C. Wilson to author, 13 Jun 53; Holliday, Notes for author, 31 Mar 53.

soldiers rode in the few jeeps, which also carried the radios, mortars, and machine guns. The battalion late in the evening headed east over the Uiryong trail. At 0200 the men reached Masang-ni, where the last north-south road that the enemy from the Chinju area could use to cut them off intersected the lateral trail they were following. Once east of this crossroad point, Wilson halted the battalion and, after security guards were posted, the men lay down to rest. During their night march, many refugees had joined them.

At 0600 the next morning, 1 August, the battalion took up the march eastward. It forded a stream and, half a mile beyond, the footsore men came on a gladsome sight: Major Arnold awaited them with a convoy of the battalion's trucks that he had led out the day before.[77]

On the last day of July the North Koreans could look back on a spectacular triumph in their enveloping maneuver through southwest Korea. Chinju had fallen. Their troops were ready to march on Masan and, once past that place, to drive directly on Pusan.

---

[77] Holliday, Notes for author, 31 Mar 53.

CHAPTER XIV

Blocking the Road to Masan

> There is still one absolute weapon ... the only weapon capable of operating with complete effectiveness—of dominating every inch of terrain where human beings live and fight, and of doing it under all conditions of light and darkness, heat and cold, desert and forest, mountain and plain. That weapon is man himself.
>
> GENERAL MATTHEW B. RIDGWAY

The impending loss of Chinju had caused Eighth Army to send its reserve regiment posthaste to the southwest. This was Colonel Michaelis' 27th Infantry, 25th Division, which had been in army reserve only one day at Waegwan after falling back through the 1st Cavalry Division above Kumch'on. During the night of 30–31 July, Eighth Army ordered Michaelis to report to General Church at Changnyong, where the 24th Division command post had moved from Hyopch'on. Colonel Michaelis left immediately with Capt. Earl W. Buchanan, his S–3, and instructed his executive officer, Maj. Arthur Farthing, to follow with the regiment.[1]

Michaelis arrived at the 24th Division command post at Changnyong during the morning of 31 July and reported to Brig. Gen. Pearson Menoher, assistant division commander. General Church was absent. General Menoher decided that Michaelis should continue on, and arranged for him to meet General Church that night at Chung-ni, a little railroad and crossroads village four miles northeast of Masan. The regiment itself passed through Changnyong in the early afternoon and continued on toward Chinju.[2]

The Two Roads to Masan

That afternoon and evening as the 27th Infantry Regiment traveled south, the 19th Infantry sought a defense position between Chinju and Masan where it could reassemble its forces and block the enemy's advance eastward from Chinju. Colonel Rhea's 1st Battalion, 19th Infantry, with supporting artillery, was in the naturally strong position at the Chinju pass.

---

[1] EUSAK WD, G–3 Stf Sec Rpt, 31 Jul 50; Ltr, Brig Gen John H. Michaelis to author, 24 Jan 53.

[2] Interv, author with Church, 25 Sep 52; Ltr, Michaelis to author, 24 Jan 53; 24th Div WD, 31 Jul 50.

Four miles east of the Chinju pass was the little village of Much'on. There the road to Masan forked. The northern route arched in a semicircle through Chungam-ni and Komam-ni to enter Masan from the north. The southern route curved in a similar semicircle through Kogan-ni and Chindong-ni to enter Masan from the south. A high mountain mass, Sobuk-san, lay enclosed in this oval area circumscribed by the two roads. (*Map IV*)

The evening of 31 July Colonel Moore established the 19th Infantry's command post one mile east of Much'on-ni on the northern road. About 2000, a military police courier arrived at his command post with a message from General Church summoning Moore to a meeting with him and Michaelis at Chung-ni.[3] Colonel Moore and his driver, guided by the courier, set out immediately and arrived at the appointed place before midnight. Church and Michaelis were already in the little railroad station.

Colonel Moore gave a detailed account of the events of the day and the location of the 19th Infantry and attached troops. There is considerable confusion as to just what orders General Church issued to Colonel Moore and Colonel Michaelis at this meeting. Since they were verbal there has been no way to check them in the records. It would appear that Moore was to hold the 1st Battalion, 19th Infantry, in its blocking position west of the Much'on-ni road fork and Colonel Michaelis was to put the 27th Infantry in a reinforcing defensive position at the pass three miles west of Chungam-ni on the northern road to Masan.[4]

After the meeting, Moore returned to his command post while Michaelis waited for his regiment, which arrived about 0300 (1 August), tired and wet. Michaelis instructed it to continue on and dig in on the high ground beyond Chungam-ni, fifteen miles westward.

Colonel Michaelis with a few staff officers left Chung-ni while it was still dark and drove to the Notch, a pass southwest of Chungam-ni, arriving there shortly after daybreak. Colonel Michaelis, Captain Buchanan, Colonel Check, and Lt. Col. Gordon E. Murch were studying the ground there and planning to occupy the position, when Capt. Elliott C. Cutler, Acting S–3, 19th Infantry, arrived. He was reconnoitering the ground for defensive positions and had selected four possible sites between the Much'on-ni crossroads and the Notch. He told Michaelis the Notch was the best site and, when he left to return to his command post, he understood that Michaelis still expected to put the 27th Infantry into the Notch position.[5]

---

[3] Intervs, author with Moore, 20 Aug 52, and Church, 25 Sep 52; Ltr, Michaelis to author, 24 Jan 53.

[4] Ltr, Michaelis to author, 24 Jan 53. In discussing this matter with the author, General Church and Colonel Moore had somewhat different recollections from those of Michaelis regarding the orders General Church gave. They recalled the orders as being that the 19th Infantry was to defend the northern road at the pass west of Chungam-ni, and that Michaelis' 27th Infantry was to move through Masan to a defensive position on the southern road near Chindong-ni. The author has concluded that the sequence of events and troop movements that followed the meeting support Michaelis' version.

[5] Ltr, Cutler to author, 9 Mar 53. Michaelis says that at the Notch about 0730 he received a message from an officer courier indicating the 19th Infantry would not hold its blocking position in front of him. Comments with ltr, Michaelis to author, 29 Sep 53.

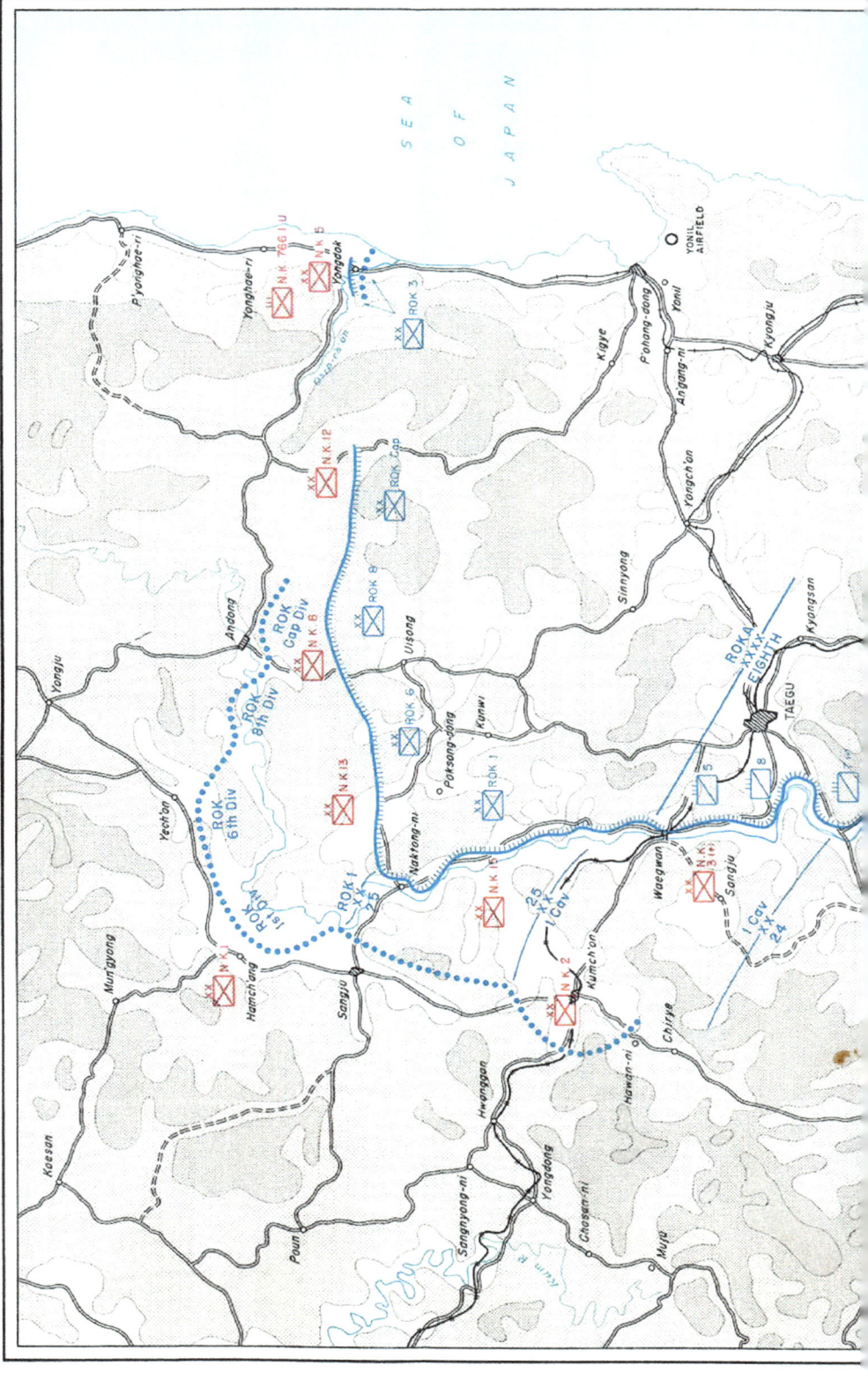

THE PUSAN PERIMETER
4 August 1950

The conversation with Cutler apparently convinced Michaelis that the 19th Infantry was on the verge of another withdrawal which would uncover the Much'on-ni road fork. After Cutler departed, Michaelis remarked to his battalion commanders, Check and Murch, "The 19th Infantry has been overrun and won't be able to do much. They are beaten. I think I will go back and cover the other road. I can't do much here."[6] Michaelis went back a mile or so to the 13th Field Artillery Battalion command post which had just been established west of Chungam-ni. There he telephoned Colonel Moore at the 19th Infantry command post.

In the conversation that followed, according to Michaelis, Moore told him the 19th Infantry could not hold the crossroads and would fall back to the Notch. Michaelis said it seemed to him imperative in that event that some force block the southern road into Masan, otherwise the North Koreans could move through Masan on Pusan and flank the entire Eighth Army. Michaelis proposed that the 19th Infantry endeavor to hold the northern road at the Chungam-ni Notch and that he take the 27th Infantry back through Masan to the vicinity of Chindong-ni to block the southern road to Masan.[7] Michaelis states that Moore concurred. Michaelis then

MOVING UP FROM CHINJU

tried, but failed, to establish communication with both the 24th Division and Eighth Army to obtain approval of this plan.

His mind made up, however, Michaelis at once gave orders to turn the 27th Regiment around and head for Chindong-ni. It was about noon.[8]

In Masan, Michaelis found the newly arrived advance command post of the 25th Division, and from it he tried to telephone General Church at the 24th Division. Unable to get the division, he then tried to reach Eighth Army. Suc-

---

[6] Interv, author with Check, 6 Feb 53.

[7] Ltr, Michaelis to author, 24 Jan 53, and Comments with ltr, 29 Sep 53; Interv, author with Maj Jack J. Kron, 1 Aug 51. Kron was formerly Executive Officer, 13th Field Artillery Battalion, and heard Michaelis' end of the conversation at his command post. He confirms the Michaelis version. Colonel Moore has no recollection of this conversation.

[8] Michaelis says he talked with Moore about 0800, but that hour seems too early. It must have been shortly before noon. Colonel Check, Colonel Murch, and Maj. Frank V. Roquemore (regimental headquarters staff) agree that Michaelis gave the order to turn around about noon. Interv, author with Check, 6 Feb 53; Interv, author with Roquemore, 6 Feb 53; Ltr and review comments, Murch to author, 2 Jan 58.

ceeding, he talked with Colonel Landrum, Chief of Staff, Eighth Army, and explained the situation. Landrum approved Michaelis' move to the southern road in the vicinity of Chindong-ni, and instructed him to continue efforts to communicate with General Church. Later in the day, when General Walker returned to the army command post, Landrum informed him of his conversation with Michaelis. Meanwhile during the day, the Eighth Army G-3 Section succeeded in getting a message to General Church informing him of Colonel Michaelis' move and the new troop dispositions west of Masan.[9]

During the afternoon, the 27th Regiment arrived at Chindong-ni. Michaelis halted the troops there while he went forward a few miles with his battalion commanders, Check and Murch, to an observation post where they conferred with General Church, who had just arrived. In the discussion there, General Church ordered Colonel Michaelis to put one battalion on the hills at the low pass where they were standing. Church decided that a reconnaissance in force should proceed westward the next morning to locate the enemy. Both the 27th Infantry and the 19th Infantry were to make this reconnaissance and the two forces were to meet at the Much'on-ni road fork. Michaelis telephoned Colonel Moore and relayed General Church's order for a reconnaissance in force with all available tanks toward Chinju at 0600 the next morning, 2 August. Moore did not favor making this attack; Michaelis did.[10]

Pursuant to General Church's instructions, Colonel Michaelis placed Murch's 2d Battalion on the high ground at Kogan-ni, where the conversation with General Church had taken place, about seven miles west of Chindong-ni, with E Company in an advanced position astride the road three miles farther west just beyond Pongam-ni. To Colonel Check was given the task of making the reconnaissance attack the next morning with the 1st Battalion. Check placed the battalion in an assembly area back of the 2d Battalion for the night. Colonel Michaelis established his command post in a schoolhouse under a high bluff in Chindong-ni.[11]

On the northern road, as Captain Cutler discovered when he returned to the 19th Infantry command post from his reconnaissance, Colonel Moore had ordered the 1st Battalion to move to the Notch in one jump instead of taking several successive delaying positions as Cutler had expected. Moore thought the one move would give the battalion more time to dig in against an expected enemy attack.[12]

The 1st Battalion left its positions at the Chinju pass and arrived at a designated assembly area two miles southwest of the Notch about 1400. Colonel Rhea remained behind at the pass with an M20

---

[9] Ltr, Landrum to author, 21 Mar 53; Ltrs, Michaelis to author, 24 Jan and 29 Sep 53; Interv, author with Roquemore, 6 Feb 53. Roquemore was responsible for preparing the 27th Infantry War Diary.

[10] Intervs, author with Church, 25 Sep 52, Check, 6 Feb 53, and Moore, 20 Aug 52; Ltrs, Michaelis to author, 24 Jan and 29 Sep 53; Ltr, Murch to author, 7 Apr 54.

[11] 2d Bn, 27th Inf, Opn Rpt, 1 Aug 50; 27th Inf WD, Activities Rpt, Aug 50; 24th Div WD, 1 Aug 50; Brig. Gen. John H. Michaelis with Bill Davidson, "This We Learned in Korea," *Collier's*, August 18, 1950, p. 39.

[12] Ltr, Cutler to author, 9 Mar 53.

armored car to protect the rear of the battalion. An hour after the battalion had moved off eastward, an American jeep carrying two North Korean scouts came up the hill from the west and stopped just short of the crest. Using small arms fire, Colonel Rhea's party killed the two enemy soldiers and recovered the jeep. Rhea's rear guard party then followed the battalion toward the Notch. Below the Notch Rhea received orders to make a reconnaissance of the high ground there. It took him about two hours to do this. Not until about 1700, after he had returned from this reconnaissance, did he receive orders to place his battalion in the position. It was evening before the 1st Battalion started to occupy the Notch position.[13]

The regimental plan called for the 1st Battalion to hold the Notch and the high ground to the right (northwest), and the ROK troops, commanded by Colonel Min, the high ground to the left (southeast) of the Notch.[14] Colonel McGrail's battalion, which had withdrawn from Chinju by a route north of the Nam River, crossed to the south side near Uiryong and arrived at the Notch ahead of the 1st Battalion. When the 1st Battalion arrived, the 2d withdrew to the northern base of the pass in regimental reserve. Late in the afternoon, the 1st Battalion, 29th Infantry, also arrived at Chungam-ni.

As the 19th and 27th Infantry Regiments made their preparations during the evening of 1 August for their reconnaissance the next morning, most welcome reinforcements arrived. They were the first medium tanks in Korea, if one excepts the three ill-fated Pershings at Chinju. About mid-July, Eighth Army activated the 8072d Medium Tank Battalion, which was to receive fifty-four old World War II medium tanks rebuilt in Japan. Detachment A (A Company) of the tank battalion, under the command of Capt. James H. Harvey, arrived at Pusan on 31 July. Railroad flatcars brought them to Masan the morning of 1 August. From there, Lt. Donald E. Barnard took the first platoon to the 19th Infantry position near Chungam-ni, and 1st Lt. Herman D. Norrell took the second platoon to the 27th Infantry at Chindong-ni. Both platoons entered action the next day.[15]

The Battle at the Notch

Colonel Moore selected Colonel Wilson's 1st Battalion, 29th Infantry, to make the reconnaissance westward from the Notch and issued his orders for it at 2000, 1 August. A platoon of five M4 medium tanks and four M8 armored cars and a platoon of engineers were to accompany the battalion.[16] Moore had available at this time a total of about 2,335 men in the 19th Infantry and attached 29th Infantry units, excluding the ROK soldiers under Colonel Min.[17]

The tanks were to lead the column. They assembled in front of the 19th In-

---

[13] Ltr, Rhea to author, 9 Apr 53.
[14] Ltr, Cutler to author, 9 Mar 53.

[15] EUSAK WD, G-1 Sec, Unit Hist Rpt, 13 Jul 50, p. 5; 8072d Med Tk Bn WD, 1-7 Aug 50 (in 25th Div WD); GHQ UNC, G-3 Opn Rpts 37, 31 Jul 50, and 38, 1 Aug 50.
[16] Ltr, Wilson to author, 25 Mar 53; Interv, author with Moore, 20 Aug 52.
[17] On 1 August the 19th Infantry strength was 1,273; the 1st Bn, 29th Inf, was 745; and the 3d Bn, 29th Inf, was 317. See 24th Div WD, 31 Jul 50; 19th Inf WD, 31 Jul 50; 19th Inf Unit Rpt 23, 1 Aug 50.

fantry regimental command post in Chungam-ni at 0530 the next morning, 2 August, and the rest of the column organized behind them. Groups of five infantrymen from C Company mounted each of the tanks and armored cars. Next came the motorized battalion in twenty-two trucks and a number of jeeps. The tanks led off from Chungam-ni at 0615 with the first good light. Half an hour later the head of the column passed through the 1st Battalion, 19th Infantry, defensive position at the Notch, its line of departure.

Excitement spread among the men at the Notch when enemy fire suddenly struck and stopped the armored column just below their position. Colonel Wilson at the time was well back in that part of the column still on the northeast incline leading up to the Notch. Hearing heavy firing forward, he jumped from his jeep and hurried up the hill. Colonel Rhea ran up as Wilson reached the crest, shouting, "You better be careful—that ground down by the pond is enemy territory. My men were fighting with them when your tanks came by."[18] Colonel Wilson's motorized column in passing through the Notch had met head-on an enemy attack just starting against the 19th Infantry.

The tanks met enemy soldiers crawling up the ditch at the side of the road, 100 yards below the crest of the pass. The tanks moved slowly ahead, firing their machine guns. Some of the enemy soldiers ran into the woods along both sides of the road. The lead tank, with its hatch open, had reached a point about 400–500 yards down the incline when an enemy mortar shell struck it, killing the crew. Fire from an enemy antitank gun hit a truck farther back in the column and set it on fire. Three enemy heavy machine guns along the road 200 yards below the crest started firing on the column as it ground to a halt. This machine gun fire almost annihilated the 1st Platoon, C Company, as the men scrambled from the trucks. Twelve or fourteen vehicles had crossed over the pass and were on the southern slope when the enemy opened fire.[19]

When the American soldiers jumped off their vehicles and ran to the roadside ditches for protection, they found the enemy already there. Several desperate struggles took place. Some North Koreans in the ditches continued to advance slowly uphill, pushing captured Americans, their hands tied, in front of them. This melee along the road resulted in about thirty American casualties.

Colonel Wilson witnessed this disastrous spectacle from a point just southwest of the Notch. Seeing that the column was effectively stopped, he placed B Company, 29th Infantry (62 men), in position with the 1st Battalion, 19th Infantry. Colonel Wilson displayed great energy and exposed himself constantly in reorganizing scattered and intermingled units west of the Notch.

---

[18] Ltr, Wilson to author, 25 Mar 53; Ltr, Rhea to author, 9 Apr 53; Ltr, Cutler to author, 3 Jul 53. Colonel Rhea states he did not know of the projected reconnaissance attack through his position by the 1st Battalion, 29th Infantry, until tanks passed through the Notch. A written order had been distributed for this attack, but by some inadvertence, Colonel Rhea did not know of it.

[19] Ltrs to author, Wilson, 25 Mar 53, Rhea, 9 Apr 53, and Cutler, 3 Jul 53; Ltr, Rhea to author, 29 Apr 53; Holliday, Notes for author, 31 Mar 53; 24th Div GO 114, 31 Aug 50.

As soon as the enemy machine gun positions were located, recoilless rifles took them under fire and either destroyed them or caused the enemy gunners to abandon them. But enemy fire in turn killed three of four crew members of the recoilless rifle on the west side of the Notch. The fourth member, Sgt. Evert E. "Moose" Hoffman, stayed with the gun and fired at every available target throughout the day. He won a battlefield commission. Another courageous noncommissioned officer, MSgt. William Marchbanks, D Company, 29th Infantry, placed his two mortars in position at the edge of the Notch and took under fire every burst of enemy fire he could locate.[20]

When the fight started, Colonel Moore came to the command post of the 1st Battalion on the west side of the Notch and stayed there most of the day, directing the defense.

The battle soon spread from the road and flared up along the high ground on either side of the Notch. The night before, B Company, 19th Infantry, had started to climb the peak on the west side of the Notch but, tired from the efforts of the past few days and the hard climb, it stopped short of the crest. On the morning of 2 August, enemy troops came upon the men in their sleep. In a swift attack the North Koreans bayoneted the company commander and several others and drove the rest off the hill. The confusion west of the Notch was heightened about noon when three American fighter planes mistakenly strafed and rocketed this company.[21]

On that (west) side of the Notch, men of the 1st Battalion, 19th Infantry, and of the 1st Battalion, 29th Infantry, became badly intermingled. The enemy force that had driven B Company, 19th Infantry, from the high ground placed cross fire from flank and rear on other units. In an effort to halt this destructive fire, C Company, 29th Infantry, gradually worked its way to a saddle short of the high ground. From there it attacked and drove the enemy force from the heights. In the attack, twelve men of C Company were killed; half of the casualties, in Colonel Wilson's opinion, were caused by American fire from neighboring positions.

During the preceding night, plans for covering the left (east) flank of the Notch position had also miscarried. Colonel Min's troops were supposed to occupy that ground and tie in with the 19th Infantry near the Notch. Morning found them too far eastward, separated by a mile and a half from the 19th Infantry. Snipers infiltrated behind some American soldiers on that side and killed five of them by shots through the back of the head. In the afternoon, enemy mortar fire on the east side also killed and wounded several men.

From his position west of the Notch, Colonel Moore saw men moving up the valley eastward, following the railroad toward Chungam-ni. Thinking they were enemy troops he directed Captain Cutler, his S–3, to send part of the 2d Battalion to block them. This force, however, turned out to be Colonel Min's

---

[20] Ltr, Rhea to author, 29 Apr 53; Interv, author with Moore, 20 Aug 52; Notes, Moore for author, Jul 53; 24th Div GO 114, 31 Aug 50.

[21] Ltrs, Rhea to author, 9 and 29 Apr 53; Ltr, Wilson to author, 25 Mar 53; Ltrs, Cutler to author, 9 Mar and 3 Jul 53.

ROK troops withdrawing because friend and foe alike had them under fire.

East of the Notch, gaps in the line produced much confusion. The 3d Battalion, 29th Infantry, had been committed next to Colonel Min's force, and B Company, 29th Infantry, also went there during the day to help hold the high ground. Enemy troops tried to advance from the railroad tunnel in front of B Company, but a platoon of F Company, 19th Infantry, counterattacked and drove them back.[22]

The fighting along the road west of the Notch died down during the afternoon. The enemy apparently had moved off to the flanks in his favorite maneuver. At midafternoon a squad from A Company, 19th Infantry, went down the road past the knocked-out vehicles and killed a few enemy soldiers still near them. The men then set up a roadblock 100 yards beyond the tanks. Other groups took out American wounded and recovered most of the vehicles. The rest of A Company swept the adjoining ridge forward of the pass for several hundred yards. By evening, the enemy had withdrawn from close contact with the 19th Infantry.

American casualties in the Notch battle numbered about ninety. North Korean losses are unknown. Nor is it known how large an enemy force was engaged there. Estimates ranged among officers present from two companies to a regiment. From information gained later concerning the location of the *6th Division*, it appears that the enemy was at least in battalion strength at the Notch on 2 August, and he may have had the greater part of a regiment.

The day's events disclosed that from Chinju elements of the enemy *6th Division* had followed closely behind the withdrawing 19th Infantry, sending the bulk of its advance units up the northern road toward Masan.

Colonel Check's Reconnaissance in Force Toward Chinju

That same morning, 2 August, Colonel Check at 0400 led the 1st Battalion, 27th Infantry, with A Battery of the 8th Field Artillery Battalion attached, westward from Chindong-ni on the southern leg of the two-pronged reconnaissance. At the head of the column a platoon of infantry rode four medium tanks (Shermans). Colonel Check's immediate objective was the road juncture at Much'on-ni.

Check's column was unopposed at first. After traveling several miles, the tanks and the lead platoon forming the point caught an enemy platoon still in their blankets along the road. When the startled North Koreans jumped up and started to run, tank machine guns and riflemen killed all but two, and these they captured.[23] Soon, enemy opposition began to develop, but it was mostly from snipers and scattered patrols.

At the Much'on-ni road fork about midafternoon, Check's column met and surprised a number of enemy soldiers. The surprise was evident, as a column of enemy supply trucks had just descended from the Chinju pass. Drivers were able to turn some of the vehicles around and

---

[22] Interv, author with Moore, 17 Feb 53; Ltr, Cutler to author, 9 Mar 53; Ltr, Wilson to author, 25 Mar 53; Holliday, Notes for author, 31 Mar 53.

[23] Interv, author with Check, 6 Feb 53; 27th Inf WD, 2 Aug 50; 1st Bn, 27th Inf, Opn Rpt, Aug 50.

escape, but the North Koreans abandoned about ten vehicles, ranging from jeeps to 2½-ton trucks. These were loaded with uniforms, food, ammunition, medicine, and other supplies. Pilots of F-51 planes overhead reported later that the appearance of Check's column caused many other vehicles to turn around at the top of the pass and head toward Chinju. They made good targets for the planes.[24]

Enemy resistance now increased. Just beyond the road fork Check dismounted his motorized battalion and sent the trucks back. He did not want to run the risk of having them captured, and he believed his men could fight their way out on foot if necessary. Only the mortar platoon and the artillery battery retained their vehicles. Having no communication with the regiment, Colonel Check sent runners back to Colonel Michaelis, but none reached their destination. Enemy forces had closed in behind Check and cut the road.

Check's battalion, now afoot, advanced westward with the tanks in the lead. In the low hills at the foot of the Chinju pass, a long hard fight with the enemy began. The North Koreans held the pass in force. Sniper fire from the right (north) caused the infantry on the tanks to dismount and take cover behind them. Suddenly, Lieutenant Norrell, tank platoon leader in the third tank, saw enemy fire hit the tank ahead of him. He could see that it was coming from three antitank guns about seventy-five yards off the road to the right. His own tank then received three hits almost immediately and started to burn. In leaving his tank, Lieutenant Norrell received machine gun and shrapnel wounds.[25] This quick burst of enemy antitank fire killed the gunner in the second tank and wounded seven other enlisted tank crew members. Very quickly, however, the artillery battery took the antitank guns under fire and silenced them. The infantry then captured the pieces. There were many enemy dead in this vicinity, and others feigning death. Check walked over to the guns and noted that they were 76-mm.[26]

Colonel Check called for volunteers to form crews for the two partly disabled but still operable tanks. Men who had operated bulldozers volunteered to drive the tanks. They received quick instruction from the drivers of the two undamaged tanks. Check used riflemen as improvised tank machine gunners. The advance continued, but in the next hour gained only a few hundred yards. About 1700 or 1730, a liaison plane reappeared and dropped a message. It was from Colonel Michaelis and read, "Return. Road cut behind you all the way. Lead with tanks if possible. Will give you artillery support when within range." [27]

That morning about 1700, Colonel Michaelis at Chindong-ni received word from Colonel Moore that enemy troops had stopped his part of the reconnais-

---

[24] Interv, author with Check, 6 Feb 53; Ltr, Col Gilbert J. Check to Lt Col Carl D. McFerren, 26 Jun 53, in OCMH files.

[25] 8072d Med Tk Bn WD, 2 Aug 50.

[26] Ibid.; Interv, author with Check, 6 Feb 53. The statement by Norrell in the report that this enemy fire came from three captured U.S. 105-mm. howitzers is incorrect.

[27] Interv, author with Check, 6 Feb 53; 8072d Med Tk Bn WD, 1-7 Aug 50; 27th Inf WD, 2 Aug 50; 1st Bn, 27th Inf, Opn Rpt, Aug 50; 24th Div WD, 2 Aug 50. The records erroneously have this final action taking place at Much'on-ni.

sance just beyond its line of departure. Moore reported that he would have all he could do to hold his defensive positions. Late in the morning and in the early afternoon, Michaelis received reports that the enemy had cut the road between Check and the rest of the regiment, and that E Company in its advance blocking position was heavily engaged. It was apparent, therefore, that strong enemy forces had moved toward Masan. He thereupon, sometime after 1600, dispatched to Colonel Check the message by liaison plane to return with the 1st Battalion.[28]

Upon receiving Colonel Michaelis' message, Colonel Check immediately set about disengaging the battalion and started back. The two damaged tanks gave trouble and had to be towed by the other tanks to start them. Check put them in the lead. The two undamaged tanks brought up the rear, behind the mortar and artillery vehicles. The infantry, moving along the sides of the ridges parallel to the road, engaged in a fire fight as the withdrawal started. Just before dark, and still west of the Much'on-ni road fork, Check decided he would have to mount his infantry on the tanks and vehicles and make a run for it. Thirty to thirty-five men crowded onto the decks of each of the four tanks. The mortar and artillery trucks likewise were loaded to capacity, but every man found a place to ride.

The tank-led column went back the way it had come, almost constantly engaged with the enemy along the road. Several times the lead tanks stopped and infantry riding the decks jumped off to rush enemy machine gun positions. Until dark, the withdrawing battalion had air cover and, when it came within range, the 8th Field Artillery Battalion and a battery of 155-mm. howitzers fired shells on either side of the road, shortening the ranges as Check's battalion neared Chindong-ni. Exhausted, the 1st Battalion reached Chindong-ni at midnight. It had suffered about thirty casualties during the day. Colonel Check's leadership on this occasion won for him the Distinguished Service Cross.[29]

During the day, an estimated enemy battalion had come in behind Check's column and attacked E Company, which held the line of departure at Pongam-ni. A relief force sent from the 2d Battalion helped E Company fight its way back to the battalion's main defensive lines at Kogan-ni, three miles eastward. Still another enemy force ambushed a platoon from A Company, 65th Engineer Combat Battalion, south of Chindong-ni on the Kosong-Sach'on road, with resulting heavy personnel losses and destruction of much equipment. Obviously, North Koreans were moving east from Chinju toward Masan on all roads.[30]

The Affair at Chindong-ni

The town of Chindong-ni, where Colonel Michaelis had his command post, lies astride the south coastal road at a point where mountain spurs from

---

[28] Ltrs, Michaelis to author, 24 Jan and 29 Sep 53.

[29] Interv, author with Check, 6 Feb 53; Ltrs, Michaelis to author, 24 Jan and 29 Sep 53; 27th Inf WD, 2 Aug 50; 1st Bn, 27th Inf, Opn Rpt, Aug 50; EUSAK WD, GO 68, 15 Sep 50.

[30] 27th Inf WD, Hist Rpt, Aug 50; 2d Bn, 27th Inf, Summ of Activities, Aug 50; Ltr with comments, Murch to author, 7 Apr 54.

the north come down to meet the sea. High finger ridges end at the northern edge of the town, one on either side of the dirt road from Chindong-ni via Haman and Komam-ni to the Nam River. The ridge on the east side of this north-south road terminates in a high, steep bluff at the northeast edge of Chindong-ni. The 27th Infantry regimental command post was in a schoolhouse under the brow of this bluff. In the school courtyard a battery of 155-mm. howitzers (A Battery, 11th Field Artillery Battalion) had emplaced. Close by was the 8th Field Artillery Battalion. Colonel Check's tired 1st Battalion and the attached four medium tanks had bivouacked there at midnight.

It was a stroke of the greatest good fortune for Colonel Michaelis and the 27th Infantry regimental headquarters that Colonel Check and his 1st Battalion had returned to Chindong-ni during the night. The next morning, 3 August, just after the regimental staff had finished breakfast in the schoolhouse command post, a sudden fusillade of small arms fire hit the building and came through the open windows.[31] This first enemy fire came from the top of the bluff above the schoolhouse. It heralded an enemy attack which came as a complete surprise.

When the attack hit Chindong-ni, some of the security guards apparently were asleep. A few outpost troops mistook some of the enemy for South Koreans from other nearby outpost positions.[32] Several Americans came running shoeless down the hill to the courtyard. Colonel Michaelis and his staff officers pulled men from under jeeps and trucks and forced them into position. One soldier went berserk and started raking his own companions with machine gun fire.[33] An officer, by a well-placed shot, wounded him and stopped his murderous fire. Michaelis and Check with other officers and noncommissioned officers gradually brought order out of the chaos.

Capt. Logan E. Weston, A Company commander, led an attack against the enemy positions on the hill overlooking the command post. He assaulted two enemy machine guns on the crest and eliminated their crews by accurate M1 rifle fire. Enemy fire wounded Weston in the thigh during this action, but after receiving first aid treatment he returned to the fight and subsequently was wounded twice more. Despite three wounds he refused to be evacuated. Ten days earlier he had likewise distinguished himself in leadership and in combat near Poun.[34]

Soon the 1st Battalion had possession of the high ground near the command post. Its mortars and recoilless rifles now joined in the fight. Before long the 105-mm. howitzers were firing white phosphorus shells on concentrations of en-

---

[31] 27th Inf Activities Rpt, S-3 Sec, Aug 50; Higgins, *War in Korea*, pp. 123-30; Harold Martin, "The Colonel Saved the Day," *The Saturday Evening Post*, September 9, 1950, pp. 32-33; Michaelis with Davidson, "This We Learned in Korea," *op. cit.* Both Higgins and Martin were present. Their accounts of the Chindong-ni action are somewhat colored.

[32] Higgins, *War In Korea*, p. 124; Martin "The Colonel Saved the Day," *op. cit.*, p. 190.

[33] Interv, author with Check, 6 Feb 53.

[34] General Order 68, 15 September 1950, awarded the Distinguished Service Cross to Weston. EUSAK WD. See also Higgins, *War in Korea*.

emy troops reported from the newly won infantry positions.[35]

At the time they launched their attack, the North Koreans undoubtedly knew that artillery was at Chindong-ni, because small groups had brought it under small arms fire during the afternoon of 2 August. But infantry were not there then, and apparently the enemy did not expect to find any there the next morning. If the North Koreans surprised the 27th's command post with their attack, they in turn were surprised by the presence of Colonel Check's battalion. Once engaged in the fight, and the initial attack failing, the local North Korean commander sent at least a second battalion to Chindong-ni to reinforce the one already there and tried to salvage the situation.

Lt. Col. Augustus T. Terry, Jr., commanding officer of the 8th Field Artillery Battalion, discovered the reinforcing battalion approaching in trucks about one thousand yards away on the Haman road from the north. The trucks stopped and the enemy battalion began dismounting.[36] Colonel Terry's artillery adjusted time fire on it. After the artillery shells began falling on them, the enemy soldiers dispersed rapidly into the hills and the threatened enemy counterattack did not materialize.

By 1300 the North Koreans had withdrawn from the immediate vicinity of Chindong-ni. American patrols counted 400 enemy dead, a large number of them in the area where the 8th Field Artillery Battalion had taken the detrucking enemy soldiers under fire. The defenders of Chindong-ni estimated they had killed and wounded 600 enemy soldiers. American casualties at Chindong-ni on 3 August were 13 killed and nearly 40 wounded in the 1st Battalion, with a total of 60 casualties for all units.[37]

Interrogation of prisoners later disclosed that two battalions of the *14th Regiment*, N.K. *6th Division*, made the attack on Chindong-ni. One battalion, with the mission of establishing a roadblock at the town, made the initial early morning attack. The other two battalions of the same regiment detoured farther to the east, with the mission of establishing roadblocks closer to Masan. One of them turned back to Chindong-ni and was dispersed by artillery fire as it was detrucking. The enemy base of operations was on Sobuk-san, north of Chindong-ni. During this engagement, the enemy used commercial telephone lines. Signal officers, tapping them through the 27th Infantry regimental switchboard, monitored the enemy conversations. That night (3 August), an operations officer and a translator heard the commanding general of the N.K. *6th Division* reprimand the commander of the *14th Regiment* for losing so many men.[38]

While the prime objective of the *14th Regiment* had been to cut the Masan road, another regiment, the *15th*, apparently had the mission of capturing Masan or the high ground around it.[39]

---

[35] 1st Bn, 27th Inf, Opn Rpt, 23 Jul–3 Aug 50.
[36] 8th FA Bn WD, Aug 50, entry for 3 Aug and Summ.
[37] *Ibid.*, 1st Bn, 27th Inf, Opn Rpt, 23 Jul–3 Aug 50; 27th Inf S–3 Activities Rpt, Aug 50.
[38] 27th Inf S–3 Activities Rpt, Aug 50; 1st Bn, 27th Inf, Opn Rpt, 4–30 Aug 50; 25th Div WD, 2–3 Aug 50; Michaelis with Davidson, "This We Learned in Korea," *op. cit.*
[39] 8th FA Bn WD, Aug 50.

When the attack on Chindong-ni failed, the *15th Regiment* withheld the attack on Masan but did infiltrate the high ground southwest of the town.

The enemy *6th Division,* which had driven so rapidly eastward from Hadong, where it first encountered American troops on 27 July, had by now, in the course of a week, suffered heavy casualties which reduced it to about half strength.[40] After the battles of the Chungam-ni Notch and Chindong-ni, both sides regrouped and made ready for a new test of strength on the approaches to Masan.

The movement around the left flank of Eighth Army in late July had been the most brilliantly conceived and executed of the North Korean tactical operations south of the Han River. It had held within it the possibilities of victory—of driving U.N. forces from the peninsula. It had compelled Eighth Army to reinforce its units in the southwest at the expense of the central front, and to redeploy the U.N. forces along a shorter line behind the Naktong River, in what came to be called the Pusan Perimeter.

In early August, General Walker received what he regarded as conclusive intelligence that the enemy plan had been to supply the North Korean enveloping force in southwestern Korea by water from the port of Kunsan and other ports southward to and including Yosu. Walker said that had the enemy force driven straight and hard for Pusan instead of occupying all the ports in southwestern Korea, he would not have had time to interpose the strength to stop it.[41]

Never afterward were conditions as critical for the Eighth Army as in the closing days of July and the first days of August 1950. Never again did the North Koreans come as close to victory as when their victorious *6th* and *4th Divisions* passed eastward through Chinju and Koch'ang. Costly, bloody battles still remained, but from a U.N. strategic point of view, the most critical phase had passed. Heavy U.N. reinforcements were then arriving, or on the point of arriving, in Korea.

---

[40] ATIS Res Supp Interrog Rpts, Issue 100 (N.K. *6th Div*), pp. 37-38.

[41] Memo, Maj Gen Doyle O. Hickey (Dep CofS, FEC) to CofS, FEC, 7 Aug 50, sub: Report of Visit to Korea.

CHAPTER XV

Establishing the Pusan Perimeter

> When I hear talk of lines I always think I am hearing talk of the walls of China. The good ones are those that nature has made, and the good entrenchments are good dispositions and brave soldiers.
> MAURICE DE SAXE, *Reveries on the Art of War*

The 25th Division Moves South

Dawn of 1 August found the U.S. 25th Division moving to new defensive positions south of Sangju on the central front. At 1500 that afternoon a telephone message from Eighth Army headquarters to General Kean abruptly changed division plans. Eighth Army alerted the division for movement south to Samnangjin on the Naktong River. There it was to deny enemy movement eastward and prepare to attack westward.[1]

An advance party of the division headquarters left Poksong-dong an hour after midnight, 2 August. That morning General Kean and his party followed by plane, stopping at Taegu for a conference at Eighth Army headquarters. At the conference, General Walker changed the destination of the division from Samnangjin to Masan. General Kean informed the division units en route of the change in orders, employing every type of communication available, from runner to radio.[2]

There was only one road for the movement of the 25th Division. This ran south from Sangju to Kumch'on and then southeast to Waegwan on the Naktong River. Travel as far as Waegwan would be by foot and motor, from Waegwan to Masan by rail. The Kumch'on Waegwan road was the main supply road to the central front. Accordingly, there was ample opportunity for conflict, confusion, and delay in the movement of supplies north and of the 25th Division south over this road. Eighth Army headquarters recognized this danger. Colonel Landrum made available from headquarters to the army G-3 Section all the officers he could spare to assist in the orderly control of the 25th Division movement. These officers concentrated their attention at points where road restrictions or the presence or movement of other units threatened trouble.[3]

Equal or even greater effort had to be

---
[1] 25th Div WD, 1 Aug 50.
[2] *Ibid.*, 2 Aug 50; 24th Inf WD, 6-31 Jul 50, p. 42; 2d Bn, 24th Inf, WD, 1-31 Aug 50.
[3] Notes by Landrum for author, recd 8 Mar 54.

made to assure that the necessary rail equipment would be at hand to carry the division from Waegwan southward. At the time, with the enemy pushing the front back everywhere, there was a great demand for rail equipment to evacuate supplies and troops. Congestion in rail yards was almost indescribable. Units seeking transportation commandeered locomotives, cars jammed the tracks, native refugees crowded into cars, and general chaos threatened. The ROK 17th Regiment, moving southwest at this time to buttress the sagging 24th Division front in the Koch'ang area, further complicated the traffic problem. Without the planning, supervision, and hard work of American transportation troops, the Korean rail system would have failed at this time.[4]

The loading of heavy equipment and weapons, such as the 155-mm. howitzers, went on all during the night of 2-3 August at Waegwan. The last of the troops arrived on trucks of the 73d Truck Company at 0530, 3 August. These dust-caked men and their equipment, loaded into boxcars and gondolas, were on their way to the new front at 0600. An hour later the last of the division equipment had been loaded into cars and was on its way to Masan.[5]

The main party of the 25th Division command post arrived at Masan at 2115, 2 August, after an all-day ride. Of the combat units, the 35th Infantry moved first, closing at Masan at 1000, 3 August. The 24th Infantry arrived at 1930 that evening. General Kean reached Masan during the day and assumed command of all the U.N. troops south of the Naktong River. The 25th Division completed the 150-mile move by foot, motor, and rail within a 36-hour period.

General Walker said that this "history making maneuver" saved Pusan. He said also that had the North Koreans attacked strongly on the Kumch'on front while the division was passing over the single road through Kumch'on, "we couldn't have done it." [6]

In recognizing the critical nature of the situation in the southwest and in acting with great energy and decisiveness to meet it, General Walker and his staff conceived and executed one of the most important command decisions of the Korean War.

United Nations Forces Withdraw Behind the Naktong

By the end of July, the enemy pressure that forced General Walker to move the 25th Division from the central to the southern front forced on him also, partly as a consequence of that move, the decision to withdraw Eighth Army across the Naktong. The withdrawal was planned to start the night of 1 August.[7]

On 30 July the 34th Infantry of the 24th Division, driven from Koch'ang, was in a defensive position near Sanje-ri astride the road to Hyopch'on and the Naktong River. That day, the 21st Infantry Regiment—except for C Company and a section of 81-mm. mortars, still at Yongdok on the east coast, and the 3d Battalion, just attached to the 1st

---

[4] See Col E. C. R. Lasher, "A Transport Miracle Saved Pusan," *Transportation Journal* (November-December, 1950), pp. 12-13.
[5] *Ibid.*

[6] New York *Times*, August 11, 1950, AP dispatch from Korea, dated 10 August, reporting conversation of General Walker.
[7] EUSAK WD, G-3 Sec, 28 and 31 Jul 50.

Cavalry Division—crossed the Naktong and took a position behind the 34th Infantry. The ROK 17th Regiment also arrived and occupied the high ground on the right (north) of the 34th Infantry. The next morning the 34th Infantry withdrew behind the 21st Infantry. Colonel Stephens then assumed command of both the 21st and the 34th Regiments on oral orders from General Church.[8]

After the 34th Infantry withdrew through the 1st Battalion, 21st Infantry, Colonel Stephens moved the ROK 17th Regiment back abreast of his troops, with one battalion on either flank and one in reserve. The next day, 1 August, North Koreans attacked both flanks. The ROK's repulsed them. General Church initially had intended that the ROK 17th Regiment would pass through the mountains around the flank of the North Koreans and attack from their rear while the 34th and 21st Regiments held them in front. But the army order for withdrawal came before this could be done. The ROK 17th Regiment at this time had a high reputation. Colonel Kim, the commander, a small man of twenty-eight years, commanded the respect of his officers and men. In a conference at this time, General Church asked Colonel Kim if his ROK's would hold their part of the line. He answered, "We will stay as long as the Americans." He was believed implicitly by those present.[9]

On 1 August Eighth Army issued an operational directive to all United Nations ground forces in Korea for their planned withdrawal behind the Naktong. It confirmed oral and fragmentary orders already issued to units on their redeployment to the main defensive positions of the Pusan Perimeter.[10]

At 0945, 2 August, Colonel Stephens received Eighth Army's order to withdraw. He at once sent the 34th Infantry across the Naktong to the Yongsan area. During the day, while the 21st Infantry and the ROK 17th Regiment fended off enemy probing attacks, he made plans to complete the withdrawal that night to the east side of the Naktong.[11]

The withdrawal east across the Naktong by the 21st Infantry proceeded smoothly during the night of 2-3 August. The last of the regiment crossed the Koryong-Taegu bridge forty-five minutes past midnight, followed by the 14th Engineer Combat Battalion two hours later. The ROK 17th Regiment, covering the withdrawal of the other units (Colonel Stephens remained with it), crossed the river at 0630, 3 August. Engineers unsuccessfully tried to blow the bridge at 0715. During the day the 3d Engineer Combat Battalion again prepared it for demolition and dropped it that night. The preceding night, at 2200, the engineers blew the other Naktong River bridge in the 24th Division sector. It was twenty air miles south of the Koryong bridge and connected

---

[8] 21st Inf WD, 30-31 Jul 50; 24th Div WD, 31 Jul 50; Interv, author with Beauchamp, 24 Sep 52; Ltr, Beauchamp to author, 7 Apr 53; Stephens, MS review comments, Dec 57.

[9] Interv, author with Church, 25 Sep 52; Interv, author with Cheek, 5 Aug 51; Interv, author with Maj Charles R. Alkire (S-2, 21st Inf), 1 Aug 51; Interv, author with Col Richard W. Stephens, 8 Oct 51.

[10] EUSAK WD, G-3 Sec, an. 3, 1 Aug 50. Annex 3 includes a copy of the directive, Plan D.

[11] 21st Inf WD, 2 Aug 50; 24th Div WD, 2 Aug 50. The 24th Division received the Eighth Army Directive, dated 1 August 1950, at 020230.

Ch'ogye with Changnyong, 24th Division headquarters.[12]

On the evening of 3 August, the third regiment of the division, the 19th Infantry, was relieved in its position at the Chungam-ni Notch west of Masan by the 35th Infantry of the 25th Division. It then moved northeast across the Naktong to the command post of the 24th Division at Changnyong, arriving there the next day. From the time of its commitment in Korea on 13 July to 4 August, the 19th Regiment had lost 80 percent of its 1/4-ton trucks, 50 percent of its 3/4-ton trucks, and 33 percent of its 2 1/2-ton trucks. Low on all supplies, it found individual clothing, hand grenades, 4.2-in. mortar ammunition, and flares and illumination shells all but impossible to obtain.[13]

Simultaneous with the movement of the 24th Division to the east side of the Naktong, the 1st Cavalry Division, next in line above it, began withdrawing on army orders from the Chirye-Kumch'on area to Waegwan on the east side of the river. The division withdrew without difficulty, except for the 5th Cavalry Regiment. This regiment, the last in the march order, was heavily engaged and one battalion nearly lost. By nightfall of 3 August, however, all units of the division were across the Naktong except the rear guard of the 1st Battalion, 8th Cavalry Regiment, which had been blocking on the Songju road, southwest of the Waegwan bridges.[14]

The main line railroad bridges and the highway bridge across the Naktong at Waegwan were to be blown as soon as all units of the 1st Cavalry Division had crossed. These bridges were the most important on the river. General Gay, in arranging for their destruction, gave orders that no one but himself could order the bridges blown. At dusk on 3 August, thousands of refugees crowded up to the bridges on the west side of the river, and repeatedly, as the rear guard of the 8th Cavalry would start across the bridge, the mass of refugees would follow. The division commander ordered the rear guard to return to the west side and hold back the refugees. When all was ready the troops were to run across to the east side so that the bridge could be blown. This plan was tried several times, but in each instance the refugees were on the heels of the rear guard. Finally, when it was nearly dark, General Gay, feeling that he had no alternative, gave the order to blow the bridge. It was a hard decision to make, for hundreds of refugees were lost when the bridge was demolished.[15]

The refugee problem was a constant source of trouble and danger to the U.N. Command during the early part of the war. During the middle two weeks of July it was estimated that about 380,000 refugees had crossed into ROK-held territory, and that this number was increasing at the rate of 25,000 daily. The refugees were most numerous in the areas of enemy advance. In July and

---

[12] 24th Div WD, 3-4 Aug 50; 21st Inf WD, 2-3 Aug 50; 24th Div G-3 Jnl, Msg 483, 022330 Aug 50; EUSAK WD, G-3 Jnl, 3 Aug 50.

[13] 19th Inf WD, 22 Jul-4 Aug 50; Ibid., 22 Jul-25 Aug 50, Logistics Sec.

[14] Ltr, Gay to author, and attached notes, 24 Aug 50; EUSAK WD, G-3 Jnl, 3 Aug 50, Msg from 1st Cav Div.

[15] Ltr, Gay to author, 24 Aug 50; EUSAK WD, G-3 Jnl, 3 Aug 50; Ibid., POR 66, 3 Aug 50. By the end of July 1950, the South Korean government had established fifty-eight refugee camps, most of them in the Pusan-Taegu area, to care for the homeless people.

August 1950, the volume of refugees moving through U.N. lines was greater than at any other time in the war.

With the destruction of the Waegwan bridges, Eighth Army by the morning of 4 August had destroyed all the bridges across the Naktong on its front. Its troops were in defensive positions on the east bank awaiting enemy crossings.

On a line curving north and east from Waegwan, the divisions of the ROK Army also withdrew across the river, co-ordinating their moves with Eighth Army on the night of 2-3 August. In this movement, the ROK forces had some severe fighting. The ROK 1st Division was heavily engaged north of the river on 2 August, while the 16th Regiment of the ROK 8th Division was even more heavily engaged by the N.K. *12th Division* at Andong.[16]

It was evident in the last days of July and the first of August that General Walker was concerned about the failure of his troops to carry out orders to maintain contact with the enemy. In preparing for the withdrawal to the Perimeter position, on 30 July he had ordered all units to maintain such contact. Three days later conditions compelled him to repeat the order with the injunction that division commanders give it their personal attention. Later in the day he thought it necessary to issue still another directive which ordered, "Daily counterattacks will be made by all units. . . . Commanders will take immediate and aggressive action to insure that these and previous instructions to this effect are carried out without delay." "Counterattack," Walker said, "is a decisive elm [element] of the defense."[17]

The Naktong River Line, as many called it, was the vital position where Eighth Army intended to make its stand. On 4 August, General Church issued to the 24th Division an order typical of those issued to American troops at this time. He directed that every man in the division know the order. It said:

Defensive and alternate positions must be prepared, routes reconnoitered, intensive patrolling of the river at night, communications perfected, and each individual know his job. There will be no withdrawal nor need there be any if each and every one contributes his share to the preparation, and, if attacked, has the will to fight it out here.

Every soldier will under all circumstances retain his weapon, ammunition, and his entrenching tool. Without these he ceases to be a soldier capable of defending himself. Many of our losses have been occasioned by failure to dig a foxhole when the time permitted.[18]

The Pusan Perimeter

The Pusan Perimeter positions taken up by the American and ROK forces on 4 August enclosed a rectangular area about 100 miles from north to south and about 50 miles from east to west. (*See Map IV.*) The Naktong River formed the western boundary of the Perimeter except for the southernmost 15 miles below the point where it turned eastward after its confluence with the Nam. The Sea of Japan formed the

---

[16] EUSAK WD, Opn Directive in G-3 an., 1 Aug 50; *Ibid.*, POR 61, 2 Aug 50; GHQ UNC G-3 Opn Rpts 38 and 39, 1-2 Aug 50; GHQ UNC, Telecon TT3619, 3 Aug 50.

[17] EUSAK WD, G-3 Jnl, Msg at 301850 Jul 50; *Ibid.*, G-3 Sec, Msg at 020845 Aug 50; *Ibid.*, G-3 Sec, 2 Aug 50.

[18] 24th Div WD, G-2 Jnl, 2-5 Aug 50, entry 232, 4 Aug 50.

eastern boundary, and the Korea Strait the southern boundary. An irregular curved line through the mountains from above Waegwan to Yongdok formed the northern boundary. Yongdok on the east coast stood at the northeast corner of the Perimeter, Pusan was at the southeast corner, Masan at the southwest corner, and Taegu near the middle from north to south, but only about 10 miles from the western and threatened side of the Perimeter. From Pusan, Masan is 30 air miles west, Taegu 55 miles northwest, P'ohang-dong 60 miles northeast, Yongdok 90 miles northeast. With the exception of the delta of the Naktong and the east-west valley between Taegu and P'ohang-dong, the ground is rough and mountainous. The mountains are particularly forbidding in the northeast above P'ohang-dong.

In planning for the defense of the Perimeter, Eighth Army believed it needed at least two reserve forces, one in the vicinity of Kyongsan, 10 miles southeast of Taegu, which it could use to bolster any part of the line in the center and in the P'ohang-dong area of the east coast, and another in the vicinity of Samnangjin-Miryang, which it could use against any threatened or actual enemy breakthrough along the lower Naktong or the Masan corridor.[19]

General Walker reported to the Far East Command at this time that he thought the 24th Division would have to be completely rehabilitated before it could be effective. He also doubted that the 25th Division had offensive capabilities. He intended to use the 30,000 ROK trainees, he said, mostly to bring the existing ROK divisions to full strength. After that was done, he would begin the organization of new ROK divisions.[20]

The deployment of U.N. forces on the arc curving from the southwest to the northeast as the battle of the Perimeter opened was as follows: U.S. 25th Infantry Division, U.S. 24th Infantry Division, U.S. 1st Cavalry Division, and then the ROK 1st, 6th, 8th, Capital, and 3d Divisions, in that order.

In the southwest, Eighth Army had hoped to anchor the line near the coast on the Chinju pass, but the enemy had forced the line eastward to a point just west of Chindong-ni, whence it ran northward from the coast to the Nam River below Uiryong, a few miles west of the confluence of the Nam and the Naktong. The 27th, 24th, and 35th Regiments of the 25th Division were on line in that order, south to north, with some ROK's (Task Force Min) interspersed among them, particularly in the 24th Infantry sector. The division command post was at Masan.[21] In addition, General Kean had at hand the 5th Regimental Combat Team, attached to the 25th Division, and the 89th Medium Tank Battalion.

Opposite the 25th Division stood the N.K. *6th Division* and the *83d Motorized*

---

[19] EUSAK WD, 4 Aug 50, Plan for Relief of 24th Inf Div.

[20] Memo, Hickey for CofS FEC, 7 Aug 50; sub: Report on Visit to Korea.
[21] 25th Div WD, 4 Aug 50; Ibid., Summ, Aug 50; 35th Inf Unit Hist, 3-4 Aug 50; 27th Inf WD, 3d Bn, 27th Inf, Hist Rpt, Aug 50; EUSAK Opn Directive 031830 Aug 50. The 25th Division now had the normal 9 battalions in its 3 regiments. An Eighth Army radio message on 3 August ordered the 1st and 3d Battalions, 29th Infantry, attached to the 25th Division. The division, in turn, on 6 August attached the 1st Battalion to the 35th Infantry and the next day attached the 3d Battalion to the 27th Regiment, as their third battalions.

Regiment of the *105th Armored Division*.

Next on the U.N. line was the U.S. 24th Division. Its zone lay north of the Nam and along the east bank of the Naktong for 25 air miles, or about 40 miles of river front. The 34th and 21st Infantry Regiments and the ROK 17th Regiment were on line in that order, south to north. The 19th Infantry was in division reserve, re-equipping after arriving from the Masan front on 4 August. The 21st Infantry front was so long that Colonel Stephens, the regimental commander, placed seven .50-caliber machine guns with crews from the 14th Engineer Combat Battalion in the main line of resistance. The division command post had now moved to Miryang.

Eighth Army on 3 August defined the boundary between the 24th and 25th Divisions as the south bank of the Naktong River, and made the commanding general of the 24th Division responsible for bridges, ferries, and small boats along the stream. General Church was to remove to the north bank, and destroy as he deemed advisable, all boats and ferries, and to prepare all bridges for demolition and blow them at his discretion. At this time, Eighth Army planned for the 9th and 23d Regiments of the 2d Infantry Division to relieve the 24th Division in its sector of the line the night of 8 August, but events were to make this impossible.[22]

Opposite the 24th Division stood the N.K. *4th Division*.

Above the 24th Division, the U.S. 1st Cavalry Division extended the line 18 air miles to a point 3 miles north of Waegwan. The actual river line was about 35 miles. The 7th Cavalry (less the 1st Battalion, which was in division reserve), the 8th Cavalry, and the 5th Cavalry Regiments were in position in the division sector, in that order from south to north. The division command post was at Taegu. Taegu, also Eighth Army headquarters, lay about 10 miles east of the Naktong River behind the center of the 1st Cavalry Division front.[23]

Opposite the 1st Cavalry Division was the N.K. *3d Division*.

The three American divisions each had fronts to defend from 20 to 40 miles long. The Naktong River Line at this time resembled closely the German front before Moscow after the first German withdrawal in 1941, when Guderian's divisions each had a front of 25 to 35 miles to defend.[24]

North of Waegwan, the ROK 1st and 6th Divisions of the ROK II Corps extended the line north along the Naktong for 20 more air miles, and thence northeast for about 10 miles toward Uisong. From there the 8th and Capital Divisions of the ROK I Corps continued the line northeast through Uisong where it turned east toward Yongdok on the coast. On the east coast the ROK 3d Division held the right anchor of the U.N. line. The ROK Army headquarters was at Taegu with a forward command post at Sinnyong. ROK I Corps headquarters was at Uisong; ROK II Corps headquarters at Kunwi.[25]

North of Waegwan, the N.K. *15th*

---

[22] EUSAK WD, G-3 Sec, 3 Aug 50, Msg at 031130; *Ibid.*, 4 Aug 50, Plan for Relief of 24th Inf Div.

[23] 1st Cav Div WD, G-2 Narr Rpt, Aug 50; EUSAK WD, POR 66, 3 Aug 50.

[24] Guderian, *Panzer Leader*, p. 265.

[25] EUSAK WD, POR 64, 3 Aug 50; GHQ UNC Sitrep, 5 Aug 50.

and part of the *13th Divisions* faced the ROK 1st Division; eastward, part of the N.K. *13th* and the *1st Division* faced the ROK 6th Division; beyond them the N.K. *8th Division* stood in front of the ROK 8th Division; next in line, the N.K. *12th Division* confronted the ROK Capital Division below Andong; and, finally, on the east coast the N.K. *5th Division* and the *766th Independent Infantry Regiment* faced the ROK 3d Division.[26]

In summary then, the ROK Army held the east half of the line from a point just above Waegwan; the U.S. Eighth Army held the west or southern part. The ROK sector extended for about 80 air miles; the Eighth Army's for about 65 air miles. The ROK troops held the most mountainous portions of the line and the part with the poorest lines of communications.

The North Korean Army comprised two corps: *I Corps* controlled operations generally along the western side of the perimeter opposite the American units; *II Corps* controlled operations along the northern or eastern half of the perimeter opposite the ROK units. This enemy corps alignment remained unchanged throughout the Pusan Perimeter period of the war.[27]

The N.K. Army had activated its *I Corps* at P'yongyang about 10 June 1950, its *II Corps* at the same place about 12 June 1950. In early August 1950, the N.K. *I Corps* included the *3d, 4th,* and *6th* (later also the *2d, 7th, 9th,* and *10th*) *Divisions; II Corps* included the *1st, 5th, 8th, 12th, 13th,* and *15th Divisions*. Tanks and personnel of the *105th Armored Division* were divided between the two corps and supported both of them.

The establishment of the Pusan Perimeter may be considered as a dividing line in viewing and appraising the combat behavior of the American soldier in the Korean War. The Pusan Perimeter for the first time gave something approaching a continuous line of troops. With known units on their left and right and some reserves in the rear, the men showed a stronger disposition to fight. Before the Pusan Perimeter, all through July and into the first days of August, there was seldom a continuous line beyond a battalion or a regimental position. Both flanks were generally wide open, and enemy troops moving through the hills could easily turn a defensive position. Supporting troops were seldom within reach. American soldiers, realizing the isolated nature of their positions, often would not stay to fight a losing battle. Few in July 1950 saw any good reason for dying in Korea; with no inspiring incentive to fight, self-preservation became the dominating factor.

U.S. Air Action and Build-up in the First Month

Air support, tactical and strategical, and the state of logistics at the end of July after the first month of war both

---

[26] ATIS Res Supp Interrog Rpts, Issues 99, 94, 104, 100, 96, 3, and 4; GHQ UNC Telecon TT3619, 3 Aug 50; TT3623, 4 Aug 50; TT3630, 7 Aug 50. GHQ UNC Sitrep, 6 Aug 50, and TT3623 have the N.K. *2d Division* opposite the ROK 1st Division. Actually, the enemy *2d Division* was in a rest area behind the line. The N.K. *1st Division* entered the Perimeter battle 8 August, after resting at Hamch'ang several days and taking in several thousand replacements.

[27] GHQ FEC, History of the N.K. Army, 31 Jul 52, pp. 41–42.

exercised continuing and pervasive influence on the course of the heavy August battles of the Pusan Perimeter.

In the first month of the Korean War, close air support of ground troops was a vital factor in preventing the North Koreans from overrunning all Korea, and in gaining for the United States the margin of time necessary to bring in reinforcements and accumulate the supplies needed to organize the Pusan Perimeter. By mid-July the U.N. Air Force had all but stopped movement of enemy troops, armor, and truck convoys during daylight. This imposed the greatest difficulties on North Korea in supporting its front-line troops, and it slowed the North Korean advance.

During the first month, the U.N. air arm comprised U.S. Air Force, Navy, and Marine planes and some Royal Australian Air Force planes and troops. By the end of July, the U.N. ground forces in Korea were receiving proportionately more air support than had General Bradley's Twelfth Army Group in World War II.[28]

In mid-July, the FEAF Bomber Command began an ever heightening attack on strategic enemy targets far behind the front. The first such target was Wonsan on the east coast. This communications center linked Vladivostok in Russia Siberia with North Korea by rail and sea. From it, rail lines ran to all the North Korean build-up centers. The great bulk of Russian supplies for North Korea in the early part of the war came in at Wonsan, and from the beginning it was considered a major military target. In the first heavy strategic bombing of the war, FEAF hit this busy port city, on 13 July, with 400 tons of demolition bombs. Three days later, thirty B-29 bombers struck the railroad marshaling yards at Seoul.[29]

One of the important bomber missions was to deny the enemy use of the ponton bridge across the Han River at Seoul, and to destroy the repaired railroad bridge there. Several attempts in July by B-29's to destroy the rail bridge failed, but on the 29th twelve bombers succeeded in hitting the ponton bridge and reported it destroyed. The next day, forty-seven B-29's bombed the Chosen Nitrogen Plant at Hungnam on the northeast coast.[30]

In the meantime, carrier-based planes from the USS *Valley Forge,* which was operating in the Yellow Sea, on 22 July destroyed at Haeju in North Korea six locomotives, exploded eighteen cars of a 33-car train, and damaged a combination highway and rail bridge.[31]

By 27 July, the FEAF Bomber Command had a comprehensive rail interdiction plan ready. This plan sought to interdict the flow of enemy troops and matériel from North Korea to the combat area. Two cut points—(1) the P'yongyang railroad bridge and marshaling yards and (2) the Hamhung bridge and Hamhung and Wonsan marshaling yards

---

[28] "Air War in Korea," *Air University Quarterly Review,* IV, No. 2 (Fall, 1950), 19-39. Fourteen fighter-bomber groups supported Bradley's 28 divisions; at the end of July 1950, 8 fighter-bomber groups supported the 3 American and 5 ROK divisions in Korea.

[29] GHQ FEC Sitrep, 12-14 Jul 50; New York *Times,* July 23, 1950. The 92d Bombardment Group was at Yokota in Japan; the 22d, at Kadena on Okinawa.

[30] GHQ UNC G-3 Opn Rpt Nr 33, 27 Jul 50; Nr 35, 29 Jul, and Nr 37, 31 Jul 50; New York *Times,* July 28, 1950.

[31] GHQ FEC Sitrep, 22 Jul 50.

—would sever rail communications with North Korea. Destruction of the rail bridges over the Han near Seoul would cut rail communication to the battle area. On 28 July the Far East Air Forces gave to the Bomber Command a list of targets in the rail interdiction program, and two days later a similar plan was ready for interdiction of highways. On the third day of August, FEAF issued to the Fifth Air Force and to the Navy lists of targets for co-ordinated interdiction attacks south of the 38th Parallel. In general, the Han River divided Fifth Air Force and FEAF Bomber Command zones.[32]

By the end of July, the Far East Air Forces had flown as many as 400 sorties in a day. Altogether, it had flown a total of 8,600 sorties—4,300 in close support missions, 2,550 in close interdiction, 57 in two strategic bombing strikes, and 1,600 in reconnaissance and cargo sorties.[33]

As the month neared an end, the first fighter plane reinforcements from the United States reached the Far East. On 23 July, the 27,000-ton Navy carrier, *Boxer*, setting a Pacific crossing record of eight days and seven hours, arrived in Japan with 145 F–51 Mustangs borrowed from National Guard air squadrons.[34] On 30 July, the Far East Air Forces had 890 planes—626 F–80's and 264 F–51's —but only 525 of them were in units and available and ready for combat.[35]

Rockets, napalm, and .50-caliber machine gun fire in strafing were the effective weapons used by the close support fighter planes. Napalm, the jellied gasoline carried in wing tanks, generated a searing heat when ignited by a contact fuze upon striking the ground. The splashing, flaming liquid is a two-edged weapon: it burns and consumes, and it strikes men with terror when it bursts on or near their positions. No one who has seen the huge, podlike tanks hurtle to the ground and burst into orange balls of flame, quickly followed by billowing clouds of dense, black smoke, would care to withstand this form of attack.

The consumption of aviation gasoline was so great in the early phase of the war, as compared to the available supply in the Far East, that it became one of the serious logistical problems. Ocean tankers could scarcely keep pace with the rate of consumption. The situation never got to the point where air operations stopped, but it came near to that. There were times when the gas terminals in Japan were empty—all the fuel was in the stations.[36]

Just as Eighth Army prepared to fall back behind the Naktong River, important ground reinforcements from Hawaii and the United States arrived in Korea. The United States had barely won the race against *space* and *time*.

The 5th Regimental Combat Team from Hawaii, commanded by Col. Godwin L. Ordway, arrived first, on 31 July,

---

[32] USAF Hist Study 71, pp. 35–37.
[33] "Air War in Korea," *op. cit.*, p. 21.
[34] *Ibid.*; Karig, *et al.*, *Battle Report: The War in Korea*, p. 104; New York *Times*, July 23, 1950. The *Boxer* also brought to the Far East 25 other planes, 1,100 Army and Air Force personnel, 190,000 gallons of aviation gasoline, 16,000 gallons of lubricating oil, and a very large cargo of shells, bombs, and other ammunition.

[35] FEAF Opns Hist, vol. 1, 25 Jun–1 Nov 50, pp. 89–90.
[36] Interv, author with Maj Gen George L. Eberle, 12 Jan 54. Eberle was GHQ UNC G–4.

after nine days at sea, with all three battalions. With the regiment came fourteen M26 Pershing tanks and the 555th (Triple Nickel) Field Artillery Battalion. Orders from Eighth Army awaited the regiment upon its arrival at Pusan to proceed at once to Masan where it was to be attached to the 24th Division. The leading element of the regiment arrived at Masan the next evening, 1 August. By the following morning the entire regiment was in an assembly area north of the town.[37]

This regiment included many Hawaiians and some former members of the famed 442d Regimental and the 100th Battalion Combat Teams, the much-decorated Nisei infantry units of World War II. Another notable characteristic of this regiment was the close bond of comradeship that existed between it and its supporting 555th Field Artillery Battalion.

Into Pusan harbor on the same day, 31 July, came the first ground troops from the United States, the 9th Infantry Regiment of the 2d Infantry Division. Known as the Manchu Regiment because of its part in suppressing the Boxer Rebellion in China in 1900, the 9th Infantry was one of the oldest regiments in the United States Army. The 2d Battalion of the regiment sailed from Tacoma, Washington, 17 July, the first Army infantry troops to depart continental United States for Korea. The 9th Infantry, commanded by Col. John G. Hill, proceeded immediately to Kyongsan, ten miles southeast of Taegu, and was placed in army reserve. The 15th Field Artillery Battalion accompanied the regiment as its artillery support unit. At 0130, 2 August, Eighth Army ordered Colonel Hill to be ready to move his regiment on 1-hour notice after 1600 that day.[38]

The 23d Infantry, 2d Division, began arriving at Pusan on 5 August. That very morning its 1st Battalion received an alert to be ready to move on an hour's notice.[39]

A third major reinforcement arrived in Korea on 2 August—the 1st Provisional Marine Brigade, commanded by Brig. Gen. Edward A. Craig. Activated on 7 July, the brigade began loading at San Diego and Long Beach, Calif., two days later and sailed for the Far East on the 14th. While still at sea it received orders to bypass Japan and head directly for Pusan. On 25 July, General Wright, Far East Command G-3, verbally ordered General Craig, who was in Japan with his advance party, to change his brigade plans from occupying the Kobe-Osaka-Kyoto area of Japan to reporting with the brigade to Eighth Army in Korea. The marines went ashore at Pusan on 3 August and proceeded immediately to Masan in Eighth Army reserve. The Marine brigade was attached to the 25th Division on 6 August. The brigade comprised the 5th Marines, commanded by Lt. Col. Raymond L. Murray, plus a brigade headquarters group. The three battalions of the regiment had only two rifle com-

---

[37] GHQ UNC Sitrep, 31 Jul 50; GHQ UNC G-3 Opn Rpt, 1-2 Aug 50; Schnabel, FEC, GHQ Support and Participation in Korean War, ch. iii, p. 23; 24th Div G-3 Jnl, 29 Jul-6 Aug 50, entry 420, 011825.

[38] 2d Div WD, 8 Jul-31 Aug 50, G-2 Hist Sec, pp. 14, 28; EUSAK WD, G-3 Sec, 30 Jul and 2 Aug 50.

[39] 2d Div WD, 8 Jul-31 Aug 50, G-2 Hist Sec, p. 28.

panies each and a Heavy Weapons Company. The brigade had a strength of 4,725 men. Most of the officers and about 65 percent of the noncommissioned officers of the Marine brigade were combat veterans.[40]

Initially, General MacArthur had planned to use the Marine brigade in an amphibious operation behind the enemy lines. The situation at the time the brigade arrived in Far Eastern waters, however, required its unloading at Pusan. Every available man, it appeared, would be needed to hold the Pusan Perimeter.

Except A Company, which already had arrived, the 8072d Medium Tank Battalion, a provisional organization equipped in Japan with repaired tanks salvaged from the Pacific island battlefields of World War II, came into Pusan harbor on 4 August. Three days later Eighth Army transferred its troops and equipment to the 89th Medium Tank Battalion. Other tanks were on the way. The SS *Luxembourg Victory* left San Francisco on 26 July carrying eighty medium tanks.[41]

Replacements from the United States also had begun to flow into the Far East Command for assignment in Korea. In July, several hundred officer and 5,287 of 5,300 promised enlisted replacements arrived in Japan and were hurried on to Korea. The Far East Command indicated that the volume of replacements would increase during August and September and reach 16,000 in October. For the last ten days of July, the airlift brought an average of 42 officers and 103 enlisted men daily from the United States west coast, about 100 less than the 240 estimated at its inception as the airlift's daily capacity.[42]

The type of war matériel coming into Pusan Harbor during July shows why the United Nations Command had to hold a defense perimeter around this vital port if the North Koreans were to be denied victory.

During the period of 2-31 July 1950, a total of 309,314 measurement tons of supplies and equipment were offloaded at Pusan, a daily average of 10,666 tons.

The first heavy lift cranes arrived on 23 July—a 60-ton crane and two crawler cranes, towed 900 miles from Yokohama. Not until the first week of August did a 100-ton crane reach Pusan. In the last half of July, Pusan was a busy port indeed, 230 ships arriving and 214 departing during the final sixteen days of the month. During this period, 42,581 troops, 9,454 vehicles, and 88,888 long tons of supplies came ashore there. Sub-

---

[40] 1st Prov Mar Brig Special Act Rpt (hereafter cited as SAR), 2 Aug-6 Sep 50, pp. 1-4; 5th Mar Regt SAR, 2 Aug-6 Sep 50; 1st Bn, 5th Mar, SAR, Aug 50, p. 1; EUSAK WD, G-4 Stf Sec, 3 Aug 50; *Ibid.*, POR 64, 3 Aug 50; GHQ UNC G-3 Opn Rpt, 3 Aug 50. Lynn Montross and Capt. Nicholas A. Canzona, USMC, *U.S. Marine Operations in Korea, 1950-1953*, vol. I, *The Pusan Perimeter* (Washington: Historical Branch, G-3, Headquarters, U.S. Marine Corps, 1954), pp. 65-89. This and succeeding volumes give a detailed account of the marines' part in the Korean War. Canzona, a participant in the Marine operations in Korea, was a member of the Marine brigade and subsequently of the 1st Marine Division.

[41] GHQ UNC G-3 Opn Rpt 41, 4 Aug 50; EUSAK GO 189, par. 1, 0001, 7 Aug 50; GHQ UNC G-3 Opn Rpt 37, 31 Jul 50.

[42] EUSAK WD, 31 Jul 50, Memo for Col Conley, sub: Projected Replacement Status; *Ibid.*, G-1 Stf Sec. Replacement quota for August was 1,900 officers, 9,500 enlisted men; for September, 1,500 officers, 11,500 enlisted men; and for October, 1,200 officers, 16,000 enlisted men.

PIER 2 AT PUSAN *where the bulk of American supplies was landed.*

ordinate ports of Ulsan and Suyong unloaded ammunition and petroleum products over the beaches from barges, tankers, and LCM's.[43]

The airlift of critically needed items from the United States tapered off at the end of July as surface transportation began to meet requirements. Some items such as the new 3.5-inch rocket were still being carried largely by airlift, 900 of them being scheduled daily for air delivery to Korea during August. The new 5-inch "shaped charge" rockets for Navy fighter planes, developed at the Navy's Inyokern, California, Ordnance Test Station, were at first delivered to Korea entirely by air. A special Air Force plane picked up at Inyokern on 29 July the first 200 of the shaped charge warheads for delivery to the Far East.[44]

After the first hectic weeks, steps were taken to reduce the necessity for the large number of airlifts to Korea from Japan. By 15 July, MacArthur's headquarters sent to Eighth Army a proposal to provide daily ferry service from the Hakata-Moji area to Pusan, and to provide this service with fast express trains from the Tokyo-Yokohama area.[45] Accordingly, a Red Ball Express was organized. It had a capacity of 300 measurement tons daily of items and supplies critically needed in Korea. The Red Ball made the run from Yokohama to Sasebo in a little more than thirty hours, and to Pusan in a total of about fifty-three hours. The first Red Ball Express train with high priority cargo left Yokohama at 1330 23 July. Regular daily runs became effective two days later. The schedule called for the Red Ball to depart Yokohama at 2330 nightly and arrive at Sasebo at 0542 the second morning thereafter, and for the cargo to be transferred directly from train to ship. Ship departure was scheduled for 1330 daily and arrival at Pusan at 0400 the next morning.[46]

Army transportation men worked almost ceaselessly during July to bring order out of near chaos in the train movements from Pusan toward the railheads at the front. By 18 July they had established a regular daily schedule of supply trains over two routes: (1) the main Pusan-Taegu-Kumch'on line with

---

[43] Pusan Logistical Command Activities Rpt, Trans Sec, Jul 50; Mossman and Middleton, Logistical Problems and Their Solution, EUSAK.

[44] GHQ UNC G-3 Opn Rpt 37, 31 Jul 50; "Air War in Korea," *op. cit.,* p. 21.
[45] GHQ FEC Sitrep, 20 Jul 50.
[46] Ibid., 23 Jul 50; EUSAK WD, Summ, 13-31 Jul 50, 25 Jul; Ibid., G-4 Stf Sec Rpt, 25 Jul 50.

a branch line from Kumch'on to Hamch'ang; and (2) the Pusan-Kyongju-Andong single track line up the east coast with a branch line from Kyongju to P'ohang-dong. As the battle front moved swiftly southward, trains after the end of July did not run beyond Taegu and P'ohang-dong. After the enemy threat developed in the southwest, a supply train ran daily from Pusan to Masan. On 1 July the U.N. Command controlled 1,404 miles of rail track in South Korea. By the end of the month this had shrunk to 431 miles of track, a loss of 973 miles, or more than two-thirds.[47]

In July, 350 mixed trains moved from Pusan toward the front. These included 2,313 freight cars loaded with 69,390 short tons of supplies. Also leaving Pusan for the front were 71 personnel trains carrying military units and replacements. Among the trains returning to Pusan from the forward area were 38 hospital trains carrying 2,581 patients, and 158 freight cars loaded largely with personal belongings taken by unit commanders from their men in trying to strip them down to only combat needs.[48]

Since the Korean railroads had been built by Japan, repair and replacement items could be borrowed from the Japanese National Railways and airlifted to Korea within a very short time after the need for them became known. One of the largest and most important of rail purchases in Japan for use in Korea was twenty-five standard-gauge locomotives. By 1 August the ROK National Police

60-TON CRANE AT PUSAN

was responsible for protecting all rail bridges and tunnels. Armed guards, their number varying with the importance of the structures, were stationed at each of them.[49]

The re-equipping of the ROK Army constituted in itself a large logistical problem in July. To meet part of the requirements, Japanese manufacturers contracted in August to produce for the ROK Army 68,000 vehicles, mostly cargo and dump trucks, with first deliveries to be made in September. Another matter of importance concerned replacing artillery losses in the early weeks of the war with World War II 105-mm. howitzers rebuilt in Japan.[50]

During the fourth week of American intervention, certain formal procedures

---

[47] Pusan Log Comd, Activities Rpt, Trans Sec, Jul 50; *Ibid.*, HQ, Plat Ldrs' Class, (B) (Provisional), Memo 1, 18 Jul 50.
[48] *Ibid.*, Trans Sec and Table V, Jul 50.

[49] GHQ FEC Ann Narr Hist Rpt, 1 Jan–31 Oct 50, p. 47; EUSAK WD, G-3 Sec, 1 Aug 50, Ltr of Instr 1, Office of Coordinator, Lines of Comm.
[50] Mossman and Middleton, *op. cit.*, pp. 8, 12.

indicated, seemingly, that the U.N. Command expected the war to continue for some time. General MacArthur, on 23 July, announced that the U.N. Command had adopted the provisions of the 1949 Geneva Prisoner of War Convention. President Syngman Rhee in a proclamation likewise accepted the provisions of the Geneva Convention on behalf of the Republic of Korea. Then, on 24 July, General MacArthur established a formal United Nations Command with headquarters in Tokyo. The next day this headquarters issued U.N. Communiqué No. 1.[51]

Strength of the Opposing Forces at the Pusan Perimeter

Although American losses were heavy in the first month of the war, the buildup of U.S. men and weapons in Korea had gone steadily forward. Initially, Americans lost as many men from heat exhaustion as from gunfire. The temperature reached 110 degrees, the Naktong hills had little vegetation, and good water was scarce. There was little shade in southern Korea. The blazing sun together with the exertion required to climb the steep slopes caused frequent throbbing headaches. The men's legs lacked the power to climb the steeply pitched mountains and buckled under the unaccustomed ordeal.[52]

The preponderance of American battle casualties was in the Army ground forces. The Navy and Air Force had few battle casualties at this time.[53] American Army casualties in Korea through 31 July 1950 totaled 6,003 men: 1,884 killed, 2,695 wounded, 523 missing, and 901 reported captured. Almost 80 percent of these casualties occurred in the last half of the month.[54] More than half the total battle losses were in the 24th Infantry Division which up to 4 August listed 85 men killed, 895 wounded, and 2,630 missing for a total of 3,610 battle casualties.[55]

ROK Army losses during the first six weeks of the war were very heavy, but the precise number is unknown. Probably the killed, wounded, and missing reached 70,000. Most ROK units were in almost continuous action during July. In the United States, where the press emphasized American battle action, the part of ROK units in checking the North Korean advance was generally under-

---

[51] GHQ FEC Ann Narr Hist Rpt, 1 Jan–31 Oct 50, p. 39; GHQ FEC Sitrep 24 Jul 50.

[52] Training Bul 3, Off, Chief of Army Field Forces, 28 Nov 50; Capt Robert K. Sawyer, Notes for author, 1 Oct 52.

[53] Typical daily battle casualty reports of this period: 30 Jul—Army, 617, including 20 KIA, 126 WIA, 417 MIA; Navy, 0; Air Force, 1 (MIA); 31 Jul—Army, 328 (20 KIA, 181 WIA, 127 MIA); Navy, 0; Air Force, 3 (1 WIA, 2 MIA). GHQ UNC G-3 Rpts 37-39, 31 Jul-2 Aug 50.

[54] DA Battle Casualties of the Army, Final Rpt, 30 Sep 54, and CTM, 31 May 52. Casualties for the last half of July totaled 4,754, including 1,265 KIA, 2,345 WIA, 971 MIA, and 173 reported captured. Eighth Army gives the total as 5,482, including 272 KIA, 1,857 WIA, and 3,353 MIA, presumably covering the period of 13–31 July. See EUSAK WD, Summ, 13–31 Jul 50.

The discrepancies between Eighth Army figures and final TAGO figures are explained in part by the fact that casualty reporting in the field is governed by regulations which provide that, unless the body is recovered or the person is actually reported in the hands of the medics, the man is reported missing in action. When additional information is received, TAGO's official casualty records are revised, and the result is reduced figures for those missing and increased figures for those killed, wounded, or captured.

[55] EUSAK WD, 4 Aug 50, CofS Slip Note 1, Plan for Relief of 24th Inf Div.

estimated and little understood. ROK Army losses were normally far greater than those of Eighth Army. On 1 August, for example, ROK casualties were 812 (84 KIA, 512 WIA, 216 MIA) in comparison with U.S. Army losses of 285, and on 3 August they were 1,133 (128 KIA, 414 WIA, 591 MIA) in comparison with U.S. Army losses of 76.[56]

If the estimate of 70,000 for ROK losses is approximately accurate, total U.N. losses up to 5 August 1950 would be about 76,000 men.

According to their own testimony, the North Korean losses were far greater for this period than U.S. military sources estimated them to be at the time. On 29 July, General MacArthur's Intelligence Section set the figure at 31,000. The Department of the Army estimated 37,500.[57] Actually, the North Korean casualties appear to have been about 58,000, according to a study of prisoner of war interrogations. This large discrepancy was due apparently to a failure on the part of American authorities to realize how great were the casualties inflicted by the ROK Army. When the enemy is advancing there is little opportunity to count his dead. In some engagements, the ROK's decimated N.K. regiments and even whole divisions.

Underestimation of enemy losses in the first five weeks of the war led in turn to an exaggerated notion of the enemy forces facing the U.N. Command along the Pusan Perimeter. The enemy had probably no more than 70,000 men in his committed eleven divisions, one independent mechanized regiment, and one independent infantry regiment, as he began crossing the Naktong River on 4-5 August to assault the U.N. forces in the Pusan Perimeter. A tabulation of estimated enemy strength by major units as of 5 August follows:[58]

Unit	Strength
1st Division	5,000
2d Division	7,500
3d Division	6,000
4th Division	7,000
5th Division	6,000
6th Division	3,600
8th Division	8,000
12th Division	6,000
13th Division	9,500
15th Division	5,000
105th Armored Division (40 tanks)	3,000
83d Motorized Regiment (detached) from 105th Armored Division)	1,000
766th Independent Infantry Regiment	1,500

No reliable figures are available for the number of enemy tanks destroyed and for tank troop casualties of the *105th Armored Division* by 5 August, but certainly they were high. There were only a few tank replacements during July.

---

[56] GHQ UNC G-3 Rpts 39, 2 Aug 50, and 41, 4 Aug 50.

[57] New York *Times*, July 30, 1950; DA Wkly Intel Rpt 76, 4 Aug 50.

[58] The estimates of both enemy losses and strength are based on enemy materials—captured documents and interrogation reports. These, taken as a body, are believed to be more reliable than estimates prepared by U.N. authorities as the battle progressed, which could be little better than guesswork. This is particularly true of the period under discussion as the enemy held the battlefield during the U.N. withdrawal movements to the Pusan Perimeter and there seldom was an opportunity to count his dead. The replacements received in the enemy combat units, as reported in prisoner interrogations, have been included in the strength figure. See ATIS Res Supp Interrog Rpts, Issue 3 (N.K. *1st Div*), p. 33; Ibid., Issue 94 (N.K. *2d Div*); Ibid., Issue 96 (N.K. *3d Div*), p. 33; Ibid., Issue 94 (N.K. *4th Div*), p. 48; Ibid., Issue 96 (N.K. *5th Div*), p. 42; Ibid., Issue 100 (N.K. *6th Div*), pp. 38-39; Ibid., Issue 99 (N.K. *12th Div*), pp. 44-46; Ibid., Issue 104 (N.K. *13th Div*), p. 60; Ibid., Issue 3 (N.K. *15th Div*), p. 42; Ibid., Issue 4 (*105th Armed Div*); 27th Inf WD, PW Interrog Rpt 10; 1st Prov Mar Brig SAR, II.

The first large tank replacement apparently took place about 15 August, when 21 new tanks and 200 tank crew men arrived at the front. Aerial action destroyed many new tanks before they could reach the battle zone. One captured major said the armored division was down to 20 percent strength by the time the battle for Taegu began.[59] The North Koreans probably had no more than 3,000 armored personnel and forty tanks at the front on 5 August.

While no exact information is available as to the number of enemy artillery pieces and heavy mortars still in action by 5 August, it probably was about one-third the number with which the North Koreans started the war. The *4th Division* artillery, for instance, reportedly had only twelve guns on 5 August when the division reached the Naktong.[60]

An official report from General MacArthur to the Department of the Army gave U.N. troop strength in Korea on 4 August 1950 as 141,808:[61]

	Strength
Total	59,238
Total Army	50,367
EUSAK	2,933
KMAG	452
1st Cavalry Division	10,276
2d Infantry Division	4,922
24th Infantry Division	14,540
25th Infantry Division	12,073
Pusan Base	5,171
1st Provisional Marine Brigade	4,713
FEAF (Korea)	4,051
Other	107
ROK Army (Estimated)	82,570

This report indicates that American ground combat units, as of 4 August, totaled more than 47,000 men. The principal ROK combat strength at this time was in five infantry divisions recently filled to a strength of approximately 45,000 men.[62]

Thus, on 4 August, the United Nations combat forces outnumbered the enemy at the front approximately 92,000 to 70,000.

The relative U.N. strength opposed to the North Koreans at the front in early August was actually much more favorable than commonly represented. A leading American newspaper on 26 July, in a typical dispatch filed in Korea, described the attack against the 1st Cavalry Division at Yongdong as being "wave after wave." A subhead in a leading article in the same newspaper a few days later said in part, "We are still outnumbered at least four to one." [63] Other American newspapers reported the Ko-

---

[59] ATIS Res Supp Interrog Rpts, Issue 4 *105th Armd Div*); 24th Div G–2 Jnl, 2–5 Aug 50, entry 256, 041010.

[60] ATIS Res Supp Interrog Rpts, Issue 106 (N.K. Arty), pp. 23, 66. This figure probably includes the 122-mm. howitzers. The standard North Korean division artillery included twenty-four 76-mm. guns and twelve 122-mm. howitzers. Most of the Russian-supplied artillery ammunition used by the North Koreans was four or five years old and verdigris deposits coated the shell casings. There were many misfires and duds. Until about October 1950, the North Koreans used only two types of artillery ammunition, high explosive and armor piercing. The shells had a point detonating fuze to which a nose cap could be attached to give a slightly delayed burst.

[61] GHQ UNC Sitrep, 4 Aug 50. The 24th Division figures include the 5th Regimental Combat Team and the 1st and 3d Battalions of the 29th Infantry. These units were attached to the 25th Division about the time the Far East Command issued the 4 August situation report.

[62] GHQ UNC G–3 Opn Rpt 41, 4 Aug 50; *Ibid.*, Sitrep to DA, 5 Aug 50. The ROK Army transferred about 14,000 of the approximately 82,000 troops listed in the estimate to labor units, so the over-all troop strength of U.N. forces would fall proportionately. This would not affect the combat forces figures.

[63] New York *Times*, July 26 and 30, 1950.

rean War in much the same vein. The claim that enemy forces outnumbered United Nations troops at least four to one had no basis in fact.

High U.S. Army sources repeated the statements that U.S. forces were greatly outnumbered. The North Korean forces had outnumbered those of the United Nations after the near collapse of the ROK Army at the end of June and until about 20 July, but never by more than two to one. By 22 July the U.N. forces in Korea equaled those of the North Koreans, and in the closing days of the month the United Nations gained a numerical superiority, which constantly increased until near the end of the year.

CHAPTER XVI

The First American Counterattack— Task Force Kean

> What is necessary to be performed in the heat of action should constantly be practiced in the leisure of peace.
> VEGETIUS, *Military Institutions of the Romans*

The enemy drive on Pusan from the west along the Chinju-Masan corridor compelled General Walker to concentrate there all the reinforcements then arriving in Korea. These included the 5th Regimental Combat Team and the 1st Provisional Marine Brigade—six battalions of infantry with supporting tanks and artillery. Eighth Army being stronger there than at any other part of the Pusan Perimeter, General Walker decided on a counterattack in this southernmost corridor of the Korean battlefront. It was to be the first American counterattack of the war.

The plan for a counterattack grew out of a number of factors—studies by the Planning Section, G-3, Eighth Army; the arrival of reinforcements; and intelligence that the North Koreans were massing north of Taegu. Although army intelligence in the first days of August seemed to veer toward the opinion that the enemy was shifting troops from the central to the southern front, perhaps as much as two divisions, it soon changed to the belief that the enemy was massing in the area above Taegu.[1]

The Army G-3 Planning Section at this time proposed two offensive actions in the near future. First, Eighth Army would mount an attack in the Masan-Chinju area between 5-10 August. Secondly, about the middle of the month, the army would strike in a general offensive through the same corridor, drive on west as far as Yosu, and there wheel north along the Sunch'on-Chonju-Nonsan axis toward the Kum River—the route of the N.K. *6th Division* in reverse. This general offensive plan was based on the expected arrival of the 2d Infantry Division and three tank battalions by 15 August. The planning study for the first attack stated that the counterattack force "should experience no difficulty in securing Chinju."[2]

---
[1] EUSAK WD, PIR 21, 2 Aug 50 and 23, 4 Aug 50.
[2] EUSAK WD, 4 Aug 50, Stf Study, G-3 Sec to the G-3.

FIRST AMERICAN COUNTERATTACK—TASK FORCE KEAN

General Walker and the Eighth Army General Staff studied the proposals and, in a conference on the subject, decided the Army could not support logistically a general offensive and that there would be insufficient troops to carry it out. The conference, however, approved the proposal for a counterattack by Eighth Army reserve toward Chinju. One of the principal purposes of the counterattack was to relieve enemy pressure against the perimeter in the Taegu area by forcing the diversion of some North Korean units southward.[3]

The attack decided upon, General Walker at once requested the Fifth Air Force to use its main strength from the evening of 5 August through 6 August in an effort to isolate the battlefield and to destroy the enemy behind the front lines between Masan and the Nam River. He particularly enjoined the commanding general of the Fifth Air Force to prevent the movement of hostile forces from the north and northwest across the Nam into the chosen battle sector.[4]

On 6 August Eighth Army issued the operational directive for the attack, naming Task Force Kean as the attack force and giving the hour of attack as 0630 the next day.[5] The task force was named for its commander, Maj. Gen. William B. Kean, Commanding General of the 25th Division.

Altogether, General Kean had about 20,000 men under his command at the beginning of the attack.[6] Task Force Kean was composed of the 25th Infantry Division (less the 27th Infantry Regiment and the 8th Field Artillery Battalion, which were in Eighth Army reserve after their relief at the front on 7 August), with the 5th Regimental Combat Team and the 1st Provisional Marine Brigade attached. It included two medium tank battalions, the 89th (M4A3) and the 1st Marine (M26 Pershings). The 25th Division now had three infantry battalions in each of its regiments, although all were understrength.[7]

The terrain and communications of this chosen field for counterattack were to some extent known to the American commanders. American units had advanced or retreated over its major roads as far as Hadong in the preceding two weeks. Certain topographic features clearly defined and limited the corridor, making it a segment of Korea where a planned operation could be executed without involving any other part of the Perimeter.

The Chinju-Masan corridor is limited on the south by the Korean Strait, on the north by the Nam River from Chinju to its confluence with the Naktong, fifteen miles northwest of Masan. Masan, at the head of Masan Bay, is at the eastern end of the corridor; Chinju, at the western end of the corridor, is 27 air miles from Masan. The shortest road

---

[3] *Ibid.*, Check Slip, 4 Aug 50, and Informal Check Slip, 5 Aug 50; Interv, author with Lt Col Paul F. Smith, 1 Oct 52.

[4] EUSAK WD, 5 Aug 50, Ltr, G-3 Air EUSAK to CG Fifth AF.

[5] *Ibid.*, 6 Aug 50, G-3 Opn Directive and ans.

[6] 25th Div WD, Summ, Aug 50, p. 7; *Ibid.*, 6-7 and 9 Aug 50. Total supported strength of the 25th Division is given as 23,080 troops, including 11,026 attached. This included the 27th Infantry Regiment, which became army reserve on 7 August. On 9 August this number had increased to 24,179, of which 12,197 were attached.

[7] 1st Prov Mar Brig, SAR, 2 Aug-6 Sep 50, pp. 1-19; 1st Bn, 5th Mar, SAR, Aug 50, p. 1.

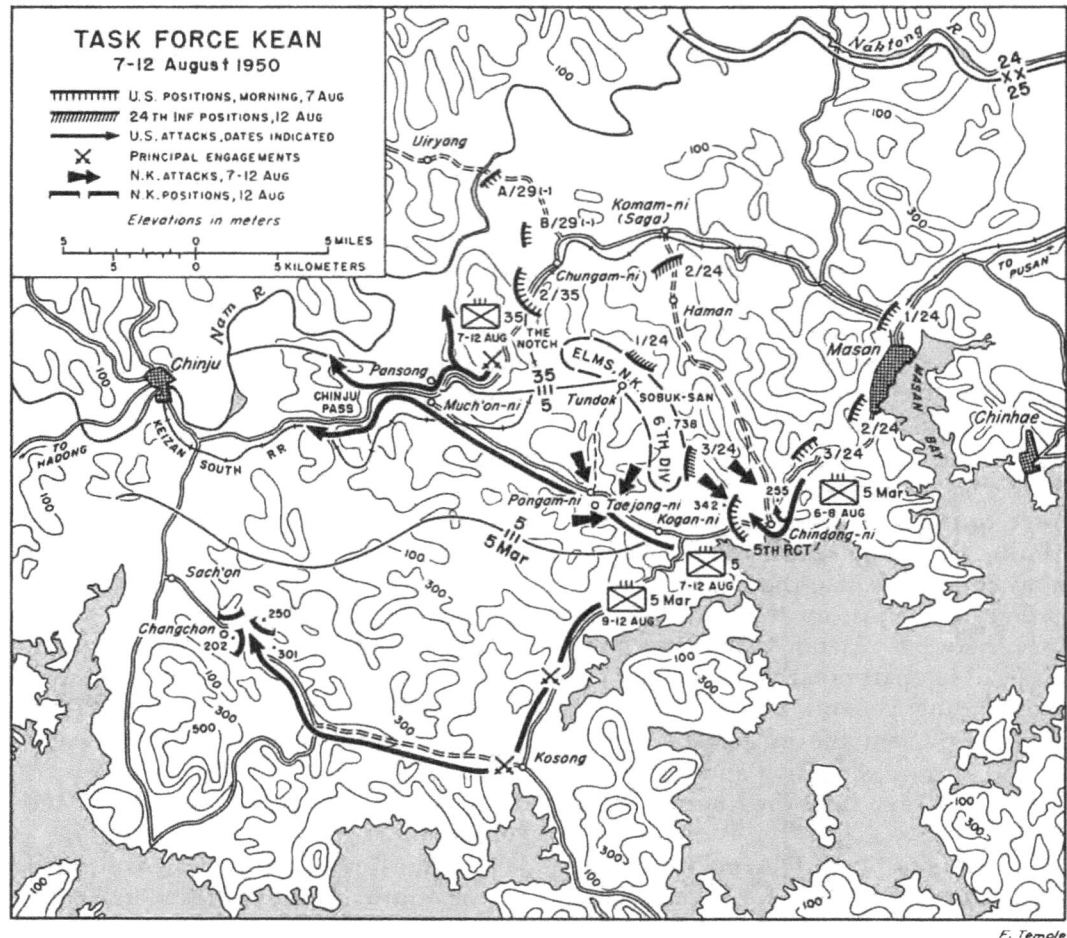

MAP 8

distance between the two places is more than 40 miles. The corridor averages about 20 miles in width. (*Map 8*)

The topography of the corridor consists mostly of low hills interspersed with paddy ground along the streams. South of the Nam, the streams run generally in a north-south direction; all are small and fordable in dry weather. In two places mountain barriers cross the corridor. One is just east of Chinju; the main passage through it is the Chinju pass. The second and more dominant barrier is Sobuk-san, about eight miles west of Masan.

The main east-west highway through the corridor was the two-lane all-weather road from Masan through Komam-ni, Chungam-ni, and Much'on-ni to Chinju. The Keizan South Railroad parallels this main road most of the way through the corridor. It is single track, standard gauge, and has numerous tunnels, cuts, and trestles.

An important spur road slanting southeast from Much'on-ni connects it with the coastal road three miles west of Chindong-ni and ten miles from Masan. The coastal, and third, road hugs the irregular southern shore line from Masan to Chinju by way of Chindong-ni, Kosong, and Sach'on.

The early summer of 1950 in Korea was one of drought, and as such was unusual. Normally there are heavy monsoon rains in July and August with an average of twenty inches of rain; but in 1950 there was only about one-fourth this amount. The cloudless skies over the southern tip of the peninsula brought scorching heat which often reached 105° and sometimes 120°. This and the 60-degree slopes of the hills caused more casualties from heat exhaustion among newly arrived marine and army units in the first week of the counterattack than enemy bullets.

The army plan for the attack required Task Force Kean to attack west along three roads, seize the Chinju pass (Line Z in the plan), and secure the line of the Nam River. Three regiments would make the attack: the 35th Infantry along the northernmost and main inland road, the 5th Regimental Combat Team along the secondary inland road to the Much'-on-ni road juncture, and the 5th Marines along the southern coastal road. This placed the marines on the left flank, the 5th Regimental Combat Team in the middle, and the 35th Infantry on the right flank. The 5th Regimental Combat Team was to lead the attack in the south, seize the road junction five miles west of Chindong-ni, and continue along the righthand fork. The marines would then follow the 5th Regimental Combat Team to the road junction, take the lefthand fork, and attack along the coastal road. This plan called for the 5th Regimental Combat Team to make a juncture with the 35th Infantry at Much'on-ni, whence they would drive on together to the Chinju pass, while the marines swung southward along the coast through Kosong and Sach'on to Chinju. The 5th Regimental Combat Team and the 5th Marines, on the night of 6–7 August, were to relieve the 27th Infantry in its front-line defensive positions west of Chindong-ni. The 27th Infantry would then revert to army reserve in an assembly area at Masan.[8]

While Task Force Kean attacked west, the 24th Infantry Regiment was to clean out the enemy from the rear area, giving particular attention to the rough, mountainous ground of Sobuk-san between the 35th and 5th Regiments. It also was to secure the lateral north-south road running from Komam-ni through Haman to Chindong-ni. Task Force Min, a regiment-sized ROK force, was attached to the 24th Infantry to assist in this mission.[9]

On the eve of the attack, Eighth Army intelligence estimated that the N.K. *6th Division,* standing in front of Task Force Kean, numbered approximately 7,500 effectives. Actually, the *6th Division* numbered about 6,000 men at this time. But the *83d Motorized Regiment* of the *105th Armored Division* had joined the *6th Division* west of Masan, unknown to Eighth Army, and its strength brought the enemy force to about 7,500 men, the Eighth Army estimate. Army intelligence estimated that the *6th Division*

---
[8] 25th Div WD, 6 Aug 50; 25th Div Opn Ord 8, 6 Aug 50.
[9] *Ibid.;* Barth MS, p. 13.

would be supported by approximately 36 pieces of artillery and 25 tanks.[10]

Who Attacks Whom?

On the right flank of Task Force Kean, the 2d Battalion of the 35th Infantry led the attack west on 7 August. Only the day before, an enemy attack had driven one company of this battalion from its position, but a counterattack had regained the lost ground. Now, as it crossed the line of departure at the Notch three miles west of Chungam-ni, the battalion encountered about 500 enemy troops supported by several self-propelled guns. The two forces joined battle at once, a contest that lasted five hours before the 2d Battalion, with the help of an air strike, secured the pass and the high ground northward.

After this fight, the 35th Infantry advanced rapidly westward and by evening stood near the Much'on-ni road fork, the regiment's initial objective. In this advance, the 35th Infantry inflicted about 350 casualties on the enemy, destroyed 2 tanks, 1 76-mm. self-propelled gun, 5 antitank guns, and captured 4 truckloads of weapons and ammunition, several brief cases of documents, and 3 prisoners. Near Pansong, Colonel Fisher's men overran what they thought had been the N.K. *6th Division* command post, because they found there several big Russian-built radios and other headquarters equipment. For the 35th Regiment, the attack had gone according to plan.[11]

The next day, 8 August, the regiment advanced to the high ground just short of the Much'on-ni road fork. There Fisher received orders from General Kean to dig in and wait until the 5th Regimental Combat Team could come up on his left and join him at Much'on-ni. While waiting, Fisher's men beat off a few enemy attacks and sent out strong combat patrols that probed enemy positions as far as the Nam River.[12]

Behind and on the left of the 35th Infantry, in the mountain mass that separated it from the other attack columns, the fight was not going well. From this rough ground surrounding Sobuk-san, the 24th Infantry was supposed to clear out enemy forces of unknown size, but believed to be small. Affairs there had taken an ominous turn on 6 August, the day preceding Task Force Kean's attack, when North Koreans ambushed L Company of the 24th Infantry west of Haman and scattered I Company, killing twelve men. One officer stated that he was knocked to the ground three times by his own stampeding soldiers. The next morning he and the 3d Battalion commander located the battalion four miles to the rear in Haman. Not all the men panicked. Pfc. William Thompson of the Heavy Weapons Company set up his machine gun and fired at the enemy until he was killed by grenades.[13]

Sobuk-san remained in enemy hands.

---

[10] EUSAK WD, 6 Aug 50, an. to Opn PIR.
[11] 25th Div WD, 6–7 Aug 50; 35th Inf WD, 7 Aug 50; Interv, author with Fisher, 5 Jan 52.
[12] 25th Div WD, 8–11 Aug 50; 35th Inf WD, 8–11 Aug 50; Barth MS, p. 14; Fisher, MS review comments, 7 Nov 57.
[13] 24th Inf WD, 6 Aug 50; EUSAK IG Rpt on 24th Inf, testimony of 1st Lt Christopher M. Gooch, S–3, 3d Bn, 24th Inf, 26 Aug 50. Department of the Army General Order 63, 2 August 1951, awarded the Medal of Honor posthumously to Pfc. William Thompson, M Company, 24th Infantry.

American units assigned to sweep the area were unable to advance far enough even to learn the strength of the enemy in this mountain fastness behind Task Force Kean. Col. Arthur S. Champney succeeded Col. Horton V. White in command of the 24th Regiment in the Sobuk-san area on 6 August.

Before beginning the account of Task Force Kean's attack in the southern sector near Chindong-ni it is necessary to describe the position taken there a few days earlier by the 2d Battalion, 5th Regimental Combat Team. Lt. Col. John L. Throckmorton, a West Point graduate of the Class of 1935, commanded this battalion. It was his first battalion command in combat. Eighth Army had moved the battalion from the docks of Pusan to Chindong-ni on 2 August to bolster the 27th Infantry. Throckmorton placed his troops on the spur of high ground that came down from Sobuk-san a mile and a half west of Chindong-ni, and behind the 2d Battalion, 27th Infantry, which was at Kogan-ni. The highest point Throckmorton's troops occupied was Yaban-san (Hill 342), about a mile north of the coastal road. A platoon of G Company occupied this point, Fox Hill, as the battalion called it. Fox Hill was merely a high point on a long finger ridge that curved down toward Chindong-ni from the Sobuk-san peak. Beyond Fox Hill this finger ridge climbed ever higher to the northwest, culminating three miles away in Sobuk-san (Hill 738), 2,400 feet high.

The next morning, 3 August, North Koreans attacked and drove the platoon off Fox Hill. That night F Company of the 5th Infantry counterattacked and recaptured the hill, which it held until relieved there by marine troops on 8 August. Nevertheless, Throckmorton's battalion was in trouble right up to the moment of the Eighth Army counterattack. There was every indication that enemy forces held the higher Sobuk-san area.[14]

On the evening of 6 August the 27th Infantry Regiment and the 2d Battalion, 5th Regimental Combat Team, held the front lines west of Chindong-ni. The 27th Regiment was near the road; the 2d Battalion, 5th Regimental Combat Team, on higher ground to the north. During the evening the rest of the 5th Regimental Combat Team relieved 27th Infantry front-line troops, and the 1st Battalion, 5th Marines, relieved the 1st Battalion, 27th Infantry, in its reserve position. The next morning the 2d Battalion, 5th Marines, was to relieve the 2d Battalion, 5th Regimental Combat Team, on the high ground north of the road. When thus relieved, the 5th Regimental Combat Team was to begin its attack west.

During the night of 6–7 August, North Koreans dislodged a platoon of Throckmorton's troops from a saddle below Fox Hill and moved to a point east and south of the spur. From this vantage point the following morning they could look down on the command posts of the 5th Marines and the 5th Regimental Combat Team, on the artillery emplacements, and on the main supply road at Chindong-ni.

That morning, 7 August, a heavy fog in the coastal area around Chindong-ni prevented an air strike scheduled to pre-

---

[14] Interv, author with Col John L. Throckmorton, 20 Aug 52; Throckmorton, MS review comments, 30 Mar 55.

cede the Task Force Kean infantry attack. The artillery fired a twenty-minute preparation. At 0720 the infantry then moved out in the much-heralded army counterattack. The 1st Battalion, 5th Regimental Combat Team, led off down the road from its line of departure just west of Chindong-ni and arrived at the road junction without difficulty. There, instead of continuing on west as it was supposed to do, it turned left, and by noon was on a hill mass three miles south of the road fork and on the road allotted to the marine line of advance. How it made this blunder at the road fork is hard to understand. As a result of this mistake the hill dominating the road junction on the northwest remained unoccupied. The 1st Battalion was supposed to have occupied it and from there to cover the advance of the remainder of the 5th Regimental Combat Team and the 5th Marines.[15]

After the 1st Battalion, 5th Regimental Combat Team, had started westward, the 2d Battalion, 5th Marines, commanded by Lt. Col. Harold S. Roise. moved out at 1100 to relieve Throckmorton's battalion on the spur running up to Fox Hill. It ran head-on into the North Koreans who had come around to the front of the spur during the night. It was hard to tell who was attacking whom. The day was furnace hot with the temperature standing at 112°. In the struggle up the slope the Marine battalion had approximately thirty heat prostration cases, six times its number of casualties caused by enemy fire. In the end its attack failed.[16]

The fight west of Chindong-ni on the morning of 7 August was in fact a general melee. Even troops of the 27th Infantry, supposed to be in reserve status, were involved. The general confusion was deepened when the treads of friendly tanks cut up telephone line strung along the roadside, causing communication difficulties. Finally at 1120, when marine troops completed relief of the 27th Infantry in its positions, Brig. Gen. Edward A. Craig, commanding the 1st Provisional Marine Brigade, assumed command, on General Kean's orders, of all troops on the Chindong-ni front. He held that command until the afternoon of 9 August.[17]

While these untoward events were taking place below it, F Company of the 5th Regimental Combat Team on the crest of Fox Hill was cut off. At 1600 an airdrop finally succeeded on the third try in getting water and small arms and 60-mm. mortar ammunition to it. The enemy got the first drop. The second was a mile short of the drop zone.

Failing the first day to accomplish its mission, the 2d Battalion, 5th Marines, resumed its attack on Fox Hill the next morning at daybreak after an air strike on the enemy positions. This time, after hard fighting, it succeeded. In capturing and holding the crest, D Company of the Marine battalion lost 8 men killed, including 3 officers, and 28 wounded. The enemy losses on Hill 342 are un-

---

[15] *Ibid.;* 5th Mar SAR, 6–7 Aug 50; Barth MS; New York *Times,* August 8, 1950, W. H. Lawrence dispatch from southern front; New York *Herald Tribune,* August 9, 1950, Homer Bigart dispatch from Korea, 7 August.

[16] 2d Bn, 5th Mar, SAR, 7 Jul–31 Aug 50, p. 6.
[17] 25th Div WD, 7 Aug 50; New York *Herald Tribune,* August 8, 1950, and August 9, 1950, Bigart dispatches; 1st Prov Mar Brig SAR, 2 Jul–6 Sep 50, p. 9; 27th Inf WD, Aug 50.

Fox Hill Position *near Masan, 7 August.*

known, but estimates range from 150 to 400.[18]

The events of 7 August all across the Masan front showed that Task Force Kean's attack had collided head-on with one being delivered simultaneously by the N.K. *6th Division.*

All of Task Force Kean's trouble was not confined to the area west of Chindong-ni; there was plenty of it eastward. For a time it seemed as if the latter might be the more dangerous. There the North Koreans threatened to cut the supply road from Masan. There is no doubt that Task Force Kean had an unpleasant surprise on the morning of 7 August when it discovered that the enemy had moved around Chindong-ni during the night and occupied Hill 255 just east of the town, dominating the road in its rear to Masan.

Troops of the 2d Battalion, 24th Infantry, and of the 3d Battalion, 5th Marines, tried unsuccessfully during the day to break this roadblock. In the

---

[18] 2d Bn, 5th Mar, SAR, 7 Jul–31 Aug 50, p. 6; Montross and Canzona, *The Pusan Perimeter,* pp. 116–17.

In a Marine infantry regiment, the 1st Battalion consisted of Headquarters and Service, A, B, C, and Weapons Companies; the 2d Battalion consisted of Headquarters and Service, D, E, F, and Weapons Companies; and the 3d Battalion consisted of Headquarters and Service, G, H, I, and Weapons Companies.

severe fighting there, artillery and air strikes, tanks and mortars pounded the heights trying to dislodge the enemy. Batteries B and C of the 159th Field Artillery Battalion fired 1,600 rounds during 7-8 August against this roadblock. Colonel Ordway, at the marines' request, also directed the fire of part of the 555th Artillery Battalion against this height. But the enemy soldiers stubbornly held their vantage point. Finally, after three days of fighting, the 3d Battalion, 5th Marines, and elements of two battalions of the 24th Infantry joined on Hill 255 east of Chindong-ni, shortly after noon on 9 August, and reduced the roadblock. There were 120 counted enemy dead, with total enemy casualties estimated at 600. On the final day of this action, the 3d Battalion, 5th Marines, which carried the brunt of the attack, had 70 casualties, half of them caused by heat exhaustion. During its two-day part in the fight for this hill, H Company of the marines suffered 16 killed and 36 wounded.[19]

When Throckmorton's 2d Battalion, 5th Regimental Combat Team, came off Fox Hill on 8 August after the 2d Battalion, 5th Marines, had relieved it there, it received the mission of attacking west immediately, to seize the hill northwest of the road junction that the 1st Battalion was supposed to have taken the day before. At this time, Throckmorton had only two companies effective after his week of combat on Fox Hill. Nevertheless, he moved against the hill but was unable to take it. His attack was weakened when supporting artillery failed to adjust on the target.

In the late afternoon, General Kean came up to the 2d Battalion position and, with Colonel Ordway present, said to Colonel Throckmorton, "I want that hill tonight." Throckmorton decided on a night attack with his two effective companies, G and E. He put three tanks and his 4.2-inch and 81-mm. mortars in position for supporting fire. That night his men gained the hill, although near the point of exhaustion.[20]

For three days the N.K. *6th Division* had pinned down Task Force Kean, after the latter had jumped off at Chindong-ni. Finally, on 9 August, the way was clear for it to start the maneuver along the middle and southern prongs of the planned attack toward Chinju.

The 5th Marines on the Coastal Road

On the afternoon of 9 August, the 1st Battalion, 5th Marines, took over from the 1st Battalion, 5th Regimental Combat Team, the hill position on the coastal road which the latter had held for three days. The army battalion then moved back to the road fork and turned down the righthand road. At last it was on the right path, prepared to attack west with the remainder of its regiment.[21]

The 5th Marines that afternoon moved rapidly down the coastal road, leapfrogging its battalions in the advance. Corsairs of the 1st Marine Air Wing, flying from the USS *Sicily* and USS *Badoeng Strait* in the waters off

---

[19] 159th FA Bn WD, 7-9 Aug 50; 3d Bn, 5th Mar, SAR, Aug 50 (Rpt of 1st Pl, G Co); 5th Mar SAR, 8-9 Aug 50; 1st Prov Mar Brig SAR, 8-9 Aug 50, pp. 10-11; Montross and Canzona, *The Pusan Perimeter*, pp. 121-22; New York *Herald Tribune*, August 9, 1950, Bigart dispatch; Col Godwin Ordway, MS review comments, 21 Nov 57.

[20] Interv, author with Throckmorton, 20 Aug 52.
[21] 25th Div WD, 9 Aug 50.

the coast, patrolled the road and adjoining hills ahead of the troops. This close air support delivered strikes within a matter of minutes after a target appeared.[22]

General Kean pushed his unit commanders hard to make up for lost time, now that the attack had at last started. The pace was fast, the sun bright and hot. Casualties from heat exhaustion on 10 August again far exceeded those from enemy action. The rapid advance that day after the frustrations of the three preceding ones caused some Tokyo spokesman to speak of the "enemy's retreat" as being "in the nature of a rout," and correspondents wrote of the action as a "pursuit." And so it seemed for a time.[23]

Just before noon on the 11th, after a fight on the hills bordering the road, the leading Marine battalion (3d) neared the town of Kosong. Its supporting artillery from the 1st Battalion, 11th Marines, adjusting fire on a crossroads west of the town, chanced to drop shells near camouflaged enemy vehicles. Thinking its position had been discovered, the enemy force quickly entrucked and started down the road toward Sach'on and Chinju. This force proved to be a major part of the *83d Motorized Regiment* of the *105th Armored Division*, which had arrived in the Chinju area to support the N.K. *6th Division*.

Just as the long column of approximately 200 vehicles, trucks, jeeps, and motorcycles loaded with troops, ammunition, and supplies got on the road, a flight of four Corsairs from the *Badoeng Strait* came over on a routine reconnaissance mission ahead of the marines. They swung low over the enemy column, strafing the length of it. Vehicles crashed into each other, others ran into the ditches, some tried to get to the hills off the road. Troops spilled out seeking cover and concealment. The planes turned for another run. The North Koreans fought back with small arms and automatic weapons and hit two of the planes, forcing one down and causing the other to crash. This air attack left about forty enemy vehicles wrecked and burning. Another flight of Marine Corsairs and Air Force F–51's arrived and continued the work of destruction. When the ground troops reached the scene later in the afternoon, they found 31 trucks, 24 jeeps, 45 motorcycles, and much ammunition and equipment destroyed or abandoned. The marine advance stopped that night four miles west of Kosong.[24]

The next morning, 12 August, the 1st Battalion, commanded by Lt. Col. George R. Newton, passed through the 3d Battalion and led the Marine brigade in what it expected to be the final lap to Sach'on, about 8 miles below Chinju. Advancing 11 miles unopposed, it came within 4 miles of the town by noon. An hour later, three and a half miles east

---

[22] 1st Prov Mar Brig SAR, 10 Aug 50; 5th Mar SAR, 10 Aug 50; Ernest H. Giusti, "Marine Air Over the Pusan Perimeter," *Marine Corps Gazette* (May, 1952), pp. 20–21; New York *Herald Tribune*, August 10, 1950.

[23] 25th Div WD, 10 Aug 50; New York *Times*, August 10, 1950.

[24] 1st Prov Mar Brig SAR, Aug 50, p. 11; 5th Mar SAR, 11 Aug 50; 3d Bn, 5th Mar SAR, 11 Aug, p. 4; Giusti, *op. cit.*; Lt Col Ransom M. Wood, "Artillery Support for the Brigade in Korea," *Marine Corps Gazette* (June, 1951), p. 18; GHQ UNC G–3 Opn Rpt 49, 12 Aug 50; 25th Div WD, 11 Aug 50. Enemy troop casualties in this action were estimated at about 200.

of Sach'on, the Marine column entered an enemy ambush at the village of Changchon or, as the troops called it, Changallon. Fortunately for the marines, a part of the *2d Battalion, 15th Regiment,* and elements of the *83d Motorized Regiment* that lay in wait in the hills cupping the valley disclosed the ambush prematurely. A heavy fight got under way and continued through the afternoon and into the evening. Marine Corsairs struck repeatedly. In the late afternoon, the 1st Battalion gained control of Hills 301 and 250 on the right, and Hill 202 on the left, of the road.

On Hill 202, before daylight the next morning, a North Korean force overran the 3d Platoon of B Company. One group apparently had fallen asleep and all except one were killed. Heavy casualties were inflicted also on another nearby platoon of B Company. Shortly after daylight the marines on Hill 202 received orders to withdraw and turn back toward Masan. During the night, B Company lost 12 men killed, 16 wounded, and 9 missing, the last presumed dead.[25]

Just before noon of the 12th, General Kean had ordered General Craig to send one battalion of marines back to help clear out enemy troops that had cut the middle road behind the 5th Regimental Combat Team and had its artillery under attack. An hour after noon the 3d Battalion was on its way back. That evening Craig was called to Masan for a conference with Kean. There he received the order to withdraw all elements of the brigade immediately to the vicinity of Chingdong-ni. Events taking place at other points of the Pusan Perimeter caused the sudden withdrawal of the Marine brigade from Task Force Kean's attack.[26]

Bloody Gulch—Artillery Graveyard

Simultaneously with the swing of the Marine brigade around the southern coastal loop toward Chinju, the 5th Regimental Combat Team plunged ahead in the center toward Much'on-ni, its planned junction point with the 35th Infantry. On 10 August, as the combat team moved toward Pongam-ni, aerial observation failed to sight enemy troop concentrations or installations ahead of it. Naval aircraft, however, did attack the enemy north of Pongam-ni and bombed and strafed Tundok still farther north in the Sobuk-san mining region.

The 1st Battalion, under the command of Lt. Col. John P. Jones, attacked down the right (north) side of the road and the 2d Battalion, under Colonel Throckmorton, down the left (south) side. The 1st Battalion on its side encountered the enemy on the hills near Pongam-ni, but was able to enter the

---

[25] 1st Bn, 5th Mar SAR, 12 Aug 50; 1st Prov Mar Brig SAR, 12 Aug 50, p. 12; 5th Mar SAR, 12 Aug 50; Maj. Francis I. Fenton, Jr., "Changallon Valley," *Marine Corps Gazette* (November, 1951), pp. 49-53; ATIS Supp, Enemy Docs, Issue 2, pp. 97-98, gives the North Korean order for the attack on Hill 202. The 1st Battalion, 5th Marines, gives its casualties for 12-13 August as 15 killed, 33 wounded, and 8 missing. Montross and Canzona, *The Pusan Perimeter,* page 155 give the Marine loss on Hill 202 in the night battle as 12 killed, 18 wounded, and 8 missing.

[26] Montross and Canzona, *The Pusan Perimeter,* page 148, quoting from General Craig's field notebook for 12 August 1950.

town and establish its command post there.

The village of Pongam was a nondescript collection of perhaps twenty mud-walled and thatch-roofed huts clustered around a road junction. It and Taejong-ni were small villages only a few hundred yards apart on the east side of the pass. The main east-west road was hardly more than a country lane by American standards. About 400 yards northeast of Pongam-ni rose a steep, barren hill, the west end of a long ridge that paralleled the main east-west road on the north side at a distance of about 800 yards. The enemy occupied this ridge. Northward from Pongam-ni extended a 500-yard-wide valley. A narrow dirt trail came down it to Pongam-ni from the Sobuk-san mining area of Tundok to the north. The stream flowing southward through this valley joined another flowing east at the western edge of Pongam-ni. There a modern concrete bridge, in sharp contrast to the other structures, spanned the south-flowing stream. West of the villages, two parallel ridges came together about 1,000 yards away, like the two sides of an inverted V. The southern ridge rose sharply from the western edge of the village. The main road ran westward along its base and climbed out of the valley at a pass where this ridge joined the other slanting in from the north. Immediately west of Pongam-ni the two ridges were separated by a 300-yard-wide valley. The northern ridge was the higher.

On 10 August the 2d Battalion, 5th Regimental Combat Team, held the southern of these two ridges at Pongam-ni and B and C Companies of the 1st Battalion held the eastern part of the northern one. The enemy held the remainder of this ridge and contested control of the pass.

During the day the regimental support artillery came up and went into positions in the stream bed and low ground at Pongam-ni and Taejong-ni. A Battery of the 555th Field Artillery Battalion emplaced under the concrete bridge at Pongam-ni, and B Battery went into position along the stream bank at the edge of the village. Headquarters Battery established itself in the village. The 90th Field Artillery Battalion, less one battery, had emplaced on the west side of the south-flowing stream. All the artillery pieces were on the north side of the east-west road. The 5th Regimental Combat Team headquarters and C Battery of the 555th Field Artillery Battalion were eastward in a rear position.[27]

That night, 10–11 August, North Koreans attacked the 1st Battalion and the artillery positions at Pongam-ni. The action continued after daylight. During this fight, Lt. Col. John H. Daly, the 555th Field Artillery Battalion commander, lost communication with his A Battery. With the help of some infantry, he and Colonel Jones, the 1st Battalion commander, tried to reach the battery. Both Daly and Jones were wounded, the latter seriously. Daly then assumed temporary command of the infantry battalion. As the day pro-

---

[27] Ltr with comments, Col Ordway to author, 18 Feb 55; Ltrs, Col John H. Daly to author, 3 Dec 54 and 10 Feb 55; Comments on Bloody Gulch, by Lt Col T. B. Roelofs, 15 Feb 55, copy furnished author by Col Ordway, 18 Feb 55. Despite an extensive search in the Departmental Records Section of the AG and elsewhere the author could not find the war diaries, journals, periodic reports, and other records of the 5th Regimental Combat Team and the 555th Field Artillery Battalion for August 1950.

gressed the enemy attacks at Pongam-ni dwindled and finally ceased.

When the 3d Battalion had continued on westward the previous afternoon the 5th Regimental Combat Team headquarters and C Battery, 555th Field Artillery Battalion, east of Pongam-ni, had been left without protecting infantry close at hand. North Koreans attacked them during the night at the same time Pongam-ni came under attack. The Regimental Headquarters and C Battery personnel defended themselves successfully. On the morning of the 11th, close-in air strikes helped turn the enemy back into the hills. Colonel Throckmorton's 2d Battalion headquarters had also come under attack. He called E Company from its Pongam-ni position to help beat off the enemy.[28]

Colonel Ordway's plan for passing the regiment westward through Pongam-ni was for the 2d Battalion to withdraw from the south ridge and start the movement, after the 1st Battalion had secured the north ridge and the pass. The regimental trains were to follow and next the artillery. The 1st Battalion was then to disengage and bring up the rear.

After Colonel Jones was evacuated, Colonel Ordway sent Lt. Col. T. B. Roelofs, regimental S–2 and formerly the battalion commander, to take command of the 1st Battalion. Roelofs arrived at Pongam-ni about 1400, 11 August, and assumed command of the 1st Battalion. Ordway had given him orders to clear the ridge north of the road west of Pongam-ni, secure the pass, protect the combat team as it moved west through the pass, and then follow it. Roelofs met Daly at Pongam-ni, consulted with him and the staff of the 1st Battalion, made a personal reconnaissance of the area, and then issued his attack order to clear the ridge and secure the pass.

Colonel Roelofs selected B Company to make the main effort. He brought it down from the north ridge to the valley floor, where it rested briefly and was resupplied with ammunition. Just before dusk, it moved to the head of the gulch and attacked the hill on the right commanding the north side of the pass. At the same time, C Company attacked west along the north ridge to effect a junction with B Company. The artillery and all available weapons of the 2d Battalion supported the attack; the artillery fire was accurate and effective. Before dusk B Company had gained and occupied the commanding ground north of the pass.[29]

One platoon of A Company, reinforced with a section of tanks, remained in its position north of Pongam-ni on the Tundok road, to protect from that direction the road junction village and the artillery positions. The remainder of A Company relieved the 2d Battalion on the south ridge, when it withdrew from there at 2100 to lead the movement westward.

His battalion's attack apparently a success, Colonel Roelofs established his command post about 300 yards west of Pongam-ni in a dry stream bed south of

---

[28] Ltr, Ordway to author, 18 Feb 55; Throckmorton, Notes for Ordway, 30 Mar 55 (forwarded by Ordway to author); Roelofs, Comments on Bloody Gulch, 15 Feb 55.

[29] Roelofs, Comments on Bloody Gulch, 15 Feb 55; Ltr and comments, Ordway to author, 18 Feb 55, and MS review comments, 21 Nov 57.

the road, crawled under the trailer attached to his jeep, and went to sleep.

As a result of the considerable enemy action during the night of 10–11 August and during the day of the 11th, Colonel Ordway decided that he could not safely move the regimental trains and the artillery through the pass during daylight, and accordingly he had made plans to do it that night under cover of darkness. That afternoon, however, Ordway was called to the radio to speak to General Kean. The 25th Division commander wanted him to move forward rapidly and said that a battalion of the 24th Infantry would come up and protect his right (north) flank. Ordway had a lengthy conversation with the division and task force commander before the latter approved the delay until after dark for the regimental movement. General Kean apparently did not believe any considerable force of enemy troops was in the vicinity of Pongam-ni, despite Ordway's representations to the contrary.

General Kean, on his part, was under pressure at this time because during the day Eighth Army had sent a radio message to him, later confirmed by an operational directive, to occupy and defend the Chinju pass line; to move Task Force Min, a regimental sized ROK unit, to Taegu for release to the ROK Army; and to be ready to release the 1st Provisional Marine Brigade and the 5th Regimental Combat Team on army order. This clearly foreshadowed that Task Force Kean probably would not be able to hold its gains, as one or more of its major units apparently were urgently needed elsewhere.

About 2100 hours, as Throckmorton's 2d Battalion, C Battery of the 555th, and the trains were forming on the road, the regimental S-3 handed Colonel Ordway a typed radio order from the commanding general of the 25th Division. It ordered him to move the 2d Battalion and one battery of artillery through the pass at once, but to hold the rest of the troops in place until daylight. Ordway felt that to execute the order would have catastrophic effects. He tried to reach the division headquarters to protest it, but could not establish communication. On reflection, Ordway decided that some aspect of the "big picture" known only to the army and division commanders must have prompted the order. With this thought governing his actions he issued instructions implementing the division order.[30]

In the meantime the 2d Battalion had moved through the pass, and once over its rim was out of communication with the regiment. Ordway tried and failed several times to reach it by radio during the night. In effect, though Throckmorton thought he was the advance guard of a regimental advance, he was on his own. Ordway and the rest of the regiment could not help him if he ran into trouble nor could he be called back to help them. In the movement of the 2d Battalion and C and Headquarters Batteries, Colonel Daly was wounded a second time and was evacuated. Colonel Throckmorton's 2d Battalion cleared

---

[30] Intervs, author with Ordway, 3 and 21 Jan 55; Ltr and comments, Ordway to author, 18 Feb 55; Ordway, MS review comments, 21 Nov 57, Roelofs, Comments on Bloody Gulch, 15 Feb 55; Ltr, Daly to author, 8 Dec 54. Roelofs and Daly confirm Ordway's account of his plan to move the regiment through the pass at night, and the division's order that all units except the 2d Battalion and C Battery, 555th Field Artillery Battalion, were to remain in position until daylight.

the pass before midnight. On the west side it came under light attack but was able to continue on for five miles to Taejong-ni, where it went into an assembly area for the rest of the night.

While these events were taking place at Pongam-ni during daylight and the evening of the 11th, the main supply road back toward Chindong-ni was under sniper fire and various other forms of attack. Three tanks and an assault gun escorted supply convoys to the forward positions.[31]

By midnight of 11 August, the 555th (Triple Nickel) Field Artillery Battalion (105-mm. howitzers), less C Battery, and Headquarters and A Batteries, 90th Field Artillery Battalion (155-mm. howitzers)—emplaced at Pongam-ni and Taejong-ni—had near them only the 1st Battalion north of the road. The regimental headquarters and the guns of the 159th Field Artillery Battalion were emplaced a little more than a mile behind them (east) along the road.[32]

Sometime after 0100, 12 August, Colonel Roelofs was awakened by his executive officer, Capt. Claude Baker. Baker informed him that the battalion had lost contact with C Company on the ridge northward and sounds of combat could be heard coming from that area. When further efforts to reach the company by telephone and radio failed, Roelofs sent runners and a wire crew out to try to re-establish contact. He then informed Colonel Ordway of this new development, and urged speedy movement of the trains and artillery westward through the pass. But Ordway reluctantly held firm to division orders not to move until after daylight.

Roelofs, taking two of his staff officers with him, set out in his jeep eastward toward Pongam-ni. He noted that the regimental trains had assembled on the road and apparently were only awaiting orders before moving. At the bridge in Pongam-ni he saw several officers of the 555th Field Artillery Battalion, who also seemed to be waiting orders to start the movement. Roelofs turned north at Pongam-ni on the dirt trail running toward the Sobuk-san mining area. He drove up that road until he came to the A Company infantry platoon and the section of tanks. They were in position. They told Roelofs they had heard sounds of small arms fire and exploding grenades in the C Company area on the ridge to their left (west), but nothing else.[33]

Upon returning to his command post Roelofs learned that contact still had not been re-established with C Company. The runners sent out had returned and said they could not find the company. The wire crew was missing. Members of the battalion staff during Roelofs' absence had again heard sounds of combat in the company area. They also had seen flares there. This was interpreted to mean that enemy troops held it and were signaling to other enemy units. From his position in the valley at regimental headquarters, Colonel Ordway could see that elements of the 1st Battalion, probably C Company, were

---

[31] 25th Div WD, 11 Aug 50; 89th Med Tk Bn WD, 7-31 Aug 50; EUSAK WD, G-3 Sec, 11 Aug 50; Ibid., POR 90, 11 Aug 50; Ltr, Lt Gen William B. Kean to author, 17 Jul 53.

[32] 25th Div WD, 12 Aug 50; 90th FA Bn WD, 11-12 Aug 50; 159th FA Bn WD, 11-12 Aug 50, and sketch 4.

[33] Roelofs, Comments on Bloody Gulch, 15 Feb 55.

being driven from the ridge. Roelofs again urged Colonel Ordway to start the trains out of the gulch.

Still unable to contact the division, Ordway now decided to move the trains and artillery out westward while it was still dark, despite division orders to wait for daylight. He felt that with the enemy obviously gaining control of the high ground above Pongam-ni, movement after daylight would be impossible or attended by heavy loss. The battalion of the 24th Infantry promised by the division had not arrived. About 0400 Ordway gave the order for the trains to move out. They were to be followed by the artillery, and then the 1st Battalion would bring up the rear. In the meantime, the battalion was to hold open the pass and protect the regimental column.[34]

Despite Ordway's use of messengers and staff officers, and his own efforts the trains seemed unable to move and a bad traffic jam developed. Movement of the trains through the pass should have been accomplished in twenty minutes, but it required hours. During the hour or more before daylight, no vehicle in Ordway's range of vision moved more than ten or twenty feet at a time. One of the factors creating this situation was caused when the Medical Company tried to move into the column from its position near the 1st Battalion command post. An ambulance hung up in a ditch and stopped everything on the road behind it until it could be pulled out.

With the first blush of dawn, enemy fire from the ridge overlooking the road began to fall on the column. At first it was light and high. Colonel Ordway got into his jeep and drove westward trying to hurry the column along. But he accomplished little. After the ambulance got free, however, the movement was somewhat faster and more orderly. Colonel Ordway himself cleared the pass shortly after daybreak. He noticed that the 1st Battalion was holding the pass and the hill just to the north of it. West of the pass, Ordway searched for a place to get the trains off the road temporarily so that the artillery could move out, but he found none suitable. He continued on until he reached Throckmorton's 2d Battalion bivouac area. The head of the regimental trains had already arrived there. He ordered them to continue on west in order to clear the road behind for the remainder of the column. Soon one of his staff officers found a schoolyard where the vehicles could assemble off the road, and they pulled in there.

About this time an artillery officer arrived from Pongam-ni and told Ordway that the artillery back at the gulch had been cut to pieces. Ordway returned to the 2d Battalion bivouac and then traveled on eastward toward Pongam-ni. On the way he met the 1st Battalion marching west on the road. The troops appeared close to exhaustion. Colonel Roelofs told Ordway that so far as he could tell the artillerymen had escaped into the hills. Ordway ordered the 1st Battalion into an assembly area and then directed the 2d Battalion to return to Pongam-ni, to cover the rear of the regiment and any troops remaining there.

That morning at dawn, after Colonel Ordway had cleared the pass, Colonel Roelofs watched the column as it tried

---

[34] Intervs, author with Ordway, 3 and 21 Jan 55; Ltr, Ordway to author, 18 Feb 55; Ordway, MS review comments, 20 Nov 57.

to clear the gulch area. To his great surprise he discovered moving with it the section of tanks and the A Company infantry platoon that he had left guarding the road entering Pongam-ni from the north. He asked the platoon leader why he had withdrawn. The latter answered that he had been ordered to do so. By the next day this officer had been evacuated, and Colonel Roelofs was never able to learn if such an order had been issued to him and, if so, by whom. Roelofs ordered the tanks and the infantry platoon to pull out of the column on to a flat spot near his command post. He intended to send them back to their original position just as soon as the road cleared sufficiently to enable them to travel. When he reported this to Colonel Ordway, he was instructed not to try it, as their movement to the rear might cause such a traffic jam that the artillery could not move.

About this time, soon after daybreak, enemy infantry had closed in so as virtually to surround the artillery. The North Korean *13th Regiment* of the *6th Division,* the enemy force at Pongam-ni, now struck furiously from three sides at the 555th and 90th Field Artillery Battalions' positions.[35] The attack came suddenly and with devastating power. Roelofs was standing in the road facing east toward Pongam-ni, trying to keep the traffic moving, when in the valley below him he saw streaks of fire that left a trail behind. Then came tremendous crashes. A truck blew up on the bridge in a mushroom of flame. The truck column behind it stopped. Men in the vehicles jumped out and ran to the ditches. Roelofs could now see enemy tanks and self-propelled guns on the dirt trail in the valley north of Pongam-ni, firing into the village and the artillery positions. To the artillerymen, this armed force looked like two tanks and several antitank guns.

The withdrawal of the section of tanks and the A Company infantry platoon from its roadblock position had permitted this enemy armor force to approach undetected and unopposed, almost to point-blank range, and with completely disastrous effects. The Triple Nickel emplacements were in the open and exposed to this fire; those of the 90th were partially protected by terrain features. The 105-mm. howitzers of the 555th Field Artillery Battalion ineffectually engaged the enemy armor. The 90th could not depress its 155-mm. howitzers low enough to engage the tanks and the self-propelled guns. Some of the Triple Nickel guns received direct hits. Many of the artillerymen of this battalion sought cover in buildings and under the bridge at Taejong-ni. Some of the buildings caught fire.

Simultaneously with the appearance of the enemy armor, North Korean small arms and automatic fire from the ridge north of the road increased greatly in volume. This fire caused several casualties among the 4.2-inch mortar crew members and forced the mortar platoon to cease firing and seek cover. The heavy machine gun platoon, fortunately, was well dug in and continued to pour heavy fire into the enemy-held ridge. An enemy machine gun opened up from the rear south of the road, but before the gunner got the range a truck driver killed him. Other sporadic efforts of a

---

[35] ATIS Supp, Enemy Docs, Issue 2, pp. 97-98, gives the enemy order for the attack at Bloody Gulch.

few infiltrating enemy troops in that quarter were suppressed before causing damage.

A lieutenant colonel of artillery came up the road with three or four men. He told Roelofs that things were in a terrible condition at the bridge and in the village. He said the guns were out of action and the trucks had been shot up and that the men were getting out as best they could. As the road traffic thinned out, enemy fire on the road subsided. Roelofs ordered the 4.2-inch mortar platoon to move on through the pass. The heavy machine gun platoon followed it. The wounded were taken along; the dead were left behind. There was no room for them on the few remaining trucks that would run.

As the last men of the 1st Battalion were moving westward toward the top of the pass, three medium tanks rolled up the road from Pongam-ni. Roelofs had not known they were there. He stopped one and ordered it to stand by. The tankers told him that everyone they saw at the bridge and along the stream was dead. To make a last check, Roelofs with several men started down anyway. On the way they met Chaplain Francis A. Kapica in his jeep with several wounded men. Kapica told Roelofs he had brought with him all the wounded he could find. Roelofs turned back, boarded the waiting tank, and started west. At the pass which his 1st Battalion men still held, he found 23 men from C Company, all that remained of 180. These survivors said they had been overrun. Roelofs organized the battalion withdrawal westward from the pass. In the advance he put A Company, then the C Company survivors. Still in contact with enemy, B Company came off the hills north of the pass in platoons. The company made the withdrawal successfully with the three tanks covering it from the pass. The tanks brought up the rear guard. The time was about 1000.

The situation in the village and at the bridge was not quite what it appeared to be to Roelofs and some of the officers and men who escaped from there and reported to him. Soon after the enemy armor came down the trail from the north and shot up the artillery positions, enemy infantry closed on the Triple Nickel emplacements and fired on the men with small arms and automatic weapons. Three of the 105-mm. howitzers managed to continue firing for several hours after daybreak, perhaps until 0900. Then the enemy overran the 555th positions.[36]

The 90th Field Artillery Battalion suffered almost as great a calamity. Early in the predawn attack the North Koreans scored direct hits on two 155-mm. howitzers and several ammunition trucks of A Battery. Only by fighting resolutely as infantrymen, manning the machine guns on the perimeter and occupying foxholes as riflemen, were the battalion troops able to repel the North Korean attack. Pfc. William L. Baumgartner of Headquarters Battery contributed greatly in repelling one persistent enemy force. He fired a truck-mounted machine gun while companions dropped all around him. Finally, a direct hit on

---

[36] 25th Div WD, 12 Aug 50; 90th FA Bn WD, 12 Aug 50; 159th FA Bn WD, 12 Aug 50; Barth MS, p. 17; Interv, Gugeler with Capt Perry H. Graves, CO, B Btry, 555th FA Bn, 9 Aug 51; Interv, author with 1st Lt Lyle D. Robb, CO, Hq Co, 5th Inf, 9 Aug 51; 1st Lt Wyatt Y. Logan, 555th FA Bn, Debriefing Rpt 64, 22 Jan 52, FA School, Ft. Sill.

his gun knocked him unconscious and off the truck. After he revived, Baumgartner resumed the fight with a rifle.[37]

At daybreak, Corsairs flew in to strafe and rocket the enemy. They had no radio communication with the ground troops but, by watching tracer bullets from the ground action, the pilots located the enemy. Despite this close air support, the artillery position was untenable by 0900. Survivors of the 90th loaded the wounded on the few serviceable trucks. Then, with the uninjured giving covering fire and Air Force F-51 fighter planes strafing the enemy, the battalion withdrew on foot.[38] Survivors credited the vicious close-in attacks of the fighter planes with making the withdrawal possible. But most of all, the men owed their safety to their own willingness to fight heroically as infantrymen when the enemy closed with them.

Meanwhile, enemy fire destroyed or burned nearly every vehicle east of the Pongam-ni bridge.

A mile eastward, another enemy force struck at B Battery, 159th Field Artillery Battalion. In this action enemy fire ignited several trucks loaded with ammunition and gasoline. At great personal risk, several drivers drove other ammunition and gasoline trucks away from the burning vehicles. The attack here, however, was not as intense as that at Pongam-ni and it subsided about 0800.[39]

After the artillery positions had been overrun, two tanks of the 25th Division Reconnaissance Company arrived from the east and tried to drive out the North Koreans and clear the road. MSgt. Robert A. Tedford stood exposed in the turret of one tank, giving instructions to the driver and gunner, while he himself operated the .50-caliber machine gun. This tank attack failed. Enemy fire killed Tedford, but he snuffed out the lives of some North Koreans before he lost his own.[40]

Meanwhile, at his assembly area five miles westward, Colonel Throckmorton had received Colonel Ordway's order to return with the 2d Battalion to the pass area west of Pongam-ni. When he arrived there the fight in the gulch and valley eastward had died down. A few stragglers came into his lines, but none after noon. Believing that enemy forces were moving through the hills toward the regimental command post at Taejong-ni, Throckmorton requested authority to return there. The regimental executive officer granted this authority at 1500.[41]

During the morning, General Barth, commander of the 25th Division artillery, tried to reach the scene of the enemy attack. But the enemy had cut the road and forced him to turn back. North Koreans also ambushed a platoon of the 72d Engineer Combat Battalion trying to help open the road. Barth telephoned General Kean at Masan and reported to him the extent of the disaster. Kean at once ordered the 3d Battalion, 5th Marines, to proceed to the scene,

---

[37] 90th FA Bn WD, 11-21 Aug 50; Barth MS, p. 18. Department of the Army General Order 36, 4 June 1951, awarded the Distinguished Unit Citation to the 90th Field Artillery Battalion.

[38] 90th FA Bn WD, 12 Aug 50; Barth MS; New York *Herald Tribune*, August 12, 1950, Bigart dispatch.

[39] 159th FA Bn WD, 11-12 Aug 50.

[40] General Order 232, 23 April 1951, awarded the Distinguished Service Cross posthumously to Sergeant Tedford. EUSAK WD.

[41] Interv, author with Throckmorton, 20 Aug 52.

and he also ordered the 3d Battalion, 24th Infantry, to attack through the hills to Pongam-ni.[42]

The Marine battalion arrived at Kogan-ni, three miles short of Pongam-ni, at 1600 and, with the assistance of air strikes and an artillery barrage, by dark had secured the high ground north of the road and east of Pongam-ni. The next morning the battalion attacked west with the mission of rescuing survivors of the 555th Field Artillery Battalion reported to be under the bridge at the village. Colonel Murray in a helicopter tried to deliver a message to these survivors, if any (there is no certainty there were any there), but was driven back by enemy machine gun fire. The marines reached the hill overlooking Pongam-ni and saw numerous groups of enemy troops below. Before they could attempt to attack into Pongam-ni itself the battalion received orders to rejoin the brigade at Masan.[43]

The 3d Battalion, 24th Infantry, likewise did not reach the overrun artillery positions. Lt. Col. John T. Corley, the much-decorated United States Army battalion commander of World War II, had assumed command of the battalion just three days before, on 9 August. Although Eighth Army sent some of the very best unit commanders in the United States Army to the 24th Regiment to give it superior leadership, the regiment remained unreliable and performed poorly. On 12 August, Corley's two assault companies in the first three hours of action against an estimated two enemy companies, and while receiving only a few rounds of mortar fire, dwindled from a strength of more than 100 men per company to about half that number. There were only 10 casualties during the day, 3 of them officers. By noon of the next day, 13 August, the strength of one company was down to 20 men and of the other to 35. This loss of strength was not due to casualties. Corley's battalion attack stopped two and a half miles from the captured artillery positions.[44]

At Bloody Gulch, the name given by the troops to the scene of the successful enemy attack, the 555th Field Artillery on 12 August lost all eight of its 105-mm. howitzers in the two firing batteries there. The 90th Field Artillery Battalion lost all six 155-mm. howitzers of its A Battery. The loss of Triple Nickel artillerymen has never been accurately computed. The day after the enemy attack only 20 percent of the battalion troops were present for duty. The battalion estimated at the time that from 75 to 100 artillerymen were killed at the gun positions and 80 wounded, with many of the latter unable to get away. Five weeks later, when the 25th Division regained Taejong-ni, it found in a house the bodies of 55 men of the 555th Field Artillery.[45]

The 90th Field Artillery Battalion lost 10 men killed, 60 wounded, and

---

[42] Barth MS, p. 19; 3d Bn, 24th Inf WD, 12 Aug 50; 25th Div WD, 12 Aug 50.

[43] 3d Bn, 5th Mar SAR, 12-13 Aug 50; 1st Prov Mar Brig SAR, 12-13 Aug 50; Montross and Canzona, *The Pusan Perimeter*, pp. 150-52.

[44] Interv, author with Corley, 6 Nov 51; Barth MS, p. 19; EUSAK IG Rpt, 24th Inf Regt, testimony of Corley, 26 Aug 50.

[45] 25th Div WD, 13 Aug 50; 90th FA Bn WD, 12 Aug 50; 27th Inf Narr Hist Rpt, Sep 50; Barth MS, p. 17; New York *Herald Tribune*, August 14, 1950, Bigart dispatch.

about 30 missing at Bloody Gulch—more than half the men of Headquarters and A Batteries present. Five weeks later when this area again came under American control, the bodies of 20 men of the battalion were found; all of them had been shot through the head.[46]

Four days after the artillery disaster, General Barth had the 555th and 90th Field Artillery Battalions reconstituted and re-equipped with weapons. Eighth Army diverted 12 105-mm. howitzers intended for the ROK Army to the 25th Division artillery and 6 155-mm. howitzers intended for a third firing battery of the 90th Field Artillery Battalion were used to re-equip A Battery. Lt. Col. Clarence E. Stuart arrived in Korea from the United States on 13 August and assumed command of the 555th Field Artillery Battalion.

West of Bloody Gulch, the 2d Battalion, 5th Regimental Combat Team, repulsed a North Korean attack at Taejong-ni on the morning of 13 August. That afternoon, the battalion entrucked and moved on to the Much'on-ni road fork. There it turned east toward Masan.

The 3d Battalion of the 5th Regimental Combat Team, rolling westward from Pongam-ni on the morning of 11 August, had joined the 35th Infantry where the latter waited at the Much'on-ni crossroads. From there the two forces moved on to the Chinju pass. They now looked down on Chinju. But only their patrols went farther. On the afternoon of 13 August and that night, the 5th Regimental Combat Team traveled back eastward. It was depleted and worn. Military police from the 25th Division were supposed to guide its units to assigned assembly areas. But there was a change in plans, and in the end confusion prevailed as most of the units were led in the darkness of 13-14 August to a dry stream bed just east of Chindong-ni. The troops were badly mixed there and until daylight no one knew where anyone else was.[47]

The next morning the 2d Battalion of the 5th Regimental Combat Team moved around west to Kogan-ni, where it relieved the 3d Battalion, 5th Marines. Colonel Throckmorton succeeded Colonel Ordway in command of the regiment on 15 August.

Task Force Kean Ended

On 14 August, after a week of fighting, Task Force Kean was back approximately in the positions from which it had started its attack. The 35th Regiment held the northern part of the 25th Division line west of Masan, the 24th Regiment the center, and the 5th Regimental Combat Team the southern part. The Marine brigade was on its way to another part of the Eighth Army line. In the week of constant fighting in the Chinju corridor, from 7 to 13 August, the units of Task Force Kean learned

---

[46] 25th Div WD, 24 Sep 50; Barth MS, p. 17. In addition to its guns, the 90th lost 26 vehicles and 2 M5 tractors. The 555th lost practically all its vehicles. Many 1st Battalion and regimental headquarters vehicles were also destroyed or abandoned. The North Korean communiqué for 12 August, monitored in a rebroadcast from Moscow, claimed, in considerable exaggeration, 9 150-mm. guns, 12 105-mm. guns, 13 tanks, and 157 vehicles captured or destroyed. See New York *Times*, August 16, 1950; Barth MS, p. 21; Interv, author with Stuart, 9 Aug 51.

[47] Interv, author with Throckmorton, 20 Aug 52; Ordway, MS review comments, 20 Nov 57.

that the front was the four points of the compass, and that it was necessary to climb, climb, climb. The saffron-colored hills were beautiful to gaze upon at dusk, but they were brutal to the legs climbing them, and out of them at night came the enemy.

While Task Force Kean drove westward toward Chinju, enemy mines and small arms fire daily cut the supply roads behind it in the vicinity of Chindong-ni. For ten successive days, tanks and armored cars had to open a road so that food supplies might reach a battalion of the 24th Infantry in the Sobuk-san area. The old abandoned coal mines of the Tundok region on Sobuk-san were alive with enemy troops. The 24th Infantry and ROK troops had been unable to clear this mountainous region.[48]

At 1550, 16 August, in a radio message to General Kean, Eighth Army dissolved Task Force Kean.[49] The task force had not accomplished what Eighth Army had believed to be easily possible—the winning and holding of the Chinju pass line. Throughout Task Force Kean's attack, well organized enemy forces controlled the Sobuk-san area and from there struck at its rear and cut its lines of communications. The North Korean High Command did not move a single squad from the northern to the southern front during the action. The N.K. *6th Division* took heavy losses in some of the fighting, but so did Task Force Kean. Eighth Army again had underestimated the N.K. *6th Division.*

Even though Task Force Kean's attack did not accomplish what Eighth Army had hoped for and expected, it nevertheless did provide certain beneficial results. It chanced to meet head-on the N.K. *6th Division* attack against the Masan position, and first stopped it, then hurled it back. Secondly, it gave the 25th Division a much needed psychological experience of going on the offensive and nearly reaching an assigned objective. From this time on, with the exception of the 24th Infantry, the division troops fought well and displayed a battle worthiness that paid off handsomely and sometimes spectacularly in the oncoming Perimeter battles. By disorganizing the offensive operations of the N.K. *6th Division* at the middle of August, Task Force Kean also gained the time needed to organize and wire in the defenses that were to hold the enemy out of Masan during the critical period ahead.

The N.K. *6th Division* now took up defensive positions opposite the 25th Division in the mountains west of Masan. It placed its *13th Regiment* on the left near the Nam River, the *15th* in the center, and the *14th* on the right next to the coast. Remnants of the *83d Motorized Regiment* continued to support the division. The first replacements for the *6th Division*—2,000 of them—arrived at Chinju reportedly on 12 August. Many of these were South Koreans from Andong, forced into service. They were issued hand grenades and told to pick up arms on the battlefield. Prisoners reported that the *6th Division* was down to a strength of between 3,000–4,000 men. Apparently it still had about twelve T34 tanks which needed fuel. The men had little food. All supplies were car-

---

[48] Interv, author with Arnold, 22 Jul 51; Interv, author with Fisher, 2 Jan 52; Fisher, MS review comments, 7 Nov 57; Barth MS, p. 15.
[49] 25th Div WD, 16 Aug 50; GHQ UNC G-3 Opn Rpt 53, 16 Aug 50.

ried to the front by A-frame porters, there placed in dumps, and camouflaged with leaves and grass.[50]

During the fighting between Task Force Kean and the N.K. *6th Division* on the Masan front, violent and alarming battles had erupted elsewhere. Sister divisions of the N.K. *6th* in the north along the Naktong were matching it in hard blows against Eighth Army's defense line. The battles of the Pusan Perimeter had started.

---

[50] ATIS Res Supp Interrog Rpts, Issue 100 (N.K. *6th Div*), pp. 38–39; 27th Inf WD, Aug 50, PW Rpt 10; EUSAK WD, 12 Aug 50, Interrog Rpt 519; 25th Div WD, Aug 50, PW Interrog.

CHAPTER XVII

The First Battle of the Naktong Bulge

> The influence of growing fire-power on tactical defense is evident. . . .
> The defensive is able more than before to carry out its original mission,
> which is to break the strength of the attacker, to parry his blows, to
> weaken him, to bleed him, so as to reverse the relation of forces and
> lead finally to the offensive, which is the only decisive form of warfare.
> RITTER VON LEEB, *Defense*

The dog days of August were at hand. The men in Eighth Army who survived that period spoke afterward of it as "the days along the Naktong." The Eighth Army no longer could withdraw when enemy pressure became oppressive. It had to stand and fight and hold, or be driven out of Korea.

General Walker's defense plan centered on holding the road and rail lines running in a large oval east of the Naktong, from Pusan north through Miryang to Taegu, and hence east through Yongch'on to Kyongju, where they turned back south to Pusan. Any further withdrawal and loss of these lines of communication would render difficult any later U.N. attempt at a counteroffensive.

The North Koreans, in preparing to attack the Pusan Perimeter and its communication system, had available four lines of advance toward Pusan: (1) through or past Masan south of the confluence of the Nam and Naktong Rivers, (2) through the Naktong Bulge to the rail and road lines at Miryang, (3) through Taegu, and (4) through Kyongju and down the east coast corridor. They tried them all simultaneously in August, apparently believing that if they did not succeed at one place they would at another.

Along the Perimeter, the most important terrain feature for both the United Nations and the North Koreans—helping the former and hindering the latter—was the Naktong River, the second largest river in Korea. It formed a huge moat in front of almost three-fourths of the Perimeter. Its numerous great folds and bends resembled a huge snake contracting its length before coiling. Along its lower course, the river is generally from one-quarter to half a mile wide and more than six feet deep. Great sand beaches appear at many places when the river is not swollen by rain. Hills come down close to the water's edge on either bank, and rice paddy valleys of varying sizes finger their way among the hills.

In Korea, the term *hill* came to mean to the soldiers anything from a knoll to a towering mountain. A few of the hills bordering the lower Naktong below Taegu on the east side rise to 1,200 feet elevation; three or four miles back from the river they climb to 2,500 feet. On the west, or enemy, side of the Naktong, the hills bordering the river are higher than on the east, reaching 2,000 feet in many instances. North of Taegu, along the upper reaches of the river, from Waegwan in a semicircle east to Andong, the hills rise still higher, many of them to elevations of 2,000 and 3,000 feet.

The line of the Naktong as organized by the American forces was a series of strongpoints on the highest hills, affording views of both the river and the natural avenues of travel from it. During the day, these points were hardly more than observation posts. At night they became listening posts and tight little defense perimeters. Some of the posts were manned only in the daytime. Others were held by no more than half a squad of men. No one expected these soldiers to fight in position; they were a form of intelligence screen, their duty being to observe and report. Jeep patrols during the daytime ran along the river road. Quite obviously, the river line was thinly held. Reserve troops some miles back from the river were ready to counterattack against any enemy crossing.

Artillery and mortars were in positions back of the river. They were laid to fire on known ferry and other probable crossing sites. The role of the artillery and the mortars was to be a vital one in the Perimeter fighting; their fire could be massed, within limits, against any major enemy effort. The infantry and the artillery together were disposed so as to hold the commanding ground and control the meager road net. The roads necessarily were all-important.

No one doubted that the North Koreans intended to force a crossing of the Naktong without delay. Time was against them. Every passing week brought closer the prospect of more American reinforcements—troops, tanks, artillery, and planes. North Korean Premier Kim Il Sung had set 15 August as the date for final victory and the liberation of all Korea. This date marked the fifth anniversary of freedom from Japanese rule.[1]

The Naktong Bulge

Seven air miles north of the point where the Naktong turns east and the Nam enters it, the Naktong curves westward opposite Yongsan in a wide semicircular loop. The bulge of land formed by this river loop measures four miles east-west and five miles north-south. This particular loop of the river and the land it enclosed on three sides became known to the American troops as the Naktong Bulge during the heavy fighting there in August and September. (*See Map IV.*)

Northward from the confluence of the Nam with the Naktong, the 24th Division held the line of the lower Naktong for a distance of sixteen air miles, or a river front of about thirty-four miles. The 34th Infantry was on the lower, southern part; the 21st Infantry was on the upper part together with the ROK 17th Regiment. The 19th Infantry, just arrived from Masan, was re-equipping in

---

[1] 1st Cav Div WD, Aug 50, G-2 Transl 0034, 191100 Aug 50.

THE FIRST BATTLE OF THE NAKTONG BULGE

the rear. In general terms, the 34th Infantry held the area west of Yongsan in the Naktong Bulge, while north of it the 21st Infantry held the area west of Changnyong.

The 3d Battalion, 34th Infantry, held the river line in its regimental front, while the 1st Battalion was in a reserve assembly area about four miles back from the river near Yongsan. (*Map 9*) The 3d Battalion front was about nine miles, or 15,000 yards long.[2] One may contrast this battalion frontage of 15,000 yards with one of 10,000 yards for a division at full strength, which U.S. Army doctrine considered normal.

The three rifle companies of the 3d Battalion—I, L, and K, in that order from north to south—were on high hills overlooking the Naktong River. An unoccupied gap of more than two miles lay between I and L Companies, and another of more than three miles lay between L and K Companies. Because of the river's course around the bulge, the three company positions resembled the points of a broad triangle; I and K were the two extremities at the eastern base and L the apex at the bulge of high ground extending westward in the big fold of the river. Along this stretch of river there were at least six ferry crossing sites.[3]

For almost the entire regimental front, hills 500 to 600 feet high rose from the narrow river valley, in some instances abruptly from the water's edge. In this nine miles of front two valleys formed entrances from the river into the hill masses stretching eastward. The northern entrance was at the Ohang village ferry crossing. This crossing lay in the gap between I and L Companies at the northern edge of the bulge. The other natural entrance into the regimental zone lay four air miles south at the under side of the bulge.

The 4.2-inch mortars supporting the 3d Battalion were about a mile and a quarter back of the river in the draw that penetrated the hills from the Ohang ferry site. The 3d Battalion command post was half a mile farther southeast in this same draw, at the village of Soesil. Commanding the battalion was Lt. Col. Gines Perez, just arrived from the United States. At Yongsan, six miles east of the river, Colonel Beauchamp had his regimental command post.

General Church ordered all civilians in the 24th Division zone to evacuate from an area five miles deep east of the river. He warned them that if they failed to do so, his troops might shoot them on sight as possible enemy agents. He said he could take no more chances with civilians; "If we are going to hold here, we cannot have any enemy behind us."[4]

The N.K. 4th Division Attacks Into the Naktong Bulge

The first enemy crossings of the Naktong River, west of the Andong mountain barrier, other than reconnaissance patrols, came on 5 August at three different places. Two were north of Waegwan in the ROK Army sector. The third was thirty miles south of Waegwan op-

---

[2] Ltr, Ayres to author, 5 June 53; Overlay of 3d Bn, 34th Inf positions, 6 Aug 50, prepared by Col Beauchamp for author.

[3] Beauchamp overlay, 6 Aug 50; Interv, author with Beauchamp, 1 Aug 52; Interv, author with Col Gines Perez, 6 Aug 51.

[4] New York *Herald Tribune*, August 6, 1950, dispatch from Korea, 5 August.

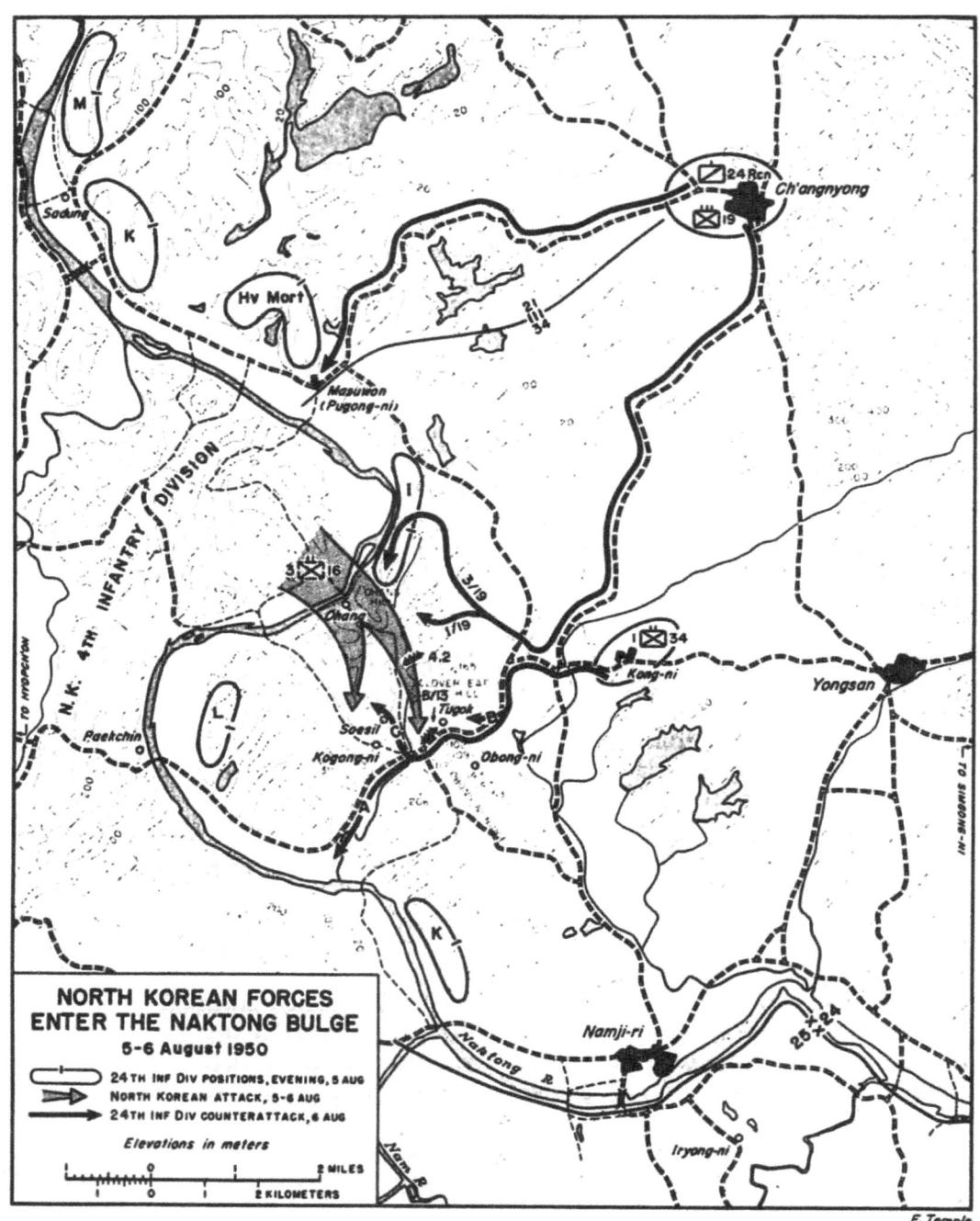

THE FIRST BATTLE OF THE NAKTONG BULGE

posite Yongsan in the 24th Division sector, in the big bulge of the Naktong. This third crossing of the river was made by the N.K. *4th Division* and was the one to have consequences which first threatened the Perimeter.

Maj. Gen. Lee Kwon Mu commanded the N.K. *4th Division*. Already he had received the highest honors, the "Hero of the Korean Democratic People's Republic" and the "Order of the National Flag, 1st Class," for achievements with his division. Forty years old, Lee had been born in Manchuria, had served in the Chinese Communist *8th Route Army*, and, according to some reports, he had been a lieutenant in the Soviet Army in World War II. After attending a school in the Soviet Union in 1948 he returned to Korea where he became Chief of Staff of the N.K. Army. Eventually he was relieved of this post. Shortly before the invasion he was recalled by Premier Kim Il Sung's personal order and given command of the *4th Division*. The division itself in August 1950 held the honorary name of "The 4th Seoul Division," "Seoul" indicating recognition of the division's part in the capture of that city.[5]

By 4 August, the N.K. *4th Division* had concentrated its three regiments in the vicinity of Hyopch'on and was studying the American dispositions and defenses opposite it on the east side of the Naktong. An officer from the division headquarters, captured later, estimated the division had a total strength of about 7,000 men at this time with about 1,500 men in each of the infantry regiments.

The division, with little or no preparation for it, intended to make an immediate crossing of the river in co-ordination with other crossings northward.[6]

On the American side, General Church considered the northern part of the 24th Division zone the more difficult to defend and reinforce because of its poor road net. He believed for this reason that the North Koreans were more likely to cross the river in that part of the division zone rather than in the southern part. Therefore, when the N.K. *4th Division* crossed in the southern part, opposite the 34th Infantry, the crossing was not where he had anticipated it would be, and it also came sooner than he had expected.[7]

Red and yellow flares burst over the Naktong at midnight 5 August, as 800 North Koreans of the *3d Battalion, 16th Regiment,* began the crossing. Most of the men stripped off their clothing, rolling it and their weapons into bundles to be carried on their heads, and stepped into the shoulder-deep water. Others made rafts to float their clothes and equipment across. This crossing was at the Ohang ferry site, three and a half miles south of Pugong-ni and due west of Yongsan. There is some evidence that the *1st Battalion* of the regiment also crossed at this time. None of the units in this initial crossing brought along mortars or heavy weapons. After reaching the east side, the enemy soldiers dressed, and in a column of platoons,

---

[5] GHQ FEC, History of the N.K. Army, pp. 41, 58, 75; 24th Div WD, 6 Aug 50; ATIS Res Supp Interrog Rpts, Issue 94 (N.K. *4th Div*), pp. 43, 49.

[6] ATIS Interrog Rpt 612, Issue 1, p. 25, Lt Jun Jai Ro; EUSAK WD, 8 Oct 50, G-2 Sec, PW Interrog, ADVATIS 1074, Jr Lt Chon Cho Hong.

[7] Interv, author with Church, 25 Sep 52; Interv, author with Stephens, 8 Oct 51; Interv, author with Maj Sammy E. Radow, CO 1st Bn, 23d Inf, 16 Aug 51.

marched southeast up the draw leading into the American lines. Their objective was Yongsan.[8]

Simultaneously with this crossing, another enemy force tried to cross the river some miles farther north in the zone of the 21st Regiment, 24th Division. This force, after running into a mine field and being shelled by artillery, was machine-gunned by infantry and driven back across the river in confusion.[9]

The enemy force that crossed at Ohang penetrated the gap between I and L Companies of the 34th Infantry, and followed the draw leading southeast to a little valley through which the Yongsan–Naktong River road passed. The battalion command post and the mortar position were approximately two miles from the enemy crossing site and directly in the line of enemy advance.[10]

At 0200, 6 August, the 34th Infantry reported to the 24th Division that an enemy force had penetrated between I and L Companies. The North Koreans moved along the draw without making any effort to attack the companies on the hills overlooking the river. They overran the 4.2-inch mortar position, but in so doing fully alerted the battalion command post near by. Aware now of the enemy penetration, most of the troops there escaped to the rear. Colonel Perez, commander of the 3d Battalion, made his way back three miles along the Yongsan road to the 1st Battalion command post and there gave Colonel Ayres his first news of the enemy crossing.[11]

Colonel Beauchamp, the 34th regimental commander, at 0520 reported to General Church: "Enemy are across river in force in center of my sector. It's pretty dark and situation is obscure. I am committing my reserve [1st Bn] at daylight to clear up the situation. Get me a liaison plane in the air at dawn."[12] Beauchamp ordered Ayres to counterattack with the 1st Battalion and restore the regimental position. At dawn there was no indication that the rifle companies of the 3d Battalion on the hills along the river, except L Company, had yet come under attack. Some elements of L Company had been forced out of position and withdrew about a mile from the river. The enemy apparently was content to leave the river line troops alone except where they lay across his axis of advance. He was concentrating on penetrating behind the river positions.

After the escape of the 3d Battalion headquarters troops, the positions of B Battery, 13th Field Artillery, eastward at the northwestern base of Obong-ni Ridge lay completely exposed to the enemy. At 0830 this battery reported small

---

[8] Interv, author with Beauchamp, 1 Aug 52; Interv, author with Perez, 6 Aug 51; 13th FA Bn WD, 6 Aug 50; 24th Div WD, 6 Aug 50; EUSAK WD, 7 Aug 50, ATIS Interrog Rpt 452, ADVATIS 307, EUSAK 342, Lee Myong Hyon; ATIS Interrog Rpt 453, Kim T'ae Mo; ATIS Interrog Rpt 453, Col Pak Kum Choi. Colonel Pak gave the strength of the N.K. *16th Regt* as follows: *1st Bn*–500, *2d Bn*–500, *3d Bn*–800, *Arty Bn*–300, all other units–200; total regimental strength, 2,300.

[9] 24th Div WD, G–3 Jnl, entry 601, 061035 Aug 50; 3d Engr (C) Bn, Unit Hist, S–2 Sec, Summ, 6 Aug 50.

[10] Ltr, Ayres to author, 3 Jun 53 and overlay showing 3d and 1st Bn, 34th Inf, positions, 5 Aug 50; AMS 1:50,000 scale map of Korea, L751, 1950, Namji-ri sheet (6820-II).

[11] Ltr, Ayres to author, 5 Jun 53; Interv, author with Ayres, 18 Nov 54; 24th Div WD, G–3 Jnl, 6 Aug 50; 34th Inf WD, 6 Aug 50.

[12] 24th Div WD, G–3 Jnl, entry 571, 060520 Aug 50.

THE FIRST BATTLE OF THE NAKTONG BULGE

arms fire in its vicinity. The 24th Division now estimated that 800 enemy were east of the river in its zone.[13]

Upon receiving the order to counterattack straight down the Yongsan–Naktong River road, Colonel Ayres directed his executive officer to mount C Company in trucks and send it down the road until he, Ayres, stopped it. Behind C Company, A, B, and the Weapons Companies under the executive officer were to follow on foot. Just the day before, 187 replacements had joined the battalion.

Ayres, his S–3, and the Assistant S–3 set off in a jeep down the road toward the river, ahead of the troops, to form an estimate of the situation. They reached the vacated 3d Battalion command post without sighting enemy troops. While looking around the command post and making plans for deployment of the 1st Battalion when it came up, Ayres and those with him received fire from the hills above them. The trucks carrying C Company now began to arrive. While the men detrucked, enemy fire hit two of them.[14]

Ayres hurried to Capt. Clyde M. Akridge, who had been in command of C Company only a few days, and directed him to attack and seize the high ground above the former 3d Battalion command post. Akridge organized his company and started forward as enemy fire gradually increased. In leading the attack, Captain Akridge was wounded three times and was finally evacuated.

Ayres took shelter at a culvert a short distance to the rear. From there he, the weapons platoon leader, and mortarmen placed 60-mm. mortar fire on the enemy-held hill until their ammunition was expended. While standing up to direct this fire, the mortar sergeant was practically cut in half by machine gun fire. Other men, lying prone, were hit. Ayres saw that he would have to get back to A and B Companies if he were to influence the actions of the battalion. With several members of the battalion staff he dashed across the rice paddy. Enemy fire hit two of the party but all reached the slopes of Obong-ni Ridge. They worked their way around the now abandoned artillery position to the rear.[15]

Before Ayres and his party escaped, B Battery, 13th Field Artillery Battalion, had come under enemy fire. At 1030 the battery commander assembled about 50 men and withdrew along a narrow road with one howitzer, four 2½-ton trucks, and three smaller vehicles. They abandoned four howitzers and nine vehicles. The battery lost 2 men killed, 6 wounded, and 6 missing.[16]

Meanwhile, in its attack, C Company had no chance of success; enemy troops were on higher ground in superior numbers. The North Koreans let loose a heavy volume of small arms and automatic fire against the company, and soon the dry creek bed in which the men were moving was strewn with dead and dying. After Colonel Ayres had dashed from the culvert across the rice paddy, Lieutenant Payne and Lt. McDonald Martin, the latter wounded, ran from the same cul-

[13] Interv, author with Beauchamp, 1 Aug 52; Interv, author with Ayres, 18 Nov 54; 13th FA Bn WD, 6 Aug 50; 24th Div WD, 6 Aug 50.
[14] Ltr, Ayres to author, 5 Jan 53; Interv, author with Beauchamp, 18 Nov 54; Ltr, Beauchamp to author, 20 May 53, and attached comments.

[15] Ltr, Ayres to author, 5 Jan 53.
[16] 13th FA Bn WD, 6 Aug 50.

vert to a grist mill a short distance away, and south of the road. There, others joined them in the next few minutes. In the fight outside, more than half the company became casualties. According to the recollection of the battalion commander, there were about thirty-five survivors in the company.[17]

While C Company met the advancing North Koreans, A and B Companies had started forward on foot from the battalion area before rations could be issued to them. When he arrived at the 1st Battalion command post at Kang-ni, Colonel Beauchamp learned that C Company had lost heavily to enemy action up ahead and had been dispersed. He went forward at once and joined A and B Companies, the latter cautiously leading the advance. The B Company point met an enemy squad and killed ten of the enemy soldiers as they tried to run back. Two antiaircraft vehicles, each mounting four .50-caliber machine guns, were in the forefront of the attack that now got under way with A Company on the left of the road and B Company on the right. Colonel Ayres rejoined the battalion at this time. Even though enemy resistance at first was light, the intense summer heat slowed the pace. Soon B Company on the right encountered strong enemy forces on Cloverleaf Hill. They halted its advance and knocked out one of the quad-50's on the road. On the left, A Company under Capt. A. F. Alfonso continued its advance with only a few casualties, passing the overrun artillery positions and reaching the area where C Company had been overwhelmed by the enemy.[18]

The light tank in the lead fired on the grist mill, supposing it to be enemy held, and scored a direct hit. This fire killed one, mortally wounded two, and wounded less severely several other C Company men inside. Then the tank and A Company men came charging up to the mill where several survivors of C Company had been fighting off North Koreans since early morning. North Korean soldiers several times had rushed to within grenade range of the building but had not succeeded in entering it. Inside, the men had stacked their dead against the walls to protect the living from small arms fire. Thus, after a daylong ordeal, the survivors were rescued by the A Company attack.

Captain Alfonso and his men set about loading dead and wounded into abandoned but still operable 2½-ton trucks. This done, he put a driver and two riflemen from his company on each truck, and, with the tank leading, he sent the vehicles back through enemy fire toward friendly lines. Lieutenant Payne, knocked unconscious when the tank shell exploded against the grist mill, regained consciousness for a few seconds when he was thrown into a truck and heard a man say, "Payne is dead as a mackerel." A little later he again regained consciousness when the truck ran into a ditch under enemy small arms fire. This

---

[17] 24th Div WD, 6 Aug 50; Interv, author with Cpl Stewart E. Sizemore (D Co, 34th Inf, 6 Aug 50), 30 Jun 51; Ltr, Maj Charles E. Payne to Ayres, 13 Dec 54, copy in OCMH; Interv, author with Ayres, 18 Nov 54.

[18] Ltr, Alfonso to Ayres, 27 Nov 54, copy in OCMH; Interv, author with Ayres, 16 Nov 54; Interv, author with Beauchamp, 18 Nov 54; Ltr, Ayres to author, 5 Jan 53; Ltr and comments, Beauchamp to author, 20 May 53. The 1st Battalion, 34th Infantry, had only 20 officers and 471 enlisted men when it began the counterattack on 6 August. See 34th Inf WD, 7 Aug 50.

THE FIRST BATTLE OF THE NAKTONG BULGE

time he was able to crawl and walk the remaining distance to safety.[19]

Following the road, Alfonso continued his attack toward the river against light resistance. Just after sunset, about 2000, A Company reached the river and joined part of L Company which was still in its position overlooking the Naktong. The combined group was only about ninety men strong. They sought temporary safety in a well dug perimeter position. Fortunately they succeeded in establishing radio contact with the 1st Battalion through an L Company artillery forward observer's radio by relay through B Company.[20]

While A Company pushed on to the river, B Company dug in on part of Cloverleaf Hill. Quiet gradually settled over the area. The day's action made it clear that the North Koreans had penetrated eastward north of the Yongsan-Naktong River road to Cloverleaf Hill, but had not yet crossed south of the road to Obong-ni Ridge. Cloverleaf and Obong-ni together formed a high backbone across the Yongsan road about three miles east of the Naktong River and nearly halfway to Yongsan.

While the 1st Battalion counterattack was in progress, I Company abandoned its hill position northward overlooking the river on the regimental right flank. The Heavy Weapons Company, a mortar platoon, and A Company, 26th Antiaircraft Automatic Weapons Battalion, joined I Company in withdrawing northeast into the zone of the 21st Infantry.

These units were not under attack. Adjacent units of the 21st Infantry saw this movement and reported it to General Church. He immediately ordered Colonel Beauchamp to stop this unauthorized withdrawal and to relieve the company commanders involved. Beauchamp sent his executive officer, Colonel Wadlington, to the scene at once. Wadlington found the men moving east, turned them around, and marched them back toward their former position. At noon General Church sent the 24th Division Reconnaissance Company to block the Naktong River–Changnyong road adjacent to I Company's former position. The Reconnaissance and I Companies then attacked an enemy force that had by now occupied a hill near Pugong-ni, but they were repulsed with considerable loss.[21]

By midmorning, General Church had become convinced that the bulk of the enemy east of the river were in the bulge area. He thereupon committed the 19th Infantry in an attack west along the northern flank of the 34th Infantry. In this attack, the 19th Infantry trapped approximately 300 enemy troops in a village east of Ohang Hill, a mile from the river, and killed most of them.[22]

The day's action had not been without creditable performances by the American troops. The counterattack of the 1st Battalion, 34th Infantry, had driven back the enemy's advanced units and regained part of Cloverleaf Hill.

---

[19] Ltr, Payne to Ayres, 13 Dec 54; Ltr, Alfonso to Ayres, 27 Nov 54; Intervs, author with Beauchamp, 18 Nov 54, and Ayres, 16 Nov 54.

[20] Ltr, Alfonso to Ayres, 27 Nov 54; Intervs, author with Beauchamp, 18 Nov 54, and Ayres, 16 Nov 54.

[21] Interv, author with Church, 25 Sep 52; Interv, author with Beauchamp, 18 Nov 54; 24th Div WD, 6 Aug 50, and G-3 Jnl, entries 593-96, 061120-061150 Aug 50; 34th Inf WD, 7 Aug 50.

[22] Interv, author with Church, 25 Sep 52; 24th Div WD, 6 Aug 50 and G-3 Jnl, entry 591, 061110 Aug 50.

This, together with the fact that K, L, and A Companies held hill positions above the Naktong without any sign of panic, prevented the enemy from seizing at the outset the road net through Yongsan. Also, it gave time for the 19th Infantry, and later the 9th Infantry, to move up for counterattack.

Artillery fire and aircraft had kept the crossing sites covered, and after daylight prevented enemy reinforcements from reaching the east side of the river. When darkness fell, the artillery continued interdiction fire on these crossing sites. The 24th Division had seventeen 105-mm. and twelve 155-mm. howitzers available to deliver supporting fires covering thirty-two miles of front.[23]

Just as the battle of the Naktong Bulge got under way, regrouping of ROK troops made it necessary for Eighth Army to order the ROK 17th Regiment released from the 24th Division. This regiment had been holding the right flank of the division line. To take its place temporarily in the emergency, General Church hastily formed Task Force Hyzer (3d Engineer Combat Battalion, less A Company; 78th Heavy Tank Battalion, less tanks; and the 24th Division Reconnaissance Company). Eighth Army allowed Church to keep the ROK 17th Regiment in line the night of 6-7 August, and before dawn it repulsed several enemy crossing attempts in its sector. On the morning of 7 August Task Force Hyzer relieved it, and the ROK 17th Regiment moved to Taegu to rejoin the ROK Army. This weakening of the line had been partly offset the previous afternoon by the arrival of the 1st Battalion, 9th Infantry, 2d Infantry Division, at Changnyong for attachment to the 24th Division.[24]

On the evening of the 6th, as the enemy held firmly to his bridgehead, General Church ordered the 34th and 19th Infantry Regiments to continue the counterattack the next morning.[25]

The Enemy Gains Cloverleaf—Obong-ni

During the night of 6-7 August, the enemy succeeded in moving an unknown number of reinforcements across to the east side of the river in the bulge area. Then, on the third night, 7-8 August, an estimated two more battalions crossed the river in four different places. Enemy units that tried to cross north of the bulge were driven back by the 21st Infantry; they then shifted southward to cross.[26]

The continuation of the American counterattack in the bulge, on the morning of 7 August, by the 19th Infantry and B Company of the 34th Infantry was a feeble effort. Extreme heat and lack of food and water were contributing factors in the failure to advance. The situation was not helped when friendly aircraft mistakenly strafed the 19th Infantry positions. In its zone, B Company, 34th Infantry, fell back after rescuing a few men of the Heavy Mortar Company who had been missing since the previous morning. On their part, the North Koreans pressed forward and occupied the greater part of Cloverleaf Hill and Obong-ni Ridge. In doing this, they

---

[23] 24th Div Arty WD, 23 Jul-25 Aug 50.

[24] 24th Div WD, 6-7 Aug 50.

[25] *Ibid.*, Opn Instr 18, 061900 Aug 50.

[26] 9th Inf WD, 8 Aug 50; 34th Inf WD, 8 Aug 50; 24th Div WD, 8 Aug 50; ATIS Interrog Rpt 602, 19 Aug 50, Issue 1, pp. 4-5, Lee Ki Sun, *2d Bn, 18th Regt, N.K. 4th Div.*

established themselves on dominating and critical terrain astride the main east-west road in the bulge area.[27]

From the crests of Cloverleaf and Obong-ni the North Koreans could see the American main supply road stretching back to Yongsan five miles away and, for a distance, beyond that town toward Miryang. Cloverleaf (Hill 165), as its name indicates, is shaped like a four-leaf clover with its stem pointing north. Cloverleaf is somewhat higher than Obong-ni Ridge across the pass to the south of it. Obong-ni Ridge is a mile and a half long, curving slightly to the southeast with a series of knobs rising from 300 to 500 feet above the rice paddies at its base. The road, where it passes between Cloverleaf and Obong-ni, follows a winding, narrow passage of low ground. The village of Tugok (Morisil) lies at the southern base of Cloverleaf just north of the road.[28] Obong village lies at the eastern base of Obong-ni Ridge half a mile south of the road. These two related terrain features, Cloverleaf Hill and Obong-ni Ridge, were the key positions in the fighting of the Naktong Bulge. The battle was to rage around them for the next ten days.

On the morning of 7 August, while the North Koreans were seizing Cloverleaf Hill and Obong-ni Ridge, Col. John G. Hill received a summons to come to the 2d Division headquarters. There he learned from the division commander that General Walker had ordered the 9th Regiment (—) to report to General Church. Hill started his troops to the bulge area at 0130, and reported to General Church about 0830, 8 August. Church told Hill he wanted him to attack at once and drive the North Koreans from the bulge salient.[29] After some discussion it was agreed that the 9th Infantry would attack at 1600.

The 9th Infantry, at full strength in troops and equipment and its men rested, contrasted strongly with the regiments of the 24th Division on the line. On 8 August, the strength of the 24th Division regiments was approximately as follows: 34th Infantry, 1,100; 19th Infantry, 1,700; 21st Infantry, 1,800.[30] The combat effectiveness of the 24th Division then was estimated to be about 40 percent because of shortage of equipment and understrength units. Fatigue and lowered morale of the men undoubtedly reduced the percentage even more.

Hill's 9th Infantry relieved B Company, 34th Infantry, on part of Cloverleaf Hill and members of the Heavy Mortar Company who were fighting as riflemen across the road near Obong-ni Ridge. Colonel Hill placed the 1st Battalion of the 9th Infantry on the left of the Yongsan road, the 2d Battalion on the right side. His command post was at Kang-ni, a mile and a half eastward toward Yongsan. Two batteries of the 15th Field Artillery Battalion (105-mm. howitzers) supported his attack, with twelve 155-mm. howitzers and additional 105-mm. howitzers of the 24th Division on call. Hill's immediate objectives were

---

[27] 19th Inf WD, 7 Aug 50; 34th Inf WD, 7 Aug 50.
[28] Tugok is represented on the 1:50,000 scale map of Korea as Morisil. To the troops at the time, however, this village was known as Tugok and that name is used in the text.

[29] Interv, author with Hill, 1 Oct 52; Brig Gen John J. Hill, MS review comments, 2 Jan 58. The designation (—) has been used to indicate a combat organization that is lacking one or more of its organic units.
[30] 24th Div WD, 8 Aug 50.

Cloverleaf Hill and Obong-ni Ridge.[31]

Colonel Hill's 9th Infantry attacked straight west late in the afternoon of 8 August against Cloverleaf and Obong-ni. On the right, the 2d Battalion succeeded in capturing part of Cloverleaf by dark, but not control of it or that side of the pass. On the left, the 1st Battalion likewise succeeded in gaining part of Obongni Ridge. But that night the North Koreans regained the ridge. This situation changed little the next day.[32]

The enemy by now had begun to show increased interest in the hill positions along the Naktong still held by American troops. At dawn on 7 August, Captain Alfonso of A Company, 34th Infantry, discovered that the enemy had occupied the ridge on his right which overlooked his position. By radio he directed artillery fire on the hill. When he started a patrol out to determine the result, enemy fire drove it back. An airdrop of supplies that afternoon was only partially successful. The company recovered little more than half the drop and lost some men to enemy fire in the process. The night passed quietly.

The next morning, 8 August, Alfonso's men could see North Koreans crossing the Naktong below them in six boats, each holding about ten to twelve men. They radioed for an air strike, and later, at a range of 1,000 yards, engaged the enemy force with their .50-caliber machine gun, causing the North Koreans to disperse along the river bank. There the air strike came in on them, with undetermined results.

That afternoon, the North Koreans began registering mortar and artillery fire on A Company's position, but ceased firing as soon as their registration was accomplished. Alfonso and his men noticed an enemy column far off, moving toward them. From this and the mortar and artillery registrations, they concluded that the enemy would deliver a co-ordinated attack against them that night. Alfonso requested permission to withdraw at 2300, and this was approved by both the battalion and regimental commanders.

At 2230, Alfonso removed his wounded to the base of the hill; the others followed. As the company started to withdraw along the road, heavy enemy fire fell on their vacated position. The North Koreans soon learned that the Americans were not there and redirected fire along the road. The company was supposed to withdraw to friendly lines south of the road at the southern end of Obong-ni Ridge. But, in a series of mistakes, one platoon kept to the road or close to it and ran into an enemy position at the northern end of Obong-ni. There it lost heavily. The rest of the company and the L Company men with it finally reached the 1st Battalion lines east of Obong-ni well after daylight, 9 August.[33]

Farther south near the river that morning, K Company received enemy attacks, one enemy group overrunning the company's forward observation post. Even though the enemy was behind it, the company received orders to hold. The next day, 10 August, reorganized L Com-

---

[31] Interv, author with Hill, 1 Oct 52; Interv, author with Beauchamp, 18 Nov 54; Ltr and comments, Beauchamp to author, 20 May 53; 9th RCT Opn Ord 4, 081315 Aug 50; *Ibid.*, Unit Rpt 1, 8 Aug 50.
[32] Interv, author with Hill, 1 Oct 52; 24th Div WD, 8–9 Aug 50.

[33] Ltr, Alfonso to Ayres, 27 Nov 54; Interv, author with Ayres, 16 Nov 54; 34th Inf WD, 9 Aug 50.

THE FIRST BATTLE OF THE NAKTONG BULGE

pany took positions behind its right flank.[34]

On 10 August, at the critical battleground within the bulge, the North Koreans on Cloverleaf Hill launched an attack which met head-on one by the 9th Infantry. Officer losses had been severe in the 2d Battalion on 8 and 9 August. On the 10th, F was the only rifle company in the battalion with more than one officer. In this fighting the North Koreans regained all the ground they had lost earlier at Cloverleaf. But north of Cloverleaf, the 2d Battalion, 19th Infantry, succeeded in capturing several hills along the Naktong, the most important being Ohang Hill. The enemy repulsed all its efforts to advance south from Ohang. The fighting on 10 August in the vicinity of Ohang Hill reduced the 2d Battalion, 19th Infantry, to about 100 effective men in the rifle companies.[35]

That evening General Church placed Colonel Hill in command of all troops in the Naktong Bulge. The troops comprised the 9th Regimental Combat Team (less the 3d Battalion), 2d Division; and the 34th and 19th Infantry Regiments, and the 1st Battalion, 21st Infantry, 24th Division, together with supporting artillery and other attached units.[36] This command was now designated Task Force Hill.

General Church ordered Colonel Hill to attack the next morning and restore the Naktong River line. Hill and the other commanders involved worked out the attack plan during the night. It called for the 9th and 19th Regiments to drive southwest through the heart of the bulge. The 1st Battalion, 21st Infantry, was to move during the night from the northern part of the division zone to a point near the southern end of Obong-ni Ridge, and from there attack southwest on the left of the 9th Regimental Combat Team. Meanwhile, the 34th Infantry would protect the left flank of the combat team at Obong-ni.[37]

As it chanced, enemy reinforcements reached the east side of the river during the night and vastly increased the difficulty of this attack. Colonel Hill had received reports as early as 8 August that the North Koreans were working at night on an underwater bridge across the Naktong at the Kihang, or Paekchin, ferry site in the middle of the bulge. The enemy *4th Division* completed this underwater bridge during the night of 10 August, and before daylight had moved trucks, heavy mortars, and approximately twelve artillery pieces to the east side of the Naktong. Some of the equipment crossed on rafts. Additional infantry units of the enemy division also crossed the river during the night. A few tanks may have crossed at this time.[38] By the morning of 11 August, therefore, five days after the initial crossing, the North

---

[34] 34th Inf WD, 9-11 Aug 50.
[35] 24th Div WD, 9-11 Aug 50; EUSAK WD, 22 Aug 50, ATIS Interrog Rpt 703, Kim Chi Ho; Hill, MS review comments, 2 Jan 58; Interv, author with Montesclaros, 1 Oct 52. In the 2d Battalion, 19th Infantry, F Company effectives numbered about 25; G Company, about 40; and E Company about 30.
[36] 24th Div WD, 10 Aug 50; EUSAK WD, Briefing for CG, 10 Aug 50; Ltr, Church to author, 7 Jul 53; Ltr, Hill to author, 15 Apr 53.

[37] 24th Div WD, 10-11 Aug 50; Intervs, author with Hill, 1 Oct 52, and Beauchamp, 18 Nov 54.
[38] 24th Div WD, 11 Aug 50; 9th RCT Unit Rpt 4, 10-11 Aug 50; ATIS Interrog Rpts, Issue Nr 1, p. 90, Nr 644, 21 Aug 50, Kim Dok Sam; *Ibid.*, Issue Nr 2, p. 8. Rpt Nr 703; EUSAK WD, 28 Sep 50, ADVATIS Interrog Rpt of Maj Choe Chu Yong, Opns Officer, N.K. *Arty Regt, 4th Div;* Ltr, Hill to author, 15 Apr 53.

Koreans had heavy weapons and equipment across into their bridgehead.

The North Koreans built many underwater bridges across the Naktong during August, 1950. They consisted of sandbags, logs, and rocks to a point about one foot below the surface of the water. In effect, they constituted shallow fords. In muddy water they were hard to detect from the air. Underwater bridges similar to them had been built, and used extensively, by the Russians in World War II, often as a surprise factor in battles on the Eastern Front. They played an important part, for instance, in the crucial battle of Stalingrad.

The attack on 11 August, intended to push the enemy into the river, failed completely. The N.K. *4th Division* fought the 9th and 19th Regiments to a standstill at their lines of departure and in their positions. Furthermore, the enemy drove the 1st Battalion, 21st Infantry, from its assembly area before it could start its part of the attack. During the morning a new feature appeared in the bulge battle—North Korean use of artillery in three groups of 6, 4, and 4 pieces, all emplaced near Kogong-ni, about a mile behind the enemy positions on Cloverleaf and Obong-ni. In the afternoon General Church found it necessary to change the order for Task Force Hill from attack to one of dig in and hold. The greater part of the N.K. *4th Division* had now crossed into the bulge area. That night the division completed its crossing of the river.[39]

Yongsan Under Attack

During 10–11 August, when the North Korean build-up on Obong-ni and Cloverleaf was increasingly apparent, enemy groups also began to appear in the extreme southern part of the 24th sector.[40] By 11 August there was unmistakable indication that enemy forces in some strength had moved around the main battle positions at Cloverleaf and Obong-ni and were behind Task Force Hill.

On that day enemy artillery fire brought Yongsan under fire for the first time. East of the town, enemy sniper fire harassed traffic on the road to Miryang. South of Yongsan, an enemy force drove back a patrol of the 24th Reconnaissance Company. And during the morning, North Koreans surprised and killed a squad of K Company, 34th Infantry, guarding the bridge over the Naktong at Namji-ri. Enemy control of this bridge cut the Yongsan-Masan road and broke the only direct vehicular communication link between the 24th and 25th Divisions. The situation was confused south of Yongsan on 11 August, at the very moment Task Force Hill's attack was being thrown back a few miles westward. In this emergency, General Church dispatched the 14th Engineer Combat Battalion to Yongsan, and General Walker ordered the 2d Battalion, 27th Infantry, in army reserve at Masan behind Task Force Kean, to attack north across the Naktong River over the Namji-ri bridge into the southern part

---

[39] 9th RCT Unit Rpt 4, 10–11 Aug 50; 24th Div WD, 11 Aug 50; EUSAK WD, 28 Sep 50, Interrog Rpt of Maj Choe Chu Yong; EUSAK WD, 18 Aug 50, G–2 Sec, ATIS Interrog Rpt 644. Kim Dok Sam, a ROK officer, monitored enemy radio conversations about N.K. artillery positions.

[40] 24th Div WD, 10–11 Aug 50; 27th Inf WD, 10 Aug 50; Ltr, Hill to author, 15 Apr 53; Ltr, Beauchamp to author, 20 May 53.

THE FIRST BATTLE OF THE NAKTONG BULGE

of the 24th Division zone.[41]

That night, 11–12 August, North Koreans built up their roadblock east of Yongsan to greater strength and extended it to a point three miles east of the town. A staff officer awakened Colonel Hill before daylight to inform him that the enemy had ambushed several ambulances and trucks two miles east of Yongsan. Although hard-pressed at Cloverleaf, Hill immediately ordered F Company, 9th Infantry, out of the line there and dispatched it together with a platoon of mortars to attack the roadblock. The 15th Field Artillery Battalion helped by turning some of its guns to fire on it.

Simultaneouly, 24th Division headquarters assembled from eight different units about 135 men, including clerks, bakers, military police, and Reconnaissance Company troops, under the command of Capt. George B. Hafemen, commanding officer of Headquarters Company. This force hurriedly moved west from Miryang and took up a position at the pass near Simgong-ni on the Yongsan-Miryang road. Its mission was to block further eastward penetration of the enemy. Two tanks accompanied Hafemen's force. Hafemen and his men held this position all afternoon against North Korean attack. Three times armored cars came through to them with food, water, and ammunition.[42]

The next day at noon, 13 August, General Church sent a plane to bring Colonel Hill for a conference with General Walker at the 24th Division command post. Walker asked Hill, "Can you raise the roadblock?" Hill replied, "Yes, I have just flown over it, and I can clear it by night." Walker seemed satisfied with this assurance.[43]

In the meantime, and pursuant to General Walker's order on the 11th, Colonel Murch's 2d Battalion, 27th Infantry, had been engaged in helping to clear the enemy from the area south of Yongsan. On the 11th Murch's battalion departed from its assembly area near Masan and rolled north toward the Naktong River. A steady stream of Korean refugees clogged the road. As the battalion pushed its way through this traffic a refugee cart overturned, exposing about fifteen rifles and several bags of ammunition. Approximately twelve North Korean soldiers disguised as refugees accompanying it fled across an open field. Infantrymen near the scene killed eight of them. Continuing on, Murch's battalion engaged and dispersed an estimated 200 enemy troops near Iryong-ni, a few miles south of the Naktong River bridge. The battalion crossed the river and by midnight had established a bridgehead on the north side against enemy small arms fire.[44]

The next day Eighth Army attached the 27th Infantry to the 24th Division with the mission of attacking north to Yongsan. Army estimates credited two enemy battalions with being east of the Yongsan-Masan road. In the fight northward during 12 August, Murch's 2d Bat-

---

[41] 19th Inf WD, 11 Aug 50; 24th Div WD, 11 Aug 50; EUSAK WD, Aug 50 Summ, 10 Aug; Interv, author with Hill, 1 Oct 52; Ltr, Murch to author, 7 Apr 54.

[42] Interv, author with Hill, 1 Oct 52; 24th Div WD, 11–12 Aug 50; New York *Herald Tribune*, August 14, 1950, Bigart dispatch. General Order 111, 30 August 1950, awarded the Silver Star to 1st Lt. William F. Coghill for gallantry in this action. 24th Div WD.

[43] Interv, author with Hill, 1 Oct 52; Ltr, Church to author, 7 Jul 53.

[44] Ltr, Murch to author, 7 Apr 54; Interv, author with Murch, 18 Mar 54; 27th Inf WD, 11 Aug 50.

talion encountered entrenched enemy who fought with mortars, machine guns, and small arms. An air strike co-ordinated with the ground attack helped it drive the enemy from his positions. In this attack, the 2d Battalion killed about 100 enemy, wounded an unknown number, and captured twelve machine guns and a number of "Buffalo" guns (14.5-caliber antitank rifles).[45]

The attack continued northward the next day with the 3d Battalion, 27th Infantry, assisting the 2d Battalion. By midafternoon of 13 August both battalions reached their objective, the high ground north and east of Yongsan. Colonels Hill and Beauchamp met Colonel Murch in Yongsan as the latter's 2d Battalion effected juncture with Task Force Hill. In this advance, the 27th Infantry troops overran four pieces of enemy artillery; two of them were captured U.S. 105-mm. howitzers.[46]

Still another American reinforcement had been converging on the enemy at Yongsan—the 1st Battalion, 23d Infantry, of the 2d Division. This battalion had just arrived at Miryang where it received orders to attack west. In this, its first action, it had nine cases of heat exhaustion but only one battle casualty.[47] Some of its troops met an advanced unit of the 27th Infantry a mile east of Yongsan.

Thus, by evening of 13 August, General Walker's prompt action in committing the 27th Infantry, together with the 24th Division's employment of headquarters and engineer troops, had eliminated the dangerous enemy penetration south and east of Yongsan.

On the 14th, a reinforced company of the 35th Infantry, 25th Division, took up a defensive position south of the Naktong River at Namji-ri bridge, relieving units of the 27th Infantry there. Responsibility for protecting the bridge passed from the 24th to the 25th Division.[48]

Enemy action in the southern part of the 24th Division sector from 10 to 13 August convinced Colonel Hill that K and L Companies were doing no good in their isolated hill positions near the Naktong. Accordingly, he issued orders —received by the 3d Battalion, 34th Infantry, at 0200, 14 August—for these companies to abandon their positions and assemble in the rear of the 1st Battalion as regimental reserve. They carried out this movement without incident.[49]

Battle at Cloverleaf-Obong-ni

During the enemy infiltration around Yongsan, fighting continued at Cloverleaf, Obong-ni, and northward. There, the 9th Regimental Combat Team, the 19th Infantry, and elements of the 34th Infantry succeeded in denying gains to the enemy division, and so tied down its main force that the N.K. *4th Division* could not exploit its penetrations southward.

Task Force Hill still had its mission of driving the enemy out of the bulge and back across the Naktong. With the North Korean penetration south and

---

[45] Ltr, Murch to author, 7 Apr 54; 24th Div WD, 12 Aug 50; 27th Inf WD, 12 Aug 50; 2d Bn, 27th Inf WD, Aug 50 Summ of Activities.
[46] 27th Inf WD, 13 Aug 60; GHQ FEC G-3 Opn Rpt 51, 14 Aug 50; 24th Div WD, 13 Aug 50.
[47] 23d Inf WD, Aug 50 Narr Summ.

[48] 27th Inf WD, 14 Aug 50.
[49] 34th Inf WD, 14 Aug 50; Interv, author with Hill, 1 Oct 52; Ltr, Hill to author, 15 Apr 53.

Point of a Combat Column *moving toward its position near Yongsan.*

east of Yongsan eliminated on 13 August, Colonel Hill planned an attack the next day with his entire force against the Cloverleaf-Obong-ni positions. One hundred aircraft were to deliver a strike on these positions. Artillery was to follow the strike with a concentrated barrage. The attacking ground formations were essentially the same, and held the same relative positions, as during their abortive attack three days earlier. The enemy division apparently had its *5th Regiment* on the north in front of the 19th Infantry, the *16th Regiment* on Cloverleaf and Obong-ni, part of the *18th Regiment* back of the *16th*, and the remainder of it scattered throughout the bulge area, but mostly in the south and east.[50]

Task Force Hill was far from strong for this attack. The two battalions of the 9th Infantry were down to approximately two-thirds strength, the 19th Infantry was very low in combat-effective troops, and the three rifle companies of the 1st Battalion, 34th Infantry, had a combined strength of less than that of one full strength rifle company.[51]

Monday, 14 August, dawned over the bulge area with a heavy overcast of clouds. Rain had been falling since 0300. This prevented the planned air strike. The 24th Division artillery, down to an estimated 40 percent combat effectiveness at this time, had massed most of its guns in the low ground just west of Yongsan under the command of Lt. Col. Charles W. Stratton, Commanding Officer, 13th Field Artillery Battalion. These guns delivered a 10-minute preparation. Then the infantry moved out. The two battalions of the 9th Regimental Combat Team, the 1st on the right and the 2d on the left, started up the slopes of Cloverleaf, while B Company, 34th Infantry, began a holding attack against Obong-ni south of the road. Although it almost reached the top of Obong-ni early in the morning, B Company was driven back by 0800.

The main battle took place northward across the road on Cloverleaf. There the American and North Korean troops locked in a close battle of attack and counterattack. The 1st Battalion lost sixty men killed or wounded in one hour of fighting. Both battalions of the 9th Regimental Combat Team gained parts of the high ground but could not control the hill mass. Northward, the 19th Infantry made no gain.[52]

That night on Cloverleaf was one of continuing combat. The North Koreans attacked and infiltrated into the 9th Infantry's dug-in defensive positions. The case of MSgt. Warren H. Jordan of E Company reflects the severity of the fighting on Cloverleaf. From 10 to 17 August, he was forced on five different occasions to take command of the company because all company officers had been killed or wounded, or had suffered heat exhaustion.[53]

---

[50] 9th RCT Opn Ord 5, 131300 Aug 50; 24th Div WD, 13 Aug 50; 19th Inf WD, 13 Aug 50; ATIS Res Supp Interrog Rpts, Issue 94 (N.K. *4th Div*), pp. 48-49.

[51] 9th RCT Unit Rpt 9, 14 Aug 50, gives the strength of its 1st Battalion as 599 enlisted men and that of the 2d Battalion as 609 enlisted men, against an authorized strength of 883 enlisted men each. Ayres, Notes for author, 24 Jan 55.

[52] 9th RCT Unit Rpt 7, 13-14 Aug 50; Overlay to accompany FO 5, 9th RCT, 131230 Aug 50; 24th Div WD, 13-14 Aug 50; Interv, author with Hill, 1 Oct 52.

[53] Capt Perry Davis, The 2d Infantry Division in Korea, July-September 1950, MS, copy in OCMH (Davis was Public Info Off, 2d Div); Interv, author with Hill, 1 Oct 52.

The enemy attack on the night of the 14th was not confined to Cloverleaf. South of Obong-ni enemy troops virtually surrounded the 1st Battalion, 21st Infantry, and inflicted numerous casualties on it. At 0300 Colonel Hill ordered Smith to withdraw. The battalion fought its way out of encirclement before dawn and took up a new defensive position. It held this new position at the south end of the main battle line with the help of a counterattack by the 3d Battalion, 34th Infantry, which had been strengthened that morning by the return of K and L Companies from their river hill positions.[54]

Very few of its members had any hope of dislodging the enemy when Task Force Hill continued the attack on the morning of 15 August. Clouds and rain still hampered air support. On the south end of Obong-ni, A and B Companies, 34th Infantry, fought a savage encounter with North Koreans on the ridge line. The 2d Platoon of A Company, led by SFC Roy E. Collins, assaulted across a shallow saddle to an enemy-held knob. Enemy troops were just over the crest of it on the reverse slope. A grenade fight immediately developed. Men exchanged rifle fire at ten paces. One enemy soldier dived over the ridge line and tackled Collins around the waist. To his amazement, Collins learned that the enemy soldier wanted to surrender. This was the only way he could do it. Within fifty minutes after launching the attack, the platoon lost 25 men killed or wounded of the 35 who had dashed across the saddle. Ten men withdrew while PFC Edward O. Cleaborn, a Negro, stubbornly stayed behind to get in one more shot. He lost his life trying to get that shot. With them the 10 able-bodied survivors took 9 wounded men, 3 of whom died before they reached an aid station.[55]

Elsewhere, the North Koreans fought Task Force Hill to a standstill. Colonel Hill had used all the resources at his command and had just barely held the enemy on his front. Having no reserve he was powerless to maneuver.

General Church came up to Colonel Hill's command post during 15 August and the two of them talked over the situation. Although they felt that the N.K. *4th Division* was growing weaker from attrition and might have exhausted its offensive power in the costly stalemate fighting at Obong-ni and Cloverleaf, they did not see how they, on their part, could continue the attack. They agreed to discontinue the attack and defend in place.[56]

General Walker had by now become most impatient at the lack of progress in driving the enemy from the bulge. Church told Walker on the 13th that the entire N.K. *4th Division* was across and in the 24th Division sector. General Walker discounted this with the curt rejoinder, "That is not my information." Church insisted nevertheless that such was the case. Intelligence later confirmed

---

[54] Interv, author with Hill, 1 Oct 52; Hill, MS review comments, 2 Jan 58; 24th Div WD, 14-15 Aug 50.

[55] Gugeler, *Combat Actions in Korea*, ch. 2, "Attack Along a Ridgeline," pp. 20-29; 24th Div WD, 15 Aug 50; Abstract of A Co, 34th Inf Morning Rpts, 14-15 Aug 50. In his account, Gugeler describes all the action as taking place on 15 August. Some of the preliminary incidents took place on the 14th, according to the morning reports of the company.

[56] Intervs, author with Church, 25 Sep 52, and Hill, 1 Oct 52.

General Church's estimate. When the attack of 15 August failed, General Walker knew he must commit more strength into the bulge if he was to drive out the enemy. Impatient and angry, he came to Church's command post during the morning and said, "I am going to give you the Marine brigade. I want this situation cleaned up, and quick." [57]

Walker returned to Taegu about noon and called a conference of some of his key staff officers to determine what forces were available to reinforce the 24th Division. The Marine brigade was en route from the Masan area to Miryang where it was to bivouac in army reserve. About 1300 Walker decided definitely that he would use the marines in the Naktong Bulge and directed Colonel Collier to fly to Miryang immediately and discuss the situation with General Craig, the Marine brigade commander, who was expected to arrive there momentarily. Collier told Craig of General Walker's instructions as the two sat talking in a jeep. General Craig immediately ordered the brigade headquarters to break bivouac and head for Yongsan.[58]

General Walker's decision on the 15th is only one of many that could be mentioned to illustrate the command problems he had to face during the two and a half months of the continuing battles of the Pusan Perimeter. Serious trouble had developed at many places at this time. A quick glance around the Perimeter for the period 11-15 August will show that Eighth Army reserves were needed almost everywhere. Task Force Kean suffered its severe setback at Bloody Gulch on 12 August. At the same time Task Force Hill had failed at Obong-ni Ridge and Cloverleaf in the Naktong Bulge and strong elements of the N.K. *4th Division* were behind it near Yongsan. In action yet to be described, the North Koreans had crossed the Naktong and were approaching Taegu north of the bulge. Eastward, the ROK forces were being driven back at a steady pace and the Perimeter was shrinking visibly in that quarter. The N.K. *5th Division* had entered P'ohang-dong on the east coast and was in position to drive down the Kyongju corridor to Pusan.

Beginning in the second week of August 1950, and continuing for the next six weeks, the two forces locked in combat at nearly all points of the Perimeter. Because it is necessary to separate the farflung conflict into parts in order to describe it, an element of distortion is thus introduced into the Pusan Perimeter story. As the reader follows each single action for this period he must constantly keep in mind, if he is to view the scene at all as the contemporary commanders did, that equally intense and costly struggles were in progress elsewhere.

Because of this multiplicity of battles taking place simultaneously at different parts of the Perimeter, it is difficult to describe satisfactorily the command problems daily confronting General Walker. He had to know, or guess correctly, where the next crisis would appear. Or, if surprised by an enemy action, he immediately had to find the means to meet it and act quickly. A commander has to think of all the actions in progress, or imminent, and make tactical decisions, balancing the

---

[57] Interv, author with Church, 25 Sep 52.
[58] Collier, MS review comments, 10 Mar 58.

needs of one part of his defense lines against those of others. A commander's viewpoint, hour by hour, is determined by changing factors of a complex situation. During the Pusan Perimeter battles in the summer of 1950 in Korea General Walker faced a trying time. As historical perspective is gained with the passing of time, Walker's chief claim to a high place in United States military history may well rest on the tactics of his masterful defensive operations on the Pusan Perimeter.

General Walker always considered the Yongsan-Miryang area just above the confluence of the Nam River with the Naktong as a very dangerous axis of enemy attack. In mid-August he considered the crisis in the Naktong Bulge to be the most serious and important of the several that faced his forces. Accordingly, he then committed there his strongest reserve. Eighth Army attached the 1st Provisional Marine Brigade to the 24th Division on 15 August, and ordered an attack as early as possible on 17 August to destroy the enemy in the bulge east of the Naktong.[59]

On 16 August, as the tired men of Task Force Hill waited in their foxholes for help, the North Koreans attacked the 9th Infantry on Cloverleaf. The attacks were intense and at close quarters. North Koreans occupied some of the American foxholes after killing their occupants. On the right, the 2d Battalion, 9th Infantry, lost ground. There was severe fighting also on Ohang Hill where elements of the 19th and 34th Regiments narrowly escaped being trapped. Captain Barszcz, commanding G Company, 34th Infantry, distinguished himself by bravery and leadership in this action.[60]

In the midst of the battle of the bulge a new enemy crossing of the Naktong occurred in the 1st Cavalry Division sector, just above the 24th Division boundary. This enemy force, estimated at two battalions, established itself on Hill 409, a mountain near Hyongp'ung. Because the area concerned was more accessible by roads from the 24th Division sector than from the 1st Cavalry Division sector, General Walker on the evening of 13 August shifted the 24th Division boundary northward to include this enemy penetration.

Just after midnight, 15-16 August, Eighth Army by telephone ordered the 24th Division to take positive action against the enemy force on Hill 409 at the division's northern extremity near Hyongp'ung. This force had now increased to an estimated regiment. Prisoners said it was the *29th Regiment* of the N.K. *10th Division,* a division not previously committed in action. Before daylight, the 1st Battalion, 23d Infantry, arrived near Hill 409 to reinforce the 21st Infantry. The regiment had arrived from the United States on 5 August and had gone to an assembly area near Taegu with the certainty that it would soon be committed at some point around the Perimeter. The enemy troops on Hill 409 posed a particular danger. At any moment they might begin a drive southeast into the already desperately hard-

---

[59] EUSAK Opn Dir, 15 Aug 50; 24th Div WD, 16 Aug 50. The 24th Division headquarters received the formal order the morning of 16 August.

[60] 24th Div WD, 16 Aug 50; 9th RCT Unit Rpt 9, 15-16 Aug 50.

pressed American forces fighting in the Naktong Bulge.[61]

But this enemy force, fortunately and most comfortingly, made no effort to leave Hill 409 where it had established itself during a most critical moment of the bulge battle. Its inactivity within the American defense perimeter demonstrated either a lack of co-ordination by the North Korean command or an inelastic adherence to plans.

Marines Attack Obong-ni

Although the situation did not look good for the American forces in the bulge on 15 August, the harsh prospect nevertheless gave a distorted view unless one knew something of the picture on the "other side of the hill." Actually, the N.K. *4th Division* was in desperate straits. Its food was in low supply. Ammunition resupply was difficult. One regiment, the *18th*, reportedly received its last ammunition resupply on 14 August. Desertion among replacements, according to prisoners, reached about 40 percent. Half the replacements did not have weapons, and they were used for labor services in digging foxholes, carrying ammunition, and foraging for food. The slightly wounded received but little medical attention, and were immediately put back into the front line. A large part of the severely wounded died from lack of medical care. Only the former Chinese Communist Forces fanatical squad and platoon leaders maintained high morale.[62]

In discussing plans for the attack with Marine brigade and regimental commanders—Craig and Murray—Church and Hill learned that they did not want to launch an attack until the carrier-based Marine Corsairs could participate. The *Badoeng Strait* and the *Sicily* would not be in position to launch their planes until 17 August. Plans were made, therefore, to attack on that day.[63]

General Church was to command the co-ordinated attack of Army and Marine troops. The attack plan placed the 1st Provisional Marine Brigade on the left in front of Obong-ni Ridge. (*Map 10*) On the extreme left, the 1st Battalion (—), 21st Infantry, was to protect the marines' left flank. The 9th Infantry stayed in front of Cloverleaf where it had been fighting for a week. The road between Cloverleaf and Obong-ni was the boundary between it and the marines. The 34th Infantry was north of the 9th Infantry. Beyond it the 19th Infantry formed the extreme right flank of the attack formations. The plan called for the 9th Infantry, after it took Cloverleaf, to be pinched out by the units on either side of it. They were to drive on to the Naktong. The 19th Infantry was to attack to the river and seize Ohang Hill, which the North Koreans had regained. The attack was to begin at 0800, 17 August. Fifty-four 105-mm. howitzers and one battalion of 155-

---

[61] 24th Div WD, 12–16 Aug 50; 21st Inf WD, 12–16 Aug 50; ATIS Res Supp Interrog Rpts, Issue 104 (N.K. *10th Div*), p. 47; Capt William M. Glasgow, Jr., Platoon Leader in Korea, MS in OCMH (Glasgow was Ldr, 2d Plat, B Co, 23d Inf, 2d Div); Interv, author with Stephens, 8 Oct 51; EUSAK WD, 5 Aug 50, G–3 Sec, Briefing for CG; 23d Inf WD, Aug 50 Summ.

[62] EUSAK WD, 30 Aug 50, ATIS Interrog Rpt 880, Paek Yong Hwan; ATIS Interrog Rpts, Issue 3, p. 180; 9th RCT Unit Rpt 7, 13–14 Aug 50.

[63] Interv, author with Church, 25 Sep 52; Interv, author with Hill, 1 Oct 52.

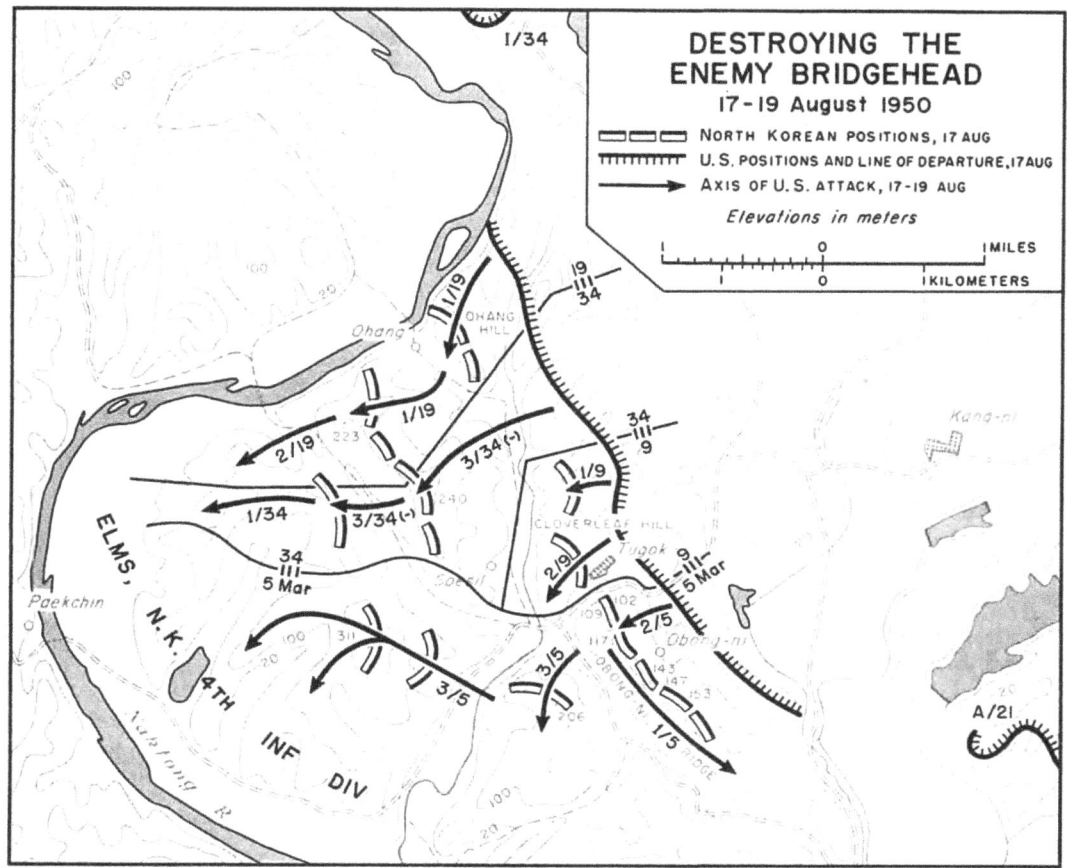

MAP 10

mm. howitzers were in place to support the attack.[64]

The 5th Marines had moved from the Masan front to Miryang, and then on 16 August it received orders to attack Obong-ni the next morning. The 2d Battalion was to lead the assault, followed by the 1st and 3d Battalions in that order. The 2d Battalion reached its assembly area in front of Obong-ni Ridge after midnight.[65]

General Church had planned to coordinate a 9th RCT attack against Cloverleaf with the Marine attack against Obong-ni Ridge. Colonel Murray, however, requested that he be allowed to attack and secure Obong-ni first before

---

[64] 24th Div Opn Directive 1, 16 Aug 50; Ibid., Opn Instr 25, 16 Aug 50; Ibid., WD, 16 Aug 50; Ibid., Div Arty WD, 23 Jul–25 Aug 50; Wood, "Artillery Support for the Brigade in Korea," Marine Corps Gazette (June, 1951), p. 19; Interv, author with Hill, 1 Oct 52; Ltr and comments, Beauchamp to author, 20 May 53.

[65] 5th Mar SAR, 2 Aug–6 Sep 50, 16 Aug; 1st Bn, 5th Mar SAR, 7 Jul–6 Sep 50, 17 Aug; 24th Div WD, 17 Aug 50.

the 9th RCT began its attack. Murray considered Obong-ni Ridge as his line of departure for the main attack and thought he could capture it with relative ease. Church, on the other hand, considered Obong-ni and Cloverleaf to be interlocking parts of the enemy position and thought they should be attacked simultaneously. However, he granted Murray's request. Between Obong-ni and the Naktong River three miles away rose two successively higher hill masses. Both Murray and Church expected the enemy to make his main effort on the second ridge, the one behind Obong-ni. Information gained later indicated that Colonel Chang Ky Dok's *18th Regiment*, reinforced by a battalion of the *16th Regiment*, defended Obong-ni Ridge. Other elements of the *16th Regiment* apparently defended Cloverleaf.[66]

Lt. Col. Harold S. Roise's 2d Battalion, 5th Marines, moved to its line of departure on the east side of a narrow valley in front of Obong-ni about 1,000 yards from the ridge crest. There it waited for the preliminaries to begin. The men studied intently the almost bare ridge opposite them, with its series of six knobs—Hills 102, 109, 117, 143, 147, and 153—rising progressively in height southward from 300 to 450 feet above the valley floor. Deep erosional gullies ran down from the saddles between the knobs leaving ribs of ground projecting from the ridge spine. About midway of the ridge a big landslide had exposed a large gash of red ground.

A 10-minute artillery preparation, falling on areas back of Obong-ni, began at 0735. Intentionally, there was no artillery preparation on Obong-ni itself. Instead, eighteen Corsairs delivered an air strike on the ridge. The strike was impressive. To observers, Obong-ni seemed to be blowing up—"was floating," as General Church described it.[67]

Two companies, E on the left and D on the right, moved out from the line of departure at 0800, using the red gash on Obong-ni as the boundary between their zones of advance. Four platoons, numbering about 120 men, constituted the assault formation that crossed the valley and started up the slope. From the ridge itself they encountered no enemy fire, but from Tugok village across the road to their right (north) came heavy small arms and machine gun fire Some fire also came from their left flank near Obong village. Mortar fire fell on the assault group when it reached the slope of Obong-ni.

At one point only did any of the marines reach the crest. This was just to the right of the red gash where a rain-formed gully led upwards. Near the crest the gully was so shallow it provided scarcely enough cover to protect one man lying down. Using this gully as cover for part of his platoon, 2d Lt. Michael J. Shinka reached the top with twenty of his original thirty men. As they scrambled into empty North Korean foxholes, grazing enemy machine gun fire from the right swept over them and North Koreans in a second row of foxholes a few yards down the reverse slope jumped up and attacked them with grenades. Five

---

[66] Interv, author with Church, 25 Sep 52; Interv, author with Canzona and Montross, Jun 54. See also Montross and Canzona, *The Pusan Perimeter*, pp. 176-77. (The text and map, page 180, incorrectly identify Cloverleaf Hill.)

[67] Interv, author with Church, 25 Sep 52; 2d Bn, 5th Mar SAR, 7 Jul-31 Aug 50, pp. 8-9.

marines were casualties in this attack; Shinka ordered the rest off the ridge. They complied quickly, pulling their wounded back on ponchos.[68]

Corsairs now returned and worked over the Obong-ni Ridge line and reverse slope with a hail of explosives. A shortage of fuel tanks prevented use of napalm. After the strike ended, the marines started upward again from halfway down the slope where they had waited. Tanks moved out into the low ground east of the ridge and supported the second attack by direct fire into Tugok village and against the ridge line. At first there was little enemy fire. Within a few minutes after the air strike had ended, however, the North Koreans moved into their forward foxholes at the crest. From these points they placed automatic fire on the climbing marines and rolled grenades down on them. Again, only Shinka's platoon reached the top. This time, starting with fifteen men, he had nine when he got there. The small group could not stay on the crest, and they fell back down the slope. Shinka crawled to the crest to see if he could find any marine wounded on top; enemy fire hit him twice, one bullet shattering his chin, another entering his right arm. He rolled down the hill. Enemy fire, inflicting heavy casualties, pinned the other units to the ground on the side of the ridge.

The heavy enemy fire from Tugok and part of Cloverleaf Hill on the right (north) was an important factor in turning back the Marine attack on Obong-ni. At 1500 the 2d Battalion held positions about halfway up the slope. In seven hours it had lost 23 killed and 119 wounded—a casualty rate of almost 60 percent of the 240 riflemen who had taken part in the attack.[69]

Because of the heavy losses in the 2d Battalion, General Craig had already decided he would have to pass the 1st Battalion through it if the attack was to continue. At 1245 Colonel Murray relayed the order to Colonel Newton to move his 1st Battalion in position to resume the attack on Obong-ni. The latter completed the relief of the 2d Battalion on the slopes by 1600.[70]

24th Division Attack Gains Cloverleaf

It was apparent during the morning that the Marine planes had failed to destroy the enemy soldiers in their deep foxholes on the reverse slope of Obong-ni. It was also clear that the heavy enemy fire from gun positions in Tugok village and on the high spurs of Cloverleaf had worked havoc among the marines trying to climb the exposed slope of Obong-ni. In the plan for resuming the attack there was one important change. Colonel Murray, now convinced that it would be necessary for the 9th Infantry on his right to attack Cloverleaf simultaneously with his attack against Obong-ni, went to General Church and told him of his changed view. Church said the 9th Infantry would

---

[68] 5th Mar SAR, 2 Aug–6 Sep 50, Incl 4, sketch of 2d Bn attack, and 17 Aug 50; Andrew C. Geer, *The New Breed: the Story of the U.S. Marines in Korea* (New York: Harper & Brothers, 1952). Geer interviewed survivors of the assault group.

[69] 2d Bn, 5th Mar SAR, 7 Jul–31 Aug 50, p. 9; Geer, *The New Breed*; Montross and Canzona, *The Pusan Perimeter*, p. 183; *Newsweek*, August 28, 1950; New York *Times*, August 18, 1950.

[70] 5th Mar SAR, 17 Aug 50; 1st Bn, 5th Mar SAR, 17 Aug 50.

attack after an artillery preparation. Murray informed Church and Hill shortly after 1500 that the 1st Battalion, 5th Marines, would be ready to launch its attack at 1600.[71]

Shortly before 1600, the 24th Division began to deliver scheduled preparatory fires on Cloverleaf, raking it from top to bottom. Part of the fire was time-on-target air bursts. The flying shell fragments of the air bursts spread a shroud of death over the crest and reverse slope. Then, at 1600, the 9th Infantry and the marines began their co-ordinated attack. The 2d Battalion, 9th Infantry, took Cloverleaf without difficulty. The artillery barrage had done its work; enemy soldiers surviving it fled down the hill. From Cloverleaf, the 9th Infantry now supported with its fire the attack of the marines against Obong-ni.[72]

At Obong-ni, the North Koreans again stopped the frontal attack of the marines. But this time, with enemy fire from Tugok and Cloverleaf almost eliminated, the righthand platoon of B Company near the boundary with the 9th RCT was able to move to the right around the northern spur of Obong-ni and reach its crest here above the road. The marines captured this knob, Hill 102, about 1700. Then the next two knobs southward, Hills 109 and 117, fell to a flanking attack from the direction of Hill 102, supported by fire from that hill. Enemy fire from the next knob southward, Hill 143, however, soon forced the A Company platoon from the crest of Hill 117 back to its eastern slope.

Just before dark the North Koreans made their first use of tanks in this battle of the Naktong Bulge. While digging in for the night, men on Hill 102 noticed three T34 tanks coming from the west. A fourth tank, not in view at first, followed. They came steadily along the road toward the pass between Obong-ni and Cloverleaf. By radio, B Company notified its battalion command post in the valley that tanks were approaching.

Three American Pershings (M26's) clanked forward to positions at a curve in the road in front of the Marine 1st Battalion command post. The 75-mm. recoilless rifles already commanded the road where it emerged from the pass. Two 3.5-inch rocket launcher teams hurried into position at the north side of the road. Three Air Force P–51's sighted the enemy tanks and made several strafing runs over them but without visible effect. Marines on Hill 102 watched with fascination as the T34's rumbled into the pass.

Down below, a dust cloud rising over a shoulder of ground warned the waiting bazooka teams that the T34's were about to come around the bend in the road. Seeing the steel hulk of the leading tank slowly come into view, one of the bazooka teams fired the first shot at a range of 100 yards, hitting the tank in its treads. The tank came on with all guns firing. A second rocket struck it just as a shell from a 75-mm. recoilless rifle tore a hole in its hull. The tank stopped but continued firing its guns. In another moment, the foremost American Pershing scored a direct hit on this T34, setting it on fire. At least one enemy crew member abandoned the

---

[71] Intervs, author with Church, 25 Sep 52, and Hill, 1 Oct 52.
[72] Ibid.; 9th RCT Unit Rpt 10, 16–17 Aug 50. The author was unable to find the 9th Regimental Combat Team War Diary for August 1950.

THE FIRST BATTLE OF THE NAKTONG BULGE

tank. Small arms fire killed him. The second enemy tank now came into view. The bazooka teams knocked it out. Two Pershing tanks destroyed the third T34 the moment it swung into sight. Air action destroyed the fourth tank before it reached the pass and dispersed enemy infantry accompanying it. In this action, Pershing tanks for the first time came face to face with the T34.[73]

When darkness fell, the marines dug in on a perimeter defense where they were. From Hill 102, B Company extended its line over Hill 109 to the saddle between it and Hill 117; there it met the defense line of A Company which bent back down the east slope of 117 to the base of the ridge. During the day the marines had 205 casualties—23 killed, 2 dead of wounds, 180 wounded.[74]

While this severe day-long battle had been in progress at Obong-ni, the 34th and 19th Infantry Regiments on the 24th Division right started their attacks late in the afternoon after repeated delays. Heavy air attacks and artillery barrages had already hit on Ohang Hill during the afternoon. This attack moved forward, but with heavy casualties in some units, notably in L Company, 34th Infantry, which came under enemy fire from the rear at one point. Ohang Hill, overlooking the Naktong River at the northern end of the bulge, fell to the 19th Infantry by dusk. That night the 24th Division intercepted an enemy radio message stating that North Korean troops in the bulge area were short of ammunition and requesting permission for them to withdraw across the Naktong.[75]

Obong-ni Falls

That evening, 17 August, American mortars and artillery registered on corridors of enemy approach to Obong-ni and Cloverleaf and on probable centers of enemy troop concentrations. Some artillery pieces fired on the river crossing sites to prevent enemy reinforcements arriving in the battle area. On Obong-ni that night, the marines, sure of an enemy counterattack, set trip flares in front of their positions. One quarter of the men stood guard while the remainder rested. On the left of the line, A Company had lost its 60-mm. mortars in the evening when four white phosphorus mortar shells struck in the mortar position, destroying the weapons and causing eighteen casualties.

At 0230, 18 August, a green flare signaled the expected enemy attack. Coming from Hill 117, the North Koreans struck A Company and isolated one platoon. Their attack formation then drove on and penetrated into B Company. The glare from bursting 81-mm. mortar illuminating shells revealed the North Korean method of attack. An enemy squad would rise from the ground, hurl grenades, and rush forward a short distance firing to front and flank with automatic weapons, and then drop to the ground. Successive enemy groups would repeat the process. The attack forced A

---

[73] 1st Bn, 5th Mar SAR, 17 Jul 50; Geer, *The New Breed*, p. 71.

[74] 1st Bn, 5th Mar SAR, 17 Aug 50; 5th Mar SAR, 2 Aug–6 Sep 50, sketch 5, N.K. counterattack, night of 17–18 August; Geer, *The New Breed*.

[75] 24th Div WD, 17 Aug 50; 34th Inf WD, Summ, 22 Jul–26 Aug 50; 13th FA Bn WD, 17 Aug 50; 19th Inf Unit Rpt 38, 17 Aug 50; Interv, author with Montesclaros, 1 Oct 52; Ltr and comments, Beauchamp to author, 20 May 53.

Company from its positions and back into the saddle south of Hill 109. In its sector, however, B Company drove the enemy from its perimeter in forty-five minutes of hard fighting. Before daylight the North Korean attack ceased.

The total North Korean losses in this night battle was not known, although 183 enemy dead were counted later around the A and B Company perimeters.

The Marine losses were heavy. Digging in that evening with 190 men and 5 officers, B Company the next morning at daylight had 110 effectives; A Company, starting the night with 185 men, had only 90 men at daylight who could take their place in the line.[76]

After daylight, the Marine 1st Battalion reorganized, and A Company prepared to attack south against Hill 117, to which the enemy attack force had withdrawn. The company crossed the saddle easily, but machine gun fire stopped it on the slope. The company commander called for an air strike. After carefully checking the designated target, a Corsair dropped a 500-pound bomb which scored a direct hit on the enemy emplacement. When bomb fragments, rocks, and dirt had settled, the 3d Platoon leaped to its feet and dashed up the slope. At the enemy emplacement they found the machine gun destroyed and its crew members dead. In five minutes A Company was on top of Hill 117.[77]

The attack now continued on across the saddle toward Hill 143. Air strikes and artillery fire greatly helped to win that point. The process was then repeated with Hills 147 and 153. At nightfall only one small pocket of enemy resistance remained on Obong-ni, and it was eliminated the next morning. The formidable ridge had been captured by an attack beginning on the right flank and moving progressively south and upward along its series of knobs and saddles.

The Enemy Bridgehead Destroyed

While the 1st Battalion was driving to the southern tip of Obong-ni on 18 August, the Marine 3d Battalion started an attack from the northern end of the ridge toward Hill 206, the next ridge line westward. The 9th Infantry supported this attack by fire from Cloverleaf. The 3d Battalion was on its objective within an hour. It met virtually no opposition.[78]

The reason for this easy advance was apparent. At the same time that the 3d Battalion was climbing Hill 206, aerial observers, forward artillery observers, and front-line infantry units all reported seeing enemy groups attempting to withdraw westward to the Naktong. They reported this movement about noon. Forward observers adjusted air bursts (VT) and quick fuze artillery fire on these groups. Part of the artillery firing on the river crossing sites employed delayed fuzes for greater effectiveness against underwater swimmers. Fighter planes ranged over the roads and trails leading down the western slopes to the

---

[76] 1st Bn, 5th Mar SAR 17–18 Aug 50; Wood, "Artillery Support for the Brigade in Korea," *op. cit.*, p. 37; Geer, *The New Breed*, p. 76. There is some discrepancy in the Marine casualty figures.

[77] 1st Bn, 5th Mar SAR, 18 Aug 50; Geer, *The New Breed*, p. 77–79; Montross and Canzona, *The Pusan Perimeter*, p. 200.

[78] 3d Bn, 5th Mar SAR, 18 Aug 50.

river and caught many enemy groups in the open.⁷⁹

After the capture of Hill 206, Colonel Murray ordered the 3d Battalion to continue the attack toward Hill 311, the last ridge line in front of the Naktong. This attack slanted northwest. At the same time, the 34th and 19th Infantry Regiments on the right flank of the 24th Division drove south and southwest into the bulge. Only in a few places was resistance moderate and as the afternoon wore on even this diminished. Troops of the 19th Infantry on Ohang Hill could see groups of 10 to 15 North Koreans in the river, totaling perhaps 75 to 100 at one time, trying to cross to the west side. Fighter planes strafed these groups all afternoon. Before dark the Marine 3d Battalion captured most of Hill 311, the 34th Infantry captured Hill 240, and the 19th Infantry captured Hill 223—the high hills fronting the river.⁸⁰

It was clear by evening, 18 August, that the enemy *4th Division* was decisively defeated and its survivors were fleeing westward across the Naktong. The next morning, 19 August, marines and 34th Infantry troops met at the Naktong. Prisoners captured that morning said most of the North Korean survivors had crossed the river during the night. By afternoon, patrols to the river found no enemy troops. The battle of the Naktong Bulge was over.⁸¹

---

⁷⁹ Wood, "Artillery Support for the Brigade in Korea," *op cit.;* ATIS Res Supp Interrog Rpts, Issue 94 (N.K. *4th Div*), p. 49.

⁸⁰ 3d Bn, 5th Mar SAR, 18 Aug 50; 24th Div WD, 18 Aug 50; Interv, author with Montesclaros, 1 Oct 52.

⁸¹ 3d Bn, 5th Mar SAR, 19 Aug 50; 24th Div WD, 19 Aug 50; 1st Prov Mar Brig SAR, 19 Aug 50, p. 13.

MARINES *moving down from Hill 311.*

The N.K. *4th Division* lost nearly all its heavy equipment and weapons in the first battle of the Naktong Bulge. The Marine ordnance section, which gathered up most of the destroyed or abandoned enemy heavier weapons, recovered 34 enemy artillery pieces, 18 of them lined up along the Yongsan–Naktong River road for supporting fires along the main axis of enemy attack. The largest enemy artillery piece was 122-mm. in size. The North Korean casualties in this battle were heavy. The 24th Division buried more than 1,200 enemy dead. According to prisoners captured at the end of the battle, each of the three rifle regiments of the N.K. *4th Division* had no more than approximately 300 to 400 men left after they recrossed to the west side of the river. These prisoners said that about one-half their wounded died for lack of medical care. The entire *4th Division* reportedly numbered about

3,500 men on 19 August at the end of the bulge battle.[82]

After the Obong-ni battle ended, a count of enemy weapons destroyed or abandoned there reportedly included 18 heavy machine guns of Russian or American manufacture, 25 light machine guns, 63 submachine guns of Russian or American manufacture, 8 antitank rifles, 1 3.5-inch rocket launcher, and quantities of ammunition and grenades. Included in the captured enemy equipment was a U.S. Army radio, SCR-300, in good operating condition, set to the frequency of the 1st Battalion, 5th Marines. This indicated that the enemy had been intercepting conversations between A and B Companies the night of 17-18 August and probably had known precisely their locations and dispositions.[83]

The destruction, for all practical purposes, of the N.K. *4th Division* in the battle of the Naktong Bulge was the greatest setback suffered thus far by the North Korean Army. The *4th Division* never recovered from this battle until after the Chinese entered the war and it was reconstituted. Ironically, on 19 August, the day its defeat became final, the division received from the North Korean headquarters the order naming it a "Guard Division" for outstanding accomplishments in battle (Taejon).[84]

On the afternoon of 19 August, the bulge battle over, Eighth Army ordered the 1st Provisional Marine Brigade released from 24th Division control. The brigade, reverting to Eighth Army reserve, assembled in the south near Changwon, east of Masan, where it remained until 1 September.[85]

---

[82] Wood, "Artillery Support for the Brigade in Korea," *op. cit.*; GHQ FEC Sitrep, 20 Aug 50; 24th Div WD, 19 Aug 50; 24th Div Arty WD, 22 Jul-25 Aug 50; ATIS Res Supp Interrog Rpt, Issue 94 (N.K. *4th Div*), p. 49; EUSAK WD, 21 Aug 50, ATIS Interrog Rpt 705, Mun Il Pun; *Ibid.*, 8 Oct 50, G-2 Sec, ADVATIS 1074, Jr Lt Chon Cho Hong, N.K. *4th Div Hq*, said the *18th Regt* had 900 men left; *Ibid.*, 28 Sep 50, ADVATIS, Maj Choe Chu Yong, Opn Off, *Arty Regt, 4th Div*, said the division artillery crossed the Naktong with 12 guns and lost them all; ATIS Interrog Rpts, Issue 2, Rpt 703, p. 8, Kim Chi Ho; Interv, author with Church, 25 Sep 52.

[83] 2d Bn, 5th Mar SAR, 19 Aug 50, p. 9 (this source says there were 36 enemy machine guns on Obong-ni); 1st Bn, 5th Mar SAR, 18 Aug 50.

[84] GHQ FEC, History of the N.K. Army, p. 75; ATIS Res Supp Interrog Rpts, Issue 94 (N.K. *4th Div*), p. 49.

[85] 24th Div WD, 19 Aug 50; 1st Prov Mar Brig SAR, 19 Aug 50; *Ibid.*, 22 Aug-1 Sep 50, p. 14.

CHAPTER XVIII

Battle for the Eastern Corridor to Pusan

> I can only advise the party on the defensive not to divide his forces too much by attempting to cover every point.
> ANTOINE HENRI JOMINI, *The Art of War*

Serious trouble for General Walker developed in the east during the threatened enemy breakthrough in the Naktong Bulge. North Korean attacks in the Kigye and P'ohang-dong area became critical as the ROK divisions there suddenly gave way and threatened to collapse. The blow came with a suddenness that contained the element of surprise. Eighth Army, low in reserves, was ill-prepared to meet an enemy breakthrough in the east, with its main forces already fully and even desperately engaged elsewhere.

Through July and into the first week of August, there were repeated rumors and reports of strong guerrilla groups in the mountains ten or fifteen miles northwest of P'ohang-dong. These reports in time were treated as casually as the repeated cry of "Wolf!" by the boy in Aesop's fable.

The Kyongju Corridor to Pusan

Throughout the Pusan Perimeter fighting, the terrain in the P'ohang-dong area exercised a dominant influence on the action there and on General Walker's tactical plans for the defense of that part of the Perimeter. A natural corridor here led straight to Pusan. (*See Map IV.*)

From Taegu a lateral highway and railroad ran east to P'ohang-dong, 50 air miles away. This lateral corridor is the first valley route to the east coast of Korea south of the Seoul-Ch'orwon-P'yonggang-Wonsan corridor, 225 miles to the north. Situated on this route about midway between Taegu and P'ohang-dong is Yongch'on. There, the only important north-south road between Taegu and the east coast comes down from Andong and Uisong through the mountains to meet the lateral valley road. East of this road for a distance of 40 air miles to the coast, lies a rugged mountain area entirely devoid of improved roads.

Twelve miles west of P'ohang-dong in the lateral Taegu corridor is the town of An'gang-ni, and 6 miles north of it is the smaller town of Kigye. The latter is situated at a point where several trails and a poor road debouch southward from the mountains into a north-south valley that enters the Taegu-P'ohang lateral corridor at An'gang-ni. This north-south valley continues on south past An'gang-ni to Pusan, 60 air miles away. Kyongju, an important rail and highway center in the Taegu-P'ohang-Pusan triangle, lies 12 miles south of An'gang-ni in this corridor. These terrain facts explain why the towns of Kigye, An'gang-ni, and Kyongju assumed importance in the eastern battles.

At P'ohang-dong the coastal road from the north swings inland along the Hyongsan-gang to a point less than 2 miles from An'gang-ni where it bends south and enters the Kyongju corridor to continue on to Pusan. Militarily, P'ohang-dong itself was of slight importance, although its port permitted a partial supply by water of the ROK and the small U.S. forces on the east coast. Rather, it was the eastern half of the Pusan Perimeter communications net, the Taegu–Yongch'on–An'gang-ni–Kyongju–Pusan route—almost a sea-level valley route the entire distance—that was of critical importance. If it should be cut by the enemy for any appreciable period of time the Taegu position would become untenable.

The eastern part of the Perimeter was not as strongly held as other parts of the line. General Walker did not have the troops and supporting heavy weapons to hold the front strongly everywhere. At some points he had to take risks. Seeing that the mountains to the north in the P'ohang area were almost a trackless waste, he thought it unlikely that the North Koreans could move forward heavy equipment and supplies in sufficient quantity to exploit a penetration there, should one be made, for a continuing drive on Pusan.[1]

Contrasting with the rugged terrain and the lack of a good communications system in the enemy's field of operations in the east, General Walker had the interior valley rail and highway net over which he could rush reinforcements to the area. He considered as another source of U.N. strength the proximity of the Yonil Airfield six miles south of P'ohang-dong, and within two to five minutes' flying time of the critical areas, should the North Koreans reach the lateral corridor.

The North Koreans Reach P'ohang-dong

On this eastern flank of the Pusan Perimeter, three North Korean divisions and an independent regiment pressed against the ROK defenders in August 1950. The *8th Division* drove down the Uisong road toward Yongch'on, the *12th Division* plunged into the mountains southeast of Andong and headed for P'ohang-dong, the *766th Independent Regiment* left the coastal road at Yongdok and swung southwest into the mountains toward Kigye and An'gang-ni, and the *5th Division* drove down the coastal road from Yongdok, with some of its infantry units infiltrating through the mountains around the ROK 3d Division.[2]

The first of these divisions, the N.K. *8th Division*, failed to penetrate to the Taegu-P'ohang lateral corridor. Near Uisong on 9 August, the ROK 8th Division caught part of its forces by surprise and almost annihilated one battalion of the *3d Regiment*, causing 700

---

[1] Interv, author with Lt Col Paul F. Smith (G–3 Opns, 8th Army), 2 Oct 52; Interv, author with Lt Col Robert G. Fergusson (G–2 Sec, 8th Army), 2 Oct 52; Ltr with comments, Landrum to author, rec'd 28 Jun 54.

[2] ATIS Res Supp Interrog Rpts, Issue 4 (N.K. *8th Div*), pp. 23–24; *Ibid.*, Issue 99 (N. K. *12th Div*), p. 46; *Ibid.*, Issue 96 (N.K. *5th Div*), p. 43.

casualties. The division's *2d Regiment* then entered the battle and itself suffered heavy losses, though it won back the ground previously lost to the ROK's.

In this fighting along the Uisong-Yongch'on road, ROK troops achieved some success against enemy armor. ROK infantry defended an antitank mine field covering both sides of the road in a narrow valley near a bridge. Two enemy tanks approaching the bridge struck mines. Three more enemy tanks and a self-propelled 76-mm. gun approached. Before they could turn around on the blocked road a flight of F-51 fighter planes came over firing rockets and dropping napalm on the six armored vehicles. All were destroyed. This affair provides a good example of multiple reporting. The Far East Air Forces claimed six kills; not to be outdone, the ROK engineers claimed the same number.[3]

The enemy *8th Division* was so badly hurt in this fighting that it was unable for a week to continue the drive on Yongch'on, and then it advanced only a few miles south of Uisong before in the face of continuing strong ROK opposition it halted to await reinforcements.[4]

Next in line eastward, the N.K. *12th Division*, now bearing the honorary name, "The Andong Division," crossed the upper Naktong at Andong and plunged into the mountains in an effort to carry out its orders to capture P'ohang-dong. Its fighting strength was only a fraction of what it had once been. At this time the *2d Battalion* of the *Artillery Regiment* sent all its artillery pieces back to Tanyang on the upper Han River because of failure to obtain ammunition for them.[5]

The ROK Capital Division was supposed to establish contact with the ROK 3d Division across this mountainous region. Reports were rife that enemy groups, the largest estimated at 2,000 men, were in the mountains inland from the coast. On 9 August, Eighth Army headquarters received a report that regular North Korean Army troops were in the "guerrilla area" northwest of P'ohang-dong, threatening the coastal road and the Yonil Airfield. On that day the 1st and 2d Battalions of the ROK 25th Regiment, a new unit just arrived from Taegu, attacked north from Kigye with orders to effect a juncture with the 3d Division south of Yongdok. Two and a half miles north of Kigye, an enemy counterattack hurled the regiment back to a point two miles southeast of the town. It was now clear that, although the ROK 3d Division held the coastal road from a point twenty miles above P'ohang-dong, there were no defenses inland in the mountains and enemy units were operating in this area.[6] (*Map 11*)

Eighth Army on 10 August organized Task Force P'ohang, consisting of the ROK 17th and 25th Regiments, the ROK 1st Anti-Guerrilla Battalion, the ROK P'ohang Marine Battalion, and C Battery of the U.S. 18th Field Artillery Battalion (75-mm.). The next day the ROK Army activated the 26th Regiment at Taegu and hurried it east to join Task Force P'ohang at An'gang-ni. Of

---

[3] Crawford, Notes on Korea, 25 Jun-5 Dec 1950.
[4] ATIS Res Supp Interrog Rpts, Issue 4 (N.K. *8th Div*), p. 24; EUSAK WD, 12 Aug 50, ATIS Interrog Rpt 507, Sr Col Han Ch'ong, CofS *8th Div*, and interrog of Sr Sgt Yung Pyong Yong.

[5] ATIS Res Supp Interrog Rpts, Issue 106 (N.K. Arty), p. 70.
[6] EUSAK WD, G-3 Sec, 8-9 Aug 50; *Ibid.*, POR 47, 10 Aug 50; GHQ FEC G-3 Opn Rpt 46, 9 Aug 50.

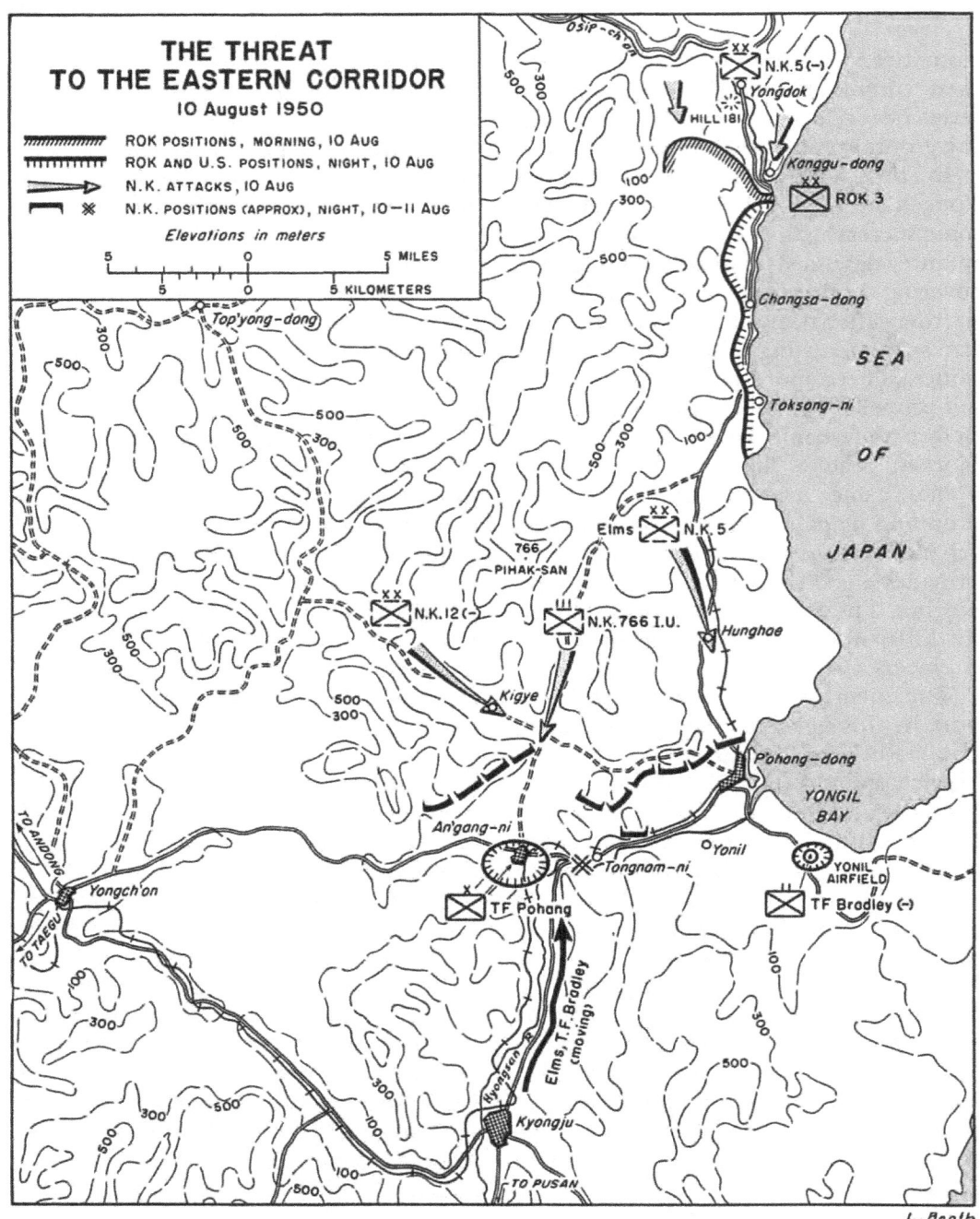

MAP 11

BATTLE FOR THE EASTERN CORRIDOR TO PUSAN

these units, only the ROK 17th Regiment was battle tested. The mission of Task Force P'ohang was to attack north from the An'gang-ni–P'ohang area and clear enemy forces from the mountains near the coast.[7]

The events around Kigye and in the mountains to the west of P'ohang-dong from this point on can be understood in their true light only if one knows what was taking place simultaneously on the east coast, only a few miles away. To bring those events into their proper perspective it is necessary now to review them.

A previous chapter recounted the series of bloody battles on the coastal road between the N.K. *5th Division* and the ROK 3d Division through the first days of August. The fighting seesawed around Yongdok for two weeks, with first one side and then the other holding the town. This action had ended with the ROK's temporarily regaining Yongdok. But they held it only briefly.

On 5 August the North Koreans attacked again and drove the ROK's south of the town to Hill 181. General Walker sent a personal message to Colonel Emmerich, the KMAG adviser with the ROK 3d Division, saying that the lost ground must be regained. Plans were made for a counterattack the next night. During the 6th, while these plans were being readied, it was possible from the ROK division command post to see, through field glasses, the North Korean and ROK troops locked in battle at grenade range on Hill 181.

The night attack got under way at 1930 with a 15-minute air attack using rockets, napalm, and bombs. Naval gunfire and an artillery preparation for another fifteen minutes followed the air attack. Then at 2000 the ROK 22d and 23d Regiments moved out in the infantry attack. They drove the North Koreans from Hill 181 and held it during the night. On the morning of 7 August the attack resumed after another naval and artillery preparation. This drove the enemy to a point just south of Yongdok.[8]

During the night attack an untoward incident occurred at the ROK 3d Division command post. An enemy mortar barrage hit close to the command post and killed several soldiers. When the KMAG adviser sent to the ROK command post for a report on the situation his messenger brought back word that he could not find anyone there. An interpreter tried to find the division commander, General Lee. He returned and said the general and his staff could not be found. Upon receiving this information Colonel Emmerich and Major Slater searched the area with flashlights and finally, with the help of some ROK soldiers, found the general and his aide in a hillside dugout. Emmerich instructed the ROK commander to assemble his staff and return to the command post. The next morning he requested that the division commander be relieved.[9]

At this time the 1st Separate Battalion and the Yongdungp'o Battalion were inactivated and their troops absorbed into the ROK 22d and 23d Regiments.

On 7 August, also, General Walker sent a message to Colonel Emmerich telling him that the bridge below Yong-

---

[7] EUSAK WD, Summ, 10–11 Aug 50, pp. 27–30; *Ibid.*, G–2 Daily Sitrep, 9 Aug 50, and Br for CG, 10 Aug 50; *Ibid.*, POR 89, 11 Aug 50.

[8] Emmerich, MS review comments, 30 Nov 57.
[9] *Ibid.*

dok at Kanggu-dong must be held. Up to this time an Engineer squad from the 24th Division had manned the demolitions on the 520-foot bridge there over the Osip-ch'on. The squad was now called back to Taegu, and control of the demolitions passed to Korean troops with directions that they were to blow the bridge only upon instructions from Major Britton of KMAG.

Just after daylight, at 0500 on 9 August, a great explosion rocked the area of the bridge. The commanding officer of the ROK 22d Regiment had ordered the bridge blown without securing approval from Major Britton. About 350 ROK soldiers of the regiment were still north of the Osip-ch'on when the bridge dropped. Many of these soldiers drowned in trying to cross the deep estuary flowing into the Japan Sea. The ROK division chief of staff demanded that the regimental commander be relieved or he would court martial him and place him before a firing squad. The Korean Army relieved the regimental commander at once.

The blowing of the Kanggu-dong bridge compelled the withdrawal southward of the ROK command post to Changsa-dong on the afternoon of 9 August to escape enemy artillery fire. On 10 August N.K. *5th Division* soldiers infiltrated around the ROK 3d Division and cut the coastal road below it at Hunghae, five miles north of P'ohang-dong. The ROK 3d Division was virtually surrounded on that date.[10]

As soon as Eighth Army learned that enemy forces had cut off the ROK 3d Division above P'ohang-dong, General Walker instructed Colonel Emmerich to meet him at Yonil Airfield. Emmerich radioed to the American cruiser *Helena*, offshore, for a helicopter to fly him to the airstrip, where he met General Walker, General Partridge, and Brig. Gen. Francis W. Farrell, Chief of KMAG.

General Walker instructed Emmerich to have the ROK 3d Division hold in place around Changsa-dong, twenty miles north of P'ohang-dong, and to prevent the enemy *5th Division* from moving its tanks and artillery down the road to the P'ohang area. If enemy tanks and artillery got through on the coastal road they would render Yonil Airfield untenable. Emmerich returned at once to Changsa-dong and relayed the orders to Brig. Gen. Kim Suk Won, the ROK 3d Division's new commander. The division then went into a perimeter defense extending along the coast from a point four miles north of Changsa-dong to a point seven miles south of the town.[11]

The sudden appearance of strong enemy army units near P'ohang-dong on 10 August surprised many American officers, including General Walker. He had just asked General Farrell if the ROK troops in the east would need American help to assure the defense of P'ohang-dong and Yonil Airfield. Farrell had advised Walker that the ROK troops would be able to protect these places. This opinion reflected that prevailing at the time—that the North Koreans would not be able to move through

---

[10] *Ibid.*; Maj. Perry Austin and Capt. Mario Paglieri (KMAG advisers with ROK 3d Div), It Can Be Done: A Lesson in Tactics, MS, copy in OCMH.

[11] Paglieri, Notes on ROK 3d Division, August 1950, MS, copy in OCMH; Interv, author with Emmerich, 4 Dec 51; Karig, *et al.*, *Battle Report: The War in Korea*, p. 147.

BATTLE FOR THE EASTERN CORRIDOR TO PUSAN

the mountains in sufficient strength to make an effective attack on P'ohang-dong from the rear.[12]

After his conference with Colonel Emmerich at Yonil Airfield, General Walker returned to Taegu. From there he sent an order by courier at 1735 to Maj. Gen. Lawrence B. Keiser, commanding the U.S. 2d Division at Kyongsan, to move the remaining elements of the 9th Regiment from that point to Yonil Airfield at once. This task force was to be commanded by Brig. Gen. Joseph S. Bradley, Assistant Division Commander, 2d Division. Task Force Bradley was to report directly to General Walker.[13]

This task force moved toward P'ohang-dong and Yonil after dark, 10 August, over the main road through Kyongju. The command group and the 3d Battalion, 9th Infantry, except K Company, reached Yonil Airfield shortly before midnight and General Bradley assumed responsibility for the ground defense of the airstrip.

Ten miles north of Kyongju and at a point about a mile east of An'gang-ni, the road bent sharply right in the Hyongsan-gang valley toward P'ohang-dong, seven miles eastward. Just after making this turn the road swung around the base of a steep mountain which crowded it close against the river near the village of Tongnam-ni. Company K and four vehicles of C Battery, 15th Field Artillery Battalion, were ambushed at this point at 0120, 11 August. Enemy fire suddenly hit the driver of the leading truck and his vehicle swerved, blocking the road. Automatic weapons fire swept over the column, bringing death and destruction. The K Company convoy fell into confusion. As many men as could fled back toward Kyongju; approximately 120 members of the company, including two officers, reached the town.[14]

Learning of the ambush, General Bradley at Yonil Airfield ordered I Company to return to An'gang-ni, to K Company's rescue. West of P'ohang-dong it, too, was ambushed. Informed by radio of this second ambush, Bradley sent two M16 vehicles, with their heavy armament of four .50-caliber machine guns each, to the scene. All but about twenty-five men of I Company got back to the airfield during the day.[15]

At the K Company ambush casualties were greater. By afternoon, 7 dead and at least 40 wounded were reported. About 25 members of C Battery, 15th

---

[12] Interv, author with Farrell, 31 Dec 52; New York Times, August 14, 1950, dispatch by W. H. Lawrence.

[13] As finally constituted, Task Force Bradley comprised the 3d Battalion, 9th Infantry; Tank Company, 9th Infantry; A Company, 2d Engineer Combat Battalion; A Battery, 82d Antiaircraft Artillery (Automatic Weapons) Battalion; C Battery, 15th Field Artillery Battalion; 3d Platoon, Heavy Mortar Company, 9th Infantry; and medical and signal detachments. EUSAK WD, 10 Aug 50, Msg at 101735, CG EUSAK to CG 2d Div; Ibid., POR 87, 10 Aug 50; Ibid., Briefing for CG, 10 Aug 50; 1st Lt Robert J. Teitelbaum, Debriefing Rpt 47, Arty School, Ft. Sill, Okla., 14 Dec 51; 82d AAA Bn WD, Summ, Aug 50; Ltr, Lt Col D. M. McMains to author, 27 May 53 (McMains commanded the 3d Bn, 9th Inf of TF Bradley); Rpt, The Korean Campaign, Arty School Rep, Army Field Forces Observer Team 2.

[14] EUSAK WD, G-3 Jnl, Msgs 110120 and 110355 Aug 50; Ibid., G-3 Jnl, 12 Aug 50; GHQ FEC G-3 Opn Rpt 48, 11 Aug 50; Interv, author with Farrell, 31 Dec 52; Ltr, McMains to author, 27 May 53; Rpt, The Korean Campaign, Arty School Rep, AFF Observer Team 2.

[15] EUSAK WD G-3 Jnl, Msg 1335, 11 Aug 50; Davis, The 2d Infantry Division in Korea, July–September 1950.

AERIAL VIEW OF P'OHANG-DONG

Field Artillery Battalion, were also lost in this ambush.

The enemy soldiers who had cut the road west of P'ohang-dong the night of 10–11 August and staged these ambushes apparently were from the *766th Independent Regiment.* This regiment, leaving the *5th Division* in the vicinity of Yongdok, had come in behind P'ohang-dong by way of mountain trails.

In the early afternoon, 11 August, General Walker ordered the Tank Company, 9th Infantry, which had stopped at Kyongju to wait upon repair of a damaged bridge, to proceed to the Yonil Airfield. He also ordered the ROK 17th Regiment released from Task Force P'ohang and to proceed from An'gang-ni to the airstrip.[16]

[16] Davis, The 2d Infantry Division in Korea July–September 1950; Rpt, The Korean Campaign, Arty School Rep, AFF Observer Team 2; EUSAK WD, G-3 Jnl, Msgs 1331 and 1700, 11 Aug 50.

Aerial reconnaissance showed the K Company ambush site was still held by enemy troops. Well aware of this, Captain Darrigo, KMAG adviser with the ROK 17th Regiment at An'gang-ni, volunteered to lead an armored patrol through to P'ohang-dong and Yonil. Darrigo rode the first of five tanks. Four F-51 fighter planes took off from Yonil Airfield and delivered a strike on the enemy positions at the ambush site just as the tanks arrived there. This air strike flushed enemy troops from concealment at just the right moment. Tank machine gun fire killed many of them; in one group about seventy North Koreans were caught in the open.

This tank column arrived at Yonil Airfield about 2030, 11 August, and were the first tanks to reach the airstrip. They were immediately placed in the perimeter defense. Darrigo was the same officer who had escaped from Kaesong at dawn, 25 June, when the North Koreans began their attack across the 38th Parallel. One who saw this courageous 30-year-old soldier when he arrived at Yonil said he looked to be fifty.[17]

While these events were taking place behind and to the east of it, Task Force P'ohang attacked north from the An'gang-ni area the morning of 11 August. (*Map 12*) It came to grief almost at once. At one place the enemy annihilated two companies of the ROK 25th Regiment. The task force, and also the ROK Capital Division, lost ground. The day was blazing hot. Great dust clouds hung over the roads. Fighter planes shuttled constantly from Yonil Airfield to the numerous nearby points where enemy troops were active, trying to stabilize the situation. One pilot, speaking of that day, said, "I barely had my wheels up before I started my strafing runs." But it was not all one-sided for the fighter planes. The day before, enemy small arms and machine gun fire had shot down four of them. By evening of 11 August, North Korean patrols reportedly were operating three miles south of P'ohang-dong. Eighth Army during the day ordered the ROK forces in the east to fall back to new positions during the nights of 12 and 13 August.[18]

The main enemy force encountered by Task Force P'ohang on 11 August seems to have been advance elements of the *12th Division*. This division had now crossed the mountains from Andong and was debouching at Kigye into the valley west of P'ohang-dong. There, in a series of battles, fought by the North Koreans almost entirely with automatic weapons and small arms, the *12th Division* drove back the ROK Capital Division and Task Force P'ohang. In this series of action the *12th* lost about 800 casualties, according to prisoner reports.[19]

That night, 11 August, the fighter planes at Yonil flew to another airfield for security, but returned the next day. From hills to the south and southwest of the airstrip enemy troops delivered long-range, ineffective fire against it. Even though this fire did no damage, it created a state of alarm. The next day, 12 August, 28-year-old Colonel Kim Hi Chun, acting on General Walker's orders, in a successful attack eastward from An'gang-ni, led his ROK 17th Regiment into Yonil, greatly to the relief of everyone there.

Enemy forces first entered P'ohang-dong on 10 or 11 August. ROK sources reported on the 11th that an estimated 300 enemy soldiers from the *766th Independent Regiment* and the *5th Division* had entered the town and seized the railroad station. But they did not remain there more than a few hours. Naval gunfire and aerial strikes drove them out to seek comparative safety in the nearby hills. The town of P'ohang-dong now became a no man's land. Patrols from ROK and North Korean units entered the town at night but neither

---

[17] Interv, author with Capt Darrigo, 5 Aug 53; Darrigo, Korean Experiences, 1950, MS, copy in OCMH; New York *Times*, August 13, 1950, dispatch by W. H. Lawrence 12 August from Yonil Airfield; *Newsweek*, August 21, 1950, pp. 16–18, article by Harold Lavine in Korea.

[18] EUSAK WD, Summ, 11 Aug 50; GHQ FEC Opn Rpt 49, 12 Aug 50; New York *Times*, August 11, 1950, Lawrence dispatch.

[19] ATIS Interrog Rpt 722, Issue 2, p. 51, Jr Lt Tu Chul Ki; ATIS Interrog Rpt 734, Issue 2, p. 80, Capt Kim Tong Il, *Trans Co, 2d Regt, 12th Div.*

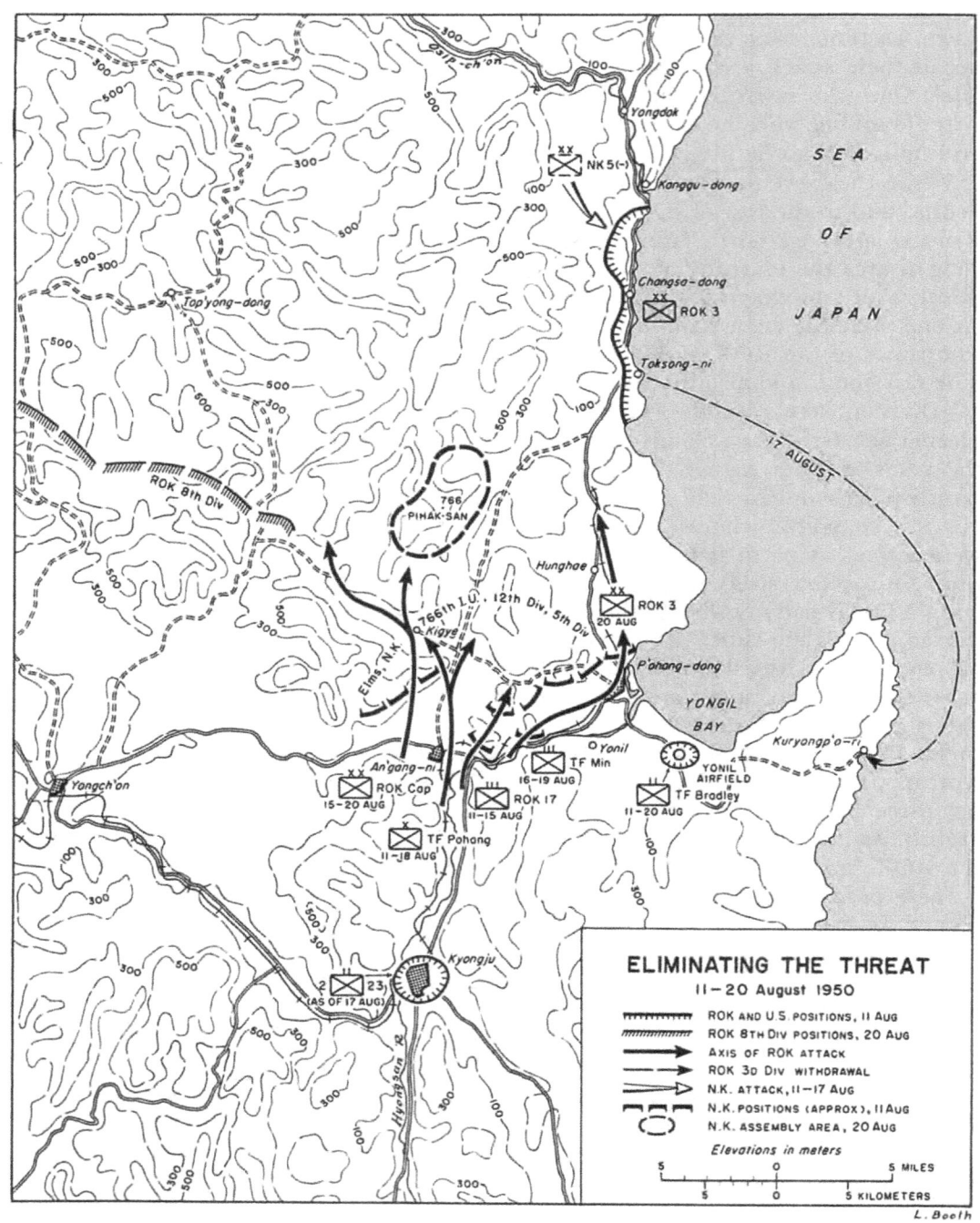

MAP 12

side held it. The battle swirled around it on the adjacent hills.[20]

The Air Force Abandons Yonil Airfield

Some United States ground and air service troops had been at Yonil Airfield before the 40th Fighter-Interceptor Squadron (35th Group) moved there on 16 July from Ashiya, Japan. On 7 August, the 39th Squadron moved to the field, and the next day the 6131st Fighter Wing was formed at the P'ohang base. But, even as these expanding air activities at Yonil were taking place, another and opposite current of events began. On 8 August, aviation engineers there received orders to evacuate their heavy equipment. In the next few days, as the North Koreans occupied the hills around P'ohang-dong and west and southwest of Yonil Airfield, FEAF officials became alarmed for the safety of their aircraft. They feared that enemy troops would be able to bring up mortars and artillery to bombard the strip, and that enemy infantry might overrun it.[21]

Even though U.S. infantry units and tanks were at Yonil on 13 August, FEAF on that day decided to abandon the field. The order came about noon. Not a single crater dented the runway as the F-51's took to the air to fly away. It appears that Colonel Witty, commanding the Air Force units at Yonil, recommended the evacuation of the field and was supported by General Partridge, commander of the Fifth Air Force. Army officials had no part in the decision to abandon the Yonil field. Army units remained at the field and it never was brought under effective enemy fire.[22]

The first news of the Fifth Air Force evacuation of Yonil Airfield came to General MacArthur's headquarters about 1600 that afternoon, 13 August, in the form of a United Press report, filed at 1320. This news report stated that an "Air Force spokesman announced that the Air Force was evacuating P'ohang air strip" because North Koreans were placing machine gun and mortar fire on the strip. A telephone call to Eighth Army headquarters at once disclosed that there was no mortar fire on the airstrip and that the report of enemy fire on the field was greatly exaggerated. It did, however, confirm that the Fifth Air Force Advance Headquarters had ordered the planes to leave the field.

General MacArthur and General Almond, his Chief of Staff, were "much upset" by the evacuation of Yonil Airfield. MacArthur instructed one of his staff officers to inform FEAF that he intended to hold the airfield and did not want the planes to return to Japan. Nevertheless, the two squadrons of F-51's (forty-five aircraft) moved from Yonil to Tsuiki Air Base on Kyushu.[23]

The heavy equipment at Yonil was

---

[20] ATIS Res Supp Interrog Rpts, Issue 106 (N.K. Arty), p. 46; EUSAK WD, 30 Aug 50, ATIS Interrog Rpt 867; *Ibid.*, POR 90, 11 Aug 50.
[21] USAF Hist Study 71, p. 20.
[22] *Ibid.*; Ltr, McMains to author, 27 May 53; New York *Times*, August 14, 1950, dispatch by W. H. Lawrence.
[23] Transcript of telephone conversation between Gen. Roderick R. Allen, Deputy CofS ROK Army, and Collier, at 1600, 13 Aug 50, CofS files, FEC; Fonecon, Allen and Lt. Gen. Lawrence C. Craigie, Vice Comdr, FEAF, at 1930, 13 Aug 50, CofS files, FEC; Memo, Capt Webster W. Plourd, ROK Air Liaison Secy to Allen, 131645 Aug 50, CofS files, FEC.

taken to the beach and loaded on LST's. The bomb supply followed, and finally Fifth Air Force personnel at the base embarked on LST's and left the next day, 14 August. A considerable supply of aviation gasoline and petroleum products remained at Yonil. Occasionally after 13 August a crippled fighter plane came down at Yonil in an emergency landing, and many fighters refueled there as long as the fuel lasted.[24]

The ROK 3d Division Evacuated by Sea

While the battles for P'ohang-dong and the entrance to the Kyongju corridor were being fought behind it, the ROK 3d Division—cut off by the N.K. *5th Division* above P'ohang-dong since 10 August—was fighting to save itself from destruction. Well aware that it had isolated the ROK division, the N.K. *5th Division* now strove to destroy it. Constant enemy attacks compelled the ROK division to reduce the extent of its perimeter. The division command post moved four miles farther south from Changsa-dong to the water's edge at Toksong-ni, where KMAG advisers thought LST's could land. The principal fire support for the shrinking ROK perimeter came from the cruiser USS *Helena* and three destroyers offshore, and from the Fifth Air Force. A tactical air control party and artillery observers directed air strikes and naval gunfire at critical points on the perimeter. Two helicopters from the *Helena* brought medical supplies for the Korean wounded.[25]

On 13 August the ROK's carried 313 of their wounded on board a supply LST at Changsa-dong. Later in the day at Toksong-ni, this LST struck rocks and opened a hole in its hull. All the wounded had to be transferred to another LST over a walkway in a heavy running sea. Dukw's (amphibious trucks) took 86 of the more critically wounded ROK's to a Korean hospital ship which arrived and anchored 500 yards offshore. The LST then sailed for Pusan.

The steadily deteriorating situation in the vicinity of P'ohang-dong caused Eighth Army on 15 August to order the ROK 3d Division evacuated by sea. The division was to land at Kuryongp'o-ri, twenty air miles southward on the cape at the south side of Yongil Bay. It was then to relieve elements of the Capital Division in the line below P'ohang-dong and join in a planned co-ordinated attack northward.[26]

Evacuation of the ROK 3d Division by LST began the night of 16 August at Toksong-ni. The division completed loading the next morning, including 125 wounded in the perimeter, and the last LST pulled away from the beach at 0700. The division at this time consisted of the 22d and 23d Regiments and 1,200 attached National Police. More than 9,000 men of the division, the 1,200 National Police, and 1,000 laborers, together with all their weap-

---

[24] USAF Hist Study 71, p. 20; Ltr, McMains to author, 27 May 53. Colonel McMains stayed at Yonil with the 3d Battalion, 9th Infantry, until 14 September 1950, when the ROK 3d Division assumed responsibility for defense of the airstrip.

[25] Paglieri, Notes on ROK 3d Div, Aug 50; Austin and Paglieri, It Can Be Done, p. 4.

[26] *Ibid.*; EUSAK WD, G-3 Sec, 15 Aug 50; GHQ FEC G-3 Opn Rpt 53, 16 Aug 50; Interv, author with Emmerich, 5 Dec 51.

ons, ammunition and equipment, escaped to the waiting vessels under cover of darkness and naval gunfire. After daylight of the 17th the Fifth Air Force helped maintain a curtain of fire around the beach. The *Helena* and several destroyers escorted the evacuation LST's to Kuryongp'o-ri where they arrived at 1030. The division unloaded at once, and received orders to move the next day into battle positions south of P'ohang-dong.[27]

The North Koreans Turned Back From the Kyongju Corridor

While it seems clear that enemy patrols and miscellaneous groups of soldiers had entered P'ohang-dong as early as 10–11 August, it was not until the 13th that the North Korean communiqué claimed its complete liberation. Large elements of the N.K. *12th Division*, advancing from the direction of Kigye, entered the town on that day. But, like others before them, they did not remain long. An officer of the enemy division, when captured later, said the *1st Regiment* withdrew from P'ohang-dong after three hours because of an intense naval bombardment and severe air strikes. The *12th Division* then took up positions on the hills west and southwest of the town. The *2d* and *3d Battalions* of the *2d Regiment* occupied the hills six miles southwest of P'ohang-dong and threatened the Yonil Airfield. Elements of the N.K. *5th Division* meanwhile had reached the hills just north of P'ohang-dong.[28]

By 14 August the Capital Division, on Eighth Army order, had moved about twenty-five miles, from near Andong to the An'gang-ni–Kigye area, where it went into the line east of the ROK 8th Division. The ROK I Corps now established its headquarters at Yongch'on.

The fighting in the vicinity of P'ohang-dong between North and South Koreans became a dog-eat-dog affair. Both sides lost heavily. The ROK's renewed their attack on 13 August when the 17th Regiment, reverting to control of the Capital Division, drove forward, supported by U.S. artillery and tanks from Task Force Bradley, to the hills north of P'ohang-dong.

Task Force P'ohang attacked northward from An'gang-ni toward Kigye. In the fighting from 15 to 17 August, the Capital Division and Task Force P'ohang pushed the North Koreans back north of the Taegu-P'ohang lateral road and away from the Kyongju corridor in the neighborhood of An'gang-ni.

About daylight, 17 August, the 2d Battalion, 23d Regiment, 2d Division, arrived at Kyongju to buttress the defense there.[29]

In the midst of this seesaw battle in the east—which also was the period of the successful enemy crossing of the

---

[27] Paglieri, Notes on ROK 3d Div, Aug 50; Austin and Paglieri, It Can Be Done, pp. 9–10; EUSAK WD G–3 Sec, 16–17 Aug 50; GHQ FEC G–3 Opn Rpt 54, 17 Aug 50; New York *Herald Tribune*, August 17, 1950.

[28] EUSAK WD, 21 Aug 50, ATIS Interrog Rpt 721, Lt. Pak Kwang Hon; *Ibid.*, 22 Aug 50, ATIS Interrog Rpt 734, Capt Kim Tong Il (*2d Regt, 12th Div*), and related interrog of Kim in ATIS Interrog Rpts, Issue 2, Rpt 734, p. 80, Rpt 723, p. 55, Sgt Im Chang Nam; ATIS Res Supp Interrog Rpts, Issue 99 (N.K. *12th Div*), p. 46; New York *Times*, August 14, 1950.

[29] Interv, author with Farrell, 31 Dec 52; EUSAK WD, 13 Aug 50; *Ibid.*, Summ, 1–31 Aug 50; GHQ FEC G–3 Opn Rpt 50, 13 Aug 50.

Naktong River into the zone of the U.S. 24th Division at the bulge—Premier Kim Il Sung of North Korean broadcast from P'yongyang an order calling on his army to drive the United States and ROK forces from Korea by the end of the month. He correctly predicted that the longer they remained the stronger they would become. He exhorted his Communist troops to "destroy the South Korean and United States [troops] to the last man." [30]

The fortunes of war in the east at last seemed to be veering in favor of the South Koreans. By nightfall of 17 August, ROK attacks in the vicinity of An'gang-ni threatened to surround the *766th Independent Regiment,* and it withdrew to the mountains north of Kigye. Battling constantly with ROK troops and suffering severely from naval gunfire and aerial strikes, the N.K. *12th Division* that night began to withdraw from the hills around P'ohang-dong. At 2000, 17 August, the *12th Division* ordered all its units to withdraw through Kigye northward to the Top'yong-dong area. The division suffered heavy casualties in this withdrawal. The next day it ordered all its units to assemble on Pihak-san on 19 August for reorganization.[31]

On Pihak-san, a 2,400-foot rugged peak six miles due north of Kigye, the *12th Division* reorganized. In this reorganization, the *766th Independent Regiment* lost its identity, its troops being distributed among the three regiments of the *12th Division.* After incorporating 2,000 replacements and the approximately 1,500 men of the *766th Independent Regiment,* the division reportedly totaled about 5,000 men. This figure shows the severe casualties suffered thus far in the war by this division, originally composed mostly of CCF veterans. Though morale was low there was little desertion.[32]

In these battles attending the withdrawal of the North Koreans from the vicinity of P'ohang-dong, the ROK Capital Division by 19 August had advanced to a point two miles north of Kigye, the 3d Division entered P'ohang-dong, and Task Force Min reached a point a mile and a half north of the town. The next day the 3d Division relieved Task Force Min and attacked to selected positions five and a half miles north of P'ohang-dong. The Capital Division also made additional gains north of Kigye. That day, 20 August, Eighth Army by radio order dissolved Task Force Bradley and redesignated the force at Yonil Airfield the 3d Battalion, 9th Infantry, Reinforced. This same day, with the emergency in the east temporarily ended, Task Force P'ohang was dissolved, and Task Force Min moved west to a position between the ROK 1st and 6th Divisions.[33]

---

[30] New York *Times,* August 15, 1950, P'yongyang broadcast monitored in Tokyo.
[31] Capt Kim Tong Il (see n. 28); ATIS Res Supp Interrog Rpts, Issue 99 (N.K. *12th Div*), pp. 46–27; 23d Inf WD, 17 Aug 50.

[32] ATIS Res Supp Interrog Rpts, Issue 99 (N.K. *12th Div*), pp. 46–47; EUSAK WD, 30 Aug 50, ATIS Interrog Rpt 869, Lee Son Chol; *Ibid.,* 734, Kim Tong Il; ATIS Interrog Rpts, Issue 2, p. 11, Rpt 704, Jr Lt Kim Dok Yong, *2d Regt, 12th Div,* Rpt 722, p. 51, Jr Lt Tu Chul Ko, *1st Regt, 12th Div,* and Rpt 724, p. 58, Lt Chang Chin Sop, *1st Regt, 12th Div.*
[33] EUSAK WD, 20 Aug 50; *Ibid.,* Aug 50 Summ, 19–20 Aug; *Ibid.,* G–3 Sec, entry 9, 20 Aug 50; *Ibid.,* G–3 Jnl, 20 Aug 50; GHQ FEC G–3 Opn Rpt 58, 21 Aug 50.

A ROK Army dispatch on 20 August claimed that its forces in the P'ohang area from 17 August on had killed 3,800 and captured 181 North Koreans. It also claimed the capture of 20 artillery pieces, 11 light mortars, 21 82-mm. mortars, 160 machine guns, 557 U.S. M1 rifles and 381 Japanese rifles.[34]

Since about the end of July, the greater part of the N.K. *12th Division* had been armed with the U.S. M1 rifle and the U.S. carbine. There was an adequate supply of ammunition for these weapons, but not always available at the front. The Japanese 99 rifles and ammunition with which the division was originally armed were turned in to the division supply dump at the end of July, when the supply of American arms captured from ROK units enabled the division to substitute them.

Not the least important of the factors that brought about the defeat of the North Koreans at P'ohang-dong and in the Kigye area in mid-August was the near exhaustion of the *12th Division* after its passage through the mountains south of Andong, and its lack of artillery and food supply. One captured officer of the division said his unit received no food after 12 August, and for five days thereafter up to the time of his capture had only eaten what the men could forage at night in the villages. His men, he said, became physically so exhausted that they were no longer combat effective. A captured sergeant of the *2d Battalion, 1st Regiment,* said that of 630 men in his battalion only 20 survived on 18 August. In the *2d Regiment,* according to a captured captain, no battalion averaged more than 250 men on 17 August. He said there was no resupply of ammunition from the rear.[35]

When the N.K. *12th Division* reached P'ohang-dong it was like a rubber band stretched to its uttermost limit. It must either break or rebound. The North Korean system of logistics simply could not supply these troops in the Kigye–P'ohang-dong area.

---

[34] New York *Times*, August 21, 1950.

[35] EUSAK WD, 22 Aug 50, ATIS Interrog Rpt 721, Lt Pak Kwang Hon, Rpt 722, Jr Lt Tu Chul Ki, Rpt 723, Im Chang Nam, Rpt 727, p. 64, Sr Sgt Choe Chol Hak, and Rpt 734, Kim Tong Il; ATIS Interrog Rpts, Issue 2, p. 51, Jr Lt Tu Chul Ki.

A survey of 825 North Korean prisoners revealed that they listed shortage of food as most important of all factors causing low morale. See USAF Hist Study 71, p. 52.

CHAPTER XIX

The Taegu Front

> Make a round of the troops immediately after a battle, or even the next day after, before the reports have been drawn up, and ask any of the soldiers and senior and junior officers how the affair went: you will be told what all these men experienced and saw, and you will form a majestic, complex, infinitely varied, depressing, and indistinct impression; and from no one—least of all from the commander in chief—will you learn what the whole affair was like.
>
> LEO TOLSTOY, *Some Words About War and Peace*

General Walker's primary objective in August was to retain a foothold in Korea. From this he intended to launch an attack later when his forces were of sufficient strength. Walker kept saying to his key staff officers and to his principal commanders substantially the following: "You keep your mind on the fact that we will win this thing by attacking. Never let an opportunity to attack pass. I want the capability and opportunity to pass to the offensive. Until that time comes I want all commanders to attack—to raid—to capture prisoners and thus keep the enemy off balance. If that is done, more and more opportunities to hurt the enemy will arise and our troops will be better prepared to pass to a general offensive when things are ripe.[1]

General Walker wanted the foothold in Korea to include the rail route from Pusan north through Miryang to Taegu, eastward to Kyongju, and back to Pusan. (*See Map IV.*) This would make possible the logistical support necessary for a breakout offensive later. To retain this circumferential communication net, General Walker had to combine a fine sense of timing with a judicious use of the small reserves he was able to assemble at any given time.[2] He had to know just when to move his limited reserves and where. They had to be at the right place and not too late. A study of the defensive fighting of the Pusan Perimeter by Eighth Army and the ROK Army will reveal that Walker proved himself a master in it.

The difficulty of forming a small reserve was one of the principal problems that confronted the Eighth Army staff

---

[1] Landrum, Comments for author, recd 23 Nov 53.

[2] Ltr, Maj Gen John A. Dabney to author, 18 Dec 53 (Dabney was Eighth Army G–3 during the summer and fall of 1950); Landrum, Comments on author's ltr to him of 1 Sep 53; Interv, author with Stebbins, 4 Dec 53.

during August and September 1950. It was a daily concern to the Eighth Army commander. Colonel Landrum, Eighth Army's chief of staff during August, considered it one of his most important daily tasks to find any unit that could be "tagged" as an army reserve. This search included both Eighth Army and ROK troops. It was considered a certainty that any troops so designated would be committed somewhere on the Perimeter within twenty-four to forty-eight hours. One of General Walker's daily greetings to his chief of staff was, "Landrum, how many reserves have you dug up for me today?"[3]

General Walker left most of the headquarters work to his staff. He spent the greater part of each day on visits to his combat units. It fell to Colonel Landrum to keep him fully informed of what had happened around the Perimeter front during his absence from headquarters. Landrum did this every day when Walker returned to Taegu. In addition to keeping in close touch with the army G-2, G-3, and G-3, Air, Colonel Landrum made it a practice to telephone each major combat unit sometime between 2200 and midnight each night and talk with the unit commander or the chief off staff about the situation on that part of the front. This provided fresh information and reflected the state of mind of the various commanders at that moment. On the basis of these nightly telephone calls, General Walker often planned his trips the next day. He went where he felt a serious situation was or might be developing.[4]

The central, or Taegu, front was to present its full measure of problems involving the use of limited reserves hastily assembled from another part of the perimeter. It was a sector where the Eighth Army commander needed to make a reasonably correct appraisal of the situation day by day. For here several corridors of approach southward converged on the valley of the Naktong, and the enemy forces advancing down these corridors were assembling in relatively great strength in close supporting distance of each other. The enemy frontal pressure against Taegu developed concurrenly with that on both flanks already described.

The North Koreans Cross the Naktong for the Attack on Taegu

The enemy forces assembled in an arc around Taegu, from south to north, were the N.K. *10th, 3d, 15th, 13th,* and *1st Divisions,* and elements of the *105th Armored Division.* They reached from Tuksong-dong on the south northward around Waegwan to Kunwi.[5] This concentration north and west of Taegu indicated that the North Koreans expected to use the natural corridor of the Naktong valley from Sangju to Taegu as a principal axis of attack in the next phase of their drive south.[6] (*Map 13*)

Across the Naktong opposite the five North Korean divisions, in early August, were, from south to north, the U.S. 1st Cavalry Division and the ROK 1st

---

[3] Landrum, Comments on author's ltr of 1 Sep 53, and Notes for author, recd 28 Jun 54.
[4] Landrum, Notes for author, recd 28 Jun 54.

[5] ATIS Res Supp Interrog Rpts, Issue 96 (N.K. *3d Div*), pp. 33-34; *Ibid.*, Issue 105 (N.K. *13th Div*), pp. 63-64; *Ibid.*, Issue 3 (N.K. *1st Div*), pp. 33-34; *Ibid.*, Issue 104 (N.K. *10th Div*), pp. 44-45; *Ibid.*, Issue 3 (N.K. *15th Div*), pp. 42-43.
[6] EUSAK WD, Summ, 5 Aug 50.

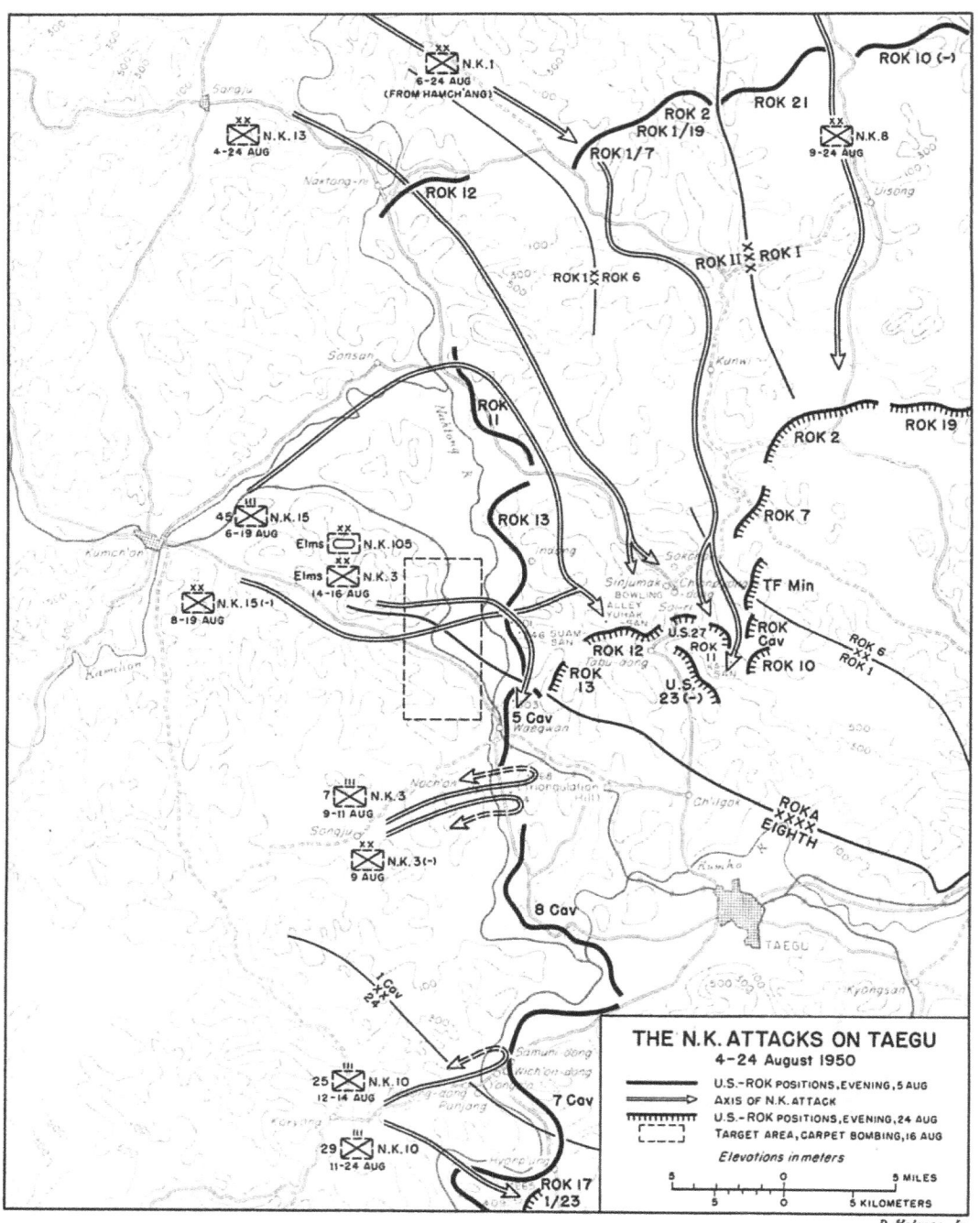

MAP 13

THE TAEGU FRONT

and 6th Divisions of the ROK II Corps. The boundary between the 1st Cavalry Division and the ROK 1st Division lay about two miles north of Waegwan and ten air miles northwest of Taegu. The *10th Division* and part of the *3d Division* were opposite the 1st Cavalry Division. Opposite the ROK 1st and 6th Divisions were part of the *3d*, and the *15th*, *13th*, and *1st Divisions*, together with supporting units of the *105th Armored Division*.

Like the 24th Infantry Division just south of it, the 1st Cavalry Division had a long front. From south to north, the 7th, 8th, and 5th Cavalry Regiments were on line in that order. The two battalions of the 8th Cavalry Regiment west of Taegu each had a front of about 10,000 yards. The 5th Cavalry Regiment at Waegwan had a front of 14,000 yards.[7] In order to provide artillery fire support for such great frontages, the artillery firing batteries were placed about 7,000 yards behind the front lines and about 6,000 to 7,000 yards apart. Each battery laid its guns on two different deflections. By shifting trails it was possible to mass the battery fire. In some instances, two batteries could mass their fire, but an entire artillery battalion could not do so because of the great flank distance within a regimental sector. The artillery tried to achieve volume of fire by rapidity of firing. In one instance, ten 105-mm. howitzers fired 120 rounds in seventy seconds, an average of one round every six seconds for each gun.[8]

In the north, the N.K. *1st Division* between 6 and 8 August crossed the Naktong River between Hamch'ang and Sangju in the zone of the ROK 6th Division. On 6 August, American planes observed ten barges engaged in ferrying troops across the river. The enemy division, although reinforced by 2,500 green replacement troops—partly at Hamch'ang and partly after crossing the river—was still only at half-strength. Many of the replacements did not have weapons and were used in rear areas in miscellaneous duties. This division, upon attacking toward Kunwi, met stubborn resistance from the ROK 6th Division and did not reach that town, twenty-five air miles due north of Taegu, until about 17 August. In battle there with the ROK 6th Division, it suffered further losses before it was able to advance south to the Tabu-dong area and the approaches to Taegu.[9]

South of the N.K. *1st Division*, the *13th Division* had started crossing the Naktong during the night of 4–5 August. On the 5th the main part of its *21st Regiment* crossed at Naktong-ni, forty air miles northwest of Taegu on the Sangju road. After the crossing was discovered, some of the enemy soldiers came under aerial strafing attacks while they were still in the water and ROK artillery and mortar fire was directed at the crossing site. On the south bank the regiment came under continuing aerial and artillery fire, but with unknown casualties. That night the *19th Regiment* crossed the river in the path of the *21st*, the men holding their weapons over their heads and wading in neck-

---
[7] 8th Cav Regt WD, 4 Aug 50; 5th Cav Regt WD, 3 Aug 50.
[8] 61st FA Bn WD, Opn Narr Summ, Aug 50.

[9] EUSAK PIR Rpt 25, 6 Aug 50; EUSAK WD, 10 Aug 50, ATIS Interrog Rpt 478, Won Sun Nam; ATIS Res Supp Interrog Rpts, Issue 3 (N.K. *1st Div*), pp. 33–34; GHQ FEC Sitrep, 9 Aug 50.

deep water. They left behind their heavy weapons and vehicles. Then the following night, 6–7 August, the third regiment of the division, the *23d*, together with two battalions of artillery, crossed below Naktong-ni on rafts. These crossings of the N.K. *13th Division* were in the zone of the ROK 1st Division, but were several miles from that division's prepared positions.[10]

ROK troops attacked the *13th Division* immediately after it crossed, forcing it into the mountains. There, the N.K. *13th Division*, its elements uniting on the east side, launched a concerted night attack, broke the ROK defenses, and began an advance that carried it twenty miles southeast of Naktong-ni on the main road to Taegu. A week after crossing the Naktong, the *13th Division* and the *1st Division* were converging on the Tabu-dong area, about fifteen miles due north of Taegu. There lay the critical terrain for the northern defense of the city.[11]

The N.K. *15th Division*, next of the enemy divisions in line southward, received approximately 1,500 replacements at Kumch'on on 5 August, which brought its strength to about 6,500 men. The next day its *45th Regiment* marched northeast toward the Naktong. The regiment passed through Sonsan on 7 August and crossed the river southeast of that town. United Nations planes strafed part of it in the crossing. Once across the river, the regiment headed into the mountains, encountering no opposition at first. The other two regiments, the *48th* and *50th*, departed Kumch'on later and began crossing the Naktong between Indong and Waegwan before dawn of 8 August. The men waded the river in four feet of water at two ferry sites, four and six miles north of Waegwan. Tanks and vehicles crossed on an underwater bridge at the upper ferry site. The major initial crossing occurred at the upper ferry site six miles from Waegwan where an estimated two battalions and at least two tanks had crossed by 0810. The North Koreans supported this crossing by direct tank fire from the west side of the river. The Air Force estimated seven tanks were in firing position there. These tanks evidently succeeded in crossing the river during the day. The N.K. *15th Division* seized Hills 201 and 346 on the east side of the river at the crossing site, before advancing eastward into the mountains toward Tabu-dong, seven air miles distant.[12]

Considering these enemy crossings the most serious threat yet to appear against Taegu, Eighth Army made plans to support the ROK Army with American troops in the event of an enemy penetration. The Air Force, in the meantime, discovered the underwater bridge six miles north of Waegwan and dropped 1,000-pound bombs on it with undetermined results.[13]

The ROK 1st Division the next day

---

[10] 1st Cav Div WD, 5 Aug 50; GHQ FEC Sitrep, 6 Aug 50; ATIS Res Supp Interrog Rpts, Issue 105 (N.K. *13th Div*), pp. 61–62.

[11] ATIS Interrog Rpts, Issue 2, Rpt 777, p. 177, 1st Lt Han Pyong Chol, *45th Regt, 15th Div;* ATIS Res Supp Interrog Rpts, Issue 105 (N.K. *13th Div*), p. 63.

[12] EUSAK WD and G–3 Jnl, 8 Aug 50; EUSAK PIR 27, 8 Aug 50; EUSAK Summ, 1–31 Aug 50; ATIS Res Supp Interrog Rpts, Issue 3 (N.K. *15th Div*), pp. 42–43; ATIS Interrog Rpts, Issue 2, Rpt 777, p. 177, Lt Han.

[13] EUSAK WD, 8 Aug 50, G–3 Jnl and Informal Checkslip, Daily Rpt from Plans Sec, G–3 Jnl; New York *Herald Tribune*, August 12, 1950.

reported it had regained the high ground at the crossing sites. The enemy force, however, had not been destroyed or driven back across the river. It had simply moved on eastward deeper into the mountains. Between 12 and 16 August the three regiments of the N.K. *15th Division* united on the east side of the Naktong in the vicinity of Yuhaksan, a towering 2,800-foot peak, five miles east of the crossing site and three miles northwest of Tabu-dong. The N.K. *13th Division* was already locked in combat on Yuhak-san with the ROK 1st Division.[14]

Opposite, and south of, Waegwan, two enemy divisions stood ready to cross the Naktong in a co-ordinated attack with the divisions to the north. The first of these, the N.K. *3d Division*, was concentrated in the vicinity of Songju, four miles southwest of Waegwan. Ten miles below the *3d*, the N.K. *10th Division* was concentrated in the Koryong area. Both these divisions were opposite the 1st Cavalry Division.

The *7th Regiment* of the *3d Division* started crossing the Naktong about 0300 9 August at a ferry site near the village of Noch'on, two miles south of the Waegwan bridge. The river at this point had a firm sandy bottom and a depth of five feet. The troops waded across holding their weapons above the water. Discovering the crossing, elements of the 5th Cavalry Regiment directed automatic weapons fire against the enemy force and called in pre-registered artillery fire on the crossing site. Although the enemy regiment suffered some casualties, the bulk of it reached the east bank safely and moved inland into the hills.[15] One of the soldiers wrote in his diary of the crossing:

Gradually advanced toward the river. Enemy shelling is fierce. Arrived at the shores of the river. The terrible enemy has sent up flares. The Naktong River is flowing quietly and evenly. Entered the river. After advancing 200 meters, shooting began with the firing of an enemy flare. The noise is ringing in my ears. Have already crossed the river. Occupied a hill. A new day is already breaking.[16]

Half an hour after the *7th Regiment* had crossed, the *8th* and *9th Regiments* started crossing the river south of it. By this time, the 5th Cavalry Regiment and all its supporting mortars and artillery were fully alerted. Flares and star shells brightly illuminated these two North Korean regiments in midstream. American fire from all supporting weapons, with the artillery playing the dominant role, decimated the enemy troops and turned them back to the west side. Only a small number reached the east side. There, either they were captured or they hid until the next night when they recrossed the river.[17]

---

[14] EUSAK POR 85, 10 Aug 50; GHQ FEC Sitrep, 9 Aug 50; ATIS Res Supp Interrog Rpts, Issue 3 (N.K. *15th Div*), p. 43; ATIS Interrog Rpts, Issue 2, p. 177, Lt Han. Geographical locations given in this portion of the text have been determined by correlating place names on the AMS Map, Korea, scale 1:50,000, with map co-ordinate readings in U.S. Army records and place names given in prisoner of war interrogations.

[15] EUSAK WD, 9 Aug 50; EUSAK, Aug 50 Summ; 1st Cav Div WD, G-2 Monthly Narr Rpt, Aug 50; 61st FA Bn WD, 9 Aug 50; ATIS Res Supp Interrog Rpts, Issue 96 (N.K. *3d Div*), p. 33.

[16] ATIS Supp Enemy Docs, Issue 2, pp. 66–67, diary from 21 Jul to 10 Aug 50 of Choe Song Hwan, entry for 9 Aug (diary captured 12 Aug).

[17] ATIS Res Supp Interrog Rpts, Issue 96 (N.K. *3d Div*), pp. 33–34; EUSAK WD, 12 Aug 50, ATIS Interrog Rpt 494, Kang Don Su.

Triangulation Hill

At daylight, 9 August, General Gay at 1st Cavalry Division headquarters in Taegu learned of the enemy crossing in his division sector south of Waegwan. As first reports were vague, he decided to withhold action until he learned more about the situation. A report informed him that 1st Lt. Harry A. Buckley, Acting S-2, 5th Cavalry Regiment, had personal knowledge of the enemy crossing. General Gay sent for the lieutenant and, while awaiting his arrival, placed the 1st Battalion, 7th Cavalry Regiment, in reserve on one-hour alert.

Upon reporting to General Gay at the division headquarters, Lieutenant Buckley stated:

> Just prior to daylight this morning, I, with a small group of men from the I&R Platoon, was on reconnaissance. Approximately 45 minutes prior to daylight, I observed enemy forces moving up the ridge line just northwest of Hill 268. The enemy were moving at a dog trot in groups of four. Every fourth man carried an automatic weapon, either a light machine gun or a burp gun. I watched them until they had all disappeared into the brush on Hill 268. In my opinion, and I counted them carefully, the enemy was in strength of a reinforced battalion, approximately 750 men. General, I am not a very excitable person and I know what I saw, when I saw it, where I was when I saw it, and where the enemy was going.[18]

A few minutes later, General Walker arrived at the division headquarters. He asked General Gay what his plans were. The latter replied that at least an enemy battalion had crossed the Naktong and was on Hill 268, that another enemy regiment was at that moment trying to cross the river under heavy fire from the 5th Cavalry Regiment, and that as soon as he was sure of his ground he was going to attack the enemy on Hill 268 and drive them back across the river. Walker commented, "Fine, be sure you are right before you move because this enemy battalion might be a feint and the real attack could well be coming farther to the left.[19] Events were later to prove this possibility correct.

At 0930, 9 August, General Gay ordered Lt. Col. Peter D. Clainos, commanding the 1st Battalion, 7th Cavalry Regiment, to eliminate the enemy penetration. The battalion moved at once from its bivouac area just outside of Taegu, accompanied by five tanks of A Company, 71st Heavy Tank Battalion. This motorized force proceeded to the foot of Hill 268, also known as Triangulation Hill, three miles southeast of Waegwan and ten air miles northwest of Taegu. The 61st Field Artillery Battalion meanwhile heavily shelled the hill. The hill was doubly important because of its proximity to lines of communication. The main Korean north-south highway from time immemorial, and the main double-track Pusan–Seoul–Harbin, Manchuria, railroad skirted its base.[20]

At noon the artillery fired a preparation on Hill 268, and the 1st Battalion then attacked it under orders to continue on southwest to Hill 154. Hill 268 was covered with thick brush about four feet high and some trees eight to ten

---
[18] Gay, Ltr and comments, 24 Aug 53.
[19] Ibid.
[20] 1st Cav Div WD, Summ, Aug 50; EUSAK WD, 9 Aug 50; 7th Cav Regt WD, 9–10 Aug 50; Engagement of 1st Bn; 61st FA Bn WD, 9 Aug 50; Interv, 1st Lt Fred L. Mitchell with Clainos, 16 Aug 50, copy in OCMH files.

TRIANGULATION HILL, *near Waegwan in the 5th Cavalry sector, under fire on 10 August.*

feet high. The day was very hot. Many 1st Battalion soldiers collapsed from heat exhaustion during the attack, which was not well co-ordinated with artillery fire. The enemy repulsed the attack.[21]

The next morning, 10 August, air strikes and artillery preparations blasted Hill 268. According to prisoners, these fires caused extremely heavy losses and created chaos in the enemy regiment.

During the morning, the assistant division commander, the chief of staff, the G–2, and several military police were ambushed and nearly all wounded on the Waegwan road at Hill 268. That afternoon, General Gay and his aide stopped near Hill 268 to talk with the 1st Battalion executive officer and a small group of men. An enemy mortar shell made a direct hit on the group, killing or wounding everyone there except Gay and his aide. Gay ordered five tanks to proceed along the Waegwan road until they could fire from the northwest into the reverse slope of the enemy-held hill. This tank fire caught the enemy soldiers there as they were seeking refuge from the artillery fire. Trapped between the two fires they started to vacate their positions. An infantry attack then reached the top of the hill without trouble and the battle was over by 1600. American artillery and mortar fire now shifted westward and cut off the enemy retreat. One time-on-target mission of white phosphorus fired by the 61st Field Artillery Battalion at this time caught a large number of enemy soldiers in a village where American ground troops later found 200 enemy dead. That evening the 1st Battalion, 7th Cavalry, reverted to division reserve, and elements of the 5th Cavalry

---

[21] Gay, Ltr and comments, 24 Aug 53; Interv, Mitchell with Lt Edward G. Deacy, 3d Plat, B Co, 7th Cav, Aug 50; Interv, Mossman with Lt Eugene E. Fells, CO B Co, 7th Cav, 24 Aug 50.

finished mopping up on Hill 268 and vicinity.[22]

When Hill 268 was examined carefully on 13 August, the enemy dead, equipment, and documents found there indicated that the *7th Regiment* of the N.K. *3d Division* had been largely destroyed. The 1st Battalion, 7th Cavalry, counted between 300 and 400 enemy dead in the battle area. The battalion itself suffered 14 men killed, and 48 wounded in the 2-day battle.[23]

Prisoners taken in the final action which cleared Hill 268 agreed substantially that about 1,000 men of the *7th Regiment* had crossed the Naktong to Hill 268, and that about 700 of them became casualties. The prisoners also agreed that artillery and mortars had inflicted most of the crippling casualties on the regiment. After crossing to the east side of the Naktong, the enemy regiment had received no food or ammunition supply. An estimated 300 survivors recrossed the river to the west side the night of 10–11 August.[24]

The N.K. *3d Division's* attempted crossing of the Naktong south of Waegwan had ended in catastrophe. When the survivors of the *7th Regiment* rejoined the division on or about 12 August, the once mighty *3d Division* was reduced to a disorganized unit of some 2,500 men. The North Korean Army placed the division in reserve to be rebuilt by re-placements.[25] This division, which had been the first to enter Seoul at the beginning of the war, fought the battle of Choch'iwon, crossed the Kum River before Taejon and defeated the 19th Infantry there, joined subsequently with the *4th Division* in the capture of Taejon, and drove the 1st Cavalry Division from Yongdong, was now temporarily out of the fight for Taegu.

The Enemy 10th Division's Crossing at Yongp'o

The North Korean plan for the attack against Taegu from the west and southwest had called for the N.K. *10th Division* to make a co-ordinated attack with the N.K. *3d Division*. The *10th Division* so far had not been in combat. It had started from Sukch'on for the front by rail about 25 July. At Ch'onan it left the trains and continued southward on foot, passing through Taejon and arriving at the Naktong opposite Waegwan on or about 8 August. There it received its combat orders two days later. Its mission was to cross the Naktong River in the vicinity of Tuksongdong, penetrate east, and cut the Taegu-Pusan main supply road. The division assembled in the Koryong area the next day, 11 August. There it was astride the main highway running northeast to Taegu over a partially destroyed Naktong bridge.[26]

Eighth Army purposely had not completely destroyed this bridge; it was passable for foot soldiers but not for

---

[22] Gay, Ltr and comments, 24 Aug 53; ATIS Res Supp Interrog Rpts, Issue 96 (N.K. *3d Div*), p. 34; 1st Cav Div WD, 10 Aug 50.
[23] 61st FA Bn WD, 10 Aug 50; 1st Cav Div WD, 10 Aug 50; 5th Cav Regt WD, 13 Aug 50.
[24] ATIS Res Supp Interrog Rpts, Issue 96 (N.K. *3d Div*), p. 34; EUSAK WD, 12 Aug 50, ATIS Interrog Rpt 505, Lee Sung Won; 1st Cav Div WD, G-2 Rpt, Aug 50, Interrog Rpt 0052, Sgt Kim Yon Hu, and Rpt 0050, Yung Tei Kwan.

[25] ATIS Res Supp Interrog Rpts, Issue 96 (N.K. *3d Div*), p. 34.
[26] *Ibid.*, Issue 104 (N.K. *10th Div*), pp. 44–45.

vehicles. In its partially destroyed condition it provided something of a trap if used by an enemy crossing force, because the bridge and its approaches channeled any enemy movement over it and were completely covered by preregistered mortar and artillery fire. To this was to be added the fire of infantry weapons located in good defensive positions on the hills near the river.

Two regiments of the N.K. *10th Division*, the *29th* on the south and the *25th* on the north, were to make the assault crossing with the *27th Regiment* in reserve. The commander of the *25th Regiment* issued an order on the eve of the crossing, stating that the objective was to "destroy the enemy in Taegu City in coordination with the *3d Infantry Division*." [27]

The 2d Battalion, 29th Regiment, was the first unit of the division to cross the river. Its troops waded unopposed to the east side, during the night of 11-12 August, at three ferry sites 3 to 5 miles due west of Hyongp'ung. This battalion climbed Hill 265, a northern spur of Hill 409, 2 miles southwest of Hyongp'ung, and set up machine gun positions. The other two battalions then crossed and occupied Hill 409. About twenty to thirty men of the *1st Battalion* reportedly drowned in the 5-foot-deep swift current in this crossing. It will be recalled that this enemy force in the Hill 409 area ambushed an I&R patrol from the 21st Infantry Regiment of the 24th Division, on the morning of 12 August, when it moved north along the river road trying to establish contact with the 7th Cavalry Regiment during the battle of the Naktong Bulge. [28]

On the north flank, the *25th Regiment* started crossing the Naktong about 0300, 12 August, in the vicinity of the partially blown highway bridge at Tuksong-dong, on the Koryong-Taegu road. The 2d Battalion, 7th Cavalry Regiment, covered this crossing site fourteen miles southwest of Taegu. By daylight, an enemy force of 300 to 400 men had penetrated to Wich'on-dong. There, H Company, 7th Cavalry Regiment, engaged it in close combat. In a grenade and automatic weapons attack, the North Koreans overran the advance positions of the company, the mortar observation post, and the heavy machine gun positions. The initial enemy objective seemed to be to gain possession of the high ground east of Yongp'o in order to provide protection for the main crossing that was to follow. By 0900, however, the 2d Battalion, with the powerful help of the 77th Field Artillery Battalion and of air strikes, drove the enemy troops back through Yongp'o toward the bridge and dispersed them. [29]

It could not be assumed that this failure would end the efforts of the N.K. *10th Division* west of Taegu. In the three days from 10 to 12 August the Naktong River had dropped three feet and was only shoulder-deep at many places. The opportunity for large-scale enemy crossings was at hand. [30]

---

[27] *Ibid.*, p. 46, reproduces this captured order.

[28] 21st Inf Regt WD, 12 Aug 50; *Ibid.*, Unit Rpt 42, an. 1; 1st Cav Div WD, G-2 Narr, Aug 50; EUSAK WD, 14 Aug 50, ATIS Interrog Rpt 551, Lee Yong Il, 1st Cav Div WD, G-2 Interrog Rpt 0038, Aug 50, Lee Yong Il; ATIS Res Supp Interrog Rpts, Issue 104 (N.K. *10th Div*), pp. 47-48.

[29] 7th Cav Regt WD, 12 Aug 50; 1st Cav Div WD, 12 Aug 50.

[30] 5th Cav Regt WD, 12 Aug 50.

A more determined enemy crossing of the Naktong in the vicinity of the blown bridge between Tuksong-dong and Yongp'o began about dawn, 14 August. Men in the outposts of the 2d Battalion, 7th Cavalry Regiment, at 0520 heard voices in the pea patches and rice paddies to their front. By 0620, an estimated 500 enemy soldiers had penetrated as far as Yongp'o. Fifteen minutes later, close combat was in progress in the 2d Battalion positions near Wich'on-dong, a mile east of the crossing site.[31]

When word of the enemy crossing reached the 1st Cavalry Division command post before daylight, General Gay alerted his division reserve, Colonel Clainos' 1st Battalion, 7th Cavalry, to move on an hour's notice. More North Koreans crossed the river in the hours after daylight, and at 0800 General Gay ordered Colonel Clainos' battalion, already loaded into trucks, to move to the Yongp'o area to support the 2d Battalion.

Enemy artillery and tank fire from the west side of the river was supporting the crossing. At midmorning, large additional enemy forces just west of the river at Tuksong-dong and Panjang apparently were about ready to attempt a crossing in support of the units already heavily engaged on the east side. Some enemy troops were crossing in barges near the bridge. Air strikes bombed the North Koreans on the west side and artillery then took them under heavy fire. The 77th Field Artillery Battalion fired approximately 1,860 rounds into the enemy concentration. In delivering this heavy, rapid fire it damaged its gun tubes.[32]

In this attack the deepest North Korean penetration reached Samuni-dong, about a mile and a half beyond the blown bridge. There the combined fire of all infantry weapons, mortars, and artillery drove the enemy back toward the river. By noon, large groups of North Koreans were trying to recross the river to the west side. Forward observers adjusted artillery and mortar fire on the retreating enemy, causing heavy casualties.

By dusk, the 7th Cavalry had eliminated the enemy bridgehead at Yongp'o. In this battle, as in the one fought two days before, the 2d Battalion distinguished itself. This was the same battalion that only three weeks earlier had performed in a highly unsatisfactory manner east of Yongdong.

In this river-crossing battle, the only major one to take place along the Naktong actually at a crossing site, the *25th and 27th Regiments* of the N.K. *10th Division* suffered crippling losses. The 7th Cavalry Regiment estimated that of 1,700 enemy who had succeeded in crossing the river, 1,500 were killed. Two days after the battle, H Company reported it had buried 267 enemy dead behind its lines, while those in the rice paddies to its front were not counted. In front of its position, G Company counted 150 enemy dead. In contrast, G Company lost only 2 men killed and 3 wounded during the battle. One of its members, Pfc. Robert D. Robertson, a machine gunner, twice had bullets pierce his helmet in the half-inch space above

---

[31] 7th Cav Regt WD, 14 Aug 50.

[32] *Ibid.*; Gay, Ltr and comments, 24 Aug 53; Interv, author with Harris, 30 Apr 54.

THE TAEGU FRONT

his scalp and tear through several letters and photographs he carried there, but leave him unhurt.[33]

Among the enemy dead were found the bodies of two colonels. Found, also, were many enemy documents. One of these documents, dated 13 August, said in part:

Kim Il Sung has directed that the war be carried out so that its final victory can be realized by 15 August, fifth anniversary of the liberation of Korea. . . .
Our victory lies before our eyes. Young soldiers! You are fortunate in that you are able to participate in the battle for our final victory. Young soldiers, the capture of Taegu lies in the crossing of the Naktong River . . . The eyes of 30,000,000 people are fixed on the Naktong River crossing operation . . .
Pledge of all fighting men: We pledge with our life, no matter what hardships and sacrifice lies before us, to bear it and put forth our full effort to conclude the crossing of the Naktong River. Young Men! Let us protect our glorious pride by completely annihilating the enemy!![34]

These words may have stirred the young soldiers of the N.K. *10th Division* but their promise was not fulfilled. Instead, the Naktong valley and surrounding hills were to hold countless North Korean graves. In its first combat mission, the crossing of the Naktong on 12–14 August, the *10th Division*, according to prisoners, suffered 2,500 casualties, some units losing as much as 50 percent of their troops.[35]

Hill 303 at Waegwan

Almost simultaneously with the major enemy crossing effort in the southern part of the 1st Cavalry Division sector at Tuksong-dong and Yongp'o, another was taking place northward above Waegwan near the boundary between the division and the ROK 1st Division. The northernmost unit of the 1st Cavalry Division was G Company of the 5th Cavalry Regiment. It held Hill 303, the right-flank anchor of the U.S. Eighth Army.

Hill 303 is an elongated oval more than two miles long on a northeast-southwest axis with an extreme elevation of about 1,000 feet. It is the first hill mass north of Waegwan. Its southern slope comes down to the edge of the town; its crest, a little more than a mile to the northeast, towers nearly 950 feet above the river. It gives observation of Waegwan, the road net running out of the town, the railroad and highway bridges across the river at that point, and of long stretches of the river valley to the north and to the south. Its western slope terminates at the east bank of the Naktong. From Waegwan a road ran north and south along the east bank of the Naktong, another northeast through the mountains toward Tabu-dong, and still another southeast toward Taegu. Hill 303 was a critical terrain feature in control of the main Pusan-Seoul railroad and highway crossing of the Naktong, as well as of Waegwan itself.

For several days intelligence sources had reported heavy enemy concentrations across the Naktong opposite the ROK 1st Division. In the first hours of 14 August, an enemy regiment crossed the Naktong six miles north of Waeg-

---

[33] 7th Cav Regt WD, 14, 16 Aug 50; 1st Cav Div WD, 14 Aug 50.
[34] 1st Cav Div WD, G–2 Rpt, Aug 50, Batch 68, Transl 0034, 19 Aug 50; Gay, Ltr and comments, 24 Aug 53.
[35] ATIS Res Supp Interrog Rpts, Issue 104 (N.K. *10th Div*), p. 48.

WAEGWAN BRIDGE *over the Naktong River. Hill 303 is below the river at lower right.*

wan into the ROK 1st Division sector, over the second underwater bridge there. Shortly after midnight, ROK forces on the high ground just north of the U.S.-ROK Army boundary were under attack. After daylight an air strike partially destroyed the underwater bridge. The North Korean attack spread south and by noon enemy small arms fire fell on G Company, 5th Cavalry Regiment, on Hill 303. This crossing differed from earlier ones near the same place in that the enemy force instead of moving east into the mountains turned south and headed for Waegwan.[36]

Before dawn, 15 August, G Company men on Hill 303 could make out about fifty enemy troops accompanied by two tanks moving boldly south along the river road at the base of the hill. They also saw another column moving to their rear and soon heard it engage F Company with small arms fire. In order to escape the enemy encirclement, F Company withdrew southward. By 0830, North Koreans had completely surrounded G Company and a supporting platoon of H Company mortarmen on Hill 303. A relief column, composed of B Company, 5th Cavalry, and a platoon of tanks tried to reach G Company, but enemy fire drove it back.[37]

[36] 2n Bn, 5th Cav Regt WD, 14 Aug 50; 5th Cav Regt WD, 14 Aug 50; EUSAK WD, Aug 50 Summ; Ibid., G-2 PIR 33, 14 Aug 50.

[37] 5th Cav Regt WD, 15 Aug 50; 1st Cav Div WD, 15 Aug 50.

Again on 16 August, B Company and the tanks tried unsuccessfully to drive the enemy, now estimated to be a battalion of about 700 men, from Hill 303. The 61st Field Artillery Battalion and three howitzers of B Battery, 82d Field Artillery Battalion, fired on the enemy-held hill during the day. Waegwan was a no man's land. For the most part, the town was deserted. Col. Marcel B. Crombez, the regimental commander, relieved the 2d Battalion commander because he had lost control of his units and did not know where they were. A new commander prepared to resume the attack. During the night, G Company succeeded in escaping from Hill 303.[38]

Before dawn of the 17th, troops from both the 1st and 2d Battalions of the 5th Cavalry Regiment, supported by A Company, 70th Tank Battalion, attacked Hill 303, but heavy enemy mortar fire stopped them at the edge of Waegwan. During the morning, heavy artillery preparations pounded the enemy positions on Hill 303, the 61st Field Artillery Battalion alone firing 1,159 rounds. The 5th Cavalry at 1130 asked the division for assistance and learned that the Air Force would deliver a strike on the hill at 1400.[39]

The air strike came in as scheduled, the planes dropping napalm and bombs, firing rockets, and strafing. The strike was on target and, together with an artillery preparation, was dramatically successful. After the strike, the infantry at 1530 attacked up the hill unopposed and secured it by 1630. The combined strength of E and F Companies on top of the hill was about sixty men. The artillery preparations and the air strike killed and wounded an estimated 500 enemy troops on Hill 303. Approximately 200 enemy bodies littered the hill. Survivors had fled in complete rout after the air strike.[40]

Tragedy on Hill 303

In regaining Hill 303 on 17 August the 5th Cavalry Regiment came upon a pitiful scene—the bodies of twenty-six mortarmen of H Company, hands tied in back, sprayed with burp gun bullets. First knowledge of the tragedy came in the afternoon when scouts brought in a man from Hill 303, Pvt. Roy Manring of the Heavy Mortar Platoon, who had been wounded in both legs and one arm by burp gun slugs. Manring had crawled down the hill until he saw scouts of the attacking force. After he told his story, some men of the I&R Platoon of the 5th Cavalry Regiment under Lt. Paul Kelly went forward, following Manring's directions, to the scene of the tragedy. One of those present has described what they saw:

The boys lay packed tightly, shoulder to shoulder, lying on their sides, curled like babies sleeping in the sun. Their feet, bloodied and bare, from walking on the rocks, stuck out stiffly . . . All had hands tied behind their backs, some with cord, others with regular issue army communica-

---

[38] 2d Bn, 5th Cav Regt WD, 16–17 Aug 50; Interv, author with Brig Gen Marcel B. Crombez, 28 Jun 55.
[39] 2d Bn, 5th Cav Regt WD, 17 Aug 50; 61st FA Bn WD, 17 Aug 50.

[40] 5th Cav Regt WD, 17 Aug 50; 1st Cav Div WD, 17 Aug 50; 2d Bn, 5th Cav Regt WD, 19 Aug 50. The North Korean communiqué for 17 August, monitored in London, claimed the complete "liberation" of Waegwan on that date. See New York *Times*, August 18, 1950.

tion wire. Only a few of the hands were clenched.[41]

The rest of the I&R Platoon circled the hill and captured two North Korean soldiers. They proved to be members of the group that had captured and held the mortarmen prisoners. From them and a third captured later, as well as five survivors among the mortarmen, have come the following details of what happened to the ill-fated group on Hill 303.[42]

Before dawn on Tuesday morning, 15 August, the mortar platoon became aware of enemy activity near Hill 303. The platoon leader telephoned the Commanding Officer, G Company, 5th Cavalry, who informed him that a platoon of some sixty ROK's would come to reinforce the mortar platoon. About breakfast time the men heard tank motors and saw two enemy tanks followed by 200 or more enemy soldiers on the road below them. A little later a group of Koreans appeared on the slope. A patrol going to meet the climbing Koreans called out and received in reply a blast of automatic weapons fire. The mortar platoon leader, in spite of this, believed they were friendly. The watching Americans were not convinced that they were enemy soldiers until the red stars became visible on their caps. They were then close upon the Americans. The North Koreans came right up to the foxholes without either side firing a shot. Some pushed burp guns into the sides of the mortarmen with one hand and held out the other as though to shake hands. One of the enemy soldiers remarked later that "the American soldiers looked dazed." [43]

The *4th Company, 2d Battalion, 206th Mechanized Infantry Regiment* of the *105th Armored Division*, apparently were the captors, although some members of *Headquarters Company* of the 45-mm. *Artillery Battalion, 105th Armored Division*, were present. The North Koreans marched the prisoners down the hill after taking their weapons and valuables. In an orchard they tied the prisoners' hands behind their backs, took some of their clothing, and removed their shoes. They told the Americans they would send them to the Seoul prisoner of war camp if they behaved well.

Apparently the original captors did not retain possession of the prisoners throughout the next two days. There is some evidence that a company of the N.K. *3d Division* guarded them after capture. It appears that the enemy force that crossed the Naktong above Waegwan on the 14th and turned south to

---

[41] Charles and Eugene Jones, *The Face of War*, pp. 45–49. At least one of the Jones brothers accompanied the I&R Platoon on this mission. See also 5th Cav Regt WD, 17 Aug 50; 1st Cav Div WD, 17 Aug 50.

[42] JAG, Korean War Crimes, Case Nr 16, 17 Jul 53.

[43] *Ibid.*, Statement of Chong Myong Tok, PW 216. The other North Korean captured with Chong on 17 August was Kim Kwon Taek, PW 217. Heo Chang Keun was the third prisoner who had personal knowledge of this incident.

It is not clear how many men were captured in the mortar platoon. The 5th Cav Regt WD, 17 Aug 50, said 41; one of the survivors said there were 43; one of the captured North Koreans said about 40; and another said about 45. For contemporary press reports of interviews with survivors see New York *Herald Tribune*, August 18, 1950, quoting Cpl. James M. Rudd; New York *Times*, August 18, 1950, account by Harold Faber based on interview with Roy Manring; *Life* Magazine, September 4, 1950, p. 36, based on interview with Cpl. Roy L. Day, Jr.; and *Newsweek*, August 28, 1950, p. 25, for personal accounts.

THE TAEGU FRONT

Hill 303 and Waegwan was part of the *3d Division* and supporting elements of the *105th Armored Division*. In any event, the first night the North Koreans gave their prisoners water, fruit, and cigarettes. They intended to move them across the Naktong that night, but American fire prevented it. During the night two of the Americans loosened the shoe laces binding their wrists. This caused a commotion. At least one of the survivors thought that a North Korean officer shot one of his men who threatened to shoot the men who had tried to free their hands.

The next day, 16 August, the prisoners were moved around a great deal with their guards. One of the mortarmen, Cpl. Roy L. Day, Jr., spoke Japanese and could converse with some of the North Koreans. That afternoon he overheard a North Korean lieutenant say that they would kill the prisoners if American soldiers came too close. That night guards took away five of the Americans; the others did not know what became of them.

On the morning of 17 August, the guards exchanged fire with U.S. soldiers. Toward noon the North Korean unit holding the Americans placed them in a gulley with a few guards. Then came the intense American artillery preparations and the air strike on the hill. At this time a North Korean officer said that American soldiers were closing in on them, that they could not continue to hold the prisoners, and that they must be shot. The officer gave the order and, according to one of those who participated, the entire company of fifty men fired into the kneeling Americans as they rested in the gulley. Some of the survivors said, however, that a group of 14 to 20 enemy soldiers ran up when 2 of their guards yelled a signal and fired into them with burp guns. Before all the enemy soldiers left the area, some of them came back to the ravine and shot again those who were groaning. Cpl. James M. Rudd escaped death from the blazing burp guns when the man at his side fell dead on top of him. Rudd, hit three times in the legs and arms, burrowed under the bodies of his fallen comrades for more protection. Four others escaped in a similar way. Two of them in making their way down the hill later were fired upon, but fortunately not hit, by 5th Cavalry soldiers attacking up the hill, before they could establish their identity.[44]

That night additional atrocities occurred near Hill 303. Near Waegwan, enemy antitank fire hit and knocked out two tanks of the 70th Tank Battalion. The next day, 18 August, American troops found the bodies of six members of the tank crews showing indications that they had been captured and executed.[45]

These incidents on Hill 303 and vicinity caused General MacArthur on 20 August to broadcast an announcement to the North Korean Army and address a leaflet to the Commander-in-Chief Armed Forces of North Korea, denouncing the atrocities. The Air Force dropped the leaflets over North Korea in large numbers. General MacArthur closed his message by saying:

---

[44] JAG, Korean War Crimes, Case Nr 16, 17 Jul 53, citing 1st Cav Div ltr, 23 Aug 50; War Diaries of 5th Cav Regt and 1st Cav Div. These and published accounts by survivors are the principal sources for the above account. Also see 2d Log Comd Activities Rpt, JA Sec, Sep 50.

[45] EUSAK WD, G-3 Jnl, 0945, 18 Aug 50.

MAJ. GEN. PAIK SUN YUP

manding the N.K. *3d Division*, transmitted an order pertaining to the treatment of prisoners of war, signed by Kim Chaek, Commander-in-Chief, and Kang Kon, Commanding General Staff, *Advanced General Headquarters* of the North Korean Army, which stated:

1. The unnecessary killing of enemy personnel when they could be taken as PsW shall be strictly prohibited as of now. Those who surrender will be taken as PsW, and all efforts will be made to destroy the enemy in thought and politically.
2. Treatment of PsW shall be according to the regulations issued by the Supreme Hq, as attached herein, pertaining to the regulation and order of PW camps.
3. This directive will be explained to and understood by all military personnel immediately, and staff members of the Cultural Section will be responsible for seeing that this is carried out.[47]

Inertia on your part and on the part of your senior field commanders in the discharge of this grave and universally recognized command responsibility may only be construed as a condonation and encouragement of such outrage, for which if not promptly corrected I shall hold you and your commanders criminally accountable under the rules and precedents of war."[46]

There is no evidence that the North Korean High Command sanctioned the shooting of prisoners during this phase of the war. What took place on Hill 303 and elsewhere in the first months of the war appears to have been perpetrated by uncontrolled small units, by vindictive individuals, or because of unfavorable and increasingly desperate situations confronting the captors. On 28 July 1950, General Lee Yong Ho, com-

Another document captured in September shows that the North Korean Army was aware of the conduct of some of its soldiers and was somewhat concerned about it. An order issued by the Cultural Section of the N.K. *2d Division*, 16 August 1950, said in part, "Some of us are still slaughtering enemy troops that come to surrender. Therefore, the responsibility of teaching the soldiers to take prisoners of war and to treat them kindly rests on the Political Section of each unit."[48]

Carpet Bombing Opposite Waegwan

In the stretch of mountain country northeast of Waegwan and Hill 303, the ROK 1st Division daily absorbed

---

[46] *Ibid.*, 22 Aug 50, has full text of MacArthur's message; see also New York *Times*, August 21, 1950.

[47] ATIS Enemy Docs, Issue 4, p. 2 (captured by U.S. 8th Cav Regt, 6 Sep 50).

[48] *Ibid.*, Issue 9, p. 102 (captured 12 Sep 50 near Changnyong, apparently by U.S. 2d Div).

North Korean attacks during the middle of August. Enemy pressure against this ROK division never ceased for long. Under the strong leadership of Maj. Gen. Paik Sun Yup, this division fought a valiant and bloody defense of the mountain approaches to Taegu. American artillery fire from the 1st Cavalry Division sector supported the division in part of its sector. The ROK 13th Regiment still held some positions along the river, while the 11th and 12th Regiments engaged the enemy in the high mountain masses of Suam-san and Yuhak-san, west and northwest of Tabu-dong and 4 to 6 miles east of the Naktong River. The North Koreans kept in repair their underwater bridge across the Naktong 6 miles north of Waegwan in front of Hills 201 and 346. Even direct hits on this bridge by 155-mm. howitzers did not seem to damage it seriously.[49]

The enemy penetration at the middle of August in the ROK 13th Regiment sector and along the boundary in the 5th Cavalry sector at Waegwan and Hill 303, together with increasingly heavy pressure against the main force of the ROK 1st Division in the Tabu-dong area, began to jeopardize the safety of Taegu. On 16 August, 750 Korean police were stationed on the outskirts of the city as an added precaution. Refugees had swollen Taegu's normal population of 300,000 to 700,000. A crisis seemed to be developing among the people on 18 August when early in the morning seven rounds of enemy artillery shells landed in Taegu. The shells, falling near the railroad station, damaged the roundhouse, destroyed one yard engine, killed one Korean civilian, and wounded eight others. The Korean Provincial Government during the day ordered the evacuation of Taegu, and President Syngman Rhee moved his capital to Pusan.[50]

This action by the South Korean authorities created a most dangerous situation. Swarms of panicked Koreans began to pour out on the roads leading from the city, threatening to stop all military traffic. At the same time, the evacuation of the city by the native population tended to undermine the morale of the troops defending it. Strong action by the Co-ordinator for Protection of Lines of Communication, Eighth Army, halted the evacuation. Twice more the enemy gun shelled Taegu, the third and last time on Sunday night, 20 August. At this time, six battalions of Korean police moved to important rail and highway tunnels within the Pusan Perimeter to reinforce their security.[51]

Just as the enemy attack on Waegwan and Hill 303 began, mounting concern for the safety of Taegu—and reports of continued enemy concentrations across the river opposite the ROK 1st and the U.S. 1st Cavalry Divisions in the Waegwan area—led to an extraordinary bomb-

---

[49] 1st Cav Div WD, 21-24 Aug 50; 1st Cav Div Arty WD, 22 Aug 50; GHQ FEC G-3 Opn Rpt 60, 23 Aug 50.

[50] EUSAK WD, G-3 Sec, 16 Aug 50; Ibid., entry 3, 18 Aug, Med Stf Sec Rpt; Ibid., G-3 Sec Rpt, entry 2; Ibid., Aug 50 Summ, p. 52; New York Times, August 18, 1950; New York Herald Tribune, August 18, 1950.

[51] EUSAK WD, Aug 50 Summ, p. 52; 1st Cav Div Arty WD, 21 Aug 50; New York Herald Tribune, August 18, 1950; New York Times, August 16 and 21, 1950. Seoul City Sue began to make propaganda broadcasts at this time. Members of the 588th Military Police Company first heard her about 10 August.

ing mission. On 14 August, General MacArthur summoned to his Tokyo office General Stratemeyer, commanding general of the Far East Air Forces, and told him he wanted a carpet bombing of the North Korean concentrations threatening the Pusan Perimeter.[52] General Stratemeyer talked with Maj. Gen. Emmett (Rosie) O'Donnell, Jr., commanding general of the Far East Bomber Command, who said a relatively good job of bombing could be done on a 3-by-5 mile area. General MacArthur's headquarters selected a 27-square-mile rectangular area 3½ miles east to west by 7½ miles north to south on the west side of the Naktong River opposite the ROK 1st Division. The southeast corner of this rectangle was just north of Waegwan. Intelligence estimates placed the greatest concentrations of enemy troops in this area, some estimates being as high as four enemy divisions and several armored regiments, totaling approximately 40,000 men.[53]

General Gay, commanding the 1st Cavalry Division, repeatedly requested that the bombing include the area northeast of Waegwan, between the Naktong River and the Waegwan–Tabu-dong road. This request was denied because of fear that bombing there might cause casualties among the 1st Cavalry and ROK 1st Division troops, even though General Gay pointed out that terrain features sharply defined the area he recommended. General Gay also offered to have 1st Cavalry Division L–19 planes lead the bombers to this target.[54]

FEAF ordered a five-group mission of B–29's from Japan and Okinawa for 16 August. Since there was no indication of enemy groupings in the target area, the bomber command divided it into twelve equal squares with an aiming point in the center of each square. One squadron of B–29's was to attack each square.

At 1158, 16 August, the first of the 98 B–29's of the 19th, 22d, 92d, 98th, and 307th Bomber Groups arrived over the target area; the last cleared it at 1224. The bombers from 10,000 feet dropped approximately 960 tons of 500- and 1,000-pound general purpose bombs. The bomber crews reported only that the bombs were on target. General O'Donnell was in the air over the target area for more than two hours, but he saw no sign of enemy activity below.[55]

General Walker reported to General MacArthur the next day that the damage done to the enemy by the "carpet bombing of 16 August could not be evaluated." Because of smoke and dust, observation, he said, was difficult from the air and the impact area was too far to the west to be observed by U.S. and ROK ground troops. Ground patrols sent out to investigate the bombed area never reached it. One 1st Cavalry Division patrol did not even get across the river, and enemy fire stopped another just after it crossed. The U.N. Command could not show by specific, concrete evi-

---

[52] Col Ethelred L. Sykes' diary. Sykes was on General Stratemeyer's staff in Tokyo in the summer of 1950.

[53] "Air War in Korea, II," *Air University Quarterly Review*, IV, No. 3 (Spring, 1951), 60; EUSAK WD, Aug 50 Summ.

[54] Gay, Ltr and comments, 24 Aug 53.

[55] "Air War in Korea," *op. cit.*; EUSAK WD, 17 Aug 50, G–3 Sec, 171115 Aug 50; GHQ FEC G–3 Opn Rpt 53, 16 Aug 50; New York *Times*, August 16, 1950, R. J. H. Johnston dispatch.

dence that this massive bombing attack had killed a single North Korean soldier.[56] Information obtained later from prisoners made clear that the enemy divisions the Far East Command thought to be still west of the Naktong had, in fact, already crossed to the east side and were not in the bombed area. The only benefit that seemingly resulted from the bombing was a sharp decrease in the amount of enemy artillery fire that, for a period after the bombing, fell in the 1st Cavalry and ROK 1st Division sectors.

Generals Walker, Partridge, and O'Donnell reportedly opposed future massive carpet bombing attacks against enemy tactical troops unless there was precise information on an enemy concentration and the situation should be extremely critical. The personal intercession of General Stratemeyer with General MacArthur caused the cancellation of a second pattern bombing of an area east of the Naktong scheduled for 19 August.[57]

Bowling Alley—The Sangju-Taegu Corridor

The 27th Infantry Regiment of the 25th Divison had just completed its mission of clearing the North Koreans from the southern part of the Naktong Bulge area in the 24th Division sector when the enemy pressure north of Taegu caused new alarm in Eighth Army headquarters. Acting on the threat from this quarter, Eighth Army on 14 August relieved the regiment from attachment to the 24th Division and the next day ordered it northward to Kyongsan in army reserve. Upon arrival at Kyongsan on 16 August, Colonel Michaelis received orders to reconnoiter routes east, north, northwest, and west of Kyongsan and be prepared on army orders to counter any enemy thrusts from these directions. During the day, two enemy tanks came through the ROK 1st Division lines twelve miles north of Taegu at Tabu-dong, but ROK 3.5-inch bazooka teams knocked out both of them.[58]

At noon the next day, 17 August, Eighth Army ordered the 27th Infantry to move its headquarters and a reinforced battalion "without delay" to a point across the Kumho River three miles north of Taegu on the Tabu-dong–Sangju road "to secure Taegu from enemy penetration" from that direction. ROK sources reported that a North Korean regiment, led by six tanks, had entered the little village of Kumhwa, two miles north of Tabu-dong.

The 1st Battalion, 27th Infantry; a platoon of the Heavy Mortar Company; and the 8th Field Artillery Battalion, less B Battery, moved north of Taegu at noon. Later in the day this force moved two miles farther north to Ch'ilgok where the ROK 1st Division command post was located. By dark, the entire 27th Regiment was north of Taegu on the Tabu-dong road, reinforced by C Company, 73d Tank Battalion. Alarm spread in Taegu where artillery fire to the north could be heard. Eighth Army

---

[56] EUSAK WD, 17 Aug 50, G-3 Sec, Msg 171115; 1st Cav Div WD, 16 Aug 50; 5th Cav Regt WD, 16 Aug 50; New York *Times*, August 17, 1950; New York *Herald Tribune*, August 17, 1950.

[57] Sykes diary; "Air War in Korea," *op. cit.*

[58] 27th Inf WD, 15–16 Aug 50; GHQ FEC Sitrep, 14 Aug 50; EUSAK WD, Opn Directive, 16 Aug 50; *Ibid.*, G-3 Sec, 16 Aug 50; *Ibid.*, Aug 50 Summ, p. 47.

ordered the 37th Field Artillery Battalion, less A Battery, to move from the Kyongju–P'ohang-dong area, where a heavy battle had been in progress for days, for attachment to the 27th Infantry Regiment in order to reinforce the fires of the 8th Field Artillery Battalion above Taegu. It arrived there the next day.[59] To the south at this same time the critical battle at Obong-ni Ridge and Cloverleaf Hill was still undecided.

In its part of the Perimeter battle, the N.K. *13th Division* had broken through into the Tabu-dong corridor and had started driving on Taegu. This division had battled the ROK 11th and 12th Regiments in the high Yuhak-san area for a week before it broke through to the corridor on 17 August. A regimental commander of the division said later it suffered 1,500 casualties in achieving that victory. On 18 August the *13th Division* was concentrated mostly west of the road just north of Tabu-dong.[60]

To the west of the *13th*, the N.K. *15th Division* also was now deployed on Yuhak-san. It, too, had begun battling the ROK 1st Division, but thus far only in minor engagements. At this critical point, the North Korean High Command ordered the *15th Division* to move from its position northwest of Tabu-dong eastward to the Yongch'on front, where the N.K. *8th Division* had failed to advance toward the Taegu lateral corridor. The *15th* left the Yuhak-san area on or about 20 August. Meanwhile, the N.K. *1st Division* on the left, or east, of the *13th* advanced to the Kunwi area, twenty-five miles north of Taegu. The North Korean command now ordered it to proceed to the Tabu-dong area and come up abreast of the *13th Division* for the attack on Taegu down the Tabu-dong corridor.

At this juncture, the North Koreans received their only large tank reinforcements during the Pusan Perimeter fighting. On or about 15 August, the *105th Armored Division* received 21 new T34 tanks and 200 troop replacements, which it distributed to the divisions attacking Taegu. The tank regiment with the N.K. *13th Division* reportedly had 14 tanks.[61]

This was the enemy situation, with the *13th Division* astride the Sangju–Taegu road just above Tabu-dong and only thirteen miles from Taegu, when Eighth Army on 18 August ordered the 27th Infantry Regiment to attack north along the road. At the same time, two regiments of the ROK 1st Division were to attack along high ground on either side of the road. The plan called for a limited objective attack to restore the ROK 1st Division lines in the vicinity

---

[59] 1st Bn, 27th Inf WD, 17 Aug 50, 27th Inf WD, 17 Aug 50; EUSAK WD, G-3 Sec, Msg 171210 Aug 50; *Ibid.*, G-3 Sec, 17 Aug 50; 37th FA Bn WD, 17–18 Aug 50; New York *Times*, August 18, 1950, Parrott dispatch from Eighth Army Hq.

[60] ATIS Res Supp Interrog Rpts, Issue 105 (N.K. *13th Div*), p. 64; ATIS Interrog Rpts, Issue 2, Rpt 771, p. 160, Lt Col Chong Pong Uk, CO, *Arty Regt*, N.K. *13th Div* (Col Chong surrendered on 22 Aug 50). Other interrog rpts on Col Chong are to be found in Issue 3, Rpt 733, p. 78 and Rpt 831, p. 66, and EUSAK WD, 24 Aug 50, G-2 Sec, Interrog Rpt 771; EUSAK WD, 5 Sep 50, ATIS Interrog Rpt 895, Maj Kim Song Jun, S-3, *19th Regt*, N. K. *13th Div*, and later CO of the regt; ATIS Interrog Rpts, Issue 3, Rpt 895, Maj Kim.

[61] ATIS Interrog Rpts, Issue 9 (N.K. Forces), Rpt 1468, pp. 158–74, Sr Col Lee Hak Ku, CofS N.K. *13th Div*, formerly G-3 N.K. *II Corps;* ATIS Res Supp Interrog Rpts, Issue 3 (N.K. *15th Div*), p. 43, Issue 3 (N.K. *1st Div*), p. 34, and Issue 4 (*105th Armord Div*), p. 39, interrog of Col Chong; ATIS Interrog Rpts, Issue 2, Rpt 777, p. 177, Lt Han.

of Sokchok, a village four miles north of Tabu-dong. The line of departure was just north of Tabu-dong. Pershing M26 tanks of C Company, 73d Tank Battalion, and two batteries of the 37th Field Artillery Battalion were to support the 27th Infantry.[62]

As the trucks rolled northward from Tabu-dong and approached the line of departure, the men inside could see the North Koreans and ROK's fighting on the high hills overlooking the road. The infantry dismounted and deployed, Colonel Check's 1st Battalion on the left of the road and Colonel Murch's 2d Battalion on the right of it. With tanks leading on the road, the two battalions crossed the line of departure at 1300. The tanks opened fire against the mountain escarpments, and the rumble of their cannonade echoed through the narrow valley. The infantry on either side of the road swept the lower hills, the tanks on the road pacing their advance to the infantry's. An enemy outpost line in the valley withdrew and there was almost no opposition during the first hour. This enemy outpost line proved to be about two and a half miles in front of the main positions. The 27th Infantry had reached a point about two miles north of Tabu-dong when Colonel Michaelis received a message stating that neither of the ROK regiments on the high ground flanking the valley road had been able to advance. He was ordered to halt and form a perimeter defense with both battalions astride the road.[63]

The two battalions of the 27th Infantry went into a perimeter defense just north of the little mud-thatched village of Soi-ri. The 1st Battalion, on the left of the road, took a position with C Company on high ground somewhat in advance of any other infantry unit, and with A Company on a ridge behind it. On their right, B Company, somewhat in advance of A Company, carried the line across the stream and the narrow valley to the road. There the 2d Battalion took up the defense line with E Company on the road and east of it and F Company on its right, while G Company held a ridge behind F Company. Thus, the two battalions presented a four-company front, with one company holding a refused flank position on either side. A platoon of tanks took positions on the front line, two tanks on the road and two in the stream bed; four more tanks were back of the line in reserve. The artillery went into firing positions back of the infantry. Six bazooka teams took up positions in front of the infantry positions along the road and in the stream bed.[64] The ROK 1st Division held the high ground on either side of the 27th Infantry positions.

In front of the 27th Infantry position, the poplar-lined Taegu-Sangju road ran northward on a level course in the narrow mountain valley. A stream on the west closely paralleled it. The road was nearly straight on a north-south axis through the 27th Infantry position and for some distance northward. Then it veered slightly westward. This stretch of

---

[62] EUSAK WD, Br for CG, 18 Aug 50; *Ibid.*, G-3 Stf Sec Rpt, 18 Aug 50, entry 2; 27th Inf WD, 18 Aug 50; GHQ FEC Sitrep, 18 Aug 50.

[63] 1st Bn, 27th Inf WD, 18 Aug 50; Ltr, Check to author, 29 Sep 53.

---

[64] 2d Bn, 27th Inf WD, Aug 50, sketch map of Soi-ri position, 18-25 Aug; Ltr, Check to author, 29 Sep 53, and attached sketch map of 27th Inf position; Interv, author with Check, 6 Feb 53.

THE BOWLING ALLEY

the road later became known as the "Bowling Alley."

A little more than a mile in front of the 27th Infantry position the road forked at a small cluster of houses called Ch'onp'yong-dong; the lefthand prong was the main Sangju road, the righthand one the road to Kunwi. At the road fork, the Sangju road bends northwestward in a long curve. The village of Sinjumak lay on this curve a short distance north of the fork. Hills protected it against direct fire from the 27th Infantry position. It was there, apparently, that the enemy tanks remained hidden during the daytime.

Rising abruptly from the valley on the west side was the Yuhak-san mountain mass which swept up to a height of 2,700 feet. On the east, a similar mountain mass rose to a height of 2,400 feet, culminating two and a half miles southward in towering Ka-san, more than 2,900 feet high at its walled summit. This high ground looks down southward into the Taegu bowl and gives observation of the surrounding country.

The Kunwi and Sangju roads from the northeast and northwest entered at Ch'onp'yong-dong the natural and easy corridor between Yuhak-san and Ka-san leading into the Taegu basin. The battles of the Bowling Alley took place just south of this road junction.

The first of seven successive enemy night attacks struck against the 27th Infantry defense perimeter shortly after dark that night, 18 August. Enemy mortars and artillery fired a heavy preparation for the attack. Two enemy tanks and a self-propelled gun moved out of the village of Sinjumak two miles in front of the 27th Infantry lines. Infantry followed them, some in trucks and others on foot. The lead tank moved slowly and without firing, apparently observing, while the second one and the self-propelled gun fired repeatedly into F Company's position. The tank machine gun fire seemed indiscriminate, as if the enemy did not know the exact location of the American positions. As the tanks drew near, a 3.5-inch bazooka team from F Company destroyed the second one in line. Bazooka teams also hit the lead tank twice but the rockets failed to ex-

plode. The crew, however, abandoned the tank. Fire from the 8th Field Artillery Battalion knocked out the self-propelled gun, destroyed two trucks, and killed or wounded an estimated hundred. Lt. Lewis Millett, an artillery forward observer, and later a Medal of Honor winner after he transferred to the infantry, directed this artillery fire on the enemy with a T34 tank within fifty yards of his foxhole. Three more enemy tanks had come down the road, but now they switched on their running lights, turned around, and went back north. Half an hour after midnight the entire action was over and all was quiet. Enemy troops made a second effort, much weaker than the first, about two hours later but artillery and mortar fire dispersed them.[65]

Certain characteristics were common to all the night battles in the Bowling Alley. The North Koreans used a system of flares to signal various actions and to co-ordinate them. It became quickly apparent to the defending Americans that green flares were used to signal an attack on a given area. So the 27th Infantry obtained its own green flares and then, after the enemy attack had begun, fired them over its main defensive positions. This confused the attacking North Koreans and often drew them to the points of greatest strength where they suffered heavy casualties. The use of mines in front of the defensive positions in the narrow valley became a nightly feature of the battles. The mines would stop the tanks and the infantry would try to remove them. At such times flares illuminated the scene and preregistered artillery and mortar fire came down on the immobilized enemy with fatal results.

On the morning of 19 August, the ROK 11th and 13th Regiments launched counterattacks along the ridges with some gains. General Walker ordered another reserve unit, a battalion of the ROK 10th Regiment, to the Taegu front to close a gap that had developed between

---

[65] 2d Bn, 27th Inf WD, Aug 50 Summ of Activities, 18 Aug; 1st Bn, 27th Inf WD, 18 Aug 50; 27th Inf WD, 18–19 Aug 50; New York *Herald Tribune*, August 21, 1950, Bigart dispatch, 20 August; Check, MS review comments, 6 Dec 57.

TANK ACTION IN THE BOWLING ALLEY, *21 August.*

the ROK 1st and 6th Divisions. In the afternoon he ordered still another unit, the U.S. 23d Infantry, to move up and establish a defense perimeter around the 8th and 37th Field Artillery Battalions eight miles north of Taegu. The 3d Battalion took up a defensive position around the artillery while the 2d Battalion occupied a defensive position astride the road behind the 27th Infantry. The next day the two battalions exchanged places.[66]

Sunday, 20 August, was a day of relative quiet on the Taegu front. Even so, United States aircraft attacked North Korean positions there repeatedly during the day. The planes began their strafing runs so close in front of the American infantry that their machine gun fire dotted the identification panels, and expended .50-caliber cartridges fell into friendly foxholes. General Walker visited the Taegu front during the day, and later made the statement that enemy fire had decreased and that Taegu "certainly is saved."[67]

By contrast, that night was not quiet. At 1700, a barrage of enemy 120-mm. mortar shells fell in the Heavy Weapons Company area. A bright moon silhouetted enemy tanks against the dark flanking mountains as they rumbled down the narrow, green valley, leading another attack. Artillery and mortar fire fell among them and the advancing enemy infantry. Waiting Americans held their small arms and machine gun fire until the North Koreans were within 150–200 yards' range. The combined fire of all weapons repulsed this attack.

The next morning, 21 August, a patrol of two platoons of infantry and

[66] 27th Inf WD, 19 Aug 50; 23d Inf WD, Aug 50 Narr Summ, p. 7; EUSAK WD, G-3 Sec, 19 Aug 50; ROK Army Hq, MS review comments, Jul 58.

[67] 1st Bn, 27th Inf WD, 20 Aug 50; EUSAK G-3 Jnl, 200955 Aug 50; New York *Herald Tribune,* August 21, 1950.

THE TAEGU FRONT

three tanks went up the road toward the enemy positions. White flags had appeared in front of the American line, and rumors received from natives alleged that many North Koreans wanted to surrender. The patrol's mission was to investigate this situation and to form an estimate of enemy losses. The patrol advanced about a mile, engaging small enemy groups and receiving some artillery fire. On its way it completed the destruction with thermite grenades of five enemy tanks disabled in the night action. The patrol also found 1 37-mm. antitank gun, 2 self-propelled guns, and 1 120-mm. mortar among the destroyed enemy equipment, and saw numerous enemy dead. At the point of farthest advance, the patrol found and destroyed an abandoned enemy tank in a village schoolhouse courtyard.[68]

That evening at dusk the 27th Infantry placed an antitank mine field, antipersonnel mines, and trip flares across the road and stream bed 150 yards in front of the infantry line. A second belt of mines, laid on top of the ground, was placed about 100 yards in front of the buried mine field.

Later that evening, 21 August, the North Koreans shelled the general area of the 27th Infantry positions until just before midnight. Then the N.K. *13th Division* launched a major attack against the ROK units on the high ground and the Americans in the valley. Nine tanks and several SP guns supported the enemy troops in the valley. Because it was on higher ground and more advanced than any other American unit, C Company on the left of the road usually was the first to detect an approaching attack. That evening the C Company commander telephoned that he could hear tanks out front. When the artillery fired an illuminating shell he was able to count nineteen vehicles in the attacking column on the road. The tanks and self-propelled guns, firing rapidly, approached the American positions. Most of their shells landed in the rear areas. Enemy infantry moved forward on both sides of the road. Simultaneously, other units attacked the ROK's on the high ridges flanking the valley.

American artillery and mortar fire bombarded the enemy, trying to separate the tanks from the infantry. Machine gun fire opened on the N.K. infantry only after they had entered the mine field and were at close range. The Pershing tanks in the front line held their fire until the enemy tanks came very close. One of the American tanks knocked out the lead enemy tank at a range of 125 yards. A 3.5-inch bazooka team from F Company knocked out a SP gun, the third vehicle in column. The trapped second tank was disabled by bazooka fire and abandoned by its crew. Artillery and 90-mm. tank fire destroyed seven more enemy tanks, three more SP guns, and several trucks and personnel carriers. This night battle lasted about five hours. The fire from both sides was intense. On the American side, a partial tabulation shows that in support of the 2d Battalion, 27th Infantry, B Battery, 8th Field Artillery Battalion (105-mm. howitzers), fired 1,661 rounds, the 4.2-inch mortar platoon fired 902 rounds, the 81-mm. mortar platoon fired 1,200 rounds, and F Company itself fired 385

---

[68] 27th Inf WD, 21 Aug 50; 1st Bn, 27th Inf WD, 21 Aug 50; Ltr, Check to author, 29 Sep 53; New York *Herald Tribune*, August 22, 1950, Bigart dispatch, 21 August.

60-mm. mortar rounds. The enemy column was destroyed. Patrols after daylight counted enemy dead in front of the perimeter position, and on that basis, they estimated the North Koreans had suffered 1,300 casualties in the night battle. Eleven prisoners captured by the patrol said the action had decimated their units and that only about one-fourth of their number remained.[69]

The men of F Company, 27th Infantry apparently coined the name Bowling Alley during the night battle of 21-22 August. The enemy T34 tanks fired armor-piercing shells straight up the road toward the American positions, hoping to knock out the American tanks. The balls of fire hurtling through the night and the reverberations of the gun reports appeared to the men witnessing and listening to the wild scene like bowling balls streaking down an alley toward targets at the other end.[70]

During the night battle, enemy forces infiltrated along the high ridge line around the east flank of the 27th Infantry and appeared the next day about noon 6 miles in the rear of that regiment and only 9 miles from Taegu. This enemy force was the *1st Regiment* of the N.K. *1st Division* which had just arrived from the Kunwi area to join in the battle for Taegu. It brought the main supply road of the 27th Infantry under small arms fire along a 5-mile stretch, beginning at a point 9 miles above Taegu and extending northward.[71]

About this time, Colonel Michaelis sent an urgent message to Eighth Army saying that the ROK troops on his left had given way and that "those people are not fighting." Prisoners told him, he said, that about 1,000 North Koreans were on his west flank. He asked for an air strike.[72]

It must not go unnoticed that all the time the 27th Infantry and supporting units were fighting along the road, the ROK 1st Division was fighting in the mountains on either side. Had these ROK troops been driven from this high ground, the perimeter position of the 27th Infantry Regiment would have been untenable. Several times the ROK troops came off the mountains in daytime looking for food in the valley and a bath in the stream. But then, supported by the American artillery, they always climbed back up the heights and reoccupied the high ground. The ROK 1st Division must receive a generous share of the credit for holding the front north of Taegu at this time.

General Paik bitterly resented Colonel Michaelis' charge that his men were not fighting. He said he would like to hold the valley position with all the tank and artillery support given the 27th Regiment while that regiment went up on the hills and fought the night battles

---

[69] 2d Bn, 27th Inf WD, Activities Rpt, 21 Aug, and Summ of Activities, 21-22 Aug 50; Ltr, Check to author, 29 Sep 53; Interv, author with Check, 6 Feb 53; ATIS Interrog Rpts,, Issue 3, Rpt 895, Maj Kim Song Jun, CO *19th Regt, 13th Div*, 21 Aug 50; EUSAK WD, 5 Sep 50, ATIS Interrog Rpt 895. The North Korean division commander blamed the *19th Regiment* for incompetence and failure to correlate its action with the rest of the division in this battle.

[70] 2d Bn, 27th Inf WD, Summ of Activities, 22 Aug 50.

[71] EUSAK WD, G-3 Sec, 22 Aug 50; 23d Inf WD, Aug 50 Summ, 22 Aug; ATIS Res Supp Interrog Rpts, Issue 3 (N.K. *1st Div*), p. 34.

[72] EUSAK WD, G-3 Sec, Msg at 1320, 22 Aug 50.

THE TAEGU FRONT

with small arms. The Eighth Army G-3 staff investigated Colonel Michaelis' charge that the ROK troops had left their positions. KMAG officers visited all the ROK 1st Division units. The Assistant G-3 went to the ROK front personally to inquire into the situation. All reports agreed that the ROK units were where General Paik said they were.[73]

The afternoon of 22 August, Lt. Col. James W. Edwards' 2d Battalion, 23d Infantry, guarding the support artillery behind the 27th Infantry, came under attack by the N.K. *1st Division* troops that had passed around the forward positions. The regimental commander, Col. Paul L. Freeman, Jr., reported to Eighth Army at 1640 that the enemy had shelled the rear battery of the 37th Field Artillery Battalion, that enemy riflemen were between the 27th and 23d Regiments on the road, and that other enemy groups had passed around the east side of his forward battalion. An intense barrage began falling on the headquarters area of the 8th Field Artillery Battalion at 1605, and 25 minutes later two direct hits on the fire direction center utterly destroyed it, killing four officers and two noncommissioned officers. The individual batteries quickly took over control of the battalion fires and continued to support the infantry, while battalion headquarters displaced under fire.[74]

Air Force, Navy, and Australian planes delivered strikes on the enemy-held ridge east of the road and on the valley beyond. These strikes included one by B-26's employing 44,000 pounds of bombs. That night, General Walker released control of the 23d Infantry, less the 1st Battalion, to the 1st Cavalry Division with orders for it to clear the enemy from the road and the commanding ground overlooking the main supply road.[75]

A bit of drama of a kind unusual in the Korean War occurred north of Tabu-dong on the 22d. About 1000, Lt. Col. Chong Pong Uk, commanding the artillery regiment supporting the N.K. *13th Division*, walked up alone to a ROK 1st Division position three miles north of Tabu-dong. In one hand he carried a white flag; over his shoulder hung a leather map case. The commanding general of the *13th Division* had reprimanded him, he said, for his failure to shell Tabu-dong. Believing that terrain obstacles made it impossible for his artillery fire to reach Tabu-dong and smarting under the reprimand, Chong had deserted.

Colonel Chong, the highest ranking prisoner thus far in the war, gave precise information on the location of his artillery. According to him, there were still seven operable 122-mm. howitzers and thirteen 76-mm. guns emplaced and camouflaged in an orchard four and a half miles north of Tabu-dong, in a little valley on the north side of Yuhak-san. Upon receiving this information, Eighth Army immediately prepared to destroy the enemy weapons. Fighter-bombers attacked the orchard site with napalm, and

---

[73] Interv, author with Brig Gen William C. Bullock, 2 Dec 53 (Bullock was Asst G-3, Eighth Army, at the time; Gay, Comments, 24 Aug 53; Ltr, Check to author, 29 Sep 53.

[74] Ltr, Check to author, 29 Sep 53; 22 Aug 50; 8th FA Bn WD, 1-31 Aug 50; 23d Inf WD, Aug 50 Narr Summ, p. 7.

[75] EUSAK WD, G-3 Sec, 22 Aug 50; 27th Inf WD, 22 Aug 50; 23d Inf WD, Aug 50 Narr Summ.

U.S. artillery took the location under fire.[76]

During the night of 22–23 August, the enemy made his usual attack against the 27th Infantry, but not in great force, and was easily repulsed. Just before noon on the 23d, however, a violent action occurred some distance behind the front line when about 100 enemy soldiers, undetected, succeeded in reaching the positions of K Company, 27th Infantry and of the 1st Platoon, C Company, 65th Engineer Combat Battalion. They overran part of these positions before being driven off with fifty killed.[77]

Meanwhile, as ordered by General Walker, the 2d Battalion, 23 Infantry, after repelling several enemy night attacks, counterattacked at dawn, 23 August, and seized the high ground overlooking the road at the artillery positions. At the same time the 3d Battalion started an all-day attack that swept a 3-mile stretch of high ground east of the road. This action largely cleared the enemy from the area behind and on the flanks of the 27th Infantry. At 1335 in the afternoon, Colonel Michaelis reported from the Bowling Alley to Eighth Army that the N.K. *13th Division* had blown the road to his front, had mined it, and was withdrawing.[78]

The next day, 24 August, the 23d Infantry continued clearing the rear areas and by night it estimated that there were not more than 200 of the enemy behind the forward positions. The Bowling Alley front was quiet on the 24th except for an unfortunate accident. An Eighth Army tank recovery team came up to retrieve a T34 tank that had stopped just in front of the forward American mine field. As the retriever began to pull the T34 forward, an American mine unseen and pushed along in some loose dirt underneath the tank, exploded, badly damaging the tank and wounding twelve men standing nearby.[79]

Shortly after midnight of 24 August the North Koreans launched what had by now become their regular nightly attack down the Bowling Alley. This attack was in an estimated two-company strength supported by a few tanks. The 27th Infantry broke up this fruitless attempt and two more enemy tanks were destroyed by the supporting artillery fire. This was the last night the 27th Infantry Regiment spent in the Bowling Alley. The confirmed enemy loss from 18 to 25 August included 13 T34 tanks, 5 self-propelled guns, and 23 vehicles.[80]

With the enemy turned back north of Taegu, General Walker on 24 August issued orders for the 27th Infantry to leave the Bowling Alley and return to the 25th Division in the Masan area. The ROK 1st Division was to assume responsibility for the Bowling Alley, but the U.S. 23d Regiment was to remain north of Taegu in its support. ROK relief of the 27th Infantry began at 1800, 25 August, and continued throughout the night

---

[76] ATIS Res Supp Interrog Rpts, Issue 106 (N.K. Arty), p. 55; ATIS Interrog Rpts, Issue 2, Rpt 771, Col Chong; New York *Times*, August 24, 1950, dispatch from Taegu, 22 August.

[77] EUSAK WD, G-3 Sec, 23 Aug 50; 3d Bn, 27th Inf WD, 23 Aug 50; 65th Engr C Bn WD, 23 Aug 50.

[78] 23d Inf WD, Aug 50 Narr Summ; EUSAK WD, G-3 Sec, 23 Aug 50; *Ibid.*, Aug 50 Summ, p. 67.

[79] 2d Bn, 27th Inf WD, Summ of Activities, 24 Aug 50; Ltr, Check to author, 29 Sep 53.

[80] 27th Inf WD, 24-25 Aug 50; 1st Bn, 27th Inf WD, 25 Aug 50; New York *Herald Tribune*, August 26, 1950.

until completed at 0345, 26 August. On 30 August the regiment received orders to move from near Taegu to Masan, and it started at 0800 the next morning, personnel going by train, vehicles by road. The Wolfhound Regiment completed the move by 2030 that night, 31 August.[81] And a very fortunate move it proved to be, for it arrived in the nick of time, as a later chapter will show.

As if to signalize the successful defense of the northern approach to Taegu in this week of fighting, a 20-year-old master sergeant of the ROK 1st Division executed a dangerous and colorful exploit. MSgt. Pea Sung Sub led a 9-man patrol 6,000 yards behind the North Korean lines to the N.K. *13th Division* command post. There his patrol killed several enemy soldiers and captured three prisoners whom they brought back with no loss to themselves. General Paik gave the daring sergeant 50,000 won ($25.00) for his exploit.[82]

Colonel Murch's 2d Battalion and Colonel Check's 1st Battalion, 27th Infantry, had gained something of a reputation for themselves in the Bowling Alley north of Taegu. The defense in depth behind their front line by the 2d and 3d Battalions, 23d Infantry, had frustrated all enemy efforts to gain control of the gateway to Taegu. The supporting tanks and the artillery had performed magnificently. During the daytime, Air Force attacks had inflicted destruction and disorganization on the enemy. And on the mountain ridges walling in the Bowling Alley, the ROK 1st Division had done its full share in fighting off the enemy thrust.

Survivors of the *1st Regiment*, N.K. *1st Division*, joined the rest of that division in the mountains east of the Taegu-Sangju road near the walled summit of Ka-san. Prisoners reported that the *1st Regiment* was down to about 400 men and had lost all its 120-mm. mortars, 76-mm. howitzers, and antitank guns as a result of its action on the east flank of the N.K. *13th Division* at the Bowling Alley.[83]

---

[81] EUSAK WD, G-3 Sec, 24-25 Aug 50; 27th Inf WD, 25-26 and 30 Aug 50. The S-3, 2d Battalion, was killed by enemy fire just as the regiment started to leave the line in the Bowling Alley. A ROK battalion commander in the relieving force was also killed about this time. 2d Bn, 27th Inf WD, 25 Aug 50; Ltr, Check to author, 29 Sep 53.

[82] New York *Times*, August 27, 1950.

[83] ATIS Res Supp Interrog Rpts, Issue 3 (N.K. *1st Div*), pp. 34-35; EUSAK WD, 28 Aug 50, ATIS Interrog Rpt 819, Chu Chae Song; *Ibid.*, 31 Aug 50, ATIS Interrog Rpt 856, Yom In Bok.

CHAPTER XX

Stalemate West of Masan

In war events of importance are the result of trivial causes.
JULIUS CAESAR, *Bellum Gallicum*

When enemy penetrations in the Pusan Perimeter at the bulge of the Naktong caused General Walker to withdraw the 1st Provisional Marine Brigade from Task Force Kean, he ordered the 25th Division to take up defensive positions on the army southern flank west of Masan. By 15 August the 25th Division had moved into these positions.

The terrain west of Masan dictated the choice of the positions. The mountain barrier west of Masan was the first readily defensible ground east of the Chinju pass. (*See Map IV.*) The two thousand-foot mountain ridges of Sobuksan and P'il-bong dominated the area and protected the Komam-ni (Saga)–Haman–Chindong-ni road, the only means of north-south communication in the army zone west of Masan.

Northward from the Masan-Chinju highway to the Nam River there were a number of possible defensive positions. The best one was the Notch and adjacent high ground near Chungam-ni, which controlled the important road junction connecting the Masan road with the one over the Nam River to Uiryong. This position, however, had the disadvantage of including a 15-mile stretch of the Nam River to the point of its confluence with the Naktong, thus greatly lengthening the line. It was mandatory that the 25th Division right flank connect with the left flank of the 24th Division at the confluence of the Nam and the Naktong Rivers. Within this limitation, it was also necessary that the 25th Division line include and protect the Komam-ni road intersection where the Chindong-ni–Haman road met the Masan-Chinju highway.

The Southern Anchor of the Army Line

From Komam-ni a 2-mile-wide belt of rice paddy land extended north four miles to the Nam River. On the west of this paddy land a broken spur of P'il-bong, dominated by 900-foot-high Sibidang-san, dropped down to the Nam. Sibidang provided excellent observation, and artillery emplaced in the Komam-ni area could interdict the road junction at Chungam-ni. Colonel Fisher, therefore, selected the Sibidang–Komam-ni position for his 35th Infantry Regiment in the northern part of the 25th Division defense line. The 35th Regiment line extended from a point two miles west of

Komam-ni to the Nam River and then turned east along that stream to its confluence with the Naktong. It was a long regimental line—about 26,000 yards.[1]

The part of the line held by the 35th Infantry—covering as it did the main Masan-Chinju highway, the railroad, and the Nam River corridor, and forming the hinge with the 24th Division to the north—was potentially the most critical and important sector of the 25th Division front. Lt. Col. Bernard G. Teeter's 1st Battalion held the regimental left west of Komam-ni; Colonel Wilkins' 2d Battalion held the regimental right along the Nam River. Maj. Robert L. Woolfolk's 3d Battalion (1st Battalion, 29th Infantry) was in reserve on the road south of Chirwon from where it could move quickly to any part of the line.

South of the 35th Infantry, Colonel Champney's 24th Infantry, known among the men in the regiment as the "Deuce-Four," took up the middle part of the division front in the mountain area west of Haman.

Below (south) the 24th Infantry and west of Chindong-ni, Colonel Throckmorton's 5th Regimental Combat Team was on the division left. On division orders, Throckmorton at first held the ground above the Chindong-ni coastal road only as far as Fox Hill, or Yabansan. General Kean soon decided, however, that the 5th Regimental Combat Team should close the gap northward between it and the 24th Infantry. When Throckmorton sent a ROK unit of 100 men under American officers to the higher slope of Sobuk-san, enemy troops already there drove them back. General Kean then ordered the 5th Regimental Combat Team to take this ground, but it was too late.[2]

The N.K. 6th Division Regroups West of Masan

In front of the 25th Division, the N.K. *6th Division* had now received orders from the North Korean command to take up defensive positions and to await reinforcements before continuing the attack.[3] From north to south, the division had its *13th, 15th,* and *14th Regiments* on line in that order. The first replacements for the division arrived at Chinju on or about 12 August. Approximately 2,000 unarmed South Koreans conscripted in the Seoul area joined the division by 15 August. At Chinju, the *6th Division* issued them grenades and told the recruits they would have to pick up weapons from killed and wounded on the battlefield and to use captured ones. A diarist in this group records that he arrived at Chinju on 13 August and was in combat for the first time on 19 August. Two days later he wrote in his diary, "I am much distressed by the pounding artillery and aerial attacks. We have no food and no water, we suffer a great deal. . . . I am on a hill close to Masan."[4]

Another group of 2,500 replacements conscripted in the Seoul area joined the *6th Division* on or about 21 August, bringing the division strength to approximately 8,500 men. In the last week

---

[1] 35th Inf Unit Hist, Aug 50.

[2] Interv, author with Throckmorton, 20 Aug 52; Throckmorton, Notes for author, 17 Apr 53.

[3] ATIS Res Supp Interrog Rpts, Issue 100 (N.K. *6th Div*), pp. 37-38.

[4] *Ibid.*, p. 38; ATIS Interrog Rpts, Issue 2, Rpt 712, p. 31, Chon Kwan O; ATIS Supp Enemy Docs, Issue 2, p. 70, Diary of Yun Hung Ki, 25 Jul-21 Aug 50.

of August and the first week of September, 3,000 more recruits conscripted in southwest Korea joined the division. The *6th Division* used this last body of recruits in labor details at first and only later employed them as combat troops.[5]

As a part of the enemy build-up in the south, another division now arrived there—the *7th Division*. This division was activated on 3 July 1950; its troops included 2,000 recruits and the *7th Border Constabulary Brigade* of 4,000 men. An artillery regiment had joined this division at Kaesong near the end of July. In Seoul on 30 July, 2,000 more recruits conscripted from South Korea brought the *7th Division's* strength to 10,000. The division departed Seoul on 1 August, the men wading the neck-deep Han River while their vehicles and heavy weapons crossed on the ponton bridge, except for the division artillery which was left behind. The *7th Division* marched south through Taejon, Chonju, and Namwon. The *1st* and *3d Regiments* arrived at Chinju on or about 15 August. Two days later some elements of the division reached T'ongyong at the southern end of the peninsula, twenty-five air miles southwest of Masan. The *2d Regiment* arrived at Yosu on or about 15 August to garrison that port. The *7th Division*, therefore, upon first arriving in southwest Korea occupied key ports to protect the *6th Division* against possible landings in its rear.[6]

The reinforced battalion that had driven the ROK police out of T'ongyong did not hold it long. U.N. naval forces heavily shelled T'ongyong on 19 August as three companies of ROK marines from Koje Island made an amphibious landing near the town. The ROK force then attacked the North Koreans and, supported by naval gun fire, drove them out. The enemy in this action at T'ongyong lost about 350 men, or about half their reinforced battalion; the survivors withdrew to Chinju.[7]

By 17 August, the reinforced North Koreans had closed on the 25th Division defensive line and had begun a series of probing attacks that were to continue throughout the month. What the N.K. *6th Division* called "aggressive patrolling" soon became, in the U.S. 24th and 35th Infantry sectors, attacks of company and sometimes of battalion strength. Most of these attacks came in the high mountains west of Haman, in the Battle Mountain, P'il-bong, and Sobuk-san area. There the *6th Division* seemed peculiarly sensitive where any terrain features afforded observation of its supply and concentration area in the deeply cut valley to the west.

Enemy Attacks at Komam-ni (Saga)

It soon became apparent that the enemy *6th Division* had shifted its axis of attack and that its main effort now would be in the northern part of the Chinju-Masan corridor just below the Nam River. General Kean had placed his strongest regiment, the 35th Infantry, in this area. Competent observers considered its commanding officer, Colonel Fisher, one of the ablest regimental com-

---

[5] ATIS Res Supp Interrog Rpts, Issue 100 (N.K. *6th Div*), p. 38.

[6] ATIS Res Supp Interrog Rpts, Issue 99 (N.K. *7th Div*), p. 34; ATIS Interrog Rpts, Issue 2, p. 94, Capt So Won Sok, *7th Div*.

[7] ATIS Res Supp Interrog Rpts, Issue 99 (N.K. *7th Div*), pp. 34-35; ATIS Interrog Rpts, Issue 2, p. 94, Capt So; GHQ FEC G-3 Opn Rpt 57, 20 Aug 50; New York *Times*, August 21, 1950.

manders in Korea. Calm, somewhat retiring, ruddy faced, and possessed of a strong, compact body, this officer was a fine example of the professional soldier. He possessed an exact knowledge of the capabilities of the weapons used in an infantry regiment and was skilled in their use. He was a technician in the tactical employment of troops. Of quiet temperament, he did not court publicity. One of his fellow regimental commanders called him "the mainstay of the division." [8]

The 35th Infantry set to work to cover its front with trip flares, but they were in short supply and gradually it became impossible to replace those tripped by the enemy. As important to the front line companies as the flares were the 60-mm. mortar illuminating shells. This ammunition had deteriorated to such a degree, however, that only about 20 percent of the supply issued to the regiment was effective. The 155-mm. howitzer illuminating shells were in short supply. Even when employed, the time lapse between a request for them and delivery by the big howitzers allowed some enemy infiltration before the threatened area was illuminated.[9]

Lt. Col. Arthur H. Logan's 64th Field Artillery Battalion, with C Battery, 90th Field Artillery Battalion, attached, and Captain Harvey's A Company, 89th Medium Tank Battalion, supported Colonel Fisher's regiment. Three medium M4A3 tanks, from positions at Komam-ni, acted as artillery and placed interdiction fire on Chungam-ni. Six other medium M26 tanks in a similar manner placed interdiction fire on Uiryong across the Nam River.[10]

In the predawn hours of 17 August an enemy attack got under way against the 35th Infantry. North Korean artillery fire began falling on the 1st Battalion command post in Komam-ni at 0300, and an hour later enemy infantry attacked A Company, forcing two of its platoons from their positions, and overrunning a mortar position. After daylight, a counterattack by B Company regained the lost ground. This was the beginning of a 5-day battle by Colonel Teeter's 1st Battalion along the southern spurs of Sibidang, two miles west of Komam-ni. The North Koreans endeavored there to turn the left flank of the 35th Regiment and split the 25th Division line. On the morning of 18 August, A Company again lost its position to enemy attack and again regained it by counterattack. Two companies of South Korean police arrived to reinforce the battalion right flank. Against the continuing North Korean attack, artillery supporting the 1st Battalion fired an average of 200 rounds an hour during the night of 19–20 August.[11]

After three days and nights of this battle, C Company of the 35th Infantry and A Company of the 29th Infantry moved up astride the Komam-ni road during the morning of 20 August to bolster A and B Companies on Sibidang. While this reinforcement was in prog-

---

[8] Interv, author with Corley, 6 Nov 51; Interv, author with Throckmorton, 20 Aug 52; Interv, author with Brig Gen Arthur S. Champney, 22 Jul 51. Throckmorton and Champney agreed substantially with Corley's opinion.

[9] 1st Bn, 35th Inf WD, 14–31 Aug 50, Summ of Supply Problem.

[10] 35th Inf WD, 1–31 Aug 50; 89th Med Tank Bn WD, 16–17 Aug 50.

[11] 35th Inf WD, 17–20 Aug 50; 1st Bn, 35th Inf WD, 19 Aug 50.

ress, Colonel Fisher from a forward observation post saw a large enemy concentration advancing to renew the attack. He directed artillery fire on this force and called in an air strike. Observers estimated that the artillery fire and the air strike killed about 350 enemy troops, half the attack group.[12]

The North Koreans made still another try in the same place. In the predawn hours of 22 August, enemy infantry started a very heavy attack against the 1st Battalion. Employing no artillery or mortar preparatory fires, the enemy force in the darkness cut the four-strand barbed wire and attacked at close quarters with small arms and grenades. This assault engaged three American companies and drove one of them from its position. After three hours of fighting A Company counterattacked at 0700 and regained its lost position. The next day, 23 August, the North Koreans, frustrated in this area, withdrew from contact in the 35th Infantry sector.[13]

Battle Mountain

At the same time that the North Koreans were trying to penetrate the 35th Infantry positions in the Sibidang-Komam-ni area, they sent strong patrols and probing attacks against the mountainous middle part of the 25th Division line. Since this part of the division line became a continuing problem in the defense of the Perimeter, more should be said about the terrain there and some of its critical features.

Old mine shafts and tunnels on the western slope of Sobuk-san provided the North Koreans in this area with ready-made underground bunkers, assembly points, and supply depots. As early as the first week of August, the North Koreans were in this mountain fastness and had never been driven out. It was the assembly area for their combat operations on the Masan front all during the month. Even when American troops had held the Notch position beyond Chungam-ni, their combat patrols had never been able to penetrate along the mountain trail that branches off the Masan road and twists its way up the narrow mountain valley to the mining villages of Ogok and Tundok, at the western base of Battle Mountain and P'ilbong, two peaks of Sobuk-san. The patrols always were either ambushed or driven back by enemy action. The North Koreans firmly protected all approaches to their Sobuk-san stronghold.[14]

When the 25th Division issued orders to its subordinate units to take up defensive positions west of Masan, the 2d Battalion, 24th Infantry, was still trying to seize Obong-san, the mountain ridge just west of Battle Mountain and P'il-bong, and across a gorgelike valley from them. At daybreak of 15 August, the 2d Battalion broke contact with the enemy and withdrew to Battle Mountain and the ridge west of Haman. The 3d Battalion of the 24th Infantry now came to the Haman area to help in the regimental defense of this sector.[15]

This high ground west of Haman on

---

[12] 1st Bn, 35th Inf WD, 20 Aug 50; 25th Div WD, 20 Aug 50.
[13] 35th Inf WD, 22 Aug 50; 25th Div WD, 23 Aug 50.

[14] Interv, author with Fisher, 5 Jan 52; 159th FA Bn WD, 12–15 Aug 50; 1st Bn, 24th Inf WD, 15 Aug 50.
[15] 2d Bn, 24th Inf WD, 15 Aug 50; 25th Div WD, 15 Aug 50.

which the 24th Infantry established its defensive line was part of the Sobuk-san mountain mass. Sobuk-san reaches its highest elevation, 2,400 feet, at P'il-bong (Hill 743), eight miles northwest of Chindong-ni and three miles southwest of Haman. From P'il-bong the crest of the ridge line drops and curves slightly northwestward, to rise again a mile away in the bald peak which became known as Battle Mountain (Hill 665). It also was variously known as Napalm Hill, Old Baldy, and Bloody Knob. Between P'il-bong and Battle Mountain the ridge line narrows to a rocky ledge which the troops called the Rocky Crags. Northward from Battle Mountain toward the Nam River, the ground drops sharply in two long spur ridges. Men who fought there called the eastern one Green Peak.[16]

At the western base (enemy side) of Battle Mountain and P'il-bong lay Ogok and Tundok, one and a quarter air miles from the crest. A generally north-south mountain road-trail crossed a high saddle just north of these villages and climbed to the 1,100-foot level of the west slope, or about halfway to the top, of Battle Mountain. This road gave the North Koreans an advantage in mounting and supplying their attacks in this area. A trail system ran from Ogok and Tundok to the crests of Battle Mountain and P'il-bong. From the top of Battle Mountain an observer could look directly down into this enemy-held valley, upon its mining villages and numerous mine shafts. Conversely, from Battle Mountain the North Koreans could look down into the Haman valley eastward and keep the 24th Infantry command post, supply road, artillery positions, and approach trails under observation. Whichever side held the crest of Battle Mountain could see into the rear areas of the other. Both forces fully understood the advantages of holding the crest of Battle Mountain and each tried to do it in a 6-week-long battle.

The approach to Battle Mountain and P'il-bong was much more difficult from the east, the American-held side, than from the west, the North Korean side. On the east side there was no road climbing halfway to the top; from the base of the mountain at the edge of the Haman valley the only way to make the ascent was by foot trail. Stout climbers required from 2 to 3 hours to reach the top of P'il-bong from the reservoir area, one and a half air miles eastward; they required from 3 to 4 hours to get on top of Battle Mountain from the valley floor. The turnaround time for porter pack trains to Battle Mountain was 6 hours. Often a dispatch runner required 8 hours to go up Battle Mountain and come back down. In some places the trail was so steep that men climbed with the help of ropes stretched at the side of the trail. Enemy night patrols constantly cut telephone lines. The wire men had a difficult and dangerous job trying to maintain wire communication with units on the mountain.

Bringing dead and seriously wounded down from the top was an arduous task. It required a litter bearer team of six men to carry a wounded man on a stretcher down the mountain. In addition, a medical aide was needed to ad-

---

[16] Interv, author with 1st Lt Louis M. Daniels, 2 Sep 51 (CO I&R Plat, 24th Inf, and during the Aug 50 action was a MSgt (Intel Sgt) in the 1st Bn, 24th Inf); Interv, author with Corley, 4 Jan 52 (Corley in Aug 50 was CO, 3d Bn, 24th Inf; in September of that year he became the regimental commander); AMS Map, Korea, 1:50,000.

minister medical care during the trip if the man was critically wounded, and riflemen often accompanied the party to protect it from enemy snipers along the trail. A critically wounded man might, and sometimes did, die before he reached the bottom where surgical and further medical care could be administered. This possibility was one of the factors that lowered morale in the 24th Infantry units fighting on Battle Mountain. Many men were afraid that if they were wounded there they would die before reaching adequate medical care.[17]

In arranging the artillery and mortar support for the 24th Infantry on Battle Mountain and P'il-bong, Colonel Champney placed the 4.2-inch mortars and the 159th Field Artillery Battalion in the valley south of Haman. On 19 August the artillery moved farther to the rear, except for C Battery, which remained in the creek bed north of Haman at Champney's insistence. Champney in the meantime had ordered his engineers to improve a trail running from Haman northeast to the main Komam-ni–Masan road. He intended to use it for an evacuation road by the artillery, if that became necessary, and to improve the tactical and logistical road net of the regimental sector. This road became known as the Engineer Road.[18]

When Colonel Champney on 15 August established his line there was a 4,000-yard gap in the P'il-bong area between the 24th Infantry and the 5th Infantry southward. The 24th Infantry had not performed well during the Task Force Kean action and this fact made a big gap adjacent to it a matter of serious concern. General Kean sent 432 ROK National Police to Champney the next day and the latter placed them in this gap.[19]

The first attack against the mountain line of the 24th Infantry came on the morning of 18 August, when the enemy partly overran E Company on the northern spur of Battle Mountain and killed the company commander. During the day, Lt. Col. Paul F. Roberts succeeded Lt. Col. George R. Cole in command of the 2d Battalion there. The next day, the enemy attacked C Company on Battle Mountain and routed it. Officers could collect only forty men to bring them back into position. Many ROK police on P'il-bong also ran away—only fifty-six of them remained in their defensive positions. American officers used threats and physical force to get others back into position. A gap of nearly a mile in the line north of P'il-bong existed in the 24th Infantry lines at the close of the day, and an unknown number of North Koreans were moving into it.[20]

On 20 August, all of C Company except the company commander and about twenty-five men abandoned their position on Battle Mountain. Upon reaching the bottom of the mountain those who had fled reported erroneously that the company commander had been killed and their position surrounded, then over-

---

[17] Interv, author with Corley, 4 Jan 52; Interv, author with Daniels, 2 Sep 51; Interv, author with Champney, 22 Jul 51; 24th Inf WD, 1–31 Aug 50, Special Problems and Lessons.

[18] Interv, author with Champney, 22 Jul 51; 159th FA Bn WD, Aug 50, and sketch maps 5 and 6.

[19] Col William O. Perry, EUSAK IG Rpt, 24th Inf Regt, 1950, testimony of Capt Alfred F. Thompson, Arty Line Off with 24th Inf, 24 Aug 50; 24th Inf WD, 15–16 Aug 50.

[20] 1st Bn, 24th Inf WD, 19 Aug 50; 159th FA Bn WD, 19 Aug 50.

run by the enemy. On the basis of this misinformation, American artillery and mortars fired concentrations on C Company's former position, and fighter-bombers, in thirty-eight sorties, attacked the crest of Battle Mountain, using napalm, fragmentation bombs, rockets, and strafing. This friendly action, based upon completely erroneous reports, forced the company commander and his remnant of twenty-five men off Battle Mountain after they had held it for nearly twenty hours. A platoon of E Company, except for eight or ten men, also left its position on the mountain under similar circumstances. On the regimental left, a ROK patrol from K Company's position on Sobuk-san had the luck to capture the commanding officer of the N.K. *15th Regiment* but, unfortunately, he was killed a few minutes later while trying to escape. The patrol removed important documents from his body. And on this day of general melee along Battle Mountain and P'il-bong, the North Koreans drove off the ROK police from the 24th Infantry's left flank on Sobuk-san.[21]

General Kean now alerted Colonel Throckmorton to prepare a force from the 5th Infantry to attack Sobuk-san. On the morning of 21 August, the 1st Battalion (less A Company), 5th Regimental Combat Team, attacked across the 24th Infantry boundary and secured Sobuk-san against light resistance. That evening a strong force of North Koreans counterattacked and drove the 1st Battalion off the mountain. At noon the next day, the 1st Battalion again attacked the heights, and five hours later B Company seized the peak. General Kean now changed the boundary line between the 5th Regimental Combat Team and the 24th Infantry, giving the Sobuk-san peak to the former. During the night, the North Koreans launched counterattacks against the 1st Battalion, 5th Regimental Combat Team, and prevented it from consolidating its position. On the morning of 23 August, A Company tried to secure the high ground 1,000 yards southwest of Sobuk and link up with B Company, but was unable to do so. The enemy considered this particular terrain feature so important that he continued to repulse all efforts to capture it, and kept A Company, 5th Regimental Combat Team, nearby, under almost daily attack.[22]

Northward from B Company's position on Sobuk, the battle situation was similar. Enemy troops in the Rocky Crags, which extended from Sobuk-san toward P'il-bong, took cover during air strikes, and napalm, 500-pound bombs, and strafing had little effect. As soon as the planes departed they reoccupied their battle positions. Elements of the 24th Infantry were not able to extend southward and join with B Company of the 5th Regimental Combat Team.[23]

Still farther northward along the mountain spine, in the Battle Mountain area, affairs were going badly for the

---

[21] 24th Inf WD, 20 Aug 50; 3d Bn, 24th Inf WD, 20 Aug 50; EUSAK IG Rpt, 24th Inf, testimony of Maj Eugene J. Carson, Ex Off, 2d Bn, 24th Inf, answer to question 141, 14 Sep 50; *Ibid.*, statement of Capt Merwin J. Camp, 9 Sep 50.

[22] Interv, author with Throckmorton, 20 Aug 52; Throckmorton, Notes and sketch maps, 17 Apr 53; 25th Div WD, 21–24 Aug 50; EUSAK WD, G–3 Sec, 21–22 Aug 50; *Ibid.*, 23 Aug 50.

[23] 1st Bn, 24th Inf WD, 23 Aug 50; Corley, Notes for author, 27 Jul 53. The code name King I was given to this rocky ledge extending from P'il-bong south toward Sobuk-san. See 159th FA Bn WD, 19 Aug 50.

ENEMY SIDE OF THE ROCKY CRAGS

24th Infantry. After C Company lost Battle Mountain, air and artillery worked over its crest in preparation for an infantry attack planned to regain Old Baldy. The hot and sultry weather made climbing the steep slope grueling work, but L Company was on top by noon, 21 August. Enemy troops had left the crest under the punishing fire of air, artillery, and mortar. They in turn now placed mortar fire on the crest and prevented L Company from consolidating its position. This situation continued until midafternoon when an enemy platoon came out of zigzag trenches a short distance down the reverse slope of Old Baldy and surprised L Company. One enemy soldier even succeeded in dropping a grenade in a platoon leader's foxhole. The other two platoons of the company, upon hearing firing, started to leave their positions and drift down the hill. The North Koreans swiftly reoccupied Old Baldy while officers tried to assemble L and I Companies on the eastern slope. Elements of E Company also left their position during the day.[24]

American air, artillery, mortar, and tank fire now concentrated on Battle Mountain, and I and L Companies prepared to counterattack. This attack made slow progress and at midnight it halted to wait for daylight. Shortly after dawn, 22 August, I and L Companies resumed the attack. Lt. R. P. Stevens led L Company up the mountain, with I Company supplying a base of fire. Lt. Gerald N. Alexander testified that, with no enemy fire whatever, it took him an hour to get

---

[24] Corley, notes for author, 27 Jul 53; Interv, author with Corley, 4 Jan 52; EUSAK IG Rpt, 24th Inf Regt, 1950, testimony of 2d Lt Gerald N. Alexander, L Co, 24th Inf, 2 Sep 50; Ibid., testimony of Maj Horace E. Donaho, Ex Off, 2d Bn, 24th Inf, 22 Aug 50; 24th Inf WD, 21 Aug 50; EUSAK WD, G-3 Sec, 21 Aug 50.

his men to move 200 yards. When they eventually reached their objective, three enemy grenades wounded six of them and at this his group ran off the hill. Alexander stopped them 100 yards down the slope and ordered them to go back up. None would go. Finally, he and a BAR man climbed back and found no defending enemy on the crest. His men slowly rejoined him. The remainder of the company reached the objective on Battle Mountain with a total loss of 17 casualties in three hours' time. A few hours later, when a small enemy force worked around its right flank, the company withdrew back down the hill to I Company's position.[25]

Fighting continued on Battle Mountain the next day, 23 August, with ROK police units arriving to reinforce I and L Companies. The American and South Korean troops finally secured precarious possession of Old Baldy, mainly because of the excellent supporting fires of the 81-mm. and 4.2-inch mortars covering the enemy's avenues of approach on the western slope. Before its relief on the mountain, L Company reported a foxhole strength of 17 men, yet, halfway down the slope, its strength had jumped to 48 men, and by the next morning it was more than 100. Colonel Corley, in command of the 3d Battalion, 24th Infantry, said, "Companies of my battalion dwindle to platoon size when engaged with the enemy. My chain of command stops at company level. If this unit is to continue to fight as a battalion it is recommended that the T/O of officers be doubled. One officer must lead and the other must drive." The situation in the Haman area caused General Walker to alert the Marine brigade for possible movement to this part of the front.[26]

On 25 and 26 August, C Company beat off a number of North Korean thrusts on Battle Mountain—all coming along one avenue of approach, the long finger ridge extending upward from the mines at Tundok. At one point in this series of actions, a flight of Air Force planes caught about 100 enemy soldiers in the open and immediately napalmed, bombed, and strafed them. There were few survivors. Task Force Baker, commanded by Colonel Cole, and comprising C Company, a platoon of E Company, 24th Infantry, and a ROK police company, defended Battle Mountain at this time. The special command was established because of the isolated Battle Mountain area and the extended regimental battle frontage. It buried many enemy dead killed within or in front of its positions during these two days.[27]

The 3d Battalion, 24th Infantry, now relieved the 1st Battalion in the Battle Mountain–P'il-bong area, except for C Company which, as part of Task Force Baker, remained on Old Baldy. Corley's battalion completed this relief by 1800, 27 August.[28]

The North Korean attacks continued. On the 28th, an enemy company-sized

---

[25] Interv, author with Corley, 4 Jan 52; EUSAK WD, G-3 Sec, 22 Aug 50; *Ibid.*, Summ, 22 Aug 50; EUSAK IG Rpt, 24th Inf Regt, 1950, testimony of Corley, 26 Aug 50, and testimony of Alexander, 2 Sep 50.

[26] 24th Inf WD, 24 Aug 50; Interv, author with Corley, 4 Jan 52; EUSAK IG Rpt, 24th Inf Regt, 1950, testimony of Alexander, 2 Sep 50, and testimony of Corley, 26 Aug 50.

[27] 1st Bn, 24th Inf WD, 26 Aug 50; 24th Inf WD, 26 Aug 50; 25th Div WD, 26 Aug 50.

[28] 3d Bn, 24th Inf WD, 27 Aug 50; 25th Div WD, 27 Aug 50.

attack struck between C and I Companies before dawn. That night, enemy mortar fire fell on C Company on Old Baldy, some of it obviously directed at the company command post. After midnight, an enemy force appeared in the rear area and captured the command post. Some men of C Company left their positions on Battle Mountain when the attack began at 0245, 29 August. The North Koreans swung their attack toward E Company and overran part of its positions. Airdrops after daylight kept C Company supplied with ammunition, and a curtain of artillery fire, sealing off approaches from the enemy's main position, prevented any substantial reinforcement from arriving on the crest. All day artillery fire and air strikes pounded the North Koreans occupying E Company's old positions. Then, in the evening, E Company counterattacked and reoccupied the lost ground.[29]

An hour before midnight, North Koreans attacked C Company. Men on the left flank of the company position jumped from their holes and ran down the mountain yelling, "They have broken through!" The panic spread. Again the enemy had possession of Battle Mountain. Capt. Lawrence M. Corcoran, the company commander, was left with only the seventeen men in his command post, which included several wounded.[30] After daylight on the 30th, air strikes again came in on Battle Mountain, and artillery, mortar, and tank fire from the valley concentrated on the enemy-held peak. A wounded man came down off the mountain where, cut off, he had hidden for several hours. He reported that the main body of the North Koreans had withdrawn to the wooded ridges west of the peak for better cover, leaving only a small covering force on Old Baldy itself. At 1100, B Company, with the 3d Battalion in support, attacked toward the heights and two hours later was on top.[31]

Units of the 24th Infantry always captured Battle Mountain in the same way. Artillery, mortar, and tank fire raked the crest and air strikes employing napalm blanketed the scorched top. Then the infantry attacked from the hill beneath Old Baldy on the east slope, where supporting mortars set up a base of fire and kept the heights under a hail of steel until the infantry had arrived at a point just short of the crest. The mortar fire then lifted and the infantry moved rapidly up the last stretch to the top, usually to find it deserted by the enemy.[32]

Battle Mountain changed hands so often during August that there is no agreement on the exact number of times. The intelligence sergeant of the 1st Battalion, 24th Infantry, said that according to his count the peak changed hands nineteen times.[33] From 18 August to the end of the month, scarcely a night passed that the North Koreans did not attack

---

[29] 24th Inf WD, 29 Aug 50.

[30] Ibid.; 25th Div WD, 29 Aug 50; EUSAK IG Rpt, 24th Inf Div, 1950, testimony of Corcoran, 1 Sep 50. Corcoran said fire discipline in his company was very poor, that his men would fire at targets out of range until they had exhausted their ammunition and at night would fire when there were no targets. He said that in his entire company he had twenty-five men he considered soldiers and that they carried the rest.

[31] 24th Inf WD, 30 Aug 50; 25th Div WD, 30 Aug 50.

[32] Interv, author with Corley, 4 Jan 52.

[33] Interv, author with Daniels, 2 Sep 51.

Old Baldy. The peak often changed hands two or three times in a 24-hour period. The usual pattern was for the enemy to take it at night and the 24th Infantry to recapture it the next day. This type of fluctuating battle resulted in relatively high losses among artillery forward observers and their equipment. During the period of 15–31 August, seven forward observers and eight other members of the Observer and Liaison Section of the 159th Field Artillery Battalion, supporting the 24th Infantry, were casualties; and they lost 8 radios, 11 telephones, and 2 vehicles to enemy action.[34]

In its defense of that part of Sobuksan south of Battle Mountain and P'ilbong, the 1st Battalion, 5th Regimental Combat Team, also had nearly continuous action in the last week of the month. MSgt. Melvin O. Handrich of C Company, 5th Regimental Combat Team, on 25 and 26 August distinguished himself as a heroic combat leader. From a forward position he directed artillery fire on an attacking enemy force and at one point personally kept part of the company from abandoning its positions. Although wounded, Sergeant Handrich returned to his forward position, to continue directing artillery fire, and there alone engaged North Koreans until he was killed. When the 5th Regimental Combat Team regained possession of his corner "of a foreign field" it counted more than seventy dead North Koreans in the vicinity.[35]

The month of August ended with the fighting in the mountains on the southern front, west of Masan, a stalemate. Neither side had secured a definite advantage. The 25th Division had held the central part of its line, at Battle Mountain and Sobuk-san, only with difficulty and with mounting concern for the future.

---

[34] 159th FA Bn WD, 1–31 Aug 50.

[35] Department of the Army General Order 60, 2 August 1951, awarded the Medal of Honor posthumously to Sergeant Handrich.

CHAPTER XXI

August Build-up and September Portents

> The impact of an army, like the total of mechanical co-efficients, is equal to the mass multiplied by the velocity . . . when you are about to give battle concentrate all your strength, neglect nothing; a battalion often decides the day.
> NAPOLEON

The Far East Air Forces in August

The Far East Air Forces probably exercised a greater relative influence in August 1950 in determining the outcome of the Korean battles than in any other month of the war. As the number of tactical air control parties increased in late July and during August, the standard practice of the Fifth Air Force was to place one with each U.S. Army regiment and division headquarters and one with each ROK division and corps headquarters. Fighter aircraft in August normally left their Japanese bases at Itazuke and Ashiya on a daily schedule of two planes every fifteen minutes. They reported to the tactical air control center at Taegu where they received specific missions. After receiving them the planes reported to the proper division TACP and then to a regimental TACP for their target assignment. By 23 August, the Fifth Air Force operated twenty-nine T-6 Mosquitoes, all using the Taegu airstrip. The Mosquitoes operated over six stations from dawn to dusk, each plane on station for a 2-hour period before being relieved by another.[1] The pilots of these planes were tactical co-ordinators. They located and controlled close support missions when TACP's did not have visual control.

At the end of the month, eight fighter squadrons were engaged in combat operations in Korea. They were about all that could be supported at the Kyushu bases. In July, FEAF flew 4,635 sorties in close support of ground troops in Korea; in August, 7,397 sorties. An average of 40 sorties daily supported each U.S. division in the August Pusan Perimeter battles. A colorful pilot from Ohio, Maj. Dean E. Hess, who had a record of 63 combat missions in Europe in World War II, had been assigned to train South Korean pilots. He was known to many as "the one man Air Force of the South Korean Army" and by his call sign "MacIntosh One." Hess was grounded by official order near the end of August

---

[1] Hq, X Corps, Analysis of the Air-Ground Operations System, 28 Jun-8 Sep 50. A tactical air control party is described above, p. 95.

after he had flown 95 combat missions in less than two months.[2]

Aviation engineer units available to the Far East Air Forces in July had been badly understrength and deficient in technical training. This slowed the construction of six planned airfields in Korea and, together with the ground reverses, prevented a deployment of fighter planes to bases there.[3]

On 4 August FEAF began B-29 interdiction attacks against all key bridges north of the 37th Parallel in Korea, and on 15 August some light bombers and fighter-bombers joined in the interdiction campaign. This campaign sought the destruction of thirty-two rail and highway bridges on the three main transportation routes across Korea: (1) the line from Sinanju south to P'yongyang and thence northeast to Wonsan on the east coast; (2) the line just below the 38th Parallel from Munsan-ni through Seoul to Ch'unch'on to Chumunjin-up on the east coast; (3) the line from Seoul south to Choch'iwon and hence east to Wonju to Samch'ok on the east coast. The interdiction campaign marked nine rail yards, including those at Seoul, P'yongyang, and Wonsan, for attack, and the ports of Inch'on and Wonsan to be mined. This interdiction program, if effectively executed, would slow and perhaps critically disrupt the movement of enemy supplies along the main routes south to the battlefront.[4]

The Air Force B-29's on 7 August bombed and largely destroyed the P'yongyang Army Arsenal and the P'yongyang railroad yards. On 7, 9, and 10 August they bombed and completely destroyed the large Chosen petroleum refinery at Wonsan. This plant, with its estimated capacity of 250,000 tons, annually produced approximately 93 percent of the North Korean petroleum products. Throughout the month the Air Force bombed the chemical complex in the Hungnam area, the largest in Asia, dropping 1,761 tons of bombs there in the period between 30 July and 19 September. It bombed the Najin docks only 17 miles south of the Siberian border and 105 air miles from Vladivostok. (Najin was an important port of entry for vessels carrying supplies from Vladivostok and it was also a rail center.) The bombers struck the metal-working industry at Songjin with 326 tons of bombs on 28 August, and three days later they heavily damaged the aluminum and magnesium plants at Chinnamp'o with 284 tons of bombs.[5]

The supremacy of the Fifth Air Force in the skies over Korea forced the North Koreans in the first month of the war to resort to night movement of supplies to the battle area. To counter this,

---

[2] USAF Hist Study 71, pp. 14, 46; 25th Div WD, 21 Aug 50; New York *Times*, August 29, 1950. Hess was an ordained minister in the Campbellite Church of the Disciples of Christ. See *Newsweek*, August 1, 1955, p. 28, for Hess' subsequent service in Korea.

[3] USAF Hist Study 71, pp. 18, 20.

[4] "Air War in Korea," *op. cit.*, IV, No. 2, 19–39; Col Raymond S. Sleeper, "Korean Targets for Medium Bombardment," *Air University Quarterly Review*, IV, No. 3 (Spring, 1951), 21–22.

[5] Sleeper, "Korean Targets for Medium Bombardment," *op. cit.*, pp. 24–26; *Air Intelligence Digest*, September 1950; Hq X Corps, A General Review of U.S. Tactical Air Support in Korea, 28 Jun–8 Sep 50, p. 61; New York *Times*, August 16, 1950.

FLAMING ROCKET *penetrating a loaded boxcar (bottom foreground) and napalm tank (right) exploding at the moment of impact.*

General Stratemeyer ordered nightly visual reconnaissance of the enemy supply routes, beginning on 6 August. On the 8th, Stratemeyer ordered Partridge to increase the night sorties to fifty; by 24 August, Fifth Air Force B-26's alone averaged thirty-five sorties nightly. Late in August the Air Force began flare missions over North Korea. B-29's would release parachute flares at 10,000 feet that ignited at 6,000 feet, whereupon co-operating B-26 bombers attacked any enemy movement discovered in the illuminated area. These M-26 parachute flares from World War II stock functioned poorly, many of them proving to be duds.[6]

Since capturing Seoul, the North Koreans had built two ponton bridges over the Han at that point, one north and one south of the rail and highway bridges. They had also started a new railroad bridge north of the old triple bridge group. The steel cantilever railroad bridge on the west still stood, defying all the efforts of the Far East Air Forces to bring it down. For almost four weeks the Air Force bombed this bridge daily with 1-, 2-, and 4-thousand-pound general purpose bombs with fuze settings, intended to damage both the superstructure and the abutments. On 19 August, nine B-29's of the 19th Group dropped 54 tons of 1,000-pound bombs on the bridge, but it still stood. The same day, Navy carrier-based planes attacked the bridge, scoring eight direct hits, and brought it down. The next day when Air Force planes returned to the bridge they found that three spans had dropped into the river.[7]

Attacks against the Han River ponton bridges at Seoul do not seem to have been successful until FEAF on 27 August ordered the Bomber Command to lay delayed action bombs alongside the bridges, set to detonate at night. This method of attack seems to have caused such heavy casualties among the North Korean labor force trying to keep the pontons in repair that the enemy finally abandoned the effort. These bridges re-

---

[6] Sleeper, "Korean Targets for Medium Bombardment," *op. cit.*, p. 66; USAF Hist Study 71, p. 45.
[7] GHQ FEC G-3, Opn Rpts 57, 20 Aug, and 62, 25 Aug 50; *Ibid.*, Sitrep, 25 Aug 50; USAF Hist Study 71, pp. 41–44; Sleeper, "Korean Targets for Medium Bombardment," *op. cit.*, p. 65. The Bomber Command made eighty-six sorties with 643 tons of demolition bombs against this bridge.

mained unfinished when the American forces recaptured Seoul.[8]

While it is clear that air power wrought great destruction of enemy equipment and troops during this period of the war, it is not possible to state accurately just how great it really was. Pilot claims are the basis of most estimates of air damage and destruction. Experience has shown that these are subject to many kinds of error. As an example, pilots often mistakenly claimed the destruction of enemy equipment if it remained immobile after attack. It is often impossible for a pilot of a high-speed aircraft to determine if his target is live or not, and three or four different pilots may claim as a "kill" a vehicle already knocked out by ground action. One study revealed a surprisingly great discrepancy between pilot claims and a ground study of destroyed enemy equipment. Pilots claimed to have destroyed ten times as many tanks with rockets as with napalm in the first three months of the Korean War, but a ground survey of destroyed enemy tanks after the Eighth Army breakout from the Pusan Perimeter showed three times as many tanks destroyed with napalm as with rockets. This gives a discrepancy factor of thirty to one in relation to pilot claims. Napalm seldom destroyed a tank by the burst of flame itself. But it did set off chain events that often led to the complete destruction of the tank. The splashing napalm on the bogie wheels set the rubber tires on fire, it heated ammunition to the point where it detonated inside the tank, or it set fuel on fire, and sometimes it

EXPLODING PHOSPHORUS BOMBS *dropped by B-29's over a North Korean barracks create an unusual pattern.*

splashed into the air intake vents and started fires inside the tank.[9]

Ground Build-up

The Far East Command's "Operation Rebuild" by August had assumed the proportions of a gigantic production of ordnance materiel. Before the end of

---

[8] USAF Hist Study 71, pp. 44-45; Operations Research Office, The Employment of Armor in Korea, ORO-R-1 (FEC), vol. 1, pp. 212-13.

[9] ORO, Close Air Support Operation in Korea, ORO-R-3 (FEC), pp. 37-38, 59, 344-45. Experiments by Eighth Army disclosed that in a napalm burst of two 110-gallon tanks, the intense flame lasted for only approximately twelve seconds and was entirely burned out in twenty seconds. The burst covered an area of about 15,000 square feet; it was considered effective in an area fifty yards square.

1950 it had expanded to employ 19,908 people in eight Japanese shops. In August, 950 2½-ton trucks alone were repaired. During the first three months of the Korean War practically all ammunition the U.N. and South Korean forces used came from rebuild stocks in Japan.

The daily rail and water Red Ball Express from Yokohama to Sasebo to Pusan, beginning on 23 July, operated with increased efficiency in August and demonstrated that it could deliver promptly to Korea any supplies available in Japan. On 5 August, for instance, it delivered 308 measurement tons; on 9 August, 403 tons; on 22 August, 574 tons; and on 25 August, 949 tons. The success of the Red Ball Express cut down the amount of airlift tonnage. This fell from 85 tons on 31 July to 49 tons on 6 August. The express eliminated the need for nearly all airlift of supplies to Korea from Japan. It delivered supplies to Korea in an average time of 60–70 hours, while the airlift delivery varied from 12 hours to 5 days. The Red Ball delivery was not only far cheaper, it was more consistent and reliable.[10]

The drop in air delivery to Korea caused General Partridge, commanding the Far East Air Forces, to complain on 10 August that the Army was not fully using the airlift's 200-ton daily capacity. That day, Eighth Army ordered curtailment of delivery by the Red Ball Express and increased use of the airlift to its maximum capacity. The reason given for this action was a sudden apprehension that the port of Pusan could not process promptly the flow of water-borne supplies. The absurdity of the logistical situation was illustrated the next day, 11 August, when, upon General Partridge's suggestion, two 2½-ton trucks were airlifted in a C–119 from Tachikawa Air Base in Japan to Taegu. The Air Force planned to airlift two trucks daily in this manner. As a result of this development, Eighth Army on 12 August ordered that, effective 15 August, the Red Ball Express be discontinued except on Tuesday and Friday of each week when it would carry cargo difficult for the planes to handle. Under this arrangement airlift tonnage greatly increased. On 16 August, transport planes carried 324 tons of cargo and 595 passengers; on 19 August, 160 tons of cargo and 381 passengers; on 28 August, 398 tons of cargo and 343 passengers; and, on 29 August, 326 tons of cargo and 347 passengers.[11]

After the Russian-built T34 tank appeared on the Korean battlefield, the Department of the Army acted as quickly as possible to correct the imbalance in armor. It alerted three medium tank battalions for immediate movement to Korea. These battalions were the 6th (M46), the 70th (M26 and M4A3), and the 73d (M26). Two of them were the school troop battalions of the Armored School at Fort Knox and of the Infantry School at Fort Benning; the third was the organic battalion of the 1st Armored Division. The Department of the Army notified General MacArthur on 10 July that it planned to ship these battalions

---

[10] GHQ FEC Sitreps, 8, 11, 23, 27 Aug 50; EUSAK WD, 8 Aug 50.

[11] EUSAK WD, G–4 Jnl, 10 Aug 50 (Rear, Yokohama); Ibid., G–4 Sec, 11–12 Aug 50; GHQ FEC Sitrep, 18 Aug 50; GHQ FEC G–3, Opn Rpts 57, 20 Aug, 66, 29 Aug, and 67, 30 Aug 50.

to the Far East as the quickest way it could devise of getting medium tanks and trained crews to the battlefield. Ships carrying these three tank battalions sailed from San Francisco on 23 July and arrived at Pusan on 7 August. The tank battalions unloaded the next day. The 6th Medium Tank Battalion served as Eighth Army reserve near Taegu in August; the 70th joined the 1st Cavalry Division on 12 August; and the 73d on army orders sent its companies to support various ground operations around the Pusan Perimeter—A Company to Ulsan guarding the eastern main supply route, B Company to Task Force Bradley at Kyongju and Kigye, and C Company to the 27th Infantry in the Bowling Alley north of Taegu. For further reinforcement of Eighth Army, the SS *Luxembourg Victory* departed San Francisco on 28 July with eighty medium tanks in its cargo. Still more armor reinforcements arrived on 16 August, when the 72d Medium Tank Battalion, organic to the 2d Infantry Division, landed at Pusan. The 2d Division also had two regimental tank companies.[12]

During August, therefore, 6 U.S. medium tank battalions landed in Korea, 5 of them in the first eight days of the month. There were, in addition, 4 regimental tank companies and about 30 light tanks for reconnaissance purposes. The tanks in the battalions were about equally divided between M26 Pershings and M4A3 Shermans, except for 1 battalion which had M46 Pattons. The tank battalions averaged 69 tanks. Through 22 August, Eighth Army had lost 20 medium tanks in action.[13] By the third week of August there were more than 500 U.S. medium tanks within the Pusan Perimeter. At the beginning of September American tanks outnumbered the enemy's on the Pusan Perimeter battlefield by at least five to one.

The Korean battle situation in August 1950 caused the Department of the Army to decide to increase its strength there by moving the 3d Infantry Division from the United States. Anticipating future offensive operations in Korea, General MacArthur on 19 August requested troops for two corps headquarters and asked that these two corps be designated I and IX Corps.[14]

Losses in the American divisions fighting in Korea had been so great in the first two months that special steps had to be taken to obtain replacements. On 19 August to help meet this demand, Eighth Army Rear in Japan ordered what it called "Operation Flushout." This required that all units in Japan reassign part of their troops as replacements for use in Korea. By 6 September, 229 officers and 2,201 enlisted men had been reassigned to Korea under this plan. Altogether, during August, 11,115 officer and enlisted replacements arrived in Ko-

---

[12] Schnabel, FEC, GHQ Support and Participation in the Korean War, ch. III, p. 29; 6th Med Tk Bn Opn Jnl, 23 Jul, 7–8 Aug 50; GHQ FEC Sitrep, 31 Jul 50.

[13] Arty School, Ft. Sill, Employment of Armor in Korea, The First Year, vol. 1, pp. 51–52; GHQ FEC G–3, Opn Rpt 64, 27 Aug 50; ORO, The Employment of Armor in Korea, ORO–R–1 (FEC), vol. 1, p. 167. The tank units in Korea in August were: 1st Marine Tank Battalion; U.S. Army 6th, 70th, 72d, 73d, and 89th Tank Battalions; Regimental tank company with the 5th RCT, three regimental tank companies with the 2d Infantry Division; and the light tanks of the reconnaissance companies of the 2d, 24th, and 25th Infantry, and the 1st Cavalry Divisions.

[14] Schnabel FEC, GHQ Support and Participation in Korean War, ch. III, pp. 24, 33.

rea from Japan and the United States.[15]

The United Nations Command had a supported strength in Korea on 1 September 1950 of nearly 180,000 men, according to figures available at the time. The major organizations reported their personnel strengths as follows:

Total	179,929
U.S. Eighth Army	78,762
2d Infantry Division 17,498	
24th Infantry Division 14,739	
25th Infantry Division 15,007	
1st Cavalry Division 14,703	
ROK Army	91,696
U.S. 1st Provisional Marine Brigade	4,290
British 27th Infantry Brigade	1,578
U.S. Fifth Air Force	3,603

Available for aerial action over Korea and naval action in the waters around it there must be counted an additional 33,651 men in the Far East Air Forces, 330 men of the Royal Australian Air Force, and 36,389 men in the U.S. Naval Forces, Far East.[16]

In early September a distinguished soldier joined the Eighth Army staff. The Department of the Army sent Maj. Gen. Leven C. Allen to Korea to serve as General Walker's chief of staff. General Allen in World War II had been General Omar N. Bradley's army group chief of staff in the European Theater of Operations. He entered on duty at Eighth Army Headquarters in Taegu on 4 September. Colonel Landrum, highly regarded by General Walker, remained as deputy chief of staff.[17]

The Korean War was more than two months old before the first United Nations troops, other than those of the United States, arrived in Korea. Since the Republic of Korea was not a member of the United Nations, the ROK Army was considered an allied force.

The British War Office on 20 August announced that it was dispatching to Korea at once from Hong Kong an infantry force of two battalions. These were regular troops and comprised the 27th Infantry Brigade headquarters, the 1st Battalion of the Middlesex Regiment, and the 1st Battalion of the Argyll and Sutherland Highlanders Regiment. Both regimental organizations dated from the American Revolution—the Middlesex Battalion from 1775, the Argylls from 1776. Since that time they had seen service in many parts of the world, including Wellington's Peninsular Campaign, India, and South Africa. Brigadier Basil A. Coad commanded the force. The British troops sailed from Hong Kong for Pusan, 1,300 miles to the north, on 25 August with bagpipes playing "Auld Lang Syne" and "The Campbells Are Coming." Five ships, including the cruiser *Ceylon* and the carrier *Unicorn*, carried the British to Pusan where they docked on 29 August. En route at sea, the rumor had spread among the troops that the North Koreans were only five miles from Pusan. Instead of the anticipated sound of gunfire the British soldiers found relative quiet in the port city. Debarking at once, the 27th In-

---

[15] Japan Logistical Comd, Hist Sec, Logistical Problems and Their Solutions, 25 Aug–31 Aug 50, p. 6 (15 Feb 52); GHQ FEC, Ann Narr Hist Rpt, 1 Jan–31 Oct 50, p. 32.

[16] EUSAK WD and PIR 50, 31 Aug 50; *Ibid.*, Sep 50 Summ; GHQ FEC Sitrep, 1 Sep 50. A postwar tabulation, ROK and UN Ground Forces Strength in Korea, 31 July 1950–31 July 1953, prepared by COA, 7 Oct 54 (copy in OCMH), shows a strength of 90,092 for Eighth Army, 126,580 for the ROK Army, and 4,468 for the 1st Provisional Marine Brigade.

[17] EUSAK WD, 4 Sep 50, sec 23, GO 52.

fantry Brigade, on Eighth Army orders, moved by train that night to an assembly area near Kyongsan, ten miles southeast of Taegu.[18]

On 24 August, General MacArthur established the Japan Logistical Command (JLC) as a major organization of the Far East Command. It relieved Eighth Army Rear of all responsibilities concerning posts, camps, and stations in Japan and assumed responsibility as well for the logistical support of all U.N. forces in Korea, except those specifically delegated to other commands. Other organizational changes came on 27 August when General MacArthur designated the Far East Air Forces and the U.S. Naval Forces, Far East, officially as part of the United Nations Command, thus clarifying his relationship to them as Commander in Chief of the United Nations Command. This action served as a precedent for subsequent attachments of other U.N. air and naval forces to the United Nations Command.[19]

The movement of refugees through the front lines and their removal from the battle area was a constant source of worry to the military authorities in August. Between 12 and 19 August, the 25th Division helped the ROK police screen and remove more than 50,000 refugees from its battlefront area between Chindong-ni and the Nam River. Altogether, the 25th Division evacuated 120,335 refugees from its sector during August. In mid-August, the 24th Division estimated there were 100,000 refugees in its southern sector seeking an opportunity to cross the Naktong River. On 24 August, about 300,000 refugees assembled in collecting points near Yongsan and Changnyong, began moving under ROK police control to areas away from the front lines. They were warned not to stray from their assigned routes of travel lest they be mistaken for guerrillas and shot. The 1st Cavalry Division and the ROK divisions eastward had similar experiences with refugees. In all cases, the ROK police, working in collaboration with the local army commanders, screened the refugees and moved them away from the combat area as quickly as possible.[20]

Occasionally, guerrillas would attack trains in rear areas of the Pusan Perimeter, usually in the Yongch'on-Kyongju area in the east or along the lower Naktong in the Samnangjin area. These attacks generally resulted in only a few persons wounded and minor damage to rail equipment. The most successful guerrilla attack behind the lines of the Pusan Perimeter occurred on 11 August against a VHF radio relay station on Hill 915, eight miles south of Taegu. A guerrilla force, estimated at 100 men, at 0515 attacked the 70 ROK police guarding the station and its American operators. They drove off the ROK police and set fire to the buildings. American casualties were 2 killed, 2 wounded, and 3 missing. When a ROK police force re-

---

[18] EUSAK WD, 29 Aug 50; *Ibid.*, G–3 Sec, Troop Control, 29 Aug 50; *Ibid.*, POR 139, 28 Aug 50; Maj Gen B. A. Coad, "The Land Campaign in Korea," *Journal of the Royal United Service Institution* (February, 1952), vol. XCVII, No. 585 (lecture given 29 Oct 51); New York *Times*, August 26, 1950; New York *Herald Tribune,* August 30, 1950, Bigart dispatch from Pusan.

[19] GHQ FEC, Ann Narr Hist Rpt, 1 Jan–21 Oct 50, ch. II.

[20] 25th Div WD, 11–19, 31 Aug 50; 2d Div Public Info Off file, Aug 50.

occupied the area later in the day the guerrillas had disappeared.[21]

How to use South Korean manpower to the greatest advantage became one of the most important problems early in the conduct of the war. An immediate need was for more troops to oppose and stop the advancing North Koreans. A longer range need was to build up the manpower of the allied forces to the point where they could drive the enemy back across the 38th Parallel. The program adopted was threefold: (1) fill the five ROK divisions to full strength with replacements; (2) activate new ROK divisions; and (3) attach large numbers of South Korean recruits to American units (a novel expedient).

As part of its projected expansion program the ROK Army opened training schools and centers for officers and replacements. On 14 July it opened the 1st Replacement Training Center at Taegu. This center at first operated on a 10-day schedule to receive and send out 1,000 men daily. The 2d Replacement Training Center at Pusan opened on 20 August. Its capacity was 500 daily, half that of the Taegu center. On 15 August, the ROK Army activated the Ground General School at Tongnae, near Pusan, which received its first class on 23 August. This school was principally a center for training infantry second lieutenant replacements. Its normal capacity was 250 candidates a week. After the pressing needs of the Pusan Perimeter battles had passed, all these schools lengthened their courses of training.[22]

On 10 August, General MacArthur, having received the necessary authority from the Department of the Army, authorized General Walker to increase the strength of the ROK Army to any practicable number.[23] Walker on 18 August requested authority to activate and equip five new ROK divisions at the rate of one a month beginning in September. The divisions were to have a strength of 10,500 men. General MacArthur denied General Walker this authority because of other needs for the available equipment, but he did concur in the recommendation to activate new divisions and service units and so reported to the Department of the Army. On 19 August the strength of the ROK tactical troops was 61,152; service troops, 23,672; total strength of the ROK Army, 84,824 men. The reported strength of ROK tactical organizations was as follows:[24]

Total	76,842
I ROK Corps Headquarters	1,275
Capital Division	16,376
8th Division	9,106
II ROK Corps Headquarters	499
1st Division	10,482
6th Division	9,300
ROK's Headquarters	2,159
3d Division	7,154
P'ohang Task Force	575
Task Force Kim	4,025
Special type troops	14,641
Training Center and Headquarters Company	1,250

The pay scale of the ROK Army in won per month was as follows, with the

---

[21] EUSAK WD, Aug 50, 25 Aug; *Ibid.*, Sig Sec and G–3 Sec, 11 Aug 50; *Ibid.*, Aug 50, 11 Aug, p. 59.
[22] ORO, Close Air Support Operations in Korea, ORO-R–3 (FEC), pp. 27–28, 42.

[23] Schnabel, FEC, GHQ Support and Participation in the Korean War, ch. IV, pp. 29, 33; GHQ FEC Sitrep, 10 Aug 50.
[24] EUSAK WD, G–4, 19 Aug 50; Schnabel, FEC, GHQ Support and Participation in the Korean War, ch. IV, pp. 31–33; ORO, Utilization of Indigenous Manpower in Korea, ORO-R–4 (FEC), Table XXII, p. 65.

exchange rate of 4,000 won to one U.S. dollar:

Pvt	3,000
Pfc	3,600
Cpl	4,500
Sgt	5,400
SSgt	6,000
MSgt	24,900
WO	29,700
2d Lt	30,900
1st Lt	33,300
Capt	35,700
Maj	41,700
Lt Col	46,500
Col	51,300
Gen	60,000

Of the five planned new divisions, the ROK Army intended to reactivate first the ROK 7th Division and second the ROK 11th Division. General MacArthur warned that the new divisions could be equipped only from stocks delivered from the United States. The ROK Army did not wait upon the planned schedule, but was in the process of reactivating the ROK 7th Division at the end of August, forming at least one battalion in each of the 3d, 5th, and 8th Regiments. Task Force Min as an organization disappeared from the ROK Army Order of Battle and became instead the 1st and 2d Battalions of the 5th Regiment, ROK 7th Division.[25]

The attachment by 10 September of a U.S. battalion of 105-mm. howitzers to each of the six ROK divisions then in action considerably increased their combat effectiveness. But even with this new artillery, it must be noted that the ROK divisions had only approximately one-fourth the artillery support of that of the American divisions in Eighth Army.[26] It should not have been surprising that sometimes the ROK divisions did not perform as satisfactorily as the U.S. divisions.

A proper ration for the ROK soldier finally evolved after experimentation and testing, and was adopted in September. It provided 3,165 calories a day for an active 130-pound man. The ration included canned fish, field biscuit, barley, rice, kelp, and tea. Supplemental items were furnished from American stocks. This diet gave promise of improving the physical stamina of the ROK soldier.[27]

Korean Augmentation to the United States Army

Concurrent with the steps taken in August to rebuild the ROK Army, the Far East Command planned to incorporate 30,000 to 40,000 ROK recruits in the four American divisions in Korea and the one still in Japan but scheduled to go to Korea. This was admittedly a drastic expedient to meet the replacement requirement in the depleted American ground forces. As early as 10 August, Eighth Army began planning for the Korean augmentation, but it was not until 15 August that General MacArthur ordered it—General Walker was to increase the strength of each company and battery of United States troops by 100 Koreans. The Koreans legally would be part of the ROK Army and would be

---

[25] GHQ FEC G-3, Opn Rpts 61, 24 Aug, and 65, 28 Aug 50; Schnabel, FEC, GHQ Support and Participation in the Korean War, ch. IV, pp. 32–33.

[26] EUSAK WD, 11 Sep 50, Arty Rpt, sec 5. Artillery was assigned to the ROK divisions as follows: 10th FA Bn to Capital Div; 17th FA Bn to 1st Div; 11th FA Bn to 3d Div; 16th FA Bn to 6th Div; 18th FA Bn to 7th Div; 50th FA Bn to 8th Div.

[27] EUSAK WD, sec 17, Quartermaster Rpt, 13 Sep 50.

paid and administered by the South Korean Government. They would receive U.S. rations and special service items. The Far East Command initially expected that each ROK recruit would pair with a United States soldier.[28]

Before the augmentation program began there had been a few cases in which American unit commanders had used volunteer South Koreans unofficially to strengthen their forces. One of the first of these officers, if not the first, was Colonel Clainos, commanding officer of the 1st Battalion, 7th Cavalry Regiment. About the first of August, just after Eighth Army had retired behind the Naktong River, four Korean officers and 133 men from the South Korean police at Taegu voluntarily joined Clainos' battalion on the unofficial basis that they would receive arms and food to the best of Colonel Clainos' ability. A Lieutenant Chung, a Tokyo-trained Korean wearing a Japanese samurai sword, marched his unit to the 1st Battalion. Colonel Clainos attached Lieutenant Chung to his staff and the other three officers to A, B and C Companies, respectively. He then attached two Korean policemen to each rifle squad in the companies. Nine days after these Koreans joined the 1st Battalion they took part in the battle at Triangulation Hill, after the North Korean crossing of the Naktong in the 1st Cavalry Division sector. Two of them were killed in this action, and seven wounded. Of the wounded, all refused evacuation except one who could not walk.[29]

The U.S. 7th Infantry Division in Japan was far understrength, having contributed key personnel to the 24th, 25th, and 1st Cavalry Divisions in succession when they mounted out for Korea. In an effort to rebuild this division, the first Korean augmentation recruits were assigned to it rather than to the divisions in Korea. The first three platoons of 313 recruits left Pusan by ship the morning of 16 August and arrived in Japan the afternoon of the 18th. Once started, the shipments of recruits left Pusan at the rate of nearly 2,000 daily. The final shipment arrived at Yokohama on the 24th and debarked the next day, making a total of 8,625 Korean officers and men for the division. The South Korean Government at first obtained many of these recruits directly from the streets of Pusan and Taegu. In the contingents shipped to Japan, schoolboys still had their schoolbooks; one recruit who had left home to obtain medicine for his sick wife still had the medicine with him.[30]

On 20 August, the American divisions in Korea received their first augmentation recruits—the 24th and 25th Divisions, 250 each; the 2d and 1st Cavalry Divisions, 249 each. For the next week each of the divisions received a daily average of 250 Korean recruits. On the 29th and 30th, the 1st Cavalry Division got an average of 740, and the 24th Division, 950 recruits daily. Near the end of August the plan changed so that every fourth day each division would receive 500 men until it had a total of 8,300 Korean recruits. Except for the first

---

[28] EUSAK WD, 10 and 20 Aug 50; *Ibid.*, Off Asst CofS, G-1, 15 Aug 50; GHQ FEC Sitreps, 10 and 19 Aug 50.
[29] Ltr, Clainos to author, n.d., but recd May 54.

[30] EUSAK WD, G-3 Sec, 19 Aug 50; *Ibid.*, 20 Aug 50; *Ibid.*, G-1 Sec Rpt, 24 Aug 50; ORO, Close Air Support Operations in Korea, ORO-R-4 (FEC), p. 54.

groups, the recruits received five days' training at the Kup'o-ri Training Center near Pusan, which was opened 20 August.[31]

Even though it initially had been the intention of the Far East Command to pair Korean augmentation recruits with American soldiers in a "buddy system," this did not work out uniformly in practice in the Eighth Army. The 1st Cavalry and the 2d Infantry Divisions used the buddy system, with the American responsible for the training of the recruit in use of weapons, drill, personal hygiene, and personal conduct. Two regiments of the 25th Division used the system, while the third placed the recruits in separate platoons commanded by American officers and noncommissioned officers. General Church directed the 24th Division to place all its augmentation recruits in separate squads and platoons commanded by selected Korean officers and noncommissioned officers. These Korean squads and platoons were attached to American units.[32]

Capt. Robert K. Sawyer who, as a 2d lieutenant, commanded a platoon of these new augmentation recruits in the Reconnaissance Company, 25th Division, has given a fair appraisal of the typical Korean recruit in the United States Army in August and September 1950:

When a fresh batch arrived our First Sergeant ran them through a brief school-

SOUTH KOREAN RECRUIT *with an American soldier.*

ing on methods of attack, and they were ready for us. Recon Company's ROK contingent ate with us (our menu plus a huge, steaming plate of rice), but otherwise was a force apart.

About sixty ROK's were assigned to each Recon platoon, under the command of an American Lieutenant, as support for the Recon platoon leader. In other words, each Recon platoon had two U.S. officers; one for the Americans, the other for the ROK's. I had the latter job for a few weeks. On some occasions I controlled forces consisting of nearly one hundred ROK's, plus ten or twelve GI's scattered throughout for control. At other times I had a fifty-fifty combination. Sometimes the Americans predominated.

It is difficult for me to evaluate the Koreans who augmented our ranks. All in all, however, I was not impressed by my charges and was happy to see the last of them. Mere recruits, they simply had not had time to become soldiers, and I used them for little more than carrying ammunition and rations. On the occasions I had to use them for fighting I spread my GI's

---

[31] 25th Div WD, 20 Aug 50; 1st Cav Div WD, 20 Aug 50; GHQ FEC Sitrep, 21 Aug 50; ORO, Close Air Support Operations in Korea, ORO-R-4 (FEC), Table XVII, pt. 1, pp. 52, 54–56, 60–62; Lt Ed. E. Balforth, "Getting Our ROK's," *U.S. Combat Forces Journal* (February, 1951), p. 23.

[32] EUSAK WD, Memo from Asst CofS G-1, 5 Sep 50, sub: Korean Augmentation; 19th Inf WD, 29 Aug 50; 35th Inf WD, 20 Aug 50; 24th Div WD, G-1 Hist Rpt, 3-4 Sep 50; 25th Div WD, 4 Sep 50.

around and prayed that nothing of consequence would happen.

My ROK's were always hungry, and never did understand that the cardboard box of C rations was meant for one day's subsistence. Often, an hour after doling out the one-box-per-man I have heard my interpreter ask me for more 'chop-chop.' The Koreans had already eaten their entire day's supply! Invariably they fell asleep when on guard, requiring constant checking by the Americans. And to make matters worse, most Koreans I have observed love to greet the morning sun with a song. This habit did not always fit into our security plan.

In one action I had spread my ROK's in a half circle position, with GI's posted here and there along the line for control. Late in the morning one lone sniper fired at us, and immediately my ROK's went to pieces. Hysterical, they lay on the ground with faces pressed into the earth, weapons pointed in the general direction of the enemy, firing madly, wasting ammunition, completely out of hand. There was only one way to straighten out the situation, so my GI's and I went from ROK to ROK, kicking them and dragging them bodily to where they could see. We eventually succeeded in quieting them down, and when the enemy attacked us later in the day my ROK's held pretty well.[33]

The buddy system of using the Korean augmentation recruits gradually broke down and was abandoned. Most American soldiers did not like the system. Most units found they could employ the recruits, organized in ROK squads and platoons with American officers and noncommissioned officers in charge, to best advantage as security guards, in scouting and patrolling, and in performing various labor details. They were particularly useful in heavy weapons companies where the hand-carrying of machine guns, mortars, and recoilless rifles and their ammunition over the rugged terrain was a grueling job. They also performed valuable work in digging and camouflaging defensive positions.[34]

There also began in August the extensive use of Korean civilians with A-frames as cargo carriers up the mountains to the front lines. This method of transport proved both cheaper and more efficient than using pack animals. American units obtained the civilian carriers through arrangements with the ROK Army. Soon the American divisions were using Korean labor for nearly all unskilled work, at an average of about 500 laborers and carriers to a division.

The U.S. divisions in Korea never received the number of Korean augmentation recruits planned for them. In September the divisions began to take steps to halt further assignments. In the middle of the month, the 24th Division requested Eighth Army not to assign to it any more such troops until the division asked for them. As one observer wrote, "The Koreans haven't had time to learn our Army technique. An American doughboy hated to have his life dependent on whether his Oriental buddy knew enough to give him covering fire at the right moment." [35] The language barrier, the difference in loyalties, the

---

[33] Sawyer, Notes on Korea, Aug-Nov 50, prepared for author in 1952.

[34] 25th Div WD, 31 Aug 50; 1st Cav Div WD, 29 Aug 50; Maj Norman F. J. Allen, Korean Army Troops, U.S.A. (KATUSA), student MS, Advanced Inf Course, Class 2, Inf School, Ft. Benning, Ga., 1952-53. This is an interesting case study of augmentation in one rifle company. The Korean carrier received a wage of 500 won daily (12½ cents) and a rice ration.

[35] Hal Boyle, "The AP Reports on the Buddy System," *U.S. Combat Forces Journal* (February, 1951), p. 23; 24th Div WD, G-1 Stf Sec Summ, 26 Aug-28 Sep 50.

lack of training in the recruits, and their relative combat ineffectiveness all put great strain on the attempt to integrate the Koreans. It was not strange that as fast as American units obtained American replacements they dispensed with their Korean replacements. By winter, the buddy system had been quietly dropped.

Eighth Army Realignment and Extension Eastward

The last of the 2d Division's regiments, the 38th, known as "The Rock of the Marne" and commanded by Col. George B. Peploe, landed at Pusan on 19 August. The next day, 20 August, Eighth Army issued an operational directive ordering the 2d Infantry Division to relieve the 24th Division as soon as the 38th Regiment closed on Miryang. The 2d Division completed relief of the 24th Division in its Naktong River positions on 24 August and Keiser, 2d Division commander, assumed responsibility for the sector at 1800 that date.

The strength of the 24th Division on 25 August was approximately 10,600 men. It needed about 8,000 replacements as well as quantities of arms, equipment, and vehicles to bring it up to war strength. The 19th Infantry and the 11th Field Artillery Battalion were attached to the 2d Division as a reserve force; the 21st Infantry became Eighth Army reserve; the rest of the division assembled in the vicinity of Kyongsan, twelve miles southeast of Taegu.[36]

General Walker, after discussing the matter with General Church on 26 August, ordered the 34th Infantry reduced to paper status and its personnel and remaining equipment transferred to the 19th and 21st Regiments. At the same time, Eighth Army also reduced to paper status the 63d Field Artillery Battalion, which had been in support of the 34th Infantry, and transferred its troops and equipment to the newly activated C Batteries of the 11th, 13th, and 52d Field Artillery Battalions. The effective dates for the transfer were 26 August for the artillery and 31 August for the infantry. The troops of the 1st Battalion, 34th Infantry, were transferred to the 19th Infantry as its newly activated 3d Battalion and the men of the 3d Battalion, 34th Infantry, were transferred to the 21st Infantry as its newly activated 2d Battalion. Out of the nearly 2,000 men who originally entered Korea with the 34th Infantry on 3 July, there were 184 left in the regiment at the end of August— the rest either had been killed, wounded, or were missing in action. Colonel Beauchamp was reassigned to the command of his old regiment, the 32d Infantry of the 7th Division.[37]

Simultaneously with this action, General Walker transferred the 5th Regimental Combat Team to the 24th Division as its third regiment. The 5th Regimental Combat Team at this time numbered about 3,500 men. The 6th Medium Tank Battalion with about 650 men also was to be attached to the 24th

---

[36] 24th Div WD, 20–26 Aug 50; 2d Div POR 64, 24 Aug 50; EUSAK WD, G–3 Sec, 24 Aug 50.

[37] EUSAK WD, GO 37, 26 Aug 50; Ibid., GO 37, 28 Aug 50; 34th Inf WD, 26 Aug 50; 24th Div WD, G–4 Opn Highlights, 26 Aug–29 Sep 50; 24th Div WD, 31 Aug 50; 19th Inf WD, Pers Summ 26 Aug–28 Sep 50; 34th Inf WD, Summ, 22 Jul–26 Aug 50; Interv, author with Beauchamp, 1 Aug 52. The 34th Infantry from 5 July to 23 August had suffered 1,714 casualties—98 KIA, 569 WIA, 773 MIA, and 274 nonbattle casualties.

Division. The division still needed approximately 4,000 replacements.[38]

The 27th and 35th Regiments of the 25th Division had received their third battalions early in August with the transfer to them of the two battalions of the 29th Infantry. The 1st Cavalry Division on 26 August received the third battalions for its regiments in organizations sent from the United States. It also received 3 provisional artillery batteries to provide the third firing battery for 3 battalions of artillery. At the end of August, therefore, the 4 U.S. divisions in Korea had finally built up their regiments to the normal 3 battalions.[39]

In Eighth Army a confused order of battle had prevailed generally throughout August. Battle conditions frequently had compelled the army to separate battalions and regiments from their parent organizations and send them posthaste to distant points of the Pusan Perimeter to bolster a threatened sector. All divisions except the 1st Cavalry at various times were broken up by this process. At the end of August, Eighth Army made an effort to unscramble the disorder. It ordered the 23d Infantry on 28 August to leave the Taegu front and return to 2d Division control at Miryang; it ordered the 27th Infantry on 30 August to rejoin the 25th Division at Masan; and it ordered the 5th Regimental Combat Team north from the Masan area to join the 24th Division.[40]

The course of battle in the ROK eastern sector of the Perimeter and the enemy advance down the Sangju-Taegu road during August caused General Walker near the end of the month to decide on a shift of the boundary eastward between the American and ROK troops. He considered the existing boundary near the Sangju-Taegu road a source of military weakness. On 26 August he ordered a new boundary line slanting southeast from a point two miles north of the Walled City of Ka-san to a point east of and below Taegu. This placed the Sangju-Taegu road and the former zone of the ROK 1st Division in the American zone. The 1st Cavalry Division was to move eastward into the ROK 1st Division zone, and the U.S. 2d Division at the same time was to extend its zone northward into the 1st Cavalry zone. The shift of units was to take place as soon as practicable, but no later than 30 August.[41]

Pursuant to the army directive, General Gay on 28 August ordered the 7th Cavalry Regiment to occupy the left (west) part of the ROK 1st Division sector and the 8th Cavalry Regiment to occupy the right (east) part. This shift placed the 7th and 8th Cavalry Regiments in mountainous terrain north of Taegu. The supply of these units now became much more difficult than it had been along the Naktong. On 29 August, the 3d Battalion, 23d Infantry, relieved

---

[38] 24th Div WD, 29 Aug 50; Interv, author with Church, 25 Sep 52. Given his choice, General Church chose to have the 5th RCT as his third regiment rather than rebuild the 34th Infantry with replacements.

[39] EUSAK WD, 26 Aug 50; 5th and 8th Cav Regts WD, 26 Aug 50; 7th Cav WD, 27 Aug 50; EUSAK GO 182, 29 Aug 50. The 3d Bn, 7th Regt, 3d Inf Div, from Fort Devens, Mass., became the 3d Bn, 8th Cav; the 2d Bn, 30th Inf Regt, 3d Div, from Fort Benning became the 3d Bn, 7th Cav, and a battalion from Camp Carson became the 3d Bn, 5th Cav Regt.

[40] EUSAK WD, 30 Aug 50; GHQ FEC G-3 Opn Rpt 65, 28 Aug 50.

[41] EUSAK WD, Opn Dir, 26 Aug 50. For a description of the Walled City of Ka-san, see pages 422-23, below.

the 7th Cavalry Regiment in the southern part of the division sector, and the 7th Cavalry in turn relieved the ROK 13th Regiment and part of the 12th. When the newly arrived 3d Battalion of the 5th Cavalry assumed responsibility on 30 August for the generally quiet 14,000-yard sector of the 8th Cavalry Regiment, the result was a 32,000-yard front for the 5th Cavalry. The 8th Cavalry Regiment then moved to the sectors of the ROK 11th and part of the 12th Regiments. The 1st Cavalry Division completed the relief of the ROK 1st Division at 1300 on 30 August, whereupon the ROK division moved to its new sector just eastward of the new boundary. The contemplated shift of the 2d Division zone of responsibility northward proved impracticable because the area could be supplied only over the road net from Taegu, and Eighth Army reestablished the old boundary between the two divisions, effective 30 August. To defend this old 7th Cavalry sector, Eighth Army attached the 3d Battalion, 23d Infantry, to the 1st Cavalry Division.[42]

On 30 August the 714th Transportation Railway Operating Battalion arrived in Korea and became responsible for operating the approximately 500 miles of rail lines within the Pusan Perimeter.[43] The rail lines usually carried supplies from Pusan to a division railhead. From there they were trucked forward to regiment and battalion.

August was a month of heavy casualties for Eighth Army. Battle casualties in its four divisions were for the 24th Division, 1,941; 25th Division, 1,800; 1st Cavalry Division, 1,503; and the 9th Regiment of the 2d Division, 827. Nonbattle casualties were high in all units, many of them caused by heat exhaustion; the 9th Regiment alone had 419 nonbattle casualties. Loss among officers was very heavy.[44]

During the same period, battle losses had been far greater in the ROK Army than in United States forces, but nonbattle casualties were fewer. On some days ROK battle losses were wholly disproportionate to American. As extreme examples, on 6 August American battle losses were 74, the ROK 1,328; on 21 August the American battle losses were 49, the ROK, 2,229.[45]

As is customary in most army and theater zones of military action, Eighth Army had prepared plans to meet all eventualities anticipated as probable. In early August, General MacArthur outlined to General Walker a defense line closer to Pusan than the Naktong River line. He wanted this line prepared for occupancy in the event Eighth Army could not stop the North Koreans at the Naktong. On 11 August, General Walker verbally instructed Brig. Gen. Garrison H. Davidson, an Engineer officer, to lay out this secondary defense line. Davidson, after looking over the ground, recommended to General Walker that because of better defensive terrain the line should be somewhat farther back toward Pusan than General MacArthur had indicated. General Walker replied that the

---

[42] 1st Cav Div WD, 28–29 Aug 50; EUSAK POR 144, 29 Aug and POR 147, 30 Aug 50; 5th Cav WD, 27 Aug 50.

[43] Mossman and Middleton, Logistical Problems and Their Solutions, p. 53.

[44] 25th Div WD, 26 and 31 Aug 50; 1st Cav Div WD, Aug 50 Summ; 2d Div WD, G–1 Sec, 9 Jul–Aug 50; Ltr, Asst CofS to CG 2d Div; 24th Div WD, AG Sec, 1–26 Aug 50, 23 Aug.

[45] GHQ FEC G–3 Opn Rpts 39–67, 2–30 Aug 50.

line would be constructed where General MacArthur had indicated it should go. General Davidson began laying out the line with very few resources. He received some help from Brig. Gen. Crump Garvin and the 2d Logistical Command at Pusan and from the 2d and 25th Divisions. This line, known as the Davidson Line, began on the east coast at Sodong-ni, approximately eight miles north of Ulsan, and extended generally west along high ground to a point northeast of Miryang, then curved down the ridge east of Muan-ni, turned south across the Naktong River and anchored on the high ground northeast of Masan. General Walker would not approve Davidson's recommendation to remove all houses from in front of the line to clear a field of fire. Davidson succeeded in laying a trace of the line on the ground, cleared fields of fire except for houses, ordered material for fortifications, and was able to have a few positions dug before he reported to the 24th Division as assistant division commander on the first of September.[46]

While General Walker had many capable staff officers at his Eighth Army headquarters at this time, perhaps none was more valuable to him than Col. John A. Dabney, Assistant Chief of Staff, G-3, who had joined the Army in Korea during July. Dabney was quiet and unassuming, possessed of a good mind, sound professional knowledge, persistent in his search of facts, and blessed with a fine judgment in evaluating combat information. He showed common sense throughout the critical Naktong battles of the Perimeter, and was a trusted and valued adviser to General Walker and his chief of staff.

At the beginning of September the United Nations had a large numerical superiority of men in the line divisions and in army reserve. In the skies over the battlefield and in the coastal waters guarding the Perimeter flanks, United Nations aerial and naval might was virtually uncontested. Approximately 600 American medium tanks mounting 90-mm. and 76-mm. guns were in the battle area on 1 September, as contrasted with probably not more than 100 North Korean Russian-built medium T34 tanks mounting 85-mm. guns. Eighth Army also had overwhelming superiority in artillery and mortar fire.

The Eighth Army intelligence officer on 30 August estimated that the twelve known enemy rifle divisions had an effective strength of 82,590 men, with combat effectiveness varying between 27 percent for the *13th* and *15th Divisions* to 96 percent for the *7th* and 100 percent for the *2d Division*. His estimate gave the North Korean divisions a loss of 26,820 men in August against a gain of only 14,770 replacements.[47] This estimate, as noted below, was not entirely correct.

The North Korean Plan

In their action against the Perimeter in August the plan and tactics of the North Koreans showed no departure from those that had characterized their

---

[46] Intcrv, author with Maj Gen Garrison H. Davidson, 28 Jan 54; Ltr, Dabney to author, 19 Jan 54.

[47] EUSAK WD and PIR 49, 30 Aug 50; *Ibid.*, Sep 50 Summ. On 1 September the United Nations held 1,753 North Korean prisoners—1,372 captured by ROK forces, 381 by Eighth Army.

advance south of the Han River in July. Their divisions simply followed the American and ROK forces on all avenues leading south and closed with them as soon as possible. Enemy action followed the familiar pattern of frontal holding attack, envelopment of the flank, and infiltration to the rear. These tactics had paid high dividends during July when the North Koreans were numerically superior to the forces opposing them and when there was no continuous and connected defense line across the width of Korea. When Eighth Army and the ROK Army withdrew into the Pusan Perimeter in early August and there stabilized a line in relatively connected although thinly held defense positions, these tactics failed for the first time in the war to accomplish their desired result.

The battle line on both flanks rested on the sea. U.N. naval forces secured these flanks. Flanking operations and a tactical decision by grand maneuver were now impossible. Success could come to the North Korean command now in only one way—by frontal attack and penetration of the Perimeter defense followed by immediate exploitation.

Generals MacArthur and Walker applied classical principles of defense in the Pusan Perimeter battles—interior lines of communications for movement of supplies and reinforcements, superior artillery fire power to break the offensive spirit of enemy soldiers and reduce their numbers, and a strong air force which is ideally suited for operational defense because it can intervene quickly in adding its fire power to turn the tide of battle.

The North Korean Army strength during August fell below the combined strength of the U.S. Eighth and the ROK Armies. It is certain also that its combat effectiveness at the first of September was considerably below what it had been a month earlier. While its numbers may have been as large, its trained troops, tanks, and heavy weapons were fewer. Many of the recruits that filled the North Korean divisions in September had no small arms.

The North Korea People's Army had shown a remarkable ability to maintain transport to its front lines over long lines of communications despite heavy and constant air attacks. This accomplishment is one of the outstanding feats of the North Korean war effort in the Pusan Perimeter period. The United Nations air effort failed to halt military rail transport. Ammunition and motor fuel, which took precedence over all other types of supply, continued to arrive at the front, though in diminished quantity. There was still a considerable resupply of heavy weapons, such as tanks, artillery, and mortars, at the front in early September, although a steady decline in artillery can be traced from the middle of August. There was a sufficient supply of small arms ammunition, but a shortage of small arms themselves became apparent by mid-August and continued to worsen with each passing week. Rear areas were able to fill only about one third of the requisitions from the front for small arms in mid-August and resupply ceased entirely about the middle of September. New trucks were almost impossible to obtain. There was no resupply of clothing. At best there were rations for only one or two meals a day. Most units had to live at least partially off the country. By 1 September the food situation was so bad in the North Korean Army at the front that most of the soldiers showed a loss of stamina with resulting impaired combat effectiveness.[48]

The North Koreans directed the Pusan Perimeter battles from their *Front Headquarters* in Kumch'on. Marshal Choe Yong Gun, the North Korean Minister of Defense, was Deputy Commander of the North Korean Armed Forces. He had formerly been associated with the Chinese Communist *8th Route Army*. In command of the *Front Headquarters* during August and September was General Kim Chaek. His chief of staff was Lt. Gen. Kang Kon until the latter was killed near Andong by a land mine explosion on 8 September.

The *II Corps* from its headquarters at Mun'gyong directed the action from north of Taegu eastward to the coast. Lt. Gen. Kim Mu Chong, a graduate of the Whampoa Military Academy under Chiang Kai-shek and a Communist veteran of the Chinese wars, commanded the *II Corps*. He had accompanied Mao Tse Tung on the "Long March" and reportedly was the only one of thirty Koreans to survive that march.

The *I Corps*, which had captured Seoul in the early days of the war, had direct charge under the *Front Headquarters* for the western half of the enemy arc around the Perimeter, from Waegwan south to the Korea Strait. Lt. Gen. Kim Ung, a spectacular soldier, commanded the *I Corps*. Kim had gone from Korea to the Whampoa Military Academy and eventually served with the Communist *8th Route Army* in North China where reportedly he became a brigade or division commander. He was generally considered the ablest of the North Korean field commanders. He was energetic and harsh, feared rather than loved by his subordinates. His *I Corps* headquarters was at Chonju.[49]

With time running against it, the North Korean High Command prepared a massive co-ordinated offensive all around the Pusan Perimeter for the first of September. As the North Korea People's Army prepared for its great effort, it brought 13 infantry divisions, 1 armored division, 2 armored brigades, and miscellaneous security forces into the line. On the *I Corps* front, reaching from opposite Taegu southward along the Naktong River, in line from north to south, were the *10th, 2d, 4th, 9th, 7th,* and *6th Infantry Divisions.* Elements of the *105th Armored Division* and the newly arrived *16th Armored Brigade* supported these troops. The *16th Armored Brigade,* really a regiment, had forty-three new T34 tanks when it left P'yongyang in August to take part in the September offensive. Back of the *6th Division* was the *104th Security Brigade.* Deployed along the *II Corps* front from northwest of Taegu eastward to the coast and in line from west to east were the *3d, 13th, 1st, 8th, 15th, 12th,* and *5th Infantry Divisions.* Elements of the *105th Armored Division* and the newly arrived *17th Armored Brigade* supported this corps. The *17th Armored Brigade,* also actually

---

[48] DA Intel Rev, Dec 50, 175, pp. 36-38; ATIS Interrog Rpts, Issue 3, Rpt 895, p. 214, Maj Kim Song Won, CO *19th Regt, 13th Div.*

[49] GHQ FEC, History of the North Korean Army, pp. 41, 84, 91-94, 98; ATIS Enemy Docs, Issue 9, p. 66, ltr, Kim Man Hwa to Col Lee Hak Ku, CofS N.K. *13th Div,* 8 Sep 50; New York *Times,* August 25 and September 11, 1950.

a regiment, had forty new tanks when it left P'yongyang. Most, if not all, of the tanks in the two brigades apparently arrived in P'yongyang on or about 23 August, coming from the Russians by way of Manchuria. Trained crews were immediately assigned to the tanks. The two armored brigades each had two battalions; each battalion was composed of four tank companies. The two new armored brigades moved to the front by rail at night.[50]

Other than the *17th Armored Brigade,* the *II Corps* had no new units along the northern and eastern front for the September offensive. In the *I Corps* sector were two new and previously uncommitted infantry formations to strengthen the assault forces there. The *9th Infantry Division,* formed around the old *3d Border Constabulary,* arrived in the Hyopch'on area from Seoul (less its *3d Regiment* which remained at Inch'on) on or about 25 August. The *7th Infantry Division,* in the Chinju-Masan area, had not been committed except for two battalions that fought briefly against ROK marines at T'ongyong.[51]

The North Korean force assembled at the front on 1 September for the assault against the Pusan Perimeter numbered about 98,000 men. Perhaps a third were raw recruits, most of them forcibly conscripted in South Korea and hastened to the front with little or no training and with few weapons. It is believed that the major organizations had personnel strength approximately as follows:[52]

Total	97,850
1st Infantry Division	5,000
2d Infantry Division	6,000
3d Infantry Division	7,000
4th Infantry Division	5,500
5th Infantry Division	7,000
6th Infantry Division	10,000
7th Infantry Division	9,000
8th Infantry Division	6,500
9th Infantry Division	9,350
10th Infantry Division	7,500
12th Infantry Division	5,000
13th Infantry Division	9,000
15th Infantry Division	7,000
104th Security Brigade	2,000
105th Armored Division	1,000
16th Armored Brigade	500
17th Armored Brigade	500

Planning for the massive attack was under way for at least the last ten days of August since the N.K. Army operational order for the *I Corps* attack was issued on or about 20 August. The enemy plan indicated five major groupings of assault units and objectives:

1. *6th* and *7th Divisions* to break through the U.S. 25th Division to Masan in the south.

2. *9th, 4th, 2d,* and *10th Divisions* to break through the U.S. 2d Division to Miryang and the Pusan-Taegu railroad and highway by way of Changnyong and Yongsan.

3. *3d, 13th,* and *1st Divisions* to break through the U.S. 1st Cavalry Division and the ROK 1st Division to Taegu.

---

[50] GHQ FEC, History of the North Korean Army; ATIS Res Supp Interrog Rpts, issues for the N.K. divisions previously cited; ORO, Employment of Armor in Korea, ORO-R-1 (FEC), vol. 1, p. 165, app. F (Apr 51); EUSAK WD, 9 Sep 50, PW Rpts, 2d Lt Won Hong Ki and Sgt Choi Soong Moon; Ibid., PIR 55, 5 Sep 50.

[51] ATIS Res Supp Interrog Rpts, Issue 100 (N.K. 9th Div), p. 49; Ibid., Issue 99 (N. K. 7th Div), p. 35.

[52] These figures are based on information derived from enemy material: ATIS Res Supp Interrog Rpts, Issues 3, 4, 94, 96, 99, 100, 104 (N.K. *1st, 2d, 3d, 4th, 5th, 6th, 7th, 8th, 9th, 10th, 12th, 13th Divs*); GHQ FEC, History of the North Korean Army.

4. *8th* and *15th Divisions* to break through the ROK 8th and 6th Divisions to Hayang and Yongch'on in the lateral corridor east of Taegu.

5. *12th* and *5th Divisions* to break through the ROK Capital and 3d Divisions to P'ohang-dong, Yonil Airfield, and the Kyongju corridor to Pusan.

Assault groupings 1 and 2 of *I Corps* were to begin their co-ordinated attacks at 2330, 31 August; assault groupings 3, 4, and 5 of *II Corps* were to attack at 1800, 2 September.[53]

---

[53] GHQ FEC, History of the North Korean Army, pp. 57, 65, 73; ATIS Res Supp Interrog Rpts, Issue 100 (N.K. *6th Div*) pp. 40–42; *Ibid.*, Issue 3 (N.K. *15th Div*), p. 44; ATIS Enemy Docs, Issue 9, p. 65, notebooks belonging to Col Lee Hak Ku, CofS *13th Div*, gives summary of order from Mu Chong, CG N.K. *II Corps*; *Ibid.*, p. 69, ltr from Choe Fam, CO *21st Regt, 13th Div*, to Col Lee Hak Ku, 2 Sep 50.

CHAPTER XXII

Perimeter Battle

> Every battle has a turning point when the slack water of uncertainty becomes the ebb tide of defeat or the flood water of victory.
>
> ADMIRAL CHARLES TURNER JOY

For most of the men who fought the battles of the Pusan Perimeter in early September 1950, it was a period of confusion. So many actions went on simultaneously that only a wide-screen view could reveal the situation as the commander had to cope with it in its totality. Since this panoramic approach is not feasible, the story in this chapter will follow the battles from the east coast near P'ohang-dong westward to Taegu and the Naktong River for the first two weeks of September. The next chapter will follow the battles for the same period of time in the southern part of the Pusan Perimeter.

It is necessary to keep in mind that not one of the battles in this phase of the war was an isolated event, but that everywhere over the extent of the Perimeter other battles of equal, greater, or lesser intensity were being waged. As an example of their impact, on 3 September 1950 General Walker faced at least five distinct and dangerous situations on the Perimeter—an enemy penetration in the east at P'ohang-dong, severance of the lateral corridor at Yongch'on between Taegu and P'ohang-dong, alarming enemy gains in the mountains north of Taegu, the threat posed by North Korean units slicing through the defenses of the Naktong Bulge area of the lower Naktong, and enemy penetration behind the greater part of the 25th Division in the Masan area in the extreme south. In addition, at this time in the east the ROK II Corps was on the point of collapse; above Taegu the 1st Cavalry Division withdrew closer to that city; and in the south disaster threatened the U.S. 2d and 25th Divisions.

Action in the East—Task Force Jackson

Although the N.K. *II Corps'* general attack in the north and east was planned for 2 September, the enemy *12th Division*, now numbering about 5,000 men, started earlier to move forward from the mountain fastnesses where it had reorganized after its defeat in the Kigye and P'ohang-dong area. (*Map 14*) The division was low in food supply, weapons, and ammunition, and its men were in a state of lowered morale. On 26 August, American and ROK officers in the P'ohang-dong–Kigye area with great optimism congratulated each other on having repulsed what they thought was the last serious threat to the Pusan Perimeter. In their view the North Koreans were now on the defensive and the war might end by Thanksgiving.

Nearest to the N.K. *12th Division* was the ROK Capital Division. At 0400, 27 August, a North Korean attack overran one company of the ROK 17th Regiment, Capital Division, north of Kigye. This caused the whole regiment to give way. Then the 18th Regiment on the right fell back because of its exposed flank. The 17th Regiment lost the town of Kigye, and the entire Capital Division fell back three miles to the south side of the Kigye valley. This enemy blow fell with startling impact on Eighth Army in the predawn hours of 27 August.[1]

At the briefing at Eighth Army headquarters in Taegu on Sunday, 27 August, General Walker showed his concern over this development. One of those present was Maj. Gen. John B. Coulter who had arrived in Korea about a month earlier. Half an hour after the briefing ended, General Walker called General Coulter to him and said, "I can't get reliable reports. I want you to go to the eastern front and represent me. I am sending a regiment from the 24th Division to help."[2]

Coulter flew to Kyongju at once, arriving there at noon. Walker in the meantime formally appointed Coulter Deputy Commander, Eighth Army, placing him in command of the ROK I Corps, the U.S. 21st Infantry, the 3d Battalion, 9th Infantry, and the 73d Medium Tank Battalion, less C Company. General Coulter designated these units Task Force Jackson and established his headquarters in the same building in Kyongju in which the ROK I Corps commander and the KMAG officers had their command post. He assumed command of Task Force Jackson at 1200, 27 August.[3]

When he arrived at Kyongju that Sunday, General Coulter found the ROK I Corps disintegrating rapidly and in low morale. Coulter talked to the ROK commanders and their staffs about the terrible effect of their failure to stop the North Koreans and the danger it posed for the entire Pusan Perimeter. General Walker had instructed him to issue his orders to the ROK I Corps commander or his chief of staff in the form of advice, which Coulter did. Coulter had the mission of eliminating the enemy penetration in the Kigye area and of seizing and organizing the high ground extending from north of Yongch'on northeasterly to the coast at Wolp'o-ri, about twelve miles north of P'ohang-dong. This line passed ten miles north of Kigye. Coulter was to attack at once with Task Force Jackson, his immediate objective being to gain the first high ground north of Kigye. The U.S. 21st Infantry Regiment on the morning of 27 August was moving to a position north of Taegu, when General Walker revoked its orders and instructed Colonel Stephens to turn the regiment around and proceed as rapidly

---

[1] EUSAK WD, G-3 Sec, Msg 0655 from KMAG, 27 Aug 50; *Ibid.*, Aug 50 Summ, p. 77; GHQ FEC G-3 Opn Rpt 64, 27 Aug 50; New York *Herald Tribune*, August 28, 1950, Bigart dispatch of 27 August.

[2] Interv, author with Lt Gen John B. Coulter, 3 Apr 53.

[3] *Ibid.*, EUSAK WD, G-3 Sec, 27 Aug 50; GHQ FEC G-3 Opn Rpt 64, 27 Aug 50; *Ibid.*, Sitrep, 28 Aug 50; Capt. George B. Shutt, Operational Narrative History of Task Force Jackson, MS in National Archives Record Service.

PERIMETER BATTLE

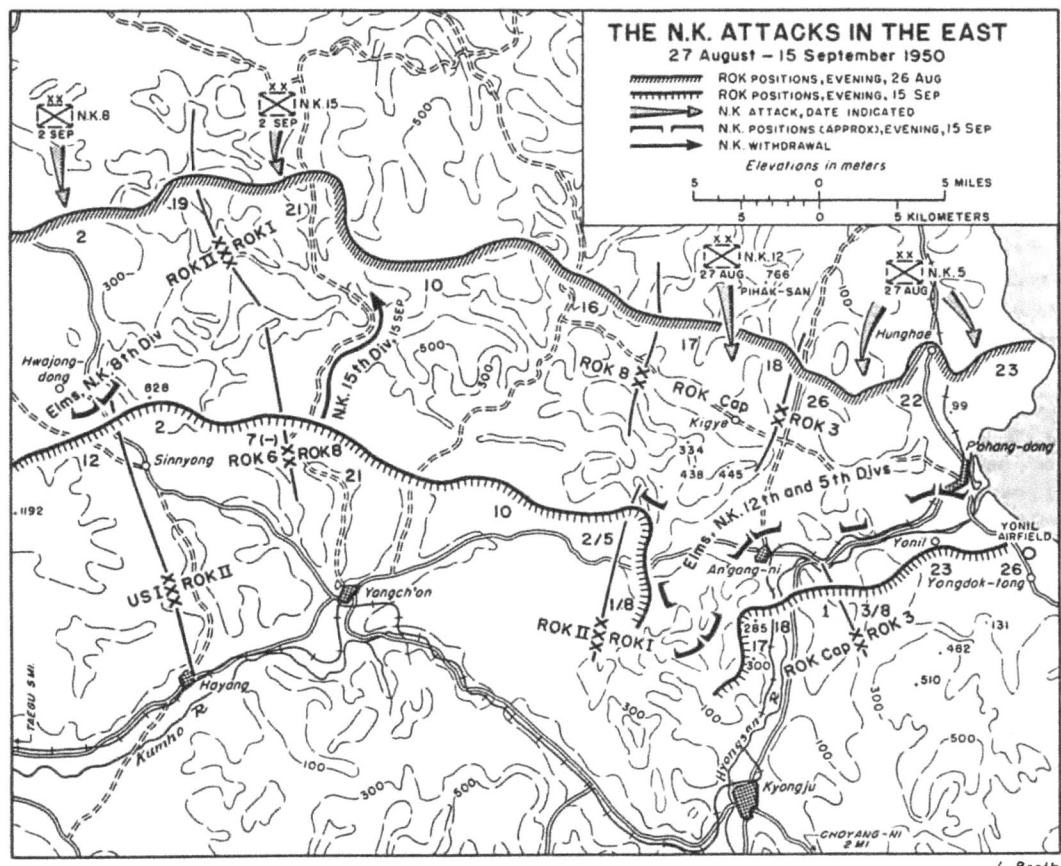

MAP 14

as possible to Kyongju and report to General Coulter. The regiment departed Taegu at 1000 and arrived at Kyongju that afternoon. Coulter immediately sent the 3d Battalion north to An'gang-ni where it went into a position behind the ROK Capital Division.[4]

General Coulter's plan to attack on 28 August had to be postponed. The ROK I Corps commander told him he could not attack, that there were "too many enemy, too many casualties, troops tired." Also, the N.K. *5th Division* above P'ohang-dong had begun to press south again and the ROK 3d Division in front of it began to show signs of giving way. On the 28th, Colonel Emmerich, the KMAG adviser to the ROK 3d Division, at a time he deemed favorable, advised Brig. Gen. Kim Suk Won, the ROK division commander, to counterattack, but General Kim refused to do so. The next day Kim said he was going to move his command post out of

---

[4] Ltr, Coulter to author, 7 Jul 53; Ltr, Stephens to author, 14 May 53; EUSAK WD, G-3 Sec, 27 Aug 50; 21st Inf WD, 27 Aug 50; 24th Div WD, 27 Aug 50.

P'ohang-dong. Emmerich replied that the KMAG group was going to stay in P'ohang-dong. Upon hearing that, Kim became hysterical but decided to stay for the time being to avoid loss of face. That day, 28 August, General Walker issued a special statement addressed to the ROK Army, and meant also for the South Korean Minister of Defense. He called on the ROK's to hold their lines in the Perimeter, and said:

It is my belief, that the over-extended enemy is making his last gasp, while United Nations forces are daily becoming stronger and stronger. The time has now come for everyone to stand in place and fight, or advance to a position which will give us greater tactical advantage from which the counter-offensive can be launched. If our present positions are pierced, we must counterattack at once, destroy the enemy and restore the positions.

To you officers and soldiers of the Army of the Republic of Korea, I ask that you rise as one and stop the enemy on your front in his tracks.[5]

The ROK disorganization was so great in the face of continued enemy pressure that Task Force Jackson could not launch its planned co-ordinated attack. Colonel Stephens' 21st Infantry was in an assembly area two miles north of An'gang-ni and ready for an attack the morning of the 28th, but during the night the ROK 17th Regiment lost its position on the high ridge northward at the bend of the Kigye valley, and the attack was canceled. The ROK's regained their position in the afternoon but that night lost it again. At the same time, elements of the enemy *5th Division* penetrated the ROK 3d Division southwest of P'ohang-dong. General Coulter directed Colonel Stephens to repel this penetration. During the 29th, B Company, 21st Infantry, supported by a platoon of tanks of B Company, 73d Medium Tank Battalion, successfully counterattacked northwest from the southern edge of P'ohang-dong for a distance of a mile and a half, with ROK troops following. The American units then withdrew to P'ohang-dong. That night the ROK's withdrew, and the next day an American infantry-tank force repeated the action of the day before. Colonel Stephens now received orders to take over from the ROK 3d Division a sector extending 1,000 yards north and 3,000 yards northwest of P'ohang-dong.[6]

Also on the 29th, the ROK Capital Division, with American tank and artillery support, recaptured Kigye and held it during the night against enemy counterattacks, only to lose it finally at dawn. American air attacks continued at an increased tempo in the Kigye area. On 31 August, the aircraft carrier USS *Sicily* alone launched 38 sorties. ROK troops reported finding the bodies of many North Koreans, apparently killed by air attack. They also found many suits of white clothing scattered on the ground, abandoned when enemy soldiers changed into uniforms.

Coincidentally with this air action in the Kigye area, U.S. naval vessels continued their efforts to help stop the N.K. *5th Division* on the east coast. A

---

[5] Ltr, Coulter to author, 7 Jul 53; EUSAK WD, G-3 Sec, 28 Aug 50; 21st Inf WD, 28 Aug 50; GHQ FEC Sitrep, 28 Aug 50; Ltr, Emmerich to Farrell, 29 Aug 50, recommending relief of Gen Kim Suk Won; New York *Times*, August 28, 1950.

[6] Ltr, Stephens to author, 14 May 53, and accompanying map of 21st Inf positions; EUSAK WD, G-3 Sec, Msg 1710 from TF Jackson; 21st Inf WD, 29 Aug 50.

cruiser and two destroyers concentrated their fire power on the Hunghae area five miles north of P'ohang-dong where the enemy division's troop assembly and forward supply center were located. On 29 and 30 August the three vessels fired almost 1,500 5-inch shells at enemy targets there in support of the ROK 3d Division. Despite this aerial and naval support, on the last day of August the battle continued to go against the ROK forces both at Kigye and P'ohang-dong.[7]

Aerial observation on 1 September disclosed that North Koreans were moving southward in the mountains above Kigye and P'ohang-dong. The next day another major enemy attack was forming north and northwest of Kigye. In the afternoon, KMAG advisers with the Capital Division estimated that 2,500 enemy soldiers had penetrated a gap between the ROK 17th and 18th Regiments.

At the same time, enemy pressure built up steadily north of P'ohang-dong, where the N.K. *5th Division* fed replacements on to Hill 99 in front of the ROK 23d Regiment. This hill became almost as notorious as had Hill 181 near Yongdok earlier because of the almost continuous and bloody fighting there for its control. Although aided by U.S. air attacks and artillery and naval gunfire, the ROK 3d Division was not able to capture this hill, and suffered many casualties in the effort. On 2 September Colonel Stephens' 21st Infantry attacked northwest from P'ohang-dong in an effort to help the ROK's recapture Hill 99. A platoon of tanks followed the valley road between P'ohang-dong and Hunghae. Stephens assigned K Company Hill 99 as its objective. The 21st Infantry made very slow progress in this attack, and in some quarters none at all. Casualties were heavy. By 1525 that afternoon K Company could account for only thirty-five men. The company was unable to take Hill 99 from the well dug-in North Koreans who threw showers of hand grenades to repel all efforts to reach the top. Two tanks of the 6th Tank Battalion were lost in this attack, one in an enemy mine field and another because of a thrown track. At dusk an enemy penetration occurred along the boundary between the ROK Capital and 3d Divisions three miles east of Kigye.[8]

The next morning, an hour and a half after midnight, the N.K. *12th Division*, executing its part of the co-ordinated N.K. *II Corps* general attack, struck the Capital Division on the high hill masses south of the Kigye valley. This attack threw back the ROK 18th Regiment on the left in the area of Hills 334 and 438, and the ROK 17th Regiment on the right in the area of Hill 445. By dawn of 3 September the enemy penetration there had reached the vital east-west corridor road three miles east of An'gangni. As a result of this 5-mile enemy gain during the night the Capital Division all but collapsed.[9]

---

[7] Interv, author with Coulter, 3 Apr 53; GHQ FEC G-3 Opn Rpts 64-68, 27-31 Aug 50; *Ibid.*, Sitreps, 28 Aug-2 Sep 50; EUSAK WD, G-3 Sec, 31 Aug 50; *Ibid.*, POR 149, 31 Aug 50; 21st Inf WD, 31 Aug 50.

[8] Ltr and marked map, Stephens to author, 14 May 53; EUSAK WD, G-3 Jnl, 2 Sep 50; 21st Inf WD, 2 Sep 50; 6th Tk Bn WD, 1-3 Sep 50; Emmerich, MS review comments, 30 Nov 57.

[9] EUSAK WD, G-3 Jnl, 0845 3 Sep 50; *Ibid.*, PIR 53, 3 Sep 50; GHQ FEC G-3 Opn Rpt 71, 3 Sep 50; *Ibid.*, Sitrep, 3 Sep 50; ROK Army Hq, MS review comments, 11 Jul 58.

This dire turn of events forced General Coulter to withdraw the 21st Infantry at once from the line northwest of P'ohang-dong and concentrate it forthwith in the vicinity of Kyongju. The 2d Battalion, commanded by Lt. Col. Gines Perez, had joined the regiment as its third battalion on 31 August, but General Coulter had held it in Task Force reserve at An'gang-ni. That battalion now took up a horseshoe-shaped defense position around the town, with some elements on high ground two miles eastward where they commanded the Kyongju–P'ohang-dong highway. The rest of the regiment closed into an assembly area north of Kyongju. At the same time, General Walker started the newly activated ROK 7th Division toward the enemy penetration. Its 5th Regiment closed at Yongch'on that afternoon, and the 3d Regiment, less its 1st Battalion, closed at Kyongju in the evening. Walker also authorized Coulter to use the 3d Battalion, 9th Infantry; the 9th Infantry Regimental Tank Company; and the 15th Field Artillery Battalion as he deemed advisable. These units, held at Yonil Airfield for its defense, had not previously been available for commitment elsewhere. The two antiaircraft batteries of automatic weapons (D Battery, 865th AAA Battalion, and A Battery, 933d AAA Battalion) were not to be moved from the airfield except in an emergency.[10]

During the day (3 September), Colonel Emmerich at P'ohang-dong sent General Coulter a message that the ROK 3d Division commander was preparing to withdraw from P'ohang-dong. Coulter went immediately to the ROK I Corps commander and had him issue an order that the ROK 3d Division would not withdraw. Coulter checked every half hour to see that the division stayed in its P'ohang-dong positions.

That night, 3–4 September, the ROK I Corps front collapsed. Three enemy tanks overran a battery of ROK artillery and then scattered two battalions of the newly arrived ROK 5th Regiment. Following a mortar preparation, the North Koreans entered An'gang-ni at 0220. An hour later the command post of the Capital Division withdrew from the town and fighting became increasingly confused. By 0400 American tanks ceased firing because remnants of the Capital Division had become hopelessly intermingled with enemy forces. Colonel Perez said, "We couldn't tell friend from foe." At daylight, G Company, 21st Infantry, discovered that it was alone in An'gang-ni, nearly surrounded by the enemy. ROK troops had disappeared. At 1810, G Company withdrew from the town and dug in along the road eastward near the rest of the 2d Battalion at the bridge over the Hyongsan-gang. North Koreans held the town and extended southward along the railroad.[11]

Receiving orders from Colonel Stephens to withdraw the 2d Battalion and join the regiment above Kyongju, Colonel Perez had to fight his way through an enemy roadblock on the east side of

---

[10] Interv, author with Coulter, 3 Apr 53; Ltr, Stephens to author, 14 May 53; EUSAK WD, G-3 Jnl 0840, 1420 3 Sep 50; *Ibid.*, G-3 Sec and Br for CG, 3 Sep 50; New York *Herald Tribune*, September 6, 1950, Bigart dispatch.

[11] EUSAK WD, G-3 Jnl, 4 Sep 50; 21st Inf WD, 28 Aug–28 Sep 50 Summ, for 3–4 Sep; GHQ FEC Sitrep, 4 Sep 50; New York *Herald Tribune*, September 6, 1950, Bigart dispatch.

ASSAULT TROOPS OF COMPANY K, *21st Infantry, under mortar fire on Hill 99, 2 September.*

the Hyongsan-gang three miles southeast of An'gang-ni. When he got through he discovered that G Company was missing. Colonel Stephens ordered Perez to turn around and get G Company. The 2d Battalion fought its way back north and found G Company at the bridge. Reunited, the battalion fought its way out again, with tanks firing down the road ahead of the column and into the hills along the sides. Enemy fire knocked the tracks off three Patton tanks. Friendly artillery then destroyed them to prevent enemy use. The 2d Battalion arrived in the Kyongju area shortly before noon.[12]

[12] 21st Inf WD, 5 Sep 50; 24th Div WD, 4 Sep 50; Ltr, Stephens to author, 14 May 53.

By noon, 4 September, enemy units had established roadblocks along the Kyongju–An'gang-ni road within three miles of Kyongju. A 2-mile-wide gap existed between the ROK 3d and Capital Divisions in the P'ohang-dong area. But the big break in the United Nations line was in the high mountain mass west of the Hyongsan valley and southwest of An'gang-ni. In this area northwest of Kyongju there was an 8-mile gap between the Capital Division and the ROK 8th Division to the west. From that direction the enemy posed a threat, General Coulter thought, to the railroad and the road net running south through the Kyongju corridor to Pusan. He was not equally concerned about enemy advances in the P'ohang-dong coastal area. Faced with this big gap on his left flank, Coulter put Stephens' 21st Infantry in the broad valley and on its bordering hills northwest of Kyongju to block any enemy approach from that direction.[13]

The situation at Kyongju during the evening of 4 September was tense. The ROK corps commander proposed to evacuate the town. He said that the North Koreans were only three miles away on the hills to the north, and that they would attack and overrun the town that night. General Coulter told him that he would not move his command post—that they were all staying in Kyongju. And stay they did. Coulter put four tanks around the building where the command posts were located. Out on the roads he stationed KMAG officers to round up ROK stragglers and get them into positions at the edge of the town. One KMAG major at pistol point stopped ROK troops fleeing southward. Most of his staff at Kyongju found Coulter irritable and hard to please, but they also say that he went sleepless and was determined to hold Kyongju.[14]

That night radio conversations between tankers on the road just north of Kyongju, overheard at Coulter's headquarters, told of knocking North Koreans off the tanks. The expected North Korean attack on Kyongju, however, never came. The enemy turned east, crossed the highway a few miles north of the town, and headed toward Yonil Airfield. The next day the Air Force, attacking enemy gun positions four miles north of Kyongju along the road, found enemy targets at many points within the triangle Kigye–Kyongju–P'ohang-dong.

North of P'ohang-dong the situation worsened. At 0200 5 September Colonel Emmerich hastened to Yonil Airfield where he conferred with Lt. Col. D. M. McMains, commanding the 3d Battalion, 9th Infantry, stationed there, and informed him of the situation in P'ohang-dong. Emmerich obtained a platoon of tanks and returned with them to the town. He placed the tanks in position and awaited the expected enemy armored attack. At 0530 he received information that elements of the ROK 22d Regiment had given way. Enemy troops entered this gap and just before 1100 the American tanks in P'ohang-dong were under heavy enemy machine gun fire. Five N.K. self-propelled guns approached and began firing. At a range of one city block the tanks knocked out the lead gun, killing three crew members. In the ensuing exchange of fire the other four withdrew. Emmerich then directed air strikes and artillery fire which destroyed the other four guns. But, nevertheless, that afternoon at 1435 the order came to evacuate all materiel and supplies from the Yonil airstrip.[15]

That night, 5–6 September, events reached a climax inside P'ohang-dong.

---

[13] Interv, author with Coulter, 3 Apr 53; Ltr, Stephens to author, 14 May 53; EUSAK WD, Br for CG, 4 Sep 50; 6th Med Tk Bn WD, 4 Sep 50.

[14] Interv, author with Coulter, 3 Apr 53; Interv, author with Col John F. Greco, 12 Aug 51 (Greco was Coulter's G-2 at Kyongju); Interv, author with Maj Wm. C. Hungate, Jr., 28 Jul 51; Interv, author with Maj George W. Flagler, 28 Jul 51 (both Hungate and Flagler were at Kyongju with Coulter); Shutt, History of Task Force Jackson.

[15] Interv, author with Coulter, 3 Apr 53; EUSAK WD, G-3 Sec, 5 Sep 50; Ibid., Br for CG, 5 Sep 50; Ibid., PIR 55, 5 Sep 50; 21st Inf WD, 5 Sep 50; GHQ FEC Opn Rpt 74, 6 Sep 50; Ibid., Sitrep, 6 Sep 50; Shutt, History of Task Force Jackson; Emmerich, MS review comments, 30 Jan 57.

At midnight, after ten rounds of enemy mortar or artillery fire struck near it, the ROK 3d Division command post moved to another location. Enemy fire that followed it to the new location indicated observed and directed fire. The ROK division commander and his G-2 and G-3 "got sick." The division withdrew from P'ohang-dong, and on 6 September this coastal town was again in enemy hands. The ROK Army relieved both the ROK I Corps and the 3d Division commanders.[16]

Because the big gap between the ROK Capital and 8th Divisions made it impossible for I Corps at Kyongju to direct the action of the 8th Division, the ROK Army at 1030, 5 September, transferred that division to the control of the ROK II Corps, and attached to it the 5th Regiment of the ROK 7th Division. This shift of command came just as the N.K. *15th Division* penetrated the ROK 8th Division lines to enter Yongch'on in the Taegu-P'ohang-dong corridor. From west of An'gang-ni the ROK 3d Regiment drove toward Yongch'on, still trying to close the gap.[17]

The startling gains of the North Koreans in the east on 4 September caused General Walker to shift still more troops to that area. The day before, he had ordered the 24th Division to move from its reserve position near Taegu to the lower Naktong River to relieve the marines in the Naktong Bulge area of the 2d Division front. It bivouacked that night in a downpour of rain on the banks of the Naktong near Susan-ni. On the morning of the 4th, before it could begin relief of the marines, the 24th received a new order to proceed to Kyongju. General Davidson, the assistant division commander, proceeding at once by jeep, arrived at Kyongju that evening. Division troops and the 19th Infantry started at 1300 the next day, 5 September, and, traveling over muddy roads, most of them arrived at Kyongju just before midnight. General Church had arrived there during the day. All division units had arrived by 0700, 6 September.[18]

General Coulter knew that the N.K. *15th Division* had crossed the Taegu lateral corridor at Yongch'on and was heading in the direction of Kyongju. On the 6th, he ordered the 21st Infantry to attack the next day up the valley and bordering hills that lead northwest from Kyongju into the high mountain mass in the direction of Yongch'on. When it attacked there on 7 September the 21st Infantry encountered virtually no opposition.

At 1230 Eighth Army redesignated Task Force Jackson as Task Force Church, and half an hour later General Coulter departed Kyongju for Taegu to resume his planning duties. General Church was now in command on the eastern front. That afternoon, 7 September, General Church canceled General Coulter's order for the 21st Infantry to attack into the mountains. He felt it was a useless dispersion of troops and he wanted the regiment concentrated near Kyongju. Church made still another change in the disposition of the

---

[16] Interv, author with Emmerich, 5 Dec 51; Interv, author with Coulter, 3 Apr 53.

[17] GHQ FEC Sitrep, 5 Sep 50; *Ibid.*, G-3 Opn Rpts 73-74, 5-6 Sep 50.

[18] Ltr, Davidson to author, 18 Feb 54; 24th Div WD, 5-6 Sep 50; EUSAK WD, G-3 Jnl, 1800 5 Sep 50; EUSAK Opn Ord for CG 24th Div and CG TF Jackson, 5 Sep 50.

task force. On the 8th he moved its command post from Kyongju to the vicinity of Choyang-ni, four miles southward. He believed the command post could be more easily defended there in the open if attacked than in a town, and that traffic congestion near it would be less.[19]

Fighting continued between the North Koreans and the ROK Capital Division on the hills bordering the valley from An'gang-ni to Kyongju. The 3d Battalion, 19th Infantry, became involved there just after midnight, 8-9 September. An enemy force attacked K Company and drove it from Hill 300, a defensive position midway between An'gang-ni and Kyongju. North Koreans held the hill during the 9th against counterattack. Farther north, on the left side of the valley, the ROK 17th Regiment attacked and, with the support of the U.S. 13th Field Artillery Battalion, captured Hill 285 and held it against several enemy counterattacks. On the opposite side of the valley (east) the ROK 18th Regiment made limited gains. These battles took place in drenching typhoon rains. Low-hanging clouds allowed very little air support. The rains finally ceased on 10 September.[20]

In this second week of September elements of the N.K. *5th Division* had spread out over the hills west, southwest, and south of P'ohang-dong. One North Korean force, estimated to number 1,600 men, reached Hills 482 and 510, four to five miles southwest of Yonil Airfield. Facing this enemy force were two regiments of the ROK 3d Division, which held a defensive position on the hills bordering the west side of the valley south of the airfield. Enemy pressure threatened to penetrate between the two ROK regiments.

On the evening of 9 September, General Church formed Task Force Davidson to eliminate this threat to Yonil. The airfield itself had not been used since the middle of August except for emergency landing and refueling of planes, but evacuation of Air Force equipment, bombs, and petroleum products was still in progress. General Davidson commanded the task force, which was composed of the 19th Infantry, less the 3d Battalion; the 3d Battalion, 9th Infantry; the 13th Field Artillery Battalion; C Battery, 15th Field Artillery Battalion; A Company, 3d Engineer Combat Battalion; the 9th Infantry Regimental Tank Company; two batteries of antiaircraft automatic weapons; and other miscellaneous units.[21]

The enemy having cut off all other approaches from the Kyongju area, the task force spent all of 10 September making a circuitous southern approach to its objective. It arrived in its assembly area at Yongdok-tong, one mile south of Yonil Airfield, at 1900 that evening. General Davidson early that morning had flown on ahead from Kyongju to Yongdok-tong. Colonel Emmerich was there to meet him when his light plane landed on the road. On the flight over, Davidson looked for but did not see any

---

[19] Ltrs, Church to author, 3 May and 26 Jul 53; Ltr, Davidson to author, 18 Feb 54; 24th Div WD, 7-8 Sep 50; EUSAK WD, G-3 Jnl, 7 Sep 50; *Ibid.*, POR 171, 7 Sep 50.
[20] 24th Div WD, 9 Sep 50; 3d Engr C Bn WD, Sep 50, Summ.

[21] Interv, author with Davidson, 28 Jan 54; Ltr, Davidson to author, 18 Feb 54; 19th Inf WD, 10 Sep 50; 24th Div WD, 9 Sep 50; EUSAK WD, G-3 Sec, 10 Sep 50; 3d Engr C Bn Unit Hist, 6 Aug-28 Sep 50.

enemy soldiers. Emmerich told Davidson the North Koreans had driven the ROK's from Hill 131. This hill was on the southern side of the boundary between the two ROK regiments holding the Yonil defensive position. Davidson and Emmerich agreed that the ROK's would have to recapture Hill 131 during the night and that then the task force would attack through the ROK 3d Division to capture the main enemy positions on Hill 482. They thought that if the task force could establish the ROK's on Hill 482 the latter should be able to hold it and control the situation themselves thereafter. Emmerich took Davidson to meet the ROK 3d Division commander. Davidson told him that he was in command in that area and informed him of his plan for the attack. That night the ROK's did succeed in recapturing Hill 131 and restoring their lines there. In this attack the ROK 3d Engineer Battalion fought as infantry, and under the leadership and guidance of Capt. Walter J. Hutchins, the KMAG adviser to the battalion, contributed heavily to the success.[22]

The next morning, 11 September, the 19th Infantry passed through the left-hand ROK regiment just south of Hill 131 and, with the 1st Battalion leading, attacked west. At 0930 it captured without opposition the first hill mass two miles west of the line of departure. The 2d Battalion then passed through the 1st Battalion and continued the attack toward Hill 482 (Unje-san), a mile westward across a steep-sided gorge. There, North Koreans held entrenched positions, and their machine gun fire checked the 2d Battalion for the rest of the day. The morning of 12 September four Australian pilots struck the enemy positions with napalm, and an artillery preparation followed the strike. The 2d Battalion then launched its attack and secured the rough and towering Hill 482 about noon. In midafternoon, ROK forces relieved Task Force Davidson on the hill mass, and the latter descended to the valley southwest of Yongdok-tong for the night. During the day, General Walker had visited the task force's command post two or three times. On 13 September, Task Force Davidson returned to Kyongju.[23]

While this action was in progress near Yonil Airfield, the week-long battle for Hill 300 north of Kyongju came to an end. A regiment of the ROK 3d Division captured the hill on 11 September. In midafternoon the 3d Battalion, 19th Infantry, relieved the ROK's there. Scattered over Hill 300 lay 257 counted enemy dead and great quantities of abandoned equipment and weapons, some of it American. In this fighting for Hill 300, the U.S. 3d Battalion, 19th Infantry, lost eight lieutenants and twenty-nine enlisted men killed.[24]

Tuesday, 12 September, may be considered as the day when the North Korean offensive in the east ended. By that date, the N.K. *12th Division* had been virtually destroyed and the *5th Division* was trying to consolidate its

---

[22] Ltr, Davidson to author, 18 Feb 54; 24th Div WD, 10 Sep 50; EUSAK WD, G–3 Sec, 10 Sep 50; Emmerich, MS review comments, 30 Nov 57.

[23] Ltr, Davidson to author, 18 Feb 54; 24th Div WD, 11–12 Sep 50; Ibid., Opn Summ, 26 Aug–28 Sept 50; EUSAK POR 186, 12 Sep 50; EUSAK WD, G–3 Jnl, 1046 12 Sep 50.

[24] 21st Inf WD, 11 Sep 50; 24th Div WD, 26 Aug–28 Sep 50, p. 40; 24th Div Arty WD, 12 Sep 50; Ltr, Stephens to author, 14 May 53. The 3d Battalion, 19th Infantry, was attached to the 21st Infantry during this action.

survivors near P'ohang-dong. Aerial observers reported sighting many enemy groups moving north and east.[25]

The ROK 3d Division followed the withdrawing *5th Division*, and the Capital Division advanced against the retreating survivors of the enemy *12th Division*. On 15 September some elements of the Capital Division reached the southern edge of An'gang-ni. Reports indicated that enemy troops were retreating toward Kigye. With the enemy threat in the east subsiding, Eighth Army dissolved Task Force Church, effective at noon 15 September, and the ROK Army resumed control of the ROK I Corps. Eighth Army also ordered the 24th Division to move to Kyongsan, southeast of Taegu, in a regrouping of forces. The 21st Infantry Regiment had already moved there on the 14th. The 19th Infantry was to remain temporarily at Kyongju in Eighth Army reserve.[26]

In the eastern battles during the first two weeks of September, the ROK troops, demoralized though they were, did most of the ground fighting. American tanks, artillery, and ground units supported them. Uncontested aerial supremacy and naval gunfire from offshore also supported the ROK's, and probably were the factors that tipped the scales in their favor. After the initial phase of their September offensive, the North Koreans labored under what proved to be insurmountable difficulties in supplying their forward units. The North Korean system of supply could not resolve the problems of logistics and communication necessary to support and exploit an offensive operation in this sector of the front.

Enemy Breakthrough at Yongch'on

In the high mountains between the Taegu sector on the west and the Kyongju–east coast sector, two North Korean divisions, the *8th* and *15th*, stood ready on 1 September to attack south and sever the Taegu–P'ohang-dong corridor road in the vicinity of Hayang and Yongch'on, in co-ordination with the North Korean offensive in the Kigye-P'ohang area. Hayang is 12, and Yongch'on 20, air miles east of Taegu. The N.K. *8th Division* was astride the main Andong–Sinnyong–Yongch'on road 20 air miles northwest of Yongch'on; the *15th* was eastward in the mountains just below Andong, 35 air miles north of Yongch'on on a poor and mountainous secondary road. The objective of the *8th Division* was Hayang; that of the *15th* was Yongch'on, which the enemy division commander had orders to take at all costs. Opposing the N.K. *8th Division* was the ROK 6th Division; in front of the N.K. *15th Division* stood the ROK 8th Division.[27]

In ten days of fighting the N.K. *8th Division* gained only a few miles, and not until 12 September did it have possession of Hwajong-dong, 14 air miles northwest of Yongch'on. In this time it

---

[25] ATIS Res Supp Interrog Rpts, Issue 106 (N.K. *12th Div*), p. 70; *Ibid.*, Issue 96 (N.K. *5th Div*), p. 43. There are many individual enemy interrogation reports in ATIS Interrogation Reports, Issues 6 and 7 (N.K. Forces), describing the condition of these two divisions at this time.

[26] 21st Inf WD, Summ, Sep 50; EUSAK WD, G-3 Jnl, 1125 14 Sep 50; *Ibid.*, Br for CG, 14 Sep 50; EUSAK PIR 64 and 65, 14-15 Sep 50; *Ibid.*, POR 192 and 195, 14-15 Sep 50; GHQ FEC G-3 Opn Rpt 83, 15 Sep 50.

[27] ATIS Res Supp Interrog Rpts, Issue 4 (N.K. *8th Div*), p. 25; *Ibid.*, Issue 3 (N. K. *15th Div*), p. 44.

lost nearly all the twenty-one new tanks of the *17th Armored Brigade* that were supporting it. Just below Hwajongdong, towering mountains close in on the road, with 3,000-foot-high Hill 928 (Hwa-san) on the east and lesser peaks 2,000 feet high on the west. At this passage of the mountains into the Taegu corridor, the ROK 6th Division decisively defeated the enemy *8th Division* and, in effect, practically destroyed it. Of these battles around Hwajongdong an enemy diarist wrote on 2 September, "Today we opened a general attack"; after 6 September, "We underwent extremely desperate battles. With no place to hide or escape from the fierce enemy artillery bombardment our main force was wiped out." On 8 September he wrote, "We suffered miserably heavy casualties from fierce enemy air, artillery, and heavy machine gun attacks. Only 20 remain alive out of our entire battalion." [28]

On the next road eastward above Yongch'on, the N.K. *15th Division* launched its attack against the ROK 8th Division on 2 September. Although far understrength, with its three regiments reportedly having a total of only 3,600 men, it penetrated in four days to the lateral corridor at Yongch'on. North of the town one regiment of the ROK 8th Division panicked when an enemy tank got behind its lines. Elements of the enemy division were in and south of Yongch'on by midafternoon 6 September. The North Koreans did not remain in the town, but moved to the hills south and southeast of it overlooking the Taegu-Kyongju-Pusan road. On 7 September some of them established a roadblock three and a half miles southeast of Yongch'on, and other elements attacked a ROK regiment a mile south of the town. During the day, however, the ROK 5th Regiment of the newly activated 7th Division, attacking from the east along the lateral corridor, cleared Yongch'on itself of enemy and then went into a defensive position north of the town. But the next day, 8 September, additional elements of the *15th Division* arrived before Yongch'on and recaptured it. That afternoon the 11th Regiment of the ROK 1st Division arrived from the Taegu front and counterattacked the enemy in and near the town. This action succeeded in clearing the enemy from most of Yongch'on, but some North Koreans still held the railroad station southeast of it. Still others were an unknown distance southeast on the road toward Kyongju.[29]

There, in the hills southeast and east of Yongch'on, the enemy *15th Division* came to grief. Its artillery regiment foolishly advanced ahead of the infantry, expended its ammunition, and, without support, was then largely destroyed by ROK counterbattery fire. The artillery commander lost his life in the action. After the ROK 5th and 11th Regiments arrived in the vicinity of Yongch'on to

---

[28] *Ibid.*, Issue 4 (N.K. *8th Div*), p. 25; ATIS Interrog Rpts, Issue 4, Rpts 922 and 923, pp. 47 and 51; ATIS Enemy Documents, Nr 28, p. 7, diary of Pak Han Pin, *83d Regt, 8th Div;* EUSAK WD, 9 Sep 50, PW Interrog Rpt, 2d Lt Wong Hong Ki; *Ibid.*, PIR 53, 3 Sep 50; New York *Herald Tribune*, September 7, 1950.

[29] EUSAK WD, G–3 Jnl, 1230 3 Sep 50, and an. to PIR 53, 3 Sep 50, and PIR 56, 6 Sep 50; *Ibid.*, Br for CG, 7 Sep 50; GHQ FEC Sitrep, 8–9 Sep 50; *Time* Magazine, September 18, 1950, J. Bell article; New York *Herald Tribune*, September 7, 1950, Bigart dispatch.

reinforce the demoralized 8th Division, ROK battle action was so severe against the enemy units that they had no chance to regroup for co-ordinating action. On 9 and 10 September ROK units surrounded and virtually destroyed the N.K. *15th Division* southeast of Yongch'on on the hills bordering the Kyongju road. The North Korean division chief of staff, Col. Kim Yon, was killed there together with many other high-ranking officers. The part played by KMAG officers in rounding up stragglers of the ROK 8th Division and in reorganizing its units was an important factor in the successful outcome of these battles. On 10 September, the ROK 8th Division cleared the Yongch'on-Kyongju road of the enemy, capturing 2 tanks, 6 howitzers, 1 76-mm. self-propelled gun, several antitank guns, and many small arms. The capture of the self-propelled gun is a revealing story in itself. The driver drove the gun, followed by a truckload of enemy infantry, from the southeast through the ROK lines to Yongch'on, where he stopped and was quietly eating dinner with ROK troops when he came under suspicion and had to make a dash for it, hotly pursued by groups of ROK's. He surrendered four miles northward to a lone ROK soldier with the explanation that he could not drive the vehicle and shoot at the same time.[30]

Advancing north of Yongch'on after the retreating survivors of the N.K. *15th Division*, the ROK 8th Division and the 5th Regiment of the ROK 7th Division encountered almost no resistance. On 12 September, elements of the two ROK organizations were eight miles north of the town. On that day they captured 4 120-mm. mortars, 4 antitank guns, 4 artillery pieces, 9 trucks, 2 machine guns, and numerous small arms. ROK forces now also advanced east from Yongch'on and north from Kyongju to close the big breach in their lines.[31]

Perhaps the most critical period of the fighting in the east occurred when the N.K. *15th Division* broke through the ROK 8th Division to Yongch'on. The enemy division at that point was in a position to turn west toward Taegu and take Eighth Army and the 1st Cavalry Division there in the rear, or to turn east and southeast and take Task Force Jackson in the rear or on its left flank. It tried to do the latter. But General Walker's quick dispatch of the ROK 5th and 11th Regiments from two widely separated sectors of the front to the area of penetration resulted in destroying the enemy force before it could exploit its breakthrough. General Walker's prompt judgment of the reinforcements needed to stem the North Korean attacks in the Kyongju-P'ohang and the Yongch'on areas, and his rapid shifting of these reinforcements to the threatened sectors from other fronts, constitute a notable command achievement in the battles of the Pusan Perimeter.[32]

---

[30] EUSAK WD, POR 180, 10 Sep 50; *Ibid.*, 14 Sep 50, interrog of Lee Yong Sil; *Ibid.*, 9, 11, 12 Sep 50, interrogs of 1st Lt Kim Yong Chul, Cpl So Yong Sik, Capt Pak Chang Yong; ATIS Res Supp Interrog Rpts, Issue 106 (N.K. Arty), p. 62; *Ibid.*, Issue 3 (N.K. *15th Div*), p. 44; GHQ FEC Sitrep, 11 Sep 50; New York *Times*, September 11 and 13, 1950. There are scores of interrogations of prisoners from the N.K. *15th Division* in ATIS Interrogation Reports, Issues 4, 5, and 9.

[31] EUSAK WD, 14 Sep 50; GHQ FEC Sitrep, 13 Sep 50; New York *Times*, September 13, 1950.

[32] Ltr, Stephens to author, 14 May 53; Interv, author with Maj Gen Edwin K. Wright (FEC G-3 at the time), 7 Jan 54; Ltr, Landrum to author, recd 28 Jun 54; Interv, author with Stebbins, 4 Dec 53.

Back on Taegu

While four divisions of the N.K. *II Corps* attacked south in the P'ohang-dong, Kyongju, and Yongch'on sectors, the remaining three divisions of the corps—the *3d*, *13th*, and *1st*, in that order from west to east—were to execute their converging attack on Taegu from the north and northwest. The *3d Division* was to attack in the Waegwan area northwest of Taegu, the *13th Division* down the mountain ridges north of Taegu along and west of the Sangju-Taegu road, and the *1st Division* along the high mountain ridges just east of the road. (*Map 15*)

Defending Taegu, the U.S. 1st Cavalry Division had a front of about thirty-five miles. General Gay outposted the main avenues of entry into his zone and kept his three regiments concentrated behind the outposts. At the southwestern end of his line General Gay initially controlled the 3d Battalion, 23d Infantry, 2d Division, which had been attached to the 1st Cavalry Division. On 5 September the British 27th Brigade, in its first commitment in the Korean War, replaced that battalion. Next in line northward, the 5th Cavalry Regiment defended the sector along the Naktong around Waegwan and the main Seoul highway southeast from there to Taegu. Eastward, the 7th Cavalry Regiment was responsible for the mountainous area between that highway and the hills bordering the Sangju road. The 8th Cavalry Regiment, responsible for the latter road, was astride it and on the bordering hills.[33]

Greatly concerned at the beginning of September over the North Korean attack and penetration of the southern sector of the Pusan Perimeter in the 2d and 25th Divisions' zone, General Walker on 1 September ordered the 1st Cavalry Division to attack north or northwest in an effort to divert to that quarter some of the enemy strength in the south. General Gay's initial decision upon receipt of this order was to attack north up the Sangju road, but his staff and regimental commanders all joined in urging that the attack instead be against Hill 518 in the 7th Cavalry zone, and they talked him out of his original intent. Only two days before, Hill 518 had been in the ROK 1st Division zone and had been considered an enemy assembly point. The 1st Cavalry Division, accordingly, prepared for an attack in the 7th Cavalry sector and for diversionary attacks by two companies of the 3d Battalion, 8th Cavalry, on the 7th Cavalry's right flank. This left the 8th Cavalry only one rifle company in reserve. The regiment's 1st Battalion was on the hill mass to the west of the Bowling Alley and north of Tabu-dong; its 2d Battalion was astride the road.

This planned attack against Hill 518 chanced to coincide with the defection and surrender on 2 September of Maj. Kim Song Jun, the S–3 of the N.K. *19th Regiment, 13th Division*. He reported that a full-scale North Korean attack was to begin at dusk that day. The N.K. *13th Division*, he said, had just taken in 4,000 replacements, 2,000 of them without weapons, and was now back to a strength of approximately 9,000 men. Upon receiving this intelligence, General Gay alerted all front-line units to

---

[33] 1st Cav Div WD, 1 Sep 50; *Ibid.*, G–3 Jnl, 2 Sep 50.

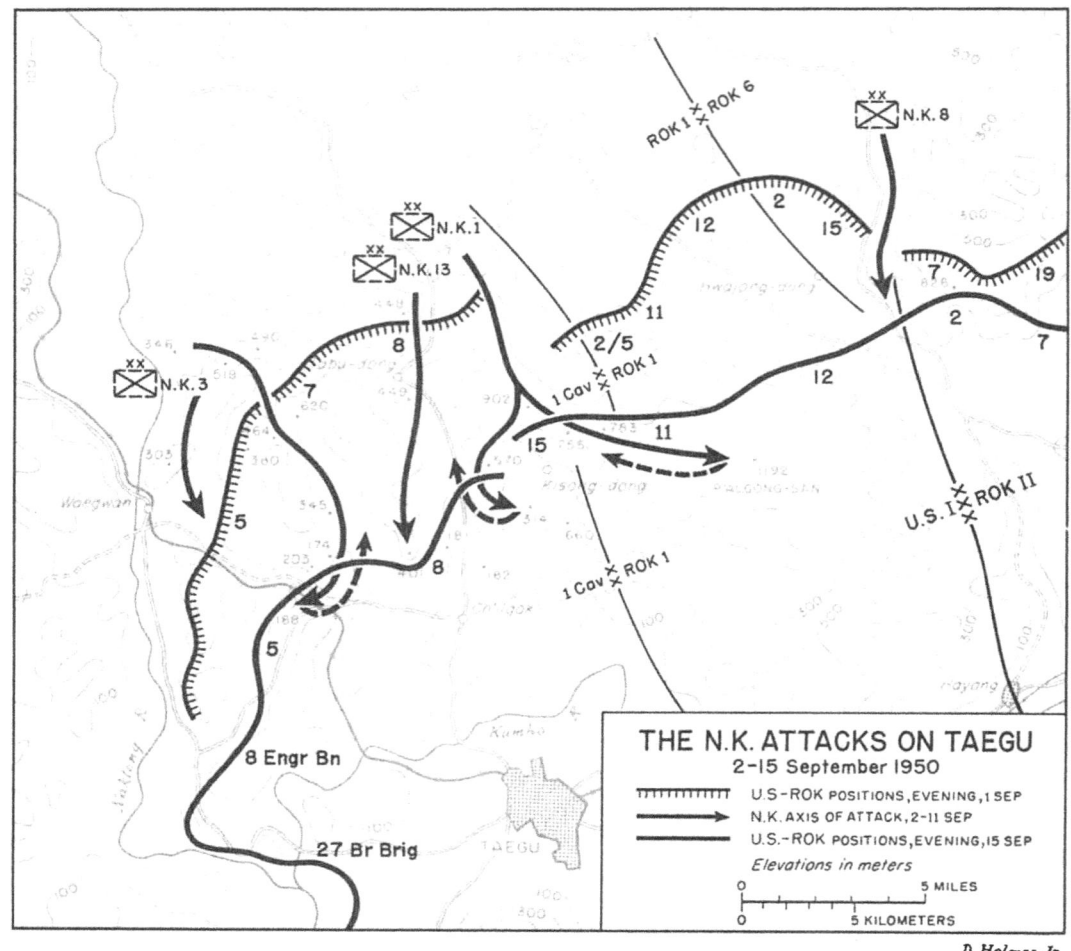

MAP 15

be prepared for the enemy attack.[34]

Complying with Eighth Army's order for what was in effect a spoiling attack against the North Koreans northwest of Taegu, General Gay on 1 September ordered the 7th Cavalry to attack the next day and seize enemy-held Hill 518. Hill 518 (Suam-san) is a large mountain mass five miles northeast of Waegwan and two miles east of the Naktong River. It curves westward from its peak to its westernmost height, Hill 346, from which the ground drops abruptly to the Naktong River. Situated north of the lateral Waegwan–Tabu-dong road, and

[34] 1st Cav Div WD, 1–2 Sep 50; GHQ FEC, History of the N.K. Army, p. 73; EUSAK WD, 5 Sep 50, ATIS Interrog Rpt 895, Maj Kim Song Jun; ATIS Interrog Rpts, Issue 3, pp. 214ff.; ATIS Res Supp Interrog Rpts, Issue 104 (N.K. *13th Div*), p. 67; Ltr and attached notes, Gay to author, 17 Jul 53; Ltr, Col Harold K. Johnson to author, n.d., but recd in Aug 54.

PERIMETER BATTLE

1st Cavalry Observation Post *overlooking the enemy-held Hill 518 complex northeast of Waegwan, 1 September.*

about midway between the two towns, it was a critical terrain feature dominating the road between the two places. After securing Hill 518, the 7th Cavalry attack was to continue on to Hill 314. Air strikes and artillery preparations were to precede the infantry attack on 2 September. Forty pieces of artillery, four-fifths of that available to the 1st Cavalry Division, were to support the attack.[35]

---
[35] Ltr, Gay to author, 17 Jul 53; 77th FA Bn Hist, Sep 50; 7th Cav WD, 1-2 Sep 50. The 77th FA Bn was in direct support of 7th Cav. To assist in firing support for the regiment were A Btry, 61st FA Bn (105-mm.); B and C Btrys, 9th FA Bn (155-mm.); and one plat, B Btry, 82d FA Bn (155-mm.)

On the morning of 2 September the Air Force delivered a 37-minute strike against Hills 518 and 346. The artillery then laid down its concentrations on the hills, and after that the planes came over again napalming and leaving the heights ablaze. Just after 1000, and immediately after the final napalm strike, the 1st Battalion, 7th Cavalry, attacked up Hill 518.

The plan of regimental attack unfortunately brought a minimum of force against the objective. While the 1st Battalion made the attack, the 2d Battalion was in a blocking position on its left (west) and the newly arrived 3d Battalion, in its first Korean operation, was to be behind the 2d Battalion and in an open gap between that battalion and Hill 518. The 1st Battalion moved up through ROK forces and, from high ground, was committed along a narrow ridge line, attacking from the southeast in a column of companies. This in turn resolved itself in a column of platoons, and finally in a column of squads. The final effect, therefore, was that of a regimental attack amounting to a one-squad attack against a strongly held position.

The attack was doomed to failure from the start. The heavy air strikes and the artillery preparations had failed to dislodge the North Koreans. From their positions they delivered mortar and machine gun fire on the climbing infantry, stopping the weak, advanced force short of the crest. In the afternoon the battalion withdrew from Hill 518 and attacked northeast against Hill 490, from which other enemy troops had fired in support of the North Koreans on Hill 518.

The next day at noon, the newly arrived 3d Battalion resumed the attack against Hill 518 from the south, over unreconnoitered ground, and, as did the 1st Battalion the day before, in a column of companies that resolved itself in the end into a column of squads. Again the attack failed. Other attacks failed on 4 September. An enemy forward observer captured on Hill 518 said that 1,200 North Koreans were dug in on the hill and that they had 120-mm. and 82-mm. mortars with ammunition.[36]

While these actions were in progress on its right, the 2d Battalion, 5th Cavalry Regiment, on 4 September attacked and captured Hill 303. The next day it had the utmost difficulty in holding the hill against enemy counterattacks. By 4 September it had become quite clear that the N.K. *3d Division* in front of the 5th and 7th Cavalry Regiments was itself attacking, and that, despite continued air strikes, artillery preparations, and infantry efforts on Hill 518, it was infiltrating large numbers of its troops to the rear of the attacking United States forces. That day the I&R Platoon reported that enemy soldiers held Hill 464, a high hill mass opposite Hill 518 on the south side of the Waegwan-Tabu-dong road, and that it had to destroy its radio and machine gun to keep them from falling into enemy hands. That night large enemy forces came through the gap between the 3d Battalion on the southern slope of Hill 518 and the 2d Battalion westward. For a time those in the 3d Battalion command post thought the attack was going to turn east and overrun them but, instead, the North Koreans turned west and occupied Hill 464 in force. By 5 September, although it was not yet known by the 7th Cavalry, Hill 464 to its rear probably had more North Koreans on it than Hill 518 to its front. North Koreans cut the Waegwan-Tabu-dong road east of the regiment so that its communications with friendly units now were only to the west. During the day the 7th Cavalry made a limited withdrawal on Hill 518. Any hope that the regiment could capture the hill vanished. One American officer described the situation north of Taegu at this time with the comment, "I'll be damned

---

[36] 7th Cav Regt WD, 4 Sep 50; 1st Cav Div WD, 5 Sep 50; 77th FA Bn Hist, 2 Sep 50; EUSAK WD, G-3 Jnl, 0400 5 Sep 50; Lt Col James B. Webel (Capt and S-3, 7th Cav, Sep 50), MS review comments, 15 Nov 57.

if I know who's got who surrounded."[37]

On the division right, Tabu-dong was in enemy hands, on the left Waegwan was a no-man's land, and in the center strong enemy forces were infiltrating southward from Hill 518. The 7th Cavalry Regiment in the center could no longer use the Waegwan–Tabu-dong lateral supply road behind it, and was in danger of being surrounded. After discussing a withdrawal plan with General Walker and Colonel Collier, General Gay on 5 September issued an order for a general withdrawal of the 1st Cavalry Division during the night to shorten the lines and to occupy a better defensive position. The movement was to progress from right to left beginning with the 8th Cavalry Regiment, then the 7th Cavalry in the Hill 518 area, and finally the 5th Cavalry in the Waegwan area. This withdrawal caused the 3d Battalion, 8th Cavalry, to give up a hill it had just attacked and captured near the Tabu-dong road on the approaches of the Walled City of Ka-san. In the 7th Cavalry sector the 1st, 3d, and 2d Battalions were to withdraw in that order, after the withdrawal of the 1st Battalion, 8th Cavalry, on their right. The 2d Battalion, 5th Cavalry, on Hill 303 north of Waegwan was to cover the withdrawal of the 7th Cavalry and hold open the escape road.[38]

---

[37] 5th Cav Regt WD, 4 Sep 50; 7th Cav Regt WD, 4–5 Sep 50; 1st Cav Div WD, 4–5 Sep 50; 77th FA Bn Hist, 5–6 Sep 50; Webel, MS review comments, 15 Nov 57; New York Times, September 5, 1950.

[38] 1st Cav Div WD, 5 Sep 50; 7th Cav Regt Opn Ord 14, 051840 Sep 50; Ltr, Gay to author, 17 Jul 53; Brig Gen Marcel G. Crombez, Notes for author, 28 Jun 55.

Crisis in Eighth Army Command

At this time, about 5 September, as the 7th Cavalry Regiment was forced into a withdrawal, and enemy penetrations in the south had opened the way to Pusan, a crisis developed in appraisals and decisions called for in the Eighth Army command. Everywhere around the Perimeter the North Koreans were penetrating the defense positions and in some places making spectacular gains. It was a question whether the Eighth Army and the ROK's could hold anything like the Pusan Perimeter based on the line of the Naktong. The ROK Army and most of the American divisions appeared to be near the breaking point. Should the United Nations line be withdrawn to the Davidson Line? That question was under debate in Eighth Army headquarters. The decision to withdraw to that line seemed near as the North Koreans captured P'ohang-dong and drove to the edge of Kyongju in the east, reached Yongch'on in the Taegu lateral corridor, captured Waegwan, Tabu-dong, and Ka-san north of Taegu, drove through the old Naktong Bulge area to Yongsan, and in the south split the U.S. 25th Division and poured into its rear areas almost to the edge of Masan. (The Naktong Bulge and Masan penetrations have not yet been described, but they had already taken place as part of the North Korean co-ordinated attack.)

General Walker discussed the issue of withdrawing to the Davidson Line one night with his principal staff officers, most of the division commanders, and General Coulter, his deputy commander in the east. Colonel Dabney, Eighth Army G-3, told General Walker that for once he did not know what to recommend, that the decision was a hard one to make, but that he hoped the Army could stay. He pointed out that North Korean penetrations in the past had waned after a few days and that they might do so again. Upon orders from Colonel Landrum, Dabney started the G-3 Section that evening working on preparing withdrawal orders for Eighth Army. The staff section worked all night long on them. They were published and ready for issuing at 0500 in the morning, but they were held in the G-3 Section pending General Walker's personal order to put them into effect. The order was not given. At some time during the night Walker reached the decision that Eighth Army would not withdraw.[39]

But at this time Eighth Army headquarters did leave Taegu. The tactical situation had deteriorated so much on the afternoon of 4 September that the 1st Cavalry Division ammunition supply point in Taegu loaded nearly all its ammunition on rail cars on Eighth Army orders and prepared for a hasty evacuation southward. The Army transportation officer placed an embargo on all rail shipments north of Samnangjin on the main line, and north and east of Kyongju on the east line. The next morning, 5 September, General Walker reached the decision to move the main army headquarters back to the old Fisheries College between Pusan and Tongnae, north of Pusan, and it made the move during the day. The ROK Army headquarters moved to Pusan. The ROK Army headquarters opened at Pusan at 0800 and Eighth Army headquarters at 1600, 6 September. Walker himself and a few staff officers remained in Taegu as an advanced echelon of the army command post, constituting a tactical headquarters. The principal reason General Walker moved Eighth Army headquarters to Pusan was for the greater protection of the army signal communication equipment. Had the Eighth Army teletype equipment been destroyed or captured by the enemy there was no other similar heavy equipment in the Far East to replace it. The Army's operations would have been seriously handicapped had this signal equipment been lost or damaged.[40]

At this time, General Garvin issued verbal orders to service troops in the 2d Logistical Command at Pusan to take

---

[39] Ltr, Dabney to author, 19 Jan 54; Notes, Landrum to author, recd 28 Jun 54; Interv, author with Wright, 7 Jan 54; Interv, author with Stebbins, 4 Dec 53; Interv, author with Tarkenton, 3 Oct 52; Interv, author with Col Robert G. Fergusson, 2 Oct 52; Interv, author with Bullock, 28 Jan 54; Collier, MS review comments, 10 Mar 58.

[40] Notes, Landrum to author, recd 28 Jun 54; Interv, author with Allen, 15 Dec 53; Collier, MS review comments, 10 Mar 58; FEC CofS files, Summ of conversation, Hickey with Landrum, 060900 Sep 50; GHQ FEC Sitrep, 7 Sep 50; EUSAK WD, G-3 Jnl, 2030 6 Sep 50; 1st Cav Div, Ordnance Act Rpt, Sep 50.
Communication between Eighth Army and the Far East Command would have suffered most if this equipment had been lost or damaged, not the tactical control of units in Korea under Eighth Army. The Marc 2, 4-van unit for teletype, and a 1,200-line switchboard could not have been replaced—there was only one each in Korea and Japan. The big teletype unit with 180 lines to Pusan and the trunk cables constituted the critical items in U.N. signal communication at this time. Interv, author with Col William M. Thames (Deputy Sig Off, FEC, 1950), 17 Dec 53; Interv, author with Col Thomas A. Pitcher (Acting EUSAK Sig Off, Sep 50), 16 Dec 53; Interv, author with Lt Col William E. Kaley, 16 Dec 50.

defensive positions on the hills bordering the port city and within the city itself if and when the tactical situation required it.[41]

What the South Korean civilian estimate of the situation was at this time can be surmised from the fact that about 5 September prominent Koreans started to leave Pusan for the island of Tsushima, midway in the Korean Strait between Korea and Japan. Operators of small 10- to 20-ton vessels smuggled them across to the island. Wealthy and influential Chinese residing in the Pusan area were planning to leave for Formosa, the first group expecting to depart about 8 September. They, too, were to be smuggled away in small vessels.[42]

This period in early September 1950 tested General Walker as perhaps no other did. Walker was generally an undemonstrative man in public, he was not popular with the press, and he was not always popular with his troops. He could be hard and demanding. He was so at this time. When many of his commanders were losing confidence in the ability of Eighth Army to stop the North Koreans he remained determined that it would. On one occasion in early September he told one of his division commanders in effect, "If the enemy gets into Taegu you will find me resisting him in the streets and I'll have some of my trusted people with me and you had better be prepared to do the same. Now get back to your division and fight it." He told one general he did not want to see him back from the front again unless it was in a coffin.[43]

By day, General Walker moved around the Perimeter defense positions either by liaison plane or in his armored jeep. The jeep was equipped with a special iron handrail permitting him to stand up so that he could observe better while the vehicle was in motion, and generally it was in rapid motion. In addition to his .45 automatic pistol, he customarily carried a repeating shotgun with him, because, as he told a fellow officer, "I don't mind being shot at, but these —— are not going to ambush me."[44] Walker was at his best in Korea in the Pusan Perimeter battles. Famous previously as being an exponent of armored offensive warfare, he demonstrated in August and September 1950 that he was also skilled in defensive warfare. His pugnacious temperament fitted him for directing the fighting of a bitter holding action. He was a stouthearted soldier.

The 7th Cavalry's Withdrawal Battle

It was in this crisis that the 7th Cavalry began its withdrawal northwest of Taegu. In his withdrawal instructions for the 7th Cavalry, Col. Cecil Nist, the regimental commander, ordered, "The 2d Battalion must clear Hill 464 of enemy tonight." This meant that the 2d Battalion must disengage from the enemy to its front and attack to its rear

---

[41] 2d Logistical Comd Activities Rpt, Sep 50, G-3 and Trans Secs. Operation Plan 4, dated 10 September, confirmed these orders.

[42] EUSAK WD, PIR 57, an. 2, 441st Counter Intelligence Corps Agent Rpt, 7 Sep 50.

[43] Notes, Landrum to author, recd 28 Jun 54; Interv, author with Maj Gen Leven C. Allen, 15 Dec 53; Interv, author with Bullock, 28 Jan 54; Interv, author with Lt Col Paul F. Smith, 1 Oct 52; Collier, MS review comments, Mar 58.

[44] Ltr, Wright to author, 12 Feb 54.

GENERAL WALKER CROSSING THE NAKTONG *in his armored jeep with handrail.*

to gain possession of Hills 464 and 380 on the new main line of resistance to be occupied by the regiment. Since efforts to gain possession of Hill 464 by other elements had failed in the past two or three days this did not promise to be an easy mission.

Heavy rains fell during the night of 5–6 September and mud slowed all wheeled and tracked vehicles in the withdrawal. The 1st Battalion completed its withdrawal without opposition. During its night march west, the 3d Battalion column was joined several times by groups of North Korean soldiers who apparently thought it was one of their own columns moving south. They were made prisoners and taken along in the withdrawal. Nearing Waegwan at dawn, the battalion column was taken under enemy tank and mortar fire after daybreak and sustained about eighteen casualties.

The 2d Battalion disengaged from the enemy and began its withdrawal at 0300, 6 September. The battalion abandoned two tanks, one because of mechanical failure and the other because it was stuck in the mud. The battalion moved to the rear in two main groups: G Company to attack Hill 464 and the rest of the battalion to seize Hill 380, half a mile farther south. The North Koreans quickly discovered that the 2d Battalion was withdrawing and attacked it. The battalion commander, Maj. Omar T. Hitchner, and his S-3, Capt. James T. Milam, were killed. In the vicinity of Hills 464 and 380 the battalion discovered at daybreak that it was virtually surrounded by enemy soldiers. Colonel Nist thought that the entire battalion was lost.[45]

Moving by itself and completely cut off from all other units, G Company, numbering only about eighty men, was hardest hit. At 0800, nearing the top of Hill 464, it surprised and killed three enemy soldiers. Suddenly, enemy automatic weapons and small arms fire struck the company. All day G Company maneuvered around the hill but never gained its crest. At midafternoon it received radio orders to withdraw that night. The company left six dead on the hill and, carrying its wounded on improvised litters of ponchos and tree branches, it started down the shale slopes of the mountain in rain and darkness. Halfway down, a friendly artillery barrage killed one of the noncommissioned officers, and a rock thrown by one of the exploding shells hit Capt. Herman L. West, G Company commander, inflicting a painful back injury. The company scattered but Captain West reassembled it. Cautioning his men to move quietly and not to fire in any circumstances, so that surrounding enemy troops might think them one of their own columns, West led his men to the eastern base of Hill 464 where he went into a defensive position for the rest of the night.[46]

On the division left, meanwhile, the 2d Battalion, 5th Cavalry, on Hill 303 came under heavy attack and the battalion commander wanted to withdraw. Colonel Crombez, the regimental commander, told him he could not do so until the 7th Cavalry had cleared on its withdrawal road. This battalion suffered heavy casualties before it abandoned Hill 303 on the 6th to the enemy.[47]

While G Company was trying to escape from Hill 464, the rest of the 2d Battalion was cut off at the eastern base of Hill 380, half a mile southward. Colonel Nist organized all the South Korean carriers he could find before dark and loaded them with water, food, and ammunition for the 2d Battalion, but the carrier party was unable to find the battalion. At dawn on 7 September the men in G Company's perimeter at the eastern base of Hill 464 saw in the dim light four figures coming down a trail toward them. Soon recognizing them as North Koreans, the men killed them. This rifle fire brought answering fire from enemy troops in nearby positions. At this time, Captain West heard what he recognized as fire from American weapons on a knob to his west. Thinking that it might be from the Weapons Platoon which had become separated from him during the night, he led his company in that direction. He was right; soon the company was reunited.

---

[45] 7th Cav Regt WD, 6-7 Sep 50; Capt Robert M. Ballard, Action of G Company on Hill 464, an. to 7th Cav Regt WD, 6 Sep 50; Webel, MS review comments, 15 Nov 57; New York *Herald Tribune*, September 8, 1950, Bigart dispatch.

[46] Ballard, Action of G Company on Hill 464; Capt. Russell A. Gugeler, *Combat Actions in Korea*, ch. 4, "Attack to the Rear," pp. 41-42.

[47] 5th Cav Regt WD, 5-6 Sep 50; Notes, Crombez for author, 28 Jul 55.

The Weapons Platoon, led by Lt. Harold R. Anderegg, had undergone a strange experience. After becoming separated from the rest of the company, three times during the night it encountered North Koreans on the trail it was following but in each instance neither side fired, each going on its way. At dawn, the platoon came upon a group of foxholes on a knoll. Enemy soldiers were occupying some of them. In a swift action which apparently surprised and paralyzed the North Koreans, the platoon killed approximately thirteen and captured three enemy soldiers. From the body of an officer the men took a brief case containing important documents and maps. These showed that Hill 464 was an assembly point for part of the N.K. *3d Division* in its advance from Hill 518 toward Taegu.[48]

Later in the day (7 September), Capt. Melbourne C. Chandler, acting commander of the 2d Battalion, received word of G Company's location on Hill 464 from an aerial observer and sent a patrol which guided the company safely to the battalion at the eastern base of Hill 380. The battalion, meanwhile, had received radio orders to withdraw by any route as soon as possible. It moved southwest into the 5th Cavalry sector. At one point it escaped ambush by turning aside when North Koreans dressed in American uniforms waved helmets and shouted, "Hey, this way, G.I.!"[49]

East of the 2d Battalion, the enemy attacked the 1st Battalion in its new position on 7 September and overran the battalion aid station, killing four and wounding seven men. That night the 1st Battalion on division order was attached to the 5th Cavalry Regiment. The rest of the 7th Cavalry Regiment moved to a point near Taegu in division reserve. During the night of 7-8 September the 5th Cavalry Regiment on division orders withdrew still farther below Waegwan to new defensive positions astride the main Seoul-Taegu highway. The enemy *3d Division* was still moving reinforcements across the Naktong. Observers sighted fifteen barges loaded with troops and artillery pieces crossing the river two miles north of Waegwan on the evening of the 7th. On the 8th the North Korean communiqué claimed the capture of Waegwan.[50]

The next day the situation grew worse for the 1st Cavalry Division. On its left flank, the N.K. *3d Division* forced the 1st Battalion, 5th Cavalry, to withdraw from Hill 345, three miles east of Waegwan. The enemy pressed forward and the 5th Cavalry was immediately locked in hard, seesaw fighting on Hills 203 and 174. The 1st Battalion, 7th Cavalry, before it left that sector to rejoin its regiment, finally captured the latter hill after four attacks.

Only with the greatest difficulty did the 5th Cavalry Regiment hold Hill 203 on 12 September. Between midnight and 0400, 13 September, the North Koreans attacked again and took Hill 203 from E Company, Hill 174 from L Company, and Hill 188 from B and F Companies. In an afternoon counterattack

---

[48] Ballard, Action of G Company on Hill 464; 7th Cav Regt WD, 7 Sep 50; Gugeler, *Combat Actions in Korea*, pp. 39-45.

[49] Ballard, Action of G Company on Hill 464; 7th Cav Regt WD, 6-7 Sep 50.

[50] 1st Bn, 7th Cav WD, 7 Sep 50; 1st Cav Div WD, 7 Sep 50; 7th Cav Regt WD, 7th Sep 50, Opn Ord 15; GHQ FEC Sitrep, 8 Sep 50.

PERIMETER BATTLE

the regiment regained Hill 188 on the south side of the highway, but failed against Hills 203 and 174 on the north side. On the 14th, I Company again attacked Hill 174, which had by now changed hands seven times. In this action the company suffered 82 casualties. Its 2d Platoon with 27 Americans and 15 ROK's at the start had only 11 Americans and 5 ROK's when it reached its objective. Even so, the company held only one side of the hill, the enemy held the other, and grenade battles between the two continued for another week. The battalions of the 5th Cavalry Regiment were so low in strength at this time as to be scarcely combat effective. This seesaw battle continued in full swing only eight air miles northwest of Taegu.[51]

Troopers in the Mountains—Walled Ka-san

Hard on the heels of Major Kim's warning that the North Korean attack would strike the night of 2 September, the blow hit with full force in the Bowling Alley area north of Taegu. It caught the 8th Cavalry Regiment defending the Sangju road badly deployed in that it lacked an adequate reserve. The North Koreans struck the 2d Battalion, 8th Cavalry, the night of 2–3 September on Hill 448 west of the Bowling Alley and two miles north of Tabu-dong, and overran it. On the right, E Company, although not under attack, was cut off and had to withdraw by a roundabout way. Lt. Col. Harold K. Johnson, commanding officer of the 3d Battalion, placed I Company in a blocking position just north of Tabu-dong astride the road. There, two enemy tanks and some enemy infantry struck it at 0200 in the morning of 3 September. In this action, I Company suffered many casualties but repelled the enemy attack. The overrun 2d Battalion withdrew through the 3d Battalion which had assembled hastily in a defensive position south of Tabu-dong. During the day, elements of the N.K. *1st Division* forced the 8th Cavalry I&R Platoon and a detachment of South Korean police from the Walled City of Ka-san on the crest of Hill 902, four miles east of Tabudong. On 3 September, therefore, Eighth Army lost to the enemy both Tabu-dong and Hill 902, locally called Ka-san, the dominant mountaintop ten miles north of Taegu.[52]

The North Koreans now concentrated artillery north of Hill 902 and, although its fire was light and sporadic, it did cause minor damage in the 99th Field Artillery positions. This sudden surge of the enemy southward toward Taegu caused concern in Eighth Army headquarters. The Army ordered a ROK battalion from the Taegu Replacement Training Center to a position in the rear of the 8th Cavalry, and the 1st Cavalry Division organized Task Force Allen, to be commanded by Assistant Division Commander Brig. Gen. Frank

---

[51] EUSAK WD, Br for CG, 130800 Sep 50; *Ibid.*, G-3 Sec, 15 Sep 50; 1st Cav Div WD, 9-10, 13-15 Sep 50; 5th Cav **Regt WD**, 13-15 Sep 50; 7th Cav Regt WD, 10 Sep 50; New York *Times*, September 9, 1950 (London rebroadcast of Moscow broadcast); I Corps WD, 15 Sep 50, Hist Narr, p. 5; ATIS Interrog Rpts, Issue 6 (N.K. Forces), Rpt 1157, Che Nak Hwan, p. 127; Allen, Korean Army Troops, USA, pp. 6-7.

[52] 8th Cav Regt WD, 3 Sep 50; 1st Cav Div WD, 3 Sep 50; EUSAK WD, G-3 Sec, 3 Sep 50; *Ibid.*, PIR 53, 3 Sep 50; Ltr, Johnson to author, recd Aug 54.

RUINS OF ANCIENT FORTRESS *and stone wall on the crest of Ka-san (Hill 902).*

A. Allen, Jr. This task force comprised two provisional battalions formed of division headquarters and technical service troops, the division band, the replacement company, and other miscellaneous troops. It was to be used in combat should the North Koreans break through to the edge of the city.[53]

Eighth Army countered the North Korean advance down the Tabu-dong road by ordering the 1st Cavalry Division to recapture and defend Hill 902. This hill, ten miles north of Taegu, gave observation all the way south through Eighth Army positions into the city, and, in enemy hands, could be used for general intelligence purposes and to direct artillery and mortar fire. Hill 902 was too far distant from the Tabu-dong road to dominate it; otherwise it would have controlled this main communication route. The shortage of North Korean artillery and mortar ammunition nullified in large part the advantages the peak held as an observation point.

Actually, there was no walled city on the crest of Ka-san. Ka-san, or Hill 902, the 3,000-foot-high mountain which differs from most high peaks in this part of Korea in having an oval-shaped semi-level area on its summit. This oval is a part of a mile-long ridgelike crest, varying from 200 to 800 yards in width, which slopes down from the peak at 902

---

[53] 1st Cav Div WD, 3 Sep 50, Ordnance Stf Sec; Ltr, Gay to author, 17 Jul 53.

PERIMETER BATTLE

D Company, 8th Engineer Combat Battalion, *position on the summit of Hill 755.*

meters to approximately 755 meters at its southeastern end. On all sides of this ridge crest the mountain slopes drop precipitously. In bygone ages Koreans had built a thirty-foot-high stone wall around the crest and had converted the summit into a fortress. One man who fought in the shadow of the wall commented later, "It looked to me like they built that wall just to keep the land from sliding down." Most of the summit in 1950 was covered with a dense growth of scrub brush and small pine trees. There were a few small terraced fields. Koreans knew Ka-san as the Sacred Mountain. Near the northern end of the crest still stood the Buddhist Poguk Temple.

When the 1st Cavalry Division on 29 August assumed responsibility for the old ROK 1st Division sector north of Taegu it sent a patrol from the I&R Platoon to the top of Ka-san. There the patrol found 156 South Korean police. There was some discussion between General Gay and Eighth Army about whether the 1st Cavalry Division or the ROK 1st Division should have the responsibility for the mountain. General Gay maintained that his understrength division with a 35-mile front was already overextended and could not extend eastward beyond the hills immediately adjacent to the Tabu-dong road. Uncertainty as to final responsibility for Ka-san ended on the afternoon of 3 September after North Koreans had seized the mountain. The Eighth Army G-3 Section telephoned Col. Ernest V. Holmes, Chief of Staff, 1st Cavalry Division, and told him that the 1st Cavalry Division had responsibility for the Walled City. Holmes replied he believed that General Gay, who was then absent from the headquarters, would not like the decision, but that pending his return he would send a company of engineers to Ka-san. When General Gay returned to his command post he said that if the army had ordered the responsibility it had to be complied with, and he approved Holmes' decision to send a company to the mountain.[54]

After his telephone conversation with Eighth Army, Colonel Holmes ordered Lt. Col. William C. Holley, commanding officer of the 8th Engineer Combat Battalion, to report to Col. Raymond D. Palmer, commanding the 8th Cavalry Regiment. That afternoon Colonel Palmer in his command post on the Tabu-dong road outlined to Holley and the commanding officers of D Company, 8th Engineer Combat Battalion, and E Company, 8th Cavalry, his attack plan to regain control of Ka-san. The Engineer company, commanded by 1st Lt. John T. Kennedy, was to lead the attack, E Company following. Once the force had gained the crest and E Company had established itself in defensive positions, the Engineer company was to come off the mountain. Luckily, many of the men in D Company had been infantrymen in World War II.[55]

That evening, D Company loaded into trucks and in a driving rain traveled north, eventually turning off the main road to the designated assembly area. On the way they met two truckloads of South Korean police going south, some of them wounded. These were the police who, together with the detachment of the I&R Platoon, had been driven off Ka-san that afternoon. After waiting in the rain awhile for orders, the Engineer company turned around and went back to camp.

The next morning (4 September) at breakfast, D Company received orders to move immediately as infantry to Ka-san. One platoon had to forego its breakfast. The company carried no rations since E Company, 8th Cavalry, was to bring food and water later. The Engineer troops arrived at their assembly area near the village of Kisong-dong two miles east of the Tabu-dong road, where Colonel Holley set up a communications command post. Sniper fire came in on the men as they moved up the trail half a mile to the base of Ka-san's steep slope. Word was given to the company that there were about seventy-five disorganized enemy troops on Ka-san. But actually, during the afternoon and evening of 3 September, the N.K. *2d Battalion, 2d Regiment, 1st Division*, had occupied the summit of Ka-san.[56]

The Engineer company started its attack up the mountain about noon, 4

---

[54] Ltr and notes, Gay to author, 17 Jul 53; Interv, author with Holmes, 27 Oct 53; 1st Cav Div WD, 29 Aug 50.

[55] Ltr, Capt John T. Kennedy to author, 2 Apr 52; Interv, author with Holley, 20 Feb 52; Interv, author with 1st Sgt Cornelius C. Kopper (D Co, 8th Engr C Bn, in 1950), 20 Feb 52.

[56] Ltr, MSgt James N. Vandygriff to author, 19 May 53 (Vandygriff was Plat Sgt, 2d Plat, D Co, 8th Engr C Bn, Sep 50); Ltr, Capt Thomas T. Jones to author, 21 Jun 53 (Plat Ldr, 3d Plat, D Co, 8th Engr C Bn, Sep 50); EUSAK WD, 11 Sep 50, interrog of Kim Choe Ski; *Ibid.*, G-3 Jnl, 0620 4 Sep 50; GHQ FEC Sitrep, 4 Sep 50.

September, following a trail up a southern spur. The 1st Platoon was in the lead, single file, followed by the 2d and 3d Platoons. Colonel Palmer considered the mission so important that he and his S-2, Capt. Rene J. Guiraud, accompanied the engineers. Platoon Sgt. James N. Vandygriff, 2d Platoon, D Company, in a brief conversation with Colonel Holley as he went ahead of the latter on his way up the trail, said he thought it was a suicide mission.

Less than a mile up the trail, D Company came under machine gun fire from its right front, which inflicted several casualties. Lieutenant Kennedy rejected Vandygriff's request to take a squad and knock out the gun, so the file got past the line of fire as best it could until BAR fire from the 3d Platoon silenced the weapon. Farther up the trail another enemy machine gun fired from the right along the trail and held up the advance until radio-adjusted artillery fire silenced it.

The file of men, with Lt. Robert Peterson of the I&R Platoon as guide, left the traillike road, which dead-ended, dropped over into a ravine on the left, and continued the climb. Enemy mortar fire killed two men and wounded eight or ten others in this phase of the ascent. At this time the 2d Platoon leader collapsed from a kidney ailment and command passed to Sergeant Vandygriff. Vandygriff led his platoon, now at the head of the company, on up the gully and finally, about 1700, came through a tunnel under a small ridge and the stone wall into the bowl-shaped summit of Hill 755, the southern arm of the Hill 902 crest. The 2d and 3d Platoons soon arrived, in that order. When he was within fifty feet of the top, Colonel Palmer received radio orders from General Gay to come off the mountain; Gay had not known that Palmer had accompanied the attack until he telephoned Holley trying to locate him.[57]

Lieutenant Kennedy quickly placed the approximately ninety men of his company in position facing in an arc from west to northeast; the 2d Platoon took the left flank near the stone wall, the 1st Platoon took the center position on a wooded knoll, and the 3d Platoon the right flank at the edge of a woods. Just as he reached the top, 2d Lt. Thomas T. Jones, commanding the 3d Platoon, saw and heard three North Korean mortars fire, approximately 1,000 yards away on a grassy ridge to the right (east). He suggested to Lieutenant Kennedy several times that he request artillery fire on these mortars, but Kennedy did not act on the suggestion. Kennedy established his command post inside the tunnel behind the 2d Platoon position. The D Company position was entirely within the area enclosed by the stone wall, which was nearly intact except on the northeast near the 3d Platoon position where it had crumbled and was covered with brush and trees. Lieutenant Jones pointed out to his platoon sergeant and squad leaders where he wanted them to take position at the edge of the woods facing the enemy mortars he had seen on the grassy ridge beyond. He then remained a few minutes

---

[57] Ltr, Jones to author, 21 Jun 53; Ltr, Vandygriff to author, 19 May 53; Ltr and notes, Gay to author, 17 Jul 53; Interv, author with Holley, 20 Feb 52; Ltr, Kennedy to author, 2 Apr 52; Interv, author with Guiraud, 21 Apr 54.

in conversation with Lieutenant Kennedy.[58]

A few minutes later Jones joined his 3d Squad men at the edge of the woods. They told him that the platoon sergeant and the rest had continued on toward the narrow grassy ridge. Just then one of the squad called Jones to the edge of the woods and pointed out ten or twelve well-camouflaged North Korean soldiers, one of them carrying a machine gun, coming down the narrow ridge toward them from the mortar position. Apparently this group was a security force for the mortars because they dropped to the ground about one-third of the way down the ridge.

Jones decided he had better bring back his other two squads to form a solid line and, expecting to be gone only a few minutes, he left his SCR-300 radio behind. That, as he said later, was his big mistake. Jones found one squad but the other had gone on farther and was not visible. While he studied the terrain and waited for a messenger he had sent to bring back that last squad, North Koreans attacked the main company position behind him. Judging by the firing and yelling, Jones thought North Koreans were all over the wooded bowl between him and the rest of the company. When the firing ended, all he could hear was North Korean voices. Jones never got back to his 3d Squad. He and the rest of the platoon dropped down off the ridge into a gully on the left, the two squads separated but for a time within sight of each other.

That night Jones and the eight men with him stayed in the ravine just under the crest. Without his radio he could not communicate with the rest of the company which he thought had been destroyed or driven off the hill. The next day when American fighter planes strafed the hilltop it confirmed his belief that no D Company men were there. Some of the men in the advanced squad made their way to safety, but North Koreans captured Jones and the eight men with him near the bottom of Ka-san on 10 September as they were trying to make their way through the enemy lines. This account of the 3d Platoon explains why—except for the 3d Squad which rejoined D Company that evening—it was out of the action and off the crest almost as soon as it arrived on top, all unknown to Lieutenant Kennedy and the rest of the company at the time.[59]

Half an hour after D Company had reached Hill 755, an estimated enemy battalion launched an attack down the slope running south to Hill 755 from the crest of Hill 902. The main attack hit Vandygriff's 2d Platoon just after Vandygriff had set up and loaded his two machine guns. These machine guns and the protection of the 15-foot wall on its left enabled D Company to turn back this attack, which left one dead and three wounded in the 2d Platoon. That night, enemy mortar and small arms fire harassed the company and there were several small probing attacks. Having

---

[58] Ltr, Jones to author, 21 Jun 53; Ltr, Kennedy to author, 2 Apr 52; Ltr, Vandygriff to author, 19 May 53.

[59] Ltrs, Jones to author, 26 May, 21 and 30 Jun 53; 1st Lt Thomas T. Jones, "Two Hundred Miles to Freedom," *The Military Engineer* (September-October 1951), pp. 351-54. The North Koreans, strangely enough, released Jones and three other soldiers later near Ch'unch'on in central Korea, where they entered the lines of the ROK 6th Division.

no communication with the 3d Platoon, Kennedy sent a patrol to its supposed position. The patrol reported back that it could find no one there but had found the rocket launchers and two light machine guns.[60]

It rained most of the night, and 5 September dawned wet and foggy on top of Hill 755. Just after daylight in a cold drizzle the North Koreans attacked. The engineers repulsed this attack but suffered some casualties. Enemy fire destroyed Vandygriff's radio, forcing him to use runners to communicate with Kennedy's command post. Ammunition was running low and three C-47 planes came over to make an airdrop. Kennedy put out orange identification panels, then watched the enemy put out similarly colored one. The planes circled, and finally dropped their bundles of ammunition and food—to the enemy. Immediately after the airdrops, two F-51 fighter planes came over and attacked D Company. It was obvious that the enemy panels had misled both the cargo and fighter planes. The fighters dropped two napalm tanks within D Company's perimeter, one of which fortunately failed to ignite; the other injured no one. The planes then strafed right through the 2d Platoon position, but miraculously caused no casualties. Soon after this aerial attack, enemy burp gun fire wounded Kennedy in the leg and ankle.[61]

Sometime between 1000 and 1100 the advanced platoon of E Company, 8th Cavalry Regiment, arrived on top of Hill 755 and came into D Company's perimeter. Some of the engineers fired on the E Company men before the latter identified themselves. The E Company platoon went into position on the right of Vandygriff, and Kennedy turned over command of the combined force to the E Company commander. Kennedy then assembled twelve wounded men and started down the mountain with them. The party was under small arms fire most of the way. A carrying party of Korean A-frame porters led by an American officer had started up the mountain during the morning with supplies. Enemy fire, killing several of the porters, turned it back.[62]

The day before, E Company had been delayed in following D Company to Hill 755. Soon after the Engineer company had started up the trail on the 4th, E Company arrived at Colonel Holley's command post at the base of the mountain. Enemy mortar fire was falling on the trail at the time and the company commander said he could not advance because of it. Holley radioed this information to Colonel Palmer who designated another company commander and said, "Tell him to come on through." This second officer broke his glasses on a rock and informed Holley that he could not go on. Holley put him on the radio to Palmer who ordered him to continue up the hill. Soon thereafter this officer was wounded in the leg. Holley then designated a third officer, who started up the mountain with E Company that evening about 2000. Enemy fire stopped the company 500 yards

---

[60] Ltr, Vandygriff to author, 19 May 53; Ltrs, Kennedy to author, 2 Apr 52 and 4 Jun 52.
[61] Ltrs, Kennedy to author, 2 Apr and 4 Jun 52; Ltr, Vandygriff to author, 19 May 53; GHQ FEC Sitrep, 5 Sep 50.

[62] Ltr, Vandygriff to author, 19 May 53; Ltrs, Kennedy to author, 2 Apr and 4 Jun 52.

short of the crest before dawn. It was this same company that the N.K. *13th Division* had cut off when it launched its attack the evening of 2 September and overran the 2d Battalion north of Tabu-dong. Tired and dispirited from this experience and their roundabout journey to rejoin the regiment, E Company men were not enjoying the best of morale.[63]

Shortly after the E Company platoon joined Vandygriff, the North Koreans attacked again. The E Company infantrymen had brought no mortars with them—only small arms. In this situation, Vandygriff took a 3.5-inch rocket launcher and fired into the North Koreans. They must have thought that it was mortar or 75-mm. recoilless rifle fire for they broke off the attack. Vandygriff checked his platoon and found it was nearly out of ammunition. He then instructed his men to gather up all the weapons and ammunition from enemy dead they could reach, and in this manner they obtained for emergency use about 30 to 40 rifles, 5 burp guns, and some hand grenades.

In the course of gathering up these enemy weapons, Vandygriff passed the dug-in position of Pfc. Melvin L. Brown, a BAR man in the 3d Squad. Brown was next to the wall on the extreme left of the platoon position at a point where the wall was only about six or seven feet high. At the bottom of the wall around Brown's position lay about fifteen or twenty enemy dead. Vandygriff asked Brown what had happened. The latter replied, "Every time they came up I knocked them off the wall." Earlier in the day, about 0800, Kennedy had visited Brown and had seen five enemy dead that Brown had killed with BAR fire. Subsequently Brown exhausted his automatic rifle ammunition, then his few grenades, and finally he used his entrenching tool to knock the North Koreans in the head when they tried to climb over the wall. Brown had received a flesh wound in the shoulder early in the morning, but had bandaged it himself and refused to leave his position.[64]

At 1330 General Gay ordered the 8th Cavalry Regiment to withdraw its men off Ka-san. Gay decided to give up the mountain because he believed he had insufficient forces to secure and hold it and that the enemy had insufficient ammunition to exploit its possession as an observation point for directing artillery and mortar fire. It is not certain that this order actually reached anyone on the hill. Colonel Holley could not reach anyone in D Company, 8th Engineer Combat Battalion.[65]

Rain started falling again and heavy fog closed in on the mountain top so that it was impossible to see more than a few yards. Again the enemy attacked the 2d Platoon and the adjacent E Company infantrymen. One of the engineers was shot through the neck and Vandygriff sent him to the company command post. In about thirty minutes he returned. "What's wrong?" asked Vandygriff. Barely able to talk from his wound

---

[63] Interv, author with Holley, 20 Feb 52; Ltrs, Kennedy to author, 2 Apr and 4 Jun 52; Ltr, Vandygriff to author, 19 May 53; Ltr, Jones to author, 21 Jun 53.

[64] Ltr, Vandygriff to author, 19 May 53; Ltrs, Kennedy to author, 2 Apr and 4 Jun 52.

[65] Interv, author with Holley, 20 Feb 52; Ltr, Gay to author, 17 Jul 53.

and shock, the man replied that there was no longer a command post, that he could not find anyone and had seen only enemy dead. Vandygriff now went to the infantry sergeant who was in command of the E Company platoon and asked him what he intended to do. The latter replied, in effect, that he was going to take his platoon and go over the wall.

Vandygriff went back to his own platoon, got his squad leaders together and told them the platoon was going out the way it came in and that he would give the wounded a 30-minute start. Enemy fire was falling in the platoon area now from nearly all directions and the situation looked hopeless. Sgt. John J. Philip, leader of the 3d Squad, started to break up the weapons that the platoon could not take out with them. Vandygriff, noticing that Brown was not among the assembled men, asked Philip where he was. The latter replied that he didn't know but that he would try to find out. Philip returned to the squad's position and came back fifteen minutes later, reporting to Vandygriff that Brown was dead. Asked by Philip if he should take the identification tags off the dead, Vandygriff said, "No," that he should leave them on because they would be the only means of identification later. Vandygriff put his platoon in a V formation and led them off the hill the same way they had come up, picking up four wounded men on the way down.[66]

At the base of the mountain, Colonel Holley and others in the afternoon saw E Company men come down from the top and, later, men from the engineer company. Each group thought it was the last of the survivors and told confused, conflicting stories. When all remaining members of D Company had been assembled, Colonel Holley found that the company had suffered 50 percent casualties; eighteen men were wounded and thirty were missing in action.[67]

Among the wounded carried off the mountain was an officer of D Company, 8th Engineer Combat Battalion. Enemy machine gun fire struck him in the leg just before he jumped off a high ledge. Two men carried him to the bottom and at his request left him in a Korean house, expecting to come back in a jeep for him. A little later, other members escaping off the mountain heard his screams. Two weeks passed before the 1st Cavalry Division recaptured the area. They found the officer's body in the house. The hands and feet were tied, the eyes gouged, a thumb pulled off, and the body had been partly burned. Apparently he had been tied, tortured, and a fire built under him.

Soldiers of the ROK 1st Division captured a North Korean near Ka-san on 4 September who said that about 800 of his fellow soldiers were in the Walled City area with three more battalions following them from the north. The Engineer company had succeeded only in establishing a perimeter briefly within the enemy-held area. By evening of 5

---

[66] Ltr, Vandygriff to author, 19 May 53. Department of the Army General Order 11, 16 February 1951, awarded the Medal of Honor posthumously to Pfc. Melvin L. Brown.

[67] Ltr, Jones to author, 21 Jun 53; Intervs, author with Holley and Kopper, 20 Feb 52; Maj Hal D. Steward, "Engineers Fight as Infantry," Ad Cosantoir (August, 1951), pp. 366-67.

September, Ka-san was securely in enemy hands with an estimated five battalions, totaling about 1,500 enemy soldiers, on the mountain and its forward slope. A North Korean oxtrain carrying 82-mm. mortar shells and rice reportedly reached the top of Ka-san during the day. The ROK 1st Division captured this oxtrain a few days later south of Ka-san.[68]

When Lieutenant Jones went back up the mountain as a prisoner on 10 September he saw at least 400–500 enemy soldiers on the ridge. A Mosquito spotter plane flew over and he felt sure it would sight the large number of enemy troops and call in fighter planes for strafing attacks. But, he said, "The pilot of the plane took one look and went away which amazed me, except that the minute they heard the plane the North Koreans all either hit the ground or squatted and ducked their heads, which attested to the effectiveness of the leaves, branches, etc., that almost every man had stuck in the string netting on the back of his shirt and the top of his cloth hat." [69]

Now, with Ka-san firmly in their possession, the N.K. *13th* and *1st Divisions* made ready to press on downhill into Taegu.

On the 6th, the day after the American troops were driven off Ka-san, an enemy force established a roadblock three miles below Tabu-dong and other units occupied Hill 570, two miles southwest of the Walled City and overlooking the Taegu road from the east side. The next morning five tanks of the 16th Reconnaissance Company prepared to lead an attack against the roadblock. The enemy troops were in a rice field west and on the hills east of the road. General Gay was at the scene to watch the action. He ordered the reconnaissance company commander to launch the attack into the rice fields at maximum speed, saying, "I don't want a damn tank moving under 25 miles per hour until you are on top of those men." [70] The tank attack speedily disposed of the enemy in the rice field, but the infantry spent several hours clearing the hills on the east side of the road.

Enemy artillery during 7 September shelled batteries of the 9th and 99th Field Artillery Battalions, forcing displacement of two batteries during the day. U.S. air strikes and artillery kept both Hills 902 and 570 under heavy attack. Even though the 1st Cavalry Division fell back nearly everywhere that day, General Walker ordered it and the ROK II Corps to attack and seize Hill 902 and the Walled City, the time of the attack to be agreed upon by the commanders concerned. He directed the ROK 1st Division and the 1st Cavalry Division to select a boundary between them and to maintain physical contact during the attack.[71]

On the morning of the 8th, Lt. Col. Harold K. Johnson's 3d Battalion, 8th Cavalry, after executing a withdrawal during the night from its former position, tried to drive the enemy from Hill 570. The three peaks of this mountain

---

[68] EUSAK WD, PIR 55, 5 Sep 50; *Ibid.*, G-3 Jnl, 0750 and 1900 5 Sep 50; *Ibid.*, interrogation of Kim Choe Ski, 11 Sep 50.
[69] Ltr, Jones to author, 30 Jun 53.

[70] Ltr, Gay to author, 17 Jul 53; 1st Cav Div WD, 7 Sep 50.
[71] EUSAK WD, G-3 Sec and G-3 Jnl, 1330 7 Sep 50; *Ibid.*, Br for CG, 7 Sep 50.

mass were under clouds, making it impossible to support the infantry attack with air strikes or artillery and mortar fire. Johnson placed all three of his rifle companies in the assault against the three peaks; two of them reached their objectives, one with little opposition, the other catching enemy soldiers asleep on the ground. But enemy counterattacks regained this second peak. The main enemy force on Hill 570 was on the third and highest of the three peaks and held it firmly against the L Company attack. The I Company commander and the L Company executive officer were killed, as were several noncommissioned officers. The Eighth Army Intelligence Section estimated that 1,000 enemy soldiers were on Hill 570, only eight air miles north of Taegu, and on 8 September it stated that the continued pressure against the eastern flank of the 1st Cavalry Division sector "represents what is probably the most immediate threat to the U.N. Forces." [72]

That same day, 8 September, the 1st Cavalry Division canceled a planned continuation of the attack against Hill 570 by the 3d Battalion, 7th Cavalry Regiment, when enemy forces threatened Hills 314 and 660, south and east of 570.

In the midst of this enemy drive on Taegu, an ammunition shortage became critical for the U.N. forces. The situation was such that General MacArthur on 9 September sent messages urging that two ammunition ships then en route to Yokohama and Pusan carrying 172,790 rounds of 105-mm. shells, with estimated arrival time 11 September, proceed at maximum speed consistent with the safety of the vessels. Eighth Army on 10 September reduced the ration of 105-mm. howitzer ammunition from fifty to twenty-five rounds per howitzer per day, except in cases of emergency. Carbine ammunition was also in critical short supply. The 17th Field Artillery Battalion, with the first 8-inch howitzers to arrive in Korea, could not engage in the battle for lack of ammunition.[73]

The N.K. *1st Division* now began moving in the zone of the ROK 1st Division around the right flank of the 1st Cavalry Division. Its *2d Regiment*, about 1,200 strong, advanced six air miles eastward from the vicinity of the Walled City on Hill 902 to the towering 4,000-foot-high mountain of P'algong-san. It reached the top of P'algong-san about daylight on 10 September, and a little later new replacements, prodded by burp guns from behind, made a wild charge toward the ROK positions. The ROK's turned back the charge, killing or wounding about two-thirds of the attacking force.[74]

The 1st Cavalry Division now had most of its combat units concentrated on its right flank north of Taegu. The 3d Battalion, 7th Cavalry, attached to the 8th Cavalry Regiment, was behind that regiment on Hills 181 and 182

---

[72] Johnson, Review notes for author on draft chapter, Aug 54; 8th Cav Regt WD, 8 Sep 50; EUSAK PIR 58, 8 Sep 50; 7th Cav Opn Ord 16 and WD overlay, 8 Sep 50.

[73] Schnabel, FEC, GHQ Support and Participation in the Korean War, ch. 4, pp. 22-23; 24th Div WD, G-4 Summ, 25-26 Aug and 10-11 Sep 50; 159th FA Bn Unit Rpt, 1-30 Sep 50; GHQ FEC Sitrep, 9 Sep 50.

[74] EUSAK WD, 14 Sep 50, interrog rpt of Kim Yong Gi; ATIS Interrog Rpts, Issue 6, Rpt 1103, p. 8; ATIS Res Supp Interrog Rpts, Issue 3 (N.K. *1st Div*), p. 36.

astride the Tabu-dong road only 6 air miles north of Taegu. The rest of the 7th Cavalry Regiment (the 1st Battalion rejoined the regiment during the day) was in the valley of the Kumho River to the right rear between the enemy and the Taegu Airfield, which was situated 3 miles northeast of the city. The 5th Cavalry was disposed on the hills astride the Waegwan road 8 air miles northwest of Taegu. On its left the entire 8th Engineer Combat Battalion was in line as infantry, with the mission of holding a bridge across the Kumho River near its juncture with the Naktong east of Taegu.[75]

The fighting north of Taegu on 11 September in the vicinity of Hills 660 and 314 was heavy and confused. For a time, the 1st Cavalry Division feared a breakthrough to the blocking position of the 3d Battalion, 7th Cavalry. The rifle companies of the division were now very low in strength. On 11 September, for instance, E Company, 5th Cavalry, in attacking Hill 203 on the division left toward Waegwan had only 3 officers and 63 men. The day before, C Company, 7th Cavalry, had only 50 men. Colonel Johnson stated later that any company of the 3d Battalion, 8th Cavalry, that had 100 men during this period was his assault company for the day.[76]

Hill 314

While the 3d Battalion, 8th Cavalry, again vainly attacked Hill 570 on 11 September, enemy soldiers seized the crest of Hill 314 two miles southeast of it and that much closer to Taegu. Actually, the two hill masses are adjacent and their lower slopes within small arms range of each other. The North Koreans drove the 16th Reconnaissance Company from the hill and only the ROK 5th Training Battalion, previously hurried into the line from Taegu in a supporting position, prevented the enemy from gaining complete control of this terrain feature. This ROK battalion still held part of the reverse slope of Hill 314 when the 3d Battalion, 8th Cavalry, hurried to the scene from its fruitless attacks on Hill 570 and tried to retake the position. The ROK battalion twice had attacked and reached the crest but could not hold it, and had dug in on the lower southern slopes. The 3d Battalion, 7th Cavalry, command post had to fight off infiltrating enemy on 12 September as it issued its attack order and prepared to attack through the 8th Cavalry lines against Hill 314.

This attack on the 12th was to be part of a larger American and ROK counterattack against the N.K. *13th* and *1st Divisions* in an effort to halt them north of Taegu. The 2d Battalion, 7th Cavalry, relieved the ROK units on Hill 660, east of Hill 314, and had the mission of securing that hill. Farther east the ROK 1st Division had the mission of attacking from P'algong-san toward the Walled City on Hill 902. The point nearest Taegu occupied by enemy forces at this time was Hill 314. Some called it the "key to Taegu." Although this may be an exaggeration, since other hills, like links in a chain, were possibly equally important, the enemy *13th Division* valued its possession and had concentrated about 700 soldiers on it. The

---

[75] Ltr, Gay to author, 17 Jul 53; 1st Cav Div WD, 11 Sep 50.

[76] 1st Cav Div WD, 11 Sep 50; 1st Bn, 7th Cav Regt WD, 10 Sep 50; 5th Cav Regt WD, Sep 50 Narr; Review notes, Johnson to author, Aug 54.

North Koreans meant to use it, no doubt, in making the next advance on Taegu. From it, observation reached to Taegu and it commanded the lesser hills southward rimming the Taegu bowl.

Hill 314 is actually the southern knob of a 500-meter hill mass which lies close to the east side of Hill 570 and is separated from that hill mass only by a deep gulch. The hill mass is shaped like an elongated teardrop, its broad end at the north. The southern point rises to 314 meters and the ridge line climbs northward from it in a series of knobs to 380 and, finally, to 500 meters. The ridge line from the 314-meter to the 500-meter point is a mile in length. All sides of the hill mass are very steep.[77]

Lt. Col. James H. Lynch's 3d Battalion, 7th Cavalry, on the eve of its attack against Hill 314 numbered 535 men, less its rear echelons. The battalion, which had been organized at Fort Benning, Ga., from the 30th Infantry Regiment of the 3d Division, had arrived in Korea at the end of August. The ill-fated action of the 7th Cavalry at Hill 518, begun nine days earlier, had been its first action. This was to be its second. The battalion attack plan this time differed radically from that employed against Hill 518 and was a direct development of that failure. The key aspect of the Hill 314 attack plan was to mass as many riflemen as possible on top of the narrow ridge line, by attacking with two companies abreast along the ridge, and not to repeat the mistakes of Hill 518 where the fire power of only a platoon, and at times of only a squad, could be brought to bear against the enemy. Because of the ammunition shortage there was no artillery preparation on Hill 314, but there was an air strike before Colonel Lynch's battalion, with L Company on the left and I Company on the right, at 1100, 12 September, started its attack. The point of departure was the front lines of the 3d Battalion, 8th Cavalry, on the lower slope of the hill.[78]

Enemy 120-mm. mortar fire was falling on and behind the line of departure as the battalion moved out. For 500 yards it encountered only sporadic small arms and machine gun fire; then enemy rifle fire became intense and preregistered mortar fire came down on the troops, pinning them to the ground. On the left, men in L Company could see approximately 400 North Koreans preparing to counterattack. They radioed for an air strike but the planes were on the ground refueling. Fortunately, they were able to repulse the counterattack with combined artillery, mortar, and small arms fire. The air strike came in at 1400, blanketing the top and the north slope of the ridge.

By this time enemy mortar fire had caused many casualties, and elements of L and I Companies became intermingled. But, in contrast to the action on Hill 518, the men continued the attack largely of their own volition after many of the officers had become casualties. The example of certain officers,

---

[77] Ltr, Johnson to author, recd Aug 54; 1st Cav Div WD, 12 Sep 50; 7th Cav Regt WD, 12 Sep 50; Attack Ord, 3d Bn, 7th Cav Regt, attached to 1st Lt Morris M. Teague, Jr.'s, Narrative and Supporting Documents Concerning Hill 314, in the 7th Cav Regt WD.

[78] Teague, Hill 314 Narr; Ltr, Gay to author, 17 Jul 53; Webel, MS review comments, 15 Nov 57; 7th Cav Regt WD, 12 Sep 50.

however, pointed the way. The commanding officer of I Company, 1st Lt. Joseph A. Fields, reorganized his company under mortar fire without regard to his own safety after the company had suffered 25 percent casualties; 1st Lt. Marvin H. Haynes led a small group which killed or drove off enemy troops that had overrun part of L Company; and Capt. Robert W. Walker, commanding officer of L Company, continued his superb personal leadership. Fields was wounded, Haynes killed. MSgt. Roy E. McCullom, the weapons platoon leader of I Company, organized his men as riflemen, and though wounded three times, in shoulders and right arm, he led them on until he received a fourth wound in the head. Wounded by mortar fragments, 2d Lt. Marshall G. Engle, I Company, refused evacuation twice, telling litter teams to go farther forward and get the more critically injured. Engle lay on the hill for twelve hours, far into the night, receiving another mortar wound during that time before a litter team finally evacuated him.[79]

Fifteen minutes after the air strike, the 3d Battalion resumed its attack toward the crest. As it neared it the North Koreans came out of their positions in a violent counterattack and engaged at close quarters. Some men gained the crest but enemy mortar and machine gun fire drove them off. They reached it a second time but could not hold it. Another air strike hit the enemy. Then, a third time, Captain Walker led a group of men of L and I Companies to the top. When Walker reached the crest he shouted back, "Come on up here where you can see them! There are lots of them and you can kill them." The men scrambled up a 60-degree slope for the last 150 yards to the top, where they closed with the North Koreans and overran their positions. Walker and the remaining men of the two companies secured the hill at 1530 and then Walker reorganized the two companies jointly under his command. There were fewer than forty effectives left in L Company and about forty in I Company; the latter had lost all its officers.[80]

General Gay caused a special study to be made of this action, so outstanding did he consider it to be. He found that the 3d Battalion suffered 229 battle casualties in the first two hours, most of them incurred during the second hour of the attack. Of these, 38 Americans were killed and 167 wounded, the remainder were attached South Koreans. The battalion aid station reported treating 130 casualties. Other wounded were treated at the 8th Cavalry aid station. Many men with minor wounds did not ask for medical attention until the battle had ended, and there were only five cases of combat shock in contrast to the eighteen on Hill 518. Enemy mortar fire caused 80 percent of the casualties.[81]

Colonel Lynch's battalion held Hill

---

[79] 1st Cav Div WD, 12 Sep 50; 7th Cav Regt WD, 12 Sep 50; Medical Log, Hill 314, attached to 3d Bn, 7th Cav Unit Rpt, 12 Sep 50; Teague, Hill 314 Narr.

[80] Medical Log with 3d Bn, 7th Cav, Unit Rpt; Teague, Hill 314 Narr.

[81] Medical Log with 3d Bn, 7th Cav, Unit Rpt; Ltr, Gay to author, 17 Jul 53; Webel, MS review comments, 15 Nov 57; Interv, author with Robert Best, ORO analyst, 3 Apr 53. Best made a study of the Hill 314 action and stated that the 3d Battalion casualties were 30 Americans killed, 119 wounded, and 10 ROK's killed or wounded. General Gay and Colonel Webel say these figures are inaccurate.

314 for the next six days and gathered up a large amount of enemy equipment and ammunition. The enemy soldiers on Hill 314 wore American uniforms, helmets, and combat boots. Many of them had M1 rifles and carbines. Two hundred of their number lay dead on the hill. Of the other 500 estimated to have been there, prisoners said most of them had been wounded or were missing.

Several atrocity cases came to light during the action on Hill 314. Capt. James B. Webel found the first one on the afternoon of the 12th while the final action on the hill was taking place. He came upon an American officer who had been bound hand and foot, gasoline poured over him, and burned. A 5-gallon can lay close to the body. Two days later members of the battalion found on the hill the bodies of four other American soldiers with their hands tied. The bodies bore evidence that the men had been bayoneted and shot while bound.[82]

After the capture of Hill 314 on 12 September, the situation north of Taegu improved. On 14 September the 2d Battalion, 8th Cavalry, attacked and, supported by fire from Hill 314, gained part of Hill 570 from the N.K. *19th Regiment, 13th Division.*

Across the army boundary on the right, the ROK 1st Division continued its attack northwest and advanced to the edge of the Walled City. The ROK 11th Regiment seized Hill 755 about dark on 14 September, and small elements of the ROK 15th Regiment reached the stone ramparts of the Walled City area at the same time. The ROK's and North Koreans fought during the night and on into the 15th at many points along the high mountain backbone that extends southeast from the Walled City to Hills 755 and 783 and on to P'algong-san. Prisoners taken by the ROK's estimated that there were about 800 North Koreans on this high ridge. The ROK 1st Division later estimated that approximately 3,000 enemy were inside the Walled City perimeter and about 1,500 or 2,000 outside it near the crest. It appears that at this time the bulk of the N.K. *1st Division* was gradually withdrawing into the Walled City and its vicinity. Indications were that the N.K. *13th Division* also was withdrawing northward. Aerial observers on the afternoon of 14 September reported that an estimated 500 enemy troops were moving north from Tabu-dong. But, while these signs were hopeful, General Walker continued to make every possible preparation for a final close-in defense of Taegu. As part of this, fourteen battalions of South Korean police dug in around the city.[83]

The fighting continued unabated north of Taegu on the 15th. The 2d Battalion, 8th Cavalry, still fought to gain control of Hill 570 on the east side of the Tabu-dong highway. On the other side, the 3d Battalion, 8th Cavalry, attacked Hill 401 where an enemy force had penetrated in a gap between the 8th and 5th Cavalry Regiments. The fighting on Hill 401 was particularly severe. Both sides had troops on the

---

[82] 7th Cav Regt WD, 12 and 15 Sep 50; Teague, Hill 314 Narr; Webel, MS review comments, 15 Nov 57; 1st Cav Div WD, 14 Sep 50.

[83] I Corps WD, Sep 50, Hist Narr, pp. 5–6; EUSAK WD, G–3 Jnl, 14 Sep 50; GHQ FEC G–3 Opn Rpts 82 and 83, 14–15 Sep 50; *Ibid.*, Sitrep, 15 Sep 50; EUSAK WD, an. to PIR 64, 14 Sep 50.

mountain when night fell. In this action, SFC Earl R. Baxter, at the sacrifice of his life, covered the forced withdrawal of his platoon (2d Platoon, L Company), killing at least ten enemy soldiers in close combat before he himself was killed by an enemy grenade.[84]

While the N.K. *II Corps* was striving to capture Taegu and penetrate behind Eighth Army toward Pusan by way of the P'ohang-Kyongju corridor, the N.K. *I Corps* along the lower Naktong and in the south had unleashed simultaneously a violent offensive to bring the entire Pusan Perimeter under assault. Of the entire Perimeter, the parts tactically most vulnerable to enemy action lay along the lower Naktong, and accordingly they promised the greatest dividends strategically to successful North Korean attack. There the battle in early September rose to great intensity and for a period the outcome hung in the balance.

---

[84] Ltr, Johnson to author, recd Aug 54; 1st Cav Div WD, 15 Sep 50. General Order 328, 20 May 1951, awarded the Distinguished Service Cross posthumously to Sergeant Baxter. EUSAK WD.

CHAPTER XXIII

North Korean Breakthrough in the South

> Exact knowledge of the terrain regulates the dispositions of the troops and the order of battle. . . . Knowledge of the country is to a general what a rifle is to an infantryman and what the rules of arithmetic are to a geometrician.
> FREDERICK THE GREAT, *Instructions for His Generals*

The dog days of August had given way to September. Casualties during the next two weeks were to be the greatest of the Korean War. To the men of Eighth Army, these were to be the worst of "the days along the Naktong." And, as if to envelop this deadly clash of arms with a misery of nature's own making, the elements brought to the battlefield blackened skies and torrential rains. It was the end of the summer monsoon season.

Aerial reconnaissance in the last week of August had disclosed to Eighth Army exceptional enemy activity behind the lines opposite the U.S. 2d and 25th Divisions in the southern part of the Pusan Perimeter. Ominously, the enemy had built three new underwater bridges across the Nam River in front of the 35th Infantry in the 25th Division sector. Aerial bombing only temporarily and partially destroyed these bridges, for they could be repaired overnight.

Eighth Army intelligence credited the North Koreans with having moved one or two new divisions and about twenty tanks to the Hyopch'on area on the west side of the Naktong River opposite the U.S. 2d Division. On 28 August the Eighth Army intelligence officer warned that a general attack "may be expected at any time along the 2d Division and 25th Division front," aimed at severing the Taegu-Pusan railroad and highway and capturing Masan.[1]

With this tense situation as the setting, the N.K. *I Corps* before midnight 31 August started its great offensive. As the final hours of August gave way to the first hours of September, North Korean soldiery crossed the lower Naktong at a number of points in a well-planned attack. From Hyongp'ung southward to the coast, in the zones of the U.S. 2d and 25th Divisions, the enemy's greatest effort struck in a single massive co-ordinated attack.

In the southern part of its sector, where the U.S. 25th Division held the U.N. line, the N.K. *I Corps* planned a crushing blow, co-ordinating it with an

---

[1] GHQ FEC Sitrep, 1 Sep 50; EUSAK PIR's 46-50, 27 Aug-1 Sep 50; EUSAK WD, entry for 30 Aug 50, and Aug 50 Summ; 25th Div WD, 28 Aug 50.

attack against the 2d Division just to the north. The North Korean *6th* and *7th Divisions* prepared for the breakthrough effort against the 25th Division after receiving their attack orders about 20 August. The operation order called for the N.K. *I Corps* to assault all along the line at 2200, 31 August. The *6th Division,* farthest south on the enemy right flank, was to attack through Haman, Masan, and Chinhae and capture Kumhae, on the west side of the Naktong River delta fifteen miles from Pusan, by 3 September. The division zone of attack was to be south of the Chinju–Komam-ni (Saga)–Masan highway. The *7th Division,* next in line north of the *6th Division,* was to attack north of the Masan highway, wheel left to the Naktong, and wait for the *6th Division* on its right and the *9th* on its left to join it. Part of the *7th Division* was concentrated in the Uiryong area west of the Nam River. This plan pitted the *6th Division* against the 24th Infantry and the *7th Division* against the 35th Infantry.[2]

On 24 August, Maj. Gen. Pang Ho San, commanding general of the N.K. *6th Division,* much decorated for the exploits of his division thus far, issued an order calculated to improve troop morale. He said the mission of the division was "to liberate Masan and Pusan within a few days." He demanded stricter discipline and more perseverance than ever before, and stated that tactics must adjust to the changes "this epoch-making conflict has introduced into the art of warfare." He summed up the battle lessons:

Our experience in night combat up to now shows that we can operate only four or five hours in the dark since we start night attacks between 2300 and 2400 hours, and, therefore, if the battle continues until dawn, we are likely to suffer losses. From now on, use daylight hours for full combat preparation, and commence attacks soon after sunset. Concentrate your battle actions mostly at night and capture enemy base positions. From midnight on, engage enemy in close combat by approaching to within 100 to 150 meters of him. Then, even with the break of dawn, the enemy planes will not be able to distinguish friend from foe, which will enable you to prevent great losses. This is the most valuable battle experience we have gained from the Chinju operation.[3]

Midnight Near Masan

On 31 August 1950 the 25th Division held a front of almost thirty miles, beginning in the north at the Namji-ri bridge over the Naktong River and extending westward on the hills south of the river to the Nam's confluence with it. (*Map V*) It then bent southwest up the south side of the Nam to where the Sobuk-san mountain mass tapered down in its northern extremity to the river. There the line turned south along rising ground to 850-foot-high Sibidang-san (Hill 276), crossed the saddle on its south face through which passed the Chinju-Masan railroad and highway, and continued southward, climbing to 2,200-foot-high Battle Mountain (Hill 665) and on to 2,400-foot-high P'il-bong (Hill 743). From P'il-bong the line dropped down

---

[2] GHQ FEC, History of the N.K. Army, p. 63; ATIS Res Supp Interrog Rpts, Issue 100 (N.K. *6th Div*), pp. 39–40; *Ibid.,* Issue 99 (N. K. *7th Div*), p. 35.

[3] ATIS Res Supp Interrog Rpts, Issue 100 (N.K. *6th Div*), pp. 41–42; GHQ FEC, History of the N.K. Army, p. 97.

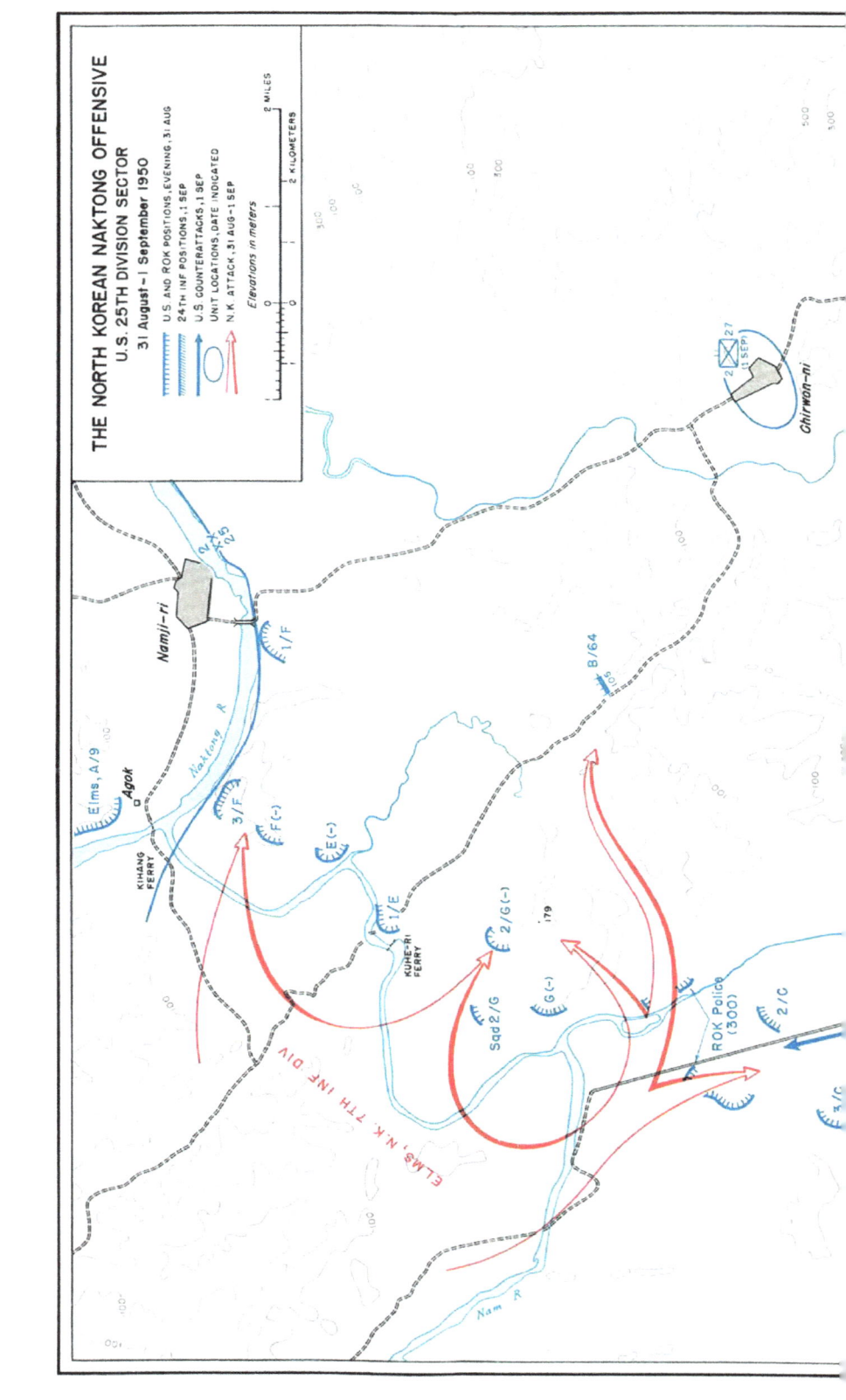

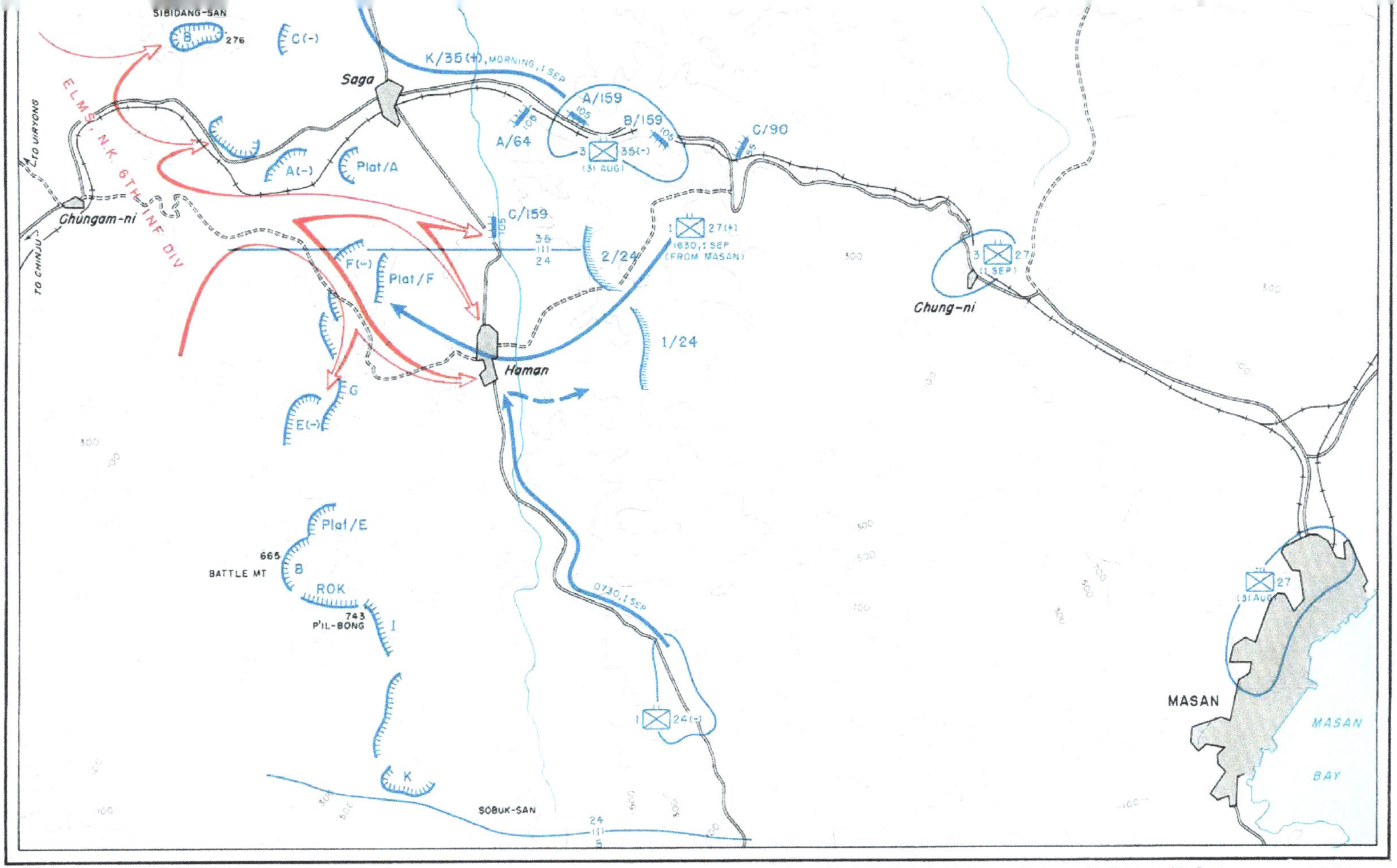

MAP V

MOUNTAIN MASS WEST OF HAMAN. *The town is in the center foreground; the 2d Battalion, 24th Regiment, position is on the crest of the second ridge west of Haman.*

spur ridge lines to the southern coastal road near Chindong-ni.

Colonel Fisher's 35th Infantry held the northern part of the division line, approximately 26,000 yards of it from the Namji-ri bridge to the Chinju-Masan highway. The regiment was responsible for the highway. Colonel Fisher considered his weakest and most vulnerable point to be a 3-mile gap along the Naktong River between most of F Company on the west and its 1st Platoon to the east. This platoon guarded the Namji-ri cantilever steel bridge on the division extreme right at the boundary with the 2d Division across the Naktong.

South of the highway, Colonel Champney's 24th Infantry held the high country west of Haman up to and including Battle Mountain and P'il-bong. Colonel Throckmorton's 5th Infantry held the southern spur of Sobuk-san to the coastal road at Chindong-ni. From Chindong-ni some ROK Marine units continued the line to the southern coast. General Kean's 25th Division command post was at Masan; Colonel Fisher's 35th Infantry command post was on the east side of the Chirwon-Chung-ni road about midway between the two towns; Colonel Champney's 24th Infantry command post was at Haman; and Colonel Throckmorton's command post was at Chindong-ni.[4]

In the left center of the 25th Division line, Lt. Col. Paul F. Roberts' 2d Bat-

---

[4] 25th Div, 35th, 24th, and 5th Inf WD's, 31 Aug 50; Interv, author with Fisher, 5 Jan 52; Interv, author with Champney, 22 Jul 51; Interv, author with Throckmorton, 20 Aug 52.

talion, 24th Infantry, held the crest of the second ridge west of Haman, a little more than a mile from the town. From Chungam-ni, in enemy territory, a secondary road zigzagged to Haman along the shoulders of low hills and across paddy ground, running generally east a mile south of the main Chinju-Masan road. It came through Colonel Roberts' 2d Battalion position in a pass a little more than a mile directly west of Haman.

Late in the afternoon of 31 August, observers with G Company, 24th Infantry, noticed a lot of activity a mile to their front. They called in two air strikes that hit this enemy area at twilight. Artillery also took it under fire. All line units were alerted for a possible enemy attack.[5]

Shortly before midnight the North Koreans struck, first hitting F Company on the north side of the pass on the Chungam-ni–Haman road. The ROK troops in the pass left their positions and fell back on G Company south of the pass. The North Koreans captured a 75-mm. recoilless rifle in the mouth of the pass and turned it on American tanks, knocking out two of them. They then overran a section of 81-mm. mortars at the east end of the pass. South of the pass, at dawn, 1st Lt. Houston M. McMurray found that only 15 out of 69 men remained with him, 8 from his own 1st Platoon, G Company, and 7 ROK's of a group he had taken into his position during the night. The enemy attacked his position at first light. They came through an opening in the barbed wire, supposedly covered by a BAR, but the BAR men had fled. Throwing grenades and spraying the area with burp gun fire, the North Koreans quickly overran the position.[6]

Farther up the slope, enemy tank fire hit E Company at midnight. The company commander, 1st Lt. Charles Ellis, an able and courageous officer, ran over to his left flank when he heard a noise there. He found that his 3d Platoon was leaving its position. Ellis threatened the platoon leader, saying he would shoot him if he did not get back in position, and fired a shot between his feet to impress him. Ellis then went to his right flank and found that platoon also leaving its position. During the night everyone in E Company ran off the hill except Ellis and eleven men. Several E Company men in fleeing their position had run through their own mine field and were killed.

It is worthwhile to anticipate a bit and tell the fate of Ellis and his small group of men who stood their ground. Enemy fire pinned them down after daylight. When three or four of the group tried to run for it, enemy machine gun fire killed them. Ellis and the rest stayed in their holes on the hill for two days, repelling several attacks in that time. Ellis was then able to withdraw southward up the mountain to the 3d Battalion's position. In his withdrawal, Ellis, discovering a man who had been injured earlier in a mine explosion, entered the mine field to rescue him.[7]

---

[5] 24th Inf WD, 31 Aug 50; Interv, author with Corley, 6 Nov 51; Fisher, MS review comments, Jan 58.

[6] 24th Inf WD, 1 Sep 50; EUSAK IG Rpt, 24th Inf Regt, Sep 50, testimony of Lt McMurray; Col John T. Corley, MS review comments, 22 Jul 53.

[7] Interv, author with Champney, 22 Jul 51; Interv, author with Corley, 6 Nov 51; EUSAK IG Rpt, testimony of Capt Charles Ellis, E Co, 24th Inf.

The fact is that shortly after the enemy attack started most of the 2d Battalion, 24th Infantry, fled its positions. The enemy passed through the line quickly and overran the 2d Battalion command post, killing many men there and destroying much equipment. Haman was then open to direct attack. As the enemy encircled Haman, Colonel Roberts, the 2d Battalion commander, ordered an officer to take remnants of the battalion and establish a roadblock at the south edge of the town. Although the officer directed a large group of men to accompany him, only eight did so. The 2d Battalion was no longer an effective fighting force.[8]

Colonel Champney at 0400, 1 September, moved the 24th Regiment command post from Haman two miles northeast to a narrow defile on the New Engineer Road. At this time, an enemy group attacked C Battery, 159th Field Artillery Battalion, a mile north of Haman. Two tanks of the 89th Tank Battalion helped defend the battery until the artillerymen could pull out the howitzers and escape back through Haman and then eastward over this recently improved trail.[9]

The enemy assault did not strike the southern part of the line held by Corley's 3d Battalion, 24th Infantry, and Colonel Throckmorton's 5th Infantry. That part of the line, however, did receive artillery and mortar fire and some diversionary light attacks. About 0200, 1 September, men in an outpost on the right flank of Colonel Corley's battalion watched an estimated 600 enemy soldiers file past at a distance of 100 yards, going in the direction of Haman. Viewed during the night from the high ground of the 3d Battalion, Haman seemed to be in flames. At dawn, men in the battalion saw an estimated 800 enemy troops enter the town.[10]

When the enemy attack broke through the 2d Battalion, Colonel Champney ordered the 1st Battalion, about three miles south of Haman on the Chindong-ni road, to counterattack and restore the line. Colonel Roberts, a superior battalion commander, assembled all the men of the disorganized 2d Battalion he could find—about forty—to join in this counterattack, which got under way at 0730. But it was of short duration. Upon contact with the enemy, the 1st Battalion broke and fled to the rear. Thus, shortly after daylight the scattered and disorganized men of the 1st and 2d Battalions of the 24th Infantry had fled to the high ground two miles east of Haman. The better part of two regiments of the N.K. *6th Division* poured into and through the 3-mile-wide Haman gap.[11]

Meanwhile, action-packed events were taking place simultaneously to the north, on the right side of the 25th Division line. Half an hour before midnight, 31 August, an enemy self-propelled high-velocity gun from across the Nam fired shells into the position of G Company, 35th Infantry, overlooking the river.

---

[8] Interv, author with Corley, 6 Nov 51; Corley, MS review comments, 22 Jul 53; EUSAK IG Rpt, testimony of 1st Lt John L. Herren.
[9] 24th Inf WD, 1 Sep 50; 159th FA Bn WD, Sep 50; Barth MS, p. 16; Interv, author with Champney, 22 Jul 51.

[10] 3d Bn, 24th Inf WD, 1 Sep 50; Corley, MS review comments, 22 Jul 53.
[11] 25th Div WD, 1 Sep 50; Interv, author with Corley, 6 Nov 51; EUSAK IG Rpt, testimony of Col Roberts.

Within a few minutes, enemy artillery had taken under fire all front-line rifle companies of the regiment from the Namji-ri bridge west. Under cover of this fire a reinforced regiment of the N.K. *7th Division* crossed the Nam River and attacked F and G Companies, 35th Infantry. Other enemy soldiers crossed the Nam on an underwater bridge in front of the paddy ground north of Komam-ni and near the boundary between the 2d Battalion, led by Lt. Col. John L. Wilkins, Jr., holding the river front and Lt. Col. Bernard G. Teeter's 1st Battalion holding the hill line that stretched from the Nam River to Sibidang-san and the Chinju-Masan highway.

In the low ground between these two battalions at the river ferry crossing site, Colonel Fisher had placed about 300 ROK police. He expected them to hold there long enough in case of a major attack to serve as a warning device. Guns from the flanking hills there could cover the low ground with fire. Back of Komam-ni he held the 3d Battalion ready for use in counterattack to stop an enemy penetration should it occur.

Unexpectedly, the ROK police companies near the ferry scattered at the first enemy fire. Half an hour after midnight enemy troops streamed through this hole in the line, some turning left to take G Company in flank and rear, and others turning right to attack C Company, which was on a spur of ground west of the Komam-ni road. The I&R Platoon and elements of C and D Companies formed a defense line along the dike at the north edge of Komam-ni where tanks joined them at daybreak. But the enemy did not drive for the Komam-ni road fork four miles south of the river as Colonel Fisher expected him to do; instead, he turned east into the hills behind Fisher's 2d Battalion.[12]

The position of B Company, 35th Infantry, on 1,100-foot-high Sibidang-san, flanking the Masan road two miles west of Komam-ni and giving observation over all the surrounding country, was certain to figure prominently in the enemy's attack. It was a key position in the 25th Division line. The enemy's preparatory barrage there lasted from 1130 to midnight. Under cover of it two battalions of the N.K. *13th Regiment, 6th Division*, moved up within 150 yards of the American foxholes. At the same time, enemy tanks, self-propelled guns, and antitank guns moved toward Komam-ni on the road at the foot of Sibidang-san. An American Sherman tank there destroyed a T34 just after midnight, and a 3.5-inch bazooka team destroyed a self-propelled gun and several 45-mm. antitank guns.

On the crest of Sibidang-san, an antipersonnel mine field stopped the first enemy infantry assault. Others followed in quick succession. They were met and turned back with the fire of all weapons. By 0230 the B Company riflemen were stripping machine gun ammunition belts for their rifles. The 1st Platoon of C Company, at the base of the mountain behind B Company, met the emergency by climbing Sibidang-san in forty-five minutes with an ammunition resupply for the company. Just before dawn the enemy attack subsided. Daylight dis-

---

[12] The Distinguished Unit Citation was awarded the 35th Infantry Regiment for action on 1–6 September 1950. Supporting Docs, AG files. 25th Div WD, 1 Sep 50; EUSAK WD, G–3 Jnl, 0120 1 Sep 50; 2d Bn, 35th Inf, Narr of Act, 31 Aug–1 Sep 50; 35th Inf WD, 31 Aug 50; I&R Plat Unit Hist, 1 Sep 50; Interv, author with Fisher, 5 Jan 52.

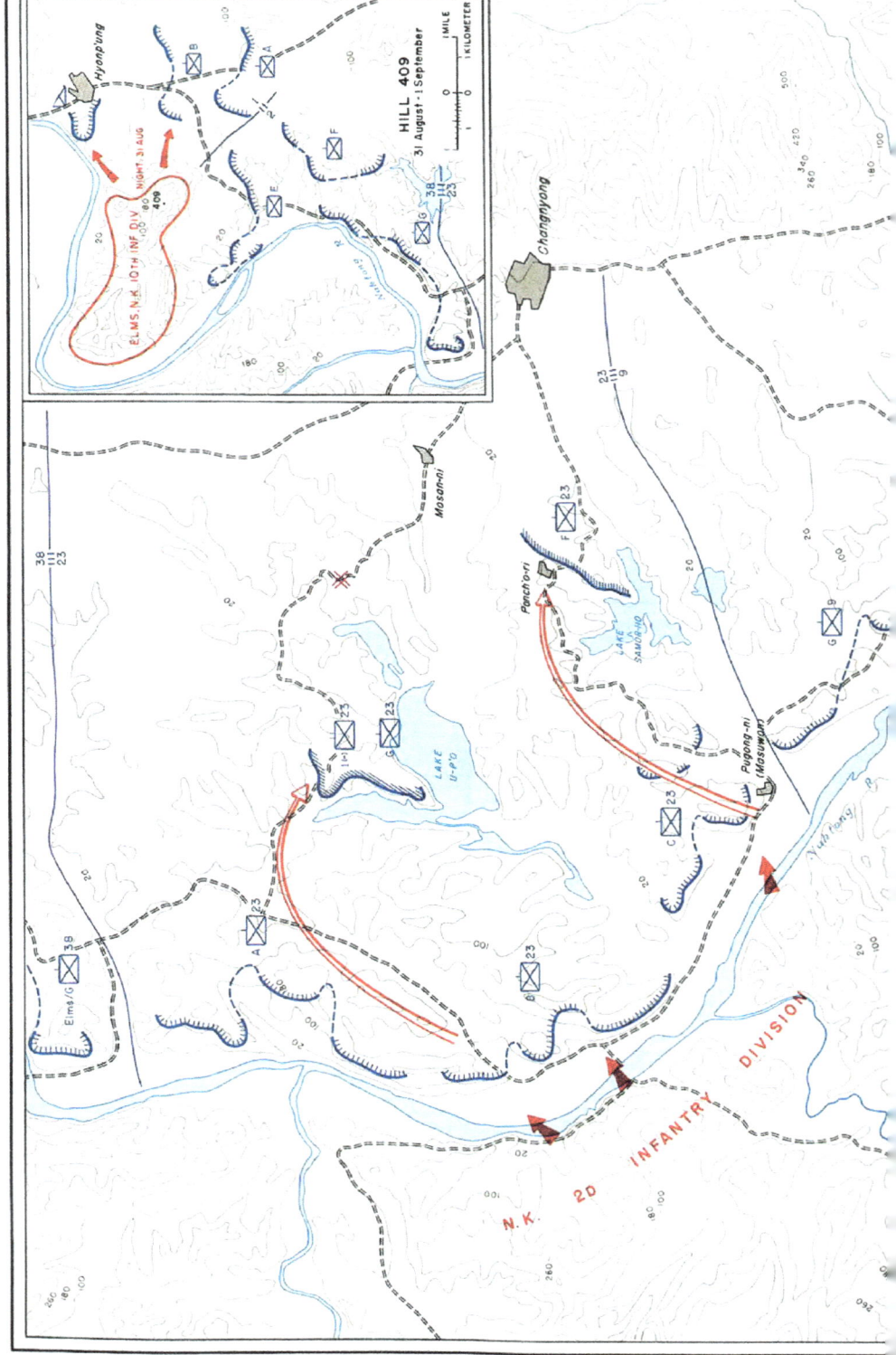

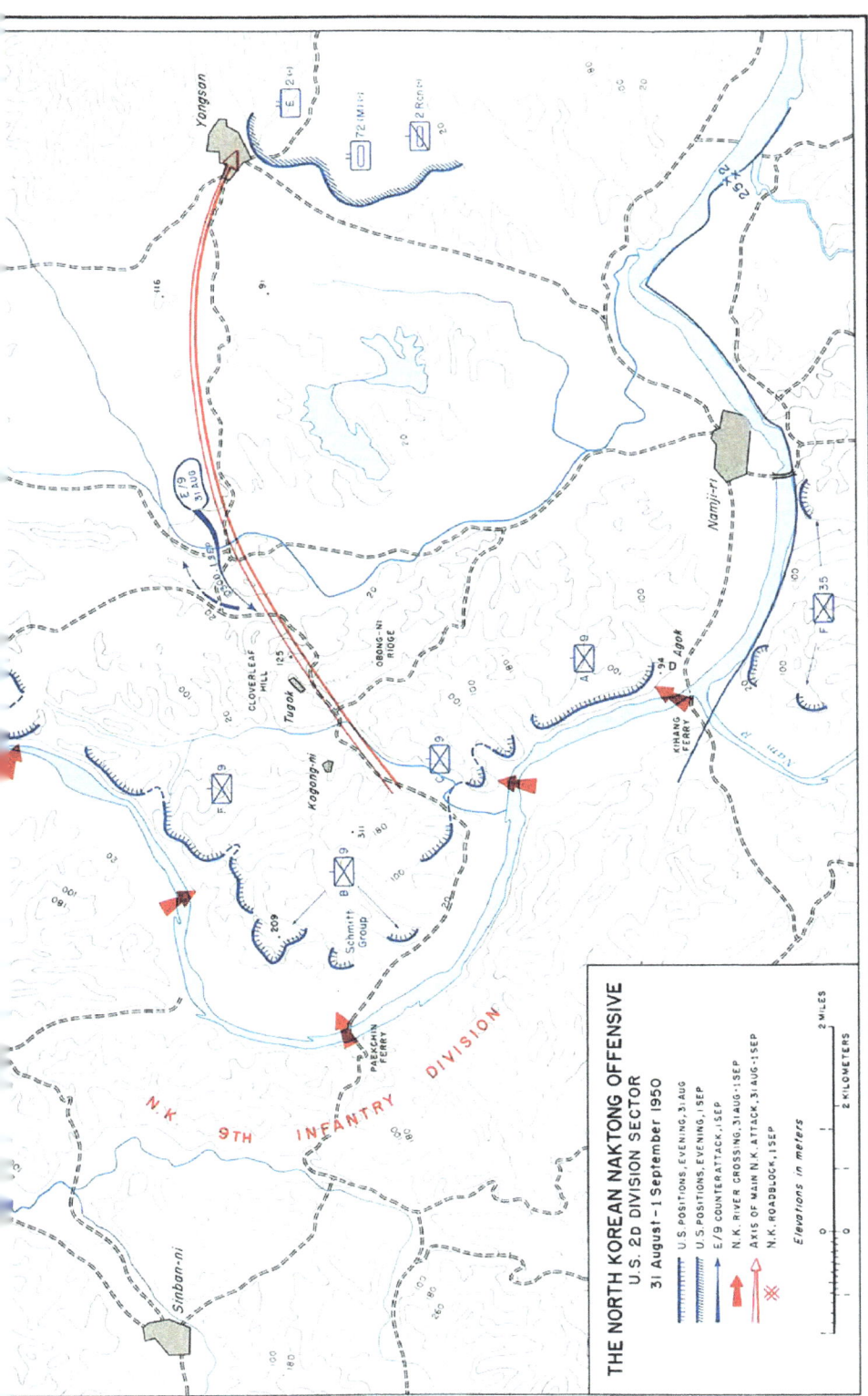

closed a great amount of abandoned enemy equipment scattered on the slope just below the crest, including thirty light and three heavy machine guns. Among the enemy dead lay the body of the commanding officer of the N.K. *13th Regiment*.[13]

At daybreak, 1 September, a tank-led relief force of C Company headquarters troops cleared the road to Sibidang-san and resupplied the 2d Platoon, B Company, with ammunition just in time for it to repel a final North Korean assault, killing seventy-seven and capturing twenty-one of the enemy.

Although Colonel Fisher's 35th Infantry held all its original positions, except that of the forward platoon of G Company, it nevertheless was in a dangerous situation. Approximately 3,000 North Korean soldiers were behind its lines. The farthest eastern penetration reached the high ground just south of Chirwon overlooking the north-south road there.

Agok

On the 35th Regiment's right flank, in the 9th Infantry, 2d Division, sector across the Naktong, the enemy also made deep penetrations. (*Map VI*) There, in the southern part of the U.S. 2d Division zone, the 9th Infantry Regiment held a sector more than 20,000 yards long, including the bulge area of the Naktong where heavy fighting had taken place earlier in August. The rifle companies on the river line here had frontages of 3,000 to 4,000 feet, and, like the units to the north and south of them, they held only key hills and observation points.

As August neared its end, men on these hills could see minor enemy activity across the river, which they interpreted as North Koreans organizing the high ground on the west side of the Naktong against a possible American attack. There was moderate enemy infiltration into the 9th Infantry forward positions, but to the men in the front line this appeared to be only normal patrol action.

Opposite, on the west side of the Naktong, General Pak Kyo Sam, commanding the N.K. *9th Division*, issued his operational order to the division on 28 August. Its mission in the forthcoming attack was stated in part as follows:

To outflank and destroy the enemy by capturing the Miryang and Samnangjin areas, thereby cutting off his [Eighth Army] route of withdrawal between Taegu and Pusan, is the mission of this division.[14]

The North Koreans apparently did not know on the eve of their attack that the U.S. 2d Division had replaced the 24th Division in this sector of the front, since they named the latter division in the attack order as being opposite it in the attack zone.

On the left and southern flank of the 9th Infantry river line, just above the junction of the Nam River with the Naktong, A Company was dug in on a long finger ridge paralleling the Naktong that terminates in Hill 94 at the Kihang ferry site. The river road from Namji-ri running west along the Naktong passes the southern tip of this ridge

---

[13] 35th Inf WD, 31 Aug 50; 35th Inf DUC award supporting docs, AG files.

[14] ATIS Enemy Documents, Issue 4, pp. 16–20, *9th Inf Div* Opn Ord concerning Naktong River crossing, signed by CG Pak Kyo Sam.

and crosses to the west side of the river at the ferry. A small village of a few huts, called Agok, lay at the base of Hill 94 and 300 yards from the river. Two medium tanks of A Company, 72d Tank Battalion and two antiaircraft vehicles of D Battery, 82d AAA Battalion, one mounting twin 40-mm. guns and the other four .50-caliber machine guns, together with two rifle squads of A Company, 9th Infantry, held a roadblock near the ferry and close to Agok. On the evening of 31 August, A Company, in accordance with orders just received, moved from its ridge positions overlooking Agok and the river to new positions along the river below the ridge line.[15]

That evening Sgt. Ernest R. Kouma took a Pershing tank to Agok to replace one that had developed gun trouble. Kouma placed his tank on the west side of Agok about forty yards from the Kihang ferry. At 2000 a heavy fog covered the river. An hour later dogs started barking on the far side of the Naktong, and continued to bark in the otherwise unbroken silence until enemy mortar shells began falling on the American-held side of the river at 2200. Fifteen minutes later a heavy enemy mortar preparation struck A Company's positions. American mortars and artillery began firing counterbattery. Some of the A Company men reported they heard noises on the opposite side of the river and splashes in the water.[16]

Suddenly at 2230 the fog lifted and Kouma saw that an enemy bridge, already two-thirds completed, was being laid across the river directly in front of him. He ordered his tank gunner to lay the 90-mm. cannon on the bridge and he himself went to the .50-caliber machine gun mounted behind the tank cupola. Kouma's gunner opened fire on the bridge and the bridging party; the other tank and the two antiaircraft vehicles joined in the action. After about a minute of this heavy fire the bridge collapsed, and after another two minutes the ponton boats used to hold the bridge in place broke loose. Machine gun fire then sank many of them. Except for the barking of the dogs across the river and an occasional mortar round, silence once again reigned as Kouma's guns fell silent after the destruction of the bridge.

At 2300 this quiet suddenly gave way to a small arms fight which flared around the left side of A Company north of the tanks. This gunfire had lasted only two or three minutes when the A Company roadblock squads near the tanks received word by field telephone that the company was withdrawing to the original ridge positions and that they should do likewise. Someone in the outpost shouted, "We are moving out, tankers!"[17] Then, as Kouma tells it:

The infantry outpost had hardly left when I spotted seven men running towards me from the direction of where Able Company's CP formerly was located. I halted them and noticed that they were wearing the division patch. [The Indianhead of 2d Division, which the newly augmented Koreans wore on their herringbone twill as did regular members of the division. Com-

---

[15] Ltr, Capt Albert J. Fern, Jr. (Plat Ldr, 2d Plat, A Co, 9th Inf, 31 Aug 50) to author, 1 Apr 56; Ltr, Maj Robert L. Cody (S-3, 1st Bn, 9th Inf, Aug-Sep 50) to author, 18 Nov 55.

[16] Ltr, MSgt Ernest R. Kouma to author, 1 May 53; Ltr, SFC Oscar V. Berry to author with location sketch map, 24 Apr 53 (Berry commanded the second tank at the Kihang ferry); Ltr, Fern to author, 1 Apr 56.

[17] Ltr, Kouma to author, 1 May 53; Ltr, Fern to author, 1 Apr 56.

pany A had some of these South Koreans.] One of them spoke excellent English. All seven came next to my tank . . . three of them crawled on the deck of the tank and informed me that a large force had crossed the river farther down approaching my position and that most of Able Company were killed or captured. At the time I had the idea that they were part of the 9th Infantry. During this time I was on top of the turret checking my 50 cal. machine gun. At a given signal they leaped from the tank and began throwing grenades on the tank and about the same time a steady spray of machine gun and rifle fire began hitting the tanks and AA guns from the crest of the high bluff about 150 yards to my right. My gunner at once took them under fire as well as SFC Berry's and the AA guns. I got back in the turret and threw about 7 or 8 grenades over the house as well as inside the house through the door which faced us.[18]

In this exchange, enemy grenades and fire wounded Kouma twice. Enemy soldiers now attacked the tanks and the antiaircraft vehicles from the rear. The group approaching the quad-50 knew the password and overran the vehicle, killing all crew members except one who escaped. Several men in the second, the dual 40-mm. gun vehicle (M19), were wounded but this tracked vehicle escaped to the rear. The two tanks were alone. They quickly changed their positions, driving out from under the cliffs and near the village to open ground with clear fields of fire for 200 yards in every direction. There they repelled repeated attacks, some enemy soldiers reaching within twenty yards of the tanks before they turned back leaving their dead and wounded. About 0130, SFC Oscar V. Berry informed Kouma his tank engine was overheating and that he was going to withdraw. A mile to the rear Berry's tank engine caught fire and he abandoned the tank. Kouma maintained his position throughout the night. With the coming of daylight the enemy attempts to destroy the tank by infantry attack ceased. At 0730 Kouma started back toward friendly lines and got through safely, firing into enemy positions on the way.[19]

In the attack against A Company, the North Koreans happened to strike the 1st Platoon, which was near Agok, but they did not find the 2d Platoon northward, commanded by 2d Lt. Albert J. Fern, Jr. Fern could tell by the sound of combat that C Company on his right and that part of A Company on his left were under heavy attack. Two stragglers from C Company soon told him the North Koreans had overrun that company. The A Company commander, 1st Lt. Adam B. Rodriguez, quickly found it necessary to abandon his command post in Agok and withdraw up the ridge to his original positions, ordering his subordinate units to do likewise. Fern's 2d Platoon had a skirmish with a small group of North Koreans in the dark in going up the slope. On top, the company reassembled and went into perimeter defense positions. For them the rest of the night passed quietly.

The N.K. *9th Division*'s infantry crossing of the Naktong and attack on its east side near midnight quickly overran the positions of C Company, north of A Company. There the North Koreans as-

---

[18] Ltr, Kouma to author, 1 May 53.

[19] Ltrs, Kouma and Berry, 1 May 53 and 24 Apr 53. Department of the Army General Order 38, 4 June 1951, awarded the Medal of Honor to Sergeant Kouma.

saulted with unusual force, to the accompaniment of green flares and blowing of whistles. The company held its positions only a short time and then attempted to escape. Many of the men moved southward, a few of them coming into A Company's ridge line positions near Agok during the night. Most of C Company moved all the way to the 25th Division positions south of the Naktong. On 2 September that division reported that 110 men of C Company had come into its lines.[20]

Task Force Manchu Misfires

Five miles north of Agok and A Company's position, B Company, 9th Infantry, held a similar position on Hill 209 overlooking the Paekchin ferry crossing of the river. This ferry was located at the middle of the Naktong Bulge where the Yongsan road came down to the Naktong and crossed it. The U.S. 2d Division, as it chanced, had planned an important reconnaissance action to start from there the night of 31 August, the very night that the N.K. *I Corps* offensive rolled across the river.

Near the end of the month two reconnaissance patrols from the 9th Infantry had crossed to the west side of the Naktong and from a hill position watched enemy tank and troop activity at a place approximately two miles west of the river, which they suspected was a division command post. Information obtained later indicated it was in fact the command post of the N.K. *9th Division*. On 25 August, Col. John G. Hill outlined projected "Operation Manchu," which was to be a company-sized combat patrol to cross the river, advance to the suspected enemy command post and communications center, destroy it, capture prisoners, and gain information of enemy plans.[21]

The 9th Infantry Regiment had planned Task Force Manchu on orders from the 2d Division, which in turn had received instructions from Eighth Army for aggressive patrolling. Colonel Hill selected three possible crossing sites for the operation. General Keiser decided on the one at the Paekchin ferry. The 9th Infantry reserve, E Company, reinforced with one section of light machine guns from H Company, was to be the attack force. The 1st Platoon, 2d Engineer Combat Battalion, was to transport it across the river in assault boats the night of 31 August. Two heavy weapons companies, D and H, were each to furnish one section of heavy machine guns, one section of 81-mm. mortars, and one section of 75-mm. recoilless rifles for supporting fires. A platoon of 4.2-inch mortars was also to give support.[22]

After dark on the evening of 31 August, 1st Lt. Charles I. Caldwell of D Company and 1st Lt. Edward Schmitt of H Company, 9th Infantry, moved their men and weapons to the base of Hill 209, which was within B Company's defense sector and overlooked the Paekchin ferry crossing of the Naktong River. The raid-

---

[20] 9th Inf WD, 2 Sep 50; Ltr, Fern to author, 1 Apr 56.

[21] Interv, author with Hill, 30 Jun 53; Cody, Operation Manchu, student MS, Advanced Inf Off Course, Class 2, Inf School, Ft. Benning, 1952-53.

[22] Interv, author with Hill, 30 Jun 50; Cody, Operation Manchu; Ltr, Capt Lee E. Beahler (CO D Co, 2d Engr C Bn, Aug-Sep 50) to author, 10 Jun 53.

ing force, E Company, was still in its regimental reserve position about two miles west of Yongsan, getting ready with the engineer platoon to move to the crossing site. Colonel Hill, the regimental commander, went forward in the evening with the 4.2-inch mortar platoon to its position at the base of Hill 209 where the mortarmen prepared to set up their weapons.

Schmitt and Caldwell took their section leaders up the hill and showed them where they wanted the weapons set up. The first of the carrying parties soon followed them. It was now a little after 2100, and dark.

The closest front line unit was B Company on top of Hill 209, approximately a mile north of the river road which curved around the hill's southern base. The regimental chaplain, Capt. Lewis B. Sheen, had gone forward in the afternoon to B Company to hold services.[23] On top of Hill 209, Chaplain Sheen and men in B Company after dark thought they could hear a swishing sound in the water below them. By straining their eyes and staring through field glasses for a long time into the near darkness, they made out a long line of North Korean soldiers wading the river.

The first enemy crossing at the Paekchin ferry caught the Heavy Mortar Platoon wholly unaware in the act of setting up its weapons. It also caught most of the D and H Company men at the base of Hill 209, only a little more than half a mile from the crossing site. The North Koreans killed or captured many of them. Colonel Hill was there, but escaped to the rear just before midnight, together with several others, when the division canceled Operation Manchu. His S–3, who was with him, delayed a bit and never got out. The first heavy weapons carrying party was on its way up the hill when the enemy engulfed the men below. It hurried on to the top where the advance group waited and there all hastily dug in on a small perimeter. This group was unmolested during the night.

Word of the enemy crossing that had caught the support elements of Task Force Manchu flat-footed had been received at the 2d Division headquarters. This news, together with the heavy enemy barrages that had developed all along the river, caused the division to cancel Operation Manchu five minutes before midnight.

From approximately 2130 until shortly after midnight the N.K. *9th Division* crossed the Naktong at a number of places and climbed the hills quietly toward the 9th Infantry river line positions. Then, when the artillery barrage preparation lifted, the North Korean infantry were in position to launch their assaults. These began in the northern part of the regimental sector and quickly spread southward. Chaplain Sheen in the B Company perimeter heard cries of "Manzai!" northward and saw many flares light the sky in that direction. At the river crossing below him he could hear enemy troops working on a bridge. By this time the sounds of enemy tanks and trucks and shouting men came up from the river. And from the hills upstream the men in B Company heard, ever so often, after a flurry of small arms

---

[23] Interv, author with Hill, 15 Apr 53; Ltr, Capt Charles I. Caldwell to author, 29 May 53, together with sketch map of positions of D and H Co units of TF Manchu, 31 Aug–4 Sep 50. Hill 209 is Hill 210 on the revised map of Korea, AMS 4, 1950.

fire, a massed shout which they interpreted as the North Korean capture of another position.²⁴

At 0200, B Company's turn came. A truck stopped at the bottom of the hill, a whistle sounded, then came a shouted order, and enemy soldiers started climbing the slope. The hills on both sides of B Company were already under attack as was also Hill 311, a rugged terrain feature a mile and a half back from the river and apparently the enemy's principal immediate objective. The North Koreans apparently were not aware of the Task Force Manchu group lower down on the hill for it remained unmolested during the night. But higher up on Hill 209 the enemy drove B Company from its position, inflicting very heavy casualties on it. Chaplain Sheen led one group of soldiers back to friendly lines on 4 September.²⁵

Approximately at 0300, 1 September, the 9th Infantry Regiment ordered its only reserve, E Company, which was to have been the striking force of Task Force Manchu, to move west along the Yongsan–Naktong River road and take a blocking position at the pass between Cloverleaf Hill and Obong-ni Ridge, about three miles from the river and six miles from Yongsan. This was the critical terrain where so much heavy fighting had taken place in the first battle of the Naktong Bulge. Fighting began at the pass at 0230 when an American medium tank of A Company, 72d Tank Battalion, knocked out a T34 at Tugok (Morisil). E Company never reached its blocking position. A strong enemy force surprised and delivered heavy automatic fire on it at 0330 from positions astride the road east of the pass. The company suffered heavy casualties, the killed including the company commander and General Keiser's aide who had accompanied the force. With the critical parts of Cloverleaf Hill and Obong-ni Ridge in enemy hands before dawn of 1 September, the best defensive terrain between Yongsan and the river was lost. The 2d Division now had to base its defense of Yongsan on relatively poor defensive terrain, the low jumbled hills at the western edge of the town.²⁶

The North Koreans Split the U.S. 2d Division

North of the 9th Infantry sector of the 2d Division front along the Naktong, the 23d Regiment on 29 August had just relieved the 3d Battalion of the 38th Infantry Regiment, which in turn had only a few days before relieved the 21st Infantry Regiment of the 24th Division. On 31 August, therefore, the 23d Regiment was in a new sector of which it had only a limited knowledge. It took over a 16,000-yard Naktong River front without its 3d Battalion which had been attached to the U.S. 1st Cavalry Division. Colonel Freeman, the regimental commander, deployed the 1st Battalion on the high ground along the river with the three companies abreast. Actually,

---

²⁴ Cody, Operation Manchu; 9th Inf WD, Sep 50, Sheen MS, From Encirclement to Safety; 9th Inf WD, 1 Sep 50, Rpt at 0040 to 9th Regt.

²⁵ Sheen, From Encirclement to Safety; Ltr, Caldwell to author, 29 May 53; Interv, author with Hill, 30 Jun 53.

²⁶ Interv, author with Hill, 30 Jun 53; 72d Tk Bn WD, 1 Sep 50; 9th Inf WD, 1 Sep 50; EUSAK WD, G–3 Jnl, 0343 1 Sep 50; Cody, Operation Manchu.

the 1st Battalion, under Lt. Col. Claire E. Hutchin, Jr., little more than outposted the hills with platoons and squads. He placed the 2d Battalion in a reserve position approximately eight miles in the rear of the 1st Battalion and in a position where it commanded the road net in the regimental sector. On the last day of the month the 2d Division moved E Company south to a reserve position in the 9th Infantry sector.[27]

Two roads ran through the regimental sector from the Naktong River to Changnyong. The main road bent south along the east bank of the river to Pugong-ni and then turned northeast to Changnyong. A northern secondary road curved around marshland and lakes, the largest of which was Lake U-p'o, to Changnyong. In effect, the 1st Battalion of the 23d Regiment guarded these two approach routes to Changnyong.

The forty-two men of the 2d Platoon, B Company, 23d Infantry, led by 1st Lt. William M. Glasgow held outpost positions on seven hills covering a 2,600-yard front along the east bank of the Naktong north of Pugong-ni. Across the river in the rice paddies they could see, in the afternoon of 31 August, two large groups of enemy soldiers. Occasionally artillery fire dispersed them.

Just before dusk turned to darkness, Glasgow and the men in his 1st Squad saw "a large and bizarre torchlight parade" come out of the hills and proceed toward the river. Glasgow immediately reported the spectacle to the battalion command post. The artillery forward observer, who estimated the crowd to number 2,000 people, thought they were refugees. When the matter was referred to Colonel Freeman, he immediately ordered the artillery to fire on the torchbearers. With each bursting shell some of the torches disappeared but others took their places and the procession continued unchecked toward the river bank.[28]

At 2100 the first shells of what proved to be a two-hour enemy artillery and mortar preparation against the American river positions jarred the fascinated Glasgow and his companions from their absorbed contemplation of the torchlight scene. As the enemy barrage rolled on, North Korean infantry crossed the river and climbed the hills in the darkness under cover of its fire. At 2300 the barrage lifted. A green flare signaled the North Korean assault. A few minutes later enemy grenades showered into Glasgow's position. After a short fight at close quarters, Glasgow and his men ran off the hill toward the rear. Similar assaults took place elsewhere along the battalion outpost line.

On the regimental left along the main Pugong-ni–Changnyong road enemy soldiers completely overran C Company by 0300, 1 September. Capt. Cyril S. Bartholdi, the company commander, and most of his men were lost. Only seven men of C Company could be accounted for, and

---

[27] 23d Inf WD, Aug 50 Summ; Freeman, Highlights of the Combat Activities of the 23d Infantry Regiment from 5 August to 30 September 1950, MS, copy in OCMH; Maj Gen Paul L. Freeman, Jr., MS review comments, 30 Oct 57.

[28] Glasgow, Platoon Leader in Korea, pp. 100ff; Glasgow, "Through Hell and Out," *Bluebook* Magazine (August, 1951), pp. 71–77 (reproduces that part of above MS covering experiences of 1–7 September 1950); 23d Inf WD, Aug 50 Summ; Interv, author with Lt Col Frank Meszar (S–3, 23d Inf, Sep 50), 15 May 53; Freeman, MS review comments, 30 Oct 57.

three days later, after all the stragglers and those cut off behind enemy lines had come in, there were fewer than twenty men in the company.[29]

As the enemy attack developed during the night, Colonel Hutchin succeeded in withdrawing a large part of the battalion, less C Company, to his command post just north of Lake U-p'o and the hills there covering the northern road into Changnyong, three miles east of the river and five air miles west of the town. B Company lost heavily in this action.

When word of Colonel Hutchin's plight and of the disaster that had overtaken C Company reached regimental headquarters, Colonel Freeman obtained the release of G and F Companies from 2d Division reserve and sent the former to help Hutchin and the latter on the southern road toward Pugong-ni and C Company. Maj. Lloyd K. Jensen, executive officer of the 2d Battalion, accompanied F Company down the Pugong-ni road. This force was unable to reach C Company, but Major Jensen collected stragglers from it and seized high ground astride this main approach to Changnyong near Ponch'o-ri above Lake Sanor-ho, and went into a defensive position there. The 2d Division released E Company to the regiment and the next day it joined F Company to build up what became the main defensive position of the 23d Regiment in front of Changnyong. Lt. Col. James W. Edwards took command of this 2d Battalion position.[30]

Enemy troops during the night passed around the right flank of Colonel Hutchin's northern blocking position and reached the road three miles behind him near the division artillery positions. The 23d Infantry Headquarters and Service Companies and other miscellaneous regimental units finally stopped this enemy penetration near the regimental command post five miles northwest of Changnyong.

Before the morning of 1 September had passed, reports coming in to 2d Division headquarters made it clear that North Koreans had penetrated to the north-south Changnyong-Yongsan road and cut the division in two; the 38th and 23d Infantry Regiments with the bulk of the division artillery in the north were separated from the division headquarters and the 9th Infantry Regiment in the south. General Keiser decided that this situation made it advisable to control and direct the divided division as two special forces. Accordingly, he placed the division artillery commander, Brig. Gen. Loyal M. Haynes, in command of the northern group. Haynes' command post was seven miles north of Changnyong. Task Force Haynes became operational at 1020, 1 September.[31] Southward, in the Yongsan area, General Keiser placed Brig. Gen. Joseph S. Bradley, Assistant Division Commander,

---

[29] 2d Div WD, JA Stf Sec Hist Rpt, 1 Sep–31 Oct 50, p. 5; 23d Inf WD, Narr Summ, Sep 50; Interv, author with Meszar, 15 May 53; EUSAK WD, 21 Sep 50, ADVATIS Interrog Rpts, Sr Lt Lee Kwan Hyon, Med Off, *17th Regt, 2d Div*; Glasgow, Platoon Leader in Korea.

[30] Interv, author with Meszar, 15 May 53; Freeman MS; Freeman, MS review comments, 30 Oct 57.

[31] 2d Div Arty WD, Narr Summ, Sep 50. Task Force Haynes remained operational until 1300, 15 September 1950. Units forming the task force were the following: 23d Inf; 38th Inf; 37th FA Bn; C Btry, 503d FA Bn; Btrys A, B, C, 82d AAA AW Bn (SP); and C Co, 72d Tk Bn.

AREA OF MAIN DEFENSIVE POSITION *in front of Changnyong.*

in charge of the 9th Infantry Regiment, the 2d Engineer Combat Battalion, most of the 72d Tank Battalion, and other miscellaneous units of the division. This southern grouping was known as Task Force Bradley.

All three regiments of the enemy *2d Division*—the *4th, 17th,* and *6th,* in line from north to south—crossed during the night to the east side of the Naktong River into the 23d Regiment sector. The enemy *2d Division,* concentrated in the Sinban-ni area west of the river, had, in effect, attacked straight east across the river and was trying to seize the two avenues of advance into Changnyong above and below Lake U-p'o. The water area of this lake and the surrounding marshland varied according to the season and the amount of rainfall. On 31 August 1950, Lake U-p'o was a large body of water although in most places only a few feet deep.[32]

General Walker's Decisions on 1 September

At daybreak of 1 September, General Keiser at 2d Division headquarters in Muan-ni, seven air miles east of Yongsan on the Miryang road, knew that his division was in the midst of a crisis. A massive enemy attack was in progress and had made deep penetrations everywhere in his sector except in the north in the zone of the 38th Infantry. The N.K. *9th Division* had effected major crossings of the Naktong at two principal points

[32] Interv, author with Meszar, 15 May 53; 2d Div WD, Aug 50 (G-3 Stf Sec Rpt is incorporated with Div Narr Summ—all G-3 supporting documents were destroyed or lost through enemy action at Kunu-ri in November 1950); 23d Inf WD, Narr Summ, Sep 50.

against the 9th Infantry; the *2d Division*, three major crossings against the 23d Infantry; and the *10th Division* had crossed more troops in the Hill 409 area near Hyongp'ung in the 38th Infantry sector. At 0810 General Keiser telephoned Eighth Army headquarters and reported the situation as he then understood it, indicating that the heaviest and deepest enemy penetrations were in the 9th Infantry sector.

The picture of the situation darkened as the morning hours passed. Liaison planes rose from the division strip every hour to observe the enemy's progress and to locate 2d Division front-line units. Communication from division and regimental headquarters to nearly all the forward units was broken. Beginning at 0930 and continuing throughout the rest of the day, the light aviation section of the division artillery located front-line units cut off by the enemy, and made fourteen drops of ammunition, food, water, and medical supplies. As information slowly built up at division headquarters it became apparent that the North Koreans had punched a hole six miles wide and eight miles deep in the middle of the division line and made lesser penetrations elsewhere. The frontline battalions of the 9th and 23d Regiments were in various states of disorganization and some companies had virtually disappeared. General Keiser hoped he could organize a defense along the Changnyong-Yongsan road, five to eight miles east of the Naktong River, and prevent enemy access to the passes eastward leading to Miryang and Ch'ongdo.[33]

On its part, the Eighth Army staff had sufficient information soon after daybreak of 1 September to realize that a big enemy attack was under way in the south. At 0900 General Walker requested the Air Force to make a maximum effort along the Naktong River from Toksong-dong, just above the 2d Division boundary, southward and to a depth of ten to fifteen miles west of the river. He wanted the Air Force to isolate the battlefield and prevent enemy reinforcements and supplies from moving across the river in support of the North Korean spearhead units. The Far East Command requested the Navy to join in the air effort, and the Seventh Fleet, pursuant to NAVFE orders, turned back from its strikes in the Inch'on-Seoul area and sped southward at full steam toward the southern battle front. General Walker came to the 2d Division front at noon and ordered a "stand or die" defense. He had already ordered ground reinforcements to the Yongsan area.[34]

For a few hours during the morning of 1 September, General Walker weighed the news coming in from his southern front, wavering in a decision as to which part of the front most needed his Pusan Perimeter reserves. Since midnight the N.K. *I Corps* had broken his Pusan Perimeter in two places—the N.K. *2d* and *9th Divisions* in the U.S. 2d Division sector, and the *7th* and *6th Divisions* in the U.S. 25th Division sector, below the junction of the Nam and Naktong Rivers. In the 2d Division sector enemy troops were at the edge of Yongsan, the

---

[33] EUSAK WD, G-3 Jnl, 1 Sep 50; *Ibid.*, PIR 51, 1 Sep 50; 2d Div WD, Hq Co, Aviation Sec, 1 Sep 50; Ibid., vol. II, Summ, 1 Sep–31 Oct 50, p. 6.

[34] EUSAK WD, G-3 Jnl, 1 Sep 50; 2d Div WD, vol. II, Summ, 1 Sep–3 Oct 50, pp. 6–7; Memo for Dept of Navy, Hist Sec, 1950, in OCMH.

gateway to the corridor leading twelve air miles eastward to Miryang and the main Pusan-Mukden railroad and highway.

Walker had a critical decision to make. He had in reserve three understrength infantry regiments and the 2-battalion British 27th Infantry Brigade which was not yet completely equipped and ready to be placed in line. Even so, this was an unusually large reserve for Eighth Army in the summer of 1950. The three U.S. regiments available to Walker were the 5th Marines at Changwon, six miles northeast of Masan, preparing for movement to the port of Pusan; the 27th Regiment of the 25th Division which had arrived at Masan only the night before at 2030 to relieve the 5th Regimental Combat Team, which was then to join the 24th Division in the Taegu area; and the 19th Infantry Regiment of the 24th Division, then with that division's headquarters at Kyongsan southeast of Taegu. Walker alerted both the 24th Division headquarters, together with its 19th Regiment, and the 1st Provisional Marine Brigade to move at a moment's notice; the 24th Division either to the 2d or 25th Division fronts, and the marines to an unannounced destination.

As the morning passed, General Walker decided that the situation was most critical in the Naktong Bulge area of the 2d Division sector. There the North Koreans threatened Miryang and with it the lifeline of the entire Eighth Army position. There, for the moment at least, was the most critical spot of the far-flung battlefield. An hour before noon General Walker ordered General Craig to prepare the marines to move at once. Just after noon the action order came and the marines made ready to depart at 1330. They were going back to the bulge area.[35]

---

[35] EUSAK WD, G-3 Sec, 1 Sep 50; 2d Div WD, 1 Sep 50; Interv, author with Hill, 30 Jun 53; Transcription and Summ of fonecon, Walker with Hickey, Deputy CofS, FEC, 020935 Sep 50, CofS files FEC.

CHAPTER XXIV

The North Korean Great Naktong Offensive

If men make war in slavish observance of rules, they will fail. . . . War is progressive, because all the instruments and elements of war are progressive.
ULYSSES S. GRANT

The situation on Eighth Army's southern front was chaotic by midday of 1 September. The North Koreans at one place had crossed at the Kihang ferry, captured Agok, engaged Kouma's tanks, and scattered A Company, 9th Infantry of the 2d Division, at its positions from Agok northward. (*See Map VI.*) Lieutenant Rodriguez succeeded in withdrawing most of A Company to its old positions on the ridge line back of the river. From there at daylight the men could see enemy soldiers on many of the ridges surrounding them, most of them moving east. After several hours, Lieutenant Fern, 2d Platoon leader, sent a patrol down the hill to Agok to obtain supplies abandoned there during the night. The patrol encountered a small enemy group in the village, killed three men and sustained two casualties, but returned with much needed water, rations, and ammunition.

Later in the morning enemy barges crossed the Naktong below A Company but they were out of range. Rodriguez sent a squad with a light machine gun to the southern tip of the ridge overlooking Agok to take these enemy troops under fire. About halfway down, the squad came upon a critically wounded Negro soldier. Around him lay ten dead North Koreans. The wounded man was evacuated to the company command post but died that afternoon. When the squad reached the tip of the ridge they saw that an enemy force occupied houses at its base. They reported this to Lieutenant Fern, who called for artillery fire through the forward observer. This artillery fire was delivered within a few minutes and was on target. The North Koreans broke from the houses, running for the river. At this the light machine gun at the tip of the ridge took them under fire, as did another across the Naktong to the south in the 25th Division sector. Proximity fuze artillery fire decimated this group. Combined fire from all weapons inflicted an estimated 300 casualties.

In the afternoon, light aircraft dropped food and ammunition to the company; only part of it was recovered.

The 1st Battalion ordered Rodriguez to withdraw the company that night.

Lieutenant Fern's 2d Platoon led the A Company withdrawal immediately after dark, moving eastward along the ridge crest. At the eastern tip the platoon started down. Near the bottom the leading men saw a column of about 400 North Koreans marching on the road some 200 yards below them with a number of machine guns mounted on wheels. Rodriguez ordered the company to circle back up the ridge and away from the road. Fern was to bring up the rear and carry with him the wounded, two of whom were litter cases. Transporting the wounded over the rough terrain in the darkness was a slow and difficult task and gradually Fern's platoon fell behind the others. By the time he reached the base of the ridge he had lost contact with the rest of the company.

At this juncture a furious fire fight erupted ahead of Fern. Enemy machine gun fire from this fight struck among the 2d Platoon and pinned it down. For their safety, Fern decided to send the wounded back into the ravine they had just descended, and put them in charge of Platoon Sgt. Herbert H. Freeman and ten men. Several stragglers from the advanced elements of the company joined Fern and reported that Rodriguez and the rest of the company had run into a sizable enemy force and had scattered in the ensuing fight. Lieutenant Rodriguez and most of the company were killed at close range. In this desperate action, Pfc. Luther H. Story, a weapons squad leader, so distinguished himself by a series of brave deeds that he was awarded the Medal of Honor. Badly wounded, Story refused to be a burden to those who might escape, and when last seen was still engaging enemy at close range. Of those with Rodriguez, approximately ten men escaped to friendly lines.

Fern decided shortly before dawn that he must try to escape before daylight. He sent word by a runner back to Freeman, who should have been about 500 yards in the rear, to rejoin the platoon. The runner returned and said he could not find Freeman. There had been no firing to the rear, so Fern knew that Freeman had not encountered enemy troops. Two men searched a second time for Freeman without success. Fern then decided that he would have to try to lead those with him to safety.

A heavy ground fog, so thick that one could hardly see twenty-five yards, developed in the early morning of 2 September and this held until midmorning. Under this cloak of concealment Fern's group made its way by compass toward Yongsan. From a hill at noon, after the fog had lifted, the men looked down on the battle of Yongsan which was then in progress. That afternoon Fern brought the nineteen men with him into the lines of the 72d Tank Battalion near Yongsan.

Upon reporting to Lt. Col. John E. Londahl, Fern asked for permission to lead a patrol in search of Sergeant Freeman's group. Londahl denied this request because every available man was needed in the defense of Yongsan. As it turned out, Freeman brought his men to safety. Upon moving back from Fern's platoon during the night battle, he had taken his group all the way back up to the top of the ridge. They had stayed there in seclusion all day, watching many enemy groups moving about in all directions below them. Freeman assumed that most of A Company had been killed or captured. For five days and nights he maintained his squad and the four wounded behind enemy lines, finally guiding them all safely to friendly lines.[1]

The End of Task Force Manchu

It will be recalled that the North Koreans who crossed near the middle of the Naktong Bulge in front of B Company, 9th Infantry, surprised the advanced support elements of Task Force Manchu at the base of Hill 209 where the Yongsan road came down to the Naktong. Some elements of the two Heavy Weapons Companies, D and H, had already started to climb the hill to emplace their weapons there when the North Korean surprise river crossing caught most of the support elements and the Heavy Mortar Company at the base of the hill. This crossing was about five miles north of the enemy crossing that had all but destroyed A Company near the division's southern boundary.

The perimeter position taken by the men of D and H Companies, 9th Infantry, who had started up the hill before the North Koreans struck, was on a southern knob (about 150 meters high) of Hill 209, half a mile south across a saddle from B Company's higher position. As the night wore on, a few more men reached the perimeter. In addition to the D and H Company men, there were a few from the Heavy Mortar Platoon and one or two from B Company.

Altogether, there were approximately 60 to 70 men, including 5 officers, in the group—an actual count was never made. An inventory of the weapons and equipment disclosed that the group had 1 SCR–300 radio; 2 heavy machine guns, 1 operable; 2 light machine guns; 1 BAR; about 20 M1 rifles; and about 40 carbines or pistols. Lieutenant Schmitt assumed command of the group.[2]

During the night Lieutenant Schmitt established radio communication with the 1st Battalion, 9th Infantry, and received promises of help on the morrow. When daylight came Schmitt and his group saw that they were surrounded by enemy. One force occupied the higher knob half a mile above them, formerly held by B Company. Below them, North Koreans continued crossing the river and moving supplies forward to their combat units, some of them already several miles eastward.

Enemy troops were not long in discovering the Task Force Manchu group. They first attacked it at 1400 that afternoon, and were repulsed. That night an estimated company attacked three times, pressing the fight to close quarters, but failed each time to penetrate the tight perimeter. Daylight of the second day disclosed many enemy dead on the steep slopes outside the perimeter.

By that morning (2 September) the

---

[1] Ltr, Fern to author, 1 Apr 56; Ltr, Cody to author, 18 Nov 55. Department of the Army General Order 70, 2 August 1951, awarded the Medal of Honor to Private Story. General Order 187, 5 December 1950, awarded the Distinguished Service Cross to Sergeant Freeman. EUSAK.

[2] Ltr, Caldwell to author, 29 May 53; Interv, author with Hill, 30 Jun 53; Hill, MS review comments, 2 Jan 58; 9th Inf WD, Sep 50, Incl B, Col Charles C. Sloane, Jr., Hill 209 (1138–1386), with sketch map; *Ibid.*, app., 1st Lt Raymond J. McDoniel, Notes (this document misspells "McDoniel" as "McDaniel"); Sheen, From Encirclement to Safety. The officers on the hill were Lt Schmitt, CO H Co; Lt McDoniel, Plat Ldr D Co; Lt Paul E. Kremser, Plat Ldr H Co; Lt Caldwell, Plat Ldr D Co; and Lt Edmund J. Lilly III, Plat Ldr B Co.

need for hand grenades was desperate. About 0900 MSgt. Travis E. Watkins of H Company shot and killed two enemy soldiers 50 yards outside the northeast edge of the perimeter. He jumped from his hole to get the weapons and grenades of the dead men; 20 yards from them three hidden enemy soldiers jumped to their feet and opened fire on him. Watkins killed them and gathered weapons, ammunition, and insignia from all five before returning to the perimeter. An hour later a group of six enemy soldiers gained a protected spot 25 yards from a machine gun position of the perimeter and began throwing hand grenades into it. Although already wounded in the head, Watkins rose from his hole to engage them with rifle fire. An enemy machine gun immediately took him under fire and hit him in the left side, breaking his back. Watkins in some manner managed to kill all six of the nearby enemy soldiers before he sank into his hole paralyzed from the waist down. Even in this condition, Watkins never lost his nerve, but shouted encouragement to his companions. He refused any of the scarce rations, saying that he did not deserve them because he could no longer fight.[3]

In the afternoon of 2 September Schmitt succeeded in radioing a request to the 1st Battalion for an airdrop of supplies. A division liaison plane attempted the drop, but the perimeter was so small and the slopes so steep that virtually all the supplies went into enemy hands. The men in the perimeter did, however, recover from a drop made later at 1900 a case of carbine ammunition, 2 boxes of machine gun ammunition, 11 hand grenades, 2½ cases of rations, part of a package of medical supplies, and 21 cans of beer. Pfc. Joseph R. Ouellette, H Company, left the perimeter to retrieve an airdrop of water cans but found on reaching them that they were broken and empty. Like Watkins, he distinguished himself by leaving the perimeter to gather weapons, ammunition, and grenades from the enemy dead. On one such occasion an enemy soldier suddenly attacked Ouellette, who killed the North Korean in hand-to-hand combat.[4]

In helping to recover the airdropped supplies on the evening of 2 September, Lieutenant Schmitt was wounded but continued to exercise his command, encouraging the diminishing group by his example. That same afternoon, the North Koreans sent an American prisoner up the hill to Schmitt with the message, "You have one hour to surrender or be blown to pieces." Failing in frontal infantry attack to reduce the little defending force, the enemy now obviously meant to take it under observed and registered mortar fire.[5]

Forty-five minutes later enemy antitank fire came in on the knob and two machine guns from positions northward and higher on the slope of Hill 209 swept the perimeter. Soon, enemy mor-

---

[3] Sworn affidavit, SSgt Grover L. Bozarth and Sgt Ralph G. Lillard, H Co, 9th Inf, 13 Sep 50, Yongsan, recommending Watkins for Medal of Honor, DA AG files.

[4] McDoniel, Notes cited n. 2, Sep 50; Ltr, Caldwell to author, 29 May 53. Department of the Army General Order 25, 25 April 1951, awarded the Medal of Honor posthumously to Private Ouellette.

[5] EUSAK WD, 9 Sep 50, an. 1 to PIR 59; 9th Inf WD, 8 Sep 50, account of Lt McDoniel; Sloane, Hill 209, Sep 50. General Order 54, 6 February 1951, awarded the Distinguished Service Cross posthumously to Lieutenant Schmitt. EUSAK.

tars emplaced on a neighboring high finger ridge eastward registered on Schmitt's perimeter and continued firing until dark. The machine gun fire forced every man to stay in his hole. The lifting of the mortar fire after dark was the signal for renewed enemy infantry attacks, all of which were repulsed. But the number of killed and wounded within the perimeter was growing, and food, water, and ammunition were needed. There were no medical supplies except those carried by one aid man.

The third day, Sunday, 3 September, was the worst of all. The weather was terrifically hot. There was no water, and only one can of C rations per man. Ammunition was almost gone. Since the previous afternoon, enemy mortar barrages had alternated with infantry assaults against the perimeter. Survivors later estimated there were about twenty separate infantry attacks—all repulsed. Two enemy machine guns still swept the perimeter whenever anyone showed himself. Dead and dying were in almost every foxhole or lay just outside. Mortar fragments destroyed the radio and this ended all communication with friendly units. Artillery fire and air strikes requested by Schmitt never came. Some enemy soldiers worked their way close to the perimeter and threw grenades into it. Six times Ouellette leaped from his foxhole to escape grenades thrown into it. Each time the enemy fired on him from close range. In this close action Ouellette was killed. Most of the foxholes of the perimeter received one or more direct mortar hits in the course of the continuing mortar fire. One of these killed Lieutenant Schmitt on 3 September. He had given his men heroic leadership and had inspired them by his example throughout three days and nights of the ordeal. The command passed now to 1st Lt. Raymond J. McDoniel of D Company, senior surviving officer.[6]

In the evening, relief came in the form of rain. McDoniel spread out two blankets recovered with airdropped supplies the day before, and wrung from them enough water to fill a 5-gallon can. The men removed their clothing and wrung water from them to fill their canteens.

The fourth night passed. At daylight on the morning of 4 September only two officers, McDoniel and Caldwell, and approximately half the men who had assembled on the hill, were alive. Some men had broken under the strain and in a state of shock had run from their holes and were killed. As the day passed, with ammunition down to about one clip per man and only a few grenades left and no help in sight, McDoniel decided to abandon the position that night. He told Caldwell that when it got dark the survivors would split into small groups and try to get back to friendly lines. That evening after dark the North Koreans tried to get their men to assault the perimeter again, but, despite shouted orders of "Manzai!" only a few grenades fell inside the perimeter—apparently the enemy soldiers had had enough and refused to charge forward.

At 2200, McDoniel and Caldwell and twenty-seven enlisted men slipped off the hill in groups of four. One poignant scene etched itself on the minds of Sergeant Watkins' comrades. Watkins, still alive in his paralyzed condition, refused efforts of evacuation, saying that he did

---

[6] Ltr, Caldwell to author, 29 May 53; McDoniel, Notes, Sep 50.

not want to be a burden to those who had a chance to get away. He asked only that his carbine be loaded and placed on his chest with the muzzle under his chin. He smiled a last farewell to his buddies and wished them well when they started off the hill.[7]

McDoniel and Caldwell started off the hill together, their plan being to make their way to the river and follow it downstream. At the road they encountered so much enemy activity that they had to wait about an hour for the supply-carrying parties, tanks, and artillery to clear so that they could cross. Once across the road the two men found themselves in the middle of a North Korean artillery battery. They escaped unobserved and hid in a field near the river at daybreak. That night the two men became separated when they ran into an enemy outpost. The next morning two enemy soldiers captured Caldwell, removed his boots and identification, smashed him on the head with a rock, and threw him over a cliff into the Naktong River. Caldwell, not critically injured, feigned death and escaped that night. Four days later, on 10 September, he entered the lines of the 72d Tank Battalion.

Of the twenty-nine men who came off the hill the night of 4 September, twenty-two escaped to friendly lines—many of them following the Naktong downstream, hiding by day and traveling by night, until they reached the lines of the 25th Division.[8]

Members of Task Force Manchu who escaped from Hill 209 brought back considerable intelligence information of enemy activity in the vicinity of the Paekchin ferry crossing site. At the ferry site the enemy had put in an underwater ford. A short distance downstream, each night half an hour after dark they placed a metal floating bridge across the river and took it up before dawn the next morning. Carrying parties of 50 civilians guarded by four soldiers crossed the river continuously at night at a dogtrot, an estimated total of 800–1,000 carriers being used at this crossing site.[9]

The Battle of Yongsan

On the morning of 1 September the *1st* and *2d Regiments* of the N.K. *9th Division* (the *3d Regiment* had been left at Inch'on), in their first offensive of the war, stood only a few miles short of Yongsan after a successful river crossing and penetration of the American line. At that point the chances of the division accomplishing its assigned mission must have looked favorable to its commanding general, Pak Kyo Sam.

As the N.K. *9th Division* approached Yongsan, its *1st Regiment* was on the

---

[7] Ltr, Caldwell to author, 29 May 53; McDoniel, Notes, Sep 50; Bozarth and Lillard Affidavit; Ltr, MSgt Robert S. Hall (1st Bn, 9th Inf, Aug–Sep 50—Hall maintained morning rpts) to author, 1 Jun 54. Department of the Army General Order 9, 16 February 1951, awarded the Medal of Honor to Sergeant Watkins posthumously.

[8] McDoniel, Notes, Sep 50; New York *Times*, September 9, 1950. Three weeks later, when the N.K. *9th Division* had been driven back across the Naktong, a party of 9th Infantry men climbed to the tragic perimeter on Hill 209. They found most of the dead had been blown to pieces in the foxholes, and it was often difficult to tell whether two or three men had occupied a particular hole. There were approximately thirty American dead at the site, fifteen of whom could be identified. Sloane, Hill 209, Sep 50.

[9] EUSAK WD, PIR 59, an. 1, 9 Sep 50.

north and its *2d Regiment* on the south. The division's attached support, consisting of one 76-mm. artillery battalion from the *I Corps*, an antiaircraft battalion of artillery, two tank battalions of the *16th Armored Brigade*, and a battalion of artillery from the *4th Division*, gave it unusual weapon support. Crossing the river behind it came the *4th Division*, a greatly weakened organization, far understrength, short of weapons, and made up mostly of untrained replacements. A captured enemy document referred to this grouping of units that attacked from the Sinban-ni area into the Naktong Bulge as "the main force" of *I Corps*. Elements of the *9th Division* reached the hills just west of Yongsan during the afternoon of 1 September.[10]

On the morning of 1 September, with only the shattered remnants of E Company at hand, the 9th Infantry had virtually no troops to defend Yongsan. General Keiser in this emergency attached the 2d Engineer Combat Battalion to the regiment. The 72d Tank Battalion and the 2d Division Reconnaissance Company also were assigned positions close to Yongsan. Colonel Hill planned to place the engineers on the chain of low hills that arched around Yongsan on the northwest.

Capt. Frank M. Reed, commanding officer of A Company, 2d Engineer Combat Battalion, led his company westward on the south side of the Yongsan–Naktong River road; Lt. Lee E. Beahler with D Company of the 2d Engineer Battalion was on the north side of the road. Approximately two miles west of Yongsan an estimated 300 enemy troops engaged A Company in a fire fight. Two quad-50's and one twin-40 gun carrier of the 82d AAA Battalion supported Reed's men in this action, which lasted several hours. Meanwhile, Lieutenant Beahler protested his position because of its long frontage and exposed flanks. With the approval of General Bradley, he moved his Engineer company to the hill immediately south of and overlooking Yongsan. A platoon of infantry went into position behind him. Captain Reed was now ordered to fall back with his company to the southeast edge of Yongsan on the left flank of Beahler's company. There, A Company went into position along the road; on its left was C Company of the Engineer battalion, and beyond C Company was the 2d Division Reconnaissance Company. The hill occupied by Beahler's D Company was in reality the western tip of a large mountain mass that lay southeast of the town. The road to Miryang came south out of Yongsan, bent around the western tip of this mountain, and then ran eastward along its southern base. In its position, D Company not only commanded the town but also its exit, the road to Miryang.[11]

North Koreans had also approached Yongsan from the south. The 2d Division Reconnaissance Company and tanks of the 72d Tank Battalion opposed them in a sharp fight. In this action, SFC

---

[10] GHQ FEC, History of the North Korean Army, p. 68; ATIS Res Supp Interrog Rpts, Issue 100 (N.K. *9th Div*), p. 49, and Issue 94 (N.K. *4th Div*), pp. 49–50; ATIS Interrog Rpts, Issue 4, p. 118, Rpt 949, 1st Lt So Chung Kun (captured 3 Sep 50, Yongsan); EUSAK WD, 14 Sep 50, an. to PIR 64, and 9 Sep 50, POW Interrog Rpt of 1st Lt So Chung Kun, *9th Div*, and Interrog Rpt of Cha Sook Wha, interpreter, *16th Regt, 4th Div*.

[11] Ltrs, Capt Lee E. Beahler to author, 10 Jun and 1 Jul 53 (sketch map of D Co positions with ltr of 1 Jul); Ltr, Reed to author, 20 Jul 53; Interv, author with Hill, 30 Jun 53.

Charles W. Turner of the Reconnaissance Company particularly distinguished himself. He mounted a tank, operated its exposed turret machine gun, and directed tank fire which reportedly destroyed seven enemy machine guns. Turner and this tank were the objects of very heavy enemy fire which shot away the tank's periscope and antennae and scored more than fifty hits on it. Turner, although wounded, remained on the tank until he was killed. That night North Korean soldiers crossed the low ground around Yongsan and entered the town from the south.[12]

About 0300, 2 September, D Company of the 2d Engineer Battalion alerted A Company that a long line of white-garbed figures was moving through Yongsan toward its roadblock. Challenged when they approached, the white figures opened fire—they were enemy troops. Four enemy tanks and an estimated battalion of North Koreans were in Yongsan.

The North Koreans now attempted a breakthrough of the Engineer position. After daylight, they were unable to get reinforcements into the fight since D Company commanded the town and its approaches. In this fight, which raged until 1100, the engineers had neither artillery nor mortar support. D Company remedied this by using its 9 new 3.5-inch and 9 old 2.36-inch rocket launchers against the enemy infantry. The fire of the 18 bazookas plus that from 4 heavy and 4 light machine guns and the rifles, carbines, and grenades of the company inflicted very heavy casualties on the North Koreans, who desperately tried to clear the way for a push eastward to Miryang. Tanks of A and B Companies, 72d Tank Battalion, at the southern and eastern edge of Yongsan shared equally with the engineers in the honors of this battle. Lieutenant Beahler was the only officer of D Company not killed or wounded in this melee, which cost the company twelve men killed and eighteen wounded. The edge of Yongsan and the slopes of the hill south of the town became a shambles of enemy dead and destroyed equipment.[13]

While this battle raged during the morning at Yongsan, Colonel Hill reorganized about 800 men of the 9th Infantry who had arrived in that vicinity from the overrun river line positions. Among them were F and G Companies, which were not in the path of major enemy crossings and had succeeded in withdrawing eastward. They had no crew-served weapons or heavy equipment. In midafternoon (2 September) tanks and the reorganized 2d Battalion, 9th Infantry, attacked through A Company, 2d Engineer Combat Battalion, into Yongsan, and regained possession of the town at 1500. Later, two bazooka teams from A Company, 2d Engineer Combat Battalion, knocked out three T34 tanks just west of Yongsan. American ground and air action destroyed other enemy tanks during the day southwest of the town. By evening the North Koreans had been driven into the hills

---

[12] Department of the Army General Order 10, 16 February 1951, awarded the Medal of Honor to Sergeant Turner posthumously.

[13] Ltrs, Beahler to author, 10 Jun and 1 Jul 53; Ltr, Reed to author, 20 Jul 53; Interv, author with Hill, 30 Jun 53; EUSAK WD, G-3 Jnl, Msg 1525, 2 Sep 50; *Ibid.*, PIR 52, 2 Sep 50. General Order 59, 8 February 1951, awarded the Distinguished Service Cross to Lieutenant Beahler for heroic leadership in this action. EUSAK.

westward. In the evening, the 2d Battalion and A Company, 2d Engineer Combat Battalion, occupied the first chain of low hills half a mile beyond Yongsan, the engineers west and the 2d Battalion northwest of the town. For the time being at least, the North Korean drive toward Miryang had been halted.[14]

At 0935 that morning (2 September), while the North Koreans were attempting to destroy the Engineer troops at the southern edge of Yongsan and clear the road to Miryang, General Walker talked by telephone with Maj. Gen. Doyle O. Hickey, Deputy Chief of Staff, Far East Command, in Tokyo. He described the situation around the Perimeter and said the most serious threat was along the boundary between the U.S. 2d and 25th Divisions. He described the location of his reserve forces and his plans for using them. He said he had started the marines toward Yongsan but had not yet released them for commitment there and he wanted to be sure that General MacArthur approved his use of them, since he knew that this would interfere with other plans of the Far East Command. Walker said he did not think he could restore the 2d Division lines without using them. General Hickey replied that General MacArthur had the day before approved the use of the marines if and when Walker considered it necessary. A few hours after this conversation General Walker, at 1315, attached the 1st Provisional Marine Brigade to the 2d Division and ordered a co-ordinated attack by all available elements of the division and the marines, with the mission of destroying the enemy east of the Naktong River in the 2d Division sector and of restoring the river line. The marines were to be released from 2d Division control just as soon as this mission was accomplished.[15]

A conference was held that afternoon at the 2d Division command post attended by Colonel Collier, Deputy Chief of Staff, Eighth Army, General Craig and Maj. Frank R. Stewart, Jr., of the Marine Corps, and General Keiser and 2d Division staff officers. A decision was reached that the marines would attack west the next morning at 0800 (3 September) astride the Yongsan–Naktong River road; the 9th Infantry, B Company of the 72d Tank Battalion, and D Battery of the 82d AAA Battalion would attack northwest above the marines and attempt to re-establish contact with the 23d Infantry; the 2d Engineer Combat Battalion, remnants of the 1st Battalion, 9th Infantry, and elements of the 72d Tank Battalion would attack on the left flank, or south, of the marines to re-establish contact with the 25th Division. Eighth Army now ordered the 24th Division headquarters and the 19th Infantry to move to the Susan-ni area, eight air miles south of Miryang and fifteen miles east of the confluence of the Nam and the Naktong Rivers. There it was to prepare to enter the battle in either the 2d or 25th Division zone. Colonel Fisher, commanding officer of the 35th Infantry, 25th Division, each morning flew along the Naktong River east of the

---

[14] Ltrs, Beahler to author, 10 Jun and 1 Jul 53; Ltr, Reed to author, 20 Jul 53; Interv, author with Hill, 30 Jun 53; Cody, Operation Manchu; EUSAK WD, G–3 Jnl, 2 Sep 50; Ibid., Br for CG, 2 Sep 50; GHQ FEC Sitrep, 2 Sep 50.

[15] Transcription and summ of fonecon, Walker with Hickey, 0935 2 Sep 50, CofS files, FEC; EUSAK WD, G–3 Sec, Opn Ord 021315 Sep 50.

U.N. TROOPS CROSS RICE PADDIES *to attack west of Yongsan.*

Namji-ri bridge to see if North Koreans had crossed from the 2d Division zone.[16]

At 1900 the evening of 2 September, Colonel Hill returned to his command post east of Yongsan where he conferred with Colonel Murray, commanding the 5th Marines, and told him that his line of departure for the attack the next morning was secure. The troops holding this line on the first hills west of Yongsan were: G Company, 9th Infantry, north of the road running west through Kogan-ni to the Naktong; A Company, 2d Engineer Combat Battalion, southward across the road; and, below the engineers, F Company, 9th Infantry. Between 0300 and 0430, 3 September, the 5th Marines moved to forward assembly areas—the 2d Battalion north of Yongsan, the 1st Battalion south of it. The 3d Battalion established security positions southwest of Yongsan along the approaches into the regimental sector from that direction.[17]

During the night, A Company of the engineers had considerable fighting with North Koreans and never reached its objective. At dawn 3 September, Reed led A Company in an attack to gain the high ground which was part of the designated Marine line of departure. The company fought its way up the slope to within 100 yards of the top, which was held by the firmly entrenched enemy. At this

---

[16] EUSAK WD, G-3 Sec, and Br for CG, 2 Sep 50; 9th Inf WD, 3 Sep 50, Opn Ord 11 and accompanying overlay, 030300 Sep 50; 1st Prov Mar Brig SAR, 2 Aug-6 Sep 50, p. 15; 2d Div Arty WD, entry 12, 2335 2 Sep 50; Fisher, MS review comments, 7 Nov 57.

[17] Interv, author with Hill, 30 Jun 53; Ltr, Beahler to author, 10 Jun 53; 1st Prov Mar Brig SAR, 2 Aug-6 Sep 50, entry for 3 Sep, p. 15; 5th Mar SAR, 3 Sep 50; 2d Bn, 5th Mar, SAR, addendum 1, 3 Sep 50; Montross and Canzona, *The Pusan Perimeter,* pp. 217-20.

point Captain Reed caught an enemy-thrown grenade and was wounded by its fragments as he tried to throw it away from his men. The company with help from Marine tank fire eventually gained its objective, but this early morning battle for the line of departure delayed the planned attack.[18]

The Marine attack started at 0855 across the rice paddy land toward enemy-held high ground half a mile westward. The 1st Battalion, south of the east-west road, gained its objective when enemy soldiers broke under air attack and ran down the northern slope and crossed the road to Hill 116 in the 2d Battalion zone. Air strikes, artillery concentrations, and machine gun and rifle fire of the 1st Battalion now caught enemy reinforcements in open rice paddies moving up from the second ridge and killed most of them. In the afternoon, the 1st Battalion advanced to Hill 91.

North of the road the 2d Battalion had a harder time, encountering heavy enemy fire when it reached the northern tip of Hill 116, two miles west of Yongsan. The North Koreans held the hill during the day, and at night D Company of the 5th Marines was isolated there. In the fighting west of Yongsan Marine armor knocked out four T34 tanks, and North Korean crew members abandoned a fifth. That night the marines dug in on a line generally two miles west of Yongsan. The 2d Battalion had lost 18 killed and 77 wounded during the day, most of them in D Company. Total Marine casualties for 3 September were 34 killed and 157 wounded. Co-ordinating its attack with that of the marines, the 9th Infantry advanced abreast of them on the north.[19]

Just before midnight, the 3d Battalion, 5th Marines, received orders to pass through the 2d Battalion and continue the attack in the morning. That night torrential rains made the troops miserable. The enemy was strangely quiet. September 4 dawned clear.

The counterattack continued at 0800, 4 September, at first against little opposition. North of the road the 2d Battalion quickly completed occupation of Hill 116, from which the North Koreans had withdrawn during the night. South of the road the 1st Battalion occupied what appeared to be a command post of the N.K. *9th Division*. Tents were still up and equipment lay scattered about. Two abandoned T34 tanks in excellent condition stood there. Tanks and ground troops advancing along the road found it littered with enemy dead and destroyed and abandoned equipment. By nightfall the counterattack had gained another three miles.[20]

That night was quiet until just before dawn. The North Koreans then launched an attack against the 9th Infantry on the right of the marines, the heaviest blow striking G Company. It had begun to rain again and the attack came in the midst of a downpour. In bringing his platoon from an outpost position to the relief of the company, SFC Loren R. Kaufman encountered an encircling en-

---

[18] Ltr, Reed to author, 20 Jul 53; Ltr, Beahler to author, 10 Jun 53; 5th Mar SAR, 3 Sep 50.

[19] Entries for 3 Sep, Marine sources cited n. 20; 1st Bn, 5th Mar, SAR, 3 Sep 50; Montross and Canzona, *The Pusan Perimeter*, pp. 220–22; Geer, *The New Breed*, p. 94.

[20] 1st Prov Mar Brig SAR, 2 Aug–6 Sep 50, pp. 15–16; 1st Bn, 5th Mar SAR, 4 Sep 50; Geer, *The New Breed*, p. 96; Montross and Canzona, *The Pusan Perimeter*, pp. 227–29.

emy force on the ridge line. He bayoneted the lead enemy scout and engaged those following with grenades and rifle fire. His sudden attack confused and dispersed this group. Kaufman led his platoon on and succeeded in joining hard-pressed G Company. In the ensuing action Kaufman led assaults against close-up enemy positions and, in hand-to-hand fighting, he bayoneted four more enemy soldiers, destroyed a machine gun position, and killed the crew members of an enemy mortar. American artillery fire concentrated in front of the 9th Infantry helped greatly in repelling the North Koreans in this night and day battle.[21]

That morning (5 September), after a 10-minute artillery preparation, the American troops moved out in their third day of counterattack. It was a day of rain. As the attack progressed, the marines approached Obong-ni Ridge and the 9th Infantry neared Cloverleaf Hill —their old battleground of August. There, at midmorning, on the high ground ahead, they could see enemy troops digging in. The marines approached the pass between the two hills and took positions in front of the enemy-held high ground.

At 1430 approximately 300 enemy infantry came from the village of Tugok and concealed positions, striking B Company on Hill 125 just north of the road and east of Tugok. Two enemy T34 tanks surprised and knocked out the two leading Marine Pershing M26 tanks. Since the destroyed Pershing tanks blocked fields of fire, four others withdrew to better positions. Assault teams of B Company and the 1st Battalion with 3.5-inch rocket launchers rushed into action, took the tanks under fire, and destroyed both of them, as well as an armored personnel carrier following behind. The enemy infantry attack was quite savage and inflicted twenty-five casualties on B Company before reinforcements from A Company and supporting Army artillery and the Marine 81-mm. mortars helped repel it.[22]

September 5 was a day of heavy casualties everywhere on the Pusan Perimeter. Army units had 102 killed, 430 wounded, and 587 missing in action for a total of 1,119 casualties. Marine units had 35 killed, 91 wounded, and none missing in action, for a total of 126 battle casualties. Total American battle casualties for the day were 1,245 men. Col. Charles C. Sloane, Jr., who had commanded part of Task Force Bradley, resumed command of the 9th Infantry, relieving Colonel Hill.[23]

During the previous night, at 2000, 4 September, General Walker had ordered the 1st Provisional Marine Brigade released from operational control of the 2d Division effective at midnight, 5 September. He had vainly protested against releasing the brigade, believing he needed it and all the troops then in Korea if he were to stop the North Korean offensive against the Pusan Perimeter. At 0015, 6 September, the marines

---

[21] Department of the Army General Order 61, 2 August 1951, awarded the Medal of Honor to Sergeant Kaufman.

[22] 9th Inf WD, 5 Sep 50; 1st Prov Mar Brig SAR, 5 Sep 50; 1st Bn, 5th Mar SAR, 5 Sep 50; Geer, *The New Breed*, pp. 97–98; Montross and Canzona, *The Pusan Perimeter*, pp. 234–37.

[23] GHQ FEC Sitrep, 5 Sep 50; 9th Inf WD, 5 Sep 50, GO 11.

began leaving their lines at Obong-ni Ridge and headed for Pusan.[24]

The American counteroffensive of 3-5 September west of Yongsan, according to prisoner statements, resulted in one of the bloodiest and most terrifying debacles of the war for a North Korean division. Even though remnants of the division, supported by the low strength *4th Division*, still held Obong-ni Ridge, Cloverleaf Hill, and the intervening ground back to the Naktong on 6 September, the division's offensive strength had been spent at the end of the American counterattack. The *9th* and *4th* enemy divisions were not able to resume the offensive.[25]

Once again the fatal weakness of the North Korean Army had cost it victory after an impressive initial success—its communications and supply were not capable of exploiting a breakthrough and of supporting a continuing attack in the face of massive air, armor, and artillery fire that could be concentrated against its troops at critical points.

The 23d Infantry in Front of Changnyong

North of the 9th Infantry and the battles that ebbed and flowed in the big bulge of the Naktong and around Yongsan, the 23d Infantry Regiment after daylight of 1 September found itself in a very precarious position. Its 1st Battalion had been driven from the river positions and isolated three miles westward. Approximately 400 North Koreans now overran the regimental command post, compelling Colonel Freeman to withdraw it about 600 yards. There, approximately five miles northwest of Changnyong, the 23d Infantry Headquarters and Headquarters Company, miscellaneous regimental units, and regimental staff officers checked the enemy in a 3-hour fight. Capt. Niles J. McIntyre of the Headquarters Company played a leading role.[26]

The infallible sign of approaching enemy troops could be seen in Changnyong itself during the afternoon of 2 September—at 1300 the native population began leaving the town. A little later a security force of 300 local police under the command of Maj. Jack T. Young and Capt. Harry H. White withdrew into the hills eastward when two groups of enemy soldiers approached from the northwest and southwest. North Koreans were in Changnyong that evening.[27]

With his communications broken southward to the 2d Division headquarters and the 9th Infantry, General Haynes during the day decided to send a tank patrol down the Yongsan road in an effort to re-establish communication. Capt. Manes R. Dew, commanding officer of C Company, 72d Tank Battalion, led the tanks southward. They had to fight their way down the road through enemy roadblocks. Of the three tanks that started, only Dew's tank got through to Yongsan. There, Captain Dew

---

[24] 2d Div Narr Summ, 1 Sep–31 Oct 50, p. 14; EUSAK WD, 4 Sep 50, Opn Ord at 042000. The removal of the Marine brigade from the Naktong front will be discussed further in the next chapter.

[25] ATIS Res Supp Interrog Rpts, Issue 100 (N.K. *9th Div*), p. 52.

[26] Freeman, MS review comments, 30 Oct 57; Highlights of the Combat Activities of the 23d Infantry Regiment from 5 August to 30 September 1950, MS, prepared in the regiment, copy in OCMH.

[27] 2d Div Arty WD, 2 Sep 50; EUSAK WD, 7 Sep 50, an. to PIR 57.

delivered an overlay of Task Force Haynes' positions to General Bradley.[28]

Still farther northward in the zone of the 38th Infantry the North Koreans were far from idle. After the enemy breakthrough during the night of 31 August, General Keiser on 1 September had ordered the 2d Battalion, 38th Infantry, to move south and help the 23d Regiment establish a defensive position west of Changnyong. In attempting to do this, the battalion found enemy troops already on the ridges along the road. They had in fact penetrated to Hill 284 overlooking the 38th Infantry command post. This hill and Hill 209 dominated the rear areas of the regiment. At 0600, 3 September, an estimated 300 North Koreans launched an attack from Hill 284 against Colonel Peploe's 38th Regiment command post. Colonel Peploe organized all officers and enlisted men present, including members of the mortar and tank companies and attached antiaircraft artillery units, to fight in the perimeter defense. Peploe requested a bombing strike which was denied him because the enemy target and his defense perimeter were too close to each other. But the Air Force did deliver rocket and strafing strikes.

This fight continued until 5 September. On that day Capt. Ernest J. Schauer captured Hill 284 with two platoons of F Company after four efforts. He found approximately 150 enemy dead on the hill. From the crest he and his men watched as many more North Koreans ran into a village below them. Directed artillery fire destroyed the village. Among the abandoned enemy matériel on the hill, Schauer's men found twenty-five American BAR's and submachine guns, a large American radio, thirty boxes of unopened American fragmentation and concussion grenades, and some American rations.[29]

Meanwhile, during these actions in its rear, the 1st Battalion, 23d Infantry, was cut off three miles westward from the nearest friendly units. On 1 September Colonel Hutchin had received instructions from the regiment to withdraw to the Changnyong area. At 1400 he sent a tank-infantry patrol to see if his withdrawal road was open. It reported that an estimated enemy battalion held the mountain pass just eastward of the battalion's defense perimeter. Upon receiving this report Colonel Hutchin requested permission by radio to remain in his present position and from there try to obstruct the movement of North Korean reinforcements and supplies. That evening Colonel Freeman approved this request, and thus began the 1st Battalion's 3-day stand as an island in a sea of enemy. During this time C-47 planes supplied the battalion by airdrops.[30]

The 2d Division, however, did not leave Colonel Hutchin to his own devices in his isolated perimeter position. Instead, on the morning of 1 September, it started the 3d Battalion, 38th Infantry, in an attack westward from the 23d Regiment command post near Mosan-ni to open the enemy-held road to the 1st Battalion. On the second day of the fighting at the enemy-held pass, the relief force, under Maj. Everett S. Stewart, the

---

[28] 2d Div Arty WD, 2 Sep 50; Interv, author with Hill, 30 Jun 53.

[29] 38th Inf Comd Rpt, Narr Summ, Sep–Oct 50; EUSAK PIR 58, 8 Sep 50; 2d Div PIR 14, 7 Sep 50.
[30] 23d Inf WD, Narr Summ, Sep 50.

battalion executive officer and temporarily acting battalion commander, broke through the enemy roadblock with the help of air strikes and artillery and tank fire. The advanced elements of the battalion joined Hutchin's battalion at 1700, 2 September. That evening, North Koreans strongly attacked the 3d Battalion, 38th Infantry, on Hill 209 north of the road and opposite Hutchin's battalion, driving one company from its position.[31]

On 4 September, General Haynes changed the boundary between the 38th and 23d Infantry Regiments, giving the northern part of the 23d's sector to the 38th Infantry, thus releasing Colonel Hutchin's 1st Battalion for movement southward to help the 2d Battalion defend the southern approach to Changnyong. The 1st Battalion, 23d Infantry, about 1,100 men strong when the enemy attack began, was now down to a strength of approximately 600 men.

The 23d Infantry now made plans to concentrate all its troops on the position held by its 2d Battalion on the Pugongni–Changnyong road. Colonel Hutchin succeeded in moving the 1st Battalion there and took a place on the left flank of the 2d Battalion. At the same time the regimental command post moved to the rear of this position. In this regimental perimeter, the 23d Infantry fought a series of hard battles. Simultaneously it had to send combat patrols to its rear to clear infiltrating enemy from Changnyong and from its supply road.

The N.K. *2d Division* made a desperate effort against the 23d Infantry's perimeter in the predawn hours of 8 September, in an attempt to break through eastward. This attack, launched at 0230 and heavily supported with artillery, penetrated F Company. It was apparent that unless F Company's position could be restored the entire regimental front would collapse. When all its officers became casualties, 1st Lt. Ralph R. Robinson, adjutant of the 2d Battalion, assumed command of the company. With North Koreans rapidly infiltrating his company's position and gaining its rear, Robinson in the darkness made his way through them 500 yards to A Company's position. There he obtained that company's reserve platoon and brought it back to F Company. He accomplished the dangerous and difficult task of maneuvering it into the gap in F Company's lines in darkness and heavy rain.[32]

The enemy attack tapered off with the coming of daylight, but that night it resumed. The North Koreans struck repeatedly at the defense line. This time they continued the fighting into the daylight hours of 9 September. The Air Force then concentrated strong air support over the regimental perimeter and gave invaluable aid to the ground troops. Casualties came to the aid stations from the rifle companies in an almost steady stream during the morning. All available men from Headquarters Company and special units were formed into squads and put into the fight at the most critical points. At one time, the regimental reserve was down to six men. When the enemy attack finally ceased

---

[31] Interv, author with Lt Col Everett S. Stewart, 19 May 53; 23d Inf WD, G–3 Jnl, entry 131, 1715 1 Sep 50. General Order 196, 14 December 1950, awarded the Distinguished Service Cross to Colonel Hutchin. 2d Div.

[32] 2d Div Arty WD, 2 Sep 50; EUSAK WD, 7 Sep 50, an. to PIR 57.

shortly after noon the 23d Regiment had an estimated combat efficiency of only 38 percent.[33]

This furious night and day battle cost the enemy division most of its remaining offensive strength. The medical officer of the *17th Regiment, 2d Division*, captured a few days later, said that the division evacuated about 300 men nightly to a hospital in Pugong-ni, and that in the first two weeks of September the *2d Division* lost 1,300 killed and 2,500 wounded in the fighting west of Changnyong.[34]

Even though its offensive strength was largely spent by 9 September, the enemy division continued to harass rear areas around Changnyong with infiltrating groups as large as companies. Patrols daily had to open the main supply road and clear the town.

A North Korean Puzzle

While the N.K. *2d Division* was making its great effort near the middle of the U.S. 2d Division line, a sister organization, the N.K. *10th Division*, on its left to the north failed to give the assistance that was expected of it in the co-ordinated corps attack. And therein lies one of the greatest North Korean failures of the war to exploit an opportunity. The singular behavior of this enemy force puzzled American commanders at the time, although they were thankful that it took the pattern it did.

The N.K. *10th Division* was the northernmost major organization of the N.K. *I Corps*. A large part of it occupied Hill 409 in a deep fold of the Naktong River just west of Hyongp'ung. Elements of this division streamed off Hill 409 the night of 31 August-1 September and struck the 1st Battalion, 38th Infantry, which formed the extreme right flank of the U.S. 2d Division. Holding the town of Hyongp'ung was C Company, which withdrew from it under enemy attack during the night of 2-3 September. Beginning with 3 September, Hyongp'ung for two weeks was either in enemy hands or a no man's land.[35]

North and east of the Hill 409 and Hyongp'ung area lay a virtually roadless, high mountain area having no fixed U.N. defensive positions. This, too, was a no man's land in early September. Four miles north of Hyongp'ung was the Yongp'o bridge across the Naktong and the 1st Cavalry Division boundary. The Yongp'o bridge site was defended by the 3d Battalion, 23d Infantry, attached to the 1st Cavalry Division for that purpose, until 0410, 5 September, when the British 27th Infantry Brigade relieved it and went into the line there. This, as previously noted, was the British brigade's first commitment in the Korean War.[36]

During the first two weeks of September large numbers of the enemy *10th*

---

[33] 23d Inf WD, Narr Summ, Sep 50; Interv. author with Meszar, 15 May 53; Highlights of Combat Activities of 23d Inf.

[34] EUSAK WD, 21 Sep 50, ADVATIS Interrog Rpts, Sr Lt Lee Kwan Hyon, Med Off, N.K. *17th Regt, 2d Div*; ATIS Interrog Rpts, Issue 6, p. 81, Kim Il Chin and Issue 7, p. 3, Yu Tong Gi; 23d Inf Comd Rpt, Sep 50, Narr Summ, p. 10.

[35] 38 Inf Comd Rpt, Sep-Oct 50, Narr Summ; EUSAK WD, G-3 Jnl, 4-5 Sep 50. Records of the 38th Infantry for September 1950 were lost in the withdrawal from Kunu-ri, 30 November, and the command report compiled later from recollections of regimental personnel lacks precise information on time, place, and overlay data for this period.

[36] GHQ FEC Sitrep, 5 Sep 50; *Ibid.*, G-3 Opn Rpt 70, 2 Sep 50.

Division came off Hill 409 and roamed the mountain mass northeast of Hyongp'ung in the gap between the U.S. 2d Division and the British 27th Brigade. This caused Eighth Army concern for the safety of Taegu. Gradually, ROK police and British combat patrols forced the North Koreans back to Hill 409. On 6 September, the day after they went into the line, the British had a taste of what the Korean War was like. A combat patrol of the Argylls under Capt. Neil A. Buchanan encountered an enemy unit and had to make its escape, leaving behind, on his own orders, Captain Buchanan badly wounded and, at his side, his wounded batman. Neither was seen again. The British company nearest Hill 409 was so isolated that airdrops of ice to it replaced carrying water cans up the hill.[37]

Had the enemy *10th Division* thrown its full weight into a drive eastward, south of Taegu, it might well have precipitated a major crisis for Eighth Army. It could have moved either northeast toward Taegu or southeast to help the *2d Division*, next in line below it, but it did neither. Its relative inactivity in the vicinity of Hill 409 when its companion divisions were engaged in desperate combat above and below it is something of a mystery. Captured enemy material and statements of prisoners indicate that its mission may have been to stay on Hill 409 until the N.K. *II Corps* had captured Taegu, but they indicated, also, that the division command was inept. The *10th Division* caused General Walker much concern at this time. He and his staff found it puzzling to reconcile the division's favorable position with its inactivity. General Walker charged Colonel Landrum, now Deputy Chief of Staff, Eighth Army, to watch the situation closely and inform him daily on it. At least twice daily Landrum insisted on a summary from the Army G-3 of activities in front of the N.K. *10th Division*.[38]

The 35th Infantry—The Rock of the Nam

On the 25th Division's right flank and north of the Haman breakthrough, the 35th Infantry Regiment at daylight, 1 September, still held all its positions except the low ground between Komam-ni and the Nam River, which the two companies of ROK police had abandoned at midnight. (*See Map V.*) In a counterattack after daylight, K Company and tanks had partially regained control of this area, but not completely. Large numbers of North Koreans, by this time, however, were behind the battle positions of the 35th Infantry as far as the Chirwon-ni and Chung-ni areas, six miles east of Komam-ni and the front positions. The North Koreans continued to cross the Nam River after daylight on 1 September in the general area of the gap between the 1st and 2d Battalions. Aerial observers saw an estimated four companies crossing there and directed proximity (VT) fuze fire of the 64th Field

---

[37] EUSAK WD, G-3 Jnl, 1330, 10 Sep 50; GHQ FEC Sitrep, 13 Sep 50; Lt Col G. I. Malcolm of Poltallock (London: Thomas Nelson & Sons, Ltd., 1952), *The Argylls in Korea*, pp. 11-12; Coad, The Land Campaign in Korea.

[38] ATIS Res Supp Interrog Rpts, Issue 104 (N.K. *10th Div*), p. 49; Interv, author with Stephens, 8 Oct 51; Interv, author with Brig Gen George B. Peploe, 12 Aug 51; Ltr and notes, Landrum to author, recd 28 Jun 54.

BATTLE TROPHY. *Men of the 35th Infantry display a North Korean flag captured in the Sibidang-san area on 5 September.*

Artillery Battalion on the crossing force, which destroyed an estimated three-fourths of it. Fighter planes then strafed the survivors. Aerial observers saw another large group in the open at the river later in the day and directed artillery proximity fuze fire on it with an estimated 200 enemy casualties.[39]

The enemy *I Corps* plan of attack below the Nam River, as indicated by the North Korean action, seemed to be for its *6th Division* to push east along the main Chinju–Komam-ni–Masan highway through the 1st Battalion, 35th Infantry, and at the same time for major elements of its *7th Division* to swing southeast behind the 2d Battalion, 35th Infantry, and cut the Chirwon road. This road crossed the Naktong River over the cantilever steel bridge at Namji-ri from the 2d Division zone and ran south through Chirwon to join the main Masan highway eight miles east of Komam-ni near the village of Chung-ni, four miles northwest of Masan. These two

---

[39] 25th Div WD, 1 Sep 50; 64th FA Bn WD, 1 Sep 50.

avenues of approach—the Komam-ni–Masan highway and the Chirwon road converging at Chung-ni—formed the axes of the enemy attack plan.

Engineer troops counterattacking up the secondary road toward Chirwon during 1 September made slow progress, and enemy troops stopped them altogether in the early afternoon. The 35th Infantry was now surrounded by enemy forces of the N.K. *6th* and *7th Divisions,* with an estimated three battalions of them behind its lines. Speaking later of the situation, Colonel Fisher, the regimental commander—a professional soldier, trained at West Point, and a regimental commander in World War II—said, "I never intended to withdraw. There was no place to go. I planned to go into a regimental perimeter and hold."[40] His regiment demonstrated its competency to do this in the September battle along the Nam, winning a Distinguished Unit Citation for its performance there.

On that first day of the enemy thrust, a critical situation existed in the 25th Division sector. Because of it, General Walker flew to General Kean's command post at Masan. In the ensuing discussion there, Kean asked Walker for authority to commit the remainder of the 27th Infantry Regiment (Walker had already released one battalion to Kean's control for use in the 24th Infantry sector) against the large enemy groups behind the 35th Infantry. Walker refused. By midafternoon, however, Kean felt that the situation was so critical that he ordered the 2d Battalion, commanded by Colonel Murch, to attack behind the 35th Infantry. A large part of the division artillery was under direct infantry attack and he felt it mandatory upon himself to commit the 2d Battalion, 27th Infantry. He gave this order on his own authority as the responsible commander on the ground, notwithstanding General Walker's earlier refusal. At a later date when General Walker knew all the facts, he approved General Kean's action.[41]

During the predawn hours of 1 September, when the N.K. *7th Division* troops had swung left after crossing the Nam River to roll up that flank, widen the gap, drive the American troops from their hill positions overlooking the Nam River, and secure a broad bridgehead for the division, the first American unit they encountered was G Company, 35th Infantry, at the north shoulder of the gap. While some enemy units peeled off to attack G Company, others continued on and engaged E Company, two miles downstream from it, and still others attacked scattered units of F Company all the way to its 1st Platoon, which guarded the Namji-ri bridge. There, at the extreme right flank of the 25th Division, this platoon drove off an enemy force after a sharp fight. By 2 September, E Company in a heavy battle had destroyed most of an enemy battalion.

Of all the 2d Battalion units, G Company received the hardest blows. Before dawn of 1 September enemy troops had G Company platoons on separate hills under heavy assault. Shortly after 0300 they overran the 3d Platoon, Heavy Mortar Company, and drove it from its position. These mortarmen climbed Hill

---

[40] Interv, author with Fisher, 5 Jan 52; 35th Inf WD, 1 Sep 50.

[41] Ltr, Kean to author, 22 Apr 53; Barth MS, p. 27.

179 and on its crest joined the 2d Platoon of G Company.

Meanwhile, the 3d Platoon of G Company, on a low hill along the Nam four miles from its juncture with the Naktong, was also under close-in attack. After daylight, Capt. LeRoy E. Majeske, G Company commanding officer, requested artillery concentrations and air strikes, but the latter were slow in coming. At 1145, the enemy had almost reached the crest of the hill, and only the narrow space covered by the air identification panel separated the two forces. A few minutes later Majeske was killed, and 2d Lt. George Roach, commanding the 3d Platoon, again reported the desperate situation and asked for an air strike. The Air Force delivered the strike on the enemy-held side of the hill, and this checked the assaults. But by this time many enemy troops had captured and occupied foxholes in the platoon position and from them they threw grenades into other parts of the position. One of the grenades killed Lieutenant Roach early in the afternoon. SFC Junius Poovey, a squad leader, now assumed command. In this close fight, one of the heroes was Cpl. Hideo Hashimoto, a Japanese-American, who edged himself forward and threw grenades into the enemy holes, some of them only ten to fifteen feet away. By 1800, Sergeant Poovey had only 12 effectives left in the platoon; 17 of the 29 men still living were wounded. With ammunition almost gone, Poovey requested and received authority to withdraw into the main G Company position. After dark, the 29 men, 3 of them carried on stretchers, escaped by timing their departure from the hill with the arrival of friendly tanks which engaged the enemy and diverted attention from the beleaguered men on top. The group reached the G Company position on Hill 179 half an hour before midnight.[42]

While G Company held its positions on Hill 179 on 2 September against enemy attack, Colonel Murch's 2d Battalion, 27th Infantry, started an attack northwest toward it at 1700 from the Chung-ni area. The battalion made slow progress against formidable enemy forces. The night was extremely dark and the terrain along the Kuhe-ri ferry road was mountainous. After fighting all that night the battalion, the next day at 1500, reached a position 1,000 yards south of the original defensive positions of G Company, 35th Infantry. A co-ordinated attack by armor, artillery, air, and infantry got under way and by 1800 the battalion had re-established the battle line. In this attack the 2d Battalion, 27th Infantry, killed 275 enemy and recovered a large part of the equipment G Company had lost earlier.

Colonel Murch's battalion remained on the regained positions during the night of the 3d. The next morning Murch received orders to attack to the rear and clear the alternate route on the western edge of the battalion zone. At 0800 G Company, 35th Infantry, relieved Murch on the regained positions

---

[42] 35th Inf WD, 1–2 Sep 50; 2d Bn 35th Inf WD, 1 Sep, and Narr story of action Sep 50; 25th Div WD, 1–2 Sep 50; New York *Herald Tribune*, September 3, 1950, Homer Bigart dispatch; New York *Times*, September 4, 1950, W. H. Lawrence dispatch.

In grenade fighting on slopes the practice of "cooking the grenade" developed. In order to avoid allowing enemy troops time to pick up and throw a grenade back, soldiers pulled the pin, released the handle in the grip for a brief period, and then threw the grenade.

2D BATTALION, 27TH INFANTRY, *on the recaptured supply road.*

and the latter started his attack back up the supply road. While this was in progress, word came that North Koreans had again driven G Company from its newly re-established position. Murch turned around, attacked, and once more restored the G Company positions. By noon of 4 September, Murch again turned over these positions to G Company and resumed his attack to the rear along the road in the gap between the 1st and 2d Battalions, 35th Infantry. Almost immediately he was in contact with enemy forces. Soon North Korean machine guns were firing on Murch's men from three directions. Torrential rains fell and observation became poor. By this time, Murch's battalion was running short of ammunition. Murch ordered the battalion to withdraw about 500 yards to favorable terrain so that he could try to effect a resupply.

But this was not easy to do. He had cleared the supply route two days previously in his attack to the G Company position but now it was closed again. With several thousand North Korean soldiers behind the 35th Infantry front, it was like pulling one's thumb from a pail of water—the space filled again immediately. Murch requested air supply and the next morning, 5 September, eight transport planes accomplished the resupply and the 2d Battalion, 27th Infantry, was ready to resume its attack to the rear. By evening that day it had cleared the supply road and adjacent terrain of enemy soldiers for a distance of 8,000 yards to the rear of G Company's front-line positions. There Murch received orders to halt and prepare to attack northeast to link up with Colonel Check's 1st Battalion, 27th Infantry.[43]

After Murch had left the Chung-ni area on 2 September in his attack toward G Company, enemy infiltrators attacked the 24th Infantry command post and several artillery positions. To meet this new situation, General Kean, again acting on his own authority as the responsible commander on the ground, ordered the remaining battalion of the 27th Infantry (technically still the 3d Battalion, 29th Infantry), commanded by Lt. Col. George H. DeChow, to attack and destroy the enemy operating there. General Kean notified Eighth Army of his action at 1250, 2 September.[44]

After an early morning struggle on 3 September against several hundred North Koreans in the vicinity of the artillery positions, DeChow's battalion launched its attack at 1500 over the high, rugged terrain west of the "Horseshoe," as the deep curve in the Masan road was called, four miles east of Komam-ni. Its mission was to seize and secure the high ground dominating the Horseshoe, and then relieve the pressure on the 24th Infantry rear. Initially only one artillery piece was in position to support the attack. After the battalion advanced some distance, an enemy force, estimated at the time to number more than 1,000 men, counterattacked it and inflicted heavy casualties, which included thirteen officers. The K Company commander, 1st Lt. Elwood F. James, was killed while leading an assault. Additional tanks moved up to help secure the exposed right flank and rear, and air strikes helped to contain the enemy force. The battalion finally succeeded in taking the high ground.[45]

The next morning, 4 September, instead of continuing the attack toward the 24th Infantry command post, DeChow, on changed orders, attacked straight ahead into the Komam-ni area where enemy troops were fighting in the artillery positions. This attack got under way at 0900 in the face of severe enemy small arms fire. In the afternoon, heavy rains slowed the attack, but after an all-day battle, I and K Companies, with the help of numerous air strikes, captured the high ground dominating the Komam-ni crossroads. Numerous casualties in the battalion had led General Kean to attach C Company, 65th Engineer Combat Battalion, to it. The next day, 5 September, the 3d Battalion turned its attack across rugged terrain toward Haman and drove through to the vicinity of the 24th Infantry command post. In its attack, the 3d Battalion counted more than 300 enemy dead in the area it traversed.[46]

The series of events that caused General Kean to change the direction of DeChow's attack toward Komam-ni began at 0100, 3 September. The 1st Battalion, 35th Infantry, protruded farther westward at this time than any other

---

[43] EUSAK WD, G-3 Jnl, 1125 and 1410, 3 Sep 50; 2d Bn, 27th Inf, WD, Unit Rpt, Sep 50; 27th Inf WD, Unit Rpt, Sep 50; Murch, MS review comments, 2 Jan 58.

[44] EUSAK WD, G-3 Jnl, 1250 2 Sep 50; 25th Div WD, 2 Sep 50; Ltr, Kean to author, 22 Apr 53. The 3d Bn, 29th Inf, became operational as the 3d Bn, 27th Inf, by 25th Div GO 134, 10 Sep 50. The 1st Bn, 29th Inf became operational as the 3d Bn, 35th Inf, the same date. EUSAK GO 49, 2 Sep 50, authorized the transfer.

[45] DeChow, MS review comments, Jul 53; Interv, author with Flynn (3d Bn. 27th Inf, Sep 50), 5 Nov 53; Barth MS, pp. 28-29.

[46] DeChow, MS review comments, Jul 53; Barth MS, pp. 28-29.

unit of the U.N. forces in Korea. Back of its positions on Sibidang-san the main supply route and rear areas were in enemy hands, and only in daylight and under escort could vehicles travel the road. On Sibidang-san the battalion had held its original positions after the heavy fighting of pre-dawn 1 September, completely surrounded by barbed wire, booby traps, and flares, with all supporting weapons inside its tight perimeters. The battalion had the advantage of calling by number for previously zeroed and numbered protective fires covering all approaches, which were quickly delivered. An hour after midnight an unusually heavy enemy assault struck the battalion. The fight there continued until dawn 3 September, when the 1st Battalion, 35th Infantry, counted 143 enemy dead in front of its positions, and on that basis estimated that the total enemy casualties must have been about 500 men.[47]

In this night battle the 64th Field Artillery Battalion gave invaluable support to the 1st Battalion and became directly involved itself in the fighting. About fifty North Koreans infiltrated before dawn to A Battery's position and delivered a banzai-type assault. Enemy soldiers employing submachine guns overran two artillery-machine gun perimeter positions, penetrating to the artillery pieces at 0300. There, Capt. Andrew C. Anderson and his men fought hand-to-hand with the North Koreans. Some of the guns fell temporarily into enemy hands and one North Korean scrawled on a howitzer tube, "Hurrah for our Company!" But the artillerymen threw the North Koreans out, aided greatly by the concentrations of fire from C Battery, 90th Field Artillery Battalion, which were placed within fifty yards of the battery and sealed off enemy reinforcements. In defending its guns in this night battle, A Battery lost seven men killed and twelve wounded—about 25 percent of its strength.[48]

The day before, the 159th Field Artillery Battalion also had distinguished itself in defending its guns in close fighting.

Fighting in support of the Nam River front in the northern part of the 25th Division sector were five batteries of the 159th and 64th Field Artillery Battalions (105-mm. howitzers) and one battery of the 90th Field Artillery Battalion (155-mm. howitzers), for a total of thirty-six guns. One 155-mm. howitzer, called by Colonel Fisher "The Little Professor," fired from Komam-ni on the Notch back of Chungam-ni, through which funneled much of the N.K. *6th Division*'s supplies. Another forward artillery piece kept the Iryong-ni bridge over the Nam under fire. The 25th Division artillery estimated it killed approximately 1,825 North Korean soldiers during the first three days of September.[49]

In this critical time, the Fifth Air Force added its tremendous fire power to that of the division artillery in support of the ground force. On 3 September, General Kean, speaking of the action during the past two days, said, "The close air support rendered by Fifth Air Force again saved this division as they

---

[47] 35th Inf WD, 3 Sep 50; 1st Bn, 35th Inf, Unit Rpt, Sep 50; EUSAK WD, G-3 Jnl, 0445, 3 Sep 50.

[48] 64th FA Bn WD, 3 Sep 50; Barth MS, p. 29; 159th FA Bn WD, Sep 50; EUSAK WD, G-3 Jnl, 0445 3 Sep 50; File supporting DUC, 35th Inf Regt, DA, AG files.

[49] 25th Div WD, 4 Sep 50; Barth MS, pp. 22, 31.

have many times before." [50] This view was supported by General Walker in an interview in November. Speaking then to a U.S. Air Force Evaluation Group, General Walker said, "I will gladly lay my cards right on the table and state that if it had not been for the air support that we received from the Fifth Air Force we would not have been able to stay in Korea." [51]

It is not possible here to follow in detail the confused ebb and flow of battle behind the 35th Infantry. Battalions, companies, and platoons, cut off and isolated, fought independently of higher control and help except for airdrops which supplied many of them. Airdrops also supplied relief forces trying to reach the front-line units. Tanks and armored cars ran the gantlet to the isolated units with supplies of food and ammunition and carried back critically wounded on the return trips.

In general, the 35th Infantry fought in its original battle line positions, while at first one battalion, and later two battalions, of the 27th Infantry fought toward it through the estimated 3,000 North Koreans operating in its rear areas.

In the confused fighting in the rear areas there were several cases of North Korean atrocities. One of the worst occurred when a group of company mess parties in jeeps pulling trailers with hot breakfast were following tanks toward the front lines. About a mile and a half from G Company, 35th Infantry, the column came under enemy fire in a defile. The tanks went on through, but most of the other vehicles under Capt. Robert E. Hammerquist, 2d Battalion S–3, turned back. At least one of the mess parties, however, pressed on after the tanks. Some of this group were captured. One of its members hid in a haystack and later escaped. He told of hearing the torture and murder of one man. He heard agonized screams, recognized the man's voice, and could hear him saying between sobs, "You might as well kill me now." Later when the area was cleared of enemy this man's body was found castrated and the fingers cut off.[52] Many soldiers of the 25th Division later saw the bodies of Americans lying in a ditch in the 35th Infantry area, their hands tied and their feet cut off. Still others saw dead Americans with their tongues cut out. Members of the N.K. *7th Division* apparently perpetrated these atrocities.[53]

During the September offensive enemy action in rear areas of the 25th Division carried right to Masan. Guerrilla activity increased, with the most tragic single incident taking place during the night of 3–4 September. That night about fifteen guerrillas, including one woman, attacked a radio relay station near Changwon, only four miles from Masan. They surprised a group of seven Americans and two South Koreans inside a tent on a hilltop. The guerrillas

---

[50] "Air War in Korea," *Air University Quarterly Review*, vol. IV, No. 3 (Spring, 1951), 61.

[51] Interv, USAF Evaluation Board with Lt Gen Walton Walker, 25 Nov 50. See also New York *Times*, September 3, 1950, for General Collins' statement quoting Walker.

[52] Interv, author with Maj Joe B. Lamb, CO 2d Bn, 35th Inf, 4 Sep 51; Intervs, author with 2d Lt Dillon Snell and 1st Lt Charles J. Hoyt, 2d Bn, 35th Inf, 4 Sep 51; Ltr, Hammerquist to author, 17 Apr 53; 35th Inf Unit Hist, 3 Sep 50.

[53] Interv, author with Lamb, 4 Sep 51; Interv, author with Sawyer (Recon Co, 25th Div, Sep 50), 27 Jun 51.

tied up the Americans, took documents from files, gathered up all weapons, and then the woman shot every one of the prisoners with a tommy gun. Two wounded Americans lived to tell the story.[54]

Even in Masan, General Kean faced a dangerous situation. The town was a nest of Communist sympathizers and agents. At the peak of the enemy offensive, Han Gum Jo, manager of the Masan branch of the Korean Press Association, confessed that he was chief of the South Korean Labor Party in Masan and that he funneled information to the enemy through a Pusan headquarters. The chief of guards of the Masan prison was the head of a Communist cell and seven of his guards were members. This and other counterintelligence information came to light at a time when desperate fighting was in progress only a few miles away. General Kean considered the situation so menacing that he ordered Masan evacuated of all people except the police, public officials, railroad and utility workers, and necessary laborers and their families. Evacuation was to be completed in five days. On 10 and 11 September alone the 25th Division evacuated more than 12,000 people by LST from Masan.[55]

Although the 25th Division generally was under much less enemy pressure after 5 September, there were still severe local attacks. On 6 September Colonel Check's 1st Battalion, 27th Infantry, moved north from the Haman area to join Murch's 2d Battalion in the cleanup of enemy troops back of the 35th Infantry and below the Nam River. Caught between the 35th Infantry on its hill positions along the river and the attacking 27th Infantry units, large numbers of North Koreans were killed. Sixteen different groups reportedly were dispersed with heavy casualties during the day. By morning of 7 September there was clear evidence that survivors of the N.K. *7th Division* were trying to escape across the Nam River. The 25th Division buried more than 2,000 North Korean dead, killed between 1 and 7 September behind its lines. This number did not include those killed in front of its positions. About 9 September Colonel Fisher traveled over these rear areas where fighting had been intense. He was astonished at the number of North Korean dead that littered the fields. Speaking of that occasion he has said, "The area of Trun in the Falaise Gap in Europe couldn't match it. Flies were so thick in some areas it limited vision."[56]

Heavy rains caused the Nam and Naktong Rivers to rise more than two feet on 8 and 9 September, thereby reducing the danger of new enemy crossings. At this juncture one of the ironies of the Korean War occurred. On the 9th, American jet planes (F-82's) mistakenly bombed the Namji-ri bridge over the Naktong and with one 500-pound bomb destroyed the 80-foot center span. Only the bridges north of the juncture of the Nam with the Naktong were supposed to be subject to aerial attack at this time. Lieutenant Vickery's 1st Platoon of F

---

[54] EUSAK WD, G-3, Coordinating Protection Lines of Communications Rear Areas, 4 Sep 50; New York *Herald Tribune*, September 4, 1950; 25th Div WD, 4 Sep 50.

[55] 25th Div WD, 3, 7, 11 and 15 Sep 50.

[56] EUSAK WD, G-3 Jnl 0720, 5 Sep 50; 27th Inf WD, 5 Sep 50; 2d Bn, 27th Inf, Unit Rpt, Sep 50; 25th Div WD, 6 Sep 50; Barth MS, p. 28; Fisher, MS review comments, Jan 58.

Company, 35th Infantry, had effectively defended the bridge—the link between the U.S. 2d and 25th Divisions—throughout the enemy offensive. The platoon had become so closely identified with this bridge that in the 25th Division it was called "Vickery's Bridge." Vickery had placed one squad on the north side of the bridge. From the south side it was supported by the rest of the platoon, a tank, and one 105-mm. howitzer, fondly called "Peg O' My Heart."

Some of the local commanders thought that had the North Koreans bypassed this bridge and crossed the Naktong farther east there would have been nothing between them and Pusan. However, North Korean attacks against Vickery's men were a nightly occurrence. The approaches to the bridge on the north side were mined. At one time there were about 100 North Korean dead lying in that area. One morning a pack of dogs were tearing the bodies when one of the animals set off a mine. That scattered the pack and the dogs in their wild flight set off more mines. Pieces of dog went flying through the air like rocks.[57]

Counterattack at Haman

In the middle of the 25th Division line, south of the 35th Infantry, the enemy breakthrough at Haman became a terrifying fact to the division headquarters after daylight, 1 September. General Kean, commanding the division, telephoned Eighth Army headquarters and requested permission to commit, at once, the entire 27th Infantry Regiment, just arrived at Masan the previous evening and still held in Eighth Army reserve. General Walker denied this request, but did release one battalion of the regiment to General Kean's control.[58]

General Kean immediately dispatched Colonel Check's 1st Battalion, 27th Infantry—which had been alerted as early as 0200—from its assembly area near Masan toward Haman, to be attached to the 24th Infantry upon arrival at Colonel Champney's command post. The 1st Platoon of the 27th Regiment's Heavy Mortar Company; a platoon of B Company, 89th Tank Battalion; and A Battery, 8th Field Artillery Battalion, reinforced Check's battalion. Check with his battalion arrived at Champney's 24th Infantry command post two miles east of Haman at 1000.[59]

The scene there was chaotic. Vehicles of all descriptions, loaded with soldiers, were moving down the road to the rear. Many soldiers on foot were on the road. Colonel Champney tried repeatedly but in vain to get these men to halt. The few enemy mortar shells falling occasionally in the vicinity did no damage except to cause the troops of the 24th Infantry and intermingled South Koreans to scatter and increase their speed to the rear. The road was so clogged with this frightened, demoralized human traffic that Colonel Check had to delay his counterattack. In the six hours he waited at this point, Check observed that none of the retreating troops of the 1st and 2d Battalions, 24th Infantry, could be assem-

---

[57] 35th Inf WD, S-2 and S-3 Jnls, item 15, 9 Sep 50; 35th Inf Unit Hist, Sep 50; EUSAK WD, G-3 Jnl, 1015, 10 Sep 50; Fisher, MS review comments, 7 Nov 57, and Jan 58.

[58] Ltr, Kean to author, 22 Apr 53; Barth MS, p. 27.

[59] 27th Inf WD, 1 Sep 50; Interv, author with Check, 6 Feb 53.

bled as units. Sgt. Jack W. Riley of the 25th Military Police Company tried to help clear the road. Men ran off the mountain past him, some with shoes off, half of them without weapons, and only a few wearing helmets. He shouted for all officers and noncommissioned officers to stop. None stopped. One man who appeared to have some rank told him, "Get out of the way." Riley pulled back the bolt of his carbine and stopped the man at gun point, and then discovered that he was a first sergeant. Asked why they would not stay in and fight, several in the group that Riley succeeded in halting simply laughed at him and answered, "We didn't see any MP's on the hill." At 1600, the 2d Battalion, 24th Infantry, assembling in the rear of the 27th Infantry, could muster only 150 to 200 men.[60]

At 1445, General Kean's orders for an immediate counterattack to restore the 24th Infantry positions arrived at Champney's command post. Check quickly completed his attack plan. For half an hour the Air Force bombed, napalmed, rocketed, and strafed Haman and adjacent enemy-held ridges. Fifteen minutes of concentrated artillery barrages followed. Haman was a sea of flames. Check's infantry moved out in attack westward at 1630, now further reinforced by a platoon of tanks from A Company, 79th Tank Battalion. Eight tanks, mounting infantry, spearheaded the attack into Haman. North Koreans in force held the ridge on the west side of the town, and their machine gun fire swept every approach—their "green tracers seemed as thick as the rice in the paddies." Enemy fire destroyed one tank and the attacking infantry suffered heavy casualties. But Check's battalion pressed the attack and by 1825 had seized the first long ridge 500 yards west of Haman; by 2000 it had secured half of the old battle position on the higher ridge beyond, its objective, one mile west of Haman. Two hundred yards short of the crest on the remainder of the ridge, the infantry dug in for the night.[61]

All day air strikes had harassed the enemy and prevented him from consolidating his gains and reorganizing for further co-ordinated attack. Some of the planes came from the carriers *Valley Forge* and *Philippine Sea*, 200 miles away and steaming toward the battlefield at twenty-seven knots. The crisis for the 25th Division was not lessened by Eighth Army's telephone message at 1045 that the 27th Infantry was to be alerted for a possible move north into the 2d Division sector.

West of Haman the North Koreans and Check's men faced each other during the night without further battle, but the North Koreans, strangely for them, kept flares over their position. In the rear areas, enemy mortar fire on the 24th Regiment command post caused Colonel Champney to move it still farther to the rear.

In the morning, under cover of a heavy ground fog, the North Koreans struck Check's battalion in a counterattack. This action began a hard fight which lasted all morning. Air strikes using na-

---

[60] 2d Bn, 24th Inf WD, 1 Sep 50; EUSAK IG Rpt, 24th Inf, Sep 50, testimony of Check, Riley, and Roberts.

[61] 1st Bn, 27th Inf WD, 1 Sep 50; A Co, 79th Hv Tk Bn WD, Sep 50; 24th Inf WD, 1 Sep 50; 25th Div WD, 1 Sep 50; EUSAK IG Rpt, Check testimony; *Newsweek*, September 11, 1950, pp. 18–20.

COMMAND POST *of the 27th Infantry under a bridge east of Haman.*

palm burned to death many North Koreans and helped the infantry in gaining the ridge. At noon, the 1st Battalion, 27th Infantry, at last secured the former positions of the 2d Battalion, 24th Infantry, and took over the same foxholes that unit had abandoned two nights before. Its crew-served weapons were still in place. During 2 September, the Air Force flew 135 sorties in the 25th Division sector, reportedly destroying many enemy soldiers, several tanks and artillery pieces, and three villages containing ammunition dumps.[62]

Early the next morning, 3 September, the North Koreans heavily attacked Check's men in an effort to regain the ridge. Artillery, mortar, and tank fire barrages, and a perfectly timed air strike directed from the battalion command post, met this attack. Part of the battalion had to face about and fight toward its rear. After the attack had been repulsed hundreds of enemy dead lay about the battalion position. A prisoner estimated that during 2-3 September the four North Korean battalions fighting Check's battalion had lost 1,000 men.[63]

Colonel Check's battalion held the ridge until dark on 4 September, then

---

[62] 1st Bn, 27th Inf WD, 2 Sep 50; 24th Inf WD, 2 Sep 50; 25th Div WD, 2 Sep 50; EUSAK IG Rpt, testimony of Check and Capt Don K. Hickman, Ex Off, 1st Bn, 27th Inf; New York *Herald Tribune*, September 2, 1950, Bigart dispatch.

[63] 1st Bn, 27th Inf WD, Sep 50 Opn Rpt, 3 Sep 50; 27th Inf WD, 3 Sep 50, and Rpt of captured documents; Barth MS, p. 27.

the 1st Battalion and F Company of the 2d Battalion, 24th Infantry, which had reorganized in the rear, relieved it. The 1st Battalion, 27th Infantry, thereupon moved back into a secondary defensive position a mile and a half east of Haman. Colonel Champney moved his command post back into Haman, placing it at the base of a hill 300 yards west of the center of the town.[64]

That night there was a repetition of the earlier disgraceful episode. Before dawn, 5 September, an enemy force of two companies, only half-armed, moved against Haman. A part of this force approached the hill at the western edge of Haman where H Company was posted as security for the 24th Regimental command post situated at its base. The H Company men left their post without firing a shot, abandoning two new machine guns. Men in the regimental command post had their first intimation that enemy troops were in the vicinity when the North Koreans opened fire on them with the captured machine guns. A small group of North Koreans infiltrated into Haman within 100 yards of the command post, where members of the I&R Platoon drove them off in a grenade battle. In the course of this action, an enemy grenade blew up an ammunition truck. The exploding shells and resulting fires gave the impression from a distance that a heavy fight was in progress.

About twenty enemy soldiers approached, undiscovered, close enough to the 1st Battalion, 24th Infantry, command post west of Haman to throw grenades and fire burp guns into it. Perhaps 45 soldiers of the battalion command group and 20 South Korean recruits were in position there at the time. The enemy was driven off at dawn, but Maj. Eugene J. Carson, battalion executive officer, then discovered that he had on position with him only 30 men, 7 of them wounded. Looking back down the hill, Carson saw approximately 40 men get up out of the rice paddies and go over to a tank at a roadblock position. These men reported to the regiment that they had been driven off the hill. Three tanks near the command post helped clear the town of North Koreans.[65]

At the time of this enemy infiltration, a white officer and from 35 to 40 Negro soldiers left their position south of Haman at a roadblock and fled to the rear until they reached Colonel Check's 1st Battalion, 27th Infantry, command post a mile and a half away. There, at 0500 this officer said 2,000 North Koreans had overrun his position and others near Haman, including the 24th Regiment command post. Check reported this story to General Kean, and then sent a platoon of tanks with a platoon of infantry toward Haman to find out what had happened. Some of his officers, meanwhile, had stopped about 220 soldiers streaming to the rear. Colonel Check ordered these men to follow his tank and infantry patrol back into Haman. Some of them did so only when threatened with a gun. The tank-led column entered Haman unopposed, where they found

---

[64] 27th Inf WD, 4 Sep 50; 24th Inf WD, 4 Sep 50; Interv, author with Champney, 22 Jul 51; Corley, MS review comments for author, 22 Jul 53.

[65] Interv, author with Champney, 22 Jul 51; EUSAK WD, 14 Sep 50, Interrog Rpt, Yun Che Gun; 24th Inf WD, 4–5 Sep 50; EUSAK IG Rpt, testimony of Champney, Roberts, and Carson.

the 24th Regiment command post intact and everything quiet.⁶⁶

The next day, 6 September, a sniper severely wounded Colonel Champney while the latter was inspecting his front-line positions west of Haman. Champney was evacuated at once. Colonel Corley, commanding officer of the 3d Battalion, succeeded to the command of the regiment.⁶⁷ Corley, known as "Cash Pays the Rent" because that was a favorite saying of his, became a highly regarded commander of the "Deuce-Four" Regiment. He was destined to fight in four campaigns of the Korean War, winning a Distinguished Service Cross, three Silver Stars, and the Legion of Merit to add to the decorations he had already won as a much-decorated battalion commander of World War II. This 36-year-old energetic West Point combat leader was soon well-known throughout the regiment.

Battle Mountain and Sobuk-san

Although the enemy *6th* and *7th Divisions* had massed their troops for the attempted breakthrough of the U.S. 25th Division positions along the Nam and Naktong Rivers as already related, the *6th Division* did not altogether ignore the mountain backbone stretching southward toward the coast. Enemy artillery and mortar fire fell on Battle Mountain, P'il-bong, and Sobuk-san during the period of the enemy offensive and there were strong local attacks and patrol actions. The 1st Battalion, 5th Infantry, never succeeded in gaining possession of the highest peak of Sobuk-san, which would have given observation into the valley below and into the enemy's rear areas. The instability of the 24th Infantry at this time made it necessary for General Kean to order Colonel Throckmorton to send his only regimental reserve, E Company, north into the 24th Infantry sector along the Haman road to protect the right flank of the 5th Regimental Combat Team. In this position, Capt. William Conger, E Company commander, collected stragglers from the 24th Infantry every night and the next morning sent them back to their units. Even the Navy entered the battle in this part of the line, for its destroyers standing off the south coast gave illumination at night by directing their searchlights against low-hanging clouds on Sobuk-san. One destroyer was on station almost continuously, supporting the ground action with the fire of six 5-inch guns. An artillery aerial observer directed this naval gunfire through the fire direction center.⁶⁸

On 7 September, a North Korean attack succeeded once again in driving ROK and American troops from Battle Mountain. The 25th Division ordered Colonel DeChow to retake the peak. DeChow, who had just counterattacked through the rear areas of the 24th Infantry to the vicinity of Haman, prepared his 3d Battalion, 27th Infantry, for the attempt. Companies K and B of the 24th Infantry were to follow him and secure the crest if he regained it. For three days,

---

⁶⁶ EUSAK IG Rpt, testimony of Check, Hickman, and Capt James D. Hunsaker, S–3, 1st Bn, 27th Inf.

⁶⁷ 24th Inf WD, 6 Sep 50; 25th Inf WD, 6 Sep 50; Interv, author with Champney, 22 Jul 51.

⁶⁸ 25th Div WD, 9 Sep 50; EUSAK WD, 5 Oct 50; Arty Sec, Arty Info Bul 8, 3 Oct 50; Throckmorton, Notes for author, 17 Apr 53.

7, 8, and 9 September, the 3d Battalion counterattacked up Battle Mountain. On the 9th, Capt. William Mitchell led his I Company to the top and engaged in hand-to-hand combat with the North Koreans. L Company followed to the crest but the dug-in enemy drove both companies off and back down the slope. An estimated two companies of enemy troops held the crest of Battle Mountain and two more companies protected their flanks. DeChow's 3d Battalion suffered heavy casualties in these three days of fighting. On the afternoon of the 9th the American counterattack force dropped back to the high ground which it had recaptured on the 7th, 1,000 yards east of Battle Mountain. Artillery, mortars, and air strikes pounded the enemy position on Battle Mountain. During this impasse, word came from the 25th Division for the battalion to move to the vicinity of Masan.[69]

With the failure of the 3d Battalion, 27th Infantry, to hold the high knob on Battle Mountain after its attacks on 8–9 September, Colonel Corley, the 24th Infantry commander, on the evening of the 9th decided to give up the attempt. He had K Company, 24th Infantry, and C Company, 65th Engineer Combat Battalion, dig in on the hill east of and lower than Battle Mountain, surrounded them with barbed wire and mine fields, and placed registered artillery and mortar fires on all enemy approaches to the position. He planned to contain the enemy on Battle Mountain by artillery and mortar fire. The North Koreans on Battle Mountain attacked the lower American defensive position many times on subsequent nights, but all their attacks were driven off. Thus, finally, after a month of almost constant battle the North Koreans gained and held possession of the crest of Battle Mountain. The defensive fires of the 24th Regiment and attached artillery, however, contained them there and they were unable to exploit the possession of this battle-torn peak.[70]

With Battle Mountain in their possession, the North Koreans set out to gain control of P'il-bong, a towering peak 250 feet higher than Battle Mountain and an air mile to the southeast. In the predawn hours of 14 September an enemy force of 400–500 men attacked I and L Companies, 24th Infantry, on P'il-bong. Several attacks were repulsed, but because of men leaving their positions L Company's strength dwindled from 100 to 40 men. Only the determined leadership of Maj. Melvin R. Blair, a replacement officer who had just assumed command of the battalion, held these men in the fight. With the remnant of L Company, Blair withdrew toward I Company's position on the crest of P'il-bong, only to find that this company under a relatively minor attack had, unknown to him, left the hill. A wounded North Korean sniper, hidden along the trail, shot Blair in the leg. Blair refused to be evacuated, but he could not hold P'il-bong with the handful of men remaining with him and it was lost.[71]

Just as soon as the crisis passed for the 25th Division, General Walker

---

[69] 25th Div WD, 8–9 Sep 50; 24th Inf WD, 9 Sep 50; EUSAK WD, G–3 Jnl, 1245, 9 Sep 50; DeChow, MS review comments, Jul 53.

[70] Interv, author with Corley, 6 Nov 51; 24th Inf WD, 9 Sep 50.

[71] Interv, author with Corley, 6 Nov 51; 3d Bn, 24th Inf WD, 14 Sep 50; EUSAK IG Rpt, testimony of Corley.

ordered it on 7 September to release the 5th Regimental Combat Team within twenty-four hours. The continuing crisis north of Taegu made it mandatory for Walker to build up his reserve there. That evening the 1st and 2d Battalions, 27th Infantry, moved from the Nam River battlefield to relieve the 5th Regimental Combat Team on the Masan front. Colonel Michaelis assumed command of the regimental zone at 1500, 9 September. The 3d Battalion, 27th Infantry, broke off its counterattacks on Battle Mountain that day, rejoined the regiment, and took its place in the southern end of the line on 11 September. Meanwhile, the 5th Regimental Combat Team began moving to Samnangjin on the 10th, the last train with its units clearing Masan at 1600 the next day. Upon arrival at Samnangjin, it passed to Eighth Army reserve.[72]

About the time the all-out North Korean assault on the Pusan Perimeter had been turned back and the 27th Infantry was relieving the 5th Regimental Combat Team in the line west of Masan, the "beer issue" came to a head and evoked strong reactions from the men who were fighting the Korean battles. Free beer had been provided U.S. soldiers on much the same basis as candy bars and cigarettes. It had been purchased with appropriated money and issued at intervals as supplementary to the food ration. Various temperance, church, and social groups, and some individuals in the United States protested the issue of beer to the soldiers. The controversy even reached the floor of Congress, with one Congressman who favored the free beer ration saying, "Water in Korea is deadlier than bullets." The pressure was sufficient to cause the Army through the Far East Command to order that 12 September would be the last day free beer could be issued to the troops. A typical infantryman's comment was, "Those organizations or whatever they are have nothing to do with us. We are doing the fighting over here and it gets pretty bad. One can of beer never hurt nobody." But henceforth, Eighth Army troops could obtain beer purchased only with nonappropriated funds and issued through the post exchanges.[73]

The defensive battles on the Masan front during August and early September brought to a head a problem that had bothered General Kean ever since the 25th Division entered the Korean War; in a larger sense, it was a problem that had concerned Eighth Army as well. Two of the division's regiments, the 27th and the 35th, had performed well in Korea. Not so the 24th Infantry, the division's third regiment. Ever since its entrance into combat in the Sangju area in July the Negro regiment had given a poor performance, although there were some exceptions and many individual acts of heroism and capable performance of duty. The unstable nature of the regiment was demonstrated in the fighting on Battle Mountain during August. Then, on the night of 31 August–1 September two battalions evaporated in the face of the enemy, and a large part of them repeated this performance four nights later. General Kean placed his

---

[72] EUSAK WD, G-3 Sec, 8-9 Sep 50; 27th Inf WD, 7-9 Sep 50; *Ibid.*, Unit Rpt, Sep 50.

[73] See 25th Div WD, 11 Sep 50; New York *Times*, September 14, and October 16, 1950; New York *Herald Tribune*, September 13, 1950.

VETERAN OF THE 5TH REGIMENTAL COMBAT TEAM *after forty-three days on the front line.*

two stronger regiments usually in the more critical terrain of the division front, but, nevertheless, the 24th Regiment constituted a weak link in the division line that might break at any time and bring disaster to the division and possibly to the army. Eighth Army and the 25th Division assigned officers of an unusually high caliber to the 24th Infantry to give it strong leadership, but this did not solve the problem.

After the enemy breakthrough in the 24th Infantry sector on 1-5 September, General Kean decided he had to seek a solution. On 9 September he recommended to General Walker the immediate removal of the 24th Infantry Regiment from combat, and that the troops of the regiment be transferred as replacements on a percentage basis to other U.S. Army units in Korea. In making these recommendations General Kean said in part, "It is my considered opinion that the 24th Infantry has demonstrated in combat that it is untrustworthy and incapable of carrying out missions expected of an infantry regiment." Nearly all officers serving in the regiment agreed with General Kean, and so did many of the Negro noncommissioned officers and enlisted men themselves. General Walker did not act on General Kean's recommendation since many considerations seemed to make such action impossible at the time.[74]

Coinciding with this heavy fighting at the Pusan Perimeter in the south a new and disturbing element appeared far to the north. In Tokyo and Washington, American military leaders studied reports they received indicating that Chinese Communist troops were moving north through China and concentrating along the Yalu River opposite Korea. An incident at this time added to the build-up of threatening storm clouds to the north. On 4 September, a twin-engine bomber wearing a red star passed over a screening ship of a U.N. naval task force operating in the Yellow Sea off the west coast of Korea, approximately at the 38th Parallel. The bomber continued on toward the center of the naval formation and opened fire on a U.N. fighter plane patrol which re-

---

[74] Ltr, Kean to CG, Eighth Army, 9 Sep 50, in EUSAK IG Rpt. The 24th Regiment continued to serve in Eighth Army as an all-Negro unit for another year. Its troops were then transferred as replacements to other infantry units of the army, integrated usually in a proportion of about 12 percent.

turned its fire and shot it down. A destroyer of the task force recovered the body of one of the bomber crew members—he was an officer of the Armed Forces of the Soviet Union.[75]

At mid-September the Eighth Army and the ROK Army were still engaged with North Korean forces at nearly all points of the Pusan Perimeter. After two weeks of the heaviest fighting of the war they had just barely turned back the great North Korean offensive on the main axes of the attack: in the east around P'ohang-dong and the Kyongju corridor, in the center at the approaches to Taegu, and in the south around Yongsan and the approaches to Masan. The battles of the Perimeter would go on, that was certain, for the issue there had not been concluded.

But overriding all other factors, favorable and unfavorable, comforting or disquieting, bearing on the Korean War at mid-September was the knowledge—now become widespread among U.N. forces in Korea—that an amphibious landing behind the enemy's lines was imminent. The date set for it was 15 September.

---

[75] New York *Times*, September 5, 1950, gives the State Department note announcing this incident. The *Times* of 7 September gives a summary of the Russian version, and the claim for damages for the bomber and three Russian crewman, which U.S. Ambassador Alan G. Kirk refused to accept.

On 31 August, Ambassador Warren Austin told the U.N. Security Council that a U.S. F-51 fighter plane on 27 August may have strafed the An-tung Airfield in Manchuria, five miles from the Korean border, and thereby have unintentionally violated the territory of Communist China.

CHAPTER XXV

The Landing at Inch'on

> The history of war proves that nine out of ten times an army has been destroyed because its supply lines have been cut off. . . . We shall land at Inch'on, and I shall crush them [the North Koreans].
>
> Douglas MacArthur

It was natural and predictable that General MacArthur should think in terms of an amphibious landing in the rear of the enemy to win the Korean War. His campaigns in the Southwest Pacific in World War II—after Bataan —all began as amphibious operations. From Australia to Luzon his forces often advanced around enemy-held islands, one after another. Control of the seas gives mobility to military power. Mobility and war of maneuver have always brought the greatest prizes and the quickest decisions to their practitioners. A water-borne sweep around the enemy's flank and an attack in his rear against lines of supply and communications appealed to MacArthur's sense of grand tactics. He never wavered from this concept, although repeatedly the fortunes of war compelled him to postpone its execution.

MacArthur's Early Plans

During the first week of July, with the Korean War little more than a week old, General MacArthur told his chief of staff, General Almond, to begin considering plans for an amphibious operation designed to strike the enemy center of communications at Seoul, and to study the location for a landing to accomplish this. At a Far East Command headquarters meeting on 4 July, attended by Army, Navy, and Air Force representatives, Generals MacArthur and Almond discussed the idea of an amphibious landing in the enemy's rear and proposed that the 1st Cavalry Division be used for that purpose. Col. Edward H. Forney of the Marine Corps, an expert on amphibious operations, was selected to work with the 1st Cavalry Division on plans for the operation.[1]

The early plan for the amphibious operation received the code name BLUEHEARTS and called for driving the North Koreans back across the 38th Parallel. The approximate date proposed for it

---

[1] Interv, author with Almond, 13 Dec 51; MS review comments, Almond for author, 23 Oct 53; Hq X Corps, Opn CHROMITE, G-3 Sec, 15 Aug-30 Sep 50, p. 1; Lynn Montross and Capt. Nicholas A. Canzona, USMC, *U.S. Marine Operations in Korea, 1950-1953*, vol. II, *The Inchon-Seoul Operation* (Washington: Historical Branch, G-3, Headquarters, U.S. Marine Corps, 1954), pp. 4-7.

was 22 July, but the operation was abandoned by 10 July because of the inability of the U.S. and ROK forces in Korea to halt the southward drive of the enemy.[2]

Meanwhile the planning for an amphibious operation went ahead in the Far East Command despite the cancellation of BLUEHEARTS. These plans were undertaken by the Joint Strategic Plans and Operations Group (JSPOG), Far East Command, which General Wright headed in addition to his duties as Assistant Chief of Staff, G–3. One of Wright's deputies, Col. Donald H. Galloway, was directly in charge of JSPOG. This unusually able group of planners developed various plans in considerable detail for amphibious operations in Korea.

On 23 July, General Wright upon MacArthur's instructions circulated to the GHQ staff sections the outline of Operation CHROMITE. CHROMITE called for an amphibious operation in September and postulated three plans: (1) Plan 100-B, landing at Inch'on on the west coast; (2) Plan 100-C, landing at Kunsan on the west coast; (3) Plan 100-D, landing near Chumunjin-up on the east coast. Plan 100-B, calling for a landing at Inch'on with a simultaneous attack by Eighth Army, was favored.[3]

This same day, 23 July, General MacArthur informed the Department of the Army that he had scheduled for mid-September an amphibious landing of the 5th Marines and the 2d Infantry Division behind the enemy's lines in co-ordination with an attack by Eighth Army.[4]

The North Korean successes upset MacArthur's plans as fast as he made them. He admitted this to the Joint Chiefs in a message on 29 July, saying, "In Korea the hopes that I had entertained to hold out the 1st Marine Division [Brigade] and the 2d Infantry Division for the enveloping counter blow have not been fulfilled and it will be necessary to commit these units to Korea on the south line rather than . . . their subsequent commitment along a separate axis in mid-September. . . . I now plan to commit my sole reserve in Japan, the 7th Infantry Division, as soon as it can be brought to an approximate combat strength." [5]

X Corps Troops Assembled

By 20 July General MacArthur had settled rather definitely on the concept of the Inch'on operation and he spoke of the matter at some length with General Almond and with General Wright, his operations officer. On 12 August, MacArthur issued CINCFE Operation Plan 100-B and specifically named the Inch'on-Seoul area as the target that a special invasion force would seize by amphibious assault.[6]

On 15 August General MacArthur es-

---

[2] Schnabel, FEC, GHQ Support and Participation in the Korean War, ch. V, pp. 1–18.

[3] *Ibid.*, ch. 5, pp. 12–13; Interv with Wright, 7 Jan 54. The landing at Kunsan called for a drive inland to Taejon; that at Chumunjin-up included a ROK division and called for an advance down the coastal road to Kangnung and then west to Wonju.

[4] GHQ FEC, Ann Narr Hist Rpt, Jan–Oct 50, p. 11.

[5] Schnabel, FEC, GHQ Support and Participation in the Korean War, ch. V, p. 25, quoting Rad C58993, CINCFE to JCS, 29 Jul 50.

[6] Diary of CG X Corps, Opn CHROMITE; Interv, author with Wright, 7 Jan 54; Interv, author with Maj Gen Clark L. Ruffner, 27 Aug 51.

tablished the headquarters group of the Special Planning Staff to take charge of the projected amphibious operation. For purposes of secrecy the new group, selected from the GHQ FEC staff, was designated, Special Planning Staff, GHQ, and the forces to be placed under its control, GHQ Reserve. On 21 August, MacArthur requested the Department of the Army by radio for authority to activate Headquarters, X Corps, and, upon receiving approval, he issued GHQ FEC General Order 24 on 26 August activating the corps. All units in Japan or en route there that had been designated GHQ Reserve were assigned to it.[7]

It appears that General MacArthur about the middle of August had made up his mind on the person he would select to command the invasion force. One day as he was talking with General Almond about the forthcoming landing, the latter suggested that it was time to appoint a commander for it. MacArthur turned to him and replied, "It is you." MacArthur told Almond that he was also to retain his position as Chief of Staff, Far East Command. His view was that Almond would command X Corps for the Inch'on invasion and the capture of Seoul, that the war would end soon thereafter, and Almond would then return to his old position in Tokyo. In effect, the Far East Command would lend Almond and most of the key staff members of the corps for the landing operation. General Almond has stated that MacArthur's decision to place him in command of X Corps surprised him, as he had expected to remain in Tokyo in his capacity as Chief of Staff, FEC. General MacArthur officially assigned General Almond to command X Corps on 26 August.[8]

General Almond, fifty-eight years old when he assumed command of X Corps, was a graduate of Virginia Military Institute. In World War I he had commanded a machine gun battalion and had been wounded and decorated for bravery. In World War II he had commanded the 92d Infantry Division in Italy. Almond went to the Far East Command in June 1946, and served as deputy chief of staff to MacArthur from November 1946 to February 1949. On 18 February 1949 he became Chief of Staff, Far East Command, and, on 24 July 1950, Chief of Staff, United Nations Command, as well.

General Almond was a man both feared and obeyed throughout the Far East Command. Possessed of a driving energy and a consuming impatience with incompetence, he expected from others the same degree of devotion to duty and hard work that he exacted from himself. No one who ever saw him would be likely to forget the lightning that flashed from his blue eyes. To his commander, General MacArthur, he was wholly loyal. He never hesitated before difficulties. Topped by iron-gray hair, Almond's alert, mobile face with its ruddy complexion made him an arresting figure despite his medium stature and the slight stoop of his shoulders.

The corps' chief of staff was Maj. Gen. Clark L. Ruffner, who had arrived from the United States on 6 August and had

---

[7] Schnabel, Theater Command, ch. VIII. This volume will treat in detail the planning of the Inch'on landing and the policy debate on it. Hq X Corps, Opn CHROMITE.

[8] Interv, author with Almond, 13 Dec 51; Hq X Corps, Opn CHROMITE; Almond biographical sketch.

THE LANDING AT INCH'ON

started working with the planning group two days later. He was an energetic and diplomatic officer with long experience and a distinguished record in staff work. During World War II he had been Chief of Staff, U.S. Army Forces, Pacific Ocean Areas, in Hawaii. The X Corps staff was an able one, many of its members hand-picked from among the Far East Command staff.

The major ground units of X Corps were the 1st Marine Division and the 7th Infantry Division. In the summer of 1950 it was no easy matter for the United States to assemble in the Far East a Marine division at full strength. On 25 July, Maj. Gen. Oliver P. Smith assumed command and on that day the Commandant of the Marine Corps issued an order to him to bring the division to war strength, less one regiment, and to sail for the Far East between 10 and 15 August. This meant the activation of another regiment, the 1st Marines, and the assembly, organization, and equipment of approximately 15,000 officers and enlisted men within the next two weeks. On 10 August, the Joint Chiefs of Staff decided to add the third regiment to the division, and the 7th Marines was activated. It was scheduled to sail for the Far East by 1 September. The difficulty of obtaining troops to fill the division was so great that a battalion of marines on duty with the Sixth Fleet in the Mediterranean was ordered to join the division in the Far East.[9]

General Smith and most of the staff officers of the 1st Marine Division arrived in Japan from the United States on 22 August. The division troops, the 1st Marines, and the staff of the 7th Marines arrived in Japan between 28 August and 6 September. A battalion of marines in two vessels, the *Bexar* and the *Montague*, departed Suda Bay, Crete, in the Mediterranean on 16 August, and sailing by way of Suez arrived at Pusan on 9 September to join the 7th Marines as its 3d Battalion. The remainder of the 7th Marines arrived at Kobe on 17 September. The 5th Marines, in Korea, received a warning order on 30 August to prepare for movement to Pusan to join the division.[10]

Bringing the 7th Infantry Division up to war strength posed an even more difficult problem. During July, FEC had taken 140 officers and 1,500 noncommissioned officers and enlisted men from the division to augment the strength of the 24th and 25th Infantry and the 1st Cavalry Divisions as they in turn had mounted out for Korea. At the end of July the division was at less than half-strength, but in noncommissioned officer weapons leaders and critical specialists the shortage was far greater than that proportion. On 27 July, the 7th Infantry Division was 9,117 men understrength—290 officers, 126 warrant officers, and 8,701 enlisted men. The day before, FEC had relieved it of all occupation duties and ordered it to prepare for movement to Korea.[11]

---

[9] 1st Mar Div SAR, Sep 50; Lt Gen Oliver P. Smith, MS review comments with ltr to Maj Gen Albert C. Smith, Chief Mil Hist, 25 Feb 54; Karig, et al., *Battle Report, The War in Korea*, pp. 123, 172.

[10] 1st Mar Div SAR, vol. III, pp. 1–2; Smith, MS review comments.
[11] EUSAK WD, 31 Jul 50, Memo for CofS, Strategic Status of 7th Inf Div; Schnabel, FEC, GHQ Support and Participation in the Korean War, ch. V, p. 5, citing Ltr, CINCFE to CG Eighth Army, 4 Aug 50; Maj Gen David G. Barr (CG 7th Inf Div), Notes, 1, 6, 31 Jul 50 (copies furnished author by Barr).

From 23 August to 3 September the Far East Command allotted to the 7th Division the entire infantry replacement stream reaching FEC, and from 23 August through 8 September the entire artillery replacement stream. By 4 September the division had received 390 officers and 5,400 enlisted replacements. General MacArthur obtained service units for the X Corps in the same way —by diverting them from scheduled assignments for Eighth Army. The Far East Command justified this on the ground that, while Eighth Army needed them badly, X Corps' need was imperative.[12]

In response to General MacArthur's instructions to General Walker on 11 and 13 August to send South Koreans to augment the 7th Infantry Division, 8,637 of them arrived in Japan before the division embarked for Inch'on. Their clothing on arrival ranged from business suits to shirts and shorts, or shorts only. The majority wore sandals or cloth shoes. They were civilians—stunned, confused, and exhausted. Only a few could speak English. Approximately 100 of the South Korean recruits were assigned to each rifle company and artillery battery; the buddy system was used for training and control.[13]

The quality of the artillery and infantry crew-served weapons troops received from the United States and assigned to the 7th Division during August and early September was high. The superior training provided by the old infantry and artillery noncommissioned officers who arrived from the Fort Benning Infantry and the Fort Sill Artillery Schools brought the 7th Division to a better condition as the invasion date approached than could have been reasonably expected a month earlier. The 7th Division strength on embarkation, including the attached South Koreans, was 24,845.[14]

The Landing Controversy

All through July and August 1950 the Joint Chiefs of Staff gave implied or expressed approval of MacArthur's proposal for an amphibious landing behind the enemy's battle lines. But while it was known that MacArthur favored Inch'on as the landing site, the Joint Chiefs had never committed themselves to it. From the beginning, there had been some opposition to and many reservations about the Inch'on proposal on the part of General Collins, U.S. Army Chief of Staff; the Navy; and the Marine Corps. The FEC senior planning and staff officers—such as Generals Almond and Hickey, Chief of Staff and Deputy Chief of Staff; General Wright, the G-3 and head of JSPOG; and Brig. Gen. George L. Eberle, the G-4—supported the plan.[15]

The Navy's opposition to the Inch'on site centered largely on the difficult tidal

---

[12] Schnabel, FEC, GHQ Support and Participation in the Korean War, ch. V, pp. 31-32; GHQ FEC, Ann Narr Hist Rpt, 1 Jan-31 Oct 50, p. 45; 7th Div WD, Aug-Sep 50; Barr, Notes, 4 Sep 50.
[13] 7th Inf Div WD, 1 Sep 50; Diary of CG X Corps, Opn CHROMITE, 1 Sep 50; Barr, MS review comments, 1957.

[14] Interv, author with Barr, 1 Feb 54; Barr, Notes, 4 Sep 50.
[15] Interv, author with Wright, 7 Jan 54; Interv, author with Eberle, 12 Jan 54; Ltr, Wright to author, 22 Mar 45; Almond, MS review comments for author, 23 Oct 53; Schabel, FEC, GHQ Support and Participation in the Korean War, ch. V, p. 23; Interv, author with Lutes (FEC Planning Sec), 7 Oct 51.

conditions there, and since this opposition continued, the Joint Chiefs of Staff decided to send two of its members to Tokyo to discuss the matter with MacArthur and his staff. A decision had to be reached. On 20 July General Collins and Admiral Forrest P. Sherman, Chief of Naval Operations, left Washington for their conference with MacArthur. Upon arrival in Japan, Collins and Sherman engaged in private conversations with MacArthur and key members of his staff, including senior naval officers in the Far East. Then, on the afternoon of 23 July, a full briefing on the subject was scheduled in General MacArthur's conference room in the Dai Ichi Building.[16]

The conference began at 1730 in the afternoon. Among those present in addition to General MacArthur were General Collins, Admiral Sherman, Vice Admirals Joy and Struble, Generals Almond, Hickey, and Wright, some members of the latter's JSPOG group, and Rear Adm. James H. Doyle and some members of his staff who were to present the naval problems involved in a landing at Inch'on.

After a short introduction by General MacArthur, General Wright briefed the group on the basic plan. Admiral Doyle then presented the naval considerations. His general tone was pessimistic, and he concluded with the remark, "The operation is not impossible, but I do not recommend it." The naval part of the briefings lasted more than an hour.

During the naval presentation MacArthur, who had heard the main arguments many times before, sat quietly smoking his pipe, asking only an occasional question. When the presentation ended, MacArthur began to speak. He talked as though delivering a soliloquy for forty-five minutes, dwelling in a conversational tone on the reasons why the landing should be made at Inch'on. He said that the enemy had neglected his rear and was dangling on a thin logistical rope that could be quickly cut in the Seoul area, that the enemy had committed practically all his forces against Eighth Army in the south and had no trained reserves and little power of recuperation. MacArthur stressed the strategical, political, and psychological reasons for the landing at Inch'on and the quick capture of Seoul, the capital of South Korea. He said it would hold the imagination of Asia and win support for the United Nations. Inch'on, he said, pointing to the big map behind him, would be the anvil on which the hammer of Walker's Eighth Army from the south would crush the North Koreans.

General MacArthur then turned to a consideration of a landing at Kunsan, 100 air miles below Inch'on, which General Collins and Admiral Sherman had favored. MacArthur said the idea was good but the location wrong. He did not think a landing there would result in severing the North Korean supply lines and destroying the North Korean Army. He returned to his emphasis on Inch'on, saying that the amphibious landing was tactically the most powerful military device available to the United Nations Command and that to employ it properly meant to strike deep and hard into enemy-held territory. He dwelt on the bitter Korean winter campaign that would become necessary if Inch'on was not undertaken. He said the North

---

[16] Schnabel, Theater Command ch. VIII; New York *Times*, August 19 1950.

Koreans considered a landing at Inch'on impossible because of the very great difficulties involved and, because of this, the landing force would achieve surprise. He touched on his operations in the Pacific in World War II and eulogized the Navy for its part in them. He concluded his long talk by declaring unequivocally for Inch'on and saying, "The Navy has never turned me down yet, and I know it will not now."

MacArthur seems to have convinced most of the doubters present. Admiral Sherman was won over to MacArthur's position. General Collins, however, seemed still to have reservations on Inch'on. He subsequently asked General Wright if the Far East Command had firm plans for a Kunsan landing which could be used as an alternate plan if the Inch'on operation either was not carried out or failed. Wright assured him that there were such plans and, moreover, that it was planned to stage a feint at Kunsan.[17]

Among the alternate proposals to Inch'on, in addition to the Kunsan plan favored by the Navy, was one for a landing in the Posung-myon area thirty miles south of Inch'on and opposite Osan. On the 23d, Admiral Doyle had proposed a landing there with the purpose of striking inland to Osan and there severing the communications south of Seoul. On the 24th, Lt. Gen. Lemuel C. Shepherd, Jr. (USMC), called on General MacArthur and asked him to change the landing site to this area—all to no avail. MacArthur remained resolute on Inch'on.

Upon their return to Washington, Collins and Sherman went over the whole matter of the Inch'on landing with the other members of the Joint Chiefs of Staff. On 28 August the Joint Chiefs sent a message to MacArthur which seemingly concurred in the Inch'on plans yet attached conditions. Their message said in part: "We concur in making preparations for and executing a turning movement by amphibious forces on the west coast of Korea, either at Inch'on in the event the enemy defenses in the vicinity of Inch'on prove ineffective, or at a favorable beach south of Inch'on if one can be located. We further concur in preparations, if desired by CINCFE, for an envelopment by amphibious forces in the vicinity of Kunsan. We understand that alternative plans are being prepared in order to best exploit the situation as it develops."[18]

MacArthur pressed ahead unswervingly toward the Inch'on landing. On 30 August he issued his United Nations Command operation order for it. Meanwhile, the Joint Chiefs in Washington expected to receive from MacArthur further details of the pending operation and, failing to receive them, sent a message to him on 5 September requesting this information. MacArthur replied the next day that his plans remained unchanged. On 7 September, the Joint Chiefs sent another message to MacArthur requesting a reconsideration of

---

[17] The account of the 23 July conference is based on the following sources: Ltr, Wright to author, 22 Mar 54; Ltr, Joy to author, 12 Dec 52; Ltr, Almond to author, 2 Dec 52; Smith, MS review comments; Montross and Canzona, *The Inchon-Seoul Operation*, pp. 40–47; Karig, et al., *Battle Report, the War in Korea*, p. 169. General MacArthur's MS review comments show no comment on this section.

[18] Schnabel, FEC, GHQ Support and Participation in the Korean War, ch. V, p. 6, citing Msg JCS 89960, JCS to CINCFE, 28 Aug 50.

the whole question and an estimate of the chances for favorable outcome. The energy and strength displayed by the North Koreans in their early September massive offensive had evidently raised doubts in the minds of the Joint Chiefs that General Walker's Eighth Army could go over successfully to the attack or that X Corps could quickly overcome the Seoul defenses. In the meantime, General MacArthur on 6 September in a letter to all his major commanders confirmed previous verbal orders and announced 15 September as D-day for the Inch'on landing.[19]

In response to the Joint Chiefs' request for a reconsideration and an estimate of the chances for a favorable landing at Inch'on, General MacArthur on 8 September sent to Washington a final eloquent message on the subject. His message said in part:

There is no question in my mind as to the feasibility of the operation and I regard its chance of success as excellent. I go further and believe that it represents the only hope of wresting the initiative from the enemy and thereby presenting an opportunity for a decisive blow. To do otherwise is to commit us to a war of indefinite duration, of gradual attrition, and of doubtful results. . . . There is no slightest possibility . . . of our force being ejected from the Pusan beachhead. The envelopment from the north will instantly relieve the pressure on the south perimeter and, indeed, is the only way that this can be accomplished. . . . The success of the enveloping movement from the north does not depend upon the rapid juncture of the X Corps and the Eighth Army. The seizure of the heart of the enemy distributing system in the Seoul area will completely dislocate the logistical supply of his forces now operating in South Korea and therefore will ultimately result in their disintegration. This, indeed, is the primary purpose of the movement. Caught between our northern and southern forces, both of which are completely self-sustaining because of our absolute air and naval supremacy, the enemy cannot fail to be ultimately shattered through disruption of his logistical support and our combined combat activities. . . . For the reasons stated, there are no material changes under contemplation in the operation as planned and reported to you. The embarkation of the troops and the preliminary air and naval preparations are proceeding according to schedule.

The next day the Joint Chiefs, referring to this message, replied tersely to MacArthur, "We approve your plan and President has been so informed." [20] It appears that in Secretary of Defense Johnson, MacArthur had in Washington a powerful ally during the Inch'on landing controversy, for Johnson supported the Far East commander.[21] Thus on 8 September Washington time and 9 September Tokyo time the debate on the projected Inch'on landing ended.

A co-ordinate part of MacArthur's Inch'on plan was an attack by the Eighth Army north from its Pusan Per-

---

[19] Schnabel, FEC, GHQ Support and Participation in the Korean War, ch. VIII; Smith MS review comments, 25 Feb 54.

[20] Rad C62423, CINCFE to JCS, 8 Sep 50, and Rad 90958, JCS to CINCFE, 8 Sep 50.

[21] In the course of the MacArthur hearings the next year, Secretary Johnson, in response to an inquiry from Senator Alexander Wiley, said, "I had been carrying along with General MacArthur the responsibility for Inch'on. General Collins—maybe the censor will want to strike this out—did not favor Inch'on and went over to try to argue General MacArthur out of it.

"General MacArthur stood pat. I backed MacArthur, and the President has always, had before backed me on it." See Senate Committees on Armed Services and Foreign Relations, 82d Cong., 1st sess., June, 1951, Hearings on *Military Situation in the Far East and the Relief of General MacArthur*, pt. 4, p. 2618.

imeter beachhead simultaneously with the X Corps landing. This action was intended to tie down all enemy forces committed against Eighth Army and prevent withdrawal from the south of major reinforcements for the North Korean units opposing X Corps in its landing area. The plan called for the Eighth Army to break out of the Perimeter, drive northward, and join forces with X Corps.

On 30 August, General Smith had sent a dispatch to X Corps requesting that the 1st Provisional Marine Brigade in Korea be released from Eighth Army on 1 September to prepare for mounting out for Inch'on. MacArthur ordered that the Marine brigade be available on 4 September for that purpose. But no sooner was this order issued than it was rescinded on 1 September because of the crisis that faced Eighth Army after the great North Korean attack had rolled up the southern front during the night.[22]

Eighth Army's use of the 1st Provisional Marine Brigade in the battle near Yongsan threatened to disrupt the Inch'on landing according to Marine and Navy opinion. A tug of war now ensued between General Smith, supported by the U.S. Naval Forces, Far East, on the one hand and General Walker on the other for control of the 5th Marines. The Marine commander insisted he must have the 5th Marines if he were to make the Inch'on landing. General Walker in a telephone conversation with General Almond said in effect, "If I lose the 5th Marine Regiment I will not be responsible for the safety of the front." Almond sided with Walker despite the fact that he was to be commander of the Inch'on landing force, taking the view that the X Corps could succeed in its plan without the regiment. He suggested that the 32d Infantry Regiment of the 7th Division be attached to the 1st Marine Division as its second assault regiment. General Smith and NAVFE remained adamant. The issue came to a head on 3 September when Admirals Joy, Struble, and Doyle accompanied General Smith to the Dai Ichi Building for a showdown conference with Generals Almond, Ruffner, and Wright.

When it became clear that the group could not reach an agreement, General Almond went into General MacArthur's private office and told MacArthur that things had reached an impasse—that Smith and the Navy would not go in at Inch'on without the 5th Marines. Hearing this, MacArthur told Almond, "Tell Walker he will have to give up the 5th Marine Regiment." Almond returned to the waiting group and told them of MacArthur's decision.[23]

The next day, 4 September, General MacArthur sent General Wright to Taegu to tell General Walker that the 1st Provisional Marine Brigade would have to be released not later than the night of 5–6 September and moved at once to Pusan. At Taegu Wright informed Walker of MacArthur's instructions and told him that the Far East Command was loading the 17th Regiment of the 7th Infantry Division for movement to Pusan, where it would be held in floating reserve and be available

---

[22] Smith, MS review comments, 25 Feb 54.

[23] Interv, author with Almond, 13 Dec 51; Smith, MS review comments, 25 Feb 54; Diary of CG X Corps, Opn CHROMITE, 2 Sep 50; Schnabel, FEC, GHQ Support and Participation in the Korean War, ch. V, pp. 26–27.

for use by Eighth Army if necessary. (It sailed from Yokohama for Korea on 6 September.) He also said that MacArthur intended to divert to Pusan for assignment to Eighth Army the first regiment (65th Infantry) of the 3d Infantry Division arriving in the Far East, the expected date of arrival being 18-20 September. General Walker, in discussing his part in the projected combined operation set for 15 September, requested that the Eighth Army attack be deferred to D plus 1, 16 September. Wright agreed with this timing and said he would recommend it to MacArthur, who subsequently approved it.[24]

Naval Plans

In making ready its part of the operation, the Commander, NAVFE outlined the tasks the Navy would have to perform. These included the following: maintain a naval blockade of the west coast of Korea south of latitude 39° 35' north; conduct pre-D-day naval operations as the situation might require; on D-day seize by amphibious assault, occupy, and defend a beachhead in the Inch'on area; transport, land, and support follow-up and strategic reserve troops, if directed, to the Inch'on area; and provide cover and support as required. Joint Task Force Seven was formed to accomplish these objectives with Admiral Struble, Commander, Seventh Fleet, as the task force commander. On 25 August, Admiral Struble left his flagship, USS *Rochester*, at Sasebo and proceeded by air to Tokyo to direct final planning.[25]

On 3 September, Admiral Struble issued JTF 7 Operational Plan 9-50. Marine aircraft from two escort carriers, naval aircraft from the U.S. carrier *Boxer*, and British aircraft from a light British carrier would provide as much support aircraft as could be concentrated in and over the landing area, and would be controlled from the amphibious force flagship (AGC) *Mt. McKinley*. An arc extending inland thirty miles from the landing site described the task force objective area.[26] In order to carry out its various missions, Joint Task Force Seven organized its subordinate parts as follows:

TF 90   Attack Force, Rear Adm. James H. Doyle, USN
TF 92   X Corps, Maj. Gen. Edward M. Almond, USA
TF 99   Patrol & Reconnaissance Force, Rear Adm. G. R. Henderson, USN
TF 91   Blockade & Covering Force, Rear Adm. W. G. Andrews, R.N.
TF 77   Fast Carrier Force, Rear Adm. E. C. Ewen, USN
TF 79   Logistic Support Force, Capt. B. L. Austin, USN
TF 70.1 Flagship Group, Capt. E. L. Woodyard, USN

For the naval phases, the command post of Admiral Struble was on the *Rochester*; that of Rear Admiral Doyle, second in command, was on the *Mt. McKinley*.

---

[24] GHQ FEC, G-3 Sec, Wright, Memo for Record, 041930K Sep 50, reporting on his discussions with Walker and subsequent report to General Almond; Barr, Notes, 6 Sep 50.

[25] Commander, Joint Task Force Seven and Seventh Fleet, Inch'on Report, September 1950, I-B-1 (hereafter cited as JTF 7, Inch'on Rpt).

[26] JTF 7, Inch'on Rpt, p. 1; Ltr, Wright to author, 22 Mar 54.

More than 230 ships were assigned to the operation. Surface vessels of JTF 7 were not to operate within twelve miles of Soviet or Chinese territory nor aircraft within twenty miles of such territory.[27]

MacArthur had selected Inch'on as the landing site for one paramount reason: it was the port for the capital city of Seoul, eighteen miles inland, and was the closest possible landing area to that city and the hub of communications centering there.

Inch'on is situated on the estuary of the Yom-ha River and possesses a protected, ice-free port with a tidal basin. The shore line there is a low-lying, partially submerged coastal plain subject to very high tides. There are no beaches in the landing area—only wide mud flats at low tide and stone walls at high tide. Because of the mud flats, the landing force would have to use the harbor and wharfage facilities in the port area. The main approach by sea is from the south through two channels 50 miles long and only 6 to 10 fathoms deep (36–60 feet). Flying Fish Channel is the channel ordinarily used by large ships. It is narrow and twisting.

The Inch'on harbor divides into an outer and an inner one, the latter separated from the former by a long breakwater and the islands of Wolmi and Sowolmi which join by a causeway. The greater part of the inner harbor becomes a mud flat at low tide leaving only a narrow dredged channel of about 12–13 feet in depth. The only dock facilities for deep draft vessels were in the tidal basin, which was 1,700 feet long, 750 feet wide, and had an average depth of 40 feet, but at mean low tide held only 14 feet of water.[28]

Inch'on promised to be a unique amphibious operation—certainly one very difficult to conduct because of natural conditions. Tides in the restricted waters of the channel and the harbor have a maximum range of more than 31 feet. A few instances of an extreme 33-foot tide have been reported. Some of the World War II landing craft that were to be used in making the landing required 23 feet of tide to clear the mud flats, and the LST's (Landing Ship, Tank) required 29 feet of tide—a favorable condition that prevailed only once a month over a period of three or four days. The narrow, shallow channel necessitated a daylight approach for the larger ships. Accordingly, it was necessary to schedule the main landings for the late afternoon high tide. A night approach, however, by a battalion-sized attack group was to be made for the purpose of seizing Wolmi-do during the early morning high tide, a necessary preliminary, the planners thought, to the main landing at Inch'on itself.[29]

Low seas at Inch'on are most frequent from May through August, high seas from October through March. Although September is a period of transition, it was considered suitable for landing operations. MacArthur and his planners had selected 15 September for D-day because there would then be a high tide giving maximum water depth over the Inch'on mud flats. Tidal range for 15 September

---

[27] JTF 7, Inch'on Rpt, p. 4, I-D-3, and ans. I and K.

[28] JTF 7, Inch'on Rpt, an. E, p. 6; Mossman and Middleton, Logistical Problems and Their Solutions. The Navy's operation plan underestimated the size of the basin.

[29] JTF 7, Inch'on Rpt. I-C-1 E-6.

THE LANDING AT INCH'ON

reached 31.2 feet at high and minus .5 feet at low water. Only on this day did the tide reach this extreme range. No other date after this would permit landing until 27 September when a high tide would reach 27 feet. On 11–13 October there would be a tide of 30 feet. Morning high tide on 15 September came at 0659, forty-five minutes after sunrise; evening high tide came at 1919, twenty-seven minutes after sunset. The Navy set 23 feet of tide as the critical point needed for landing craft to clear the mud flat and reach the landing sites.[30]

Another consideration was the sea walls that fronted the Inch'on landing sites. Built to turn back unusually high tides, they were 16 feet in height above the mud flats. They presented a scaling problem except at extreme high tide. Since the landing would be made somewhat short of extreme high tide in order to use the last hour or two of daylight, ladders would be needed. Some aluminum scaling ladders were made in Kobe and there were others of wood. Grappling hooks, lines, and cargo nets were readied for use in holding the boats against the sea wall.

The initial objective of the landing force was to gain a beachhead at Inch'on, a city of 250,000 population. The 3d Battalion, 5th Marines, was to land on Wolmi-do on the early morning high tide at 0630, 15 September (D-day, L-hour). With Wolmi-do in friendly hands, the main landing would be made that afternoon at the next high tide, about 1730 (D-day, H-hour), by the 1st and 5th Marines.

Three landing beaches were selected —Green Beach on Wolmi-do for the preliminary early morning battalion landing, and Red Beach in the sea wall dock area of Inch'on and Blue Beach in the mud flat semiopen area at the south edge of the city for the two-regimental-size force that would make the main landing in the evening. Later, 7th Infantry Division troops would land at Inch'on over what was called Yellow Beach.

The 5th Marines, less the 3d Battalion, was to land over Red Beach in the heart of Inch'on, north of the causeway which joined Wolmi-do with Inch'on, and drive rapidly inland 1,000 yards to seize Observatory Hill. On the left of the landing area was Cemetery Hill, 130 feet high, on which three dual-purpose guns reportedly were located. On the right, a group of buildings dominated the landing area. The 5th Marines considered Cemetery and Observatory Hills as the important ground to be secured in its zone.

Simultaneously with the 5th Marines' landing, the 1st Marines was to land over Blue Beach at the base of the Inch'on Peninsula just south of the city. This landing area had such extensive mud flats that heavy equipment could not be brought ashore over it. It lay just below the tidal basin of the inner harbor and an adjacent wide expanse of salt evaporators. Its principal advantage derived from the fact that the railroad and main highway to Seoul from Inch'on lay only a little more than a mile inland from it. A successful landing there could quickly cut these avenues of escape or access at the rear of Inch'on.[31]

---

[30] 1st Mar Div SAR, Inch'on-Seoul, 18 Sep–7 Oct 50, p. 12, and G–3 Sec, an. C.

[31] JTF 7, Inch'on Rpt, B–2 Opn Plan and an. B; 1st Mar Div SAR, vol. III, p. 4, and vol. I, p. 13.

An early objective of the 1st Marine Division after securing the beachhead was Kimpo Airfield, sixteen road miles northeast of Inch'on. Then would follow the crossing of the Han River and the drive on Seoul.

As diversions, the battleship *Missouri* was to shell east coast areas on the opposite side of the Korean peninsula, including the rail center and port of Samch'ok, and a small force was to make a feint at Kunsan on the west coast, 100 air miles south of Inch'on.

Intelligence Estimate

General MacArthur's view at the end of August that the North Koreans had concentrated nearly all their combat resources against Eighth Army in the Pusan Perimeter coincided with the official G-2 estimate. On 28 August the X Corps G-2 Section estimated the enemy strength in Seoul as approximately 5,000 troops, in Inch'on as 1,000, and at Kimpo Airfield as 500, for a total of 6,500 soldiers in the Inch'on-Seoul area. On 4 September the estimate remained about the same except that the enemy force in the Inch'on landing area was placed at 1,800-2,500 troops because of an anticipated build-up there. This estimate remained relatively unchanged four days later, and thereafter held constant until the landing.[32]

American intelligence considered the enemy's ability to reinforce quickly the Inch'on-Seoul area as inconsequential. It held the view that only small rear area garrisons, line of communications units, and newly formed, poorly trained groups were scattered throughout Korea back of the combat zone around the Pusan Perimeter. Aerial reconnaissance reported heavy movement of enemy southbound traffic from the Manchurian border, but it was not clear whether this was of supplies or troops, or both. Although reports showed that the Chinese Communist Forces had increased in strength along the Manchurian border, there was no confirmation of rumors that some of them had moved into North Korea.[33]

The Far East Command considered the possibility that the enemy might reinforce the Inch'on-Seoul area from forces committed against Eighth Army in the south. If this were attempted, it appeared that the North Korean *3d, 13th,* and *10th Divisions,* deployed on either side of the main Seoul-Taejon-Taegu highway, could most rapidly reach the Inch'on area.

North Korean air and naval elements were considered incapable of interfering with the landing. On 28 August the Far East Command estimated there were only nineteen obsolescent Soviet-manufactured aircraft available to the North Korean Air Force. The U.N. air elements, nevertheless, had orders to render unusable any known or suspected enemy air facilities, and particularly to give attention to new construction at Kimpo, Suwon, and Taejon. North Korean naval elements were almost nonexistent at this time. Five divisions of small patrol-type vessels comprised the North Korean Navy; one was on the west coast at Chinnamp'o, the others at Wonsan on the east coast. At both places

---

[32] Hq X Corps, Opn CHROMITE, p. 5; X Corps WD, G-2 Sec, Hist Rpt, 15 Aug-30 Sep 50, p. 1; 1st Mar Div SAR, vol. III, p. 5.

[33] X Corps WD, G-2 Sec, Hist Rpt, 15 Aug-30 Sep 50; JTF 7, Inch'on Rpt, II, E-2.

they were bottled up and rendered impotent. On the morning of 7 September a ROK patrol vessel (PC boat) north of Inch'on discovered and sank a small craft engaged in mine laying; thus it appeared that some mines were to be expected.[34]

As a final means of checking on conditions in Inch'on harbor, the Navy on 31 August sent Lt. Eugene F. Clark to Yonghung-do, an island at the mouth of the ship channel ten sea miles from Inch'on. There, Clark used friendly natives to gather the information needed. He sent them on several trips to Inch'on to measure water depths, check on the mud flats, and to observe enemy strength and fortifications. He transmitted their reports by radio to friendly vessels in Korean waters. Clark was still in the outer harbor when the invasion fleet entered it.[35]

The Ships Load Out

At the end of August the ports of Kobe, Sasebo, and Yokohama in Japan and Pusan in Korea had become centers of intense activity as preparations for mounting the invasion force entered the final stage. The 1st Marine Division, less the 5th Marines, was to outload at Kobe, the 5th Marines at Pusan, and the 7th Infantry Division at Yokohama. Most of the escorting vessels, the Gunfire Support Group, and the command ships assembled at Sasebo.

The ships to carry the troops, equipment, and supplies began arriving at the predesignated loading points during the last days of August. In order to reach Inch'on by morning of 15 September, the LST's had to leave Kobe on 10 September and the transports (AP's) and cargo ships (AK's) on 12 September. Only the assault elements were combat-loaded. Japanese crews manned thirty-seven of the forty-seven LST's in the Marine convoy.[36]

The loading of the 1st Marine Division at Kobe was in full swing on 2 September when word came that the next morning a typhoon would strike the port, where more than fifty vessels were assembled. All unloading and loading stopped for thirty-six hours. At 0600 on 3 September, Typhoon *Jane* screeched in from the east. Wind velocity reached 110 miles an hour at noon. Waves forty feet high crashed against the waterfront and breakers rolled two feet high across the piers where loose cargo lay. Seven American ships broke their lines and one of the giant 200-ton cranes broke loose. Steel lines two and a half inches thick snapped. Only by exhausting and dangerous work did port troops and the marines fight off disaster. By 1530 in the afternoon the typhoon began to blow out to sea. An hour later relative calm descended on the port and the cleanup work began. A few vessels had to go into drydock for repairs, some vehicles were flooded out, and a large quantity of clothing had to be cleaned, dried, and repackaged.[37]

---

[34] JTF 7, Inch'on Rpt, an. E; Schnabel, FEC, GHQ Support and Participation in the Korean War, ch. V, pp. 36–37; Karig, *et al.*, *Battle Report, The War in Korea*, p. 195.

[35] Karig, *et al.*, *Battle Report, The War in Korea*, pp. 176–91, relates the Clark mission in detail.

[36] 1st Mar Div SAR, 15 Sep–7 Oct 50, an. D, p. 4; 7th Inf Div WD, Sep 50.

[37] JTF 7, Inch'on Rpt, I–D–3; 1st Mar Div SAR, 15 Sep–7 Oct 50, an. D, p. 6; SFC William J. K. Griffen, "Typhoon at Kobe," *Marine Corps Gazette* (September, 1951); "Operation Load-up," *The Quartermaster Review* (November–December, 1950), p. 40.

Despite the delay and damage caused by *Jane*, the port of Kobe and the 1st Marine Division met the deadline of outloading by 11 September. On the 10th and the 11th, sixty-six cargo vessels cleared Kobe for Inch'on. They sailed just ahead of another approaching typhoon. This second typhoon had been under observation by long-range reconnaissance planes since 7 September. Named *Kezia*, it was plotted moving from the southwest at a speed that would put it over the Korean Straits on 12-13 September.

On the 11th, the 1st Marine Division sailed from Kobe and the 7th Infantry Division from Yokohama. The next day the 5th Marines departed Pusan to rendezvous at sea. The flagship *Rochester* with Admiral Struble aboard got under way from Sasebo for Inch'on at 1530, 12 September. That afternoon a party of dignitaries, including Generals MacArthur, Almond, Wright, Maj. Gen. Alonzo P. Fox, Maj. Gen. Courtney Whitney, and General Shepherd of the Marine Corps, flew from Tokyo to Itazuke Air Base and proceeded from there by automobile to Sasebo, arriving at 2120. Originally, the MacArthur party had planned to fly from Tokyo on the 13th and embark on the *Mt. McKinley* at Kokura that evening. But Typhoon *Kezia*'s sudden change of direction caused the revision of plans to assure that the party would be embarked in time. The *Mt. McKinley*, sailing from Kobe with Admiral Doyle and General Smith aboard, had not yet arrived at Sasebo when MacArthur's party drove up. It finally pulled in at midnight, and departed for the invasion area half an hour later after taking MacArthur's party aboard.[38]

Part of the invasion fleet encountered very rough seas off the southern tip of Kyushu early on 13 September. Winds reached sixty miles an hour and green water broke over ships' bows. In some cases, equipment shifted in the holds, and in other instances deck-loaded equipment was damaged. During the day the course of *Kezia* shifted to the northeast and by afternoon the seas traversed by the invasion fleet began to calm. The aircraft carrier *Boxer*, steaming at forced speed from the California coast with 110 planes aboard, fought the typhoon all night in approaching Japan. At dusk on the 14th, it quickly departed Sasebo and at full speed cut through the seas for Inch'on.[39]

Preliminary Bombardment

Air attacks intended to isolate the invasion area began on 4 September and continued until the landing. On the 10th, Marine air elements struck Wolmi-do in a series of napalm attacks. Altogether, sixty-five sorties hit Inch'on during the day.[40]

The main task of neutralizing enemy batteries on Wolmi-do guarding the Inch'on inner harbor was the mission of Rear Adm. J. M. Higgins' Gunfire Support Group. This group, composed of 2

---

[38] JTF 7, Inch'on Rpt, II, 1; 1st Mar Div SAR, vol. I, pp. 15-18; Diary of CG X Corps, Opn CHROMITE, 12 Sep 50; Ltr, Wright to author, 22 Mar 54; Barr, Notes, 11 Sep 50.

[39] Diary of CG X Corps, Opn CHROMITE, 13 Sep 50; Karig, *et al.*, *Battle Report, The War in Korea*, p. 197.

[40] GHQ FEC, G-3 Opn Rpt 79, 11 Sep 50; Ernest H. Giusti, "Marine Air Over Inchon-Seoul," *Marine Corps Gazette* (June, 1952), p. 19.

THE LANDING AT INCH'ON

United States heavy cruisers, 2 British light cruisers, and 6 U.S. destroyers, entered the approaches to Inch'on harbor at 1010, 13 September. Just before noon the group in Flying Fish Channel sighted an enemy mine field, exposed at low water. It destroyed some of the mines with automatic fire. At 1220, the 4 cruisers anchored from seven to ten miles offshore, while 5 destroyers—the *Mansfield, DeHaven, Swenson, Collett,* and *Gurke*—proceeded on to anchorages close to Wolmi-do under cover of air strikes by planes from Fast Carrier Task Force 77. The destroyers began the bombardment of Wolmi-do at 1230.[41]

Five enemy heavily revetted 75-mm. guns returned the fire. In the intense ship-shore duel, the *Collett* received nine hits and sustained considerable damage. Enemy shells hit the *Gurke* three times, but caused no serious damage. The *Swenson* took a near miss which caused two casualties: one was Lt. (jg.) David H. Swenson, the only American killed during the bombardment. The destroyers withdrew at 1347.

At 1352 the cruisers, anchored out of range of the Wolmi-do batteries, began an hour and a half bombardment. Planes of Task Force 77 then came in for a heavy strike against the island. After the air strike terminated, the cruisers resumed their bombardment at 1610 for another half hour. Then at 1645 the Gunfire Support Group got under way and withdrew back down the channel.[42]

The next day, D minus 1, the Gunfire Support Group returned. Just before 1100, planes of Task Force 77 again delivered heavy strikes against the island. The heavy cruisers began their second bombardment at 1116, this time also taking under fire targets within Inch'on proper. The destroyers waited about an hour and then moved to their anchorages off Wolmi-do. The cruisers ceased firing while another air strike came in on the island. After it ended, the five destroyers began their bombardment at 1255 and in an hour and fifteen minutes fired 1,732 5-inch shells into Wolmi-do and Inch'on. When they left there was no return fire—the Wolmi-do batteries were silent.[43]

Securing the Inch'on Beachhead

The X Corps expeditionary troops arriving off Inch'on on 15 September numbered nearly 70,000 men.[44] At 0200

---

[41] JTF 7, Inch'on Rpt, I-E-1, Recon in Force; EUSAK WD, 24 Oct 50, G-2 Sec, ADVATIS 1225, Interrog of Sr Lt Cho Chun Hyon.

[42] JTF 7, Inch'on Rpt, I-E-1, and II-1; GHQ FEC Sitrep, 14 Sep 50.

[43] JTF 7, Inch'on Rpt, I-E-2; Karig, *et al.*, *Battle Report, The War in Korea*, p. 210.

[44] Hq X Corps, Opn CHROMITE, G-3 Sec Hist Rpt, (gives strength of X Corps as 69,450); 1st Mar Div SAR, vol. I, an. A, 5.

The major units were the 1st Marine Division, the 7th Infantry Division, the 92d and 96th Field Artillery Battalions (both 155-mm. howitzers), the 50th Antiaircraft Artillery (Automatic Weapons) Battalion (SP), the 56th Amphibious Tank and Tractor Battalion, the 19th Engineer Combat Group, and the 2d Engineer Special Brigade. The 1st Marine Division on invasion day had a strength of 25,040 men—19,494 organic to the Marine Corps and the Navy, 2,760 Army troops attached, and 2,786 Korean marines attached. Later, after the 7th Marines arrived, the organic Marine strength increased about 4,000 men. On invasion day the GHQ UNC reserve consisted of the 3d Infantry Division and the 187th Airborne Regimental Combat Team (composed of troops from the 11th Airborne Division). The ROK 17th Regiment was in the act of moving from Eighth Army to join X Corps.

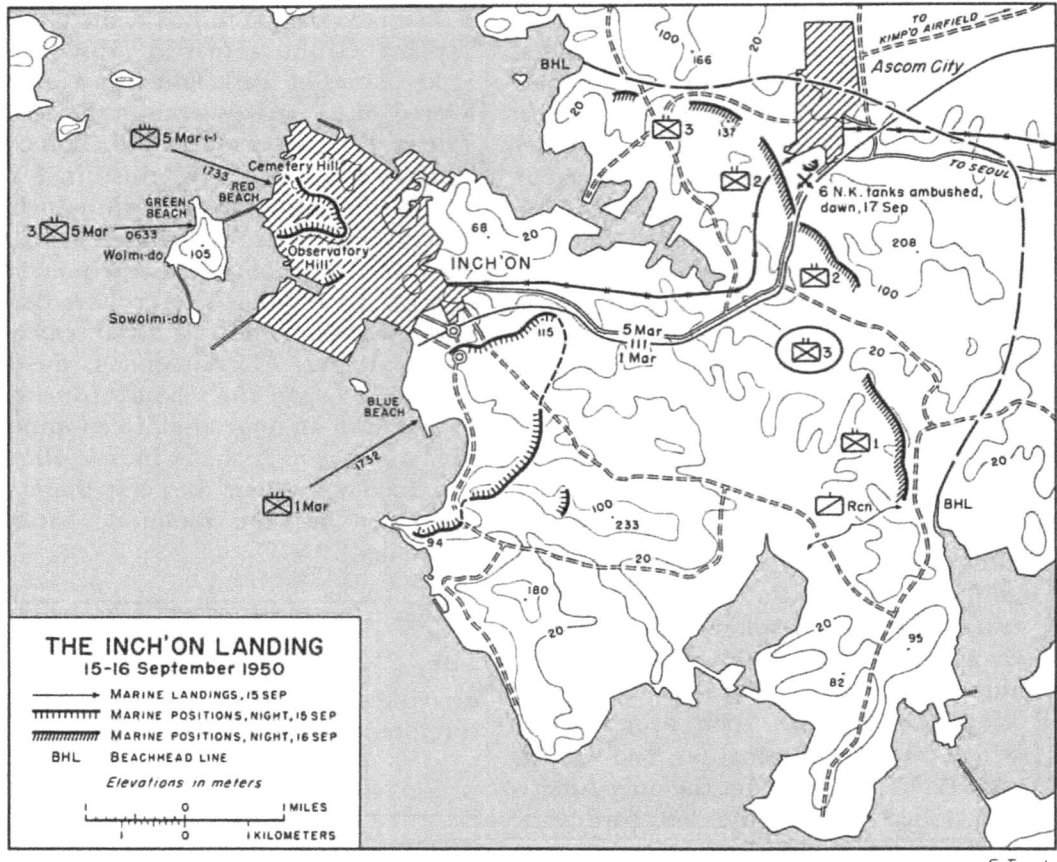

MAP 16

the Advance Attack Group, including the Gunfire Support Group, the rocket ships (LSMR's) and the Battalion Landing Team, began the approach to Inch'on. A special radar-equipped task force, consisting of three high speed transports (APD's) and one Landing Ship Dock (LSD), carried the Battalion Landing Team—Lt. Col. Robert D. Taplett's 3d Battalion, 5th Marines, and a platoon of nine M26 Pershing tanks from A Company, 1st Tank Battalion—toward the transport area off Wolmi-do.

Dawn of invasion day came with a high overcast sky and portent of rain.[45]

Wolmi-do, or Moon Tip Island, as it might be translated, is a circular hill (Hill 105) about 1,000 yards across and rising 335 feet above the water. A rocky hill, it was known to be honeycombed with caves, trenches, gun positions, and dugouts. (*Map 16*)

The first action came at 0500. Eight

---

[45] JTF 7, Inch'on Rpt, I-L-1 and I-F-1; 1st Mar Div SAR, vol. I, p. 13.

THE LANDING AT INCH'ON

WOLMI-DO

Marine Corsairs left their escort carrier for a strike on Wolmi-do. The first two planes caught an armored car crossing the causeway from Inch'on and destroyed it. There was no other sign of life visible on the island as the flight bombed the ridge line. At 0530 the Special Task Force was in its designated position ready to land the assault troops. Twenty minutes later, Taplett's 3d Battalion began loading into 17 landing craft (LCVP's); the 9 tanks loaded into 3 landing ships (LSV's). L-hour was fifty minutes away.

Air strikes and naval gunfire raked Wolmi-do and, after this, three rocket ships moved in close and put down an intense rocket barrage. The landing craft straightened out into lines from their circles and moved toward the line of departure. Just as a voice announced over the ship's loud speaker, "Landing force crossing line of departure," MacArthur came on the bridge of the *Mt. McKinley*. It was 0625. The first major amphibious assault by American troops against an enemy since Easter Sunday, 1 April 1945, at Okinawa was under way. About one mile of water lay between the line of departure and the Wolmi-do beach.[46]

The 3d Battalion moved toward Wolmi-do with G and H Companies in assault and I Company in reserve. Even after the American rocket barrage lifted there was still no enemy fire. The first wave of troops reached the bathing beach on the northern arm of the island unopposed at 0633.

The first troops ashore moved rapidly inland against almost no resistance. Within a few minutes the second wave landed. Then came the LSV's carrying

[46] X Corps WD, Opn CHROMITE, 15 Sep 50: 1st Mar Div SAR, vol. III, an. P, p. 4; Lynn Montross, "The Inchon Landing," *Marine Corps Gazette* (July, 1951), pp. 26ff; Geer, *The New Breed*, pp. 213–25.

the tanks, three of which carried dozer blades for breaking up barbed wire, filling trenches, and sealing caves; three other tanks mounted flame throwers. One group of marines raised the American flag on the high ground of Wolmi-do half an hour after landing. Another force crossed the island and sealed off the causeway leading to Inch'on. The reduction of the island continued systematically and it was secured at 0750.[47]

A little later in the morning, Colonel Taplett sent a squad of marines and three tanks over the causeway to Sowolmi-do where they destroyed an estimated platoon of enemy troops; some surrendered, others swam into the sea, and still others were killed. Taplett's battalion assumed defensive positions and prepared to cover the main Inch'on landing later in the day.

In the capture of Wolmi-do and Sowolmi-do the Battalion Landing Team killed 108 enemy soldiers and captured 136. About 100 more in several caves refused to surrender and were sealed by tank dozers into their caves. Marine casualties were light—seventeen wounded.[48]

The preinvasion intelligence on Wolmi-do proved to be essentially correct. Prisoners indicated that about 400 North Korean soldiers, elements of the *3d Battalion, 226th Independent Marine Regiment,* and some artillery troops of the *918th Artillery Regiment* had defended Wolmi-do.

After the easy capture of Wolmi-do came the anxious period when the tide began to fall, causing further activity to cease until late in the afternoon. The enemy by now was fully alerted. Marine and naval air ranged up and down the roads and over the countryside isolating the port to a depth of twenty-five miles, despite a rain which began to fall in the late afternoon. Naval gunfire covered the closer approaches to Inch'on.

Assault troops of the 5th and 1st Marines began going over the sides of their transports and into the landing craft at 1530. After a naval bombardment, rocket ships moved in close to Red and Blue Beaches and fired 2,000 rockets on the landing areas. Landing craft crossed lines of departure at 1645, and forty-five minutes later neared the beaches. The first wave of the 5th Marines breasted the sea wall on Red Beach at 1733. Most of the A Company men in the fourteen boats of the first three waves climbed over the sea wall with scaling ladders; a few boats put their troops ashore through holes in the wall made by the naval bombardment.[49]

On the left flank of the landing area, the 3d Platoon of A Company encountered enemy troops in trenches and a bunker just beyond the sea wall. There in an intense fight the marines lost eight men killed and twenty-eight wounded. Twenty-two minutes after landing, the company fired a flare signaling that it held Cemetery Hill. On top of Cemetery Hill, North Koreans threw down their arms and surrendered to the 2d Pla-

---

[47] 3d Bn, 5th Mar, Special Act Rpt, an. P to 5th Mar Special Rpt, in 1st Mar Div SAR; JTF 7, Inch'on Rpt, I-F-1, 15 Sep 50.

[48] 1st Mar Div SAR, vol. I, an. B, App. 1, 1; JTF 7, Inch'on Rpt, I-H-2; X Corps WD, G-2 Sec, Hist Rpt, Intel Estimate 8.

[49] 1st Bn, 5th Mar SAR, p. 3; 1st Mar Div SAR, vol. III; Geer, *The New Breed,* pp. 24-25. Montross and Canzona, *The Inchon-Seoul Operation,* covers the 1st Marine Division part of the Inch'on operation in detail. Much of this fine work is based on extensive interviews with participants.

THE LANDING AT INCH'ON

LANDING CRAFT AND BULLDOZERS *stuck in the Wolmi-do mud after the tide fell.*

toon. Other elements of the battalion by midnight had fought their way against sporadic resistance to the top of Observatory Hill.

The 2d Battalion, 5th Marines, landing on the right side of Red Beach, encountered only spotty resistance and at a cost of only a few casualties gained its objective.

Assault elements of the 1st Marines began landing over Blue Beach at 1732, one minute ahead of the 5th Marines at Red Beach. Most of the men were forced to climb a high sea wall to gain exit from the landing area. One group went astray in the smoke and landed on the sea wall enclosing the salt flats on the left of the beach. The principal obstacle the 1st Marines encountered was the blackness of the night. Lt. Col. Allan Sutter's 2d Battalion lost one man killed and nineteen wounded in advancing to the Inch'on-Seoul highway, one mile inland. The landing force had taken its final D-day objectives by 0130, 16 September.[50]

Following the assault troops, eight specially loaded LST's landed at Red Beach just before high tide, and unloading of equipment to support the forces ashore the next day continued throughout the night. Beaching of the LST's brought tragedy. Just after 1830, after receiving some enemy mortar and machine gun fire, gun crews on three of the LST's began firing wildly with 20-mm. and 40-mm. cannon, and, before they could be stopped, had killed 1 and wounded 23 men of the 2d Battalion, 5th Marines. The Marine landing force casualties on D-day were 20 men killed, 1 missing in action, and 174 wounded.[51]

The U.N. preinvasion estimate of en-

---

[50] 1st Mar Div SAR, Vol. I, an. P, p. 6, and an. C, p. 6; X Corps WD, Opn CHROMITE, 15 Sep 50; Diary of CG X Corps, 15 Sep 50.

[51] Montross and Canzona, *The Inchon-Seoul Operation*, pp. 110–11; Geer, *The New Breed*, p. 128.

MARINES MOPPING UP *on Wolmi-do*.

emy strength at Inch'on was accurate. Prisoners disclosed that about 2,000 men had comprised the Inch'on garrison. Some units of the N.K. *22d Regiment* moved to Inch'on to reinforce the garrison before dawn of the 15th, but they retreated to Seoul after the main landing that evening. To the rank and file of the North Korean soldiers in Seoul the landing came as a surprise.[52]

On the morning of 16 September the two regiments ashore established contact with each other by 0730. Thereafter a solid line existed around Inch'on and escape for any enemy still within the city became unlikely. The ROK Marines now took over mop-up work in Inch'on and went at it with such a will that hardly anyone in the port city, friend or foe, was safe.[53]

Early in the morning of the 16th, Marine aircraft took off from the carriers to aid the advance. One flight of eight Corsairs left the *Sicily* at 0548. Soon it sighted six enemy T34 tanks on the

---

[52] ATIS Supp Enemy Documents, Issue 2, pp. 114–16, Opn Ord 8–10 Sep 50, CO *226th Unit*, captured 16 Sep 50; ATIS Interrog Rpt (N.K.) Issue 10, p. 7; *Ibid.*, Issue 8, Rpt 1345, Lt Il Chun Son, and Rpt 1346, Lt Lee San Kak; X Corps WD, Opn CHROMITE, p. 26, interrog of Capt Chan Chul, and p. 30, interrog of Lt Col Kim Yonh Mo.

[53] Diary of CG X Corps, 16 Sep 50; Montross, "The Inchon Landing," *op. cit.*

THE LANDING AT INCH'ON

Seoul highway three miles east of Inch'on moving toward the latter place. Ordered to strike at once, the Corsairs hit the tanks with napalm and 500-pound bombs, damaging three of them and scattering the accompanying infantry. The enemy returned the fire, hitting one of the Corsairs. Capt. William F. Simpson's plane crashed and exploded near the burning armor, killing him. A second flight of eight Corsairs continued the attack on the tanks with napalm and bombs and, reportedly, destroyed them all. Later in the morning, however, when the advance platoon of the 1st Marines and accompanying tanks approached the site, three of the T34's began to move, whereupon the Pershings engaged and destroyed them.[54]

Both Marine regiments on the second day advanced rapidly against light resistance and by evening had reached the Beachhead Line, six miles from the landing area. Their casualties for the day were four killed and twenty-one wounded.

Thus, within twenty-four hours of the main landing, the 1st Marine Division had secured the high ground east of Inch'on, occupied an area sufficient to prevent enemy artillery fire on the landing and unloading area, and obtained a base from which to mount the attack to seize Kimpo Airfield. In the evening of 16 September General Smith established his command post east of Inch'on and from there at 1800 notified Admiral Doyle that he was assuming responsibility for operations ashore.[55]

Capture of Kimpo Airfield and Advance to the Han River

During the advance thus far the boundary between the 5th and 1st Marines had followed generally the main Inch'on-Seoul highway, which ran east-west, with the 5th Marines on the north and the 1st Marines astride and on its south side. Just beyond the beachhead line the boundary left the highway and slanted northeast. This turned Colonel Murray's 5th Marines toward Kimpo Airfield, seven miles away, and the Han River just beyond it. Col. Lewis B. Puller's 1st Marines, astride the Inch'on-Seoul highway, headed toward Yongdungp'o, the large industrial suburb of Seoul on the south bank of the Han, ten air miles away.

During the night of 16-17 September, the 2d Battalion, 5th Marines, occupied a forward defensive position commanding the Seoul highway just west of Ascom City. Behind it the 1st Battalion held a high hill. From a forward roadblock position, members of an advanced platoon of D Company, at 0545 on the 17th, saw the dim outlines of six tanks on the road eastward. Infantry accompanied the tanks, some riding on the armor.

The enemy armored force moved past the hidden outpost of D Company. At 0600, at a range of seventy-five yards, rockets fired from a bazooka set one of

---

[54] X Corps WD, G-3 Sec, Msgs J-2, 4, 6, 7 from 160705 to 160825, Sep 50; 1st Mar Div SAR, vol. II, an. OO, p. 15; Geer, *The New Breed*, p. 128; ATIS Enemy Documents, Issue 10, Rpt 1529, Hang Yong Sun, and Rpt 1534, Lt Lee Song Yol.

[55] 1st Mar Div SAR, vol. I, p. 22, and an. C, p. 7; Smith, MS review comments, 25 Feb 54.

DESTROYED ENEMY TANKS *on the road to Seoul.*

the tanks on fire. Pershing tanks now opened fire on the T34's. The recoilless rifles joined in. Within five minutes combined fire destroyed all six enemy tanks and killed 200 of an estimated 250 enemy infantry. Only one man in the 2d Battalion was wounded.[56]

Early that morning, General MacArthur, accompanied by Admiral Struble, and Generals Almond, Wright, Fox, Whitney, and others came ashore and proceeded to General Smith's command post, and from there went on to the position of the 2d Battalion, 5th Marines, where they saw the numerous enemy dead and the still-burning T34 tanks. On the way they had passed the six tanks destroyed the morning before. The sight of twelve destroyed enemy tanks seemed to them a good omen for the future.[57]

The 5th Marines advanced rapidly on the 17th and by 1800 its 2d Battalion was at the edge of Kimpo Airfield. In the next two hours the battalion seized

---

[56] 5th Mar SAR, pp. 7–8, in 1st Mar Div SAR, vol. III; 1st Mar Div SAR, vol. II, an. OO, p. 16; Montross and Canzona, *The Inchon-Seoul Operation*, pp. 147–51.

[57] Ltr, Wright to author, 22 Mar 54; Diary of CG X Corps, 17 Sep 50.

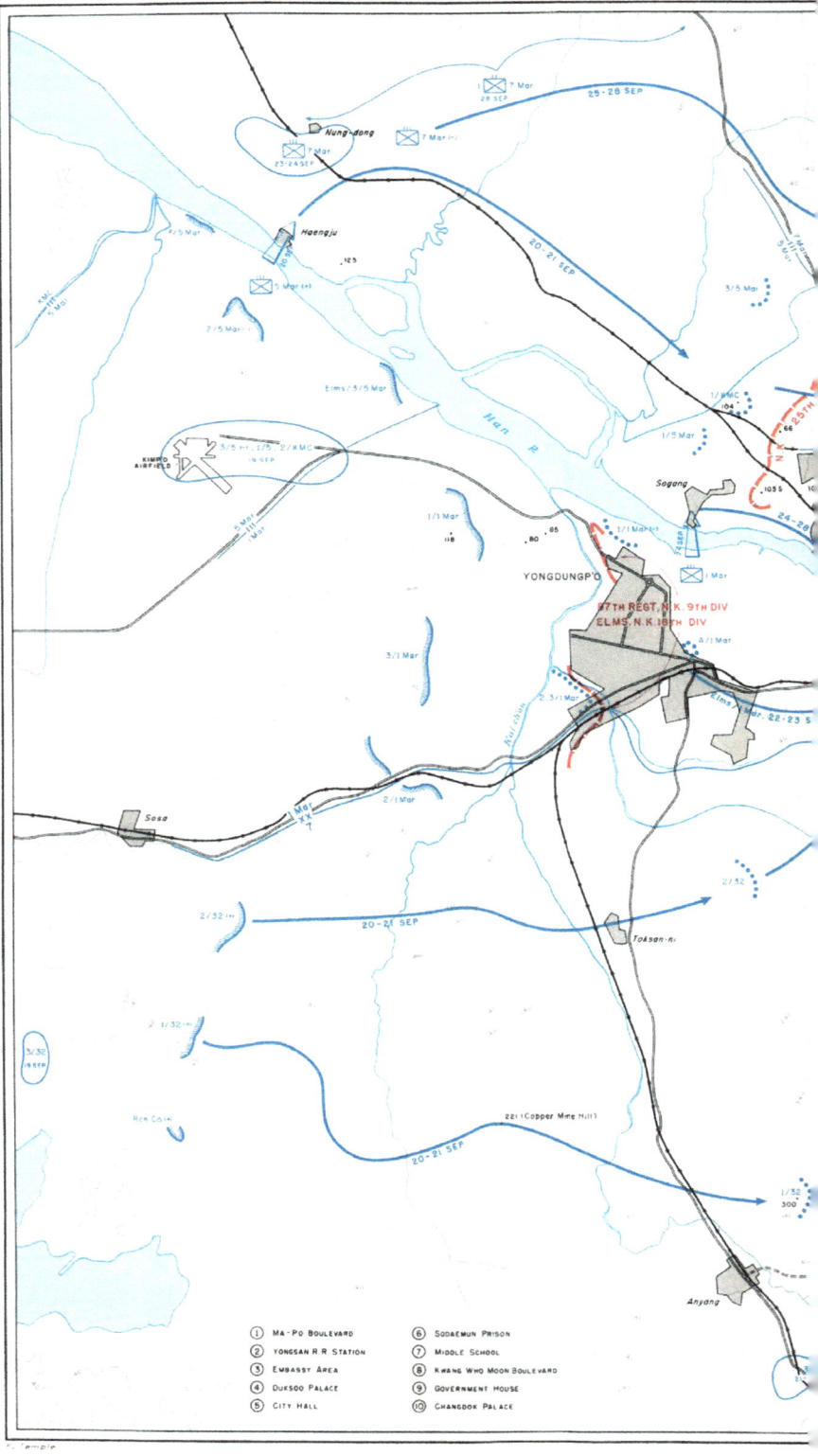

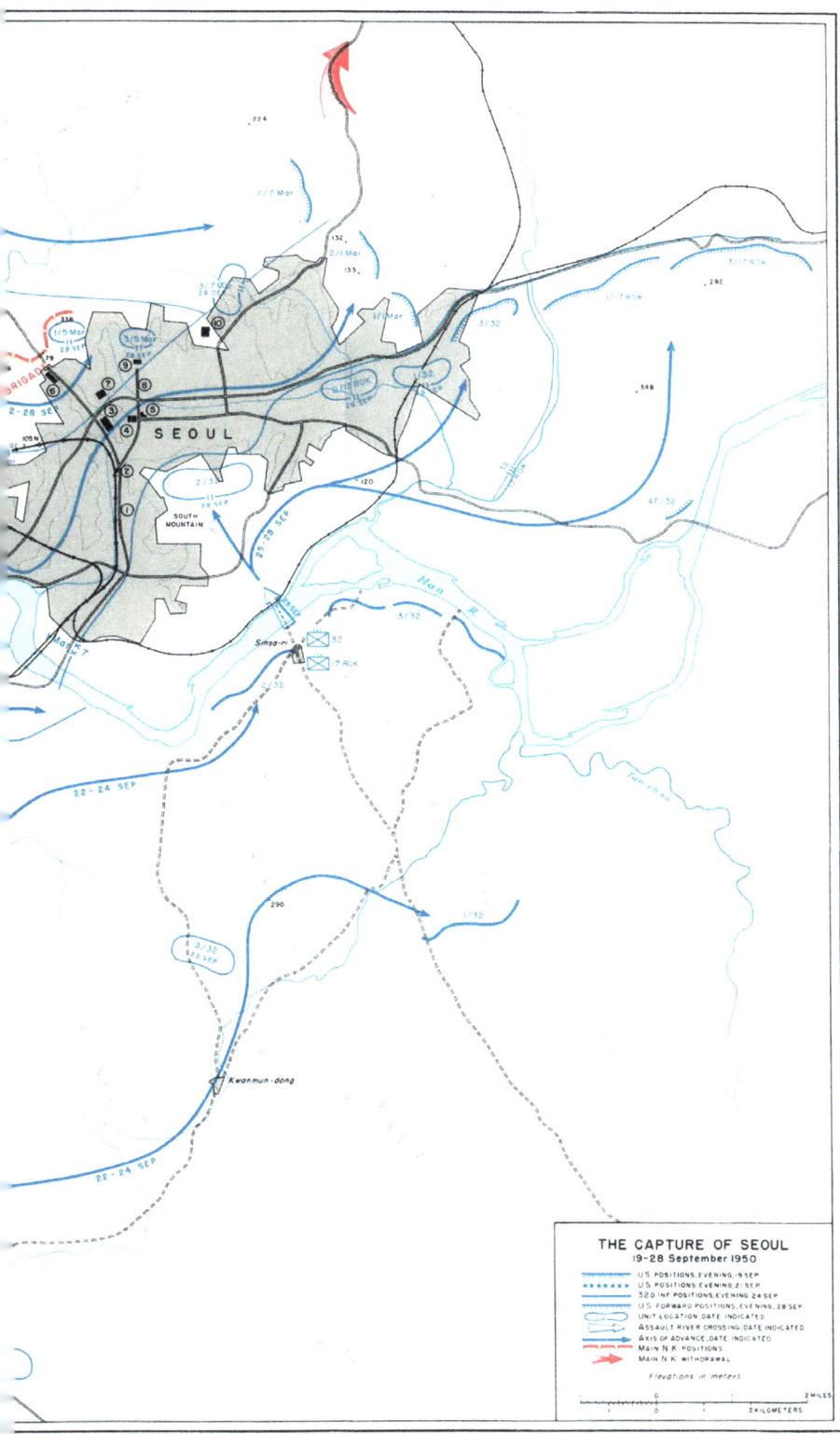

THE LANDING AT INCH'ON

the southern part of the airfield. The 400-500 enemy soldiers who ineffectively defended it appeared surprised and had not even mined the runway. During the night several small enemy counterattacks hit the perimeter positions at the airfield between 0200 and dawn, 18 September. The marines repulsed these company-sized counterattacks, inflicting heavy casualties on the enemy troops, who finally fled to the northwest E Company and supporting tanks played the leading role in these actions. Kimpo was secured during the morning of 18 September.[58]

The capture on the fourth day of the 6,000-foot-long, 150-foot-wide, hard surfaced Kimpo runway, with a weight capacity of 120,000 pounds, gave the U.N. Command one of its major objectives. It broadened greatly the capability of employing air power in the ensuing phases of the attack on Seoul; and, more important still, it provided the base for air operations seeking to disrupt supply of the North Korean Army.

On the 18th, the 2d Battalion, 5th Marines, sent units on to the Han River beyond the airfield, and the 1st Battalion captured Hill 99 northeast of it and then advanced to the river. At 1409 in the afternoon a Marine Corsair landed at Kimpo and, later in the day, advance elements of Marine Air Group 33 flew in from Japan. The next day more planes came in from Japan, including C-54 cargo planes, and on 20 September land-based Corsairs made the first strikes from Kimpo.[59]

Continuing its sweep along the river, the 1st Battalion, 5th Marines, on the 19th swung right and captured the last high ground (Hills 118, 80, and 85) a mile west of Yongdungp'o. At the same time, the 2d Battalion seized the high ground along the Han River in its sector. At nightfall, 19 September, the 5th Marines held the south bank of the Han River everywhere in its zone and was preparing for a crossing the next morning. (*Map VII*)

Meanwhile, the 2d Engineer Special Brigade relieved the ROK Marines of responsibility for the security of Inch'on, and the ROK's moved up on the 18th and 19th to the Han River near Kimpo. Part of the ROK's Marines extended the left flank of the 5th Marines, and its 2d Battalion joined them for the projected crossing of the Han River the next day.[60]

In this action, the 1st Marines had attacked east toward Yongdungp'o astride the Seoul highway. Its armored spearheads destroyed four enemy tanks early on the morning of the 17th. Then, from positions on high ground (Hills 208, 107, 178), three miles short of Sosa, a village halfway between Inch'on and Yongdungp'o, a regiment of the N.K. *18th Division* checked the advance. At nightfall the Marine regiment dug in for the night a mile from Sosa. At Ascom

---

[58] 5th Mar SAR, 17 Sep 50, pp. 7-8, in the 1st Mar Div SAR, vol. III; 1st Mar Div SAR, vol. I, p. 18; X Corps WD, G-3 Sec, 18 Sep 50; New York *Herald Tribune*, September 18, 1950, Bigart dispatch.

[59] 1st Mar Div SAR, G-3 an. C, vol. I, p. 10; JTF 7, Inch'on Rpt, 18 Sep 50; USAF Hist Study 71, p. 66; New York *Herald Tribune*, September 19, 1950, Bigart dispatch.

[60] 1st Mar Div SAR, vol. I, G-3 Sec, an. C, pp. 10-13, 18-19 Sep 50; Geer, *The New Breed*, pp. 133-34.

City, just west of Sosa, American troops found 2,000 tons of ammunition for American artillery, mortars, and machine guns, captured there by the North Koreans in June, all still in good condition.[61]

Not all the action that day was on and over land. Just after daylight, at 0550, two enemy YAK planes made bombing runs on the *Rochester* lying in Inch'on harbor. The first drop of four 100-pound bombs missed astern, except for one which ricocheted off the airplane crane without exploding. The second drop missed close to the port bow, causing minor damage to electrical equipment. One of the YAK's strafed H.M.S. *Jamaica*, which shot down the plane but suffered three casualties.[62]

Ashore, the 1st Marines resumed the attack on the morning of the 18th and passed through and around the burning town of Sosa at midmorning. By noon the 3d Battalion had seized Hill 123, a mile east of the town and north of the highway. Enemy artillery fire there caused many casualties in the afternoon, but neither ground nor aerial observers could locate the enemy pieces firing from the southeast. Beyond Sosa the North Koreans had heavily mined the highway and on 19 September the tank spearheads stopped after mines damaged two tanks. Engineers began the slow job of removing the mines and, without tank support, the infantry advance slowed. But at nightfall advanced elements of the regiment had reached Kal-ch'on Creek just west of Yongdungp'o.[63]

Other elements of the X Corps had by now arrived to join in the battle for Seoul. Vessels carrying the 7th Infantry Division arrived in Inch'on harbor on the 16th. General Almond was anxious to get the 7th Division into position to block a possible enemy movement from the south of Seoul, and he arranged with Admiral Doyle to hasten its unloading. The 2d Battalion of the 32d Regiment landed during the morning of the 18th; the rest of the regiment landed later in the day. On the morning of 19 September, the 2d Battalion, 32d Infantry, moved up to relieve the 2d Battalion, 1st Marines, in its position on the right flank south of the Seoul highway. It completed the relief without incident by noon. The total effective strength of the 32d Infantry when it went into the line was 5,114 men—3,241 Americans and 1,873 ROK's. Responsibility for the zone south of the highway passed to the 7th Division at 1800, 19 September. During the day, the 31st Regiment of the 7th Division came ashore at Inch'on.[64]

The Navy had supported the ground action thus far with effective naval gunfire. The *Rochester* and *Toledo* had

---

[61] 1st Mar Div SAR, vol. I, G-3 Sec, an. C, p. 8 and an. B, app. 2, p. 1; New York *Herald Tribune*, September 18, 1950, Bigart dispatch; CINCFE, Sitrep, 250600-260600 Sep 50.

[62] JTF 7, Inch'on Rpt, I-F-2 and IV-1.

[63] 1st Mar Div SAR, vol. I, G-3 Sec, an. C, pp. 10-13, 18-19 Sep 50; Geer, *The New Breed*, p. 136; Montross and Canzona, *The Inchon-Seoul Operation*, p. 178.

[64] 32d Inf WD, 16-19 Sep 50; Diary of CG X Corps, 18-19 Sep 50; JTF 7, Inch'on Rpt, I-F-2; 1st Mar Div SAR, G-3 Sec, an. C, p. 13, 19 Sep 50; Almond, MS review comments for author, 23 Oct 53; 7th Inf Div WD, 16-19 Sep 50; 31st Inf WD, 19 Sep 50.

THE LANDING AT INCH'ON

KIMPO RUNWAY *after capture by the 5th Marines.*

been firing at ranges up to 30,000 yards in support of the marines and the ROK's on their left flank. Now, on the 19th, the *Missouri* arrived in Inch'on harbor from the east coast of Korea and began delivering naval gunfire support to the 7th Division on the right flank. Despite difficult tide conditions and other restrictive factors in Inch'on harbor, the Navy by the evening of 18 September had unloaded 25,606 persons, 4,547 vehicles, and 14,166 tons of cargo.[65]

The battle for Seoul lay ahead. Mounting indications were that it would be far more severe than had been the action at Inch'on and the advance to the Han. Every day enemy resistance had increased on the road to Yongdungp'o. Aerial observers and fighter pilots reported large bodies of troops moving toward Seoul from the north. The N.K. *18th Division*, on the point of moving from Seoul to the Naktong front when the landing came at Inch'on, was instead ordered to retake Inch'on, and its advanced elements had engaged the 1st Marines in the vicinity of Sosa. On the 17th, enemy engineer units began mining the approaches to the Han River near Seoul. About the same time, the N.K. *70th Regiment* moved from Suwon to join in the battle. As they prepared to cross the Han, the marines estimated that there might be as many as 20,000 enemy troops in Seoul to defend the city. The X Corps intelligence estimate on 19 September, however, undoubtedly expressed the opinion prevailing among American commanders—that the enemy was "capable of offering stubborn resistance in Seoul but unless substantially reinforced, he is not considered

[65] JTF 7, Inch'on Rpt, 18 Sep 50, and II–6.

TOP-LEVEL BRIEFING, *1st Marine Division Headquarters, Inch'on, 17 September. Seated in front row, from left: Generals MacArthur and Smith, Admiral Struble, and Generals Whitney and Wright.*

capable of making a successful defense."[66]

Not until their 18 September communiqué did the North Koreans mention publicly anything connected with the Inch'on landing and then they merely stated that detachments of the coastal defense had brought down two American fighter planes.[67]

---

[66] JTF 7, Inch'on Rpt, I-F-2 and an. B, app. 2, p. 2, 18 Sep 50; ATIS Interrog Rpts (N.K.) Issue 8, Rpt 1300, p. 1, Hon Gun Mun, p. 40, Kim So Sung; Rpt 1336, p. 45, Kim Won Yong; Rpt 1365, p. 90, Kan Chun Kil; Rpt 1369, p. 96, Maj Chu Yong Bok; *Ibid.*, Issue 9, p. 29, Kim Te Jon; X Corps PIR 1, 19 Sep 50; Giusti, "Marine Air Over Inchon-Seoul, " *op. cit.*, p. 19.

[67] New York *Times*, September 19, 1950.

CHAPTER XXVI

The Capture of Seoul

> By the grace of a merciful Providence our forces fighting under the standard of that greatest hope and inspiration of mankind, the United Nations, have liberated this ancient city of Seoul.
>
> DOUGLAS MACARTHUR (at Seoul, 29 September 1950)

With the crossing of the Han River projected for 20 September, the drive on Seoul was about to begin. During the planning stages for the Inch'on landing, MacArthur had prophesied to Almond, "You will be in Seoul in five days." Almond replied, "I cannot do that but I will have the city in two weeks." [1]

The plan for crossing the Han River called for Colonel Murray's 5th Marines to cross at the ferry site three miles northeast of Kimpo Airfield and eight miles west of Seoul. (*See Map VII.*) A swimming party of fourteen men, mostly from the Reconnaissance Company, stepped into the Han at 2000 on the evening of the 19th, crossed safely to the north side, and found that the crossing site was suitable for LVT's. A 5-man patrol then continued up the slope of Hill 125 but turned back short of the crest. The swimming party gave the signal for the rest of the company to cross. When eight of nine amphibious tractors carrying the Reconnaissance Company were in the water enemy mortar and machine gun fire suddenly struck among them. The tractors turned around and made for the south bank. An hour later the swimming party arrived there with three wounded and one missing. Its plans disrupted, the 5th Marines now began preparing for an assault crossing of the Han after daylight.[2]

After a heavy artillery preparation against Hill 125, I Company, 5th Marines, began the assault crossing at 0645, 20 September. Enemy fire from automatic weapons and small arms on Hill 125 caused rather heavy casualties in I Company but it secured the hill by 0940. Other elements of the 3d Battalion, still riding LVT's, encountered little or no resistance and proceeded a mile inland to cut the Seoul-Kaesong railroad and a road at the village of Nung-dong by 0830. Still riding in LVT's they now turned right and moved southeast along the railroad track toward Seoul.[3]

---

[1] Interv, author with Almond, 13 Dec 51.

[2] 5th Mar SAR in 1st Mar Div SAR, vol. III, p. 9, 19 Sep 50; Diary of CG X Corps, 19 Sep 50; Montross and Canzona, *The Inchon-Seoul Operation*, pp. 191-93.

[3] 1st Mar Div SAR, vol. I, an. B, app. 2, pp. 5, 19; *Ibid.*, an. C, G-3 Sec, p. 14, 20 Sep 50; *Ibid.*, vol. III, p. 10.

The 2d Battalion followed the 3d Battalion across the river at 1000, passed through it, and continued the advance. By nightfall the 5th Marines with twelve tanks, and the 2d Battalion, ROK Marines, were across the river. Engineers had begun constructing a ponton ferry at the crossing site.

On the morning of 21 September, the 5th Marines, after repulsing an enemy company-sized counterattack, advanced southeast astride the rail and road lines paralleling the Han River. Resistance, at first light, steadily increased. The 3d Battalion captured and turned over to Korean marines Hill 104, north of the rail line and five and a half miles from the crossing site, and then turned northeast toward Hill 296 at the northwest edge of Seoul. In the meantime, the 1st Battalion attacked and captured a series of lower hills south of the rail and road lines. That evening the 5th Marines faced a line of hills running generally north-south along the western edge of Seoul. At the southern end of the line, near the village of Sogang, the 1st Battalion was within three miles of the main (Yongsan) railroad station in Seoul.[4]

Although unaware of the fact as they rested on their arms that night at the gate to the city, the men of the 5th Marines were to be held at this line of hills for four days of bloody battle. There the North Koreans had chosen to fight their battle for the western approaches to the city.

After receiving word of the rapid advance of the 5th Marines toward Seoul, General MacArthur returned to Tokyo on 21 September.[5]

The Capture of Yongdungp'o

Advancing on the right (south) of the 5th Marines, the 1st Marines gradually approached Yongdungp'o. Relieved by the 32d Infantry Regiment, 7th Infantry Division, in the early afternoon of 19 September, the 1st Battalion, 1st Marines, was ready to shift northeast to hill positions captured during the day by the 5th Marines at the west edge of Yongdungp'o. Because its transportation was late in arriving, darkness had fallen before the 1st Battalion reached its detrucking point. Company A climbed to the summit of Hill 118 to relieve the occupying force. Later C Company joined it there. Meanwhile, elements of the 1st Battalion, 5th Marines, had departed at 2100 from Hills 80 and 85 nearby, because there was a deadline set for their departure that would enable them to march the six to eight miles to the 5th Marines' Han River crossing site.

After having lost these hills that afternoon to the 5th Marines, the North Koreans counterattacked just before daylight. Their attack groups left Yongdungp'o, crossed the rice paddies and Kal-ch'on Creek, and arrived on Hills 80 and 85 to find them undefended. Part of the enemy force continued on to Hill 118 where A and C Companies of the 1st Marines repulsed them. The unfortunate loss of Hills 80 and 85 at

---

[4] *Ibid.*, vol. I, an. C, G–3 Sec, 21 Sep 50, p. 15; ATIS Interrog Rpts, Issue 8, p. 108, Rpt 1376, Lt Chai Chan Ya; Geer, *The New Breed*, p. 155.

[5] Diary of CG X Corps, 21 Sep 50.

MARINES ON HILL 125 *under heavy enemy fire.*

the edge of Yongdungp'o that night made it necessary for the 1st Battalion, 1st Marines, to assault them again in the morning. It recaptured Hill 85 only after intense close combat in which there were many Marine casualties.[6]

Simultaneously with the North Korean predawn attack against Hills 80, 85, and 118, a battalion-size force led by five T34 tanks left Yongdungp'o on the Inch'on highway to counterattack the 1st Marines. It ran headlong into the Marine position before daylight and in a flaming battle in the darkness the North Koreans were all but annihilated.

In this fight, Pfc. Gonegan boldly approached the T34 tanks. He knocked out two of them with his 3.5-inch bazooka and was in the act of firing on a third when he was killed. Dawn disclosed 300 dead North Korean soldiers on the road, in the ditches, and strewn about on the adjacent slopes.

By 0945, the main body of the 1st Marines reached the high ground overlooking Yongdungp'o from the west side of Kal-ch'on Creek, a sizable stream flowing north past the west edge of the city into the Han. General Almond arrived there at 1000 and in a conference with Colonel Puller, the Marine regimental commander, authorized him to shell Yongdungp'o. For the rest of the day the regiment held its place on the west side of the stream while artillery shelled Yongdungp'o and planes bombed it. The

---

[6] Montross and Canzona, *The Inchon-Seoul Operation*, pp. 216–19; Geer, *The New Breed*, pp. 136–37.

artillery barrage continued into the night.[7]

The arc of high ground west of Yongdungp'o was nearest to the city at its northern and southern extremities. At the center, a wide expanse of rice paddies and dikes, as well as Kal-ch'on Creek, separated the hills from the city. Accordingly, the best points from which to attack seemed to be the two extremities of the arc. The 1st Battalion was on the north, closest to the Han; the 2d Battalion was on the south along the Inch'on highway; the 3d Battalion was in reserve.

At daybreak, 21 September, the artillery resumed its preparation against Yongdungp'o, the big industrial suburb on the south bank of the Han, three miles southwest of Seoul. Then, at 0630, the marines attacked. At the northern end of the arc the 1st Battalion moved off Hills 85 and 80 onto the flat rice paddy ground and across Kal-ch'on Creek into the edge of Yongdungp'o. There enemy fire caused many casualties and slowed its advance. North Koreans held the dikes at the northwest approach to the city.

In its part of the attack, the 2d Battalion at the southern end of the arc had even harder going. Enemy mortar and artillery fire from high ground on that flank took a heavy toll in Marine casualties. By early afternoon, the 2d Battalion had suffered 85 casualties in crossing the rice paddies bordering Kal-ch'on Creek. Here at the edge of Yongdungp'o, large parts of which were now burning, the North Koreans fought the battalion to a standstill. The 3d Battalion, 1st Marines, passed through the hard-hit 2d Battalion late in the afternoon and continued the attack under heavy artillery fire.[8]

The North Koreans had held off the attacks at either end of their line, when in an unexpected manner the key to Yongdungp'o fell into the marines' hands. While the heavy battles were in progress on either flank, A Company left Hill 118 and moved behind low, masking hills to approach the dike system in the rice fields near the center of the line directly west of the main part of Yongdungp'o. The company formed an assault line behind a high dike, crossed it, and then advanced through chest-high rice to the deep mud of Kal-ch'on Creek, crossed the stream, reformed in front of another dike on the far side, and then entered the city streets undiscovered. As A Company moved through the empty heart of the town the men could hear sounds of heavy fighting on their right and left. Capt. Robert Barrow, the company commander, soon found that he and his men were 700 yards inside the town without contact with other friendly units. His reaction was not, as is so often the case when troops are in such a situation, that he and his company were alone, isolated, and surrounded. Instead, he realized that he was in the enemy's rear and proceeded to exploit the situation.[9]

Soon Barrow's advanced platoon on the left saw enemy troops hurrying west-

---

[7] 1st Mar Div SAR, vol. I, Annex Charlie, G-3 Sec, 20 Sep 50, p. 14; Diary of CG X Corps, 20 Sep 50; X Corps WD, Opn CHROMITE, 20 Sep 50.

[8] 1st Mar Div SAR, vol. I, G-3 Sec, 21 Sep 50, pp. 15, 19; Diary of CG X Corps, 21 Sep 50; Montross and Canzona, *The Inchon-Seoul Operation*, pp. 221-25.

[9] Geer, *The New Breed*, p. 149.

THE CAPTURE OF SEOUL

ward along the concrete highway from Seoul—reinforcements for the battle in progress. Its fire surprised and either destroyed or dispersed these troops. The company moved on. Shortly before noon, and after passing almost through the city, Barrow stopped at its eastern side. There he placed his men in a defensive perimeter on both sides of a 30-foot-high dike upon whose crest ran a surfaced road which joined at this point with the Seoul-Inch'on highway.

That afternoon the North Koreans apparently were too busy in the battle at the western edge of the city to give much attention to the unit in their rear, although small groups did make feeble efforts against it. But at dusk five tanks attacked A Company. In the battle between bazooka and tank the bazooka was victorious, the latter knocking out one and damaging two of the tanks. The two undamaged tanks, with machine guns blazing and cannon booming, made five passes along the deeply dug-in infantry at thirty yards' distance from the levee. Then the tanks withdrew into the city. At 2100 an enemy infantry force attacked the 3d Platoon at the northern end of the company perimeter. The platoon repulsed five separate attacks there before midnight. Morning disclosed more than 275 enemy dead in the vicinity of the dike and road intersection and many automatic weapons scattered about on the ground.[10]

On 21 September two developments behind the front occurred that were to affect future tactical operations. First, the third regiment of the 1st Marine Division, the 7th Marines, arrived in Inch'on harbor and began unloading. Second, command of the operation passed from Admiral Struble to General Almond, who at 1800 assumed command of the Seoul operation ashore at the X Corps command post in Inch'on. At this time there were 49,568 persons, 5,356 vehicles, and 22,222 tons of cargo ashore.[11]

The North Koreans, after their failure during the night of 21–22 September to drive Captain Barrow's company from its advanced position at the eastern edge of Yongdungp'o, apparently abandoned the city before daybreak. The 1st Marines occupied the city the next morning. On the left near the river they reached the destroyed railroad and highway bridges over the Han River two miles east of Yongdungp'o.[12]

The *87th Regiment* of the N.K. *9th Division* and elements of the N.K. *18th Division* had defended Yongdungp'o. One battalion of the *87th Regiment* reportedly suffered 80 percent casualties in the fighting there. Prisoners revealed that this regiment had left Kumch'on on 16 September to reinforce the Seoul area, traveling in trains that hid in tunnels during the day, and had arrived in the Yongdungp'o area on 20 September, barely in time to enter the fight there.[13]

On the 22d, the 1st Marine Division issued an operations order setting forth its plan for the seizure of Seoul. The

---

[10] Montross and Canzona, *The Inchon-Seoul Operation*, pp. 228–31; Geer, *The New Breed*, pp. 151–53.

[11] TF 7, Inch'on Rpt, I-F-3; Diary of CG X Corps, 21 Sep 50.

[12] 1st Mar Div SAR, vol. I, an. C, G–3 Sec, 22–23 Sep 50, pp. 17–19; X Corps WD, G–2 Sec Hist Rpt, PIR 4, 22 Sep 50.

[13] GHQ FEC, History of the North Korean Army (section of *9th Div*), 31 Jul 52; ATIS Res Supp Interrog Rpts, Issue 100, p. 53; X Corps WD, PIR 4, 22 Sep 50.

1st Marines was to cross the Han in the Yongdungp'o area and join the 5th Marines north of the river, forming the division right, while the 7th Marines was to move up from Inch'on and go into the line north of the 5th Marines, which then would form the center of a 3-regiment line. The plan contemplated that the 1st Marine Division, without the help of other ground units, would capture the city. But that same day, General Almond introduced one change in the plan—he indicated that the ROK Marines and the ROK 17th Regiment were also to be committed in securing the city.[14]

Securing the Southern Flank

As the 1st Marines fought its way along the Inch'on-Seoul highway and into Yongdungp'o, the 7th Infantry Division protected its right flank and engaged enemy units moving toward the battle area from the south. An extensive mine field delayed the 32d Regiment on the 20th as it attacked toward Anyang-ni where it was to cut the Seoul-Suwon highway. Exploding mines damaged three tanks of A Company, 73d Tank Battalion, and completely blocked the narrow dirt road the column was following. Colonel Beauchamp, the regimental commander, had a narrow escape. A mine destroyed his jeep, killing the driver and wounding the radio operator a few minutes after he had left it. Engineer troops removed more than 150 mines from this field. The regiment during the day captured T'ongdok Mountain and part of Copper Mine Hill.[15]

On the 21st, the 32d Infantry seized the rest of Copper Mine Hill. It also captured the high ground two miles south of Yongdungp'o and Hill 300, the high ground immediately northeast of Anyang-ni. The 7th Division Reconnaissance Company arrived at Anyang-ni at 1430. When darkness fell, the 3d Battalion, 32d Infantry, held blocking positions astride the Suwon highway two miles south of Anyang-ni, the 1st Battalion held the road east and the high ground northeast of the town, and elements of the regimental combat team had established contact northward at Toksan-ni with the 2d Battalion, where the latter had captured a considerable quantity of ordnance and medical supplies.[16]

After arriving at Anyang-ni with the Reconnaissance Company, Maj. Irwin A. Edwards, Assistant G-2, 7th Division, received radio orders from the division to turn south to Suwon and secure the airfield below the town. Approximately at 1600, 2d Lt. Jesse F. Van Sant, commanding a tank platoon, took the point with his tanks and, followed by the Reconnaissance Company and Major Edwards, started toward Suwon. Naval aircraft bombed Suwon just before they arrived there at 1800 and destroyed a large wooden structure on top of the ancient great stone wall at its East Gate. Debris from this structure blocked the gateway and forced the company to turn

---

[14] Diary of CG X Corps, 22 Sep 50; 1st Mar Div SAR, vol. I, an. C, G-3 Sec, p. 17, Opn Plan 3-50, 22 Sep 50.

[15] 32d Inf WD, 20 Sep 50; 7th Div POR 2, overlay, 202200 Sep 50; Interv, author with Beauchamp, 1 Aug 52.

[16] Ltr, Lt Col Irwin A. Edwards to author, 5 Aug 53; Interv, author with Barr, 1 Feb 54; Beauchamp, MS review comments for author, 19 Jan 54.

THE CAPTURE OF SEOUL

aside to find another entrance into the town. At this point, Lt. Col. Henry Hampton, 7th Division G-3, arrived from Anyang-ni with a platoon of B Company, 18th Engineer Combat Battalion, and joined the group.

Hampton and Edwards with two enlisted men led the column through the streets. Near the center of Suwon the four men surprised two North Korean officers in the act of trying to escape in an American jeep. Edwards shot the driver; the other officer, a major of the N.K. *105th Armored Division*, surrendered. The armored column engaged in some street fighting with scattered groups of enemy soldiers, capturing altogether, thirty-seven North Koreans. Three miles south of Suwon the column went into a perimeter defense astride the highway. Being without maps, it had unwittingly passed the airfield a mile back up the road.[17]

About 2100 a full moon rose and Maj. Gen. David G. Barr, having lost radio contact with the Reconnaissance Company, decided to send an armored force toward Suwon to find it. Colonel Hampton and the platoon of engineers had already loaded into a truck and gone ahead. Task Force Hannum, named after its commander, Lt. Col. Calvin S. Hannum, commanding the 73d Tank Battalion, started from Anyang-ni at 2125. This motorized force—comprised of B Company, 73d Tank Battalion, and the battalion Advance Command Group; K Company, 32d Infantry; C Battery, 48th Field Artillery Battalion; and a medical detachment—hurried south in the moonlight with all possible speed. Lt. Col. John W. Paddock, 7th Division G-2, accompanied it. On the way to Suwon, Colonel Paddock established radio contact with Major Edwards and asked for guides to direct him and his force into the perimeter.[18]

Hannum's armored column reached Suwon near midnight, found the East Gate blocked, and turned aside to enter the town from another point through the ancient stone wall that girds the town on that side. Inside the town an enemy tank hidden behind a building opened fire on the leading American tank, knocking it out with one shot and killing Capt. Harold R. Beavers, the B Company tank commander who was inside it. In the fight that flared in the next few minutes other American tanks destroyed this T34, but a second enemy tank escaped. Hannum's force tried to follow it but became lost at the edge of town. Hannum decided to wait for daylight rather than to risk another enemy tank ambush in the darkness.

Meanwhile, Edwards' party in its perimeter south of Suwon heard the sound of tanks northward. Lieutenant Van Sant thought their clatter sounded like T34's, but the others discounted his comments and hastened preparations to send a party to meet Hannum. Major Edwards put a Korean civilian and eight men from the Reconnaissance Company into two jeeps. Colonel Hampton said he would go along and possibly continue on to rejoin the 7th Division headquarters at Anyang-ni. The party started with Edwards driving the first of four jeeps. A mile northward Ed-

---

[17] Ltr, Edwards to author, 5 Aug 53; X Corps WD, G-2 Hist Rpt, PIR 4, 22 Sep 50.

[18] Interv, author with Hannum, 21 Jul 53; 7th Div WD, Narr, 21-22 Sep 50; Ltr, Edwards to author, 5 Aug 53.

wards saw four tanks approaching in the moonlight. He flicked his lights in a recognition signal for what he thought was Hannum's lead tank. The tank stopped. Then suddenly its machine guns started firing, and it came on toward the halted vehicles. The men jumped from the jeeps and scrambled into the ditches. Colonel Hampton, however, started toward the tank waving his arms, evidently still thinking them friendly. Machine gun fire cut him down and the oncoming tank crunched into Edwards' jeep. Edwards escaped and rejoined the Reconnaissance Company the next morning.

The North Korean tanks rumbled on south and a few minutes later the first one entered the Reconnaissance Company's perimeter. Just ahead of it, an escapee from the jeep party ran into the perimeter and gave the alarm. The second enemy tank reached the edge of the perimeter. Van Sant gave the order to fire. The American M26 tanks destroyed both T34's at point-blank range of forty yards or less. The other two T34's turned and clattered back toward Suwon.[19]

At daylight Hannum led his armored column south through the town, now deserted. Below it he passed the crushed jeeps and the bodies of Hampton and two or three other men killed there. At midmorning Hannum's armored force joined the Reconnaissance Company at Suwon Airfield where Major Edwards had moved it and Van Sant's tanks at daybreak. Before noon, Col. Richard P. Ovenshine's 31st Infantry Regiment of the 7th Division (less the 3d Battalion in division reserve) arrived at Suwon and relieved Task Force Hannum at the airfield. The Reconnaissance Company then reconnoitered south toward Osan. Task Force Hannum rejoined the 7th Division in the Anyang-ni area.[20]

The big event of 22 September was securing Suwon Airfield and opening it to United Nations air traffic. This field, 21 miles south of Seoul, could accommodate the large C-54 transport planes with its 5,200-foot runway.

Meanwhile, 7 miles northeast of Anyang-ni, enemy forces succeeded in ambushing the lead platoon of B Company, 32d Infantry, and badly disorganized it. Lt. Col. Don C. Faith, Jr., the 1st Battalion commander, withdrew B Company 2 miles, to the vicinity of Kwanmundong, closely pursued by the enemy. There the battalion checked the North Koreans. During the day, Lt. Col. Charles M. Mount's 2d Battalion, 32d Infantry, seized the series of hills from 1 to 2 miles south of the rail and highway bridges that crossed the Han into Seoul.

On 23 September, the 1st Battalion captured its objective, Hill 290. This hill, 3 miles below the Han River and 7 miles southeast of Yongdungp'o, dominates the approaches to the Han River and Seoul from that direction.[21]

On the morning of 24 September,

---

[19] Interv, author with Hannum, 21 Jul 53; Ltrs, Edwards to author, 5 and 13 Aug 53; Ltr, Beauchamp to author, 15 Jul 53; Beauchamp, MS review comments for author, 19 Jan 54; 7th Div WD, 21 Sep 50; 32d Inf WD, 21 Sep 50; New York Herald Tribune, September 23, 1950, Bigart dispatch.

[20] Interv, Hannum with author, 21 Jul 53; Ltrs, Edwards to author, 5 and 13 Aug 53; 7th Inf Div WD, 22 Sep 50; 31st Inf Narr Rpt, 22 Sep 50; X Corps WD, 21-22 Sep 50.

[21] 32d Inf WD, 22 Sep 50; 7th Div WD, 22 Sep 50; 7th Div POR's 4 and 5 and accompanying overlays, 22-23 Sep 50; Beauchamp, MS review comments for author, 19 Jan 54; Ltr, Mount to author, 12 Mar 56.

THE CAPTURE OF SEOUL

Mount's battalion in a predawn attack caught North Koreans asleep in their positions and overran them. In this surprise action the battalion captured a regimental headquarters and much equipment, and broke the remaining enemy strength close to the south bank of the river opposite Seoul. During the day the battalion cleared the south bank of the Han in the fold of the river southeast of the city. This made possible an important action the next morning.[22]

Seoul's Western Rampart

While the 7th Division was securing X Corps' southern flank, the heaviest fighting in the battle for Seoul began at the city's western edge on 22 September and lasted four days.

The North Korean defense line at the western edge of Seoul was anchored at the north on Hill 296 just south of the Kaesong highway and west of Seoul's Sodaemun Prison. From the crest of Hill 296 the North Korean line curved in a gentle half-moon eastward and southward down spur ridges two and a half miles to the Han River, the concave side facing west toward the United Nations troops. The greater part of this uneven ridge line was dominated by three hills, each 105 meters high, and accordingly known as Hills 105. Hills 105 North and 105 Center lay north of the rail and highway lines running into Seoul along the northern bank of the Han River; Hill 105 South lay between the rail and road lines and the river. Hills 105 Center and 105 South completely dominated the Pusan-to-Manchuria Kyonggi main rail line and the road that passed through the saddle between them to enter the city. These hills had been a training area for Japanese troops during the period of Japanese domination and since then of both South and North Korean soldiers. The area was well covered with various types of field fortifications and susceptible to quick organization for defense. The main railroad station and Government House lay in the center of Seoul two miles east of these positions.

The principal enemy unit manning this line was the N.K. *25th Brigade*. Newly formed a month earlier at Ch'orwon, it had started moving by train from that place to Seoul on the day of the Inch'on landing, most of it arriving there four days later on 19 September. Maj. Gen. Wol Ki Chan, forty-five years of age and formerly a student in Russia, commanded the brigade. Most of the brigade's officers and noncommissioned officers had had previous combat experience with the Chinese Communist Forces. The brigade numbered about 2,500 men, and apparently was composed of two infantry battalions, four heavy machine gun battalions, an engineer battalion, a 76-mm. artillery battalion, a 120-mm. mortar battalion, and miscellaneous service troops. It and the *78th Independent Regiment* defended both the military and topographic crests. Foxholes, undercut into the slopes, gave protection from overhead shell air bursts. Concrete caves held supplies. More than fifty heavy machine guns with interlocking fields of fire dotted this defensive position.[23]

---

[22] 7th Div WD, 24 Sep 50.

[23] 1st Mar Div SAR, vol. I, an. B, p. 17, and vol. III, 5th Mar SAR, an. B, app. 1, pp. 5–6, and an. O, p. 9.

On the morning of 22 September the 5th Marines set out to capture these last hills in front of Seoul. On the north flank the 3d Battalion's objective was Hill 296. In the center, the objective of the 2d Battalion, ROK Marines, was Hill 105 Center, but the battalion had to take two knobs called Hills 66 and 88 before reaching the main hill behind them. On the south flank across the railroad track the 1st Battalion, 5th Marines, objective was Hill 105 South. The attack began at 0700. Two hours later the 3d Battalion on the north reported it had captured its objective against only moderate resistance, but this report was misleading because the battalion did not have control of the southern slopes and ridges of Hill 296 where the North Korean strength was concentrated. On the southern flank heavy enemy fire stopped the 1st Battalion for a while, but late in the day it took Hill 105 South after a smashing artillery and mortar preparation. But enemy artillery scored too, some of its fire landing in the 1st Battalion rear areas and inflicting thirty-nine casualties there during the day, including six killed.[24]

In the center, enemy fire decimated the ROK Marine battalion in its attack against Hills 66 and 88. The fighting was heavy there all day long. Marine air strikes tried in vain to destroy the enemy positions. Later, North Korean prisoners said that the *25th Brigade* had 40 percent casualties that day. The next morning, 23 September, the Korean marines resumed the battle in the center and suffered continuing heavy casualties, while accomplishing little. At midafternoon the 2d Battalion, 5th Marines, on orders from Colonel Murray, took over the attack in the center. After sustaining many casualties with little gain, the lead company (D) dug in for the night, short of the enemy-held ridge. In another furious fight, one platoon of F Company suffered so many casualties it had only seven men left for duty at nightfall. Meanwhile, the rest of the regiment had held in place on the flanks and repelled counterattacks during the day.[25]

At noon on 23 September General Smith had ordered the 7th Marines, which had begun unloading at Inch'on on the 21st, to cross the Han and come up behind the 5th Marines. During the day X Corps headquarters moved from Inch'on to Ascom City, about halfway to Seoul on the main Inch'on-Seoul highway.

After daylight on the 24th, elements of the 3d Battalion, 5th Marines, started down the finger ridge from Hill 296, hoping to outflank the enemy in front of the 2d Battalion in the center. Simultaneously, D Company moved out in assault against the ridge line. A heavy morning mist shrouded the company as it crossed the low ground and reached the base of Hill 66. Unexpectedly, the lead elements came upon enemy troops in their trenches. Neither side saw the other because of the fog and smoke until they were at close quarters. A grenade battle started immediately. One

---

[24] 1st Mar Div SAR, vol. III, p. 9, 22 Sep 50, and vol. I, an. C, G–3 Sec, p. 17, 22 Sep 50, and an. B, app. 2, p. 8; Geer, *The New Breed*, pp. 155–57; New York *Herald Tribune*, September 23, 1950, Bigart dispatch.

[25] 1st Mar Div SAR, vol. I, an. C, G–3 Sec, pp. 17–19, 22–23 Sep 50, and an. B, app. 2, p. 10; *Ibid.*, vol. III, an. B, app. 1, 1st Mar Div Opn Ord 9–50, 231200 Sep 50, p. 6; X Corps WD, 23 Sep 50; Giusti, "Marine Air Over Inchon-Seoul," *Marine Corps Gazette* (June 1952).

squad of twelve marines in trying to maneuver around the southern tip of the ridge was wiped out except for three wounded who escaped.

In an effort to break the deadlock, Marine air strikes came in repeatedly. In the course of two such attacks, North Korean antiaircraft fire damaged five of ten planes. Enemy automatic and mortar fire became intense after the fog lifted.

In the early afternoon the 30 remaining effectives in D Company's rifle platoons and 14 other men assembled from the Weapons Platoon, ammunition carriers, and company headquarters prepared for a desperate assault against the ridge line of Hill 66. Thirty-three men were to make the assault up the last 150 yards of the slope—11 others were to follow with machine guns and ammunition. Corsairs came over for final strafing runs, bombing, and napalming of the enemy position. This done, the 33 men, at a prearranged signal of a Corsair's second dry run over the enemy, jumped from their holes and charged forward in a 100-yard-long line. The D Company commander, 1st Lt. H. J. Smith, was killed in front of his men. The others kept going and 26 of them reached the top. The headlong charge surprised the North Koreans; in a sudden panic many ran down the back slope, others feigned death, and some fought back. Enemy dead were stacked up everywhere—in foxholes, in bunkers —and many were strewn about over the ground. When all of D Company's men reached the top there were 56 men to defend it, 26 of them wounded but refusing evacuation. They held the hill against a counterattack. During this day, D Company suffered 176 casualties among its 206 men—36 killed, 116 wounded and evacuated, and 26 more wounded but present for duty.[26]

Events were to prove that D Company's capture of Hill 66 on the afternoon of the 24th was the decisive action in the battle at the western gate to Seoul. The 2d Battalion on the morning of the 25th resumed the attack toward Hill 105 Center. Artillery and fighter bombers pounded the enemy-held hill line all morning. From recently captured Hill 66, D Company advanced northward slowly during the morning up the shank of the fishhook ridge line that slanted southwest from Hill 296, and then turned southeast to capture Hill 88 at the point of the hook just after noon. By midafternoon other elements of the 2d Battalion had captured Hill 105 Center, and the 3d Battalion had gained control of Hill 105 North after very heavy fighting. According to prisoners, three enemy battalions lost 500 men during the day trying to hold the northern hill. The western defenses of Seoul had fallen. More than 1,200 dead enemy soldiers lay on their stubbornly defended positions. Marine estimates placed the total number of enemy killed there by all arms at 1,750.[27]

When the enemy defenses at the western edge of Seoul fell on 25 September, the 1st Marine Division had all its regi-

---

[26] 1st Mar Div SAR, vol. I, an. C, G–3 Sec, p. 21, 24 Sep 50; *Ibid.*, vol. III, 5th Mar SAR, p. 11, 24 Sep 50; X Corps WD, 24 Sep 50; Montross and Canzona, *The Inchon-Seoul Operation*, pp. 245–50; Geer, *The New Breed*, pp. 161–62; Giusti, "Marine Air Over Inchon-Seoul," *op. cit.*

[27] 1st Mar Div SAR, vol. III, an. B, app. 1, p. 6 and an. P, 5th Mar SAR, p. 9; *Ibid.*, vol. I, an. C, G–3 Sec, p. 24, 25 Sep 50; X Corps WD, G–2 Hist Rpt, PIR 7, 25 Sep 50. Montross and Canzona, *The Inchon-Seoul Operation*, pages 239–59, has a detailed account of this battle.

AMERICAN TROOPS MOVE ON SEOUL *along the north bank of the Han River.*

ments together north of the Han River. At 2200 on the night of 23 September, the division had issued an operations order, confirming earlier verbal orders, directing the 1st Marines to cross the Han River early the next morning.[28]

During the morning of 24 September the 1st Marines began crossing the Han from Yongdungp'o in the shadow of Hill 105 South, where the 1st Battalion, 5th Marines, protected the crossing site. Before dark the regiment had crossed to the north side and the 1st and 2d Battalions had taken over from the 1st Battalion, 5th Marines, the southern flank of the Marine line at the western edge of Seoul. By now the 7th Marines had moved up on the left flank of the 5th Marines, with the mission of cutting across the northern edge of Seoul and blocking escape routes there. The 3d Battalion of the 187th Airborne Regiment airlifted from Ashiya, Japan, to Kimpo Airfield on the 24th and upon arrival there assumed responsibility for the airfield.[29]

On the morning of 25 September, two platoons of tanks from B Company, 1st Tank Battalion, including two dozer tanks and a section of flame-throwing tanks, accompanied by a platoon of engineers and another of infantry set out to join the 1st Marines in Seoul. Near the base of Hill 105 South, an enemy force with several antitank guns ambushed the column. The fighting was heavy and the outcome in doubt for several minutes until a flame-thrower tank reached a point from which it

---

[28] 1st Mar Div Opn Ord 9-50, 231200 and Opn Ord 10-50, 232200 Sep 50.

[29] 1st Mar Div SAR, vol. I, an. C, G-3 Sec, p. 21, 24 Sep 50, and an. B, G-2 Sec, p. 11, 24 Sep 50; 187th RCT Act Rpt, 22 Sep-2 Oct 50.

spurted flame into the enemy trenches. Many North Korean soldiers broke from cover. Machine gun fire from other tanks cut them down as they ran. Several North Koreans came out of a previously undiscovered cave and surrendered. When a large group inside the cave saw these men unhurt they too surrendered. Of the nearly 300 North Koreans that attacked this armored column, approximately 150 were killed, 131 captured. The tank column joined Colonel Puller's 1st Marines in Seoul at noon.[30]

During the morning the 3d Battalion, 1st Marines, made a 90-degree turn northward to change the regimental direction of attack from eastward to northward toward the heart of the city. While it was doing this, the 1st Battalion on its right held a blocking position at the southern edge of Seoul. Once the 3d Battalion had turned northward, the 1st Battalion pivoted to orient its attack northward abreast of and on the right of it. Street fighting now began in Seoul, 25 September, in the zone of the 1st Marines just as the 5th Marines completed its capture of the North Korean defensive hill line at the western edge of the city.[31]

The 32d Infantry Enters Seoul

By this time an important change had taken place in the plan to capture Seoul. The original operations plan required the 1st Marine Division to clear the city. But the expected capture of Seoul by the marines was moving behind schedule. The stubborn enemy defense had denied the Marine division any important advance for three days. General Almond, the corps commander, had been growing increasingly impatient. Seoul was a symbol in the Korean War, just as Paris, Rome, and Berlin had been in World War II. It was a political and psychological as well as a military target. General MacArthur desired to capture the city as soon as possible and restore the Korean capital to its people.[32]

Dissatisfied with the marines' progress, General Almond on 23 September told General Smith that he could continue his frontal assaults but that he strongly urged him to use the space south of the Han River for an envelopment maneuver by the 1st Marines. Smith was unwilling to act on Almond's suggestion because he wanted to unite the 1st and 5th Marines on the north side of the Han instead of having them on opposite sides of the river. Almond told Smith that he would give him twenty-four hours longer to make headway. If Smith could not, Almond said, he would change division boundaries and bring the 7th Infantry Division and its 32d Regiment into the battle for the envelopment of the enemy defenses in Seoul.[33]

On the morning of 24 September the North Koreans still held the marines at

---

[30] 1st Mar Div SAR, vol. II, an. OO, p. 8, Rpt 1st Tk Bn, 25 Sep 50; Geer, *The New Breed*, p. 165; Montross and Canzona, *The Inchon-Seoul Operation*, pp. 259-61.

[31] 1st Mar Div SAR, vol. I, an. C, G-3 Sec, p. 23, 25 Sep 50, and situation overlay 251800 Sep.

[32] Most of the responsible Marine officers felt that X Corps hurried them too much in the Seoul operation. Col John H. Chiles (G-3 X Corps Sep 50), MS review comments for author, 15 Dec 53; Lt Gen Oliver P. Smith, MS review comments, 25 Feb 54; Almond, MS review comments for author, 15 Dec 53; Interv, author with Lt Col Earle W. Williamson (G-3 Sec, X Corps), 28 Aug 51.

[33] Interv, author with Almond, 13 Dec 51; Smith, MS review comments, 25 Feb 54.

the west edge of Seoul. About 0930 General Almond arrived at 7th Division headquarters and conferred with General Barr, the 7th Division commander, Brig. Gen. Henry I. Hodes, assistant 7th Division commander, and Col. Louis T. Heath, the division chief of staff. Almond told Barr he had tentatively decided that the 7th Division would attack across the Han River into Seoul the next morning. Almond then returned to his command post and there told Colonel Paik, commander of the ROK 17th Regiment, that he expected to attach his regiment to the 32d Infantry for the attack on Seoul.[34]

His mind now made up, Almond called a commanders' conference to meet with him at 1400 at Yongdungp'o Circle. Present besides Almond were Generals Smith, Barr, and Hodes, Colonels Forney and Beauchamp, and Col. John H. Chiles. In this open-air meeting, Almond quickly told the assembled commanders that he was changing the boundary between the 1st Marine Division and the 7th Infantry Division, and that the 32d Regiment, with the ROK 17th Regiment attached, would attack across the Han River into Seoul at 0600 the next morning. The meeting was brief. At its conclusion the officers dispersed at once to make their respective plans.[35]

In the afternoon and evening, X Corps attached the ROK 17th Regiment, the Marine 1st Amphibious Tractor Battalion (less one company), and two platoons of A Company, 56th Amphibious Tank and Tractor Battalion, to the 7th Division to support the crossing.[36]

The crossing was to be at the Sinsa-ri ferry, three miles east of the main rail and highway bridges over the Han River. On the opposite (north) bank, South Mountain (Nam-san) extended from the river northwest two miles into the heart of Seoul, culminating in a peak 900 feet high, the highest point in the city, about one mile east of the main Seoul rail station. A long, ridgelike, shallow saddle connected this peak with a slightly lower one. On a western finger ridge of the main peak, near the 350-foot elevation and only half a mile from the rail station, was a large shrine and a formally landscaped park. From the western base of South Mountain a long series of steps led up to this shrine and park. Viewing Seoul on a north-south axis, the peak of South Mountain was halfway into the city. Government House, at the northern edge of the city, lay two miles away. The main highway and rail line running east out of the city passed about a mile beyond the northern base of South Mountain. On this mountain nearly three months before, a company of ROK soldiers had conducted the last action in the defense of Seoul, dying, it has been said, to the last man.

The 32d Infantry's mission was first to seize and secure South Mountain, then to secure Hill 120 situated two miles eastward at the southeast edge of Seoul, and finally to seize and secure

---

[34] 7th Div WD, 24 Sep 50; Diary of CG X Corps, 24 Sep 50; Hist, Off CofS, X Corps, 24 Sep 50.

[35] Interv, author with Almond, 13 Dec 51; Ltr, Beauchamp to author, 15 Jul 53; Diary of CG X Corps, 24 Sep 50; 7th Div WD, 24 Sep 50; 32d Inf WD, 24 Sep 50. Forney, a Marine officer, was X Corps Deputy CofS.

[36] 32d Inf WD, 24 Sep 50; 7th Div WD, 24 Sep 50; Diary of CG X Corps, 24 Sep 50; Hist, Off CofS, X Corps, 24 Sep 50.

THE CAPTURE OF SEOUL

SEOUL AS SEEN FROM THE AIR. *Government House is in the center.*

Hill 348, a large, high hill mass five miles east of Seoul and dominating the highway and rail line entering the city from that side. The regiment had a strength of 4,912 men as it prepared for the crossing—3,110 Americans and 1,802 ROK's.[37]

Before daybreak of the 25th, General Hodes established an advanced division command post near the river from which he was to direct the crossing operation. At 0400, General Almond, Admiral Struble, and members of the corps staff departed the X Corps headquarters at Ascom City to watch the crossing of the 32d Regiment. General Barr went forward at 0430 to the 32d Infantry's command post and an hour later he and Colonel Beauchamp left for an observation post near the river. At 0600, the 48th Field Artillery Battalion began firing a 30-minute artillery preparation, and the heavy mortars joined in to

---

[37] 7th Div WD, 25 Sep 50; 32d Inf WD, 25 Sep 50.

pound the cliffs lining the opposite side beyond the river bank.[38]

Colonel Mount's 2d Battalion, selected to make the assault crossing, loaded into amphibious tractors in its assembly area and at 0630 F Company started across the Han. A ground fog obscured the river area. The entire 2d Battalion reached the north bank without loss of personnel or equipment. The 2d Battalion hurried across the narrow river beach, scaled the 30- to 60-foot cliffs, and moved rapidly to the slopes of South Mountain. An hour after the first troops had crossed the river the bright morning sun dispersed the ground fog. Air strikes then came in on South Mountain and Hill 120. Apparently this crossing surprised the North Koreans. Their works on South Mountain were only lightly manned.

The 1st Battalion, commanded by Colonel Faith, followed the 2d across the Han and at 0830 started to move east along the river bank toward Hill 120. Just after noon the 3d Battalion crossed the river, followed the 1st Battalion eastward, and passed through it to occupy Hill 120. The 1st Battalion then took a position between the 3d and 2d Battalions. The ROK 17th Regiment crossed the Han immediately behind the 3d Battalion and moved to the extreme right flank of the 32d Infantry line where, at 2150, it began an all-night attack toward Hill 348.[39]

While the rest of the regiment crossed the Han behind it and moved eastward, the 2d Battalion climbed the slopes of South Mountain, reaching and clearing the summit against moderate resistance by 1500. Once there, it immediately began digging in on a tight perimeter.

The North Koreans did not counterattack South Mountain as quickly as expected. The night passed tensely but quietly for the waiting 2d Battalion. Finally, at 0430 on the morning of the 26th, the soldiers heard tanks moving about and the sound of automatic weapons fire to their front. In semidarkness half an hour later a large enemy force, estimated to number approximately 1,000 men, violently counterattacked the 2d Battalion perimeter on top of South Mountain. On the higher western knob of the mountain, G Company held its position against this attack, but on the lower eastern knob North Koreans overran F Company. Using all its reserves, Colonel Mount's battalion finally restored its positions at 0700 after two hours of battle and drove the surviving enemy down the slopes. Mount's men counted 110 enemy dead within its perimeter and 284 more outside for a total of 394 enemy killed. They took 174 prisoners.[40]

E Company mopped up enemy troops on the rear slopes of the mountain and in the area at its base near the river. Later in the morning, elements of the 1st Battalion had a sharp engagement in the streets immediately north of South Mountain, capturing there some eighty enemy soldiers, apparently a remnant

---

[38] 32d Inf WD, 25 Sep 50; Diary of CG X Corps, 25 Sep 50.

[39] 32d Inf WD, 25 Sep 50; 7th Div WD, 25 Sep 50; Diary of CG X Corps, 25 Sep 50; Beauchamp, MS review comments for author, 19 Jan 54. Where time for events differs in the various levels of command records, the author has followed that of the lower unit, the one closest to the action, unless other evidence supports another choice.

[40] 32d Inf WD, 26 Sep 50; Ltr, Beauchamp to author, 15 Jul 53.

of the force that had counterattacked South Mountain.

To the east, the 1st Battalion on the morning of the 26th engaged in a heavy fire fight while the 3d Battalion, commanded by Lt. Col. Heinrich G. Schumann, advanced from Hill 120 toward Hill 348, four miles farther east. In this advance, L Company saw a large column of enemy troops on the highway leaving Seoul. The company commander, 1st Lt. Harry J. McCaffrey, Jr., seized the opportunity for surprise and immediately ordered his men to attack. His initiative paid off. In the ensuing action, L Company killed about 500 North Korean soldiers, destroyed 5 tanks, destroyed or captured more than 40 vehicles, 3 artillery pieces, 7 machine guns, 2 ammunition dumps, much clothing and POL products, and overran and captured a large headquarters of corps size, which may have been the principal enemy headquarters in the defense of Seoul.[41]

By midafternoon (26 September) the ROK 17th Regiment had captured Hills 348 and 292 dominating the highway four miles east of Seoul. That evening the 32d Infantry and the ROK 17th Regiment cleared their zone of the enemy, and E Company established contact with the marines on the regimental left at the western base of South Mountain.

Battle of the Barricades

On 25 September, while the 32d Infantry crossed the Han and seized South Mountain, the 1st Marine Division entered Seoul proper. When the 1st Marine Regiment turned north that day, ahead of it lay the main Seoul railroad station. the French, American, and Russian consulates, the City Hall, the Duk Soo Palace of ancient rulers of Korea and Museum of Art, and the main business and hotel area. The 5th Marines, on the other hand, was just entering the city in the northwest quarter, pointed generally eastward toward Government House two miles away. Its course would take it past big Sodaemun Prison. Beyond Government House lay Changdok Palace and the Royal Gardens. That evening the 1st and 5th Marines made plans for a co-ordinated attack the next morning.

Just before dusk an air report claimed that enemy columns were streaming north out of the city. General Almond at X Corps headquarters immediately sent a message to the Far East Air Forces requesting a flare mission to illuminate the roads so that Marine night fighters could attack the enemy troops. A B-29 dropped flares for several hours and two long columns of enemy soldiers came under air attack. Corps artillery placed interdiction fire on the closer portions of the escape route.[42]

At 2040 that evening a X Corps flash message from General Almond came over the teletype to the 1st Marine Division saying, "X Corps TACAir Commander reports enemy fleeing city of Seoul on road north. . . . He is conducting heavy air attack and will con-

---

[41] Ltr, Beauchamp to author, 15 Jul 53, and MS review comments, 19 Jan 54; 32d Inf WD, 26 Sep 50; 7th Div WD, Narr, 26 Sep 50, and Narr, 7th Div POR 8, 26 Sep 50. Headquarters, 7th Infantry Division, General Order 69, 13 October 1950, awarded the Silver Star to Lieutenant McCaffrey.

[42] Hist, Off CofS, X Corps, 25 Sep 50; USAF Hist Study 71, p. 76.

tinue same. You will push attack *now* to the limit of your objective in order to insure maximum destruction of enemy forces."[43] Col. Alpha L. Bowser, 1st Marine Division operations officer, doubted that the enemy was fleeing the city. He telephoned the X Corps operations officer and questioned the order to "attack now," but that officer told him to attack as ordered. Bowser then gave the message to General Smith who in turn telephoned General Ruffner, X Corps chief of staff, objecting to the order. Smith did not believe the enemy was leaving Seoul and he did not want to attack through the city at night. Ruffner told him that Almond personally had dictated the order and that it was to be executed without delay. General Smith then telephoned Colonels Puller and Murray at 2200 and transmitted the order. He told them to concentrate their advance along avenues that could be identified easily at night, and ordered the three Marine regiments to establish contact with each other.[44]

Within a few minutes after the 5th Marines received the order for the night attack, an enemy force of approximately 200 men struck its 3d Battalion. Fighting continued until 0445 when the battalion repulsed the North Koreans. Meanwhile, regimental patrols sent south and southeast to establish contact with the 1st Marines failed to do so. Likewise, patrols of the 7th Marines from the north failed to establish contact with the 5th Marines. Except for its patrols, the 5th Marines did not move forward during the night from its evening positions.[45]

After receiving the order for the night attack, Colonel Puller ordered the 1st Marines to prepare to attack at 0145 after a 15-minute artillery preparation. A patrol from the 3d Battalion moved out at the conclusion of this preparation and a short distance away encountered a large enemy force preparing to counterattack. Some members of the patrol escaped and gave the alarm. The battalion at 0153 sent a flash message to Colonel Puller that an enemy tank-led force was on the point of attacking it. Puller thereupon ordered a second 15-minute artillery barrage to be fired directly in front of the 3d Battalion, the Marine attack to follow that.

This second barrage, together with mortar, tank, and automatic fire caught an estimated force of 700 North Koreans, supported by twelve tanks, two self-propelled guns, and 120-mm. mortar fire, attacking straight down the main boulevard, and decimated it. The lead enemy tank struck a mine at a Marine street block and bazookas destroyed others. Burning buildings illuminated the street scene in front of the 3d Battalion. The enemy attack continued until daylight although it became progressively weaker. After daylight the marines captured 83 prisoners, counted 250 enemy dead, and saw four tanks and two self-propelled guns knocked out in front of them.[46]

Because of the enemy counterattack

---

[43] 1st Mar Div SAR, vol. I, an. C, G-3 Sec, p. 25, 25 Sep 50.
[44] Ibid.
[45] Ibid., p. 26, 26 Sep 50.
[46] Ibid., vol. I, an. C and an. B, app. 2, p. 14, 26 Sep 50; Ibid., vol. II, an. PP, p. 9; X Corps WD, 26 Sep 50; Diary of CG X Corps, 26 Sep 50; Geer, *The New Breed*, pp. 168-70.

THE CAPTURE OF SEOUL

TANKS ENTERING SEOUL *through cleared barricade.*

during the night and the lack of contact between its regiments, the Marine division did not launch a night attack as ordered. Its lines after daylight, 26 September, were substantially the same as they had been the evening before.

It appears that after the seizure of South Mountain by the 32d Infantry and the reduction of the hill defenses at the western edge of the city by the 5th Marines during the 25th, the North Korean commander in Seoul decided the city was doomed and began the withdrawal of certain units that evening while leaving others to fight desperate delaying actions. The aerial reports of enemy columns fleeing the city and General Almond's conclusion that the North Koreans were evacuating Seoul were therefore not without foundation. The major enemy unit withdrawing at this time was the N.K. *18th Division* which had fought south of the Han River in the Yongdungp'o area. On 24 September it had assembled in Seoul, and the next evening the approximately 5,000 men remaining in the division retreated northward on the Uijongbu road, headed for Ch'orwon. At the same time, to cover this withdrawal, the North Korean commander struck with desperate counterattacks at every point of American advance into the city. Against the 2d Battalion, 32d Infantry, on South Mountain he struck with one battalion and at other elements of the regiment eastward with another battalion. The heavy counterattack against the 3d Battalion, 1st Marines, he launched in reinforced battalion strength; while against the 3d Battalion, 5th Marines, he sent a reinforced company.[47]

After the enemy attacks died away with the coming of daylight on the 26th, the marines launched their attack. In a day-long effort down Ma-Po Boulevard the 2d Battalion, 1st Marines, gained less than a mile, and very little at all after 1400. Snipers fired from houses along the way and enemy soldiers manned barricades, making of each one a small battlefield. The 5th Marines had even stronger opposition in trying to advance from a spur of Hill 296 into the city and made only slight gains, but it did establish contact with the 1st Marines.

Just after noon, the Marine division brought Col. Homer L. Litzenberg's 7th Marines into the fight for Seoul proper, directing it to seize the mountain pass north of the city, and to cut the highway running northeast out of Seoul for Uijongbu and Ch'orwon at a point one mile northeast of Government House. The regiment's D Company turned down the Kaesong-Seoul highway toward the city, seeking to establish contact with the 5th Marines, but came under heavy enemy fire at 0830 opposite Sodaemun Prison at the northwest corner of Seoul. The company suffered many casualties there and, unable to advance farther, withdrew to a road cut between Hills 296 and 338 where it established a perimeter defense. That afternoon two planes dropped ammunition and medical supplies to it. Enemy fire hit both planes, and one crash-landed at Kimpo. Friendly tanks succeeded in reaching D Company's perimeter and carried out the wounded. At dusk on Tuesday, 26 September, X Corps troops held approximately half the city.[48]

About twenty hours earlier, just before midnight of the 25th, General Almond had announced the liberation of Seoul, three months to the day after the North Koreans began the invasion. Almond apparently based his announcement on air reports of North Korean evacuation of the city and the seizure of South Mountain during the day. On the 26th, General MacArthur signed and released United Nations Command Communiqué 9 at 1410 announcing the fall of Seoul. The communiqué said in part, "Seoul, the capital of the Republic of Korea, is again in friendly hands. United Nations forces, including the 17th Regiment of the ROK Army and elements of the U.S. 7th and 1st Marine Divisions, have completed the envelopment and seizure of the city." [49] In subsequent communiqués MacArthur made no mention of further fighting in Seoul, confining comment to combat operations in the Suwon area south of the city.

But on 27 September, the battle of the barricades in Seoul continued. In the middle part of Seoul the barricades stretched across the streets from side to side and were usually placed at intersections. Mostly they were chest-high and made of rice and fiber bags filled with earth. From behind them and at their

---

[47] FEC, Inf Order of Battle, N.K. Army, Supp, Gen Hist of N.K. Army Units, Chart 14 (N.K. *18th Div*), 16 Sep 51; ATIS Interrog Rpts, Issue 10, p. 78, Rpt 1534, Lt Lee Song Yol.

[48] 1st Mar Div SAR, vol. I, an. C, G-3 Sec, pp. 26-28, 26 Sep 50; *Ibid.*, vol. III, 5th Mar SAR, p. 13, 27 Sep 50; X Corps WD, 26 Sep 50; Geer, *The New Breed*, p. 176; New York *Herald Tribune*, September 27, 1950, Bigart dispatch from Seoul.

[49] UNC Communiqué 9, 26 Sep 50; GHQ UNC G-3 Opn Rpt, 26 Sep 50; X Corps WD, 26 Sep 50; New York *Times*, September 26, 1950, Lawrence dispatch.

THE CAPTURE OF SEOUL

sides enemy soldiers fired antitank guns and swept the streets with machine gun fire. Other soldiers were posted in adjacent buildings. Antitank mines belted the streets in front of the barricades.

The Marine attack settled into a routine for reducing the barricades. Navy and Marine planes would rocket and strafe them, mortarmen and infantry would set up a base of fire covering the engineers while they exploded the mines, two or three Pershing tanks would advance to the barricade, take it under fire destroying antitank guns and automatic weapons, and breach it. Occasionally, flame-throwing tanks rumbled up to stubbornly held positions and helped reduce the barrier. Infantry accompanying and following the tanks gave them protection, destroyed snipers, and cleared the area. A single barricade might hold up a battalion advance as much as an hour.

On the 27th, the 2d Battalion, 1st Marines, drove down Ma-Po Boulevard into the heart of the city, capturing the French Embassy and raising the American flag over it just before 1100. Richard J. H. Johnston, a correspondent for the New York *Times* who had lived in Seoul for four years, guided Capt. Charles D. Frederick and his E Company men in the afternoon to the Soviet Embassy, where they pulled down the Red flag and raised the American at 1530. They then crossed over to the adjacent American Embassy and raised the American flag over it seven minutes later. North Korean machine gunners at the gate of the American Embassy surrendered without firing. The 1st Battalion meanwhile captured the railroad station in the morning in fairly heavy action and then encountered a series of strongly defended barricades along the main thoroughfare leading northward into the center of the city. ROK marines followed the 1st Battalion, mopping up behind it.[50]

In the northwestern part of the city, the 5th Marines advanced on the 27th against relatively light resistance. Overnight the opposition of the previous day had largely vanished. On the regimental north flank, E Company without opposition entered Sodaemun Prison. Earlier a tank-led force from the 7th Marines had relieved D Company in its perimeter just beyond the prison. A Korean civilian informed troops of E Company, 5th Marines, that about five days earlier approximately 400 American prisoners held in the prison had been removed and taken northward. At midafternoon, the 5th Marines established contact with the 7th Marines in the northwest corner of Seoul.

The main axis of attack of the 5th Marine Regiment, however, was farther south. There the 3d Battalion secured the Seoul Middle School and Hill 79 just to the north of it by 1015, and reorganized for the attack toward Government House, its major objective. From the Seoul Middle School the battalion advanced due east to Kwang Who Moon Circle, where a memorial shrine stood. From behind a barricade at this intersection the North Koreans put up their last organized resistance in the heart of the city. A flame-throwing tank clanked across the large circular plaza and ended this resistance.

---

[50] 1st Mar Div SAR, vol. I, an. C, p. 29; *Ibid.*, vol. II, 1st Mar Regt SAR, an. PP, p. 10, 27 Sep 50; X Corps WD, G-3 Sec, Msg J-17, 271145 Sep 50; New York *Times*, September 28, and Johnston dispatch from Seoul, September 27, 1950.

From Kwang Who Moon Circle a broad and, in peacetime, imposingly beautiful, modern boulevard also named Kwang Who Moon runs north one-half mile, terminating in front of the modern and handsome Government House. After the tanks had reduced the barricade at Kwang Who Moon Circle, G Company, 5th Marines, advanced without opposition down the boulevard to Government House "as fast as they could walk," as one who was present has written. The company had possession of the building at 1508, and immediately thereafter struck the North Korean flags flying from the flag poles on either side of the Court of Lions in front of the building and raised in their place the American flag.

The breakthrough to Government House apparently caught some North Korean officials or stragglers there by surprise, compelling a hasty getaway, for upon entering the troops found hot food ready for eating. The battalion cleared the area of snipers and stragglers during the afternoon, and that night the 3d Battalion established its command post in the building.[51]

During that morning, the 1st Battalion, 5th Marines, following behind the 3d Battalion, turned off to the left after reaching the Seoul Middle School and attacked north to Hill 338, a key terrain feature a mile northwest of Government House. At 1900 it secured the hill which dominated the Seoul-Pyongyang highway at the northwest corner of the city. Except for scattered snipers and stragglers, the last defenders of Seoul withdrew from the city that night.

The next day, 28 September, although its 1st Battalion had to contend with many mines, the 1st Marines swept through the northeast corner of Seoul against only light resistance to complete its occupation. By evening the regiment had taken Hills 132 and 133, at the northeast edge of Seoul, dominating the Seoul-Uijongbu-Ch'orwon highway. A mile farther north, the enemy held the 7th Marines in check short of its objective, Hill 224, the key terrain feature on the other, west, side of the highway.[52]

Enemy resistance in Seoul had ended —the North Korean forces were withdrawing northward in the direction of Uijongbu just ninety days after they had victoriously entered the city in their bid for conquest of South Korea.

MacArthur Re-establishes Syngman Rhee in Seoul

After his return to Tokyo, General MacArthur on 23 September sent a message to the Joint Chiefs of Staff in Washington saying in part, "I plan to return President Rhee, his cabinet, senior members of the legislature, the U.N. Commission and perhaps others of similar official category to domicile in Seoul as soon as conditions there are sufficiently stable to permit reasonable security."[53] The combat situation in Seoul did not permit final plans for the ceremony until 27 and 28 September.

General MacArthur and his party ar-

---

[51] 5th Mar Regt SAR in 1st Mar Div SAR, vol. III, an. P, 10–13, 27 Sep 50; 1st Mar Div SAR, vol. I, an. C, G–3 Sec, p. 30; New York *Herald Tribune*, September 28, 1950, Bigart dispatch from Seoul, 27 September.

[52] 1st Mar Div SAR, vol. I, p. 19, an. C, G–3 Sec, pp. 30–31; and an. B, app. 2, p. 16, 28 Sep 50; X Corps WD, G–2 Sec Hist Rpt, PIR 10, 28 Sep 50.

[53] Msg C64159, MacArthur to JCS, 23 Sep 50, CM-IN 14748.

THE CAPTURE OF SEOUL

rived at Kimpo Airfield from Tokyo at 1000, 29 September. General Almond and other high-ranking officers met the party and proceeded with it to Seoul. During the night bulldozers had worked to clear the main streets of barricades and the litter of battle. Wildly cheering throngs of South Koreans assembled and lined the streets in the shell-torn, burning city. The 3d Battalion, 1st Marines, provided security along the route from the Han River ponton bridge; the 3d Battalion, 5th Marines, provided security around Government House.[54]

The National Assembly Hall in Government House was packed with selected South Korean officials and citizens and representatives of the combat units that had liberated Seoul. At 1200, General MacArthur came into the chamber with President Rhee and proceeded to the dais where important officers and officials were seated, including General Walker and a few Eighth Army officers who had flown to Seoul on MacArthur's invitation. The Austrian-born wife of President Rhee took her place beside her husband. MacArthur began forthwith to deliver his short address in sonorous voice and unhurried words:

Mr. President: By the grace of a merciful Providence our forces fighting under the standard of that greatest hope and inspiration of mankind, the United Nations, have liberated this ancient capital city of Korea.

He spoke of the ravages of war that had visited the land, of the righteous wrath and indignation that had caused fifty-three nations to pledge their aid to the Republic of Korea, and of the spiritual revulsion against Communism. Then, turning to President Rhee, he continued:

In behalf of the United Nations Command I am happy to restore to you, Mr. President, the seat of your government that from it you may better fulfill your constitutional responsibilities.

The assemblage then joined MacArthur in reciting the Lord's Prayer. While MacArthur spoke slivers of glass fell from the partially shattered glass-paneled roof, but he gave them no heed.[55]

Aging but indomitable, Syngman Rhee rose to express the gratitude of the Republic of Korea for the liberation of its capital city. All but overcome with emotion, he departed from his prepared text and stretching out his hands, clenching and unclenching them, spoke to that part of the audience made up of American soldiers, "How can I ever explain to you my own undying gratitude and that of the Korean people?"

The short ceremony over, General MacArthur left at once for Kimpo Airfield and at 1335 departed for Tokyo.

The capture of Seoul led to a series of exchanges between officials of the United States Government and MacArthur. President Truman sent a message which said in part, "Few operations in military history can match either the delaying action where you traded space for time in which to build up your forces, or the brilliant maneuver which has now resulted in the liberation of Seoul." From the Joint Chiefs of Staff

---

[54] Diary of CG X Corps, 29 Sep 50; New York *Herald Tribune*, September 30, 1950; 1st Mar Div SAR, vol. I, an. C, G-3 Sec, 28-29 Sep 50.

[55] DA Public Info Div (PID) file, Miscellaneous Public Statements, Letters, and Documents relating to the Korean War, September 1950; New York *Herald Tribune*, September 30, 1950.

MacArthur received a message which read in part, "Your transition from defensive to offensive operations was magnificently planned, timed, and executed. . . . We remain completely confident that the great task entrusted to you by the United Nations will be carried to a successful conclusion." [56]

MacArthur sent his thanks to the President and the Joint Chiefs of Staff, saying he would publish their messages to all elements of his command.

The Blocking Force South of Seoul

While the greater part of X Corps concentrated its strength before Seoul and was preoccupied with its capture, the blocking force of the 31st Infantry Regiment, 7th Division, thirty miles below the city, was not without action. On 23 September, when Colonel Ovenshine's 31st Infantry Regiment assumed responsibility for Suwon and Suwon Airfield, its mission was to clear the enemy from Suwon and to seize and hold the high ground south of the airfield. Prisoners captured in Suwon by the Reconnaissance Company reported that a regiment of the *105th Armored Division* was in Choch'iwon on the 18th, only fifty air miles to the south, and on its way north to help the Seoul garrison. If this was true, it had to be assumed that this armored force must be approaching the 31st Infantry position. Accordingly, the regiment kept the area south of Suwon under close observation.[57]

During the night of 24 September, the 2d Battalion, 31st Infantry, on high ground (Hill 142) two miles south of the Suwon Airfield came under attack an hour before midnight, and enemy armor struck the battalion's left flank resting on the Suwon-Osan highway. The battalion, with the supporting artillery fire of the 57th Field Artillery Battalion and of B Battery, 15th Field Artillery Battalion, repulsed the attack and knocked out four T34 tanks. The next day the 92d Field Artillery Battalion moved to Suwon to strengthen the forces there. Aerial reconnaissance on the 25th and 26th reported enemy entrenchments in the hills dominating both sides of the highway and rail line just north of Osan, eight to ten miles south of Suwon and two to three miles south of the American position.[58]

On the 26th, Colonel Ovenshine ordered the 2d Battalion to attack and seize the high ground held by the North Koreans near Osan. Interestingly enough, this included the positions where Task Force Smith had met and delayed the North Koreans briefly on 5 July in the first American ground action of the war. The 3d Battalion, less I Company, stood ready to reinforce the 2d Battalion. Ovenshine started the 2d Battalion Task Force—composed of E, F, and part of G Companies and two platoons of tanks—on a wide, flanking movement southeastwardly toward Osan to attack the enemy positions from the rear. At the same time, he formed another attack force composed of elements of G and H Companies, and A

---

[56] DA PID file, Miscellaneous Public Statements, Letters, and Documents relating to the Korean War, September 1950.

[57] 31st Inf WD, 23 Sep 50; 7th Div WD, 23 Sep 50; X Corps WD, G-2 Hist Rpt, PIR 6, 24 Sep 50; Interrog of Maj Lee Ki J'un.

[58] 31st Inf WD, overlay to POR 10, 24 Sep 50; 7th Div WD, 24-25 Sep 50.

Company, 73d Tank Battalion, to attack south along the highway.

By daylight of the 27th, the flanking force arrived at Osan. A bazooka team destroyed an enemy tank that fired on the column. The force then moved through Osan and engaged the enemy on the hills northward. Attacking down the road simultaneously from the north, the second force was stopped by strong enemy tank, antitank gun, mortar, and small arms fire. Fighting continued throughout the clear, warm autumn day, with the 31st Infantry making only small gains. Prisoners captured in the action said that the enemy force was indeed from the *105th Armored Division*. While its ground gains were slight, the 31st Infantry claimed the destruction or immobilization of 14 tanks, 6 antitank guns, and several mortars, and the infliction of 300 North Korean casualties. The 31st Infantry's two attack forces dug in that night around Hill 113 where the main enemy force was concentrated. Maj. Lester K. Olson, the regimental S-3, and Lt. Col. Robert R. Summers, the 2d Battalion commander, were both seriously wounded during the day.[59]

On the morning of the 28th, the American infantry withdrew at 0830 almost a mile westward from their overnight positions to make sure that they would not suffer casualties from air strikes scheduled to come in against Hills 113 and 92. Beginning at noon and continuing for fifty minutes, seven Navy planes attacked both hills and the railroad tunnel area just east of Hill 92, using napalm extensively. When the air strikes ended, the 57th and 92d Field Artillery Battalions pounded the hills for thirty minutes, the Heavy Mortar Company joining in the preparation. When it ended, K and L Companies attacked eastward against Hill 113. By 1515 they had secured the hill against only light resistance, and from there L Company attacked across the saddle to Hill 92, 600 yards away, supported by K Company fire from Hill 113. An hour later the 31st Infantry held both hills—taken without a single casualty to itself. Surviving enemy troops withdrew eastward. The road between Suwon and Osan was open. The next day the 31st Infantry buried more than a hundred enemy dead on the captured positions.[60]

While the 31st Infantry was clearing the Osan highway, the 2d Battalion, 17th Infantry, 7th Division, fought its first battle of the war on 29 September in a heavy fire fight against an enemy force at the southeast side of Seoul. In this action, which continued after dark, the battalion suffered seventy-nine casualties. That night the 49th Field Artillery Battalion laid down a barrage which effectively broke up an attempted enemy counterattack. The North Koreans reportedly suffered more than 400 men killed.[61]

On 30 September the 1st Marine Di-

---

[59] 31st Inf WD, 26–28 Sep 50; 7th Div WD, 26–27 Sep 50; X Corps WD, G–3 Sec, Msg J–52, 2315 27 Sep 50; Interv, author with Barr, 1 Feb 54.

[60] 31st Inf WD, and PIR 9, an. 2, 28 Sep 50; 7th Div WD, 28–29 Sep 50. General Almond was dissatisfied with Colonel Ovenshine's handling of the 31st Infantry in the action below Suwon and relieved him of command on 5 October. Intervs, author with Almond, 13 Dec 51, and Barr, 1 Feb 54.

[61] 7th Div WD, 29 Sep 50; 17th Inf WD, 28–29 Sep 50; Barr, Notes, 29 Sep 50, and MS review comments, Nov 57. The third regiment of the 7th Division, the 17th Infantry, arrived at Inch'on on the 24th from Pusan, where it had been held in floating reserve for Eighth Army, and began unloading the next day.

vision assumed responsibility for the 32d Infantry zone in Seoul and that unit then crossed back to the south side of the Han River.

The X Corps Situation

After the capture of Seoul, the 1st Marine Division cleared enemy troops from the northern environs of the city. On 1 October, elements of the 5th Marines patrolled the P'yongyang highway as far as Munsan-ni and the Imjin River. They encountered only scattered individual enemy riflemen except in the vicinity of Munsan-ni.

The 7th Marines, at the same time, advanced up the Uijongbu road north of the city against almost no resistance, hampered only by mines. But the next day, 2 October, the regiment made virtually no gains. Three battalions of the *31st Regiment, N.K. 31st Division,* well dug-in on either side of the highway, stopped the regiment in hard fighting three miles south of Uijongbu in the vicinity of Nuwon-ni. There high mountains closing in on either side of the highway created a natural fortress.[62]

During the night, the enemy blocking force withdrew northward, and on 3 October tanks led the 2d Battalion into Uijongbu in the afternoon. Marine and Navy air strikes had completely destroyed the town. The 7th Marines occupied the high ground just north of Uijongbu and consolidated its position around the town for the night. The fighting of 2–3 October in front of Uijongbu was the last organized resistance the 1st Marine Division encountered in the Inch'on-Seoul operation.[63]

Before being driven from Seoul, the North Koreans had taken ghastly revenge on men, women, and children in the families of South Korean soldiers, policemen, and guerrillas.

The Seoul operation disclosed that the preinvasion estimate of 5,000 organized troops in the city was low and that, instead, there were approximately 8,000 such troops in Seoul and 5,000 more in the Yongdungp'o area. Reinforcements after the landing at Inch'on brought the total enemy troops in Seoul to at least 20,000. And there were at least 10,000 enemy soldiers between the Han River and Suwon. Below Suwon in the Osan area there were from 2,000 to 3,000 more. It appears that altogether somewhat more than 30,000 North Korean troops entered battle in the Inch'on-Suwon-Seoul area, and that there were perhaps 10,000 more miscellaneous soldiers in the vicinity, uncommitted or who arrived too late to be used. The X Corps reported 7,000 North Korean prisoners taken in the fighting and estimated enemy troops killed at 14,000.[64]

The 1st Marine Division did not lose a single tank to enemy tank action in the Seoul operation but lost several to enemy infantry action. An accurate

---

[62] 1st Mar Div SAR, vol. I, an. C, G-3 Sec, pp. 36–37, 1–2 Oct 50; *Ibid.*, vol. III, an. RR, p. 24.

[63] 1st Mar Div SAR, an. C, G-3 Sec, p. 38, 3 Oct 50; Interv, author with Col Harold K. Johnson, 4 Jan 52.

[64] 1st Mar Div SAR, vol. I, p. 21, and an. B, app. 2, p. 16, 28 Sep, and p. 24, 5 Oct 50; X Corps WD, 30 Sep 50; 32d Inf WD, 30 Sep 50. The 1st Marine Division captured 4,792 prisoners and claimed to have inflicted 13,666 enemy casualties. In the 7th Division the 32d Infantry Regiment captured 1,203 prisoners and estimated it had killed 3,000 enemy troops; the 31st and 17th Infantry Regiments each inflicted several hundred casualties. Estimates of enemy casualties inflicted by ROK units are not available.

THE CAPTURE OF SEOUL

count of the enemy tanks destroyed in the X Corps operation is hard to make, but it appears that approximately 45 to 50 were destroyed in the Inch'on-Yongdungp'o-Seoul area and about 10 to 15 more in the Suwon-Osan area, or about 60 altogether. The North Koreans lost a great amount of other military equipment in the Seoul operation. The 1st Marine Division alone reported that it had destroyed or captured 23 120-mm. mortars, 19 45-mm. antitank guns, 56 heavy machine guns, 337 light and submachine guns, 59 14.5 antitank rifles, and 7,543 rifles.[65]

The Inch'on-Seoul victory cost the United Nations forces approximately 3,500 casualties. The 7th Infantry Division suffered 572 battle casualties, including 106 killed, 409 wounded, and 57 missing in action. Of the total, 166 were ROK soldiers integrated into the division. Within the division, the 32d Regiment lost 66 killed, 272 wounded, and 47 missing. The heaviest losses in X Corps occurred in the 1st Marine Division which suffered total casualties of 2,383 men—364 killed, 53 who died of wounds, 1,961 wounded, and 5 missing. Marine losses were heaviest for the six days from 21 to 27 September. During that time it suffered 1,482 battle casualties, the greatest single day's loss being 285 on 24 September.[66]

---

[65] 1st Mar Div SAR, vol. II, an. OO, p. 42, 7 Oct 50, and an. PP, p. 14; Ibid., vol. I, an. B, app. 2, p. 24, 5 Oct 50; 7th Div WD, 18–30 Sep 50.

[66] X Corps WD, 30 Sep 50; 7th Div WD, Narr, 30 Sep 50; 32d Inf WD, 30 Sep 50; 1st Mar Div SAR, vol. I, p. 20, and an. A, G–1 Sec, p. 6; Smith, MS review comments, 25 Feb 54. In a letter to the author, 13 February 1954, General Smith claimed the 1st Marine Division suffered 2,430 battle casualties in the Inch'on-Seoul operation. Montross and Canzona, The Inchon-Seoul Operation, page 297, gives Marine casualties as 366 KIA, 49 DOW, 6 MIA, and 2,029 WIA, for a total of 2,450. The figure 2,383 is that given in Marine records cited.

CHAPTER XXVII

Breaking the Cordon

> Tactics are based on weapon-power . . . strategy is based on movement . . . movement depends on supply.
> J. F. C. FULLER, *The Generalship of Ulysses S. Grant*

The Inch'on landing put the United States X Corps in the enemy's rear. Concurrently, Eighth Army was to launch a general attack all along its front to fix and hold the enemy's main combat strength and prevent movement of units from the Pusan Perimeter to reinforce the threatened area in his rear. This attack would also strive to break the enemy cordon that had for six weeks held Eighth Army within a shrinking Pusan Perimeter. If Eighth Army succeeded in breaking the cordon it was to drive north to effect a juncture with X Corps in the Seoul area. The battle line in the south was 180 air miles at its closest point from the landing area in the enemy's rear, and much farther by the winding mountain roads. This was the distance that at first separated the anvil from the hammer which was to pound to bits the enemy caught between them.

Most Eighth Army staff officers were none too hopeful that the army could break out with the forces available. And to increase their concern, in September critical shortages began to appear in Eighth Army's supplies, including artillery ammunition. Even for the breakout effort Eighth Army had to establish a limit of fifty rounds a day for primary attack and twenty-five rounds for secondary attack. Fortunately, the *Aripa* arrived in the Far East with a cargo of 105-mm. howitzer shells in time for their use in the offensive. But, despite some misgivings, General Walker and his chief of staff, General Allen, believed that if the Inch'on landing succeeded Eighth Army could assume the offensive and break through the enemy forces encircling it.[1]

The Eighth Army Plan

The Eighth Army published its attack plan on 6 September and the next day General Allen sent it to Tokyo for approval. Eighth Army revised the plan on 11 September, and on the 16th made it an operations directive. It set the hour for attack by United Nations and ROK forces in the Perimeter at 0900, 16 September, one day after the Inch'on landing. The U.S. Eighth and the ROK Armies were to attack "from present

---

[1] Interv, author with Lt Col Paul F. Smith, 7 Oct 52; Ltr, Maj Gen Leven C. Allen to author, 10 Jan 54; Brig Gen Edwin K. Wright, FEC, Memo for Record, 4 Sep 50; Interv, author with Stebbins (EUSAK G-4 Sep 50), 4 Dec 53; Interv, author with Maj Gen George L. Eberle, 12 Jan 54.

bridgehead with main effort directed along the Taegu-Kumch'on-Taejon-Suwon axis," to destroy the enemy forces "on line of advance," and to effect a "junction with X Corps." [2]

The operations directive required the newly formed United States I Corps in the center of the Perimeter line to strive for the main breakthrough. The following reasons dictated this concept: (1) the distance to the link-up area with X Corps was shorter than that from elsewhere around the Perimeter, (2) the road net was better and had easier grades, (3) the road net offered the armor better opportunity to exploit a breakthrough, and (4) supply to advancing columns would be easier. The plan called for the 5th Regimental Combat Team and the 1st Cavalry Division to seize a bridgehead over the Naktong River near Waegwan. The 24th Division would then cross the river and drive on Kumch'on-Taejon, followed by the 1st Cavalry Division which would patrol its rear and lines of communications. While this breakthrough attempt was in progress, the 25th and 2d Infantry Divisions in the south on the army left flank and the ROK II and I Corps on the east and right flank were to attack and fix the enemy troops in their zones and to exploit any local breakthrough. The ROK 17th Regiment was to move to Pusan for water movement to Inch'on to join X Corps.

Supplementing the 5th Regimental Combat Team's mission of establishing a bridgehead across the Naktong, the U.S. 2d and 24th Divisions were to strive for crossings of the river below Waegwan and the ROK 1st Division above it. Execution of this plan was certain to run into difficulties because the Engineer troops and bridging equipment available to General Walker were not adequate for several quick crossings. Eighth Army had equipment for only two ponton treadway bridges across the Naktong.

To help replace the Marine Air squadrons taken from the Eighth Army front for the X Corps operation at Inch'on, General Stratemeyer obtained the transfer from the 20th Air Force on Okinawa to Itazuke, Japan, of the 51st Fighter-Interceptor Wing and the 16th and 25th Fighter-Interceptor Squadrons.

The situation at the Pusan Perimeter did not afford General Walker an opportunity to concentrate a large force for the breakout effort in the center. The enemy held the initiative and his attacks pinned down all divisions under Eighth Army command except one, the U.S. 24th Infantry Division, which Walker was able to move piecemeal from the east to the center only on the eve of the projected attack. The problem was to change suddenly from a precarious defense to the offensive without reinforcement or opportunity to create a striking force. In theater perspective, Eighth Army would make a holding attack while the X Corps made the envelopment. A prompt link-up with the X Corps along the Taejon-Suwon axis was a prerequisite for cutting off a large force of North Koreans in the southwestern part of the peninsula.

Eighth Army anticipated that the news of the Inch'on landing would have a demoralizing effect on the North Koreans in front of it and an opposite effect on the spirit of its own troops. For this rea-

---

[2] EUSAK Opn Plan 10, 6 Sep 50, and Revision, 11 Sep 50; EUSAK WD, G-3 Plans Sec, 7 Sep 50; Ibid., 15-16 Sep 50; I Corps WD, G-3 Sec, 2 Aug-30 Sep 50.

son, General Walker had requested that the Eighth Army attack not begin until the day after the Inch'on landing. While the news of the successful landing spread to Eighth Army troops at once on the 15th, apparently it was not allowed to reach the enemy troops in front of Eighth Army until several days later.

The corridors of advance in the event of a breakout from the Perimeter necessarily would be the same that the North Korean Army had used in its drive south. Enemy forces blocked every road leading out of the Perimeter. The axis of the main effort required the use of the highway from the Naktong opposite Waegwan to Kumch'on and across the Sobaek Range to Taejon. A second corridor, the valley of the Naktong northward to the Sangju area, could be used if events warranted it. The Taegu–Tabudong–Sangju road traversed this corridor, with crossings of the Naktong River possible at Sonsan and Naktong-ni. From Sangju the line of advance could turn west toward the Kum River above Taejon or bypass Taejon for a more direct route to the Suwon-Seoul area.

Eastward in the mountainous central sector, the ROK's would find the best route of advance by way of Andong and Wonju. On the east coast they had no alternative to a drive straight up the coastal road toward Yongdok and Wonsan.

An important step taken by the Far East Command in preparation for the offensive was the establishment of corps organization within Eighth Army. Up to this time Eighth Army had controlled directly the four infantry divisions and other attached ground forces of regimental and brigade size. Beginning in August, preparations were made to provide Eighth Army with two corps.

On 2 August, I Corps was activated at Fort Bragg, N.C., with General Coulter in command. Eleven days later General Coulter and a command group arrived in Korea and began studies preparatory to a breakout effort from the Perimeter. The main body of the corps staff arrived in Korea on 6 September, but it still had no troops assigned to it.[3]

The IX Corps was activated on 10 August at Fort Sheridan, Ill., with Maj. Gen. Frank W. Milburn in command. General Milburn and a small group of staff officers departed Fort Sheridan on 5 September by air for Korea. The main body of the corps staff, however, did not reach Korea until the end of September and the first part of October. Both I and IX Corps had previously been part of Eighth Army in Japan, the I Corps with the 24th and 25th Divisions with headquarters in Kyoto, and the IX Corps with the 1st Cavalry and the 7th Divisions with headquarters in Sendai.[4]

General Walker had decided to group the main breakout forces under I Corps. He gave long and serious thought to the question of a commander for the corps. Walker eventually shifted General Milburn on 11 September from IX Corps to I Corps and General Coulter from I Corps to IX Corps. Milburn assumed command of I Corps that day at Taegu and Coulter assumed command of IX Corps the next day at Miryang. I Corps

---

[3] I Corps WD, Hist Narr, 2 Aug–30 Sep 50; EUSAK WD, Aug 50 Summ.

[4] IX Corps WD, Hist Narr, 23–30 Sep 50. It is interesting to note that I and IX Corps had been deactivated in Japan only a few months before, in the early part of 1950, in line with maintaining the framework of four divisions and remaining within reduced army personnel ceilings.

became operational at 1200, 13 September, with the U.S. 1st Cavalry Division, the 5th Regimental Combat Team (−), and the ROK 1st Division attached. On 15 and 16 September the 5th Regimental Combat Team and the 24th Division moved to the Taegu area, and by the evening of 16 September I Corps comprised the U.S. 24th and 1st Cavalry Divisions, the 5th Regimental Combat Team, the British 27th Infantry Brigade, the ROK 1st Division, and supporting troops.[5]

During the first week of the Eighth Army offensive the IX Corps was not operational. It became so at 1400, 23 September, on Eighth Army orders which attached to it the U.S. 25th and 2d Infantry Divisions and their supporting units. Until 23 September, therefore, these two divisions operated directly under Eighth Army command.[6]

IX Corps was not made operational at the same time as I Corps principally because of a critical lack of communications personnel and equipment. The Signal battalion and the communications equipment intended for this corps had been diverted to X Corps. Even after IX Corps became operational the lack of proper communications facilities hampered its operations.[7]

The Enemy Strength

On the eve of Eighth Army's attack, the intelligence annex to the army order presented an elaborate estimate of the enemy's strength, order of battle, and capabilities. This gave the North Koreans 13 infantry divisions on line supported by 1 armored division and 2 armored brigades, with the N.K. *I Corps* on the southern half of the front having 6 infantry divisions with armored support—a strength of 47,417 men, and the *II Corps* on the northern and eastern half of the front having 7 infantry divisions with armored support—a strength of 54,000 men. This made a total of 101,417 enemy soldiers around the Perimeter. Eighth Army intelligence estimated enemy organizations at an average of 75 percent strength in troops and equipment.[8]

The Eighth Army estimate credited the enemy with sufficient strength to be able to divert three divisions from the Pusan Perimeter to the Seoul area without endangering his ability to defend effectively his positions around the Perimeter. The estimate stated, "Currently the enemy is on the offensive and retains this capability in all general sectors of the Perimeter. It is not expected that this capability will decline in the immediate future."

With respect to both enemy troop strength and equipment the Eighth Army estimate was far too high. Although it is not possible to state precisely the strength of the North Korean units facing Eighth Army in mid-September and the state of their equipment, an examination of prisoner of war inter-

---

[5] Landrum, Notes for author, recd 8 Mar 54; EUSAK Special Ord 49, 11 Sep 50; EUSAK WD, G-3 Sec, 13 and 16 Sep 50; I Corps WD, G-3 Sec, 12-19 Sep 50; EUSAK POR 195, 15 Sep 50; 24th Div WD, 15-16 Sep 50. The 3d Battalion of the 19th Regiment, 24th Division, remained at Samnangjin on the lower Naktong as a left flank guard force.

[6] IX Corps WD, Hist Summ, 23-30 Sep 50; EUSAK WD, POR 217, 22 Sep 50 (POR erroneously dated 200001).

[7] Landrum, Notes for author, recd 8 Mar 54.

[8] EUSAK WD, 16 Sep 50, app. 1 to an. A (Intel) to Opn Plan 10 (as of 10 Sep 50).

rogations and captured documents reveals that it was far less than Eighth Army thought it was. The Chief of Staff, N.K. *13th Division*, Col. Lee Hak Ku, gave the strength of that divison as 2,300 men (not counting 2,000 untrained and unarmed replacements not considered as a part of the division) instead of the 8,000 carried in the Eighth Army estimate. The N.K. *15th Division*, practically annihilated by this time, numbered no more than a few hundred scattered and disorganized men instead of the 7,000 men in the Eighth Army estimate. Also, the N.K. *5th Division* was down to about 5,000 men instead of 6,500, and the N.K. *7th Division* was down to about 4,000 men instead of the 7,600 accorded it by the Eighth Army estimate. The N.K. *1st, 2d,* and *3d Divisions* almost certainly did not begin to approach the strength of 7,000-8,000 men each in mid-September accorded to them in the estimate.[9]

Enemy losses were exceedingly heavy in the first half of September. No one can accurately say just what they were. Perhaps the condition of the North Korean Army can best be glimpsed from a captured enemy daily battle report, dated 14 September, and apparently for a battalion of the N.K. *7th Division*. The report shows that the enemy battalion on 14 September had 6 officers, 34 noncommissioned officers, and 111 privates for a total of 151 men. There were 82 individual weapons in the unit: 3 pistols, 9 carbines, 57 rifles, and 13 automatic rifles. There was an average of somewhat more than 1 grenade for every 2 men—a total of 92 grenades. The unit still had 6 light machine guns but less than 300 rounds of ammunition for each.[10]

A fair estimate of enemy strength facing Eighth Army at the Perimeter in mid-September would be about 70,000 men. Enemy equipment, far below the Eighth Army 75 percent estimate of a few days earlier, particularly in heavy weapons and tanks, was probably no more than 50 percent of the original equipment.

Morale in the North Korean Army was at a low point. No more than 30 percent of the original troops of the divisions remained. These veterans tried to impose discipline on the recruits, most of whom were from South Korea and had no desire to fight for the North Koreans. It was common practice in the North Korean Army at this time for the veterans to shoot anyone who showed reluctance to go forward when ordered or who tried to desert. Food was scarce, and undernourishment was the most frequently mentioned cause of low morale by prisoners. Even so, there had been few desertions up to this time because the men were afraid the U.N. forces would kill them if they surrendered and that their own officers would shoot them if they made the attempt.[11]

---

[9] ATIS Interrog Rpts, Issue 9 (N.K. Forces), Rpt 1468, pp. 158ff, Col Lee Hak Ku; *Ibid.,* Issue 7, Rpt 1253, p. 112, Sr Lt Lee Kwan Hyon; ATIS Res Supp Interrog Rpts, Issue 3 (N.K. *15 Div*), p. 44; *Ibid.,* Issue 96 (N.K. *5th Div*), pp. 43-44; *Ibid.,* Issue 99 (N.K. *7th Div*), p. 38; *Ibid.,* Issue 4 (N.K. *105th Armored Div*), p. 39; *Ibid.,* Issue 100 (N.K. *9th Div*), p. 52; ATIS Interrog Rpts, Issue 22 (N.K. Forces), p. 4; EUSAK WD, 30 Sep 50, G-2 Sec, interrog of Maj Lee Yon Gun, Asst Regt CO, *45th Regt, 15th Div.*

[10] 35th Inf WD, PW Interrrog Team Rpt by Lt Herada, 151500 Sep 50.

[11] U.N. forces had captured and interned at the Eighth Army enclosure 3,380 N.K. prisoners by 15 September. The ROK Army had captured 2,254 of them; Eighth Army, 1,126. See EUSAK WD, Incl 16, Provost Marshal Rpt, 15 Sep 50.

United Nations' Perimeter Strength

Standing opposite approximately 70,000 North Korean soldiers at the Pusan Perimeter in mid-September were 140,000 men in the combat units of the U.S. Eighth and ROK Armies. These comprised four U.S. divisions with an average of 15,000 men each for a total of more than 60,000 men, to which more than 9,000 attached South Korean recruits must be added, and six ROK divisions averaging about 10,000 men each with a total of approximately 60,000 men. The three corps headquarters added at least another 10,000 men, and if the two army headquarters were counted the total would be more than 150,000 men. The major U.N. units had an assigned strength at this time as follows: [12]

U.S. Eighth Army	84,478
U.S. I Corps	7,475
(plus attached Koreans, 1,110)	
U.S. 1st Cavalry Division	13,904
(plus attached Koreans, 2,338)	
U.S. 24th Division	16,356
(plus attached Koreans, 2,786)	
U.S. 2d Division	15,191
(plus attached Koreans, 1,821)	
U.S. 25th Division	15,334
(plus attached Koreans, 2,447)	
British 27th Infantry Brigade	1,693
ROK Army	72,730

[12] GHQ FEC Sitrep, 16 Sep 50; GHQ FEC G-3 Opn Rpt, 16 Sep 50. U.S. Air Force strength in Korea was 4,726 men. The total U.N. supported strength in Korea was 221,469 men, of which about 120,000 were in the ROK Army, 83,000 assigned, and 30,000-odd in training. See EUSAK POR 65, G-4 Sec, 15 Sep 50. NAVFE strength was 52,011 men.

Since it marked a turning point in the Korean War, the middle of September 1950 is a good time to sum up the cost in American casualties thus far. From the beginning of the war to 15 September 1950, American battle casualties totaled 19,165 men. Of this number, 4,280 men were killed in action, 12,377 were wounded, of whom 319 died of wounds, 401 were reported captured, and 2,107 were reported missing in action. The first fifteen days of September brought higher casualties than any other 15-day period in the war, before or afterward, indicating the severity of the fighting at that time.[13]

The assigned strength of the U.S. divisions belied the number of men in the rifle companies, the men who actually did the fighting. Some of the rifle companies at this time were down to fifty or fewer effectives—little more than 25 percent strength. The Korean augmentation recruits, virtually untrained and not yet satisfactorily integrated were of little combat value at this time.

While perhaps 60,000 of the 70,000 ROK Army soldiers were in the line, most of the ROK divisions, like those of the North Korean Army, had sunk to a low level of combat effectiveness because of the high casualty rate among the trained commissioned and noncommissioned officers and the large percentage of recruits among the rank and file. After taking these factors into account, however, any realistic analysis of the strength of the two opposing forces must

[13] Battle Casualties of the Army, 31 May 52, DA TAGO.

give a considerable numerical superiority to the United Nations Command.[14]

In the matter of supporting armor, artillery, and heavy weapons and the availability of ammunition for these weapons, the United Nations Command had an even greater superiority than in troops, despite the rationing of ammunition for most artillery and heavy weapons. Weapon fire power superiority was probably about six to one over the North Koreans. In the air the Far East Air Forces had no rival over the battleground, and on the flanks at sea the United Nations naval forces held unchallenged control.[15]

The 38th Infantry Crosses the Naktong

The morning of 16 September dawned over southern Korea with murky skies and heavy rain. The weather was so bad the Air Force canceled a B-29 saturation bombing scheduled against the enemy positions in the Waegwan area.

The general attack set for 0900 did not swing into motion everywhere around the Perimeter at the appointed hour for the simple reason that at many places the North Koreans were attacking and United Nations troops defending. In most sectors an observer would have found the morning of 16 September little different from that of the 15th or the 14th or the 13th. It was the same old Perimeter situation—attack and counterattack. The battle for the hills had merely gone on into another day. Only in a few places were significant gains made on the first day of the offensive. (*Map 17*) The 15th Regiment of the ROK 1st Division advanced to the right of the North Korean strongpoint at the Walled City north of Taegu in a penetration of the enemy line. Southward, the U.S. 2d Division after hard fighting broke through five miles to the hills overlooking the Naktong River.[16]

The most spectacular success of the first day occurred in the 2d Division zone. There, west of Yongsan and Changnyong, the 2d Division launched a 3-regiment attack with the 9th Infantry on the left, the 23d Infantry in the center, and the 38th Infantry on the right. Its first mission was to drive the enemy *4th, 9th,* and *2d Divisions* back across the Naktong. The attack on the left failed as the enemy continued to hold Hill 201 against all attacks of the 9th Infantry. In the center, a vicious enemy predawn attack penetrated the perimeter of C Company, 23d Infantry, and caused twenty-five casualties, which included all company officers and the platoon leader of the attached heavy weapons platoon.

On the 15th, the 3d Battalion had returned to regimental control from attachment to the 1st Cavalry Division, and because it had not been involved in the preceding two weeks of heavy fighting, Colonel Freeman assigned it the main attack effort in the 23d Infantry zone. After the early morning attack on

---

[14] Lt. Gen. Chung Il Kwon commanded the ROK Army. The six ROK divisions were the following: 1st Division—11th, 12th, 15th Regiments; 3d Division—22d, 23d, 26th Regiments; 6th Division—2d, 7th, 19th Regiments; 7th Division—3d, 5th, 8th Regiments; 8th Division—10th, 16th, 21st Regiments; and Capital Division—1st, 17th, 18th Regiments. See EUSAK WD, Br for CG, 12 Sep 50.

[15] EUSAK WD, Arty Rpt, 11 Sep 50.

[16] EUSAK POR 198, 16 Sep 50; I Corps WD, 16 Sep 50; 2d Inf WD, Sep 50; 38th Inf WD, 16 Sep 50.

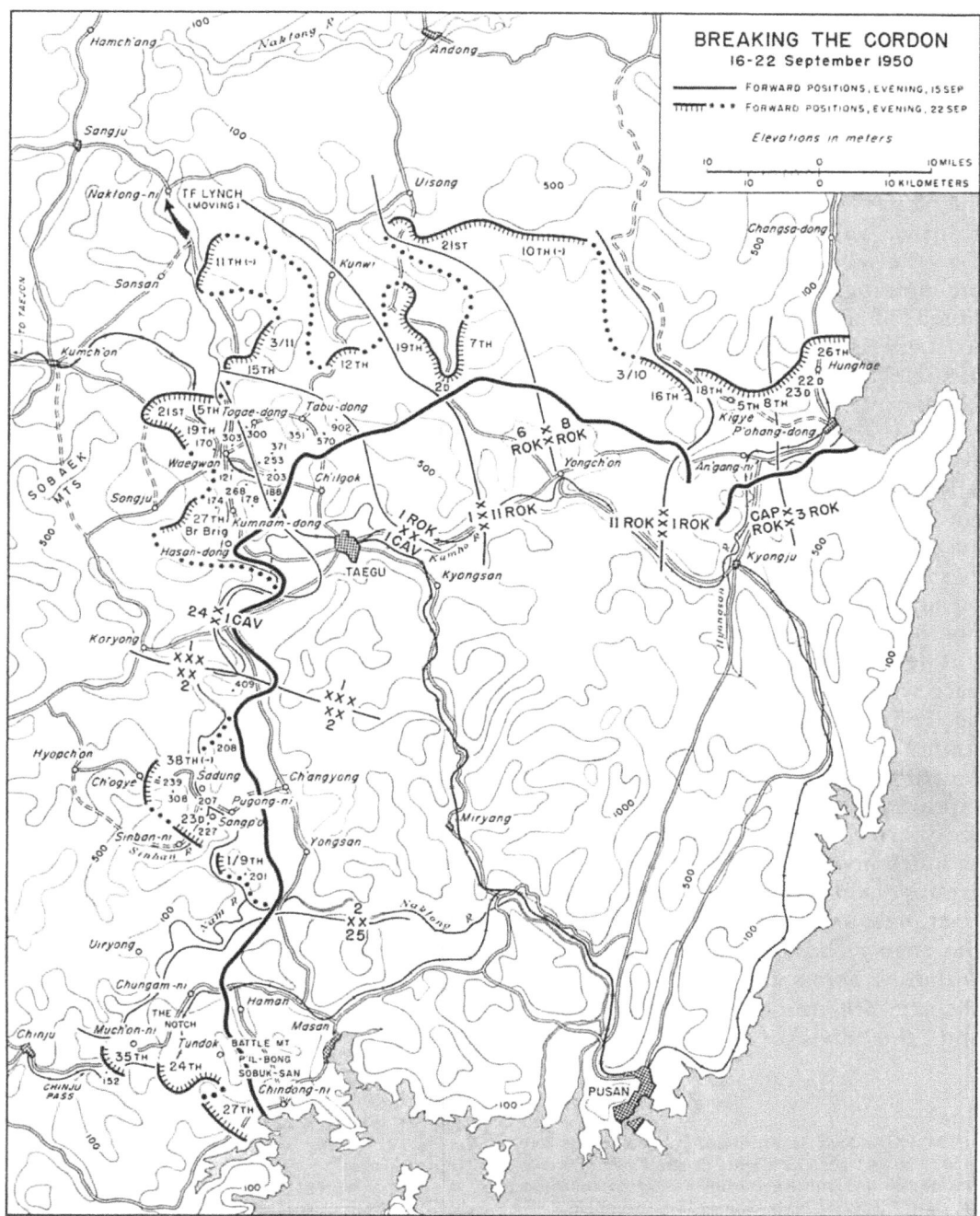

MAP 17

the 16th was repulsed, Lt. Col. R. G. Sherrard ordered his 3d Battalion to move out at 1000 in attack, with C Company of the 72d Tank Company in support. Enemy resistance was stubborn and effective until about midafternoon when the North Koreans began to vacate their positions and flee toward the Naktong. To take advantage of such a break in the fighting, a special task force comprised of B Battery, 82d Antiaircraft Artillery Battalion, and the 23d Regimental Tank Company had been formed for the purpose of advancing rapidly to cut off the North Korean soldiers. From about 1600 until dark this task force with its heavy volume of automatic fire cut down large numbers of fleeing enemy along the river. The weather had cleared in the afternoon and numerous air strikes added to the near annihilation of part of the routed army.[17]

The 38th Infantry on the right kept pace with the 23d Infantry in the center. Four F-51's napalmed, rocketed, and strafed just ahead of the 38th Infantry, contributing heavily to the 2d Battalion's capture of Hill 208 overlooking the Naktong River. Fighter planes operating in the afternoon caught and strafed large groups of enemy withdrawing toward the river west of Changnyong. That night the enemy's *2d Division* command post withdrew across the river, followed by the *4th, 6th,* and *17th Rifle Regiments* and the division artillery regiment.

Their crossings continued into the next day.[18]

On the 17th, air attacks took a heavy toll of enemy soldiers trying to escape across the Naktong in front of the 2d Division. During the day, fighter planes dropped 260 110-gallon tanks of napalm on the enemy in this sector and strafed many groups west of Changnyong. The fleeing enemy troops abandoned large quantities of equipment and weapons. In pursuit the 23d Infantry captured 13 artillery pieces, 6 antitank guns, and 4 mortars; the 38th Infantry captured 6 artillery pieces, 12 antitank guns, 1 SP gun, and 9 mortars. General Allen, Eighth Army chief of staff, in a telephone conversation with General Hickey in Tokyo that evening said, "Things down here [Pusan Perimeter] are ripe for something to break. We have not had a single counterattack all day."[19]

During the morning of 18 September patrols of the 2d and 3d Battalions, 38th Infantry, crossed the Naktong near Pugong-ni, due west of Changnyong, and

---

[17] Maj Gen Paul L. Freeman, Jr., MS review comments, 30 Oct 57; Highlights of the Combat Activities of the 23d Inf Regt from 5 Aug 50 to 30 Sep 50; 23d Inf WD, Narr Summ, Sep 50; *Ibid.,* G-3 Jnl, entry 151, 160207 Sep 50. Task Force Haynes, which had defended the Changnyong area since 1 September, was dissolved on 15 September.

[18] 2d Div WD, G-3 Sec, Sep 50; 23d Inf WD, Narr Summ, Sep 50; *Ibid.,* G-3 Jnl, entry 151, 160207 Sep 50; EUSAK PIR 66, 16 Sep 50; 38th Inf Comd Rpt, Sep-Oct 50; FEAF Opns Hist, vol. I, 25 Jun-31 Oct 50, p. 168; ATIS Res Supp Interrog Rpts, Issue 94 (N.K. 2d Div), p. 38; ATIS Interrog Rpts, Issue 7 (N.K. Forces), Rpts 1208, 1233, 1242, pp. 19, 69, 82 and 131. The senior medical officer of the *17th Regiment,* captured on the 17th, estimated that each of the three regiments of the 2d *Division* had only approximately 700 men left. See EUSAK WD, 21 Sep 50, ADVATIS Interrog Rpt of Sr Lt Lee Kwan Hyon.

[19] FEAF Opns Hist, vol. I, 25 Jun-31 Oct 50, p. 170; "Air War in Korea," *Air University Quarterly Review* IV, (Spring, 1951), No. 3, 70; 23d Inf Comd Rpt, Jnl entry 175, 17 Sep 50, and Pers Rpt 13, 17 Sep 50; 38th Inf Comd Rpt, Sep-Oct 50, p. 8; ATIS Res Supp Interrog Rpts, Issue 106 (N.K. Arty), p. 51; Fonecon, Allen with Hickey, GHQ FEC CofS, 17 Sep 50; EUSAK WD, G-3 Air, 17 Sep 50.

found the high ground on the west side of the river clear of enemy troops. Colonel Peploe, regimental commander, thereupon ordered Lt. Col. James H. Skeldon, 2d Battalion commander, to send two squads across the river in two-man rubber boats, with a platoon to follow, to secure a bridgehead. Peploe requested authority to cross the river in force at once. At 1320 Col. Gerald G. Epley, 2d Division chief of staff, authorized him to move one battalion across the river.

Before 1600, E and F Companies and part of G Company had crossed the 100-yard-wide and 12-foot-deep current. Two hours later the leading elements secured Hill 308 a mile west of the Naktong, dominating the Ch'ogye road, against only light resistance. This quick crossing clearly had surprised the enemy. From Hill 308 the troops observed an estimated enemy battalion 1,000 yards farther west. That evening Colonel Skeldon requested air cover over the bridgehead area half an hour after first light the next morning.

During the day, the 38th Infantry captured 132 prisoners; 32 of them were female nurses, 8 were officers—1 a major. Near the crossing site on the east bank buried in the sand and hidden in culverts, it found large quantities of supplies and equipment, including more than 125 tons of ammunition, and new rifles still packed in cosmoline.[20]

The 38th Infantry's crossing of the Naktong by the 2d Battalion on 18 September was the first permanent crossing of the river by any unit of Eighth Army in the breakout, and it was the most important event of the day. The crossing was two days ahead of division schedule.

On the 19th the 3d Battalion, 38th Infantry, crossed the river, together with some tanks, artillery, and heavy mortars. The 3d Battalion was to protect the bridgehead while the 2d Battalion pushed forward against the enemy. In order to support the two battalions now west of the river it was necessary to get vehicles and heavy equipment across to that side. The two destroyed spans of the Changnyong-Ch'ogye highway bridge across the Naktong could not be repaired quickly, so the 2d Engineer Combat Battalion prepared to construct a floating bridge downstream from the crossing site.

By the end of the third day of the attack, 18 September, the U.S. 2d Division had regained control of the ground in its sector east of the Naktong River except the Hill 201 area in the south and Hill 409 along its northern boundary. Elements of the N.K. *9th Division* had successfully defended Hill 201 against repeated air strikes, artillery barrages, and attacks of the 9th Infantry. At its northern boundary Eighth Army, for the moment, made no effort to capture massive Hill 409. There, air strikes, artillery barrages, and patrol action of the 1st Battalion, 38th Infantry, merely attempted to contain and neutralize this enemy force of the *10th Division*. Behind the 2d Division lines there were many enemy groups, totaling several hundred soldiers, cut off and operating as far as twenty miles east of the river. During the 18th, a 22-man patrol of the 23d Infantry came to grief in trying to

---

[20] Interv, author with Peploe, 12 Aug 51; 2d Div POR 132, 18 Sep 50; 2d Div WD, 18 Sep 50 and CofS Log entries 121 and 124, 18 Sep 50; 38th Inf Comd Rpt, Sep–Oct 50, pp. 9–10; 2d Div WD, G–3 Jnl, Msg 74, 181625 Sep 50; EUSAK WD, 18 Sep 50 and G–3 Jnl, Msg 181745; 2d Div WD, G–2 Jnl, entry 2107, 181525 Sep 50, and PIR 25, 18 Sep 50.

THE BATTLE FOR HILL 201. *This photograph, taken on 18 September, shows 9th Infantry soldiers helping a wounded man to the rear.*

cross the Naktong, partly because of the river's depth. Enemy fire from the west bank killed three, wounded another, and drove the rest of the patrol back to the east side.[21]

The 5th Regimental Combat Team Captures Waegwan

The 5th Regimental Combat Team was attached to the 1st Cavalry Division on 14 September. It went into an assembly area west of Taegu along the east bank of the Naktong River six miles below Waegwan and prepared for action. On 16 September it moved out from its assembly area to begin an operation that was to prove of great importance to the Eighth Army breakout. Numbering 2,599 men, the regiment was 1,194 short of full strength. The three battalions were nearly equal, varying between 586 and 595 men in strength. On the 16th only the 2d Battalion engaged the enemy as it attacked north along the Naktong River road toward Waegwan. But by the end of the second day the 3d Battalion had joined in the battle and the 1st Battalion was deployed to enter it.[22]

---

[21] 2d Div POR 132, 18 Sep 50; 2d Div WD, G–3 Sec, 18 Sep 50; 2d Div PIR 24, 17 Dec 50; see Capt. Russell A. Gugeler, Small Unit Actions in Korea, ch. V, "Patrol Crossing of the Naktong, I&R Platoon, 23d Infantry, 18 September 1950," gives details of this incident. MS in OCMH. For an account of a typical rear area action, see Capt. Edward C. Williamson, Attack of the 38th Ordnance Medical Maintenance Company by a Guerrilla Band, 20 September 1950. MS in OCMH.

[22] 24th Div WD, G–1 Hist Rpt, 26 Aug–28 Sep 50; 1st Cav Div WD, 14–16 Sep 50. The earliest 5th RCT document found in the official records is the Personnel Report for 17 September and is included in the 24th Division records.

The next day, 19 September, as the 38th Infantry crossed the Naktong, the 5th Regimental Combat Team began its full regimental attack against Hill 268, southeast of Waegwan.

An estimated 1,200 soldiers of the N.K. *3d Division*, supported by tanks, defended this southern approach to Waegwan. The hills there constituted the left flank of the enemy *II Corps*. If the North Koreans lost this ground their advanced positions in the 5th Cavalry zone eastward along the Taegu highway would become untenable. The tactical importance of Hill 268 and related positions was made the greater by reason of the gap in the enemy line to the south. At the lower side of this gap the British 27th Infantry Brigade held vital blocking positions just above strong forces of the N.K. *10th Division*.

In hard fighting all day the 5th Regimental Combat Team gained Hill 268, except for its northeast slope. By night the 3d Battalion was on the hill, the 1st Battalion had turned northwest from it toward another enemy position, and the 2d Battalion had captured Hill 121, only a mile south of Waegwan along the river road. Air strikes, destructive and demoralizing to the enemy, had paced the regimental advance all the way. In this important action along the east bank of the Naktong, the 5th Cavalry and part of the 7th Cavalry protected the 5th Regimental Combat Team's right flank and fought very heavy battles co-ordinated with the combat team on the adjoining hills east of Waegwan.[23] At 1800 that evening, 18 September, the 5th Regimental Combat Team and the 6th Medium Tank Battalion reverted to 24th Division control.

The next morning the battle for Hill 268 continued. More than 200 enemy soldiers in log-covered bunkers still fought the 3d Battalion. Three flights of F-51's napalmed, rocketed, and strafed these positions just before noon. This strike enabled the infantry to overrun the enemy bunkers. Among the North Korean dead was a regimental commander. About 250 enemy soldiers died on the hill. Westward to the river, other enemy troops bitterly resisted the 2d and 1st Battalions, losing about 300 men in this battle. But Colonel Throckmorton's troops pressed forward. The 2d Battalion entered Waegwan at 1415. Fifteen minutes later it joined forces there with the 1st Battalion. After surprising an enemy group laying a mine field in front of it, the 2d Battalion penetrated deeper into Waegwan and had passed through the town by 1530.[24]

On 19 September the N.K. *3d Division* defenses around Waegwan broke apart and the division began a panic-stricken retreat across the river. At 0900 aerial observers reported an estimated 1,500 enemy troops crossing to the west side of the Naktong just north of Waegwan, and in the afternoon they reported roads north of Waegwan jammed with enemy groups of sizes varying from 10 to 300 men pouring out of the town. By midafternoon observers reported enemy soldiers in every draw and pass north of Waegwan. During the day the 5th Regimental Combat Team captured 22 45-mm. antitank guns, 10 82-mm. mor-

---

[23] 5th RCT WD, 18 Sep 50.

[24] 5th RCT WD, 19 Sep 50; *Ibid.*, Unit Rpt 38, 19 Sep 50; 24th Div Opn Instr 44, 17 Sep 50; 24th Div WD, G-1 Sec, 19 Sep 50; Throckmorton, MS review comments, recd 16 Apr 54.

tars, 6 heavy machine guns, and approximately 250 rifles and burp guns.[25]

On 20 September the 5th Regimental Combat Team captured the last of its objectives east of the Naktong River when its 2d Battalion in the afternoon seized important Hill 303 north of Waegwan. In securing its objectives, the 5th Regimental Combat Team suffered numerous casualties during the day—18 men killed, 111 wounded, and 3 missing in action. At 1945 that evening the 1st Battalion started crossing the river a mile above the Waegwan railroad bridge. By midnight it had completed the crossing and advanced a mile westward. The 2d Battalion followed the 1st Battalion across the river and dug in on the west side before midnight. During the day the 3d Battalion captured Hill 300, four miles north of Waegan. The following afternoon, 21 September, after the 2d Battalion, 5th Cavalry Regiment, relieved it on position, the 3d Battalion crossed the Naktong. The 5th Regimental Combat Team found large stores of enemy ammunition and rifles on the west side of the river.[26]

The 5th Regimental Combat Team in five days had crushed the entire right flank and part of the center of the N.K. *3d Division*. This rendered untenable the enemy division's advanced positions on the road to Taegu where it was locked in heavy fighting with the 5th Cavalry Regiment.

From 18 to 21 September, close air support reached its highest peak in the Korean campaign. Fighters and bombers returned several times a day from Japanese bases to napalm, bomb, rocket, and strafe enemy strongpoints of resistance and to cut down fleeing enemy troops caught in the open.[27]

The 24th Division Deploys West of the Naktong

The Eighth Army and I Corps plans for the breakout from the Pusan Perimeter called for the 24th Division to make the first crossings of the Naktong River. Accordingly, General Church on 17 September received orders to force a crossing in the vicinity of the Hasandong ferry due west of Taegu. The 5th Regimental Combat Team had just cleared the ground northward and secured the crossing site against enemy action from the east side of the river. The 21st Infantry was to cross the river after dark on 18 September in 3d Engineer Combat Battalion assault boats. Once landed on the other side, the regiment was to attack north along the west bank of the Naktong to a point opposite Waegwan where it would strike the main highway to Kumch'on. The 24th Reconnaissance Company and the 19th Infantry Regiment were to cross at the same time a little farther south and block the roads leading from Songju, an enemy concentration point, some six miles west of the river. The unexpected crossing of the Naktong during the day by the 2d Battalion, 38th Infantry, farther south

---

[25] 24th Div WD, 19 Sep 50; 5th RCT WD, 19 Sep 50 and Unit Rpt 38, 19 Sep 50; EUSAK PIR 69, 19 Sep 50; ATIS Interrog Rpts, Issue 13 (N.K. Forces), Rpt 1880, p. 189. MSgt Son Tok Hui, *105th Armored Division*.

[26] 5th RCT WD, 20–21 Sep 50; EUSAK WD, Br for CG, 20 Sep 50; Throckmorton, MS review comments, recd 16 Apr 54.

[27] EUSAK WD, Sep 50 Summ, p. 30; "Air War in Korea," *Air University Quarterly Review*, IV, No. 2 (Fall, 1950), 19–39.

In moving up to the Naktong, the 24th Division had to cross one of its tributaries, the Kumho River, that arched around Taegu. On the morning of the 18th, Colonel Stephens, the 21st Infantry regimental commander, discovered that the I Corps engineers had not bridged the Kumho as planned. The division thereupon hurried its own Engineer troops to the stream and they began sandbagging the underwater bridge that the 5th Regimental Combat Team had already used so that large vehicles could cross. A makeshift ferry constructed from assault boats moved jeeps across the Kumho. Constant repair work on the underwater sandbag bridge was necessary to keep it usable. By nightfall there was a line of vehicles backed up for five miles east of the Kumho, making it clear that the regiment would not be in position to cross the Naktong that evening after dark as planned. As midnight came and the hours passed, General Church began to fear that daylight would arrive before the regiment could start crossing and the troops consequently would be exposed to possibly heavy casualties. He repeatedly urged on Stephens the necessity of crossing the Naktong before daylight. During the night supporting artillery fired two preparations against the opposing terrain.[29]

Despite nightlong efforts to break the traffic jam and get the assault boats, troops, and equipment across the Kumho and up to the crossing site, it was 0530, 19 September, before the first wave of assault boats pushed off into the Naktong. Six miles below Waegwan and just south of the village of Kumnan-dong on the west side, Hill 174 and its long southern finger ridge dominated the crossing site. In the murky fog of dawn there was no indication of the enemy on the opposite bank. The first wave landed and started inland. Almost at once enemy machine gun fire from both flanks caught the troops in a crossfire. And now enemy mortar and artillery fire began falling on both sides of the river. The heaviest fire, as expected, came from Hill 174 and its long southern finger ridge.

For a while it was doubtful that the crossing would succeed. The 1st Battalion, continuing its crossing under fire, suffered approximately 120 casualties in getting across the river. At 0700 an air strike hit Hill 174. On the west side the 1st Battalion reorganized and, supported by air napalm and strafing strikes, attacked and captured Hill 174 by noon. That afternoon the 3d Battalion crossed the river and captured the next hill northward. During the night and the following morning the 2d Battalion crossed the Naktong. The 1st Battalion on 20 September advanced north to Hill 170, the high ground on the west side of the river opposite Waegwan, while the 3d Battalion occupied the higher hill a mile northwestward.[30]

Meanwhile, two miles south of the 21st Infantry crossing site, the 2d Battalion,

---

[28] 24th Div WD, 17 Sep 50 and an. B, overlay accompanying 24th Div Opn Instr 44, 17 Sep 50.
[29] 24th Div WD, 18–19 Sep 50; 21st Inf WD, 18–19 Sep 50, and Summ, 26 Aug–28 Sep 50; Throckmorton, MS review comments, recd 16 Apr 54; Col Emerson C. Itschner, "The Naktong Crossings in Korea," *The Military Engineer*, XLIII, No. 292 (March–April, 1951), 96ff; Interv, author with Alkire (21st Inf), 1 Aug 51.

[30] 24th Div WD, 19 Sep 50; 21st Inf Unit Rpts 73–74, 18–20 Sep 50; 3d Engr C Bn WD, Narr Summ, Sep 50.

19th Infantry, began crossing the Naktong at 1600 on the afternoon of the 19th and was on the west side by evening. Enemy mortar and artillery fire inflicted about fifty casualties while the battalion was still east of the river. Beach operations were hazardous. Once across the river, however, the battalion encountered only light enemy resistance.

In the 24th Division crossing operation the engineers' role was a difficult and dangerous one, as their casualties show. The 3d Engineer Combat Battalion lost 10 Americans and 5 attached Koreans killed, 37 Americans and 10 Koreans wounded, and 5 Koreans missing in action.[31]

On 20 September the 19th Infantry consolidated its hold on the high ground west of the river along the Songju road. The 24th Reconnaissance Company, having crossed the river during the night, passed through the 19th Infantry and started westward on the Songju road. During the day I Corps attached the British 27th Infantry Brigade to the 24th Division and it prepared to cross the Naktong and take part in the division attack. Relieved in its position by the 2d Battalion, 7th Cavalry Regiment, the British 27th Brigade moved north to the 19th Infantry crossing site and shortly after noon started crossing single file over a rickety footbridge that Engineer troops had thrown across the river. An enemy gun shelled the crossing site sporadically but accurately all day, causing some British casualties and hampering the ferrying of supplies for the 19th Regiment. Despite special efforts, observers could not locate this gun because it remained silent while aircraft were overhead.[32]

Thus, on 20 September, all three regiments of the 24th Division and the attached British 27th Brigade were across the Naktong River. The 5th Regimental Combat Team held the high ground north of the Waegwan-Kumch'on highway, the 21st Infantry that to the south of it, the 19th was below the 21st ready to move up behind and support it, and the 24th Reconnaissance Company was probing the Songju road west of the Naktong with the British brigade preparing to advance west on that axis. The division was ready to attack west along the main Taegu-Kumch'on-Taejon-Seoul highway.

With the 24th Division combat elements west of the river, it was necessary to get the division transport, artillery, tanks, and service units across to support the advance. The permanent bridges at Waegwan, destroyed in early August by the 1st Cavalry Division, had not been repaired by the North Koreans except for ladders at the fallen spans to permit foot traffic across the river. A bridge capable of carrying heavy equipment had to be thrown across the Naktong at once. Starting on 20 September and working continuously for thirty-six hours, the 11th Engineer Combat Battalion and the 55th Engineer Treadway Bridge Company completed at 1000, 22 September, an M2 ponton float treadway bridge

---

[31] 24th Div WD, 19 Sep 50; 3d Engr C Bn WD, Narr Summ, Sep 50.

[32] 21st Inf Unit Rpts, 19-20 Sep 50; Ltr, Gay to author, 30 Sep 53; 2d Bn, 7th Cav Jnl, 20 Sep 50; 24th Div WD, 21-22 Sep 50; EUSAK WD, 22 Sep 50; 19th Inf WD, 19-21 Sep 50 and Summ, 19-21 Sep; Maj. Gen. B. A. Coad, "The Land Campaign in Korea," *op. cit.*, p. 4; Eric Linklater, *Our Men in Korea, The Commonwealth Part in the Campaign, First Official Account* (London: Her Majesty's Stationery Office, 1952), p. 18.

CROSSING THE KUMHO RIVER *via underwater bridge and makeshift ferry.*

across the 700-foot-wide and 8-foot-deep stream at Waegwan. Traffic began moving across it immediately. Most 24th Division vehicles were on the west side of the Naktong by midnight. Many carried signs with slogans such as "One side, Bud—Seoul Bound," and "We Remember Taejon." [33]

In the action of 20–21 September near Waegwan the North Koreans lost heavily in tanks, as well as in other equipment and troops on both sides of the Naktong. In these two days the 24th Division counted 29 destroyed enemy tanks, but many of them undoubtedly had been destroyed earlier in August and September. According to enemy sources, the *203d Regiment* of the *105th Armored Division* retreated to the west side of the Naktong with only 9 tanks, and the *107th Regiment* with only 14. Nevertheless, the enemy covered his retreat toward Kumch'on with tanks, self-propelled guns, antitank guns, and small groups of supporting riflemen.[34]

Except for the muddle in bridging the Kumho River and the resulting delayed crossing of the Naktong by the 21st Infantry Regiment, the 5-day operation of the 24th Division beginning on 18 Sep-

---

[33] 24th Div WD, 21–22 Sep 50; 61st FA Bn WD, 20 Sep 50; I Corps WD, Engr Sec, 22 Sep 50; 3d Engr C Bn WD, Narr Summ, Sep 50; Itschner, "The Naktong River Crossings in Korea," *op. cit.*

[34] 24th Div WD, 20–22 Sep 50; 5th RCT WD, 21 Sep 50; EUSAK WD, G–3 Air, 22 Sep 50; GHQ FEC Sitrep, 22 Sep 50; ATIS Res Supp Interrog Rpts, Issue 4 (*105th Armored Div*), pp. 39–40; *Ibid.*, Issue 14 (N.K. Forces), p. 4, Rpt 1901, Lt Lee Kim Chun.

PONTON TREADWAY BRIDGE *across the Naktong, built in thirty-six hours.*

tember left little to be desired. On the 22d the division was concentrated and poised west of the river ready to follow up its success. Its immediate objective was to drive twenty miles northwest to Kumch'on, headquarters of the North Korean field forces.

The Indianhead Division Attacks West

Below the 24th Division, the 2d Division waited for the 9th Infantry to capture Hill 201. On the 19th, the 1st and 2d Battalions, 23d Infantry, were put into the fight to help reduce the enemy stronghold. While the 1st Battalion helped the 9th Infantry at Hill 201, the 2d Battalion attacked across the 9th Infantry zone against Hill 174, a related enemy defense position. In this action Sgt. George E. Vonton led a platoon of tanks from the regimental tank company to the very top of Hill 201 in an outstanding feat which was an important factor in driving the enemy from the heights. That evening this stubbornly held enemy hill on the 2d Division left flank was in 9th Infantry hands and the way was open for the 2d Division crossing of the Naktong.

In predawn darkness, 20 September, the 3d Battalion, 23d Infantry, without opposition slipped across the river in assault boats at the Sangp'o ferry site, just south of where the Sinban River enters the Naktong from the west. The battalion achieved a surprise so complete that its leading element, L Company, captured a North Korean lieutenant colonel and his staff asleep. From a map captured at this time, American troops learned the locations of the N.K. *2d, 4th,* and *9th Divisions* in the Sinban-ni area. By noon the 3d Battalion had captured Hill 227, the critical terrain dominating the crossing site on the west side.[35]

In the afternoon, the 1st Battalion, 23d Infantry, crossed the river. Its objective was Hill 207, a mile upstream from the crossing site and dominating the road which crossed the Naktong there. In moving toward this objective, the lead company soon encountered the Sinban River which, strangely enough, no one in the company knew was there. After several hours of delay in attempting to find a method of crossing it, the troops finally crossed in Dukw's and, in a night attack, moved up the hill which they found undefended.[36]

Meanwhile, the 3d Battalion had dug in on Hill 227. That night it rained hard and, under cover of the storm, a company of North Koreans crept up near the crest. The next morning (21 September) while L Company men were eating breakfast the enemy soldiers charged over the hill shooting and throwing grenades. They drove one platoon from its position and inflicted twenty-six casualties. Counterattacks regained the position by noon.[37]

While this action was taking place on the hill south of it, the 1st Battalion, 23d Infantry, with a platoon of tanks from the 72d Tank Battalion, attacked up the road toward Sinban-ni, a known enemy headquarters command post five miles west of the river. The advance against strong enemy opposition was weakened by ineffective co-ordination between tanks and infantry. The great volume of fire from supporting twin-40 and quad-50 self-propelled AA gun vehicles was of greatest help, however, in enabling the troops to make a two-and-a-half mile advance which bypassed several enemy groups.

The next morning an enemy dawn attack drove B Company from its position and inflicted many casualties. Capt. Art Stelle, the company commander, was killed. During the day an estimated two battalions of enemy troops in heavy fighting held the 23d Infantry in check in front of Sinban-ni. The 2d Battalion of the regiment crossed the Naktong and moved up to join the 1st Battalion in the battle north of the road. South of it the 3d Battalion faced lighter resistance. The next day, 23 September, the 23d Regiment gained Sinban-ni, and was ready then to join the 38th Infantry in a converging movement on Hyopch'on.[38]

On the next road northward above the 23d Infantry, six miles away, the 38th Infantry had hard fighting against strong enemy delaying forces as it attacked toward Ch'ogye and Hyopch'on. An air strike with napalm and fragmentation bombs helped its 2d Battalion on 21 September break North Korean resistance

---

[35] 23d Inf Comd Rpt, Narr, Sep 50, p. 12; *Ibid.,* Jnl entry 183, 19 Sep 50, and entries 192 and 197, 20 Sep 50; 2d Div WD, G–3 Sec, Sep–Oct 50, p. 18 and PIR 27, 20 Sep 50; EUSAK WD POR 206, 19 Sep 50; Freeman, MS review comments, 30 Oct 57; Combat Activities of the 23d Infantry.

[36] 23d Inf WD, entries 199–202, 20 Sep 50; EUSAK WD, G–3 Sec, 20 Sep 50; Glasgow, Platoon Leader in Korea, pp. 207–24.

[37] Interv, author with Radow (M Co, 23d Inf, Sep 50), 16 Aug 50; 23d Inf WD, entries 206–10, 20 Sep 50.

[38] 23d Inf WD, 20–22 Sep 50, entries 206–210, 214–222, and 226; 23d Inf POR 26, 20–21 Sep 50; and an. 1, Overlay; Glasgow, Platoon Leader in Korea, pp. 234–62. Glasgow, a platoon leader in B Company and critically wounded in the fight, indicates that part of the company behaved poorly in the enemy dawn attack.

ADVANCING TO THE CREST OF HILL 201

on Hill 239, the critical terrain overlooking Ch'ogye. The next day the battalion entered the town in the early afternoon. Before midnight the 1st Battalion turned over its task of containing elements of the N.K. *10th Division* on Hill 409 east of the Naktong to the 2d Battalion, 9th Infantry, and started across the river to join its regiment.[39]

[39] 38th Inf Comd Rpt, Sep–Oct 50, pp. 10–12; 2d Div PIR 18, 21 Sep 50; 2d Div WD, G–3 Sec, Sep–Oct 50, p. 20; *Ibid.*, G–4 Sec; EUSAK WD, G–3 Jnl, entry 1456, 22 Sep 50. An enemy sketch captured on the 21st near Ch'ogye showed accurately every position the 1st Battalion, 38th Infantry, had occupied east of the Naktong.

Although it had only 276 feet of bridging material, the 2d Division, by resorting to various expedients, completed a bridge in the afternoon of 22 September across the 400-foot-wide stream at the Sadung ferry site, and was ready to start moving supplies to the west side of the river in support of its advanced units.

Encirclement Above Taegu

In the arc above Taegu and on the right of the 5th Regimental Combat Team, the 1st Cavalry Division and the ROK 1st Division had dueled for days

BREAKING THE CORDON

VIEW FROM CREST OF HILL 201

with the N.K. *3d, 1st,* and *13th Divisions* in attack and counterattack. The intensity of the fighting there in relation to other parts of the Perimeter is apparent in the casualties. Of 373 casualties evacuated to Pusan on 16 September, for instance, nearly 200 came from the Taegu area. The fighting centered, as it had for the past month, on two corridors of approach to Taegu: (1) the Waegwan-Taegu highway and railroad, where the 5th Cavalry Regiment blocked the advanced elements of the N.K. *3d Division* five miles southeast of Waegwan and eight miles northwest of Taegu, and (2) the Tabu-dong road through the mountains north of Taegu where other elements of the 1st Cavalry Division and the ROK 1st Division had been striving to hold off the N.K *13th* and *1st Divisions* for nearly a month. There the enemy was still on hills overlooking the Taegu bowl and only six miles north of the city.

General Gay's plan for the 1st Cavalry Division in the Eighth Army breakout effort was (1) to protect the right flank of the 5th Regimental Combat Team as it drove on Waegwan by having the 5th Cavalry Regiment attack and hold the enemy troops in its zone east of the Waegwan-Taegu highway; (2) to maintain pressure by the 8th Cavalry Regiment on the enemy in the Ch'ilgok area north of Taegu, and be prepared on order to make a maximum effort to drive north to Tabu-dong; and (3) the 7th Cavalry Regiment on order to shift, by successive battalion movements, from the division right flank to the left flank and make a rapid encirclement of the enemy over a trail and secondary road between Waegwan and Tabu-dong. If the plan worked, the 7th and 8th Cavalry Regiments would meet at Tabu-dong and enclose a large number of enemy troops in the Waegwan–Taegu–Tabu-dong triangle. General Gay started shifting forces from right to left on 16 September by moving the 2d Battalion, 7th Cavalry, to Hill 188 in the 5th Cavalry area.[40]

North of Taegu on the Tabu-dong road enemy units of the N.K. *13th Division* fought the 8th Cavalry Regiment to a standstill during the first three days of the Eighth Army offensive. Neither side was able to improve its position materially. The enemy attacked the 2d Battalion, 8th Cavalry, repeatedly on Hill 570, the dominating height east of the mountain corridor, ten miles north of Taegu. West of the road, the 3d Battalion made limited gains in high hills closer to Taegu. The North Koreans on either side of the Tabu-dong road had some formidable defenses, with a large number of mortars and small field pieces dug in on the forward slopes of the hills. Until unit commanders could dispose their forces so that they could combine fire and movement, they had to go slow or sacrifice the lives of their men.

General Walker was displeased at the slow progress of the 8th Cavalry Regiment. On the 18th he expressed himself on this matter to General Gay, as did also General Milburn, commander of I Corps. Both men believed the regiment was not pushing hard. The next day the division attached the 3d Battalion, 7th Cavalry, to the 8th Cavalry Regiment, and Colonel Holmes, the division chief of staff, told Colonel Palmer that he must take Tabu-dong during the day. But the enemy *13th Division* frustrated the 8th Cavalry's attempt to reach Tabu-dong. Enemy artillery, mortar, and automatic weapons crossfire from the Walled City area of Ka-san east of the road and the high ground of Hill 351 west of it turned back the regiment with heavy casualties. On 20 September the 70th Tank Battalion lost seven tanks in this fight.[41]

But on the right of the 1st Cavalry Division, the ROK 1st Division made impressive gains. General Paik's righthand regiment, the 12th, found a gap in the enemy's positions in the high mountains and, plunging through it, reached a point on the Tabu-dong–Kunwi road ten miles northeast of Tabu-dong, and approximately thirteen miles beyond the most advanced units of the 1st Cavalry Division. There the ROK troops were in the

---

[40] Ltr, Gay to author, 30 Sep 53; 2d Bn, 7th Cav, Unit Jnl, 16 Sep 50.

[41] 8th Cav Regt WD, 16–20 Sep 50; 1st Cav Div WD, 16–20 Sep 50; *Ibid.*, PIR 181, 20 Sep 50; I Corps WD, 16–20 Sep 50; EUSAK WD, G-3 Sec, 18 Sep 50, situation overlay 0630, 18 Sep 50; Ltr, Gay to author, 30 Sep 53; Col Harold K. Johnson, MS review comments for author, Aug 54. Department of the Army General Order 38, 16 April 1952, awarded the Distinguished Unit Citation to the 2d Battalion, 8th Cavalry Regiment, and attached units for defense of Hill 570.

rear of the main body of the N.K. *1st* and *13th Divisions* and in a position to cut off one of their main lines of retreat. The U.S. 10th AAA Group accompanied the ROK 12th Regiment in its penetration and the artillerymen spoke glowingly of "the wonderful protection" given them, saying, "The 10th AAA Group was never safer than when it had a company of the 12th Regiment acting as its bodyguard. Everywhere the Group moved, Company 10 of the 12th Regiment moved too." This penetration caused the N.K. *1st Division* on 19 September to withdraw its *2d* and *14th Regiments* from the southern slopes of Kasan (Hill 902) to defend against the new threat. That day also a ROK company penetrated to the south edge of the Walled City.[42]

Along the Waegwan-Taegu road at the beginning of the U.N. offensive on 16 September, the 5th Cavalry Regiment attacked North Korean positions, centering on Hills 203 and 174 north of the road and Hill 188 opposite and south of it. Approximately 1,000 soldiers of the *8th Regiment, 3d Division,* held these key positions. The 1st Battalion, 5th Cavalry, began the attack on the 16th. The next day the 2d Battalion, 7th Cavalry, joined in, moving against Hill 253 farther west. There North Koreans engaged F and G Companies of the 7th Cavalry in heavy combat. When it became imperative to withdraw from the hill, G Company's Capt. Fred P. DePalina, although wounded, remained behind to cover the withdrawal of his men. Ambushed subsequently by enemy soldiers, DePalina killed six of them before he himself died. The two companies were forced back south of the road.[43]

For three days the North Koreans on Hill 203 repulsed every attempt to storm it. "Get Hill 203" was on every tongue. In the fighting, A Company of the 70th Tank Battalion lost nine tanks and one tank dozer to enemy action on 17 and 18 September, six of them to mines, two to enemy tank fire, and two to enemy antitank fire. In one tank action on the 18th, American tank fire knocked out two of three dug-in enemy tanks. Finally, on 18th September, Hill 203 fell to the 1st Battalion, 5th Cavalry, but the North Koreans continued to resist from the hills northwest of it, their strongest forces being on Hill 253. In this battle the three rifle companies of the 2d Battalion, 7th Cavalry, were reduced to a combined strength of 165 effective men—F Company was down to forty-five effectives. The enemy's skillful use of mortars had caused most of the casualties. At the close of 18 September the enemy *3d Division* still held the hill mass three miles east of Waegwan, centering on Hills 253 and 371.[44]

---

[42] EUSAK WD, G-3 Sec, 18 Sep 50, situation overlay 0630 18 Sep; I Corps WD, Narr Hist, 19 Sep 50; ATIS Interrog Rpts, Issue 9 (N.K. Forces), Interrog Rpt 1468, pp. 158-74, Col Lee Hak Ku, CofS *13th Div*, captured 21 Sep 50; Capt. Arthur C. Brooks, Jr., "From Pusan to Unsan with the 10th AAA Group," *Antiaircraft Journal*, XCIV, No. 1 (January-February, 1951), 14.

[43] 2d Bn, 7th Cav, Unit Jnl, 17-18 Sep 50; 1st Cav Div WD, 17 Sep 50. General Order 182, 30 March 1951, awarded the Distinguished Service Cross posthumously to Captain DePalina. EUSAK. (The order is apparently in error on the date of his death, giving it as 19 September.)

[44] 1st Cav Div WD, 16-18 Sep 50; 1st Cav Div Arty Unit Hist, 17 Sep 50; 5th Cav Regt WD, 16-18 Sep 50; *Ibid.*, Narr Rpt; 7th Cav Regt WD, 17-18 Sep 50; 1st Cav Div, G-2 Hist, Sep 50; Summ of Act, A Co, 70th Tk Bn, 17-24 Sep 50; I Corps WD, 18 Sep 50; USAF Hist Study 71, p. 66.

40-MM. ANTIAIRCRAFT BATTERY *attached to the ROK 1st Division fighting north of Tabu-dong.*

On 18 September forty-two B–29 bombers of the 92d and 98th Groups bombed west and northwest of Waegwan across the Naktong but apparently without damage to the enemy.

The battle on the hills east of Waegwan reached a climax on the 19th when the 1st Battalion, 5th Cavalry, and the 2d Battalion, 7th Cavalry, engaged in very heavy fighting with fanatical, die-in-place North Koreans on Hills 300 and 253. Elements of the 1st Battalion, 5th Cavalry, gained the crest of Hill 300. On that hill the 1st Battalion suffered 207 battle casualties—28 American soldiers killed, 147 wounded, and 4 missing in action, for a total of 179, with 28 additional casualties among the attached South Koreans. At noon, F Company reported 66 men present for duty; E and G Companies between them had 75 men. That afternoon the battalion reported it was only 30 percent combat effective. The 5th Cavalry's seizure of the 300 and 253 hill mass dominating the Taegu road three miles southeast of Waegwan unquestionably helped the 5th Regimental Combat Team to capture Waegwan that day. But one mile to the north of these hills, the enemy on Hill 371 in a stubborn holding action turned back for the moment all efforts of the 5th Cavalry to capture that height.[45]

---

[45] 2d Bn, 7th Cav, Unit Jnl, 19 Sep 50; 7th Cav Regt WD, 19 Sep 50; 1st Cav Div WD, 19–20 Sep 50. There were 205 counted enemy dead on Hill 300.

In its subsequent withdrawal from the Waegwan area to Sangju the N.K. *3d Division* fell from a strength of approximately 5,000 to about 1,800 men. Entire units gave way to panic. Combined U.N. ground and air action inflicted tremendous casualties. In the area around Waegwan where the 5th Cavalry Regiment reoccupied the old Waegwan pocket a count showed 28 enemy tanks—27 T34's and one American M4 refitted by the North Koreans—as destroyed or captured.[46]

During the 19th General Gay started maneuvering his forces for the encirclement movement, now that the hard fighting east of Waegwan had at last made it possible. Colonel Clainos led his 1st Battalion, 7th Cavalry, from the division right to the left flank, taking position in front of the 2d Battalion, 7th Cavalry, to start the movement toward Tabu-dong. Gay ordered the 3d Battalion, 7th Cavalry, to shift the next morning from the right flank to the left, and prepare to follow the 1st Battalion in its dash for Tabu-dong. On the morning of 20 September the 3d Battalion entrucked north of Taegu and rolled northwest on the road toward Waegwan. The regimental commander, apparently fearing that enemy mortar and artillery fire would interdict the road, detrucked his troops short of their destination. Their foot march tired the troops and made them late in reaching their assembly area. This overcaution angered General Gay because the same thing had happened when the 2d Battalion of the same regiment had moved to the left flank four days earlier.[47]

In the meantime, during the morning the 1st Battalion, 7th Cavalry, led off down the road toward Waegwan past Hill 300. Two miles short of Waegwan the lead elements at 0900 turned off the main highway onto a poor secondary road which cut across country to a point three miles east of Waegwan, where it met the Waegwan–Tabu-dong road. This latter road curved northeast, winding along a narrow valley floor hemmed in on both sides by high mountains all the way to Tabu-dong, eight miles away.

Even though an armored spearhead from C Company, 70th Tank Battalion, led the way, roadblocks and enemy fire from the surrounding hills held the battalion to a slow advance. By midafternoon it had gained only two miles, and was only halfway on the cutoff road that led into the Waegwan–Tabu-dong road. The column stopped completely when a tank struck a mine. General Gay showed his irritation over the slow progress by ordering the regimental commander to have the 1st Battalion bypass enemy on the hills and "high-tail it" for Tabu-dong.[48]

Acting on General Gay's orders, the 1st Battalion pushed ahead, reached the Tabu-dong road, and turned northeast on it toward the town eight miles away. This road presented a picture of devastation—dead oxen, disabled T34 tanks, wrecked artillery pieces, piles of abandoned ammunition, and other military

---

[46] ATIS Res Supp Interrog Rpts, Issue 96 (N.K. *3d Div*), pp. 34-35; I Corps WD, Narr Hist, 20 Sep 50 and G-2 Sec, 22 Sep 50; 5th Cav Regt WD, 22 Sep 50; EUSAK WD, 22 Sep 50, and POR 216, 22 Sep 50.

[47] 1st Bn, 7th Cav, Unit Jnl, 19 Sep 50; 3d Bn, 7th Cav, Unit Jnl, Msg 5, 191920, and Msg 6, 201400 Sep 50; Ltr, Gay to author, 30 Sep 53.

[48] 7th Cav Regt WD, 20 Sep 50 (entries for 19 and 20 Sep are run together with no date entry for the 20th).

equipment and supplies littered its course. As the battalion halted for the night, an exploding mine injured Colonel Clainos. He refused evacuation, but the next day was evacuated on orders of the regimental commander. That evening the 1st Battalion, with the 3d Battalion following close behind, advanced to the vicinity of Togae-dong, four miles short of Tabu-dong.

The premature detrucking of the 3d Battalion during the day was the final incident that caused General Gay to replace the 7th Cavalry regimental commander. That evening General Gay put in command of the regiment Colonel Harris, commanding officer of the 77th Field Artillery Battalion, which had been in support of the regiment. Harris assumed command just before midnight.[49]

Colonel Harris issued orders about midnight to assembled battalion and unit commanders that the 7th Cavalry would capture Tabu-dong on the morrow, and that the element which reached the village first was to turn south to contact the 8th Cavalry Regiment and at the same time establish defensive positions to secure the road.

The next morning, 21 September, the 1st Battalion resumed the attack and arrived at the edge of Tabu-dong at 1255. There it encountered enemy resistance, but in a pincer movement from southwest and northwest cleared the village by 1635. An hour later the battalion moved out of Tabu-dong down the Taegu road in attack southward toward the 8th Cavalry Regiment.

Late that afternoon, General Gay was accompanying the 1st Battalion, 8th Cavalry, advancing northward toward Tabu-dong. He and Colonel Kane, the battalion commander, were standing close to a tank when a voice came over its radio saying, "Scrappy, this is Skirmish Red, don't fire." A few minutes later a sergeant, commanding the lead platoon of C Company, 7th Cavalry, came into the position and received the personal congratulations of the division commander upon completing the encircling movement.[50]

Meanwhile, the 3d Battalion, 7th Cavalry, arrived at Tabu-dong and turned north to deploy its troops in defensive positions on both sides of the road. By this time, elements of the ROK 1st Division had cut the Sangju road above Tabu-dong and were attacking south toward the village. The ROK 12th Regiment, farthest advanced, had a roadblock eight miles to the northeast below Kunwi. It appeared certain that the operations of the 1st Cavalry Division and the ROK 1st Division had cut off large numbers of the N.K. *3d, 13th,* and *1st Divisions* in the mountains north of Taegu. The next day, 22 September, the 11th Regiment of the ROK 1st Division and units of the ROK National Police captured the Walled City of Ka-san, and elements of the ROK 15th Regiment reached Tabu-dong from the north to link up with the 1st Cavalry Division.[51]

___

[49] 7th Cav Regt WD, 20 Sep 50; 1st Bn, 7th Cav, Unit Jnl, 20 Sep 50; 3d Bn, 7th Cav, Unit Jnl, Msgs 10, 12, 14, 20 Sep 50; 77th FA Bn WD, 20 Sep 50; Ltr, Gay to author, 30 Sep 53.

[50] 7th Cav WD, 20-21 Sep 50; 3d Bn, 7th Cav, Unit Jnl, Msg 15, 20 Sep 50; 1st Bn, 7th Cav, Unit Jnl, 21 Sep 50; I Corps WD, 21 Sep 50; 1st Cav Div WD, 21 Sep 50; Ltr, Gay to author, 30 Sep 53; Interv, author with Harris, 30 Apr 54; Interv, author with Clainos, 30 Apr 54.

[51] 3d Bn, 7th Cav, Unit Jnl, Msgs 22 and 26, 211500 and 211700 Sep 50; 61st FA Bn WD, 21 Sep 50; EUSAK WD, 21 Sep 50.

The Right Flank

In the mountainous area of the ROK II Corps the enemy *8th Division* was exhausted and the *15th* practically destroyed. The ROK divisions were near exhaustion, too, but their strength was greater than the enemy's and they began to move slowly north again. The ROK 6th Division attacked against the N.K. *8th Division*, which it had held without gain for two weeks, and in a 4-day battle destroyed the division as a combat force. According to enemy sources, the N.K. *8th Division* suffered about 4,000 casualties at this time. The survivors fled north toward Yech'on in disorder. By 21 September the ROK 6th Division was advancing north of Uihung with little opposition.[52]

Eastward, the ROK 8th Division, once it had gathered itself together and begun to move northward, found little resistance because the opposing enemy *15th Division* had been practically annihilated.

In the battle-scarred Kigye–An'gang-ni–Kyongju area of the ROK I Corps sector, units of the Capital Division fought their way through the streets of An'gang-ni on 16 September, the day the U.N. offensive got under way. Beyond it, the ROK 3d Division had moved up to the north bank of the Hyongsan-gang just below P'ohang-dong. The next day a battalion of the ROK 7th Division, advancing from the west, established contact with elements of the Capital Division and closed the 2-week-old gap between the ROK II and I Corps.

Retiring northward into the mountains, the N.K. *12th Division* fought stubborn delaying actions and did not give up Kigye to the Capital Division until 22 September. It then continued its withdrawal toward Andong. This once formidable organization, originally composed largely of Korean veterans of the Chinese Communist Army, was all but destroyed—its strength stood at approximately 2,000 men. The North Korean and ROK divisions on the eastern flank now resembled exhausted wrestlers, each too weak to press against the other. The ROK divisions, however, had numerical superiority, better supply, daily close air support and, in the P'ohang-dong area, naval gunfire.[53]

On the 16th, naval support was particularly effective when Admiral Charles C. Hartman's Task Group, including the battleship USS *Missouri*, appeared off P'ohang-dong. The big battleship pounded the enemy positions below the town, along the dike north of the Hyongsan-gang, with 2,000-pound shells from its 16-inch guns. Two days later the battleship again shelled these dike positions under observed radio fire direction by Colonel Emmerich, KMAG adviser to the ROK 3d Division. ROK troops then assaulted across the bridge, but enemy machine gunners cut them down. The number killed is unknown, but 144 were wounded in trying to cross the bridge. In a final desperate step, thirty-one ROK

---

[52] EUSAK WD, G-3 Jnl, entry 1050, 21 Sep 50; Ibid., G-3 Sec, 19 Sep 50; ATIS Res Supp Interrog Rpts, Issue 4 (N.K. *8th Div*), p. 25; ATIS Interrog Rpts, Issue 10 (N.K. Forces), Rpt 1517, p. 44, Lt Choe Yun Ju.

[53] ATIS Res Supp Interrog Rpts, Issue 99 (N.K. *12th Div*), pp. 48–49; EUSAK WD, G-2 Stf Sec Rpt, 14 Sep 50, and Summ, 19 Sep 50, p. 31; Ibid., POR 217, 22 Sep 50.

soldiers volunteered to die if necessary in trying to cross the bridge. Fighter planes helped their effort by making dummy strafing passes against the enemy dike positions. Of the thirty-one who charged, nineteen fell on the bridge. Other ROK soldiers quickly reinforced the handful of men who gained a foothold north of the river. There they found dead enemy machine gunners tied to their dike positions.[54]

As a preliminary move in the U.N. offensive in the east, naval vessels on the night of 14–15 September had transported the ROK Miryang Guerrilla Battalion, specially trained and armed with Russian-type weapons, to Changsa-dong, ten miles above P'ohang-dong, where the battalion landed two and a half hours after midnight in the rear of the N.K. *5th Division*. Its mission was to harass the enemy rear while the ROK 3d Division attacked frontally below P'ohang-dong. That evening the enemy division sent a battalion from its *12th Regiment* to the coastal hills where the Miryang Battalion had taken a position and there engaged it. The ROK guerrilla battalion's effort turned into a complete fiasco. The U.S. Navy had to rush to its assistance and place a ring of naval gunfire around it on the beach, where enemy fire had driven the battalion. This saved it from total destruction. Finally, on 18 September, with great difficulty, the Navy evacuated 725 of the ROK's, 110 of them wounded, by LST. Thirty-nine dead were left behind, as well as 32 others who refused to try to reach the evacuating ships.[55]

Although this effort to harass the enemy rear came to nothing and gave the ROK 3d Division little help, elements of that division had combat patrols at the edge of P'ohang-dong on the evening of 19 September. The next morning at 1015 the division captured the destroyed fishing and harbor village. One regiment drove on through the town to the high ground north of it. And in the succeeding days of 21 and 22 September the ROK 3d Division continued strong attacks northward, supported by naval gunfire and fighter planes, capturing Hunghae, and driving the N.K. *5th Division* back on Yongdok in disorder.[56]

The Left Flank—The Enemy Withdraws From Sobuk-san

At the other end of the U.N. line, the left flank in the Masan area, H-hour on 16 September found the 25th Division in an embarrassing situation. Instead of being able to attack, the division was still fighting enemy forces behind its lines, and the enemy appeared stronger than ever on the heights of Battle Mountain, P'il-bong, and Sobuk-san.

General Kean and his staff felt that the division could advance along the roads toward Chinju only when the mountainous center of the division front

---

[54] Interv, author with Emmerich, 5 Dec 51; EUSAK WD, 18 Sep 50; GHQ FEC, G–3 Opn Rpt, 17 Sep 50; Karig, *et al.*, *Battle Report, The War in Korea*, pp. 254–55.

[55] EUSAK WD, G–3 Sec, 14–15 Sep 50; *Ibid.*, Br for CG, 15 Sep 50; GHQ FEC, History of the N.K. Army, pp. 51, 61; GHQ FEC Sitrep, 19–20 Sep 50; Karig, *et al.*, *Battle Report, The War in Korea*, pp. 243–55.

[56] Interv, author with Emmerich, 5 Dec 51; EUSAK WD, Summ, 20 Sep 50, p. 32; *Ibid.*, Br for CG, and G–3 Sec, 20 Sep 50; EUSAK WD, 21–22 Sep 50; USAF Hist Study 71, p. 67; ATIS Res Supp Interrog Rpts, Issue 96 (N.K. *5th Div*), p. 44.

ENEMY-HELD AREA, *showing high ground north of P'ohang-dong.*

was clear of the enemy. The experience of Task Force Kean in early August, when the enemy had closed in behind it from the mountains, was still fresh in their minds. They therefore believed that the key to the advance of the 25th Division lay in its center where the enemy held the heights and kept the 24th Infantry Regiment under daily attack. The 27th Infantry on the left and the 35th Infantry on the right, astride the roads between Chinju and Masan, could do little more than mark time until the situation in front of the 24th Infantry improved.

To carry out his plan, General Kean on 16 September organized a composite battalion-sized task force under command of Maj. Robert L. Woolfolk, commanding officer of the 3d Battalion, 35th Infantry, and ordered it to attack the enemy-held heights of Battle Mountain and P'il-bong the next day, with the mission of restoring the 24th Infantry positions there. On the 17th and 18th the task force repeatedly attacked these heights, heavily supported by artillery fire from the 8th and 90th Field Artillery Battalions and by numerous air strikes, but enemy automatic fire from the heights drove back the assaulting troops every time with heavy casualties. Within twenty-four hours, A Company, 27th Infantry, alone suffered fifty-seven casualties. Woolfolk's force abandoned its effort to drive the enemy from the peaks after its failure on the 18th, and the task group was dissolved the next day.[57]

During the morning of 19 September it was discovered that the enemy had abandoned the crest of Battle Mountain during the night, and the 1st Battalion, 24th Infantry, moved up and occupied it. On the right, the 35th Infantry began moving forward. There was only light resistance until it reached the high ground in front of Chungam-ni where cleverly hidden enemy soldiers in spider holes shot at 1st Battalion soldiers from the rear. The next day the 1st Battalion captured Chungam-ni, and the 2d Battalion captured the long ridge line running northwest from it to the Nam River. Meanwhile, the enemy still held strongly against the division left where the 27th Infantry had heavy fighting in trying to move forward.[58]

On 21 September the 35th Infantry Regiment captured the well-known Notch, three miles southwest of Chungam-ni, and then swept westward eight air miles without resistance, past the Much'on-ni road fork, to the high ground at the Chinju pass. There at 2230 the lead battalion halted for the night. At the same time, the 24th and 27th Regiments in the center and on the division left advanced, slowed only by the rugged terrain they had to traverse. They passed abandoned position after position from which the North Koreans previously had fought to the death, and saw that enemy automatic positions had honeycombed the hills.[59]

The events of the past three days made it clear that the enemy in front of the 25th Division in the center and on the right had started his withdrawal the night of 18–19 September. The N.K. *7th Division* withdrew from south of the Nam River while the *6th Division* sideslipped elements to cover the entire front. Covered by the *6th Division*, the *7th* had crossed to the north side of the Nam River by the morning of the 19th. Then the N.K. *6th Division* had withdrawn from its positions on Sobuk-san.[60]

Although the North Korean withdrawal had been general in front of the 25th Division, there were still delaying groups and stragglers in the mountains. Below Tundok on the morning of 22 September some North Koreans slipped into the bivouac area of A Company, 24th Infantry. One platoon leader awoke to find an enemy soldier standing over him. He grabbed the enemy's bayonet and struggled with the North Korean until someone else shot the man. Nearby another enemy dropped a grenade into a foxhole on three sleeping men, killing

---

[57] EUSAK WD, 16 Sep 50; 24th Inf WD, 16 Sep 50; 27th Inf WD, 17 Sep 50; 1st Bn, 27th Inf Unit Rpt, Sep 50; 25th Div WD, Narr Rpt, Sep 50, p. 31; Barth MS, p. 33. Woolfolk's task group: Hq, 3d Bn, 35th Inf; I Co, 35th Inf; A Co, 27th Inf; B Co and 1 plat, C Co, 65th Engr C Bn. The 25th Reconnaissance Company and the Heavy Weapons Company, 24th Infantry, gave support.

[58] 24th Inf WD, 19 Sep 50; 35th Inf WD, 19–20 Sep 50; 1st Bn, 35th Inf WD, 19–20 Sep 50; 27th Inf WD, Act Rpt, Sep 50, p. 3; 25th Div WD, Narr, Sep 50, p. 25; EUSAK WD, G–3 Jnl, entry 1610, 20 Sep 50.

[59] 35th Inf Unit Rpt, 21 Sep 50; 1st Bn, 35th Inf, Unit Rpt, 21 Sep 50; 27th Inf Act Rpt, Sep 50, p. 3; 2d Bn, 24th Inf, WD, 21 Sep 50; Barth MS, p. 35.

[60] 25th Div WD, 19 Sep 50, and Narr Rpt, Sep 50, p. 31.

two and wounding the third. A little later mortar fire fell on a company commanders' meeting at 1st Battalion headquarters and inflicted seven casualties, including the commanding officer of Headquarters Company killed, and the battalion executive officer, the S-1, and the S-2 wounded.[61]

Up ahead of the division advance, elements of the N.K. *6th Division* at the Chinju pass blocked the 35th Infantry all day on 22 September, covering the withdrawal of the main body across the Nam River and through Chinju, six miles westward. The assault companies of the 1st Battalion, 35th Infantry, got within 200 yards of the top of Hill 152 at the pass but could go no farther.[62]

Just before the Eighth Army breakout MacArthur had revived a much debated proposal. On 19 September General Wright sent a message from Inch'on to General Hickey, Acting Chief of Staff, FEC, in Tokyo, saying General MacArthur directed that Plan 100-C, which provided for a landing at Kunsan, be readied for execution. He indicated that MacArthur wanted two U.S. divisions and one ROK division prepared to make the landing on 15 October. This proposal indicates quite clearly that on the 19th General MacArthur entertained serious doubts about the Eighth Army's ability to break out of the Pusan Perimeter. In truth it did not look very promising. General Walker, when informed of this plan, opposed taking any units out of the Eighth Army line in the south. By the 22d the situation had brightened considerably for a breakout there, and after discussing the matter with Walker that day General MacArthur gave up the idea of a Kunsan landing; General Hickey penciled on the plan, "File."[63]

Aerial observers' reports on 22 September gave no clear indication of enemy intentions. While there were reports of large enemy movements northward there were also large ones seen going south. Eighth Army intelligence on that day estimated the situation to be one in which, "although the enemy is apparently falling back in all sectors, there are no indications of an over-all planned disengagement and withdrawal."[64] This estimate of enemy intentions was wrong. Everywhere, even though it was not yet apparent to Eighth Army, the enemy units were withdrawing, covering their withdrawal by strong blocking and delaying actions wherever possible.

In any analysis of Eighth Army's unanticipated favorable position at this time it is imperative to calculate the effect of the Inch'on landing on the North Koreans fighting in the south. There can be little doubt that when this news reached them it was demoralizing in the extreme and was perhaps the greatest single factor in their rapid deterioration. The evidence seems to show that news of the Inch'on landing was kept from most of the North Korean officers as well as nearly all the troops at the Pusan Perimeter for nearly a week. It would appear that the North Korean

---

[61] Interv, author with 1st Lt Robert J. Tews (Plat Ldr A Co, 24th Inf), 21 Sep 51; 24th Inf WD, 22 Sep 50; 25th Div WD, Narr, p. 27, Sep 50.

[62] 35th Inf WD, 22-23 Sep 50; 25th Div WD, 22 Sep 50 and Narr, p. 40.

[63] Msg 063180, CINCUNC to CINCFE (Wright to Hickey), 19 Sep 50, FEC CofS file.

[64] EUSAK PIR 72, 22 Sep 50.

High Command did not decide on a withdrawal from the Perimeter and a regrouping somewhere farther north until three or four days after the landing when it became evident that Seoul was in imminent danger. The pattern of fighting and enemy action at the Perimeter reflects this fact.

Nowhere on 16 September, when Eighth Army began its offensive, did it score material gains except in certain parts of the 2d Division zone where the 38th and 23d Infantry Regiments broke through decimated enemy forces to reach the Naktong River. Until 19 September there was everywhere the stoutest enemy resistance and no indication of voluntary withdrawal, and, generally, U.N. advances were minor and bought only at the cost of heavy fighting and numerous casualties. Then during the night of 18–19 September the enemy *7th* and *6th Divisions* began withdrawing in the southern part of the line where the enemy forces were farthest from North Korean soil. The *6th Division* left behind well organized and effective delaying parties to cover the withdrawals.

On 19 September Waegwan fell to the U.S. 5th Regimental Combat Team, and the ROK 1st Division in the mountains north of Taegu penetrated to points behind the enemy *1st* and *13th Divisions'* lines. These divisions then started their withdrawals. The next day the ROK 3d Division on the east coast recaptured P'ohang-dong and in the ensuing days the *5th Division* troops in front of it fell back rapidly northward on Yongdok. And at the same time the ROK Army made sweeping advances in the mountains throughout the eastern half of the front. The 1st Cavalry Division was unable to make significant gains until 20 and 21 September. On the 21st it finally recaptured Tabu-dong. West of the Naktong the U.S. 2d Division fought stubborn enemy delaying forces on 21 and 22 September.

The effect of the Inch'on landing and the battles around Seoul on enemy action at the Pusan Perimeter from 19 September onward was clearly apparent. By that date the North Korean High Command began to withdraw its main forces committed in the south and start them moving northward. By 23 September this North Korean retrograde movement was in full swing everywhere around the Perimeter. This in itself is proof of the theater-wide military effectiveness of the Inch'on landing. The Inch'on landing will stand as MacArthur's masterpiece.

By 23 September the enemy cordon around the Pusan Perimeter was no more —Eighth Army's general attack combined with the effect of the Inch'on landing had rent it asunder. The Eighth Army and the ROK Army stood on the eve of pursuit and exploitation, a long-awaited revenge for the bitter weeks of defeat and death.

CHAPTER XXVIII

Pursuit and Exploitation

> Once the enemy has taken flight, they can be chased with no better weapons than air-filled bladders . . . attack, push, and pursue without cease. All maneuvers are good then; it is only precautions that are worthless. MARSHAL MAURICE DE SAXE, *Reveries on the Art of War*

By 23 September the North Korean Army was everywhere in retreat from the Pusan Perimeter. Eighth Army, motorized and led by armored spearheads, was ready to sweep forward along the main axes of advance.

The Eighth Army decision to launch the pursuit phase of the breakout operation came suddenly. On 20 September General Allen, in a telephone conversation with General Hickey in Tokyo, reported, "We have not had any definite break yet. They [the North Koreans] are softening but still no definite indication of any break which we could turn into a pursuit."[1] The next day General Allen thought the break had come, and on 22 September General Walker issued his order for the pursuit.

The Eighth Army order stated:

Enemy resistance has deteriorated along the Eighth Army front permitting the assumption of a general offensive from present positions. In view of this situation it is mandatory that all efforts be directed toward the destruction of the enemy by effecting deep penetrations, fully exploiting enemy weaknesses, and through the conduct of enveloping or encircling maneuver get astride enemy lines of withdrawal to cut his attempted retreat and destroy him.[2]

The order directed a full-scale offensive: I Corps to continue to make the main effort along the Taegu-Kumch'on-Taejon-Suwon axis and to effect a juncture with X Corps; the 2d Infantry Division to launch an unlimited objective attack along the Hyopch'on-Koch'ang-Anui-Chonju-Kanggyong axis; the 25th Division on the army's southern flank to seize Chinju and be ready to attack west or northwest on army order; and the ROK Army in the east to destroy the enemy in its zone by deep penetrations and enveloping maneuvers. An important section of the Eighth Army order and a key to the contemplated operation stated, "Commanders will advance where necessary without regard to lateral security."

Later in the day, Eighth Army issued radio orders making IX Corps, under General Coulter, operational at 1400, 23

---

[1] Fonecon, Gen Allen with Gen Hickey, 1145 20 Sep 50, CofS GHQ files.

[2] Eighth Army Opn Ord 101, 22 Sep 50, copy in EUSAK WD, G-3 Sec, 22 Sep 50.

September, and attaching the U.S. 2d and 25th Infantry Divisions to it. This order charged IX Corps with the responsibility of carrying out the missions previously assigned to the 2d and 25th Divisions. In preparing for the pursuit, Eighth Army moved its headquarters from Pusan back to Taegu, reopening there at 1400, 23 September.[3]

The U.N. forces around the Pusan Perimeter at this time numbered almost 160,000 men, of whom more than 76,000 were in Eighth Army and about 75,000 in the ROK Army. United Nations reinforcements had begun arriving in Korea by this time. On 19 September the Philippine 10th Infantry Battalion Combat Team began unloading at Pusan, and on 22 September the 65th Regimental Combat Team started unloading there, its principal unit being the 65th Puerto Rican Infantry Regiment. The next day Swedish Red Cross Field Hospital personnel arrived at Pusan. On the 19th, the Far East Command deactivated the Pusan Logistical Command and reconstituted it as the 2d Logistical Command—its mission of logistical support unchanged.[4]

Since pursuit of the enemy along any one of the several corridors leading away from the Pusan Perimeter did not materially affect that in any other, except perhaps in the case of the Taejon and Poun-Ch'ongju central roadways, the pursuit phase of the breakout operation will be described by major corridors of advance. The story will move from south to north and northeast around the Perimeter. It must be remembered that the various movements were going on simultaneously all around the Perimeter.

The 25th Division Crosses Southwest Korea

On the day he assumed command of operational IX Corps, 23 September, General Coulter in a meeting with General Walker at the 25th Division command post requested authority to change the division's axis of attack from southwest to west and northwest. He thought this would permit better co-ordination with the 2d Division to the north. Walker told Coulter he could alter the division boundaries within IX Corps so long as he did not change the corps boundaries.[5]

The change chiefly concerned the 27th Regiment which now had to move from the 25th Division's south flank to its north flank. General Kean formed a special task force under Capt. Charles J. Torman, commanding officer of the 25th Reconnaissance Company, which moved through the 27th Infantry on the southern coastal road at Paedun-ni the evening of the 23d. The 27th Regiment then began its move from that place to the division's north flank at Chungam-ni. The 27th Infantry was to establish a bridgehead across the Nam River and attack through Uiryong to Chinju.[6] (*Map VIII*)

On the morning of 24 September Task

---

[3] EUSAK WD, G-3 Sec, 22-23 Sep 50.
[4] GHQ FEC, G-3 Opn Rpt, 22 Sep 50. The assigned strength as of 1800, 21 September 1950, was: Eighth Army, 76,837; British 27th Infantry Brigade, 1,679; Air Force in Korea, 4,794; Philippine 10th Battalion Combat Team, 1,200; ROK Army, 74,987. EUSAK WD, 19-23 Sep 50; 2d Log Comd Act Rpt, Sep 50.

[5] Intervs, author with Coulter, 20 Jul 51 and 2 Apr 53; IX Corps WD, Sep 50, Personal Recollections of Coulter.
[6] 27th Inf Hist Rpt, Sep 50, p. 10; 25th Div WD, 23 Sep 50; EUSAK WD, 23 Sep 50; 25th Recon Co WD, 23 Sep 50.

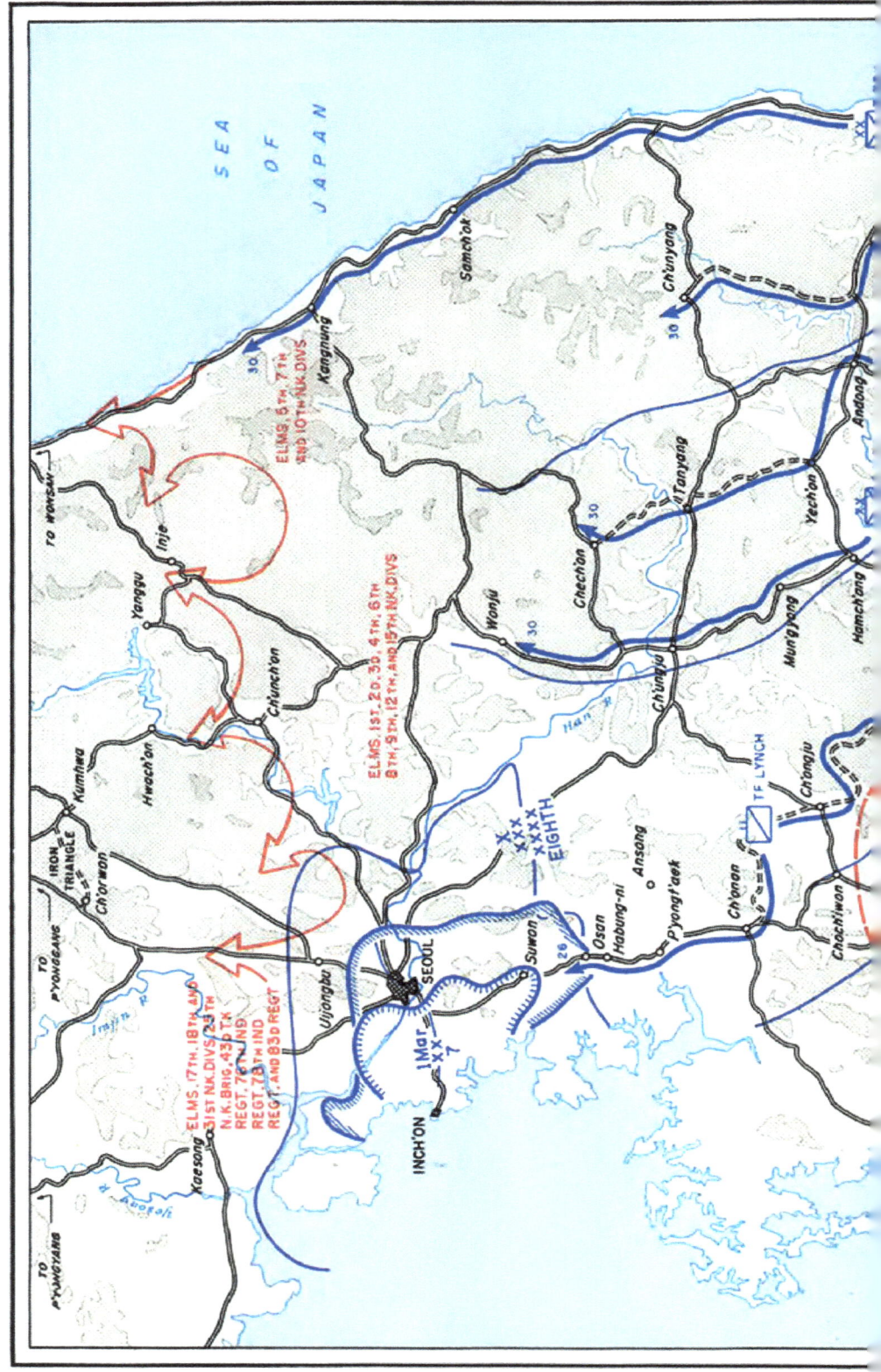

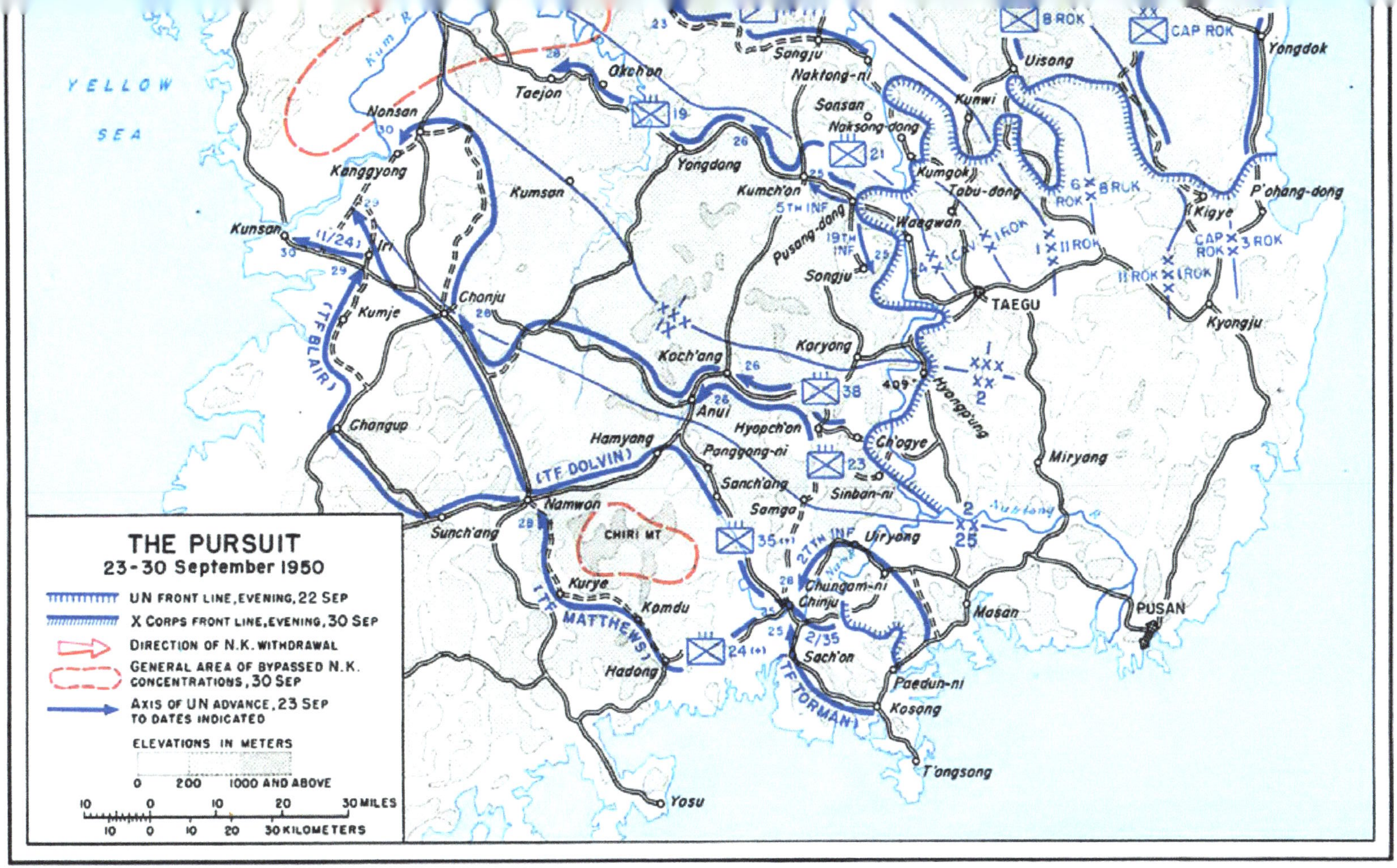

MAP VIII

THE PURSUIT
23-30 September 1950

- UN FRONT LINE, EVENING, 22 SEP
- X CORPS FRONT LINE, EVENING, 30 SEP
- DIRECTION OF N.K. WITHDRAWAL
- GENERAL AREA OF BYPASSED N.K. CONCENTRATIONS, 30 SEP
- AXIS OF UN ADVANCE, 23 SEP TO DATES INDICATED

ELEVATIONS IN METERS: 200, 1000 AND ABOVE

Printed by Defense Mapping Agency Hydrographic/Topographic Center

F. Temple

Force Torman attacked along the coastal road toward Chinju. North of Sach'on the task force engaged and dispersed about 200 enemy soldiers of the *3d Battalion, 104th Security Regiment*. By evening it had seized the high ground at the road juncture three miles south of Chinju. The next morning the task force moved up to the Nam River bridge which crossed into Chinju. In doing so one of the tanks hit a mine and fragments from the explosion seriously wounded Captain Torman, who had to be evacuated.[7]

Meanwhile, on the main inland road to Chinju the N.K. *6th Division* delayed the 35th Infantry at the Chinju pass until the evening of 23 September, when enemy covering units withdrew. The next day the 35th Infantry consolidated its position at the pass. That night a patrol reported that enemy demolitions had rendered the highway bridge over the Nam at Chinju unusable.

On the strength of this information the 35th Regiment made plans to cross the Nam downstream from the bridge. Under cover of darkness at 0200, 25 September, the 2d Battalion crossed the river two and a half miles southeast of Chinju. It then attacked and seized Chinju, supported by tank fire from Task Force Torman across the river. About 300 enemy troops, using mortar and artillery fire, served as a delaying force in defending the town. The 3d and 1st Battalions crossed the river into Chinju in the afternoon, and that evening Task Force Torman crossed on an underwater sandbag ford that the 65th Engineer Combat Battalion built 200 yards east of the damaged highway bridge. Working all night, the engineers repaired the highway bridge so that vehicular traffic began crossing it at noon the next day, 26 September.[8]

Sixteen air miles downstream from Chinju, near the blown bridges leading to Uiryong, engineer troops and more than 1,000 Korean refugees worked all day on the 25th constructing a sandbag ford across the Nam River. Enemy mortars fired sporadically on the workers until silenced by counterbattery fire of the 8th Field Artillery Battalion. Before dawn of the 26th the 1st Battalion, 27th Infantry, crossed the Nam. Once on the north bank, elements of the regiment attacked toward Uiryong, three miles to the northwest, and secured the town just before noon after overcoming an enemy force that defended it with small arms and mortar fire. The regiment pressed on to Chinju against negligible resistance on 28 September.[9]

On 24 September Eighth Army had altered its earlier operational order and directed IX Corps to execute unlimited objective attacks to seize Chonju and Kanggyong. To carry out his part of the order, General Kean organized two main task forces with armored support centered about the 24th and 35th Infantry Regiments. The leading elements of these two task forces were known respectively as Task Force Matthews and Task Force Dolvin. Both forces were to start their drives from Chinju. Task Force

---

[7] 25th Recon Co WD, G-3 Sec, Sep 50; 25th Div WD, 23-24 Sep 50; ATIS Interrog Rpts, Issue 12, p. 193, Rpt 1769, Lt Col Pak Chong Song, CO, *3d Bn, 104th Security Regt*.

[8] 35th Inf Unit Rpt, 25-26 Sep 50; 25th Recon Co WD, Sep 50; 25th Div WD, Hist Narr, p. 44; IX Corps WD, 25 Sep 50; 65th Engr C Bn WD, 25-26 Sep 50.

[9] 1st Bn, 27th Inf, Unit Rpt, 26 Sep 50; 27th Inf Hist Rpt, 25-26 Sep 50, p. 11; 25th Div WD, Sep 50, Narr Hist, p. 46.

Matthews, the lefthand column, was to proceed west toward Hadong and there turn northwest to Kurye, Namwon, Sunch'ang, Kumje, Iri, and Kunsan on the Kum River estuary. Taking off at the same time, Task Force Dolvin, the righthand column, was to drive north out of Chinju toward Hamyang, there turn west to Namwon, and proceed northwest to Chonju, Iri, and Kanggyong on the Kum River.[10]

Three blown bridges west of Chinju delayed the departure of Task Force Matthews (formerly Task Force Torman) until 1000, 27 Septebmer. Capt. Charles M. Matthews, commanding officer of A Company, 79th Tank Battalion, replaced Torman in command of the latter's task force after Torman had been wounded and evacuated. He led the advance out of Chinju with the 25th Reconnaissance Company and A Company, 79th Tank Battalion. The 3d Battalion, 24th Infantry, followed Task Force Matthews, and the rest of the regiment came behind it. Matthews reached Hadong at 1730.[11]

In a sense, the advance of Task Force Matthews became a chase to rescue a group of U.S. prisoners that the North Koreans moved just ahead of the pursuers. Korean civilians and bypassed enemy soldiers kept telling of them being four hours ahead, two hours ahead—but always ahead. At Hadong the column learned that some of the prisoners were only thirty minutes ahead. From Hadong, in bright moonlight, the attack turned northwest toward Kurye. About ten miles above Hadong at the little village of Komdu the advanced elements of the task force liberated eleven American prisoners. They had belonged to the 3d Battalion, 29th Infantry Regiment. Most of them were unable to walk and some had open wounds.[12]

Just short of Namwon about noon the next day, 28 September, several vehicles at the head of the task force became stuck in the river crossing below the town after Sgt. Raymond N. Reifers in the lead tank of the 25th Reconnaissance Company had crossed ahead of them. While the rest of the column halted behind the stuck vehicles Reifers continued on into Namwon.

Entering the town, Reifers found it full of enemy soldiers. Apparently the North Koreans' attention had been centered on two F-84 jet planes that could be seen sweeping in wide circles, rocketing and strafing the town, and they were unaware that pursuing ground elements were so close. Surprised by the sudden appearance of the American tank, the North Koreans in wild disorder jumped over fences, scurried across roof tops, and dashed madly up and down the streets.

---

[10] Eighth Army, Ltr of Inst to CG, I and IX Corps, 24 Sep 50; EUSAK WD, 23 Sep 50; 25th Div WD, 24-25 Sep 50.

[11] The name Task Force Torman is used frequently in the official records when TF Matthews is meant. TF Matthews consisted of the 25th Rcn Co; A Co, 79th Tk Bn; a platoon of B Co, 67th Engr C Bn; an air TAC Party; and the medical section of the 27th Inf Regt.
There were three separate task forces in this movement: (1) TF Matthews which formed the point; (2) TF Blair, named after Maj Melvin R. Blair, CO 3d Bn, 24th Inf, which followed close behind Matthews; and (3) TF Corley, named for Col John T. Corley, CO 24th Inf Regt, which included the rest of the RCT, following TF Blair. See 24th Inf WD, 26-30 Sep 50; 3d Bn, 24th Inf Unit Rpt, 26-30 Sep 50.

[12] Sawyer, Notes for author, 1 Oct 52 (Sawyer, then a 1st lieutenant, commanded the 3d Plat, 25th Recon Co, in TF Matthews); 25th Div WD, Med Co Unit Rpt (24th Inf), 28 Sep 50; 3d Bn, 24th Inf WD, 27 Sep 50; Corley, MS review comments, Oct 57.

Reifers said later that the scene would have appeared ludicrous if his own plight had not been so precarious. Suddenly he heard American voices calling out, "Don't shoot! Americans! GI's here!" A second later a gateway leading into a large courtyard burst open and the prisoners—shouting, laughing, and crying—poured out into the street.

Back at the head of the stuck column, 1st Lt. Robert K. Sawyer over his tank radio heard Reifer's voice calling out, "Somebody get up here! I'm all alone in this town! It is full of enemy soldiers and there are American prisoners here." Some of the tanks and vehicles now pushed ahead across the stream. When Sawyer's tank turned into the main street he saw ahead of him, gathered about vehicles, "a large group of bearded, haggard Americans. Most were bare-footed and in tatters, and all were obviously half starved. We had caught up with the American prisoners," he said, "there were eighty-six of them." [13]

Task Forces Matthews and Blair cleared Namwon of enemy soldiers. In midafternoon Task Force Dolvin arrived there from the east. Task Force Matthews remained overnight in Namwon, but Task Force Blair continued on toward Chongup, which was secured at noon the next day, 29 September. That evening Blair's force secured Iri. There, with the bridge across the river destroyed, Blair stopped for the night and Task Force Matthews joined it. Kunsan, the port city on the Kum River estuary, fell to the 1st Battalion, 24th Infantry, without opposition at 1300, 30 September.[14]

Eastward of and generally parallel to the course of Task Force Matthews and the 24th Infantry, Task Force Dolvin and the 35th Infantry moved around the eastern and northern sides of the all but impenetrable Chiri-san area, just as the 24th Infantry had passed around its southern and western sides. This almost trackless waste of 750 square miles of 6,000 to 7,000-foot-high forested mountains forms a rough rectangle northwest of Chinju about thirty by twenty-five miles in dimension, with Chinju, Hadong, Namwon, and Hamyang at its four corners. This inaccessible area had long been a hideout for Communist agents and guerrillas in South Korea. Now, as the North Korean forces retreated from southwest Korea, many enemy stragglers and some organized units with as many as 200 to 400 men went into the Chiri Mountain fastnesses. There they planned to carry on guerrilla activities.[15]

---

[13] Intervs, author with Sawyer at numerous times in the fall of 1951 and in 1952; Sawyer, Notes for author, 1 Oct 52; 24th Inf WD, 28 Sep 50; 25th Div WD, Med Co Unit Rpt (24th Inf), 28 Sep 50; 3d Bn, 24th Inf WD, 28 Sep 50. Sawyer is the source for details of the Reifers incident; his information was based on personal experience and numerous extended conversations held with Reifers at the time of and shortly after the event. Reifers was later killed near Unsan in North Korea on 27 November 1950 in the CCF offensive.

Most of the official Army records erroneously give credit to TF Dolvin for liberating these prisoners (EUSAK WD, G-3 Jnl, 28 Sep 50; IX Corps PIR, Msg 281645 Sep 50; 25th Div WD, Narr, Sep 50, p. 49). The 3d Bn, 24th Inf Unit Rpt, the Med Co Rpt, and Sawyer's Notes, however, leave no doubt that TF Matthews effected the liberation. TF Dolvin did not reach the outskirts of Namwon until midafternoon, about 1515, nearly three hours after TF Matthews had entered the town. See 89th Med Tk Bn WD, Sep 50.

[14] 3d Bn, 24th Inf, Unit Rpt, 28-30 Sep 50; 24th Inf WD, 30 Sep 50.

[15] ATIS Interrog Rpts, Issue 12 (N.K. Forces), Rpt 1728, p. 86, Jr Lt Ku Sung Son, *110th Security Regt;* Rpt 1764, p. 175, Jr Lt Kang Myong Ho, *110th Security Regt;* Rpt 1711, p. 36, Jr Lt Kim Tok Ho, *102d Security Regt.*

Lt. Col. Welborn G. Dolvin, commanding officer of the 89th Tank Battalion, led Task Force Dolvin out of Chinju at 0600, 26 September, on the road northwest toward Hamyang, the retreat route taken by the main body of the N.K. *6th Division*. The tank-infantry task force included as its main elements A and B Companies, 89th Medium Tank Battalion, and B and C Companies, 35th Infantry. It had two teams, A and B, each formed of an infantry company and a tank company. The infantry rode the rear decks of the tanks. The tank company commanders commanded the teams.[16]

Three miles out of Chinju the lead M26 tank struck a mine. While the column waited, engineers removed eleven more from the road. Half a mile farther on, a second tank was damaged in another mine field. Still farther along the road a third mine field, covered by an enemy platoon, stopped the column again. After the task force dispersed the enemy soldiers and cleared the road of mines, it found 6 antitank guns, 9 vehicles, and an estimated 7 truckloads of ammunition in the vicinity abandoned by the enemy. At dusk, the enemy blew a bridge three miles north of Hajon-ni just half an hour before the task force reached it. During the night the task force constructed a bypass.[17]

The next morning, 27 September, a mine explosion damaged and stopped the lead tank. Enemy mortar and small arms fire from the ridges near the road struck the advanced tank-infantry team. Tank fire cleared the left side of the road, but an infantry attack on the right failed. The column halted, and radioed for an air strike. Sixteen F-51 fighter-bombers came in strafing and striking the enemy-held high ground with napalm, fragmentation bombs, and rockets. General Kean, who had come forward, watched the strike and then ordered the task force to press the attack and break through the enemy positions. The task force broke through on the road, bypassing an estimated 600 enemy soldiers. Another blown bridge halted the column for the night while engineers constructed a bypass.

Continuing its advance at first light on the 28th, Task Force Dolvin an hour before noon met elements of the 23d Infantry, U.S. 2d Division, advancing from the east, at the road junction just east of Hamyang. There it halted three hours while engineers and 280 Korean laborers constructed a bypass around another blown bridge. Ever since leaving Chinju, Task Force Dolvin had encountered mine fields and blown bridges, the principal delaying efforts of the retreating N.K. *6th Division*.

When it was approaching Hamyang the task force received a liaison plane report that enemy forces were preparing to blow a bridge in the town. On Colonel Dolvin's orders the lead tanks sped ahead, machine-gunned enemy troops who were placing demolition charges, and seized the bridge intact. This success upset the enemy's delaying plans. The rest of the afternoon the task force dashed ahead at a speed of twenty miles

---

[16] Interv, author with 1st Lt Francis G. Nordstrom (89th Med Tk Bn elements of TF), 31 Aug 51; 89th Med Tk Bn Unit Rpt, 25-26 Sep 50; 25th Div WD, 24 Sep 50; Joseph M. Quinn, "Catching the Enemy Off Guard," *Armor*, vol. 60 (July-August, 1951), pp. 47-48.
TF Dolvin also included the 1st Plat, A Co, 65th Engr C Bn; 2d Plat, Hv Mort Co, 35th Regt; Medical Det, 89th Med Tk Bn; and TF trains.

[17] 89th Med Tk Bn WD, 26 Sep 50.

an hour. It caught up with numerous enemy groups, killing some of the soldiers, capturing others, and dispersing the rest. At midafternoon Task Force Dolvin entered Namwon to find that Task Force Matthews and elements of the 24th Infantry were already there.

Refueling in Namwon, Task Force Dolvin just after midnight continued northward and in the morning reached Chonju, already occupied by elements of the 38th Infantry Regiment, and continued on through Iri to the Kum River. The next day at 1500, 30 September, its mission accomplished, Task Force Dolvin was dissolved. It had captured or destroyed 16 antitank guns, 19 vehicles, 65 tons of ammunition, 250 mines, captured 750 enemy soldiers, and killed an estimated 350 more. It lost 3 tanks disabled by mines and 1 officer and 45 enlisted men were wounded in action.[18]

In crossing southwest Korea from Chinju to the Kum River, Task Force Matthews had traveled 220 miles and Task Force Dolvin, 138 miles. In the wake of Task Force Dolvin the 27th Regiment moved north from Chinju to Hamyang and Namwon on 29 September and maintained security on the supply road. This same day, 29 September, ROK marines captured Yosu on the south coast.

The 2d Division Pushes West

Opposite the old Naktong Bulge area, the N.K. *9th*, *4th*, and *2d Divisions* retreated westward. At Sinban-ni the *4th Division* turned toward Hyopch'on. The *9th* withdrew on Hyopch'on, and the *2d*, after passing through Ch'ogye, continued on to the same place. Apparently the *9th Division*, in the lead, had passed through Hyopch'on before elements of the U.S. 2d Division closed in on the place.[19]

On 23 September the 38th Infantry of the U.S. 2d Division had hard fighting in the hills around Ch'ogye before overcoming enemy delaying forces. The next day the 23d Infantry from the southeast and the 38th Infantry from the northeast closed on Hyopch'on in a double envelopment movement. Elements of the 38th Infantry established a roadblock on the north-south Chinju-Kumch'on road running northeast out of Hyopch'on and cut off an estimated two enemy battalions still in the town. During the day the 3d Battalion, 23d Infantry, entered Hyopch'on after a rapid advance of eight miles from the southeast. As the North Koreans fled Hyopch'on in the afternoon, 38th Infantry fire killed an estimated 300 of them at the regiment's roadblock northeast of the town. Two flights of F-51 fighter planes caught the rest in the open and continued their destruction. The surviving remnant fled in utter disorder for the hills. The country around Hyopch'on was alive with hard-pressed, fleeing North Koreans on 24 September, and the Air Force, flying fifty-three sorties in the area, wrought havoc among them. That night elements of the 1st Battalion, 38th

---

[18] 89th Med Tk Bn WD, 28-30 Sep 50; A Co, 79th Tk Bn, Unit Rpt, Sep 50; IX Corps WD, Hist Narr, 23-30 Sep 50; 25th Div WD, Narr, Sep 50, pp. 49, 58; EUSAK WD, Recommendation for Distinguished Unit Citation, 89th Med Tk Bn, Armor Sec, 11 Mar 51.

[19] ATIS Res Supp Interrog Rpts, Issue 100 (N.K. *9th Div*), p. 53; *Ibid.*, Issue 94 (N.K. *4th Div*), p. 50; *Ibid.*, Issue 94 (N.K. *2d Div*), p. 38; EUSAK WD, G-2 Sec, 3 Oct 50.

Infantry, entered Hyopch'on from the north.[20]

At daylight on the 25th, the 38th Infantry started northwest from Hyopch'on for Koch'ang. The road soon became impassable for vehicles and the men had to detruck and press forward on foot.

In retreating ahead of the 38th Infantry on 25 September the N.K. *2d Division*, according to prisoners, abandoned all its remaining vehicles and heavy equipment between Hyopch'on and Koch'ang. This apparently was true, for in its advance from Hyopch'on to Koch'ang the 38th Infantry captured 17 trucks, 10 motorcycles, 14 antitank guns, 4 artillery pieces, 9 mortars, more than 300 tons of ammunition, and 450 enemy soldiers, and killed an estimated 260 more. Division remnants, numbering no more than 2,500 men, together with their commander, Maj. Gen. Choe Hyon, who was ill, scattered into the mountains.

Up ahead of the ground troops, the Air Force in the late afternoon bombed, napalmed, rocketed, and strafed Koch'ang, leaving it virtually destroyed. After advancing approximately thirty miles during the day, the 38th Infantry stopped at 2030 that night only a few miles from the town.[21]

Elements of the 38th Infantry entered Koch'ang at 0830 the next morning, 26 September, capturing there a North Korean field hospital containing forty-five enemy wounded. Prisoners disclosed that elements of the N.K. *2d, 4th, 9th, and 10th Divisions* were to have assembled at Koch'ang, but the swift advance of the U.S. 2d Division had frustrated the plan.[22]

The 23d Infantry was supposed to parallel the 38th Infantry on a road to the south, in the pursuit to Koch'ang, but aerial and road reconnaissance disclosed that this road was either impassable or did not exist. General Keiser then directed Colonel Freeman to take a road to the north of the 38th Infantry. Mounted on organic transportation, the regiment, less its 1st Battalion, started at 1600 on the 25th and made a night advance to Koch'ang, fighting three skirmishes and rebuilding four small bridges on the way. It arrived at Koch'ang soon after the 38th Infantry, in daylight on 26 September.

That evening the 23d Infantry continued the advance to Anui, fourteen miles away, which it reached at 1930 without enemy opposition. Except for the small town itself, the area was a maze of flooded paddies. The regimental vehicles could find no place to move off the roads except into the village streets where they were dispersed as well as possible. At least one enemy group remained in the vicinity of Anui. At 0400 the next morning, 27 September, a heavy enemy artillery and mortar barrage struck in the town. The second round

---

[20] 38th Inf Comd Rpt, 24 Sep 50; 2d Div WD, G-3 Sec, 24 Sep 50; EUSAK WD, Br for CG, 24 Sep 50, and PIR 74, 24 Sep 50; Interv, author with Peploe, 12 Aug 51. The Air Force claimed it destroyed on 24 September in the Hyopch'on area 3 tanks, 5 artillery pieces, 1 antitank gun, an ammunition dump, a supply dump, a POL dump, and an estimated 1,400 enemy soldiers. See EUSAK WD, G-3 Air Br Rpt, 24 Sep 50.

[21] ATIS Interrog Rpts, Issue 12 (N.K. Forces), Rpt 1741, p. 118, Lt Ko Kon Su, Aide to CG, N.K. *2d Div*; EUSAK WD, 25 Sep 50; 38th Inf Comd Rpt, 25 Sep 50; 2d Div PIR 32, 25 Sep 50; ATIS Res Supp Interrog Rpts, Issue 94 (N.K. *2d Div*), p. 38.

[22] 38th Inf Comd Rpt, Sep–Oct 50, p. 13; 23d Inf Comd Rpt, 26 Sep 50; EUSAK WD, 26 Sep 50; IX Corps PIR, Msg 332, 261700 Sep 50.

hit the 3d Battalion command post, killing the battalion executive officer, the S-2, the assistant S-3, the motor officer, the artillery liaison officer, and an antiaircraft officer. Lt. Col. R. G. Sherrard, the battalion commander, was severely wounded; also wounded were twenty-five enlisted men of the Regimental and Headquarters Companies.[23]

At least passing notice should be taken of another event on 27 September. The last organized unit of the North Korean forces east of the Naktong River, elements of the N.K. *10th Division*, withdrew from notorious Hill 409 near Hyongp'ung and crossed to the west side of the river before daylight. Patrols of the 9th Infantry Regiment entered Hyongp'ung in the afternoon, and two companies of the 2d Battalion occupied Hill 409 without opposition. On 28 September the 2d Battalion, 9th Infantry, crossed the Naktong to join the 2d Division after the newly arrived 65th Regimental Combat Team of the U.S. 3d Division relieved it on Hill 409.[24]

At 0400, 28 September, Colonel Peploe started the 38th Infantry, with the 2d Battalion leading, from Koch'ang in a motorized advance toward Chonju, an important town in the west coastal plain seventy-three miles away across the mountains. The 25th Division also was approaching Chonju through Namwon. Meeting only light and scattered resistance, the 2d Battalion, 38th Infantry, entered Chonju at 1315, having covered the seventy-three miles in nine and a half hours. At Chonju the battalion had to overcome about 300 enemy soldiers of the *102d* and *104th Security Regiments,* killing about 100 of them and taking 170 prisoners.

There the 38th Infantry ran out of fuel for its vehicles. Fortunately, a 2d Division liaison plane flew over the town and the pilot learned the situation. He reported it to the 2d Division and IX Corps which rushed gasoline forward. At 1530 on 29 September, after refueling, the 3d Battalion departed Chonju for Nonsan and continued to Kanggyong on the Kum River, arriving there without incident at 0300 the morning of 30 September.

The IX Corps had only two and a half truck companies with which to transport supplies to the 25th and 2d Divisions in their long penetrations, and the distance of front-line units from the railhead increased hourly. When the 2d Division reached Nonsan on the 29th the supply line ran back more than 200 road miles, much of it over mountainous terrain and often on one-way roads, to the railhead at Miryang. The average time for one trip was forty-eight hours. In one 105-hour period, Quartermaster truck drivers supporting the 2d Division got only about thirteen hours' sleep.[25]

At the end of September the 2d Division was scattered from the Kum River southward, with the 38th Infantry in

---

[23] 23d Inf Comd Rpt, 26-27 Sep 50; 2d Div WD, G-3 Sec, 26-27 Sep 50; Freeman, MS review comments, 30 Oct 57; Combat Activities of the 23d Infantry.

[24] 2d Div PIR 34, 27 Sep 50; EUSAK POR 232 and PIR 77, 27 Sep 50; EUSAK WD, Br for CG, 27-28 Sep 50; 2d Div Hist, vol. II, p. 31.

[25] Intervs, author with Coulter, 20 Jul and 2 Apr 53; Interv, author with Peploe, 12 Aug 51; 2d Div Comd Rpt Hist, vol. II, 28 Sep 50; 2d Div WD, G-4 Sec, Sep-Oct 50; 38th Inf Comd Rpt, Sep-Oct 50, p. 14; Capt Perry Davis, The 2d Infantry Division in Korea, July-September 1950, MS, copy in OCMH; Coulter, MS review comments, 22 Nov 57.

the Chonju-Kanggyong area, the 23d Infantry in the Anui area, and the 9th Infantry in the Koryong-Samga area.

Taejon Regained

On the right flank of the U.S. 2d Division, the British 27th Infantry Brigade, attached to the U.S. 24th Division for the pursuit, was to move against Songju while the 24th Division simultaneously attacked parallel to and north of it on the main highway toward Kumch'on. After passing through Songju, the British brigade was to strike the main highway halfway between the Naktong River and Kumch'on. Its path took it along the main retreat route of the N.K. *10th Division.* The brigade was across the Naktong and ready to attack before daylight on 22 September.

At dawn the 1st Battalion, Middlesex Regiment, seized a small hill, called by the men Plum Pudding Hill, on the right of the road three miles short of Songju. The battalion then attacked the higher ground immediately to the northeast, known to the British as Point 325 or Middlesex Hill. Supported by American tank fire and their own mortar and machine gun fire, the Middlesex Battalion took the hill from dug-in enemy soldiers before dark.[26]

While the Middlesex Battalion attacked Hill 325, the Scottish Highlander Argyll Battalion moved up to attack neighboring Hill 282 on the left of the road. Starting before dawn on 23 September, B and C Companies after an hour's climb seized the crest of Hill 282, surprising there a North Korean force at breakfast. Across a saddle, and nearly a mile away to the southwest, higher Hill 388 dominated the one they had just occupied. C Company started toward it.

But enemy troops occupying this hill already were moving to attack the one just taken by the British. The North Koreans supported their attack with artillery and mortar fire, which began falling on the British. The action continued throughout the morning with enemy fire increasing in intensity. Shortly before noon, with American artillery fire inexplicably withdrawn and the five supporting U.S. tanks unable to bring the enemy under fire because of terrain obstacles, the Argylls called for an air strike on enemy-held Hill 388.[27]

Just after noon the Argylls heard the sound of approaching planes. Three F-51 Mustangs circled Hill 282 where the British displayed their white recognition panels. The enemy on Hill 388 also displayed white panels. To his dismay, Captain Radcliff of the tactical air control party was unable to establish radio contact with the flight of F-51's. Suddenly, at 1215, the Mustangs attacked the wrong hill; they came in napalming and machine-gunning the Argyll position.

The terrible tragedy was over in two minutes and left the hilltop a sea of orange flame. Survivors plunged fifty feet down the slope to escape the burning napalm. Maj. Kenneth Muir, second

---

[26] 24th Recon Co (24th Div) WD, Summ, 22 Sep 50; Linklater, *Our Men in Korea,* p. 19. Linklater was with the British brigade in Korea and used its records in preparing this small book. Middlesex Hill is shown on revised maps as Hill 341.

[27] Linklater, *Our Men in Korea;* Malcolm, *The Argylls in Korea,* pp. 17-22.

in command of the Argylls, who had led an ammunition resupply and litter-bearing party to the crest before noon, watching the flames on the crest die down, noticed that a few wounded men still held a small area on top. Acting quickly, he assembled about thirty men and led them back up the hill before approaching North Koreans reached the top. There, two bursts of enemy automatic fire mortally wounded him as he and Maj. A. I. Gordon-Ingram, B Company commander, fired a 2-inch mortar. Muir's last words as he was carried from the hilltop were that the enemy "will never get the Argylls off this ridge." But the situation was hopeless. Gordon-Ingram counted only ten men with him able to fight, and some of them were wounded. His three Bren guns were nearly out of ammunition. At 1500 the survivors were down at the foot of the hill.

The next day a count showed 2 officers and 11 men killed, 4 officers and 70 men wounded, and 2 men missing for a total of 89 casualties; of this number, the mistaken air attack caused approximately 60.[28]

That night, after the Argyll tragedy, the 1st Battalion, 19th Infantry, attacked south from Pusang-dong on the Waegwan-Kumch'on highway and captured Songju at 0200, 24 September. From there it moved to link up with the British 27th Brigade below the town. That day and the next the 19th Infantry and the British brigade mopped up in the Songju area. On the afternoon of 25 September the British brigade, released from attachment to the U.S. 24th Division, reverted to I Corps control.

The N.K. *10th Division* which had been fighting in the Songju area, its ammunition nearly gone and its vehicles out of fuel, withdrew on the 24th and 25th after burying its artillery. A captured division surgeon estimated the *10th Division* had about 25 percent of its original strength at this time. The N.K. *I Corps,* about 25 September, ordered all its units south of Waegwan to retreat northward.[29]

On 23 September, the day that disaster struck the British from the air near Songju, the U.S. 24th Division started its attack northwest along the Taejon-Seoul highway. General Church had echeloned his three regiments in depth so that a fresh regiment would take the lead at short intervals and thus maintain impetus in the attack. Leading off for the division, the 21st Infantry headed for Kumch'on, the N.K. headquarters. Elements of the N.K. *105th Armored Division* blocked the way with dug-in camouflaged tanks, antitank guns, and extensive mine fields.

---

[28] Malcolm, *The Argylls in Korea*, pp. 22-23; Linklater, *Our Men in Korea*, pp. 20-21; I Corps WD, G-3 Sec, 2 Aug-30 Sep 50, Rpt of Lt Col Thomas C. Gillis; I Corps WD, 23 Sep 50; FEAF Opn Hist, I, 25 Jun-31 Oct 50, p. 184 (23 Sep). The British Government awarded Major Muir posthumously the Victoria Cross, England's highest military award for valor. Text of citation in Brig. C. N. Barclay, *The First Commonwealth Division* (Aldershot: Gale and Polden, 1954), app. D, p. 218.

[29] 24th Div WD, 23 Sep 50; 19th Inf WD, 23-26 Sep 50; EUSAK WD, British Forces, 23-24 Sep 50; *Ibid.*, POR 228, 26 Sep 50; *Ibid.*, G-2 Sec, 5 Oct 50, Interrog ADVATIS 1039, Pak In Hyok, Surgeon *10th Div* Hosp; GHQ FEC, History of the N.K. Army, pp. 41 and 69; ATIS Res Supp Interrog Rpts, Issue 106 (N.K. Arty), pp. 68 and 76.

KUMCH'ON FROM THE AIR

In the afternoon a tank battle developed in which D Company, 6th Medium Tank Battalion (Patton M46), lost four tanks to enemy tank and antitank fire. During a slow advance, American tanks and air strikes in turn destroyed three enemy tanks.[30]

Just as this main Eighth Army drive started it was threatened with a supply breakdown. Accurate enemy artillery fire during the night of the 22d destroyed the only raft at the Naktong River ferry and cut the footbridge three times. The ferrying of vehicles and supplies during the day practically stopped, but at night local Koreans carried across the river the supplies and ammunition needed the next day.

Shortly after midnight, 23–24 September, the 5th Regimental Combat Team passed through the 21st Infantry to take the lead. Enemy troops in positions on Hill 140, north of the highway, stopped the regiment about three miles east of Kumch'on. There the North Koreans fought a major delaying action to permit large numbers of their retreating units to escape. The North Korean command diverted its *9th Division*, retreating from the lower Naktong toward Taejon, to Kumch'on to block the rapid Eighth Army advance. Remaining tanks of two regiments of

---

[30] 21st Inf WD, 23 Sep 50; 6th Med Tk Bn WD, 22–24 Sep 50; EUSAK WD, G–3 Jnl, 1715, 23 Sep 50; 24th Div WD, 23 Sep 50.

ON THE OUTSKIRTS OF KUMCH'ON *infantrymen take a brief rest.*

the N.K. *105th Armored Division* and the *849th Independent Anti-Tank Regiment,* the latter recently arrived at Kumch'on from the north, also joined in the defense of the town.

In the battle that followed in front of Kumch'on, the 24th Division lost 6 Patton tanks to enemy mines and antitank fire, while the North Koreans lost 8 tanks, 5 to air attack and 3 to ground fire. In this action the enemy *849th Regiment* was practically destroyed. The 5th Regimental Combat Team and supporting units lost approximately 100 men killed or wounded, most of them to tank and mortar fire. Smaller actions flared simultaneously at several points on the road back to Waegwan as bypassed enemy units struck at elements of the 19th Infantry bringing up the rear of the 24th Division advance.[31]

As a result of the battle in front of Kumch'on on 24 September, the 21st Infantry swung to the north of the highway and joined the 5th Regimental Combat Team that night in a pincer attack on the town. The 3d Battalion of the 5th Regimental Combat Team entered Kumch'on the next morning, and by 1445 that afternoon the town, a mass of rubble from bombing and artillery barrages, was cleared of the enemy.

---

[31] I Corps WD, Narr Hist, 24 Sep 50; EUSAK WD, G-2 Sec, 30 Sep 50, interrog Lt Kim Chong Song (N.K. *9th Div*); 24th Div WD, 24 Sep 50, and G-1 Hist Rpt, 25 Sep; 5th RCT Unit Rpt 43, 24 Sep 50; 6th Med Tk Bn WD, 24-25 Sep 50; New York *Times,* September 26, 1950.

That evening the 21st Infantry continued the attack westward. The 24th Division was interested only in the highway. If it was clear, the column went ahead. With the fall of Kumch'on on the 25th, enemy resistance melted away and it was clear that the North Koreans were intent only on escaping.[32]

On 26 September the 19th Infantry took the division lead and its 2d Battalion entered Yongdong without resistance. In the town jail the troops found and liberated three American prisoners. The regiment continued on and reached Okch'on, ten miles east of Taejon, at 0200, 27 September. There it halted briefly to refuel the tanks and give the men a little rest.

At 0530 the regiment resumed the advance—but not for long. Just outside Okch'on the lead tank hit a mine and enemy antitank fire then destroyed it. The 1st Battalion deployed and attacked astride the road but advanced only a short distance. The North Koreans held the heights west of Okch'on in force and, as at Kumch'on three days earlier, were intent on a major delaying operation. This time it was to permit thousands of their retreating fellow soldiers to escape from Taejon. An American tank gunner moving up to join the fight in front of Taejon sang, "The last time I saw Taejon, it was not bright or gay. Today I'm going to Taejon and blow the place away."[33]

This fight in front of Taejon on 27 September disclosed that the city, as expected, was an assembly point for retreating North Korean units south and west of Waegwan. The 300 prisoners taken during the day included men from seven North Korean divisions. The reports of enemy tanks destroyed in the Taejon area during the day are confusing, conflicting, and, taken together, certainly exaggerated. The ground forces reported destroying 13 tanks on the approaches to the city, 3 of them by A Company, 19th Infantry, bazooka teams. The Air Force claimed a total of 20 tanks destroyed during the day, 13 of them in the Taejon area, and another 8 damaged.[34]

On the morning of the 28th an air strike at 0700 hit the enemy blocking position. When the 2d Battalion advanced cautiously up the slopes, it was unopposed. It then became clear that the North Koreans had withdrawn during the night. Aerial reconnaissance at the time of the air strike disclosed approximately 800 North Korean troops moving out of Taejon on the road past the airstrip. At noon aerial observers saw more enemy troops assembling at the railroad station and another concentration of them a few miles west of Taejon turning toward Choch'iwon. The Air Force napalmed and strafed still another force of 1,000 enemy soldiers west of the city.

Scouts of the 2d Battalion, 19th Infantry, and engineers of C Company, 3d Engineer Combat Battalion, entered the outskirts of Taejon at 1630. An hour later the 19th Infantry secured the city

---

[32] 21st Inf WD, 25 Sep 50; 24th Div WD, 25 Sep 50; I Corps WD, Narr Hist, 25 Sep 50; EUSAK POR 226, 25 Sep 50; ATIS Res Supp Interrog Rpts, Issue 4 (N.K. *105th Armd Div*), pp. 39–40; Interv, author with Alkire, 1 Aug 51.

[33] 24th Div WD, 26–28 Sep 50 and G-1 Summ, 26 Sep; 19th Inf WD, Opn Summ, 26 Sep 50.

[34] 19th Inf WD, 27 Sep 50; 24th Div WD, 27 Sep 50; EUSAK WD, G-3 Sec and G-3 Air Br Rpt, 27 Sep 50; GHQ FEC Sitrep, 271603 Sep 50.

after engineers had cleared mines ahead of tanks leading the main column. At 1800 a 24th Division artillery liaison plane landed at the Taejon airstrip.[35]

On 28 September, the day it entered Taejon, the 19th Infantry captured so many North Korean stragglers that it was unable to keep an accurate count of them. The capture of large numbers of prisoners continued during the last two days of the month; on the 30th the 24th Division took 447 of them. At Taejon the division captured much enemy equipment, including four U.S. howitzers lost earlier and fifty new North Korean heavy machine guns still packed in cosmoline. At Choch'iwon the North Koreans were destroying equipment to prevent its capture.[36] Already other U.S. forces had passed Taejon and Choch'iwon on the east to cut the main highway farther north at Ch'onan and Osan.

With the capture of Taejon, the 24th Division accomplished its mission in the pursuit. And sweet revenge it was for the Taro Leaf Division to re-enter this now half-destroyed town where it had suffered a disastrous defeat nine weeks earlier. Fittingly enough, it was the 19th Infantry Regiment and engineers of the 3d Engineer Combat Battalion, among the last to leave the burning city on that earlier occasion, who led the way back in. But there was bitterness too, for within the city American troops soon discovered that the North Koreans had perpetrated there one of the greatest mass killings of the entire Korean War.

American soldiers were among the victims.

While this is not the place to tell in detail the story of the North Korean atrocities perpetrated on South Korean civilians and soldiers and some captured American soldiers, an account of the breakout and pursuit would not be complete without at least a brief description of the grisly evidence that came to light at that time. Everywhere the advancing columns found evidence of atrocities as the North Koreans hurried to liquidate political and military prisoners held in jails before they themselves retreated in the face of the U.N. advance. At Sach'on the North Koreans burned the jail, causing some 280 South Korean police, government officials, and landowners held in it to perish. At Anui, at Mokp'o, at Kongju, at Hamyang, at Chonju, mass burial trenches containing the bodies of hundreds of victims, including some women and children, were found, and near the Taejon airstrip the bodies of about 500 ROK soldiers, hands tied behind backs, lay in evidence of mass killing and burial.

Between 28 September and 4 October a frightful series of killings and burials were uncovered in and around the city. Several thousand South Korean civilians, estimated to number between 5,000 and 7,000, 17 ROK Army soldiers, and at least 40 American soldiers had been killed. After Taejon fell to the North Koreans on 20 July civilian prisoners had been packed into the Taejon city jail and still others into the Catholic Mission. Beginning on 23 September, after the first U.S. troops had crossed the Naktong, the North Koreans began executing these people. They were

---

[35] 24th Div WD, 28 Sep 50; EUSAK WD, G-3 Air Br Rpt, PIR 78, G-3 Jnl 1715 and 1920, 28 Sep 50; 3d Engr C Bn Unit Rpt, Narr Summ, Sep 50.
[36] 24th Div WD, 28-30 Sep 50; EUSAK WD, G-2 Sec, 10 Oct 50, PW Rpt, ADVATIS 1028, Lt Pak Kyu, *I Corps Rear Command.*

taken out in groups of 100 and 200, bound to each other and hands tied behind them, led to previously dug trenches, and shot. By 26 September American forces had approached so close to Taejon that the N.K. Security Police knew they had to hurry. The executions were speeded up and the last of them took place just before the city fell.

Of the thousands of victims only six survived—two American soldiers, one ROK soldier, and three South Korean civilians. Wounded and feigning death, they had been buried alive. The two wounded Americans had only a thin layer of loose soil over them, enabling them to breathe sufficiently to stay alive until they could punch holes to the surface, one of them with a lead pencil. Still wired to their dead comrades beneath the soil and partially buried themselves, they were rescued when the city fell to the 24th Division. Hundreds of American soldiers, including General Milburn, the I Corps commander, and General Church, the 24th Division commander, saw these ghastly burial trenches and the pathetic bodies of the victims.[37]

On 29 September the 24th Division command post moved to Taejon. From there the division had the task of protecting the army line of communications back to the Naktong River. Its units were strung out for nearly 100 miles: the 19th Infantry held the Taejon area up to the Kum River, the 21st Infantry extended from Taejon southeast to Yongdong, the 5th Regimental Combat Team was in the Kumch'on area, and the 24th Reconnaissance Company secured the Waegwan bridges.

From Tabu-dong to Osan—Eighth Army Link-up With X Corps

The Eighth Army breakout plans initially required the 1st Cavalry Division to cross the Naktong River at Waegwan and follow the 24th Division toward Kumch'on and Taejon. As the breakout action progressed, however, I Corps changed the plan so that the 1st Cavalry Division would cross the river at some point above Waegwan, pursue a course east of and generally parallel to that of the 24th Division, and seize Sangju. General Milburn left to General Gay the decision as to where he would cross. General Gay, the 1st Cavalry Division commander, and others, including Colonel Holmes, his chief of staff, and Colonel Holley of the 8th Engineer Combat Battalion, had proposed a crossing at Naktong-ni where a North Korean underwater bridge was known to exist. General Walker rejected this proposal. He himself flew in a light plane along the Naktong above Waegwan and selected the ferry site at Sonsan as the place the division should cross.[38]

In front of the 1st Cavalry Division

---

[37] The documentation on these atrocities is voluminous in the official records of the Army. Only a few citations will be given here: 25th Div WD, 5 Oct 50; 24th Div WD, Stf Secs, 29 Sep–31 Oct and G–1 Hist Rpt, 4 Oct 50; 2d Div WD, JA Stf Sec Rpt, Sep–Oct 50; Interim Hist Rpt, War Crimes Div, JA Sec, Korean Communications Zone (cumulative to 30 Jun 53); Lt Gen Frank W. Milburn, MS review comments, Nov 57; New York *Times*, October 3, 1950.

[38] Ltrs, Gay to author, 30 Sep and 21 Oct 53; Interv, author with Holmes, 27 Oct 53; Interv, author with Holley, 20 Feb 52; 1st Cav Div WD, 21 Sep 50; 7th Cav Regt Opn Plan 18; EUSAK WD, Br for CG, 21 Sep 50; Milburn, MS review comments, Nov 57.

Col. Lee Hak Ku, *Chief of Staff, N.K. 13th Division, being transported to 1st Cavalry Division headquarters for questioning.*

two enemy divisions were retreating on Sangju. The N.K. *3d Division* reportedly had only 1,800 men when its survivors arrived there. The other division, the *13th*, was in complete disorder in the vicinity of Tabu-dong and northward along the road to Sangju when the 1st Cavalry Division prepared to engage in the pursuit.[39]

Shortly before noon, 21 September, General Walker telephoned from Taegu to General Hickey in Tokyo. He had important news—the chief of staff of the N.K. *13th Division* had surrendered that morning. Walker told Hickey that, based on the prisoner's testimony, the N.K. *II Corps* had ordered its divisions on 17 September to go on the defensive and that the *13th Division* knew nothing of the Inch'on landing.[40]

The *13th Division*'s chief of staff had indeed surrendered that morning. Shortly after daylight Sr. Col. Lee Hak Ku gently shook two sleeping American soldiers of the 8th Cavalry Regiment on the roadside near the village of Samsandong, four miles south of Tabu-dong. Once they were awake, the 30-year-old North Korean surrendered to them.

---

[39] ATIS Res Supp Interrog Rpts, Issue 96 (N.K. *3d Div*), p. 35; *Ibid.*, Issue 106 (N.K. Arty), p. 76; GHQ FEC, History of the N.K. Army, p. 57.

[40] Fonecon, Walker with Hickey, 1145, 21 Sep 50, GHQ CofS files.

Colonel Lee had slipped away from his companions during the night and approached the American lines alone. He was the ranking North Korean prisoner at the time and remained so throughout the war. Before he became chief of staff of the *13th Division*, Lee had been operations officer (G-3) of the N.K. *II Corps*. Later he was to become notorious as the leader of the Communist prisoners of the Compound 76 riots on Koje Island in 1952.

Now, however, on the day of his voluntary surrender, Colonel Lee was most co-operative. He gave a full report on the deployment of the *13th Division* troops in the vicinity of Tabu-dong, the location of the division command post and the remaining artillery, the status of supply, and the morale of the troops. He gave the strength of the division on 21 September as approximately 1,500 men. The division, he said, was no longer an effective fighting unit, it held no line, and its survivors were fleeing from the Tabu-dong area toward Sangju. The regiments had lost communication with the division and each, acting on its own impulse and according to necessity, was dispersed in confusion. Many other *13th Division* prisoners captured subsequently confirmed the situation described by Colonel Lee.

Colonel Lee said the *19th Regiment* had about 200 men, the *21st Regiment* about 330, the *23d* about 300; that from 70 to 80 percent of the troops were South Korean conscripts and this condition had existed for a month; that the officers and noncommissioned officers were North Korean; that all tanks attached to the division had been destroyed and only 2 of 16 self-propelled guns remained; that there were still 9 122-mm. howitzers and 5 120-mm. mortars operational; that only 30 out of 300 trucks remained; that rations were down one-half; and that supply came by rail from Ch'orwon via Seoul to Andong.[41]

At the time of Colonel Lee's surrender, General Gay had already directed Lt. Col. William A. Harris, Commanding Officer, 7th Cavalry Regiment, to lead the pursuit movement for the 1st Cavalry Division. Colonel Harris, now with a 2-battalion regiment (the 2d Battalion had relieved the British 27th Brigade on the Naktong), organized Task Force 777 for the effort. Each digit of the number represented one of the three principal elements of the force: the 7th Cavalry Regiment, the 77th Field Artillery Battalion, and the 70th Tank Battalion. Harris assigned Lt. Col. James H. Lynch's 3d Battalion as the lead unit, and this force in turn was called Task Force Lynch. In addition to the 3d Battalion, 7th Cavalry, it included B Company, 8th Engineer Combat Battalion; two platoons of C Company, 70th Tank Battalion (7 M4 tanks); the 77th Field

---

[41] The first extensive interrogation report on Colonel Lee is in EUSAK WD, 21 Sep 50. Others more complete include ATIS Interrog Rpts, Issue 9 (N.K. Forces), Interrog Rpt 1468, pp. 158–74. See also ATIS Interrog Rpts, Issue 14 (N.K. Forces), Rpt 1915, Col Mun Che Won, CO *23d Regt, 13th Div*, p. 43; *Ibid.*, Issue 27 (N.K. Forces), p. 82, Rpt 2978, Lt Col Yun Bong Hun, CO *19th Regt, 13th Div*; *Ibid.*, Issue 10 (N. K. Forces), p. 38, Interrog Rpt 1516, Maj Yu Pong Sun, Medical Off of *19th Regt*; *Ibid.*, p. 52, Lt Kim Pyon Jon. There is a very large number of prisoner interrogation reports from the N.K. *13th Division* available in the ATIS documents not cited here which, collectively, give a detailed picture of the nearly complete destruction of this division by 22 September 1950. Capt Jones N. Epps, Reduction of Compound 76, UN POW Camp, Koje-do, Korea, Student MS, Advanced Inf Course, Ft. Benning, Class 1, 1952–53, is of interest relative to Colonel Lee in the prisoner riots in 1952.

Artillery Battalion (less one battery); the 3d Platoon, Heavy Mortar Company; the regimental I&R Platoon; and a tactical air control party.[42]

After helping to repel an attack by a large force of North Koreans cut off below Tabu-dong and seeking to escape northward, Task Force Lynch started to move at 0800, 22 September from a point just west of Tabu-dong. Brushing aside small scattered enemy groups, Colonel Lynch put tanks in the lead and the column moved forward. Up ahead flights of planes coursed up and down the road attacking fleeing groups of enemy soldiers.

Near Naksong-dong, where the road curved over the crest of a hill, enemy antitank fire suddenly hit and stopped the lead tank. No one could see the enemy guns. General Gay, who was with the column, sent the remaining four tanks in the advance group over the crest of the hill at full speed firing all weapons. In this dash they overran two enemy antitank guns. Farther along, the column halted while men in the point eliminated a group of North Koreans in a culvert in a 10-minute grenade battle.[43]

After the task force had turned into the river road at the village of Kumgok but was still short of its initial objective, the Sonsan ferry, a liaison plane flew over and dropped a message ordering it to continue north to Naktong-ni for the river crossing. The column reached the Sonsan ferry at 1545. There, before he turned back to the division command post in Taegu, General Gay approved Lynch's decision to stop pending confirmation of the order not to cross the river there but to proceed to Naktong-ni. At 1800 Lynch received confirmation and repetition of the order, and an hour later he led his task force onto the road, heading north for Naktong-ni, ten miles away.

A bright three-quarter moon lit the way as the task force hastened forward. Five miles up the river road it began to pass through burning villages, and then suddenly it came upon the rear elements of retreating North Koreans who surrendered without resistance.

An hour and a half before midnight the lead tanks halted on the bluff overlooking the Naktong River crossing at Naktong-ni. Peering ahead, men in the lead tank saw an antitank gun and fired on it. The round struck a concealed enemy ammunition truck. Shells in the truck exploded and a great conflagration burst forth. The illumination caused by the chance hit lighted the surrounding area and revealed a fascinating and eerie sight. Abandoned enemy tanks, trucks, and other vehicles littered the scene, while below at the underwater bridge several hundred enemy soldiers were in the water trying to escape across the river. The armor and other elements of the task force fired into them, killing an estimated 200 in the water.[44]

Task Force Lynch captured a large

---

[42] Ltrs, Harris to author, 25 Nov 52 and 23 Dec 53; Ltr, Col James H. Lynch to author, 11 Dec 53; 1st Cav Div WD, 21 Sep 50.

[43] 3d Bn, 7th Cav Regt, G-3 Jnl, Msg 4, 220800 Sep 50; 1st Cav Div, G-3 Jnl, 22 Sep 50; Lt. Col. James H. Lynch, "Task Force Penetration," *Combat Forces Journal* (January, 1951), pp. 11-16; Lynch, "Tie-in in Korea," *Armor*, vol. 59, No. 6 (November-December 1950), pp. 34-36; Ltr, Gay to author, 30 Sep 53.

[44] Ltr, Gay to author, 30 Sep 53; Ltr, Lynch to author, 11 Dec 53; 3d Bn, 7th Cav Regt, Unit Jnl, 22 Sep 50; 1st Cav Div WD, 22 Sep 50; C Co, 70th Tk Bn, Summ of Action, 17-24 Sep 50; EUSAK WD, Br for CG, 22 Sep 50.

amount of enemy equipment at the Naktong-ni crossing site, including 2 abandoned and operable T34 tanks; 50 trucks, some of them still carrying U.S. division markings; and approximately 10 artillery pieces. According to prisoners taken at the time, this enemy force consisted principally of units of the N.K. *3d Division,* but it included also some men from the *1st* and *13th Divisions.*

Reconnaissance parties reported the ford crossable in waist-deep water and the far bank free of enemy troops. Colonel Lynch then ordered the infantry to cross to the north bank. At 0430, 23 September, I and K Companies stepped into the cold water of the Naktong and began wading the river. The crossing continued to the accompaniment of an exploding enemy ammunition dump at the other end of the underwater bridge. At 0530 the two companies secured the far bank. Altogether, in the twenty-two hours since leaving Tabu-dong, Task Force Lynch had advanced thirty-six miles, captured 5 tanks, 50 trucks, 6 motorcycles, 20 artillery pieces, secured a Naktong River crossing site, and had killed or captured an estimated 500 enemy soldiers.[45]

During the 23d, Maj. William O. Witherspoon, Jr., led his 1st Battalion across the river and continued on ten miles northwest to Sangju, which he found abandoned by the enemy. Meanwhile, Engineer troops put into operation at Naktong-ni a ferry and raft capable of transporting trucks and tanks across the river, and on the 24th they employed 400 Korean laborers to improve the old North Korean underwater bridge. Tanks were across the river before noon that day and immediately moved forward to join the task force at Sangju.

As soon as the tanks arrived, Colonel Harris sent Capt. John R. Flynn with K Company, 7th Cavalry, and a platoon of tanks thirty miles farther up the road to Poun, which they entered before dark. Colonel Harris had authority only to concentrate the regiment at Poun; he was not to go any farther.

On the 24th also, General Gay sent a tank-infantry team down the road from Sangju toward Kumch'on where the 24th Division was engaged in a hard fight on the main Waegwan-Taejon-Seoul highway. Since this took the force outside the 1st Cavalry Division zone of action, I Corps ordered it to withdraw, although it had succeeded in contacting elements of the 24th Division.[46]

On 24–25 September General Gay concentrated the 1st Cavalry Division in the Sangju–Naktong-ni area while his advanced regiment, the 7th Cavalry, stayed at Poun. About dark on the 25th he received a radio message from I Corps forbidding him to advance his division farther. Gay wanted to protest this message but was unable to establish radio communication with the corps. He was able, however, to send a message to Eighth Army headquarters by liaison plane asking for clarification of what he

---

[45] 3d Bn, 7th Cav Regt, S–3 Jnl, 222230 Sep 50; 1st Cav Div WD, 23 Sep 50, EUSAK WD, Br for CG, 22 Sep 50; Lynch, articles cited n. 44.

[46] 1st Cav Div WD, 23–24 Sep 50; C Co, 70th Tk Bn Unit Rpt, 17–24 Sep 50; EUSAK WD, G–3 Jnl, 0201 and 1345 24 Sep 50; Ltr, Gay to author, 30 Sep 52; Ltr, Harris to author, 23 Dec 53; Interv, author with Holley, 20 Feb 52; Itschner (CO I Corps Engrs Sep 50), "The Naktong River Crossings in Korea," *op. cit.,* pp. 96ff; Lynch, articles cited n. 44; 70th Tk Bn WD, 23–27 Sep 50.

thought was a confusion of General Walker's orders, and requesting authority to continue the breakthrough and join X Corps in the vicinity of Suwon. During the evening, field telephone lines were installed at Gay's forward echelon division headquarters at the crossing site, and there, just before midnight, General Gay received a telephone call from Col. Edgar T. Conley, Jr., Eighth Army G-1, who said General Walker had granted authority for him to go all the way to the link-up with X Corps if he could do so.[47]

Acting quickly on this authority, General Gay called a commanders' conference in a Sangju schoolhouse the next morning, 26 September, and issued oral orders that at twelve noon the division would start moving day and night until it joined the X Corps near Suwon. The 7th Cavalry Regiment was to lead the advance by way of Poun, Ch'ongju, Ch'onan, and Osan. Division headquarters and the artillery would follow. The 8th Cavalry Regiment was to move on Ansong via Koesan. At noon the 5th Cavalry Regiment, to be relieved by elements of the ROK 1st Division, was to break off its attack toward Hamch'ang and form the division rear guard; upon reaching Choch'iwon and Ch'onan it was to halt, block enemy movement from the south and west, and await further orders.[48]

On the right of the 1st Cavalry Division the ROK 1st Division, as part of the U.S. I Corps and the only ROK unit operating as a part of Eighth Army, had passed through Tabu-dong from the north on 22 September and headed for the Sonsan ferry of the Naktong. It crossed the river there on the 25th, and moved north on the army right flank to relieve elements of the 1st Cavalry Division, and particularly the 5th Cavalry Regiment, in the Hamch'ang-Poun area above Sangju. The 1st Cavalry Division was now free to employ all its units in the pursuit.[49]

Upon receiving General Gay's orders at the commanders' conference in Sangju, Colonel Harris in turn ordered Colonel Lynch at Poun to lead northwest with his task force as rapidly as possible to effect a juncture with 7th Division troops of the X Corps somewhere in the vicinity of Suwon. This task force was the same as in the movement from Tabu-dong on the 22d, except that now the artillery contingent comprised only C Battery of the 77th Field Artillery Battalion.

The regimental I&R Platoon and 1st Lt. Robert W. Baker's 3d Platoon of tanks, 70th Tank Battalion, led Task Force Lynch out of Poun at 1130, 26 September. Baker had orders from Lynch to move at maximum tank speed and not to fire unless fired upon. For mile after mile they encountered no enemy opposition—only cheers from South Korean villagers watching the column go past. Baker found Ch'ongju deserted except for a few civilians when he entered it at midafternoon.

Approximately at 1800, after traveling sixty-four miles, Baker's tanks ran out of gasoline and the advance stopped at

---

[47] Ltrs, Gay to author, 30 Sep 52 and 31 Dec 53; Ltr, Harris to author, 23 Dec 53; Ltr, Brig Gen Edgar T. Conley, Jr., to author, 26 Mar 56; I Corps WD, 22 and 24 Sep 50.

[48] Ltrs, Gay to author, 30 Sep 52 and 31 Dec 53; Ltrs, Harris to author, 8 and 23 Dec 53.

[49] Ltr, Gay to author, 30 Sep 53; Itschner, "The Naktong River Crossings in Korea," op. cit.; I Corps WD, Narr Hist, 25 Sep 50; EUSAK WD, G-3 Sec, and Br for CG, 29 Sep 50.

Ipchang-ni. For some reason the refuel truck had not joined the tank-led column. Three of the six tanks refueled from gasoline cans collected in the column.

Just after these three tanks had refueled, members of the I&R Platoon on security post down the road ran up and said a North Korean tank was approaching. Instead, it proved to be three North Korean trucks which approached quite close in the near dark before their drivers realized that they had come upon an American column. The drivers immediately abandoned their vehicles, and one of the trucks crashed into an I&R jeep. On the trucks was enough gasoline to refuel the other three tanks. About 2000 the column was at last ready to proceed.[50]

Colonel Harris ordered Colonel Lynch, at the latter's discretion, to drive on in the gathering darkness with vehicular lights on. This time Baker's platoon of tanks, rather than the I&R Platoon, was to lead the column. The other platoon of three tanks was to bring up the rear. At his request, Colonel Lynch gave Baker authority to shoot at North Korean soldiers if he thought it necessary. Shortly after resuming the advance at 2030 the task force entered the main Seoul highway just south of Ch'onan.

It soon became apparent that the task force was catching up with enemy soldiers. Ch'onan was full of them. Not knowing which way to turn at a street intersection, Baker stopped, pointed, and asked a North Korean soldier on guard, "Osan?" He received a nod just as the soldier recognized him as an American and began to run away. The rest of the task force followed through Ch'onan without opposition. Groups of enemy soldiers just stood around and watched the column go through. Beyond Ch'onan, Baker's tanks caught up with an estimated company of enemy soldiers marching north and fired on them with tank machine guns. Frequently they passed enemy vehicles on the road, enemy soldiers on guard at bridges, and other small groups.

Soon the three lead tanks began to outdistance the rest of the column, and Colonel Lynch was unable to reach them by radio to slow them. In this situation, he formed a second point with a platoon of infantry and a 3.5-inch bazooka team riding trucks, the first truck carrying a .50-caliber ring-mounted machine gun. Actions against small enemy groups began to flare and increase in number. When they were ten miles south of Osan men in the task force heard from up ahead the sound of tank and artillery fire. Lynch ordered the column to turn off its lights.[51]

Separated from the rest of Task Force Lynch, and several miles in front of it by now, Baker's three tanks rumbled into Osan at full speed. After passing through the town, Baker stopped just north of it and thought he could hear vehicles of the task force on the road behind him, although he knew he was out of radio communication with it. T34 tank tracks in the road indicated that enemy armor might be near.

---

[50] Ltrs, Harris to author, 25 Nov 52 and 23 Dec 53; Ltr, Lynch to author, 11 Dec 53; 70th Tk Bn WD, Act Rpt of 1st Lt Robert W. Baker, C Co, Oct 50.

[51] Baker Rpt, C Co, Oct 50; Lynch, articles cited n. 44; 3d Bn, 7th Cav Regt, S–3 Jnl, 262000 Sep 50; 61st FA Bn WD, 26 Sep 50; EUSAK WD, G–3 Jnl, 0350 27 Sep 50.

Starting up again, Baker encountered enemy fire about three or four miles north of Osan. His tanks ran through it and then Baker saw American M26 tank tracks. At this point fire against his tanks increased. Antitank fire sheared off the mount of the .50-caliber machine gun on the third tank and decapitated one of its crew members. Baker's tanks, now approaching the lines of the U.S. 31st Infantry, X Corps, were receiving American small arms and 75-mm. recoilless rifle fire. American tanks on the line held their fire because the excessive speed of the approaching tanks, the sound of their motors, and their headlights caused the tankers to doubt that they were enemy. One tank commander let the first of Baker's tanks go through, intending to fire on the second, when a white phosphorus grenade lit up the white star on one of the tanks and identified them in time to avoid a tragedy. Baker stopped his tanks inside the 31st Infantry lines. He had established contact with elements of X Corps. The time was 2226, 26 September; the distance, 106.4 miles from the starting point at Poun at 1130 that morning.[52]

That Baker ever got through was a matter of great good luck for, unknown to him, he had run through a strong enemy tank force south of Osan which apparently thought his tanks were some of its own, then through the North Korean lines north of Osan, and finally into the 31st Infantry position just beyond the enemy. Fortuitously, American antitank and antipersonnel mines on the road in front of the American position had just been removed before Baker's tanks arrived, because the 31st Infantry was preparing to launch an attack.

Baker's tanks may have escaped destruction from American weapons because of a warning given to X Corps. Shortly after noon of 26 September MacArthur's headquarters in Tokyo had radioed a message to X Corps, to NAVFE, and to the Far East Air Forces saying that elements of Eighth Army might appear at any time in the X Corps zone of action and for the corps to take every precaution to prevent bombing, strafing, or firing on these troops. A little later, at midafternoon, Generals Walker and Partridge, flying from Taegu unannounced, landed at Suwon Airfield and conferred with members of the 31st Infantry staff for about an hour. Walker said that elements of the 1st Cavalry Division attacking from the south would probably arrive in the Osan area and meet the 7th Division within thirty-six hours.[53]

After his miraculous escape, Baker and the 31st Infantry tank crews at the front line tried unsuccessfully to reach Task Force Lynch by radio.

Instead of being right behind Baker at Osan, the rest of Task Force Lynch was at least an hour behind him. After turning out vehicular lights approximately ten miles south of Osan, Task Force Lynch continued in blackout. Just south of the village of Habong-ni, Colonel Lynch, about midnight, noticed a T34 tank some twenty yards off the road and commented to Captain Webel, the regimental S–3 who accompanied the task force, that the Air Force must have destroyed it. Many men in the column

---

[52] Baker Rpt, C Co, Oct 50; 70th Tk Bn WD, Oct 50, Opn Rpt, 23–27 Sep.

[53] X Corps WD, G–3 Sec, Msgs J–5 at 0200, J–33 at 1400, and J–39 at 1738; 31st Inf WD, 26 Sep 50; 7th Div WD, Narr, 26 Sep 50.

saw the tank. Suddenly it opened fire with cannon and machine gun. A second enemy tank, unnoticed up to that time, joined in the fire. Task Force Lynch's vehicular column immediately pulled over and the men hit the ditch.

Lt. John G. Hill, Jr., went ahead to the point to bring back its rocket launcher team. This bazooka team destroyed one of the T34's, but the second one moved down the road firing into vehicles and running over several of them. It finally turned off the road into a rice paddy where it continued to fire on the vehicles. A 75-mm. recoilless rifle shell immobilized the tank, but it still kept on firing. Captain Webel had followed this tank and at one point was just on the verge of climbing on it to drop a grenade down its periscope hole when it jerked loose from a vehicle it had crashed into and almost caught him under its tracks. Now, with the tank immobilized in the rice paddy, a 3.5-inch bazooka team moved up to destroy it but the weapon would not fire. Webel pulled a 5-gallon can of gasoline off one of the vehicles and hurried to the side of the tank. He climbed on it and poured the gasoline directly on the back and into the engine hatch. A few spurts of flame were followed by an explosion which blew Webel about twenty feet to the rear of the tank. He landed on his side but scrambled to his feet and ran to the road. He had minor burns on face and hands and two ribs broken. The burning tank illuminated the entire surrounding area.

Up at the head of the halted column, Colonel Lynch heard to the north the sound of other tank motors. He wondered if Baker's three tanks were returning. Watching, he saw two tanks come over a hill 800 yards away. Fully aware that they might be enemy tanks, Lynch quickly ordered his driver, Cpl. Billie Howard, to place the lead truck across the road to block it. The first tank was within 100 yards of him before Howard got the truck across the road and jumped from it. The two tanks halted a few yards away and from the first one a voice called out in Korean, "What the hell goes on here?" A hail of small arms fire replied to this shout.

The two tanks immediately closed hatches and opened fire with cannon and machine guns. The truck blocking the road burst into flames and burned.

The three tanks still with Task Force Lynch came up from the rear of the column and engaged the enemy tanks. Eight more T34's quickly arrived and joined in the fight. The American tanks destroyed one T34, but two of them in turn were destroyed by the North Korean tanks. Webel, in running forward toward the erupting tank battle, came upon a group of soldiers who had a 3.5-inch bazooka and ammunition for it which they had just pulled from one of the smashed American trucks. No one in the group knew how to operate it. Webel took the bazooka, got into position, and hit two tanks, immobilizing both. As enemy soldiers evacuated the tanks, he stood up and fired on them with a Thompson submachine gun.

Sgt. Willard H. Hopkins distinguished himself in this tank-infantry melee by mounting an enemy tank and dropping grenades down an open hatch, silencing the crew. He then organized a bazooka team and led it into action against other tanks. In the tank-infantry battle that raged during an hour or more, this bazooka team was credited by some sources with destroying or helping to destroy 4 of the enemy tanks. Pfc. John R. Muhoberac was an outstanding member of this team. One of the enemy tanks ran all the way through the task force position shooting up vehicles and smashing into them as it went. At the southern end of the column a 105-mm. howitzer had been set up and there, at a point-blank range of twenty-five yards, it destroyed this tank. Unfortunately, heroic Sergeant Hopkins was killed in this exchange of crossfire as he was in the act of personally attacking this tank. Combined fire from many weapons destroyed another tank. Of the 10 tanks in the attacking column, 7 had been destroyed. The 3 remaining T34's withdrew northward. In this night battle Task Force Lynch lost 2 men killed, 28 wounded, and 2 tanks and 15 other vehicles destroyed.[54]

After the last of the enemy tanks had rumbled away to the north, Colonel Harris decided to wait for daylight before going farther. At 0700 the next morning, 27 September, the task force started forward again. The men were on foot and prepared for action. Within a few minutes the point ran into an enemy tank which a 3.5-inch bazooka team destroyed. An enemy machine gun crew opened fire on the column but was quickly overrun and the gunners killed in a headlong charge by Lt. William W. Woodside and two enlisted men. A little later the column came upon two abandoned enemy tanks and blew them up. The head of Task Force Lynch reached Osan at 0800.

At 0826, 27 September, north of Osan at a small bridge, Platoon Sgt. Edward C. Mancil of L Company, 7th Cavalry, met elements of H Company, 31st Infantry, 7th Division. Task Force 777 sent a message to General Gay which said in part, "Contact between H Company, 31st Infantry Regiment, 7th Division, and forward elements of Task Force 777 established at 0826 hours just north of Osan, Korea."[55]

After the link-up with elements of the 31st Infantry, elements of Task Force 777 did not actually participate in this regiment's attack against the North Koreans on the hills north of Osan. Their communication equipment, including the forward air controllers, and their medical troops, however, did assist the 31st Infantry. General Gay arrived at Osan before noon and, upon seeing the battle in progress on the hills to the north, conferred with a 31st Infantry battalion commander. He offered to use the 8th Cavalry Regiment as an enveloping force and assist in destroying the enemy. He also offered to the 31st Infantry, he said, the use of the 77th and 99th Field Artillery Battalions and one tank company. The battalion com-

---

[54] 7th Cav Regt WD, 27 Sep 50; Lynch, articles cited n. 44; Ltr, Lynch to author, 11 Dec 53; Ltrs, Harris to author, 8 and 23 Dec 53; Lt Col James B. Webel, MS review comments, 15 Nov 57. Eighth Army General Order 132, 11 March 1952, awarded Colonel Lynch the Oak Leaf Cluster to the Distinguished Service Cross. Department of the Army General Order 35, 8 April 1952, awarded the Distinguished Unit Citation to the 3d Battalion, 7th Cavalry Regiment, and attached units. GHQ FEC General Order 21, 3 February 1951, awarded the Distinguished Service Cross to Captain Webel and the Distinguished Service Cross posthumously to Sergeant Hopkins.

[55] Brig Gen William A. Harris, MS review comments, 29 Oct 57, quoting copy of message in his possession; 7th Cav Regt WD, 27 Sep 50; Lynch, articles cited n. 44. It would appear that some elements of K Company, 7th Cavalry, were also in the contacting group.

mander said he would need concurrence of higher authority. Just what happened within the 31st Infantry after General Gay made this offer has not been learned. But elements of the 1st Cavalry Division stood idly by at Osan while the 31st Infantry fought out the action which it did not win until the next afternoon, 28 September. General Barr, commanding general of the 7th Infantry Division, has said he was never informed of General Gay's offer of assistance.[56]

In this rapid advance to Osan, the 1st Cavalry Division cut off elements of the *105th Armored Division* in the Ansong and P'yongt'aek area and miscellaneous units in the Taejon area. On the 28th, elements of C Company, 70th Tank Battalion, and K Company, 7th Cavalry, with the strong assistance of fighter-bombers, destroyed at least seven of ten T34's in the P'yongt'aek area, five by air strikes. Elements of the 16th Reconnaissance Company barely escaped destruction by these enemy tanks, and did suffer casualties.[57]

As late as 29 September, L Company of the 5th Cavalry Regiment ambushed approximately fifty enemy soldiers in nine Russian-built jeeps driving north from the vicinity of Taejon.

The ROK Army Arrives at the 38th Parallel

Eastward, the ROK Army made advances from Taegu that kept pace with Eighth Army, and in some instances even outdistanced it. This performance is all the more remarkable because the ROK Army, unlike the Eighth Army, was not motorized and its soldiers moved on foot.

In the ROK II Corps, the 6th and 8th Divisions on 24 September gained approximately sixteen miles. The 6th Division advanced on Hamch'ang and entered it the night of 25 September. By the 27th it was advancing across the roughest part of the Sobaek Range, past Mun'gyong in the high passes, on its way to Chungju. On the last day of the month the 6th Division encountered enemy delaying groups as it approached Wonju.

The ROK 8th Division made similarly rapid advances on the right of the 6th Division. Its reconnaissance elements entered Andong before midnight of the 24th. Five spans of the 31-span bridge over the Naktong there were down. Remnants of two enemy divisions, the N.K. *12th* and *8th*, were retreating on and through Andong at this time. The *12th Division* was pretty well through the town, except for rear guard elements, when advanced units of the ROK 8th Division arrived, but the main body of the N.K. *8th Division* had to detour into the mountains because ROK troops arrived there ahead of it. After two days of fighting, during which it encountered extensive enemy mine fields, the ROK 8th Division secured Andong on 26 September. That evening the division's advanced elements entered Yech'on, twenty miles northwest of Andong. The next day some of its troops were at Tanyang preparing to cross the

---

[56] Ltr, Gay to author, 31 Dec 53; Harris, MS review comments, 29 Oct 57; Interv, author with Barr, 1 Feb 54.

[57] 70th Tk Bn WD, Oct 50, Opn Rpt, C Co, 23–27 Sep 50; Ltr, Capt Charles A. Rogers to author, 1 Feb 54 and his attached MS on 16th Recon Co action in Korea, 1950 (written May 1951 in Korea); Webel, MS review comments, 15 Nov 57.

upper Han River.[58] On the last day of the month the division met strong enemy resistance at Chech'on and bypassed the town in the race northward.

The ROK Capital Division was keeping pace with the others in the pursuit. On the 27th it had entered Ch'unyang, about thirty-one miles east of the ROK 8th Division, and was continuing northward through high mountains.

On the night of 1-2 October, shortly after midnight, an organized North Korean force of from 1,000 to 2,000 soldiers, which had been bypassed some place in the mountains, struck with savage fury as it broke out in its attempt to escape northward. Directly in its path was Wonju where the ROK II Corps headquarters was then located. This force overran the corps headquarters and killed many of its men, including five American officers who were attached to the corps or who had come to Wonju on liaison missions. The North Koreans ran amok in Wonju until morning, killing an estimated 1,000 to 2,000 civilians.[59]

Along the east coast the ROK 3d Division, with heavy U.S. naval gunfire support, captured Yongdok on 25 September. A huge cloud of black smoke hung overhead from the burning city.

The fall of the town apparently caught the N.K. *5th Division* by surprise. Some Russian-built trucks were found with motors running, and artillery pieces were still in position with ammunition at hand. Horse-drawn North Korean signal carts were found with ponies hitched and tied to trees. After the fall of Yongdok it appears that remnants of the *5th Division*, totaling now no more than a regiment, turned inland for escape into the mountains. One North Korean regimental commander divided his three remaining truckloads of ammunition and food among his men and told them to split into guerrilla bands.

In the pursuit up the coastal road above Yongdok, Maj. Curtis J. Ivey, a member of KMAG, with the use of twenty-five 2½-ton trucks made available for the purpose through the efforts of Colonel McPhail, KMAG adviser to the ROK I Corps, led the ROK's northward in shuttle relays. When a roadblock was encountered it was Major Ivey who usually directed the action of the point in reducing it.[60]

The impressive gains by the ROK units prompted General Walker to remark on 25 September, "Too little has been said in praise of the South Korean Army which has performed so magnificently in helping turn this war from the defensive to the offensive." [61]

---

[58] EUSAK WD, Br for CG, 25-26 Sep 50; GHQ FEC Sitrep, 26 Sep 50; EUSAK WD, 5 Oct, G-2 Sec, PW Interrog ADVATIS 1038, and ATIS Interrog Rpts, Issue 12 (N.K. Forces), Rpt 1753, p. 148, Lt Col Kim Chong Ung, Supply Officer, *31st Regt, N. K. 12th Div.*

[59] EUSAK WD, 2 Oct 50. Eighth Army General Order 35, 21 January 1951, awarded the Distinguished Service Cross posthumously to Capt. Walt W. Bundy and 2d Lt. George E. Mannan, 205th Signal Repair Company, who were killed in Wonju while covering the escape of seventeen enlisted men.

[60] EUSAK WD, G-3 Sec, 24-26 Sep 50; *Ibid.*, POR 229, 26 Sep 50; *Ibid.*, Br for CG, 24-26 Sep 50; *Ibid.*, Engr Hist Rpt, 24 Sep 50; *Ibid.*, G-2 Sec, 30 Sep 50, interrogs of Lt Kim Kun Bong, Arty Maintenance Off, *11th Regt, N.K. 5th Div*, and of Sr Lt Pak Kwan Hyok, Medical Off, *2d Regt, N.K. 8th Div*; ATIS Interrog Rpts, Issue 13 (N.K. Forces), Rpt 1865, p. 153, Lt Han Si Hong; GHQ FEC G-3 Opn Rpt, 25 Sep 50; Emmerich, MS review comments, Dec 57.

[61] New York *Times*, September 26, 1950.

On up the coast road raced the ROK 3d Division. It secured Samch'ok on the morning of 29 September, and then continued on toward Kangnung. It moved north as fast as feet and wheels could take it over the coastal road. It led all ROK units, in fact, all units of the United Nations Command, in the dash northward, reaching a point only five miles below the 38th Parallel on the last day of the month.[62]

The Invaders Expelled From South Korea

The last week of September witnessed a drastic change in the pattern of North Korean military activity. Enemy targets were disappearing from the scene. On 24 September some fighter pilots, unable to find targets, returned to their bases without having fired a shot. Survivors of the once victorious North Korea People's Army were in flight or in hiding, and, in either case, they were but disorganized and demoralized remnants. On 1 October there occurred an incident illustrating the state of enemy demoralization. An Air Force Mosquito plane pilot dropped a note to 200 North Korean soldiers northeast of Kunsan ordering them to lay down their arms and assemble on a nearby hill. They complied. The pilot then guided U.N. patrols to the waiting prisoners.

The virtual collapse of the North Korean military force caused General MacArthur on 1 October to order the Air Force to cease further destruction of rail, highway, bridge, and other communication facilities south of the 38th Parallel, except where they were known to be actively supporting an enemy force. Air installations south of the 40th Parallel were not to be attacked, and he halted air action against strategic targets in North Korea.[63]

The extent of his collapse was truly a death blow to the enemy's hopes for continuing the war with North Korean forces alone. Loss of weapons and equipment in the retreat north from the Pusan Perimeter was of a scope equal to or greater than that suffered by the ROK Army in the first week of the war. For the period 23–30 September, the IX Corps alone captured 4 tanks, 4 self-propelled guns, 41 artillery pieces, 22 antitank guns, 42 mortars, and 483 tons of ammunition. In I Corps, the 24th Division on one day, 1 October, captured on the Kumsan road below Taejon 7 operable tanks and 15 artillery pieces together with their tractors and ammunition. On the last day of September the 5th Cavalry Regiment captured three trains complete with locomotives hidden in tunnels. A few miles north of Andong advancing ROK forces found approximately 10 76-mm. guns, 8 120-mm. mortars, 5 trucks, and 4 jeeps, together with dead enemy soldiers, in a tunnel—all had been destroyed earlier by air force napalm attacks at either end of the tunnel. At Uisong, ROK forces captured more than 100 tons of rice, other supplies, and most of the remaining equipment of one North Korean division. The North Koreans had abandoned

---

[62] EUSAK WD, G-3 Sec, 27-30 Sep 50; *Ibid.,* Summ, p. 43, Sep 50; *Ibid.,* Br for CG, 29-30 Sep 50. Beginning on 25 September, LST's from Pusan helped supply the ROK 3d Division in this advance. Sixty tons a day were required for a ROK division. See 2d Log Comd Activities Rpt Sep 50.

[63] USAF Study 71, pp. 66-67; "Air War in Korea," *Air University Quarterly Review,* IV (Fall, 1950), p. 35.

Captured Enemy Equipment

76-mm. howitzer

Chinese grenades

Russian-made SU76

Small arms (front to rear): Russian 7.62-mm. submachine (burp) gun; Russian 7.62-mm. carbine M1944; Japanese 7.7-mm. rifle; Russian 7.62 Tokarev semiautomatic rifle with flash hider; Russian 14.5-mm. antitank rifle PTRD-1941 (Degtyarev).

120-mm. mortar

76-mm. gun

Coryunov heavy machine gun

many tanks, guns, vehicles, ammunition, and other equipment because they lacked gasoline to operate their vehicles.[64]

During the approximately three months of the war up to the end of September, all U.N. combat arms had made various claims regarding destroyed enemy equipment, especially tanks and self-propelled guns. Air Force claims for the period, if totaled from daily reports, would be extravagantly high. After the U.N. breakout from the Pusan Perimeter, in the period from 26 September to 21 October 1950, seven survey teams traveled over all major routes of armored movement between the Perimeter line and the 38th Parallel, and also along the Kaesong-Sariwon-P'yongyang highway above the Parallel. This survey disclosed 239 destroyed or abandoned T34 tanks and 74 self-propelled 76-mm. guns. The same survey counted 60 destroyed U.S. tanks.[65]

According to this survey, air action destroyed 102 (43 percent) of the enemy tanks, napalm accounting for 60 of them or one-fourth the total enemy tank casualties; there were 59 abandoned T34's without any visible evidence of damage, also about one-fourth the total; U.N. tank fire accounted for 39 tanks (16 percent); and rocket launchers were credited with 13 tanks (5 percent). The number credited to bazooka fire is in error, for the number certainly is much higher. Very likely air action is credited in this survey with many tanks that originally were knocked out with infantry bazooka fire. There are many known cases where aircraft attacked immobilized tanks after bazooka fire had stopped them. There was an almost complete absence of enemy tanks destroyed by U.S. antitank mines.

No reliable information is available concerning the number of damaged tanks the North Koreans were able to repair and return to action. But the figure of 239 found destroyed or abandoned comes close to being the total number used by the North Korea People's Army in South Korea. Very few escaped from the Pusan Perimeter into North Korea at the end of September.

From July through September 1950 United States tank losses to all causes was 136. A survey showed that mine explosions caused 70 percent of the loss. This high rate of U.S. tank casualties in Korea to mines is all the more surprising since in World War II losses to mines came to only 20 percent of tank losses in all theaters of operations.[66]

In the two weeks beginning with 16 September, the breakout and pursuit period, the U.N. forces in the south placed 9,294 prisoners in the Eighth Army stockade. This brought the total to 12,777. Eighth Army had captured 6,740 of them and the ROK Army 6,037. Beginning with 107 prisoners on 16 September the number had jumped to 435

---

[64] IX Corps WD, sec. IV, Sep 50; EUSAK PIR 81, 1 Oct 50; GHQ FEC Sitrep, 1 Oct 50; 1st Cav Div WD, 30 Sep 50; 5th Cav Regt Unit Hist, 30 Sep 50; USAF Hist Study 71, p. 40; 24th Div WD, Narr Summ, 29 Sep–31 Oct 50.

[65] ORO, The Employment of Armor in Korea, ORO–R–1 (FEC), vol. II, and app. K, 8 Apr 51. The figures for 239 tanks and 74 SP guns are adjusted from a larger total in overlapping reports from the seven surveys.

As late as July 1951, the author counted 74 enemy T34 tanks and 14 76-mm. SP guns rusting along the main highway running from Waegwan on the Naktong River to Seoul; 30 of the T34's were between the river and Taejon.

[66] ORO, The Employment of Armor in Korea, 8 Apr 51; DA Intelligence Review, March 1951, No. 178, p. 53.

on 23 September and passed the 1,000 mark daily with 1,084 on 27 September, 1,239 the next day, and 1,948 on 1 October.[67]

The rapid sweep of the U.N. forces northward from the Pusan Perimeter in the last week of September bypassed thousands of enemy troops in the mountains of South Korea. One of the largest groups, estimated to number about 3,000 and including soldiers from the N.K. *6th* and *7th Divisions* with about 500 civil officials, took refuge initially in the Chiri Mountains of southwest Korea. At the close of the month, of the two major enemy concentrations known to be still behind the U.N. lines, one was south of Kumch'on in the Hamyang area and the other northeast and northwest of Taejon.

Just before midnight, 1 October, a force of approximately sixty North Korean riflemen, using antitank and dummy mines, established and maintained a roadblock for nearly ten hours across the main Seoul highway about fifteen miles northwest of Kumch'on. A prisoner said this roadblock permitted about 2,000 North Korean soldiers and a general officer of the N.K. *6th Division* to escape northward. The *6th* at the time apparently still had its heavy machine guns and 82-mm. mortars but had discarded all heavier weapons in the vicinity of Sanch'ong.[68]

Enemy sources make quite clear the general condition of the North Korean Army at the end of September. The *6th Division* started its withdrawal in good order, but most of its surviving troops scattered into the Chiri Mountain area and elsewhere along the escape route north so that only a part reached North Korea. The *7th Division* commander reportedly was killed in action near Kumch'on as the division retreated northward; remnants assembled in the Inje-Yanggu area above the 38th Parallel in mid-October. In the *2d Division*, Maj. Gen. Choe Hyon, the division commander, had only 200 troops with him north of Poun at the end of September. Other elements of the division had scattered into the hills.

Parts of the *9th* and *10th Divisions* retreated through Taejon, and other parts cut across the Taejon highway below the city in the vicinity of Okch'on when they learned that the city had already fallen. Only a handful of men of the *105th Armored Division* reached North Korea. The commanding general of the N.K. *I Corps* apparently dissolved his headquarters at Choch'iwon during the retreat and then fled with some staff officers northeast into the mountains of the Taebaek Range on or about 27 September. From the central front near Taegu, 1,000 to 1,800 men of the *3d Division* succeeded in reaching P'yonggang in what became known as the Iron Triangle at the beginning of October. The *1st Division*, retreating through Wonju and Inje, assembled approximately 2,000 men at the end of October.

Of all the North Korean divisions fighting in South Korea perhaps no other suffered destruction as complete as the *13th*. Certainly no other yielded so many

---

[67] EUSAK WD, Provost Marshal Sec, 16 Sep–1 Oct 50; U.S. Military Academy, Operations in Korea (25 Jun 50–1 Apr 51), p. 12. As contrasted with the number of prisoners in the stockade, the total number reported captured by 20 September, however, was 23,620 (4,305 by 15 September), and by 1 October approximately 30,000.

[68] 25th Div WD, Sep 50; *Ibid.*, G–2 Sec, 8 Oct 50, ADVATIS 1069, Maj Chi Ki Chol, N.K. *6th Div Arty Regt;* EUSAK PIR 79 and 80, 29 and 30 Sep 50; 24th Div WD, Enemy Situation, 29 Sep–31 Oct 50; Throckmorton, Notes for author.

high-ranking officers as prisoners of war. In August the *13th Division* artillery commander surrendered; on 21 September Col. Lee Hak Ku, the chief of staff, surrendered; three days later the commander of the self-propelled gun battalion surrendered; the division surgeon surrendered on the 27th; and Col. Mun Che Won, a 26-year-old regimental commander, surrendered on 1 October after hiding near Tabu-dong for nearly a week. The commander of the *19th Regiment*, 22-year-old Lt. Col. Yun Bong Hun, led a remnant of his command northward by way of Kunwi, Andong, and Tanyang. Near Tanyang, finding his way blocked by ROK troops, he marched his regiment, then numbering 167 men, into a ROK police station at Subi-myon and surrendered. A few members of the division eventually reached the P'yonggang area in the Iron Triangle.

Remnants of the *8th Division*, numbering perhaps 1,500 men, made their way northeast of P'yonggang and continued on in October to a point near the Yalu River. Some small elements of the *15th Division* escaped northward through Ch'unch'on to Kanggye in North Korea. From Kigye about 2,000 men of the *12th Division* retreated through Andong to Inje, just north of the 38th Parallel, picking up stragglers from other divisions on the way so that the division numbered about 3,000 to 3,500 men upon arrival there. Remnants of the *5th Division* infiltrated northward above Yongdok along and through the east coast mountains in the direction of Wonsan.

The bulk of the enemy troops that escaped from the Pusan Perimeter assembled in the Iron Triangle and the Hwach'on-Inje area of east-central North Korea just above the 38th Parallel. On 2 October an Air Force pilot reported an estimated 5,000 enemy marching in small groups along the edge of the road north of the 38th Parallel between Hwach'on and Kumhwa.

The commanding general of the N.K. *II Corps* and his staff apparently escaped to the Kumhwa area in the Iron Triangle, and the best available evidence indicates that the commanding general and staff of the N.K. *Army Front Headquarters* at Kumch'on also escaped northeast to the Iron Triangle. From there in subsequent months this headquarters directed guerrilla operations on U.N. lines of communications.

It appears that not more than 25,000 to 30,000 disorganized North Korean soldiers reached North Korea from the Pusan Perimeter after the U.N. breakout in late September. For all practical purposes the North Korea People's Army had been destroyed. That was the real measure of the success of the Inch'on landing and Eighth Army's correlated attack—General MacArthur's strategy for winning the war.[69]

---

[69] This summary of the condition of the North Korean Army at the end of September 1950 is based upon an analysis of a large body of enemy materials. The most important of them are GHQ FEC, History of the N.K. Army; ATIS Res Supp Interrog Rpts, Issues 3 (*1st and 15th Divs*), 94 (*2d and 4th Divs*), 96 (*3d and 5th Divs*), 100 (*6th and 9th Divs*), 99 (*7th and 12th Divs*), 4 (*8th Div and 105th Armd Div*), 104 (*10th and 13th Divs*), and 106 (N.K. Arty); ATIS Interrog Rpts (N.K. Forces), Issues 9, 10, 12, 13, 14, 15, 18, 20, 25; ATIS Enemy Documents, Issue 16, p. 48; ATIS Interrog Rpts (Korean Opns), Issue 27, p. 82; FEC, Order of Battle Information, 16 Sep 51. N.K. Army Supp, Chart 9; EUSAK WD, G-2 Sec, PW Interrog, 16 Sep–31 Oct 50.

TABLE 3—ESTIMATED U.N. STRENGTH AS OF 30 SEPTEMBER 1950[a]

Organization	U.N. Forces	Attached Koreans
Total Ground Combat Forces	198,211	22,404
Total U.S. Ground Combat Forces	113,494	22,404
Combat		
Eighth Army	1,120	
I Corps	4,141	267
1st Cavalry Division	13,859	2,961
24th Infantry Division	15,591	3,606
IX Corps	4,224	1,009
2d Infantry Division	14,122	2,756
25th Infantry Division	14,617	3,230
X Corps	8,344	600
7th Infantry Division	15,865	7,975
1st Marine Division (reinforced)	21,611	
ROK Army	81,644	
British Ground Combat Forces	1,704	
Philippine Ground Combat Forces	1,369	
FEAF	36,677	
Other U.N. Air Forces	330	
NAVFE	59,438	7,045
Total Ground Service Forces	20,608	444
Service		
Eighth Army	2,820	
I Corps	1,235	305
IX Corps	187	110
X Corps	2,039	29
Pusan Base	9,792	
Inch'on Base	4,452	
Seoul Area Command	83	

[a] Figures are adjusted and do not include personnel previously carried as wounded, missing, or injured who had returned to duty by 30 September.
Source: EUSAK WD, 30 Sep 50; GHQ FEC Sitrep, 29–30 Sep 50.

The war in Korea by the end of September had cost Eighth Army 24,172 battle casualties—5,145 killed in action; 16,461 wounded in action, of whom 422 died of wounds; 402 reported captured; and 2,164 missing in action. Many of the latter were prisoners of war.[70]

Estimated U.N. strength in Korea as of 30 September 1950 is shown in Table 3.

[70] Battle Casualties of the Army, 31 May 52, DA TAGO.

TABLE 4—POSTWAR TABULATION OF U.N. STRENGTH IN KOREA AS OF 30 SEPTEMBER 1950

Organization	Strength
Total Ground Combat Forces	229,772
U.S. Army	103,601
1st Cavalry Division	14,472
2d Infantry Division	17,656
7th Infantry Division	15,620
24th Infantry Division	11,876
25th Infantry Division	14,824
Nondivisional units	29,153
U.S. 1st Marine Division (reinforced)	21,525
ROK Army	101,573
Korean divisions	82,786
Attached to U.S. Army combat units	18,787
British Brigade	1,704
Philippine Battalion Combat Team	1,369
Total Ground Service Forces	119,559
U.S. Army	28,507
ROK Army	91,052
Korean Service units	90,608
Attached to U.S. Army service units	444
U.S. Far East Air Forces	36,677
U.S. Naval Forces, Far East	59,438
Other U.N. Air Forces	330

Source: ROK and UN Ground Forces Strength in Korea, 31 July 1950-31 July 1953, DA, COA, 7 Oct 54, and GHQ FEC Sitrep, 29-30 Sep 50.

CHAPTER XXIX

The Plan for Complete Victory

It is better to abandon a whole province than to divide an army.
                                                        VON SCHLIEFFEN

The question whether U.N. forces should cross the 38th Parallel became a most difficult one as soon as the Inch'on landing succeeded and the Eighth Army broke out from the Pusan Perimeter. As a result of long and detailed consideration at high levels on the future course of action, the government in Washington decided Eighth Army should cross into North Korea.

Pursuant to this decision, the Joint Chiefs of Staff on 27 September sent to General MacArthur a comprehensive directive to govern his future actions. They stated that his first objective was to be the destruction of the North Korean forces. He was to unite all of Korea under Syngman Rhee if possible. But they warned him that he was not to consider the directive final since developments might require its modification. They particularly enjoined him to make special efforts to determine whether Soviet or Chinese intervention appeared likely, and to report any such threat to them at once.

Subject to these injunctions, the directive stated that MacArthur's mission was "the destruction of the North Korean Armed Forces" and authorized him to conduct military operations for that purpose north of the 38th Parallel, provided that at the time there was no major Chinese Communist Forces or Soviet entry into North Korea or announced intention to enter in order to counter U.N. military operations there. The Joint Chiefs added that in no circumstances would any of the U.N. forces cross the Manchurian or Soviet borders of Korea and that non-Korean ground forces, as a matter of policy, should not be used in the area along the Manchurian border or in the northeast provinces bordering the Soviet Union. They instructed MacArthur to submit his plan for operations north of the 38th Parallel to them for approval. Thus the Joint Chiefs of Staff in Washington held in their own hands final approval for any operation north of the 38th Parallel.[1]

Upon receiving this directive MacArthur urged on the JCS removal of the restriction requiring specific approval from the United States Government before his forces crossed the 38th Parallel. He urged that he be allowed to cross the Parallel and seek out and

---

[1] JCS 92801, 27 Sep 50, Personal for MacArthur, from JCS to CINCUNC.

destroy the remaining parts of the North Korean Army if North Korea did not surrender in accordance with a proclamation he intended to issue.

Two days later Secretary of Defense George C. Marshall sent him a personal message, marked for his eyes only, which stated that he should feel free tactically and strategically to proceed north of the 38th Parallel. President Truman himself had approved this message.[2]

It is clear that on 29 September MacArthur had authority from the United States Government to cross the 38th Parallel. In a communication to the Secretary of Defense on 30 September, MacArthur said, "Unless and until the enemy capitulates, I regard all of Korea open for our military operations."[3]

The next day, 1 October, in order to remove any obscurity that might still exist in Washington regarding his plan, MacArthur sent a message that was crystal clear as to his intentions. He said:

I plan to issue and make public the following general directive to all elements of the United Nations Command at 1200 hours, Monday, 2 October, unless I receive your instructions to the contrary. "Under the provisions of the United Nations Security Council Resolution of 27 June, the field of our military operations is limited only by military exigencies and the international boundaries of Korea. The so-called 38th Parallel, accordingly, is not a factor in the military employment of our forces. To accomplish the enemy's complete defeat, your troops may cross the border at any time, either in exploratory probing or exploiting local tactical conditions. If the enemy fails to accept the terms of surrender set forth in my message to him of 1 October, our forces, in due process of campaign will seek out and destroy the enemy's armed forces in whatever part of Korea they may be located."[4]

MacArthur stated later that the temporary U.N. halt at the 38th Parallel that occurred in early October was due to logistical difficulties.[5]

From the Communist side certain storm signals appeared. In a speech in Peiping on 1 October, the first anniversary of the Chinese Communist state, Premier Chou En-lai warned that the Chinese people "will not tolerate foreign aggression and will not stand aside should the imperialists wantonly invade the territory of their neighbor."[6] This clearly was a threat to intervene in the Korean War if U.N. forces crossed the 38th Parallel. In the United Nations the Soviet delegate proposed on 2 October a plan which called for a cease fire in Korea and the withdrawal of all foreign troops. The next day Sir Benegal Rau, the Indian delegate, stated his government's view that U.N. forces should not cross the 38th Parallel. The Indian view was undoubtedly influenced by a report to Prime Minister Jawaharlal Nehru from India's Ambassador to Peiping

---

[2] JCS 92985, 29 Sep 50, Marshall to MacArthur; JCS 92975, JCS to CINCFE, 29 Sep 50, Memo for Secy Def from Bradley, Chmn, JCS, 29 Sep 50; S. Comm. on Armed Services and S. Comm. on Foreign Relations, 82d Cong., 1st Sess., 1951, Joint Hearings, *Military Situation in the Far East*, pt. 1, pp. 245, 339-40, and 488 (hereafter cited as Senate MacArthur Hearings), testimony of Marshall.

[3] Msg C65034, CINCFE to DA for Secy Def, 30 Sep 50, and Msg C65035, CINCFE to CG Eighth Army, 30 Sep 50, quoted in Schnabel, FEC, GHQ Support and Participation in the Korean War, ch. VI, pp. 16-17.

[4] Msg C65118, CINCUNC to DA, 1 Oct 50, quoted in Schnabel, *op. cit.*, p. 17.

[5] Senate MacArthur Hearings, pt. 1, p. 245.

[6] New York *Times*, October 2, 1950, a London dispatch; New York *Herald Tribune*, October 1, 1950.

THE PLAN FOR COMPLETE VICTORY

that China would enter the war if the U.N. forces crossed the Parallel.[7]

Meanwhile, MacArthur on 1 October issued his demand that North Korea surrender. He addressed his message to the Commander in Chief of the North Korean forces. He called upon the North Koreans to lay down their arms and cease hostilities under such military supervision as he might direct in order that the decisions of the United Nations might be carried out with a minimum of further loss of life and destruction of property, and to liberate U.N. prisoners of war and civilian internees. There was no answer from North Korea.

On 9 October General MacArthur issued an ultimatum calling "for the last time" for North Korean surrender. There was no official response from North Korea to this demand, but Kim Il Sung in a radio broadcast in P'yongyang on the morning of 10 October, which was monitored in Tokyo, rejected it.[8]

MacArthur's Plan of Operations in North Korea

As Eighth Army approached a junction with X Corps near Seoul, General Walker became concerned about the future relationship of Eighth Army and X Corps. He and his staff felt that X Corps should become part of Eighth Army and that all U.N. forces in Korea should operate under a unified field command.[9] It is not known with certainty whether General Walker ever discussed with General MacArthur his own ideas about operations north of the 38th Parallel. It appears, however, that he never submitted them to him in writing.

So far as is known, the nearest General Walker ever came to broaching the subject to MacArthur in writing was on 26 September when he sent a discreetly worded message to him suggesting that he would like to be informed of X Corps' progress and plans so that he could plan better for the approaching juncture of the two forces. General MacArthur dashed Walker's hopes in a reply the next day, informing him that X Corps would remain in GHQ Reserve, in occupation of the Inch'on-Seoul area ready to undertake a GHQ-directed operation "of which you will be apprised at an early date."[10]

When General MacArthur flew to Seoul on 29 September to return the South Korean capital to the government of Syngman Rhee he already had formulated in his mind plans for the next phase of Korean operations. On 26 September, General Hickey had sent a check sheet to General Wright stating that General MacArthur wanted plans developed for further operations in North Korea which would employ the X Corps in an amphibious landing at Wonsan. Because the Far East Command's Joint Strategic Plans and Opera-

---

[7] New York *Times*, October 3 and 4, 1950; Msg 031344Z, DA to SCAP, 3 Oct 50, cited in Schnabel, *op. cit.*, ch. VII, p. 13.

[8] Dept of State Pub 4015, app. A, *United Nations Command Seventh Report to the Security Council, United Nations, 1–15 October 1950.* See also New York *Times*, October 9 and 11, 1950.

[9] Interv, author with Maj Gen Leven C. Allen, 15 Dec 53.

[10] Msg CX64410, 27 Sep 50, CINCFE to CG Eighth Army, and Msg G25090 KG, CG Eighth Army to CINCFE, 26 Sep, both quoted in Schnabel, *op. cit.*, ch. VI, pp. 9–10; Interv, author with Allen, 15 Dec 53.

tions Group had kept active its studies for amphibious operations in areas other than Inch'on, including one for a corps-size landing in the Wonsan-Hamhung area of the east coast, it was only a matter of a few hours until General Wright had the outline of such a plan in MacArthur's hands.

This plan proposed that the advance into North Korea would consist of a "main effort of Eighth Army on the west in conjunction with an amphibious landing at Wonsan or elsewhere." [11] This was the beginning officially of the Far East Command decision that led quickly to the establishment of two separate field commands in Korea for the next phase of the war, and which almost at once became the subject of controversy.

For a period prior to 26 September, it appears that General MacArthur had intended to place X Corps under Eighth Army command once Seoul had fallen. Generals Hickey and Wright favored this course of action, and Maj. Gen. George L. Eberle, the Far East Command G–4, agreed with them. But apparently they did not actively advocate it to General MacArthur. Eberle held the view that although it would be possible to support X Corps logistically in an amphibious operation on the east coast, it could more easily be supported as part of Eighth Army. But if MacArthur ever had been uncertain on the future role of the X Corps, he had decided the point in his own mind by the last week of September. The reasoning which led General MacArthur to decide on two commands in Korea can best be understood by reference to the terrain map of North Korea and the problem of logistics.[12]

Above the Seoul-Wonsan corridor the northern Taebaek Range rises to rugged heights in the east central part of the peninsula, forming an almost trackless mountainous waste in the direction of the Manchurian border. The principal routes of travel follow the deep mountain valleys in a generally north-south direction. The only reasonably good lateral road from east to west in North Korea lay just north of the 39th Parallel, connecting P'yongyang with Wonsan, on the east coast. A rail line also crossed the peninsula here. Any plan for a military campaign north of the P'yongyang-Wonsan corridor in the interior of North Korea would encounter most difficult logistical and supply problems.

In surveying the logistical problems attending any future military operations in Korea, General MacArthur had to note the condition of transport communications in South Korea. U.N. aerial action, together with enemy demolitions, had destroyed nearly all the rail and highway bridges north of the Pusan Perimeter. Weeks of concentrated work by all available Engineer troops would be required to repair the rail lines from the Pusan Perimeter to the 38th Parallel. Aerial action had also badly shattered the communication and transport system of North Korea. In considering this state of affairs, General MacArthur apparently decided that he could

---

[11] Interv, author with Maj Gen Edwin K. Wright, 7 Jan 54; Check Sheet, Gen Hickey to JSPOG, 26 Sep 50, sub: Plans for Future Operations, quoted in Schnabel, *op. cit.*, ch. VI, pp. 19–20.

[12] Interv, author with Wright, 7 Jan 54; Lt Gen Doyle O. Hickey, MS review comments, 14 Feb 56; Almond, MS review comments, 4 May 55; Interv, author with Eberle, 12 Jan 54.

not supply both Eighth Army and X Corps from Inch'on for a quick continuation of the pursuit northward. He also wanted to get military forces behind the North Koreans retreating from the Pusan Perimeter through the central mountains and up the east coast. MacArthur reasoned that a landing on the northeast coast might accomplish this. The base for operations in Korea actually was Japan. MacArthur believed that two separate forces co-ordinated from there could operate in Korea without impairing the effectiveness of either.

Involved also in his decision was the idea of encirclement of the North Korean capital. While Eighth Army attacked north from the Seoul area toward P'yongyang, MacArthur's plan called for the X Corps, upon landing at Wonsan, to drive west along the P'yongyang corridor and to take the city from the flank and rear.

The first outline of the operational plan for the projected movement into North Korea set the target date for the Wonsan assault, for planning purposes, at twelve days after Eighth Army passed through the X Corps in the Seoul-Inch'on area. It was thought that Eighth Army could initiate its attack three to seven days before the X Corps amphibious assault on Wonsan. General MacArthur approved this plan on 29 September.[13]

After the GHQ plan to move the X Corps by water to Wonsan became known to Eighth Army, Colonel Dabney, Eighth Army G-3, prepared a message to GHQ setting forth a concept to replace it. This plan would have assigned X Corps to Eighth Army and provided for early movement against P'yongyang and Wonsan overland. The Eighth Army staff felt that the GHQ plan to outload X Corps would unnecessarily delay pursuit of the defeated North Korean Army and would impede the advance of Eighth Army northward. It also believed that the ROK advance on the east coast would capture Wonsan before the X Corps could be landed there. Dabney took the message to General Walker who read it and said that he agreed with the plan, but that it was not to be sent to GHQ. According to Dabney, Walker said he had already made his views known and had received contrary orders. In connection with the possible escape into North Korea of large numbers of enemy soldiers from the Pusan Perimeter, Eighth Army earlier had requested X Corps to block the central mountain route through Wonju and Ch'unch'on with at least a regiment, but X Corps had replied that it could not extend "the anvil" to that point.[14] On 11 October a radio message from General MacArthur shattered any remaining hope Walker may have had of directing future operations in the east. It informed him that MacArthur intended to use Wonsan Airfield for land-based aircraft under X Corps control and that the ROK I Corps in the east, then under Eighth Army control, would come under X Corps command as soon as that corps landed.[15]

---

[13] JSPOG file, FEC, Opn Plan 9-50, 29 Sep 50, cited in Schnabel, op. cit., ch. 6, pp. 21-22.

[14] Intervs, author with Gens Allen, 15 Dec 53, Wright, 7 Jan 54, and Eberle, 12 Jan 54; Hickey, MS review comments, 14 Feb 56; Dabney, MS review comments, 26 Nov 57.

[15] Msg CX66169, 11 Oct 50, CINCFE to CG Eighth Army, quoted in Schnabel, op. cit., ch. VI, p. 27.

It appears that General Walker believed that X Corps, after the fall of Seoul, should continue the attack north to P'yongyang under Eighth Army command, with Eighth Army moving up behind it. He reasoned that this should save a lot of time as X Corps was already in position for continuing the attack in the west, and Eighth Army was not. In such an attack the corps could continue to be supplied from Inch'on. General Walker and most Eighth Army senior officers felt that not to continue the pursuit at once—to halt for a period of almost two weeks while X Corps loaded out at Inch'on and Eighth Army moved into position below the 38th Parallel—would permit the escape of a large part of the remaining North Korean forces retreating northward which might otherwise be destroyed or captured.

In Walker's view, once the X Corps reached P'yongyang, with or without Eighth Army help as the case might be, Eighth Army could then move laterally along the P'yongyang-Wonsan corridor to the east coast where it would join the ROK I Corps already there and advancing northward. This plan contemplated the X Corps continuing the attack in the west from P'yongyang toward the Yalu. An alternate course would be for the X Corps to cross to the east coast by the P'yongyang-Wonsan corridor, while Eighth Army attacked north from P'yongyang. The operations of both forces would be co-ordinated under Walker's command, and both would be supplied from Inch'on and Pusan and by airlift until Wonsan fell. Then the force operating in the east could be supplied largely by sea through that port and Hungnam farther to the north. Generals Hickey, Wright, and Eberle of MacArthur's staff favored such a plan of operations.[16]

Admiral Joy, Commander, NAVFE, and key members of his staff, had objected to the Wonsan amphibious operation as being unnecessary, holding the view that X Corps could march overland from Seoul to Wonsan much faster than it could be lifted and landed there by water. General Smith, commanding the 1st Marine Division, had many reservations about the proposed operations of his division in northeast Korea.[17]

The prediction of the Eighth Army commander and staff that Wonsan would fall to the ROK I Corps before the X Corps could land there became a fact on 10 October. And their view that the North Korean capital of P'yongyang would also fall to Eighth Army attack before the X Corps could move west from Wonsan also proved to be correct. General MacArthur officially acknowledged this fact by issuing on 17 October a new United Nations Command Operations Order which drew a boundary between Eighth Army and X Corps. This boundary, starting at the 39th Parallel, followed generally the watershed of the high Taebaek Range that extended through the eastern part of Korea up to the Yalu River.[18]

Eighth Army Deploys for the Attack

Based on General MacArthur's United

---

[16] General MacArthur says these officers never expressed any such views to him at the time. MacArthur MS review comments, 15 Nov 57.

[17] Ltr, Smith to author, 13 Feb 54; Smith, MS review comments, 15 Nov 57; Karig, et al., *Battle Report: The War in Korea*, pp. 298-99.

[18] UNC Opn Ord 4, 17 Oct 50, cited in Schnabel, *op. cit.*, ch. 6, pp. 31-32.

THE PLAN FOR COMPLETE VICTORY

TANK TROOPS *of the 1st Cavalry Division pursuing the enemy fourteen miles north of Kaesong on 13 October.*

Nations Command Operations Order 2, dated 2 October, Eighth Army the next day issued an operations order to implement its part in the plan for the attack into North Korea. The army order called for the U.S. I Corps to seize a line west of the Imjin River with not less than a division, and to concentrate the corps in an assembly area there as rapidly as IX Corps could relieve it. The U.S. I Corps was then to conduct operations northward on army orders, making the main effort with the 1st Cavalry Division leading the attack. The 24th Division and the ROK 1st Division were to protect the corps flanks and form a reserve.[19]

In addition to relieving the U.S. I Corps in its zone, the U.S. IX Corps was to protect the line of communications, Seoul-Suwon-Taejon-Taegu-Pusan and, together with ROK police, destroy the remaining enemy forces in South Korea.

The ROK Army was directed to move its II Corps, consisting of the 6th, 7th, and 8th Divisions, to the area between Ch'unch'on and Uijongbu in central Korea, and its I Corps, composed of the Capital and 3d Divisions, to the area between Yongp'o and Chumunjin-up on the east coast, all prepared to attack northward. The ROK Army was also to provide a new division (the 11th) by 5 October to help IX Corps in the rear areas of South Korea.

Pursuant to orders, the 1st Cavalry

---

[19] EUSAK Opn Ord 103, 3 Oct 50; EUSAK WD, G-3 Sec, 3 and 4 Oct 50.

Division on 5 October advanced north of Seoul for the purpose of securing the U.S. I Corps assembly area near the 38th Parallel. Led by I Company, the 5th Cavalry Regiment in the evening crossed to the north side of the Imjin River at Munsan-ni.

At noon on the 7th, the 16th Reconnaissance Company entered Kaesong, and that evening elements of the 1st Battalion, 8th Cavalry Regiment, arrived there. By evening of 8 October the 7th and 8th Cavalry Regiments of the 1st Cavalry Division had secured the I Corps assembly area in the vicinity of Kaesong. Some of the troops were within small arms range of the 38th Parallel. Behind the 1st Cavalry Division, the 24th Division concentrated in the Seoul area.[20]

At this juncture a new military organization appeared in Korea, and it also concentrated near Seoul. The 3d Battalion, Royal Australian Regiment, commanded by 30-year-old Lt. Col. Charles H. Green, a veteran of World War II, arrived at Pusan on 28 September. It joined the British 27th Brigade at Kumch'on on 3 October, which was then renamed the 27th British Commonwealth Brigade. Two days later the bulk of the brigade moved by air to Kimpo Airfield as part of the I Corps concentration near the 38th Parallel.[21]

With its I Corps concentrated to the north of Seoul, Eighth Army took over control of the Inch'on-Seoul area from X Corps at 1200, 7 October. The command posts of both Eighth Army and the ROK Army moved from Taegu and opened in Seoul on 12 October.[22]

Earlier, on 4 October, the Far East Air Forces and the Fifth Air Force, acting on a directive of 8 July, had assumed control of the Marine squadrons at Kimpo. This was highly displeasing to X Corps, and particularly so to the marines. But the change in control actually made little difference in air operations since FEAF directed that the 1st Marine Air Wing continue to support X Corps. The Fifth Air Force headquarters moved to Seoul on 15 October. As a result of the September victories, the Japan-based fighters and fighter-bombers of the Fifth Air Force moved to Korean bases. This permitted an increase in their armament load, more time over target and combat area, and lengthened flight ranges into North Korea.[23]

The ROK I Corps Captures Wonsan and Hungnam

Regardless of whether the U.N. forces did or did not cross the 38th Parallel, there was always the strong probability that the ROK troops would. Syngman Rhee had often stated his intention of halting the South Korean Army only at the Yalu. Speaking at a mass meeting at Pusan on 19 September he said, "We have to advance as far as the Manchurian border until not a single enemy soldier is left in our country." He said that he did not expect the U.N. forces to stop at the 38th Parallel, but if they

---

[20] EUSAK POR 259, 6 Oct, and 265, 8 Oct 50; EUSAK PIR 262, 7 Oct 50; 1st Cav Div WD, 6-7 Oct 50; 5th Cav Regt WD, 6 Oct 50; EUSAK WD, G-3 Sec, 7 Oct 50; 24th Div WD, 4-6 Oct 50.

[21] EUSAK WD, G-3 Sec, 28 Sep and 5 Oct 50; Ibid., Br for CG, 5-6 Oct 50; I Corps WD, 3 Oct 50; GHQ UNC, G-3 Opn Rpt, 3 Oct 50.

[22] EUSAK POR No. 277, 12 Oct 50; EUSAK PLR No. 84, 6 Oct 50; EUSAK WD, 7 Oct 50.

[23] USAF Hist Study 71, 1 Jul 52.

THE PLAN FOR COMPLETE VICTORY

did, he continued, "we will not allow ourselves to stop." [24] And stop the ROK troops did not.

A message dropped by a KMAG G-3 officer from a light plane at Samch'ok and delivered to Colonel Emmerich at Kangnung on the afternoon of 29 September ordered the ROK 3d Division to cross the 38th Parallel and proceed to Wonsan as soon as possible. Advanced patrols of the ROK 3d Division crossed the parallel on 30 September. The next day just before noon two rifle companies crossed the border and came under fire from enemy troops in old fixed positions north of the Parallel. On 2 October the ROK 3d and Capital Divisions established their command posts in Yangyang, eight miles north of the parallel. Although General MacArthur made the first official public announcement of forces under U.N. command crossing the 38th Parallel on 3 October, the American press had reported the incident the day before. Anticipating that ROK forces would cross the Parallel, newspaper correspondents flew to Kangnung, just south of the border on the east coast, to get the news.[25]

Now began a remarkable phase of the pursuit. The ROK 3d Division traveled northward night and day, on foot and by vehicle, out of communication most of the time with higher headquarters, without flank protection to the west, and bypassing many enemy groups which often attacked their supply points in the rear. There were some costly fire fights on the road north. The N.K. *5th Division* with about 2,400 survivors, retreating as best it could ahead of the ROK's, kept the pursuing advanced elements under mortar and 76-mm. antitank fire. The road was heavily mined and lead vehicles had many casualties. From fortified positions, including connecting trenches, caves, and dug-in gun positions, North Koreans tried to stop or slow the ROK advance. The 3d Division averaged about fifteen miles a day. Many of its men had no shoes and large numbers trudged ever northward on bloody feet.

The Capital Division followed the 3d, and at intervals sent some of its units inland into the Diamond Mountains, the lofty and beautiful Kumgang-san, which crowded close upon the coast line. In happier days these mountains had been the vacation grounds of people from all parts of Korea.

In central Korea, troops of the ROK II Corps crossed into North Korea later than did the troops of the I Corps on the coast. On 6 October the ROK 6th Division crossed the parallel from the vicinity of Ch'unch'on and advanced on Hwach'on. For three days it fought two regiments of the N.K. *9th Division* which stubbornly defended that town. Late on the afternoon of 8 October the division entered Hwach'on, driving two enemy battalions northwest.

The 8th Division crossed the 38th Parallel on 7 October. On its right, the 7th Division crossed a day or two later. Both divisions headed for the Iron Triangle. ROK troops arrived at the Iron Triangle on 10 October. There in the

---

[24] FEC, CofS files, Associated Press dispatch from Pusan, 1450 19 Sep 50.
[25] Ltr, Emmerich to author, 12 Feb 54; Emmerich, MS review comments, 12 Dec 57; EUSAK WD, G-3 Jnl, Msgs at 2000, 2215, 2305 1 Oct, and Msg at 2030 2 Oct 50; EUSAK WD, Summ, 4 Oct 50; CINCFE Korean Release 522, 031545 Oct 50; New York *Times*, October 2, 1950.

Ch'orwon area a large force of North Koreans attacked the ROK 16th Regiment during the day but was repulsed and forced to withdraw. Elements of the 8th Division then entered Ch'orwon.

The Iron Triangle, a place whose name became famous later in the Korean War, was an area of relatively flat terrain, shaped like an equilateral triangle, in the mountains of east central North Korea. It is situated 20 to 30 miles above the 38th Parallel, halfway across the peninsula, and 50 air miles northeast of Seoul. It is bounded at its three corners by the towns of Ch'orwon at its western base, Kumhwa at its eastern base, and P'yonggang at its northern apex. The Iron Triangle is an important North Korean rail and road communication center, linking east and west coastal areas with each other, and in turn connecting them with the communication net leading south through central South Korea.

On 11 October the ROK 8th Division and the 7th Regiment of the 6th Division converged on P'yonggang. On 13 October the 7th Division arrived there by way of Kumhwa.

All the ROK divisions, except the 1st, which was part of the U.S. I Corps and accordingly under direct American command, were across the Parallel before any of the American divisions crossed.[26]

On 9 October, the ROK 3d and Capital Divisions were at the south edge of Wonsan, 110 air miles up the coast above the 38th Parallel. That day the Capital Division on the Wonsan–Iron Triangle road south of the city captured 6 tanks, 4 artillery pieces, 10 82-mm. mortars, 1 120-mm. mortar, 30 heavy machine guns, 500 submachine guns, 5,000 Russian rifles, 1 boxcar of medical supplies, and another of miscellaneous supplies. The bulk of the ROK 3d Division arrived in front of Wonsan by the coastal road. The N.K. *24th Mechanized Artillery Brigade*, the *945th Regiment* (naval amphibious troops), and other units subordinate to the naval headquarters at Wonsan defended the city. Enemy artillery pieces emplaced behind dikes just south of it delivered direct fire against the ROK's.[27]

Troops of both the ROK 3d and Capital Divisions entered Wonsan on 10 October, with the 3d Division on the coastal road making the greater effort. About two miles long and of irregular, narrow width, the city is shaped by the 450-foot-high hills that rise abruptly from the narrow coastal strip. In order to settle rival claims as to which division entered the city first, the corps commander, Brig. Gen. Kim Baik Yil decreed that both divisions got there simultaneously at 0600 and that both secured it at 1000. But the city was not secured then. Colonel Emmerich, KMAG senior adviser with the 3d Division, entered the city with the front line troops of the ROK 23d Regiment just after noon. The North Koreans had maintained a heavy artillery fire from the city until almost noon. Then, after withdrawing most of their guns from Wonsan, they fired into the city all after-

---

[26] EUSAK WD, Summ, Oct 50; *Ibid.,* Daily News Bulletin, 4 Oct 50; EUSAK POR's, 7-9 Oct 50; EUSAK WD, G-3 Sec, 4 Oct and 7 Oct 50; *Ibid.,* Br for CG, 4, 5, 9, 10, 11-14 Oct 50; *Ibid.,* PIR's 86-88, 6-8 Oct, and 91, 11 Oct 50.

[27] EUSAK WD, Br for CG, 090001 Oct 50; GHQ FEC, History of the N.K. Army, pp. 81-82.

THE PLAN FOR COMPLETE VICTORY

3D ROK DIVISION OFFICERS AND KMAG ADVISERS

noon from its northwest sector and the hills behind it. That afternoon the 3d Division captured the heavily mined airfield on the peninsula east of the city. At nightfall both ROK divisions were still engaged in street fighting within the city. During the night an enemy armored task force, including about ten 76-mm. self-propelled antitank guns, returned to the airfield and did a good job of shooting it up, burning out most of the buildings and hangars.[28]

The next day, 11 October, the ROK 3d Division fought through Wonsan against enemy artillery, mortar, and small arms fire. It secured the city, and by evening had troops one mile north of it. The Capital Division helped clear the city and occupied the airfield. Generals Walker and Partridge flew into the Wonsan Airfield on the 11th. Finding it in good condition, General Partridge had twenty-two planes of the Combat Cargo Command fly in 131 tons of supplies for the ROK troops the next day.[29]

In the week after the capture of Wonsan the ROK 3d Division remained in the vicinity, securing the area for the expected landing of X Corps. The Capital Division meanwhile moved on

---

[28] Ltr, Emmerich to author, 12 Feb 54; EUSAK WD, Br for CG, 100001–110800 Oct 50.

[29] EUSAK WD, 11 Oct 50, Aide de Camp Diary; Schnabel, *op. cit.*; USAF Hist Study 71, p. 76.

ROK TROOPS *marching past the Diamond Mountains.*

north fifty air miles up the coast, and, against light resistance, secured both Hamhung and its port, Hungnam, on 17 October.[30]

During its great success in advancing northward into North Korea the ROK Army expanded and reorganized. On 8 October it reactivated the 5th Division at Taegu and once again counted eight divisions, the same number that it had when the war began. Simultaneously, the ROK Army activated the 1st Guerrilla Group of five battalions (1st, 2d, 3d, 5th, 6th). Eight days later, on 16 October, it activated the ROK III Corps. This new corps, to which the 5th and 11th Divisions were attached, was to assume responsibility for the ROK Army zone south of the Seoul-Ch'unch'-on-Inje-Yangyang axis, and destroy remaining enemy troops and guerrillas in that part of Korea.[31]

The X Corps Prepares To Move Amphibiously to Northeast Korea

About the time the ROK I Corps crossed the 38th Parallel and started north toward Wonsan, General Almond and Admiral Struble received on 1 October preliminary instructions from GHQ, Far East Command, for the projected landing at Wonsan. Joint Task Force 7 had been re-established to land the X Corps at Wonsan, and Admiral Struble had been named to command it. He received from Admiral Joy the mis-

---

[30] Interv, author with Emmerich, 5 Dec 51; EUSAK WD, G-3 Sec, 12, 15, and 16 Oct 50; *Ibid.*, Br for CG, 14, 17 Oct 50.

[31] EUSAK POR 300, 20 Oct 50; EUSAK WD, G-4 Sec, 5 Oct 50; GHQ UNC, G-3 Opn Rpt, 20 Oct 50; IX Corps WD, bk. 1, 13 Oct 50. The 5th Division was supposed to move to the Andong area in the east, but it actually stayed in northwest Korea. The 11th Division established headquarters at Namwon in southwest Korea.

THE PLAN FOR COMPLETE VICTORY

sion of JTF 7. This was (1) to maintain a naval blockade of the east coast of Korea south from Ch'ongjin; (2) to load and transport X Corps to the Wonsan area and provide cover and support en route; (3) to conduct pre-D-day naval operations as required; (4) on D-day to seize by amphibious assault, occupy, and defend a beachhead in the Wonsan area; (5) to provide naval gunfire, air, and initial logistic support to X Corps in the Wonsan area.[32]

General MacArthur on 2 October formalized in his United Nations Operation Order 2 instructions for U.N. military operations north of the 38th Parallel, and set forth therein the plan of movement and the mission of X Corps. The X Corps was to revert to GHQ Reserve when Eighth Army passed through it in the Seoul area. The 1st Marine Division and X Corps headquarters were to load at Inch'on while the 7th Infantry Division and most of the X Corps troops moved to Pusan for loading. The problem of outloading X Corps at Inch'on in adverse tidal conditions with the limited amount of amphibious craft available, concurrently with the expected partial use of the port by Eighth Army, was so complicated and difficult that MacArthur decided that part of the force would have to outload at Pusan if the entire corps was to be loaded within two weeks.[33]

The selection of Wonsan as the site of the projected X Corps landing in northeast Korea had been based on a number of factors. Situated at the southwest side of a large bay which bulges inland from the Japan Sea, Wonsan is the principal port on the east coast of Korea; it is the eastern terminus of the easiest route across North Korea; and it is a road and rail communications center. In 1950 when the war started the city had a population of approximately 150,000. The Japanese had developed Wonsan as a naval base, and the North Koreans had continued to use it for the same purpose. It was the principal port of entry for Russian supplies and military equipment received by sea from the Vladivostok area, and it was a key point on the rail line running southwest into Korea from the Soviet Vladivostok base. It was the petroleum refining capital of Korea. From Wonsan a military force could move inland and west across the peninsula to P'yongyang, or north to the Hamhung-Hungnam area, fifty air miles away, the most important industrial area of all Korea.[34]

On 30 September General Smith, commander of the 1st Marine Division, was first informed of the projected X Corps landing at Wonsan. The next day he was requested to submit loading plans by 3 October with a proposed D-day at Wonsan of 15 October. Since ships for the lift had not yet been designated it was impossible to meet these dates. On 7 October, Admiral Doyle, in command of the Attack Force, recommended 20 October as the earliest

---

[32] Act Rpt, JTF 7, Wonsan Opn, I-A-1; *Ibid.*, I-B-1, COMNAVFE Opn Plan 113-50; X Corps WD, Oct 50, CofS Sec, p. 10.

[33] Act Rpt, JTF 7, Wonsan Opn, I-C-1; X Corps WD, Oct 50, CofS Sec, p. 10; Schabel, *op. cit.*, ch. VI, pp. 23-24; 2d Log Comd, Oct 50 Act Rpt, G-4 Sec.

[34] Joint Intel Study Pub Board, JANIS 75, ch. VIII (Korea—Cities and Towns), pp. 52-53; GHQ FEC, Terrain Study 6, Northern Korea, sec. XIV, pp. 26-27 and Map 760, Wonsan City Plan, Plate 12; X Corps WD, Oct 50, Opns, pp. 18-19; Diary of CG X Corps, 24 Oct 50.

D-day which the amphibious assault forces could meet. Admirals Struble and Joy concurred and forwarded this recommendation to General MacArthur. He accepted it as a tentative D-day but indicated that every effort should be made to achieve an earlier one. Two days later Admiral Struble published his operation plan outlining the task force organization. JTF 7 was organized as follows:

90	Attack Force, Rear Adm. James H. Doyle
95	Advance Force, Rear Adm. Allan E. Smith
95.2	Covering and Support Group, Rear Adm. Charles C. Hartman
95.6	Minesweeping Group, Capt. Richard T. Spofford
92	X Corps, Maj. Gen. Edward M. Almond
96.2	Patrol and Reconnaissance Group, Rear Adm. George R. Henderson
96.8	Escort Carrier Group, Rear Adm. Richard W. Ruble
77	Fast Carrier Force, Rear Adm. Edward C. Ewen
70.1	Flagship Group (USS *Missouri*), Capt. Irving T. Duke
79	Logistics Support, Capt. Bernard L. Austin

On 10 October General MacArthur ordered U.N. Operations Plan 2 put into effect, thereby canceling all other tentative plans.[35]

General MacArthur's Operation Plan 9–50 of 29 September assigned priority of outloading at Inch'on to the 1st Marine Division, the amphibious assault element of X Corps. On 3 October, X Corps ordered the Marine division to initiate movement to an assembly area in Inch'on. On 4 October, General Almond issued a corps order for the projected operations at Wonsan. The 1st Marine Division had the mission of seizing a corps base of operations while the 7th Infantry Division was to start an attack west to join with Eighth Army in front of P'yongyang. By 6 October the 1st, 5th, and 11th Marines had virtually completed their movement to Inch'on; the next day the 7th Marines began its movement from Uijongbu to the Inch'on assembly area. As it assembled at Inch'on for outloading, the 1st Marine Division numbered 23,591 men, with 40 U.S. Army troops and 4,516 Korean marines attached, for a total of 28,147.[36]

At noon on 6 October the 3d Logistical Command assumed responsibility for all unloading at Inch'on. During the day the X Corps requested it to halt all unloading activities not directly concerned with the corps, because otherwise X Corps outloading would be delayed for an estimated six to twenty days. X Corps reverted to GHQ Reserve at noon on 7 October when Eighth Army assumed responsibility for the Inch'on-Seoul area.

---

[35] Act Rpt, JTF 7, Wonsan Opn, app. D, Opn Ord Comdr 7th Flt, 16–50, 5 Oct 50; *Ibid.*, I–C–3–4; *Ibid.*, II–3; X Corps WD, Oct 50, CofS Notes, 10 Oct 50.

[36] CINCFE Opn Plan 9–50, 29 Sep 50; X Corps Opn Instr 9, 031600 Oct 50; X Corps WD, catalogue of Plans and Orders, p. 44; X Corps WD, Summ of Opns, 3–5 Oct 50, and POR 18, 6 Oct 50; 1st Mar Div SAR, 15 Sep–7 Oct 50, an. C, pp. 39–42; and vol. I, an. A, G–1 Sec; X Corps Opn Ord 4, 4 Oct 50; X Corps WD, Diary of CG X Corps, 4, 7 Oct, and Notes of CofS, 4, 7 Oct 50.

THE PLAN FOR COMPLETE VICTORY

The 31-foot tides and the great mud banks at low tide made the outloading exceedingly difficult and required carefully co-ordinated schedules in moving troops and supplies. There were only seven berths where LST's or landing craft could beach at Inch'on and these could be used only at high tide. Moreover, there was no adequate staging area. There was only one small pier from which vehicles could be loaded into an LCM, and then only at high tide. Vehicles were loaded on the top decks of LST's and ferried out to the ships in the harbor, and there lifted by crane from the LST's to the APA's and AKA's. The tidal basin was used to outload all bulk cargo for ferrying to the ships in the harbor. This unexpectedly developed into a major and difficult task. The 1st Marine Division had been informed that the 1st Logistical Command would bottom load all the shipping dispatched to Inch'on to outload the division with 10 days' level of supply, Classes I, III, and V. But this was not done, and it resulted in the necessity of unloading from ships in the harbor and reloading on others, and also of reloading on X Corps shipping considerable supplies from the dumps ashore that otherwise could have been left for Eighth Army. From Japan by air came 32,000 assault rations and 100,000 C rations to Kimpo Airfield, and from there they were taken to the port for outloading.

Troops began loading at Inch'on on the 9th. The 1st and 3d Battalions, 1st Marines, went aboard their LST's on 10 October, and were in these cramped quarters for sixteen days before they again got ashore. On 11 October the X Corps command post closed ashore and opened aboard the *Mt. McKinley*. Bulk loading of cargo began on 8 October and continued to 16 October when all X Corps loading at Inch'on was completed. Already the U.S. Eighth Army had crossed the Parallel in the west and was fighting its way north.

CHAPTER XXX

Eighth Army and X Corps Enter North Korea

Wherever the enemy goes let our troops go also.
ULYSSES S. GRANT, dispatch to Halleck, 1 August 1864

*Eighth Army Crosses the Parallel—
The Kumch'on Pocket*

On 5 October Eighth Army issued its operations order for the movement across the 38th Parallel, but withheld the date for the attack. Two days later General Allen telephoned General Hickey and told him that General Walker wanted to know when A-day (date for crossing the Parallel) was to be given. Hickey replied, "Your A-day will be at such time as you see it ready." Allen replied, "That's fine, because we're on the verge of it now." A message from Tokyo the same day confirmed the call. Eighth Army at once implemented its order of the 5th by radio messages to General Milburn at U.S. I Corps and to the Chief of Staff, ROK Army. The attack on P'yongyang was about to begin.[1]

Eighth Army expected strong enemy resistance at the 38th Parallel and a stubborn defense of P'yongyang. According to ROK Army combat intelligence, the North Koreans had three known lines of defense across the peninsula, each consisting of pillboxes, gun emplacements, trenches, and barbed wire entanglements. The first line was along the 38th Parallel and was about 500 yards in depth; the second line was about three miles behind the first; the third lay farther back and was based on locally situated critical terrain features. All three lines were oriented to defend against southern approaches.[2]

North of the Parallel the U.N. Command expected to meet newly activated divisions that had been training in North Korea or elements of units that had engaged in the fighting around Seoul. Some intelligence sources indicated there might be as many as six divisions totalling 60,000 men in North Korean training centers. Actually, only

---

[1] Fonecon, Allen with Hickey, 1115 7 Oct 50, and Msg CX65711, CINCUNC to CG Eighth Army, 7 Oct 50, both quoted in Schnabel, FEC, GHQ Support and Participation in the Korean War, ch. VI, pp. 24-25; EUSAK WD, G-3 Sec, 7 Oct 50, Opn Ord 104, 5 Oct 50.

[2] EUSAK PIR's 82, 2 Oct, 89, 9 Oct, 90, 10 Oct, and 93, 13 Oct 50.

the N.K. *19th* and *27th Divisions* defended the Kumch'on-Namch'onjom area north of Kaesong. Both had been brigades activated in the summer and expanded in September to division status. They engaged in combat for the first time when U.N. forces crossed the Parallel. On the right (west) of these divisions, the *74th Regiment* of the *43d Division* defended the Yesong River crossing site west of Kaesong. The *43d Division,* organized in mid-September, had the task of defending the coastal area beyond the Yesong River. Some elements of the N.K. *17th Armored Division* engaged in action just north of the Parallel in the zone of the ROK 1st Division, east of the 1st Cavalry Division.[3]

Ready for the attack, the 1st Cavalry Division was deployed in three regimental combat teams just below the Parallel in the vicinity of Kaesong. In the center, Colonel Palmer's 8th Cavalry Regiment was to attack frontally along the main highway axis from Kaesong to Kumch'on; on his right, Colonel Crombez' 5th Cavalry Regiment was to swing eastward, then west, in a circular flanking movement designed to envelope enemy forces south of Kumch'on, fifteen miles north of the Parallel. Meanwhile, on the division left, Colonel Harris' 7th Cavalry Regiment faced the task of crossing the Yesong River to get on the road running north from Paekch'on to the little town of Hanp'o-ri, six miles north of Kumch'on, where the main P'yongyang road crossed the Yesong River. At Hanp'o-ri the 7th Cavalry was to establish a blocking position to trap the large enemy forces that General Gay expected the 8th and 5th Cavalry Regiments to be driving northward. These were the maneuvers involved in the action of the Kumch'on Pocket. Because the prospects of forcing a crossing of the Yesong River did not appear very promising with the support available, General Gay and the division staff relied principally on the 8th and 5th Cavalry Regiments for initial success in the attack.

The 1st Cavalry Division sent patrols across the Parallel late on the afternoon of the 7th, and others crossed Sunday night, 8 October. Then on Monday, 9 October, at 0900 General Gay issued his orders, and the division moved up to the Parallel and started fighting its way northward. (*Map 18*)

In the division center along the main highway, the advance was very slow. The highway was heavily mined and the armored spearhead repeatedly came to a halt, waiting for Engineer troops to remove the mines. On 12 October, halfway to Kumch'on, an enemy strongpoint defended with tanks, self-propelled guns, and antiaircraft weapons again stopped the regiment. An air strike by sixteen planes and a 155-mm. howitzer barrage failed to dislodge the enemy. In this action, Lt. Col. Robert W. Kane, the 1st Battalion commander, was severely wounded.[4]

---

[3] EUSAK PIR 85, 5 Oct 50, and PIR 89, Incl No. 3, 9 Oct 50; FEC, Ord of Battle Info, N.K. Army, Chart 14 (N.K. *19th Div*) and Chart 13 (N.K. *17th Div*); ATIS Interrog Rpts, Issue 14 (N.K. Forces), p. 138, and Issue 15, pp. 100, 149, 191, 192; ATIS Enemy Documents, Issue 16, p. 45, diary of Sr Col Chang Tong Mu; GHQ FEC, History of the N.K. Army, p. 27.

[4] 8th Cav Regt WD, S-3 Jnl, Msg 091226 Oct 50; Capt. Charles A. Rogers, History of the 16th Reconnaissance Company in Korea, 18 July 1950-April 1951, MS, May 1951, copy in OCMH; 1st Cav Div WD, 11-12 Oct 50.

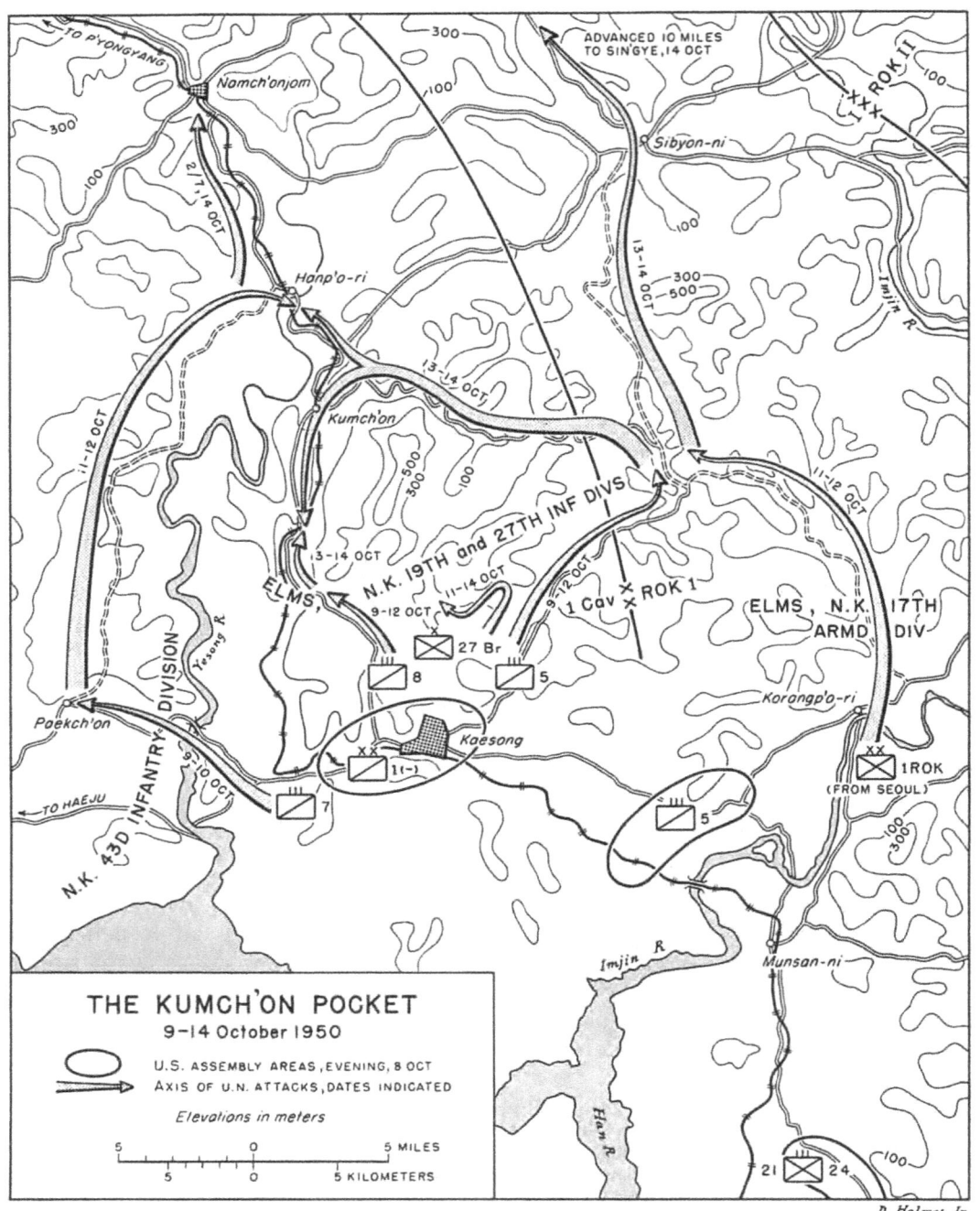

On the division right the 5th Cavalry Regiment also had difficulty. It reached the Parallel at 1930 9 October but did not cross until the next morning. In its initial attack it captured the hills flanking and dominating the road on both sides just above the Parallel. Fifteen miles northeast of Kaesong an enemy force held a long ridge with several knobs (Hills 179, 175, 174) dominating a pass. There it stopped the 1st Battalion. The next day, 12 October, the 2d Battalion joined in the battle. The 5th Cavalry drove the North Koreans from the ridge during the afternoon. In the fighting at Hill 174, 1st Lt. Samuel S. Coursen, a platoon leader in C Company, went to the aid of a soldier who had entered an enemy emplacement mistakenly thinking it was empty. The soldier escaped with a wound, but Coursen was later found dead there together with seven enemy soldiers whom he had killed in a desperate hand-to-hand struggle. Several of the North Koreans had crushed skulls from rifle butt blows.[5]

The day before, 11 October, the 27th British Commonwealth Brigade, with tanks of B Company, 6th Medium Tank Battalion, in support, had crossed the Imjin River and followed the 5th Cavalry Regiment northeast out of Kaesong. General Gay's plan was for the brigade to move northwest through the mountains for a close-in envelopment of Kumch'on. His aerial observer, hitherto very reliable, wrongly reported that the roads were as shown on the maps and that the plan was feasible. The road taken by the British, little more than a cart track, dead-ended in the mountains. The Middlesex Battalion got lost on this trail, turned back, and tried another. Despite an arduous effort in the mountains, the British troops never got into the fight for Kumch'on.[6]

While the British were crossing the Imjin, the ROK 1st Division crossed it at Korangp'o-ri at dawn on the 11th, eastward of the 1st Cavalry Division, and attacked northwest on a road that converged with the one taken by the 5th Cavalry Regiment. The 5th Cavalry in the late afternoon of 12 October was engaged in a fire fight with the enemy at the objective crossroads when advance elements of the ROK 1st Division arrived there from the southeast. In a conference on the spot Colonel Crombez and General Paik, the ROK division commander, agreed that the 5th Cavalry would have precedence on the road until Crombez' troops turned west, five miles northward on a lateral road leading into Kumch'on. The ROK 1st Division, following behind the 5th Cavalry, would then continue its attack north to Sibyon-ni where it would veer northwest toward P'yongyang. Tanks of C Company, 6th Medium Tank Battalion, supported the ROK 1st Division.[7]

Of the three regimental attack forces, the 7th Cavalry Regiment on the divi-

---

[5] 5th Cav POR 23, 091800–101800 Oct 50; 5th Cav Reg WD, 9 Oct 50 and Oct Narr Summ; 1st Cav Div WD, 11–12 Oct 50. Department of the Army General Order 57, 2 August 1951, awarded the Medal of Honor posthumously to Lieutenant Coursen.

[6] Ltr, Gay to author, 23 Jan 54; Interv, author with Crombez, 12 Jan 56; 1st Cav Div WD, 12 Oct 50.

[7] Crombez, MS review comments, 12 Jan 56; 6th Med Tk Bn WD, 29 Sep–Oct 50 (with 24th Div records); EUSAK POR 272, 11 Oct 50; 1st Cav Div WD, 12–13 Oct 50.

sion left flank had the most difficult assignment, and in fact General Gay and his staff expected it to accomplish little. The regiment had to cross the wide Yesong River against defending enemy forces before it could turn north as the lefthand column in the Kumch'on Pocket maneuver. Since all of I Corps' bridging troops and equipment were committed to establishing bridges across the Imjin River at Munsan-ni to support the main effort northward, river crossing support could not be supplied for the 7th Cavalry Regiment at the Yesong River.

On 8 October the regiment received orders to move up to the Yesong River, search for crossing sites, and clear enemy troops from the area southwest of Kaesong. The I&R Platoon found that the high, 800-yard-long combination highway and rail bridge over the river on the Kaesong-Paekch'on route was standing, although damaged. It was so weakened, however, that it could support only foot traffic. The I&R Platoon received small arms, automatic, and mortar fire from the enemy on the far side of the river. Colonel Clainos, commander of the 1st Battalion, also personally reconnoitered the area with a platoon of A Company on the afternoon of the 8th and received fire from the west bank of the stream. The I&R Platoon leader told him that enemy forces held the west side of the river from the southern tip of the peninsula to a point one-half mile northeast of the Yesong River bridge. Colonel Harris, the regimental commander, upon receiving the I&R Platoon report that the bridge was usable for foot troops, ordered the platoon to prevent further destruction of the bridge. He then called upon the 1st Battalion to seize the bridge and crossing area.[8]

A full report of the situation was given to the 1st Cavalry Division with the recommendation that the 7th Cavalry Regiment seize this unexpected opportunity for a quick crossing of the river. General Gay feared that the North Koreans had set a trap in leaving the bridge usable for foot troops, and that enemy zeroed-in mortar and artillery fire and automatic weapons would decimate any troops caught on it. The division staff said also that a regimental attack west of the Yesong River northward could not be supported logistically. The untiring efforts of Colonel Harris and his S–3, Captain Webel, however, succeeded in winning from General Gay authority to attempt the crossing on the 9th.

On the afternoon of 9 October the 7th Cavalry Regiment delivered three hours of preparatory artillery fire against enemy positions on the west bank of the river. At 1500, Colonel Clainos ordered a platoon of C Company to cross the bridge under cover of the barrage. In crossing the bridge and seizing the immediate approaches on the far side, the platoon suffered a few casualties from small arms fire. Following this platoon, B Company, 8th Engineer Combat Battalion, went on the bridge and spent all night under fire repairing holes in the roadway. After the first troops reached the far side, Clainos sent the rest of C Company across and it occupied the hill on the right of the

---

[8] Ltr, Webel (7th Cav S–3 Oct 50) to author, 13 Apr 54; Ltr, Col Peter D. Clainos to author, 24 May 54; Ltrs, Gay to author, 23 Jan and 19 Apr 54; Ltr, Harris to author, 7 Apr 54.

bridge. Next to cross was B Company, which seized the hill just south of the bridge. The artillery and mortar barrage had been unable to silence enemy mortars, and these fired heavy concentrations on the bridge during the 1st Battalion crossing, which took several hours to complete. The overhead steel girders of the bridge gave excellent protection from fire and prevented many casualties. When the supporting artillery barrage had to be lifted from the immediate environs of the bridge, once the 1st Battalion troops crossed to that side, casualties began to increase rapidly from enemy fire. In this crossing attack, the 1st Battalion had 78 casualties; C Company alone had 7 killed and 36 wounded.

After dark the North Koreans launched a counterattack against the 1st Battalion, and Colonel Harris ordered Lt. Col. Gilmon A. Huff to hasten his crossing with the 2d Battalion. Just before midnight Huff's battalion started infiltrating across the bridge which was still under some mortar and small arms fire. On the other side, Huff assembled his battalion on the south flank of the 1st Battalion, approximately 100 yards west of the bridge. He then attacked west along the Paekch'on road in a column of companies with G Company leading. This attack progressed only a short distance when a heavy enemy counterattack from the south struck the flank of G Company. The enemy counterattack threw the 2d Battalion into momentary confusion. In the beginning of the fight enemy small arms fire hit Huff in the shoulder, but he remained with his battalion throughout the night battle. The largest weapons the battalion had at hand were 57-mm. recoilless rifles and 60-mm. mortars. Huff showed superb leadership in this difficult night battle and eventually seized the high ground southeast of the bridge and the road. By dawn it was clear that the battle was all but over and that the 2d Battalion would be able to move forward. Huff then turned over command of the battalion to the executive officer who led it in a continuation of the attack westward. The battalion seized Paekch'on and the high ground north of the town in the afternoon.[9]

The next morning, 11 October, the 3d Battalion, 7th Cavalry, crossed the Yesong River and headed north. Thus, by that morning all three regiments of the 1st Cavalry Division had crossed the 38th Parallel and were driving into North Korea. The 3d Battalion, 7th Cavalry, on the morning of 12 October, seized its objective—the railroad and highway bridges at Hanp'o-ri north of Kumch'on, and the road junction there. This closed the western escape route of an estimated 1,000 enemy troops in Kumch'on. Friendly fighter-bombers mistakenly strafed and rocketed the 3d Battalion at Hanp'o-ri, wounding several men. That evening the 2d Battalion joined the 3d Battalion at Hanp'o-ri.[10]

During the night at the 3d Battalion roadblock, the pressure from the 8th and 5th Cavalry Regiments on the North Koreans was made evident. MSgt. John H. Smith and his platoon of L Company ambushed 11 enemy trucks running with

---

[9] Ltr, Huff to author, 28 Apr 54; Ltr, Webel to author, 13 Apr 54; Fonecon, Webel with author, 20 May 54; Ltr, Clainos to author, 24 May 54; Ltr, Gay to author, 19 Apr 54; 2d Bn, 7th Cav Unit Jnl, 0355–0700 10 Oct 50; 7th Cav Regt WD, 9–10 Oct 50.

[10] 7th Cav Regt WD, 12 Oct 50; 1st Cav Div WD, 11–12 Oct 50; Webel, MS review comments for author, 13 Apr 54.

their lights on. They destroyed 4 trucks loaded with ammunition, captured 6 others, killed about 50 enemy soldiers, and captured an equal number. Among the latter was a mortally wounded regimental commander who had in his possession a document indicating that two North Korean divisions, the *27th* and *19th,* intended to break out of Kumch'on the night of 14 October. Before he died the officer said part of the enemy force had been ordered to withdraw to Namch'onjom, a fortified area fifteen miles north of Kumch'on.[11]

The drive of the 7th Cavalry Regiment northward to Hanp'o-ri after crossing the Yesong River could not have taken place without one of the most successful logistical supply operations of the Korean War. In the discussions before the 7th Cavalry attack at the Yesong River bridge, the 1st Cavalry Division G-4 had told Colonel Harris and Maj. Lucian Croft, the regimental S-4, that he could not provide the gasoline, rations, and certain types of ammunition for the drive north from Paekch'on even if the river crossing attempt was successful. Colonel Harris and Captain Webel decided to try to obtain the needed logistical support from the 3d Logistical Command at Inch'on by amphibious transport through the Yellow Sea and up the Yesong River. Capt. Arthur Westburg, an assistant regimental S-3 officer, went to Inch'on and presented the matter to Brig. Gen. George C. Stewart, the port commander. General Stewart and his staff loaded 500 tons of supplies on thirteen LCV's. They arrived at the 7th Cavalry crossing site at the Yesong River bridge late in the afternoon of the 10th. Engineer troops from I Corps on the 12th constructed a ponton ferry at the bridge site and it transported the tanks of C Company, 70th Tank Battalion, across the river for support of the regiment.[12]

The 13th of October promised to be a critical day in the efforts of the 1st Cavalry Division to close the Kumch'on Pocket. With the 7th Cavalry blocking the exit road from Kumch'on, the decisive action now rested with the 8th and 5th Cavalry Regiments which were trying to compress the pocket from the south and the east.

After it turned west from the Sibyonni road the 5th Cavalry encountered an almost continuous mine field in its approach to Kumch'on, and it also had to fight and disperse an enemy force estimated to number 300 soldiers, eight miles from the town. Overcoming these difficulties, the regiment pressed ahead and by the evening of the 13th it was approaching Kumch'on.

Strong opposition confronted the 8th Cavalry Regiment on the main highway where the enemy apparently had concentrated most of his available forces and weapons. There, on the morning of the 13th, an artillery preparation employing proximity fuze air bursts blanketed the North Korean positions. Because of the closeness of the American

---

[11] 7th Cav Regt WD, 12 Oct 50; 7th Cav Regt Opn Ord 28, 141015 Oct 50; EUSAK WD, G-3 Jnl, 1100 13 Oct 50.

[12] Ltr, Webel to author, 13 Apr 54; Ltr, Harris to author, 7 Apr 54; 7th Cav Regt WD, 10-11 Oct 50; 3d Log Comd Hist Opn Rpt, G-4 Sec (Hist Memo: Yesong River Supply and Ferry Mission), 10-12 Oct 50. During the 12th, the 1st Cavalry Division received reinforcements which were attached to it for the drive on P'yongyang. These were B Co, 6th Med Tk Bn; the 89th Tk Bn; the the 13th FA Bn; and the 90th FA Bn.

troops to the enemy, a planned B-26 bomber strike was canceled, but a new flight of fighter planes appeared over the enemy positions every thirty minutes. The North Koreans resisted stubbornly with tanks, artillery, mortars, small arms fire, and counterattacks. In one of the counterattacks, enemy tanks rumbled out of the early morning mist to strike an outpost of B Company, 70th Tank Battalion. Sgt. Marshall D. Drewery said his tank gunner first fired on the lead enemy tank at a range of fifty yards. A second round hit it at a range of twenty yards. Still the T34 came on and rammed into the American tank. Drewery's driver put his tank in reverse, jerked loose, and backed away. At a few yards' range the gunner fired a third round into the enemy tank which now had a split gun muzzle and was burning. Amazingly, the tank rumbled forward and rammed Drewery's tank a second time. The fourth round finally knocked out this stubborn enemy tank. In the day's series of attacks and counterattacks the 8th Cavalry and supporting arms destroyed eight enemy tanks; B Company, 70th Tank Battalion, accounted for seven of them without loss to itself.[13]

While the enemy force south of Kumch'on fought desperately and successfully to prevent the 8th Cavalry from closing in on the town, a large enemy column of trucks and carts with an estimated 1,000 soldiers moved northward out of it on the road toward Namch'onjom. At the Hanp'o-ri bridge it ran into the 7th Cavalry roadblock. In the ensuing action, the 7th Cavalry, aided by air strikes, killed an estimated 500 and captured 201 of this force. Many enemy troops, however, escaped into the hills northeast of the town.

At the same time, elements of the N.K. *43d Division* cut off below Paekch'on were moving around that town and fleeing north. One such group in company strength occupied old North Korean defensive positions just north of the 38th Parallel the night of 12-13 October. The following day it ambushed the tail end of the 1st Battalion, 7th Cavalry, column moving north from Paekch'on. Part of A Battery, 77th Field Artillery Battalion, and B Company, 8th Engineer Combat Battalion, were in the ambushed column. A soldier who escaped raced back into Paekch'on to the 3d Battalion, 21st Infantry, command post. Colonel Stephens, the regimental commander, happened to be there. Upon hearing what had happened, he directed Lt. Col. John A. McConnell, Commanding Officer, 3d Battalion, to send a company to the scene. Colonel McConnell thereupon directed I Company, 21st Infantry, which was on a blocking mission south of the ambush site, to go there. On arrival it engaged and dispersed the enemy force with mortar and small arms fire, and captured 36 North Koreans. In this ambush the North Koreans killed 29 American and 8 South Korean soldiers and wounded 30 Americans and 4 South Koreans. They also destroyed 4 and damaged 14 vehicles. In this episode, as in so many others like it, those caught in the roadblock apparently made little effort to defend themselves. In another ambush on the road that night enemy troops captured the 2d Battalion, 7th Cavalry, supply

---

[13] 1st Cav Div WD, 13-14 50; 8th Cav Regt WD, Jnl file 0643 to 0800 13 Oct 50; New York *Herald Tribune*, October 14, 1950.

officer and 11 men; subsequently, however, the officer and 5 men escaped.[14]

At midnight of the 13th, the 2d Battalion, 5th Cavalry Regiment, resumed its attack on Kumch'on from the east. After dispersing an enemy force near the town, the battalion then entered and seized the northern part of it. The 3d Battalion following behind seized the southern part. At 0830, 14 October, Colonel Crombez and the regimental command group arrived in Kumch'on. Crombez ordered the 2d Battalion to turn north toward the 7th Cavalry at Hanp'o-ri and the 3d Battalion to turn south to meet the 8th Cavalry on the Kaesong road. The 1st Battalion remained behind to secure the town.

Advancing northwest, the 2d Battalion joined elements of the 7th Cavalry above Hanp'o-ri at noon. An enemy force, estimated to number 2,400 men, which had been attacking the 7th Cavalry roadblock position at Hanp'o-ri, escaped into the hills when the 2d Battalion approached from the south. Meanwhile, attacking south from Kumch'on, the 3d Battalion neared a special task force of the 8th Cavalry Regiment which had attacked north during the morning and already had lost two tanks to enemy action. The two columns, the 3d Battalion, 5th Cavalry, and the special 8th Cavalry task force met just after noon about four miles south of Kumch'on. Even though the 1st Cavalry Division envelopment and capture of Kumch'on had been carried out in five days, a large part of the enemy force in the Kumch'on Pocket escaped, mostly to the north and northwest.[15]

The day Kumch'on fell to the 1st Cavalry Division, 14 October, the North Korean Premier and Commander in Chief, Kim Il Sung, issued an order to all troops of the North Korea People's Army explaining the reasons for the army's defeat and outlining harsh measures for future army discipline. Alluding to the recent reverses, Kim Il Sung said, "Some of our officers have been cast into utter confusion by the new situation and have thrown away their weapons and left their positions without orders." He commanded; "Do not retreat one step farther. Now we have no space in which to fall back." He directed that agitators and deserters be executed on the spot, irrespective of their positions in the Army. To carry out this order, he directed that division and unit commanders organize, by the following day, a special group, which he termed the "Supervising Army," its men to be recruited from those who had distinguished themselves in battle.[16]

At the close of 14 October, with U.S. I Corps troops through the principal prepared enemy positions between the 38th Parallel and the North Korean capital, enemy front lines as such had ceased to exist. The North Korean forces were in a state of utter confusion.

In these auspicious circumstances President Truman on 15 October met

---

[14] 1st Cav Div WD, 13 Oct 50; 7th Cav Regt WD, 13 Oct 50; 24th Div WD, 14 Oct 50; Webel, MS review comments for author, 13 Apr 54; Stephens, MS review comments, Dec 57.

[15] 1st Cav Div WD, 13–14 Oct 50; 7th Cav Regt WD, 13–14 Oct 50; 8th Cav Regt Jnl, 141310–141315 Oct 50; Crombez, MS review comments, 12 Jan 56; Stephens MS review comments, Dec 57.

[16] ATIS Supp, Enemy Docs, Issue 19, pp. 1–4, order dated 14 Oct 50, issued to all NKPA personnel by Kim Il Sung and Pak Hon Yong, Chief of Supreme Political Bureau, NKPA.

KUMCH'ON, NORTH KOREA, *after the battle.*

General MacArthur on Wake Island. A few days earlier, in announcing his intention to make the trip, President Truman had said he would discuss with General MacArthur "the final phase of U.N. action in Korea." [17]

The X Corps Moves to Northeast Korea

While the I Corps of Eighth Army was driving into North Korea on the P'yongyang axis and the 1st Marine Division was loading at Inch'on, the 7th Infantry Division was assembling at Pusan to outload there in the X Corps amphibious movement to northeast Korea. On 30 September the division had been relieved of its responsibilities in the Seoul area and its units began to shift south and southeast to the Suwon and Ich'on areas preparatory to the long overland move to Pusan. Ten LST's were reserved at Inch'on for the division's tanks and heavy equipment.

On 4 October Eighth Army indicated the route it wanted the 7th Division to take through its zone, specifying the road through Ch'ungju, Hamch'ang, Kumch'on, Taegu, and Kyongju to Pusan, a road distance of 350 miles from Ich'on. At Taegu the troops were to load on trains for the final part of the journey, whereupon the trucks would return to Suwon and Ich'on for others. [18]

---

[17] EUSAK WD, 21 Oct 50, has transcript of Truman's address at San Francisco, 17 Oct; New York Times, October 11, 1950.

[18] X Corps WD, CofS Notes, 2, 4 Oct 50; 7th Inf Div WD, G-3 Jnl, 2-4 Oct 50, and Msg 17, 5 Oct 50; X Corps WD, Opn Sec, pp. 16-18; Barr, Notes, 30 Sep-2 Oct 50.

The 3d Battalion, 31st Infantry, led the 7th Division movement, passing the initial point at Ich'on at 0350 5 October, with the rest of the regiment following. The command group of the 32d Infantry led the movement of that regiment through Ich'on four hours later. The 17th Regiment remained at Ich'on, holding its blocking position there until relieved on 8 October, and it then began the motor movement to Pusan. Both the 31st and 32d Regiments closed at Pusan on 7 October. On 8 October the 7th Division command post closed at Anyang-ni and opened at Pusan, although most of the headquarters was still on the road.

The movement to Pusan was not without incident. On two occasions enemy forces ambushed convoys in the mountains near Mun'gyong. The first ambush caught the head of the 2d Battalion, 31st Infantry, at 0200, 6 October, and inflicted nine casualties; the second ambush at 0230, 9 October, caught the division headquarters convoy in the pass three miles northwest of Mun'gyong. Enemy machine gun fire killed six men and destroyed several vehicles. Elements of the 1st Battalion, 17th Infantry, succeeded in clearing the pass area that afternoon. This battalion thereafter patrolled the pass above Mun'gyong until it was relieved on 11 October by the 27th Infantry Regiment of the 25th Division.[19]

The division artilllery was the last major unit to leave Ich'on, clearing there at 1700 on 10 October. It and the 1st Battalion, 17th Infantry, arrived at Pusan on 12 October to complete the division movement to the port. About 450 division troops had been airlifted on 11 October from Kimpo Airfield to Pusan. In addition to the 7th Division, the X Corps Medical, Engineer, Ordnance, Transportation, Quartermaster, Chemical, and Signal units moved overland to Pusan for outloading. Altogether, in seven days, approximately 1,460 tons of supplies and equipment and 13,422 troops had moved overland in division vehicles and those of the 52d Truck Battalion.[20]

The loading of the 7th Division vehicles and equipment at Pusan began on 14 October and that of the men two days later. The division was completely loaded on 17 October, the deadline set by X Corps nine days earlier. The loading of corps troops at Pusan began on 19 October.

In its order of 8 October, X Corps had required the 2d Logistical Command to furnish 15 days' supply of all classes for the 25,000 troops outloading at Pusan, 10 days of Class II and IV supplies for the troops outloading at Inch'on, and, for the entire corps, 15 days' resupply to arrive in the Wonsan area on D-day plus 8 (28 October). Except for Class I supply, the 2d Logistical Command had no reliable information as to the requirements of the various units. Providing the 15 days of supply depleted depot stocks in that area, particularly of winter clothing, operational rations, POL, and post exchange comfort items. This resulted in subsequent logistical

---

[19] 7th Inf Div WD, 6–11 Oct 50; X Corps WD, 6–11 Oct 50; X Corps POR 19, 7 Oct 50; Barr Notes, 9 Oct 50; X Corps WD, G–3 Jnl, Msg 46, 2215 9 Oct 50.

[20] X Corps WD, Oct 50, Log Sec, p. 22.

difficulties for Eighth Army. Much of the 15 days' resupply for X Corps had to be requisitioned on the Japan Logistical Command.[21]

The difficult logistical and outloading problem given the 2d Logistical Command on such short notice was worked out successfully only by the constant mutual effort and co-operation of the staffs of the logistical command and of the 7th Infantry Division. The outloading was completed in time. It was an outstanding performance. On 16 October the 7th Division advance command post opened aboard the USS *Eldorado*. But because mine fields in Wonsan Harbor now delayed sailing of the convoys for nearly two weeks, the hectic work at the port to meet the loading deadline was largely in vain.

Mines at Wonsan Harbor

After the Inch'on landing and Eighth Army's successful breakout from the Pusan Perimeter, evidence began to mount that the North Koreans were mining the coastal waters of North Korea. Three U.S. ships, the *Brush, Mansfield,* and *Magpie,* struck mines and suffered heavy damage. Although intelligence sources indicated enemy mines were being laid in coastal waters, little was known about the location and extent of these mine fields. North Korean interests certainly dictated, however, that the sea approaches to Wonsan should be mined.

In a series of conferences from 2 to 4 October, Admiral Struble and his staff decided to form the Advance Force JTF 7, which would proceed to the objective area and begin minesweeping at the earliest possible date. All minesweepers available were to be concentrated for the task. The group comprised 21 vessels, including 10 American and 8 Japanese minesweepers, and 1 South Korean vessel used as a minesweeper. Minesweeping operations at Wonsan began on 10 October. A search by helicopter over the harbor channel showed it to be heavily mined inside the 30-fathom curve. The plan to sweep this channel was canceled and another substituted—to sweep from the 100-fathom curve down the Russian Hydropac Channel passing between Yo-do and Hwangt'o-do Islands. By 12 October this channel had been swept a distance of twenty-four miles from the 100-fathom curve. Ten miles remained to the inner harbor.[22]

At this point the novel idea was advanced of exploding mines along a narrow passageway by aerial bombing which would permit the lead sweeps to pass. On 12 October thirty-nine planes from the carriers *Philippine Sea* and *Leyte* flew down the Russian channel dropping 1,000-pound bombs.

Three minesweepers, the *Pirate, Pledge,* and *Incredible,* then entered the bombed channel to resume minesweeping. Northwest of Yo-do Island the *Pirate* struck a mine at 1209; the *Pledge* hit one six minutes later. Both vessels sank. As the *Incredible*, third in line, maneuvered into safe water, enemy shore

---

[21] 7th Inf Div WD, 14 Oct 50; 2d Log Comd Monthly Act Rpt, G-4 Sec, Oct 50; Barr Notes, 14 Oct 50; Interv, author with Col A. C. Morgan, CofS 2d Log Comd, 21 Jul 51; Interv, author with Lt Col Robert J. Fuller, 2d Log Comd, G-4 Sec, 21 Jul 51.

[22] Act Rpt, JTF 7, Wonsan Opn, I-C-2 and 3, and VI-D-1.

batteries opened fire. Twelve men went down with the two sunken ships. One enlisted man died later from wounds. At least 33 others were wounded and injured in varying degrees; some sources place the number of wounded as high as 99. The *Incredible* itself rescued 27 survivors.[23]

The menace of shore batteries was removed on 17 October when ground forces of the ROK I Corps, which had already captured Wonsan, gained control of the peninsulas and islands commanding the harbor approaches.

Casualties from mines continued. On 18 October two ROK Navy vessels struck mines in the Wonsan area; one was disabled at the entrance to the harbor, and the other, a minesweeper, was sunk. The next day a Japanese minesweeper struck a mine and sank.

The risk of sending transports with troops to the beaches was still great. The presence of ground mines in the shallow water made necessary a thorough magnetic sweep of the close-in approaches to the landing beaches. Because troops of the ROK I Corps were now well past Wonsan, the military situation did not warrant an unnecessary risk in unloading the Marine units. Admiral Struble, therefore, recommended that they not be unloaded on 20 October as planned, but that D-day be deferred until the minesweeping could be completed. Admiral Joy and General MacArthur concurred.

A report from the minesweeper group on 23 October indicated that a channel free of mines had been swept to Blue-Yellow Beach, but that sweeping of the beach area itself was being continued. At a conference on board the *Missouri* the next day, Admiral Struble decided that landings could start on the 25th; actually they did not begin until the morning of the 26th. The conference on the 24th also decided that the minesweepers should clear the Wonsan inner harbor. Then they were to sweep the approaches to Hungnam to clear that port. General Almond had urged this so that logistical support could be centered there for the X Corps operations in northeast Korea. Not until 4 November did the minesweepers complete their work in the Wonsan inner harbor. Ships of the task force then stood into the harbor and pulled up alongside the dock.

Their dangerous work finished at Wonsan, the minesweepers still had to continue it in the Hungnam area. There they swept a channel 32 miles long and 1,600 yards wide, as well as an anchorage in the inner harbor. Actually, the minesweepers were busy as long as X Corps was in northeast Korea. Floating mines were common sights at this time off the east coast of Korea in the Wonsan-Hungnam area. One of the worst mine disasters occurred on 16 November, when an Army tug with a crane barge in tow struck a mine off the entrance to Wonsan Harbor and sank, with approximately thirty men lost out of forty.[24]

While the minesweeping was progress-

---

[23] *Ibid.*, pts. V, IV, and I-D-1 to I-D-3; Karig, et al., *Battle Report, The War in Korea*, pp. 317-18; Lt. Comdr. R. N. Hartmann, USNR, "Minesweepers Go In First," *Armed Forces Chemical Journal*, vol. V, No. 2 (October, 1951), pp. 19, 46.

[24] Act Rpt, TF 90, Amphib Group 1, Hungnam Redeployment, 9-25 Dec 50, Status of Sweep Operations, 7 Dec 50; 3d Inf Div Comd Rpt, CofS Jnl, entry at 1637 17 Nov 50.

ing offshore, Lt. Col. William J. McCaffrey, Deputy Chief of Staff, X Corps, on 16 October brought the X Corps Advance Command Post to Wonsan by air, flying from Kimpo Airfield. He immediately established communications with the ROK I Corps and the commander of the minesweeping operations. McCaffrey's staff set to work at once with the ROK I Corps G-2 to learn who had laid the mines in the harbor and to find the warehouses where they had been stored. This was done successfully by the ROK I Corps intelligence section. The ROK's found a villager who had worked in the mine depot. After his fears were quieted, he guided a party to a depot north of Wonsan where the mines had been stored and assembled. He also provided information enabling the investigators to take into custody one of the sampan captains who had helped plant the mines. The information gained from these sources indicated that thirty Russians had been in Wonsan until 4 October assembling the mines and supervising laying the mine fields. Working almost entirely at night, from about thirty-two small boats, North Korean crews and their supervisors had laid approximately 3,000 mines.[25]

The North Koreans and their helpers had not confined laying mines at Wonsan to the waters in the harbor. The beaches were also heavily planted with land mines. This had been expected, and as soon as the ROK I Corps had secured Wonsan it cleared the beaches of mines.

An unusual incident growing out of this work occurred the night of 16 October. At the north end of the Wonsan Harbor ROK troops had stacked about 1,000 20-pound box mines they had just lifted from the beaches. A ROK lieutenant and five enlisted men decided to have a private celebration, and, moving off about 200 yards, the lieutenant fired into the stacked mines. The mines exploded, shattering panes of glass in the provincial capital building two miles away. Unfortunately, they also killed the six ROK's.

The X Corps Ashore

The ships of Amphibious Group One and the LST's of the tractor group sailed from Inch'on late in the afternoon of 16 October. At 0800 on the 17th, the main body of the Attack Force with the 1st Marine Division aboard departed Inch'on, moved into the Yellow Sea, and headed south to round the tip of Korea. From Inch'on it was 830 miles to Wonsan by the shortest sea route.[26]

After arriving off the objective area, the flotilla carrying the 1st Marine Division steamed slowly back and forth from 19 to 25 October in the Sea of Japan just outside the Wonsan channel. The restless marines called it "Operation Yo-yo." It was a great relief to everyone afloat when twenty-one transports and

---

[25] Act Rpt, JTF 7, I-D-1 to I-D-3; Karig, *et al.*, *Battle Report, The War in Korea*, pp. 327–30; New York *Times*, October 21, 1950, dispatch from Hanson Baldwin on USS *Missouri* off Wonsan, 20 Oct 50; Ltr, Col William J. McCaffrey to Almond, 1 Dec 54, and forwarded by latter to author.

[26] X Corps WD, Diary of CG, 17 Oct 50; *Ibid.*, Notes of CofS X Corps, 17–19 Oct 50; 1st Mar Div SAR, 8 Oct–13 Dec 50, vol. I, p. 20 and vol. II, an. C, p. 4; 2d Log Comd Rpt, Oct 50, G-4 Sec, pp. 3–6; 3d Log Comd Hist Rpt, Oct 50; Karig, *et al., Battle Report, The War in Korea*, pp. 301–05.

LANDING CRAFT APPROACHING BEACH *at Wonsan on 26 October.*

fifteen LST's came into the harbor on 25 October and dropped anchor off Blue and Yellow Beaches. The X Corps began a quiet, administrative landing at 0730 on 26 October. At 1000 27 October the command post of the 1st Marine Division closed aboard the USS *Mt. McKinley* and opened in Wonsan. By the close of 28 October all combat elements of the division were ashore.

Meanwhile, the 7th Division had remained idly afloat at Pusan for ten days. Finally, on October it received orders to proceed to Iwon, 150 miles above Wonsan, and to unload there across the beaches.

Because the X Corps mission by now had been changed to advancing northward instead of westward from Wonsan, General Almond decided to land the 7th Division as close as possible to its axis of advance inland toward North Korea's northern border. This was to be the Pukch'ong-P'ungsan-Hyesanjin road to the Yalu. On receipt of the changed orders, the 17th Regimental Combat Team, which was to be first ashore, had to unload its unit equipment from its transports at Pusan and reload combat equipment on LST's, in order to be prepared to land on a possibly hostile beach. This done, seven LST's with the 17th Regimental Combat Team aboard left Pusan on 27 October and headed up the coast for Iwon. The landing proved to be without danger for the minesweepers found no mines there, and the ROK Capital Division had captured and passed through the town several days earlier. The 17th Infantry landed over the beaches at Iwon unopposed on the morning of the 29th. Except for most of its tanks, the 7th Division completed unloading there on 9 November.[27]

---

[27] 7th Div WD, 17, 29 Oct 50 and G-3 Jnl, 26-28 Oct; *Ibid.*, POR, 9 Nov 50; X Corps WD, Summ, 29 Oct 50; Barr Notes, 26, 29 Oct and 9 Nov 50.

CHAPTER XXXI

The Capture of P'yongyang

To the devil with history and principles! After all, what is the problem?
Verdy du Vernois at battle of Nachod, anecdote told by Foch

The Logistical Situation

The Eighth Army advance into North Korea had begun under great logistical difficulties and was supported only on the narrowest margin. On 10 October, the day after the attack began, General Milburn expressed himself as being disturbed by the logistical situation of I Corps. He felt that at least 3,000 tons of balanced stocks should be in the Kaesong ammunition supply points. But Col. Albert K. Stebbins, Jr., Eighth Army G-4, informed him that this could not be accomplished unless all the truck companies were diverted to that task. The unfavorable supply situation largely grew out of the fact that during the first half of October (1-17 October) unloading activities at Inch'on for Eighth Army were negligible. Practically all the port capabilities at that time were engaged in mounting out the 1st Marine Division for the Wonsan operation. Levels of some supplies for I Corps were at times reduced to one day, and only selective unloading enabled the supply sections to meet troop requirements. Most combat vehicles, such as tanks, operated in the forward zone without knowing whether they would have enough fuel at hand to continue the attack the next day.

Because it could not support any more troops north of the Han River at this time, Eighth Army had been compelled to undertake the movement north of the 38th Parallel with only one corps (I Corps), leaving IX Corps below the river. As rapidly as the logistical situation permitted, General Walker intended to move IX Corps into North Korea to help in the drive to the border. On 23 October, General Walker informed General Coulter that the ROK III Corps (5th and 11th Divisions) would relieve IX Corps in its zone as soon as practicable for this purpose, and not later than 10 November.[1]

On 19 October the army forward distributing point was at Kaesong. Hence, for most units supplies had to be trucked more than a hundred miles—a most difficult logistical situation even with good roads, and those in Korea were far from that. During this time Eighth Army used about 200 trucks daily to transport food,

---
[1] IX Corps WD, bk. I, sec. II, Oct 50; EUSAK WD, 23 Oct 50; Ltr of Instr, CofS to CG IX Corps, 23 Oct 50.

THE CAPTURE OF P'YONGYANG

gasoline, and lubricants to dumps 50 miles north of Seoul.

A pipeline, completed in October, carried aviation gasoline from Inch'on to Kimpo Airfield and helped immensely in supplying the planes with fuel.[2]

The 3d Logistical Command at Inch'on was assigned to Eighth Army on 7 October with the primary mission of providing it with logistical support in North Korea. Eighth Army in turn attached the 3d Logistical Command to the 2d Logistical Command. From Pusan the 2d Logistical Command continued of necessity to forward by rail and truck supplies for Eighth Army.

The solution to Eighth Army's logistical problems rested in the last analysis on the railroads. Airlift and long-distance trucking were emergency measures only; they could not supply the army for an offensive operation several hundreds of miles from its railhead.

At the end of September, rail communications for Eighth Army did not extend beyond the old Pusan Perimeter. Yet the army itself was then at the Han River, 200 miles northward. Because of the resulting logistical strain, the repair of the rail line north of Waegwan was of the greatest importance.

The reconstruction of the railroad bridges over the major rivers north of Taegu constituted the greatest single problem. To rebuild these bridges Eighth Army marshaled all available bridging equipment and matériel. Engineer construction troops, aided by great numbers of Korean laborers, worked to the limit of their endurance to restore the rail lines northward. The Koreans assumed responsibility for repairing minor bridges, I Corps most of the highway bridges, and Eighth Army the rail bridges and the largest highway bridges.

The first great task was to repair the 165-foot break in the Waegwan rail bridge over the Naktong. Working fifty feet above the water, the engineers, after some preliminary work, in 7 days completed the major repairs. Rail traffic crossed the bridge on 5 October. At first all effort was concentrated on opening single track communications over the 200 miles of rail from the Naktong to the Han River. This was accomplished on 10 October, 17 days after reconstruction work started at the Naktong River bridge. It was not until 11 days later that a shoofly bridge carried rail traffic across the Han into Seoul.[3]

But even after trains crossed into Seoul they could proceed only as far as Munsan-ni on the south bank of the Imjin River. This was still 200 miles below the Eighth Army front at the Ch'ongch'on River in late October. Thus, at that time the railhead was still as many miles south of the Eighth Army front

---

[2] 3d Log Comd Hist Rpt, Oct 50; 2d Log Comd Rpt, G-4 Sec, Oct 50, pp. 3-6; EUSAK WD, G-4 Sec Rpt, 10 Oct 50; Ibid., G-3 Jnl, 15 Oct 50; Interv, author with Eberle (FEC UNC G-4, 1950), 12 Jan 54; Interv, author with Maj Gen Leven C. Allen, 15 Dec 53; ORO, *An Evaluation of Service Support in the Korean Campaign*, ORO-T-6 (FEC), 1 Mar 51, p. 8.

[3] EUSAK WD, Engr Off Rpt, 30 Sep and 15 Oct 50; Ibid., Trans Sec, 26 Oct, G-4 Staf Sec, 12 Nov, and G-1 Daily Hist Rpt, 20 Nov 50; Dept of State Pub 4051, *United Nations Command Eighth Report to the Security Council, United Nations, 16-31 October 1950*, p. 6; Col. Paschal N. Strong, "Army Engineers in Korea," *Military Engineer*, vol. 44, No. 302 (November-December, 1952), 405-10, and "Engineers in Korea—Operation Shoestring," vol. 43, No. 291 (January-February, 1951); Interv, author with Strong (Eighth Army Engr Off), 17 Sep 51.

as it had been a month earlier when the front was in the Seoul area and the railhead was at Waegwan. At Munsan-ni the supplies were unloaded, trucked across the Imjin, and reloaded on trains on the north side. Meanwhile, Engineer troops were at work repairing the Imjin River rail bridge. The water span was 1,600 feet long, with a length of several thousand feet of earth fill required in its approaches. As a generalization, it may be said that the railhead lagged 200 miles behind the Eighth Army front in October 1950.

The daily "must" trains from Pusan at this time were (1) a train of 9 cars to Taejon for the 25th Division, (2) a ration train of 20 cars (200,000 rations) to Yongdungp'o, (3) 2 ammunition trains of 20 cars each, (4) 1 hospital train, (5) 1 POL train of 30 cars, and (6) 1 train of 20 cars every other day in support of ROK troops based in the Seoul area.[4]

Repair of the major highway bridges presented a problem just as pressing as repair of the rail bridges. In some respects it was an even more immediate problem because, in general, the highway bridges could be repaired more quickly, and they were the first used to keep supplies moving forward to the troops. The 207-foot span break in the Naktong River highway bridge at Waegwan was closed with pile bents and a 100-foot triple single-panel Bailey bridge. The first traffic crossed the repaired bridge on 30 September. To provide a vehicular bridge across the Han River at Seoul quickly, the FEAF Combat Cargo Command, using seventy C-119 flights, flew in a ponton bridge from Japan. This 50-ton floating bridge was 740 feet long. On 30 September, 3,034 vehicles crossed it, and thereafter traffic passed over it day and night. A second bridge was completed across the Han on 7 October. The next afternoon two-way traffic resumed across the river.

At every turn in the operations in North Korea during October, Eighth Army's effort was limited by an adverse logistical situation. And it must be borne in mind that Eighth Army's troops had almost reached the North Korean capital of P'yongyang before it could get any supplies through the port of Inch'on, where facilities were still devoted exclusively to outloading the X Corps.

Sariwon Scramble

With action in the Kumch'on Pocket ended, in the first phase of Eighth Army's drive into North Korea, the 2d Battalion, 7th Cavalry, marched from Hanp'o-ri on Namch'onjom. *(Map 19)* Air strikes on that town at 0700, 15 October, preceded the attack. The 2d Battalion then launched its assault, supported by artillery, against fiercely defending North Koreans. After hard fighting the 2d Battalion overcame the enemy force and entered Namch'onjom at noon, losing ten men killed and thirty wounded in the battle. North Korean prisoners said that strafing attacks on Namch'onjom during the morning had destroyed the *19th Division* command post and killed the division chief of staff.[5]

---

[4] EUSAK WD, G-3 Jnl, 15 Oct 50 and Surgeon's Rpt, 12-13 Oct 50.

[5] 7th Cav Regt Opn Ord 28, 141015 Oct 50; 5th Cav Regt WD, 15 Oct 50; 1st Cav Div WD, 14-16 Oct 50; 7th Cav Regt WD, 15-16 Oct 50; EUSAK WD, G-3 Jnl, 1130 15 Oct 50; Webel, MS review comments, 13 Apr 54; Ltr, Harris to author, 7 Apr 54; Crombez, MS review comments, 12 Jan 56; Interv, author with Crombez, 12 Jan 56.

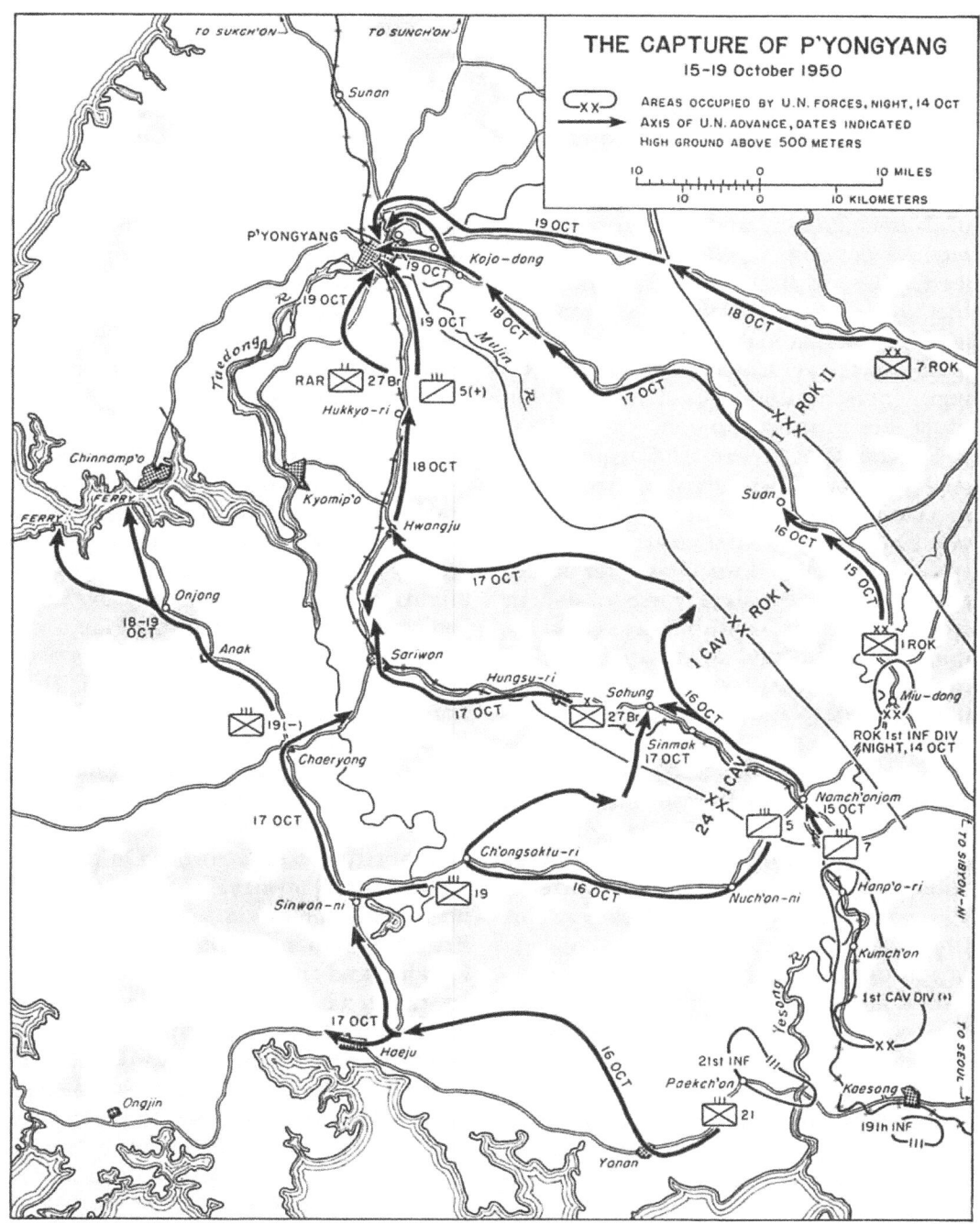

Torrential rains now turned the dusty roads into seas of mud, and maneuvers planned to put the 5th Cavalry in front of the retreating enemy came to naught.

On 16 October, Colonel Lynch's 3d Battalion, 7th Cavalry, led the attack out of Namch'onjom, and by noon it had secured Sohung, seventeen miles northwest. The 1st Battalion passed through the town, turned north on a secondary road, and prepared to advance on Hwangju the next day. Colonel Harris and the regimental headquarters arrived at Sohung late in the afternoon.

On the right of the 1st Cavalry Division the ROK 1st Division had made spectacular progress. On the 13th it entered Sibyon-ni, a vital crossroads northeast of Kaesong. Two days later it engaged a regiment-sized force of North Koreans, which was supported by six tanks and artillery, in heavy battle in the vicinity of Miu-dong, twelve miles northeast of Namch'onjom. Air strikes helped the ROK's. With his men following the high ground and his tanks on the road, Paik moved ahead. His division fought another battle the next day, 16 October, after which its leading elements entered Suan, forty air miles southeast of P'yongyang. General Paik said at this time that his tactics were "no stop." It began to look as if his division, the infantry afoot and traveling over secondary roads, was going to beat the American motorized columns to P'yongyang.[6]

On 15 October General Milburn reflected General Walker's impatience with what Walker thought was a slow advance. Milburn ordered the 24th Division to move into attack position on the left (west) of the 1st Cavalry Division and to seize Sariwon from the south, and then attack north toward the North Korean capital. On the same day General Gay ordered the 27th British Commonwealth Brigade to assemble behind the 7th Cavalry Regiment and be prepared to pass through it and seize Sariwon. Thus the stage was set for a continuation of the I Corps drive for P'yongyang. General Gay has said of that period, "The situation was tense, everybody was tired and nervous."[7]

Colonel Stephen's 21st Infantry of the 24th Division met just enough opposition as it moved from Paekch'on toward Haeju to prevent the infantry from mounting the trucks and rolling along rapidly as a motorized column. Its tank-infantry teams on 17 October overcame 300 North Koreans defending Haeju and secured the town that afternoon.[8]

The 19th Regiment of the 24th Division, meanwhile, trailed the 5th Cavalry Regiment. Both of them turned westward off the main highway at Namch'onjom. The 19th Infantry was to continue westward beyond Nuch'on-ni and then turn north toward Sariwon. On the 16th a bad traffic jam developed on the road up to Namch'onjom where the 27th British Commonwealth Brigade, the 5th Cavalry, and the 19th Regiment were all on the road. For long periods the vehicles moved slowly, bumper to bumper. From Namch'onjom westward, the 19th Infantry, behind the 5th Cavalry Regiment, was powerless to accelerate its pace although General Church had ordered it

---

[6] EUSAK WD, POR 279, 13 Oct and POR 289, 16 Oct 50; *Ibid.*, G–3 Jnl, 1130 15 Oct 50.

[7] Ltr, Gay to author, 23 Jan 54; I Corps Opn Dir 12, 151000 Oct 50; 24th Div WD, 15 Oct 50; Linklater, *Our Men in Korea*, p. 22.

[8] 24th Div WD, 16–19 Oct 50; EUSAK WD, G–3 Sec, 17 Oct 50.

to do so. Word came at this time that General Milburn had told Generals Gay and Church that whichever division—the 1st Cavalry or the 24th Infantry—reached Sariwon first would thereby win the right to lead the corps attack on into P'yongyang. The 24th Division was handicapped in this race for Sariwon, as it had a roundabout, longer route over inferior roads and poorer supply routes.[9]

A dominant characteristic of all units in the advance at this time was the strong rivalry prevailing between divisions, and even between units within a division, to gain the most ground and be the first to reach the North Korean capital. Flare-ups between units were frequent and nerves were taut.

One such flare-up occurred before dawn of 17 October. On the preceding afternoon two battalions and the regimental headquarters of the 7th Cavalry reached Sohung. The 3d Battalion held the town and together with F Company established roadblocks there. The 27th British Commonwealth Brigade was to pass through it the next morning in attack along the main highway to Sariwon. Holding a roadblock south of Sohung was Capt. Arthur H. Truxes, Jr., with F Company. Colonel Harris in posting his roadblock forces gave them orders to shoot at anything moving in front of the perimeter during the hours of darkness. He says he had no information that the 5th Cavalry was making a night approach toward his position. Captain Webel, S-3 of the 7th Cavalry Regiment, says that he told the 5th Cavalry liaison officer with the regiment of the roadblock forces and their orders to shoot, and asked him to return to the 5th Cavalry and inform it of the situation. This officer did not do that, however, but stayed in the 7th Cavalry command post overnight. The leading elements of the 1st Battalion, 5th Cavalry Regiment, approached the 7th Cavalry outpost one mile south of Sohung at 0300 the morning of 17 October, and a fire fight broke out between them, each thinking the other an enemy force. Before the mistake could be corrected, 7th Cavalry fire wounded seven men of the 5th Cavalry.[10]

On 17 October, with the 1st Battalion in the lead, the 7th Cavalry Regiment followed the secondary "cow path" road north from Sohung in a circuitous route toward Hwangju where it would strike the main P'yongyang highway north of Sariwon. The 27th British Commonwealth Brigade passed through the lines of the 7th Cavalry that morning at Sohung and took up the advance along the main highway toward Sariwon.

Sariwon lay some thirty miles up the highway almost due west from Sohung. At Sariwon the highway and railroad debouched from the mountains, turned north and ran through the coastal plain

---

[9] 24th Div WD, 16 Oct 50; 1st Cav Div WD, 16 Oct 50; 7th Cav Regt WD, 16 Oct 50; Crombez, MS review comments, 12 Jan 56; Ltr, Crombez to author, 12 Oct 54; Interv, author with Crombez, 12 Jan 56.

[10] 5th Cav Regt Unit Jnl, msg 181, 0630 17 Oct 50; 5th Cav Regt WD, 16–17 Oct 50; Ltrs, Harris to author, 23 Dec 53 and 7 Apr 54; Gay, MS review comments for author, 13 Mar 54; Ltr, Crombez to author, 12 Oct 54; Interv, author with Crombez, 12 Jan 56; Crombez, MS review comments, 12 Jan 56; Interv, author with Maj Gen Frank A. Allen, Jr., 28 Jan 54; Webel, MS review comments, 15 Nov 57. This episode is confused and the principals do not agree on all details. Captain Truxes' account of this incident was unobtainable as he was killed in action when the Chinese entered the war.

to P'yongyang, thirty-five miles away. Only occasional low hills lay across the road between Sariwon and P'yongyang. It was generally expected that the North Koreans would make their stand for the defense of P'yongyang, short of the city itself, on the heights before Sariwon.

A platoon of Maj. David Wilson's A Company of the Argyll 1st Battalion, mounted on American Sherman tanks, formed the point as the Argylls led the attack. Brig. Gen. Frank A. Allen, Jr., Assistant Division Commander, 1st Cavalry Division, accompanied the Argylls. Groups of haggard and hungry North Korean soldiers stood along the roadside waiting for a chance to surrender, and Russian-made trucks, their gas tanks empty, stood abandoned. Four miles short of Sariwon, on the hills guarding the approach to the town, it looked for a while as if the anticipated big battle had started. Enemy rifle fire suddenly burst on the column from a hillside apple orchard, 200 yards away. The column stopped and the men sought cover.

Behind the lead tanks, General Allen jumped from his jeep, stamped along the road, waved a map and shouted, "They're in that orchard, rake 'em, blast them out of there!" The general's aide, 1st Lt. John T. Hodes, climbed on one of the tanks and trained his glasses on the orchard to give fire direction. The pilot of a spotter plane above the ridge dipped his wings to indicate the presence of the enemy in force. A few North Koreans started running from the orchard when the tanks began firing into it. Suddenly, a mass of North Koreans broke from the orchard, rushed for the ridge line, and vanished over the top. Wilson's A Company of the Argylls moved on the orchard and swept it clean of remaining enemy troops. They killed about 40 and captured others in this brief action. The fleeing North Koreans left behind ten machine guns and, in the pass, they abandoned a battery of antitank guns. The British now entered Sariwon, a large town, which they found to be badly damaged by bombing. Their loss thus far for the day was 1 man killed and 3 wounded.[11]

About 1700 in the afternoon the Australian 3d Battalion passed through the Argylls in the town and advanced five miles north of it toward Hwangju. There the Australians went into a perimeter blocking position in front of a range of hills strongly held by the enemy, and prepared to attack in the morning.

Now began a succession of weird events in what proved to be a chaotic night in Sariwon. A British reconnaissance group south of the town encountered a truckload of North Korean soldiers driving north. The North Koreans shot their way through and continued into the town, but, finding the northern exit closed, they turned back and met the reconnaissance group again. In this second encounter, the reconnaissance party killed about twenty of the enemy troops.

A little later, Lt. Col. Leslie Nielson, commanding officer of the Argyll 1st Battalion, driving in the gloom near the southern end of Sariwon, was suddenly amazed to see coming toward him on either side of the road a double file of

---

[11] Maj Gen B. A. Coad, "The Land Campaign in Korea," *op. cit.;* Linklater, *Our Men in Korea,* pp. 22–23; Bartlett, *With the Australians in Korea,* pp. 27–28; Ltr, Gay to author, 23 Jan 54; 1st Cav Div WD, 17 Oct 50; Charles and Eugene Jones, *The Face of War,* pp. 150–51; New York *Herald Tribune,* October 17, 1950.

North Korean soldiers. The leading soldiers fired at him but missed. Nielson shouted to his driver, "Put your foot on it!" The driver did, and raced four miles through the marching North Koreans. Clearing the last of them, Nielson and his driver took to the hills and stayed there until morning. This enemy force, fleeing in front of the 19th Infantry, 24th Division, and approaching Sariwon from the south, did not know the town had already fallen to U.N. units.

There were many times during that wild night in Sariwon when U.N. soldiers thought the North Koreans were South Koreans coming up from the south with the 24th Division, and the North Koreans thought the British were Russians. There were several instances of mutual congratulations and passing around of cigarettes. One group of North Koreans greeted a platoon of Argylls with shouts of "Comrade!" and, rushing forward in the dim light, slapped the Scots on the back, offered cigarettes, and gave them the red stars from their caps as souvenirs. The ensuing fight was at very close quarters.

Lt. Robin D. Fairrey, the Argylls' mortar officer, walked around a corner into a group of North Koreans. Maintaining his composure, he said to them, "Rusky, Rusky," and after receiving several pats on the back, turned another corner and got away.

During this scrambled night at Sariwon about 150 North Koreans were killed; strangely enough, the British lost only one soldier. Most of the North Koreans passed through the town. North of it the Australian 3d Battalion reaped a harvest, capturing 1,982 North Korean soldiers at its roadblock. Maj. I. B. Ferguson played a leading role in capturing this large number of enemy troops. When the first of them came up to the Australian outpost a night battle seemed imminent. Ferguson mounted a tank and called out in the gloom for the North Koreans to surrender, telling them they were surrounded. After some hesitation, the leading enemy unit dropped its arms and surrendered, and most of the others followed its example.[12]

During the day, while the 27th British Commonwealth Brigade advanced on Sariwon along the main highway, the 7th Cavalry Regiment, with Colonel Clainos' 1st Battalion in the lead, hurried along the poor secondary roads through the hills north of it. This column was about three miles from Hwangju and the main highway above Sariwon when at 1600 in the afternoon it received a message General Gay dropped from a light plane. The message said that the roads out of Sariwon were crowded with hundreds of North Korean soldiers, and it directed Colonel Clainos to have one battalion of the 7th Cavalry turn south at Hwangju on the main highway to meet the British and help trap the large numbers of enemy soldiers in the Sariwon area, while another battalion turned right and held the town of Hwangju. Clainos and the two battalion commanders agreed that the 1st Battalion would turn to meet the British and the 2d Battalion would hold Hwangju.[13]

Soon after turning south on the Sariwon-P'yongyang highway the leading

---

[12] Coad, "The Land Campaign in Korea," *op. cit.;* Linklater, *Our Men in Korea;* 1st Cav Div WD, 17–18 Oct 50; Bartlett, *With the Australians in Korea,* p. 29; New York *Herald Tribune*, October 20, 1950.

[13] Ltrs, Gay to author, 23 Jan and 13 Mar 54; Clainos, MS review comments, 24 May 54.

elements of the 1st Battalion captured an enemy cavalry detachment and thirty-seven horses.

A little later the battalion came under fire from the enemy on the hill barrier ahead and separating it from the Australians. The battalion's motorized point had a short skirmish with an enemy group during which its South Korean interpreter, although wounded, tried and indeed succeeded in reaching the North Korean forward position. He told the North Koreans that the column they were fighting was Russian. The enemy platoon thereupon came up to the 7th Cavalry's point, which Colonel Clainos had just joined. Clainos turned the enemy group over to a squad leader who proceeded to disarm it. Finding that they had been tricked, some of the enemy tried to resist. This ended when the squad leader knocked one of the North Koreans into a ditch.

The enemy platoon's surrender took place in clear daylight and was observed by hundreds of North Korean soldiers in the nearby hills. Almost immediately, enemy soldiers from the eastern side of the position began pouring in to surrender. On the western side, however, small arms fire continued until dark when many there also came out to surrender. Altogether, more than 1,700 North Korean soldiers and thirteen female nurses surrendered to the 1st Battalion that evening.

Colonel Clainos had established radio communication with the Australians about 1800. At 2230, he radioed Colonel Green of the Australian battalion that, with vehicle lights on, he was coming through the pass with his battalion and prisoners. An hour before midnight the 1st Battalion, 7th Cavalry, reached the Australian perimeter. There, Colonel Clainos overheard one Australian soldier saying to another, "Now what do you make of this? Here we are all set for a coordinated attack in the morning, and the bloody Yanks come in at midnight from the north, with their lights burning, and bringing the whole damned North Korean Army as prisoners." [14]

Into P'yongyang

It had become clear by the time the U.N. troops reached Sariwon that the remaining North Korean forces could not attempt a strong defense of P'yongyang without incurring total destruction or capture. The North Koreans by this time not only had to contend with the U.S. I Corps, approaching the capital city along the main Seoul axis from the south, but also the enveloping movements of the ROK Army forces from the southeast and east. Some of these forces, if they continued their rapid advance for a few days more, would almost certainly cut on the north the highways and exits from the doomed city. P'yongyang would then be surrounded and any forces retained in and around the city for its defense would face either destruction or surrender.

The flanking operation originally conceived by General MacArthur for the X Corps after it had landed on the east coast at Wonsan had, in fact, been carried out by ROK Army units under Eighth Army control before a single soldier of X Corps landed in the east. By

---

[14] Clainos, MS review comments for author, 24 May 54; Coad, "The Land Campaign in Korea," *op. cit.*; Linklater, *Our Men in Korea*; 7th Cav Regt WD, 17 Oct 50; 1st Cav Div WD, 17 Oct 50; Ltrs, Gay to author, 23 Jan and 13 Mar 54.

THE CAPTURE OF P'YONGYANG

evening of 17 October four ROK divisions were racing each other, as well as the American and British units of the U.S. I Corps, to be first in reaching P'yongyang. The ROK 1st Division, only fifteen miles away to the southeast, was closest of all U.N. units to the city. On its right flank, the ROK 7th Division was swinging toward P'yongyang from the east. Still farther east the ROK 8th Division had almost reached Yangdok in the central mountains where it would turn west on the P'yongyang-Wonsan lateral road. And, finally, the ROK 6th Division was just short of Yangdok on this road, fifty air miles east of P'yongyang, after having turned west on 15 October from Wonsan on the coast, which it had reached by the road from Hwach'on. Thus, the U.S. I Corps was nearing P'yongyang from the south and southeast, the ROK 7th Division from the southeast, and the ROK 8th and 6th Divisions from the northeast. With approximately seven U.N. divisions converging on P'yongyang, obviously the North Korean Army in its state of depletion, disorganization, and demoralization could not hold the city.[15]

The Eighth Army G–2 estimated on 17 October that less than 8,000 effectives of the N.K. *32d* and *17th Divisions* were available for defense of P'yongyang. The estimate concluded that the enemy would undertake a token defense of the city while the main force withdrew northward across the Ch'ongch'on River for further operations.[16]

The 1st Cavalry Division had won the honor of leading the attack into P'yongyang when the British 27th Brigade, attached to it, beat the 24th Division into Sariwon. Leading elements of the 19th Infantry Regiment, 24th Division, were still several miles south of Sariwon when orders came at 1700 on 17 October to stop and hold up the attack because U.N. troops were already in the town. Morale in the 1st Cavalry Division was high. Most of the soldiers heard and passed on a rumor that the city was their final objective in the war, and once it was taken the American troops would leave Korea. Most of them expected to eat Thanksgiving Day dinner in Japan.[17]

Since the 7th Cavalry Regiment was the unit farthest north, General Gay ordered it to resume the advance on P'yongyang at daylight 18 October. The 3d Battalion at Hwangju became the assault battalion even though its men were tired from their long night movement to the town. At daylight on the 18th the battalion crossed the ford in Hwangju and began the advance. Resistance was light until the leading elements of the battalion arrived in front of the high ground south of Hukkyo-ri, halfway to P'yongyang. There enemy high velocity gun and heavy 120-mm. mortar fire struck the column. Captain Webel, the regimental S–3, estimated that a reinforced battalion of about 800 men held the prepared enemy defensive positions.

Twenty tanks of C Company, 70th Tank Battalion supported the battalion, but they had to contend with fire from three or four dug-in enemy tanks and a mined roadway. In the midst of the fighting, enemy small arms fire shot down an F–51 fighter plane. General Milburn, the corps commander, watched the ac-

---

[15] See EUSAK WD and POR's, 12–17 Oct 50, for movements and positions of ROK units.

[16] EUSAK PIR's 95, 15 Oct, and 97, 17 Oct 50.

[17] 1st Cav Div WD, 18 Oct 50; Interv, author with Crombez, 12 Jan 56; 24th Division WD, 17 Oct 50.

TANK-SUPPORTED CONVOY *winds through the safety channel of a mined area en route to P'yongyang.*

tion from an apple orchard at the side of the road, and about midafternoon General Gay came up and joined him. Dissatisfied with the progress of the attack, Gay ordered the regimental commander, Col. James K. Woolnough, who had temporarily replaced Colonel Harris, to start the other two battalions on flank movements against the enemy-held ridge. Captain Webel protested to General Gay that the enemy position was all but taken and that commitment of the other two battalions was unnecessary. But Gay let the order stand when he learned from Woolnough that the latter had already started to implement it. The two battalions upon coming up moved off toward the enemy flanks in what proved to be a nightlong movement. The next morning they found the enemy positions abandoned.

After giving the order on the 18th for a full regimental attack on the Hukkyo-ri position, General Gay informed Colonel Woolnough that the 5th Cavalry Regiment would pass through the 7th Cavalry the next morning and take up the attack on P'yongyang. He then went back and found Colonel Crombez and gave him the order. The 5th Cavalry Regiment was still strung out on the mountainous secondary road it had been traveling behind the 7th Cavalry from Sohung to Hwangju. Crombez did not have the last battalion in bivouac until 2300 that night.[18]

At 0500 on 19 October Lt. Col. Paul Clifford's 2d Battalion, 5th Cavalry Regiment, led north out of Hwangju. When it arrived at the 7th Cavalry lines at Hukkyo-ri those troops had just repulsed an enemy counterattack. At this point three enemy tanks rumbled up. A 5th Cavalry bazooka team led by a young Italo-American boy knocked out these tanks. Questioned about the exploit a little later, the boy explained, "Me and my two buddies were sitting over there behind that rock. These tanks came up toward us and stopped right out there on the road. They raised their turrets and started talking to each other. One of my buddies said, 'Christ, them ain't GI's, them are Gooks,' and I said, 'Let's shoot the S.O.B.'s' and that is what we did."[19]

---

[18] Webel, MS review comments, 13 Apr 54; Interv, author with Lynch, 9 Jun 54 (Lynch commanded the 3d Bn at Hukkyo-ri); Interv, author with Crombez, 28 Jun 55; Ltr, Harris to author, 8 Dec 53; Ltrs, Gay to author, 23 Jan and 19 Apr 54; Interv, author with Clainos, 30 Apr 54; 1st Cav Div WD, 17–18 Oct 50.

[19] Ltr, Gay to author, 23 Jan 54; Ltr, Capt James H. Bell (CO F Co, 5th Cav Regt Oct 50) to author, 11 Apr 56; Interv, author with Crombez, 28 Jun 55; 5th Cav Div Regt WD, 19 Oct 50.

The author has been unable to identify this boy, who reportedly was killed later.

THE CAPTURE OF P'YONGYANG

F Company, led by 1st Lt. James H. Bell, reinforced with five tanks, a platoon of engineers, and a section of heavy machine guns, now passed through the 7th Cavalry and led the 5th Cavalry Regiment toward P'yongyang. Just as Bell was passing the first of the burning enemy tanks a friendly plane swooped down and rocketed it. The concussion almost made him a casualty.

Flights of jet planes coursed overhead in advance of F Company and, on at least two occasions, they helped supporting artillery reduce enemy forces that threatened to delay its advance. The regimental commander, Colonel Crombez, and a small command group followed immediately behind F Company most of the morning and pushed it hard.

At 1102, Lieutenant Bell's F Company reached the 20-yard-wide Mujin-ch'on River, a tributary of the Taedong at the southern edge of P'yongyang. North Korean troops from behind a 20-foot embankment on the north side defended the highway bridge over it with three antitank guns. Bell's troops were delayed there for about half an hour until their mortar fire caused the North Korean gun crews to abandon the antitank guns. Bell's F Company then crossed the Mujin-ch'on and entered the southwestern edge of P'yongyang just after 1100.[20]

P'yongyang is the oldest city in Korea, and for a long time was its capital.

BURNING ENEMY TANK *knocked out by 5th Cavalry bazooka team at Hukkyo-ri, 19 October.*

Its population at the outbreak of the war was approximately 500,000. The city is situated astride the Taedong River, one of the larger streams of Korea, forty miles from where it empties into the Yellow Sea. The main part of the city with the important public buildings lay on the north side of the river. A large, relatively new industrial suburb sprawled opposite on the south side. Two railroad bridges of the Pusan-Seoul-Mukden railroad cross the Taedong River here. Upstream from them about two miles was the main highway bridge. The Taedong at P'yongyang averages about 400–500 yards in width. As the current is swift, it constitutes a major military obstacle to north-south movement.

Bell received orders to turn west and seize certain factory buildings, the railroad bridges, and a bridgehead on the north bank of the Taedong. In about

---

[20] Ltr, Bell to author, 8 Mar 54; Ltr, Crombez to author, 12 Oct 54; Interv, author with Crombez, 28 Jun 55; 5th Cav Regt WD, 19 Oct 50; 1st Cav Div WD, 19 Oct 50; EUSAK WD, Br for CG, 19–20 Oct 50.

Bell estimates the time he entered the south edge of P'yongyang as 1330. The official records, based on an aerial observer's report, give it as 1102.

5TH CAVALRY TROOPS *at the southern edge of P'yongyang, 19 October.*

half an hour he reached the river's southern bank and found that only one span of each of the two railroad bridges (each 3-span) was intact. After a hasty examination of the eastern bridge, Bell decided that infantry could cross on one of its spans to an island in the river. Leaving some riflemen and the Engineer platoon at its southern end to guard the tanks which gave supporting fire, he led the rest of F Company across to the island and secured it by midafternoon. While F Company was crossing to the island, enemy on the north bank destroyed a section of the bridge still intact there. During the afternoon the 3d Battalion, 5th Cavalry, crossed to the island and relieved F Company, which then moved back to the airfield on the south bank.

While F Company was trying to seize the railroad bridges over the Taedong, the rest of the 2d Battalion crossed the Mujin-ch'on and turned right toward the main highway bridge which crossed the Taedong River about midway on the city waterfront. This was the only bridge still intact on 19 October when U.N. troops entered P'yongyang. When the leading elements of E and G Companies neared the bridge the North Koreans blew up the center span.

Almost simultaneously with the 1st Cavalry Division's arrival at P'yongyang the ROK 1st Division entered the city on the Sibyon-ni–P'yongyang road at a point northeast of the 1st Cavalry Division. On the night of 18 October the chances had appeared excellent for the ROK 1st Division to be first into P'yongyang. After a day of very heavy fighting in which it gained two miles, it was only eight miles away. The leading elements of the 1st Cavalry Division were about 30 miles away. But the North Koreans made a stronger fight against the ROK 1st Division than against the 1st Cavalry Division, possibly because it was closer to the city and the more immediate threat. Also, the road on which the ROK's approached P'yongyang was heavily mined with both antipersonnel and antitank mines. Paik's division fought throughout the rainy night and finally overcame an enemy strongpoint an hour or two after daybreak. Enemy emplacements and automatic fire stopped the ROK infantry again about six miles from the city near Kojo-dong. Tanks of C Company, 6th Tank Battalion, in the ensuing ROK attack enveloped the enemy positions from both flanks, destroyed self-propelled guns, and overran the North Korean entrenchments, physically crushing machine guns and enemy soldiers. It was estimated that the tanks in this action killed nearly 300 North Koreans.

According to General Paik, extensive mine fields in the street behind the overrun enemy positions delayed the tanks, but the infantry of the ROK 2d Battalion, 12th Regiment, kept moving and General Paik affirms that they arrived at the edge of the Taedong River just before 1100 and deployed along the south bank northeast of the highway bridge. Leading elements of the 2d Battalion, 5th Cavalry Regiment, arrived at the traffic circle 100 yards east of the highway bridge almost at the same time. The leading tanks of C Company, 6th Tank Battalion, were in the southern edge of the city, according to their own records, at 1245. Tanks of D Company, 6th Medium Tank Battalion, entered the city along the same approach a little later, turned north, and together with troops of the ROK 11th Regiment secured the airfield at 1440. Other ROK units earlier had secured a smaller airfield a few miles to the east.[21]

After the North Koreans blew the highway bridge across the Taedong, elements of the 2d Battalion, 5th Cavalry, continued northeast along the river searching for a ford reported to be located there. When they found it a few miles east of the city they discovered that elements of the 15th Regiment, ROK 1st Division, already had crossed the river there, and others were then in

CAPITOL BUILDING IN P'YONGYANG. *The men having coffee are members of Task Force Indianhead.*

the act of crossing into the main part of the city. Later, Colonel Crombez asked General Paik how his troops found the ford so quickly. Paik answered, "I am a native of P'yongyang. I know the fords."[22]

By dark most of the ROK 1st Division was in the main part of P'yongyang north of the Taedong River. Nor was that all. The 8th Regiment of the ROK 7th Division swung into north P'yongyang from the east and was in possession of Kim Il Sung University in the northern part of the city by 1700.[23]

The next day, 20 October, the ROK

---

[21] 6th Med Tk Bn WD, 19 Oct 50; EUSAK PIR 99, 19 Oct 50; EUSAK WD, 19 Oct 50, and G-3 Jnl, 1300-1600 19 Oct 50; 5th Cav Regt WD, 19 Oct 50; 10th AAA Group WD, 19-20 Oct 50; 1st Cav Div WD, 19 Oct 50; I Corps WD, Oct 50, p. 18; Gen Paik Sun Yup (CofS ROKA), MS review comments, 11 Jul 58.

[22] Ltr, Bell to author, 11 Apr 56; Interv, author with Crombez, 12 Jan 56.

[23] Interv, author with Schwarze (KMAG adviser with ROK 7th Div Oct 50), 3 Feb 54; 5th Cav Regt WD, 19-20 Oct 50; EUSAK WD, Br for CG, 190001-200800 Oct 50; EUSAK POR 299, 20 Oct 50.

1st Division advanced into the heart of the city and took the strongly fortified administrative center with ease. The enemy troops posted there were too demoralized to fight and they abandoned both guns and entrenchments. At 1000 the ROK 1st Division reported the entire city had been secured, including the City Hall, the Provincial Government offices, and the N.K. People's Committee offices. The ROK 8th Regiment aided the 1st Division by sweeping through the northwest section of the city and clearing it of the enemy. As soon as Engineer assault boats could be brought up, the 3d Battalion, 5th Cavalry, began crossing to the north side of the Taedong, and by noon that regiment, with the 3d Battalion, 7th Cavalry, attached to it, was across the river. Bells in Christian churches pealed a welcome. The people appeared friendly and there were no disturbances.[24]

When the operations of Eighth Army had progressed to the point where it appeared probable that P'yongyang would fall in the near future, the army on 16 October had organized a special task force known as Task Force Indianhead. Its name derived from the shoulder patch of the 2d Infantry Division. This task force was to enter the North Korean capital with the advance units of the 1st Cavalry Division. Its mission was to secure and protect specially selected government buildings and foreign compounds until they could be searched for enemy intelligence materials. Lt. Col. Ralph L. Foster, Assistant Chief of Staff for G-2, 2d Division, commanded the task force, which was built around K Company, 38th Infantry Regiment, and six tanks of C Company, 72d Medium Tank Battalion, and included Engineer demolition troops, automatic weapons vehicles of the 82d AAA Battalion, and counterintelligence troops. The task force secured most of its assigned objectives in P'yongyang on 20 October. It obtained a considerable amount of intelligence material, both military and political, which was turned over to a special team from GHQ, Far East Command, and transported by air to Tokyo.[25]

Twenty American prisoners escaped or were rescued from the North Koreans in the capture of P'yongyang. Most of the large number of prisoners held there, however, had been taken northward several days before the U.N. forces entered the city.

General Gay established his 1st Cavalry Division headquarters in the granite buildings of the North Korean Military Academy ten miles southwest of P'yongyang on the Chinnamp'o road. He was responsible for the internal security and order of P'yongyang after its capture. On 23 October he appointed Colonel Crombez civil assistance officer in the city because of the latter's special knowledge of the country and its people. Colonel Johnson, a veteran of Bataan, replaced Crombez in command of the 5th Cavalry Regiment until 14 December.

---

[24] EUSAK WD, G-3 Jnl, 1200 20 Oct 50; *Ibid.*, Br for CG, 20-21 Oct 50; I Corps WD, 20 Oct 50; Ltr, Crombez to author, 12 Oct 54.

[25] Ltrs, Foster to author, 11 and 21 May 54; Ltr, Gay to author, 13 Feb 54; EUSAK POR 292, 17 Oct 50; EUSAK WD, Br for CG, 190001-200800 Oct 50; 2d Div WD, Summ, 1 Sep-31 Oct 50, vol. II, pp. 47-49.

THE CAPTURE OF P'YONGYANG

The 5th Cavalry Regiment was disposed in the southern outskirts of P'yongyang, the 8th Cavalry Regiment in the northern outskirts, and the 7th Cavalry Regiment at Chinnamp'o, P'yongyang's port. After the fall of P'yongyang, Colonel Harris had led the 7th Cavalry Regiment in a forced night movement from the city thirty-five miles southwest to Chinnamp'o. The regiment entered the port city in the dead of night, 22 October.

On 24 October, General Walker took personal command of his advance Eighth Army headquarters, established two days earlier by Colonel Collier of his staff, in the attractive and undamaged gray brick building in P'yongyang which had been the headquarters of Premier Kim Il Sung.[26]

On 21 October a touching and revealing ceremony occurred on the P'yongyang airfield. General MacArthur had flown in from Tokyo to confer briefly with Generals Walker and Stratemeyer after the fall of the North Korean capital. In the course of his brief visit he reviewed F Company, 5th Cavalry Regiment, which had been the first American unit to enter P'yongyang. He asked all men in the company who had landed with it in Korea ninety-six days earlier, when it numbered nearly 200 men, to step forward. Only five men stepped forward; three of them had been wounded.[27]

KIM IL SUNG'S DESK. *Colonel Foster occupies the North Korean Premier's office in P'yongyang. Note portrait of Stalin.*

---

[26] 5th Cav Regt WD, 22-23 Oct 50; GHQ UNC press release, 25 Oct 50. Ltr, Harris to author, 7 Apr 54; EUSAK WD, Br for CG, 22 Oct 50; 7th Cav Regt WD, 22-23 Oct 50.

[27] Ltr, Gay to author, 23 Jan 54; Crombez, MS review comments, 28 Jun 55.

CHAPTER XXXII

Up to the Ch'ongch'on

> It is only common sense to say that we cannot hope to build up a true doctrine of war except from true lessons, and the lessons cannot be true unless based on true facts, and the facts cannot be true unless we probe for them in a purely scientific spirit.
> Basil Henry LIDDELL HART, *The Ghost of Napoleon*

Airborne Attack: Sukch'on and Sunch'on

When Eighth Army crossed the 38th Parallel and drove on P'yongyang, General MacArthur held the 187th Airborne Regiment, commanded by Col. Frank S. Bowen, Jr., in GHQ reserve at Kimpo Airfield near Seoul. He planned to employ the airborne troops in a drop north of P'yongyang in an attempt to cut off North Korean officials and enemy troops, and to rescue American prisoners of war who it was assumed would be evacuated northward when the fall of the North Korean capital seemed imminent.

After changing the date a time or two, General MacArthur set the airdrop for the morning of 20 October. There were to be two drop zones 30 air miles north of P'yongyang, the principal one at Sukch'on and the other at Sunch'on.[1] Two highways run north from P'yongyang like the sides of a narrow capital letter V, each roughly paralleling a rail line. The main highway from P'yongyang to the Yalu River and the Manchurian border at Sinuiju forms the left-hand side of the V. Sukch'on on this highway is situated in a wide valley surrounded by low hills, about 35 road miles north of P'yongyang. The right-hand road passes through rougher terrain to reach Sunch'on on the Taedong River, 17 air miles east of Sukch'on. (*Map 20*)

The airborne regiment turned out in a heavy rain for reveille at 0230 in the after-midnight darkness of 20 October. The men ate breakfast and then went to the airfield where they waited in the downpour for the weather to improve. Shortly before noon the sky began to clear. The regiment loaded into 113 planes, C-119's and C-47's of the 314th and 21st Troop Carrier Squadrons based in Japan. The planes were crowded—a typical C-119 carried 46 men in 2 sticks of 23 men each, 15 monorail bundles, and 4 door bundles. Each man had a main parachute, a .45-caliber pistol, and a carbine or M1 rifle.

The first aircraft, carrying Colonel

---
[1] 187th Abn RCT Unit Hist, pt. II, 17-19 Oct 50; I Corps WD, 20 Oct 50; EUSAK WD, 20 Oct 50.

UP TO THE CH'ONGCH'ON

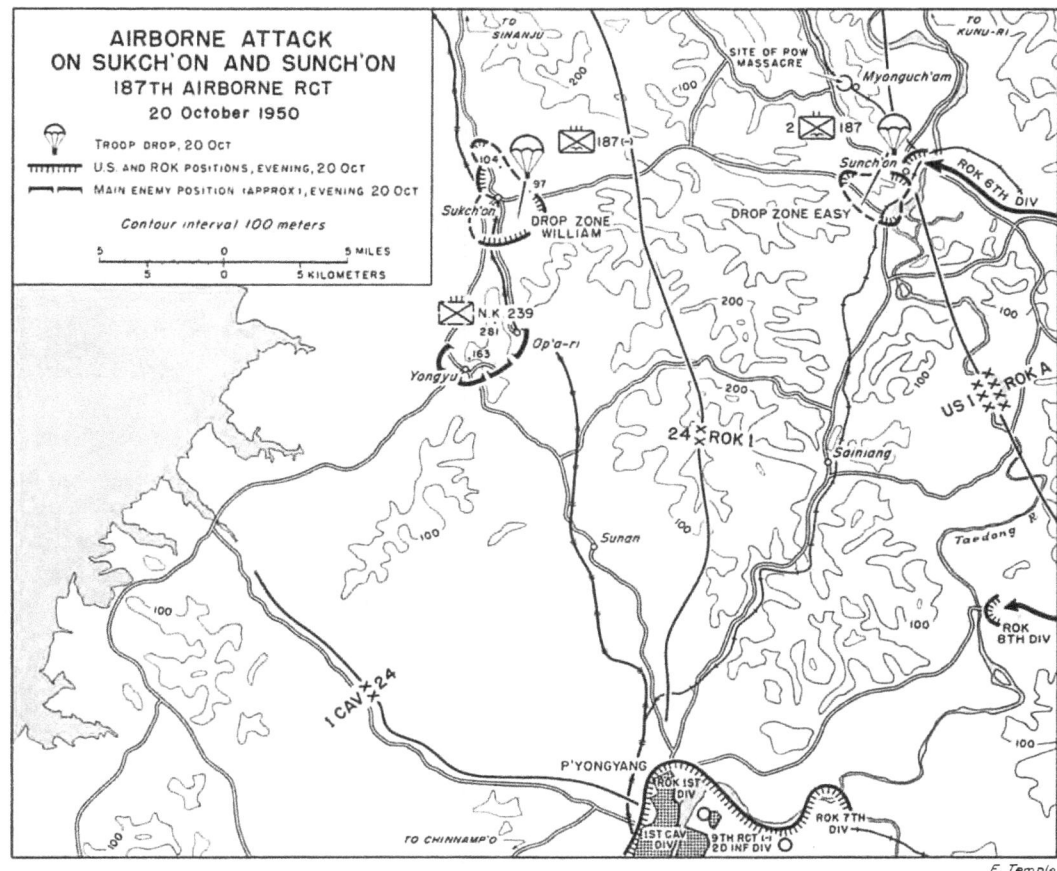

MAP 20

Bowen, was airborne at noon. When all the planes had assembled over the Han River estuary, they turned north along the west coast of Korea. This flight carried about 2,800 men. Recent intelligence had informed the airborne force that a trainload of American prisoners, traveling only at night and then slowly, was on its way north from P'yongyang. Colonel Bowen's men hoped to intercept this train and rescue the prisoners.

As the troop carriers approached the drop zone, fighter planes preceded them rocketing and strafing the ground. At approximately 1400 the first troops began dropping from the lead planes over Sukch'on. There was no enemy antiaircraft fire and only occasional sniper fire came into the drop zone. This first drop put Colonel Bowen and 1,470 men of the 1st Battalion, regimental Headquarters and Headquarters Company, and supporting engineer, medical, and service troops on the ground in Drop Zone William, southeast of Sukch'on. Twenty-five men were injured in this jump. One group landed a mile and a half east of the drop zone and lost one man killed

MASS AIRDROP NEAR SUNCH'ON

in his parachute by attacking enemy soldiers. Seventy-four tons of equipment were dropped with the men.[2]

After the troop drop came that of the heavy equipment—equipment organic to an airborne infantry regiment, including jeeps, 90-mm. towed antitank guns, 105-mm. howitzers, and a mobile radio transmission set equivalent in weight to a 2½-ton truck. Seven 105-mm. howitzers of the 674th Field Artillery Battalion and 1,125 rounds of ammunition were in the drop. Six of the howitzers were recovered in usable condition.

About 90 percent of the shells were undamaged and none exploded. This was the first time heavy equipment had been dropped in combat, and it was the first time C-119's had been used in a combat parachute operation.

The 1st Battalion, against only light resistance, seized Hill 97 east of Sukch'on, where Colonel Bowen established his command post, and Hill 104 north of the town, cleared the town of Sukch'on itself, and set up a roadblock north of it.

In the meantime, the 3d Battalion had jumped in the same zone, turned south, taken up defensive positions on low hills two miles south of the town, and established roadblocks across the

[2] 187th Abn RCT Unit Hist, pts. I and II, 20 Oct 50.

ARTILLERY AIRDROP NEAR SUKCH'ON

highway and railroad at that point. It seized its objectives by 1700, killing five enemy soldiers and capturing forty-two others without loss to itself.

In the second jump area the 2d Battalion at 1420 began parachuting onto Drop Zone Easy, two miles southwest of Sunch'on. Twenty men were injured in this jump. The battalion secured its objective by night against virtually no resistance. Two companies established roadblocks south and west of Sunch'on. A third advanced to the town and established contact there with elements of the ROK 6th Division which had reached Sunch'on from the southeast in its push toward the Ch'ongch'on River.

During this and succeeding days, a total of approximately 4,000 troops and more than 600 tons of equipment and supplies were dropped at Sukch'on and Sunch'on. Included in the equipment were 12 105-mm. howitzers, 39 jeeps, 38 ¼-ton trailers, 4 90-mm. antiaircraft guns, 4 ¾-ton trucks, and 584 tons of ammunition, gasoline, water, rations, and other supplies.

On the morning after the airdrop, the 1st Battalion, 187th Airborne Regiment gained the dominant terrain it needed directly north of Sukch'on to carry out its mission of blocking the main highway running north. Strong enemy rear guard forces held the next line of hills northward. That afternoon elements of the 1st Battalion established contact with the 2d Battalion at Sunch'on.

General MacArthur, accompanied by Generals Stratemeyer, Wright, and Whitney, had flown from Japan to watch the airdrop. After seeing the parachute troops land and assemble successfully, he flew to P'yongyang. There he commented to reporters that the airborne landing seemed to have been a complete surprise to the enemy. He estimated that 30,000 North Korean troops, perhaps half of those remaining in North Korea, were caught in the trap between the 187th Airborne Regiment on the north and the 1st Cavalry and ROK 1st Divisions at P'yongyang on the south, and that they would be destroyed or captured. He termed the airdrop an "expert performance" and said, "This closes the trap on the enemy." The next day in Tokyo MacArthur predicted that "the war is very definitely coming to an end shortly." [3]

General MacArthur's optimism was not supported by the events of succeeding days. The airborne troops had not cut off any sizable part of the North Korean forces. The main body of the enemy had already withdrawn north of Sukch'on and Sunch'on and were either north of the Ch'ongch'on River or in the act of crossing it. No important North Korean Army or government officials were cut off and killed or captured. Civilians in P'yongyang said that the principal North Korean government officials had left P'yongyang on 12 October for Manp'ojin on the Yalu. The best information indicated, however, that the North Korean Government had moved to Kanggye in the mountains twenty air miles southeast of Manp'ojin. Most of the American and South Korean prisoners had been successfully removed into the remote part of North Korea.[4]

The Enemy Blocking Force Destroyed

The most important action growing out of the airdrop occurred on 21–22 October in the zone of the 3d Battalion, 187th Regimental Combat Team, about eight miles south of Sukch'on in the vicinity of Op'a-ri. At 0900, 21 October, the 3d Battalion started south from its roadblock position toward P'yongyang in two combat teams: one (I Company) along the railroad, the other (K Company) along the highway. Following the railroad, I Company at 1300 reached Op'a-ri. There an estimated enemy battalion, employing 120-mm. mortars and 40-mm. guns, attacked it. After a battle lasting two and a half hours, the North Koreans overran two platoons and forced I Company, with ninety men missing, to withdraw to Hill 281 west of the railroad. The North Koreans did not press their advantage but withdrew to their own defensive positions on the high ground around Op'a-ri.[5]

Meanwhile, K Company, advancing south along the highway, encountered an estimated enemy battalion a mile

---

[3] *Stars and Stripes* (Pacific), October 21, 1950, p. 1, col. 6; New York *Times*, October 21, 1950 (including editorial); EUSAK WD, 22 Oct 50, Daily News Bul.

[4] GHQ FEC, History of the N.K. Army, pp. 41, 77–78; ATIS Interrog Rpts (N.K. Forces), Issue 17, p. 1, Rpt 2200, Bak Tong Hyon; *Ibid.*, Issue 19, p. 111, Rpt 2449, Jr Lt Chong Kil Hwan; EUSAK PIR's 99, 100, and 101, 19–21 Oct 50.

[5] 187th Abn RCT Unit Hist, 21 Oct 50.

north of Yongyu. After a sharp fight this enemy force withdrew south and east of the town to defensive positions on high ground, and K Company continued on into Yongyu and to Hill 163, just north of the town. Yongyu on the highway and Op'a-ri on the railroad are three miles apart and almost opposite each other.

The 3-mile gap separating the railroad and the highway here is the greatest distance between them at any point between P'yongyang and Sukch'on. Extending on a southwest to a northeast axis, and cutting across both the highway and railroad at Yongyu and Op'a-ri, is a line of high hills offering the best defensive ground between P'yongyang and the Ch'ongch'on River. Here, the N.K. *239th Regiment,* about 2,500 strong, had taken up defensive positions. This regiment had been the last force to leave P'yongyang. Its mission was to fight a delaying action against U.N. troops expected to advance north from P'yongyang. Now, suddenly, it found itself attacked by two separate forces from the rear.

At midnight the N.K. *239th Regiment* attempted to break out to the north. In its first attack a small group got into the K Company command post. In the close-quarter fight there Capt. Claude K. Josey, K Company commander, although wounded twice by an enemy burp gun, sprang on the gunner and wrested the gun from him before collapsing. The company executive officer was also wounded. Eventually, the enemy soldiers were either killed or driven off.

In two other attacks after midnight enemy soldiers forced the men at the roadblock near Hill 163 to withdraw after they had expended their ammunition. Aware of this withdrawal, the North Koreans attacked again at 0400. Then, at 0545, they ran blindly into the 3d Battalion command post and the L Company perimeter, and suffered very heavy casualties from direct and enfilading fire. In spite of these heavy losses the enemy renewed his attack, about 300 men striking L Company and 450 men assaulting Headquarters Company. At this point the airborne troops sent a radio message describing their situation and requesting help. Pfc. Richard G. Wilson, a medical aide, gave his life in heroic action in trying to reach and care for the wounded.[6]

Help was to come from close at hand as a result of a general advance northward of the U.S. I Corps. On 20 October, the day P'yongyang was secured, General Milburn had ordered the corps to continue the attack to the MacArthur Line, a line roughly thirty-five miles south of the Yalu River. The 24th Division, with the 27th British Commonwealth Brigade attached, was to lead this attack. On the right of the 24th Division three ROK divisions—the 1st, under I Corps, and the 6th and 8th under ROK II Corps, in that order eastward—were ready to join in the attack northward.[7]

---

[6] Department of the Army General Order 36, 4 June 1951, awarded the Distinguished Unit Citation to the 3d Battalion, 187th Airborne Regiment, and the 2d Section, Antitank Gun Platoon, Support Company, for this action. Department of the Army General Order 64, 2 August 1951, awarded the Medal of Honor posthumously to Pfc. Richard G. Wilson, Medical Company, 187th Airborne Regiment, for action near Op'a-ri, 21 October 1950. Eighth Army General Order 135, 12 March 1951, awarded the Distinguished Service Cross to Capt. Claude K. Josey for action near Yongyu.

[7] 24th Div WD, 20 Oct 50; EUSAK WD, 21 Oct and Br for CG, 210001–220800 Oct 50; EUSAK WD, G–3 Jnl, 0700 22 Oct 50.

At noon on 21 October, in this general Eighth Army advance, the British brigade crossed the Taedong River at P'yongyang and headed north on the main highway running toward Sukch'on, with the immediate mission of reaching the Ch'ongch'on River. Approaching Yongyu that evening, Brigadier Coad decided to halt for the night.

The British could hear the heavy night battle taking place a mile or two north of them. At first light on the 22d, two companies of the Argyll 1st Battalion advanced into Yongyu. There the Australian 3d Battalion passed through them, with Capt. A. P. Denness and his C Company in the lead riding tanks of D Company, U.S. 89th Tank Battalion. The tankers had orders not to fire because of the known proximity of the 187th Airborne troops.

Just north of Yongyu enemy rifle fire suddenly came from an orchard that spread out on both sides of the road. Captain Denness and his men jumped from the tanks and charged with fixed bayonets into the apple orchard. They went into it with a dash that brought forth admiration from all who witnessed it. One American officer present told of seeing a big, red-haired Australian jump into an enemy trench and come out later, his hands streaming blood from many cuts and his clothes slashed from head to foot. An inspection of the trench later revealed eight dead North Koreans there.

Colonel Green deployed a second company to seize high ground on the right of the road. Soon he had to send a third company to follow the second as the enemy fired on it from the rear. Then he sent his fourth company on the left of the road to follow C Company. The enemy was now using mortar as well as rifle and automatic fire. This action for the Australians was one of rifle, grenade, and bayonet. After committing all his rifle companies, Colonel Green moved his small headquarters into the orchard. There he was immediately attacked by a sizable group of North Koreans. In this fight his group killed thirty-four enemy soldiers. Among his own wounded were three men of his personal staff. One platoon of Australians crossed a rice field, kicked over stacks of straw, and shot the North Korean soldiers they found hiding in them.

In this hand-to-hand infantry fight the North Koreans lost about 270 killed and more than 200 captured; incredibly, the Australians had only approximately 7 wounded. Enemy survivors fled westward. The Middlesex 1st Battalion now passed through the Australians and, with the tanks, joined the 187th Airborne force at 1100.[8]

The 3d Battalion, 187th Airborne Regiment, reported that it had killed 805 of the enemy and captured 681 prisoners in the Yongyu battle. Caught between the airborne troops and the British 27th Brigade, the N.K. *239th Regiment* was practically destroyed at Yongyu. That afternoon the 3d Battalion returned to Sukch'on with the

---

[8] Linklater, *Our Men in Korea*, pp. 24-25; Bartlett, *With the Australians in Korea*, pp. 30-31; Barclay, *The First Commonwealth Division*, p. 23; 187th Abn RCT Unit Hist, 21-22 Oct 50; Ibid., POR 10, 21 Oct 50; Interv, author with 1st Lt Francis Nordstrom (tk plat ldr, D Co, 89th Tk Bn), 31 Aug 51; Interv, author with Maj James W. Deloach (I Corps liaison off), 28 Jul 51. Both Nordstrom and Deloach witnessed the C Company bayonet attack. GHQ FEC General Order 54, 1 November 1950, awarded the Silver Star to Lt. Col. Charles H. Green.

British following it. There the British brigade relieved the 187th Airborne Regiment in its positions.

While the Yongyu battle was in progress, the 2d Battalion, 187th Airborne Regiment, remained relatively inactive in its drop zone at Sunch'on. The ROK 6th Division performed most of the work in clearing the town and its vicinity of enemy stragglers.

The 187th Airborne Regimental Combat Team returned to P'yongyang on 23 October, traveling by the secondary road through Sunch'on. This left the main highway free for the movement of the British 27th Brigade and the 24th Division. Altogether, the 187th Airborne Regiment suffered 46 jump casualties and 65 battle casualties in the Sukch'on-Sunch'on operations. It captured 3,818 North Korean prisoners in this operation.[9]

Death in the Evening

After the airdrop a new task force, formed around the 1st Battalion, 8th Cavalry Regiment, and a company of tanks, 70th Tank Battalion, started from P'yongyang to make junction with the airborne troops at Sunch'on. Lt. Col. William M. Rodgers of the tank battalion commanded the task force. It arrived at Sunch'on at 0900 21 October, picking up on the way five American prisoners who had recently escaped their North Korean captors. At the bridge just south of Sunch'on a few enemy troops hiding in holes under it opened fire as Task Force Rodgers came up and killed two men of the 8th Cavalry. The North Koreans had remained unobserved even though some airborne troops were on the bridge.

General Gay and Brig. Gen. Frank A. Allen, Jr., from an L-5 plane had watched Task Force Rodgers successfully establish contact with the airborne troops. Upon returning to P'yongyang, General Allen climbed into his jeep and accompanied by his aide, his driver, and two war correspondents (Don Whitehead of the Associated Press and Richard Tucker of the Baltimore *Sun*), started for Sunch'on, arriving there about noon.

Allen had been in the command post of the 2d Battalion, 187th Airborne Regiment, only a short time when a Korean civilian came in and excitedly told a story of North Koreans murdering about 200 Americans the night before at a railroad tunnel northwest of the town. Allen determined to run down this story at once.

His group set out with the Korean civilian and, on the way, stopped at the ROK 6th Division command post in Sunch'on. There a ROK colonel, an interpreter, and a driver in a second jeep joined Allen and drove with him to a railroad tunnel just beyond the village of Myonguch'am, five air miles northwest of Sunch'on. They arrived there at 1500. The railroad ran along a hillside cut and entered the tunnel some distance above the dirt road the men had followed. While the rest waited on the road, the ROK colonel climbed the hillside and entered the tunnel. He came back and said he had found seven dead Americans inside. Allen and the others now climbed to the tunnel. Inside it near the far end they found the seven emaciated bodies on straw mats beside

---

[9] 187th Abn RCT Unit Hist, 23-24 Oct 50; EUSAK WD, G-3 Jnl, Msg 1945 22 Oct 50.

NORTH KOREAN ATROCITY SITE *is marked by graves of American soldiers who were shot down as they waited for their evening meal.*

the rail track. These men had either starved to death or died from disease. Some had old wounds, apparently battle wounds.

The ROK colonel had walked on through the tunnel. He reappeared at the end and called out that he could see five Americans on the ridge top. Everyone hurried outside and started down the track. A little distance beyond the tunnel, a thin, wounded American soldier staggered from the brush. He was Pfc. Valdor John. Allen placed his coat around the shivering boy, who broke into tears and protested that he was too dirty to wear it. He then stammered out, "They are over there," and pointed into the brush. Seventeen dead Americans, all shot, lay there in a gulley. John had escaped by feigning death. Allen started climbing the ridge to the Americans who could be seen on top. Whitehead, sickened by the sight he had just seen, walked off alone across the railroad track into a cornfield on the other side. There he accidentally stumbled upon a semicircle of fifteen more dead Americans. They had been shot as they sat on the ground with rice bowls in hand expecting to receive food. Whitehead turned back to report to Allen; on his way back three American survivors came from among some bushes to him. Allen brought six more Americans who had escaped down off the ridge.

These survivors told the story of what had happened. Two trains, each carrying about 150 American prisoners of war, had left P'yongyang Tuesday night, 17 October, making frequent stops to repair the tracks, and crawling north at a snail's pace. Each day five or six men died of dysentery, starvation, or exposure. Their bodies were removed from the train. A few men escaped as the train traveled north. On the afternoon of the 20th, while the parachute jump was in progress, the second of the two trains stayed in the tunnel northwest of Sunch'on to escape the air activity in the vicinity. The group of 100 prisoners of this train, crowded into open coal gondolas and boxcars, was the remnant of 370 whom the North Koreans had marched north from Seoul more than a month earlier. That evening, the prisoners had been taken from the train in three groups to receive their evening meal. They were shot down as they waited for it. The train and the North Korean guards left that night.

From this story it appeared that there was another group of murdered men yet to be found. A search revealed a fresh burial place, and, upon removal of a thin covering of earth, the men discovered 34 more bodies. Altogether there were 66 dead (exclusive of the seven found in the tunnel) and 23 survivors, some of the latter critically wounded. Two of these died during the night, leaving only 21 who survived. A ROK detachment safely convoyed the rescued Americans and the dead to P'yongyang, where C-54's carried them to Japan.[10]

The Advance Continues

Even as the airborne troops came to ground at Sukch'on the Eighth Army G-2 was preparing his estimate that the North Koreans would be incapable of making more than a token defense of the Ch'ongch'on River barrier, forty-five air miles north of P'yongyang. He predicted that the enemy withdrawal would continue on to the north along the axes of two rail and highway routes, the first bending to the right and leading northeast from Sinanju and Anju on the Ch'ongch'on through Huich'on to Kanggye deep in the rugged mountains of central North Korea, twenty-two air miles from the Yalu River; and the second, the west coastal route, bending left and running northwest from the Ch'ongch'on River to Sinuiju near the mouth of the Yalu River at the Manchurian border.[11]

The Communist radio on 21 October announced that Premier Kim Il Sung's government had established a new capital at Sinuiju, on the south bank of the Yalu and opposite the Chinese city

---

[10] Interv, author with Maj Gen Frank A. Allen, Jr., 28 Jan 54; Interv, author with Whitehead, 27 Apr 56; Memphis *Commercial Appeal*, October 23, 1950 (detailed account by Whitehead, dateline Sunch'on, Korea, 22 Oct 50); Ltr, Lt Col Harry Fleming to author, 9 Mar 54 (Fleming was KMAG adviser with ROK 7th Regt, 6th Div, and joined Allen's party at the tunnel); 187th Abn RCT Unit Rpt, 21 Oct 50; EUSAK WD, G-3 Jnl, Msg 1930 22 Oct 50; Interim Hist Rpt, War Crimes Div, JAG, cumulative to 30 Jun 53. The author has relied principally on interviews with Allen and Whitehead and Whitehead's detailed account written at the time from notes made on the spot.

[11] EUSAK PIR 101, 21 Oct 50.

THE MIDDLESEX 1ST BATTALION *starts across the Ch'ongch'on River at Sinanju.*

of An-tung on the north bank.[12] But the fugitive North Korean capital soon moved on to Kanggye, and it was there in the mountains that the remnants of the North Korean Government and military power assembled. The Kanggye-Manp'ojin area, mountainous in the extreme and heavily wooded, was an ideal area in which to fight defensive delaying actions. It had been a stronghold of Korean guerrilla operations during Japanese rule. Many crossings of the Yalu were near at hand, it was centrally located, and it had lateral road communications to both northeast and northwest Korea.

On 22 October, C Company, 6th Medium Tank Battalion, designated Task Force Elephant, started from P'yongyang by way of Sunch'on for Kujang-dong to block the railroad there. Passing through Sunch'on, the task force arrived at its objective at 2200 and then turned west to Kunu-ri (Kaech'on on some maps), twenty miles downstream in the valley of the Ch'ongch'on. The ROK 1st Division followed behind the task force. *(Map 21)* The ROK's recovered 40 escaped American prisoners whom they evacuated at once to P'yongyang. Two more escaped prisoners came in at Kunu-ri the next morning, 23

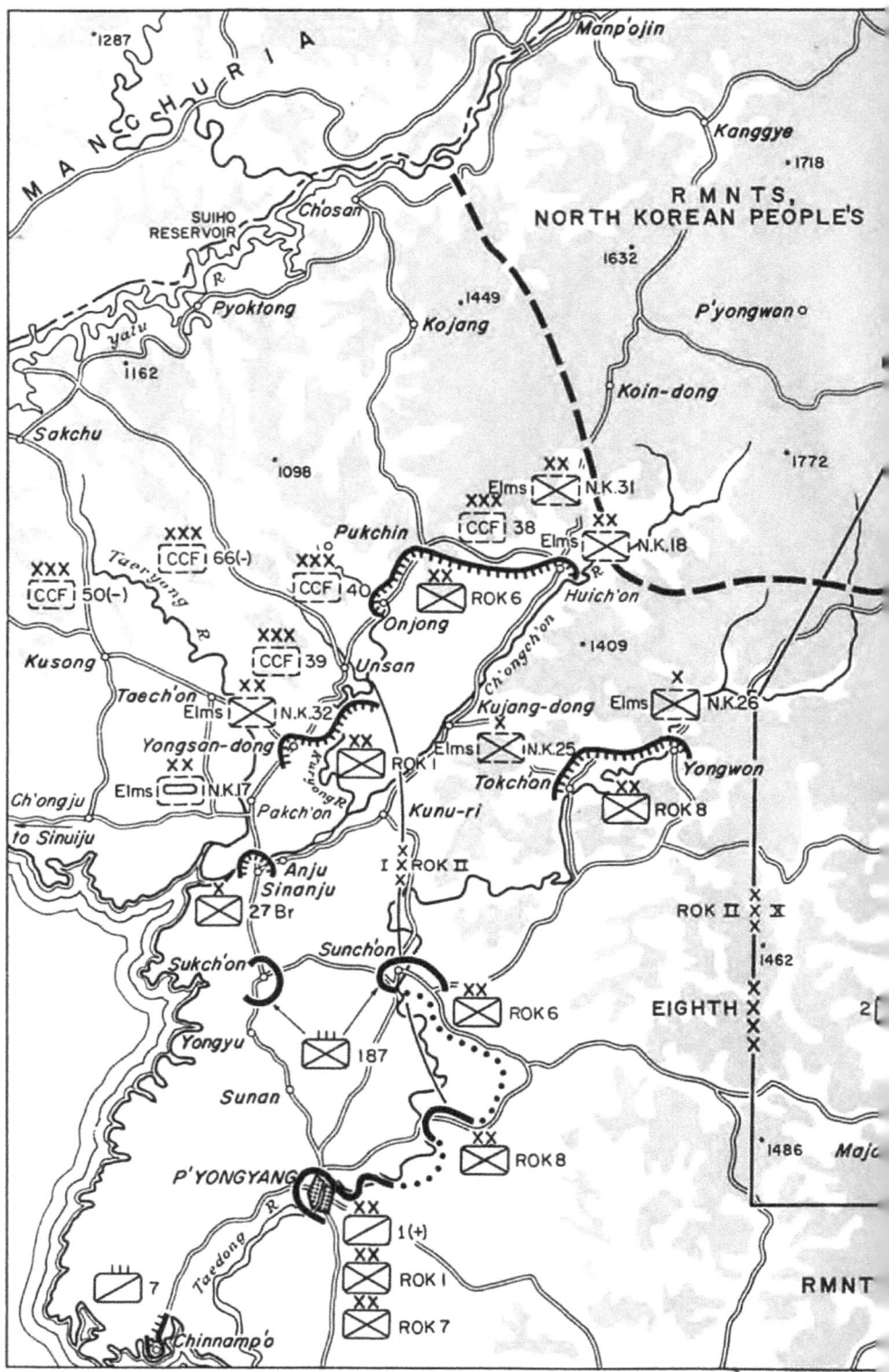

MAP 21

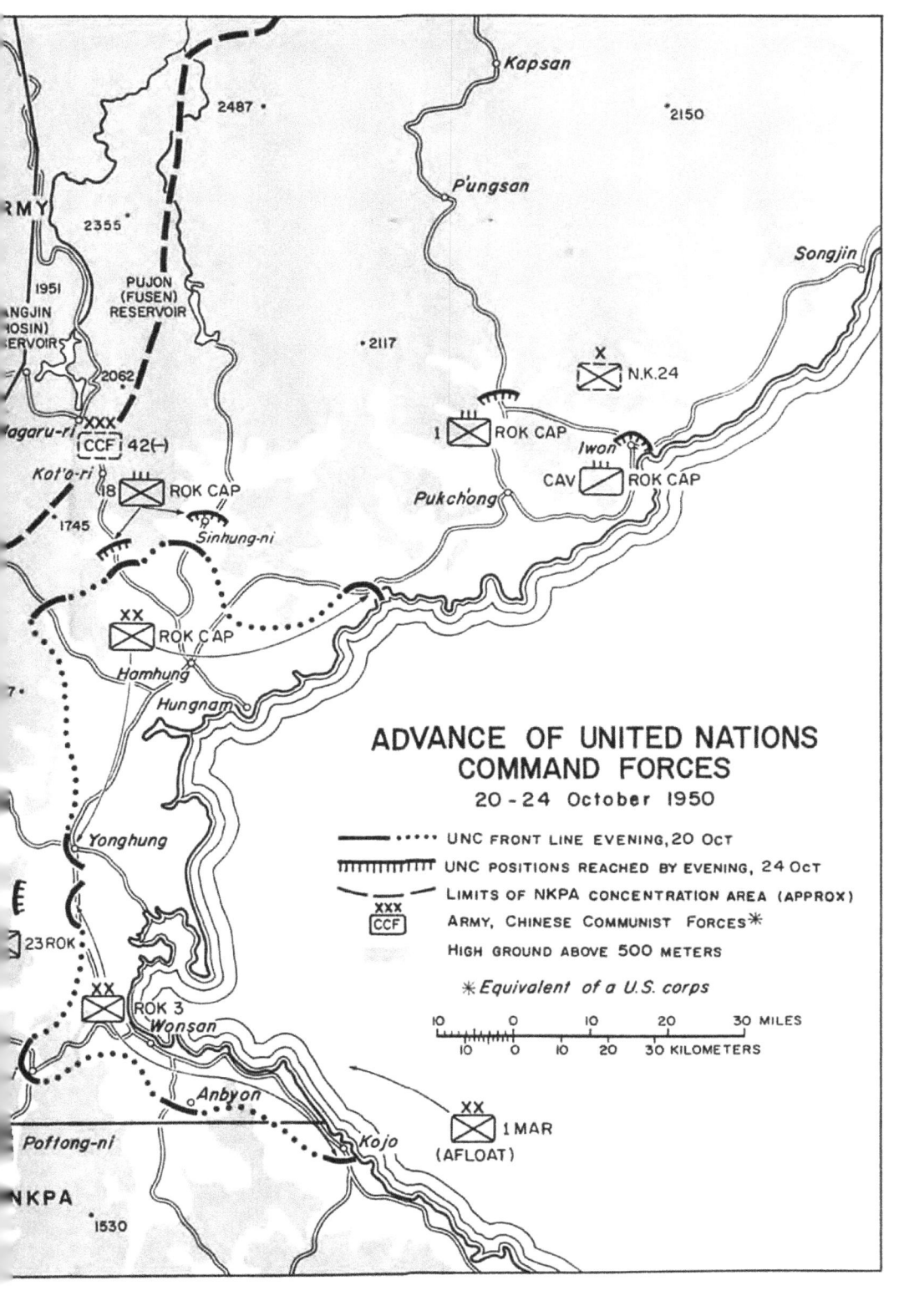

October. That afternoon, a sergeant of the ROK 6th Division found the bodies of 28 American prisoners on the railroad track, and 3 men still alive, four miles north of Kujang-dong.[13]

On 23 October General Paik led his division from Kunu-ri down the valley of the Ch'ongch'on. Near Anju, D Company tanks knocked out two T34 tanks and two self-propelled guns, and captured one tank intact. Just before noon a platoon of tanks seized the damaged wooden bridge over the Ch'ongch'on River three miles northeast of Anju. A tank patrol continued downstream to Sinanju, which it found deserted by the enemy and the bridges there across the Ch'ongch'on destroyed.

Repair of the Anju bridge began at once and continued through the night. By 0900 24 October wheeled traffic, including 2½-ton trucks, could cross on it. During that morning a reconnaissance party found a tank ford three miles east of the bridge, and the 6th Medium Tank Battalion crossed the river there. All three regiments of the ROK 1st Division crossed the Ch'ongch'on on 23-24 October. The division then attacked northeast toward Unsan.[14]

Complying with I Corps' order to continue the advance beyond P'yongyang, advance elements of the 24th Division arrived in an assembly area north of the city the evening of 22 October, and there the division assumed control of the 27th British Commonwealth Brigade, the 89th Medium Tank Battalion, and the 90th Field Artillery Battalion. Meanwhile, the British Brigade had hurried on northward from Sukch'on. On 23 October it arrived at Sinanju only a few hours after the ROK 1st Division tank patrol entered the town. It also secured the airstrip five miles to the southwest. By this time the 24th Division completed its move to Sunan, twelve miles north of P'yongyang.[15]

The Ch'ongch'on River at Sinanju, not far from the sea, is wide, has 12-foot tides, and deep mud along its edges. On the 24th the British Middlesex 1st Battalion started crossing in assault boats. The rest of the brigade and the vehicles crossed that night over the ROK 1st Division bridge at Anju. The 3d Engineer Combat Battalion now worked to clear the highway to Sinanju, and to improve it for carrying the main part of Eighth Army's logistical support in the projected drive to the Manchurian border.[16]

While the U.S. I Corps on the U.N. left advanced to the Ch'ongch'on, two divisions of the ROK Army on its right also took up the advance. The ROK 6th Division turned northeast from Kunu-ri up the Ch'ongch'on River on the road that led through Huich'on to Kanggye.

---

[12] *Ibid.*; EUSAK WD, 23 Oct 50, Daily News Bul, dispatch of 21 Oct 50.

[13] 6th Med Tk Bn WD, 22-23 Oct 50; 10th AAA Group WD, Oct 50; Interv, author with Maj Roy M. Gramling (KMAG adviser with the ROK 6th Div), 17 Feb 54.

[14] 6th Med Tk Bn WD, 22-24 Oct 50; EUSAK WD, G-3 Sec and Br for CG, 24 Oct 50; EUSAK POR's 306 and 307, 22 Oct, and 309, 23 Oct 50.

[15] I Corps WD, 22 Oct 50; 24th Div WD, 22-25 Oct 50; EUSAK WD, G-4 Stf Sec, 22 Oct and G-3 Sec, 23 Oct 50; EUSAK PIR 103, 23 Oct 50. At Sunan staff officers investigated and confirmed a civilian report that General Dean had been held a prisoner in the town before being moved farther north.

[16] 24th Div WD, 23-24 Oct 50; British 27th Brig Unit Rpt, Sitrep 241800-261800 Oct 50; EUSAK WD, G-3 Sec, 24 Oct 50; 3d Engr Bn WD, Narr Summ, 29 Sep-Oct 50.

East of it the ROK 8th Division reached Tokch'on at midnight of 23 October. There it turned north and struck the Ch'ongch'on at Kujang-dong two days later. Both the ROK 6th and 8th Divisions (ROK II Corps) were now in exceedingly mountainous country. Near Kunu-ri the ROK 6th Division captured two trains, one carrying 8 tanks, and, farther on, near Kujang-dong, it captured 50 boxcars of ammunition. The division had a hard fight with an estimated regiment of North Koreans south of Huich'on but dispersed this force and entered Huich'on on the night of the 23d. There it captured 20 T34 tanks needing only minor repairs. At Huich'on the ROK 6th Division turned west, and later north, its objective being Ch'osan on the Yalu River. It was now far in front of any U.N. division.[17]

On 24 October, when Eighth Army troops crossed the Ch'ongch'on River and the ROK 6th Division passed through Huich'on and headed for the Yalu, less than six weeks had passed since that army had battled desperately to hold its lines 320 air miles to the south along the Pusan Perimeter. The Inch'on landing likewise was less than six weeks in the past. The capture of Seoul was about four weeks in the past. Since then, the Eighth Army, moving up from the south after breaking out of its embattled Perimeter, had penetrated 160 air miles north of Seoul and 130 air miles into North Korea. In doing this it had overrun the enemy's capital and breached the last important river barrier south of the northern border of the country.

At the same time the ROK I Corps under its command had fought its way northward equally far on the east coast to capture Wonsan. And in the closing days of this period the U.S. X Corps had moved amphibiously around the length of Korea to appear off Wonsan for an imminent landing and subsequent operations in that part of Korea. This Eighth Army–ROK–X Corps attack which moved the front northward more than 300 miles in less than six weeks had virtually destroyed the North Korean Army.

---

[17] EUSAK WD, Br for CG, 22–25 Oct 50; *Ibid.*, POR 307 and PIR 102, 22 Oct 50; Gen Paik Sun Yup, MS review comments, 11 Jul 58.

CHAPTER XXXIII

The Chinese Intervene

> O divine art of subtlety and secrecy! Through you we learn to be invisible, through you inaudible; and hence hold the enemy's fate in our hands.
>
> SUN TZU, *The Art of War*

The Far East Command near the end of October changed its policy with respect to Koreans attached to United States Army units, authorizing a strength of only twenty-five Koreans to an American infantry company or unit of similar size, instead of the 100 per company previously authorized. The resulting release of several thousand Korean soldiers who had been assigned to U.S. Army divisions since August made possible the activation of a new ROK division. On 25 October the ROK Army activated the 9th Division, composed of the 28th, 29th, and 30th Regiments, of two battalions each. On 30 October, three battalions of the 1st Anti-Guerrilla Group became the third battalion of each of these regiments. By 7 November, 8,272 Korean soldiers had been released and turned back to the ROK Army and several thousand more were on the point of being released. On that day the ROK Army reactivated in Seoul the 2d Infantry Division which had been shattered in the early days of the war. This division at first had only two regiments, the 17th and the 31st, but on 13 November the 32d Regiment was activated at Seoul as the division's third regiment.[1]

Other new military forces began making their appearance in Korea at this time, just when it began to look as if they would not be needed. The scheduled arrival of several United Nations troop organizations in Korea made necessary arrangements to equip and train them so that they could become effective parts of the Eighth Army command. In an attempt to accomplish this, General Walker on 8 October ordered the 2d Logistical Command to establish a United Nations Reception Center (UNRC) at Taegu University as soon as EUSAK moved from it. Its mission was "to clothe, equip, and provide familiarization training with U.S. Army weapons and equipment to U.N. troops as determined essential for operations in Korea by the Reception Center Commander." Not more than 6,200 troops were expected to be in training at the center at any one time. The first unit to

---

[1] EUSAK WD, G-1 Daily Hist Rpt, 26 Oct 50; Ibid., POR 389, 19 Nov 50; Ibid., Br. for CG, 9 Nov 50; GHQ UNC, G-3 Rpts, 27 and 30 Oct 50; 25th Div WD, 30 Oct 50.

make use of it was the 1st Turkish Armed Forces Command which arrived there on 18 October.[2]

The first of the new forces to arrive in Korea was the Thailand Battalion whose advance party arrived at Pusan on 3 October; the main party arrived more than a month later on 7 November. Following closely after the Thailand advance party came the advance party of the Turkish Brigade which arrived at Pusan on 12 October. The main body of the brigade (5,190 troops) arrived at Pusan five days later and began unloading on the 18th. The Turkish troops were fully equipped except for certain weapons. On 24 October, the advance parties of the Netherlands Battalion and the British 29th Brigade arrived in Korea. In Canada a special force of 10,000 men had volunteered and trained for combat service in Korea, and on 7 November an advance party of 345 of them arrived at Pusan to prepare the way for the main body. But with the war seemingly near an end, only a battalion followed; the main body was held in Canada.[3]

It should be emphasized that at this time when Eighth Army was making ready to continue the pursuit north of the Ch'ongch'on River, its logistical situation was not good. The breakdown of rail transportation in October, coincident with Eighth Army's rapid advance northward, caused an extraordinarily heavy burden to fall on truck transport operating over bad roads with long hauls from ports and railheads. At the end of October the 24th Division railhead was still at Yongdungp'o on the south side of the Han River, while the division service elements were in the vicinity of Pakch'on, 205 miles farther north. The longer the trucks ran over the rough Korean roads, the greater grew the number that became inoperable. It was a type of logistical support that promised soon to wear itself to destruction since the spare parts needed for repairs were not available.

During September, October, and on into November, 76 percent of Eighth Army's trucks operated on a 24-hour basis. In order to supply I Corps north of the 38th Parallel, Eighth Army had to take away from the 2d and 25th Divisions large numbers of their trucks, thereby virtually immobilizing these divisions. The 2d Division at one time furnished 320 trucks that were organized into a Red Ball Express to supply I Corps from the Han River. The need for trucks was so critical, and normal methods of delivering them to the tactical units so uncertain, that divisions and corps sent men back to Pusan by air and rail to drive the trucks 400 miles north over atrocious roads to the fronts.[4]

As soon as P'yongyang fell to Eighth Army an airlift of supplies to the airfield there got under way from Ashiya Air Base in Japan and from Kimpo Airfield near Seoul. The Kimpo airlift sought to attain a goal of transporting 1,000 tons daily to P'yongyang or north-

---

[2] Maj William F. Fox, History of the Korean War, Inter-Allied Co-operation During Combat Operations, vol. III, pt. 2, sec. B, pp. 10–11, MS in OCMH; Ltr Ord, Hq, EUSAK to CG, 2d Log Comd, 8 Oct 50, sub: Establishment of UNRC.

[3] Log Comd Monthly Act Rpt, G–3 and G–4 Secs, Oct and Nov 50.

[4] Interv, author with Maj Gen Leven C. Allen, 15 Dec 53; EUSAK WD, Trans Sec, 18 Nov and G–4 Jnl, Msg 9, 241430 Nov 50; 24th Div WD, G–4 Daily Summ, 29–30 Oct 50; 2d Div WD, Narr Summ, Nov 50, p. 11.

ward. A large part of this airlift at the end of October carried ammunition. On 28 October, for instance, cargo planes carried 1,037 tons of ammunition from Kimpo to P'yongyang, and, as early as 31 October, planes carried ammunition to the hastily repaired fighter strip near Sinanju for the ROK units fighting along and above the Ch'ongch'on.[5]

American Optimism at End of October

Offsetting the bad logistical situation at the end of October was the general belief among U.S. commanders that the war in Korea was all but ended. Viewed in this light, the situation looked so favorable that the Department of the Army and the Commander in Chief, Far East, made plans for the redeployment of Eighth Army units, including the return of the 2d Infantry Division to the United States or to Europe, and of other organizations later. On 25 October the Department of the Army notified General MacArthur that it planned to cancel shipment of enlisted reserve corps troops to the Far East scheduled for October and November, except 17,000 noncommissioned officers. All this was in accordance with general agreements reached at the Wake Island Conference earlier in the month.[6]

Even in Korea this cutback fever had taken hold. On 22 October General Walker requested authority from General MacArthur to divert to Japan all bulk-loaded ammunition ships arriving thenceforth in Korea from the United States, as he felt there was enough ammunition in Korea to satisfy future needs. MacArthur approved this request, and he also took steps to have six ammunition ships, en route to the Far East carrying 105-mm. and 155-mm. shells and Air Force bombs, diverted to Hawaii or returned to the United States. And General Weible, Commanding General, Japan Logistical Command, requested the Commanding General, San Francisco Port of Embarkation, to cancel all outstanding requisitions for ground ammunition and to unload any ships still in port.[7]

Morale was high in the U.N. forces as they crossed the Ch'ongch'on and set out on what most of them though would be the last, brief phase of the war. In the 1st Cavalry Division many men thought they would parade on the Plaza in Tokyo wearing yellow cavalry scarves on Thanksgiving Day. The division even started turning in its equipment in expectation of being the first organization to return to Japan. Others throughout the army threw away handbills listing prices of gifts available at post exchanges, saying they were going to do their Christmas shopping in Japan.

In the United States the New York *Times* probably expressed the prevailing opinion there at this stage of the war when it stated editorially, "Except for unexpected developments along the frontiers of the peninsula, we can now be easy in our minds as to the military outcome."[8]

---

[5] EUSAK WD, Ord Daily Act Rpts, 27, 28, 31 Oct and 6 Nov 50; *Ibid.*, Trans Sec, 25 Oct 50; 3d Log Comd Act Rpt, Nov 50, p. 8.

[6] Schnabel, FEC, GHQ Support and Participation in the Korean War, ch. VII, pp. 3–5, citing Msg 94651, JCS to CINCFE, 21 Oct 50, Msg C67065, CINCFE to DA for JCS, 21 Oct 50, and Msg S94985, DA to CINCFE, 25 Oct 50.

[7] *Ibid.*, ch. VII, pp. 6–7, citing Msg CX67506, CINCFE to CG Eighth Army and CG JLC, 26 Oct 50, and Msg CX7702, CINCFE to DA, 28 Oct 50.

[8] New York *Times*, October 29, 1950.

Looking ahead to the task of rehabilitating the people of the Republic of Korea, General MacArthur took steps to establish a Civil Assistance Command in Eighth Army. On 30 October General Walker activated this command with an authorized staff of 161 officers and 117 enlisted men, to become effective 1 November.[9]

Until 17 October General MacArthur's orders, based on the Joint Chiefs of Staff directive of 27 September, had restrained U.N. ground forces other than ROK troops from operating north of a line extending from Ch'ongju on the west through Kunu-ri and Yongwon to Hamhung on the east coast. On 17 October General MacArthur, in his UNC Operations Order 4, lifted this restriction and advanced northward the line below which all U.N. ground forces could operate. This new line, confirmed in a message to all commanders on 19 October, extended generally from Sonch'on through Koin-dong–P'yongwon–P'ungsan to Songjin on the east coast. (*See Map 21.*) It was generally thirty to forty miles south of the Manchurian border across the greater part of the peninsula, and was within the spirit and meaning of the Joint Chiefs of Staff directive of 27 September, which was still in effect. In the policy laid down in this directive only ROK forces were to be used in the provinces of Korea bordering on the Yalu River.[10]

But on 24 October, as the leading U.N. forces crossed the Ch'ongch'on River, General MacArthur issued an order to his ground commanders in Korea which changed all earlier orders drastically. He now removed all restrictions on the use of U.N. ground forces south of the border, and instructed his commanders to press forward to the northern limits of Korea, utilizing all their forces.[11] Thus, when Eighth Army began what it thought would be the last series of maneuvers to end the war it did so under orders radically different from those that had so far guided its operations in Korea.

The day it was issued, this order brought a message from the Joint Chiefs of Staff to MacArthur stating that it was not in accord with the directive of 27 September and asking for an explanation. General MacArthur's reply the next day justified lifting the restriction as a matter of military necessity. He said that the ROK forces could not handle the situation by themselves, that he felt he had enough latitude under existing directives to issue the order, and that, furthermore, the whole subject had been covered in the Wake Island Conference.[12]

While it is clear that the Joint Chiefs of Staff felt that MacArthur had violated their basic 27 September directive, they did not countermand his orders to go to the Yalu. When the 27th British Commonwealth Brigade crossed the Ch'ong-

---

[9] EUSAK WD, G-3 Sec, 30 Oct 50; *Ibid.*, G-1 Sec, Civil Assistance Stf Sec Rpt, 1 Nov 50.

[10] Schnabel, FEC, GHQ Support and Participation in the Korean War, ch. VI, pp. 31-32, citing Msg CX66705, CINCUNC to all comdrs, 17 Oct 50, and CX66839, CINCUNC to all comdrs, 19 Oct 50.

[11] *Ibid.*, p. 34, citing Msg CX67291, CINCUNC to all comdrs, 24 Oct 50.

[12] C67397, CINCFE to JCS, 25 Oct 50; Senate MacArthur Hearings, MacArthur's testimony, pp. 97-98; Gen. of the Army Omar N. Bradley's testimony, pt. 1, p. 757, and Gen Collins' testimony, pt. 2, pp. 1216-17, 1229-30, 1235, 1239-41, 1312-13.

ch'on, that unit, the U.S. 24th Infantry Division which followed, and all the other U.N. troops deployed in Korea, were authorized to go to the Yalu River —to the extreme northern limits of the country.

General Walker on 25 October was quoted as saying, "Everything is going just fine." [13] And so it was—just then.

Continuation of the Pursuit

The Ch'ongch'on River and its tributaries, the Kuryong and Taeryong Rivers, all flowing from the north, together form the last major water barrier in the western part of North Korea short of the border. The Ch'ongch'on valley is a wide one for Korea, varying in width from 3 to 20 miles. The Ch'ongch'on, like the Yalu, flows from the northeast to the southwest and it generally parallels the Yalu at a distance of approximately 65 air miles. The Ch'ongch'on River, the principal terrain feature in the field of operations for Eighth Army during late October and November 1950, largely dictated the army's deployment and tactical maneuvers.

The main P'yongyang highway crosses the Ch'ongch'on at Sinanju and runs west and northwest in the coastal area to Sinuiju at the North Korean border. Inland from the west coast, mountainous spines run down from the Yalu to the valley of the Ch'ongch'on and the terrain becomes ever rougher and more forbidding. These mountains reach their greatest heights and become almost trackless wastes in central Korea between the Changjin (Chosin) [14] Reservoir and the Yalu. The Yalu itself, save for its lower west coast reaches, runs through a gorgelike channel rimmed by high mountains on both sides. The great Suiho hydroelectric dam on the middle Yalu impounds a reservoir of the same name that extends upstream for sixty air miles, pushing water into hundreds of little lateral fjordlike mountain valleys.

Above the reservoir there is a major crossing of the Yalu at Manp'ojin. Twenty air miles southeast of Manp'ojin, situated in the very heart of the mountain fastness, is Kanggye. There the North Korean governmental officials and high military commanders assembled. From there, if necessary, they could retreat across the Yalu at Manp'ojin to the sanctuary of Manchuria.

From the valley of the Ch'ongch'on the principal road to Kanggye and Manp'ojin ran northeast from the Sinanju-Anju-Kunu-ri area through Huich'on. A railroad followed the same passageway. From the lower valley of the Ch'ongch'on, fifty air miles inland from the west coast, an important secondary road network ran north through Unsan to the Yalu. The events of the next few weeks were to give this particular road net special importance.

The configuration of the valley of the lower Ch'ongch'on in relation to the mountain ridges that approach it from the Yalu must be noted. North of the lower Ch'ongch'on for a distance of approximately fifteen air miles the ground is flat or only slightly rising with occasional low hills. A lateral road extending eastward from Yongsan-dong and generally paralleling the river marks the

---

[13] EUSAK WD, Daily News Bul, 25 Oct 50.

[14] See p. 729, n. 1, below.

cleavage line between this low ground, which in a broad sense can be described as the valley of the Ch'ongch'on, and the mountain spurs that rise rather abruptly from it and extend to the Yalu. The southern extremities of these mountain ranges with their limited corridors of passage form a natural defensive barrier to a military advance northward. The towns of Taech'on, Unsan, and Onjong stand at the entrances to these mountain corridors. There, the logical implications of the terrain were soon to be translated by an enemy into harsh and unwonted military reality.

The Eighth Army operation above the Ch'ongch'on began essentially as a continuation of the pursuit that had started with the breakout from the Pusan Perimeter; the U.S. I Corps was on the left, the ROK II Corps on the right. Within Milburn's I Corps, the 24th Division (British 27th Brigade attached) was on the left, the ROK 1st Division on the right. The U.N. Command expected little organized opposition from the enemy and emphasized a speedy advance to the northern border. Several columns were to strike out northward with little or no physical contact between them. The advance was not to be closely co-ordinated; each column was free to advance as fast and as far as possible without respect to gains made by others.

ROK Troops Reach the Yalu

As Eighth Army resumed its general advance toward the North Korean border, the ROK 6th Division of the ROK II Corps appeared to have the greatest success of any front-line U.N. division. (*Map* 22) Meeting virtually no opposition and traveling fast up the valley of the Ch'ongch'on, it reached Huich'on the night of 23 October. There it left the valley of the Ch'ongch'on and turned west, the 7th Regiment leading. Its advanced battalion marched northwest over a cart trail, but the remainder of the regiment had to turn west from Huich'on on a road to Onjong. The night of 24-25 October, the 7th Regiment passed through Onjong, then turned north and joined its advanced battalion.[15] Finding the road clear, it headed north for its objective, the town of Ch'osan, fifty air miles away on the Yalu. Late in the afternoon the regiment stopped at Kojang, a sizable town eighteen air miles south of Ch'osan, and bivouacked there for the night.

The next morning, 26 October, Maj. Harry Fleming, KMAG adviser with the ROK 7th Regiment, accompanied the Reconnaissance Platoon, reinforced, into Ch'osan. The remainder of the regiment stayed at its overnight position. In Ch'osan the Reconnaissance Platoon found North Koreans retreating into Manchuria across a narrow floating footbridge that spanned the Yalu. Fleming and the ROK officers directed the setting up of machine guns to halt this foot traffic into Manchuria, but so placed the weapons that the impact area of their fire would not be in China across the river. After a thorough reconnaissance of the town, Fleming and the main body of the Reconnaissance Platoon returned to the regimental position. They left a small party in Ch'osan because the next morning the main force of the ROK 7th

---

[15] Interv, author with Gramling, 17 Feb 54; Ltrs, Fleming to author, 9 and 18 Mar 54; EUSAK WD, G-3 Jnl, 23-24 Oct 50.

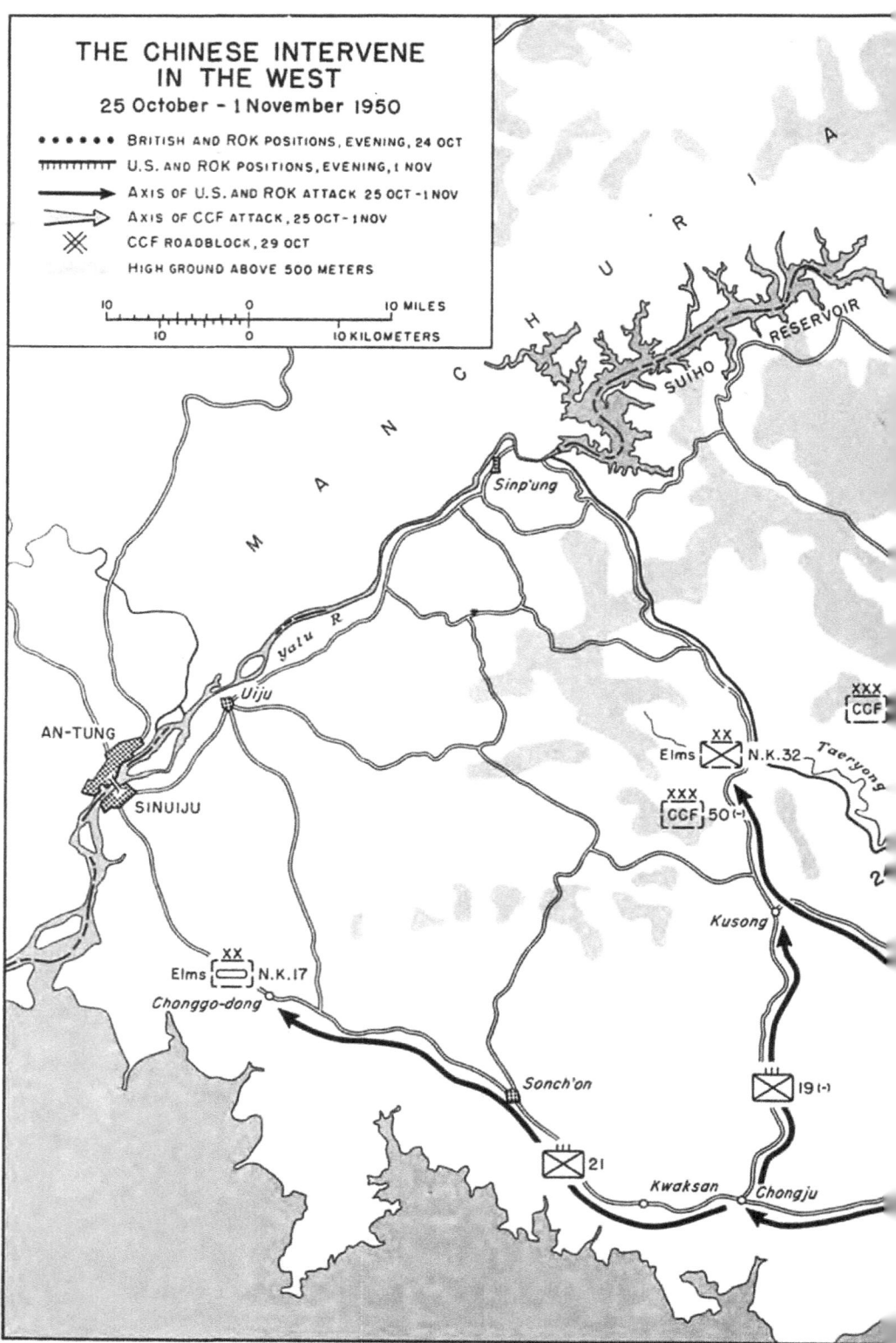

MAP 22

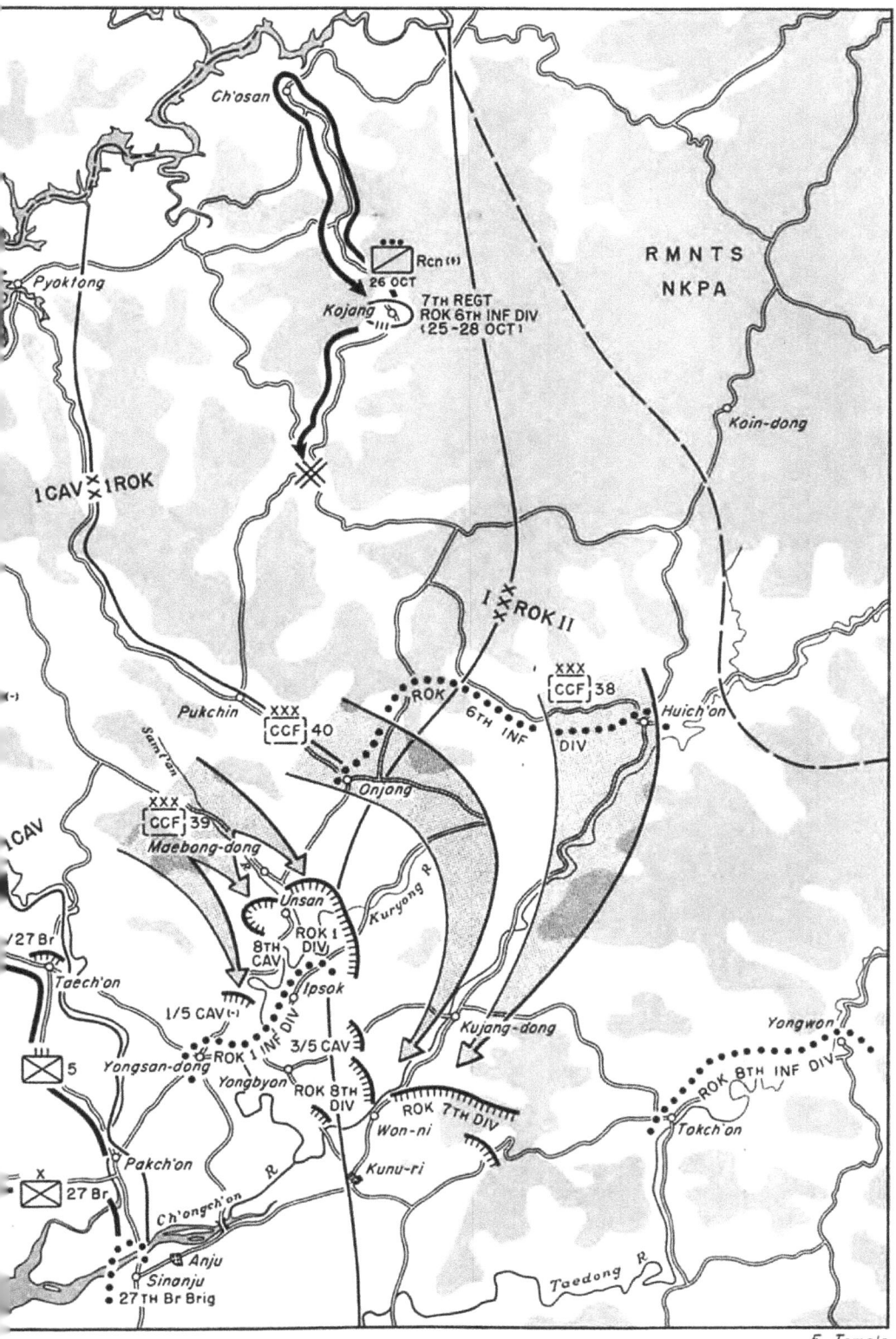

Regiment was to come into the town.[16]

The Reconnaissance Platoon from the 7th Regiment, ROK 6th Division, was the first U.N. unit to reach the northern border of North Korea, and, as events turned out, it was the only element operating under Eighth Army command ever to get there during the war.

Following behind the 6th Division, the ROK 8th Division had reached the valley of the Ch'ongch'on at Kujang-dong the night of 25–26 October, marching from Sunch'on through Tokch'on. On the 26th, the day the advanced elements of the 6th Division reached the Yalu, the 8th turned up the Ch'ongch'on Valley toward Huich'on for the purpose of joining the 6th Division.

Chinese Strike the ROK II Corps

The day before, on 25 October, the 3d Battalion, 2d Regiment, ROK 6th Division, had started northwest from the little crossroads village of Onjong, ten air miles northeast of Unsan, headed for Pukchin. There the 2d Regiment expected to turn north to Pyoktong on the Yalu. Eight miles west of Onjong the 3d Battalion came under enemy fire. The troops dismounted from their vehicles to disperse what they thought was a small force of North Koreans. But the roadblock turned out to be a Chinese trap. In the action that followed the Chinese destroyed the battalion as an organized force. Approximately 400 of 750 ROK's in the battalion escaped, however, and in the afternoon infiltrated back to Onjong. Among those captured in this action was Lt. Glen C. Jones, KMAG adviser to the battalion, who later died in a prison camp.[17]

Meanwhile, back at Onjong the 2d Battalion of the ROK 2d Regiment learned that the 3d Battalion had become heavily engaged, and moved out to support it. On the way, members of the battalion saw enemy troops moving about on the hills to the north. Patrols sent out to investigate came back with a Chinese prisoner. He said that Chinese forces had been waiting in the mountains around Pukchin since 17 October. Another Chinese soldier, badly wounded, was captured on the road ahead. That evening Chinese troops cut off the 2d Battalion from Onjong, but it escaped southward cross-country and succeeded in rejoining the 1st Battalion and regimental headquarters in the town.

At 0330 that night, the Chinese attacked Onjong. The ROK troops there broke in panic, but officers succeeded in stopping them at the southeast edge of town. When the Chinese penetrated this position at 0600 the ROK's started withdrawing eastward. They had gone only three miles when they came to a roadblock—the Chinese had cut them off. At this time not a single company of the ROK 2d Regiment was intact. The ROK's now scattered into the hills. Maj. Roy M. Gramling, KMAG adviser to

---

[16] This account of the ROK's at Ch'osan is based largely on Ltrs, Fleming to author, 9 and 18 Mar 54; also, Interv, author with Lt Col Willard G. Pearson, 1 Aug 51; EUSAK POR 319, 26 Oct 50; EUSAK WD, Br for CG, 26 Oct 50.

[17] Interv, author with Gramling, 17 Feb 54; EUSAK POR 319, 26 Oct 50. Unless otherwise noted, the Onjong narrative is based on the author's interview with Gramling. Army records have only a few fragmentary references to the ROK II Corps action at Onjong.

the regiment, and another KMAG officer escaped to Huich'on, but a third, Capt. Paul V. S. Liles, fell captive to the Chinese. That the 2d Regiment apparently did little determined fighting in its first encounter with the Chinese is indicated by the fact that about 2,700 men out of approximately 3,100 in the regiment eventually escaped to the Ch'ongch'on.

When the ROK 2d Regiment came under Chinese attack at Onjong, the 19th Regiment, except for one battalion, was in Huich'on. The 10th Regiment of the ROK 8th Division also was there. Maj. Gen. Yu Jae Hung, commanding the ROK II Corps, ordered these troops, less the 1st Battalion, 10th Regiment, which was to remain in Huich'on, to attack west in an attempt to recover the abandoned vehicles and artillery pieces of the 2d Regiment. These two regiments reached a point on 28 October from which advanced units could look down on Onjong and see some of the abandoned equipment, but they never got any farther. The next day these two regiments suffered the same fate that had overtaken the 2d Regiment. Heavily defeated, they lost their vehicles and three batteries of artillery—all they had.[18]

These startling developments in the Onjong area cut off the 7th Regiment of the ROK 6th Division to the north. At its headquarters at Kojang on the evening of the 26th, the regiment was making plans to occupy Ch'osan on the Yalu in the morning when it received a radio message from the ROK 6th Division. This message said that the 2d Regiment had been defeated and scattered, and ordered it, the 7th Regiment, to start south to rejoin the division. Major Fleming replied by radio that the regiment could not move unless it was resupplied with gasoline, food, and ammunition. An airdrop of supplies was successfully accomplished two days later at 1100.

The following morning, 29 October, the ROK 7th Regiment started south. Before noon, when approximately twenty miles south of Kojang, it ran into an enemy roadblock. In a very short time the entire regiment was committed against an enemy force. The tactical air control party called in strong air support and, according to Major Fleming, "with the tremendous help of the close air support we received, we were able to hold our own during the daylight hours, but after night fell and without the support of the fighter planes we could not hold the enemy off." [19]

During the night large numbers of ROK soldiers scattered into the hills in an effort to make their way south; some, however, stayed in position to the end. By daylight resistance had ended. It appears probable, from a hand-drawn operations map of the *373d Regiment, CCF 125th Division,* captured in March 1951, that one battalion of this regiment set the trap and fought the action that destroyed the ROK 7th Regiment. Major Fleming, wounded in fifteen places and the only American to survive the battle, was captured at 0630 by the Chinese. Almost three years later Major Fleming returned to the United States in the pris-

---

[18] Interv, author with Gramling, 17 Feb 54; EUSAK WD, 28 Oct 50, Memo to CofS, G-2, *et al.,* from Acting CofS, G-3 (Rpt of Lt Col F. J. Lagasse after visiting Hq ROK II Corps); *Ibid.,* 29 Oct 50.

[19] Ltrs, Fleming to author, 9 and 18 Mar 54; EUSAK WD, Br for CG, 28 Oct 50; Lagasse Rpt, cited n. 17.

oner exchange in the fall of 1953.[20]

Eventually, about 875 officers and men of the 3,552 in the regiment escaped to Kunu-ri and rejoined the 6th Division. Col. Lim Bu Taik, the regimental commander, and two of his battalion commanders escaped, but the other principal regimental staff officers and the KMAG advisers were either killed or captured.[21]

The collapse of the ROK II Corps on the right of Eighth Army and the frightening, but confused, reports of Chinese troops in the action caused Eighth Army on 29 October to order the ROK 7th Division released from U.S. I Corps' control to revert to the ROK II Corps. It ordered the ROK II Corps to place the 8th Division in a defensive position north of the Ch'ongch'on, extending from Yongbyon eastward to the river at Kujang-dong, and then for the 7th Division to extend the line south toward Tokch'on.[22]

By 31 October Chinese forces were pressing against the ROK II Corps defensive line north and east of Kunu-ri. That morning they broke through the 16th Regiment of the 8th Division, near its boundary with the ROK 1st Division, causing one battalion to scatter.

On the south side of the Ch'ongch'on, Chinese forces by 1 November had pushed the ROK 7th Division back to the vicinity of Won-ni. The ROK II Corps of necessity by this time had pivoted to face generally east. This resulted in a gap between its left flank and Eighth Army. The U.S. 2d Division, attached by Eighth Army to I Corps, was assembled hurriedly in the vicinity of Sunch'on to meet a possible emergency in this gap.[23]

Thus matters stood on 1 November. Within a few days after its first action on 25 October, the CCF had driven back the ROK II Corps, crippling it disastrously, and was south of the Ch'ongch'on on the open right flank of Eighth Army. And disaster was also threatening in the center of the Eighth Army front at Unsan.

Unsan—Prelude

In its part of the general advance, the ROK 1st Division on 25 October was strung out on the road running from the Ch'ongch'on River to Unsan. Its 15th Regiment passed through Yongbyon and continued on without opposition toward Unsan, fifteen air miles northward. Elements of D Company, 6th Medium Tank Battalion, led the way and passed through Unsan. A mile and a half northeast of the town, just before 1100, enemy mortar fire suddenly interdicted a bridge as the American tanks were approaching it. ROK troops deployed and engaged the enemy force. Half an hour later they reported 300 Chinese troops in the hills just north of Unsan. A little later they captured the first Chinese soldier taken prisoner by U.N. forces in the Korean War. American tank crewmen at the

---

[20] Ltrs, Fleming to author, 9 and 18 Mar 54; EUSAK WD, G-3 Jnl, Msg 0130 30 Oct 50; Interv, author with Gramling, 17 Feb 54; ATIS Enemy Documents, Korean Operations, Issue 42 (11 Jun 51), item 52, opposite p. 162.

[21] Interv, author with Lt Col Thomas E. Bennett (KMAG adviser to ROK 7th Regt in early Nov 50), 11 Dec 53; Paik Sun Yup, MS review comments, 11 Jul 58.

[22] EUSAK WD, G-3 Sec, 29 Oct 50; US I Corps WD, Oct 50, p. 45.

[23] EUSAK PIR 111, 31 Oct 50; EUSAK WD, G-3 Sec, 31 Oct and 1 Nov 50.

interdicted bridge learned at 1144 of the captured Chinese. The prisoner said there were 10,000 Chinese Communist troops in the hills north and northwest of Unsan and another 10,000 eastward toward Huich'on.[24]

During the afternoon the fighting north of town gradually intensified and just after 1400 the ROK troops in contact with the Chinese estimated them to be two reinforced companies. The TACP controller, who had been pinned down by enemy fire for more than an hour, finally established radio communication with the Mosquito plane overhead and informed its pilot of the Chinese prisoner and his story that 10,000 to 20,000 Chinese soldiers were in the vicinity of Unsan. The pilot related the alarming story at Eighth Army headquarters. That evening I Corps headquarters received a message from a G-2 liaison officer with the ROK 1st Division reporting the capture of the Chinese prisoner. Special arrangements were made to take the captive to the Eighth Army advance command post at P'yongyang for interrogation. The prisoner was interrogated there the next morning. There could be no doubt that he was Chinese. By midafternoon three more Chinese were brought into P'yongyang. They, too, looked Chinese, spoke Chinese, and understood neither Korean nor Japanese.[25]

The ROK 12th Regiment, second in the division column, turned west when it arrived at Unsan. Just beyond the town it, too, found Chinese troops blocking the way. The ROK 11th Regiment, bringing up the division rear, halted for the night a few miles below Unsan. The report spread rapidly among the ROK's during the afternoon that the enemy troops on their front were Chinese.[26]

Ironically, that same afternoon, 25 October, the U.S. I Corps headquarters at 1600 published its order directing its forces to go all the way to the Yalu. For its part, the ROK 1st Division was "to continue the destruction of North Korean forces."[27]

The 25th of October had been a cold day and carried promise of the bitter North Korean winter that lay ahead. All night the fight above Unsan continued with the sound of small arms and machine guns and the booming of supporting 155-mm. howitzers echoing through the darkness. A small flurry of snow fell early in the morning, the first snow of the winter for these troops. But it was a minor worry compared to the startling fact that during the night enemy forces had nearly surrounded Unsan. Morning brought more information that the forces were Chinese. One report told of thirty-three Chinese dead found north of the town.

Northeast of Unsan, ROK infantry of the 15th Regiment during the morning of the 26th fell back under enemy attack. At 1030 Lt. Col. John S. Growden, commanding the 6th Medium Tank Battalion, thinking that his tanks holding the road northeast of Unsan were in danger of being overrun, ordered D Company to fall back to high ground south-

---

[24] I Corps WD, 25 Oct 50; I Corps Intel Summ 122, 25 Oct 50; I Corps PIR 40, 25 Oct 50; 6th Med Tk Bn WD, 25 Oct 50.

[25] 6th Med Tk Bn WD, 25 Oct 50; EUSAK WD, G-3 Jnl, Msg at 1715 25 Oct 50; Ltr, Col Percy W. Thompson (G-2, I Corps Oct 50) to author, 9 Apr 54; Collier, MS review comments, 10 Mar 58.

[26] EUSAK POR 316, 25 Oct 50.
[27] I Corps Opn Dir 14, 251600 Oct 50.

east of the town. West of Unsan the ROK 12th Regiment held fast. The 11th Regiment moved up to join the 12th Regiment in the battle, but almost at once had to move back south of Unsan to combat an enemy force that cut the main supply road there in an envelopment from the west. Instead of driving off this enemy roadblock force, the 11th Regiment itself was pushed north to the edge of Unsan. An entry in the supporting U.S. 10th Antiaircraft Artillery Group War Diary at this time states, "Due to the seriousness of the situation around Unsan, the Group was prepared to move out on a moment's notice." The ROK's estimated that a full enemy division confronted them.[28]

The reaction of Eighth Army intelligence to this development was that the Chinese troops in the Onjong and Unsan areas indicated "some further reinforcement of North Korean units with personnel taken from the Chinese Communist Forces, in order to assist in the defense of the border approaches." The estimate stated there were "no indications of open intervention on the part of Chinese Communist Forces in Korea."[29]

On the 27th the situation at Unsan improved somewhat. An airdrop shortly after 1100 by ten C-119 planes flying from Ashiya Air Base eased the critical supply situation within the ROK 1st Division, the two supporting tank companies of the 6th Tank Battalion, and the 10th AAA Group. Freshly supplied with ammunition, the ROK 15th and 12th Regiments attacked and made slight gains north and west of the town. To the south of the town two battalions of the 11th Regiment cleared the road, and in the late afternoon reported the enemy there had withdrawn to the northwest. In these attacks the ROK's found the Chinese well dug-in, exceptionally well camouflaged, and very hard to locate.

When the ROK 1st Division first encountered the Chinese above Unsan on 25 October, General Paik, the division commander, was at P'yongyang attending a celebration. He had by now returned to his command post at Yongbyon. Going forward to the scene of fighting, Paik examined enemy dead. He said they were all Chinese. Paik had served with the Japanese Manchurian Army in World War II and he knew the Chinese well. He estimated there was a Chinese division of 10,000 soldiers—a solid organization and not just Chinese mixed with North Koreans—in front of him. He told General Milburn, the I Corps commander, there were "many, many Chinese."[30]

On the 28th the fighting at Unsan quieted down, although the ROK's captured two more Chinese prisoners. They repeated the same story told by previous

---

[28] 10th AAA WD, 25-31 Oct 50; U.S. units supporting the ROK 1st Division at this time were the 17th Field Artillery Battalion (105-mm.), 10th Antiaircraft Artillery Group (included 155-mm. howitzers and 90-mm. guns), and two companies of the 6th Medium Tank Battalion. EUSAK WD, Br for CG, 26-27 Oct 50; EUSAK PIR 106, 26 Oct 50; EUSAK WD, G-3 Jnl, Msgs at 1340, 1530, 1700, and 2115, 26 Oct, and Jnl, 27 Oct 50; I Corps WD, 26 Oct 50; 6th Med Tk Bn WD, 26-27 Oct 50; Arty Rpt 12, 27 Oct 50.

[29] I Corps Opn Dir 15, 26 Oct 50; EUSAK PIR 106, 26 Oct 50.

[30] Interv, author with Col William H. Hennig (CO, 10th AAA Group, Oct 50), 23 Mar 54; Interv, author with Milburn, 4 Jan 52; I Corps WD, 27 Oct 50; New York Times, October 27, 1950.

Supply by Air *to the ROK 1st Division in the Unsan area.*

prisoners—that they were members of large Chinese organizations that had entered the war.

General Walker and the Eighth Army staff at P'yongyang had, of course, followed closely the many reports that came in concerning the puzzling and disturbing news from north of the Ch'ongch'on, particularly the information given by the first prisoners alleged by the ROK's to be Chinese. But, as would be natural in such a newly developing situation, the intelligence officials did not accept at face value all the information the prisoners related about the Chinese troop organizations they said were in Korea. As the extent of reverses north of the Ch'ongch'on mounted quickly within a day or two, General Walker and his staff, however, were forced to question the correctness of their initial reaction that the Chinese troops there represented only reinforcement of North Korean units.

By the morning of 28 October General Walker had become sufficiently concerned over events to order the 1st Cavalry Division relieved of its security mission at P'yongyang and to move north, pass through the ROK 1st Division at Unsan, and attack to the Yalu. General Gay ordered the 8th Cavalry Regiment to begin the division movement. It departed P'yongyang the next morning,

29 October. During the day it crossed the Ch'ongch'on at Anju and went into an assembly area at Yongsan-dong that evening.[31]

The ROK attack that began at first light on the morning of 29 October quickly developed into a stubborn fight against dug-in enemy using mortars, automatic weapons, and small arms. Even with the help of the artillery barrages and Fifth Air Force strafing attacks, the ROK's could not dislodge the Chinese.

Because Chinese forces had engulfed the ROK II Corps to the east in the Onjong and Huich'on areas, the ROK 1st Division now constituted a northern salient in the U.N. line. On its left there was a gap of fifteen air miles between it and elements of the U.S. 24th Division, the nearest Eighth Army unit on the west.

The next morning Lt. Col. Harold K. Johnson's 5th Cavalry Regiment arrived at Yongsan-dong. Johnson's mission was to protect the rear of the 8th Cavalry Regiment, which that morning had continued on north to Unsan where it was to relieve part of the ROK 1st Division. The 1st Battalion, 8th Cavalry, under Maj. John Millikin, Jr., arrived at Unsan that afternoon, 30 October. In conferring with KMAG officers attached to the ROK 12th Regiment, Millikin and his company commanders learned that the ROK line, about 8,000 yards north of Unsan, was under attack and being pushed back.[32]

On 31 October, the 2d and 3d Battalions, 8th Cavalry, relieved the ROK 12th Regiment. But on the right an enemy attack during the night had driven back the ROK 2d Battalion more than a mile. Its commander wanted his troops to regain the lost ground before they were relieved. Millikin's 1st Battalion, however, moved into a defensive position behind this part of the ROK line north of Unsan. That afternoon, General Milburn, U.S. I Corps commander, visited the 8th Cavalry regimental command post and was told everything was all right.

On the morning of 1 November the ROK's tried to regain their lost ground. Though assisted by elements of the 6th Tank Battalion they made only a slight gain. In this situation, elements of B Company of Millikin's battalion and an attached platoon of tanks from B Company, 70th Tank Battalion, attacked north along the west bank of the Samt'an River. In this fight tank fire greatly assisted the ROK's, but three of the tanks were damaged. By noon the 2d Battalion of the ROK 12th Regiment had regained something more than half a mile of ground. But it seemed that it would make no further gain as heavy enemy 120-mm. mortar fire started falling, forcing the tanks to withdraw. Eastward across the river, at a distance of about two miles, the ROK 15th Regiment could be seen under very heavy attack.

The ROK 2d Battalion commander gave notice in the afternoon that if he was not relieved by 1600 his battalion would leave its position anyway. Apparently Col. Raymond D. Palmer, the 8th Cavalry commander, refused to effect the relief of the ROK battalion while heavy

---

[31] I Corps WD, 28 Oct 50; EUSAK POR 325, 28 Oct 50; Ltr, Gay to author, 19 Feb 54.

[32] Ltr, Gay to author, 19 Feb 54; Ltr, Millikin (CO, 1st Bn, 8th Cav Regt, Oct 50) to author, 6 May 54; I Corps WD, 29-30 Oct 50; EUSAK WD, Br for CG, 29 Oct 50; EUSAK WD, G-3 Sec, 30 Oct 50; 6th Med Tk Bn WD, 30 Oct 50; 8th Cav Regt Unit Jnl, entry at 301915 Oct 50.

fighting was in progress. The 1st Battalion, 8th Cavalry, actually relieved the ROK's north of Unsan at 1600 when the latter fell back through its lines, thus requiring Millikin's men to hold where they were. Watching the action across the river in the area held by the ROK 15th Regiment, while this change was taking place in his own front, Colonel Millikin saw through his field glasses that the hillside seemed alive as waves of enemy troops moved along the ridge leading into the ROK lines.[33]

The positions held in the late afternoon of 1 November by the 8th Cavalry were anchored on the right, about a mile northwest of Unsan, on the road below the village of Maebong-dong near the west bank of the Samt'an River. The line extended from there in an arc southwest across the mountain to a point three miles west of Unsan. There it crossed the east-west road out of Unsan and curved southeast to strike the main supply road, the Yongsan-dong and Yongbyon road, about three miles below Unsan. The 1st, 2d, and 3d Battalions were on this line in that order from east to west and southeast. This semicircle had a radius of about three miles from Unsan at the center, except on the north where the 1st Battalion was only a mile distant from the town. The 8th Cavalry regimental command post was on the main supply road south of Unsan between the town and the 3d Battalion command post. The day before, General Gay had established the 1st Cavalry Division command post at Yongsan-dong, twelve miles to the south.[34]

The arrival of the U.S. 8th Cavalry Regiment at Unsan had set in motion a redeployment of the ROK 1st Division. Upon being relieved west of Unsan on 31 October, the ROK 11th Regiment had shifted southeast to establish contact with the ROK 8th Division on the corps boundary. The ROK 12th Regiment moved to a rest and reserve assembly area at Ipsok south of the Kuryong River, six air miles from Unsan. Still engaged in the battle at Unsan, the ROK 15th Regiment was desperately trying to hold its position across the Samt'an River east of the 8th Cavalry Regiment. In short, the U.S. 8th Cavalry Regiment was to the north, west, and south of Unsan; the ROK 1st Division to the northeast, east, and southeast of it.

On the morning of 1 November, pursuant to I Corps and division orders, Colonel Johnson, the 5th Cavalry regimental commander, made ready to move a battalion of the 5th Cavalry eastward to bolster the disintegrating ROK II Corps lines near the I Corps boundary. Johnson alerted the 3d Battalion to move at 1230. At noon, Lt. Col. Hallett D. Edson, the 8th Cavalry regimental executive officer, arrived at the 5th Cavalry command post from Unsan. He told Johnson that about halfway between the two regiments, near the Nammyon River where it flows into the Camel's Head Bend of the Kuryong, he had encountered a great number of Korean refugees. They told him that a large force of Chi-

---

[33] Ltr, Millikin to author, 6 May 54; Interv, author with Hennig, 23 Mar 54; 70th Tk Bn WD, 1 Nov 50, Msg file, 1210, 1435; 8th Cav Regt Jnl file, 31 Oct–1 Nov 50, and 8th Cav POR 181, Msgs 311730, 011413, 011645, 31 Oct–1 Nov 50.

[34] Ltr, Millikin to author, 6 May 54 and attached sketch map; Ltr, Lt Col William Walton (CO, 2d Bn, 8th Cav, Nov 50) to author, 27 Aug 54 and attached sketch map; I Corps POR's 150 and 151, 1 Nov 50; 8th Cav Regt Unit Jnl, 011430 Nov 50.

THE CHINESE INTERVENE

nese was approaching behind them from the west. Since it was the 5th Cavalry's mission to protect the rear of the 8th Cavalry, Edson asked Johnson what he would do about the report. Johnson at once directed the 1st Battalion to send at least a platoon-sized patrol to investigate it.[35]

Johnson then departed with the 3d Battalion and placed it in a defensive position six miles northeast of Yongbyon on a low line of hills astride the Yongbyon–Kujang-dong road, facing east. This accomplished, he and the battalion commander proceeded on eastward some miles until they encountered a mass of retreating troops of the ROK II Corps. Johnson said of them: "They were a solid mass of soldiers on the road—indifferent to vehicles moving, indifferent to all that was around them. They were a thoroughly defeated outfit at this particular time." Johnson had served in the Philippines during the fall of Bataan in World War II and he likened the appearance and behavior of these ROK's to what he had seen on Bataan just before the American surrender there.[36]

Johnson turned back, passed through the picturesque walled city of Yongbyon, and that evening, shortly after dark, arrived at his command post at Yongsandong. There he learned that the 1st Battalion patrol in the early afternoon had found Chinese soldiers astride the road opposite the Turtle Head Bend of the Kuryong River, four air miles south of the 3d Battalion, 8th Cavalry, positions. During the afternoon two companies of the 1st Battalion had moved to the scene and were now engaged in battle there with a large enemy force.

On the West Coastal Road

Westward in the coastal area, the pursuit seemed to be going forward with success. On the evening of 25 October the 27th British Commonwealth Brigade crossed the Taeryong River at and near Pakch'on. On the west side it met enemy opposition. On the 27th the Middlesex 1st Battalion led the brigade attack, and three miles west of the river engaged an enemy force in a severe battle. In the course of it, air strikes and artillery preparations helped the infantry by knocking out ten North Korean T34 tanks and two self-propelled guns. After this battle, Brigadier Coad was convinced that the days of "rolling" were over, and he adopted a brigade formation better suited to heavy combat. On the 28th, after a 15-mile advance, the brigade stopped three miles from Ch'ongju.[37]

The next morning, 29 October, the Australian 3d Battalion attacked toward Ch'ongju. Aerial observers reported at least four enemy tanks with infantry on the ridge overlooking the road at the pass. In strikes against these positions with napalm and rockets, the Air Force destroyed four tanks. The Australian attack then gained the pass and the adjacent ridge lines. That evening the North Koreans attacked the Australians there in the two hours preceding midnight,

---

[35] Interv, author with Col Harold K. Johnson, 28 Apr 54; Johnson, MS review comments, recd Aug 54.

[36] Ibid.; Ltr, Millikin to author, 6 May 54.

[37] 27th British Commonwealth Brig Sitrep, 24–28 Oct 50; 24th Div WD, 26–28 Oct 50; EUSAK POR 316, 25 Oct 50; Bartlett *With the Australians in Korea*, pp. 32–34.

employing self-propelled gun and tank support. Australian bazooka teams destroyed three enemy T34's. Supporting American tank fire helped repel the attack. The Australians lost nine killed and thirty wounded in the battle before Ch'ongju. The next morning the Argylls entered Ch'ongju.

That evening, 30 October, North Korean high velocity shells landed in the vicinity of the town, six of them in the headquarters area of the Australian 3d Battalion. One of the six shells cleared a crest, hit a tree, and exploded outside Colonel Green's tent. Colonel Green was asleep inside on a stretcher. Strangely enough, although there were numerous soldiers in the area at the time, no one was injured except Colonel Green, who was struck in the stomach by a shell fragment. The seriously wounded officer was taken to the surgical hospital at Anju. There three days later the much admired Lt. Col. Charles H. Green, the Australian 3d Battalion commander, died. Lt. Col. I. B. Ferguson succeeded him in command of the battalion. The same night that North Korean fire struck down Colonel Green, similar artillery or tank fire killed Major Reith of the 27th Brigade.

Brigadier Coad on the 30th asked General Church, commanding the 24th Division, to pass a regiment through his British troops at Ch'ongju because they were very tired. Acceding at once, Church ordered the 21st Infantry Regiment to lead the advance.

At dark that evening, Lt. Col. Gines Perez' 2d Battalion, 21st Infantry, passed through the British lines and headed north past the burning houses of Ch'ongju. The moon was up and the silvery light promised to aid the night attack.

Beyond Ch'ongju the men could hear the rumble of withdrawing North Korean tanks. At 0200 on high ground two and a half miles west of the village of Kwaksan seven enemy tanks and about 500 North Korean infantry troops tried to ambush the battalion column. The nearest enemy tank opened fire with its cannon at 300 yards' range. Other enemy tanks joined the fire, their shells looking like big orange balls as they came streaking down the road. Several of them hit American tanks, but all bounced off. These tanks returned fire at the enemy gun flashes. Colonel Stephens, the regimental commander, and Colonel Perez, the battalion commander, from their radio jeeps directed the battle that was now joined. By dawn the North Koreans abandoned their position, leaving behind fifty dead, 5 knocked-out tanks, 1 self-propelled gun, and 7 antitank guns. After daylight an air attack destroyed 2 more enemy tanks, and the infantry captured 2 on flatcars.[38]

After this night of battle, the regiment encountered only light resistance. Its advanced troops, Lt. Col. Charles B. Smith's 1st Battalion, by noon of 1 November reached the outskirts of Chonggo-dong, eighteen air miles from Sinuiju and the Yalu River.

There, acting on orders from the 24th Division, Colonel Stephens ordered the battalion to halt, consolidate its position, and be prepared to defend in depth. The order from the 24th Division for the

---

[38] Interv, author with Col Gines Perez, 6 Aug 51; Interv, author with Maj Charles R. Alkire (S–2, 21st Inf Regt), 6 Aug 51; 24th Div WD, 29–31 Oct 50; 21st Inf Unit Rpt 115, 31 Oct 50. Eighth Army General Order 244, 26 April 1951, awarded the Distinguished Service Cross to Colonel Perez.

regiment to halt, which in turn had come from I Corps, hit the 1st Battalion, 21st Infantry, "like a bolt out of the blue." [39]

At midafternoon seven enemy tanks and an estimated 500 infantry attacked the 1st Battalion at Chonggo-dong. Capt. Jack G. Moss, commanding A Company, 6th Medium Tank Battalion, led his tanks out to meet the enemy armor. In a blazing tank battle that lasted half an hour, they destroyed it. Two of the American tanks were slightly damaged. The fire of infantry, tanks, and artillery turned back the North Korean infantry and inflicted on it an estimated 100 casualties.[40]

This was the northernmost action fought by a unit of the United States Eighth Army in the Korean War. By a strange coincidence, the infantry element engaged was Colonel Smith's 1st Battalion, 21st Infantry, part of which had fought the first American ground battle near Osan nearly four months earlier. In a geographical sense at least, the action near Chonggo-dong on the afternoon of 1 November was the high-water mark of Eighth Army's effort to reach the Manchurian border and consolidate all of Korea for a unified government.

Advancing behind the 27th British Commonwealth Brigade, the 5th Regiment had been the first unit of the 24th Division to cross the Ch'ongch'on River. It continued on and crossed the Taeryong River above Pakch'on on 28 October. From there it marched northward on the right of the British troops toward Taech'on. On the 29th in a heavy battle it and supporting air units destroyed nine enemy tanks and four self-propelled guns. The 5th Regimental Combat Team then entered Taech'on. Two of 89 prisoners taken were Chinese, the first captured by American troops in the Korean War. They turned out to be deserters or stragglers from their units. There were no CCF units in contact with the 5th Regimental Combat Team at Taech'on.[41]

From Taech'on, Colonel Throckmorton's 5th RCT turned northwest toward Kusong. An enemy force estimated to number 5,000 to 6,000 men, supported by tanks, self-propelled guns, artillery, and mortars stubbornly opposed the advance. But the 5th RCT, strongly supported by tactical air, captured Kusong just after noon on the 31st. The regimental attack the next day secured the road junction a few miles north of Kusong. In this action the regiment killed an estimated 300 to 400 enemy soldiers, and destroyed 2 self-propelled guns, 8 76-mm. howitzers, 8 mortars, 6 antitank guns, and 5 machine guns. Advanced elements of the 5th RCT were about ten miles north of Kusong at midday when a liaison plane came over and dropped a message, as it had to the 21st Infantry along the coastal road. This ordered the regiment to stop and hold in place.[42]

---

[39] 21st Inf WD, 1 Nov 50; EUSAK WD, G-3 Sec, 1 Nov 50; 24th Div WD, 1 Nov 50.

[40] 21st Inf Unit Rpt 116, 31 Oct-1 Nov 50; Interv, author with Lt Col Charles B. Smith, 6 Nov 51; *Armor* (May-June, 1951), article by 1st Lt. Robert D. Wilcox (tk plat ldr in the action), p. 28.

[41] Interv, author with Col John L. Throckmorton, 16 Apr 54; Ltr, Thompson to author, 9 Apr 54.

[42] 24th Div WD, 30 Oct-2 Nov 50; EUSAK WD, Br for CG, 30 Oct 50; Interv, author with Maj Gen Garrison H. Davidson, 28 Jan 54.

The uncertainty of the 21st and 5th Regiments during the afternoon and evening of 1 November over their future courses of action was resolved an hour before midnight when the 24th Division ordered them to withdraw toward the Ch'ongchon.[43] Mystified and disappointed, the men of the two regimental combat teams traveled back toward the Ch'ongch'on the night of 1–2 November. They were to learn later that the explanation for this, to them, puzzling development lay in events that had taken place in the east. The day before, 31 October, General Walker verbally had ordered General Milburn to limit the 24th Division attack in keeping with the situation in the Unsan area. There lay the controlling events.

The X Corps' Changing Mission

Contemporary events unfolding at the X Corps front in northeast Korea complete the view of the whole situation at the time the Chinese were first appearing in the suddenly changed picture of the almost ended war. As late as 16 October General Almond had received orders from General MacArthur's headquarters in Tokyo that, upon landing, X Corps would attack west along the Wonsan-P'yongyang axis. But the next day he received an alert order from General MacArthur stating that if Eighth Army had captured P'yongyang before X Corps landed, the corps would advance north instead of west. On the 18th came an alternate order from MacArthur which provided that, if P'yongyang was captured before D-day, X Corps would advance north in a zone parallel to Eighth Army, with the watershed of the Taebaek Range as the boundary between the two forces. The next day, 19 October, X Corps received the final and definite order to advance north.[44]

On 20 October General Almond flew from the USS *Missouri* by helicopter to the Wonsan Airfield. At noon he assumed command of troops in the X Corps area north of latitude 39° 10′ north and east of the Taebaek Range. The X Corps command post was now officially in Wonsan. By the end of October, X Corps had teletype communications with Eighth Army and the 2d Logistical Command, and radio communications with GHQ in Tokyo.[45]

The troops which General Almond found in his corps area on 20 October consisted of his own small command group of approximately 10 officers and 30 men, ROK I Corps troops numbering more than 23,000 men, and the few hundred troops of the 1st Marine Air Wing already at the airfield. His own X Corps troops still afloat would bring the total to nearly 84,000 men. In addition, there was the U.S. 3d Division which he expected would soon join the corps. Of the approximately 84,000 men then in the corps, more than a third—32,000— were South Korean soldiers. The major tactical organizations were the U.S. 1st Marine and 7th Infantry Divisions, and the 3d and Capital Divisions of ROK I

---

[43] 24th Div WD, 1–2 Nov 50; 21st Inf Unit Jnl, Msg 31, 012211 and Msg 35, 012300 Nov 50; EUSAK WD, G-3 Sec, 31 Oct 50.

[44] X Corps WD, Oct 50 Summ, p. 3; *Ibid.*, Opns, p. 19, citing CINCUNC Msg CX66705, 17 Oct 50, and CINCUNC Msg CX66739, 19 Oct 50; *Ibid.*, Diary, CG X Corps, 16 and 18 Oct 50.

[45] X Corps WD, Summ and Diary, CG X Corps, 20 Oct '50; *Ibid.*, Oct 50 Summ, Sig Sec, pp. 29–30.

THE CHINESE INTERVENE

Corps.[46] The only known organized enemy groups in the X Corps area at this time were north and northeast of Hungnam.

Rough terrain characterized the area in northeast Korea assigned to the X Corps. (*See Map 21.*) Even the coastal plain hardly deserved that name; the only level or semilevel land there consisted of isolated pockets extending inland generally for a distance of from three to five miles. These were separated from each other by hill spurs that came down to the sea. The Wonsan-Hamhung pocket is by far the largest of these northeast coast semilevel areas. Wonsan and Hamhung, and the latter's port of Hungnam, were the largest centers of population in the X Corps zone of operation. Wonsan in 1949 had a population of 150,000, but it had fallen to an estimated 90,000 in October 1950. Hamhung's population in October 1950 was placed at 80,000, at least 40 percent of it Communist or Communist-inclined. Chemical, dye, medical, gunpowder, and fertilizer plants in the Hungnam-Hamhung area made it the outstanding industrial area of Korea. At the ports of Wonsan and Hungnam ice is unusual, and when it occurs it is so thin as to be unimportant.

Back of the coastal strip lies the northern Taebaek Range with its steep slopes and narrow, twisting valleys. The peaks in the highest parts of the range reach an altitude of 6,000 feet or more. In the interior part of the northern Taebaeks the winter temperatures often reach 20° to 30° below zero. Snow in October and November is normally infrequent, and in December not usually heavy enough to form deep, permanent drifts. But rivers in the Taebaek Range usually freeze over by mid-December. Beginning forty air miles northward from Hamhung and extending another forty miles north in the heart of the Taebaek Range lies the Changjin Reservoir. Fifteen air miles east of it lies the smaller Pujon (Fusen) [47] Reservoir.

The principal road north from the Wonsan-Hamhung plain climbs the Taebaek Range to the Kot'o-ri plateau and then continues on to Hagaru-ri at the southern end of the Changjin Reservoir. From the Hamhung area a second important road, the east coast road, curves northeast toward the border of the Soviet Union. Inland from this coastal road the communication routes were poor—in places scarcely more than mountain trails.

Almond's general plan of deployment in this mountainous waste of northeast Korea was for the ROK I Corps to advance to the northeast border along the coastal and adjacent roads; the U.S. 7th Infantry Division, southwest of the ROK's, to advance to the northern border over the Iwon-Pukch'ong-Hyesanjin corridor; southwest of the 7th Division,

---

[46] X Corps POR 24, 20 Oct 50. The actual strengths of the various organizations were as follows:

X Corps	U.S.	ROK
Total	51,489	33,692
Hq and Hq and Service Group	3,870	80
X Corps Combat Troops	1,479	
1st Marine Div	24,031	
Army Attached Marine Div	93	
Engr Special Brig	1,393	
X Corps Tactical Air	1,786	
7th Div	18,837	7,804
1st and 5th ROK Marines		2,159
Hq and Hq Co. ROK I Corps		664
Capital Div (ROK)		11,626
3d Div (ROK)		11,359

[47] See p. 729, n. 1, below.

the U.S. 1st Marine Division to advance northward from Hamhung to the Changjin Reservoir, with its specific route beyond that point dependent on tactical developments in its front; and the U.S. 3d Division, when it arrived, to secure the Wonsan-Hamhung area, keep open the corps lines of communication, and protect the corps rear and left flank from guerrilla interference. Until the 3d Division arrived, the 1st Marine Division would have the responsibility of securing the Wonsan-Hungnam area. Accordingly it would not be entirely free to concentrate for the advance northward. As General Almond himself said a little later of X Corps, "We are scattered all over the landscape." But, generally, the deployment was controlled by the road net of the area in which the corps was to operate.[48]

On 26 October General Almond issued orders for his plan of operation. In its zone, the 1st Marine Division was split into three regimental combat teams: (1) the 1st Marines to relieve ROK I Corps elements in the Kojo and Majonni areas south and west of Wonsan; (2) the 5th Marines to secure the Wonsan area, the Yonp'o Airfield south of Hungnam, and the X Corps west flank; and (3) the 7th Marines to relieve the ROK 3d Division along the Hamhung-Changjin Reservoir corridor, and to secure the power installations of the Changjin and Pujon Reservoirs.[49]

The CCF Block the Way to Changjin Reservoir

Acting upon its orders, the ROK I Corps had attacked north from the Hamhung area—the 3d Division north toward the Changjin Reservoir and the Capital Division northeast up the coastal road. The 26th Regiment led the advance for the ROK 3d Division. On the morning of 25 October two battalions of the regiment approached the first and second hydroelectric plants of the Changjin Reservoir area, about thirty road miles inland from Hungnam, and halfway to the reservoir itself. A message from Maj. Malcolm Smith, KMAG adviser with the regiment, to Colonel Emmerich that evening informed him that the regiment had captured a prisoner definitely identified as a Chinese soldier who said he belonged to the *5th Regiment* of the Chinese *8th Army*. This prisoner said there were 4,000 to 5,000 Chinese in the immediate vicinity.

During the next two days the ROK regiment moved ahead very slowly against increasing resistance. On the morning of 28 October the ROK's attacked in the vicinity of Sudong in what proved to be a very costly action, and suffered heavy casualties. ROK patrols to the Sinhung-ni and Koto-ri areas brought back news that they had seen at both places what they believed to be Chinese soldiers. That day two Chinese

---

[48] X Corps WD, 4 Nov 50, G-1 Rpt, Notes on Conference between CG X Corps and Partridge, 4 Nov 50; X Corps WD, 26 Oct 50; *Ibid.*, Catalogue of Plans and Orders, p. 50, Opn Instr 13, 261000 Oct 50.
The corps boundary was changed slightly on 28 October to run from the Sea of Japan at the 38th Parallel to longitude 128° east, thence northwest to Poftong-ni, longitude 127° 5' east, latitude 38° 58' north, thence north on that parallel to the 39th Parallel, thence west on that parallel to longitude 126° 45' east. See EUSAK WD, G-3 Sec, 28 Oct 50.

[49] X Corps WD, Oct 50, Opns, p. 20; 1st Mar Div SAR, 8 Oct-13 Dec 50, an. C, pp. 9-10.

THE CHINESE INTERVENE

soldiers were captured one mile west of Sudong.

All day of the 29th small arms close combat continued in the large fields around the second hydroelectric plant. In the afternoon enemy 120-mm. fire increased. The ROK troops at the same time began to show signs of demoralization as their supply of grenades ran low. In the fighting on this day, the ROK's captured sixteen more Chinese soldiers and learned from them that the *370th Regiment, CCF 124th Division, 42d Army, XIII Army Group*, blocked the way north, with the rest of the division nearby. North Korean tanks supported these Chinese. The Chinese division and regimental headquarters reportedly were at Hagaru-ri at the southern end of the Changjin Reservoir. On the 30th, after a heavy battle with the CCF, the ROK 26th Regiment withdrew a short distance to a stronger defensive position.[50]

The capture of the sixteen Chinese on the 29th was a considerable prize, and General Kim, the ROK I Corps commander, telephoned the news to General Almond. The next day, 30 October, General Almond went to the ROK I Corps command post at Hamhung and personally inspected the captives and interviewed them through an interpreter. The Chinese told him they had not eaten for three days. They said they had crossed the Yalu River at Manp'ojin on 16 October (later they said they had crossed on the 14th) and had marched from there on foot at night, their mortars being carried on packhorses and mules. Most of the sixteen soldiers were members of the *Mortar Company, 370th Regiment*. At the time of their capture they said three of their four mortars had been destroyed and the fourth had been withdrawn. The men were well-clothed, healthy, and averaged twenty-eight to thirty years in age. They asserted that their entire division had crossed into Korea and marched to the front. Most of the men in this division had been in Chiang Kai-shek's Nationalist Army, stationed near Peiping, until about a year earlier, they said. Their division had surrendered there to the Communists and was immediately taken into the Red Army. General Almond at once sent a personal radio message to General MacArthur informing him of the presence of CCF units in northeast Korea and giving such details as he had learned in the course of his interview with the prisoners.[51]

The *370th Regiment* apparently arrived at its positions near Sudong on 23 or 24 October and first encountered ROK troops on the 25th. Behind it came the other two regiments of the *124th Division*, the *371st* and *372d*, one a few days behind the other. When General Almond visited General Kim again on 31 October, he learned that seven more CCF prisoners had been captured to make a total of twenty-five now in the X Corps zone. Some of them said a second CCF division was near the Changjin Reservoir.[52]

---

[50] X Corps WD, Oct 50, p. 15; X Corps PIR 33, 29 Oct, and 35, 31 Oct 50; Emmerich, MS review comments, 30 Nov 57.

[51] X Corps WD, Diary, CG X Corps, 30 Oct 50; Ibid., G-1 Rpt, Notes on Conference between CG X Corps and Partridge, 4 Nov 50; X Corps PIR 34, 30 Oct 50; Interv, author with Almond, 13 Dec 51; Ltr, McCaffrey to Almond, 1 Dec 54, forwarded to author.

[52] X Corps WD, Diary, CG X Corps, 31 Oct 50; Ibid., PIR 36, 1 Nov 50; ATIS Interrog Rpts (N.K. Forces), Issue 18, 2324, p. 57.

A search of enemy dead showed they carried no official identification, although a few had written their names and units in ink on the left inside of their blouses. The officer's uniform differed from that of the rank and file only by a vertical red piping on trousers, on the left side of the jacket, around the collar, and a diagonal across the sleeve cuff. The uniforms were heavily quilted cotton, usually a mustard brown color, although some of the Chinese wore dark blue. The quilted uniform was warm until it became water-soaked; then it was difficult to dry. Underneath it the soldiers wore the summer uniform and any other clothing they owned. Their laceless shoes were of cloth, low-cut, rubber-soled, and worn with sets of cotton socks. Heavy cotton caps had ear flaps that gave neck protection. These soldiers were armed mostly with Japanese rifles confiscated in Manchuria at the end of World War II. The greater part of their mortars, machine guns, and Thompson submachine guns were American-made, having been captured from the Nationalists. Approximately 70 percent of the *124th Division* had formerly been Nationalist soldiers in Chiang Kai-shek's army. Having left its artillery behind because of the mountains, the *124th Division* in the battle below the reservoir used nothing larger than 82-mm. mortars.[53]

North Koreans as well as the newly arrived CCF fought in the Sudong area. On the 29th, for instance, in addition to the sixteen Chinese, the ROK 26th Regiment captured sixty North Korean prisoners. There, as in front of Eighth Army at the same time, the North Koreans fought delaying actions while they backed up to a point where they met the approaching Chinese or the latter lay in wait. It was perhaps a coincidence that the Chinese entered action on both fronts, first against ROK troops as it chanced, at almost the same moment. In both east and west that fateful day was 25 October.

---

[53] X Corps PIR 43, 8 Nov and 46, an. 2, 11 Nov 50; 1st Mar Div SAR, vol. I, pp. 15, 19, 20, 30, an. B, 6-8 Nov 50; SSgt Robert W. Tallent, "New Enemy," *Leatherneck*, vol. XXXIV, No. 2 (February 22, 1951), pp. 12-14.

CHAPTER XXXIV

Unsan

So ends the bloody business of the day.
HOMER, *Odyssey*

In the Unsan and Onjong area at the end of October, great smoke clouds hung in the skies. What did these smoke clouds portend? Everyone in the area noticed them. Capt. Jack Bolt, commanding officer of C Battery, 99th Field Artillery Battalion, counted ten different forest fires burning in the mountains when his unit moved up on the 30th to support the 3d Battalion, 8th Cavalry Regiment, south of Unsan. The next day Colonel Johnson witnessed much the same thing during his visit to the 8th Cavalry regimental command post. And General Allen, the 1st Cavalry Division assistant commander, likewise saw them on 1 November when he drove to Unsan. These great smoke clouds north and northeast of Unsan came from forest fires set by the enemy. They obscured U.N. aerial observation and masked enemy troop movements.

The evidence on 1 November particularly indicated that some large enemy movement was in progress. That morning a Korean civilian reported that 2,000 Chinese soldiers were in a valley nine miles southwest of Unsan and that their mission was to move eastward and cut the road below the town. A member of a Home Guard unit reported there were 3,000 Chinese on Obong-san, six miles southwest of Unsan. Colonel Edson, in talking to Colonel Johnson, apparently referred to this force. At noon, air and artillery had dispersed an enemy column eight miles southeast of Unsan, killing approximtaely 100 horses and an unknown number of men. This column was approaching the ROK 11th Regiment positions which were then near the ROK II Corps boundary. In the afternoon aerial observers reported sighting large columns of enemy troops in motion northeast and southwest of Unsan. An air strike hit one of these columns, containing twenty-one vehicles loaded with troops, nine miles northeast of Unsan.[1]

At his command post at Yongsan-dong in the afternoon, General Gay and Brig. Gen. Charles D. Palmer, the division artillery commander, were listening to the chatter on the artillery radio set. Suddenly the voice of an observer in an L–5 plane directing fire of the 82d Field

---

[1] I Corps WD, Intel Summs, 142–43, and POR 150, 1 Nov 50.

Artillery Battalion (155-mm. howitzers) came in: "This is the strangest sight I have ever seen. There are two large columns of enemy infantry moving southeast over the trails in the vicinity of Myongdang-dong and Yonghung-dong. Our shells are landing right in their columns and they keep coming." The two places mentioned were about seven and five air miles respectively southwest and west of Unsan. General Palmer broke in on the radio to order the 99th Field Artillery Battalion to join in the fire on these enemy columns. General Gay, who had become uneasy about the dispersion of the 1st Cavalry Division, telephoned I Corps headquarters to request that the 7th Cavalry Regiment, which I Corps was holding south of the Ch'ongch'on, be ordered to join him at Yongsan-dong and that he be allowed to withdraw the 8th Cavalry Regiment a distance of several miles from Unsan. He also protested the use of the 3d Battalion, 5th Cavalry, at the corps boundary on the east. His requests were denied.[2]

While the record indicates general reluctance on the part of the American command to accept the accumulating evidence of Chinese intervention, at least one responsible staff officer seems to have agreed with the ROK interpretation of events at an early date. Col. Percy W. Thompson, G-2 of I Corps, briefed troops of the advanced party of the 1st Cavalry Division at I Corps headquarters when the division was committed in the Unsan area. He pointed out that they might be fighting Chinese forces. Their reaction was one of disbelief and indifference. This same attitude was apparent in the staff of the 8th Cavalry Regiment and some of the division officers when Colonel Hennig, who had been with the ROK 1st Division throughout the Unsan fighting, tried to tell them that they were up against Chinese forces. General Gay maintained that his first information on Chinese intervention came on 1 November when he visited General Paik at the latter's ROK 1st Division headquarters at Yongbyon. This is hard to reconcile with the fact that in the last two days of October officers and men of the 8th Cavalry Regiment at Unsan heard a great deal about the Chinese from the ROK 1st Division troops and the attached KMAG officers. Apparently most of the officers and men of the 8th Cavalry Regiment received this information with skepticism or disbelief.[3]

In the early afternoon of 1 November General Walker telephoned to General Milburn and told him the ROK II Corps had ceased to be an organized fighting organization, and that his right flank was unprotected. Walker told Milburn to take measures to protect his flank and to assume command of any ROK units that came into the U.S. I Corps area. General Milburn set out immediately for Kunu-ri to see the ROK corps commander, after giving orders to his chief of staff, Brig. Gen. Rinaldo Van Brunt, to organize a blocking force to take a position on the Kunu-ri–Anju road southwest of Kunu-ri. This blocking force was composed principally of Engineer and Ordnance troops. Its mission was to protect the I Corps right flank and the ponton bridges over the Ch'ongch'on River.

---

[2] Ltr, Gay to author, 19 Feb 54.

[3] Ltrs, Gay to author, 19 Feb, 15 Mar, and 24 June 54; Interv, author with Hennig, 23 Mar 54; Ltr, Thompson to author, 9 Apr 54.

When Milburn arrived at the ROK II Corps headquarters he found it in the act of moving to Sunch'on. The ROK corps commander told him that he had lost contact with and did not know the location of most of his subordinate units, that they were disorganized, and that so far as he knew he had only three battalions of the ROK 7th Division in the vicinity of Kunu-ri capable of fighting. Milburn told the ROK commander that he must hold Kunu-ri, and that a blocking force of U.S. troops west of the town would support him.[4]

Meanwhile, other disquieting events were taking place south of Unsan and behind the 8th Cavalry Regiment. When the platoon-sized combat patrol from the 1st Battalion, 5th Cavalry, in the early afternoon of 1 November moved north from Yongsan-dong it found its way blocked at a point four air miles, or six to seven road miles, below the position of the 3d Battalion, 8th Cavalry Regiment. (Map 23) As radio reports told him of the enemy's strength, the battalion commander rapidly reinforced the platoon with the full strength of A and B Companies. The enemy force held a position on the ridge extending across the road just south of the Turtle Head Bend of the Kuryong River.

Upon Colonel Johnson's return to the 5th Cavalry command post in the evening, the 1st Battalion commander requested him to release the third rifle company. Johnson approved the request, and C Company moved north. In the meantime, shortly after dark, the Chinese at the roadblock attacked the two companies in front of them and drove B Company from its position with the loss of four 81-mm, mortars and other equipment. Colonel Johnson then directed the withdrawal of A Company to the defensive position C Company established near midnight. There, A and B Companies assembled for reorganization. Johnson alerted the 2d Battalion at 2300, and two hours later ordered it north to support the 1st Battalion.[5]

By noon of 1 November, therefore, the Chinese had cut and blocked the main road six air miles south of Unsan with sufficient strength to turn back two rifle companies which had been strongly supported by air strikes during daylight hours. The CCF had set the stage for an attack that night against the 8th Cavalry Regiment and the ROK 15th Regiment. When dusk fell that evening enemy soldiers were on three sides of the 8th Cavalry—the north, west, and south. Only the ground to the east, held by the ROK 15th Regiment, was not in Chinese possession.

North of the Town

The Chinese attack north of Unsan had gained strength in the afternoon of 1 November against the ROK 15th Regiment on the east, and gradually it extended west into the zone of the 8th Cavalry Regiment. The first probing attacks there, accompanied by mortar barrages, came at 1700 against the right flank unit, the 1st Battalion. There was also something new in the enemy fire support—rockets fired from trucks. These

---

[4] MS review comments, Milburn, Nov 57.

[5] Interv, author with Johnson, 28 Apr 54; Johnson, MS review comments, Aug 54; I Corps WD, 1 Nov 50 Intel Summ 142; 5th Cav WD, 1 Nov 50; I Corps POR 153, 2 Nov 50.

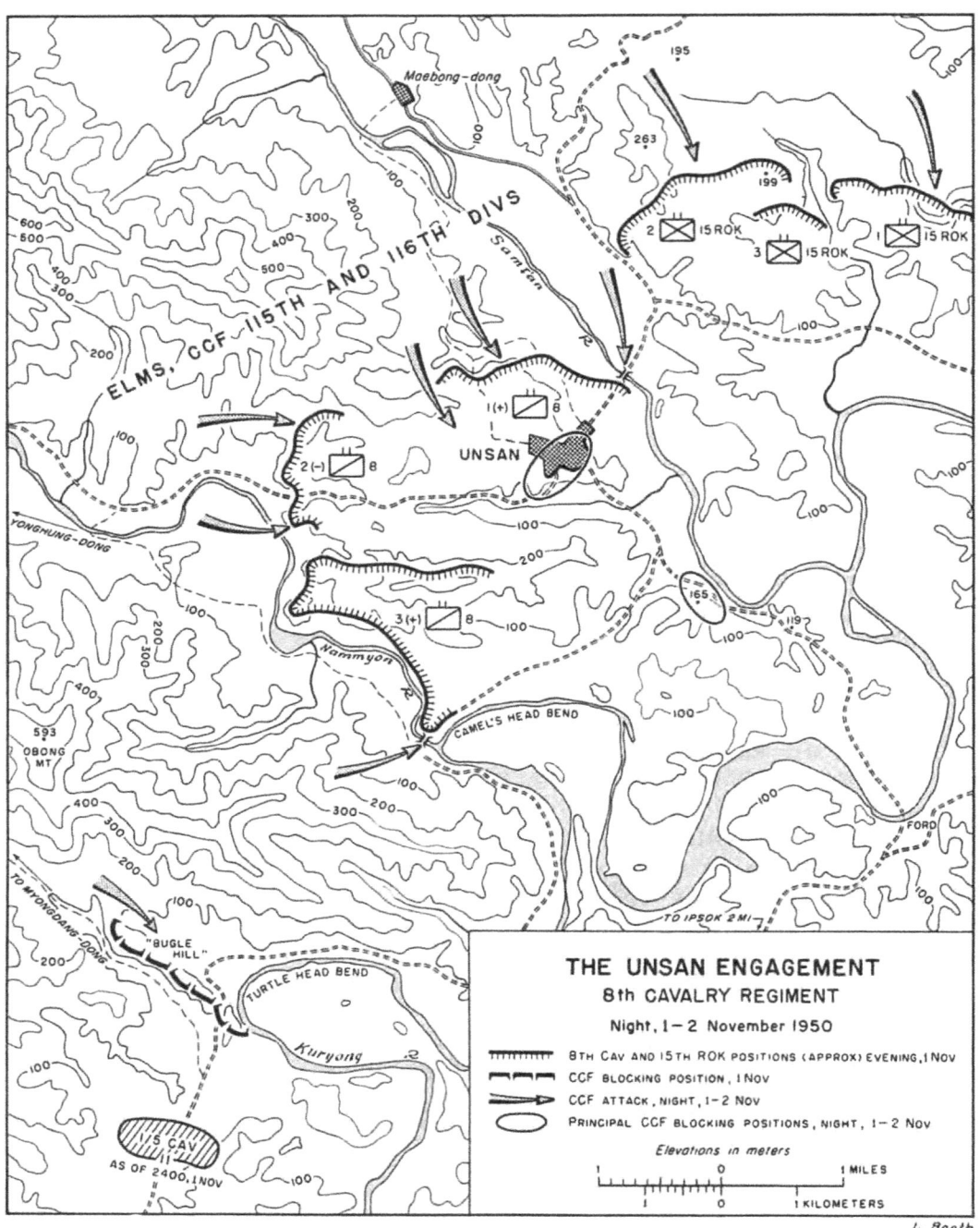

MAP 23

rocket vehicles were to the northeast, across the Samt'an River. Supporting artillery soon located and forced the rocket vehicles to move, but not before their rockets had struck an ammunition truck at the battalion command post. Major Millikin's men recovered one of the rocket shells and found that it was of the Russian Katushka 82-mm. type fired from four multiple tubes, truck-mounted.

At dusk Millikin's 1st Battalion controlled the river approaches from the north except for portions in the ROK 15th Regiment zone on the east side. Millikin's position was weak on the left, however, where troop strength did not permit him to extend far enough to reach the main ridge leading into Unsan. He had physical contact with the 2d Battalion in that direction only by patrols. Neither battalion held this ridge except for outposts.[6]

East of the river the ROK's were under heavy attack. In this action the ROK's captured two 57-mm. recoilless rifles and two automatic rifles with Chinese markings. At 1900 the 10th AAA Group, supporting the ROK's, issued a march order and in a tense atmosphere began packing its equipment. An hour and a half later the group closed its fire direction center, and at 2100 its motor convoy moved south under blackout conditions. The 78th AAA Battalion's 90-mm. guns, which were tractor-drawn and could be moved quickly, remained behind and continued to fire in support of the ROK's for an hour or two longer; then they too withdrew on corps orders. After about 2300 the ROK 15th Regiment disintegrated rapidly, and shortly after midnight ceased to exist as a combat force. Very few of these ROK troops escaped; they were either killed or captured.[7]

A lull in the fighting at Millikin's position ended at 1930 when the Chinese struck his battalion all along its line. They drove the right flank back 400 yards. The left flank then withdrew half that distance. Millikin rushed fifty men from the Engineer platoon and the Heavy Mortar Company to the right flank, and with this reinforcement he held there. Heavy action continued. About 2100 the Chinese found the weak link on the ridge line and began moving through it down the ridge behind the 2d Battalion.

At 2200 the tanks holding the bridge northeast of Unsan in the right rear of Millikin's 1st Battalion reported large groups of men across the Samt'an River, moving south. The 4.2-inch mortars supporting the ROK 15th Regiment in that area had now quit firing. Radio reports from the ROK's made it clear that they were being defeated and pushed back. In order to ascertain what the situation was there, Millikin sent his assistant S–3 across the river in a jeep to locate the mortarmen. That officer, after crossing the river, was fired on but escaped and reported back to Millikin. The moon was now coming up. Night visibility was good.

Since it was apparent that enemy groups were passing him on the east, Millikin ordered the battalion trains and all noncombat vehicles to move south through Unsan to the road fork and be

---

[6] Ltr, Millikin to author, 6 May 54.

[7] Intervs, author with Hennig, 23–24 Mar 54; 10th AAA Group WD, 1–2 Nov 50.

prepared to move from there southeast across the Kuryong River ford in the ROK 1st Division zone to Ipsok. About the same time, Lt. Col. William Walton, commanding officer of the 2d Battalion, ordered his motor officer to take all vehicles in the motor pool across the river by this same route. These vehicles from the two battalions arrived safely at Ipsok.

With much sounding of bugles and whistles the Chinese extended their strong attacks westward to the 2d Battalion, and in a short time penetrated its right and encircled its left. At the same time the fight with the 1st Battalion went on. Near the battalion boundary, A Company reported that it was engaged in hand-to-hand combat with the enemy in two directions, had pulled back its left flank, and was withdrawing to the next ridge. On Millikin's right the tanks holding the ground along the river were being pressed back. By 2300 both the 1st and 2d Battalions had been forced back and their positions penetrated. The 1st Battalion had expended its basic load of ammunition and most of the reserve ammunition the regiment had sent forward. Millikin reported by radio to the regimental commander the increasingly desperate situation of the two front-line battalions and the fact that he was almost out of ammunition.[8]

While this night battle was increasing in intensity, an important conference was in progress at I Corps headquarters. During the afternoon, General Milburn and his staff had become more and more disturbed at reports of what was happening to the ROK II Corps eastward and of the increasing tempo of the action near Unsan. At noon on 1 November I Corps had ordered the 24th Division to halt its advanced units, then only a few miles from the North Korean border. Some hours later, about 1800 in the afternoon, General Milburn sent out a call for a meeting at corps headquarters that night to be attended by the commanding generals and certain staff members of the 24th Division, the 1st Cavalry Division, and the ROK 1st Division. Before General Gay left his command post for the I Corps meeting at Anju, he ordered Col. Ernest V. Holmes, his chief of staff, to send a warning order to the 8th Cavalry Regiment to be prepared to withdraw from Unsan.

The meeting at I Corps headquarters got under way about 2000. In this meeting General Milburn directed the corps to go from the attack to the defensive immediately. This was the first time I Corps had gone on the defensive since its breakout from the Pusan Perimeter. Milburn returned the 8th Cavalry Regiment to division control, and ordered that it and the ROK 15th Regiment withdraw at once from Unsan to positions above the Yongsan-dong–Yongbyon–Unhung east-west road. This would amount to a general withdrawal of approximately twelve air miles. Generals Gay and Paik were to co-ordinate the withdrawals of their advanced regiments, the ROK 15th Regiment to be the last to withdraw. General Gay telephoned Colonel Holmes from Anju, instructing him to issue the withdrawal order to the 8th Cavalry Regiment. Then he and General Paik and their parties

---

[8] Ltr, Millikin to author, 6 May 54; Ltr, Walton to author, 27 Aug 54; 8th Cav Unit Hist Rpt, 1 Nov 50; 70th Tk Bn Jnl, 10 Nov 50 (a report from CO B Co, 70th Tk Bn, for period 1–9 Nov 50).

started back to their headquarters. A little after midnight they reached the 1st Cavalry Division command post. There they learned the bad news from the Unsan front.[9]

Colonel Palmer received the withdrawal order from the 1st Cavalry Division about 2300. Fifteen minutes before midnight he issued a warning order alerting all battalions and the regimental trains for a withdrawal south. At midnight he issued the withdrawal order. The withdrawal route indicated was the only one possible—east from the road fork south of Unsan, across the ford of the Kuryong River, and then by the main supply route of the ROK 1st Division to Ipsok and Yongbyon. Major Millikin telephoned Colonel Walton that he would try to hold Unsan until the 2d Battalion cleared the road junction south of it. Then he would withdraw. The 3d Battalion, south of Unsan, was to bring up the regimental rear.[10]

In the 2d Battalion, Colonel Walton had lost communication by this time with all his companies except H Company. He gave that company the withdrawal order with instructions to relay it to the rifle companies since it still had communication with them. The 2d Battalion headquarters group, under ineffective enemy small arms fire, began withdrawing eastward to the sound of heavy firing in Unsan.

In Major Millikin's 1st Battalion area just north of Unsan, A Company had been forced from its left flank position and Chinese were infiltrating south along the ridge line into Unsan behind the battalion. At the same time, the Chinese were pressing hard against B Company on the right and the tanks of B Company, 70th Tank Battalion, along the river where they guarded the battalion's right flank. Millikin soon received word that the tanks had been forced back to the road junction at the northeast edge of the town. The tankers reported they would try to hold there until the 1st Battalion could withdraw past that point. Millikin issued orders for A and B Companies each to leave one platoon behind as rear guard, and for them and D Company to withdraw through C Company to the tank-held road junction. When Millikin himself arrived at the road juncture he found there two tanks and the D Company mortar vehicles. Other tanks had already passed on into Unsan. A din of small arms fire from Unsan indicated that the enemy held the town.

A few minutes later, about half an hour after midnight, elements of A and B Companies arrived at the road fork at the northeast edge of Unsan. Enemy troops in the town began firing at them and caused some casualties. Millikin then sent these A and B Company men around to the east of Unsan with instructions to wait for him at the road fork and bridge south of the town. Mil-

---

[9] Ltr, Gay to author, 19 Feb 54; Interv, author with Holmes, 26 Feb 54; Interv, author with Col Robert T. Hazlett (KMAG adviser to ROK 1st Div and present with Paik at I Corps conference), 25 Feb 54; Ltr, Thompson to author, 9 Apr 54; I Corps WD, 1 Nov 50. The verbal orders given at the conference were confirmed by I Corps in Operation Directive 19, published at 2200, 1 November.

[10] Ltrs, Millikin and Walton to author, 6 May and 27 Aug 54; Ltr, Col Hallett D. Edson, 16 Apr 54, and attached Exhibit A, Maj. William S. Coleman (S-3, 8th Cav Regt), Operations of the 8th Cavalry Regiment, 1-2 November 1950, in the Vicinity of Unsan (15 Nov 50); I Corps WD, Intel Summ 146; 1st Cav Div POR 182, 011700-021700 Nov 50; 8th Cav Unit Hist Rpt, 1 Nov 50; 70th Tk Bn Jnl, 10 Nov 50 (1-9 Nov 50, 70th Tk Bn Rpt).

likin and most of his staff remained at the northeast edge of Unsan. They hoped to direct the rest of the battalion on the escape route, and to send the mortar carriers with wounded, escorted by the two remaining tanks, through Unsan to the road fork southward.

Four tanks of the 1st Platoon of B Company, 70th Tank Battalion, already had fought their way through the town and arrived at the road fork south of it. It was the noise of this conflict in Unsan that Millikin and his men heard from the northeast edge of the town. Fifteen minutes later Millikin ordered the last two tanks and the mortar vehicles with the wounded to try to get through Unsan. A burning truck at the first turn going west into the town halted the column. In trying to get around the truck the first tank slid into a shell crater and got stuck. Chinese soldiers killed the tank commander as he struggled to free the tank. Other Chinese placed a satchel charge on the tracks of the second tank and disabled it. Of the ten tank crewmen, two were killed and five wounded. Apparently none of the wounded on the mortar carriers escaped.[11]

A little later, about 0100, a miscellaneous assortment of men, including elements of C Company, South Koreans attached to the 1st Battalion, ROK stragglers from the 15th Regiment, and Chinese soldiers, arrived at the road junction northeast of town at about the same time. Millikin still waited there. In the confusion that now spread out of control the men tried to escape in groups. Millikin and a small group went westward north of Unsan and then circled to the southwest. At 0200, they encountered parts of H Company from the 2d Battalion also trying to reach the road fork south of Unsan.

Roadblock South of Town

When Colonel Palmer ordered the regimental withdrawal he placed Colonel Edson, the regimental executive officer, in charge of co-ordinating it and sent him to the road junction a mile and a half south of Unsan and a mile north of the regimental command post. That road junction was the critical point to be reached and passed by the scattered elements of the command. Accompanied by Capt. Rene J. Guirard, the regimental S-2, and two squads of the I&R Platoon, Edson arrived at the road junction just before midnight. Capt. Filmore W. McAbee, S-3 of the 3d Battalion, took one platoon of I Company and the company commander to the road fork about midnight, and after conferring there with Edson, he personally placed the platoon in position to protect the junction from the north.

The regimental trains passed through, as did the trains of the 1st and 2d Battalions; numerous groups of the 1st Battalion and some from the 2d Battalion also came through. The four 1st Platoon tanks arrived there about 0030. Edson placed them in defensive positions at the road junction. They remained there until two tanks of the 2d Platoon arrived. Then Edson ordered the first group of tanks to go southeast to the ford over the Kuryong River, and to protect it for the last part of the withdrawal. The two tanks that had just come through Unsan remained at the road junction.

---

[11] 70th Tk Bn, S-3 Jnl, Msgs at 0015 and 0030 2 Nov 50.

It was now about 0130, 2 November.[12]

As yet there had been no enemy action south of Unsan in the 3d Battalion area. Artillery elements supporting that battalion began withdrawing north through the road junction at this time. Headquarters and Service Battery and B Battery of the 99th Field Artillery Battalion passed eastward through the road junction. Next came C Battery. Captain Bolt, the battery commander, reached the road fork about 0220 at the head of his column of twenty vehicles, which included six prime movers towing six 105-mm. howitzers. He stopped briefly to talk with Colonel Edson who told him everything was all right and to go on.

The withdrawal route ran generally east from the road fork for a mile before it turned southeast to the ford across the Kuryong River and hence to Ipsok, four miles south of the river. Immediately east of the road fork the road ran on an embankment built above rice paddies with ditches on either side. North of the road, a considerable expanse of paddy ground extended to the Samt'an River at a point just before it turned east in a sharp bend to flow into the Kuryong a mile away. On the south side the paddy ground gave way to high ground which culminated in Hills 165 and 119. They crowded close on the road beginning at a point about 200 yards east of the road fork.

Captain Bolt turned east on this road and had proceeded about 200 yards when, upon glancing back, he saw that the second vehicle was not behind him. He told his driver to stop the jeep; they waited. The second vehicle had continued on past the turn at the road fork, had had to back up, and in doing so had jammed the column and caused the delay.

As he waited, Captain Bolt happened to glance to his left across the paddy ground, and in the moonlight he saw a line of men coming toward the road. He thought they were retreating 8th Cavalry infantrymen and remarked about them to his driver. When the oncoming soldiers were about fifty to seventy-five yards away the entire group opened fire on the road. Bolt shouted to his driver to get going, and upon rounding a curve where the hill came down to the road they lost sight of the rest of the battery at the road fork. Just around the curve from 15 to 20 enemy soldiers stood in the road. They opened fire on the jeep as it raced toward them. Bolt returned it with his submachine gun. The enemy group scattered to the sides of the road. The jeep raced on and passed 2 other small enemy groups, the last one numbering no more than 3 or 4 soldiers. Bolt soon caught up with the end of the regimental column, which he found consisted of B Battery and the four tanks of the 1st Platoon, B Company, 70th Tank Battalion. He tried to get one of the tanks to go back and fire down the road, but the tank commander said he was out of ammunition.[13]

---

[12] Coleman, Opns of 8th Cav, 1–2 Nov; Ltr, Edson to author, 16 Apr 54; Interv, author with Guirard, 21 Aug 54; Ltr, Maj Filmore W. McAbee to author, 8 Feb 57; 70th Tk Bn WD, 10 Nov and S–3 Jnl Msg at 0030 2 Nov 50; 8th Cav Unit Hist Rpt, 2 Nov 50.

[13] Details of Bolt's encounter with the CCF east of the road fork are based on Interv, Capt Edward C. Williamson with Bolt, 11 Jul 51, as reported in Williamson, Ambush of Battery C, 99th Field Artillery ,Battalion, 29 Oct–2 Nov 50, MS, copy in OCMH.

The enemy force at the road apparently had followed the 1st Battalion from north of Unsan, coming down along the west bank of the Samt'an River, although it is possible that they had crossed the river from the ROK 15th Regiment zone on the east.

As Bolt's jeep disappeared around the turn of the road the enemy soldiers reached the road embankment and opened fire on the next vehicle when it approached. This caused the driver to lose control and the 2½-ton truck upset over the side of the embankment, dragging the 105-mm. howitzer it was towing crosswise on the road and blocking it. One of the two tanks at the road fork went forward to try to break the roadblock, but the upset truck and howitzer blocked the way and the tank came under attack. Crewmen abandoned the tank after disabling its weapons. There is some evidence that a Chinese satchel charge had already broken the tank treads. Bolt's jeep was the last vehicle to pass eastward from the road fork below Unsan. Thus, at 0230 the Chinese had effectively cut the only remaining escape road from Unsan.[14]

At the road fork confusion swept over bewildered and frightened men. No one, it seems, was able to gather together enough men to fight the enemy roadblock force. Colonel Edson apparently made such an effort but it failed, and in the end he and his group escaped by circling around and through the roadblock force eastward and then south into the hills. Captain Guirard had several personal encounters with Chinese in this escape. Most of the artillerymen caught in the roadblock disappeared into the hill mass south of the road. A few officers, including one from I Company, and some of the noncommissioned officers, tried to assemble the men who had abandoned their vehicles and equipment on the road. But the few men they were able to bring together disappeared as soon as they turned their backs on them to look for others. A few Chinese soldiers came down among the vehicles and threw grenades, but most of them stayed at their roadblock position. Soon enemy machine gun and mortar fire began falling on the road junction area from the adjacent high ground.[15]

After watching Colonel Edson and his party disappear to the east, Colonel Walton, who meanwhile had arrived from west of Unsan, returned to his own 2d Battalion group at the road junction and led them southward across the hills. He came in through ROK lines at Ipsok after daylight with 103 men. When Major Millikin and his 1st Battalion group met elements of H Company west of the town, Millikin placed his wounded in their vehicles, and the combined party came on to the road fork. They found it a shambles of wrecked and abandoned vehicles and equipment.

Behind Millikin and the H Company group, the rest of the 2d Battalion never succeeded in reaching the road fork south of Unsan. Half a mile west of it, at the edge of the town, an enemy force cut the east-west road. There the Chi-

---

[14] 70th Tk Bn, S-3 Jnl, Msg at 0230 2 Nov 50.

[15] Williamson, Ambush of Battery C; Interv, author with Guirard, 21 Aug 54; Ltr, Edson to author, 16 Apr 54.

nese stopped A Battery, 99th Field Artillery Battalion, and the 3d Platoon, B Company, 70th Tank Battalion. Soon abandoned vehicles clogged the road at this point. The congestion was so bad that even the tanks could not get through and their crew members abandoned them after destroying their weapons. A few of these men filtered through to the road fork, but most of them went south over the hills. The infantry elements of the 2d Battalion for the most part scattered into the hills. Many of them reached ROK lines near Ipsok. Others came in to the position of the 3d Battalion, 8th Cavalry, the next morning. The sound of the 9th Field Artillery Battalion at Ipsok firing in support of the ROK 1st Division served as a guide for most of the men caught in the Unsan roadblock, and they moved in that direction.

When Major Millikin and his group arrived at the road fork they found Maj. Robert J. Ormond, commanding officer of the 3d Battalion, 8th Cavalry, there with a platoon of infantry. This was the I Company platoon McAbee earlier had posted north of the road fork blocking the road from Unsan. Millikin queried Ormond to find out what the latest orders were, as he had been out of communication with everyone since directing the 1st Battalion withdrawal. Ormond replied that he had no recent information, that his last orders were to try and hold the road fork until the 1st and 2d Battalions had gone through, and that he believed large portions of them had already passed eastward. Ormond then turned back south to his own battalion to start its withdrawal. The whole general area of the road fork was now under enemy small arms fire, some of it coming from the south which at first had been free of enemy soldiers.

Millikin found scattered elements of the 1st Battalion near the road fork and he collected about forty men, including Capt. Robert B. Straight of B Company who was wounded. Straight had stayed behind with one platoon north of Unsan when the rest of his company had withdrawn. There was one operable tank still at the road fork. Using its radio, Millikin tried to communicate with elements of the regiment, but was able to reach only one tank which was then engaged in running a roadblock near the ford over the Kuryong. The 1st Battalion commander then ordered the tank to start toward the enemy roadblock. He was following it with his men when enemy fire scattered them. The small groups infiltrated the Chinese lines and headed south. Millikin and the men with him crossed the Kuryong just before daylight and reached Ipsok about 0800. There he found his battalion trains and about 200 men of the 1st Battalion, most of them from those parts of A and B Companies that he had sent southeast around Unsan at the beginning of the withdrawal.

About noon on 2 November practically all men of the 1st Battalion who were to escape had reached the Ipsok area, and a count showed that the battalion had lost about fifteen officers and 250 enlisted men to all types of casualties. About half the battalion's mortars and heavy weapons had been lost to the enemy. Most of the regimental headquarters; the regimental trains; four tanks of B company, 70th Tank Battalion; and five artillery pieces crossed the Kuryong River ford safely and assembled in the vicinity of Yongbyon. From there they rejoined the 1st Cavalry Division at Yongsan-dong.[16]

Ordeal Near Camel's Head Bend

During the evening and first part of the night of 1 November the troops of the 3d Battalion, 8th Cavalry, south of Unsan and their supporting artillery and tanks had enjoyed undisturbed quiet. Some of them in the late afternoon had noticed airplanes strafing a few miles to the south and were aware that an enemy force in that vicinity was on their main supply road. Major Ormond just before midnight had passed on to his company commanders word of the impending withdrawal. Lt. Col. Robert Holmes, commanding officer of the 99th Field Artillery Battalion, gave instructions for the two batteries of artillery (B and C) to withdraw. Battalion headquarters and B Battery departed at 0115 and cleared the road fork south of Unsan. Last of the artillery to march was Captain Bolt with C Battery at 0200, and, as already noted, he encountered the first of the enemy roadblock force. A platoon of twenty-five men from K Company accompanied C Battery.[17]

The 3d Battalion had taken a position just north of the Nammyon River, where it flowed into the nose of the Camel's Head Bend of the Kuryong three air miles southwest of Unsan. Its mission was to guard the regimental rear. Major Ormond had established his command post in a flat plowed field with a tight perimeter formed by headquarters and M Company command groups. Two squads of M Company held the bridge immediately in the rear (south) of the battalion headquarters, and the 4th Platoon of B Company, 70th Tank Battalion, was disposed in position there on either side of the road north of the river. The tree line extending west along the Nammyon was held by L Company with one platoon on a high hill on the south side; I and K Companies in that order were on a ridge line running from northeast to southwest overlooking the stream northwest of the battalion command post. The communications switchboard and the S-2 and S-3 sections of the battalion headquarters found just off the road a ready-made dugout for their use in a 20-by-20-foot hole with a log and straw roof over it which the North Koreans had dug at some earlier date to hide vehicles from aircraft.[18]

Upon receiving the regimental order to withdraw, with the 3d Battalion assigned the mission of guarding the regimental rear, Major Ormond issued instructions for K and I Companies to withdraw from their positions to the battalion command post. Company L was to cover their withdrawal. None of the rifle companies was engaged with the

---

[16] Ltr, Millikin to author, 6 May 54; I Corps POR 153, 2 Nov 50; EUSAK WD, G-3 Jnl, 0840 2 Nov 50; 8th Cav Unit Hist Rpt, 2 Nov 50.

[17] Williamson, Ambush of Battery C; 99th FA Bn WD, 1 Nov 50.

[18] Ltr, Lt Col Veale F. Moriarty (Ex Off, 3d Bn, 8th Cav, Nov 50) to author, and attached sketch map, 11 Jun 54; Ltrs, McAbee (S-3 3d Bn, 8th Cav, Nov 50) to author, 20 Aug 54 and 8 Feb 57; Ltr, SSgt Elmer L. Miller to Capt Carlos L. Fraser, CO B Co, 70th Tk Bn, 6 Nov 50, from 4th Field Hospital (Miller was a tank commander at the 3d Bn command post); Ltr, Capt Walter L. Mayo, Jr. (Arty Liaison Off, C Btry, 99th FA Bn, with L Co) to author, 15 Jan 58, together with notes prepared by him for Unit Historian, 8th Cav Regt, in 1954. These sources form the principal basis for the following account of the 3d Battalion except as otherwise noted.

enemy, and no difficulty was expected. Major Ormond then drove northward to the regimental command post and subsequently to the road fork south of Unsan where Major Millikin saw him.

Ormond started back south just a few minutes before enemy troops cut the road below the fork. As it was, he returned to his command post without trouble. There he told certain members of his staff that the 3d Battalion could not withdraw northward through the road fork below Unsan as planned because that road was now held by enemy forces. Using a map Ormond showed Maj. Veale F. Moriarty, the battalion executive officer, the cross-country route he intended the battalion to follow and sent the motor officer off to find a ford by which the vehicles could cross the river. He then gave instructions to SSgt. Elmer L. Miller, in charge of a section of tanks near the command post, to cover the battalion withdrawal. Miller passed this word on to the 4th Platoon tank commander, and then went to examine the ford selected for the vehicular crossing. All the vehicles in the battalion area, except the tanks, were lined up on the road bumper to bumper ready to begin the withdrawal.

At this time, close to 0300, a company-sized column of men (one source said platoon-sized) from the south approached the bridge over the Nammyon River below the battalion command post. The two squads of M Company charged with security of the bridge let the column pass over the bridge thinking they were ROK's. When this column was even with the command post one of its leaders sounded a bugle. This was the signal for a deadly surprise assault on the battalion command post from all sides. At the same time, other enemy forces engaged L Company along the stream bank to the southwest, and still others crossed the stream directly south of the command post and attacked the tanks there. Sergeant Miller crawled back to his tank in time to help fight enemy troops off the decks with a pistol. The tanks on both sides of the road backed up to the road except one which was first damaged by a satchel charge and then, in a few minutes, blew up. At the road the tanks held off other enemy troops trying to cross the stream from the south.[19]

In the command post itself the greatest confusion reigned after the onset of the Chinese attack. Hand-to-hand encounters took place all over the battalion headquarters area as the Chinese soldiers who had marched across the bridge fanned out, firing on anyone they saw and throwing grenades and satchel charges into the vehicles, setting many of them on fire. Part of the men around the command post were still in their foxholes or shelters, some of them apparently asleep awaiting the order to start the withdrawal. One man later said, "I woke up when the shooting started." Another said, "Someone woke me and asked if I could hear a bunch of horses on the gallop . . . then bugles started playing taps, but far away. Someone blew a whistle, and our area was shot to hell in a matter of minutes." Still another man was awakened by an exploding hand grenade. Lt. W. C. Hill said, "I thought I was dreaming when I heard a bugle

---

[19] The 70th Tk Bn S-3 Jnl, Msg at 0300 2 Nov, reporting Miller's radio message on the destruction of this tank is the most reliable evidence on the time of the CCF attack against the 3d Battalion.

sounding taps and the beat of horses' hooves in the distance. Then, as though they came out of a burst of smoke, shadowy figures started shooting and bayoneting everybody they could find."[20]

When the shooting started, Major Ormond and Captain McAbee left the command dugout to determine the extent of what they thought was a North Korean attack. Major Moriarty, battalion executive officer, who was in the dugout at the time never saw Ormond again.

Once outside the dugout, Captain McAbee started for the roadblock at the bridge and Major Ormond veered off to the right to go to L Company by the river. As McAbee approached the bridge small arms fire knocked off his helmet and a few seconds later another bullet shattered his left shoulder blade. He turned back toward the command post and ran into a small group of enemy soldiers. He dodged around a jeep, with the enemy in pursuit. As they came around the jeep he shot them. In the field along the road he saw about thirty more enemy troops attempting to set a tank on fire. McAbee emptied his carbine into this group, and then, growing weak from loss of blood, he turned again toward the dugout. A few steps farther and three enemy soldiers stepped from the roadside ditch and prodded him with bayonets. Not trying to disarm him, they jabbered to each other, seemingly confused. McAbee pointed down the road, and after a little argument among themselves they walked away. Once more on his way to the dugout McAbee fell into the hands of a small group of Chinese, and repeated his earlier experience. After this second group walked off up the road, McAbee finally reached the command post.

Meanwhile, a few minutes after Ormond and McAbee had left the dugout, Capt. Clarence R. Anderson, the battalion surgeon, and Father Emil J. Kapaun, the chaplain, brought in a wounded man. The small arms fire continued unabated and Major Moriarty stepped outside to investigate. Visibility was good, and in the bright moonlight he saw Captain McAbee stagger toward him. Just beyond McAbee, Moriarty saw three or four uniformed figures wearing fur headgear. He grabbed McAbee and thrust him into the dugout. Close at hand someone called for help. Responding to the call, Moriarty clambered over the dugout ramp leading from the road and found the battalion S-4 rolling on the ground grappling with an enemy soldier. Moriarty shot this soldier with his pistol and another who was crouching nearby. For the next fifteen or twenty minutes he was one of the many in the command post area waging a "cowboy and Indian" fight with the Chinese, firing at close range, and throwing grenades.[21]

Seeing a center of resistance developing around Miller's tank, Moriarty ran to it and found about twenty other men crouching around it. When enemy mortar fire began falling near the tank, Moriarty took these men and with them crossed the stream to the south. They destroyed a small group of enemy troops at the stream bank. The south side appearing free of the enemy at that point,

---

[20] New York *Herald Tribune*, November 3, 1950, dispatches written at Ipsok, 2 November, by a correspondent who escaped from the Unsan area.

[21] Ltr, Moriarty to author, 11 Jun 54; Ltrs, McAbee to author, 20 Aug 54 and 8 Feb 57.

they proceeded southeast. During the night this party was joined by others from different units of the regiment. When they reached friendly ROK lines near Ipsok after daylight there were almost a hundred men in the group.

After perhaps half an hour of hand-to-hand fighting in the battalion command post area the Chinese were driven out. In the meantime, most of L Company had withdrawn from the stream's edge back to the command post. Making its way toward the command post, pursuant to the earlier withdrawal order, K Company ran into an enemy ambush and lost its command group and one platoon. The remainder reached the battalion area closely followed by the Chinese. There on the valley floor the disorganized men of the 3d Battalion formed a core of resistance around Sergeant Miller's three tanks and held the enemy off until daylight.

Another island of resistance had formed at the ramp to the command post dugout. Three men who manned the machine gun there in succession were killed by Chinese grenades. When daylight came only five of the twenty or more men who had assembled there were left. After a final exchange of grenades with these men, the Chinese in the nearby ditches withdrew. The group at the ramp then joined the others in the small perimeter around the three tanks.

Enemy mortar fire kept everyone under cover until an hour after daylight. Then a Mosquito plane and fighter-bomber aircraft came over and began a daylong series of strikes against the Chinese. This kept the enemy under cover during the rest of the day and gave the men at the command post a chance to take stock of their situation and to gather in the wounded. They found Major Ormond, the battalion commander, very badly wounded and the rest of the battalion staff wounded or missing. There were approximately 6 officers and 200 men of the battalion still able to function. Within 500 yards of the 200-yard-wide perimeter there were more than 170 wounded. As they were brought inside the small perimeter the wounded were counted; the dead apparently were not.

The beleaguered men also used the daylight respite gained from the air cover to dig an elaborate series of trenches and retrieve rations and ammunition from the vehicles that had escaped destruction. An L-5 plane flew over and dropped a mail bag of morphine and bandages. A helicopter also appeared and hovered momentarily a few feet above the 3d Battalion panels, intending to land and evacuate the more seriously wounded, but enemy fire hit it and it departed without landing. The battalion group was able to communicate with the pilot of a Mosquito plane overhead who said a relief column was on its way to them.[22]

The relief column the pilot of the Mosquito plane referred to was the 5th Cavalry force that, after having been repulsed during the previous afternoon and night, resumed its effort at daylight to break through to the 3d Battalion of the 8th Cavalry. Just before 0400, 2 No-

---

[22] Ltrs, McAbee to author, 20 Aug 54 and 8 Feb 57; I Corps WD, 2 Nov 50, Surg Sec Daily Rpt; 8th Cav Unit Hist Rpt, 2 Nov 50; EUSAK WD, G-3 Jnl, Msg at 0840 2 Nov 50; 70th Tk Bn WD, 10 Nov 50 (Rpt, B Co, 70th Tk Bn, 1-9 Nov 50); Ltr, Miller to Fraser, 6 Nov 50. Two helicopters did evacuate twenty-two critically wounded from Ipsok.

vember, the 2d Battalion, 5th Cavalry, arrived at the defensive position the 1st Battalion had held during the latter part of the night. On General Gay's order, the 1st Battalion, 7th Cavalry, now also became available to Colonel Johnson. Gay directed that it strike off across country in an effort to flank the enemy position on the left while the 5th Cavalry attacked frontally. For the frontal attack, Colonel Johnson placed the 1st Battalion, 5th Cavalry, on the left of the road and the 2d Battalion on the right. His plan called for these two battalions to capture the enemy-held ridge in their front on a sufficient frontage to allow the 3d Battalion—which had been released that morning to his control and was then moving to join him, spearheaded by a tank company—to move through to the relief of the 3d Battalion, 8th Cavalry. The 3d Battalion would be up and ready for this effort by afternoon.

Colonel Johnson had a special interest in rescuing the 3d Battalion, 8th Cavalry. He had brought it to Korea from Fort Devens, Mass., where only two months earlier it had been part of the 7th Regiment of the 3d Division. It became the 3d Battalion of the 8th Cavalry Regiment, and he had commanded it through the Pusan Perimeter breakout battles. By right of this earlier association it was "his own battalion."

The two lead attack companies of the 5th Cavalry failed to reach and seize their objectives on 2 November. The 1st Battalion of the 7th Cavalry really contributed nothing to the effort as it merely moved off into rough country and never entered the fight. The attack had almost no support from artillery, since only two 155-mm. howitzers could reach the enemy positions and higher headquarters would not authorize moving up the lighter artillery. The repeated strikes by strong air cover against the enemy ridge positions probably did little damage because the dense smoke haze hanging over the area obscured the objective. The 2d Battalion in the afternoon made the last effort after an air strike had strafed the enemy-held ridge. But again the smoke haze was so heavy that the pilots could not see any targets and it is doubtful whether their strikes caused much damage. The dug-in Chinese did not budge. A prisoner said that five Chinese companies of the *8th Route Army* were holding the ridge.

In this night and day battle with the Chinese at the Turtle Head Bend of the Kuryong River the two battalions of the 5th Cavalry suffered about 350 casualties, 200 of them in Lt. Col. John Clifford's 2d Battalion which carried the brunt of the fighting on 2 November. The 5th Cavalry Regiment always thereafter referred to this ridge where it first encountered the CCF as "Bugle Hill." The name was well chosen for during the night and on into the day the Chinese had used bugles, horns, and whistles as signaling devices. No doubt they also hoped that these sounds would terrorize their enemy during the eerie hours of night battle.

With the battle still in progress against this Chinese force, General Milburn, the corps commander, after conferring with General Gay, at 1500 verbally instructed the latter to withdraw the 1st Cavalry Division. The two had agreed that with the forces available they could not break the roadblock. Approximately two hours later Gay received confirmation of the order from corps. General Gay at dusk made what he has described as the most difficult decision he was ever called on to make—to order the 5th Cavalry Regiment to withdraw and leave the 3d Battalion, 8th Cavalry, to its fate.[23] Thus, at dark on 2 November the 3d Battalion, 8th Cavalry, had no further hope of rescue.

At the 3d Battalion perimeter Chaplain Kapaun and Captain Anderson had risked their lives constantly during the day in attending the wounded. Many men not previously injured had been hit by sniper and machine gun fire in carrying wounded into the perimeter. Although wounded several times, and seriously, Major Ormond had refused treatment until all other wounded had been cared for. At dusk Chaplain Kapaun left the perimeter and went to join the fifty to sixty wounded who had been placed in the old dugout battalion command post. This dugout, initially at the southeast corner of the original perimeter, was now approximately 150 yards outside the new one. The three tanks moved inside the infantry position.

Just before dusk a division liaison plane flew over the 3d Battalion perimeter and dropped a message ordering it to withdraw under cover of darkness. Over his tank radio Miller received from a liaison pilot a similar message stating that the men were on their own and to use their own judgment in getting out. But, after talking over the situation, the tankers and the infantry in the little perimeter decided to stay and try to hold out during the night.[24]

As dusk settled over the beleaguered group and the last of the protecting air cover departed, the Chinese bombarded the little island of men with 120-mm. mortars which had been brought into position during the day. The tankers, thinking the mortar barrage was directed at them, moved the tanks outside the perimeter to divert it away from the infantry. The barrage followed them, but part of it soon shifted back to the infantry inside the perimeter. All the tanks were hit two or three times, and one of them started to burn. A crewman was killed in putting out the fire. His ammunition almost gone and his gasoline low, Miller decided that his tanks would not last out the night if they stayed where they were. He called the infantry over their SCR-300 radio and told them his conclusion that in the circumstances the tanks would be of no help to them. They agreed. Miller led the tanks off to the southwest. Three miles from the perimeter Miller and the other crew members had to abandon the tanks in the valley of the Kuryong. After some desperate encounters, Miller and a few of his men reached friendly lines.[25]

At the 3d Battalion perimeter the Chinese followed their mortar barrage with an infantry attack. To meet this, the men inside the perimeter fired bazooka rounds into the vehicles to start fires and light up the area. Attacking across the open field in successive waves and silhouetted against the burning vehicles, the Chinese made easy targets and were shot down in great numbers. Six times during the night the Chinese at-

---

[23] Ltr, Gay to author, 19 Feb 54; Interv, author with Johnson, 28 Apr 54; 5th Cav WD, 2-4 Nov 50; Milburn, MS review comments, Nov 57.

[24] Ltr, McAbee to author, 20 Aug 54; Ltr, Miller to Fraser, 6 Nov 50; 70th Tk Bn WD, Msg at 1620 2 Nov 50.

[25] Ltr, Miller to Fraser, 6 Nov 50; 70th Tk Bn WD, Msg (from S-2, 5th Cav, to G-2, 1st Cav Div) 081140 Nov 50, and Msg at 1050 3 Nov 50; EUSAK PIR 113, 2 Nov 50.

tacked in a strength of approximately 400 men, but each time they were beaten back from the perimeter. During the night about fifty men from the 2d Battalion who had been in the hills all day broke through to join those in the besieged 3d Battalion perimeter.

In this heavy action, the Chinese early in the evening, by mortar fire and grenades, knocked out the two machine gun positions at the old command post dugout. Then they overran it. Inside the dugout were between 50 and 60 badly wounded men. The Chinese took 15 of the wounded who were able to walk with some help, including Captain McAbee and Chaplain Kapaun, and removed them to the Nammyon River outside the range of fire. The others, unable to walk, were left inside the dugout. In getting out of the field of fire with their captors, the 15 men had to crawl over the dead. Major McAbee has stated that at the edge of the perimeter where he passed the enemy dead they were piled three high and he estimated there must have been 1,000 enemy dead altogether.[26] But this number seems excessive.

On the morning of 3 November a 3-man patrol went to the former battalion command post dugout and discovered that during the night the Chinese had taken out some of the wounded. That day there was no air support. Remaining rations were given to the wounded. Enemy fire kept everyone under cover. The night was a repetition of the preceding one, with the Chinese working closer all the time. After each enemy attack had been driven back men would crawl out and retrieve weapons and ammunition from the enemy dead. Their own ammunition was almost gone.

Daylight of 4 November disclosed that there were about 200 men left able to fight. There were about 250 wounded. A discussion of the situation brought the decision that those still physically able to make the attempt should try to escape. Captain Anderson, the battalion surgeon, volunteered to stay with the wounded. 1st Lt. Walter L. Mayo, Jr., and 1st Lt. Philip H. Peterson, accompanied by two enlisted men, left the perimeter to scout a way out. They crawled up the irrigation ditches to the old command post and talked with some of the American wounded the Chinese had left there. They found the ramp covered with dead Chinese and Americans. They then crawled up the roadside ditches to the small village farther north and found only some wounded Chinese in it. In reaching the village, Lieutenant Mayo has estimated that he crawled over the bodies of 100 Chinese. From there the four men scouted the ford across the river. That done, the two officers sent the two enlisted men back to the 3d Battalion perimeter with instructions to lead the group out, while they continued to scout the river crossing area. It was about 1430.

After the two enlisted men returned to the perimeter and reported on the escape route, Capt. George F. McDonnell of the 2d Battalion group and Capt. William F. McLain of E Company, together with 1st Lt. Paul F. Bromser of L Company and the able-bodied men, withdrew to the east side of the perimeter just as the Chinese let loose a terrific barrage of white phosphorus shells. These bursting shells completely covered the perimeter area and obscured it with

---

[26] Ltr, McAbee to author, 8 Feb 57.

smoke. There was no doubt that the Chinese were trying to screen an attack. Within five minutes the 200 men cleared the perimeter on the east side where an open field had prevented the enemy from taking positions. They left the wounded with Captain Anderson who was to surrender them. As they left the wounded behind, one who was present said none of the latter shed tears but, instead, simply said to come back with reinforcements and get them out. The wounded knew there was no alternative for those who still might escape.

The escaping group traveled all that night east and northeast and then south and southwest through a rain storm. In the morning from a mountainside they watched a few battalions of Chinese horse cavalry and infantry pass by on a road below them. Later in the day the battalion group went south through more hills and crossed the valley near Ipsok. The next day, within sight of bursting American artillery shells, Chinese forces surrounded them and the battalion group, on the decision of the officers, broke up into small parties in the hope that some of them would escape. At approximately 1600 on the afternoon of 6 November the action of the 3d Battalion, 8th Cavalry, as an organized force came to an end. Most of these men were either killed or captured that day, apparently in the vicinity of Yongbyon.[27]

The heroic 3d Battalion commander, Major Ormond, was among the wounded captured by the Chinese in the perimeter beside the Kuryong. He subsequently died of his wounds and, according to some reports of surviving prisoners, was buried beside the road about five miles north of Unsan. Of his immediate staff, the battalion S-2 and S-4 also lost their lives in the Unsan action. About ten officers and somewhat less than 200 enlisted men of the 3d Battalion escaped to rejoin the regiment. There were a few others who escaped later, some from captivity, and were given the status of recovered allied personnel.[28]

It is difficult to arrive at precise figures in totaling the losses at Unsan. In the night battle the troop loss in the ROK 15th Regiment was admittedly very heavy. The regiment's loss in weapons and equipment was virtually total, and included four liaison planes of the 9th Field Artillery Battalion and the 6th Tank Battalion which U.S. fighter planes subsequently demolished on the ground.

At first, more than 1,000 men of the 8th Cavalry Regiment were missing in action, but as the days passed, some of these returned to friendly lines along the Ch'ongch'on. Two weeks after the Unsan action tank patrols were still bringing in men wounded at Unsan and fortunate enough to have been sheltered and cared for by friendly Koreans. On 22 November the Chinese themselves, in a propaganda move, turned free 27 men who had been prisoners for two weeks or longer, 19 of them captured from the 8th Cavalry Regiment at Unsan. After all the stragglers and those who had

---

[27] The account of the 3d Battalion after the tanks left the perimeter is based on McAbee's and Mayo's letters to author. McAbee and Anderson lived to return to the United States in the prisoner exchange after the Korean armistice. Chaplain Kapaun died in 1951 while a prisoner of war.

[28] Ltr, Moriarty to author, 11 Jun 54; Ltr, McAbee to author, 8 Feb 57; Interv, author with Johnson, 28 Apr 54; Interv, Guirard, 21 Aug 54. The figures are from Moriarty, who remained as executive officer of the battalion.

walked south through the hills had reported in, the losses were found to total about 600 men. Enemy sources later indicated the Chinese captured between 200 and 300 men at Unsan. The principal officer casualties included a battalion commander and most of his staff, 5 company commanders, 2 medical officers, and 1 chaplain. In addition to the infantry losses, about one-fourth of the men of B Company, 70th Tank Battalion, were casualties. The Heavy Mortar Company also suffered heavily. The regiment's loss in weapons and equipment was very heavy indeed. It included 12 105-mm. howitzers and 9 tanks and 1 tank recovery vehicle. On 3 November the 8th Cavalry Regiment reported it had 45 percent of its authorized strength. The division G-4 considered the regiment inoperable until troops and equipment losses could be replaced.[29]

The Eighth Army announced on 5 November that "as a result of an ambush" the 1st Cavalry Division would receive all the new replacements until further notice. In the next twelve days, Eighth Army assigned 22 officers and 616 enlisted men as replacements to the 1st Cavalry Division. Nearly all of them went to the 8th Cavalry Regiment.[30]

To cover the withdrawal to the south side of the Ch'ongch'on of the 1st Cavalry Division and the ROK 1st Division, I Corps organized a special force known as Task Force Allen. The 2d and 3d Battalions, 7th Cavalry Regiment, and the 19th Engineer Combat Group were the principal organizations in the task force. Brig. Gen. Frank A. Allen, Jr., Assistant Division Commander, 1st Cavalry Division, commanded it. In addition to covering the withdrawal, it also had the mission of protecting the I Corps east flank in the Kunu-ri area.[31]

The Chinese force that brought disaster to the 8th Cavalry Regiment at Unsan was the *116th Division* of the *39th Army*. Elements of the *347th Regiment* imposed the roadblock east of the road fork south of Unsan that thereafter halted all vehicular traffic. The *115th Division* also fought in the Unsan action. It appears, therefore, that from first to last—from 25 October to 2 November—two Chinese divisions, or elements of them, engaged the ROK 1st Division and the U.S. 8th and 5th Cavalry Regiments in the Unsan area.[32]

---

[29] 1st Cav Div WD, 5, 6, and 17 Nov 50; 7th Cav Hist Rpt, 22 Nov 50; 8th Cav Unit Hist Rpt, 3 Nov 50; 70th Tk Bn WD, Jnl, 10 Nov 50; EUSAK WD, G-3 Daily Hist Rpt, 6 Nov 50; Ltr, Gay to author, 19 Feb 54.
The equipment loss figures are based on the following sources: EUSAK POR 339, 2 Nov 50; 70th Tk Bn WD, Summ, 2 Nov, and Jnl, Msg 4, 101000 Nov 50; 1st Cav Div WD, G-4 Jnl, 12 Oct 50, Div Arty and 70th Tk Bn battle losses, 27 Oct-4 Nov 50; 1st Cav Div POR 190, 10 Nov 50, an. A; 1st Cav Div WD, 5 Nov 50; EUSAK WD, 7 Nov 50, Ltr, CG EUSAK to CINCFE, sub: ROKA and U.S. Equipment Losses, 1-3 Nov 50; I Corps WD, POR 153, 2 Nov 50. These sources also gave losses in small arms, automatic weapons, and vehicles.
In a study of combat experience at Unsan prepared and distributed by *Headquarters, XIX Army Group, CCF*, the Chinese command, after recounting the large amount of equipment captured, apologized for what it considered relatively few prisoners. The study stated, "As a result of lack of experience in mopping-up operations in mountainous areas, only 200 odd were captured." See ATIS Enemy Documents, Issue 47, pp. 139ff, mimeographed booklet in Chinese, A Collection of Combat Experiences.

[30] EUSAK WD, G-1 Daily Hist Rpt, 5 and 17 Nov 50.
[31] Ltr, Gay to author, 19 Feb 54; Interv, Johnson, 28 Apr 54; 7th Cav Unit Hist Rpt, 1-4 Nov 50; I Corps WD, 2 Nov 50.
[32] ATIS Enemy Documents, Issue 47, pp. 139ff; I Corps, Armor Combat Bul 27, 15 Jun 51, quoting from captured Chinese notebook, Experiences in the Unsan Operation.

CHAPTER XXXV

Eighth Army Holds the Ch'ongch'on Bridgehead

The whole art of war consists in getting at what is on the other side of the hill.
                                                DUKE OF WELLINGTON

Action North of the River

Monday, 2 November, was a day of hectic activity and some confusion in the command posts of Eighth Army and its subordinate organizations. Orders and changes to orders came in an almost endless stream as steps were taken to withdraw U.S. I Corps below the Ch'ongch'on River. In the final instructions the 27th British Commonwealth Brigade and the 19th Infantry Regiment of the 24th Division were to remain north of the river in a bridgehead that encompassed and protected the bridges and tank fords over the Ch'ongch'on and Taeryong Rivers in the Anju-Pakch'on areas. General Walker wished to hold these river crossing sites for the purpose of resuming the offensive.[1]

By evening of 3 November the 27th Brigade had moved from Taech'on into its assigned defensive positions around Pakch'on at the northwest corner of the bridgehead. (*Map 24*) The fine fur boots on the feet of some of the enemy dead at Taech'on, and three Chinese deserters who entered their lines there, revealed to the British that they already had had minor brushes with the Chinese. Following close behind the departing British, Chinese forces entered Taech'on less than an hour after the British rear guard had left it.[2]

The other part of the bridgehead force, the 19th Infantry Regiment, also moved during 3 November to its defensive positions just north of the Ch'ongch'on and northeast of Anju. Once the 19th Infantry was in its defensive positions, the ROK 1st Division, still in contact with the enemy, withdrew through it to the south side of the Ch'ongch'on, completing its crossing before noon of 4 November.[3]

---

[1] 24th Div WD, 2 Nov 50; 27th British Commonwealth Brig Sitrep, 1-4 Nov 50; EUSAK POR 340, 2 Nov 50; I Corps WD, 1-2 Nov 50.

[2] 24th Div WD, G-2 Jnl, 4 Nov 50, Rpt from Home Guards of Taech'on; 27th British Commonwealth Brig Sitrep, 1-4 Nov 50; Coad, "The Land Campaign in Korea," *op. cit.*, p. 7; Linklater, *Our Men in Korea*, pp. 26-27; Bartlett, *With the Australians in Korea*, p. 39.

[3] 19th Inf Unit Rpt 114, 2-3 Nov 50; 24th Div WD, Nov 50 Summ; I Corps WD, 3 Nov 50.

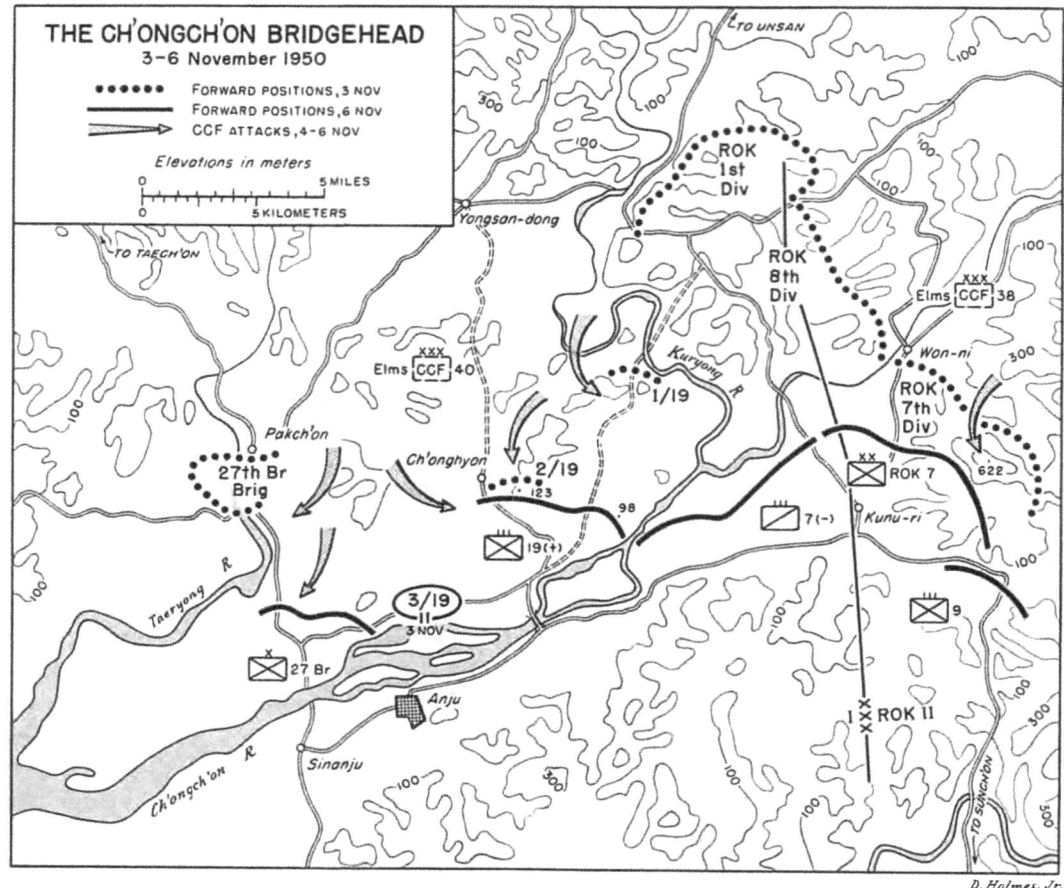

MAP 24

The boundary between the ROK Army and the U.S. I Corps crossed the Ch'ongch'on on a north-south line at Kunu-ri. Already the Chinese had crowded the ROK II Corps into a restricted defensive area near Won-ni about four miles northeast of Kunu-ri. On 3 November the 5th Regimental Combat Team of the 24th Division took a position at Kunu-ri behind the ROK II Corps. The 9th Regiment of the U.S. 2d Infantry Division was in position south of Kunu-ri protecting the road to Sunch'on. Enemy forces during the day advanced within two and a half miles of Kunu-ri.[4]

The next day, 4 November, enemy forces drove hard for Kunu-ri. Hill 622, a large mountain cresting three miles northeast of Kunu-ri, dominated the town, the valley of the Ch'ongch'on, and the rail and highway communication lines passing along it. The 3d and 5th

[4] 5th RCT WD, 3 Nov 50; 24th Div WD, 3 Nov 50; I Corps WD, 3 Nov 50; EUSAK WD, 3 Nov 50.

Regiments of the ROK 7th Division held this key terrain feature, with the 5th RCT, 24th Division, in blocking position just behind them. The ROK 8th Regiment was in reserve along the road east of Kunu-ri. That morning a strong CCF attack broke the ROK 3d Regiment position on the mountain and the South Koreans began streaming back through the 5th RCT. Capt. Hubert H. Ellis, commanding officer of C Company, stopped and reorganized these ROK troops and sent them back to retake the hill. The ROK 8th Regiment was now also committed to the battle. The hill changed hands several times throughout the day, but at dark ROK troops held its vital northwest ridge.

The 5th RCT itself had heavy fighting in this battle to hold Kunu-ri, and was forced to withdraw about 1,000 yards. Part of the fighting was at close quarters. Some men, like 1st Lt. Morgan B. Hansel of C Company who gave his life to prevent the disintegration of a platoon, charged Chinese machine gun emplacements alone. By evening the enemy attack in estimated division strength (elements of the CCF *38th Army*) had been repulsed. The ROK 7th Division and Col. "Rocky John" Throckmorton's 5th Regimental Combat Team had saved Kunu-ri and successfully protected the right flank of Eighth Army.[5]

Simultaneously with this attack south of the Ch'ongch'on against Kunu-ri, the enemy struck the bridgehead force north of the river. On 4 November both ground and aerial observers reported approximately 1,000 enemy soldiers crossing the Kuryong River two miles northwest of the 1st Battalion, 19th Infantry, and moving south through wooded terrain, evidently intent on getting into the rear of the battalion. The enemy maneuver succeeded. Chinese troops captured the battalion's radio while the operator was using it to report the situation to the regimental headquarters. The battalion did not make much of a fight, and, after destroying and abandoning its heavy equipment and vehicles, it withdrew eastward and infiltrated across the Kuryong and Ch'ongch'on Rivers to friendly positions. Nearly all the men escaped.[6]

Meanwhile, a task force of the 3d Battalion, 19th Infantry, subsequently reinforced by the entire battalion, tried to drive through to the 1st Battalion's position, but strong enemy forces on the road repelled it. With these difficulties developing in the bridgehead area, General Church ordered Brig. Gen. Garrison H. Davidson, the assistant division commander of the 24th Division, to assume command of all 24th Division troops north of the Ch'ongch'on and to co-ordinate the actions of the 27th British Commonwealth Brigade and the division troops. Davidson arrived at the 19th Infantry command post shortly after noon of the 4th to assume command of Task Force Davidson. The worsening situation caused General Church at 1630 also to order the 21st Infantry Regiment to

---

[5] I Corps WD, 4 Nov 50; 5th RCT WD, 4 Nov 50; Interv, author with Maj Grady R. Hamilton (S-3 5th RCT Aug 51), 10 Aug 51; ATIS Interrog Rpts (Enemy Forces), Issue 24, Interrog 2811, p. 29, Sgt Chon Song Hyon. Eighth Army General Order 397, 4 June 1951, awarded the Distinguished Service Cross posthumously to Lieutenant Hansel.

[6] 19th Inf Unit Rpt 115, 4-5 Nov 50; 19th Inf WD, Opn Summ, Nov 50; 24th Div WD, 4-5 Nov 50; 24th Div PIR 115, 3-4 Nov 50; Interv, Maj Gen Garrison H. Davidson (Asst Div Comdr 24th Div Nov 50), 28 Jan 54.

cross to the north side of the Ch'ongch'on River during the night and attack the next day, to clear the enemy from the 19th Infantry area and restore the bridgehead line.[7]

An enemy force made a further penetration in the 19th Infantry zone during the night, but the next morning, 5 November, the 2d and 3d Battalions, 21st Infantry, attacked and restored the position. Once again, as in the days on the Naktong, the 3d Engineer Combat Battalion assumed an infantry role in taking positions to protect the Anju bridges over the Ch'ongch'on. Fleeing the battle area, hordes of refugees crossed the Ch'ongch'on; 20,000 of them passed through the checking points on the south side of the river on 4–5 November.[8]

On the west, there was a 5-mile gap between the left flank of the 19th Infantry bridgehead position and the 27th British Commonwealth Brigade position. A large mountain mass lay in this no man's land, and over and through it enemy forces could move at will to the flank and rear of either the 27th Brigade or the 19th Infantry. On the 19th Infantry's extreme left flank at the edge of this gap the 2d Battalion held Hill 123 which overlooked a valley near the little village of Ch'onghyon, four miles above the Ch'ongch'on.

On the night of 5–6 November the enemy made a co-ordinated attack all along the bridgehead line. At Hill 123 the attack achieved surprise against E and G Companies, 19th Infantry. At least part of the enemy assault force came up to E Company's position from the rear, apparently following field telephone wire. The Chinese caught many men asleep in their sleeping bags and killed them where they lay. Others were shot in the back of the head. The Chinese virtually overran the battalion positions on Hill 123.

Cpl. Mitchell Red Cloud, an Indian from Wisconsin, gave the first alarm to E Company from his position on the point of the ridge where a trail climbed to the company command post. A group of Chinese suddenly charged him from a brush-covered area 100 feet away. Corporal Red Cloud sprang to his feet and fired his BAR into them. Enemy fire wounded and felled him, but he pulled himself to his feet, wrapped one arm around a small tree, and again delivered point-blank BAR fire until Chinese bullets cut him down. Later, American officers found a string of Chinese dead in front of his body.[9]

Another BAR man in E Company, Pfc. Joseph W. Balboni, was equally heroic. Chinese soldiers approached unnoticed within seventy-five feet of him. From this short distance they charged forward. Balboni met them with bursts from his BAR and stood in his tracks until killed. Two days later when a friendly patrol visited the spot seventeen enemy dead were found in front of Balboni's body.[10]

---

[7] 19th Inf WD, 4 Nov 50; 24th Div WD, 4 Nov 50; Interv, author with Davidson, 28 Jan 54.

[8] 19th Inf WD, 5 Nov 50; 19th Inf Unit Rpt 116, 4–5 Nov 50; 24th Div WD, 5 Nov 50; I Corps WD, 4–5 Nov 50; EUSAK WD, Br for CG, 5 Nov 50; EUSAK PIR 116, 5 Nov 50.

[9] Department of the Army General Order 26, 25 April 1951, awarded the Medal of Honor posthumously to Red Cloud. Interv, author with Davidson, 28 Jan 54; 19th Inf Unit Rpt 117, 5–6 Nov, and Rpt 119, 7–8 Nov 50; 24th Div WD, 6 Nov 50; 19th Inf Opn Summ, Nov 50.

[10] Eighth Army General Order 63, 10 February 1951, awarded the Distinguished Service Cross posthumously to Private Balboni.

By 0300 the battalion had withdrawn 1,000 yards. There it was only barely able to hold its new position. After daylight the enemy withdrew from contact with the 2d Battalion. Elsewhere the other battalions on the 19th Infantry front repulsed the attacks on them after hard fighting. Artillery firing from the south side of the Ch'ongch'on supported the 19th Infantry during the bridgehead battles.

After daylight the re-equipped 1st Battalion, 19th Infantry, which had re-crossed to the north side of the Ch'ongch'on during the night, counterattacked and closed the gap between the 2d Battalion and the rest of the regiment on its right. The 19th Regiment then began restoring its original bridgehead line.

In these night battles of predawn 6 November the enemy had lost heavily. Two days later, the 2d Battalion alone counted 474 enemy dead in the vicinity of Hill 123, and it found evidence that many more dead had been buried. The 3d Battalion, 19th Infantry, counted more than 100 enemy dead. Interrogation of prisoners disclosed that the *355th Regiment, CCF 119th Division;* the *358th Regiment, CCF 120th Division;* and a North Korean regiment had attacked the 19th Infantry on the east side of the bridgehead.[11]

Simultaneously with its attacks against the Eighth Army right flank at Kunu-ri and the eastern side of the Ch'ongch'on bridgehead, the enemy struck with equal force against the western side of the bridgehead at Pakch'on on the Taeryong River. The Australian 3d and Argyll 1st Battalions were in defensive positions on the west side of the Taeryong River opposite Pakch'on, except A Company of the Argylls which was on the east side of the river south of Pakch'on. The Middlesex 1st Battalion was also on the east side in and around Pakch'on. Two and a half miles south of Pakch'on the 61st Field Artillery Battalion of the 1st Cavalry Division had emplaced to support the British.

During the night of 4–5 November an enemy force moved east around Pakch'on toward the support artillery where it could cut the road behind the brigade. By daylight these enemy troops were in position to launch their attack.

An estimated battalion of Chinese opened fire from the east with mortars and small arms on the 61st Field Artillery Battalion. Immediately, each battery commander placed all his men, except the gun crews who remained with their weapons, in a tight perimeter around the battery positions, manning every automatic weapon. Word of the attack reached the British, and A Company of the Argylls started south at once to the aid of the artillerymen. The brigade commander then ordered the remainder of the Argyll 1st Battalion to cross to the east side of the river.

The most severe attack fell on C Battery. Capt. Howard M. Moore, commanding officer of the battery, wheeled one 105-mm. howitzer around and fired point-blank into enemy troops in the rice paddies to the east. Forty-five minutes later he got a second howitzer turned around. The battery fired 1,400 rounds, some at a range of 50 yards, although the average range was about 300 yards. An aerial observer directed the fire of another battery in support of C Battery. Part of the enemy plan was to blow a

---

[11] 19th Inf Unit Rpts 117, 118, 119, 5–8 Nov 50; Interv, author with Davidson, 28 Jan 54.

critical bridge at the artillery position. If this had succeeded it is unlikely that the brigade would have saved a single tank or vehicle. The artillerymen killed one member of a demolition squad within twenty yards of the bridge.

At 0900 two tanks arrived at the C Battery perimeter. Before the Argylls arrived with more armored support, C Battery had lost 2 men killed and 18 wounded. The rest of the artillery battalion had 17 men wounded. Enemy action had destroyed 1 howitzer, 6 vehicles, 1 radio, and some other miscellaneous equipment. There were about 70 enemy dead in the vicinity of the gun positions. Speaking later before an English audience, Brigadier Coad said of C Battery, 61st Field Artillery Battalion, "I would like to say how magnificently these American gunners fought. Dead Chinese were lying thirty yards from the gun shields. . . . It was up to the very highest traditions of any artillery regiment." [12]

Upon arriving at the artillery position, A Company of the Argylls attacked a nearby hill, first winning, then losing it. Air reports now indicated that approximately one Chinese division had passed east around and below Pakch'on, virtually surrounding the brigade. While heavy air strikes went in to impede and disrupt the Chinese maneuver and attack, Brigadier Coad ordered the Australian 3d Battalion, still on the west side of the Taeryong, to withdraw to the east side.

Once on the east side, the Australians passed through the Argylls and in the early afternoon attacked north toward Pakch'on. In a bayonet charge they regained high ground the Argylls had lost two miles below the town. In this desperate battle the Australians lost twelve killed and sixty-four wounded. It now became apparent that the brigade could not hold the Pakch'on bridgehead. Under cover of the Australian attack, and a simultaneous one by the Middlesex 1st Battalion which cleared the road southward, the rest of the brigade and the artillery withdrew under fire toward the Ch'ongch'on River.

That evening the Australians joined the rest of the brigade in a defense perimeter astride the Pakch'on road on the first line of hills, 4,000 to 6,000 yards north of the Ch'ongch'on River. The Australians occupied the most advanced and exposed position. Soon after dark the Chinese struck them in an attack which continued unabated for four hours, forcing two companies to withdraw. By dawn of 6 November, however, the Chinese themselves had withdrawn from contact. The British estimated the Chinese lost 300 men to ground action and 600 to 1,000 to air action during the day and that night.

After daylight on Monday, 6 November, Australians in their positions could see enemy forces withdrawing northward up a valley. The predawn attacks of 6 November against the bridgehead area and Kunu-ri proved to be the last heavy engagements of the Chinese in their First Phase Offensive. During the day they withdrew generally out of contact. Aerial

---

[12] Department of the Army General Order 33, 31 March 1952, awarded the Distinguished Unit Citation to the 61st Field Artillery Battalion, 1st Cavalry Division. 61st FA Bn WD, 5 Nov 50; 1st Lt Hal W. Chaney (C Btry, 61st FA Bn), Debriefing Rpt 64, Arty School, Ft. Sill, Okla., 22 Jan 52; 27th British Commonwealth Brig Sitrep 4-Nov 50; Coad, "The Land Campaign in Korea," op. cit.; Linklater, *Our Men in Korea*, pp. 26-27; Bartlett, *With the Australians in Korea*, pp. 39-40.

observers reported many sightings of large enemy forces moving northward. Limited objective attacks by the 24th Division on 7 November all reached their goals against light opposition, and seemed to indicate that the violent enemy attacks of the past twelve days had ended for the present.[13]

MIG's and Jets Over the Yalu

Coinciding with the appearance of the Chinese in the Korean War came a new turn in air action over Korean territory. Except for its opening weeks, the Korean War had been characterized by the U.S. Fifth Air Force's complete dominance of the skies. Now, suddenly, Russian-built MIG's began crossing over into North Korea from Manchurian bases and challenging the Fifth Air Force when its planes approached the Yalu border. In the closing days of October, American planes had for the first time been allowed to approach the border.

At the beginning of the month, Fifth Air Force planes were prohibited from flying within fifty miles of the border. On 17 October this restriction was eased, and finally on 25 October it was lifted to allow close support missions, under control of a tactical air control party or a Mosquito observer, as near the border as necessary. Pilots of these missions were carefully selected and flew under experienced leaders, for there was to be no bombing within five miles of the border.[14]

On 31 October the famous Russian-built MIG–15 jet first entered combat over Korean territory when a number of them attacked American propeller-driven aircraft in the Sinuiju area. The Fifth Air Force reportedly destroyed several MIG's at this time. It was not known then whether the enemy plane build-up was North Korean or some "volunteer" air force.[15]

On 5 November General MacArthur gave a new turn to the course of the war by ordering aerial bombing to destroy the Yalu River bridges from the Korean side halfway into the stream. He felt this action necessary to stop or greatly reduce the flow of Chinese troops and equipment into Korea. The order came at the time the CCF attack threatened to overrun Eighth Army's Ch'ongch'on River bridgehead and to capture Kunu-ri on the south side. The Joint Chiefs of Staff in Washington received from MacArthur a radio report of the order. They immediately countermanded it, repeating their directive not to bomb targets within five miles of the border.[16]

General MacArthur replied at once to the JCS message in one of the strongest protests he ever dispatched to Washington. He said the only way to halt the reinforcement of the enemy was to destroy the bridges. Paraphrased, his message continued, "Under the gravest protest that I can make I am carrying

---

[13] EUSAK WD, G–3 Sec, 6 Nov 50; I Corps WD, 6 Nov 50; 24th Div WD, 6 Nov 50; 5th Cav WD, Narr Rpt, Nov 50; Ltr, Gay to author, 19 Feb 54. Task Force Allen was dissolved at 1700, 6 November.

[14] USAF Hist Study 71, p. 80.

[15] FEAF Opn Hist, II, 19; Dept of State Pub 4051, *United Nations Command Ninth Report to the Security Council, United Nations, 1–15 November 1950*, pp. 11–12; EUSAK WD, 4 Nov 50, EUSAK Daily News Bul, UP dispatch, 1 November, quoting General Partridge.

[16] Msg, JCS 95878, JCS Personal for MacArthur, 5 Nov 50, quoted in Schnabel, FEC, GHQ Support and Participation in the Korean War, ch. VII, pp. 16–17;, Senate MacArthur Hearings, pt. 1, p. 20, testimony of MacArthur, 3 May 51.

out your instructions and suspending this strike." He argued that what he proposed to do was within the rules of war and the resolutions and directions he had received, and that it constituted no act of belligerency against Chinese territory. He asked that the matter be brought immediately to the attention of the President, "as I believe your instructions may result in a calamity of major proportions for which, without his personal and direct understanding of the situation, I cannot accept responsibility." [17]

This message produced the result MacArthur desired. The Joint Chiefs of Staff on 6 November authorized MacArthur to proceed with the planned bombing of the Korean end of the Yalu bridges, provided that he still considered such action essential to the safety of his forces. MacArthur was expressly forbidden, however, to bomb any dams or power plants on the Yalu River or to violate Manchurian property and airspace.[18]

Along the Manchurian border there were known to be at least seven major bridges across the Yalu River and three across the Tumen River. The most important Yalu structures were the 3,000-foot-long rail and highway bridges connecting Sinuiju and An-tung, the 2,000-foot-long rail and highway bridges thirty-five air miles northeast of Sinuiju near Sakchu, and the 1,500-foot-long rail bridge at Manp'ojin.

The first bomber strike against the Yalu River bridges at Sinuiju went in on 8 November, seventy-nine B–29's under fighter escort executing the mission. The date is memorable also for the first battle between jet planes in aerial warfare. Lt. Russell Brown, pilot of an F–80 in the fighter escort, shot a MIG–15 down in flames.

Thereafter, land-based and carrier-based planes attacked the Yalu bridges almost daily during the rest of the month, and the doctrine of "hot pursuit" into the enemy's Manchurian sanctuary soon became a burning issue, not only in the battle zone but in the diplomatic capitals of the world.

---

[17] Msg C68396, CINCFE to DA, 6 Nov 50.
[18] Msg, JCS 95949, JCS to CINCFE, 6 Nov 50.

CHAPTER XXXVI

The Chinese Appraise Their First Phase Korean Action

Those who wage war in mountains should never pass through defiles without first making themselves masters of the heights.
MAURICE DE SAXE, *Reveries on the Art of War*

What were the Chinese Communist Forces that fought the battles in late October and early November, and just when and how did they come to Korea? What did they think of their own efforts in their first actions against American troops?

The Chinese troops that appeared suddenly in the Korean fighting near the end of October had crossed the Yalu River from Manchuria in the period from 13 or 14 to 20 October. Hiding from aerial observation during the day and marching at night, they had reached their chosen positions on the southern fringe of the high mountain mass fifty air miles south of the Yalu. There they lay in wait overlooking the corridors that entered these mountains from a point near Huich'on on the east along a line extending sixty air miles westward through Onjong and Unsan.

Three Chinese armies, the *38th*, *40th*, and *39th*, each composed of three infantry divisions, were deployed in that order from Huich'on westward, on this line of battle in front of Eighth Army and the ROK II Corps. The *38th Army* was northwest of Huich'on, the *40th* in the Onjong area, and the *39th* above Unsan. Two more armies, the *66th* and the *50th*, of three divisions each, remained hidden in reserve and out of action in the west during the Chinese First Phase Offensive. This made a total of fifteen divisions. Elements of another division, the *125th*, apparently were the troops that cut off and dispersed the 7th Regiment of the ROK 6th Division below Ch'osan.[1]

The CCF *39th Army* arrived at Antung on the north side of the Yalu River in Manchuria in mid-October and immediately crossed the river into Korea

---

[1] ATIS Enemy Documents, Issue 47, pp. 139ff, booklet, A Collection of Combat Experiences, issued by Hq XIX Army Group, CCF, 29 Mar 51 (also partially reproduced by Hq U.S. I Corps, G-2 Sec, Aug 51); Ibid., Issue 11, pp. 74-82, Primary Conclusions of Battle Experiences at Unsan, issued by Hq 66th Army, 20 Nov 50; Ibid., Issues 6, 2 Sep 51, A-9 and 35, 1-15 Nov 52, p. 45; FEC Intel Digest, vol. I, Nr 4, p. 26 (17 Feb 53), *XIII Army Group*, CCF; FEC, Order of Battle Information, CCF, 15 Jun 51.

at Sinuiju. There it came under the operational control of the *XIII Army Group*. The *38th* and *40th Armies* crossed into Korea about the same time. Later in the month, the *50th* and *66th Armies* crossed into Korea in support of the others. It may be concluded that if the U.S. I Corps had not withdrawn when it did, elements of these two CCF armies would have engaged the 5th and 19th Regiments of the 24th Division above Kusong. As it was, small parts of the *66th Army* did accidentally encounter the 19th Regiment there on 1 November and exchanged shots with it.[2]

While the CCF *39th Army* stopped the ROK 1st Division at Unsan, the *40th* engaged and virtually destroyed the ROK 6th Division at Onjong. On the second day of the action, 26 October, the CCF *38th Army* joined the *40th Army* in the battle against the ROK 6th and 8th Divisions between Onjong and Huich'on. These two Chinese armies then rolled the ROK II Corps back southwest along the valley of the Ch'ongch'on to the edge of Kunu-ri.

Simultaneously with the deployment of these Chinese divisions in front of Eighth Army, others deployed in front of the X Corps in northeast Korea. Three CCF divisions, the *124th*, *125th*, and *126th*, forming the *42d Army*, entered Korea at Manp'ojin. The first to cross the border was the *124th Division*. On 14 October it left T'ung-hua in southern Manchuria, about fifty air miles from the North Korean border, and proceeded by train to Chi-an on the Yalu opposite Manp'ojin, where it crossed the river the same day. On the 16th it started on foot from Manp'ojin, marching southeast through Kanggye and Yudam-ni to Hagaru-ri. From there its advanced elements proceeded to the point south of the Changjin Reservoir where they met the ROK 26th Regiment on 25 October. The remainder of the division moved up to the point of contact and joined in the battle near Sudong against the U.S. 1st Marine Division troops that replaced the ROK 26th Regiment. The other two CCF divisions that followed the *124th* into Korea at Manp'ojin remained out of action behind the *124th* in this phase of the fighting, but assumed defensive positions in the Changjin Reservoir area, blocking the roads to Kanggye.

Except for the action against the *124th Division*, it would appear that the ROK and U.S. troops had not reached the points in northeast Korea where the CCF intended to block their advance. While the *124th Division* at first drove back the ROK troops it encountered, and then slowed the advance of the U.S. Marine troops that replaced them on the road to the reservoir, it did not have the success that attended the CCF action against the ROK II Corps and part of the U.S. I Corps in the west. In fact, this CCF division was virtually destroyed.

In the First Phase Offensive, highly skilled enemy light infantry troops had carried out the Chinese attacks, generally unaided by any weapons larger than mortars. Their attacks had demonstrated that the Chinese were well-trained disciplined fire fighters, and particularly adept at night fighting. They were masters of the art of camouflage.

---

[2] FEC Intel Digest, vol. I, Nr 4, 1-15 Feb 53, Histories of CCF Army Groups Active in Korea: XIII Army Group, pp. 30-37; EUSAK PIR 109, 29 Oct 50.

Their patrols were remarkably successful in locating the positions of the U.N. forces. They planned their attacks to get in the rear of these forces, cut them off from their escape and supply roads, and then send in frontal and flanking attacks to precipitate the battle. They also employed a tactic which they termed Hachi Shiki, which was a V-formation into which they allowed enemy forces to move; the sides of the V then closed around their enemy while another force moved below the mouth of the V to engage any forces attempting to relieve the trapped unit. Such were the tactics the Chinese used with great success at Onjong, Unsan, and Ch'osan, but with only partial success at Pakch'on and the Ch'ongch'on bridgehead.

The Chinese soldiers engaging in the First Phase Offensive were well-fed, in excellent physical condition, well-clothed, and well-equipped. As the British had noted, some of them even wore fur-lined boots. Despite numerous American intelligence conjectures at the time that the first Chinese were integrated and scattered throughout the North Korean units, this was not the fact. From the very beginning the Chinese fought in Chinese organizations and were never mixed as individuals into North Korean organizations.

In the offensive against the Eighth Army and the ROK II Corps at the end of October and the first week of November the action was almost entirely by Chinese troops. The delaying action along the west coast against the 24th Division, however, was by North Koreans. Only in rare instances, such as in the final action to the east against the 19th Infantry and the 27th British Commonwealth Brigade, were North Korean infantry troops involved, and then they apparently constituted only a relatively small part of the total attacking enemy force. The North Korean *105th Armored Division,* partly reconstituted since the Naktong battles, was committed to help the Chinese and did so with tank fire in a few instances, but it played a negligible role in the fighting. The Fifth Air Force destroyed most of its tanks back of the battle front. On 7 November, for instance, U.N. aircraft reportedly destroyed 6 tanks, 3 armored cars, and 45 vehicles in Pakch'on and the area eastward.[3]

At the same time in northeast Korea the ROK I Corps encountered Chinese forces at only one point on the road to the reservoir. Within a few days elements of the 1st Marine Division relieved the ROK's there, and they had a stubborn fight for nearly a week in gaining the Kot'o-ri plateau south of the Changjin Reservoir. The Chinese intervention in northeast Korea had not been on the same scale as in the west central part, nor had it had the same success. It is to be noted that the Chinese appeared only in the mountainous, inland part of the peninsula; on neither coast were there any Chinese contacts at this time.

Since the First Phase Offensive was the first engagement in the Korean War between American and Chinese troops, the opinion the Chinese formed of their adversary as a result of it may be of interest. On 20 November, less than three weeks after the CCF *39th Army* had driven the U.N. forces from the Unsan area, the headquarters of the

---

[3] 24th Div WD, 7 Nov 50; GHQ FEC, History of the N.K. Army, p. 80.

66th Army, "Chinese Peoples' Volunteer Army," published a pamphlet entitled, "Primary Conclusions of Battle Experiences at Unsan." In it the Chinese listed what they considered the strengths and weaknesses of the American forces, based on their experience with the 8th Cavalry Regiment. On the favorable side the pamphlet described in some detail the American method of making an attack and said:

The coordinated action of mortars and tanks is an important factor. . . . Their firing instruments are highly powerful. . . . Their artillery is very active. . . . Aircraft strafing and bombing of our transportation have become a great hazard to us . . . their transportation system is great. . . . Their infantry rate of fire is great and the long range of fire is still greater.[4]

Not so favorable was the Chinese estimate of the American infantry. The pamphlet said that American soldiers when cut off from the rear

. . . abandon all their heavy weapons, leaving them all over the place, and play opossum. . . . Their infantrymen are weak, afraid to die, and haven't the courage to attack or defend. They depend on their planes, tanks, and artillery. At the same time, they are afraid of our fire power. They will cringe when, if on the advance, they hear firing. They are afraid to advance farther. . . . They specialize in day fighting. They are not familiar with night fighting or hand to hand combat. . . . If defeated, they have no orderly formation. Without the use of their mortars, they become completely lost . . . they become dazed and completely demoralized. . . . At Unsan they were surrounded for several days yet they did nothing. They are afraid when the rear is cut off. When transportation comes to a standstill, the infantry loses the will to fight.

After analyzing the Americans' strength and weakness, the Chinese set forth certain principles for future operations:

As a main objective, one of the units must fight its way rapidly around the enemy and cut off their rear. . . . Route of attack must avoid highways and flat terrain in order to keep tanks and artillery from hindering the attack operations. . . . Night warfare in mountainous terrain must have a definite plan and liaison between platoon commands. Small leading patrol groups attack and then sound the bugle. A large number will at that time follow in column.

The Chinese admitted they did not have an effective weapon against the American tank, but said that 20-pound TNT charges placed on the tracks or under the tank would disable it. Antitank sections consisted of four men carrying two 20-pound and two 5-pound charges.

The Chinese summed up their viewpoint on the first phase of their intervention:

Our Army [39th] was the first expeditionary force ordered to hurry to the I-Ung-pong area of Unsan to relieve the North Korean Army and intercept the enemy advancing northwards at Unsan. We deployed our main force to encircle and annihilate the enemy at Hichon [Huichon], Onjong, and Chosan. At that time, we did not fully comprehend the tactical characteristics and combat strength of the enemy, and we lacked experience in mountain warfare. Moreover, we engaged the enemy (first, in the form of interdiction, then in that of attack) without sufficient preparation; yet the result was satisfactory.

---

[4] ATIS Enemy Documents, Issue 11, pp. 74–82, reproduces this document, captured by ROK 1st Div, 26 Nov 50. See also ATIS Enemy Documents, Issue 47.

CHAPTER XXXVII

Guerrilla Warfare Behind the Front

Do not now go into such dangerous and difficult places, but order your guides to lead you by the easiest road, unless it is much too long; for the easiest road is the shortest for an army. XENOPHON, *Cyropaedia*

In late October and during November, guerrilla warfare was increasing in intensity behind the United Nations front lines in North Korea. Remnants of the North Korea People's Army retreating into North Korea from the Pusan Perimeter and, to a lesser degree, miscellaneous guerrillas carried on this action.

While the U.S. I Corps advanced beyond the 38th Parallel into North Korea together with the bulk of the ROK Army, the U.S. IX Corps in early October assembled in the Taejon-Chonju area, well south of the Han River. There it prepared to secure the supply routes from the old Pusan Perimeter, repair the railroad, and hunt down and destroy bypassed enemy groups. The IX Corps command post opened at Taejon on 5 October. The 2d Infantry Division assumed responsibility generally for the area west and southwest of Taejon, and the 25th Division for the Taejon area and that south and east of it. The newly activated ROK 11th Division was attached to IX Corps on 5 October to help with security in rear areas. On 10 October the Eighth Army Ranger Company was attached to IX Corps, and it joined with the 25th Division Reconnaissance Company in antiguerrilla activity in the Poun area, northeast of Taejon.[1]

During October the 25th Division was the American organization most actively employed in antiguerrilla warfare. It had 6,500 square miles of mountainous country in its zone of responsibility. This lay athwart the escape routes from the old Pusan Perimeter of the larger part of the enemy units cut off or bypassed. On occasion, large groups of enemy soldiers were cornered and either destroyed or captured. On 7 October the 1st Battalion, 35th Infantry, largely as a result of unusually effective artillery fire, killed or wounded about 400 of an enemy force estimated to number approximately 500 men. On another occasion the 3d Battalion of the same regiment captured 549 prisoners in one day.[2]

Enemy guerrilla action, in fact, extended all the way to the southern tip

---

[1] IX Corps WD, Sep 50, Personal Recollections of General Coulter; *Ibid.*, bk. I, sec. II, Oct 50; 2d Inf Div Hist, vol. II, Sep 50, p. 44; 25th Div WD, 7 Oct 50; IX Corps WD, 10 and 15 Oct 50.
[2] EUSAK WD, Br for CG, 24 Oct 50; 25th Div WD, Hist, bk. I, 7-8 Oct 50.

of Korea. Reportedly it was co-ordinated and directed by Kim Chaek, the commander of the North Korean *Front Headquarters*. The guerrillas harassed isolated villages, ambushed patrols, fired on trains, cut telephone lines, and attacked South Korean police stations.

In South Korea bands of guerrillas ambushed vehicles on both the Green Diamond (east coast) and Red Diamond (mountainous western) routes between Pusan and Taegu, and at night raided villages for food, clothing, and hostages. In the latter part of November an estimated 20,000 guerrillas operated in the southwest corner of Korea. The Chirisan area there between Hadong and Koch'ang continued to be a center of guerrilla activity despite the efforts of the newly organized ROK 11th Division and the National Police to suppress it.[3]

Near the 38th Parallel in the central part of Korea there was serious guerrilla action. A long series of incidents occurred in the Ch'unch'on-Hwach'on area north of Wonju. On 22 October an enemy force attacked and dispersed sixty ROK soldiers and police guarding the Hwach'on Dam. The North Koreans then opened the dam's control gates and the Pukhan River rose four feet by the next day and one pier of a railroad bridge many miles below was washed out. On the 25th when a ROK police battalion reoccupied Hwach'on and the hydroelectric dam east of it they found the turbine and control panels at the dam seriously damaged. In November the 1st, 3d, 5th, and 7th ROK Anti-Guerrilla Battalions were almost constantly engaged with North Korean forces in the Hwach'on area. Most of them apparently were elements of the N.K. *10th Division*. At one time the North Koreans held Ch'unch'on, cutting off all its communications with Seoul only forty-five miles to the southwest.[4]

In the east, in the high Taebaek Mountains southwest of Samch'ok, in mid-November there were 4,000 bypassed soldiers of the N.K. *3d, 4th,* and *5th Divisions,* with miscellaneous guerrillas, according to the report of a North Korean regimental commander who surrendered there. Guerrillas even operated at the edge of Seoul. On 15 October a group of them attacked a radio relay station four and a half miles north of the Capital building.

In northeast Korea there was guerrilla action behind the X Corps front from the very moment troops came ashore at Wonsan and it continued until the corps left that part of the country.

Within a few hours after it landed there on 26 October, the 1st Battalion, 1st Marine Regiment, loaded onto gondola cars and just after noon started for Kojo, thirty-nine miles down the coast. There it relieved ROK troops guarding a supply dump. That first night passed quietly, and the next afternoon the ROK's loaded into a train and departed northward.

In a few hours the deceptive quiet at Kojo exploded into a wild night battle

---

[3] 2d Log Comd Act Rpt, G-2 Sec, Nov 50; EUSAK WD, Br for CG, 23 Nov 50; IX Corps WD, bk. 1, 17-18 Oct 50.

[4] EUSAK WD, G-3 Jnl, Msg 2100 23 Oct 50; *Ibid.*, G-3 Jnl, Msg at 1200 12 Nov 50; *Ibid.*, G-3 Sec, 13 Nov 50; *Ibid.*, Br for CG, 25 Oct 50; GHQ FEC, History of the N.K. Army, p. 69 (N.K. *10th Div*); ATIS Res Supp Interrog Rpts, Issue 104 (N.K. *10th Div*), p. 50; ATIS Interrog Rpts, Issue 27 (Korean Opns), p. 81ff, Lt Col Yun Bong Hun, CO *19th Regt*, N.K. *13th Div*.

that began soon after dark and continued after daylight of the 28th. An organized force of North Koreans, later determined by prisoner interrogations to have been three battalions of the N.K. *5th Division,* had silently crept close to the hill positions of the marines south and northwest of Kojo. The enemy attack came so swiftly at one platoon position that fifteen marines were killed there—seven in their sleeping bags. For a time two Marine companies were cut off, but they eventually fought off the enemy and re-established contact with the battalion.[5]

Upon receiving word of the enemy attack, General Almond requested the dispatch of two destroyers to Kojo where they delivered naval gunfire in support of the marines, and on his orders the 1st Marine Air Wing delivered strikes on Kojo that almost completely demolished and burned it. In the afternoon the 1st Marine Division started the 2d Battalion, 1st Marines, from Wonsan for Kojo, and that evening a tank company began loading into an LST at Wonsan, its destination, Kojo. Before noon of the 28th, however, the North Koreans moved off west into the hills and the fight was over. The marines recovered their dead and counted their losses—27 killed, 39 wounded, 3 missing.[6]

Other guerrilla actions south and west of Wonsan, apparently by elements of the N.K. *5th Division,* followed the Kojo incident. On 2 November, an enemy force ambushed a supply convoy behind the 3d Battalion, 1st Marines, near Wonsan, killing nine and wounding fifteen men.

Some of the most destructive of the attacks behind the lines occurred along the main rail and highway route between Wonsan and Hungnam. On the night of 6–7 November, after dark, an enemy force ambushed a convoy south of Kowon, thirty-five miles north of Wonsan, and, after the drivers fled into the adjacent rice paddies, burned three jeeps and twenty trucks. North of town another group ambushed a military police patrol and then attacked a signal unit, inflicting casualties on both.

At the town of Kowon itself, before midnight, North Koreans attacked a northbound Marine Corps supply train. Thirty marines were riding the train as guards. The night was dark, and snow flurries increased the poor visibility. After the train had stopped at a water tank, a North Korean soldier violently flung open the door of the front coach and burst inside. A marine killed him instantly. Enemy burp gun and rifle fire now ripped into the coaches. Outside, enemy soldiers blew the track ahead and killed the engineer when he started to back the train. The North Koreans persisted in their efforts to enter the coaches despite heavy losses until they finally succeeded, shooting and clubbing every marine they thought still alive. But 2 wounded marines inside the coach successfully feigned death and escaped later. In this action the train engineer and 6 marines were killed, and 8 marines wounded.[7]

---

[5] 1st Mar Div SAR, 8 Oct–13 Dec 50, vol. I, p. 23; *Ibid.,* vol. II, an. C, pp. 6–8, 26–28 Oct 50; Geer, *The New Breed,* pp. 196–203.

[6] X Corps WD, G–3 Jnl, Msg 39, 28 Oct 50; Diary of CG, X Corps, 28 Oct 50; 1st Mar Div SAR, vol. II, an. C, pp. 10–15, 29 Oct–2 Nov 50.

[7] 1st Mar Div SAR, vol. II, an. C, p. 27, 7 Nov 50; X Corps WD, 7–8 Nov 50; *Ibid.,* PIR 42, 7 Nov 50; Geer, *The New Breed,* pp. 248–51.

Later in the night, at 0230, an estimated 500 North Koreans attacked a battalion of the 65th Infantry Regiment, 3d Division, which just the previous day had occupied Yonghung, eight miles farther north and midway between Wonsan and Hungnam, and inflicted 40 casualties. This same enemy force then struck a detachment of the 4th Signal Battalion nearby, and, in moving northward from it, stumbled into the camp of the 96th Field Artillery Battalion. There the North Koreans penetrated the battalion positions and by mortar fire destroyed six 155-mm. howitzers and the battalion trains containing all the ammunition supply, inflicting about 40 casualties. The enemy withdrew after daylight. Aerial observers later discovered an estimated 2,000 enemy troops moving on secondary roads into the mountains northwest of Yonghung. Two heavy air strikes on them caused an estimated 300 casualties.[8]

To the west, elements of the N.K. *15th Division* held the upper Imjin River valley and centered their harassing action against Majon-ni. From the beginning this area was one of the worst centers of North Korean guerrilla action in the X Corps zone of operations. The Wonsan–Majon-ni road was the eastern end of the main lateral road across the peninsula to the North Korean capital city of P'yongyang. From Wonsan, ridge after ridge of the Taebaek Range rose westward for an airline distance of 60 miles. The road twisted along narrow gorges and climbed zigzag over mountain passes. Majon-ni, only 16 air miles from Wonsan, is 28 by road. The little village of 300 population is located at the junction of the lateral Wonsan–P'yongyang road and the north-south road following the Imjin River from Sibyon-ni. For 60 air miles this latter road followed the cramped, twisting gorge of the Imjin River through the heart of the Taebaek Range. It was a favorite route of travel for cutoff North Koreans and traversed one of the most important centers of guerrilla activity in all Korea.

The 3d Battalion, 1st Marines, commanded by Lt. Col. Thomas Ridge, drew the task of holding the Majon-ni road junction, and relieved ROK 3d Division troops there on 28 October. Ridge established a tight perimeter defense line around the village with a roadblock on each of the three roads coming into the Y-shaped junction. On 7 November the 3d Battalion came under general attack at Majon-ni and lost some outpost positions. Air strikes after daylight helped repel the North Koreans. That same day enemy forces on the Majon-ni–Wonsan road ambushed a convoy in Ambush Alley, as it came to be known, on the east side of the 3,000-foot pass. E Company, 1st Marines, accompanying the convoy as guard, lost eight men killed and thirty-one wounded.[9]

On 12 November the 1st Battalion, 15th Infantry, left Wonsan to relieve the marines at Majon-ni. Because of enemy roadblocks it did not arrive there until the next day. On the 14th, the ROK 3d Korean Marine Corps (KMC) Battalion, which had landed at Wonsan four days earlier, arrived at Majon-ni and proceeded fourteen air miles westward to

---

[8] X Corps PIR 42, 7 Nov 50 and PIR 43, 8 Nov 50; X Corps WD, Diary of CG, 7 Nov 50.

[9] 1st Mar Div SAR, vol. II, an. C, pp. 8–26, 28 Oct–7 Nov 50.

Tongyang where it established a blocking position at another north-south road intersection with the Wonsan-P'yongyang road, near the U.S. X Corps–Eighth Army boundary. Relieved at the isolated Majon-ni mountain crossroads, the 3d Battalion, 1st Marines, joyfully departed on 14 November for Wonsan.[10]

On the night of 20–21 November, an estimated 200 enemy soldiers with armored support again attacked the Majon-ni perimeter. After penetrating it at one point the enemy was repulsed just before daylight.

That day, 21 November, a motorized patrol consisting of two officers and ninety-one men of the 1st Battalion, 15th Infantry, moved west from Majon-ni to establish contact with the 3d KMC Battalion at Tongyang. In an 8-mile gorge about midway between the two places a hidden enemy force ambushed the column. In this action the patrol lost twenty-eight men and most of its vehicles and heavy weapons. A platoon of tanks and a company of infantry from the 2d Battalion arrived to reinforce the Majon-ni garrison. A second attempt to get through to Tongyang on the 22d also failed when a tank-led column turned back because, overnight, the enemy had badly cratered and mined the road. It now became necessary to supply the 3d KMC Battalion at Tongyang by airdrop.

Again, on the 23d, a reinforced rifle company left Majon-ni with the task of repairing the cratered road and proceeding west to contact the ROK marines.

The ROK's at the same time were instructed by an airdropped message to send a force eastward on the road to meet the 15th Infantry force. The westbound column had just passed the point of the ambush two days earlier when an estimated 300 enemy troops opened fire on it. Fortunately, the ROK force arrived from the opposite direction and joined in the fight. But both the ROK and the 15th Infantry forces withdrew after the latter had lost sixteen wounded and three missing in action.

Finally, on 25 November the 1st Battalion, 15th Infantry, and the 3d KMC Battalion made a co-ordinated attack against the enemy force that had cut the road between them and decisively defeated it, killing 150, capturing four 120-mm. mortars, and destroying a large ammunition cache. This action temporarily reopened the supply road to Tongyang. But determined and destructive enemy activity in this area never ceased as long as U.N. forces were there.[11]

Between the U.S. 65th Regiment and the ROK 26th Regiment to the north, a large gap existed in the U.S. 3d Division zone that was also a center of guerrilla activity. Near the Eighth Army–X Corps boundary there the 5,600-foot-high mountain mass of Paek-san interposed its trackless waste between the two regiments and the lateral roads they had to use for communication and supply. Between 18 and 22 November B Company, 65th Infantry, tried to establish contact with the ROK 26th Regiment to the north but was driven back after two engagements with enemy forces on Paek-san. The 3d Division estimated that the bulk of 25,000 North Korea

---

[10] 1st Mar Div SAR, Oct–Dec 50, vol. II, an. C, pp. 26–40, 7–14 Nov 50; 3d Inf Div Comd Rpt, sec. III, Narr of Opns, pp. 5–14, Nov 50; 1st Lt. Charles R. Stiles, "The Dead End of Ambush Alley," *Marine Corps Gazette* (November, 1951), p. 39; Geer, *The New Breed*, pp. 206–15.

[11] 3d Div Comd Rpt, sec. III, pp. 5–9.

People's Army guerrillas in its zone were within a 10-mile radius of Paek-san.[12]

Because there were no usable roads in the northern part of its zone, the U.S. 3d Division could supply the ROK 26th Regiment only with great difficulty. Because of this, Maj. Gen. Robert H. Soule on 21 November requested General Almond to move the boundary between the 3d Division and the 1st Marine Division northward a few miles so as to place the Huksu-ri–Sach'ang-ni road within the 3d Division zone. The next day the X Corps granted the request and changed the boundary. General Soule thereupon ordered the ROK 26th Regiment to establish blocking positions at Huksu-ri and Sach'ang-ni. In the course of capturing these places, the ROK's fought several engagements. An enemy battalion defending Sach'ang-ni was driven away only after it had lost more than 100 men killed or captured.

The ROK's then attacked north and west out of Sach'ang-ni for several miles, encountering enemy delaying forces. On 24 November in this continuing action, the ROK 26th Regiment captured twenty-six CCF soldiers in the vicinity of Sach'ang-ni, the first Chinese soldiers encountered in the X Corps zone with the exception of those in the reservoir area. The road on which this action occurred ran south from Yudam-ni and the west shore of the Changjin Reservoir. Their presence here indicated that Chinese forces were working southward along the X Corps left flank. Information obtained from prisoners indicated that Chinese forces had been in position there for approximately three weeks to check any U.N. attempt to advance north over this road. It chanced that the ROK 26th Regiment on 24 November was the first organization to reach the point where Chinese of the *125th Division* stood guard. This was the newly developed situation when on 25 November the 1st Battalion, 7th Infantry, relieved the ROK 26th Regiment at Sach'ang-ni.[13]

A survey of 110 enemy prisoners taken in one 24-hour period early in November in the X Corps rear areas showed they came from sixty-two different organizations. In the latter part of November, X Corps intelligence estimated that 25,000 North Korean Army guerrillas operated south and west of Hungnam in the X Corps rear areas. The pattern of guerrilla activity gradually shifted northward during November, from below Wonsan to the mountains west of Hungnam. A special report prepared by X Corps listed 109 separate guerrilla attacks in the corps zone during the month, an average of better than three and a half a day.[14]

In the west coastal area of North Korea in the Eighth Army zone, guerrilla activity at this time was not as great as in northeast and central Korea. Patrols, nevertheless, were necessary.

In the hills north and east of P'yongyang these patrols uncovered large quantities of enemy war supplies in caves,

---

[12] 3d Div Comd Rpt, sec. II, p. 2, and sec. III, p. 7, Nov 50; 65th Inf Comd Rpt, Nov 50, p. 3.

[13] 3d Div Comd Rpt, sec. III, pp. 10–13; X Corps PIR 60, 25 Nov 50; FEC Intel Digest, vol. I, Nr 4, 1–15 Feb 53, Histories of CCF Army Groups Active in Korea, pt. III, *XIII Army Group*, pp. 32–33.

[14] 1st Mar Div SAR, vol. I, pp. 23, 28; X Corps PIR's 38, 3 Nov, 43, 8 Nov, and 46, 11 Nov 50; 3d Inf Div Comd Rpt, Nov 50, sec. II, Intel Summ, p. 2; X Corps, Guerrilla Activities, X Corps Zone, Nov 50, with location map of attacks.

tunnels, and other hiding places. Much of this was found in the mining area east of P'yongyang in old mine shafts and tunnels accessible to spur rail lines. The most important find of all was made by Lt. Doric E. Ball's patrol from M Company, 23d Infantry Regiment, 2d Division on 6 November. With the aid of a local chief of police, the patrol found a huge arsenal in an old lead mine nine miles northeast of Kangdong. In it were about 400 lathes of mixed American, English, and Russian manufacture; all the machinery needed to make Russian-type burp guns and 120-mm. mortars was there. The arsenal consisted of nineteen large rooms used variously as machine shop, storage room, office space, and an auditorium. This armament factory, known as Arsenal No. 65, had originally been above ground in P'yongyang, but aerial bombing had caused the North Koreans to move it to the mine.

East of the main supply road strong guerrilla bands were active in the Sibyon-ni area. One of the worst incidents in this area occurred on 6 November about midway between Kumch'on and Sibyon-ni when an enemy force ambushed the I&R Platoon and a platoon of L Company, 27th Infantry, reinforced by C Battery, 8th Field Artillery Battalion. The 1st Battalion hurried to the scene and at midnight rescued several wounded and missing men, but the enemy had disappeared. Three days later the bodies of fifteen men from the ambushed patrol were found in a shallow grave. According to a survivor, the North Koreans had murdered these men when they followed the example of 1st Lt. Harold G. Parris, an officer captured with them, in refusing to give their captors information beyond their name, rank, and serial number.[15]

At the same time, an enemy force estimated at 1,000 men held control of the Ich'on area some miles eastward. It required a combined attack of the U.S. 27th Infantry from the southwest and of the ROK 17th Regiment from the east on 7 November to drive this force into the hills. A week earlier, on 28 October, North Koreans had killed all the ROK wounded and hospital personnel in a field hospital at Ich'on.[16]

It was inevitable that the Iron Triangle of central North Korea would become the scene of enemy guerrilla and harassing action since it was a principal assembly area for North Korean soldiers retreating northward. The U.N. effort to open the railroad from Seoul through the Iron Triangle to Wonsan encountered almost unceasing guerrilla attacks. Most of them occurred just north of P'yonggang at the apex of the Triangle. ROK troops rode all trains as guards, and pitched battles often were fought between them and the guerrillas.

On the morning of 2 November one of the largest of these actions occurred when a force of about 1,000 guerrillas ambushed a work train ten miles north of P'yonggang. Fortunately, 200 soldiers of the ROK 17th Regiment were riding the train as guards and they succeeded in beating off the attackers, killing 40 and capturing 23 of them. These prison-

---

[15] 27th Inf WD, 6, 9 Nov 50; 8th FA Bn WD, 5-9 Nov 50. Eighth Army General Order 484, 1 July 1951, awarded the Distinguished Service Cross posthumously to Lieutenant Parris. The sixteen captured men were from C Battery, 8th Field Artillery Battalion.

[16] EUSAK WD, Br for CG, 7 Nov 50; Ministry of National Defense, ROK, *Korea in War*, vol. I, 1 May 1950-June 1951, p. A-67.

ers said there were 4,000 guerrillas in the vicinity and that they planned to attack every train going toward Wonsan. Enemy activity became so intense in this area that the entire ROK 17th Regiment was sent there, and gradually elements of the U.S. 25th Division also entered the fight in the Iron Triangle.[17]

On 9 November about 1,400 enemy troops of the *18th Regiment, N.K. 4th Division,* attacked Ch'orwon in the Iron Triangle, driving away 800 South Korean police. The next day about 500 men of the *5th Regiment* of the same division occupied Yonch'on, ten miles to the south on the road to Seoul. Elements of the 24th Infantry Regiment, 25th Division, tried but failed to regain the town. That evening a North Korean roadblock force ambushed an I&R Platoon and A Company, 24th Infantry, column near there. The next day when the regiment retook Yonch'on it found the bodies of thirty-eight American soldiers at the ambush site and all vehicles burned.

Co-ordinated with the enemy action at Ch'orwon and Yonch'on, an enemy regiment, supported by mortars, attacked the 1st and 2d Battalions, ROK 17th Regiment, at P'yonggang on 10 November, and had surrounded them by daylight the next morning. Maj. Robert B. Holt, a KMAG adviser with the regiment, radioed a request for the 3d Battalion of the ROK regiment at Ich'on to attack eastward, and he also arranged for an airdrop of ammunition. During the day a Mosquito plane landed at P'yonggang and picked up Holt, who directed air strikes on the enemy positions with reportedly heavy casualties to the North Koreans. The enemy force withdrew from around P'yonggang during the night of 11–12 November. But two nights later part of it returned and again attacked the airstrip and the town. The ROK's cleared both places of enemy troops before noon of the 14th at a cost of 11 men killed and 23 wounded, as against 141 enemy killed and 20 captured. The enemy pressure in this area never ceased and the situation there became more precarious when the 25th Division troops moved north to participate in the 24 November Eighth Army attack.[18]

---

[17] EUSAK WD, G-3 Jnl, Msg at 2315, 2 Nov, and Off for Co-ordination of Protection of Lines of Comm, Rear Areas, Daily Rpt, 28 Oct and 2 Nov 50.

[18] EUSAK WD, G-3 Jnl, Msg 0700 9 Nov 50; EUSAK PIR's 121–25, 10–14 Nov 50; EUSAK POR 370, 12 Nov 50; 25th Div WD, 11–14 Nov 50; GHQ FEC, History of the N.K. Army, pp. 59, 68; ATIS Res Supp Interrog Rpts, Issue 94 (N.K. *4th Div*), p. 50; ATIS Res Supp Interrog Rpts, Issue 100 (N.K. *9th Div*), p. 54; ATIS Interrog Rpts, Issue 18 (Enemy Forces), p. 94 and p. 152; Interv, author with 1st Lt Robert J. Tews (Plt Ldr A Co, 24th Inf, at time of incident and present at scene of ambush, 11 Nov), 3 Sep 51.

CHAPTER XXXVIII

The X Corps Advances to the Yalu

> Water shapes its course according to the ground over which it flows; the soldier works out his victory in relation to the foe whom he is facing. Therefore, just as water retains no constant shape, so in warfare there are no constant conditions.
> SUN TZU, *The Art of War*

ROK I Corps Attacks up the Coastal Road

After the landing of the X Corps at Wonsan on 26 October, the ROK Capital Division, already north of Hungnam, continued its attack northward in three regimental combat teams. (*Map 25*) The ROK Cavalry Regiment of the division, a motorized organization, constituted what General Almond called the "flying column." It was to advance as rapidly as possible toward the border. Almond made arrangements for supplying this flying column from an LST at sea, and he provided it with a tactical air control party from the 7th Infantry Division. Two days after the X Corps landing at Wonsan, the ROK Cavalry Regiment against strong opposition captured Songjin, 105 air miles northeast of Hungnam. At the same time, the 1st Regiment of the Capital Division approached P'ungsan, inland halfway to the border on the Iwon–Sinch'ang-ni–Hyesanjin road. Two days later the third regiment of the division, the 18th, reached the south end of Pujon Reservoir.[1]

In front of the ROK Cavalry Regiment on the coastal road an estimated North Korean battalion retreated northward toward Kilchu, a sizable town twenty miles north of Songjin. Kilchu is fourteen air miles inland from the coast, the farthest point inland for a town of any size along the whole length of the east coastal road. Situated beyond the reach of effective naval gunfire, it was a favorable place for the North Koreans to fight a delaying action. The ROK attack before daylight of 3 November developed into a day-long battle which

---

[1] X Corps PIR 34, 30 Oct 50; X Corps WD, Summ, 28 Oct 50 and WD, 4 Nov 50, G-1 Rpt, Rpt on Almond-Partridge Conference.
Like both AMS maps of Korea, scales 1:250,000 and 1:50,000, the text uses the Korean place names Pujon and Changjin for the two reservoirs that figure prominently in the narrative hereafter. Hagaru-ri is used for the combined areas of the town of Changjin and the village of Hagaru-ri. Because the American forces were using Japanese maps (some early maps gave dual names), they used the Japanese names Chosin and Fusen rather than the Korean Changjin and Pujon for the reservoirs.

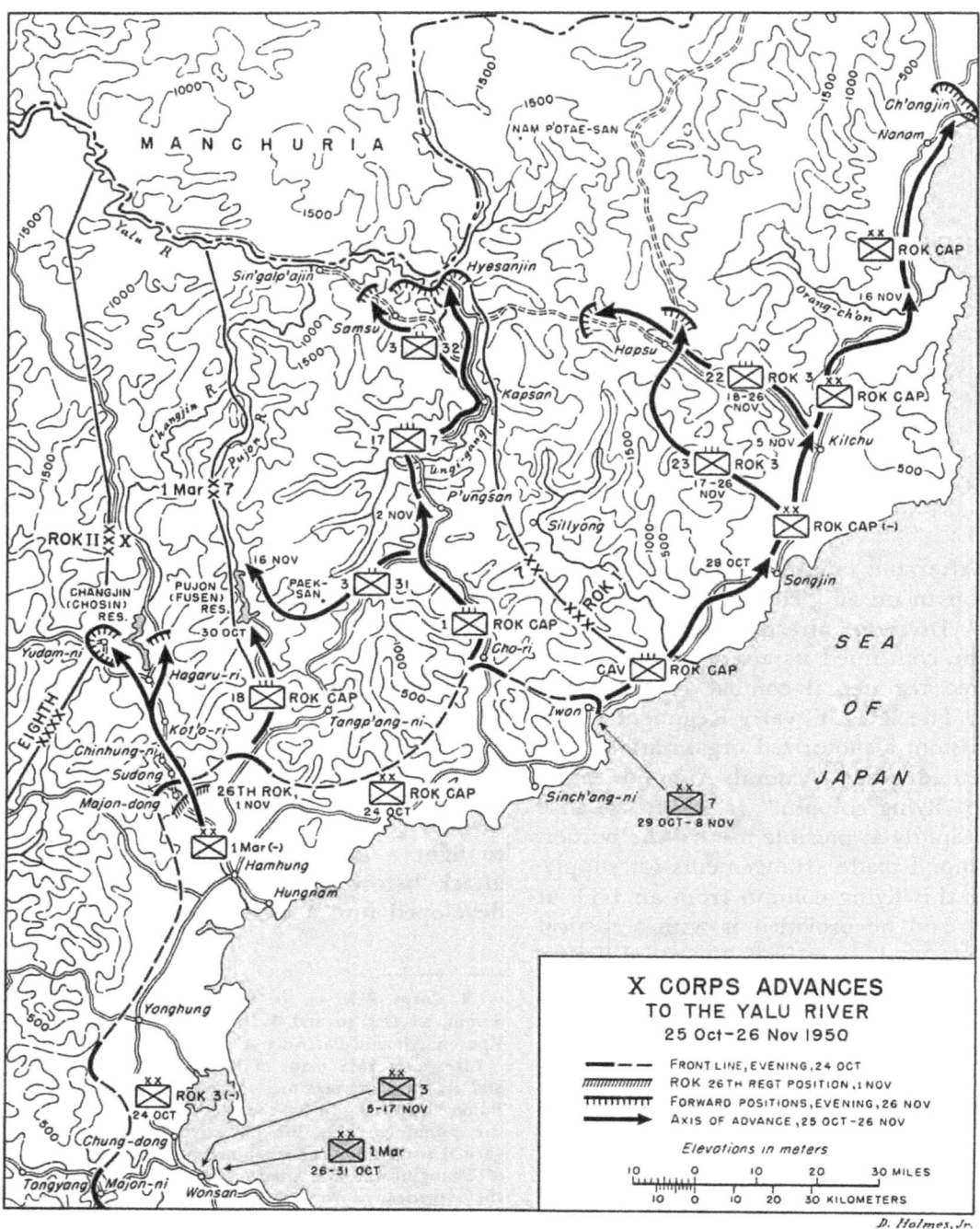

MAP 25

failed to win the town. The ROK 1st Regiment joined the Cavalry Regiment in the battle. By daylight of 5 November the two ROK regiments had encircled Kilchu, and they captured it before noon. On the day of Kilchu's capture Corsair air strikes from the 1st Marine Air Wing were credited with destroying 2 enemy tanks, 4 artillery pieces, and 350 counted enemy dead. The next day a count of all the North Korean dead reached 530. In the Kilchu battle the ROK's captured 9 45-mm. antitank guns, 6 82-mm. mortars, and 10 heavy machine guns. The ROK Cavalry Regiment lost 21 killed and 91 wounded. Prisoners said the N.K. *507th Brigade* had defended the town. The local North Korean commander reportedly ordered the execution of a battalion commander whose unit had retreated.[2]

After the Kilchu battle, aerial reports indicated that fresh enemy troops were moving south along the coastal road from the Ch'ongjin-Nanam area. Supported by tanks, this force, estimated at six to seven battalions, met the Capital Division on 12 November just north of the Orang-ch'on, thirty miles above Kilchu. In the resulting battle it forced the ROK 18th Regiment to withdraw south of the stream. Bad weather prevented effective close air support, and, since the scene of action was beyond the range of destroyers' guns, the heavy cruiser *Rochester* was sent to provide naval gunfire support. Clearing weather enabled Corsairs to join in the battle on the 13th, and that afternoon an air strike destroyed two tanks, damaged a third, and forced another to withdraw. Six inches of snow covered the Orang-ch'on battlefield.[3]

The enemy attack resumed and made further penetrations in the positions of the 18th Regiment on 14 November. The next day it compelled the 18th and the 1st Regiments to withdraw again. Close air support for the ROK's prevented the North Koreans from exploiting this success and during the day destroyed 3 more tanks, 2 self-propelled guns, and 12 trucks. At the same time, thirty B-29's dropped 40,000 incendiary bombs on Hoeryong, a rail and road communication center of 45,000 population on the Tumen River at the Manchurian border, 100 miles southwest of Vladivostok. By 16 November the four days of ground battle and three of aerial attack had so weakened the enemy force that it faltered, and the ROK 18th Regiment once more advanced slowly.

A delayed report covering the three days from the evening of 14 November to that of 17 November listed 1,753 enemy killed, 105 prisoners, and the capture of 4 rapid-fire guns, 62 light machine guns, 101 burp guns, and 649 rifles. On the 19th, air attacks destroyed 2 more tanks and 2 artillery pieces. The USS *St. Paul* now gave naval gunfire support to the ROK's. The enemy force that fought the battle of the Orang-ch'on consisted of about 6,000 troops of the N.K. *507th Brigade* and a regiment of the N.K. *41st Division*, supported by a battalion of 8 tanks.[4]

---

[2] X Corps WD, Summ of Opns, 3-6 Nov 50; *Ibid.*, PIR's 39, 4 Nov, 40, 5 Nov, and 41, 6 Nov 50.

[3] X Corps POR 48, 13 Nov 50; X Corps PIR 47, 12 Nov, and 48, 13 Nov 50.

[4] X Corps POR 50, 15 Nov, and 57, 22 Nov 50; X Corps PIR 49, 14 Nov, 51, 16 Nov, and 54, 19 Nov 50; X Corps WD, 25 Nov 50, app. 1, Intel Est to an. AO 7, p. 2; GHQ UNC, G-3 Opn Rpt, 14 Oct 50; EUSAK WD, 16 Nov 50, EUSAK Daily News Bul.

The ROK troops fought these battles in northeast Korea under great physical hardship from the cold. On 16 November the temperature in their zone already had dropped to 16° below zero. Their uniforms in most cases consisted of one old suit of fatigues, worn-out shoes, one half blanket per man, and an old U.S. Army overcoat. The situation was about to improve, however, for the next day at Songjin an LST unloaded 26,000 sets of ROK winter clothing. Another LST loaded with shoes, wool socks, underwear, shirts, and field jackets was to sail from Pusan that same day.

By 17 November the ROK 3d Division had moved up behind the Capital Division on the coastal road and had started its 23d Regiment inland from Songjin toward Hapsu. The next day its 22d Regiment started for the same objective from farther north at Kilchu. The larger part of the ROK 3d Division, therefore, was now deployed on the left of and inland from the Capital Division. Six LST's of the Korean Navy supplied the ROK I Corps.[5]

Able at last to resume its advance after the battle of the preceding week, the Capital Division on 20 November crossed the Orang-ch'on and resumed its drive toward Ch'ongjin, the big industrial center 30 miles north of the river and 65 air miles southwest of the Siberian border. A little more than a month earlier a naval task force had heavily bombarded Ch'ongjin with 1,309 rounds of 6-inch, 400 rounds of 8-inch, and 163 rounds of 16-inch shells. ROK troops, following behind a rolling barrage of naval gunfire, enveloped Ch'ongjin on 25 November. That evening the 1st Regiment moved around the city to a point 5 miles north of it; the Cavalry Regiment seized the airfield on its western edge; and the 18th Regiment was on its southern outskirts. The next day, Ch'ongjin fell to the Capital Division. The ROK's now planned to turn due north and inland along the highway and railroad leading to Hoeryong at the Manchurian border.[6]

U.S. 7th Infantry Division Reaches Manchurian Border

The U.S. 7th Infantry Division, in its zone of operations between the ROK I Corps to the north and the 1st Marine Division to the south, likewise made important gains in carrying out its part of the X Corps mission in northeast Korea. On 29 October the 17th Infantry Regiment of the division landed unopposed at Iwon. That same day the 1st Battalion of the regiment; the 49th Field Artillery Battalion; and A Company, 13th Engineer Combat Battalion moved from the beachhead to Cho-ri, a distance of 50 miles. From Cho-ri the 7th Division was to strike north for the Manchurian border at Hyesanjin, 70 air miles away. But over the poor dirt road that twisted its way through the mountains and the Korean upland the distance was much greater. On the last day of the month the 1st Battalion and regimental headquarters moved on to P'ungsan, 120 road miles from the Iwon beaches and approximately halfway between the coast and Hyesanjin. The 1st Regiment of the

---

[5] X Corps POR's 52-55, 17-20 Nov 50.

[6] X Corps POR's 55-61, 20-26 Nov 50; X Corps PIR's 59-61, 24-26 Nov 50; 2d Log Comd Hist Rpt, Water Div, Trans Sec, Nov 50.

ROK Capital Division had cleared the road of enemy troops that far. When the 7th Division got all its elements ashore its total strength would exceed 26,600 men. The division on 1 November counted 18,837 men, almost full-strength, and to this were added 7,804 attached South Korean soldiers.[7]

The U.S. 7th Infantry Division had its initial action in northeast Korea on 1 November when the 1st Battalion, 17th Infantry, helped the ROK 1st Regiment repulse a strong North Korean attack two miles north of P'ungsan. Col. Herbert B. Powell, commander of the 17th Infantry Regiment, ordered an attack by the 1st Battalion the next morning at 0800 to clear the enemy force from in front of the town. But the North Koreans in approximately regimental strength attacked first, at 0700, starting an action that continued throughout the day. Except for one company, all units of the 17th Regiment arrived at P'ungsan by the end of the day. Colonel Powell's regiment now relieved the ROK 1st Regiment, which turned back to join the Capital Division on the coastal road.[8]

Because the open beaches were wholly at the mercy of the weather and high seas, unloading of the 7th Infantry Division at Iwon went forward slowly. The relatively few vehicles ashore, the long haul, and the low stockpile on the beach combined to cause the 17th Infantry on 4 November to request an airdrop at P'ungsan of 4.2-inch, 81-mm., and 60-mm. mortar ammunition. An airdrop the next day had considerable breakage loss. Patrols on the 4th discovered the enemy had withdrawn from in front of P'ungsan, and the 17th Infantry advanced unopposed to the Ungi River. The temperature stood at 2° below zero.[9]

At the Iwon beachhead, the 3d Battalion, 31st Infantry Regiment, landed on 3 November and the rest of the regiment followed ashore the next day. The regimental mission was to move to the left (west) flank of the 17th Infantry. This would place it in the mountainous country extending to the Pujon Reservoir. ROK troops previously had advanced into that region.[10]

Carrying out its mission, the 31st Infantry Regiment advanced on the division left flank toward the reservoir. On 8 November it encountered Chinese soldiers on the eastern slopes of Paek-san, a 7,700-foot peak twelve miles east of the southern end of the reservoir. This was the U.S. 7th Division's first contact with the CCF. There, during the afternoon, elements of the regiment engaged in a battle with an estimated battalion of Chinese, later identified as part of the CCF *376th Regiment, 126th Division*. Before nightfall the 31st Infantry seized that part of Paek-san, and the Chinese force withdrew with at least 50 killed. On this same day a patrol of the regiment met a Marine patrol about midway between Hamhung and the Pujon Reservoir, thus establishing the first contact between the two divisions in northeast Korea.[11]

---

[7] 7th Inf Div WD, 29-31 Oct 50; X Corps POR 36, 1 Nov 50.
[8] 7th Inf Div WD, 1-2 Nov 50; 17th Inf WD, 1-2 Nov 50; Interv, author with Brig Gen Herbert B. Powell, 13 Apr 54.

[9] 7th Inf Div WD, G-4 Jnl, 4-5 Nov 50; *Ibid.*, 5-7 Nov 50; Barr Notes, 6-7 Nov 50.
[10] 7th Inf Div WD, 2-4 Nov 50.
[11] 7th Inf Div WD, 7-10 Nov 50.

THE 1ST BATTALION, 17TH INFANTRY, *enters Hyesanjin on the Yalu River on the morning of 21 November.*

On the division right flank the next day, 9 November, the 7th Reconnaissance Company moved to Sillyong, east of P'ungsan, to protect a power installation.

On 12 November the division received orders from X Corps to continue the advance northward. The 17th Infantry was to seize Kapsan, and then go to Hyesanjin on the Yalu; the 31st Infantry was to advance on the left of the 17th; and the 32d Infantry was to seize the southeast shore of the Pujon Reservoir. The 32d Infantry, which began unloading on 4 November and was the last of the regiments to come ashore at Iwon, moved southwest from the beach along the coast through Hamhung and there turned northeast to Tangp'ang-ni in preparation for its part in the operation.[12]

In accordance with the corps order, the 17th Infantry prepared to attack across the Ungi River on 14 November. To replace the bridge which the North Koreans had blown, Colonel Powell had ROK troops in the regiment construct a floating footbridge made of planking extending between empty oil drums. En-

---

[12] 7th Inf Div WD, 9–12 Nov 50; X Corps Opn Ord 9, 12 Nov 50.

Looking Across the Yalu, *from left to right: Brig. Gen. Homer Kiefer, Generals Hodes, Almond, and Barr, and Colonel Powell.*

emy fire on the bridge site was at long range and ineffective. The 2d Battalion, 17th Infantry, crossed over this footbridge without difficulty on the 14th and proceeded to the attack.

The 3d Battalion was scheduled to cross the river at the same time over a shallow ford a few miles to the east. During the night of 13-14 November enemy forces apparently opened dams upstream. The water level rose two feet, making the river waist-deep. In the face of heavy small arms and some mortar fire, six men of L Company waded the stream in weather 7° below zero. A few other men entered the water, but it soon became apparent that all who crossed the stream would be frozen and out of action in a few minutes unless they were specially cared for. The battalion commander ordered the men who had crossed to the north side to return. Their clothes had to be cut from them. They were then wrapped in blankets and taken to the 3d Battalion command post tent to warm. Casualties from this abortive crossing attempt were 1 killed, 6 wounded, and 18 men suffering frostbite from exposure in the river. Colonel Powell agreed with the battalion commander that the 3d Battalion could not cross by wading the icy water. Both Generals Barr and Almond concurred in this decision. The battalion subsequently crossed over the oil drum footbridge.[13]

The need for shelters and warming areas for the front-line troops led the 7th Division the next day to request the immediate delivery of 250 squad tents and 500 oil-burning stoves. In order to keep vehicle gasoline lines and carburetors from freezing it was necessary to mix alcohol or alcohol-base antifreeze with gasoline.

On 15 November, the 1st Battalion crossed the Ungi River behind the 2d Battalion and moved up on its left, but the two battalions made only small gains. On the 16th, aerial observers reported the enemy forces separating into small groups and withdrawing toward Kapsan. That day the 17th Regiment gained about eight miles. On the 19th, the 1st Battalion seized Kapsan at 1030 after a co-ordinated infantry, tank, and artillery attack. In this action the 17th Tank Company overran enemy troops in their foxholes, while the heavy fire of the 15th AAA Battalion 40-mm. weapons drove other North Koreans from log-covered trenches and pillboxes and then cut them down. Under cover of the combined fire of the tanks and the antiaircraft weapons the infantry then crossed the river. That night the 1st Battalion was eight miles north of Kapsan, only twenty-three road miles from Hyesanjin on the Yalu. The 2d and 3d Battalions followed behind the 1st Battalion. The regimental command post set up in Kapsan for the night.[14]

The next day, 20 November, the 17th Regiment in a column of battalions—the 1st, 3d, and 2d, in that order—advanced on foot nineteen miles over icy roads through and over the mountains to a point only a few miles from the Yalu. Small enemy groups opposed the advance with only brief exchanges of fire, and then fled. On the morning of 21 November, without opposition, the 1st Battalion, 17th Infantry, led the way into Hyesanjin, and by 1000 had occupied the town and surrounding ground to the banks of the Yalu River. General Almond had flown into Kapsan on the 20th and, together with General Barr and Colonel Powell, accompanied the leading elements of the 17th Infantry Regiment into the town. A week earlier, on the 13th, Navy carrier planes had attacked the military camp at Hyesanjin, burning the barracks buildings and warehouses. The town was now about 85 percent destroyed by this and earlier aerial action.[15]

Upon receiving word that elements of the 7th Division had reached the Yalu, General MacArthur immediately sent a message to General Almond saying, "Heartiest congratulations, Ned, and tell Dave Barr that the 7th Division hit the jackpot." Almond added his own congratulations to Barr on the 22d, saying in part, "The fact that only twenty days ago this division landed amphibiously over the beaches at Iwon and advanced 200 miles over tortuous mountain terrain and fought successfully against a determined foe in subzero

---

[13] 17th Inf WD, 14 Nov 50; 7th Div WD, 14 Nov 50; Barr Notes, 14–15 Nov 50; Interv, author with Powell, 13 Apr 54; Interv, author with Lt Col Walter Gunthorp (2d Bn, 17th Inf, Nov 50), 13 Apr 54.

[14] 7th Div WD, 15–19 Nov 50; Barr Notes, 19 Nov 50; Capt George H. Worf, "Enroute to the Yalu," *Antiaircraft Journal* (March–April, 1951), p. 22.

[15] 17th Inf WD, 21 Nov 50; 7th Inf Div WD, 20–21 Nov 50; X Corps WD, Diary of CG, 21 Nov 50; X Corps POR 55–56, 20–21 Nov 50; X Corps PIR 56, 21 Nov 50; Barr Notes, 21 Nov 50.

weather will be recorded in history as an outstanding military achievement." [16]

The Yalu River at Hyesanjin is not the great river it becomes near its mouth at Sinuiju. At Hyesanjin, near its source on the southwest slopes of 8,000-foot-high Nam P'otae-san, the White Head Mountain famous in Korean history, the Yalu was approximately 50 to 75 yards wide. On the day the 17th Infantry first stood on its banks the river was frozen over except for a 6-foot-wide channel; four days later it was completely frozen over. The bridge across the stream at Hyesanjin had been destroyed before the 17th Infantry arrived there. Upstream about 300 yards on the north side of the Yalu in Manchuria there was an undamaged Chinese village larger than Hyesanjin. Officers and men of the 17th Infantry had mixed emotions, some apprehensive, as they looked across the ribbon of ice and water into Manchuria. There they saw CCF sentries walk their rounds and their officers come and go.[17]

Meanwhile, to the southwest, the 31st Infantry Regiment patrolled extensively and advanced in its zone. This mountainous waste was virtually roadless, and ox-drawn carts were used to transport supplies and evacuate wounded. On 15 November a patrol from the 3d Battalion, 31st Infantry, reached the eastern shore of Pujon Reservoir. The next day another patrol encountered about 200 CCF soldiers at the northern end of the reservoir and drove them away after a brief fight. On the 18th, patrols ranged both sides of the reservoir. Leaving strong detachments to guard the mountain passes from the reservoir eastward into the division's rear along the Cho-ri–P'ungsan road, General Barr on 20 November began moving the bulk of the 31st and 32d Regiments to the P'ungsan-Kapsan area behind the 17th Infantry. On the division right, ROK troops finally arrived at Sillyong shortly before midnight of the 20th to relieve I Company, 32d Infantry. Unfortunately, in the darkness each group at first thought the other the enemy and a brief fire fight resulted in the wounding of five ROK's.

The 32d Infantry Regiment, concentrating now at Kapsan, prepared to strike northwest through Samsu to Sin'galp'a-jin on the Yalu. This would put it on the Manchurian border to the left or west of the 17th Regiment at Hyesanjin. Task Force Kingston, commanded by 2d Lt. Robert C. Kingston, a platoon leader of K Company, started for Samsu on 22 November and entered the town unopposed at midafternoon, followed later by the rest of the 3d Battalion, less I Company.[18]

The 17th Infantry at Hyesanjin was to co-operate with the 32d Infantry by attacking west to meet it. On 22 November, the first day that it attempted to move west to join the 32d Infantry, one of its combat patrols encountered a force of North Koreans about seven miles west of Hyesanjin, and a stubborn fight developed. This set a pattern of

---

[16] Schnabel, FEC, GHQ Support and Participation in the Korean War, ch. VII, p. 2, quoting Msg U/CX2867, CG X Corps to CG 7th Div, 21 Nov 50, and Msg U/CX2859, CG X Corps to CG 7th Div, 22 Nov 50.

[17] Interv, author with Almond, 23 Nov 54; Interv, author with Barr, 1 Feb 54; Interv, author with Powell, 13 Apr 54.

[18] 7th Div WD, 22 Nov 50; X Corps PIR 57, 22 Nov 50; 1st Lt Martin Blumenson, Task Force Kingston (32d Infantry Regiment, 22–29 November 50), copy in OCMH.

ON THE BANKS OF THE YALU, *two soldiers look across the valley into the mountains of Manchuria.*

action that occupied the 17th Infantry during the next week, as long as it was in that part of Korea—daily fights with small but stubborn enemy forces that blew bridges, cratered roads, all but immobilized the regiment, and kept it from making any appreciable gains. At the same time, in front of the 32d Infantry, enemy forces fought effective delaying actions north of Samsu so that not until 28 November did Task Force Kingston, reinforced, reach Sin'galp'ajin.[19]

The intense cold of northeast Korea in late November took its toll in frost- bite casualties in the 7th Division. The worst to suffer was the 31st Infantry which operated in the remote mountain regions east of the Pujon Reservoir. A total of 142 men in the division were treated for frostbite up to 23 November; 83 of them were from the 31st Regiment. Of the 58 men evacuated because of frostbite, 33 were from that regiment.[20]

3d Infantry Division Joins X Corps

During November the U.S. 3d Infantry Division joined the X Corps in Ko-

---

[19] X Corps PIR 59, 24 Nov 50; 7th Div WD, 22–28 Nov 50; Senate MacArthur Hearings, pt. 4, p. 2954, testimony of Gen Barr.

[20] 7th Div WD, G–1 Rpt, 23 Nov 50.

Ox-Drawn Sleds *replace trucks for the movement of supplies west of P'ungsan across the icy wastes.*

rea. One of its regiments, the 65th, had been in South Korea for more than two months. It had embarked on two transports in Puerto Rico on 25 August, passed through the Panama Canal, and sailed directly for Korea. It arrived at Pusan on 22 September and disembarked the next day. The other two regiments, the 7th and 15th, and the division headquarters sailed from San Francisco between 30 August and 2 September. The last ship of the division transports arrived at its destination, Moji, Japan, on 16 September.

Because the division was greatly understrength it was scheduled to receive large numbers of Koreans (KATUSA) for integration into its units. The division, minus the 65th Infantry Regiment, had an actual strength of only 7,494 men on 15 September. Beginning the first of October and continuing through the month, the 3d Division in Japan received 8,500 Korean draftees. Squads often consisted of two American enlisted men and eight Koreans.[21]

The 65th Infantry was the first part of the 3d Division to join X Corps in

---

[21] EUSAK WD, G-1 Hist Rpt, 15 Sep 50; 3d Div Comd Rpt, Nov 50, sec. 1, p. 1; Maj. James A. Huston, Time and Space, ch. IV, p. 117, MS in OCMH; ORO, Utilization of Indigenous Manpower in Korea, ORO (FEC), pp. 54-56.

northeast Korea. Its 2d Battalion, the first to land, came ashore at Wonsan on 5–6 November and was thereupon attached to X Corps for operations. The regiment was composed of white Puerto Ricans, Virgin Islands Negroes, white soldiers from the United States, Negroes from the United States (tank company), Americans of Japanese descent, and, finally, integrated South Koreans. When it sailed from Puerto Rico all the enlisted men in the infantry regiment were Puerto Rican, as were sixty-four of the 206 officers.[22]

In Japan the main body of the 3d Division made ready to outload at the port of Moji the first week of November. A division advance party opened the 3d Division tactical command post at Wonsan on 10 November. The 15th Regimental Combat Team began unloading there on the 11th, and the 7th RCT finished landing on 17 November.

The 3d Division's primary mission was to relieve all 1st Marine Division troops in the Wonsan area and south of Hamhung, to block the main roads in the southern part of the corps zone against guerrillas and bypassed North Koreans, and to protect the Wonsan-Hungnam coastal strip. The 3d Division zone of responsibility measured approximately ninety by thirty-five miles, an area so large as to make centralized division control impracticable. Therefore, General Soule, the division commander, decided to establish four regimental combat teams and to assign sectors and missions to each. These were the 7th RCT, commanded by Col. John S. Guthrie; the 15th RCT, commanded by Col. Dennis M. Moore; the 65th RCT, commanded by Col. William W. Harris; and the ROK 26th Regiment of the ROK 3d Division (attached to the U.S. 3d Division for operations), commanded by Col. Rhee Chi Suh. The 10th Field Artillery Battalion supported the 7th RCT; the 39th Field Artillery Battalion, the 15th RCT; the 58th Armored Artillery Battalion (self-propelled guns) and C Company, 64th Heavy Tank Battalion, the 65th RCT; and A Battery, 96th Field Artillery Battalion, the ROK 26th Regiment.[23]

The 15th RCT had the mission of protecting Wonsan and the area south and west of the city, with the Wonsan–Majon-ni–Tongyang road the probable axis of major enemy activity. North of the 15th RCT, the 65th RCT was to hold the west central part of the division zone, with the Yonghung–Hadongsan-ni lateral road the principal route into the regimental sector from the coast. The northern sector of the division zone, west of Hamhung, fell to the ROK 26th Regiment; included among its missions was that of patrolling west to the Eighth Army–X Corps boundary. The 7th RCT was in 3d Division reserve with the mission of securing the coastal area from Chung-dong, a point about eight miles north of Wonsan, to Hungnam. The 64th Heavy Tank Battalion (–) was also in division reserve.[24]

---

[22] 3d Div Comd Rpt, Nov 50, sec. III, p. 3; *Ibid.*, G–3 Jnl, entry 1225, 10 Nov 50; X Corps POR 52, 17 Nov 50; X Corps PIR 46, 11 Nov 50; 2d Log Comd Hist Rpt, G–3 and G–4 Secs., Nov 50; MS review comments, Col John H. Chiles to author, Nov 54.

[23] 3d Div Comd Rpt, Nov 50, sec. III, p. 4; X Corps Opn Ord 6, 11 Nov 50.

[24] 3d Div Comd Rpt, Nov 50, sec. III, p. 5.

The 3d Division did not engage in any major military operation during the November period covered in this volume, but beginning on 12 November it did have a number of engagements with North Korean forces in ambushes and roadblocks along the regimental main supply routes, particularly in the sector of the 15th RCT west of Wonsan between Majon-ni and Tongyang. Several of these were serious and resulted in heavy losses of men and equipment. They grew progressively worse toward the end of November; apparently the North Korean actions were co-ordinated with Chinese intervention in the reservoir area of northeast Korea.

7th Marines Clear Road to Reservoir

While the ROK I Corps and the U.S. 7th Infantry Division advanced toward the northeast border of Korea against scattered and ineffective North Korean opposition, the 1st Marine Division began moving up its assigned axis of advance toward the Changjin Reservoir to the southwest of them. Its rate of advance was not to be as rapid as theirs, nor was it to go as far.

At 0730 Sunday, 29 October, the 1st Battalion, 7th Marines, began loading into trucks at the Wonsan Agricultural College, and an hour later it started on the 83-mile trip to Hamhung. The next day X Corps ordered the 1st Marine Division to relieve the ROK I Corps in the reservoir area. At the end of the month the 7th Marines was in an assembly area north of Hamhung, and the 5th Marines was en route there from Wonsan.

From Hamhung to the southern tip of the Changjin Reservoir the road climbs for 56 miles. For slightly more than half the distance, to Chinhung-ni, the climb is easy and gradual over a two-lane road. From there a one-lane dirt road zigzags up precipitous slopes to the 4,000-foot-high plateau lying just south of the reservoir. In an air-line distance of 4 miles, and a road distance of 8 miles, north of Chinhung-ni, the road climbs 2,500 feet in elevation to the rim of the plateau, two and a half miles south of Kot'o-ri. A narrow-gauge railroad paralleled the road from Hamhung to Chinhung-ni, but from that point to the top of the plateau a cable car' incline replaced it. Once on top of the plateau, the railroad track continued north to Hagaru-ri and the Changjin Reservoir. There were four mountain power plants on the road to the reservoir.

Six road miles below Chinhung-ni is the village of Sudong. There, just below the steep climb to the plateau, the CCF *124th Division* held its blocking position. Three miles south of Sudong the road, climbing northward, crosses from the west to the east side of a mountain stream. The bridge at this crossing was of importance; if it were destroyed the U.N. forces north and south of it would be separated and those on the north cut off from their source of supply. Hill 698 dominated this bridge from the west, as did Hill 534 from the east. These two hills were critical terrain features.

Early on 1 November the 7th Marines entrucked at its Hamhung assembly area and, together with its attached artillery, the 2d Battalion, 11th Marines, it moved north 26 road miles to defensive positions behind the ROK 26th Regiment, 3 miles below Changjin Power Plant 3. The ROK troops had fallen back more than 5 miles since they first met the Chinese.[25]

At 1030, 2 November, the 7th Marines relieved the ROK 26th Regiment in its position and the 1st Battalion, followed by the 2d Battalion, attacked north. By noon it had confirmed that Chinese troops opposed it, and during the day captured three of them—one from the *370th Regiment* and two from the *372d*. The 1st Battalion at 1630 began to prepare defensive positions for the night about one mile south of Sudong. The 2d Battalion, nearly a mile behind the 1st Battalion, meanwhile had engaged in a hard struggle for Hill 698 west of the road. Three miles behind the 2d Battalion the regimental headquarters and the 3d Battalion were at the Majon-dong road fork.[26]

Shortly after midnight the CCF launched a co-ordinated attack, calculated to separate the 1st and 2d Battalions from each other and from the regiment behind them. The enemy infantry cut in between the 1st and 2d Battalions and almost overran the 4.2-inch mortar company in position along the road. Fighting was close and at grenade range for both battalions. In the course of the battle the Chinese gained a position dominating the crucial bridge in the 2d Battalion area. With the coming of daylight, Marine aircraft went into feverish action, repeatedly attacking the Chinese and eventually forcing them from their roadblock positions. Sandbagged trucks successfully brought sixty-six wounded marines through CCF small arms fire to the rear. During the day combined ground and air action killed about 700 enemy soldiers. Identification on the dead showed that nearly all of them were members of the *370th Regiment*.[27]

After the heavy battle on the 3d, the CCF apparently withdrew, for the marines encountered only light opposition on the 4th as they entered and passed through Sudong and continued on to the higher ground around Chinhung-ni. At Samgo railroad station, just north of Chinhung-ni, the marines destroyed the last four tanks of the N.K. *344th Tank Regiment*.

Less than a mile beyond Chinhung-ni the steep climb began through the Funchilin pass to the Kot'o-ri plateau. The marines could see enemy troops on the heights flanking the road at the pass. Farther north, according to aerial observers, an estimated 400 soldiers and three tanks were moving south from the Changjin Reservoir. Strafing reportedly caused heavy casualties in this column. A critical terrain feature, Hill 750, or How Hill as it came to be called, a mile and a half beyond Chinhung-ni, dominated the road where it made a hairpin loop of 1,000 yards eastward in starting the climb. This hill was, in fact, the

---

[25] 1st Mar Div SAR, Oct–Dec 50, vol. II, an. C, 1–2 Nov, pp. 14–16; *Ibid.*, vol. III, an. RR, 2 Nov, p. 12; X Corps POR 34, 30 Oct 50.

[26] 1st Mar Div SAR, Oct–Dec 50, vol. III, p. 12, an. RR, 2 Nov 50; X Corps WD, 2 Nov 50, Msg at 1730 from Maj Sayre; X Corps PIR 37, 2 Nov 50; Lynn Montross and Capt. Nicholas A. Canzona, USMC, *U.S. Marine Operations in Korea, 1950–1953*, vol. III, *The Chosin Reservoir Campaign* (Washington: Historical Branch, G–3, Headquarters, U.S. Marine Corps, 1954), is an excellent detailed account of the 1st Marine Division in northeast Korea in 1950.

[27] 1st Mar Div SAR, Oct–Dec 50, vol. II, p. 19, an. C, 3 Nov 50; X Corps WD, PIR 39, 4 Nov 50; Geer, *The New Breed*, pp. 234–36; Montross and Canzona, *The Chosin Reservoir Campaign*, pp. 103–09.

southern knob of a long finger ridge that extended southward from the rim of the Kot'o-ri plateau, on the east side of the road.

The 3d Battalion on 5 November moved through the 1st Battalion to start the attack up the pass. From How Hill the CCF stopped its advance. A map taken from a dead CCF officer showed that reinforced battalions on either side of the road were holding the high ground. Marine aircraft repeatedly attacked How Hill but failed to force the enemy from his positions.

The marines had to take How Hill before they could advance farther. The next day H Company made a long flanking march to approach the hill from the southeast. At 1600 in the afternoon of the 6th, H Company reached the position from which it was to make its assault. After half an hour of air strikes and an artillery preparation, two platoons started for the top. Four times the CCF drove them back. When darkness fell the Chinese still held the hill, and H Company withdrew. All night artillery and mortars pounded How Hill, the 81-mm. mortars firing 1,800 rounds.[28]

Meanwhile, west of the road a Marine force had seized Hill 611 without difficulty. A prisoner taken there supplied the second report X Corps had received that two more Chinese organizations, the CCF *125th* and *126th Divisions*, were in the reservoir area.

The next morning, patrols from the 3d Battalion found that the enemy had withdrawn from the heights behind Chinhung-ni, including How Hill,

CHINESE COMMUNIST POW'S, *wearing quilted cotton winter uniforms and fleece-lined caps.*

leaving behind many dead and some wounded. Information gained later from prisoners disclosed that the artillery and mortar barrage against How Hill during the night had caused crippling casualties in the *372d Regiment* (possibly the *371st*) of the *124th Division* while it was moving up to reinforce the line. These losses had caused the CCF to withdraw. On the afternoon of 7 November the 3d Battalion moved ahead and reached the village of Pohujang and Power Plant 1.[29]

During the marines' six days of battle with the Chinese *124th Division* the 1st Marine Air Wing had inflicted great numbers of casualties on the Chinese. But according to prisoners, the support-

---

[28] 1st Mar Div SAR, vol. II, pp. 23–25, an. C, 5–6 Nov 50; X Corps PIR's 40–41, 5–6 Nov 50; Geer, *The New Breed*, pp. 239–41.

[29] 1st Mar Div SAR, vol. II, pp. 27–28, an. C, 7 Nov 50; ATIS Interrog Rpts (Enemy Forces), Issue 19, Nr 2400, p. 1, Wang Fu Tien, *372d Regt*, *124th Div*.

ing artillery and mortars had taken an even greater toll. After 7 November the CCF *124th Division* reportedly was down to a strength of about 3,000 men. Except for its stragglers, the *124th Division* did not again enter the fighting in the reservoir area.

Thus far the action against the CCF *124th Division* from 2 through 7 November had cost the 7th Marines 46 men killed, 262 wounded, and 6 missing in action.[30]

For two days after reaching Power Plant 1, the 7th Marines sent out patrols which failed to contact the enemy. On 10 November the regiment moved up over the pass without opposition and occupied Kot'o-ri. Only seven miles now separated it from Hagaru-ri.

In its fight to reach the Kot'o-ri plateau the 7th Marines had captured 58 Chinese prisoners, 54 of them from the *124th Division* and 4 from the *126th Division*. It had taken its first prisoner from the *126th Division* on 7 November.[31]

During the time the 7th Marines was heavily engaged in combat with the CCF *124th Division*, a controversy between General Almond and General Partridge over the control of the 1st Marine Air Wing came to a head. Under existing procedure the Fifth Air Force Joint Operations Center at Seoul controlled the assignment of missions to the 1st Marine Air Wing. General Almond felt that, during a period of active ground combat when the local ground tactical situation could change drastically within an hour or two, he, the local commander, should have complete command over the air units supporting the ground troops. On 4 November General Partridge flew to Wonsan to hold a conference with General Almond on the subject. General Almond won his point; the Fifth Air Force ordered the 1st Marine Air Wing to assume direct responsibility for close support of X Corps without reference to the Joint Operations Center. Close support requests beyond the capabilities of the 1st Marine Air Wing were to be reported to the Fifth Air Force.[32]

The first night on the Kot'o-ri plateau, 10–11 November, was to be one painfully unforgettable to the men of the 7th Marines. During the afternoon and night the temperature dropped 40 degrees to 8° below zero—and with it came a wind of 30 to 35 miles an hour velocity. Although the weather later became colder, with the temperature dropping to from 20° to 25° below zero, it did not affect the men as did this first shock of subzero temperature. During the succeeding three or four days more than 200 men of the regiment collapsed from severe cold and were placed in sick bays for medical treatment. Stimulants had to be used to accelerate depressed respiration. Water-soluble medicines froze, and morphine could be maintained in satisfactory condition only when kept against the body. Plasma could be used only after a 60- to 90-minute preparation in a warm tent.[33]

---

[30] 1st Mar Div SAR, vol. III, an. RR, p. 34.
[31] X Corps PIR 47, 12 Nov 50.

[32] X Corps WD, 4 Nov 50, G–1 Rpt, Notes on Conference between CG X Corps and Gen Partridge, 4 Nov 50; USAF Hist Study 71, pp. 76–78.
[33] 1st Mar Div SAR, Oct–Dec 50, vol. III, p. 79, an. RR, app. 3, Cold Weather Rpt, and p. 95, app. H, Medical Rpt.

On the plateau and at the reservoir the men found that they needed more energy-giving food. Candy was at a premium. One veteran of the Changjin Reservoir operation said later, "I think we consumed more [candy] in one cold Korea week than we averaged in a Stateside year. . . . I saw many others do as I did—eat six or seven large Tootsie Rolls within a 10 to 15 minute period." [34]

The Gap Between Eighth Army and X Corps

A glance at a map of North Korea which shows the locations across the breadth of the peninsula of forces under United Nations command at this time, in mid-November, would reveal to any student of war a situation at once startling and perhaps bewildering. In northeast Korea, forces under X Corps command were far to the north, and in some places stood at the northern boundary of the country. In west and central North Korea the forces under Eighth Army command were far south of these latitudes. A line drawn due east from the Eighth Army front after the battle to hold the Ch'ongch'on River bridgehead in early November would cross the X Corps rear areas far behind the corps front. Not only was the X Corps front far north of Eighth Army's, but it was also separated from it by a wide lateral gap. Virtually all of North Korea west or northwest of the X Corps front in November was in enemy hands.

This great gap, seldom penetrated even by army or corps patrols, extended a minimum distance of 20 air miles from the northernmost right flank positions of Eighth Army to the nearest left flank positions of X Corps. Farther south the gap was greater, being about 35 air miles on a line east of P'yongyang and west of Wonsan. This was the distance after the Korean Marine Corps 3d Battalion established its blocking position at Tongyang on 14 November; before that the distance was about 50 air miles when the X Corps' westernmost position was at Majon-ni. The road-mile distances of this gap over exceedingly bad mountain trails—they hardly could be called roads—were far greater. The 20 air miles, for instance, between Maengsan, the easternmost position of Eighth Army beyond Tokch'on, and that of the X Corps at Kwangch'on just across the X Corps boundary was about 50 road miles.

On any line projected westward north of Hamhung there were no Eighth Army troops opposite X Corps. The enemy held all the territory there from the X Corps boundary west to the Yellow Sea. Accordingly, physical contact between the two commands would have to be made in the southern part of the X Corps zone if it was to be accomplished at all.

This wide gap between the two major tactical organizations of the U.N. Command in Korea caused great concern to Eighth Army and some to the Joint Chiefs of Staff in Washington; but less concern in X Corps, and very little, apparently, to General MacArthur. He believed that the mountainous backbone of North Korea was so destitute of roads and usable means of communication that it would be impossible for the U.N. forces to maintain a continuous line

---

[34] 1st Lt. William J. Davis, "Lessons Learned Up North," *Marine Corps Gazette* (April, 1952), p. 45.

across the peninsula that far north, and that the enemy would be unable to use this mountainous spine for effective military operations. Indeed, it seems quite clear that it was principally because of this forbidding terrain and the lack of lateral communications between the western and eastern parts of North Korea that General MacArthur established the two separate commands in North Korea.[35]

Many times it has been alleged that the Chinese in late November and in December 1950 took advantage of this great gap between Eighth Army and X Corps to defeat the U.N. forces in Korea. But this concept can be refuted. First, a study of CCF troop movements and deployments in November and December 1950, and the subsequent military action, will show that the Chinese forces did not use the area of this gap for extensive or decisive military operations. Instead, they operated against the Eighth Army right flank where the ROK II Corps was on line, just as they had in their First Phase Offensive in late October and early November. In short, they crushed and rolled up the Eighth Army right flank; they did not attack it from the gap, nor did they move around and behind it through the gap between Eighth Army and X Corps. Second, the unified line formed later across Korea by Eighth Army and X Corps under Eighth Army command was farther south where the terrain and communication facilities were much more favorable for a continuous line than in the area which was the scene of operations in November 1950.

While General MacArthur never expected solid and continuous physical contact between Eighth Army and X Corps in North Korea, he did expect communication and co-ordination between them by radio and personal liaison to the extent possible. There was radio communication between the two commands, and there was a daily trip by air of a liaison officer from X Corps to Eighth Army and back. As early as 25 October, before X Corps troops had landed on the east coast, arrangements had been made by the Fifth Air Force Joint Operations Center for two reconnaissance flights daily between the ROK II Corps right flank and X Corps left flank, which were to report on front lines and enemy concentrations.[36]

The two commands made many attempts to establish physical contact between them by means of patrols scheduled to meet at designated points along the Eighth Army–X Corps boundary. The first of these efforts was made on 6 November when the 2d Infantry Division of Eighth Army sent a reinforced patrol from K Company, 23d Infantry, to the designated point (the village of Songsin-ni) on the boundary five miles east of Yangdok. The patrol reached this point the next day but there were no elements of the X Corps there to meet it. At Yangdok the K Company patrol found and destroyed 16 boxcars of 120-mm., 80-mm., and 47-mm. ammunition;

---

[35] Senate MacArthur Hearings, pt. 1, p. 246, testimony of MacArthur, and pt. 2, pp. 972–75, testimony of Bradley.

[36] EUSAK WD, G–3 Jnl, Msg 1700, 25 Oct 50; Interv, author with Col LeRoy Lutes, Jr. (Planning Off G–3, X Corps, 1950), 7 Oct 51; Interv, author with Maj Gen Frank A. Allen, Jr., 28 Jan 54.

6 self-propelled guns; 16 47-mm. antitank guns; 30 57-mm. antitank guns; 1 120-mm. mortar; 3 heavy machine guns; and 3 antitank rifles. The X Corps sent a radio message to Eighth Army saying that marines from the 3d Battalion, 1st Marines, at Majon-ni, 30 air miles to the east, could not meet the Eighth Army patrol because of the distance and intensive guerrilla action in the area to be traversed. It suggested other contact points on roads to the north—at Hadongsan-ni and at Sach'ang-ni.[37]

Upon receiving this message Eighth Army withdrew the 23d Infantry patrol and prepared to send another one from the 38th Infantry Regiment, 2d Division, to Hadongsan-ni on the next lateral road northward. General Almond meanwhile had ordered Colonel Harris, commanding officer of the 65th Infantry Regiment, 3d Division, to place one battalion near the boundary to establish contact there with elements of Eighth Army. For this purpose the 1st Battalion, 65th Infantry Regiment, on 10 November after some delay rolled west and established its patrol base at Kwangch'on, about four air miles from the boundary, but double that in road miles.[38]

On 9 November IX Corps of Eighth Army had ordered the 38th Infantry to send a patrol to Hadongsan-ni. But the patrol of the 2d Reconnaissance Company which tried to reach that point was turned back by craters and boulders in the road. The next day patrols discovered all roads leading east from the 38th Infantry area were cratered or blocked by boulders. From the X Corps zone a patrol of the 65th Infantry went to the boundary on 11 November, and the next day it went two miles beyond its boundary without meeting a patrol from Eighth Army. On the 12th the pilot of a liaison plane working with the patrol discovered a ROK force westward and dropped a message to it arranging a meeting for the next day. On the 13th, however, even though it went nine miles beyond the boundary to a point where the road became impassable, the 65th Infantry patrol failed to meet an Eighth Army patrol. Eighth Army had tried to keep the rendezvous at Hadongsan-ni, but its strong motorized patrol built around E Company, 38th Infantry, was stopped by road craters ten miles east of Maengsan. All the mountain roads and trails leading eastward from this area were examined by 38th Infantry patrols but none were found that would permit passage of motorized vehicles. Some of the craters were about fifteen feet deep and thirty-five feet in diameter. Although work was started on a bypass it appears that it was never completed.[39]

While the 38th Infantry patrol failed to get through to the contact point on

---

[37] EUSAK WD, G-3 Jnl, Msg at 1335 6 Nov, G-3 Sec, 7 Nov 50, and Br for CG, 10 Nov 50. Songsin-ni does not appear on the 1:250,000 revised map of Korea, but the village of Yakhyon-dong is at the map co-ordinates given in the records for Songsin-ni.

[38] X Corps WD, Summ, 10 Nov 50; Ibid., Diary of CG; 65th Inf Comd Rpt, Nov 50, p. 5; Interv, author with Almond, 23 Nov 54.

[39] 2d Inf Div WD, Narr Summ, Nov 50; 2d Inf Div POR's 300, 13 Nov 50, and 303, 14 Nov 50; IX Corps WD, bk. I, sec. IV, Opns, Nov 50; 3d Inf Div WD, G-3 Jnl, 13 Nov 50; EUSAK WD, Br for CG, 13 and 16 Nov 50; 38th Inf WD, 12-18 Nov 50.

the 14th, there was success from another quarter. On the 13th an Eighth Army liaison plane dropped two messages to the X Corps patrol saying that a patrol from the 10th Regiment, ROK 8th Division, was working its way to the contact point along a different route. On 14 November at 1000 the two friendly patrols, a platoon from the 2d Battalion, 10th Regiment, ROK 8th Division, and a patrol from the 1st Battalion, 65th Infantry, did meet near the village of Songha-dong just west of the boundary. The ROK patrol had come on foot from its patrol base at Maengsan, forty-five miles to the west. En route it had encountered an estimated total of 400 North Korean guerrillas and had fought several minor engagements. The round trip of the ROK patrol to the boundary and back to its base took ten days. This should explain why there were not daily meetings between Eighth Army and X Corps patrols at the boundary contact point.[40]

On 18 November, just before noon, a patrol from the 3d Battalion, 38th Infantry, reportedly reached Hadong-san-ni on the boundary where it found a blown bridge which it could not bypass. There were no patrols there at that time from the 65th Infantry in the X Corps zone. Only once, therefore, on 14 November, did patrols from the Eighth Army (ROK II Corps) and the X Corps make physical contact with each other at the army-corps boundary.[41]

---

[40] 3d Inf Div WD, G-3 Jnl, Msg CG X Corps to Eighth Army, 1500, and entries at 1020, 2220 13 Nov 50; *Ibid.*, G-3 Jnl entry at 141330 Nov 50; X Corps PIR 49, 14 Nov 50; 65th Inf Comd Rpt, Nov 50, p. 4; EUSAK POR 379, 15 Nov 50; EUSAK WD, G-3 Sec, 14 Nov 50; Lt. Col. Robert C. Cameron, "The Lost Corps," *Military Review*, vol. XXXIII, No. 2 (May, 1953), p. 11. Cameron was KMAG adviser to the 10th Regt, ROK 8th Div.

[41] 2d Inf Div WD, POR 315, 18 Nov 50; 38th Inf WD, 16-18 Nov 50.

CHAPTER XXXIX

The Big Question

> A bold operation is one which has no more than a chance of success but which, in case of failure, leaves one with sufficient forces in hand to cope with any situation. A gamble, on the other hand, is an operation which can lead either to victory or to the destruction of one's own forces.
>
> IRWIN ROMMEL, "Account of the War in Africa," *Rommel Papers*

By the end of the first week of November it was clear that Chinese Communist Forces had intervened in the Korean War. This intervention, long feared and by some expected, had become a fact. The intervention came in sufficient force to drive Eighth Army back to the Ch'ongch'on River and to delay the advance of X Corps in the east toward the Changjin Reservoir. After accomplishing this, the Chinese Communist Forces withdrew from immediate contact with Eighth Army behind a screen of North Korean soldiers. The big question now loomed—what was the purpose and extent of the Chinese intervention? The U.N. command and intelligence agencies had to ponder and answer it in determining the future conduct of military operations.

The Chinese Communist Forces

A look at the background of the Chinese Communist Forces seems necessary to an understanding of the problem. While the Chinese Communist Party itself dates from 1921, Chinese Communist fighting forces may be said to have come into existence with the outbreak of the Nanchang rebellion in China on 1 August 1927. This date is commemorated as the founding date of the Chinese Communist Forces by the Chinese ideograms in the upper lefthand corner of the CCF flag and insignia.[1] A month before the Nanchang rebellion, Generalissimo Chiang Kai-shek had expelled the Communist Party from the Kuomintang. From that time on the two groups became increasingly hostile toward each other and engaged in an intermittent civil war lasting for two decades, until at last Chiang Kai-shek's Nationalist Government in 1949 was driven from the China mainland to Formosa.

For a time in 1934 it had appeared that Chiang Kai-shek was on the point of destroying the Communist forces in China. But in a series of battles, be-

---

[1] GHQ FEC, MI Sec, Order of Battle Information, Chinese Communist Forces in Korea, 15 Jun 51 (hereafter cited as FEC MIS, Order of Battle Info, CCF), p. 1.

ginning on 21 October of that year and lasting through the 29th, the Communists broke through the Nationalist forces that had surrounded them in Kiangsi Province and started out on what has since been called the "Long March" to Yenan in Shensi Province, far to the northwest. Approximately 100,000 Communist soldiers began this march with Lin Piao leading the *First Army Corps.*

Finally, on 20 October 1935, a year after they had started from Kiangsi, 20,000 survivors of the Long March met units of the *25th, 26th,* and *27th Red Armies* in Shensi that had been there since 1933. The veterans of the Long March had traveled more than 6,000 miles; they had crossed 18 mountain ranges, 24 rivers, 12 different provinces, and had averaged nearly 24 miles a day for the 235 days and 18 nights of actual travel.[2]

In Shensi Province the Chinese Communists then began a reorganization and consolidation of their forces. They established there a secure base that became the foundation for their future operations. Survivors of the Long March were organized into the *8th Route Army,* commanded by Chu Teh. By 1947 the Chinese Communist Army was entrenched in North China and Manchuria with about 600,000 troops. The Soviet withdrawal from Manchuria had taken place in April of the preceding year. Chu Teh, commander of the Chinese Communist Army, at that time announced the primary mission of his force was the piecemeal annihilation of the Nationalist Armies by guerrilla-type action.

The Chinese Communist Army in Manchuria was called the North-East People's Liberation Army (NEPLA). Lin Piao commanded this army, which by the end of 1947 had cut Nationalist lines of communication to Manchuria and isolated that important area from the rest of China. In the spring of 1949 NEPLA was redesignated the *Fourth Field Army,* incorporating five army groups, the *XII* through *XVI,* which in turn comprised the CCF *38th* through *58th Armies,* a total of 60 divisions of about 10,000 men each. This gave a total of approximately 600,000 men in the *Fourth Field Army.* The Korean volunteers and Manchurian Korean veterans in this army numbered about 145,000.

Lin Piao's *Fourth Field Army* played a prominant role in the Chinese Communist Forces' great triumph of wresting control of the China mainland from the Nationalists in 1949. Some elements of his army marched all the way from Manchuria to South China where they made the amphibious attack against Hainan Island in the spring of 1950 and began preparations for a similar attack against Formosa. The *Fourth Field Army* had fought from Manchuria to Hainan Island in the China Civil War without a major defeat. In June 1950 these elements of the *Fourth Field Army* marched to Canton and entrained there for Antung, Manchuria, across the Yalu River from Korea. Lin Piao was now taking them back to the Korean border to stand ready for any eventuality arising from the impending Communist invasion of South Korea. Still other elements of the *Fourth Field Army* moved during the

---

[2] *Ibid.,* pp. 1-2; Edgar Snow, *Red Star Over China* (New York: Modern Library, 1944), pp. 207-16.

summer from other points in China back to Manchuria. A part of the army had always remained there.[3]

Following on the heels of the *Fourth Field Army*, elements of the *Third Field Army*, which consisted of the *20th* through the *37th Armies*, moved to Manchuria in the late summer and early autumn of 1950. By mid-October the Chinese forces of the *Third* and *Fourth Field Armies* had concentrated more than 400,000 troops in Manchuria close to Korea. A Chinese Communist army comprised normally three divisions, although a few of them had four. A full-strength Chinese division had approximately 10,000 soldiers. It was elements of the *Fourth Field Army*, the best field army of the Chinese Communist Forces, that first intervened in the Korean War.[4]

Eighth Army Estimate of CCF Intervention

On 25 October, Col. Percy W. Thompson, G–2 of U.S. I Corps, made special arrangements to transport the first Chinese prisoner, captured that day at Unsan by the ROK 1st Division, to the Eighth Army advanced command post at P'yongyang for interrogation. There could be no doubt that he was Chinese; he spoke neither Korean nor Japanese. His story seemed straightforward and credible.[5] With this first interrogation of a captured Chinese soldier in Korea by U.S. Army intelligence officials be-

CHINESE COMMUNIST FLAG

gan the build-up of a large body of information on Chinese Communist units in Korea. The Chinese Communist prisoners captured in the Eighth Army zone of responsibility grew steadily in number from the 3 captured at Unsan and Onjong on 25 October. By 29 October 10 had been captured; by 2 November, 55; by 20 November, 84; and by 23 November, as Eighth Army assumed its final deployment for the attack designed to reach the Yalu, 96 CCF prisoners had been captured. They identified six Chinese Communist armies—the *38th, 39th, 40th, 42d, 50th,* and *66th,* of which they were members—as being in Korea. (Each army had three divisions, thus the six totaled eighteen divisions.) Eastward in its zone, X Corps had captured prisoners from the *42d Army*.[6] As events

---

[3] FEC MIS, Order of Battle Info, CCF, CCF *Fourth Field Army*, pp. 1–9; FEC Intel Digest, vol. 1, No. 4, 1–15 Feb 53, CCF XIII Army Group, pp. 30–37.

[4] FEC MIS, Order of Battle Info, CCF, pp. 9, 171; FEC Intel Digest 10, 2 Nov 51.

[5] Ltr and attached statement, Col Percy W. Thompson to author, 9 Apr 54.

[6] EUSAK PIR's 109, 29 Oct; 11, 31 Oct; 113, 2 Nov; 116, 5 Nov; 120, 9 Nov; 121, 10 Nov; 124, 13 Nov; and 134, 23 Nov 50.

CHU TEH

were to prove, the *42d Army* near the end of this period had sideslipped from the X Corps area southwest into the Eighth Army zone.

Within the first week of CCF intervention in Korea, prisoners had been taken from four different Chinese armies in the Eighth Army zone. Eighth Army interrogated these first Chinese prisoners intensively, even using a lie detector on three selected and flown to P'yongyang.[7] But in evaluating the interrogations, Eighth Army intelligence officials were skeptical of the stories of large Chinese forces in Korea and, lacking what they believed adequate confirmation, did not accept the substance of the prisoners' accounts. One intelligence item reproduced at different headquarters minimized the scale of Chinese intervention, stating that of 344 prisoners taken at Unsan in two days only two were Chinese. This statement was certainly inaccurate because that number of prisoners was never captured at Unsan. This figure could have been obtained only by counting the many disorganized and retreating North Koreans captured on the road from the Ch'ongch'on River to Unsan. After the Chinese entered the fight against the ROK 1st Division just above Unsan, very few prisoners were captured and these were wounded Chinese.[8]

The initial estimate at Eighth Army headquarters based on prisoners' reports was that the presence of Chinese troops at Unsan and Onjong indicated some reinforcement of North Korean units with troops taken from the Chinese Communist Forces in order to assist in defense of the border approaches, but that there were "no indications of open intervention on the part of Chinese Communist Forces in Korea."[9] On 30 October the 1st Cavalry quoted in one of its

---

[7] Interv, author with Col Robert G. Fergusson (Deputy ACofS G-2, Eighth Army Oct–Nov 50), 23 Jun 52.

[8] EUSAK PIR 107, 27 Oct 50; 1st Cav Div PIR 100, OB an., 30 Oct 50. Colonel Thompson says that at the time this report appeared he had objected to the statistical statement appearing in the 1st Cavalry Division PIR which allegedly was based on a I Corps report. Colonel Thompson, I Corps G–2; Colonel Hennig, Commanding Officer, 10th AAA Group, supporting the ROK 1st Division at Unsan; and Colonel Hazlett, KMAG adviser to the ROK 1st Division, all have told the author there was no such number as 344 prisoners taken at Unsan. And there is no indication in the combat records that that many prisoners were taken there.

[9] EUSAK PIR 106, 26 Oct 50; 1st Cav Div WD, 30 Oct 50; I Corps WD, Intel Summ 135, 30 Oct 50; New York *Times*, October 28, 1950.

reports from a I Corps estimate of a day or two earlier, "There are no indications at this time to confirm the existence of a CCF organization or unit, of any size, on Korean soil."

The first week of Chinese action in Korea, however, did cause General Walker to restrain I Corps, which, acting on his warning, ordered the 24th Division back to the Ch'ongch'on River from its advanced position. This order on 1 November disturbed the Far East Command. General Hickey telephoned General Allen about the withdrawal and the latter had to explain why General Walker and his staff considered it advisable.[10]

During the first phase of Chinese intervention the units involved tried to conceal their identity by using code names. This succeeded rather well at first. The *54th Unit*, for instance, was not suspected of being in reality the *38th Army*, which prisoners said it was, but was accepted as being only a small part of it. Similar evaluations were made of the *55th, 56th, 57th,* and *58th Units*, each of which represented a CCF army. In point of fact, the *54th Unit* was the *38th Army;* the *55th Unit*, the *39th Army;* and the *56th Unit*, the *40th Army*. This misconception was further deepened by the Chinese use of a battalion code to represent a full division; thus the *1st Battalion, 55th Unit*, was actually the *115th Division, 39th Army*. Chinese officials maintained from the first the fiction that the Chinese fighting in Korea were volunteers. Thousands of

LIN PIAO

interrogations of Chinese prisoners later and scores of captured Chinese documents proved this contention false.[11]

Eighth Army intelligence noted on 31 October that out of a total of eleven Chinese prisoners taken in the Eighth Army zone by that date, six claimed to belong to the *56th Unit* and two claimed the *55th Unit*. The army intelligence estimate on that date spoke of these two units as "token units" and surmised that they probably were concerned with protecting the approaches to the Kanggye area. By 1 November, however, on the

---

[10] Interv, author with Maj Gen Leven C. Allen, 15 Dec 53; Ltr, Thompson to author, 9 Apr 54; Ltr, Lt Gen Doyle O. Hickey to author, 14 Feb 56.

[11] EUSAK WD, 31 Oct 50, G-2 Sec, Interrog of Yang Jun-tzu, 164-MISDI-1171; Ibid., 28 Oct 50, G-2 Sec, Interrog of Yen Shu-cheng, 164-MISDI-1167; Ibid., 1 Nov 50, Interrog of Huang Che-chan, 164-MISDI-1174; Ibid., PIR 113, 2 Nov 50; FEC Intel Digest, vol. 1, Nr 4, 17 Feb 53, XIII Army Group, CCF; FEC MIS, Order of Battle Info, CCF.

eve of the 8th Cavalry disaster at Unsan, Eighth Army intelligence had changed its view so far as to say that the enemy forces in the vicinity of Unsan included "possibly at least two Chinese units of regimental size." [12]

By 4 November, Eighth Army intelligence had accepted two Chinese units of division size in Korea. The next day it raised this estimate to "three divisional sized Task Units," tentatively identified as the *54th, 55th,* and *56th Units,* totaling approximately 27,000 men. It will be noted that the Chinese code unit still was underestimated—now being accepted as of division size rather than army size, which it in fact was.[13]

On 6 November, at the very time as it chanced that the CCF withdrew from general contact with Eighth Army, General Walker wrote a letter to General MacArthur in which he expressed his views of the tactical situation on his front. He said in part:

There has never been and there is now no intention for this army to take up or remain in passive perimeter or any other type of defense. Every effort is being made to retain an adequate bridgehead to facilitate the resumption of the attack as soon as conditions permit. All units continue to execute local attacks to restore or improve lines. Plans have been prepared for the resumption of the offensive employing all forces available to meet the new factor of organized Chinese Communist forces. These plans will be put into execution at the earliest possible moment and are dependent only upon the security of the right flank, the marshalling of the attack troops and the restoration of vital supplies.[14]

On 13 November Eighth Army received its first report of a prisoner from the CCF *42d Army*. The report came from the ROK II Corps on the right flank of the army front. In the next few days other Chinese prisoners from the *42d Army* were taken in this same general area around Tokch'on. All came from the *374th Regiment, 125th Division, 42d Army.*[15] This Chinese army at the time was sideslipping southwest from the Changjin Reservoir area in the X Corps zone to the right flank of Eighth Army, while elements of the CCF *Third Field Army* were replacing it in northeast Korea.

At the end of the third week in November, as U.N. forces made ready to resume their attack toward the border of Korea, Eighth Army intelligence estimated there were about 60,000 Chinese troops in Korea. Various field reports reaching the Department of the Army in Washington differed in their estimates, their figures ranging from 46,700 to 70,000.[16]

The opinions held by the ranking members of the Eighth Army staff on the extent of Chinese intervention, capability, and intention seem to have varied. General Walker apparently shared the view held by Lt. Col. James C. Tarkenton, his G-2, that the Chinese in Korea

---

[12] EUSAK PIR's 109, 29 Oct; 111, 31 Oct; and 112, 1 Nov 50.

[13] EUSAK PIR 115, 4 Nov, and 116, 5 Nov 50; Ltr, Thompson to author, 9 Apr 54.

[14] MacArthur, MS review comments, with Ltr to Maj Gen Richard W. Stephens, Chief, OCMH, 15 Nov 57. MacArthur's comments on the copy of the manuscript on file in OCMH are in pencil and each one is initialed by him.

[15] EUSAK PIR's 124, 13 Nov; 129, Incl 2, 18 Nov; and 131, 20 Nov 50.

[16] Interv, author with Fergusson, 23 Jun 53; DA *Intel Rev,* 175, Dec 50, p. 33; Ltr, Maj Gen John A. Dabney to author, 3 Feb 54.

numbered only a few divisions composed possibly of volunteers; that there were no organized CCF armies, as such, in Korea; and that China would not enter the war.[17] Colonel Dabney, Eighth Army G-3, was skeptical of this view. He arrived at the conclusion that the Chinese might well have crossed the Yalu River in great strength, but he too was still searching for final answers.

In the two weeks after the Chinese broke off their First Phase Offensive and withdrew from contact with Eighth Army, the impact of the Chinese menace on the American command gradually subsided. Among Eighth Army staff members, the motive generally ascribed for the first CCF intervention in October and early November was that the Chinese wanted to protect the power plants south of the Yalu River. Many now thought they would dig in on a defensive line to do this. As the days passed and the front remained quiet, fear of massive Chinese intervention dwindled.

A careful study of Eighth Army daily intelligence reports for the month of November 1950 reveals that, despite daily reference to the Chinese potential north of the Yalu River in Manchuria, there was a tapering off of concern about full Chinese intervention from about 10 November until 24 November, when Eighth Army resumed its offensive. In this connection it should be noted that the controlling Eighth Army viewpoint could scarcely avoid being influenced somewhat by that of the Far East Command, which seems to have been that China would not intervene with major forces.

The X Corps Estimate

The capture of sixteen prisoners from the *370th Regiment* of the *124th Division* by the ROK 26th Regiment on 29 October convinced the X Corps G-2 that "integral CCF units have been committed against U.N. forces."[18] General Almond said at this time he intended to attack with sufficient strength to find out if the Chinese were in only regimental or in greater strength. The 7th Marines' attack on the road to the Changjin Reservoir disclosed that the Chinese were there in at least division strength.

Elements of X Corps encountered and captured only a few Chinese soldiers from another division, the *126th*, near the Changjin Reservoir. On the east side of the Pujon Reservoir, a few more were captured who said they were from the same division. These prisoners reported that a third division, the *125th*, was in the Changjin Reservoir area. Because this division guarded the road and rail line approaching Yudam-ni and the reservoir from the southwest—the central part of the peninsula—X Corps was not in contact with it until the third week of November. By then most of this enemy division had already moved southwestward into the Eighth Army zone.

Although X Corps did not have as harsh an experience with Chinese forces

---

[17] Interv, author with Lt Gen Frank W. Milburn, 4 Jan 52; Ltr, Dabney to author, 3 Feb 54; Interv, author with Fergusson, 23 Jun 53; Interv, author with Allen, 15 Dec 53; Interv, author with Brig Gen William C. Bullock (Asst G-3 EUSAK, Nov 50), 28 Jan 54. The author has considered carefully and taken into account the MS review comments of Col. Tarkenton (Eighth Army G-2 at the time), Dec 57, in making final revisions in this chapter.

[18] X Corps PIR 34, 30 Oct 50; Pacific *Stars and Stripes*, November 1, 1950.

in the First Phase Offensive as did Eighth Army, it nevertheless received intelligence which indicated large-scale Chinese intervention. In mid-November, for instance, two civilian draftsmen, formerly employed by the Traffic Department of the P'yongyang Railway Bureau, reported on what they saw and heard of Chinese intervention before they left Manp'ojin on 26 October. According to them, there had been a continuous flow of CCF soldiers through Manp'ojin beginning on 12 October. One of the men estimated 80,000 Chinese had passed south through the border town. Chinese officers had variously told the two men that 200,000 and 400,000 Chinese soldiers were to enter Korea.[19]

The lack of enemy activity in front of X Corps during the second and third weeks of November prompted the corps intelligence officer to state officially on 18 November that "the enemy's recent delaying operations are apparently concluded and he is once again withdrawing to the north. The speed of his movements has caused a loss of contact at most points." General Almond himself at this time did not think that the Chinese had intervened in the Korean War in force.[20]

As the date approached for the U.N. attack intended to complete the occupation of all Korea, X Corps, like Eighth Army, seemed to take the view that enemy forces in front of it would fight only a delaying defensive action. On 22 November, corps intelligence reported that the enemy was "apparently preparing to make a defensive stand in his present positions," and that there was "no evidence to indicate any considerable number of CCF units have crossed the border since the initial reinforcement."[21]

The next day, however, elements of the 7th Marines captured two Chinese soldiers seven miles west of Hagaru-ri who said they belonged to the *267th Regiment, 89th Division*, which had crossed the Yalu ten days earlier. The men had deserted from their unit the night before and walked toward the U.N. lines.[22] The most interesting and important thing about these two deserters was that, if their story was true, not only was there another new Chinese division in Korea, but it came from a new army, the *20th*, a new army group, *IX*, and, most important of all, from a new field army, the CCF *Third Field Army*, which in the summer had been in the Shanghai area.

In preparing for its part in the impending U.N. offensive, X Corps anticipated that when the Eighth Army advance reached Huich'on, and X Corps itself neared the Kanggye road above Huich'on in the U.N. double envelopment attack, the enemy would react violently, and the possibility of enemy ground and air reinforcements from Manchuria could not be overlooked.[23]

While X Corps recognized the capabilities of CCF strength beyond the border, it seems clear that on the eve of

---

[19] X Corps PIR 49, 14 Nov 50.
[20] X Corps PIR's 53, 18 Nov, and 54, 19 Nov 50; X Corps POR 54, 19 Nov 50; Interv, author with Almond, 13 Dec 51.
[21] X Corps PIR 57, 22 Nov 50.
[22] X Corps PIR 58, 23 Nov 50.
[23] X Corps PIR 59, 24 Nov 50; X Corps WD, 25 Nov 50, app., an. A to X Corps Order 7, pp. 2, 5–6.

THE BIG QUESTION

the impending U.N. attack—set for 24 November in the west and 27 November in the northeast—corps believed that not more than one or two CCF divisions were on its front and that the enemy's efforts in the near future would be wholly defensive in character. General Almond, the corps commander, held this view. As in the case of Eighth Army, the controlling X Corps view was probably influenced by that of the Far East Command.

The Far East Command's and MacArthur's Estimates

Of all the intelligence levels of the U.N. command and the American government, perhaps the most decisive in evaluating the intention and capability of Chinese intervention in the Korean War was that of the Far East Command in Tokyo. The evaluation by General MacArthur and his intelligence officers of Chinese intervention and Chinese military capability in Korea in October and November 1950 seems to have been the determining factor in shaping the future course of U.N. military action in that country.

Why this was so requires explanation, for normally the intelligence evaluation of whether a foreign power has decided to intervene in a war in national force involves political intelligence at the highest level. Field and theater commanders could expect such an evaluation to be made by the government in Washington with the advice of its Central Intelligence Agency. The intelligence responsibility of Eighth Army and X Corps was tactical; strategic intelligence responsibility rested with the Central Intelligence Agency, the Department of the Army, and the theater headquarters, with the ultimate political intelligence the responsibility of the President and his immediate advisers. But apparently the Central Intelligence Agency and the administration generally did not evaluate the available intelligence so as to reach a conviction on the question of whether the Chinese intended to intervene in the Korean War different from that held by General MacArthur. It must be inferred that either Washington was undecided or that its view coincided with that of the Commander in Chief, Far East, since it did not issue directives to him stating a different estimate. The conclusion, then, is that in the developing situation of November the views of the Far East Command were decisive on the military course to be taken in Korea at that time.

The Korean War had scarcely started when the Far East Command began to consider the threat of CCF intervention. On 28 June its daily intelligence summary stated that the possibility existed that North Korea might receive Chinese Communist reinforcements from Manchuria. In early July General MacArthur informed the Joint Chiefs of Staff in Washington that if Chinese combat forces did become involved in the war the assistance of the Strategic Air Command would be required to destroy communications into and through North Korea from China. At this time the Far East Command estimated there were 116,000 CCF regular troops in Manchuria. An increase in CCF troop strength there became perceptible during the month and continued steadily thereafter. Much of the information concerning CCF troop movements from south to north China came from Chinese

CHOU EN-LAI

Nationalist sources on Formosa. Chiang Kai-shek's government received a steady stream of intelligence from its agents on the China mainland, and it, in turn, provided General MacArthur's command with numerous reports.[24]

Many of the intelligence reports received at Tokyo, as is usual in such matters, were inaccurate and unreliable. Such were several reports in August and September that CCF troops had crossed the border into North Korea. One of these reports, on 29 August, alleged that four CCF armies had crossed the Yalu and were deployed in North Korea.[25]

On 8 September the daily intelligence summary included a report of the Chinese Nationalist Ministry of Defense G–2 that if the outcome of the war seemed doubtful, elements of Lin Piao's *Fourth Field Army* probably would be committed. This report further indicated that such troops would not be used as CCF units but would be integrated into the North Korea People's Army.[26]

The Far East Command learned in mid-September of an alleged conference in mid-July in Peiping where it was decided to support North Korea short of war. Chou En-lai was quoted, however, as having said that if the North Koreans were driven back to the Yalu, the CCF would enter Korea. Far East Command intelligence, in commenting on this report, said that the Chinese Communist authorities apparently were worried over Korea and would regard a U.N. advance to the Yalu as a "serious threat to their regime."[27] Two weeks later, on the last day of September, the daily intelligence summary reported on an alleged high-level conference in Peiping on 14 August, at which it had been decided to provide 250,000 CCF troops for use in Korea.[28]

A new note of more official character entered into the intelligence clamor on 3 October. The Chinese Communist Foreign Minister, Chou En-lai, summoned Ambassador Sardar K. M. Panikkar of India to his office in Peiping and told him that if the United States or United Nations forces crossed the 38th Parallel, China would send troops to de-

---

[24] FEC, Daily Intel Summ, 28 Jun 50 (hereafter cited as FEC DIS); *Ibid.*, Nr 6, 2 Sep 51, p. A–3; FEC telecon with DA, TT3467, 6 Jul 50.
[25] FEC DIS 2915, 2 Sep 50; X Corps PIR 22, an. 2, 10 Oct 50.

[26] FEC DIS 2921, 8 Sep 50.
[27] FEC DIS 2929, 16 Sep 50.
[28] FEC DIS 2943, 30 Sep 50.

fend North Korea. He said this action would not be taken if only South Korean troops crossed the 38th Parallel. This information was communicated quickly by the Indian Ambassador to his government, which in turn informed the United States and the United Nations. The government at Washington immediately dispatched the message to General MacArthur in Tokyo.[29] Representatives of other nations reported similar statements coming from Chinese officials in Peiping. Then, on 10 October, the Peiping radio broadcast as a declaration of Chinese Communist intentions a statement to the same effect. On 15 October the Department of the Army informed MacArthur's headquarters of another report from a reliable source that Moscow was preparing a surprise for American troops when they approached the northern border.[30]

In early October an escaped American officer informed American intelligence authorities that he had been interrogated in North Korea by three Soviet officers and that one of them, a senior colonel, told him on 22 September that if U.S. forces crossed the 38th Parallel new Communist forces would enter the war in support of North Korea.[31]

On 5 October for the first time Far East Command intelligence listed as number one priority in enemy capabilities "Reinforcement by Soviet Satellite China." But this estimate did not long remain in first priority; it dropped to second place the next day, to third place on 9 October, and remained there through 13 October. On 14 October the intelligence estimate again raised the reinforcement of North Korea to first priority. There it remained during the Wake Island Conference.[32]

The Far East Command daily intelligence summary for 14 October carried a lengthy analysis of the problem and presumably represented the official view of Maj. Gen. Charles A. Willoughby, Far East Command G-2. This intelligence estimate accepted a total strength of thirty-eight CCF divisions in nine armies in Manchuria. It expressed the view that Russia would find it convenient and economical to stay out of the conflict and let the Chinese provide the troops if there was to be intervention. It went on to say that the interest of all intelligence agencies was focused on the "elusive Lin Piao" and the Yalu River. One significant paragraph stated:

Recent declarations by CCF leaders, threatening to enter North Korea if American forces were to cross the 38th Parallel, are *probably in a category of diplomatic blackmail.* [Italics supplied.] The decision, if any, is beyond the purview of collective intelligence: it is a decision for war, on the highest level; i.e. the Kremlin and Peiping. However, the numerical and troop potential in Manchuria is a fait-accompli. A total of 24 divisions are disposed along the Yalu River at crossing points. In this general deployment, the grouping in the vicinity of Antung is the most immediately available Manchurian force, astride a suitable road net for deployment southward.[33]

---

[29] FEC DIS 2947, 4 Oct 50; Senate MacArthur Hearings, pt. 3, p. 1833, testimony of Secy of State Dean Acheson.
[30] Schnabel, FEC, GHQ Support and Participation in the Korean War, ch. VII, p. 13, citing Msg 94214, DA to CINCFE, 15 Oct 50.
[31] FEC DIS 2950, 7 Oct 50.

[32] FEC DIS 2948, 5 Oct, and 2949-60, 6-17 Oct 50.
[33] FEC DIS 2957, 14 Oct 50.

This same report pointed to the recent fall of Wonsan as a serious loss to the enemy and one jeopardizing his entire defense structure. It went on to say, "This open failure of the enemy to rebuild his forces suggests that the CCF and Soviets, in spite of their continued interest and some blatant public statements, have decided against further expensive investment in support of a lost cause."

Meanwhile, President Truman on 10 October had announced his intention to fly to the Pacific for a meeting with General MacArthur over the coming weekend to discuss "the final phase of U.N. action in Korea." The conference between the President, General MacArthur, and selected advisers of each took place on Wake Island, Sunday, 15 October. Most of the talk concerned plans for the rehabilitation of Korea after the fighting ceased. General MacArthur said he expected formal resistance to end throughout North and South Korea by Thanksgiving Day and that he hoped to get the Eighth Army back to Japan by Christmas. In response to President Truman's question, "What are the chances for Chinese or Soviet interference?", notes of the conference indicate that General MacArthur replied substantially as follows:

Very little. Had they interfered in the first or second months it would have been decisive. We are no longer fearful of their intervention. We no longer stand with hat in hand. The Chinese have 300,000 men in Manchuria. Of these probably not more than 100,000 to 200,000 are distributed along the Yalu River. Only 50,000 to 60,000 could be gotten across the Yalu River. They have no Air Force. Now that we have bases for our Air Force in Korea, if the Chinese tried to get down to Pyongyang there would be greatest slaughter.[34]

General MacArthur then discussed briefly the chance of Russian intervention, holding the view that it was not feasible and would not take place.

General MacArthur has challenged the accuracy of the notes of the conversations at the Wake Island Conference. He maintains that the question concerning possible Chinese or Soviet intervention was low on the President's agenda, and that while he replied that the chances of such intervention were "very little," he added that this opinion was purely speculative and derived from the military standpoint, while the question fundamentally was one requiring a political decision. His view, he states, was also conditioned by the military assumption that if the Chinese did intervene United States forces would retaliate, and in a peninsular war could work havoc with their exposed lines of communication and bases of supply. He says, in effect, that he took it for granted that Chinese knowledge of this capability would be a powerful factor in keeping them from intervening.[35]

---

[34] Substance of Statements Made at Wake Island Conference on October 15, 1950, compiled by General of the Army Omar N. Bradley, Chairman, JCS, from notes kept by the conferees from Washington. Copies of this Substance of Statements were forwarded to General MacArthur by the JCS on 19 October 1950, and receipted for by his aide on 27 October. Neither General MacArthur nor his headquarters advised the JCS of any nonconcurrence with this record of the conference. See Bradley, Letter of Submittal, 2 May 1951, to Senator Richard Russell, Chairman, Senate Armed Services Committee, included as part of the document (printed by the Committee on Armed Services and the Committee on Foreign Relations, U.S. Senate (Washington, 1951); New York Times, October 11, 1950; Dept of State Pub 4263, United States Policy in the Korean Conflict, July 1950–February 1951, p. 19.

[35] MacArthur, MS review comments, 15 Nov 57.

It must be noted that General MacArthur's opinion on the subject was not questioned by the President or any of the others present, who must be assumed to have had knowledge of the highest level of intelligence bearing on the matter. In fact, so thoroughly did they seem to agree with his opinion that the Chairman of the Joint Chiefs of Staff asked him when he could spare a division for European duty. So it would seem that General MacArthur in responding to the President's question merely voiced the consensus of the highest officials from the seat of government. This is how matters stood at mid-October.

On 20 October the Far East Command daily intelligence summary carried a report from a source it regarded as reliable that 400,000 CCF troops were at the border alerted to cross on the 18th or 20th. The Far East Command stated that precautionary measures had been taken of conducting daily air reconnaissance flights over all avenues of approach to the U.N. forces from the Yalu but that "so far no positive movements except intermittent though large-scale truck convoys have been picked up."[36] On this same date, the Far East Command issued CINCFE Plan 202, which was to be the basis for withdrawal of U.N. forces from Korea when the fighting ended. This plan assumed there would be no intervention either by Chinese or Soviet forces.[37]

Strangely enough, beginning on 25 October and continuing throughout the month, and at a time when the U.N. forces were actually fighting the Chinese Communist Forces in North Korea and capturing Chinese prisoners, the Far East Command daily intelligence summary placed Chinese intervention second in priority to guerrilla operations in enemy capabilities. The intelligence summary for 27 October carried the story of the first CCF prisoners captured two days earlier. The G–2 comment on the prisoners' account of Chinese intervention was that it was "based on PW reports and is unconfirmed and thereby unaccepted."[38]

The next day, 28 October, after discussing further the question of possible CCF intervention, the intelligence estimate said:

From a tactical viewpoint, with victorious U.S. Divisions in full deployment, it would appear that the auspicious time for such [Chinese] intervention has long since passed; it is difficult to believe that such a move, if planned, would have been postponed to a time when remnant North Korean forces have been reduced to a low point of effectiveness.[39]

On 31 October the daily summary discussed the fact that ten Chinese prisoners had been taken by Eighth Army and that the ROK II Corps had suffered reverses. It then said that the situation "may signify the commitment of Chinese Communist Forces in the Korean conflict." The United Nations Command report to the Security Council covering the period 16–31 October, in mentioning the capture of Chinese prisoners, said there was no positive evidence

---

[36] FEC DIS 2963, 20 Oct 50.
[37] Schnabel, FEC, GHQ Support and Participation in the Korean War, ch. VII, pp. 1–2, citing CINCFE Opn Plan 202, 20 Oct 50, JSPOG files.

[38] FEC DIS 2968–2974, 25–31 Oct 50.
[39] FEC DIS 2971, 28 Oct 50.

that Chinese units as such had entered Korea.[40]

On 3 November, however, the Far East Command accepted the estimate that 16,500 CCF troops were in contact with U.N. forces in Korea and that possibly the total might be 34,000. This intelligence report listed CCF strength in Manchuria totaling 833,000 men, of whom 415,000 were Chinese Communist regular ground forces. On this same day the Joint Chiefs of Staff in Washington dispatched a message to MacArthur expressing their concern over what appeared to be "overt intervention in Korea by Chinese Communist units," and asked his views on the matter. He replied the next day that while it was a distinct possibility, "there are many fundamental logical reasons against it and sufficient evidence has not yet come to hand to warrant its immediate acceptance."[41]

On the same day, 3 November, that MacArthur received the inquiry from the Joint Chiefs of Staff, the Peiping radio broadcast a joint communiqué in Chinese by the Chinese Communist Party and various political parties participating in the Peiping government. It declared the Korean War was a direct threat to the safety of China and that the Chinese people should take the initiative and exert utmost efforts to resist the United States and assist North Korea. The Far East Command G-2, in commenting on this broadcast, said that preceding ones had sounded like "bombast and boasting. The above does not."[42] Two days later, on 5 November, the daily intelligence summary stated that the Chinese Communist Forces had the potential to launch a large-scale counteroffensive at any time and without warning.[43]

On the heels of this estimate came General MacArthur's well-publicized special communiqué on 6 November which charged the Communists with having "committed one of the most offensive acts of international lawlessness of historic record by moving without any notice of belligerency elements of alien Communist forces across the Yalu River into North Korea," and of massing a great concentration of possible reinforcements behind the sanctuary of the Manchurian border. Concerning the future, he said, "Whether and to what extent these reserves will be moved forward to reinforce units now committed remains to be seen and is a matter of the gravest international significance."[44]

The Far East Command intelligence report the next day raised its accepted number of CCF troops in Korea to 34,500; 27,000 in the Eighth Army zone and 7,500 in the X Corps zone.[45] On the 9th it carried a rather detailed analysis of the CCF in Korea. It accepted 8 CCF divisions from 4 armies with a strength of 51,600 men as being in contact with U.N. forces; it accepted 2 more

---

[40] FEC DIS 2974, 31 Oct 50; Dept of State Pub 4051, *United Nations Command Eighth Report to the Security Council, United Nations, 16–31 October 1950*, p. 2.

[41] FEC DIS 2977, 3 Nov 50; Schnabel, FEC, GHQ Support and Participation in the Korean War, ch. VII, p. 14, quoting Msg W95790 CSUSA to CINCFE, 3 Nov 50, and Msg C68285 CINCFE to DA, 4 Nov 50.

[42] FEC DIS 2980, 6 Nov 50.

[43] FEC DIS 2979, 5 Nov 50.

[44] GHQ FEC Communiqué 11, 6 Nov 50; see also New York *Times*, November 6, 1950; Dept of State Pub 4263, pp. 20–22.

[45] FEC DIS 2981, 7 Nov, and 2982, 8 Nov 50.

divisions with 12,600 men as probably in contact, and still another 2 divisions with 12,600 men as possibly being in the X Corps zone but not in contact with U.N. forces. This analysis gave a total of 76,800 CCF troops as probably being in North Korea.[46]

The report of a conference in Peiping on 17 October when Chinese officials allegedly decided to go to war received further consideration on 12 November, in the light of more information, and the G-2 comment was that "this information may be evaluated as probably true." Reports continued to reach Tokyo from the Chinese Nationalist government on Formosa that the Chinese Communists intended to throw their main forces against the United Nations in Korea and also to increase their participation in the Indochina fighting.[47]

At mid-month, the U.N. Command reported to the Security Council that elements of twelve CCF divisions had been identified in forward areas, nine in Eighth Army zone, three in X Corps. As the third week of November passed, the Korean front was relatively quiet. Far East Command intelligence took notice of the continuing propaganda actively being carried on in Peiping and elsewhere by radio broadcasts, letters to newspaper editors, rallies, and other devices, in what seemed to be a campaign to prepare the nation for a defensive intervention war in Korea. The Far East Command now apparently accepted Chinese Communist strength in Korea at a maximum of 70,051 and a minimum of 44,851. Apparently this estimate did not change up to the beginning of the U.N. attack on 24 November.[48]

The Department of the Army estimate of CCF strength in Korea was essentially the same as that of the Far East Command, Eighth Army, and X Corps. In the week preceding the resumption of the U.N. attack on 24 November it accepted the estimate of 51,600 CCF troops in Korea, and a probable total of 76,800 CCF troops in Korea. It credited these troops to four CCF armies (the *38th, 39th, 40th,* and *42d*) with twelve divisions, giving each division a strength of 6,300 men.[49]

It is obvious that the Far East Command was in possession of a great amount of intelligence concerning the Chinese and their relation to the Korean War. But the vital questions still remained. Just what did General Willoughby, MacArthur's G-2, think, and, most important, what did General MacArthur himself think, of the probability of full-scale Chinese intervention?

While General Willoughby frequently pointed out in his intelligence summaries the potentialities of CCF intervention, it appears on all the evidence

---

[46] FEC DIS 2983, 9 Nov, and 2988, 14 Nov 50.
[47] FEC DIS 2989, 15 Nov 50.

[48] Dept of State Pub 4051, *United Nations Command Ninth Report to the Security Council, United Nations, 1–15 November 1950*, p. 9; FEC DIS 2993, 19 Nov 50. The original CCF strength in Korea before casualties was given as between 50,400 and 76,600. This indicated that FEC intelligence believed that approximately 5,500 CCF soldiers had become casualties in the fighting up to that time. See also FEC DIS 2994–2998, 20–24 Nov 50.
[49] See DA Wkly Intel Rpts 91, 17 Nov 50, pp. 19–21, and 92, 24 Nov 50, p. 32. A full treatment of the Department of the Army and the Joint Chiefs of Staff levels in the Korean War may be found in Schnabel, Theater Command.

that he did not think it would take place. When Maj. Gen. Leven C. Allen passed through Tokyo in early September on his way to Korea to assume the post of Chief of Staff, Eighth Army, Willoughby in a conversation with him played down the possibility of Chinese intervention and said the Chinese were sensible and would keep out of the Korean affair.[50] When General Ruffner, Chief of Staff, X Corps, in talking with General Willoughby in November, expressed concern about the great number of CCF divisions identified in the Eighth Army and X Corps zones, Willoughby answered they may have been only elements of that many divisions—not that many full divisions.[51] And in November when General Hickey, Acting Chief of Staff, Far East Command, with the G-2, G-3, and G-4 of that command, visited the X Corps in Korea to form a firsthand estimate of the degree of Chinese intervention, he asked General Willoughby substantially the following question: "If, as General Almond states, Chinese forces have intervened, how many Chinese troops do you estimate are now in Korea?" General Willoughby reiterated that only volunteers had entered Korea and that probably only a battalion of volunteers of each division identified was actually in Korea. In this same conversation, in response to a question from General Almond about what had happened to the 8th Cavalry Regiment in the Eighth Army zone, General Willoughby reportedly replied that the regiment had failed to put out adequate security, been overrun by a small, violent surprise attack, and had scattered during the hours of darkness.[52]

The Far East Command intelligence reports themselves during October and November 1950, although filled with intelligence data and estimates of the CCF capabilities, seem never to reflect the evaluated opinion that the Chinese would intervene in full force.

General MacArthur's view seems to have paralleled closely that reflected in the Far East Command intelligence evaluations, but he may have been somewhat more apprehensive of massive Chinese intervention. On 7 November he sent a report to the Joint Chiefs of Staff, in response to their request for one, that reflects his views and outlook at the time. His message, paraphrased, said:

Unquestionably . . . organized units of CCF have been and are being used against U.N. forces; that while it is impossible to determine accurately the precise strength, it is enough to have taken the initiative in the west and to have slowed appreciably our offensive in the east. The pattern seems established that such forces will be used and increased at will, probably without a formal declaration of hostilities. If this enemy build-up continues, it can easily reach a point preventing our resumption of the offensive and even force a retrograde movement. An attempt will be made in the west, possibly within 10 days, again to assume the initiative if the flow of enemy reinforcements can be checked. Only through such an offensive can an accurate measure of the enemy strength be taken.[53]

Despite this somewhat somber view, MacArthur two days later expressed himself optimistically in a message to the JCS with respect to future possible

---

[50] Interv, author with Gen Allen, 15 Dec 53.
[51] Interv, author with Maj Gen Clark L. Ruffner, 27 Aug 51.
[52] Ltr, Col William J. McCaffrey (X Corps Deputy CofS, Nov 50) to Lt Gen Edward M. Almond, 1 Dec 54, and forwarded by Almond to author.
[53] CINCFE to DA for JCS, C68465, 7 Nov 50.

THE BIG QUESTION

military operations against the Chinese Communist Forces. He said:

> I believe that with my air power, now unrestricted so far as Korea is concerned except as to hydroelectric installations, I can deny reinforcements coming across the Yalu in sufficient strength to prevent the destruction of those forces now arrayed against me in North Korea.[54]

On the day the U.N. attack began, 24 November, General MacArthur gave further evidence of the degree to which this view guided his thinking. In a communiqué that day he announced:

> The United Nations massive compression envelopment in North Korea against the new Red Armies operating there is now approaching its decisive effort. The isolating component of the pincer, our Air Forces of all types, have for the past three weeks, in a sustained attack of model coordination and effectiveness, successfully interdicted enemy lines of support from the North so that further reinforcement therefrom has been sharply curtailed and essential supplies markedly limited.[55]

Perhaps even more revealing of MacArthur's state of mind was his special communiqué to the United Nations later the same day in which he said:

> The giant U.N. pincer moved according to schedule today. The air forces, in full strength, completely interdicted the rear areas and an air reconnaissance behind the enemy line, and along the entire length of the Yalu River border, showed little sign of hostile military activity. The left wing of the envelopment advanced against stubborn and failing resistance. The right wing, gallantly supported by naval air and surface action, continued to exploit its commanding position.
> Our losses were extraordinarily light. The logistic situation is fully geared to sustain offensive operations. The justice of our course and promise of early completion of our mission is reflected in the morale of troops and commanders alike.[56]

In these dispatches General MacArthur expressed a viewpoint which apparently dominated his thinking during most of the critical period of October and November 1950 while he and the United Nations wrestled with the problem of CCF intervention. He seems to have believed, first, that the Chinese would not intervene in full force, and, second, that should they do so, his air power would destroy them. General MacArthur very likely expected to fight a battle with the Chinese Communist Forces short of the Yalu, but he expected to win it through the decisive effect of the interdiction and close support capabilities of his air power. This reliance on air power in dealing with the CCF was perhaps the crucial factor in MacArthur's calculations.

Actuality

The statement of Chou En-lai to the Indian Ambassador on 3 October, the announcements made over the Peiping radio, the timing of CCF troop movements as learned from prisoners, and other forms of intelligence, taken in connection with later events, make it seem reasonably clear that the Chinese Communist government had decided by early

---

[54] CINCFE to DA for JCS, C68572, 9 Nov 50.
[55] GHQ UNC Communiqué 12, 24 Nov 50, in EUSAK WD, 24 Nov 50. EUSAK Daily News Bul, 24 Nov 50.

[56] Senate MacArthur Hearings, pt. 3, p. 1834, testimony of Acheson, quoting MacArthur's message.

October on intervention in North Korea if United Nations troops other than ROK's crossed the 38th Parallel. Whether the Chinese Communists believed the United Nations Command would cross the Parallel is unknown, but there is at least one good reason to think the North Korean Government believed the U.N. Command would stop at the 38th Parallel. Kim Il Sung, Commander in Chief of the North Korea People's Army, in an order to the army dated 14 October 1950, stated in part, "Other reasons that we have failed are that many of us felt that the 38th Parallel would be as far as the US Forces would attack...." [57]

Within a few days after the leading elements of the U.S. forces crossed the 38th Parallel at Kaesong on 9 October, elements of the CCF were crossing the Yalu River at the Manchurian border into North Korea. The first of these troops apparently crossed the boundary on 13 or 14 October, although it is possible that some may have crossed on the 12th.

Four CCF armies, each of three divisions, crossed the Yalu River between 14 and 20 October. Two of them, the *39th* and the *40th,* crossed from An-tung, Manchuria, to Sinuiju, North Korea; the other two, the *38th* and *42d,* crossed from Chi-an, Manchuria, to Manp'ojin, North Korea. All four armies were part of Lin Piao's *Fourth Field Army* and upon arrival in Korea were subordinated to the CCF *XIII Army Group.* The *1st Motorized Artillery Division,* two regiments of the *2d Motorized Artillery Division,* and a cavalry regiment also crossed into Korea at An-tung about 20–22 October in support of the four armies already across. [58]

Three of the four CCF armies entering Korea deployed in front of Eighth Army, the fourth deployed in front of X Corps. From west to east these armies took the following positions: the *39th Army* was in front of Unsan, the *40th Army* in front of Onjong. The *38th Army,* marching from Manp'ojin through Kanggye, reached a position on Eighth Army's right flank in the Huich'on area. Very likely it was troops from this CCF army that General Dean saw in the early dawn one morning in mid-October twenty miles north of Huich'on as he was being taken by his captors to Manp'ojin. The *39th* and *40th Armies* entered combat with U.N. forces for the first time on 25 October; the *38th* entered combat on the 26th.

The fourth army, the *42d,* moved from Manp'ojin through Kanggye to the Changjin Reservoir area in front of the X Corps main axis of advance in northeast Korea. It, like the *39th* and *40th Armies,* first entered combat against forces under U.N. command on 25 October. The west flank units of this army, elements of the CCF *125th Division,* overlapped into the Eighth Army zone and apparently constituted the enemy force that dispersed the ROK 7th Regi-

---

[57] X Corps PIR 55, 20 Nov 50, reproduces this captured document, Order 1-1, 14 Oct 50, signed by Kim Il Sung and Pak Kun Yon, Chief, Korean People's Supreme Political Bureau.

[58] FEC Intel Digest, vol. 1, Issue 4, 1–15 Feb 53 pp. 26–38; *Ibid.,* Issue 26, 16–30 Jun 52, Individual Histories, Chinese Communist Support and Service Units, pp. 46–47; FEC MIS, Order of Battle Info CCF, p. 9.

ment below Ch'osan at the end of October.[59]

At the time, then, that General MacArthur was expressing to President Truman and his advisers at Wake Island on 15 October his belief that there was very little likelihood that the Chinese Communist Forces would intervene, that, if they did, no more than 60,000 could get across the Yalu and that his air force would destroy them, approximately 120,000 CCF soldiers either had already crossed, were in the act of crossing, or were moving from their assembly and training areas to the crossing sites for the purpose of crossing.

Following the first four armies in approximately ten days, two more CCF armies crossed into North Korea at the end of October. These were the *50th* and *66th Armies* which, crossing from An-tung to Sinuiju, had completed their crossing into North Korea by 31 October. Each of these armies was composed of three divisions recently brought up to war strength. In these two armies approximately 60,000 more CCF troops came into North Korea, to make a total during the month of approximately 180,000 troops. The *50th Army* deployed southward on the CCF west flank and remained in reserve during the CCF First Phase Offensive. An element of this army did, however, exchange fire with the 19th Infantry Regiment on 1 November near Kusong.[60]

KIM IL SUNG

Also, before the end of October the CCF *42d Truck Regiment* entered Korea at Sinuiju from An-tung, and the *5th Truck Regiment* and the *8th Artillery Division* entered Manp'ojin from Ch-ian. Both truck units supported the First Phase Offensive.[61]

In the X Corps zone, the *42d Army* had sent the *124th Division* south of the Changjin Reservoir where it fought the delaying battle in late October and the first part of November with elements of the ROK 3d Division and the U.S. 7th Marines. The *126th Division* remained in reserve in the reservoir area, but it had a number of minor engagements and patrol actions with the U.S. 7th Division in the Pujon Reservoir area. The *125th Division* moved southward from Yudam-ni to block the axis of approach from

---

[59] FEC Intel Digest, vol. 1, Nr 4, 1–15 Feb 53, pp. 28–33; EUSAK WD, G–2 Sec, 12 Nov 50, interrog of Ma Yu-fu; *Ibid.*, 14 Nov 50, ATIS Interrog Rpts (Enemy Forces), Issue 17, 2279, p. 186, interrog of Lin Piao Wu (a company grade officer); 1st Mar Div SAR, 8 Oct–15 Dec 50, vol. 1, an. B, p. 23.

[60] FEC Intel Digest, vol. 1, Nr 4, 1–15 Feb 53, pp. 36–37.

[61] *Ibid.*, Issue 26, 16–30 Jun 52, pp. 48, 52.

TABLE 5—ORGANIZATION OF THE
XIII ARMY GROUP

Armies	Divisions	Regiments
38th	112th	334th, 335th, 336th
	113th	337th, 338th, 339th
	114th	340th, 341st, 342d
39th	115th	343d, 344th, 345th
	116th	346th, 347th, 348th
	117th	349th, 350th, 351st
40th	118th	352d, 353d, 354th
	119th	355th, 356th, 357th
	120th	358th, 359th, 360th
42d	124th	370th, 371st, 372d
	125th	373d, 374th, 375th
	126th	376th, 377th, 378th
50th	148th	442d, 443d, 444th
	149th	445th, 446th, 447th
	150th	448th, 449th, 450th
66th	196th	586th, 587th, 588th
	197th	589th, 590th, 591st
	198th	592d, 593d, 594th

Source: FEC Intel Digest, vol. 1, Nr 4, 17 Feb 53; FEC MIS, Order of Battle Info, CCF, 15 Jun 51; Ibid., Nr 35, 1-15 Nov 52, p. 45; Ibid., Nr 6, 2 Sep 51, p. A-9.

Sach'ang-ni to the north. By 13 November it had moved southwest across the X Corps–Eighth Army boundary into the Eighth Army zone where it appeared before the ROK 8th Division in the Tokch'on area on the Eighth Army east flank.

These six armies, five in the Eighth Army zone and one in the X Corps zone, composed the CCF *XIII Army Group* with a total of 18 divisions, each division at the standard strength of about 10,000 men. In the Chinese Army the division and regiment numeration proceeds progressively in sequence. The organization of the *XIII Army Group* illustrates this. (*Table 5*)

A third major CCF entry into North Korea now took place. The *IX Army Group, Third Field Army*, entered Korea during the first half of November. This army group had come by rail directly to the border from Shantung Province, China, in late October and early November and had started crossing at once. It comprised three armies, the *20th, 26th,* and *27th,* each of three divisions. Each of these armies was reinforced by a division taken from the *30th Army*, this giving each army four divisions.[62] The *IX Army Group* entering Korea in the first part of November, therefore, added 12 infantry divisions to the 18 already there, for a total now of 30 divisions. In addition to these 30 infantry divisions, the Chinese Communist Forces also had in North Korea a number of artillery, cavalry, and support units.

The *IX Army Group* moved southeast to the Changjin Reservoir area, large units of it arriving there on or before 13 November. On that date, elements of the *IX Army Group* relieved the *42d Army* of its responsibility in that sector, and the *124th* and *126th Divisions* of the *42d Army* followed the *125th* southwest into the Eighth Army zone. By the end of the third week of November, therefore, the *XIII Army Group* of the CCF *Fourth Field Army*, with 18 divisions of infantry (180,000 men), was concentrated in front of Eighth Army, and the *IX Army Group* of the CCF *Third Field Army*, with 12 divisions of infantry (120,000 men), was concentrated in front of X Corps. A formidable total of approximately 300,000 CCF infantry troops

---

[62] The *89th Division* reinforced the *20th Army;* the *88th Division,* the *26th Army;* and the *90th Division,* the *27th Army.*

THE BIG QUESTION

were now deployed in North Korea.[63]

The entry of the Chinese Communists into the Korean War necessarily brought changes in the enemy command. It appears that Peng Teh-huai, Deputy CCF Commander, established a joint *CCF-NKA Headquarters* in Mukden and there made basic decisions concerning enemy operations. A subordinate headquarters, called the *N.K. Army–CCF Combined Headquarters,* under Kim Il Sung, Commander in Chief of the North Korean Army, was publicly given credit for controlling military operations in Korea, but it seems certain that actual control rested in Mukden. There is some indication that the CCF *XIII Army Group* at first may have been under Kim Il Sung's North Korean command. The *IX Army Group* apparently was under complete CCF control from the beginning.

Conclusion

Starting with an acceptance of only a few Chinese "volunteers" mixed with North Korean units, the U.N. Command in the course of a month had gradually raised its estimate to accept about 60,000 to 70,000 Chinese troops in Korea by 24

PENG TEH-HUAI

November, less than one-fourth the number actually there. How was it possible for the U.N. Command to mistake so grossly the facts in the situation, even after it had met a considerable part of these Chinese forces in combat?

The answer seems clear enough. First, although the Chinese Communist government had several times openly stated it would intervene if U.N. forces other than ROK troops crossed the 38th Parallel, American authorities were inclined to disbelieve this and to consider these statements to be in the nature of threats and diplomatic blackmail. Second, the actual troop movements across the Yalu and deployment south were made at night and so in the main were not subject to aerial observation. During the day, aerial observation failed to discover

---

[63] The approximate figure of 300,000 for the Chinese was arrived at only after careful study of the intelligence information. Although the 30 regular divisions may not all have been precisely 10,000 strong, the round figure takes into account the miscellaneous service, cavalry, and artillery units. FEC Intel Digest, vol. 1, Nr 3, 16–31 Jan 53, *IX Army Group*, pp. 32–37; *Ibid.*, vol. 1, Nr 4, 1–15 Feb 53, *XIII Army Group*, p. 33; FEC Intel Digest, Nr 8, 16–30 Sep 51, and Nr 6, 16–31 Aug 51, p. A–12; FEC MIS, Order of Battle Info, CCF, pp. 9–10, 87–91, and *Third Field Army*, 1 Mar 51; ATIS Enemy Docs, Issue 29, p. 84, Chinese Notebook, 11–24 Nov 50; 1st Mar Div SAR, vol. 1, an. B, 8 Oct–15 Dec 50, pp. 25, 32.

the troops, who remained hidden in the hills under perfect camouflage discipline. Third, because they were not adequately confirmed, the reports from prisoners and Korean civilians of mass CCF movements across the border were not accepted by intelligence authorities. The intelligence system of Eighth Army, for various reasons, did not work as well in North Korea as it had in South Korea during the days of the Pusan Perimeter.

A word should be said about the CCF march discipline and capabilities, which in large part accounted for the secrecy with which the Chinese Communists entered and deployed in North Korea. This march capability and performance equaled the best examples of antiquity. In Xenophon's account of the retreat of the 10,000 Greeks, a day's march on the average came to a little less than 24 miles. The Roman military pace was set to cover 20 miles in 5 hours, the usual day's march for a Roman legion. In normal training exercises the Roman legions had to make three such marches every month. On occasion the legions were required to march 24 miles in 5 hours. When Caesar besieged Gergovia in Gaul, he marched 50 miles in 24 hours.[64]

In a well-documented instance, a CCF army of three divisions marched on foot from An-tung in Manchuria, on the north side of the Yalu River, 286 miles to its assembly area in North Korea, in the combat zone, in a period ranging from 16 to 19 days. One division of this army, marching at night over circuitous mountain roads, averaged 18 miles a day for 18 days. The day's march began after dark at 1900 and ended at 0300 the next morning. Defense measures against aircraft were to be completed before 0530. Every man, animal, and piece of equipment were to be concealed and camouflaged. During daylight only bivouac scouting parties moved ahead to select the next day's bivouac area. When CCF units were compelled for any reason to march by day, they were under standing orders for every man to stop in his tracks and remain motionless if aircraft appeared overhead. Officers were empowered to shoot down immediately any man who violated this order.[65]

These practices, especially the march and bivouac discipline, explain why United Nations aerial observation never discovered the CCF deployment into Korea. The Chinese Communist Forces moved 300,000 men into position in October and November and none of them was ever discovered by the U.N. Command prior to actual contact. While the planes were overhead searching for possible Chinese movement into Korea, the Chinese, perfectly camouflaged, lay hidden below. The aerial observers did not see them nor did the aerial photographs reveal their presence.

The Pregnant Military Situation

On 6 November General MacArthur took official notice of the recent CCF offensive and summed up his estimate of the changing situation in Korea. He said

---

[64] See Xenophon, *The Anabasis*, and William Duncan's *Caesar* (includes Caesar's Commentaries), pp. 46–50.

[65] FEC Intel Digest 16, 16–31 Jan 52, March of a CCF Army, pp. 33–39; I Corps WD, 30 Oct 50, Intel Summ 135, 30 Oct 50. Although the march described actually occurred early in 1951, a few months after the initial CCF intervention, the initial CCF troops entering Korea apparently marched at an equal rate of speed at night to reach their assembly areas.

the defeat of the North Koreans had been decisive when the Chinese intervened in "one of the most offensive acts of international lawlessness of historic record." Speaking in high praise of General Walker, he said the possible trap "surreptitiously laid calculated to encompass the destruction of the United Nations Forces" was avoided, "with minimum losses only by the timely detection and skillful maneuvering of the United States commander responsible for that sector." General MacArthur announced his future intentions in these words, "Our present mission is limited to the destruction of those forces now arrayed against us in North Korea with a view to achieving the United Nations' objective to bring unity and peace to the Korean nation and its people." He intended, obviously, to destroy the Chinese forces in Korea as well as the remaining North Koreans. To accomplish this he considered it necessary to establish an integrated continuous front in western and central Korea for co-ordinated large-scale offensive action.[66]

That same day, 6 November, General Walker issued Eighth Army's operation plan for a renewal of the offensive. It called for an advance to the Korean border with three corps abreast—the U.S. I Corps on the west, the U.S. IX Corps in the center, and the ROK II Corps on the east in the army zone.[67] In preparing for the projected offensive, tentatively set for 15 November, Eighth Army had to bring the IX Corps into the line. Steps

GENERAL MACARTHUR

had already been taken to accomplish this. On 2 November the ROK III Corps had assumed responsibility for the then IX Corps zone, and IX Corps completed its move to Sunch'on on 4 November. The next day at noon the IX Corps became operational there with control of the 2d Infantry Division.[68]

Colonel Stebbins, Eighth Army G–4, estimated that Eighth Army needed 3,000 tons of supplies daily for passive defensive operations and 4,000 daily for active combat. At no time in October or up to about 20 November was Eighth Army able to supply this minimum need for active offensive combat. The 4,000

---

[66] GHQ FEC Communiqué 11, 6 Nov 50; Dept of State Pub 4051, *United Nations Command Ninth Report to the Security Council, United Nations, 1–15 November 1950*, p. 10.

[67] EUSAK Opns Plan 14, 6 Nov 50; EUSAK WD, G–3 Sec, 6 Nov 50.

[68] EUSAK POR 342, 3 Nov 50; EUSAK WD, G–3 Sec, 4 Nov 50; IX Corps WD, Nov 50, bk. I, sec. IV, Opns.

tons daily was finally achieved by bringing forward approximately 2,000 tons daily to P'yongyang by rail from the south, by unloading 1,000 tons daily at Chinnamp'o, and by bringing approximately 1,000 tons daily into North Korea by airlift.[49]

While Eighth Army was striving to overcome the logistical difficulties that delayed its resumption of the attack in mid-November, X Corps in northeast Korea continued its headlong rush to the border against scattered and ineffective opposition except in the 1st Marine Division sector below the Changjin Reservoir. There the Marine division and regimental commanders, much to the X Corps commander's dissatisfaction, deliberately slowed their advance.

From the very beginning of X Corps operations in northeast Korea, General Smith had looked with disfavor on the wide dispersal of the subordinate units of the Marine division. On 7 November in a conference with General Almond, he again urged the concentration of the division. The recent experience of X Corps with the CCF *124th Division* and Eighth Army's encounter with the CCF in the west apparently caused General Almond to be more amenable to General Smith's arguments for concentrating the Marine division, and he agreed to it. Smith then went further and argued that the division should not advance to the Kot'o-ri plateau at the south end of the Changjin Reservoir with winter at hand, but General Almond felt that the marines should hold Hagaru-ri at the southern end of the reservoir. With the withdrawal of the CCF from contact both in the west and northeast Korea about 7 November, confidence soon reasserted itself in both Eighth Army and X Corps, and X Corps on 11 November reiterated its directive to proceed to the Yalu. Both Eighth Army and X Corps were still enjoined under General MacArthur's directive of 24 October to proceed to the Yalu. Apparently General Almond hoped that the troops could reach the border quickly, turn over the area to ROK troops, and withdraw before winter really set in.[70]

After the 7th Marines reached the Kot'o-ri plateau on 10 November, neither Colonel Litzenberg, the regimental commander, nor General Smith, the division commander, showed any inclination to hurry the advance. General Smith plainly indicated that he was apprehensive about his western exposed flank, that he wanted to improve the road up the pass from the division railhead at Chinhung-ni, that he wanted to develop a secure base at Hagaru-ri, and that he wanted to garrison key points on the main supply road back south. And most of all he wanted to concentrate the full strength of the Marine division in the Hagaru-ri area before trying to advance further toward the Yalu.

Winter struck early in the Changjin

---

[49] Interv, author with Stebbins, 4 Dec 53; Interv, author with Maj Gen Leven C. Allen, 15 Dec 53; Ltr, Allen to author, 27 Nov 54; EUSAK WD, G-3 Sec, 13 Nov 50, and G-4 Jnl, Msg 7, 241015 Nov 50.

[70] Interv, author with Ruffner, 15 Aug 51; Interv, author with Lynn Montross and Capt Nicholas Canzona, Marine Corps Hist Sec, 6 Apr 54; Interv, author with Almond, 13 Dec 51; Lt Gen Oliver P. Smith, MS review comments, 15 Nov 57; X Corps Special Rpt on Chosin Reservoir, Nov 50; Schnabel, FEC, GHQ Support and Participation in the Korean War, ch. VII, pp. 21-23.

Reservoir area of Korea in 1950. It arrived with violent force and subzero temperatures on 10 November, the day the marines reached the Kot'o-ri plateau. From that day on the troops there were involved in a winter campaign. Patrols sent out from Kot'o-ri on 11 and 12 November found only small scattered enemy groups in the hills, and the next day a Marine unit advanced to Pusong-ni, halfway to the reservoir. On 14 November the 7th Marines, wearing their heavy arctic parkas, trudged in subzero weather toward Hagaru-ri over a road now covered with an inch of snow. Vehicles froze up on the move, brakes grabbed, transmissions were stiff, and the men themselves had difficulty in moving forward. Entering Hagaru-ri, the marines found it burned out by previous bombing attacks and practically deserted. Natives told them that the 3,000 Chinese soldiers occupying the town had departed three days earlier, going north and west. A Chinese soldier from the *377th Regiment, 126th Division*, captured near Hagaru-ri during the day, said elements of his division were east of the reservoir. That night, 14–15 December, the temperature dropped to 15 degrees below zero.[71]

The next day the 7th Marines completed its movement into Hagaru-ri, and Colonel Litzenberg made arrangements for a perimeter defense. The 1st Battalion protected the northwest approaches, the 2d Battalion the southern, and the 3d Battalion the northeast approaches to the town. That same day the 2d Battalion, 5th Marines, arrived at Kot'o-ri, beginning the concentration of the rest of the 1st Marine Division in the Changjin Reservoir area behind the 7th Marines. The 5th Marines now guarded the main supply route back to Hamhung.

Two days after the first Marine units entered Hagaru-ri, General Smith and Maj. Gen. Field Harris (Commanding General, 1st Marine Air Wing) on 16 November looked over the ground there and selected the site for a C-47 airstrip. Smith felt that such an airstrip would be needed to supplement supply by road and for fast evacuation of casualties. Engineer troops began work on the airstrip on 19 November, and others continued work on improving the road up the pass from Chinhung-ni. The first trucks climbed through the pass to Hagaru-ri on the 18th. Smith held the Marine advance to Hagaru-ri while this work continued.

Thus it was, that with virtually no enemy opposition, the marines advanced at an average rate of only a mile a day between 10 and 23 November. But this caution on the part of General Smith.in concentrating the division and his insistence on securing its supply lines and of establishing a base for further operations in the frigid, barren wastes of the Changjin Reservoir area were to prove the division's salvation in the weeks ahead.

Although the projected Eighth Army attack on the 15th had to be postponed because of logistical difficulties, the army on the 14th ordered an attack to be made, on a day and hour to be announced, to seize a line running generally from Napch'ongjong, on the west coastal road, eastward through Taech'on–

---

[71] 1st Mar Div SAR, vol. II, pp. 38, 40, an. C, 13–14 Nov 50; X Corps PIR 49, 14 Nov 50; ATIS Interrog Rpts (Enemy Forces), Issue 18, Nr 2304, Cheng Cheng Kwo.

Onjong–Huich'on to Inch'o-ri. This was to be the line of departure for the projected co-ordinated attack. The army was then to be prepared to continue the advance on order to the northern border of Korea. General Walker's order reflects an intention to proceed with a closely co-ordinated attack in order to have the army under control at all times. It also reflects a considerable degree of caution and a certain respect for the enemy forces. It appears on the weight of the evidence that General Walker wanted to make the attack. He expected opposition, but apparently believed he could reach the border. His chief of staff, General Allen, shared this view.[72]

On 17 November, with the logistical situation improved, Eighth Army announced to its subordinate organizations that the attack north would start on 24 November. General MacArthur notified the Joint Chiefs of Staff at the same time of the tentative attack date, emphasizing that the delay in mounting the offensive had been due to logistical difficulties. He optimistically reported that the intensified air attacks of the past ten days had isolated the battlefield from added enemy reinforcements and had greatly reduced the flow of enemy supplies.[73]

Up to the launching of the 24 November attack the U.S. Eighth Army and the X Corps had suffered a total of 27,827 battle casualties in the Korean War; 21,529 in Eighth Army and 6,298 in X Corps. Of the Eighth Army total, 4,157 had been killed in action, 391 more had died of wounds, and 4,834 were missing in action.[74]

On the afternoon of 21 November Eighth Army advised I and IX Corps and the ROK Army that H-hour for the army attack was 1000 24 November. Word of the attack hour had reached the front-line units by 23 November. That was Thanksgiving Day. The army front was generally quiet. Patrols went out several thousand yards in front of the line with little enemy contact. Nearly everywhere the enemy seemed to have withdrawn during the past week, leaving behind light outpost and covering positions. At no place did U.N. forces uncover what could be considered a main line of resistance.[75]

As Eighth Army units moved out in attack on 24 November they encountered only a few small enemy squad- and platoon-sized groups employing small arms fire. Even in the ROK II Corps zone of attack enemy opposition was unexpectedly light. In most places the U.N. advance was unopposed.

Generals MacArthur, Stratemeyer, Wright, Willoughby, and Whitney, to-

---

[72] EUSAK Opn Plan 15, 14 Nov 50; EUSAK WD, G-3 Sec, 11, 14 Nov 50; Interv, author with Allen, 15 Dec 53; Interv, author with Stebbins, 4 Dec 53. Colonel Stebbins, the Eighth Army G-4 at the time, however, told the author that General Walker did not want to make the attack.

[73] EUSAK WD, G-3 Sec, Msg 172100 to CG I and IX Corps and CG ROK; I Corps WD, 18 Nov 50; Schnabel, FEC, GHQ Support and Participation in the Korean War, ch. VII, p. 26, citing Msg C69211, CINCUNC to DA, 18 Nov 50.

[74] EUSAK WD, AG Sec, Statistical Casualty Rpt, 24 Nov 50; X Corps POR 59, 24 Nov 50; TAGO Rpt, May 52, shows Korean casualties through 15 Nov 50 as 28,159: 5,702 KIA; 18,909 WIA, of which 482 were DOW; and 3,548 missing or captured.

[75] EUSAK WD, G-3 Sec, Opn Instr, 211645 Nov 50; EUSAK PIR 133, 22 Nov 50; 24th Div WD, 23 Nov 50; 89th Med Tk Bn Unit Hist, Nov 50, p. 3; I Corps WD, 22 Nov 50.

Insignia of Major U.S. Ground Force Units in Korean War in 1950

gether with several chiefs of U.S. press bureaus in Tokyo, had flown to Korea the morning of the 24th to witness the beginning of the attack. General Walker joined them in visits to I Corps, IX Corps, and 24th Division headquarters along the Ch'ongch'on. At I Corps headquarters General Milburn cast a momentary shadow over the bright picture being drawn when he told the party that his patrols had found the Unsan area heavily defended, and in his opinion the projected IX Corps attack there would not progress easily. General Church briefed the party at the 24th Division headquarters shortly after noon on the progress of the attack. Optimism and enthusiasm as to chances of the attack succeeding seemed to prevail.[76]

In the afternoon when General Leven Allen returned to Eighth Army headquarters from the airstrip where he had accompanied the party, he remarked to some of the staff members, "I think the attack will go. General MacArthur would not have come over if he did not think so."[77]

---

[76] EUSAK PIR 135, 24 Nov 50; EUSAK WD, CG memo for record (aide-de-camp), 24 Nov 50; IX Corps WD, bk. I, 24 Nov 50; I Corps WD, Nov 50; Interv, author with Maj Gen Edwin K. Wright, 7 Jan 54.

[77] Interv, author with Brig Gen William C. Bullock, 28 Jan 54; Ltr, Maj Gen Leven C. Allen to author, 4 Dec 54.

The Sources

There is little need for extended comment on the sources used in preparing this volume. Their nature will be evident in the footnote citations. With the exception of a few passages, and these largely in the first chapters, the entire work is based on primary sources. These consist of the official records of the United States and United Nations armed forces bearing on the land, sea, and air action. ROK records were also consulted, but generally they were scant and sometimes nonexistent.

The U.S. Army ground organizations kept war diaries from army level down through infantry regiments and artillery and tank battalions. They also maintained daily periodic intelligence and operations reports and journal message files. Separate battalions kept similar records. Although not required by the Adjutant General for record purposes, infantry battalion war diaries in some instances were attached to regimental war diaries and in that manner found their way into the permanent records of the Department of the Army. Included in the daily Eighth Army War Diary was a useful G-3 Air report.

Some contemporary army records were lost in combat. The most important of these were the records of the 34th Infantry Regiment, lost in the battle of Taejon in July 1950, and the records of the 2d Infantry Division and of its 9th and 38th Regiments, lost at Kunu-ri in late November 1950. Substitutes were made up from memory of individuals and scattered sources bearing on the period. The records of the 5th Regimental Combat Team for its first month of combat, August 1950, were never located, although a thorough search for them was made in the Adjutant General's Office.

The Marine combat units kept records called special action reports that were similar to the Army war diaries, together with annexes covering subordinate units and staff sections. They also maintained G-2 and G-3 journal files.

For the Inch'on landing and the Wonsan-Hungnam operation, the naval records of Joint Task Force Seven were indispensable sources.

All the war diaries, special action reports, periodic reports, and journal files of combat units and headquarters at all levels were read and studied, as well as similar reports of logistical and service organizations.

Supplementing the records, and often more important, as indicated in the Preface, were the firsthand accounts of participants. These have come from army commanders, corps and division commanders, regimental and battalion commanders, company commanders, platoon leaders, staff officers, platoon sergeants, other noncommissioned officers, and privates in personal interviews, correspondence, and their review of early manuscript drafts on actions in which they fought. Each such personal account was checked against the others and the records, and all were used in the framework of the time sequence and map locations given in the operations journals and periodic reports of the various command echelons. Discrepancies abounded. Often it was not easy to reconcile conflicting evidence and arrive at a narrative in which one could have confidence.

Enemy sources used consisted of captured North Korean and Chinese Communist Forces documents and thousands of reports of interrogations of prisoners from both the North Korean Army and the Chinese Communist Forces. The value of the interrogation reports varied widely depending upon the rank and position in the enemy organization held by the prisoner. Many were entirely valueless, but one could never know in advance what little scrap of information any report might yield. The most useful body of enemy material was in the collections of the Allied Translator and Interpreter Section (ATIS) of General MacArthur's Far East Headquarters, although a sizable amount of similar material was included as attachments to the S-2 and G-2 periodic reports of regiments, divisions, corps, and army. Interrogation of prisoner reports found with the records of combat units had a particular value because they often represented the best information available to the troops on the enemy situation in their immediate front, although later interrogation reports might be more complete.

Names of enemy organizations, whether North Korean or Chinese Communist Forces, are italicized in the text.

The writer believes that good military history cannot be written without a clear knowledge of the terrain involved in action. He studied the terrain on the ground itself whenever possible, and gave to map study a proportionately large allotment of time. The Army Map Service map of Korea, scale 1:50,000, fourth edition, February 1951, was the standard terrain map used, although earlier editions and maps at both larger and smaller scales were also consulted. Special maps were employed in the case of actions involving towns and cities of any size.

Glossary

AAA	Antiaircraft Artillery
Abn	Airborne
Act	Action
ADCOM	Advance Command and Liaison Group in Korea
ADVATIS	Advanced Allied Translator & Interpreter Section
AFF	Army Field Forces
AGC	Amphibious force flagship equipped with special communication facilities
AK	Cargo ship
Amphib	Amphibious
AMS	Army Map Service
an.	Annex
AP	Armor-piercing
AP	Transport
APA	Attack transport
APD	High-speed transport
Armd	Armored
Arty	Artillery
ATIS	Allied Translator & Interpreter Section
AW	Automatic Weapons
BAR	Browning Automatic Rifle
BC	N.K. Border Constabulary (called *Bo An Dae*)
BLUEHEARTS	Code name for the original plan for an amphibious landing behind enemy lines, abandoned by 10 July 1950. Succeeded by CHROMITE
Bn	Battalion
Br	Briefing
Brig	Brigade
Btry	Battery
Bul	Bulletin
C	Combat
CCF	Chinese Communist Forces
CCS	Combined Chiefs of Staff
CG	Commanding General
Chmn	Chairman
CHROMITE	Code name for amphibious operations in September 1950, one of which was a landing at Inch'on
CINCFE	Commander in Chief, Far East
CINCUNC	Commander in Chief, United Nations Command
CM-IN	Classified message—In
CO	Commanding Officer

Comd	Command
Comdr	Commander
Comm	Communication
COMNAVFE	Commander, U.S. Naval Forces Far East
CP	Command post
CofS	Chief of Staff
CSGPO	Chief of Staff, G–3, Plans & Operations Div.
CSUSA	Chief of Staff, U.S. Army
DA	Department of the Army
Det	Detachment
Dir	Director
DIS	Daily Intelligence Summary
Div	Division
DOW	Died of wounds
DUKW	Amphibious truck
EDT	Eastern Daylight Time
Engr	Engineer
Est	Estimate
EST	Eastern Standard Time
EUSAK	Eighth United States Army in Korea
Ex Off	Executive Officer
FA	Field Artillery
FDC	Fire Direction Center
FEAF	Far East Air Forces
FEC	Far East Command
FO	Field Order
Fonecon	Telephone conversation
G–2	Intelligence section of divisional or higher staff
G–3	Operations and training section of divisional or higher staff
Gen	General
GO	General Orders
GS	General Staff
HE	High explosive
HEAT	High explosive, antitank
Hist	History, Historical
Hq	Headquarters
Hv	Heavy
IG	Inspector General
I&R	Intelligence & Reconnaissance
Incl	Inclosure
Inf	Infantry
Info	Information
Instr	Instruction
Intel	Intelligence
Interrog	Interrogation
Interv	Interview
JAG	Judge Advocate General
JCS	Joint Chiefs of Staff

GLOSSARY

JLC	Japan Logistical Command
Jnl	Journal
JOC	Joint Operations Center
JSPOG	Joint Strategic Plans and Operations Group
JTF 7	Joint Task Force Seven
KIA	Killed in action
KMAG	U.S. Korean Military Advisory Group
KMC	Korean Marine Corps
LCVP	Landing craft, vehicle, personnel
Ldr	Leader
Log	Logistical
LSD	Landing ship, dock
LSMR	Landing ship, medium (rocket)
LST	Landing ship, tank
LSV	Landing ship, vehicle
Ltr	Letter
LVT	Landing vehicle, tracked
MATS	Military Air Transport Service
Med Stf	Medical Staff
Med Tk	Medium Tank
MIA	Missing in action
Mil	Military
MIS	Military Intelligence Service
(−)	Minus
Mort	Mortar
MS	Manuscript
Msg	Message
MSgt	Master Sergeant
Narr	Narrative
Natl	National
NAVFE	U.S. Naval Forces, Far East
NKPA	North Korea People's Army
Nr	Number
OCMH	Office of the Chief of Military History
Ofc	Office
Off	Officer, Officers
Opns	Operations
Ord	Order
OSAF	Office of the Secretary of the Air Force
PC	Patrol vessel
Pers	Personnel
PIR	Periodic Intelligence Report
Plat	Platoon
PLR	Periodic Logistics Report
POL	Petroleum, oil, and lubricants
POR	Periodic Operations Report
Pub	Publication
PW	Prisoner of War

Rad	Radio
RCT	Regimental Combat Team
Rec	Recoilless
Recd	Received
Recon	Reconnaissance
Regt	Regiment
Rep	Representative
Res	Research
Rev	Review
Rpt	Report
RTO	Rail Transportation Office
S-1	Adjutant
S-2	Intelligence Officer
S-3	Operations and Training Officer
S-4	Supply Officer
S. Comm.	Senate Committee
SAR	Special Action Report
SCAP	Supreme Commander for the Allied Powers
SCR	Set complete radio
Sec	Section
Secy	Secretary
Sep	Separate
SFC	Sergeant First Class
Sig	Signal
Sitrep	Situation Report
SO	Special Order
SP	Self-propelled
Stf	Staff
Summ	Summary
Supp	Supplement
Surg	Surgical
TACP	Tactical air control party
TAGO	The Adjutant General's Office
Telecon	Teletypewriter conference
TF	Task Force
Tk	Tank
T/O	Tables of Organization
Trans	Transport, Transportation
Transl	Translation
UNC	United Nations Command
UNRC	United Nations Reception Center
USAFIK	U.S. Army Forces in Korea
USSR	Union of Soviet Socialist Republics
VHF	Very High Frequency
VT	Variable Time Fuze
WD	War Diary
WIA	Wounded in action
Wkly	Weekly

Basic Military Map Symbols

Symbols within a rectangle indicate a military unit, within a triangle an observation post, and within a circle a supply point.

Military Units—Identification

Antiaircraft Artillery	◁△▷
Armored Command	◯
Army Air Forces	∞
Artillery, except Antiaircraft and Coast Artillery	•
Cavalry, Horse	╱
Cavalry, Mechanized	∅
Chemical Warfare Service	G
Coast Artillery	◇
Engineers	E
Infantry	⊠
Medical Corps	⊞
Ordnance Department	⚭
Quartermaster Corps	Q
Signal Corps	S
Tank Destroyer	TD
Transportation Corps	⊛
Veterinary Corps	▽

Airborne units are designated by combining a gull wing symbol with the arm or service symbol:

Airborne Artillery	⌒•
Airborne Infantry	⌒⊠

Size Symbols

The following symbols placed either in boundary lines or above the rectangle, triangle, or circle inclosing the identifying arm or service symbol indicate the size of military organization:

Squad	•
Section	• •
Platoon	• • •
Company, troop, battery, Air Force flight	I
Battalion, cavalry squadron, or Air Force squadron	I I
Regiment or group; combat team (with abbreviation CT following identifying numeral)	I I I
Brigade, Combat Command of Armored Division, or Air Force Wing	X
Division or Command of an Air Force	XX
Corps or Air Force	XXX
Army	XXXX
Group of Armies	XXXXX

EXAMPLES

The letter or number to the left of the symbol indicates the unit designation; that to the right, the designation of the parent unit to which it belongs. Letters or numbers above or below boundary lines designate the units separated by the lines:

Company A, 137th Infantry	A ⊠ 137
8th Field Artillery Battalion	• 8
Combat Command A, 1st Armored Division	A ▭ 1
Observation Post, 23d Infantry	△ 23
Command Post, 5th Infantry Division	⊠ 5
Boundary between 137th and 138th Infantry	—137 / III / 138—

Weapons

Machine gun	•→
Gun	●
Gun battery	⊔⊔⊔
Howitzer or Mortar	✦
Tank	◇
Self-propelled gun	⬡

Index

A-day, 38th Parallel crossing: 622
A-frames: 183
Adams, 1st Lt. Raymond "Bodie": 74
Advance Attack Group: 504
Advance Command and Liaison Group in Korea (ADCOM): 42–44, 55–57
Advance Force, 95: 620
Advance Force, Joint Task Force 7: 620
Aerial bombing of mines: 633
Aerial observation: 101, 126, 130, 133, 153, 166, 211–12, 212n, 227, 228, 276, 316, 326, 401, 408, 420, 435, 437, 452, 470–71, 483, 500, 513, 531, 533, 538, 553, 571, 586, 625, 633, 644, 649n, 681, 689, 711, 713, 714–15, 717, 724, 731, 736, 742, 761, 769–70. *See also* Tactical air control parties.
Agok battle: 443–46
Air attacks, effectiveness of: 123
Air attacks, enemy: 45, 51, 152, 512
Air Force in Korea: 574n
Air forces, build-up: 118–19
Air-ground co-operation. *See* Air support.
Air strikes, friendly: 24, 62–63, 94, 140, 165, 241, 298, 371, 426, 478, 582–83, 627
Air supply. *See* Airdrops; Airlifts.
Air support: 51, 376–79
  acknowledged by Generals Kean and Walker: 476–77
  at Battle Mountain: 371, 372, 373, 374, 484, 569
  at Bowling Alley: 361, 363
  carrier-based: 52
  Changjin Reservoir: 742, 743
  Changnyong area: 467, 468
  Chinju: 227, 231, 578
  Ch'ongju area: 681, 682
  Chonui: 90–92, 93
  close: 95–96, 255–57, 256n, 567–68
  cover, evacuation of Seoul: 39
  flare missions, 378, 531
  Fox Hill: 272–76
  Haman area: 475, 480–81
  Hills 66 and 68: 524, 525
  Hills 92 and 113: 539
  Hill 116: 464
  Hill 117: 316–17
  Hill 120: 530
  Hill 303: 347
  Hill 314: 433, 434
  Hills 518 and 346: 413–14
  Hwanggan battle: 201
  Hyesanjin: 736
  Hyongsan-gang valley ambush: 326
  Hyopch'on area: 579–80, 580n

Air support—Continued
  for Inch'on landing: 497, 502, 503, 504–05, 506, 508–09, 511
  interdiction attacks: 376–79, 379n
  Kigye area: 400–401, 404
  Kilchu area: 731
  Komam-ni: 368
  Kum River Line: 130, 133, 134, 140
  Kumch'on Pocket: 623, 629
  lack of: 137
  Majon-ni: 724
  Masan area: 440
  Much'on-ni road fork: 244
  Mun'gyong plateau: 195
  Naktong River crossing sites: 298, 300, 304, 316, 317, 337, 338, 343, 346, 452
  Nam River: 471, 473
  Nanch'onjom: 640, 642
  the Notch: 270
  Obong-ni ridge line: 312, 313
  Pakch'on: 714
  P'ohang-dong area: 330, 332, 408
  Pongam-ni: 276, 278, 284, 285
  Pusan Perimeter: 550, 551, 553, 554, 559
  P'yongt'aek: 95, 598
  P'yongyang area: 649
  South Mountain: 530
  Taech'on area: 683
  Taegu front: 358
  Taejon: 152–53, 154, 165, 586
  Taeryong River: 681
  Triangulation Hill: 341
  Uijongbu: 540
  Unsan: 689, 691, 700, 703, 704
  Yalu River: 715–16
  Yongdok: 184–85, 186–87, 188, 192
  Yongdungp'o: 517
  Yonghung area: 724
  Yongsan-dong area: 679
  Yonil: 107
Airborne attacks: 654–58
Airborne battalions
  1st, 187th: 654–56
  2d, 187th: 657–58, 661
  3d, 187th: 526, 656, 658–61, 659n
Airborne Regiment, 187th: 654–61
Aircraft
  reconnaissance: 50
  reinforcements: 257, 257n
  transport: 50
Airdrops: 272, 300, 374, 452, 454, 457, 467, 470, 474, 477, 534, 654–61, 674, 677, 725, 728, 733

Airlifts: 56, 59, 60, 61, 61n, 115, 260, 380, 526, 612, 614, 617, 621, 632, 635, 639, 640, 668-69
Airsman, Capt. John: 184
Akridge, Capt. Clyde M.: 295
Alexander, Lt. Gerald N.: 372-73
Alfonso, Capt. A. F.: 296-98, 300
Alkire, Capt. Charles R.: 90, 91n
All-Weather Fighter Squadron, 68th: 39
All-Weather Fighter Squadron, 339th: 39
Allen, Brig. Gen. Frank A., Jr.: 421-22, 573, 622, 644, 661-63, 663n, 689, 708, 753. *See also* Task Force Allen.
Allen, Maj. Gen. Leven C.: 177n 382, 542, 550, 764, 774, 776
Almond, Maj. Gen. Edward M.: 56, 57, 120, 497, 634, 636, 723, 726, 772. *See also* Corps, X.
  and abandonment of Yonil Airfield: 329
  and amphibious landing controversy: 492-96
  and amphibious landing plans: 488
  appointed commander of X Corps: 490
  and capture of Seoul: 515-41, 539n
  estimates of CCF: 755-56, 764
  and Inch'on landing: 502, 510, 512
  at MacArthur-Walker conference: 206-07
  operational plans: 685-86
  and X Corps: 618, 620, 684
  and X Corps advance to Yalu: 729-48
Ambush Alley: 724-25
Ambushes, enemy: 326, 629-30, 632
Ambushes, guerrilla: 721-28
American Mission in Korea: 13
American troops, Chinese evaluation of: 719-20
Ammunition: 61, 68, 70
  shortages: 180, 228, 431, 474, 542
  smokeless powder, enemy use of: 140
  supply: 55-56, 149, 442, 452, 728, 733
Amphibious landings
  Inch'on: 488-514, 572
  P'ohang-dong: 196
  T'ongyong: 366
  Wonsan: 609-12, 618-21, 635-37
Amphibious landings, enemy: 106
Amphibious movement of X Corps: 631-35
Anderegg, Lt. Harold R.: 420
Anderson, Capt. Andrew C.: 476
Anderson, Capt. Clarence R.: 702, 705, 706-07, 707n
Anderson, Capt. Monroe: 136
Andong, battle of: 187-88
Andrews, Rear Adm. W. G.: 497
An'gang-ni area, battles in: 319-33
Ansong: 77-78, 80, 81
Antiaircraft Artillery Battalions
  15th: 736
  26th: 133
  40th: 50n
  50th: 503n
  76th: 693
  82d: 325n, 444, 450n, 460, 462, 550, 652

Antiaircraft Artillery Battalions—Continued
  92d: 199
  507th: 46
  865th: 402
  933d: 402
Antiaircraft Artillery Group, 10th: 677, 677n, 693
Antiguerrilla activities: 16, 27, 107, 721-28
Antitank mines: 72
Anui, battle of: 223-24, 224n
Applegate, MSgt. James A.: 219, 220
Arawaka, Cpl. Jack: 139
Argyll Regiment. *See* British Battalion, 1st, Argyll and Sutherland Highlanders Regiment.
Armored Artillery Battalion, 58th: 740
Armored Division, 1st: 380
Armored School, Fort Knox: 380
Arnold, Maj. Charles E.: 233-34
Artillery, Chinese evaluation of: 720
Artillery, enemy: 11-12, 17-18, 18n, 25, 53, 154, 264, 264n, 301, 302, 344
Artillery Battalions. *See* Field Artillery Battalions.
Artillery strikes, friendly: 84, 93, 135, 199, 229, 241-42, 290, 371, 419
Artillery support
  Battle Mountain: 368-75, 484, 569-70
  Changnyong: 468
  Ch'ongch'on bridgehead: 713
  Chonui: 93
  Cloverleaf Hill: 306, 314, 315
  Haman area: 480, 481
  Hill 99: 401, 404
  Hill 201: 551
  Hill 518: 413, 414
  How Hill: 743-44
  Kuhe-ri ferry road: 473
  Kum River Line: 132-37
  Kumch'on Pocket: 623, 628
  Masan area: 274
  Naktong River crossing sites: 298, 316, 555
  Nam River: 470-71
  Ohang Hill: 310-11, 315
  Pongam-ni area: 285
  Sangju area: 194
  Seoul: 515, 517-18, 525, 529-30, 531, 532, 538, 539
  Siban-ni: 559
  Sibidang-san: 476
  Taegu front: 337, 339, 340-41, 344, 347, 359-60, 363
  Taeryong River area: 681
  of Task Force Smith: 65-76
  of 35th Infantry: 721
  Unsan area: 679, 689, 691-93
  Yesong River: 626-27
  Yongdok: 185, 187
  Yongsan: 464, 465
Artillery-tank battles: 30, 68-72, 68n, 69n, 81, 86, 90
Atrocities: 94, 143, 347-50, 348n, 435, 477-78, 540, 587-88, 588n, 661-63, 663n

INDEX

Attack Force: 635
Attack Force 90: 620
Augmentation. *See* Korean augmentation.
Austin, Capt. Bernard L. (USN): 497, 620
Austin, Warren: 487n
Australian Air Force: 58
Australian Battalion, 3d: 614, 644–46, 660, 660n, 681–82, 713–15
Aviation gasoline, supply of: 257, 257n
Ayres, Lt. Col. Harold B.: 77, 79–83, 100, 129, 129n, 154–56, 166–68, 166n, 178, 294–98

B–26's: 50, 95, 118, 361
B–29's: 50, 51, 118, 119, 256, 352, 376–79, 531
B rations, 5-in-1: 115
Babb, 1st Lt. Earl: 91n
Badoeng Strait: 274–75
Baker, Capt. Claude: 280
Baker, 1st Lt. Robert W.: 593–98
Balboni, Pfc. Joseph W.: 712, 712n
Baldwin, Hanson W.: 209
Ball, Lt. Doric E.: 727
Baltimore Sun: 661
Barnhard, Lt. Donald E.: 239
Barr, Maj. Gen. David G.: 521, 528, 735–37. *See also* Infantry Division, 7th.
Barricade fighting: 531–36
Barrow, Capt. Robert: 518–19
Barszcz, Capt. Michael: 142–44, 161, 177–78, 220–21, 227–28, 229–30, 309
Barter, Maj. Charles T.: 126
Barth, Brig. Gen. George B.: 65, 65n, 79–80, 82, 284, 286
Bartholdi, Capt. Cyril S.: 449
Battalion Landing Team: 504, 506
Battalions. *See* Antiaircraft Artillery Battalions; Cavalry Battalions; Engineer Combat Battalions; Field Artillery Battalions; Infantry Battalions; Marine Battalions; Tank Battalions.
Battle Mountain (Hill 665): 368–75, 438, 439, 483–87, 568–70
Baumgartner, Pfc. William L.: 283–84
Baxter, SFC Earl R.: 436, 436n
Bazooka-tank battles: 69–72, 86–87, 156–57, 162–64, 163n, 193, 197–98, 201, 314–15, 353, 356–57, 359, 461, 465, 509–10, 517, 519, 532, 539, 596–97, 602, 648, 682
Bazookas, 2.36-inch: 69–72
Beachhead Line: 509
Beahler, Lt. Lee E.: 460–61, 461n
Beauchamp, Col. Charles E.: 147–81, 150n, 213, 225–26, 291–98, 389, 520, 528, 529
Beavers, Capt. Harold R.: 521
Beech, Keyes: 33, 40
"Beer issue": 485
Belfast: 185
Belgian Government: 115

Bell, 1st Lt. James H.: 649, 649n
Bernard, 2d Lt. Carl F.: 74
Berry, SFC Oscar V.: 444n, 445
Best, Robert: 434n
Bexar: 491
Bigart, Homer: 91n
Bissett, Maj. David, A., Jr.: 147, 154
Bixler, Lt. Ray: 92–94
Blair, Maj. Melvin R.: 484, 576n
Bloody Gulch: 276–86, 308
Bloody Knob. *See* Battle Mountain.
Blue Beach: 499, 506–07, 634, 636
BLUEHEARTS: 488–89
Bo An Dae. *See under* North Korean units.
Bolt, Capt. Jack: 689, 697–98, 697n, 700
Bombardment Group, 19th: 51
Bomber Command, Far East Air Forces: 256–57
Bomber Group, 19th: 352
Bomber Group, 22d: 352
Bomber Group, 92d: 352
Bomber Group, 98th: 352
Bomber Group, 307th: 352
Bombing. *See* Air support.
Bombing, carpet. *See* Carpet bombing.
Bowen, Col. Frank S., Jr.: 654–58
Bowling Alley: 353–63, 363n, 411, 421
Bowser, Col. Alpha L.: 532
Boxer: 497, 502
Boyd, 2d Lt. Ralph C.: 172–73, 173n
Bradley, Brig. Gen. Joseph S.: 325–27, 450–51, 460, 467. *See also* Task Force Bradley.
Bradley, General of the Army Omar N.: 382, 760
Bridges: 81, 152, 153, 342–44, 377
  blowing of: 65, 80, 90, 100, 121–22, 123, 131, 131n, 134, 175, 182, 184, 226, 250–52, 324, 378, 575, 578, 650, 734, 748
  construction of: 556–57, 560
  destroyed: 598, 610, 665, 737
  floating: 551, 556–57, 640, 734
  repairing of: 580, 626, 639–40, 665
  underwater: 555, 575, 591, 592
Bridges, enemy
  destroyed: 444
  floating: 459
  underwater: 301–02, 338, 345–46, 351, 437, 442, 459, 588
British Battalion, 1st, Argyll and Sutherland Highlanders Regiment: 382, 470, 582–83, 644–46, 660, 682, 713–14
British Battalion, 1st, Middlesex Regiment: 382, 582, 625, 660, 665, 681, 713–14
British Commonwealth Brigade, 27th: 614, 625, 642–46, 647, 659–61, 665, 670–72, 681, 683, 709–15, 719. *See also* British Brigade, 27th Infantry.
British Brigade, 27th Infantry: 382–83, 411–15, 453, 469–70, 545, 547, 553, 556, 574n, 582–83, 582n, 606, 613. *See also* British Commonwealth Brigade, 27th.

British Brigade, 29th: 668
British troops in Korea: 382-83
Bromser, 1st Lt. Paul F.: 706
Bronze Star Medal: 154n
Brown, Lt. Frank: 22
Brown, Pfc. Melvin L.: 428-29, 429n
Brown, Lt. Russell: 716
Brush: 633
Buchanan, Capt. Earl W.: 235, 236
Buchanan, Capt. Neil A.: 470
Buckley, 1st Lt. Harry A.: 340
Buckley, 1st Lt. John A.: 200-201
Buddy system: 387-89, 388n, 492
"Buffalo" guns: 304
"Bugle Hill": 704
Build-up: 149
 air: 255-57, 376-79
 ground: 379-89
 ROK forces: 384-86
 supplies and equipment: 259-60
 tanks: 380-81, 381n
Build-up, enemy: 365-66
Bundy, Capt. Walt W.: 599n
Burp guns: 69, 347-49

C-47's: 45, 153, 654
C-54's: 44, 61, 61n, 663
C-119's: 380, 654-56
C rations: 115
Caldwell, 1st Lt. Charles I.: 446-47, 456n, 458-59
Camel's Head Bend: 680, 700-708
Canadian forces: 668
Cannon, 85-mm.: 69, 70, 71
Canzona, Capt. Nicholas A.: 259n
Carpet bombing: 350-53
Carson, Maj. Eugene J.: 482
Cashe, Lt.: 98
Casualties: 260-63, 262n, 275, 662-63
 Airborne Regiment, 187th: 658, 661
 Australian: 682, 714
 Cavalry: 199-200, 205, 342, 344-45, 421, 434, 434n, 561, 563, 627, 699, 704, 707-08
 Eighth Army: 391, 605, 606, 774
 Engineer: 244, 556
 Field Artillery: 128-29, 241, 285-86, 295, 325-26, 375
 Infantry: 88, 93, 94, 98, 98n, 122, 141, 161, 179-80, 194-95, 202-03, 221, 221n, 224, 240, 246, 306, 307, 325, 373, 389n, 407, 448, 449-50, 459n, 468-69, 475, 484, 554, 555, 570
 Marine: 272, 274, 276, 276n, 313, 315, 316, 316n, 464, 506, 507, 509, 517, 518, 524, 525, 534, 541, 541n, 723, 744
 from mines: 633-34, 635
 nonbattle: 262, 269, 272, 275, 304, 391, 735, 738, 744
 on Pusan Perimeter: 437, 465

Casualties—Continued
 ROK: 22, 34, 35, 188, 262-63, 391, 434, 434n, 524, 561, 686, 707, 728, 731, 774n
 Seoul battle: 541, 541n
 X Corps: 774
 United Nations: 263, 437, 547
Casualties, enemy: 27, 29, 34-35, 55, 76, 76n, 95, 102, 103, 106, 179, 185, 187, 188, 193, 195, 200, 203, 205, 246, 247, 263, 263n, 270, 272-73, 274, 275n, 316, 317, 327, 332, 341, 342, 344, 354, 360, 363, 366, 454, 461, 469, 471, 478, 481, 519, 524, 525, 527, 530, 531, 539, 540, 540n, 546, 553, 564n, 565, 567, 579, 659, 660, 683, 713, 714, 724, 731, 742, 743-44
Cavalry Battalions
 1st, 5th Cavalry: 198, 205, 347, 563, 564, 625, 681, 691, 704
 2d, 5th Cavalry: 199, 347, 414, 419-21, 554, 625, 630, 648-50, 651, 691, 703-05
 3d, 5th Cavalry: 390n, 391, 630, 650, 652, 680-81, 690, 704
 1st, 7th Cavalry: 185, 186, 340-41, 342, 344, 413-15, 418-20, 565-66, 592, 626-27, 629, 642, 643, 645-46, 704
 2d, 7th Cavalry: 203, 343-45, 413-14, 417-20, 432, 562, 563-66, 627, 629-30, 640, 645, 708
 3d, 7th Cavalry: 390n, 413-15, 418-20, 431-35, 434n, 562, 565-66, 627, 642, 643, 647, 652, 708
 1st, 8th Cavalry: 197-98, 411, 566, 614, 623, 661, 679-80, 691-94, 695-96, 698-700
 2d, 8th Cavalry: 197, 198-99, 411, 421, 427-29, 435, 562, 562n, 679, 680, 693, 694, 695, 696, 698-99
 3d, 8th Cavalry: 390n, 411, 421, 430-31, 432, 562, 679, 680, 681, 691, 695, 697, 699, 700-707, 700n, 701n
Cavalry Division, 1st: 206, 208, 235, 253, 254, 309, 382, 383, 390, 391, 395, 397, 613-14, 658, 669, 678, 680, 752n. *See also* Gay, Maj. Gen. Hobart R.
 and buddy system: 385-89
 at Inch'on: 488, 491
 Naktong River withdrawal: 251
 Parallel crossing: 623-30, 628n
 P'ohang-dong landing: 195-97
 Pusan Perimeter breakout: 543, 545, 547, 548, 552, 556, 560-66, 588-98
 P'yongyang, capture of: 640-53
 strength: 49, 50n, 547, 605, 606
 Taegu: 335-36, 339, 340-42, 345-47, 351-53, 361, 410, 411-36
 Taejon: 149, 150, 165, 177, 179, 181
 Yongdong: 197-200, 203-05
Cavalry Regiments
 5th: 99n, 196, 197, 198, 199-200, 204, 254, 337, 339, 341-42, 345-50, 348n, 411-15, 419-21, 432, 435, 553, 554, 561-62, 563, 565, 593, 598, 614, 623-25, 627, 628, 630, 642, 643, 643n, 648-53, 679, 680-81, 691-708

INDEX

Cavalry Regiments—Continued
  7th: 196, 202, 204, 205, 254, 337, 343-45, 390-91, 411-15, 413n, 417-20, 431-32, 433, 553, 556, 562, 590-98, 597n, 614, 623, 625-28, 629-30, 640, 642, 643, 645-46, 647-53, 690, 704
  8th: 196, 197, 198, 199, 204, 254, 337, 390-91, 411-15, 421-32, 432-36, 562, 562n, 565-66, 593, 597, 614, 623, 627, 628-29, 630, 678-80, 690-708, 720
Cavalry, ROK: 128
Cemetery Hill: 499, 506
Chae Byong Duk, Maj. Gen.: 12, 29, 30, 31, 32, 33, 40, 43-44, 56, 215, 216
Chai Ung Jun, General: 19
Champney, Col. Arthur S.: 271, 365-75, 367n, 438-441, 479-83
Chandler, Lt. Col. Homer B.: 141
Chandler, Capt. Melbourne C.: 420
Chang Chang Kuk, Maj. Gen.: 16n, 32-33
Chang Ky Dok: 312
Changdok Palace: 531
Changhowon-ni battle: 104
Changjin Power Plant 3: 741
Changjin (Chosin) Reservoir: 671, 685, 686-88, 718, 726, 729n, 741-45, 755, 766, 767, 768, 772-73
Changnyong battle: 466-69
Chech'on, fall of: 103-04
Check, Lt. Col. Gilbert J.: 200-201, 236, 237-38, 237n, 242-44, 245-46, 475, 478, 479-83
Cheek, Maj. Leon B.: 226
Chiang Kai-shek: 749, 758
Chiles, Col. John H.: 528
Chinch'on, fall of: 102
Chindong-ni: 236-39, 236n, 242, 243, 244-47, 271-74. *See also* Chinju-Masan corridor.
Chinese Communist Forces (CCF): 9-10, 310, 486, 500
  at Changjin Reservoir: 686-88
  enter Korean War: 673-88
  extent of intervention: 749-70
  veterans of, in N.K. forces: 332, 523, 567
Chinese Communist Forces units
  Army, Third Field: 751, 754, 756, 768
  Army, Fourth Field: 750-51, 758, 766, 768
  Army, 8th: 686
  Army, 8th Route: 293, 394, 704, 750
  Army, 20th: 756, 768, 768n
  Army, 26th: 768, 768n
  Army, 27th: 768, 768n
  Army, 38th: 711, 717, 751, 753, 763, 766, 768
  Army 39th: 708, 717-20, 751, 753, 763, 766, 768
  Army, 40th: 717-19, 751, 753, 763, 766, 768
  Army, 42d: 687, 718, 751-52, 754, 763, 766, 767, 768
  Army, 50th: 717, 751, 767, 768
  Army, 66th: 717-20, 751, 767, 768
  Army Corps, First: 750
  Army Group, IX: 756, 768-69
  Army Group, XIII: 687, 718, 766, 768-69

Chinese Communist Forces units—Continued
  Army Group, XIX: 708n
  Division, 1st Motorized Artillery: 766
  Division, 2d Motorized Artillery: 766
  Division, 8th Artillery: 767
  Division, 89th: 756, 768n
  Division, 115th: 708, 753
  Division, 116th: 708
  Division, 119th: 713
  Division, 120th: 713
  Division, 124th: 687-88, 718, 741, 743-44, 755, 767, 768
  Division, 125th: 674, 717, 718, 743, 754, 766, 767-68
  Division, 126th: 718, 733, 743, 755, 767, 768, 773
  Division, 139th: 10
  Division, 140th: 10
  Division, 141st: 10
  Division, 156th: 10
  Division, 164th: 9
  Division, 166th: 9
  Headquarters, CCF-NKA: 769
  Regiment, 5th: 686
  Regiment, 5th Truck: 767
  Regiment, 42d Truck: 767
  Regiment, 267th: 756
  Regiment, 347th: 708
  Regiment, 355th: 713
  Regiment, 358th: 713
  Regiment, 370th: 687, 742, 755
  Regiment, 371st: 687, 742, 743
  Regiment, 372d: 687, 743
  Regiment, 373d: 674
  Regiment, 374th: 754
  Regiment, 376th: 733
  Regiment, 377th: 773
  Unit, 54th. See Army, 38th.
  Unit, 55th. See Army, 39th.
  Unit, 56th. See Army, 40th.
Chinese Communist government: 765-66, 769
Chinese Communist threat to intervene: 607
Chinese evaluation of American troops: 719-20
Chinese First Phase Offensive. *See* First Phase Offensive (CCF).
Chinese intervention not credited: 690
Chinese Manchurian Army: 10
Chinese prisoners, interrogation of: 751-53, 754-56, 761
Chinese soldier, description of: 718-19
Chinju: 213-15, 222-23, 227-33, 242-44, 574-75, 577-79
Chinju-Masan corridor: 266, 267-68, 270-74
Chinju pass: 235, 236, 242-43, 268, 269, 286, 287, 570-71
Chiri-san area: 577, 722
Chirye: 203-05
Choch'iwon battle: 96-100
Choe Chu Yong, Maj.: 318n

Choe Hyon, Maj. Gen.: 580, 603
Choe Yong Gun, Marshal: 7, 31
Chon U, Maj. Gen.: 103
Ch'onan night battle: 80, 81, 82–88, 83n
Chong Myong Tok: 348n
Chong Pong Uk, Lt. Col.: 361
Ch'ongch'on River
    bridgehead: 709–15
    crossed: 683
    drive to: 654–66
Chonggo-dong: 682–83
Ch'ongjin, capture of: 732
Ch'ongju, fall of: 102
Ch'ongju battle: 681–82
Chonju, fall of: 210
Chonui battle: 89–95
Chosin Reservoir. *See* Changjin (Chosin) Reservoir.
Chou En-lai: 608, 758, 765
Christenson, Sgt. Jerry C.: 87, 87n
CHROMITE: 489
Chu Teh: 750
Ch'unch'on: 26–27, 103
Chung, Lt.: 386
Chung Il Kwon, Lt. Gen.: 56, 548n
Chungam-ni: 236, 236n, 239, 240. *See also* Notch, the.
Ch'ungju: 102, 103–104
Church, Maj. Gen. John H.: 44–45, 61, 62–63, 83, 188–89, 250, 252, 390n, 583, 588, 642–43, 682, 711–12, 776. *See also* Infantry Division, 24th.
    and ADCOM: 43–44, 43n, 44n, 55–58, 110
    and buddy system: 387
    commander, attack on Cloverleaf-Obong-ni: 310–18
    commander, 24th Division: 180
    Deputy Commander, USAFIK: 64
    and Masan action: 235–38, 236n
    and Naktong Bulge battle: 291–317
    and Naktong River action: 554–58
    and southwest Korea action: 213–14, 221, 225, 226, 231
    and Task Force Church: 405–06
    Task Force Davidson, sets up: 406
CINCFE Plan 202: 761
Civil Assistance Command: 670
Clainos, Lt. Col. Peter D.: 186, 340, 344, 386, 565–66, 626–27, 645–46
Claire, Sister Mary: 42n
Clark, Lt. Eugene F.: 501
Clarke, 1st Lt. Arthur M.: 79, 147, 162–63, 162n, 172, 176–77
Cleaborn, PFC Edward O.: 307
Clifford, Lt. Col. John: 704
Clifford, Lt. Col. Paul: 648
Cloverleaf Hill (Hill 165): 296–97, 298–302, 306–18, 448, 465, 466, 697
Coad, Brigadier Basil A.: 382, 660, 681, 682, 714
Code names, CCF use of: 753

Coghill, 1st Lt. William F.: 303n
Cold-weather fighting: 732, 735, 738, 744–45, 772–73
Cole, Lt. Col. George R.: 370
Collett: 503
Collier, Col. William A.: 109–10, 177n, 202, 308, 415, 462, 653
Collins, General Lawton J.: 47, 477n, 492–94, 495n
Collins, SFC Roy E.: 307
Collins, Sgt. Roy F.: 80–81
Combat Cargo Command: 617
Command
    changes in: 83–84
    estimates: 117–20
    problems, Eighth Army and X Corps: 609–12
    ROK forces, U.S.-U.N. relations between: 111–13
Commander in Chief, Far East: *See* MacArthur, General of the Army Douglas.
Communications: 248, 334, 416, 416n 593, 684. *See also* Lines of communication.
    at Battle Mountain: 369
    at Chinju-Masan corridor: 267
    inadequacy of: 110, 218
    lack of: 81, 123, 180, 215, 222, 225, 284, 426–27, 545, 592
    loss of: 70, 73–74, 92, 98, 127, 138, 272, 277, 280, 414, 452, 458, 466
    in North Korea: 610, 746
    for Pusan Perimeter: 105, 116–17
    at Taejon: 156, 157, 159, 161, 164, 167, 179
Conger, Capt. William: 483
Conley, Col. Edgar T., Jr.: 593
Connor, 2d Lt. Ollie D.: 69
Conscription, enemy, of South Koreans: 365–66, 590
Cook, Maj. John M.: 136
Cooper, Maj. Curtis: 166
Copper Mine Hill: 520
Corcoran, Capt. Lawrence M.: 374, 374n
Corley, Lt. Col. John T.: 285, 373, 441, 483–86, 576n
Corps, I: 112, 613–14, 622, 630, 642, 646–47, 659, 665, 672, 690, 694, 695n, 710, 718, 721, 753. *See also* Coulter, Maj. Gen. John B.; Milburn, Maj. Gen. Frank W.
    Pusan Perimeter, pursuit phase of breakout: 573, 592, 593
    Pusan Perimeter breakout: 543, 544–45, 544n, 547, 556
    strength: 605
    supply situation: 638, 668
Corps, IX: 613, 638, 771. *See also* Coulter, Maj. Gen. John B.; Milburn, Maj. Gen. Frank W.
    activated: 544–45, 544n
    and antiguerrilla activities: 721
    Pusan Perimeter, pursuit phase: 573–606
    Pusan Perimeter breakout: 573–74
    strength: 605
Corps, X: 112, 614, 666, 718, 772. *See also* Almond, Maj. Gen. Edward M.

INDEX

Corps, X—Continued
  amphibious landing, Wonsan: 618–21, 635–37
  amphibious movement: 631–35
  casualties: 774
  command relations with Eighth Army: 609–12
  Commanding General. *See* Almond, Maj. Gen. Edward M.
  disposition vis-à-vis Eighth Army: 745–48
  guerrilla activities against: 722–26
  intelligence estimate of CCF: 755–57
  link-up with Eighth Army: 588–98
  North Korea, moves into: 622–37
  operational plans: 684–86
  Pusan Perimeter, pursuit phase of breakout: 573, 593
  and Seoul, capture of: 515–41
  strength: 605, 684–85, 685n
  Yalu, advance to: 729–48
Corps, XXIV: 3
Corsairs: 312, 313, 508–09, 511
Coulter, Maj. Gen. John B.: 398–405, 404n, 544–45, 573–74. *See also* Corps, I; Corps, IX.
Counterattacks
  first American: 266–88
  Naktong Bulge battle: 294–98
Coursen, 1st Lt. Samuel S.: 625, 625n
Covering and Support Group, 95.2: 620
Cox, Capt. O'Dean T.: 98
Crabb, Brig. Gen. Jared V.: 36
Craig, Brig. Gen. Edward A.: 258, 272, 276, 308, 310, 313, 453, 462
Crane, Burton: 33, 33n, 40
Crawford, Maj. Richard I.: 31n
Croft, Maj. Lucian: 628
Crombez, Col. Marcel B.: 347, 623, 625, 630, 648–53
Cutler, Capt. Elliott C.: 236–37, 238, 241

D-day, Inch'on: 495, 498–99
Dabney, Col. John A.: 392, 415–16, 611
Dai Ichi Building: 493
Daly, Lt. Col. John H.: 277–78, 279, 279n
Dare, SFC Robert E.: 157, 157n
Darrigo, Capt. Joseph R.: 23, 23n, 326–27
Dashmer, Capt. Richard: 75
Davidson, Brig. Gen. Garrison H.: 391–92, 406–07, 711
Davidson Line: 391–92, 415–16
Dawson, Lt. Col. Robert H.: 126
Day, Cpl. Roy L., Jr.: 349
Dean, Maj. Gen. William F.: 59, 65, 106, 108, 110, 119, 188–89, 213, 766. *See also* Infantry Division, 24th.
  ambushed by "friendly" Koreans: 176–77
  awarded Medal of Honor: 177n
  commands USAFIK: 64
  and east coast defense: 106, 108
  estimate of enemy: 119

Dean, Maj. Gen. William F.—Continued
  General Dean's Story: 177
  gets him a tank: 162–63, 163n
  and Kum River Line: 122, 129, 130, 131, 136–37, 141, 142, 144
  and P'yongt'aek-Choch'iwon delaying action: 77–100
  and Taejon: 147–51, 152–55, 156–63, 164–79, 181
DeChow, Lt. Col. George H.: 475, 483–84
Defection of troops: 479–80, 482–83
Defense perimeters: 73, 128, 230, 308–09, 310, 315, 326, 330, 355, 358, 445, 447, 456–59, 701–07, 713–14, 724–25
DeHaven: 185, 503
Deloach, Maj. James W.: 660n
Democratic People's Republic of Korea: 5
Demolitions. *See under* Bridges.
Denness, Capt. A. P.: 660
DePalina, Capt. Fred P.: 563, 563n
Department of the Army: 669, 759, 763, 763n
Detachment X: 46
Dew, Capt. Manes R.: 466–67
Discipline, enemy: 546, 718–19
Distinguished Service Cross: 71n, 87, 98n, 128n, 157n, 244, 245n, 436n, 456n, 457n, 461n, 468n, 483, 563n, 597n, 599n, 659n, 682n, 711n, 712n, 727n
Distinguished Service Cross, Oak Leaf Cluster: 597n
Distinguished Unit Citation: 284n, 442n, 472, 562n, 597n, 659n, 714n
Dolvin, Lt. Col. Welborn G.: 578–79
Donahue, Capt. Joseph K.: 218, 221
Double envelopments: 73, 145, 201–02, 579, 756. *See also* Envelopments; Envelopments, enemy.
Doyle, Rear Adm. James H.: 196, 493, 494, 496, 497, 502, 509, 512, 619–20
Dressler, Maj. William E.: 126, 128
Drewery, Sgt. Marshall D.: 629
Drop Zone Easy: 657
Drop Zone William: 655
Duk Soo Palace: 531
Duke, Capt. Irving T. (USN): 620
Dukw's: 330, 559
Dunham, Maj. Leland R.: 156, 158–59, 166
Dunn, Maj. John J.: 81–82, 84–85, 87n
Dysentery, prevalence of: 180

Early, 2d Lt. Charles C.: 134, 136
East coastal road battle: 105–08, 182–87
Eberle, Maj. Gen. George L.: 257n, 492, 610, 612
Edson, Lt. Col. Hallett D.: 680–81, 689, 696–98
Edwards, Maj. Irwin A.: 520–22
Edwards, Lt. Col. James W.: 361, 450
Eighth Army: 55, 59, 88, 110–11, 113, 120, 177n, 227, 330, 675, 676, 718, 719
  assumes operational control of Korean campaign: 109–20

Eighth Army—Continued
  boundary lines shifted: 390
  casualties: 605, 774
  and CCF intervention: 751–55
  Ch'ongch'on River, drive to: 654–66
  and Ch'ongch'on River bridgehead: 709–15
  Civil Assistance Command in: 670
  command crisis: 415–17
  command relations with X Corps: 609–12
  commander. See Walker, Lt. Gen. Walton H.
  Coulter appointed deputy commander: 398
  disposition in North Korea vis-à-vis X Corps: 745–47
  and guerrilla activities: 726
  headquarters move to Pusan: 416, 416n
  intelligence estimates: 213, 303, 431, 437, 571, 647, 663, 677, 678
  and July crisis: 247
  North Korea, deploys for attack into: 612–14
  North Korea, moves into: 622–37
  orders attack to Yalu: 773–74
  Pusan Perimeter, breakout of: 542–72
  Pusan Perimeter breakout, pursuit after: 573–606
  realignment: 389–91
  reserve: 235, 253, 258, 267, 267n, 269, 302, 308, 318, 319, 353, 381, 389, 453, 479, 539n
  and ROK augmentation: 385–89, 388n
  and "stand or die" order: 205–06
  strength: 605, 606
  supply: 584, 638–40, 668–69, 771–72
  and Task Force Church: 405, 408
  and Task Force Jackson: 405
  and Task Force Kean: 267, 287
  withdrawal across Naktong: 249–52
Eighth Army Rear: 80, 381, 383
Eldorado: 633
Ellis, 1st Lt. Charles: 440
Ellis, Capt. Hubert H.: 711
Emery, Maj. Jack R.: 230
Emmerich, Lt. Col. Rollins S.: 40, 61, 107, 182–85, 323–25, 399–400, 402, 404, 406–07, 567, 615, 616, 686
Enemy
  attack routes to Pusan Perimeter: 289
  attack tactics: 315
  casualties. See Casualties, enemy.
  claims: 88, 129n, 188, 347n
  conscription of South Koreans: 590
  deserters: 361
  equipment. See Equipment, enemy.
  expulsion of, from South Korea: 600–604
  operations in central mountains: 101–05
  operations on east coast: 105–08
  units. See North Korean units; Chinese Communist Forces units.
Engineer Combat Battalions
  2d: 325n, 446, 451, 460–61, 362–64, 551

Engineer Combat Battalions—Continued
  3d: 90, 99, 100, 123, 152, 156–57, 162–63, 173, 250, 298, 406, 554, 556, 665, 712
  8th: 205, 424–30, 432, 588, 590, 626–27, 629
  11th: 556
  13th: 732
  14th: 250, 254, 302
  18th: 521
  65th: 244, 362, 475, 484
  67th: 576n
  72d: 284
Engineer Combat Group: 19th: 503n, 708
Engineer Special Brigade, 2d: 503n, 511, 685n
Engle, 2d Lt. Marshall G.: 434
English, Lt. John A.: 136
Envelopments: 194, 623–30, 646, 650, 731, 732. See also Double envelopments.
Envelopments, enemy: 92, 98, 101, 154, 158, 178, 179, 181, 185, 212, 222–24, 677. See also Double envelopments.
Epley, Col. Gerald G.: 551
Equipment: 113–14
  abandoned: 82, 85, 194, 199, 203, 208, 219, 295, 674, 698–99, 711
  airdropped: 656–57
  deliberate destruction of: 143, 172, 414, 711
  enemy use of: 318, 333, 435, 467, 688
  losses: 88, 98–99, 128, 144, 179, 221, 244, 251, 285, 286n, 375, 381, 563, 602, 699, 707–08, 708n
Equipment, enemy
  abandoned: 226, 243, 443, 550, 580, 591–92, 603
  captured: 410, 587, 616, 666, 725
  destroyed: 30, 359, 628, 629, 719, 731, 746–47
  losses: 27, 29–30, 46, 72, 90, 91n, 95, 102, 103, 163–64, 179, 201, 205, 270, 275, 317, 318, 318n, 362, 363, 531, 539, 540–41, 550, 551, 553–54, 557, 565, 579, 586, 590, 600–602, 602n, 682, 683
Equipment, Soviet-manufactured. See Soviet-manufactured equipment.
Escort Carrier Group, 96.8: 620
Estimate of enemy situation, July: 212
Evacuation of U.S. nationals from Korea: 38–40
Everest, Maj. Gen. Frank F.: 118–19
Eversole, Sgt. Edwin A.: 71
Ewen, Rear Adm. Edward C.: 497, 620
Exchange rate: 115, 384–85

F4U Corsair description: 96. See also Corsairs.
F–51's (Mustang): 17, 51, 96, 153, 257, 321, 329
F–80's: 39, 51, 95
  description: 96
  MIG, first battle with: 716
F–80C: 51
F–82's: 39, 95
Faber, Harold: 348n
Fairrey, Lt. Robin D.: 645
Faith, Lt. Col. Don C., Jr.: 522, 530–31

INDEX 793

Far East Air Forces (FEAF): 36, 39, 44, 50, 51, 62–63, 95, 120, 256–57, 321, 329, 352–53, 376–79, 531, 548, 605, 606, 614. *See also* Stratemeyer, Lt. Gen. George E.
Far East Bomber Command: 352-53
Far East Command: 46, 56, 101, 120, 211, 753. *See also* MacArthur, General of the Army Douglas.
   deactivates Pusan Logistical Command: 574
   decision on two separate field commands: 609–10
   establishes corps organization: 544
   estimate of CCF intervention: 757–65, 763n
   evacuation plan: 39
   and intelligence of enemy strength in Seoul: 500–501
   intelligence, faulty: 353
   and July crisis: 214
   naval strength: 50
   and plans for amphibious landing: 195–96, 488–89
   policy on Koreans attached to U.S. units: 667
   requests naval support: 452
   and ROK augmentation: 385–89, 388n
   "roll-up" plan: 114
Farrell, Brig. Gen. Francis W.: 324. *See also* Korean Military Advisory Group (KMAG).
Farthing, Maj. Arthur: 235
Fast Carrier Force, 77: 620
Felhoelter, Chaplain Herman G.: 143
Fenstermacher, Capt. Edgar R.: 140, 143, 143n
Fentriss: 214
Ferguson, Lt. Col. I. B.: 645, 682
Fern, 2d Lt. Albert J., Jr.: 445, 454–56
Ferry crossing sites: 122, 134, 136, 291, 293, 337, 338, 339, 343, 442, 443–44, 444n, 446–47, 459, 515, 528, 554, 555, 558, 584, 591–92, 593
Field, Lt. Col. Eugene J.: 198
Field Artillery Battalions
   8th: 242, 244, 245–46, 267, 353–63, 479, 575, 727, 727n
   9th: 413n, 430, 699
   10th: 385n, 740
   11th: 90, 126, 132–33, 134, 135, 138, 144, 144n, 147, 179, 230, 231, 245, 385n, 389
   13th: 99, 132–33, 138, 141, 144, 152, 179, 219, 225, 226, 228, 230, 231, 237, 237n, 294–98, 306, 389, 406
   15th: 258, 299, 303, 325-26, 402, 406, 538
   16th: 385n
   17th: 385n, 431, 677n
   18th: 321, 385n
   37th: 354–63, 450n
   39th: 740
   48th: 521, 529–30
   49th: 732
   50th: 385n
   52d: 63, 68, 76n, 132, 137–38, 143, 144, 175, 389
   57th: 538
   61st: 198–99, 340, 341, 347, 413n, 713–14, 714n
   63d: 86, 100, 123–30, 129n, 154n, 179, 389

Field Artillery Battalions—Continued
   64th: 194, 367–75, 470–71, 476
   77th: 199, 343, 344, 413n, 566, 590, 593, 597, 629
   82d: 196, 347, 413n, 689–90
   90th: 192, 194, 277, 280, 282, 283, 284n, 285–86, 367–75, 476, 569, 665
   92d: 503n
   96th: 503n, 724, 740
   99th: 198–99, 205, 421, 430, 597, 689, 690, 697, 697n, 699, 700
   159th: 49, 194, 274, 280, 284, 370, 375, 441, 476
   503d: 450n
   555th (Triple Nickel): 258, 274, 277–78, 277n, 279, 279n, 280, 282–83, 285–86
   674th: 656
Fielder, Wilson, Jr.: 166
Fields, 1st Lt. Joseph A.: 434
Fifth Air Force: 39, 51, 95–96, 212–13, 329–31, 476–77, 614, 715–16, 719, 744. *See also* Partridge, Maj. Gen. Earl E.
Fifth column activity in Seoul: 34
Fighter-Bomber Squadron, 35th: 39, 106, 107, 184
Fighter-Interceptor Squadron, 16th: 543
Fighter-Interceptor Squadron, 25th: 543
Fighter-Interceptor Squadron, 40th: 184–85, 329
Fighter-Interceptor Wing, 51st: 543
Fighter Wing, 6131st: 329
Fire discipline: 374n
First Phase Offensive (CCF): 714, 717–20, 746, 755–56, 767
Fisher, Col. Henry G.: 108, 191–93, 191n, 364–75, 438–43, 462–63, 470–79
Flagler, Maj. George W.: 404n
Flagship Group, 70.1: 620
Flare missions: 378, 531
Flares: 339, 357, 359, 367
Fleet Marine Force: 50
Fleming, Lt. Col. Harry: 663n, 672–75
Flying Fish Channel: 498, 503
Flynn, Capt. John R.: 216–20, 592
Forney, Col. Edward H.: 488, 528, 528n
Fort Benning Infantry School: 380, 492
Fort Sill Artillery School: 492
Foster, Lt. Col. Ralph L.: 652
Fowler, 1st Lt. Samuel R.: 231–33
Fox, Maj. Gen. Alonzo P.: 502, 510
Fox Hill: 271–74
Frederick, Capt. Charles D.: 535
Freeman, Sgt. Herbert H.: 455–56, 456n
Freeman, Col. Paul L., Jr.: 361, 448–50, 466, 467, 548, 580
Front lines, length of: 337
Frostbite: 735, 738
Fusen Reservoir: *See* Pujon (Fusen) Reservoir.

Galloway, Col. Donald H.: 489
Garvin, Brig. Gen. Crump: 116, 149, 392, 416–17

Gay, Maj. Gen. Hobart R.: 390, 661, 678, 680. *See also* Cavalry Division, 1st.
   and blowing of Waegan bridge: 251
   and North Korean drive: 623–30
   and plans for 1st Cavalry Division: 195–97
   and Pusan Perimeter battle: 397–436, 434n
   and P'yongyang, capture of: 642–53
   requests bombing in Waegan area: 352
   and Tabu-dong to Osan drive: 588–98
   and Taegu, encirclement above: 561–66
   at Triangulation Hill: 340–42
   and Unsan battle: 689–708
   and Yongdong battle: 203–06
   and Yongp'o battle: 344
General Headquarters, Far East Command: 51. *See also* MacArthur, General of the Army Douglas.
General Headquarters Reserve: 490, 503n, 619, 654
General Headquarters, Special Planning Staff: 490
General Headquarters, United Nations Command: 51. *See also* MacArthur, General of the Army Douglas.
Geneva Prisoner of War Convention: 262
Geography of Korea: 1–2, 101–02, 104–05, 121, 190
Gibney, Frank: 33, 40
Gilbert, 1st Lt. Leon A.: 195, 195n
Glasgow, 1st Lt. William M.: 449
Gonegan, Pfc.: 517
Gordon-Ingram, Maj. A. I.: 583
Government House, Seoul: 4, 523, 528, 531, 534, 535, 536, 537
Gramling, Maj. Roy M.: 673–74
Greco, Col. John F.: 404n
Green, Lt. Col. Charles H.: 614, 646, 660, 660n, 682
Green Beach: 499
Green Diamond route: 722
Green Peak: 369. *See also* Sobuk-san.
Greenwood, Col. Walter, Jr.: 21n, 32, 40
"Grenade, cooking the": 473n
Grenades, thermite: 359
Griffin, Lt.: 233
Ground General School: 384
Group, 92d: 564
Group, 98th: 564
Growden, Lt. Col. John S.: 676
Guerrilla activities: 27, 477–78, 577, 721–28, 747, 748, 761
Guerrillas: 7, 8, 105, 106, 211, 319, 383–84, 599, 740
Guiraud, Capt. Rene J.: 425, 696, 698
Gunfire Support Group: 503
Guns. *See also* Artillery; Howitzers; Mortars; Recoilless rifles.
   37-mm.: 114
   40-mm.: 114
   75-mm.: 114
   76-mm.: 114
   76-mm., divisional: 17, 18n
   105-mm.: 114

Gurke: 503
Guthrie, Col. John S.: 740

H-hour, 24 November attack: 774
Hachi Shiki: 719
Hackett, Capt. Alan: 136
Hadong, trap at: 215–21
Hadongsan-ni: 747, 748
Haeju: 21, 642
Hafemen, Capt. George B.: 303
Hagaru-ri: 729n
Haman counterattack: 479–83
Hamch'ang: 191–93
Hamilton, Maj. William E.: 23n
Hammerquist, Capt. Robert E.: 477
Hampton, Lt. Col. Henry: 521–22
Han River
   advance toward: 511–14
   bridges, blowing of: 32–34
   crossing: 105, 526–31
   description: 101–02
Handrich, MSgt. Melvin O.: 375, 375n
Hannum, Lt. Col. Calvin S.: 521–22
Hansel, 1st Lt. Morgan B.: 711, 711n
Hare, 1st Lt. Percy R.: 68n
Harris, Maj. Gen. Field: 773
Harris, Lt. Col. William A.: 199, 566, 590–98, 626–28, 642, 643, 648
Harris, Col. William W.: 740, 747
Hartman, Rear Adm. Charles C.: 567, 620
Harvey, Capt. Charles V. H.: 204–05
Harvey, Capt. James H.: 239
Hasan-dong ferry crossing site: 554
Hashimoto, Cpl. Hideo: 473
Haskins, 1st Sgt. James W. R.: 143
Hatfield, Capt. Raymond D.: 147, 168–69
Hausman, Maj. James W.: 14n, 16n, 24n, 29, 33, 43
Haynes, Brig. Gen. Loyal M.: 450, 466, 468
Haynes, 1st Lt. Marvin H.: 434
Hazlett, Col. Robert T.: 31n, 33, 43, 57, 695n, 572n
Heat exhaustion: 139, 262, 269, 272, 274, 275, 298, 304, 341, 391
Heater, Pvt. Leotis E.: 86
Heath, Col. Louis T.: 528
Helicopters used to evacuate wounded: 703n
Henderson, Rear Adm. George R.: 497, 620
Hennig, Col.: 690, 752n
Heo Chang Keun: 348n
Herbert, 2d Lt. Robert L.: 159–60, 162, 167, 170, 171n
Hess, Maj. Dean E.: 17, 376–77, 377n
Hickey, Maj. Gen. Doyle O.: 462, 492, 493, 550, 571, 573, 589, 609, 610, 612, 622, 753, 764
Hicks, Lt. Joseph E.: 130
Higbee: 185
Higgins, Rear Adm. J. M.: 185, 502–03
Higgins, Marguerite: 40
Highways. *See* Roads.

INDEX

Hill, Col. John G.: 258, 299–307, 446–47, 463, 465
Hill, Lt. John G., Jr.: 596
Hill, Lt. W. C.: 701–02
Hill 66: 524–25
Hill 79: 535
Hill 80: 511, 516
Hill 85: 511, 516
Hill 88: 524, 525
Hill 91: 464
Hill 92: 539
Hill 94: 443–44
Hill 97: 656
Hill 99: 401, 511
Hill 102: 312, 314, 315
Hill 104: 516, 656
Hill 105: 523–25, 526
Hill 107: 511
Hill 109: 312, 314, 315, 316
Hill 113: 539
Hill 116: 464
Hill 117: 312, 314, 315, 316
Hill 118: 511, 516–17, 518
Hill 119: 697
Hill 120: 528, 530–31
Hill 121: 553
Hill 123: 512, 712
Hill 125: 465, 515
Hill 131: 407
Hill 132: 536
Hill 133: 536
Hill 138: 151
Hill 140: 584
Hill 142: 538
Hill 143: 312, 316
Hill 143: 314
Hill 147: 312, 316
Hill 152: 571
Hill 153: 312, 316
Hill 163: 659
Hill 165. *See* Cloverleaf Hill.
Hill 174: 420–21, 555, 558, 563, 625
Hill 175: 625
Hill 178: 511
Hill 179: 472–73, 625
Hill 181: 186, 323, 401, 431–32
Hill 182: 431–32
Hill 188: 262–63, 420–21
Hill 200: 131, 131n, 134, 135, 139, 145
Hill 201: 338, 351, 548, 551, 558
Hill 202: 276
Hill 203: 420–21, 432, 563
Hill 206: 316–17
Hill 207: 559
Hill 208: 511, 550
Hill 209: 446–48, 447n, 456–59, 459n, 467, 468
Hill 223: 317
Hill 224: 536
Hill 227: 559

Hill 239: 560
Hill 240: 317
Hill 250: 276
Hill 253: 563–64
Hill 255: 273–74
Hill 268: 340–42, 553
Hill 276. *See* Sibidang-san.
Hill 281: 658
Hill 282: 582
Hill 284: 467
Hill 285: 406
Hill 296: 516, 523, 524–25, 534
Hill 300: 406, 407, 520, 564, 564n, 565
Hill 301: 276
Hill 303: 345–50, 414, 415, 419, 554
Hill 308: 551
Hill 311: 317, 448
Hill 314: 431, 432–36, 434n
Hill 325. *See* Middlesex Hill.
Hill 334: 401
Hill 338: 534, 536
Hill 345: 420
Hill 346: 338, 351, 412–13
Hill 342. *See* Fox Hill.
Hill 348: 529–30, 351
Hill 351: 562
Hill 371: 564
Hill 380: 418–20
Hill 388: 582
Hill 401: 435
Hill 409: 309–10, 343, 452, 469–70, 551, 560, 581
Hill 438: 401
Hill 445: 401
Hill 448: 421
Hill 464: 414, 417–20
Hill 475. *See* Songak-san.
Hill 482: 406, 407
Hill 490: 414
Hill 510: 406
Hill 518: 411–15, 420, 433, 434
Hill 534: 741
Hill 570: 430–31, 432–33, 435, 562, 562n
Hill 611: 743
Hill 622: 710–11
Hill 660: 431, 432
Hill 665. *See* Battle Mountain.
Hill 698: 741
Hill 738. *See* Sobuk-san.
Hill 743. *See* P'il-bong.
Hill 750. *See* How Hill battle.
Hill 755: 425, 426–29, 435
Hill 902. *See* Ka-san.
Hill 915: 383
Hill 928: 409
Hillery, Lt.: 165
Hitchner, Maj. Omar T.: 419
Hodes, Brig. Gen. Henry I.: 528, 529
Hodes, 1st Lt. John T.: 644

Hodge, Lt. Gen. John R.: 3, 4
Hoeryong: 731
Hoffman, Sgt. Evert E. "Moose": 241
Holley, Lt. Col. William C.: 424–29, 588
Holliday, 1st Lt. Sam C.: 223
Holmes, Col. Ernest V.: 423–29, 562, 588, 694
Holmes, Lt. Col. Robert: 700
Holt, Maj. Robert B.: 728
Holt, Capt. Vyvyan: 42n
Hongch'on: 103
Hopkins, Sgt. Willard H.: 596–97, 597n
"Horseshoe," the: 475
"Hot pursuit" doctrine: 716
How Hill battle: 742–43
Howard, Cpl. Billie: 596
Howitzers, 105-mm: 16–17, 55–56, 66–72, 68n, 119, 261, 298
Howitzers, 122-mm: 17, 18n
Howitzers, 155-mm: 135, 282, 298, 476
Howitzers, 8-inch: 431
Hutchin, Lt. Col. Claire E., Jr.: 448–50, 467–68, 468n
Hutchins, Capt. Walter J: 407
Huff, Lt. Col. Gilmon A: 627
Hughes, 1st Lt. John C: 222–24, 224n
Hughes, Capt. Kenneth W: 217n
Huich'on, capture of: 666
Hull, Lt. Gen. John E.: 2–3
Hungate, Maj. William C., Jr: 404n
Hungnam, capture of: 614–18
Hunt, Father Charles: 42n
Hunt, Lt. Col. Lewis A.: 116
Hwa-san. See Hill 928.
Hwach'on Dam: 722
Hwanggan battle: 200–203
Hyesanjin, capture of: 736
Hyopch'on: 293, 579–80

Imjin River battle: 23–24
In Min Gun. See North Korea People's Army.
Inch'on: 4, 55
Inch'on Base: 605
Inch'on landing: 488–514, 572
Incredible: 633–34
Infantry Battalions
 1st, 5th Infantry: 272, 274, 276–84, 371, 375, 483, 553
 2d, 5th Infantry: 271–74, 276–84, 279n, 286, 553
 3d, 5th Infantry: 286, 553, 585
 1st, 7th Infantry: 517
 3d, 7th Infantry: 390n
 1st, 9th Infantry: 298, 299–301, 306, 454, 462
 2d, 9th Infantry: 258, 298–301, 306, 309, 314, 454–55, 461–62, 560, 583
 3d, 9th Infantry: 316, 325, 325n, 330n, 332, 398, 402, 404, 406
 1st, 15th Infantry: 724–25
 2d, 15th Infantry: 725

Infantry Battalions—Continued
 1st, 17th Infantry: 632, 732–33, 736
 2d, 17th Infantry: 539, 735, 736
 3d, 17th Infantry: 735–36
 1st, 19th Infantry: 132, 133, 137, 138, 139–40, 144–45, 213, 221, 227–31, 235, 238–39, 240–42, 407, 583, 586, 711, 713
 2d, 19th Infantry: 132, 144, 152, 153–54, 157, 158–59, 160–61, 164–79, 213, 221, 227–31, 239, 301, 301n, 407, 555–56, 586, 711–13
 3d, 19th Infantry: 106, 185, 289, 406, 407–08, 407n, 545n, 711
 1st, 21st Infantry: 60, 82, 89, 96–97, 99–100, 134–36, 168, 174, 226–27, 301, 307, 310, 555, 682–83
 2d, 21st Infantry: 389, 402, 555, 682, 712
 3d, 21st Infantry: 89, 90–94, 96–99, 204, 205, 398, 555, 629, 712
 1st, 23d Infantry: 258, 304, 309, 448–49, 466, 467–68, 558–59
 2d, 23d Infantry: 331, 358, 361–62, 448–49, 468, 558–59
 3d, 23d Infantry: 358, 361–62, 390–91, 411, 468–69, 548, 550, 558–59, 579–81
 1st, 24th Infantry: 194, 373, 374, 441, 479–83, 569–70, 577
 2d, 24th Infantry: 193–94, 273–74, 368, 370, 439–41, 479–83
 3d, 24th Infantry: 190–91, 194, 285, 368, 373, 374, 440, 441, 576
 1st, 27th Infantry: 200–201, 238, 242–44, 245–46, 353, 355–63, 475, 478, 479–82, 485, 575, 727
 2d, 27th Infantry: 185–86, 201–02, 238, 244, 271, 303–04, 355–63, 472–75, 478, 485
 3d, 27th Infantry: 304, 483–84, 485
 1st, 29th Infantry: 214–21, 222–23, 227, 233–34, 238, 239–42, 240n, 253n, 365
 3d, 29th Infantry: 214–21, 227, 228, 231, 238, 242, 253n, 342
 2d, 30th Infantry: 390n
 2d, 31st Infantry: 538–39, 632
 3d, 31st Infantry: 538, 632, 733, 737
 1st, 32d Infantry: 520, 522, 530–31
 2d, 32d Infantry: 512, 520, 522–23, 530–31, 533
 3d, 32d Infantry: 520, 530–31
 1st, 34th Infantry: 77, 79–82, 88, 100, 123, 129, 129n, 151, 154, 155–56, 157, 158–59, 161, 164–79, 225–27, 291, 294–98, 304, 389
 3d, 34th Infantry: 77, 80, 81–82, 83–85, 86–88, 123, 125, 151, 157–58, 164–79, 225–27, 291–98, 304, 307, 389
 1st, 35th Infantry: 113, 185, 192, 195, 202, 365, 367–68, 442, 470–74, 475–76, 570, 571, 721
 2d, 35th Infantry: 191–93, 195, 270, 442, 470–74, 570, 575
 3d, 35th Infantry: 113, 442, 569, 721
 1st, 38th Infantry: 469, 560, 579–80
 2d, 38th Infantry: 467, 550–51, 559–60, 581
 3d, 38th Infantry: 448, 467–68, 550–51, 581, 748

INDEX

Infantry Battalions—Continued
- 1st, 65th Infantry: 747, 748
- 2d, 65th Infantry: 740

Infantry Division, 2d: 119, 298, 301, 381, 382, 389, 390, 391, 392, 395, 397, 467–68, 470, 489, 573–74, 652, 667, 668, 669, 675, 710, 746, 771. *See also* Keiser, Maj. Gen. Lawrence B.
- antiguerrilla activities: 721, 727
- and buddy system: 386–88
- and Pusan Perimeter fighting: 437–53, 542–43, 545, 547, 548, 551, 558–59, 572
- strength: 264, 605–06
- in west: 579–82

Infantry Division, 3d: 381, 503n, 581, 684, 724, 725–26, 738–41, 747–48. *See also* Soule, Maj. Gen. Robert H.

Infantry Division, 7th: 4, 5, 386, 489, 499, 501–02, 503n, 512, 593, 595,; 619, 620, 684, 685n, 729, 767. *See also* Barr, Maj. Gen. David G.
- amphibious movement: 631–33, 636–37
- build-up: 491–92
- reaches Manchurian border: 732–38
- at Seoul: 520–23, 527–31
- strength: 49, 50n, 605–06

Infantry Division, 24th: 88, 89, 90, 101, 102, 108, 119–20, 134, 144, 195, 196, 253, 254, 382, 389, 390, 392, 405, 408, 613, 672, 679, 682, 684, 694, 718, 719, 753. *See also* Church, Maj. Gen. John H.
- and buddy system: 385–89
- and Chinju area defense: 212–15
- at Ch'ongch'on bridgehead: 709–15
- condition of: 122, 213
- deployment on Kum: 110–111
- at Naktong Bulge: 290–318
- in Pusan Perimeter breakout: 588, 592
- in Pusan Perimeter fighting: 438–43, 543, 545, 547, 554–58
- and P'yongyang capture: 642–53
- strength: 49, 50n, 605–06
- in Taejon battle: 146–81, 582–88
- withdrawal across Naktong: 249–50

Infantry Division, 25th: 108, 111, 185, 188, 199, 202, 206, 208, 248–49, 253, 253n, 267, 267n, 304, 382, 383, 390, 392, 395, 479, 632, 668. *See also* Kean, Maj. Gen. William B.
- and antiguerrilla activity: 721, 728
- at Battle Mountain: 483–87
- and buddy system: 386–88
- at Masan: 364–75
- in Pusan Perimeter breakout: 574–79, 581
- and Pusan Perimeter fighting: 437–53, 543, 545, 547, 568–71
- at Sangju: 190–95
- strength: 49, 50n, 605–06

Infantry Regiments
- 5th: 365, 370, 371, 389–90, 389n, 439, 441, 718. *See also* 5th Regimental Combat Team.

Infantry Regiments—Continued
- 7th: 739
- 9th: 254, 258, 298, 299–301, 303, 306, 309, 310, 313–16, 325–26, 325n, 443–48, 450–51, 454, 456–59, 460–66, 548, 558–59, 583, 710
- 15th: 739–40
- 17th: 496–97, 539, 539n, 540n, 632, 732–37
- 19th: 99, 106, 122, 125, 130–45, 132n, 147–48, 155, 159, 185, 213, 215, 220, 223, 227–31, 235–42, 236n, 251, 254, 290–317, 389, 405–08, 453, 462, 555–56, 586–88, 642, 645, 647, 709–15, 718, 719, 767
- 21st: 60, 63–64, 76n, 88–94, 96–100, 122, 130, 131, 133, 134, 147, 148, 150, 152, 165, 168, 173, 174–76, 186, 249–50, 254, 290, 294, 297, 298, 309, 343, 389, 398, 400–402, 405, 407n, 408, 448, 554–55, 556, 584–86, 588, 629, 642, 682–84, 712
- 23d: 184, 254, 258, 361–62, 390, 448–51, 450n, 466–69, 548, 550–52, 552n, 558–59, 572, 578, 579, 580–81, 727, 746
- 24th: 49, 108, 113, 190–95, 253, 269, 270, 279, 285, 287, 365–75, 438–43, 479–86, 486n, 491, 569–70, 570n, 575, 577, 579, 728
- 25th: 491
- 27th: 108, 192, 193, 199–204, 235–39, 236n, 244–47, 253, 253n, 271, 272, 353–63, 390, 453, 472, 480, 569–70, 574, 576n, 579, 632, 727
- 29th: 49, 214, 224, 367
- 31st: 522, 538–39, 540n, 595, 597–98, 733, 737
- 32d: 389, 496, 512, 516, 520–23, 527–31, 632, 734, 737
- 34th: 63, 77–100, 122–30, 133, 145, 146–81, 213, 222, 223, 225–27, 249–50, 254, 290–310, 315–17, 389
- 35th: 108, 191–93, 253, 253n, 269, 270, 276, 286, 304, 364–75, 390, 437–43, 442n, 470–79, 569–70, 575, 577, 578
- 38th: 389, 450, 467–68, 469n, 548–52, 559–60, 572, 579–81, 652, 747–48
- 65th: 497, 724, 725, 739–40, 747–48

Infantry-tank actions. *See* Tank-infantry actions.

Intelligence: 20, 210, 211, 212, 459, 478, 622, 633, 635, 677–78, 757–58

Intelligence estimates: 222, 227
- of CCF: 751–65
- of enemy dispositions: 345, 352, 353
- of enemy strength: 269–70, 392, 431, 437, 501, 507–08, 622
- of guerrillas: 726

Invasion south across 38th Parallel: 21–28
Iron Triangle: 604, 615–16, 727–28
Itazuke Air Base: 51, 95
Ivey, Maj. Curtis J.: 599
Iwanczyk, 2d Lt. Frank: 223
Iwon beachhead: 733

Jacques, Lt. Leon J., Jr.: 98
Jamaica: 512

James, 1st Lt. Elwood F.: 475
Japan Logistical Command. *See* Logistical Command, Japan.
Japanese 99 rifles: 333
Japanese *17th Area Army in Korea:* 3
Japanese surrender in World War II: 2-3
Jensen, Lt. Col. Carl C.: 89, 90, 94, 97-98
Jensen, Maj. Lloyd K.: 450
Jet planes, first battle between: 716
John, Pfc. Valdor: 662
Johnson, Lt. Col. Harold K.: 430-31, 652, 679, 680-81, 689-708
Johnson, 1st Lt. Jasper R.: 190
Johnson, Louis A.: 46, 495, 495n
Johnston, Richard J. H.: 535
Joint Chiefs of Staff: 38, 118, 119, 491, 492-95, 536, 537-38, 607, 670, 715-16, 745, 757, 760n, 761, 762, 763n, 764-65, 774
Joint Operations Center, Far East Air Forces: 95, 744, 746
Joint Strategic Plans and Operations Group (JSPOG): 51, 489, 609-10
Joint Task Force Seven: 497-98, 618-21, 633-34
Jones, Lt. Glen C.: 673
Jones, Lt. Col. John P.: 276-78
Jones, Cpl. Robert D.: 154n
Jones, 2d Lt. Thomas T.: 425-26, 426n, 430
Jordan, MSgt. Warren H.: 306
Josey, Capt. Claude K.: 659, 659n
Joy, Vice Adm. Charles Turner: 50, 52, 493, 496, 612, 618-20, 634
Juneau: 52, 184, 185

Kaesong battle: 22-23
Kal-ch'on Creek: 517-18
Kane, Lt. Col. Robert W.: 199, 566, 623
Kang Kon, Lt. Gen.: 350, 394
Kapaun, Father Emil J.: 702, 705, 706
Kap-ch'on River: 131, 147, 151, 153-54
Kapica, Chaplain Francis A.: 283
Kapsan, capture of: 736
Ka-san: 356, 390, 415, 421-32, 435, 562, 563, 566
Kaufman, SFC Loren R.: 464-65, 465n
Kean, Maj. Gen. William B.: 108, 191, 195, 206, 207, 248, 439, 472, 475, 479, 568-70. *See also* Infantry Division, 25th.
  on air support: 476-77
  assumes command of U.N. forces south of Naktong: 249
  and Battle Mountain: 370, 371
  and Masan: 365, 478
  and performance of 24th Infantry: 485-86
  and Task Force Dolvin: 575
  and Task Force Kean: 266-288
  and Task Force Matthews: 575
  and Task Force Torman: 574
  and Yongdok battle: 185

Keiser, Maj. Gen. Lawrence B.: 325, 389, 446, 450, 450-52, 460, 462, 580. *See also* Infantry Division, 2d.
Keizan South Railroad: 268
Kelly, Lt. Paul: 347
Kennedy, 1st Lt. John T.: 424-29
Kessler, Maj. George D.: 27-28
Kigye area, battles in: 319-33
Kihang ferry: 443-44, 444n
Kilchu, capture of: 729-31
Kim, Col.: 186
Kim Baik Yil, Brig. Gen.: 616
Kim Chaek, General: 350, 394, 722
Kim Chong Won ("Tiger"), Col.: 106, 107, 186
Kim Dok Sam: 302n
Kim Hi Chun, Col.: 250, 327
Kim Il Sung: 5, 7, 19, 21-22, 332, 345, 609, 630, 653, 663, 766, 769
Kim Il Sung University: 651
Kim Kwang Hyop, Lt. Gen.: 104, 187
Kim Mu Chong, Lt. Gen.: 104, 187, 394
Kim Paik Il, General: 32-33, 34
Kim Song Jun: 411
Kim Suk Won, Brig. Gen.: 324, 399-400, 687
Kim Ung, Lt. Gen.: 394
Kim Yon, Col.: 410
Kimpo Airfield: 36, 39, 53, 500, 509-11
Kingston, 2d Lt. Robert C.: 737
Kirk, Alan G.: 487n
Koch'ang: 222, 225-27, 580
Koesan, fall of: 104
Kogan-ni: 236, 238
Koman-ni (Saga): 236, 366-68
Kongju: 88, 89-90, 121-29, 146
Korangp'o-ri: 22
Korea, description of: 1-4
Korean augmentation: 385-89, 388n, 739
Korean Government: 31, 351
Korean Military Advisory Group (KMAG): 13, 13n, 16-18, 20-21, 22, 30, 31, 32, 34, 38-42, 55, 62, 324
  advisers: 22, 27, 28-29, 32, 32n, 33, 40, 43, 56, 57, 104, 107, 182-84, 186, 323-24, 330, 361, 398, 401, 404, 406-07, 410, 567, 599, 615, 616, 663n, 672, 673-74, 675, 679, 686, 690, 695n, 728, 752n
Korean National Assembly: 4
Kot'o-ri plateau: 744-45, 772-73
Kouma, Sgt. Ernest R.: 444-45, 445n
Kozuki, Lt. Gen. Yoshio: 3
Kremser, Lt. Paul E.: 456n
Kristanoff, 1st Lt. George W.: 155, 155n
Kron, Maj. Jack J.: 237n
Kuhe-ri ferry: 473
Kum River: 88, 90, 99-100, 108, 121
Kum River Line battle: 121-46
Kumch'on: 203-05
Kumch'on Pocket: 622-31, 640
Kumsan—Taejon battle: 150, 153, 166, 169, 172, 175

INDEX

Kunsan, fall of: 210
Kup'o-ri Training Center: 387
Kuryong River: 700–708
Kuryong River crossing, enemy: 711
Kusong, capture of: 683
Kwang Who Moon Boulevard: 536
Kwang Who Moon Circle: 535–36
Kyongju battle: 404–08
Kyongju corridor: 102, 319–20, 331–33

L–19's: 352
Landrum, Col. Eugene M.: 109, 110, 120, 148–50, 202, 207, 212, 238, 248, 335, 382, 416, 470
Lantron, Maj. Newton W.: 88, 158, 167
Lauer, Lt. Lester: 204
Lawrence, William H.: 208
LCM's: 260, 621
LCV's: 628
Lee Chi Yep, Lt. Col.: 41
Lee Chu Sik, Brig. Gen.: 107, 182, 185, 323
Lee Hak Ku, Sr., Col.: 28n, 72–73, 546, 589–90, 590n, 604
Lee Hyung Koon, Brig. Gen.: 29, 30, 32
Lee Kwon Mu, Maj. Gen.: 20, 293
Lee Kyu Hyun: 177n
Lee Yong Ho, Gen.: 350
Legion of Merit: 483
Lester, Lt.: 98
Leyte: 633
Libby, Sgt. George D.: 173, 173n
Liles, Capt. Paul V. S.: 674
Lilly, Lt. Edmund J., III: 456n
Lim Bu Taik, Col.: 675
Lin Piao: 750, 758, 759, 766
Lindsay, Lt.: 160
Lines of communication: 101, 104, 116–17, 150–51, 152, 289, 319–20, 340, 364, 393. *See also* Communications.
Little, Lt.: 159
"Little Professor, The": 476
Litzenberg, Col. Homer L.: 534, 772, 773
Logan, Lt. Col. Arthur H.: 367
Logan, Maj. Edward O.: 137, 138–41, 139n, 143–44, 143n, 215, 221
Logistical Command, 1st: 621
Logistical Command, 2d: 392, 416–17, 574, 632, 639, 684
Logistical Command, 3d: 620, 628, 639
Logistical Command, Japan: 81, 633, 383, 669
Logistical Command, Pusan: 574
Logistical problems in North Korea: 610–611
Logistics: 114–15, 383. *See also* Supply.
Logistics Support, 79: 620
Londahl, Lt. Col. John E.: 455
"Long March": 394, 750
Lovless, Col. Jay B.: 77, 81–84, 83n
Lowe, Pfc. Jack E.: 162
LSD's: 504

LSMR's: 504
LST's: 77, 330, 501, 621, 636–37, 729–32
Lutes, Lt. Col. LeRoy: 61
LVT's: 515
Lynch, Lt. Col. James H.: 433–35, 590–92, 593–98, 597n, 642, 648n

M1 rifle: 333
McAbee, Capt. Filmore: 696, 699, 702, 706, 707n
MacArthur, General of the Army Douglas: 3, 13, 13n, 40, 52, 55, 59, 73, 106, 195–96, 380, 391–92, 745–46, 754, 754n, 774–76
 and abandonment of Yonil Airfield: 329
 and ADCOM: 42–43
 announces crossing of Parallel: 615
 announces liberation of Seoul: 534
 assumes control of British naval forces: 48
 authorized to intervene in South Korea: 38
 authorized to use U.S. ground troops in South Korea: 46
 and bombing of Yalu: 715–16
 and carpet bombing: 352–53
 and CCF intervention: 687, 757–65
 command, June 1950: 50–51
 and command relations with ROK's: 111–12
 as Commander in Chief, U.N. Command: 383
 congratulates Almond on reaching Yalu: 736
 and defense tactics at Pusan Perimeter: 393
 demands North Korean surrender: 609
 denounces North Korean atrocities: 349–50
 designates FEAF and NAVFE in U.N. Command: 383
 desire to capture Seoul: 527
 establishes Civil Assistance Command: 670
 establishes Japan Logistical Command: 383
 flies to Korea: 44–46
 flies to P'yongyang: 653
 and Inch'on landing: 502, 505, 510, 516, 572
 and intelligence estimate of enemy in Pusan Perimeter: 500
 and July crisis: 214
 and landing controversy: 492–97, 495n
 and Marine units: 259, 462
 and messages from President and JCS: 537–38
 and operational plans: 488–92, 571, 607–12, 612n, 619, 620, 646, 654, 670–71, 684, 771
 and redeployment plans: 669
 re-establishes Syngman Rhee in Seoul: 536–38
 requests additional troops: 381
 requests ammunition ships: 431
 requests reinforcements: 118–20
 and ROK Army: 384–86
 stops air attacks south of Parallel: 600
 strategy for victory: 117–18
 successful strategy in Korean War: 604
 at Sukch'on and Sunch'on airdrops: 658
 and tactics and strategy: 148
 and U.N. Command: 51, 112, 112n, 262

MacArthur, General of the Army Douglas—Cont.
  and Wake Island meeting with President: 630–31, 760–61, 760n
  and Walker, conference with: 207, 207n
  and Walker, praise of: 771
  and Wonsan landing: 634
MacArthur Line: 659
McCaffrey, 1st Lt. Harry J., Jr.: 531
McCaffrey, Lt. Col. William J.: 635
McCall, Cpl. Edward L.: 128
McCullom, MSgt. Roy E.: 434
McDaniel, Maj. William T.: 164, 169–71, 170n, 171n
McDoniel, 1st Lt. Raymond J.: 456n, 458–59
McDonnell, Capt. George F.: 706
McGill, Lt. Henry T.: 135
McGrail, Lt. Col. Thomas M.: 133, 137, 141–42, 153–54, 159–60, 178, 227, 229, 239
Machine guns
  .50-caliber: 68
  7.62-mm.: 69, 70
McIntyre, Capt. Niles J.: 466
MacLean, Col. Allan D.: 182, 197, 214
McLain, Capt. William F.: 706
McMains, Lt. Col. D. M.: 325, 330n, 404
McMurray, 1st Lt. Houston M.: 440
McPhail, Lt. Col. Thomas D.: 26, 599
Magpie: 633
Maher, Lt. Thomas A.: 135
Mahoney, Lt. Col. William J.: 41
Majeske, Capt. LeRoy E.: 473
Majon-ni, guerrilla activities around: 724
Makarounis, 1st Lt. Alexander G.: 218–19, 221
Manchu Regiment. See Infantry Regiment, 9th.
Manchurian Korean veterans: 750
Mancil, Sgt. Edward C.: 597
Mannan, 2d Lt. George E.: 599n
Manpower, South Korean, use of: 384
Manring, Pvt. Roy: 347, 348n
Mansfield: 185, 503, 633
Mao Tse Tung: 394
March discipline: 123, 180, 228, 770, 770n
Marchbanks, MSgt. William: 241
Marine Corps infantry regiment: 273n
Marine Corps squadrons: 614
Marine Corps units
  Air Wing, 1st: 274–75, 614, 723, 731, 743–44, 773
  Battalion, 1st, 1st Marines: 516–19, 527, 536, 621, 722–23
  Battalion, 1st Amphibious Tractor: 528
  Battalion, 1st Medium Tank: 267
  Battalion, 2d, 1st Marines: 507, 512, 518–19, 535, 536, 723
  Battalion, 3d, 1st Marines: 512, 518–19, 527, 533, 535–36, 621, 723, 724–25, 747
  Battalion, 1st, 5th Marines: 271, 274, 275–76, 310–18, 463–65, 509–11, 516, 524, 526, 536
  Battalion, 2d, 5th Marines: 271–73, 310–18, 463–65, 507, 509–11, 516, 524–25, 773

Marine Corps units—Continued
  Battalion, 3d, 5th Marines: 273–74, 275–76, 276n, 284–85, 286, 310–18, 463, 464, 499, 505–06, 515–16, 524, 525, 533–34, 537
  Battalion, 1st, 7th Marines: 741, 742–43, 773
  Battalion, 2d, 7th Marines: 540, 742, 773
  Battalion, 3d, 7th Marines: 742, 743, 773
  Battalion, 2d, 11th Marines: 741
  Brigade, 1st Provisional: 258–59, 259n, 266, 267, 272, 279, 308, 309, 310–18, 382, 453, 462, 496
  Division, 1st: 50, 259n, 619, 621, 684, 686, 718, 719, 723, 726. See also Smith, Maj. Gen. Oliver P.
    at Changjin Reservoir: 772–73
    Inch'on landing: 491, 496, 501–13, 503n, 506n
    in North Korea: 732, 740, 741–45, 742n
    Seoul, capture of: 515–41
    troop strength: 620, 685n
    Wonsan landing: 635–37
  Division, 2d: 50
  Regiment, 1st: 491, 499, 506–14, 516–20, 526–27, 531–36, 620, 621, 686
  Regiment, 5th: 258–59, 269, 271, 274–76, 310–18, 453, 463–65, 489, 491, 496, 499, 501–02, 509–11, 515–16, 520, 524–26, 527, 531–36, 540, 620, 686, 741, 773
  Regiment, 7th: 491, 503n, 519, 520, 524, 526, 532, 534–36, 540, 620, 686, 741–45, 755, 756, 767, 772–73
  Regiment, 11th: 620
Marks, Capt.: 178
Marshall, General of the Army George C.: 2–3, 608
Martin, Maj. Floyd: 73
Martin, Lt. McDonald: 295–96
Martin, Col. Robert R.: 83–84, 85, 86–88
Masan. See also Chinju-Masan corridor.
  approaches to: 235–47
  battle: 438–43
  Communist sympathizers in: 478
  stalemate: 364–75
Matériel: 519. See also under Equipment.
Matthews, Capt. Charles M.: 576
Mayo, Capt. Walter L., Jr.: 700n, 706
Medal of Honor: 173, 173n, 177n, 270n, 357, 375n, 429n, 445n, 455, 456n, 457n, 461n, 465n, 625n, 659n, 712n
Meloy, Col. Guy S., Jr.: 130–37, 137–45, 143n
Menoher, Brig. Gen. Pearson: 83, 122, 141, 142, 168, 173, 174, 175, 235
Michaelis, Lt. Col. John H. "Mike": 108, 200–203, 235–39, 236n, 243–45, 353, 355, 360–61, 362, 485
Middlesex Hill: 582, 582n
Middlesex Regiment. See British Battalion, 1st, Middlesex Regiment.
MIG's: 715–16
Milam, Capt. James T: 419
Milburn, Maj. Gen. Frank W.: 544, 562, 588, 622, 638, 642, 643, 647–48, 659, 672, 677, 679, 684,

INDEX

Milburn, Maj. Gen. Frank W.—Continued
690–91, 694, 704, 776. *See also* Corps, I; Corps, IX.
Military Air Transport Service (MATS): 115
Miller, SSgt. Elmer L.: 700n, 701–05, 701n
Millett, Lt. Lewis: 357
Milleson, Capt. Hugh P.: 221
Millikin, Maj. John, Jr.: 679–80, 691–94, 695–96, 698–99, 701
Min Ki Sik, Col.: 224, 239, 241–42
Mines: 173, 357, 359, 603, 628, 633–35, 650, 651
Minesweeping: 633–35
Minesweeping Group, 95.6: 620
Missouri: 500, 513, 567
Mitchell, Cpl. Harry D.: 204
Mitchell, Capt. William: 220, 484
Montesclaros, Capt. Melicio: 25, 132, 142, 160, 167, 178, 221
Moore, Col. Dennis M.: 740
Moore, Capt. Howard M.: 713
Moore, Col. Ned D.: 213, 215–33, 236–38, 236n, 237n, 239–42, 243
Moore, William R.: 232–33
Morale: 147, 180–81, 255, 287, 299, 370, 428, 647, 669
Morale, enemy: 310, 332, 397, 546, 600, 647, 652
Moriarty, Maj. Veale F.: 700n, 701–03, 707n
Morisil. *See* Tugok.
Morrissey, 2d Lt. J.: 217–20
Mortars
 60-mm.: 61
 4.2-inch: 50, 59, 61, 66, 92
Mosquito. *See* T–6's.
Moss, Capt. Jack G.: 683
Mott, Lt. Col. Harold W.: 214–21
Mount, Lt. Col. Charles M.: 522, 530
Mountain fighting: 101–05, 187–88
Mountain marches: 105–06
Mt. Kinley: 196, 497, 502, 621, 636
Muccio, John J.: 4, 5, 13, 16, 31, 36–37, 39, 40, 43, 44, 55
Much'on-ni: 236–38, 242–44
Muhoberac, Pfc. John R.: 597
Muir, Maj. Kenneth: 582–83, 583n
Mun Che Won, Col.: 604
Mun'gyong pass battle: 104–05
Mun'gyong plateau: 190–95
Munsan-ni: 23–24
Murch, Lt. Col. Gordon E.: 202, 236, 237, 238, 303–04, 355–63, 472–75, 478
Murray, Lt. Col. Raymond L.: 258, 285, 310, 313, 463–65, 509–11, 515, 524, 532
Mustang. *See* F–51's (Mustang).

Najin docks: 377
Naktong Bulge, first battle of: 289–318
Naktong offensive, enemy: 454–87

Naktong River
 crossing: 548–60
 description: 101–02
 Line: 252–54
 upper, battle: 187–88
Naktong-ni ferry crossing site: 591–92
Nam P'otae-san: 737
Nam River: 364–65
Nam River battle: 470–79
Namch'onjom, capture of: 640
Namji-ri bridge: 302–03, 304, 438–42, 471–72, 478–79
Nam-san. *See* South Mountain.
Napalm, use of: 321, 347, 361, 371, 373, 374, 379, 379n, 407, 413, 480–81, 502, 509, 525, 550, 553, 559, 578, 582, 586, 681
Napalm Hill. *See* Battle Mountain.
Nash, 2d Lt. Robert E.: 137, 141, 161n
Naval forces: 107, 501–05, 548
Naval Forces, Far East (NAVFE): 38, 39, 50, 52, 378, 497–500, 605, 618–21
Naval gunfire support: 184, 185, 186, 187, 331, 332, 366, 401, 408, 483, 502–09, 512–13, 567, 599, 723, 731, 732
Naval support: 184, 452, 483, 568
Negro units
 3d Battalion, 9th Infantry: 316, 325, 325n, 330n, 332, 398, 402, 404, 406
 1st Battalion, 24th Infantry: 194, 373, 374, 441, 479–83, 569–70, 577
 2d Battalion, 24th Infantry: 193–94, 273–74, 368, 370, 439–41, 479–83
 3d Battalion, 24th Infantry: 190–91, 194, 285, 368, 373, 374, 440, 441, 576
Nehru, Jawaharlal: 608–09
Nelson, Pvt. James H.: 169
Netherlands Battalion: 668
Newton, Lt. Col. George R.: 275, 313
Niblo, Brig. Gen. Urban: 114
Nielson, Lt. Col. Leslie: 644–45
Night fighting: 357–62, 438–43, 531–34, 693–94, 701–03, 705–06, 722–23
Nist, Col. Cecil: 417–19
Nonsan: 129, 130, 146, 150–51, 153, 158, 159
Nordstrom, 1st Lt. Francis: 660n
Norrell, 1st Lt. Herman D.: 239, 243, 243n
North-East People's Liberation Army (NEPLA): 750
North Korea: 4, 5–6, 42n, 673
North Korea People's Army: 7–12, 8n, 9n, 11n, 21, 34n, 600, 721, 725–26, 758, 766. *See also* North Korean Army.
North Korean Air Force: 500
North Korean Army: 17–18, 18n, 53, 210, 255, 318, 350, 395–96, 600–604, 604n, 666. *See also* North Korea People's Army.
North Korean artillery: 17, 18n
North Korean Border Constabulary (BC): 8, 18

North Korean Government: 5, 21, 658, 663-64, 671, 766
North Korean High Command: 19, 103, 350, 394
North Korean Ministry of Defense: 7
North Korean Navy: 12, 500
North Korean People's Council: 5
North Korean Security Police: 588
North Korean units. See also Chinese Communist Forces (CCF) units.
  Battalion, 2d, 1st Regiment, 12th Division: 333
  Battalion, 2d, 2d Regiment, 12th Division: 331, 424
  Battalion, 3d, 2d Regiment, 12th Division: 331
  Battalion, 2d, 15th Regiment, 6th Division: 276
  Battalion, 1st, 16th Regiment, 4th Division: 293
  Battalion, 3d, 16th Regiment, 4th Division: 293
  Battalion, 1st, 29th Regiment, 10th Division: 343
  Battalion, 2d, 29th Regiment, 10th Division: 343
  Battalion, 2d, 206th Mechanized Regiment: 348
  Battalion, 3d, 226th Independent Marine: 506
  Battalion, 2d Artillery: 188, 348, 321
  Battalion, 105th Armored: 9. See also Brigade, 105th Armored; Division, 105th Armored; Regiment, 105th Armored.
  BC Brigade, 1st: 8
  BC Brigade, 2d: 8
  BC Brigade, 3d: 8, 20, 22, 395
  BC Brigade, 5th: 8
  BC Brigade, 7th: 8, 366
  Brigade, 16th Armored: 394, 395n, 460
  Brigade, 17th Armored: 394-95, 395n
  Brigade, 24th Mechanized Artillery: 616
  Brigade, 25th: 523, 524
  Brigade, 104th Security: 394, 395n
  Brigade, 105th Armored: 10, 11, 24, 30. See also Battalion, 105th Armored; Division, 105th Armored; Regiment, 105th Armored.
  Brigade, 507th: 731
  Corps, I: 11, 11n, 26, 255, 394-95, 396, 436, 437-53, 460, 471-72, 545, 583, 603
  Corps, II: 11, 11n, 26, 72-73, 104, 187, 255, 394-95, 396, 397-436, 470, 545, 553, 589-90, 604
  Division, 1st: 9, 20, 24, 31, 102-05, 193, 195, 255, 255n, 335-38, 354-63, 395, 395n, 411-15, 421, 430, 431, 432-36, 546, 561-66, 572, 592, 603-04
  Division, 2d: 20, 26, 27, 102, 103, 122, 146, 178, 200-203, 255, 255n, 350, 394, 395, 395n, 437-53, 466-69, 546, 548, 550, 550n, 559, 579-80, 603
  Division, 3d: 8, 20, 24-25, 29-30, 31-35, 53, 55, 88, 94, 99, 102, 122, 130-37, 144, 145, 146-81, 197-99, 203-05, 210, 254, 255, 335-42, 350, 394, 395, 395n, 411-15, 420, 500, 546, 553-54, 561-66, 589, 592, 603, 722
  Division, 4th: 8, 9, 20, 24, 25, 29, 31-35, 53-55, 58, 72, 76, 81, 88, 94, 99, 102, 122, 123-30, 129n, 146-81, 210, 211, 213, 222-24, 225-27, 247, 254, 255, 289-318, 394, 395, 395n, 460-66, 548, 559, 579, 580, 722, 728

North Korean units—Continued
  Division, 5th: 8, 9-10, 12, 20, 27, 28, 105-07, 182-87, 255, 308, 323-33, 394, 395n, 396, 399-408, 407n, 568, 572, 599, 604, 614-15, 722-23, 723
  Division, 6th: 9, 20, 53, 55, 210-34, 242, 246-47, 253, 255, 266-88, 365-75, 394, 395, 395n, 438-53, 470-79, 483-87, 570-71, 572, 575, 578, 603
  Division, 7th: 8, 9, 10, 20, 26-27, 103, 255, 366, 394-95, 395, 395n, 438-53, 470-79, 483, 546, 570, 572, 603. See also Division, 12th.
  Division, 8th: 105, 191, 255, 320-21, 394, 395n, 396, 408-10, 567, 598, 603, 604
  Division, 9th: 255, 394, 395, 395n, 438-53, 459-56 459n, 519, 548, 551, 559, 579, 580, 584, 603, 615
  Division, 10th: 10, 255, 309, 335, 337, 339, 342-45, 394, 395, 395n, 452, 500, 551, 553, 560, 580, 581, 582, 583, 604, 722
  Division, 12th: 9, 11n, 103, 104, 105, 187-88, 190, 255, 319-33, 394, 395n, 397-408, 407n, 567, 598, 604. See also Division, 7th.
  Division, 13th: 10, 105, 193, 195, 255, 335, 337, 338, 339, 354-63, 394, 395, 395n, 411-15, 428, 430, 432-36, 500, 546, 561-66, 572, 589-90, 590n, 592, 604
  Division, 15th: 10, 104, 105, 195, 255, 337, 338-39, 354, 394, 395n, 396, 405, 408-10, 546, 567, 604, 724
  Division, 17th Armored: 623
  Division, 18th: 511, 513, 519, 533
  Division, 19th: 623, 628, 640
  Division, 27th: 623, 628
  Division, 31st: 540
  Division, 41st: 731
  Division, 43d: 623, 629
  Division, 105th Armored: 10, 72, 88, 105, 178, 254, 255, 275, 335, 337, 348-49, 354, 394, 395n, 521, 538-39, 557, 583, 585, 598 603, 719. See also Battalion, 105th Armored; Brigade, 105th Armored; Regiment, 105th Armored.
  Headquarters: 11, 11n, 394, 604, 722, 769
  Regiment, 1st, 1st Division: 360, 363
  Regiment, 1st, 7th Division: 10, 366
  Regiment, 1st, 9th Division: 459-60
  Regiment, 1st, 12th Division: 331
  Regiment, 2d, 1st Division: 431, 563
  Regiment, 2d, 7th Division: 10, 366
  Regiment, 2d, 8th Division: 321
  Regiment, 2d, 9th Division: 459-60
  Regiment, 2d, 12th Division: 333
  Regiment, 3d, 7th Division: 10, 366
  Regiment, 3d 8th Division: 320-21
  Regiment, 3d, 9th Division: 459
  Regiment, 4th Rifle, 2d Division: 26, 451, 550
  Regiment, 5th, 4th Division: 57, 72n, 153, 158, 178, 306, 728
  Regiment, 6th Rifle, 2d Division: 26, 27, 451, 550
  Regiment, 7th, 3d Division: 30, 198, 203, 204, 339-42

INDEX 803

North Korean units—Continued
  Regiment, 8th, 3d Division: 53, 205, 339, 563
  Regiment, 9th, 3d Division: 32, 198, 339
  Regiment, 10th Rifle, 5th Division: 9, 107–08
  Regiment, 11th Rifle, 5th Division: 9, 105
  Regiment, 12th Motorcycle: 20
  Regiment, 12th Rifle, 5th Division: 9, 568
  Regiment, 13th, 6th Division: 9, 23, 211, 282, 287, 365, 442–43
  Regiment, 14th, 1st Division: 563
  Regiment, 14th, 6th Division: 9, 22, 211, 246, 287, 365
  Regiment, 15th, 6th Division: 9, 23, 211, 230, 246–47, 276, 287, 365, 371
  Regiment, 16th, 4th Division: 29, 72, 88, 122–23, 127–29, 129n, 153, 178, 306, 312–18
  Regiment, 17th Motorcycle: 11n, 28n
  Regiment, 17th Rifle, 2d Division: 26, 451, 469, 550, 550n
  Regiment, 18th, 4th Division: 72, 88, 153, 178, 226, 306, 310–18, 728
  Regiment, 19th, 13th Division: 337–38, 360n, 435, 590, 604
  Regiment, 21st, 13th Division: 337, 590
  Regiment, 22d: 508
  Regiment, 23d, 13th Division: 338, 590
  Regiment, 25th, 10th Division: 343–45
  Regiment, 27th, 10th Division: 343, 344
  Regiment, 29th, 10th Division: 309, 343–45
  Regiment, 31st, 12th Division: 188
  Regiment, 31st, 31st Division: 540
  Regiment, 45th, 15th Division: 338
  Regiment, 48th, 15th Division: 338
  Regiment, 50th, 15th Division: 338
  Regiment, 70th, 18th Division: 514
  Regiment, 74th, 43d Division: 623
  Regiment, 78th Independent: 523
  Regiment, 83d Motorized, 105th Armored Division: 253–54, 275, 287
  Regiment, 87th, 9th Division: 519
  Regiment, 102d Security: 581
  Regiment, 104th Security: 575, 581
  Regiment, 105th Armored: 10. *See also Battalion, 105th Armored; Brigade, 105th Armored; Division, 105th Armored.*
  Regiment, 107th Tank: 10, 24, 72, 178, 557
  Regiment, 109th Tank: 10, 24–25, 105
  Regiment, 203d Tank: 10, 178, 557
  Regiment, 206th Mechanized: 10
  Regiment, 239th: 659–60
  Regiment, 344th Tank: 742
  Regiment, 766th Independent: 27, 28, 105, 106, 255, 319–33
  Regiment 849th Independent Anti-Tank: 585
  Regiment, 918th Artillery: 506
  Regiment, 945th: 616
  Regiment, Artillery: 153
Northwest Airlines: 36

Notch, the: 236–42, 236n, 270, 364, 476, 570. *See also* Chungam-ni.
Nugent, Capt. Ambrose H.: 76n

Obong-ni Ridge: 294–95, 297, 298–302, 304–18, 465–66
Observatory Hill: 499, 507
O'Donnell, Maj. Gen. Emmett (Rosie): 352
Ogok: 368, 369
Ohang ferry crossing site: 293–94
Ohang Hill: 297, 301, 309, 310, 315, 317
Okada, Cpl. Richard: 93
Okch'on: 133–34, 147, 148, 150, 158, 168, 170, 172, 174, 178
Old Baldy. *See* Battle Mountain.
Olson, Maj. Lester K.: 387
Ongjin Peninsula: 21–22
Onjong battle: 673–75, 673n
"Operation Flushout": 381–82
"Operation Manchu": 446–47
"Operation Rebuild": 379–80
"Operation Yo-yo": 635
Operational Plan 9-50: 497–98
Operational plans. *See also* Strategy; Tactics.
  airborne attack: 654
  amphibious landings: 195–96, 488–500, 609–12, 618–21
  breakout and pursuit: 588
  for Cavalry Division, 1st: 195–97
  Chinju, counterattack toward: 266–67
  Chinju pass: 269
  Ch'ongch'on bridgehead: 709
  Ch'ongch'on River, north of: 672
  Cloverleaf-Obong-ni: 310–12
  counterattack: 266–67
  Davidson Line, withdrawal to: 415–16
  Han River crossing: 515
  Hill 314: 433
  Inch'on landing: 497–500, 498n
  MacArthur's: 117–18, 488–92, 607–12, 612n, 619–20, 646, 654, 684, 771
  Naktong River Line: 252
  North Korea: 607–21, 771
  Pusan Perimeter: 253, 542–43, 573–74
  river crossings: 554–55
  Seoul, capture of: 519–20, 527
  Taebaek Range, withdrawal across: 28
  Taegu, encirclement above: 561–62
  Taejon defense: 147–51
  for Task Force Kean: 269
  X Corps: 684–86
  Uijongbu Corridor: counterattack: 29
  Walker's: 110–11, 148–50, 150n, 152, 289, 542–45, 588–89, 709, 754, 771
  Yalu, attack to: 773–74
  Yongsan battle: 462
Operational plans, enemy. *See also* Envelopments, enemy; Tactics, enemy.

Operational plans, enemy—Continued
 Nam River: 471–72
 Pusan Perimeter: 392–96, 437–38
 Taejon: 146
 38th Parallel, attack across: 19–20
Orang-ch'on River, crossed by ROK's: 732
Ordway, Col. Godwin L.: 257, 274, 278–82, 279n, 286
Ormond, Maj. Robert J.: 699, 700–707
Orr, 2d Lt. Augustus B.: 139–40
Osan: 538–39
 battle: 65–76
 pursuit phase fighting: 588–98
Osburn, Capt. Leroy: 80, 81
Ouellette, Pfc. Joseph R.: 457, 457n, 458
Oum Hong Sup, Lt. Col.: 31
Ovenshine, Col. Richard P.: 522, 538–39, 539n

P–51's: 314
Pace, Frank, Jr.: 47
Paddock, Lt. Col. John W.: 521
Paekchin ferry: 446–47, 459
Paek-san, capture of: 733
Paik In Yup, Col.: 22, 22n
Paik Sun Yup, Maj. Gen. 15, 16n, 22, 23–24, 351, 360–61, 363, 562, 625, 642, 650–51, 665, 677, 690–708, 695n
Pak Kyo Sam, General: 443, 459
Palmer, Brig. Gen. Charles D.: 196–97, 198, 689–90
Palmer, Col. Raymond D.: 424–25, 427, 562, 623, 679–80, 695, 696
Pang Ho San, Maj. Gen.: 211, 438–53
Panikkar, Sardas K. M.: 758–59
Parachute flares: 378
Parris, 1st Lt. Harold G.: 727, 727n
Parrott, Lindsay: 21n
Partridge, Maj. Gen. Earl E.: 44, 185, 207, 324, 329, 353, 378, 380, 595, 617, 744. *See also* Fifth Air Force.
Patrol and Reconnaissance Group, 96.2: 620
Patrols between Eighth Army and X Corps: 746–48
Pay scale, ROK Army: 384–85
Payne, Lt. Charles E.: 79, 295–97
Pea Sung Sub, MSgt.: 363
Peace Preservation Corps. *See* North Korean Border Constabulary.
Peacock Mountain: 26
"Peg O' My Heart": 479
Peiping radio broadcasts: 759, 762–63, 765
Peng Teh-huai: 769
Peploe, Col. George B.: 389, 467, 551, 581
Perez, Lt. Col. Gines: 291–98, 402–03, 682, 682n
Perimeter, Pusan. *See* Pusan Perimeter.
Perimeter defense. *See* Defense perimeters.
Perry, Lt. Col. Miller O.: 63, 65–76, 71n, 79–80, 137–38
Pershing tanks. *See* Tanks. M26 (Pershing).

Peterson, Lt. Robert: 425
Philip, Sgt. John J.: 429
Philippine Sea: 633
Philippine 10th Infantry Battalion Combat Team: 574, 574n, 606
Philips, 2d Lt. Ernest: 219
P'il-bong: 364–75, 438–39, 483, 484, 568
Pirate: 633
Plan 100-B: 489
Plan 100-C: 489, 489n
Plan 100-D: 489
Plans. *See* Operational plans.
Pledge: 633
Plum Pudding Hill: 582
P'ohang-dong: 102, 187, 196, 319–33, 397–410, 568
Pohujang, capture of: 743
Pongam-ni: 276–85
Ponton ferries, constructed: 628
Poovey, SFC Junius: 473
Potsdam Conference: 2–3
Poun: 200–202
Powell, Col. Herbert B.: 733–38
Powers, 1st Lt. Lawrence C.: 69n
Prisoners
 American: 76n, 664–65
 enemy: 546n, 587, 602–03, 603n, 645, 646, 660, 675–76, 688, 721, 731, 751–53, 752n, 754–56, 761
Puerto Rican Infantry Regiment, 65th: 574
Pujon (Fusen) Reservoir: 686, 729–38, 729n, 755, 767
Puller, Col. Lewis B.: 509, 517, 527, 532
P'ungsan: 732–33
Pusan, port of: 116–17
Pusan Base: 605
Pusan Base Command: 116. *See also* Logistical Command, 2d; Logistical Command, Pusan.
Pusan defense line. *See* Davidson Line.
Pusan Logistical Command. *See* Logistical Command, Pusan.
Pusan-Mukden railroad: 174
Pusan Perimeter: 208, 308–10, 352, 666, 672, 694, 704, 721. *See also* Naktong Bulge, first battle of; Naktong River Line.
 battles, east coast to Taegu: 397–436
 battles, in the south: 437–53
 breakout: 542–72
 breakthrough of, by enemy: 437–53
 communications: 320
 establishment of: 252–55, 253n
 enemy tactics for: 392–96
 influence of terrain on fighting in: 319–20
 and pursuit phase of breakout: 573–606
 tactics: 200
Pusan-Seoul railroad: 345
Putnam, Capt. Gerald D.: 107
P'yongt'aek, withdrawal from: 77–82
P'yongyang, capture of: 646–53, 652n
P'yongyang Army Arsenal: 377

INDEX

Quad-50's: 136, 559

Radcliff, Capt.: 582
Radford, Admiral Arthur W.: 50
Raibl, Maj. Tony J.: 214–21
Railroads: 150, 183, 248–49, 260–61, 268–69, 319, 340, 377, 378, 499–500, 639–40, 741
Rations: 115, 184, 385
Rau, Sir Benegal: 608
Ray, Cpl. Lawrence A.: 128–29, 128n
Recoilless rifles
  57-mm.: 50
  75-mm.: 50, 59, 61, 66, 69, 314
Reconnaissance, aerial. *See* Aerial observation.
Recruits: 385–89, 388n, 547
Recruits, enemy: 366, 395, 546
Red Ball Express: 260, 380, 668
Red Beach: 499, 506–07
Red Cloud, Cpl. Mitchell: 712, 712n
Red Diamond route: 722
Redeployment plans: 669
Reed, Capt. Frank M.: 460–62, 464
Refugee movements: 66, 81, 82, 83, 89, 199, 211, 228n, 230, 233–34, 249, 251–52, 251n, 303, 351, 383, 466, 681, 712
Regimental Combat Team, 5th: 49, 253, 257–58, 266–74, 276–86, 277n, 453, 483, 485, 543, 545, 552–54, 555, 564, 572, 584–86, 588, 683–84, 710–11. *See also* Infantry Regiments, 5th.
Regimental Combat Team, 7th: 740. *See also* Infantry Regiments, 7th.
Regimental Combat Team, 9th: 301, 304, 306. *See also* Infantry Regiments, 9th.
Regimental Combat Team, 15th: 740–41. *See also* Infantry Regiments, 15th.
Regimental Combat Team, 17th: 636–37. *See also* Infantry Regiments, 17th.
Regimental Combat Team, 65th: 574. *See also* Infantry Regiments, 65th.
Regimental Combat Team, 187th Airborne: 503n
Regimental Combat Team, 442d: 258
Reifers, Sgt. Raymond N.: 576–77, 577n
Reinforcements, aircraft: 257, 257n
Reinforcements, ground: 257–59
Reinforcements, U.N.: 574, 574n, 667–68
Reith, Maj.: 682
Replacements: 180, 196, 228–29, 259, 259n, 295, 381–82
Replacements, enemy: 222, 287, 310, 337, 354, 365–66, 411, 431, 460
Republic of Korea Air Force: 13–14, 17
Republic of Korea (ROK) Army: 65, 107, 572, 622, 721
  as Allied force: 382
  artillery assigned to: 385, 385n
  augmentation to U.S. Army: 385–89, 388n, 492, 667
  bravery: 24

Republic of Korea (ROK) Army—Continued
  casualties. *See under* Casualties.
  Chief of Staff. *See* Chae Byong Duk, Maj. Gen.; Chung Il Kwon, Lt. Gen.; Paik Sun Yup, Maj. Gen.
  Chonju Training Command: 191
  Commanding General. *See* Chung Il Kwon, Lt. Gen.
  counterattack in Uijongbu Corridor: 28–30
  deployment for attack north: 613
  deployment along Perimeter: 254
  disposition, July 1950: 102
  forces: 12–18, 35
  headquarters: 31, 32, 40, 41, 43, 57, 58, 110, 416
  KMAG's opinion of: 20–21
  Kwangu Training Command: 191
  operations in central mountains: 101–05
  operations on east coast: 105–08
  origins and development: 12–13
  pay scale: 384–85
  Pusan Training Command: 191
  ration: 115–16, 183, 385
  recruiting: 183
  re-equipping of: 261
  relieves I Corps and 3d Division commanders: 405
  reorganization: 188–91, 618, 667
  Replacement Training Center: 421
  Replacement Training Center, 1st: 384
  Replacement Training Center, 2d: 384
  Replacement Training Command: 191
  strength: 13, 15, 16n, 35n, 190, 191, 384, 547, 547n, 574, 574n, 605, 606
  tactical situation at Seoul: 30–31
  38th Parallel reached by: 598–600
  Training Center and Headquarters Company: 384n
  and United Nations: 112
  and withdrawal across Naktong: 252
  Yalu, reached by: 672–73
Republic of Korea Army units
  Battalion, 1st, 1st Guerrilla Group: 618
  Battalion, 2d, 1st Guerrilla Group: 618
  Battalion, 3d, 1st Guerrilla Group: 618
  Battalion, 5th, 1st Guerrilla Group: 618
  Battalion, 6th, 1st Guerrilla Group: 618
  Battalion, 1st, 2d Regiment: 673
  Battalion, 2d, 2d Regiment: 763
  Battalion, 3d, 2d Regiment: 673
  Battalion, 1st, 10th Regiment: 674
  Battalion, 2d, 10th Regiment: 531
  Battalion, 2d, 12th Regiment: 651, 679
  Battalion, 1st, 17th Regiment: 728
  Battalion, 2d, 17th Regiment: 728
  Battalion, 1st Separate, 23d Regiment: 107, 186, 323
  Battalion, 1st, 25th Regiment: 321
  Battalion, 2d, 25th Regiment: 321

Republic of Korea Army units—Continued
  Battalion, 1st Anti-Guerrilla: 321, 722
  Battalion, 3d Anti-Guerrilla: 722
  Battalion, 5th Anti-Guerrilla: 722
  Battalion, 7th Anti-Guerrilla: 722
  Battalion, 3d Engineer: 28, 407
  Battalion, 2d Marine: 516, 524
  Battalion, 3d Marine: 516, 529
  Battalion, 5th Training: 432
  Battalion, Miryang Guerrilla: 568
  Battalion, P'ohang Marine: 321
  Battalion, Yongdungp'o: 323
  Battalion Combat Team, 100th: 258
  Corps, I: 89, 189–90, 191, 254, 331, 384, 398, 405, 543, 612, 613–18, 634, 635, 666, 685, 686, 687, 729–32, 741
  Corps, II: 189–90, 191, 254, 337, 384, 397, 405, 430, 543, 567, 598, 599, 613, 615, 672–75, 679, 680, 681, 690, 694, 710, 718, 719, 748, 754, 761, 771
  Corps, III: 618, 638, 771
  Division, 1st: 22, 24, 31, 53, 112, 189–90, 191, 193, 253, 254, 255, 255n, 332, 335–36, 338–39, 345–46, 350–63, 384n, 385n, 390–91, 395, 409, 430, 431, 432, 435, 545, 548, 548n, 560–63, 566, 572, 593, 613, 623, 625, 642–53, 658, 659, 664–65, 672, 675–81, 677n, 690–708, 709, 718, 752
  Division, 2d: 28–30, 31, 53, 102, 189, 193, 667
  Division, 3d: 28–29, 53, 102, 107, 182–87, 190, 191, 253, 254, 255, 321–24, 330–32, 330n, 384n, 385n, 396, 399–408, 548n, 567, 568, 572, 599–600, 600n, 615–17, 684, 685n, 686, 732, 767
  Division, 5th: 28, 31, 53, 618, 618n, 638
  Division, 6th: 27, 28, 53, 102, 103, 104, 189–90, 191, 193, 195, 253, 254, 255, 332, 336–37, 358, 384n, 385n, 396, 408–10, 548n, 567, 598, 613, 615–16, 647, 657, 659, 661, 665–66, 672, 673–75, 717, 718
  Division, 7th: 29–30, 31, 53, 104, 210–11, 223–24, 228, 385, 385n, 402, 405, 409, 548n, 567, 613, 616, 651, 675, 691, 711. See also Task Force Min.
  Division, 8th: 28, 28n, 53, 102–06, 187–91, 253, 254, 255, 320–21, 331, 384, 385n, 396, 403, 405, 408–10, 548n, 567, 598–99, 613, 615–16, 647, 659, 666, 672, 673, 674, 680, 718, 768
  Division, 9th: 667
  Division, 11th: 385, 613, 618, 618n, 638, 721, 722
  Division, Capital: 29, 31, 53, 102, 188–89, 191, 253, 254, 255, 321, 327, 330, 331, 332, 384, 385n, 396, 398–408, 548n, 567, 599, 615–16, 637, 684, 685n, 686, 729–33
  Group, 1st Anti-Guerrilla: 667
  Group, 1st Guerrilla: 618
  Regiment, 1st: 25, 191, 548n, 729–33
  Regiment, 1st Cavalry: 191
  Regiment, 1st Marine: 685n
  Regiment, 2d: 191, 548n, 673–74

Republic of Korea Army units—Continued
  Regiment, 3d: 25, 385, 405, 548n, 710–11
  Regiment, 5th: 28, 29, 385, 402, 405, 409–10, 548n, 710–11
  Regiment, 5th Marine: 685n
  Regiment, 7th: 26, 191, 548n, 616, 672–75, 717, 766–67
  Regiment, 8th: 385, 548n, 651, 652, 711
  Regiment, 9th: 25
  Regiment, 10th: 27, 28, 191, 357–58, 548n, 674, 748
  Regiment, 11th: 22, 23, 191, 351, 354, 357–58, 391, 409–10, 435, 548n, 566, 651, 676–77, 680, 689
  Regiment, 12th: 22, 23, 23n, 191, 351, 354, 391, 548n, 562–63, 566, 676–77, 679, 680
  Regiment, 13th: 22, 23–24, 351, 357–58, 391
  Regiment, 15th: 191, 435, 548, 548n, 566, 651, 675, 677, 679, 680, 691–94, 696, 698, 707
  Regiment, 16th: 191, 548n, 616, 675
  Regiment, 17th: 22, 102, 112, 191, 193–94, 226–27, 250, 254, 290, 298, 321, 323, 326, 327, 398–408, 503n, 520, 528–31, 543, 548n, 667, 727–28. See also Task Force P'ohang.
  Regiment, 18th: 191, 398–408, 548n, 728–32
  Regiment, 19th: 191, 548n, 674
  Regiment, 21st: 27, 28, 191, 548n
  Regiment, 22d: 28, 185, 191, 323–24, 330, 404, 548n, 732
  Regiment, 23d: 53, 102, 106, 107, 184, 189, 191, 323, 330, 401, 548n, 616, 732
  Regiment, 25th: 321, 327
  Regiment, 26th: 321, 548n, 686–88, 718, 725–26, 740, 741, 742, 755
  Regiment, 28th: 667
  Regiment, 29th: 667
  Regiment, 30th: 667
  Regiment, 31st: 667
  Regiment, 32d: 667
  Regiment, Cavalry: 729–32
Task Force Kim: 384
Task Force Min: 228, 239–40, 241, 253, 269, 279, 332, 385. See also Division, 7th.
Task Force P'ohang: 321, 323, 326, 327, 331–32, 384. See also Regiment, 17th.
Republic of Korea Coast Guard: 13
Republic of Korea Constitution: 4
Republic of Korea marines: 211, 224, 230, 366, 439–40, 508, 511, 520, 535, 579, 620
Republic of Korea naval combat team: 185
Republic of Korea National Police: 14, 261, 330, 367, 370, 373, 383–84, 423, 424, 435, 442, 470, 566, 722
Republic of Korea Navy: 17, 52, 634
Reserves: 145, 335. See also under Eighth Army.
Rhea, Lt. Col. Robert L.: 213, 222–23, 227–31, 239, 240, 240n
Rhee, Syngman: 4, 12, 21, 44, 55, 111, 112, 262, 351, 536–38, 614
Rhee Chi Suh, Col.: 740

INDEX

Ridge, Lt. Col. Thomas: 724
Ridge line fighting: 313–18
Riley, Sgt. Jack W.: 480
Riots, Compound 76: 590, 590n
River crossings
  Ch'ongch'on: 665, 666, 679, 683
  Han: 515–16, 526–30
  Imjin: 614, 625
  Naktong: 192, 303, 548–59, 591–92, 593
  Nam: 575
  Orang-ch'on: 732
  Taedong: 650–52, 660
  Taeryong: 681
  Ungi: 734–36
  Yesong: 626–28
River crossings, enemy
  Han: 52–55, 105, 187
  Kum: 123–26, 130–37
  Kuryong: 711
  Naktong: 291–94, 298, 301–02, 309, 335–39, 342–45, 420, 437, 442, 447, 449, 451–52, 454, 456, 459, 460
  Nam: 470–71
  at P'yongt'aek: 81
Roach, 2d Lt. George: 473
Roadblocks: 80, 90, 153–55, 204, 225, 233, 303, 579, 627–30, 643, 656–57, 724–25
Roadblocks, enemy: 98, 137–43, 155, 164–79, 174n, 273–74, 303, 430, 603, 673, 674, 691, 696–99, 700–707, 741–42
Roberts, Lt. Col. Paul F.: 370, 439–40
Roberts, Brig. Gen. William L.: 18, 20, 21n
Robertson, Pfc. Robert: 344–45
Robinson, 1st Lt. Ralph R.: 468
Rochester: 497, 502, 512, 513, 731
Rocket launchers: 86. *See also* Bazooka-tank battles.
  2.36-inch: 69–72, 119
  3.5-inch: 119, 156–57, 162–64, 163n, 197–98, 314–15, 428
Rockets: 323, 371, 505, 506
  enemy use of: 691–93
  5-inch "shaped charge": 260
Rockwell, Lt. Col. Lloyd H.: 22, 23–24
Rocky Crags: 369, 371, 371n. *See also* Sobuk-san.
Rodgers, Lt. Col. William M.: 661
Rodriguez, 1st Lt. Adam B.: 445, 454–55
Roelofs, Lt. Col. T. B.: 278–83, 279n
Roise, Lt. Col. Harold S.: 272, 312
Roquemore, Maj. Frank V.: 237n
Round Top. *See* Hill 181.
Rowlands, Capt. Richard A.: 147
Royal Australian Air Force 77th Squadron: 48
Royal Canadian Air Force Squadron: 115
Royal Gardens: 381
Ruble, Rear Adm. Richard W.: 620
Rudd, Cpl. James M.: 348n, 349
Ruffner, Maj. Gen. Clark L.: 490–91, 496, 532, 764
Russian Hydropac Channel: 633

Saga. *See* Komam-ni.
Samsu, capture of: 737
Samyo: 126
San Francisco Port of Embarkation: 669
Sangju fighting: 190–95
Sangju-Taegu corridor. *See* Bowling Alley.
Sangp'o ferry crossing site: 558–59
Sariwon, capture of: 640–46
Sawyer, Capt. Robert K.: 387–88, 576n, 577, 577n
Schauer, Capt. Ernest J.: 467
Schmitt, 1st Lt. Edward: 446–47, 456–58, 456n, 457n
Schumann, Lt. Col. Heinrich G.: 531
Scott, 1st Lt. Dwain L.: 71, 71n
Scott, Lt. Col. Peter W.: 32, 57n
Security Council. *See under* United Nations.
Sedberry, Maj. George R., Jr.: 32, 32n
Seegars, Maj. Boone: 84
Self-propelled guns, 76-mm.: 17, 18n
Seoul: 19, 20, 30–35, 513–41
Seoul Area Command: 605
Seoul City Sue: 351n
Seoul Middle School: 535–36
Seoul-Pusan highway: 131, 133, 147, 150, 174, 200
Seventh Fleet: 38, 50
Shadrick, Pvt. Kenneth: 79, 79n
Sharra, Capt. George F.: 216–17, 221n
Sheen, Chaplain Lewis B.: 447–48
Shells, illuminating: 367
Shepherd, Lt. Gen. Lemuel C., Jr.: 494, 502
Sherman, Admiral Forrest P.: 493–94
Sherrard, Lt. Col. R. G.: 550, 581
Shinka, 2d Lt. Michael J.: 312–13
Shortages, ammunition: 180, 228, 431, 474, 542
Shrader, MSgt. Bryant E. W.: 232–33
Shtykov, Col. Gen. Terenty F.: 7
Sibidang-san: 438, 442–43
Sibyon-ni, capture of: 642
Sibyon-ni area, guerrilla activities in: 727
Sicily: 274, 400, 508
Signal Battalion, 4th: 724
Sihn Sung Mo: 12
Silver Star: 71n, 138n, 155n, 171n, 173n, 303n, 483, 660n
Silver Star Oak Leaf Cluster: 176n
Simpson, Capt. William F.: 509
Sinch'on, bridge blown at: 131
Sinsa-ri ferry: 528
Sixth Fleet: 491
Skeldon, Lt. Col. James H.: 551
Slack, Capt.: 178
Slater, Maj. Harold: 107, 184, 323
Sloane, Col. Charles C., Jr.: 465
Smith, Rear Adm. Allan E.: 620
Smith, Lt. Col. Charles B.: 60–76, 79, 80, 97, 99, 307, 682. *See also* Task Force Smith.
Smith, Lt. Col. David H.: 77, 84, 88
Smith, 1st Lt. H. J.: 525
Smith, Capt. Jack E.: 158, 169–71, 175–76

Smith, MSgt. John H.: 627–28
Smith, Lt. Loyd D.: 140
Smith, Maj. Malcolm: 686
Smith, Maj. Gen. Oliver P.: 491, 496, 509, 510, 524, 527–28, 527n, 532, 541n, 612, 619, 772–73. *See also* Marine Corps units, Division, 1st.
Sobaek Mountains: 121, 150
Sobuk-san: 236, 246, 268, 269, 270–71, 287, 364–75, 483–87, 568–71
Sodaemun Prison: 523, 531, 534, 535
Songak-san (Hill 475): 22–23
Songhwan-ni: 77, 80, 81
Songjin, capture of: 729
Songsin-ni: 746, 747n
Sonsan ferry crossing site: 591, 593
Sorties. *See* Air support.
Soule, Maj. Gen. Robert H.: 726, 740. *See also* Infantry Division, 3d.
South Korea: 4–6. *See also* Republic of Korea.
South Mountain: 528–31, 533
Southerland, Capt. Lundel M.: 128
Soviet activity in Korean War: 635
Soviet Army: 3
Soviet intervention, consideration of: 607
Soviet-manufactured equipment: 10, 11–12, 12n, 17–18, 18n, 24–25, 270, 318, 380, 395, 500, 598, 599, 644, 693, 715–16 727. *See also under* Tanks, enemy.
Soviet officers in North Korea: 759
Soviet-trained North Korean officers: 523
Soviet troops in Korean War: 486–87, 487n
Soviet Union: 1, 2, 5, 7–8, 11–12, 46, 48, 607, 759
Soviet Union Armed Forces: 487
Sowolmi-do: 506
Spaulding, Capt. Malcolm C.: 166
Spear, Pvt. Paul R.: 98, 98n
Special Task Force: 505
Spofford, Capt. Richard T. (USN): 620
Stahelski, Capt. Anthony F.: 128
"Stand or die" order: 205–09, 208n
Star shells: 339
Starling, 1st Lt. Herman W.: 129n
Stebbins, Col. Albert K., Jr.: 638, 771, 774n
Steele, 1st Lt. William H.: 138, 138n
Stelle, Capt. Art: 559
Stevens, Lt. R. P.: 372
Stephens, Col. Richard W.: 60, 88–91, 91n, 92–94, 94n, 96–97, 99, 130, 133, 148, 152, 174–75, 250, 398–99, 400–404, 405, 555, 629, 642, 682–83
Stewart, Maj. Everett S.: 467–68
Stewart, Maj. Frank R., Jr.: 462
Stewart, Brig. Gen. George C.: 628
Stith, 1st Lt. Archie L.: 123, 126
Story, Lt. Col. Anthony F.: 44, 44n
Story, Pfc. Luther H.: 455, 456n
Straight, Capt. Robert B.: 699
Strategic Air Command: 757
Strategic bombing. *See* Air support.

Strategy: 104–05, 117–18, 607–21. *See also* Operational plans; Tactics.
Stratemeyer, Lt. Gen. George E.: 44, 50, 51, 120, 352, 353, 378, 543, 653, 658, 774, 776. *See also* Far East Air Forces (FEAF).
Stratton, Lt. Col. Charles W.: 132, 137, 306
Street fighting: 86–87, 527, 534–36
Strengths. *See* Troop strengths.
Struble, Vice Adm. Arthur D.: 50, 493, 497, 502, 510, 519, 529, 618–21, 633–34
Stuart, Lt. Col. Clarence E.: 286
Suam-san. *See* Hill 518.
Sukch'on, airborne attack on: 654–58
Summers, Lt. Col. Robert R.: 539
Sunch'on, airborne attack on: 654–58
Supply: 442, 600n, 638–40
 of aviation gasoline: 257, 257n
 by airdrop: 452, 656, 657, 674, 677, 725, 728, 733
 by airlift: 612, 617, 621, 640, 668–69, 773
 by amphibious transport: 628
 difficulties: 89, 668, 726, 771–72, 774
 by LST: 729–32
 by rail: 248–49, 260–61, 380
 roads: 248, 287, 668, 773
 ROK: 17, 182–83
 by truck: 632, 668
Supply, enemy: 12, 393–94, 408
Supreme People's Assembly of Korea: 5
Sutter, Lt. Col. Allan: 507
Suwon: 55–58, 520–22, 538–39, 539n
Suwon Airfield: 45, 51, 56, 522, 538–39
Suwon-Osan highway: 538–39
Swedish Red Cross Field Hospital: 574
Swenson: 185, 503
Swenson, Lt. (jg) David H.: 503
Swink, Maj. Lloyd: 22
Szito, SFC Joseph S.: 172

T–6's: 95–96, 376
T19's: 114
T34's. *See under* Tanks, enemy.
Tabor, Cpl.: 135
Tabu-dong: 351, 421, 588–98
Tactical air control center: 95
Tactical air control parties (TACP's): 51, 90–91, 95–96, 165, 166, 167, 216, 217, 220, 330, 376, 576n, 582, 591, 674, 676, 715, 729. *See also* Aerial observation.
Tactics: 143. *See also* Operational Plans; Strategy.
 amphibious landing: 488–92
 at Battle Mountain: 374–75
 on Hill 314: 433
 in night fighting: 357
 Pusan Perimeter: 393, 542–45
 in street fighting: 535
 at Taejon: 147–51
 at Yongdok: 186

INDEX

Tactics, enemy: 10, 200, 210, 222, 347, 445–46, 469, 718–19, 746, 769–70. See also Envelopments, enemy; Operational plans, enemy.
  at Choch'iwon: 98
  delaying: 737–38
  mistakes, east coast: 106
  in night fighting: 357, 438, 694, 704
  at Obong-ni: 315–16
  at Pusan Perimeter: 392–93, 437–38
  at Taejon: 146, 158, 178, 179
  U.N. air supremacy effect on: 377–78
  use of forest fires: 689
Taebaek Mountains: 101–05, 685, 722
Taedong River crossings: 649–52
Taegu: 102
  attack toward: 397–436
  battle above: 560–66
  Eighth Army headquarters: 110
  front battle: 334–63
Taejon: 90, 130, 133, 144, 146–81
  ADCOM command post established at: 57
  battle, first day: 151–55
  battle, second day: 155–64
  defensive plans for: 147–51
  enemy attack on: 102
  enemy enters: 161–62
  regained: 164–70
  terrain: 121, 150–51
  troop dispositions at: 122
  withdrawal from: 164–79
Taejon Airfield: 147, 151, 152, 154, 157–58
Taep'yong-ni, blowing of bridges at: 121, 131
Takasago Maru: 214
Talley, Pvt. Sidney D.: 223
Tank-artillery battles. See Artillery-tank battles.
Tank Battalions
  1st: 504
  1st Marine: 381n
  6th: 380, 381, 381n, 389–90, 401, 553, 560, 561, 584, 625, 664, 665, 675, 676, 677, 677n, 679, 707
  64th Heavy: 740
  70th: 347, 349, 380, 381, 381n, 562, 563, 565, 590, 593–98, 628, 629, 647, 661, 679, 695–99, 701–05, 708
  71st Heavy: 340
  72d: 381, 381n, 444, 448, 450n, 451, 455, 459, 460–61, 462, 466, 550, 559, 652
  73d: 353, 355, 380, 381, 381n, 398, 400, 520, 521–22, 539
  78th Heavy: 90, 98, 100, 133, 298
  79th: 192, 202, 480, 576, 576n
  89th: 253, 259, 267, 367–75, 381n, 441, 479, 578, 660, 665
  8072d: 239, 259
  and Tractor Battalion, 56th Amphibious: 503n, 528
Tank-bazooka fights. See Bazooka-tank fights.

Tank-infantry actions: 239–42, 243–44, 346–47, 355, 400, 430, 590–98, 642, 644, 647–49, 660
Tanks
  M4A3: 114, 367, 380–81
  M15A1: 114
  M19: 445
  M24: 50, 100
  M26: 380–81, 444–45
    as artillery: 367
    at Chinju: 231–33
    as dozers: 505–06
    versus T34's: 314–15, 359–60, 509–10, 522
  M46: 380–81
  build-up in Korea: 380–81, 381n
  Chinese evaluation of: 720
  medium: 259
  performance: 94, 94n, 144
Tanks, enemy: 30, 69–72, 86–87, 97–98, 263–64
  T34: 11–12, 12n, 31–32, 32n, 35, 57–58, 68, 157, 162–64, 163n, 197–98, 314–15, 380, 508–09, 522
  and infantry actions: 80–81, 90–92, 156–64, 356–59, 362
  role of, in tactics: 146
Tanyang: 101–02, 104
Tanyang corridor: 104
Tanyang Pass: 104–05
Taplett, Lt. Col. Robert D.: 504–06
Tarkenton, Lt. Col. James C.: 754–55, 755n
Taro Leaf Division. See Infantry Division, 24th.
Task Forces
  Allen: 421–22, 708, 715n
  Blair: 576n, 577
  Bradley: 325–27, 325n, 332, 451. See also Infantry Regiments, 9th.
  Church: 405–08. See also Task Forces, Jackson.
  Corley: 576n
  Davidson: 406–07, 711
  Dolvin: 575–79, 577n, 578n
  Elephant: 664
  Hannum: 521–23
  Haynes: 450, 450n, 466–67, 550n
  Hill: 301–07, 309. See also Infantry Regiments, 9th.
  Hyzer: 298
  Indianhead: 652
  Jackson: 397–405, 410. See also Task Forces, Church.
  Kean: 266–88, 308, 370, 569
  Kingston: 737–38
  Lynch: 590–98
  Manchu: 446–48, 456–59
  Matthews: 575–79, 576n, 577n
  90: 196
  90 Attack Force: 497
  91 Blockade and Covering Force: 497
  92: 497
  99 Patrol and Reconnaissance Force: 497
  Rodgers: 661

Task Forces—Continued
  Smith: 60–76, 79–80, 81, 82, 92, 96–97, 538
  70.1 Flagship Group: 497
  77 Fast Carrier Force: 497, 503–05
  79 Logistic Support Force: 497
  777: 590–98
  Torman: 574–75, 576n
Task Group: 567
Tedford, MSgt. Robert A.: 284
Teeter, Lt. Col. Bernard G.: 365, 367, 442
Terrain
  Agok area: 443–44
  Battle Mountain area: 368–69
  Bowling Alley: 355–56
  Camel's Head Bend: 700
  central Korea: 101–02
  Changjin (Chosin) Reservoir: 741–42
  Chinju-Masan corridor: 267–69
  Ch'ongch'on River area: 663, 671, 710–11, 712
  Chonui area: 92
  Cloverleaf Hill: 298–99, 312
  Hill 303 area: 345
  Hill 314: 432
  Hill 409 area: 469
  Hill 518: 412–13
  Imjin River Area: 724
  Inch'on area: 498–99
  Iron Triangle: 615–16
  Kaesong area: 22–23
  Kanggye-Manp'ojin area: 664
  Ka-san: 356, 422–23
  Kigye area: 319–20
  Kot'o-ri area: 742–43
  Kum River area: 121, 131–32
  Kyongju corridor: 102, 319–20
  Masan area: 364–65
  Naktong Bulge: 290–91
  Naktong River–Changnyong area: 448–49
  North Korea: 610, 732–33, 745–46
  Obong-ni Ridge: 299, 312
  Paek-san area: 725
  P'ohang-dong area: 319–20
  Pongam-ni area: 277
  Pujan (Fusen) Reservoir area: 733
  Pusan Perimeter: 252–53, 289–91, 438
  P'yongt'aek-Ansong line: 77, 79
  P'yongyang area: 643–44, 649, 654, 658–59
  Seoul area: 523, 528–29
  Taebaek Range area: 685
  Taegu: 408, 411, 412–13
  Taejon: 121, 150–51
  Unsan area: 671–72, 680
  Waegwan area: 345
  Wolmi-do: 504
  Wonsan: 619, 685
  Yalu River area: 671–72, 716, 736–37
  Yongsan area: 448
Terry, Lt. Col. August T., Jr.: 246

Thailand Battalion: 668
38th Parallel: 5, 13, 37, 105, 113, 638, 721, 758–59, 766, 769
  as boundary between occupation forces: 3, 3n
  crossed by Eighth Army: 622–31
  crossing plans: 607–21
  deployment of ROK Army along: 16, 20
  enemy preparations and invasion across: 19–28, 20n
  incidents along: 5
  reached by ROK Army: 598–600
  Soviet forces advance south of: 3
Thompson, Col. Percy W.: 690, 751, 752n
Thompson, Pfc. William: 270, 270n
Throckmorton, Lt. Col. John L.: 271–74, 276–84, 286, 365, 367n, 371, 439, 441, 483, 553, 683–84, 711
Tides at Inch'on: 498–99, 513, 621
"Tiger Kim." See Kim Chong Won, Col.
Time: 21n
Time Magazine: 40
Time-on-target fire: 314, 341
Tokyo Ordnance Depot: 114
Toledo: 512–13
T'ongdok Mountain: 520
Torman, Capt. Charles J.: 574–75
Training: 113, 384. See also Buddy system.
Transportation Railroad Operating Battalion, 714th: 391
Triangulation Hill. See Hill 268.
Triple Nickel. See Field Artillery Battalions, 555th.
Troop Carrier Squadron, 21st: 654
Troop Carrier Squadron, 314th: 654
Troop dispositions
  Agok area: 443–44
  Battle Mountain: 370
  Bowling Alley: 353–54
  Ch'ongch'on River area: 672
  Ch'ongch'on River bridgehead: 709–11, 713
  Cloverleaf-Obong-ni: 310–11
  Han River: 519–20
  Hill 518: 413–14
  Inch'on landing: 499
  Kaesong area: 22
  Kum River: 123
  Masan area: 364–65
  Naktong Bulge: 290–91, 298
  Naktong River: 448–49, 462–63
  Nam River: 442
  North Korea, attack into: 613–14
  North Korea offensive: 771
  Pusan Perimeter: 253–54, 438–40, 543, 573–74
  P'yongyang: 647, 653
  Taegu area: 335–36, 390–91, 411, 431–32, 561–62
  Taejon: 122, 150–51, 152
  X Corps: 685–86
  38th Parallel: 20, 623
  Unsan area: 700

INDEX

Troop dispositions—Continued
  Wonsan: 740–41
Troop dispositions, enemy
  Bowling Alley: 354
  Cloverleaf Hill: 306
  Huich'on-Unsan: 717–18
  Masan: 365–66
  mountain corridors: 105
  Northeast Korea: 718, 766–68
  Pusan Perimeter: 253–55, 255n, 394–96, 438
  Taegu: 335–36, 411
  38th Parallel: 19–20, 622–23
  Yongsan area: 459–60
Troop strengths: 110, 110n, 197n, 264–65, 264n, 267n, 299, 382, 384, 389, 491–92, 503, 503n, 547–48, 547n, 574, 574n, 605, 606, 620, 684, 685n, 733, 739
Troop strengths, enemy: 263–64, 263n, 269–70, 293, 294n, 332, 365–66, 395, 395n, 409, 507–08, 540, 545–46, 589, 590, 647, 768–69, 769n
Truck Battalion, 52d: 632
Truck transport: 668
Truman, Harry S.: 3, 5, 42–43, 716, 757, 760, 767
  action on North Korean invasion: 37–38
  authorizes use of U.S. ground troops: 46–48
  designates MacArthur Commanding General of the Military Forces: 112
  message to MacArthur on liberation of Seoul: 537–38
  and Wake Island meeting: 630–31
Truxes, Capt. Arthur H., Jr.: 643, 643n
Tucker, Richard: 661
Tufts, Capt. Ben L.: 64, 177n
Tugok: 299, 299n, 312, 313, 314
Tuksong-dong bridge: 342–44
Tuman-ni: 132, 137–38
Tundok: 368, 369, 373
Tunnels: 148, 150, 165, 168, 169, 174, 175, 182
Tunnels, use by enemy: 368
Turkish Armed Forces Command, 1st: 668
Turkish Brigade: 668
Turner, SFC Charles W.: 460–61, 461n
Turtle Head Bend: 681, 691
Twentieth Air Force: 51
Twin-40 self-propelled antiaircraft gun vehicles: 559
Typhoons. See Weather, Inch'on landing.

Uijongbu Corridor: 19, 20, 24–25, 28–30
Underwater bridges. See under Bridges.
Ungi River, crossed: 734–36
Union of Soviet Socialist Republics (USSR). See Soviet Union.
United Democratic Patriotic Front Central Committee: 19
United Nations: 1, 392, 608–09
  assigns military observers to Parallel: 6
  Communiqué No. 1: 262

United Nations—Continued
  General Assembly: 4, 5
  member nations offer support in Korean War: 48
  and North Korea: 5
  and pamphlets dropped over South Korea: 53
  reaction to North Korean invasion: 37–38
  Reception Center: 667–68
  reinforcements: 667–68
  Security Council: 761–62, 763
  Temporary Commission on Korea (UNCOK): 4, 20
  troop strength: 605, 606
United Nations Command: 262, 352–53, 383, 547–48, 622–23, 761–62, 763, 766, 769

Van Brunt, Brig. Gen. Rinaldo: 690
Van Sant, 2d Lt. Jesse F.: 520–22
Vandygriff, Sgt. James N.: 425–29
Vehicles, repair of: 114
Vickery, Lt.: 478–79
"Vickery's Bridge." See Namji-ri bridge.
Victoria Cross: 583n
Vieman, Col. Jewis D.: 32n, 41
Vladivostok: 377
Vonton, Sgt. George E.: 558

Wadlington, Lt. Col. Robert L.: 86, 88, 100, 125, 129, 158, 169, 170–71, 171n, 174, 297
Waegwan: 291, 345–47
  capture of: 552–54
  carpet bombing: 350–53
Wagnebreth, Sgt. Wallace A.: 126
Wake Island Conference: 539, 540, 545, 630–31, 669, 670
Walker: 214
Walker, Capt. Robert W.: 434
Walker, Lt. Gen. Walton H.: 49, 59, 120, 595, 617, 653, 690, 776. See also Eighth Army.
  on air support: 477, 477n
  and alteration of boundary lines: 574
  appoints Coulter Deputy Commander, Eighth Army: 398
  and Assistant Chief of Staff: 392
  assumes command in Korea: 110–13
  biography: 109–10
  and briefing, 27 August: 398
  on carpet bombing: 352–53
  at Ch'onan: 88
  and Civil Assistance Command: 670
  and command crisis: 415–16
  and command problems: 308–09, 609–12
  concentrates reinforcements, Chinju-Masan: 267
  and daily visits to combat units: 335
  and Davidson Line: 391–92
  decisions, 1 September: 451–53
  defense tactics: 289, 334, 393, 435
  and disposition of troops, Masan: 364–65
  dissatisfied with 8th Cavalry: 562

Walker, Lt. Gen. Walton H.—Continued
    and east coast situation: 131, 182, 185, 186–87, 188–89
    and Eighth Army realignment: 389–92
    establishes United Nations Reception Center: 667
    and impatience with drive on P'yonghang: 642
    and intelligence on CCF: 678–79, 754–55
    and marines, use of: 465–66
    and Masan action: 238
    and movement of 25th Division: 248–49
    operational plans: 110–11, 148–50, 150n, 152, 542–45, 588–89, 709, 754, 771
    and order for counterattacks: 252
    orders release of 5th Regimental Combat Team: 484–85
    orders 24th Division withdrawal: 753
    and performance of 24th Infantry: 486
    personality sketch: 417
    and Plan 100–C: 571
    and P'ohang-dong area battle: 319–33
    praised by MacArthur: 771
    and pursuit order after Perimeter breakout: 573–74
    and Pusan Perimeter situation: 397
    and puzzle of *10th Division:* 470
    and relief of IX Corps: 638
    requests support from Fifth Air Force: 267
    reserves, use of: 335, 405, 410
    and ROK Army, 28 August message to: 400
    and ROK Army augmentation: 385–89, 388n
    and ROK Army increase: 384
    and ROK divisions, plan for: 253
    and ROK units, praise of: 599
    and Sangju: 190
    at Seoul ceremony: 537
    shifts commanders of I and IX Corps: 544–45
    situation report to Hickey: 462
    "stand or die" order: 205–09, 207n
    tactics: 200, 319–20, 334
    at Taegu with Gay: 197
    and threat to southwest Korea: 212–13, 226–27
    and tug of war over marines: 496
    and 25th Division crisis: 472
    and 24 November attack: 774, 774n
Walled City of Ka-san. *See* Ka-san.
Walton, Lt. Col. William: 680n, 694, 695, 698
Watkins, Cpl. Robert B.: 162
Watkins, MSgt. Travis E.: 457, 457n, 458, 458n
Weapons. *See entries for various types of weapons.*
Weather: 107, 139, 437, 455, 685
    effect of, on troops: 262, 269, 272, 275, 298, 304, 341, 372, 391, 732, 735–36, 738, 744, 772–73
    hampering effects of: 74, 92, 97, 212, 228, 271–72, 306, 406, 418, 428, 431, 474, 475, 548, 642, 654, 731, 733
Weather, Inch'on landing: 501–02

Weather hampers enemy: 478
Webel, Lt. Col. James B.: 414n, 434, 435n, 595–96, 597n, 626, 628, 643, 647
Weible, Maj. Gen. Walter L.: 114, 669
Weigle, 1st Lt. Tom.: 160
West, Capt. Herman L.: 419
Westburg, Capt. Arthur: 628
Weston, Capt. Logan E.: 201, 245, 245n
Whampoa Military Academy: 394
White, Capt. Harry H.: 466
White, Col. Horton V.: 108, 194, 195, 271
White Head Mountain: 737
Whitehead, Don: 661–63, 663n
Whitney, Maj. Gen. Courtney: 502, 510, 658, 774, 776
Wiley, Alexander: 495n
Wilkins, Lt. Col. John L., Jr.: 192, 365, 442
Williamson, Lt. Col. Earle W.: 527n
Willoughby, Maj. Gen. Charles A.: 759, 763–64, 774, 776
Wilson, Maj. David: 644
Wilson, Pfc. Richard G.: 659, 659n
Wilson, Brig. Gen. Vennard: 192
Wilson, Lt. Col. Wesley C.: 214, 222, 223, 224, 233–34, 239–42
Wilcox, 2d Lt. George W.: 167n
Winningstad, Col. Olaf P.: 231
Winstead, Lt. Col. Otho: 132, 135, 136, 137, 139, 139n
Witherspoon, Maj. Willian O., Jr.: 592
Witty, Col. Robert: 106, 184, 329
Wol Ki Chan, Maj. Gen.: 523
Wolmi-do: 503, 504–06
Wonjon: 215–16
Wonju, fall of: 102
Wonsan, capture of: 614–21
Wonsan Agricultural College: 741
Woods, Capt. Kenneth Y.: 161
Woodside, Lt. Col. William W.: 597
Woodyard, Capt. E. L. (USN): 497
Woolfolk, Maj. Robert L.: 365, 569–70
Woolnough, Col. James K.: 648
Woolridge, Maj. John R.: 194–95
World War II: 2–3
    equipment used in Korea: 11, 16–17, 96, 113–14, 239, 259, 261, 378, 498, 688
    rations: 115
    use of underwater bridges in: 302
    veterans of, in Korea: 8–9, 61, 77, 83, 109, 135, 206, 216, 258, 259, 285, 293, 376, 382, 424, 472, 483, 490–91, 614, 652, 677, 681, 687
Wounded, difficulties in care of: 369–70
Wright, Brig. Gen. Edwin K.: 36, 39, 258, 489, 492–97, 502, 510, 571, 609–10, 612, 658, 774, 776
Wright, Col. William H. S.: 30, 31, 32, 40–42, 43, 56, 57
Wygal, Lt. William: 167

INDEX

Yaban-san. *See* Fox Hill.
YAK's: 26, 39, 45, 512
Yalu River, air battles over: 715-16
Yalu River, reached: 671-73
Yech'on, battle at: 190-91, 191n
Yellow Beach: 499, 634, 636
Yesong River crossing sites: 623
Yongch'on: 408-10
Yongdok battles: 106-08, 182-87, 599
Yongdong battle: 196-200
Yongdungp'o battles: 55, 516-20
Yongdungp'o Separate Battalion: 107
Yongin road: 102
Yongju-Andong corridor, defense of: 104

Yongsan: 293-94, 448
   battles: 302-03, 459-66
Yongsan-Naktong River road: 295, 297, 299
Yongsu River: 142
Yonil Airfield: 107, 184, 185, 320-33, 402, 404, 406
   abandoned: 329-30, 330n
Young, Maj. Jack T.: 466
Yu Jae Hung, Maj. Gen.: 674
Yu Jai Hyung, Brig. Gen.: 29
Yuhak-san: 351, 354, 356, 361
Yun Bong Hun, Lt. Col.: 604
Yusong: 144, 145, 147

Zimmerman, Pvt. Charles T.: 173

Lightning Source UK Ltd.
Milton Keynes UK
UKOW07n1643040915

258091UK00005B/42/P